MAP PAGES

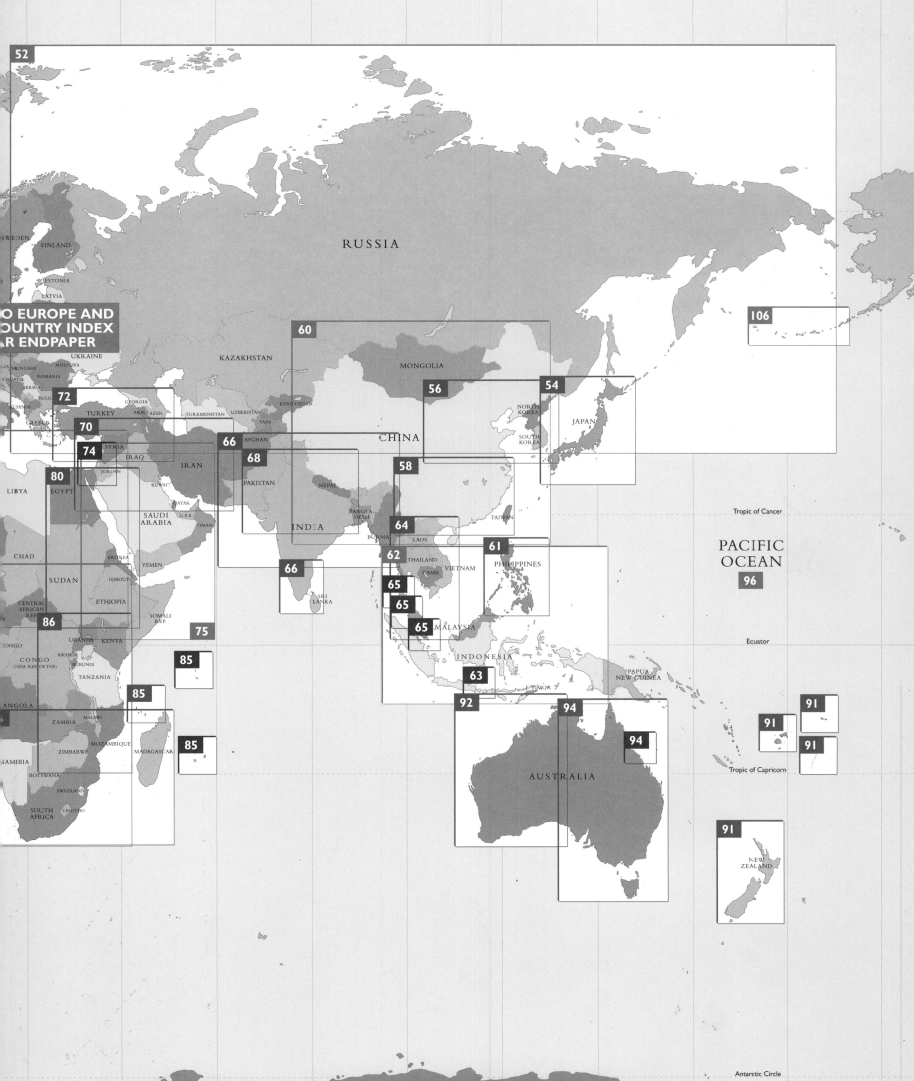

OXFORD

NEW CONCISE
WORLD ATLAS

OXFORD

NEW CONCISE

WORLD ATLAS

THIRD EDITION

THE EARTH IN SPACE
Cartography by Philip's

Text
Keith Lye

Illustrations
Stefan Chabluk

Star Charts
Wil Tirion

PICTURE ACKNOWLEDGEMENTS
Mike Brown 46 (top left), 48 (top left), 50 (top left), 56 (top left), 60 (top left)
Corbis /William Caram 59, /Ed Eckstein 58 (bottom), /Colin Garratt; Milepost 92 1/2 60 (bottom),
/Aaron Horowitz 40 (top left), /Wolfgang Kaehler 37, /Manoocher/Webistan 48 (top right),
/Kevin R Morris 48 (bottom), /Galen Rowell 62 (bottom), /Royalty-Free 36 (top left), 44 (top left),
47, 52 (top left), 54 (top left), 58 (top left), 62 (top left), /Peter Turnley 51, /Nik Wheeler 46
(bottom), /Tim Wright 61
Corbis Saba /Shepard Sherbell 56 (bottom)
Corbis Sygma /Thorne Anderson 63
Michael P. Doukas/USGS/CVO 32 (top left)
Akira Fujii/David Malin Images 27
Getty Images/The Image Bank /Peter Hendrie 36 (top right), /Pete Turner 55
Getty Images/Stone /James Balog 32 (bottom), /Simeone Huber 49, /Gary John Norman 52 (bottom),
/Frank Oberle 41 (top), /Dennis Oda 33, /Donovan Reese 34–5, /Michael Townsend 45
Robert Harding Picture Library /Bill Ross 57
Images Colour Library Limited 31
NASA 18 (top left), 20 (top left), 22 (top left), 24 (top left), 26 (top left), 26 (bottom), /Jacques
Descloitres, MODIS/GSFC 28 (top left), /ESA, S. Beckwith (STScI) and the HUDF Team 18 (bottom),
/GSFC 24 (top right), /Hubble Heritage Team (STScI/AURA)/R.G. French (Wellesley College)/J. Cuzzi
and J. Lissauer (NASA/Ames Research Center)/L. Dones (SwRI) 25 (bottom left), /JPL 24 (centre left),
24 (bottom left), 25 (top right), 25 (centre right), /JPL/Univ. Arizona 25 (top left), /JPL/USGS
24 (bottom right), /JSC 38 (top left), 42 (top left), /Hal Pierce/GSFC 40 (top right), /A. Stern (SwRI),
M. Buie (Lowell Observatory)/ESA 25 (bottom right), /Reto Stöckli, Robert Simmon/GSFC 17
NPA Group, Edenbridge, UK 28 (bottom), 29, (top), 29 (bottom), 64
Caroline Ohara 34 (top left)
Christopher Rayner 30 (top left), 35 (top)
Rex Features /Sipa 50 (bottom)
Robin Scagell/Galaxy 27 (bottom)
Science Photo Library /Martin Bond 30 (bottom), /CNES, 1992 Distribution SPOT Image 43 (top),
/Luke Dodd 19, 21, /Earth Satellite Corporation 41 (bottom), /Simon Fraser 54 (bottom), /NASA 38
(bottom), 39, /David Parker 42 (bottom), /Peter Ryan 43 (bottom), /Jerry Schad 20 (bottom)
Still Pictures /François Pierrel 44 (bottom)
Tony Stone Images /Nigel Press 53

Copyright © 2009 Philip's

Philip's,
a division of Octopus Publishing Group Limited,
2–4 Heron Quays, London E14 4JP
An Hachette UK Company

Cartography by Philip's

Published in North America by
Oxford University Press, Inc.
198 Madison Avenue,
New York, NY 10016

www.oup.com/us

OXFORD
UNIVERSITY PRESS   Oxford is a registered trademark of Oxford University Press

Library of Congress Cataloging-in-Publication Data available

ISBN 978–0–19–539329–3

Printing (last digit): 9 8 7 6 5 4 3 2 1

Printed in Hong Kong

USER GUIDE

The reference maps which form the main body of this atlas have been prepared in accordance with the highest standards of international cartography to provide an accurate and detailed representation of the Earth. The scales and projections used have been carefully chosen to give balanced coverage of the world, while emphasizing the most densely populated and economically significant regions. A hallmark of Philip's mapping is the use of hill shading and relief coloring to create a graphic impression of landforms: this makes the maps exceptionally easy to read. However, knowledge of the key features employed in the construction and presentation of the maps will enable the reader to derive the fullest benefit from the atlas.

MAP SEQUENCE

The atlas covers the Earth continent by continent: first Europe; then its land neighbor Asia (mapped north before south, in a clockwise sequence), then Africa, Australia and Oceania, North America, and South America. This is the classic arrangement adopted by most cartographers since the 16th century. For each continent, there are maps at a variety of scales. First, physical relief

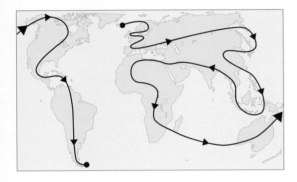

and political maps of the whole continent; then a series of larger-scale maps of the regions within the continent, each followed, where required, by still larger-scale maps of the most important or densely populated areas. The governing principle is that by turning the pages of the atlas, the reader moves steadily from north to south through each continent, with each map overlapping its neighbors.

MAP PRESENTATION

With very few exceptions (for example, for the Arctic and Antarctica), the maps are drawn with north at the top, regardless of whether they are presented upright or sideways on the page. In the borders will be found the map title; a locator diagram showing the area covered; continuation arrows showing the page numbers for maps of adjacent areas; the scale; the projection used; the degrees of latitude and longitude; and the letters and figures used in the index for locating place names and geographical features. Physical relief maps also have a height reference panel identifying the colors used for each layer of contouring.

MAP SYMBOLS

Each map contains a vast amount of detail which can only be conveyed clearly and accurately by the use of symbols. Points and circles of varying sizes locate and identify the relative importance of towns and cities; different styles of type are employed for administrative, geographical and regional place names to aid identification. A variety of pictorial symbols denote landforms such as glaciers, marshes and coral reefs, and man-made structures including roads, railroads, airports, and canals. International borders are shown by red lines. Where neighboring countries are in dispute, for example in parts of the Middle East, the maps show the *de facto* boundary between nations, regardless of the legal or historical situation. The symbols are explained on the first page of the World Maps section of the atlas.

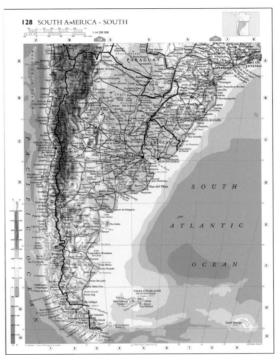

MAP SCALES

1:16 000 000
1 inch = 252 statute miles

The scale of each map is given in the numerical form known as the "representative fraction." The first figure is always one, signifying one unit of distance on the map; the second figure, usually in millions, is the number by which the map unit must be multiplied to give the equivalent distance on the Earth's surface. Calculations can easily be made in centimeters and kilometers, by dividing the Earth units figure by 100 000 (i.e. deleting the last five 0s). Thus 1:1 000 000 means 1 cm = 10 km. The calculation for inches and miles is more laborious, but 1 000 000 divided by 63 360 (the number of inches in a mile) shows that 1:1 000 000 means approximately 1 inch = 16 miles. The table below provides distance equivalents for scales down to 1:50 000 000.

LARGE SCALE		
1:1 000 000	1 cm = 10 km	1 inch = 16 miles
1:2 500 000	1 cm = 25 km	1 inch = 39.5 miles
1:5 000 000	1 cm = 50 km	1 inch = 79 miles
1:6 000 000	1 cm = 60 km	1 inch = 95 miles
1:8 000 000	1 cm = 80 km	1 inch = 126 miles
1:10 000 000	1 cm = 100 km	1 inch = 158 miles
1:15 000 000	1 cm = 150 km	1 inch = 237 miles
1:20 000 000	1 cm = 200 km	1 inch = 316 miles
1:50 000 000	1 cm = 500 km	1 inch = 790 miles
SMALL SCALE		

MEASURING DISTANCES

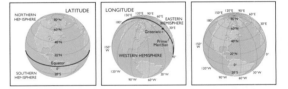

Although each map is accompanied by a scale bar, distances cannot always be measured with confidence because of the distortions involved in portraying the curved surface of the Earth on a flat page. As a general rule, the larger the map scale (that is, the lower the number of Earth units in the representative fraction), the more accurate and reliable will be the distance measured. On small-scale maps such as those of the world and of entire continents, measurement may only be accurate

along the "standard parallels," or central axes, and should not be attempted without considering the map projection.

MAP PROJECTIONS

Unlike a globe, no flat map can give a true scale representation of the world in terms of area, shape, and position of every region. Each of the numerous systems that have been devised for projecting the curved surface of the Earth on to a flat page involves the sacrifice of accuracy in one or more of these elements. The variations in shape and position of land masses such as Alaska, Greenland, and Australia, for example, can be quite dramatic when different projections are compared. For this atlas, the guiding principle has been to select projections that involve the least distortion of size and distance. The projection used for each map is noted in the border. Most fall into one of three categories – conic, azimuthal, or cylindrical – whose basic concepts are shown above. Each involves plotting the forms of the Earth's surface on a grid of latitude and longitude lines, which may be shown as parallels, curves, or radiating spokes.

LATITUDE AND LONGITUDE

Accurate positioning of individual points on the Earth's surface is made possible by reference to the geometrical system of latitude and longitude. Latitude *parallels* are drawn west–east around the Earth and numbered by degrees north and south of the equator, which is designated 0° of latitude. Longitude *meridians* are drawn north–south and numbered by degrees east and west of the *prime meridian*, 0° of longitude, which passes through Greenwich in England. By referring to these coordinates and their subdivisions of minutes (1/60th of a degree) and seconds (1/60th of a minute), any place on Earth can be located to within a few hundred yards. Latitude and longitude are indicated by blue lines on the maps; they are straight or curved according to the projection employed. Reference to these lines is the easiest way of determining the relative positions of places on different maps, and for plotting compass directions.

NAME FORMS

For ease of reference, both English and local name forms appear in the atlas. Oceans, seas, and countries are shown in English throughout the atlas; country names may be abbreviated to their commonly accepted form (for example, Germany, not The Federal Republic of Germany). Conventional English forms are also used for place names on the smaller-scale maps of the continents. However, local name forms are used on all large-scale and regional maps, with the English form given in brackets only for important cities – the large-scale map of Russia and Central Asia thus shows Moskva (Moscow). For countries which do not use a Roman script, place names have been transcribed according to the systems adopted by the British and US Geographic Names Authorities. For China, the Pin Yin system has been used, with some more widely known forms appearing in brackets, as with Beijing (Peking). Both English and local names appear in the index, the English form being cross-referenced to the local form.

CONTENTS

WORLD STATISTICS

COUNTRIES	10
CITIES	11
CLIMATE	12–13
PHYSICAL DIMENSIONS	14–15

THE EARTH IN SPACE

THE UNIVERSE	18–19
THE CONSTELLATIONS	20–21
STAR CHARTS	22–23
THE SOLAR SYSTEM	24–25
THE EARTH: TIME AND MOTION	26–27
THE EARTH FROM SPACE	28–29
THE DYNAMIC EARTH	30–31
EARTHQUAKES AND VOLCANOES	32–33
FORCES OF NATURE	34–35
OCEANS AND ICE	36–37
THE EARTH'S ATMOSPHERE	38–39
CLIMATE AND WEATHER	40–41
WATER AND LAND USE	42–43
THE NATURAL WORLD	44–45
THE HUMAN WORLD	46–47
LANGUAGES AND RELIGIONS	48–49
INTERNATIONAL ORGANIZATIONS	50–51
AGRICULTURE	52–53
ENERGY AND MINERALS	54–55
WORLD ECONOMIES	56–57
TRADE AND COMMERCE	58–59
TRAVEL AND COMMUNICATIONS	60–61
THE WORLD TODAY	62–63

WORLD MAPS

MAP SYMBOLS	1
THE WORLD: POLITICAL 1:84 000 000	2–3
ARCTIC OCEAN 1:31 100 000	4
ANTARCTICA 1:31 100 000	5

EUROPE

EUROPE: PHYSICAL 1:17 800 000	6
EUROPE: POLITICAL 1:17 800 000	7

SCANDINAVIA
1:5 300 000
Iceland 1:5 300 000
Færoe Islands 1:5 300 000

8–9

DENMARK AND SOUTHERN SWEDEN
1:2 200 000

10–11

IRELAND
1:1 800 000

12

SCOTLAND
1:1 800 000
Orkney Islands 1:1 800 000
Shetland Islands 1:1 800 000

13

ENGLAND AND WALES
1:1 800 000
Isles of Scilly 1:1 800 000

14–15

BRITISH ISLES
1:4 400 000

16

NETHERLANDS, BELGIUM AND LUXEMBOURG
1:2 200 000

17

NORTHERN FRANCE
1:2 200 000

18–19

SOUTHERN FRANCE
1:2 200 000

20–21

CENTRAL EUROPE
1:4 400 000

22–23

GERMANY AND SWITZERLAND
1:2 200 000

24–25

AUSTRIA, CZECH REPUBLIC
AND SLOVAK REPUBLIC
1:2 200 000

26–27

HUNGARY, ROMANIA AND THE LOWER DANUBE
1:2 200 000

28–29

POLAND AND THE SOUTHERN BALTIC
1:2 200 000

30–31

BALTIC STATES, BELARUS AND UKRAINE
1:4 400 000

32–33

THE VOLGA BASIN AND THE CAUCASUS
1:4 400 000

34–35

WESTERN SPAIN AND PORTUGAL
1:2 200 000

36–37

EASTERN SPAIN
1:2 200 000
Menorca 1:2 200 000

38–39

NORTHERN ITALY, SLOVENIA AND CROATIA
1:2 200 000

40–41

SOUTHERN ITALY
1:2 200 000

42–43

THE BALKANS
1:2 200 000

44–45

SOUTHERN GREECE AND WESTERN TURKEY
1:2 200 000

46–47

THE BALEARICS, THE CANARIES AND MADEIRA
1:900 000 / 1:1 800 000

48

MALTA, CRETE, CORFU, RHODES AND CYPRUS
1:900 000 / 1:1 200 000

49

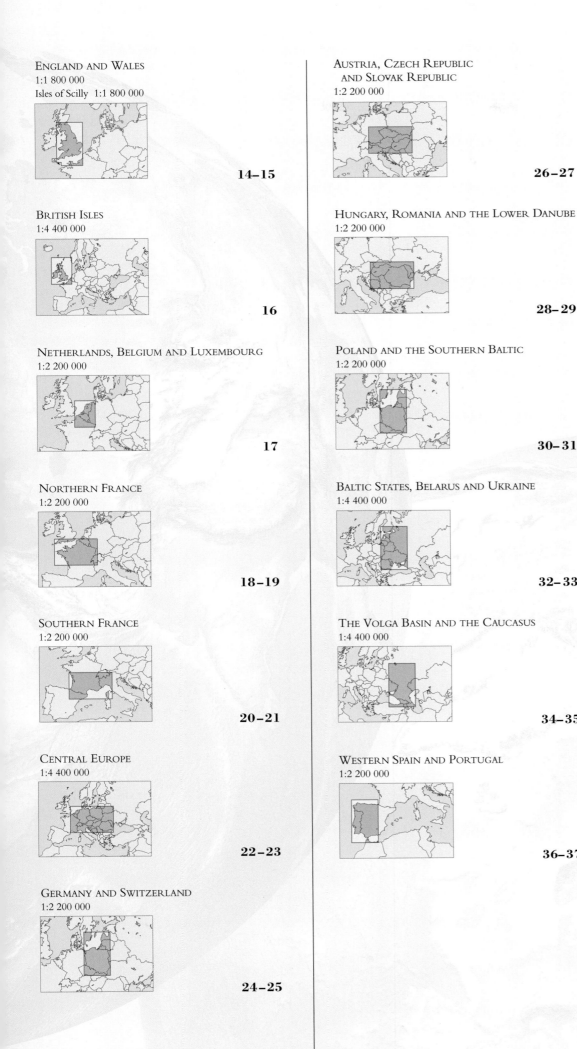

ASIA

ASIA: PHYSICAL
1:44 400 000   **50**

ASIA: POLITICAL
1:44 400 000   **51**

RUSSIA AND CENTRAL ASIA
1:17 800 000

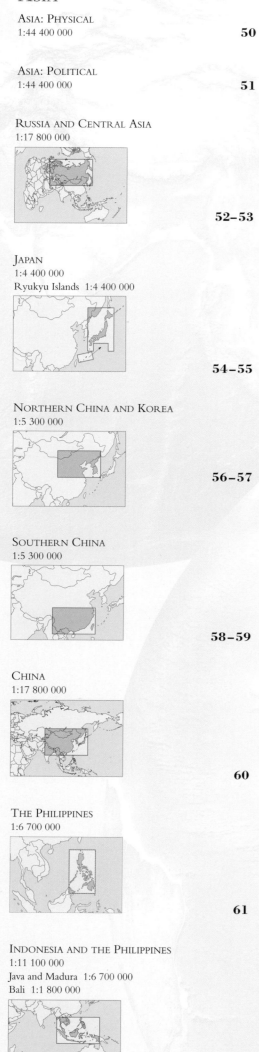

                                                52–53

JAPAN
1:4 400 000
Ryukyu Islands 1:4 400 000

                                                54–55

NORTHERN CHINA AND KOREA
1:5 300 000

                                                56–57

SOUTHERN CHINA
1:5 300 000

                                                58–59

CHINA
1:17 800 000

                                                60

THE PHILIPPINES
1:6 700 000

                                                61

INDONESIA AND THE PHILIPPINES
1:11 100 000
Java and Madura 1:6 700 000
Bali 1:1 800 000

                                                62–63

MAINLAND SOUTHEAST ASIA
1:5 300 000
Ko Phuket 1:900 000
Ko Samui 1:900 000
Pinang 1:900 000
Singapore 1:900 000

                                                64–65

SOUTH ASIA
1:8 900 000

                                                66–67

NORTHERN INDIA, PAKISTAN AND NEPAL
1:5 300 000
Jammu and Kashmir 1:5 300 000

                                                68–69

THE MIDDLE EAST
1:6 200 000

                                                70–71

TURKEY AND TRANSCAUCASIA
1:4 400 000

                                                72–73

THE NEAR EAST
1:2 200 000

                                                74

ARABIA AND THE HORN OF AFRICA
1:13 300 000

                                                75

AFRICA

AFRICA: PHYSICAL
1:37 300 000   **76**

AFRICA: POLITICAL
1: 37 300 000   **77**

NORTHERN AFRICA
1:13 300 000
The Azores 1:13 300 000
Cape Verde Islands 1:8 900 000

                                                78–79

THE NILE VALLEY
1:7 100 000
The Nile Delta 1:3 600 000

                                                80–81

WEST AFRICA
1:7 100 000

                                                82–83

CENTRAL AND SOUTHERN AFRICA
1:13 300 000
Seychelles 1:2 200 000
Réunion 1:2 200 000
Mauritius 1:2 200 000
Comoros 1:7 100 000

                                                84–85

EAST AFRICA
1:7 100 000

                                                86–87

SOUTHERN AFRICA
1:7 100 000
Madagascar 1:7 100 000

                                                88–89

AUSTRALIA AND OCEANIA

AUSTRALIA AND OCEANIA:
 PHYSICAL AND POLITICAL
1:44 400 000   **90**

NEW ZEALAND
1:5 300 000
Fiji 1:5 300 000
Samoan Islands 1:5 300 000
Tonga 1:5 300 000
Tahiti and Moorea 1:1 100 000
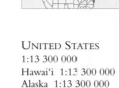
                                      91

WESTERN AUSTRALIA
1:7 100 000

                                      92–93

EASTERN AUSTRALIA
1:7 100 000
Whitsunday Islands 1:2 200 000
Tasmania 1:7 100 000
Torres Strait 1:7 100 000
                                      94–95

PACIFIC OCEAN
1:48 000 000   **96–97**

NORTH AMERICA

NORTH AMERICA: PHYSICAL
1:31 100 000   **98**

NORTH AMERICA: POLITICAL
1:31 100 000   **99**

CANADA
1:13 300 000
                                      100–101

WESTERN CANADA
1:6 200 000
                                      102–103

EASTERN CANADA
1:6 200 000
                                      104–105

UNITED STATES
1:13 300 000
Hawai'i 1:13 300 000
Alaska 1:13 300 000
                                      106–107

UNITED STATES – WEST
1:6 250 000
                                      108–109

CENTRAL AND SOUTHERN CALIFORNIA
 AND WESTERN WASHINGTON
1:2 200 000

                                      110–111

UNITED STATES MIDWEST AND
 NORTHEAST
1:6 250 000

                                      112–113

NORTHEASTERN UNITED STATES
1:2 200 000

                                      114–115

UNITED STATES – SOUTH
1:6 250 000

                                      116–117

MEXICO
1:7 100 000
                                      118–119

CENTRAL AMERICA AND THE WEST INDIES
1:7 100 000
Jamaica 1:2 700 000
Guadeloupe 1:1 800 000
Martinique 1:1 800 000
Puerto Rico 1:2 700 000
Virgin Islands 1:1 800 000
St Lucia 1:890 000
Barbados 1:890 000
                                      120–121

SOUTH AMERICA

SOUTH AMERICA: PHYSICAL
1:31 100 000   **122**

SOUTH AMERICA: POLITICAL
1:31 100 000   **123**

SOUTH AMERICA – NORTH
1:14 200 000
Trinidad and Tobago 1:2 200 000

                                      124–125

CENTRAL SOUTH AMERICA
1:7 100 000
                                      126–127

SOUTH AMERICA – SOUTH
1:14 200 000
                                      128

INDEX TO WORLD MAPS
                                      129–224

WORLD STATISTICS: COUNTRIES

This alphabetical list includes the principal countries and territories of the world. If a territory is not completely independent, the country it is associated with is named. The area figures give the total area of land, inland water, and ice. The population figures are 2008 estimates where available. The annual income is the Gross Domestic Product per capita in US dollars. The figures are the latest available, usually 2008 estimates.

Country/Territory	Area km² Thousands	Area miles² Thousands	Population Thousands	Capital	Annual Income US $
Afghanistan	652	252	32,738	Kabul	800
Albania	28.7	11.1	3,620	Tirana	6,000
Algeria	2,382	920	33,770	Algiers	7,000
American Samoa (US)	0.20	0.08	65	Pago Pago	8,000
Andorra	0.47	0.18	83	Andorra La Vella	42,500
Angola	1,247	481	12,531	Luanda	8,800
Anguilla (UK)	0.10	0.04	14	The Valley	8,800
Antigua & Barbuda	0.44	0.17	85	St John's	19,000
Argentina	2,780	1,074	40,482	Buenos Aires	14,200
Armenia	29.8	11.5	2,969	Yerevan	6,400
Aruba (Netherlands)	0.19	0.07	102	Oranjestad	21,800
Australia	7,741	2,989	21,007	Canberra	38,100
Austria	83.9	32.4	8,206	Vienna	39,200
Azerbaijan	86.6	33.4	8,178	Baku	9,000
Azores (Portugal)	2.2	0.86	236	Ponta Delgada	15,000
Bahamas	13.9	5.4	307	Nassau	28,600
Bahrain	0.69	0.27	718	Manama	37,200
Bangladesh	144	55.6	153,547	Dhaka	1,500
Barbados	0.43	0.17	282	Bridgetown	19,300
Belarus	208	80.2	9,686	Minsk	11,800
Belgium	30.5	11.8	10,404	Brussels	37,500
Belize	23.0	8.9	301	Belmopan	8,600
Benin	113	43.5	9,248	Porto-Novo	1,500
Bermuda (UK)	0.05	0.02	67	Hamilton	69,900
Bhutan	47.0	18.1	682	Thimphu	5,600
Bolivia	1,099	424	9,248	La Paz/Sucre	4,500
Bosnia-Herzegovina	51.2	19.8	4,590	Sarajevo	6,500
Botswana	582	225	1,842	Gaborone	13,300
Brazil	8,514	3,287	196,343	Brasília	10,100
Brunei	5.8	2.2	381	Bandar Seri Begawan	53,100
Bulgaria	111	42.8	7,263	Sofia	12,900
Burkina Faso	274	106	15,265	Ouagadougou	1,200
Burma (= Myanmar)	677	261	47,758	Rangoon/Naypyidaw	1,200
Burundi	27.8	10.7	8,691	Bujumbura	400
Cambodia	181	69.9	14,242	Phnom Penh	2,000
Cameroon	475	184	18,468	Yaoundé	2,300
Canada	9,971	3,850	33,213	Ottawa	39,300
Canary Is. (Spain)	7.2	2.8	1,682	Las Palmas/Santa Cruz	19,900
Cape Verde Is.	4.0	1.6	427	Praia	3,800
Cayman Is. (UK)	0.26	0.10	48	George Town	43,800
Central African Republic	623	241	4,444	Bangui	700
Chad	1,284	496	10,111	Ndjaména	1,600
Chile	757	292	16,454	Santiago	14,900
China	9,597	3,705	1,330,045	Beijing	6,000
Colombia	1,139	440	45,014	Bogotá	8,900
Comoros	2.2	0.86	732	Moroni	1,000
Congo	342	132	3,903	Brazzaville	4,000
Congo (Dem. Rep. of the)	2,345	905	66,515	Kinshasa	300
Cook Is. (NZ)	0.24	0.09	12	Avarua	9,100
Costa Rica	51.1	19.7	4,196	San José	11,600
Croatia	56.5	21.8	4,492	Zagreb	16,100
Cuba	111	42.8	11,424	Havana	9,500
Cyprus	9.3	3.6	793	Nicosia	28,600
Czech Republic	78.9	30.5	10,221	Prague	26,100
Denmark	43.1	16.6	5,485	Copenhagen	37,400
Djibouti	23.2	9.0	506	Djibouti	3,700
Dominica	0.75	0.29	73	Roseau	9,900
Dominican Republic	48.5	18.7	9,507	Santo Domingo	8,100
East Timor	14.9	5.7	1,109	Dili	2,400
Ecuador	284	109	13,928	Quito	7,500
Egypt	1,001	387	81,714	Cairo	5,400
El Salvador	21.0	8.1	7,066	San Salvador	6,200
Equatorial Guinea	28.1	10.8	616	Malabo	4,100
Eritrea	118	45.4	5,502	Asmara	700
Estonia	45.1	17.4	1,308	Tallinn	21,200
Ethiopia	1,104	426	82,545	Addis Ababa	800
Faroe Is. (Denmark)	1.4	0.54	49	Tórshavn	31,000
Fiji	18.3	7.1	932	Suva	3,900
Finland	338	131	5,245	Helsinki	37,200
France	552	213	64,148	Paris	32,700
French Guiana (France)	90.0	34.7	200	Cayenne	8,300
French Polynesia (France)	4.0	1.5	283	Papeete	18,000
Gabon	268	103	1,486	Libreville	14,400
Gambia, The	11.3	4.4	1,735	Banjul	1,300
Gaza Strip (OPT)*	0.36	0.14	1,500	–	2,900
Georgia	69.7	26.9	4,631	Tbilisi	4,700
Germany	357	138	82,370	Berlin	34,800
Ghana	239	92.1	23,383	Accra	1,500
Gibraltar (UK)	0.006	0.002	28	Gibraltar Town	38,200
Greece	132	50.9	10,723	Athens	32,000
Greenland (Denmark)	2,176	840	58	Nuuk	20,000
Grenada	0.34	0.13	90	St George's	13,400
Guadeloupe (France)	1.7	0.66	453	Basse-Terre	7,900
Guam (US)	0.55	0.21	176	Agana	15,000
Guatemala	109	42.0	13,002	Guatemala City	5,200
Guinea	246	94.9	9,807	Conakry	1,100
Guinea-Bissau	36.1	13.9	1,503	Bissau	600
Guyana	215	83.0	771	Georgetown	3,900
Haiti	27.8	10.7	8,925	Port-au-Prince	1,300
Honduras	112	43.3	7,639	Tegucigalpa	4,400
Hungary	93.0	35.9	9,931	Budapest	19,800
Iceland	103	39.8	304	Reykjavik	39,900
India	3,287	1,269	1,147,996	New Delhi	2,800
Indonesia	1,905	735	237,512	Jakarta	3,900
Iran	1,648	636	65,875	Tehran	12,800
Iraq	438	169	28,221	Baghdad	4,000
Ireland	70.3	27.1	4,156	Dublin	46,200
Israel	20.6	8.0	7,112	Jerusalem	28,200
Italy	301	116	58,145	Rome	31,000
Ivory Coast (= Côte d'Ivoire)	322	125	20,180	Yamoussoukro	1,700
Jamaica	11.0	4.2	2,804	Kingston	7,400
Japan	378	146	127,288	Tokyo	34,200
Jordan	89.3	34.5	6,199	Amman	5,000
Kazakhstan	2,725	1,052	15,341	Astana	11,500
Kenya	580	224	37,954	Nairobi	1,600
Kiribati	0.73	0.28	110	Tarawa	3,200
Korea, North	121	46.5	23,479	Pyŏngyang	1,700
Korea, South	99.3	38.3	48,379	Seoul	26,000
Kosovo	10.9	4.2	2,127	Pristina	2,300
Kuwait	17.8	6.9	2,597	Kuwait City	57,400
Kyrgyzstan	200	77.2	5,357	Bishkek	2,100
Laos	237	91.4	6,678	Vientiane	2,100
Latvia	64.6	24.9	2,245	Riga	17,800
Lebanon	10.4	4.0	3,972	Beirut	11,100
Lesotho	30.4	11.7	2,128	Maseru	1,600
Liberia	111	43.0	3,335	Monrovia	500
Libya	1,760	679	6,174	Tripoli	14,400
Liechtenstein	0.16	0.06	34	Vaduz	25,000
Lithuania	65.2	25.2	3,565	Vilnius	17,700
Luxembourg	2.6	1.0	486	Luxembourg	81,100
Macedonia (FYROM)	25.7	9.9	2,061	Skopje	9,000
Madagascar	587	227	20,043	Antananarivo	1,000
Madeira (Portuga)	0.78	0.30	241	Funchal	22,700
Malawi	118	45.7	13,932	Lilongwe	800
Malaysia	330	127	25,274	Kuala Lumpur/Putrajaya	15,300
Maldives	0.30	0.12	386	Malé	3,900
Mali	1,240	479	12,324	Bamako	5,000
Malta	0.32	0.12	404	Valletta	24,200
Marshall Is.	0.18	0.07	63	Majuro	2,500
Martinique (France)	1.1	0.43	436	Fort-de-France	14,400
Mauritania	1,026	396	3,365	Nouakchott	2,100
Mauritius	2.0	0.79	1,274	Port Louis	12,100
Mayotte (France)	0.37	0.14	216	Mamoudzou	4,900
Mexico	1,958	756	109,955	Mexico City	14,200
Micronesia, Fed. States of	0.70	0.27	108	Palikir	2,200
Moldova	33.9	13.1	4,324	Chişinău	2,500
Monaco	0.001	0.0004	33	Monaco	30,000
Mongolia	1,567	605	2,996	Ulan Bator	3,200
Montenegro	14.0	5.4	678	Podgorica	9,700
Morocco	447	172	34,343	Rabat	4,000
Mozambique	802	309	21,285	Maputo	900
Namibia	824	318	2,089	Windhoek	5,400
Nauru	0.02	0.008	14	Yaren District	5,000
Nepal	147	56.8	29,519	Katmandu	1,100
Netherlands	41.5	16.0	16,645	Amsterdam/The Hague	40,300
Netherlands Antilles (Neths)	0.80	0.31	225	Willemstad	16,000
New Caledonia (France)	18.6	7.2	225	Nouméa	15,000
New Zealand	271	104	4,173	Wellington	27,900
Nicaragua	130	50.2	5,786	Managua	2,900
Niger	1,267	489	13,273	Niamey	700
Nigeria	924	357	146,255	Abuja	2,300
Northern Mariana Is. (US)	0.46	0.18	87	Saipan	12,500
Norway	324	125	4,644	Oslo	55,200
Oman	310	119	3,312	Muscat	20,200
Pakistan	796	307	172,800	Islamabad	2,600
Palau	0.46	0.18	21	Melekeok	8,100
Panama	75.5	29.2	3,310	Panamá	11,600
Papua New Guinea	463	179	5,932	Port Moresby	2,200
Paraguay	407	157	6,831	Asunción	4,200
Peru	1,285	496	29,181	Lima	8,400
Philippines	300	116	96,062	Manila	3,300
Poland	323	125	38,501	Warsaw	17,300
Portugal	88.8	34.3	10,677	Lisbon	22,000
Puerto Rico (US)	8.9	3.4	3,958	San Juan	17,800
Qatar	11.0	4.2	825	Doha	29,400
Réunion (France)	2.5	0.97	788	St-Denis	6,200
Romania	238	92.0	22,247	Bucharest	12,200
Russia	17,075	6,593	140,702	Moscow	15,800
Rwanda	26.3	10.2	10,186	Kigali	900
St Kitts & Nevis	0.26	0.10	40	Basseterre	19,700
St Lucia	0.54	0.21	160	Castries	11,300
St Vincent & Grenadines	0.39	0.15	118	Kingstown	10,500
Samoa	2.8	1.1	217	Apia	4,900
San Marino	0.06	0.02	30	San Marino	41,900
São Tomé & Príncipe	0.96	0.37	206	São Tomé	1,300
Saudi Arabia	2,150	830	28,147	Riyadh	20,700
Senegal	197	76.0	12,147	Dakar	1,600
Serbia	77.5	29.9	10,159	Belgrade	10,900
Seychelles	0.46	0.18	82	Victoria	17,000
Sierra Leone	71.7	27.7	6,295	Freetown	700
Singapore	0.68	0.26	4,608	Singapore City	52,000
Slovak Republic	49.0	18.9	5,455	Bratislava	21,900
Slovenia	20.3	7.8	2,008	Ljubljana	29,500
Solomon Is.	28.9	11.2	581	Honiara	1,900
Somalia	638	246	9,559	Mogadishu	600
South Africa	1,221	471	48,783	Cape Town/Pretoria	10,000
Spain	498	192	40,491	Madrid	34,600
Sri Lanka	65.6	25.3	21,129	Colombo	4,300
Sudan	2,506	967	40,218	Khartoum	2,200
Suriname	163	63.0	476	Paramaribo	8,900
Swaziland	17.4	6.7	1,129	Mbabane	5,100
Sweden	450	174	9,045	Stockholm	38,500
Switzerland	41.3	15.9	7,582	Bern	40,900
Syria	185	71.5	19,748	Damascus	4,800
Taiwan	36.0	13.9	22,921	Taipei	31,900
Tajikistan	143	55.3	7,212	Dushanbe	2,100
Tanzania	945	365	40,213	Dodoma	1,300
Thailand	513	198	65,493	Bangkok	8,500
Togo	56.8	21.9	5,859	Lomé	900
Tonga	0.65	0.25	119	Nuku'alofa	4,600
Trinidad & Tobago	5.1	2.0	1,231	Port of Spain	18,600
Tunisia	164	63.2	10,384	Tunis	7,900
Turkey	775	299	71,893	Ankara	12,000
Turkmenistan	488	188	5,180	Ashkhabad	6,100
Turks & Caicos Is. (UK)	0.43	0.17	22	Cockburn Town	11,500
Tuvalu	0.03	0.01	12	Fongafale	1,600
Uganda	241	93.1	31,368	Kampala	1,100
Ukraine	604	233	45,994	Kiev	6,900
United Arab Emirates	83.6	32.3	4,621	Abu Dhabi	40,000
United Kingdom	242	93.4	60,944	London	36,600
United States of America	9,629	3,718	303,825	Washington, DC	47,000
Uruguay	175	67.6	3,478	Montevideo	12,200
Uzbekistan	447	173	27,345	Tashkent	2,600
Vanuatu	12.2	4.7	215	Port-Vila	4,600
Venezuela	912	352	26,415	Caracas	13,500
Vietnam	332	128	86,117	Hanoi	2,800
Virgin Is. (UK)	0.15	0.06	24	Road Town	38,500
Virgin Is. (US)	0.35	0.13	110	Charlotte Amalie	14,500
Wallis & Futuna Is. (France)	0.20	0.08	15	Mata-Utu	3,800
West Bank (OPT)*	5.9	2.3	2,408	–	2,900
Western Sahara	266	103	394	El Aaiún	2,500
Yemen	528	204	23,013	Sana'	2,400
Zambia	753	291	11,670	Lusaka	1,500
Zimbabwe	391	151	11,350	Harare	200

*OPT = Occupied Palestinian Territory

World Statistics: Cities

This list shows the principal cities with more than 750,000 inhabitants. The figures are taken from the most recent census or estimate available, usually 2007, and as far as possible are the population of the metropolitan area or urban agglomeration (for example, greater New York, Mexico, or Paris). All the figures are in thousands. Local name forms have been used for the smaller cities (for example, Thessaloniki).

AFGHANISTAN	
Kabul	3,288
ALGERIA	
Algiers	3,260
ANGOLA	
Luanda	2,839
ARGENTINA	
Buenos Aires	13,349
Córdoba	1,592
Rosario	1,312
Mendoza	1,072
San Miguel de Tucumán	837
ARMENIA	
Yerevan	1,103
AUSTRALIA	
Sydney	4,388
Melbourne	3,663
Brisbane	1,769
Perth	1,484
Adelaide	1,137
AUSTRIA	
Vienna	2,260
AZERBAIJAN	
Baku	1,856
BANGLADESH	
Dhaka	12,560
Chittagong	4,171
Khulna	1,497
Rajshahi	1,035
BELARUS	
Minsk	1,778
BELGIUM	
Brussels	1,012
BOLIVIA	
La Paz	1,533
Santa Cruz	1,352
Cochabamba	797
BRAZIL	
São Paulo	18,333
Rio de Janeiro	11,469
Belo Horizonte	5,304
Pôrto Alegre	3,795
Recife	3,527
Brasília	3,341
Salvador	3,331
Fortaleza	3,261
Curitiba	2,871
Campinas	2,640
Belém	2,097
Goiânia	1,878
Manaus	1,673
Santos	1,634
Vitória	1,602
Maceió	1,137
Natal	1,049
São Luís	982
São José dos Campos	972
João Pessoa	931
Teresina	895
Campo Grande	821
BULGARIA	
Sofia	1,093
BURKINA FASO	
Ouagadougou	870
BURMA (MYANMAR)	
Rangoon	4,107
Mandalay	927
CAMBODIA	
Phnom Penh	1,364
CAMEROON	
Douala	1,980
Yaoundé	1,727
CANADA	
Toronto	5,312
Montréal	3,640
Vancouver	2,188
Ottawa	1,156
Calgary	1,058
Edmonton	1,015
CHILE	
Santiago	5,683
CHINA	
Shanghai	14,503
Beijing	10,717
Guangzhou	8,425
Shenzhen	7,233
Wuhan	7,093
Hong Kong	7,041
Tianjin	7,040
Chongqing	6,363
Shenyang	4,720
Dongguan	4,320
Chengdu	4,065
Xi'an	3,926
Harbin	3,695
Nanjing	3,621
Guiyang	3,447
Dalian	3,073
Changchun	3,046
Zibo	2,982
Kunming	2,837
Hangzhou	2,831
Qingdao	2,817
Taiyuan	2,794
Jinan	2,743
Zhengzhou	2,590
Fuzhou	2,453
Changsha	2,451
Lanzhou	2,411
Xiamen	2,371
Shijiazhuang	2,275
Jinxi	2,268
Jilin	2,255
Wenzhou	2,212
Nanchang	2,188
Zaozhuang	2,096
Nanchong	2,046
Nanning	2,040
Linyi	2,035
Ürümqi	2,025
Yantai	1,991
Wanxian	1,963
Xuzhou	1,960
Baotou	1,920
Hefei	1,916
Suzhou	1,849
Nanyang	1,830
Tangshan	1,825
Ningbo	1,810
Datong	1,763
Yancheng	1,678
Tianmen	1,676
Shangqiu	1,650
Lu'an	1,647
Wuxi	1,646
Luoyang	1,644
Hohhot	1,644
Anshan	1,611
Qiqihar	1,607
Tai'an	1,598
Daqing	1,594
Xinghua	1,587
Pingxiang	1,562
Handan	1,535
Xiantao	1,528
Zhanjiang	1,514
Weifang	1,498
Shantou	1,495
Fushun	1,456
Xianyang	1,450
Luzhou	1,447
Neijiang	1,441
Changde	1,429
Huainan	1,420
Liuzhou	1,409
Suining, Sichuan	1,401
Quanzhou	1,377
Xintai	1,334
Mianyang	1,322
Heze	1,318
Yiyang	1,318
Yueyang	1,286
Suqian	1,258
Changzhou	1,249
Huaian	1,243
Chifeng	1,238
Jingmen	1,228
Yuzhou	1,226
Zaoyang	1,210
Huzhou	1,203
Tianshui	1,199
Yongzhou	1,182
Mudanjiang	1,171
Liupanshui	1,149
Leshan	1,143
Jining, Shandong	1,143
Xiaoshan	1,130
Yixing	1,129
Zigong	1,087
Xianyang	1,072
Fuyu	1,068
Yulin	1,060
Baoding	1,042
Xinyi, Jiangsu	1,022
Zhuzhou	1,016
Jixi	1,012
Linqing	1,009
Jiamusi	1,006
Xiangfan	1,006
Zhangjiakou	1,001
Benxi	967
Xiangxiang	936
Zhangjiagang	936
Xinyu	932
Yichun, Heilongjiang	916
Yichun, Jiangxi	890
Jinzhou	888
Zhaotong	879
Yuyao	876
Anshun	864
Hengyang	853
Xuanzhou	851
Tongliao	847
Huaibei	830
Jiaxing	817
Kaifeng	810
Fuxin	807
Hunjiang	798
COLOMBIA	
Bogotá	7,594
Medellín	3,236
Cali	2,583
Barranquilla	1,918
Bucaramanga	1,069
Cartagena	1,002
Cúcuta	883
CONGO	
Brazzaville	1,173
CONGO (DEM. REP. OF THE)	
Kinshasa	6,049
Kolwezi	1,207
Lubumbashi	1,179
Mbuji-Mayi	1,024
COSTA RICA	
San José	1,217
CROATIA	
Zagreb	1,067
CUBA	
Havana	2,192
CZECH REPUBLIC	
Prague	1,171
DENMARK	
Copenhagen	1,091
DOMINICAN REPUBLIC	
Santo Domingo	2,563
Santiago de los Caballeros	804
ECUADOR	
Guayaquil	2,387
Quito	1,514
EGYPT	
Cairo	11,146
Alexandria	3,760
Shubrâ el Kheima	937
EL SALVADOR	
San Salvador	1,517
ETHIOPIA	
Addis Ababa	2,899
FINLAND	
Helsinki	1,091
FRANCE	
Paris	9,820
Lyons	1,403
Marseilles	1,382
Lille	1,029
Nice	889
Toulouse	761
Bordeaux	754
GEORGIA	
Tbilisi	1,406
GERMANY	
Berlin	3,389
Hamburg	1,740
Munich	1,263
Cologne	963
GHANA	
Accra	1,981
Kumasi	1,517
GREECE	
Athens	3,238
Thessaloniki	824
GUATEMALA	
Guatemala City	3,242
GUINEA	
Conakry	1,465
HAITI	
Port-au-Prince	2,129
HONDURAS	
Tegucigalpa	1,061
HUNGARY	
Budapest	1,693
INDIA	
Mumbai	18,336
Delhi	15,334
Kolkata	14,299
Chennai	6,915
Bangalore	6,532
Hyderabad	6,145
Ahmedabad	5,171
Pune	4,485
Surat	3,671
Kanpur	3,040
Jaipur	2,796
Lucknow	2,589
Nagpur	2,359
Patna	2,066
Indore	1,941
Vadodara	1,686
Bhopal	1,656
Coimbatore	1,628
Ludhiana	1,583
Agra	1,526
Vishakhapatnam	1,468
Cochin	1,461
Nashik	1,408
Meerut	1,340
Faridabad	1,330
Varanasi	1,300
Ghaziabad	1,277
Asansol	1,272
Jamshedpur	1,246
Madurai	1,245
Jabalpur	1,234
Rajkot	1,205
Dhanbad	1,195
Amritsar	1,162
Allahabad	1,153
Vijayawada	1,093
Srinagar	1,093
Aurangabad	1,065
Bhilainagar-Durg	1,051
Solapur	1,012
Ranchi	999
Jodhpur	954
Guwahati	941
Gwalior	939
Trivandrum	918
Calicut	917
Tiruchchirapalli	913
Chandigarh	896
Hubli-Dharwad	854
Mysore	851
INDONESIA	
Jakarta	13,215
Bandung	4,126
Surabaya	2,992
Medan	2,287
Palembang	1,733
Ujung Pandang	1,284
Bandar Lampung	915
Malang	898
Tegal	898
Semarang	816
Bogor	761
IRAN	
Tehran	7,352
Mashhad	2,147
Esfahan	1,547
Tabriz	1,396
Karaj	1,235
Shiraz	1,230
Qom	1,045
Ahvaz	967
Bakhtaran	771
IRAQ	
Baghdad	5,910
Mosul	1,236
Basra	1,187
Irbil	840
IRELAND	
Dublin	1,037
ISRAEL	
Tel Aviv-Yafo	3,025
Haifa	948
ITALY	
Rome	3,348
Milan	2,953
Naples	2,245
Turin	1,660
Genoa	803
IVORY COAST (CÔTE D'IVOIRE)	
Abidjan	3,516
JAPAN	
Tokyo	12,064
Yokohama	6,427
Osaka	2,599
Nagoya	2,172
Sapporo	1,922
Kobe	1,493
Kyoto	1,468
Fukuoka	1,341
Kawasaki	1,250
Hiroshima	1,126
Kitakyushu	1,011
Sendai	1,008
Chiba	887
Sakai	792
JORDAN	
Amman	1,292
KAZAKHSTAN	
Almaty	1,156
KENYA	
Nairobi	2,818
KOREA, NORTH	
Pyŏngyang	3,351
N'ampo	1,102
Hamhung	821
KOREA, SOUTH	
Seoul	9,888
Busan	3,830
Incheon	2,884
Daegu	2,675
Daejeon	1,522
Gwangju	1,379
Seongnam	1,353
Ulsan	1,340
Ansan	984
Pucheon	900
Suwon	876
Pohang	790
KUWAIT	
Kuwait City	1,810
KYRGYZSTAN	
Bishkek	828
LATVIA	
Riga	719
LEBANON	
Beirut	2,070
LIBYA	
Tripoli	2,098
Benghazi	1,114
MADAGASCAR	
Antananarivo	1,808
MALAYSIA	
Kuala Lumpur	1,405
MALI	
Bamako	1,379
MEXICO	
Mexico City	19,013
Guadalajara	3,905
Monterrey	3,517
Toluca	1,987
Puebla	1,880
Tijuana	1,570
Ciudad Juárez	1,469
León	1,438
Torreón	1,057
San Luis Potosí	927
Mérida	919
Querétaro	913
Mexicali	840
Culiacán	799
MONGOLIA	
Ulan Bator	842
MOROCCO	
Casablanca	3,743
Rabat	1,859
Fès	1,032
Marrakesh	951
MOZAMBIQUE	
Maputo	1,316
NEPAL	
Katmandu	1,176
NETHERLANDS	
Amsterdam	1,157
Rotterdam	1,112
NEW ZEALAND	
Auckland	1,152
NICARAGUA	
Managua	1,165
NIGER	
Niamey	997
NIGERIA	
Lagos	11,135
Kano	2,884
Ibadan	2,375
Kaduna	1,329
Benin City	1,022
Ogbomosho	959
Port Harcourt	942
NORWAY	
Oslo	808
PAKISTAN	
Karachi	11,819
Lahore	6,373
Faisalabad	2,533
Rawalpindi	1,794
Gujranwala	1,466
Multan	1,459
Hyderabad	1,392
Peshawar	1,255
Islamabad	791
PANAMA	
Panamá	1,216
PARAGUAY	
Asunción	1,858
PERU	
Lima	8,180
PHILIPPINES	
Manila	10,677
Davao	1,326
POLAND	
Warsaw	1,680
Lódz	815
PORTUGAL	
Lisbon	2,761
Porto	1,309
PUERTO RICO	
San Juan	2,604
ROMANIA	
Bucharest	1,934
RUSSIA	
Moscow	10,672
Saint Petersburg	5,315
Novosibirsk	1,425
Nizhniy Novgorod	1,288
Yekaterinburg	1,281
Samara	1,140
Omsk	1,132
Kazan	1,108
Rostov	1,081
Chelyabinsk	1,067
Ufa	1,035
Volgograd	1,016
Perm	1,014
Voronezh	918
Saratov	881
Simbirsk	864
Krasnoyarsk	840
Togliatti	771
SAUDI ARABIA	
Riyadh	5,514
Jedda	3,807
Mecca	1,529
Medina	1,044
Dammam	920
SENEGAL	
Dakar	2,313
SERBIA	
Belgrade	1,116
SIERRA LEONE	
Freetown	1,007
SINGAPORE	
Singapore City	4,372
SOMALIA	
Mogadishu	1,320
SOUTH AFRICA	
Johannesburg	3,254
Cape Town	3,083
Durban	2,631
Pretoria	1,271
Vereeniging	1,027
Port Elizabeth	1,006
SPAIN	
Madrid	5,608
Barcelona	4,795
SUDAN	
Khartoum	4,518
SWEDEN	
Stockholm	1,729
Gothenburg	829
SWITZERLAND	
Zürich	1,144
SYRIA	
Aleppo	2,505
Damascus	2,317
Homs	915
TAIWAN	
Taipei	2,606
Kaohsiung	1,515
T'aichung	1,033
TANZANIA	
Dar es Salaam	2,683
THAILAND	
Bangkok	6,604
TOGO	
Lomé	1,337
TUNISIA	
Tunis	2,063
TURKEY	
Istanbul	9,712
Ankara	3,573
Izmir	2,487
Bursa	1,414
Adana	1,245
Gaziantep	862
Konya	761
UGANDA	
Kampala	1,345
UKRAINE	
Kiev	2,621
Kharkov	1,521
Dnepropetrovsk	1,122
Donetsk	1,065
Odessa	1,027
Zaporozhye	863
Lvov	794
UNITED ARAB EMIRATES	
Dubai	1,330
Abu Dhabi	928
UNITED KINGDOM	
London	8,505
Birmingham	2,280
Manchester	2,228
Liverpool	1,519
Glasgow	1,159
UNITED STATES OF AMERICA	
New York	18,718
Los Angeles	12,298
Chicago	8,814
Miami	5,434
Philadelphia	5,392
Dallas–Fort Worth	4,655
Boston	4,361
Houston	4,320
Atlanta	4,304
Washington	4,238
Detroit	4,034
Phoenix–Mesa	3,416
San Francisco	3,385
Seattle	2,989
San Diego	2,852
Minneapolis–St Paul	2,556
Tampa–St Petersburg	2,252
Denver	2,239
Baltimore	2,205
St Louis	2,159
Cleveland	1,855
Portland	1,810
Pittsburgh	1,806
Las Vegas	1,720
San Bernardino	1,690
San Jose	1,631
Cincinnati	1,599
Sacramento	1,555
Norfolk–Virginia Beach	1,460
Kansas City	1,437
San Antonio	1,436
Indianapolis	1,387
Milwaukee	1,316
Orlando	1,306
Providence	1,248
Columbus	1,236
Austin	1,107
Memphis	1,053
New Orleans	1,010
Buffalo	977
Stamford	889
Salt Lake City	888
Jacksonville	882
Louisville	864
Hartford	852
Richmond	819
Charlotte	759
URUGUAY	
Montevideo	1,353
UZBEKISTAN	
Tashkent	2,181
VENEZUELA	
Caracas	3,276
Valencia	2,330
Maracaibo	2,182
Maracay	1,138
Ciudad Guayana	966
Barquisimeto	923
VIETNAM	
Ho Chi Minh City	5,065
Hanoi	4,164
Haiphong	1,873
YEMEN	
Sana'	1,801
ZAMBIA	
Lusaka	1,450
ZIMBABWE	
Harare	1,527
Bulawayo	824

WORLD STATISTICS: CLIMATE

Rainfall and temperature figures are provided for more than 70 cities around the world. As climate is affected by altitude, the height of each city is shown in meters beneath its name. For each location, the top row of figures shows the total rainfall or snow in millimeters, and the bottom row the average temperature in degrees Celsius; the average annual temperature and total annual rainfall are at the end of the rows. The map opposite shows the city locations.

CITY	JAN.	FEB.	MAR.	APR.	MAY	JUNE	JULY	AUG.	SEPT.	OCT.	NOV.	DEC.	YEAR
EUROPE													
Athens, Greece	62	37	37	23	23	14	6	7	15	51	56	71	402
107 m	10	10	12	16	20	25	28	28	24	20	15	11	18
Berlin, Germany	42	33	41	37	54	69	56	58	45	37	44	55	571
55 m	-1	0	4	9	14	17	19	18	15	9	5	1	9
Istanbul, Turkey	87	71	63	43	33	25	24	24	44	71	85	107	655
14 m	5	6	7	11	16	20	23	23	20	16	12	8	14
Lisbon, Portugal	111	110	69	54	44	16	3	4	33	62	93	103	702
77 m	11	12	14	16	17	20	22	23	21	18	14	12	17
London, UK	54	40	37	37	46	45	57	59	49	57	64	48	593
5 m	4	5	7	9	12	16	18	17	15	11	8	5	11
Málaga, Spain	61	51	62	46	26	5	1	3	29	64	64	62	474
33 m	12	13	16	17	19	29	25	26	23	20	16	13	18
Moscow, Russia	39	38	36	37	53	58	88	71	58	45	47	54	624
156 m	-13	-10	-4	6	13	16	18	17	12	6	-1	-7	4
Odesa, Ukraine	57	62	30	21	34	34	42	37	37	13	35	71	473
64 m	-3	-1	2	9	15	20	22	22	18	12	9	1	10
Paris, France	56	46	35	42	57	54	59	64	55	50	51	50	619
75 m	3	4	8	11	15	18	20	19	17	12	7	4	12
Rome, Italy	71	62	57	51	46	37	15	21	63	99	129	93	744
17 m	8	9	11	14	18	22	25	25	22	17	13	10	16
Shannon, Ireland	94	67	56	53	61	57	77	79	86	86	96	117	929
2 m	5	5	7	9	12	14	16	16	14	11	8	6	10
Stockholm, Sweden	43	30	25	31	34	45	61	76	60	48	53	48	554
44 m	-3	-3	-1	5	10	15	18	17	12	7	3	0	7
ASIA													
Bahrain	8	18	13	8	3	0	0	0	0	0	18	18	81
5 m	17	18	21	25	29	32	33	34	31	28	24	19	26
Bangkok, Thailand	8	20	36	58	198	160	160	175	305	206	66	5	1,397
2 m	26	28	29	30	29	29	28	28	28	28	26	25	28
Beirut, Lebanon	191	158	94	53	18	3	3	3	5	51	132	185	892
34 m	14	14	16	18	22	24	27	28	26	24	19	16	21
Colombo, Sri Lanka	89	69	147	231	371	224	135	109	160	348	315	147	2,365
7 m	26	26	27	28	28	27	27	27	27	27	26	26	27
Harbin, China	6	5	10	23	43	94	112	104	46	33	8	5	488
160 m	-18	-15	-5	6	13	19	22	21	14	4	-6	-16	3
Ho Chi Minh, Vietnam	15	3	13	43	221	330	315	269	335	269	114	56	1,984
9 m	26	27	29	30	29	28	28	28	27	27	26	28	28
Hong Kong, China	33	46	74	137	292	394	381	361	257	114	43	31	2,162
33 m	16	15	18	22	26	28	28	28	27	25	21	18	23

CITY	JAN.	FEB.	MAR.	APR.	MAY	JUNE	JULY	AUG.	SEPT.	OCT.	NOV.	DEC.	YEAR
ASIA (continued)													
Jakarta, Indonesia	300	300	211	147	114	97	64	43	66	112	142	203	1,798
8 m	26	26	27	27	27	27	27	27	27	27	27	26	27
Kabul, Afghanistan	34	60	68	72	23	1	6	2	2	4	19	22	313
1,815 m	-3	-1	6	13	18	22	25	24	20	14	7	3	12
Karachi, Pakistan	13	10	8	3	3	18	81	41	13	<3	3	5	196
4 m	19	20	24	28	30	31	30	29	28	28	24	20	26
Kazalinsk, Kazakhstan	10	10	13	13	15	5	5	8	8	10	13	15	125
63 m	-12	-11	-3	6	18	23	25	23	16	8	-1	-7	7
Kolkata, India	10	31	36	43	140	297	325	328	252	114	20	5	1,600
6 m	20	22	27	30	30	30	29	29	29	28	23	19	26
Mumbai, India	3	3	3	3	18	485	617	340	264	64	13	3	1,809
11 m	24	24	26	28	30	29	27	27	27	28	27	26	27
New Delhi, India	23	18	13	8	13	74	180	172	117	10	3	10	640
218 m	14	17	23	28	33	34	31	30	29	26	20	15	25
Omsk, Russia	15	8	8	13	31	51	51	51	28	25	18	20	318
85 m	-22	-19	-12	-1	10	16	18	16	10	1	-11	-18	-1
Shanghai, China	48	58	84	94	94	180	147	142	130	71	51	36	1,135
7 m	4	5	9	14	20	24	28	28	23	19	12	7	16
Singapore	252	173	193	188	173	173	170	196	178	208	254	257	2,413
10 m	26	27	28	28	28	28	28	27	27	27	27	27	27
Tehran, Iran	46	38	46	36	13	3	3	3	3	8	20	31	246
1,220 m	2	5	9	16	21	26	30	29	25	18	12	6	17
Tokyo, Japan	48	74	107	135	147	165	142	152	234	208	97	56	1,565
6 m	3	4	7	13	17	21	25	26	23	17	11	6	14
Ulan Bator, Mongolia	3	3	3	5	10	28	76	51	23	5	5	3	208
1,325 m	-26	-21	-13	-1	6	14	16	14	8	-1	-13	-22	-3
Verkhoyansk, Russia	5	5	3	5	8	23	28	25	13	8	8	5	134
100 m	-50	-45	-32	-15	0	12	14	9	2	-15	-38	-48	-17
AFRICA													
Addis Ababa, Ethiopia	3	3	25	135	213	201	206	239	102	28	3	0	1,151
2,450 m	19	20	20	20	19	18	18	19	21	22	21	20	20
Antananarivo, Madag.	300	279	178	53	18	8	8	10	18	61	135	287	1,356
1,372 m	21	21	21	19	18	15	14	15	17	19	21	21	19
Cairo, Egypt	5	4	4	1	1	0	0	0	0	1	4	6	26
116 m	13	15	18	21	25	28	28	28	26	24	20	15	22
Cape Town, S. Africa	15	8	18	48	79	84	89	66	43	31	18	10	508
17 m	21	21	20	17	14	13	12	13	14	16	18	19	17
Jo'burg, S. Africa	114	109	89	38	25	8	8	8	23	56	107	125	709
1,665 m	20	20	18	16	13	10	11	13	16	18	19	20	16

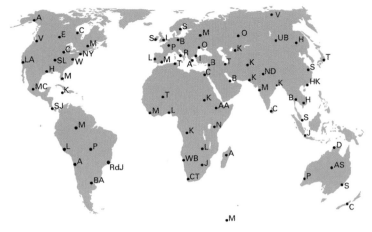

CITY	JAN.	FEB.	MAR.	APR.	MAY	JUNE	JULY	AUG.	SEPT.	OCT.	NOV.	DEC.	YEAR
AFRICA (continued)													
Khartoum, Sudan	3	3	3	3	3	8	53	71	18	5	3	0	158
390 m	24	25	28	31	33	34	32	31	32	32	28	25	29
Kinshasa, Congo (D.R.)	135	145	196	196	158	8	3	3	31	119	221	142	1,354
325 m	26	26	27	27	26	24	23	24	25	26	26	26	25
Lagos, Nigeria	28	46	102	150	269	460	279	64	140	206	69	25	1,836
3 m	27	28	29	28	28	26	26	25	26	26	28	28	27
Lusaka, Zambia	231	191	142	18	3	3	3	0	3	10	91	150	836
1,277 m	21	22	21	21	19	16	16	18	22	24	23	22	21
Monrovia, Liberia	31	56	97	216	516	973	996	373	744	772	236	130	5,138
23 m	26	26	27	27	26	25	24	25	25	25	26	26	26
Nairobi, Kenya	38	64	125	211	158	46	15	23	31	53	109	86	958
820 m	19	19	19	19	18	16	16	16	18	19	18	18	18
Timbuktu, Mali	1	0	0	1	4	16	54	74	29	4	0	0	183
301 m	22	24	28	32	34	35	32	30	32	31	28	23	29
Tunis, Tunisia	64	51	41	36	18	8	3	8	33	51	48	61	419
66 m	10	11	13	16	19	23	26	27	25	20	16	11	18
Walvis Bay, Namibia	3	5	8	3	3	3	3	3	3	3	3	3	23
7 m	19	19	19	18	17	16	15	14	14	15	17	18	18
AUSTRALIA, NEW ZEALAND AND ANTARCTICA													
Alice Springs, Aust.	43	33	28	10	15	13	8	8	8	18	31	38	252
579 m	29	28	25	20	15	12	12	14	18	23	26	28	21
Christchurch, N.Z.	56	43	48	48	66	66	69	48	46	43	48	56	638
10 m	16	16	14	12	9	6	6	7	9	12	14	16	11
Darwin, Australia	386	312	254	97	15	3	3	3	13	51	119	239	1,491
30 m	29	29	29	29	28	26	25	26	28	29	30	29	28
Mawson, Antarctica	11	30	20	10	44	180	4	40	3	20	0	0	362
14 m	0	-5	-10	-14	-15	-16	-18	-18	-19	-13	-5	-1	-11
Perth, Australia	8	10	20	43	130	180	170	149	86	56	20	13	881
60 m	23	23	22	19	16	14	13	13	15	16	19	22	18
Sydney, Australia	89	102	127	135	127	117	117	76	73	71	73	73	1,181
42 m	22	22	21	18	15	13	12	13	15	18	19	21	17
NORTH AMERICA													
Anchorage, USA	20	18	15	10	13	18	41	66	66	56	25	23	371
40 m	-11	-8	-5	2	7	12	14	13	9	2	-5	-11	2
Chicago, USA	51	51	66	71	86	89	84	81	79	66	61	51	836
251 m	-4	-3	2	9	14	20	23	22	19	12	5	-1	10
Churchill, Canada	15	13	18	23	32	44	46	58	51	43	39	21	402
13 m	-28	-26	-20	-10	-2	6	12	11	5	-2	-12	-22	-7
Edmonton, Canada	25	19	19	22	43	77	89	78	39	17	16	25	466
676 m	-15	-10	-5	4	11	15	17	16	11	6	-4	-10	3
Honolulu, USA	104	66	79	48	25	18	23	28	36	48	64	104	643
12 m	23	18	19	20	22	24	25	26	26	24	22	19	22
Houston, USA	89	76	84	91	119	117	99	99	104	94	89	109	1,171
12 m	12	13	17	21	24	27	28	29	26	22	16	12	21

CITY	JAN.	FEB.	MAR.	APR.	MAY	JUNE	JULY	AUG.	SEPT.	OCT.	NOV.	DEC.	YEAR
NORTH AMERICA (continued)													
Kingston, Jamaica	23	15	23	31	102	89	38	91	99	180	74	36	800
34 m	25	25	25	26	26	28	28	28	27	27	26	26	26
Los Angeles, USA	79	76	71	25	10	3	3	3	5	15	31	66	381
95 m	13	14	14	16	17	19	21	22	21	18	16	14	17
Mexico City, Mexico	13	5	10	20	53	119	170	152	130	51	18	8	747
2,309 m	12	13	16	18	19	19	17	18	18	16	14	13	16
Miami, USA	71	53	64	81	173	178	155	160	203	234	71	51	1,516
8 m	20	20	22	23	25	27	28	28	27	25	22	21	24
Montréal, Canada	72	65	74	74	66	82	90	92	88	76	81	87	946
57 m	-10	-9	-3	-6	13	18	21	20	15	9	2	-7	6
New York City, USA	94	97	91	81	81	84	107	109	86	89	76	91	1,092
96 m	-1	-1	3	10	16	20	23	23	21	15	7	2	11
St Louis, USA	58	64	89	97	114	114	89	86	81	74	71	64	1,001
173 m	0	1	7	13	19	24	26	26	22	15	8	2	14
San José, Costa Rica	15	5	20	46	229	241	211	241	305	300	145	41	1,798
1,146 m	19	19	21	21	22	21	21	21	21	20	20	19	20
Vancouver, Canada	154	115	101	60	52	45	32	41	67	114	150	182	1,113
14 m	3	5	6	9	12	15	17	17	14	10	6	4	10
Washington, DC, USA	86	76	91	84	94	99	112	109	94	74	66	79	1,064
22 m	1	2	7	12	18	23	25	24	20	14	8	3	13
SOUTH AMERICA													
Antofagasta, Chile	0	0	0	3	3	3	5	3	3	3	3	0	13
94 m	21	21	20	18	16	15	14	14	15	16	18	19	17
Buenos Aires, Arg.	122	123	154	107	92	50	53	63	78	139	131	103	1,215
27 m	23	23	21	17	13	9	10	11	13	15	19	22	16
Lima, Peru	3	3	3	3	5	5	8	8	8	3	3	3	41
120 m	23	24	24	22	19	17	16	17	18	19	21	22	20
Manaus, Brazil	249	231	262	221	170	84	58	38	46	107	142	203	1,811
44 m	28	28	28	28	28	28	28	28	29	29	29	28	28
Paraná, Brazil	287	236	239	102	13	3	3	5	28	127	231	310	1,582
260 m	23	23	23	23	23	21	21	24	24	24	24	23	23
Rio de Janeiro, Brazil	125	122	130	107	79	53	41	43	66	79	104	137	1,082
61 m	26	26	25	24	22	21	21	21	22	23	23	25	23

WORLD STATISTICS: PHYSICAL DIMENSIONS

Each topic list is divided into continents and within a continent the items are listed in order of size. The bottom part of many of the lists is selective in order to give examples from as many different countries as possible. The order of the continents is as in the atlas, Europe through to South America. The world top ten are shown in square brackets; in the case of mountains this has not been done because the world top 30 are all in Asia. The figures are rounded as appropriate.

WORLD, CONTINENTS, OCEANS

THE WORLD	km²	miles²	%
The World	509,450,000	196,672,000	–
Land	149,450,000	57,688,000	29.3
Water	360,000,000	138,984,000	70.7
Asia	44,500,000	17,177,000	29.8
Africa	30,302,000	11,697,000	20.3
North America	24,241,000	9,357,000	16.2
South America	17,793,000	6,868,000	11.9
Antarctica	14,100,000	5,443,000	9.4
Europe	9,957,000	3,843,000	6.7
Australia & Oceania	8,557,000	3,303,000	5.7
Pacific Ocean	155,557,000	60,061,000	46.4
Atlantic Ocean	76,762,000	29,638,000	22.9
Indian Ocean	68,556,000	26,470,000	20.4
Southern Ocean	20,327,000	7,848,000	6.1
Arctic Ocean	14,056,000	5,427,000	4.2

SEAS

PACIFIC	km²	miles²
South China Sea	2,974,600	1,148,500
Bering Sea	2,268,000	875,000
Sea of Okhotsk	1,528,000	590,000
East China & Yellow	1,249,000	482,000
Sea of Japan	1,008,000	389,000
Gulf of California	162,000	62,500
Bass Strait	75,000	29,000

ATLANTIC	km²	miles²
Caribbean Sea	2,766,000	1,068,000
Mediterranean Sea	2,516,000	971,000
Gulf of Mexico	1,543,000	596,000
Hudson Bay	1,232,000	476,000
North Sea	575,000	223,000
Black Sea	462,000	178,000
Baltic Sea	422,170	163,000
Gulf of St Lawrence	238,000	92,000

INDIAN	km²	miles²
Red Sea	438,000	169,000
Persian Gulf	239,000	92,000

MOUNTAINS

EUROPE		m	ft
Elbrus	Russia	5,642	18,510
Dykh-Tau	Russia	5,205	17,076
Shkhara	Russia/Georgia	5,201	17,064
Koshtan-Tau	Russia	5,152	16,903
Kazbek	Russia/Georgia	5,047	16,558
Pushkin	Russia/Georgia	5,033	16,512
Katyn-Tau	Russia/Georgia	4,979	16,335
Shota Rustaveli	Russia/Georgia	4,860	15,945
Mont Blanc	France/Italy	4,808	15,774
Monte Rosa	Italy/Switzerland	4,634	15,203
Dom	Switzerland	4,545	14,911
Liskamm	Switzerland	4,527	14,852
Weisshorn	Switzerland	4,505	14,780
Taschorn	Switzerland	4,490	14,730
Matterhorn/Cervino	Italy/Switzerland	4,478	14,691
Mont Maudit	France/Italy	4,465	14,649
Dent Blanche	Switzerland	4,356	14,291
Nadelhorn	Switzerland	4,327	14,196
Grandes Jorasses	France/Italy	4,208	13,806
Jungfrau	Switzerland	4,158	13,642
Barre des Ecrins	France	4,103	13,461
Gran Paradiso	Italy	4,061	13,323
Piz Bernina	Italy/Switzerland	4,049	13,284
Eiger	Switzerland	3,970	13,025
Grossglockner	Austria	3,797	12,457
Mulhacén	Spain	3,478	11,411
Etna	Italy	3,340	10,958
Zugspitze	Germany	2,962	9,718
Olympus	Greece	2,917	9,570
Galdhøpiggen	Norway	2,469	8,100
Ben Nevis	UK	1,342	4,403

ASIA		m	ft
Everest	China/Nepal	8,850	29,035
K2 (Godwin Austen)	China/Kashmir	8,611	28,251
Kanchenjunga	India/Nepal	8,598	28,208
Lhotse	China/Nepal	8,516	27,939
Makalu	China/Nepal	8,481	27,824
Cho Oyu	China/Nepal	8,201	26,906
Dhaulagiri	Nepal	8,167	26,795
Manaslu	Nepal	8,156	26,758
Nanga Parbat	Kashmir	8,126	26,660
Annapurna	Nepal	8,078	26,502
Gasherbrum	China/Kashmir	8,068	26,469
Broad Peak	China/Kashmir	8,051	26,414
Xixabangma	China	8,012	26,286
Gayachung Kang	Nepal	7,897	25,909
Himalchuli	Nepal	7,893	25,896
Disteghil Sar	Kashmir	7,885	25,869
Nuptse	Nepal	7,879	25,849
Kangbachen	Nepal	7,858	25,781
Khunyang Chhish	Kashmir	7,852	25,761
Masherbrum	Kashmir	7,821	25,659
Nanda Devi	India	7,817	25,646
Rakaposhi	Kashmir	7,788	25,551
Batura	Kashmir	7,785	25,541
Namche Barwa	China	7,782	25,531
Kamet	India	7,756	25,447
Soltoro Kangri	Pakistan	7,742	25,400
Gurla Mandhata	China	7,728	25,354
Trivor	Pakistan	7,720	25,328
Kongur Shan	China	7,719	25,324
Jannu	Nepal	7,710	25,295
Tirich Mir	Pakistan	7,690	25,229
K'ula Shan	Bhutan/China	7,543	24,747
Pik Imeni Ismail Samani	Tajikistan	7,495	24,590
Demavend	Iran	5,604	18,386
Ararat	Turkey	5,165	16,945
Gunong Kinabalu	Malaysia (Borneo)	4,101	13,455
Yu Shan	Taiwan	3,997	13,113
Fuji-San	Japan	3,776	12,388

AFRICA		m	ft
Kilimanjaro	Tanzania	5,895	19,340
Mt Kenya	Kenya	5,199	17,057
Ruwenzori			
(Margherita)	Uganda/Congo (D.R.)	5,109	16,762
Meru	Tanzania	4,565	14,977
Ras Dashen	Ethiopia	4,533	14,872
Karisimbi	Rwanda/Congo (D.R.)	4,507	14,787
Mt Elgon	Kenya/Uganda	4,321	14,176
Batu	Ethiopia	4,307	14,130
Guna	Ethiopia	4,231	13,882
Toubkal	Morocco	4,165	13,665
Irhil Mgoun	Morocco	4,071	13,356
Mt Cameroun	Cameroon	4,070	13,353
Amba Ferit	Ethiopia	3,875	13,042
Pico del Teide	Spain (Tenerife)	3,718	12,198
Thabana Ntlenyana	Lesotho	3,482	11,424
Emi Koussi	Chad	3,415	11,204
Mt aux Sources	Lesotho/South Africa	3,282	10,768
Mt Piton	Réunion	3,069	10,069

OCEANIA		m	ft
Puncak Jaya	Indonesia	5,029	16,499
Puncak Trikora	Indonesia	4,730	15,518
Puncak Mandala	Indonesia	4,702	15,427
Mt Wilhelm	Papua New Guinea	4,508	14,790
Mauna Kea	USA (Hawai'i)	4,205	13,796
Mauna Loa	USA (Hawai'i)	4,169	13,678
Aoraki Mt Cook	New Zealand	3,753	12,313
Mt Balbi	Solomon Islands	2,439	8,002
Orohena	French Polynesia (Tahiti)	2,241	7,352
Mt Kosciuszko	Australia	2,228	7,310

NORTH AMERICA		m	ft
Mt McKinley			
(Denali)	USA (Alaska)	6,194	20,321
Mt Logan	Canada	5,959	19,551
Pico de Orizaba	Mexico	5,610	18,405
Mt St Elias	USA/Canada	5,489	18,008
Popocatépetl	Mexico	5,452	17,887

NORTH AMERICA (continued)		m	ft
Mt Foraker	USA (Alaska)	5,304	17,401
Iztaccihuatl	Mexico	5,286	17,343
Mt Lucania	Canada	5,226	17,146
Mt Steele	Canada	5,073	16,644
Mt Bona	USA (Alaska)	5,005	16,420
Mt Blackburn	USA (Alaska)	4,996	16,391
Mt Sanford	USA (Alaska)	4,940	16,207
Mt Wood	Canada	4,840	15,880
Nevado de Toluca	Mexico	4,670	15,321
Mt Fairweather	USA (Alaska)	4,663	15,298
Mt Hunter	USA (Alaska)	4,442	14,573
Mt Whitney	USA	4,418	14,495
Mt Elbert	USA	4,399	14,432
Mt Harvard	USA	4,395	14,419
Mt Rainier	USA	4,392	14,409
Blanca Peak	USA	4,372	14,344
Longs Peak	USA	4,345	14,255
Tajumulco	Guatemala	4,220	13,845
Grand Teton	USA	4,197	13,770
Mt Waddington	Canada	4,019	13,186
Mt Robson	Canada	3,959	12,989
Chirripó Grande	Costa Rica	3,837	12,589
Pico Duarte	Dominican Rep.	3,175	10,417

SOUTH AMERICA		m	ft
Aconcagua	Argentina	6,962	22,841
Bonete	Argentina	6,872	22,546
Ojos del Salado	Argentina/Chile	6,863	22,516
Pissis	Argentina	6,779	22,241
Mercedario	Argentina/Chile	6,770	22,211
Huascarán	Peru	6,768	22,205
Llullaillaco	Argentina/Chile	6,723	22,057
Nevado de Cachi	Argentina	6,720	22,047
Yerupaja	Peru	6,632	21,758
Nevado de Tres Cruces	Argentina/Chile	6,620	21,719
Incahuasi	Argentina/Chile	6,601	21,654
Cerro Galan	Argentina	6,600	21,654
Tupungato	Argentina/Chile	6,570	21,555
Sajama	Bolivia	6,520	21,391
Illimani	Bolivia	6,485	21,276
Coropuna	Peru	6,425	21,079
Ausangate	Peru	6,384	20,945
Cerro del Toro	Argentina	6,380	20,932
Siula Grande	Peru	6,356	20,853
Chimborazo	Ecuador	6,267	20,561
Alpamayo	Peru	5,947	19,511
Cotapaxi	Ecuador	5,896	19,344
Pico Cristóbal Colón	Colombia	5,800	19,029
Pico Bolivar	Venezuela	5,007	16,427

ANTARCTICA		m	ft
Vinson Massif		4,897	16,066
Mt Kirkpatrick		4,528	14,855
Mt Markham		4,349	14,268

OCEAN DEPTHS

ATLANTIC OCEAN	m	ft	
Puerto Rico (Milwaukee) Deep	8,604	28,232	[7]
Cayman Trench	7,680	25,197	[10]
Gulf of Mexico	5,203	17,070	
Mediterranean Sea	5,121	16,801	
Black Sea	2,211	7,254	
North Sea	660	2,165	
Baltic Sea	463	1,519	
Hudson Bay	258	846	

INDIAN OCEAN	m	ft	
Java Trench	7,450	24,442	
Red Sea	2,635	8,454	
Persian Gulf	73	239	

PACIFIC OCEAN	m	ft	
Mariana Trench	11,022	36,161	[1]
Tonga Trench	10,882	35,702	[2]
Japan Trench	10,554	34,626	[3]
Kuril Trench	10,542	34,587	[4]
Mindanao Trench	10,497	34,439	[5]
Kermadec Trench	10,047	32,962	[6]

PACIFIC OCEAN (continued)

		m	ft	
Peru–Chile Trench		8,050	26,410	[8]
Aleutian Trench		7,822	25,662	[9]

ARCTIC OCEAN

	m	ft
Molloy Deep	5,608	18,399

SOUTHERN OCEAN

	m	ft
South Sandwich Trench	7,235	23,737

LAND LOWS

		m	ft
Caspian Sea	Europe	−28	−92
Dead Sea	Asia	−418	−1,371
Lake Assal	Africa	−156	−512
Lake Eyre North	Oceania	−16	−52
Death Valley	North America	−86	−282
Laguna del Carbón	South America	−105	−344

RIVERS

EUROPE

		km	miles	
Volga	Caspian Sea	3,700	2,300	
Danube	Black Sea	2,850	1,770	
Ural	Caspian Sea	2,535	1,575	
Dnepr (Dnipro)	Black Sea	2,285	1,420	
Kama	Volga	2,030	1,260	
Don	Black Sea	1,990	1,240	
Petchora	Arctic Ocean	1,790	1,110	
Oka	Volga	1,480	920	
Belaya	Kama	1,420	880	
Dnister (Dniester)	Black Sea	1,400	870	
Vyatka	Kama	1,370	850	
Rhine	North Sea	1,320	820	
N. Dvina	Arctic Ocean	1,290	800	
Desna	Dnepr (Dnipro)	1,190	740	
Elbe	North Sea	1,145	710	
Wisla	Baltic Sea	1,090	675	
Loire	Atlantic Ocean	1,020	635	

ASIA

		km	miles	
Yangtze	Pacific Ocean	6,380	3,960	[3]
Yenisey–Angara	Arctic Ocean	5,550	3,445	[5]
Huang He	Pacific Ocean	5,464	3,395	[6]
Ob–Irtysh	Arctic Ocean	5,410	3,360	[7]
Mekong	Pacific Ocean	4,500	2,795	[9]
Amur	Pacific Ocean	4,442	2,760	
Lena	Arctic Ocean	4,402	2,735	
Irtysh	Ob	4,250	2,640	
Yenisey	Arctic Ocean	4,090	2,540	
Ob	Arctic Ocean	3,680	2,285	
Indus	Indian Ocean	3,100	1,925	
Brahmaputra	Indian Ocean	2,900	1,800	
Syrdarya	Aral Sea	2,860	1,775	
Salween	Indian Ocean	2,800	1,740	
Euphrates	Indian Ocean	2,700	1,675	
Vilyuy	Lena	2,650	1,645	
Kolyma	Arctic Ocean	2,600	1,615	
Amudarya	Aral Sea	2,540	1,578	
Ural	Caspian Sea	2,535	1,575	
Ganges	Indian Ocean	2,510	1,560	
Si Kiang	Pacific Ocean	2,100	1,305	
Irrawaddy	Indian Ocean	2,010	1,250	
Tarim–Yarkand	Lop Nor	2,000	1,240	
Tigris	Indian Ocean	1,900	1,180	

AFRICA

		km	miles	
Nile	Mediterranean	6,695	4,160	[1]
Congo	Atlantic Ocean	4,670	2,900	[8]
Niger	Atlantic Ocean	4,180	2,595	
Zambezi	Indian Ocean	3,540	2,200	
Oubangi/Uele	Congo (D.R.)	2,250	1,400	
Kasai	Congo (D.R.)	1,950	1,210	
Shaballe	Indian Ocean	1,930	1,200	
Orange	Atlantic Ocean	1,860	1,155	
Cubango	Okavango Delta	1,800	1,120	
Limpopo	Indian Ocean	1,770	1,100	
Senegal	Atlantic Ocean	1,640	1,020	
Volta	Atlantic Ocean	1,500	930	

AUSTRALIA

		km	miles
Murray–Darling	Southern Ocean	3,750	2,330
Darling	Murray	3,070	1,905
Murray	Southern Ocean	2,575	1,600
Murrumbidgee	Murray	1,690	1,050

NORTH AMERICA

		km	miles	
Mississippi–Missouri	Gulf of Mexico	5,971	3,710	[4]
Mackenzie	Arctic Ocean	4,240	2,630	
Missouri	Mississippi	4,088	2,540	

NORTH AMERICA (continued)

		km	miles
Mississippi	Gulf of Mexico	3,782	2,350
Yukon	Pacific Ocean	3,185	1,980
Rio Grande	Gulf of Mexico	3,030	1,880
Arkansas	Mississippi	2,340	1,450
Colorado	Pacific Ocean	2,330	1,445
Red	Mississippi	2,040	1,270
Columbia	Pacific Ocean	1,950	1,210
Saskatchewan	Lake Winnipeg	1,940	1,205
Snake	Columbia	1,670	1,040
Churchill	Hudson Bay	1,600	990
Ohio	Mississippi	1,580	980
Brazos	Gulf of Mexico	1,400	870
St Lawrence	Atlantic Ocean	1,170	730

SOUTH AMERICA

		km	miles	
Amazon	Atlantic Ocean	6,450	4,010	[2]
Paraná–Plate	Atlantic Ocean	4,500	2,800	[10]
Purus	Amazon	3,350	2,080	
Madeira	Amazon	3,200	1,990	
São Francisco	Atlantic Ocean	2,900	1,800	
Paraná	Plate	2,800	1,740	
Tocantins	Atlantic Ocean	2,750	1,710	
Orinoco	Atlantic Ocean	2,740	1,700	
Paraguay	Paraná	2,550	1,580	
Pilcomayo	Paraná	2,500	1,550	
Araguaia	Tocantins	2,250	1,400	
Juruá	Amazon	2,000	1,240	
Xingu	Amazon	1,980	1,230	
Ucayali	Amazon	1,900	1,180	
Uruguay	Plate	1,610	1,000	

LAKES

EUROPE

		km²	miles²
Lake Ladoga	Russia	17,700	6,800
Lake Onega	Russia	9,700	3,700
Saimaa system	Finland	8,000	3,100
Vänern	Sweden	5,500	2,100

ASIA

		km²	miles²	
Caspian Sea	Asia	371,000	143,000	[1]
Lake Baikal	Russia	30,500	11,780	[8]
Tonlé Sap	Cambodia	20,000	7,700	
Lake Balqash	Kazakhstan	18,500	7,100	
Aral Sea	Kazakhstan/Uzbekistan	17,160	6,625	
Lake Dongting	China	12,000	4,600	
Lake Ysyk	Kyrgyzstan	6,200	2,400	
Lake Orumiyeh	Iran	5,900	2,300	
Lake Koko	China	5,700	2,200	
Lake Poyang	China	5,000	1,900	
Lake Khanka	China/Russia	4,400	1,700	
Lake Van	Turkey	3,500	1,400	

AFRICA

		km²	miles²	
Lake Victoria	East Africa	68,000	26,300	[3]
Lake Tanganyika	Central Africa	33,000	13,000	[6]
Lake Malawi/Nyasa	East Africa	29,600	11,430	[9]
Lake Chad	Central Africa	25,000	9,700	
Lake Bangweulu	Zambia	9,840	3,800	
Lake Turkana	Ethiopia/Kenya	8,500	3,290	
Lake Volta	Ghana	8,480	3,270	
Lake Kariba	Zambia/Zimbabwe	5,380	2,150	
Lake Albert	Uganda/Congo (D.R.)	5,300	2,050	
Lake Nasser	Egypt/Sudan	5,250	2,030	
Lake Mweru	Zambia/Congo (D.R.)	4,920	1,900	
Lake Kyoga	Uganda	4,430	1,710	
Lake Tana	Ethiopia	3,620	1,400	
Lake Cabora Bassa	Mozambique	2,750	1,070	
Lake Rukwa	Tanzania	2,600	1,000	
Lake Mai-Ndombe	Congo (D.R.)	2,300	890	

AUSTRALIA

		km²	miles²
Lake Eyre	Australia	8,900	3,400
Lake Torrens	Australia	5,800	2,200
Lake Gairdner	Australia	4,800	1,900

NORTH AMERICA

		km²	miles²	
Lake Superior	Canada/USA	82,350	31,800	[2]
Lake Huron	Canada/USA	59,600	23,010	[4]
Lake Michigan	USA	58,000	22,400	[5]
Great Bear Lake	Canada	31,800	12,280	[7]
Great Slave Lake	Canada	28,500	11,000	[10]
Lake Erie	Canada/USA	25,700	9,900	
Lake Winnipeg	Canada	24,400	9,400	
Lake Ontario	Canada/USA	19,500	7,500	
Lake Nicaragua	Nicaragua	8,200	3,200	
Lake Athabasca	Canada	8,100	3,100	
Smallwood Reservoir	Canada	6,530	2,520	
Reindeer Lake	Canada	6,400	2,500	
Nettilling Lake	Canada	5,500	2,100	

SOUTH AMERICA

		km²	miles²
Lake Titicaca	Bolivia/Peru	8,300	3,200
Lake Poopo	Bolivia	2,800	1,100

ISLANDS

EUROPE

		km²	miles²	
Great Britain	UK	229,880	88,700	[8]
Iceland	Atlantic Ocean	103,000	39,800	
Ireland	Ireland/UK	84,400	32,600	
Novaya Zemlya (N.)	Russia	48,200	18,600	
W Spitzbergen	Norway	39,000	15,100	
Novaya Zemlya (S.)	Russia	33,200	12,800	
Sicily	Italy	25,500	9,800	
Sardinia	Italy	24,000	9,300	
N. E. Spitzbergen	Norway	15,000	5,600	
Corsica	France	8,700	3,400	
Crete	Greece	8,350	3,200	
Zealand	Denmark	6,850	2,600	

ASIA

		km²	miles²	
Borneo	Southeast Asia	744,360	287,400	[3]
Sumatra	Indonesia	473,600	182,860	[6]
Honshu	Japan	230,500	88,980	[7]
Sulawesi (Celebes)	Indonesia	189,000	73,000	
Java	Indonesia	126,700	48,900	
Luzon	Philippines	104,700	40,400	
Mindanao	Philippines	101,500	39,200	
Hokkaido	Japan	78,400	30,300	
Sakhalin	Russia	74,060	28,600	
Sri Lanka	Indian Ocean	65,600	25,300	
Taiwan	Pacific Ocean	36,000	13,900	
Kyushu	Japan	35,700	13,800	
Hainan	China	34,000	13,100	
Timor	Indonesia	33,600	13,000	
Shikoku	Japan	18,800	7,300	
Halmahera	Indonesia	18,000	6,900	
Ceram	Indonesia	17,150	6,600	
Sumbawa	Indonesia	15,450	6,000	
Flores	Indonesia	15,200	5,900	
Samar	Philippines	13,100	5,100	
Negros	Philippines	12,700	4,900	
Bangka	Indonesia	12,000	4,600	
Palawan	Philippines	12,000	4,600	
Panay	Philippines	11,500	4,400	
Sumba	Indonesia	11,100	4,300	
Mindoro	Philippines	9,750	3,800	

AFRICA

		km²	miles²	
Madagascar	Indian Ocean	587,040	226,660	[4]
Socotra	Indian Ocean	3,600	1,400	
Réunion	Indian Ocean	2,500	965	
Tenerife	Atlantic Ocean	2,350	900	
Mauritius	Indian Ocean	1,865	720	

OCEANIA

		km²	miles²	
New Guinea	Indonesia/Papua NG	821,030	317,000	[2]
New Zealand (S.)	Pacific Ocean	150,500	58,100	
New Zealand (N.)	Pacific Ocean	114,700	44,300	
Tasmania	Australia	67,800	26,200	
New Britain	Papua New Guinea	37,800	14,600	
New Caledonia	Pacific Ocean	19,100	7,400	
Viti Levu	Fiji	10,500	4,100	
Hawai'i	Pacific Ocean	10,450	4,000	
Bougainville	Papua New Guinea	9,600	3,700	
Guadalcanal	Solomon Islands	6,500	2,500	
Vanua Levu	Fiji	5,550	2,100	
New Ireland	Papua New Guinea	3,200	1,200	

NORTH AMERICA

		km²	miles²	
Greenland	Atlantic Ocean	2,175,600	839,800	[1]
Baffin Is.	Canada	508,000	196,100	[5]
Victoria Is.	Canada	212,200	81,900	[9]
Ellesmere Is.	Canada	212,000	81,800	[10]
Cuba	Caribbean Sea	110,860	42,800	
Newfoundland	Canada	110,680	42,700	
Hispaniola	Dominican Rep./Haiti	76,200	29,400	
Banks Is.	Canada	67,000	25,900	
Devon Is.	Canada	54,500	21,000	
Melville Is.	Canada	42,400	16,400	
Vancouver Is.	Canada	32,150	12,400	
Somerset Is.	Canada	24,300	9,400	
Jamaica	Caribbean Sea	11,400	4,400	
Puerto Rico	Atlantic Ocean	8,900	3,400	
Cape Breton Is.	Canada	4,000	1,500	

SOUTH AMERICA

		km²	miles²
Tierra del Fuego	Argentina/Chile	47,000	18,100
Falkland Is. (East)	Atlantic Ocean	6,800	2,600
South Georgia	Atlantic Ocean	4,200	1,600
Galapagos (Isabela)	Pacific Ocean	2,250	870

Niagara Falls, USA/Canada
Lake Erie can be seen at the bottom of this image, with Lake Ontario at the top. Flowing northward between them is the Niagara River; just to the north of Grand Island, the river dissects the Niagara escarpment and has formed the Horseshoe (Canadian) and American Falls, 182 ft (55 m) and 173 ft (53 m) high, respectively. Toronto is at the northwest of the image. [Map page 113]

THE EARTH
IN SPACE

THE UNIVERSE 18

THE CONSTELLATIONS 20

STAR CHARTS 22

THE SOLAR SYSTEM 24

THE EARTH: TIME AND MOTION 26

THE EARTH FROM SPACE 28

THE DYNAMIC EARTH 30

EARTHQUAKES AND VOLCANOES 32

FORCES OF NATURE 34

OCEANS AND ICE 36

THE EARTH'S ATMOSPHERE 38

CLIMATE AND WEATHER 40

WATER AND LAND USE 42

THE NATURAL WORLD 44

THE HUMAN WORLD 46

LANGUAGES AND RELIGIONS 48

INTERNATIONAL ORGANIZATIONS 50

AGRICULTURE 52

ENERGY AND MINERALS 54

WORLD ECONOMIES 56

TRADE AND COMMERCE 58

TRAVEL AND COMMUNICATIONS 60

THE WORLD TODAY 62

THE UNIVERSE

In early 2003, NASA scientists produced an image of the Universe as it was about 380,000 years after its creation. The image was produced by an American satellite called the Wilkinson Microwave Anisotropy Probe (WMAP), which was launched in June 2001.

The probe measures small variations in the cosmic microwave background (CMB) radiation, left over from the creation of the Universe. By measuring the size of hot and cold spots in the CMB, scientists have calculated how far away they are, and this data has enabled them to calculate the age of the Universe. It has also established the proportions of its three ingredients, namely 4% ordinary matter (made up of atoms), 23% of "cold dark matter," whose nature is unknown, and 73% of the mysterious "dark energy," which seems to be accelerating the expansion of space.

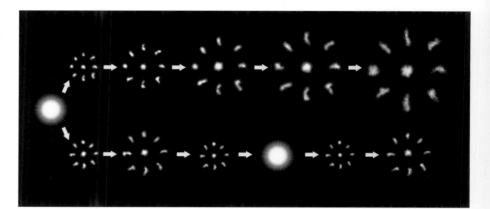

▼ *The depths of the Universe*
In this segment of sky, just one-tenth the area of the full Moon, the Hubble Space Telescope recorded an estimated 10,000 galaxies in 2003–4.

Scientists have established that our Universe was created, or "time" began, about 13.7 billion years ago (disproving earlier estimates that ranged from 8 billion to 24 billion years), that it is flat, and that the first stars did not appear until it was 200 million years old.

THE BIG BANG

Most scientists agree that the Universe was formed by a colossal explosion, called the "Big Bang." In the first millionth of a second after the Big Bang, the Universe expanded from a dimensionless point of infinite mass and

▲ *The end of the Universe*
The diagram shows two theories concerning the fate of the Universe. One theory, top, suggests that the Universe will expand indefinitely, becoming an immense dark graveyard. Another theory, bottom, suggests that the galaxies will fall back until everything is again concentrated in one point in a so-called Big Crunch. This might then be followed by a new Big Bang.

THE NEAREST STARS

The 22 nearest stars, excluding the Sun, with their distance from the Earth in light-years.*

Proxima Centauri	4.2
Alpha Centauri A	4.4
Alpha Centauri B	4.4
Barnard's Star	5.9
Wolf 359	7.8
Lalande 21185	8.3
Sirius A	8.6
Sirius B	8.6
UV Ceti A	8.7
UV Ceti B	8.7
Ross 154	9.7
Ross 248	10.3
Epsilon Eridani	10.5
HD 217987	10.7
Ross 128	10.9
L789-6	11.2
61 Cygni A	11.4
Procyon A	11.4
Procyon B	11.4
61 Cygni B	11.4
HD 173740	11.5
HD 173739	11.7

* A light-year is about 5,900 billion miles [9,500 billion km].

density into a fireball about 19 billion miles [30 billion km] across. The Universe has been expanding ever since, as demonstrated in the 1920s by Edwin Hubble, the American astronomer after whom the Hubble Space Telescope, which has also been shedding light on the origins of the Universe, was named.

The temperature at the end of the first second was perhaps 10 billion degrees – far too hot for composite atomic nuclei to exist. As a result, the fireball consisted mainly of radiation mixed with microscopic particles of matter. Almost a million years passed before the Universe was cool enough for atoms to form.

In regions where matter was relatively dense, atoms began, under the influence of gravity, to move together to form protogalaxies – masses of gas separated by empty space. The proto-galaxies were dark, because the Universe had cooled. But 200 million years after its creation, stars began to form within the protogalaxies as particles were drawn together. The internal pressure produced as matter condensed created the high temperatures required to cause nuclear fusion. Stars were born and later destroyed. Each gener-ation of stars fed on the debris of extinct ones. Each generation pro-duced larger atoms, increasing the number of different chemical elements.

▲ The Home Galaxy

This schematic plan shows that our Solar System is located in one of the spiral arms of the Milky Way galaxy, a little less than 30,000 light-years from its center. The center of the Milky Way galaxy is not visible from Earth. Instead, it is masked by light-absorbing clouds of interstellar dust.

THE GALAXIES

At least a billion galaxies are scattered through the Universe, though the discoveries made by the Hubble Space Telescope suggest that there may be far more than once thought, and some estimates are as high as 100 billion. The largest galaxies contain trillions of stars, while small ones contain less than a billion.

Galaxies tend to occur in groups or clusters, while some clusters appear to be grouped in vast superclusters. Our Local Cluster includes the spiral Milky Way galaxy, whose diameter is about 100,000 light-years; one light-year, the distance that light travels in one year, is about 5,900 billion miles [9,500 billion km]. The Milky Way is a huge galaxy, shaped like a disk with a bulge at the center. It is larger, brighter and more massive than many other known galaxies. It contains about 100 billion stars, which rotate around the center of the galaxy in the same direction as the Sun does.

One medium-sized star in the Milky Way galaxy is the Sun. After its formation, about 5 billion years ago, there was enough leftover matter around it to create the planets, asteroids, moons, and other bodies that together form our

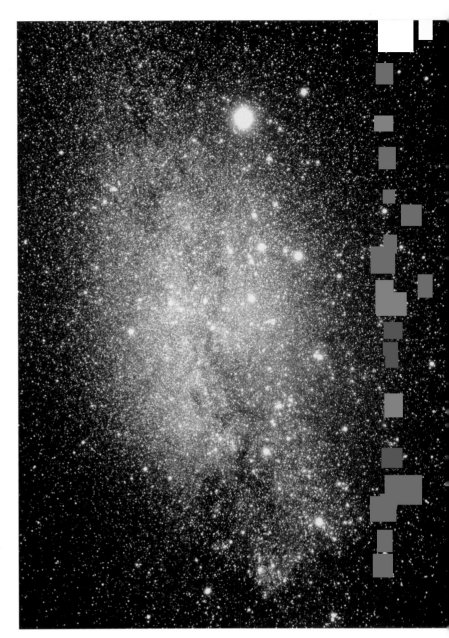

▲ The Milky Way

This section of the Milky Way is dominated by Sirius, the Dog Star, top center, in the constellation of Canis Major. Sirius is the brightest star in the sky.

Solar System. The Solar System rotates around the center of the Milky Way galaxy approx-imately every 225 million years.

Stars similar to our Sun are known to have planets orbiting around them. By 2009, about 300 of these extrasolar planets had been reported, most of them being gas giants like Jupiter. Evidence from the Hubble Space Telescope suggests that the raw materials from which planets are formed are common in dusty disks around many stars. This raises one of the most intriguing questions that has ever faced humanity: if other planets exist, are they home to living organisms?

Before the time of Galileo, people thought that the Earth lay at the center of the Universe. But we now know that our Solar System and even the Milky Way galaxy are tiny specks in the Universe as a whole. Perhaps our planet is also not unique in its ability to support intelligent life.

THE CONSTELLATIONS

On a clear night, under the best conditions and far away from the glare of city lights, a person in northern Europe can look up and see about 2,500 stars. In a town, however, light pollution can reduce visibility to 200 stars or fewer. Over the whole celestial sphere it is possible to see about 8,500 stars with the naked eye and it is only when you look through a telescope that you begin to realize that the number of stars is countless.

SMALL AND LARGE STARS

Stars come in many sizes. Some, called neutron stars, are compact, with the same mass as the Sun but with diameters of only about 12 miles [20 km]. Larger than neutron stars are the small white dwarfs. Our Sun is a medium-sized star, but many visible stars in the night sky are giants with diameters typically 20 times that of the Sun, or supergiants with diameters from 50 to several hundred times that of the Sun.

Two bright stars in the constellation Orion are Betelgeuse (also known as Alpha Orionis) and Rigel (or Beta Orionis). Betelgeuse is an orange-red supergiant, whose diameter is about

500 times that of the Sun. Rigel is also a supergiant. Its diameter is about 50 times that of the Sun, but its luminosity is estimated to be 40,000 times that of the Sun.

The stars we see in the night sky all belong to our home galaxy, the Milky Way. This name is also used for the faint, silvery band that arches across the sky. This band, a slice through our galaxy, contains an enormous number of stars.

▼ *The Big Dipper*

The Big Dipper, or Plough, seen above glowing yellow clouds lit by city lights. It is part of a larger group called Ursa Major, one of the best-known constellations of the northern hemisphere. The two bright stars to the lower right of the photograph (Merak and Dubhe) are known as the Pointers because they show the way to the Pole Star.

THE CONSTELLATIONS

The constellations and their English names. Constellations visible from both hemispheres are listed.

Andromeda	Andromeda	Delphinus	Dolphin	Perseus	Perseus
Antlia	Air Pump	Dorado	Swordfish	Phoenix	Phoenix
Apus	Bird of Paradise	Draco	Dragon	Pictor	Easel
Aquarius	Water Carrier	Equuleus	Little Horse	Pisces	Fishes
Aquila	Eagle	Eridanus	River Eridanus	Piscis Austrinus	Southern Fish
Ara	Altar	Fornax	Furnace	Puppis	Ship's Stern
Aries	Ram	Gemini	Twins	Pyxis	Mariner's Compass
Auriga	Charioteer	Grus	Crane	Reticulum	Net
Boötes	Herdsman	Hercules	Hercules	Sagitta	Arrow
Caelum	Chisel	Horologium	Clock	Sagittarius	Archer
Camelopardalis	Giraffe	Hydra	Water Snake	Scorpius	Scorpion
Cancer	Crab	Hydrus	Sea Serpent	Sculptor	Sculptor
Canes Venatici	Hunting Dogs	Indus	Indian	Scutum	Shield
Canis Major	Great Dog	Lacerta	Lizard	Serpens*	Serpent
Canis Minor	Little Dog	Leo	Lion	Sextans	Sextant
Capricornus	Sea Goat	Leo Minor	Little Lion	Taurus	Bull
Carina	Ship's Keel	Lepus	Hare	Telescopium	Telescope
Cassiopeia	Cassiopeia	Libra	Scales	Triangulum	Triangle
Centaurus	Centaur	Lupus	Wolf	Triangulum Australe	Southern Triangle
Cepheus	Cepheus	Lynx	Lynx		
Cetus	Whale	Lyra	Lyre	Tucana	Toucan
Chamaeleon	Chameleon	Mensa	Table Mountain	Ursa Major	Great Bear
Circinus	Compasses	Microscopium	Microscope	Ursa Minor	Little Bear
Columba	Dove	Monoceros	Unicorn	Vela	Ship's Sails
Coma Berenices	Berenice's Hair	Musca	Fly	Virgo	Virgin
Corona Australis	Southern Crown	Norma	Level	Volans	Flying Fish
Corona Borealis	Northern Crown	Octans	Octant	Vulpecula	Fox
Corvus	Crow	Ophiuchus	Serpent Bearer		
Crater	Cup	Orion	Hunter		
Crux	Southern Cross	Pavo	Peacock		
Cygnus	Swan	Pegasus	Winged Horse		

* In two halves: Serpens Caput, the head, and Serpens Cauda, the tail.

THE BRIGHTEST STARS

The 15 brightest stars visible from northern Europe. Magnitudes are given to the nearest tenth.

Sirius	−1.4
Arcturus	0.0
Vega	0.0
Capella	0.1
Rigel	0.2
Procyon	0.4
Betelgeuse	0.4
Altair	0.8
Aldebaran	0.9
Spica	1.0
Antares	1.0
Pollux	1.2
Fomalhaut	1.2
Deneb	1.2
Regulus	1.4

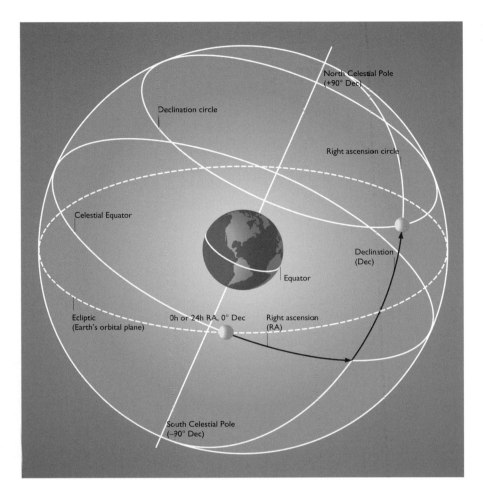

Celestial sphere

The diagram shows the imaginary surface on which astronomical positions are measured. The celestial sphere appears to rotate about the celestial poles, as though an extension of the Earth's own axis. The Earth's axis points toward the celestial poles.

The nucleus of the Milky Way galaxy cannot be seen from Earth. Lying in the direction of the constellation Sagittarius in the southern hemisphere, it is masked by clouds of dust.

THE BRIGHTNESS OF STARS

Astronomers use a scale of magnitudes to measure the brightness of stars. The brightest visible to the naked eye were originally known as first-magnitude stars, ones not so bright were second-magnitude, down to the faintest visible, which were rated as sixth-magnitude. The brighter the star, the lower the magnitude. With the advent of telescopes and the development of accurate instruments for measuring brightnesses, the magnitude scale has been refined and extended. Very bright bodies, such as Sirius, Venus, and the Sun, have negative magnitudes. The nearest star is Proxima Centauri, part of a multiple star system, which is 4.2 light-years away. Proxima Centauri is very faint and has a magnitude of 11.0. Alpha Centauri A, one of the two brighter members of the system, is the nearest visible star to Earth. It has a magnitude of 1.7.

These magnitudes are known as apparent magnitudes – measures of the brightnesses of the stars as they appear to us. These are the magnitudes indicated on the star charts on pages 22–23. But the stars are at very different distances. The star Deneb, in the constellation Cygnus, for example, is 3,200 light-years away. So astronomers also use absolute magnitudes – measures of how bright the stars really are. A star's absolute magnitude is

the apparent magnitude it would have if it could be placed 32.6 light-years away. So Deneb, with an apparent magnitude of 1.2, has an absolute magnitude of –8.7.

The brightest star in the night sky is Sirius, the Dog Star, with a magnitude of –1.4. This medium-sized star is 8.6 light-years distant but it gives out about 20 times as much light as the Sun. After the Sun and the Moon, the brightest objects in the sky are the planets Venus, Mars, and Jupiter. For example, Venus has a magnitude of up to –4. The planets have no light of their own, however, and shine only because they reflect the Sun's rays. But while stars have fixed positions, the planets shift nightly in relation to the constellations, following a path called the ecliptic (shown on the star charts overleaf). As they follow their orbits around the Sun, their distances from the Earth vary, and therefore so also do their magnitudes.

While atlas maps record the details of the Earth's surface, star charts are a guide to the heavens. An observer at the equator can see the entire sky over the course of a year, but an observer at one of the poles can see only the stars in a single hemisphere.

The Southern Cross

The Southern Cross, or Crux, in the southern hemisphere, was classified as a constellation in the 17th century. It is as familiar to Australians and New Zealanders as the Big Dipper (or Plough) is to people in the northern hemisphere. The vertical axis of the Southern Cross points toward the South Celestial Pole.

STAR CHARTS

Star magnitudes

Apparent visual magnitudes

Magnitudes: -1 0 1 2 3 4 5

⊙ Variable star   ✴ Open Cluster
⊕ Globular Cluster   ▢ Nebula   ⬭ Galaxy

The Milky Way is shown in light blue on the chart.

These pages show a star chart for each hemisphere. The northern hemisphere chart is centered on the North Celestial Pole, while the southern hemisphere chart is centered on the South Celestial Pole.

In the northern hemisphere, the North Pole is marked by the star Polaris, or Pole Star. Polaris lies within a degree of the point where an extension of the Earth's axis meets the sky. Polaris appears to be almost stationary, and navigators throughout history have used it as a guide. Unfortunately, the South Celestial Pole has no convenient reference point.

Star charts of the two hemispheres are bounded by the celestial equator, an imaginary line in the sky directly above the terrestrial equator. Astronomical coordinates, which give the location of stars, are normally stated in terms of

▲ *Star chart of the northern hemisphere*

When you look into the sky, the stars seem to be on the inside of a huge dome. This gives astronomers a way of mapping them. This chart shows the sky as it would appear from the North Pole. To use the star chart above, an observer in the northern hemisphere should face south and turn the chart so that the current month appears at the bottom. The chart will then show the constellations on view at about 11 p.m. Greenwich Mean Time. The map should be rotated clockwise 15° for each hour before 11 p.m. and counterclockwise for each hour after 11 p.m.

right ascension (the equivalent of longitude) and declination (the equivalent of latitude). Because the stars appear to rotate around the Earth every 24 hours, right ascension is measured eastward in hours and minutes. Declination is measured in degrees north or south of the celestial equator.

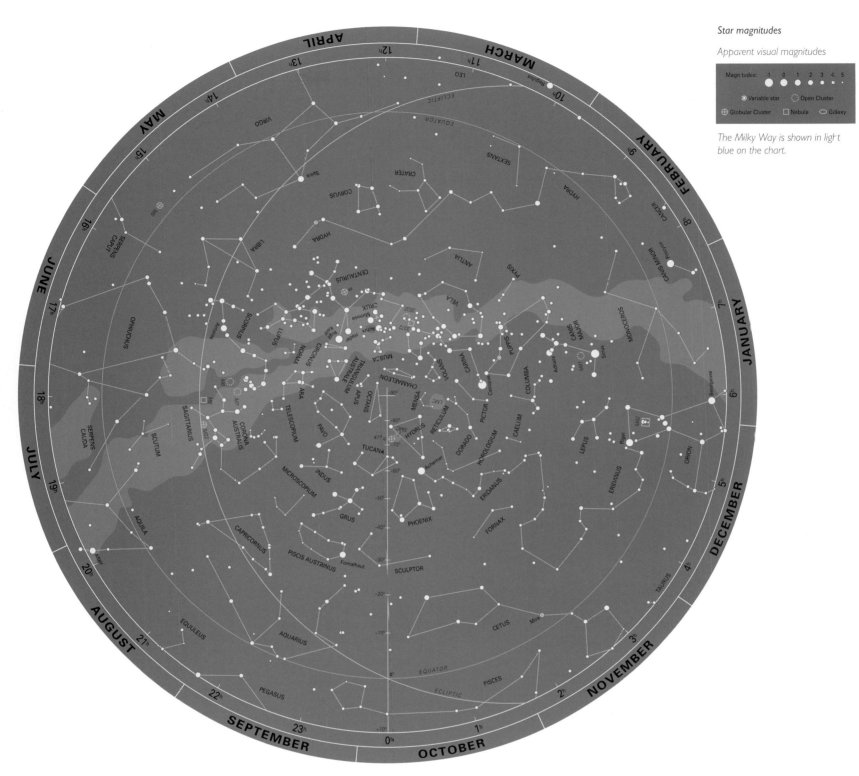

Star magnitudes

Apparent visual magnitudes

Magnitudes: -1 0 1 2 3 4 5

⊙ Variable star ⊙ Open Cluster

⊕ Globular Cluster ☐ Nebula ◯ Galaxy

The Milky Way is shown in light blue on the chart.

CONSTELLATIONS

Every star belongs to a particular constellation. There are 88 constellations, many of which were named by the ancient Greeks, Romans, and other early peoples after animals and mythological characters, such as Orion and Perseus. More recently, astronomers invented names for constellations seen in the southern hemisphere, in areas not visible from around the Mediterranean Sea.

Some groups of easily recognizable stars form parts of a constellation. For example, seven stars form the shape of the Big Dipper, or Plough, within the constellation Ursa Major. Such groups are called asterisms.

The stars in constellations lie in the same direction in space, but normally at vastly different distances. Hence, there is no real connection

▲ **Star chart of the southern hemisphere**

Many constellations in the southern hemisphere were named not by the ancients but by later astronomers and thus have modern names. The Large and Small Magellanic Clouds (LMC, SMC) are small "satellite" galaxies of the Milky Way. To use the chart, an observer in the southern hemisphere should face north and turn the chart so that the current month appears at the bottom. The map will then show the constellations on view at about 11 p.m. Greenwich Mean Time. The chart should be rotated clockwise 15° for each hour before 11 p.m. and counterclockwise for each hour after 11 p.m.

between them. The positions of stars seem fixed, but in fact the shapes of the constellations are changing slowly over very long periods of time. This is because the stars have their own "proper motions," which because of the huge distances involved are imperceptible to the naked eye.

THE SOLAR SYSTEM

Our knowledge of the Solar System has increased greatly since the start of the Space Age in 1957, with the launch of the Soviet satellite Sputnik 1. Research continues and, in 2006, studies of the outer Solar System led the International Astronomical Union to reclassify Pluto as a "dwarf planet." It now belongs to a group of orbiting bodies, including the asteroid Ceres, and, beyond Pluto, Eris (once called UB313 or Xena), which was discovered in 2003.

Scientists believe that the Solar System was formed from a rotating disk of gas and dust, the remains of a previous generation of stars. About 5 billion years ago, a new star, the Sun, was born, containing 99.8% of the mass of our Solar System. The remaining material makes up the planets and other bodies in the Solar System.

THE PLANETS

Mercury is the closest planet to the Sun and the fastest moving. Space probes have revealed that its surface is covered by craters, and looks much like the Earth's Moon. Mercury is a hostile place, with no significant atmosphere and temperatures ranging between 750°F [400°C] by day and −275°F [−170°C] by night. It seems unlikely that anyone will ever want to visit this planet.

Venus is much the same size as Earth, but it is the hottest of the planets, with temperatures reaching 885°F [475°C], even at night. The reason for this scorching heat is the atmosphere, which consists mainly of carbon dioxide, a gas that traps heat thus creating a greenhouse effect. The density of the atmosphere is about 90 times that of Earth, and dense clouds permanently mask the planet's surface. Active volcanic regions discharging sulfur dioxide may account for the haze of sulfuric-acid droplets in the upper atmosphere. Seen from Earth, Venus is brighter than any other star or planet and is

easy to spot. It is often the first object to be seen in the evening sky and the last to be seen in the morning sky. It can even be seen in daylight.

Earth, seen from space, looks blue (because of the oceans which cover more than 70% of the planet) and white (a result of clouds in the atmosphere). The atmosphere and water make Earth the only planet known to support life. The Earth's hard outer layers, including the crust and the top of the mantle, are divided into rigid plates. Forces inside the Earth move the plates, modifying the land-scape, and causing earthquakes and volcanic activity. Weathering and erosion also change the surface.

Mars has many features in common with the Earth, including an atmosphere with clouds and polar caps that partly melt in summer. Scientists once considered that it was the most likely planet on which other life might exist, but the two Viking space probes that went there in the 1970s found only a barren rocky surface, with no trace of water. But NASA probes, such as Phoenix in 2008, have revealed the presence of ice and other evidence that Mars was once potentially habitable, at least by simple microbes.

PLANETARY DATA								
Planet	Mean distance from Sun (million miles)	Mass (Earth=1)	Period of orbit (Earth days/yrs)	Period of rotation (Earth days)	Equatorial diameter (miles)	Average density (water=1)	Surface gravity (Earth=1)	Number of known satellites*
Sun	−	332,946	−	25.38	865,000	1.41	27.9	−
Mercury	36.0	0.06	87.97d	58.65	3,032	5.43	0.38	0
Venus	67.2	0.82	224.7d	243.02	7,521	5.24	0.91	0
Earth	93.0	1.00	365.3d	1.00	7,926	5.52	1.00	1
Mars	141.6	0.11	687.0d	1.029	4,220	3.94	0.38	2
Jupiter	483.7	317.8	11.86y	0.411	88,848	1.33	2.36	63
Saturn	886.6	95.2	29.45y	0.428	74,900	0.69	0.91	60
Uranus	1,784.0	14.5	84.02y	0.720	31,764	1.27	0.89	27
Neptune	2,795.2	17.2	164.8y	0.673	30,776	1.64	1.13	13

* Number of known satellites at mid-2009

Asteroids are small, rocky bodies. Most of them orbit the Sun between Mars and Jupiter, but some small ones can approach the Earth. The largest is Ceres, 567 miles [913 km] in diameter. There may be around a million asteroids bigger than 0.6 miles [1 km].

Jupiter, the giant planet, lies beyond Mars and the asteroid belt. Its mass is almost three times as much as all the other planets combined and, because of its size, it shines more brightly than any other planet apart from Venus and, occasionally, Mars. Jupiter is made up mostly of hydrogen and helium, covered by a layer of clouds. Its Great Red Spot is a high-pressure storm. The planet also has a faint ring system. The four largest moons of Jupiter were discovered by Galileo. They are worlds in their own right: Io is the most volcanic body yet discovered; Europa and Ganymede have icy surfaces, perhaps with liquid oceans below; and Callisto has an ancient, cratered terrain. Jupiter made headline news when it was struck by fragments of Comet Shoemaker–Levy 9 in July 1994, creating huge fireballs that caused scars on the planet that remained visible for months after the event.

Saturn is structurally similar to Jupiter but it is best known for its rings. The rings measure about 170,000 miles [270,000 km] across, yet they are no more than a few hundred yards thick. Seen from Earth, the rings seem divided into three main bands of varying brightness, but photographs sent back by space probes showed that they are broken up into thousands of thin ringlets composed of ice particles ranging in size from a snowball to an iceberg. The origin of the rings is still a matter of debate.

Uranus was discovered in 1781 by William Herschel, who first thought it was a comet. It is broadly similar to Jupiter and Saturn in composition, though its distance from the Sun makes its surface even colder. Uranus is circled by thin rings which were discovered in 1977. Unlike the rings of Saturn, the rings of Uranus are black, which explains why they cannot be seen from Earth.

Neptune, named after the mythological sea god, was discovered in 1846 as the result of mathematical predictions made by astronomers to explain irregularities in the orbit of Uranus, its near twin. Little was known about this distant body until Voyager 2 came close to it in 1989. Neptune has thin rings, like those of Uranus. Its atmosphere features blue-green clouds and the occasional prominent dark spot.

Pluto, once regarded as the smallest planet in the Solar System, has been reclassified as a "dwarf planet" since 2006. Discovered in 1930 by Clyde Tombaugh, the American astronomer, Pluto's orbit is odd and it sometimes comes closer to the Sun than Neptune. Pluto lies in the Kuiper Belt, a vast region beyond the orbit of Neptune. Pluto and Eris, another dwarf planet, are the largest known objects in the Kuiper Belt.

Comets are small icy bodies that orbit the Sun in highly elliptical orbits. When a comet swings in toward the Sun some of its ice evaporates, and the comet brightens and may become visible from Earth. The best known is Halley's Comet, which takes 76 years to orbit the Sun.

THE EARTH: TIME AND MOTION

The Earth is constantly moving through space like a huge, self-sufficient spaceship. First, with the rest of the Solar System, it moves around the center of the Milky Way galaxy. Second, it rotates around the Sun at a speed of more than 60,000 mph [100,000 km/h], covering a distance of nearly 600 million miles [1,000 million km] in a little over 365 days. The Earth also spins on its axis, an imaginary line joining the North and South Poles, via the center of the Earth, completing one turn in a day. The Earth's movements around the Sun determine our calendar, though accurate observations of the stars made by astronomers

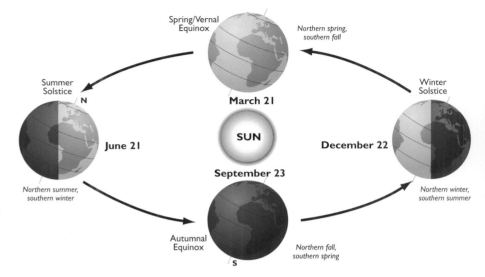

▼ The Earth from the Moon

In 1969, Neil Armstrong and Edwin "Buzz" Aldrin, Jr, were the first people to set foot on the Moon. This photograph of the Earth was taken by the crew of Apollo 11 as they orbited the Moon.

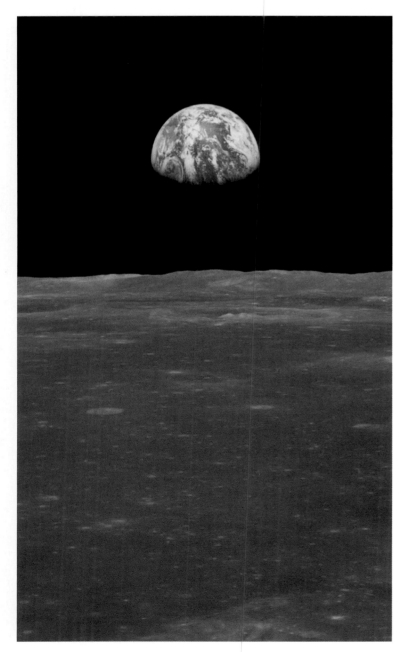

help to keep our clocks in step with the rotation of the Earth around the Sun.

THE CHANGING YEAR

The Earth takes 365 days, 6 hours, 9 minutes, and 9.54 seconds to complete one orbit around the Sun. We have a calendar year of 365 days, so allowance has to be made for the extra time over and above the 365 days. This is allowed for by introducing leap years of 366 days. Leap years are generally those, such as 1992 and 1996, which are divisible by four. Century years, however, are not leap years unless they are divisible by 400. Hence, 1700, 1800, and 1900 were not leap years, but the year 2000 was one. Leap years help to make the calendar conform with the solar year.

Because the Earth's axis is tilted by approximately 23½°, the middle latitudes enjoy four distinct seasons. On March 21, the vernal or spring equinox in the northern hemisphere, the Sun is directly overhead at the equator and everywhere on Earth has about 12 hours of daylight and 12 hours of darkness. But as the Earth continues on its journey around the Sun, the northern hemisphere tilts more and more toward the Sun. Finally, on June 21, the Sun is overhead at the Tropic of Cancer (latitude 23½° North). This is the summer solstice in the northern hemisphere.

▲ The Seasons

The approximate 23½° tilt of the Earth's axis remains constant as the Earth orbits around the Sun. As a result, first the northern and then the southern hemispheres lean toward the Sun. Annual variations in the amount of sunlight received in turn by each hemisphere are responsible for the four seasons experienced in the middle latitudes.

▼ Tides

The daily rises and falls of the ocean's waters are caused by the gravitational pull of the Moon and the Sun. The effect is greatest on the hemisphere facing the Moon, causing a "tidal bulge." The diagram below shows that the Sun, Moon, and Earth are in line when the spring tides occur. This causes the greatest tidal ranges. On the other hand, the neap tides occur when the pull of the Moon and the Sun are opposed. Neap tides, when tidal ranges are at their lowest, occur near the Moon's first and third quarters.

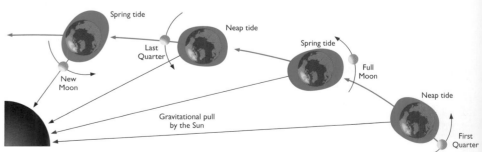

SUN DATA

DIAMETER	865,000 miles
VOLUME	3.388×10^{17} cu miles
VOLUME (EARTH=1)	1.303×10^{6}
MASS	1.989×10^{30} kg
MASS (EARTH=1)	3.329×10^{5}
MEAN DENSITY (WATER=1)	1.409
ROTATION PERIOD:	
AT EQUATOR	25.4 days
AT POLES	about 35 days
SURFACE GRAVITY (EARTH=1)	28
MAGNITUDE:	
APPARENT	−26.9
ABSOLUTE	+4.71
TEMPERATURE:	
AT SURFACE	9,932°F [5,800 K]
AT CORE	15×10^{6} K

MOON DATA

DIAMETER	2,159 miles
MASS (EARTH=1)	0.0123
DENSITY (WATER=1)	3.34
MEAN DISTANCE FROM EARTH	238,856 miles
MAXIMUM DISTANCE (APOGEE)	252,712 miles
MINIMUM DISTANCE (PERIGEE)	221,457 miles
SIDEREAL ROTATION AND REVOLUTION PERIOD	27.322 days
SYNODIC MONTH (NEW MOON TO NEW MOON)	29.531 days
SURFACE GRAVITY (EARTH=1)	0.165
MAXIMUM DAYTIME SURFACE TEMPERATURE	+243°F [390 K]
MINIMUM NIGHTTIME SURFACE TEMPERATURE	−261°F [110 K]

▶ *Phases of the Moon*

The Moon rotates more slowly than the Earth, making one complete turn on its axis in just over 27 days. This corresponds to its period of revolution around the Earth and, hence, the same hemisphere always faces us. The interval between one full Moon and the next (and also between new Moons) is about 29½ days, or one lunar month. The apparent changes in the appearance of the Moon are caused by its changing position in relation to the Earth. Like the planets, the Moon produces no light of its own. It shines by reflecting the Sun's rays, varying from a slim crescent to a full circle, and back again.

The overhead Sun then moves south again until, on September 23, the autumnal equinox in the northern hemisphere, the Sun is again overhead at the Equator. The overhead Sun then moves south until, on around December 22, it is overhead at the Tropic of Capricorn. This is the winter solstice in the northern hemisphere, and the summer solstice in the southern, where the seasons are reversed.

At the poles, there are two seasons. During half of the year, one of the poles leans toward the Sun and has continuous sunlight. For the other six months, the pole leans away from the Sun and is in continuous darkness.

Regions around the equator do not have marked seasons. Because the Sun is high in the sky throughout the year, it is always hot or warm. When people talk of seasons in the tropics, they are usually referring to other factors, such as rainy and dry periods.

DAY, NIGHT, AND TIDES

As the Earth rotates on its axis every 24 hours, first one side of the planet and then the other faces the Sun and enjoys daylight, while the opposite side is in darkness.

The length of daylight varies throughout the year. The longest day in the northern hemisphere falls on the summer solstice, June 21, while the longest day in the southern hemisphere is on December 22. At 40° latitude, the length of daylight on the longest day is 14 hours, 30 minutes. At 60° latitude, daylight on that day lasts 18 hours, 30 minutes. On the shortest day, December 22 in the northern hemisphere and June 21 in the southern, daylight hours at 40° latitude total 9 hours and 9 minutes. At latitude 60°, daylight lasts only 5 hours, 30 minutes in the 24-hour period.

Tides are caused by the gravitational pull of the Moon and, to a lesser extent, the Sun on the waters in the world's oceans. Tides occur twice every 24 hours, 50 minutes – one complete orbit of the Moon around the Earth.

▲ *Total eclipse of the Sun*

A total eclipse is caused when the Moon passes between the Sun and the Earth. With the Sun's bright disk completely obscured, the Sun's corona, or outer atmosphere, can be viewed.

The highest tides, the spring tides, occur when the Earth, Moon, and Sun are in a straight line, so that the gravitational pulls of the Moon and Sun are combined. The lowest, or neap, tides occur when the Moon, Earth, and Sun form a right angle. The gravitational pull of the Moon is then opposed by the gravitational pull of the Sun. The greatest tidal ranges occur in the Bay of Fundy in Canada. The greatest mean spring range is 47.5 ft [14.5 m].

The speed at which the Earth is spinning on its axis is gradually slowing down, because of the movement of tides. As a result, experts have calculated that, in about 200 million years, the day will be 25 hours long.

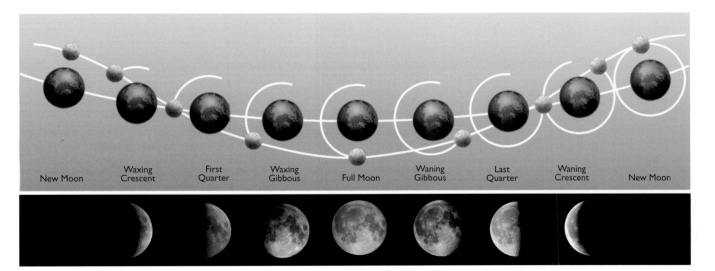

| New Moon | Waxing Crescent | First Quarter | Waxing Gibbous | Full Moon | Waning Gibbous | Last Quarter | Waning Crescent | New Moon |

THE EARTH FROM SPACE

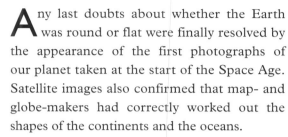

Any last doubts about whether the Earth was round or flat were finally resolved by the appearance of the first photographs of our planet taken at the start of the Space Age. Satellite images also confirmed that map- and globe-makers had correctly worked out the shapes of the continents and the oceans.

More importantly, images of our beautiful, blue, white, and brown planet from space impressed on many people that the Earth and its resources are finite. They made people realize that if we allow our planet to be damaged by such factors as overpopulation, pollution, and irresponsible overuse of resources, then its future and the survival of all the living things upon it may be threatened.

VIEWS FROM ABOVE

The first aerial photographs were taken from balloons in the mid-19th century and their importance in military reconnaissance was recognized as early as the 1860s during the American Civil War.

Since the end of World War II, photographs

▼ *Mount Etna, Sicily*
The most active volcano in Europe, Mount Etna, 10,906 ft [3,323 m] high, is shown here during the 2002–3 eruption, its plume of ash and smoke spreading southward over the Mediterranean, east of Malta.

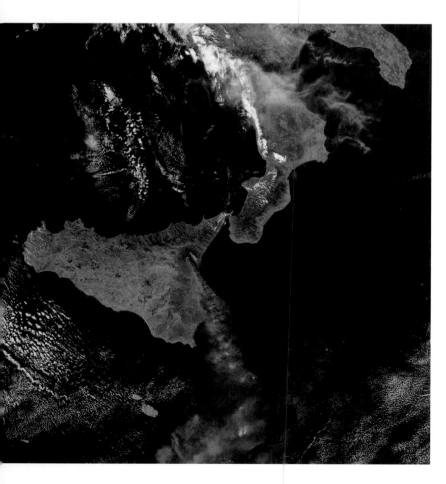

taken by aircraft have been widely used in map-making. The use of air photographs has greatly speeded up the laborious process of mapping land details and they have enabled cartographers to produce maps of the most remote parts of the world.

Aerial photographs have also proved useful because they reveal features that are not visible at ground level. For example, circles that appear on many air photographs do not correspond to visible features on the ground. Many of these mysterious shapes have turned out to be the sites of ancient settlements previously unknown to archeologists.

IMAGES FROM SPACE

Space probes equipped with cameras and a variety of remote-sensing instruments have sent back images of distant planets and moons. From these images, detailed maps have been produced, rapidly expanding our knowledge of the Solar System.

Images from space are also proving invaluable in the study of the Earth. One of the best known uses of space imagery is the study of the atmosphere. Polar-orbiting weather satellites that circle the Earth, together with geostationary satellites, whose motion is synchronized with the Earth's rotation, now regularly transmit images showing the changing patterns of weather systems from above. Forecasters use these images to track the development and paths of hurricanes, enabling them to issue storm warnings.

Remote-sensing devices are now monitoring changes in temperatures over the land and sea, while photographs indicate the melting of ice sheets. In 2006, Indian scientists announced that satellite images showed that a once populated island in the Ganges delta had vanished, probably as a result of global warming. Such methods also reveal polluted areas and areas suffering deforestation.

In recent years, remote-sensing devices have been used to monitor the damage being done to the ozone layer in the stratosphere, which prevents most of the Sun's harmful ultraviolet radiation from reaching the surface. The discovery of "ozone holes," where the protective layer of ozone is being thinned by chlorofluorocarbons (CFCs), chemicals used in the manufacture of such things as air conditioners and refrigerators, has enabled governments to take concerted action to save our planet from imminent danger.

EARTH DATA

MAXIMUM DISTANCE FROM SUN (APHELION)
94,508,166 miles

MINIMUM DISTANCE FROM SUN (PERIHELION)
91,403,477 miles

LENGTH OF YEAR – SOLAR TROPICAL (EQUINOX TO EQUINOX)
365.24 days

LENGTH OF YEAR – SIDEREAL (FIXED STAR TO FIXED STAR)
365.26 days

LENGTH OF DAY – MEAN SOLAR DAY
24 hours, 3 minutes, 56 seconds

LENGTH OF DAY – MEAN SIDEREAL DAY
23 hours, 56 minutes, 4 seconds

SUPERFICIAL AREA
197,000,000 sq miles

LAND SURFACE
57,500,000 sq miles (29.2%)

WATER SURFACE
139,500,000 sq miles (70.8%)

EQUATORIAL CIRCUMFERENCE
24,901 miles

POLAR CIRCUMFERENCE
24,860 miles

EQUATORIAL DIAMETER
7,926 miles

POLAR DIAMETER
7,900 miles

EQUATORIAL RADIUS
3,963 miles

POLAR RADIUS
3,950 miles

VOLUME OF THE EARTH
$259,880 \times 10^6$ cu miles

MASS OF THE EARTH
5.97×10^{24} kg

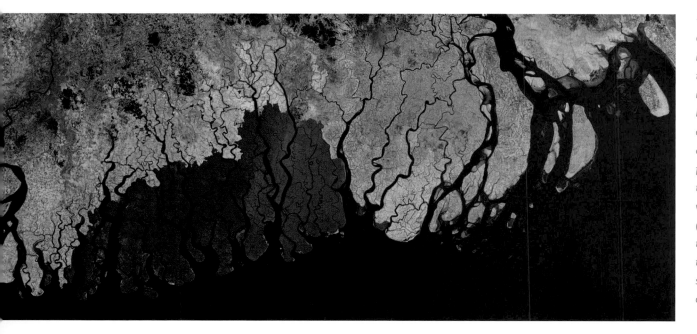

◀ *Ganges Delta, India/Bangladesh*
*Over 186 miles [300 km] wide, this
is the world's largest delta, created by
the River Ganges depositing sediment
it has carried from the Himalayas.
It is extremely vulnerable to frequent
cyclones and tidal surges, but is
densely populated because of the
fertile land. On the western side of
the image is the mouth of the Hugli,
with the elongated city of Kolkata
(Calcutta) showing as dark gray just to
the north. The large red area indicates
the presence of mangrove forests and
swamps, and is divided between the
countries of India and Bangladesh.*

▶ *Imperial Valley, USA/Mexico*
*The Salton Sea is the dark area
at the top left of the image.
It was inadvertently created in
1905 during an attempt to divert
the flow of the Colorado River for
irrigation. It lies 236 ft [72 m]
below sea level and is very saline.
To the south is a large area of
productive land, showing bright
red on this image. The abrupt
color change toward the
bottom of this area marks
the US–Mexico boundary.*

THE DYNAMIC EARTH

The Earth was formed about 4.6 billion years [4,600 million years] ago from the ring of gas and dust left over after the formation of the Sun. As the Earth took shape, lighter elements, such as silicon, rose to the surface, while heavy elements, notably iron, sank toward the center.

Gradually, the outer layers cooled to form a hard crust. The crust enclosed the dense mantle which, in turn, surrounded the even denser liquid outer and solid inner core. Around the Earth was an atmosphere, which contained abundant water vapor. When the surface cooled, rainwater began to fill hollows, forming the first lakes and seas. Since that time, our planet has been subject to constant change – the result of powerful internal and external forces that still operate today.

THE HISTORY OF THE EARTH

From their study of rocks, geologists have pieced together the history of our planet and the life forms that evolved upon it. They have dated the oldest known crystals, composed of the mineral zircon, at 4.2 billion years. But the oldest rocks are younger, around 4 billion years old. This is because older rocks have been recycled or weathered away by natural processes.

The oldest rocks that contain fossils, which

▼ *Lulworth Cove, southern England*

When undisturbed by earth movements, sedimentary rock strata are generally horizontal. But lateral pressure has squeezed the Jurassic strata at Lulworth Cove into complex folds.

are evidence of once-living organisms, are around 3.5 billion years old. Fossils of soft-bodied creatures have been found in rocks of the Ediacaran period. But by the start of the Cambrian period, which followed the Ediacaran around 540 million years ago, life was abundant in the world's oceans.

The Cambrian is the first period in the Paleozoic (or ancient life) era. The Paleozoic era is followed by the Mesozoic (middle life) era, which witnessed the spectacular rise and fall of the dinosaurs, and the Cenozoic (recent life) era, which was dominated by the evolution of mammals. Each of the eras is divided into periods, and the periods in the Cenozoic era, covering the last 65 million years, are further divided into epochs.

THE EARTH'S CHANGING FACE

While life was gradually evolving, the face of the Earth was constantly changing. By piecing together evidence of rock structures and fossils, geologists have demonstrated that around 250 million years ago, all the world's land areas were grouped together in one huge land mass called Pangaea. Around 180 million years ago, the supercontinent Pangaea began to break up. New oceans opened up as the continents began to move toward their present positions.

Evidence of how continents drift came from studies of the ocean floor in the 1950s and 1960s. Scientists discovered that the oceans are young features. By contrast with the continents, no part of the ocean floor is more than 200 million years old. The floors of oceans older than 200 million years have completely vanished.

Studies of long undersea ranges, called ocean ridges, revealed that the youngest rocks occur along their centers, which are the edges of huge plates – rigid blocks of the Earth's lithosphere, which is made up of the crust and the solid upper layer of the mantle. The Earth's lithosphere is split into six large and several smaller plates. The ocean ridges are "constructive" plate margins, because new crustal rock is being

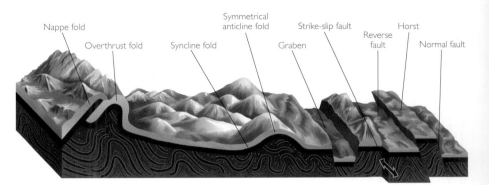

Nappe fold · Overthrust fold · Syncline fold · Symmetrical anticline fold · Graben · Strike-slip fault · Reverse fault · Horst · Normal fault

▲ *Mountain building*

Lateral pressure, which occurs when plates collide, squeezes and compresses rocks into folds. Simple symmetrical upfolds are called anticlines, while downfolds are synclines. As the pressure builds up, strata become asymmetrical and they may be tilted over to form recumbent folds. The rocks often crack under the intense pressure and the folds are sheared away and pushed forward over other rocks. These features are called overthrust folds or nappes. Plate movements also create faults along which rocks move upward, downward, and sideways. The diagram shows a downfaulted graben, or rift valley, and an uplifted horst, or block mountain.

The Himalayas are a young fold mountain range formed by a collision between two plates. The earthquakes felt in the region testify that the plate movements are still continuing.

▼ Geological time scale

The geological time scale was first constructed by a study of the stratigraphic, or relative, ages of layers of rock. But the absolute ages of rock strata could not be fixed until the discovery of radioactivity in the early 20th century. Some names of periods, such as Cambrian (Latin for Wales), come from places where the rocks were first studied. Others, such as Carboniferous, refer to the nature of the rocks formed during the period. For example, coal seams (containing carbon) were formed from decayed plant matter during the Carboniferous period.

formed there from magma that wells up from the mantle as the plates gradually move apart. The deep-ocean trenches are "destructive" plate edges where two plates are pushing against each other. One plate descends beneath the other into the mantle where it is melted. These areas are called "subduction zones."

A third type of plate edge is called a transform fault. Here two plates are moving alongside each other. The best known of these plate edges is the San Andreas fault in California, which separates the Pacific plate from the North American plate.

Slow-moving currents in the partly molten asthenosphere, which underlies the solid lithosphere, are responsible for moving the plates, a process called plate tectonics.

MOUNTAIN BUILDING

The study of plate tectonics has helped geol-

ogists to understand the mechanisms that are responsible for the creation of mountains. Many of the world's greatest ranges were created by the collision of two plates and the bending of the intervening strata into huge loops, or folds. For example, the Himalayas began to rise around 50 million years ago, when a plate supporting India collided with the huge Eurasian plate. Rocks on the floor of the intervening and long-vanished Tethys Sea were squeezed up to form the Himalayan Mountain Range.

Plate movements also create tension that cracks rocks, producing long faults along which rocks move upward, downward, or sideways. Block mountains are formed when blocks of rock are pushed upward along faults. Steep-sided rift valleys are formed when blocks of land sink down between faults. For example, the basin and range region of the southwestern United States has both block mountains and downfaulted basins, such as Death Valley.

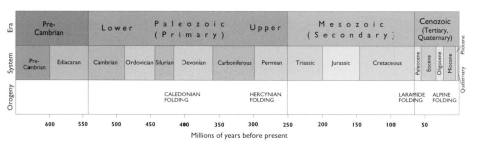

Era	Pre-Cambrian		Lower	Paleozoic (Primary)		Upper		Mesozoic (Secondary)			Cenozoic (Tertiary, Quaternary)			
System	Pre-Cambrian	Ediacaran	Cambrian	Ordovician	Silurian	Devonian	Carboniferous	Permian	Triassic	Jurassic	Cretaceous	Paleocene / Eocene / Oligocene / Miocene	Pliocene / Quaternary		
Orogeny					CALEDONIAN FOLDING		HERCYNIAN FOLDING					LARAMIDE FOLDING	ALPINE FOLDING		
	600	550	500	450	400	350	300	250	200	150	100	50			

Millions of years before present

EARTHQUAKES AND VOLCANOES

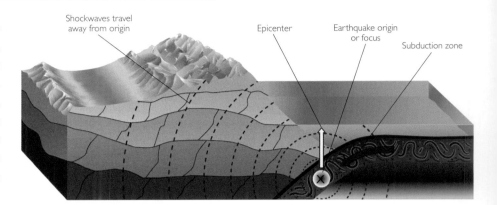

On October 8, 2005, a massive earthquake occurred along the converging Indian and Eurasian plates in northern Pakistan's Northwest Frontier province and Indian-ruled Kashmir. Measuring 7.6 on the Richter scale, it caused about 87,000 deaths. Thousands were injured and 3 million people were left homeless at the onset of winter. The relief work was hampered by landslides, which blocked the roads leading to remote village communities.

THE RESTLESS EARTH

Earthquakes can occur anywhere, whenever rocks move along faults. But the most severe and most numerous earthquakes occur near

▼ San Andreas Fault, United States

Geologists call the San Andreas fault in southwestern California a transform, or strike-slip, fault. Sudden movements along it cause earthquakes. In 1906, shifts of about 15 ft [4.5 m] occurred near San Francisco, causing a massive earthquake.

the edges of the plates that make up the Earth's lithosphere. Japan, for example, lies in a particularly unstable region above subduction zones, where plates are descending into the Earth's mantle. It lies in a zone encircling the Pacific Ocean, called the "Pacific ring of fire."

Plates do not move smoothly. Their edges are jagged and for most of the time they are locked together. However, pressure gradually builds up until the rocks break and the plates lurch forward, setting off vibrations ranging from slight tremors to terrifying earthquakes. The greater the pressure released, the more destructive the earthquake.

Earthquakes are also common along the ocean trenches where plates are moving apart, but they mostly occur so far from land that they do little damage. Far more destructive are the earthquakes that occur where plates are moving alongside each other. For example, the earthquakes that periodically rock southwestern California are caused by movements along the San Andreas Fault.

The spot where an earthquake originates is called the focus, while the point on the Earth's surface directly above the focus is called the epicenter. Two kinds of waves, P-waves or compressional waves and S-waves or shear waves, travel from the focus to the surface where they make the ground shake. P-waves travel faster than S-waves and the time difference between their arrival at recording stations enables scientists to calculate the distance from a station to the epicenter.

Earthquakes are measured on the Richter scale, which indicates the magnitude of the shock. The most destructive earthquakes are shallow-focus, that is, the focus is within 37 miles [60 km] of the surface. A magnitude of 7.0 is a major earthquake, but lower magnitude 'quakes can cause great damage if their epicenters are close to densely populated areas.

Scientists have been working for years to find effective ways of forecasting earthquakes but

▲ Earthquakes in subduction zones
Along subduction zones, one plate is descending beneath another. The plates are locked together until the rocks break and the descending plate lurches forward. From the point where the plate moves – the origin – seismic waves spread through the lithosphere, making the ground shake. The earthquake in Mexico City in 1985 occurred in this way.

NOTABLE EARTHQUAKES
(since 1900)

Year	Location	Mag.
1906	San Francisco, USA	8.3
1906	Valparaiso, Chile	8.6
1908	Messina, Italy	7.5
1915	Avezzano, Italy	7.5
1920	Gansu, China	8.6
1923	Yokohama, Japan	8.3
1927	Nan Shan, China	8.3
1932	Gansu, China	7.6
1934	Bihar, India/Nepal	8.4
1935	Quetta, India[†]	7.5
1939	Chillan, Chile	8.3
1939	Erzincan, Turkey	7.9
1964	Anchorage, Alaska	8.4
1968	N. E. Iran	7.4
1970	N. Peru	7.7
1976	Guatemala	7.5
1976	Tangshan, China	8.2
1978	Tabas, Iran	7.7
1980	El Asnam, Algeria	7.3
1980	S. Italy	7.2
1985	Mexico City, Mexico	8.1
1988	N. W. Armenia	6.8
1990	N. Iran	7.7
1993	Maharashtra, India	6.4
1994	Los Angeles, USA	6.6
1995	Kobe, Japan	7.2
1995	Sakhalin Is., Russia	7.5
1996	Yunnan, China	7.0
1997	N. E. Iran	7.1
1998	N. E. Afghanistan	7.0
1999	Izmit, Turkey	7.4
1999	Taipei, Taiwan	7.6
2001	El Salvador	7.7
2001	Gujarat, India	7.7
2002	Baghlan, Afghanistan	6.1
2003	Mexico	7.8
2003	Bam, Iran	6.7
2004	N. Morocco	6.5
2004	Sumatra, Indonesia	9.1
2005	N. Pakistan	7.6
2006	Java, Indonesia	6.4
2007	S. Peru	8.0
2008	Sichuan, China	7.8
2009	L'Aquila, Italy	6.3

[†] now Pakistan

with limited success. But in the early 2000s, some scientists claimed that they had successfully forecast eruptions by identifying tremors, called "long-period events." They believe these relatively minor but long-lasting tremors are caused when magma surges up underground passages but fails to reach the surface.

VOLCANIC ERUPTIONS

Most active volcanoes also occur on or near plate edges. Many undersea volcanoes along the ocean ridges are formed from magma that wells up from the asthenosphere to fill the gaps created as the plates, on the opposite sides of the ridges, move apart. Some of these volcanoes reach the surface to form islands. Iceland is a country which straddles the Mid-Atlantic Ocean Ridge. It is gradually becoming wider as magma rises to the surface through faults and vents. Other volcanoes lie alongside subduction zones. The magma that fuels them comes from the melted edges of the descending plates.

A few volcanoes lie far from plate edges. For example, Mauna Loa and Kilauea on Hawai'i are situated near the center of the huge Pacific plate. The molten magma that reaches the surface is created by a source of heat, called a "hot spot," in the Earth's mantle.

Magma is molten rock at temperatures of about 2,012°F to 2,192°F [1,100°C to 1,200°C]. It contains gases and superheated steam. The chemical composition of magma varies. Viscous magma is rich in silica and superheated steam, while runny magma contains less silica and steam. The chemical composition of the magma affects the nature of volcanic eruptions.

Explosive volcanoes contain thick, viscous magma. When they erupt, they usually hurl clouds of ash (shattered fragments of cooled magma) into the air. By contrast, quiet volcanoes emit long streams of runny magma, or lava. However, many volcanoes are intermediate in type, sometimes erupting explosively and sometimes emitting streams of fluid lava. Explosive and intermediate volcanoes usually have a conical shape, while quiet volcanoes are flattened, resembling upturned saucers. They are often called shield volcanoes.

One dangerous type of eruption is called a *nuée ardente*, or "glowing cloud." It occurs when a cloud of intensely hot volcanic gases, dust particles, and superheated steam are exploded sideways from a volcano, often following a violent explosion which hurls ash high into the air. Pyroclastic surges and flows are similar. The clouds sweep downhill, destroying all in their paths. Pyroclastic surges and flows killed many people during the Vesuvius eruption in AD 79. The bodies were later buried by ash falls.

▲ Cross-section of a volcano

Volcanoes are vents in the ground, through which magma reaches the surface. The term volcano is also used for the mountains formed from volcanic rocks. Beneath volcanoes are pockets of magma derived from the semimolten asthenosphere in the mantle. The magma rises under pressure through the overlying rocks until it reaches the surface. There it emerges through vents as pyroclasts, ranging in size from large lumps of magma, called volcanic bombs, to fine volcanic ash and dust. In quiet eruptions, streams of liquid lava run down the side of the mountain. Side vents sometimes appear on the flanks of existing volcanoes.

▲ Kilauea Volcano, Hawai'i

The volcanic Hawaiian islands in the North Pacific Ocean were formed as the Pacific plate moved over a "hot spot" in the Earth's mantle. Kilauea on Hawai'i emits blazing streams of liquid lava.

FORCES OF NATURE

On December 26, 2004, a sudden movement of the plates beneath the Indian Ocean triggered a magnitude 9.1 earthquake. The 'quake created a tsunami, a fast-moving wave that battered the coasts of southern and southeastern Asia, and was even felt in East Africa. Entire communities were wiped out and the death toll was about 280,000. The worst damage occurred in Indonesia, Thailand, Sri Lanka, and India. Such events remind us of the great forces that operate inside our planet. But other forces are operating continuously, forever changing the landscape.

The chief forces acting on the surface of the Earth are weathering, running water, ice, and winds. The forces of erosion seem to act slowly. One estimate suggests that an average of only 1.4 inches [3.5 cm] of land is removed by natural processes every 1,000 years. But over millions of years, the highest mountains are eroded away.

WEATHERING
Weathering occurs in all parts of the world, but the most effective type of weathering in any area depends on the climate and the nature of the

▼ *Grand Canyon, Arizona, at dusk*

The Grand Canyon in the United States is one of the world's natural wonders. Eroded by the Colorado River and its tributaries, it is up to 1 mile [1.6 km] deep and 18 miles [29 km] wide.

RATES OF EROSION

	SLOW ← WEATHERING RATE → FAST		
Mineral solubility	low (e.g. quartz)	moderate (e.g. feldspar)	high (e.g. calcite)
Rainfall	low	moderate	heavy
Temperature	cold	temperate	hot
Vegetation	sparse	moderate	lush
Soil cover	bare rock	thin to moderate soil	thick soil

Weathering is the breakdown and decay of rocks in situ. It may be mechanical (physical), chemical, or biological.

rocks. For example, in cold mountain areas, when water freezes in cracks in rocks, the ice occupies 9% more space than the water. This exerts a force which, when repeated over and over again, can split boulders apart. By contrast, in hot deserts, intense heating by day and cooling by night causes the outer layers of rocks to expand and contract until they break up and peel away like layers of an onion. These are examples of what is called mechanical weathering.

Chemical weathering involves chemical reactions in various rocks. These reactions usually involve water. For example, rainwater containing carbon dioxide dissolved from the air or soil is a weak acid that reacts with limestone, wearing out pits, tunnels, and complex networks of caves. Water also combines with some minerals, such as feldspar in granite, to create kaolin, a soft white clay.

▲ *Rates of erosion*

The chart shows that the rates at which weathering takes place depend on the chemistry and hardness of rocks, climatic factors, especially rainfall and temperature, the vegetation, and the nature of the soil cover in any area. The effects of weathering are increased by human action, particularly the removal of vegetation and the exposure of soils to the rain and wind.

▼ Glaciers

During Ice Ages, ice spreads over large areas but, during warm periods, the ice retreats. The chart shows that the volume of ice in many glaciers is decreasing. Experts estimate that, between 1850 and the early 21st century, more than half of the ice in Alpine glaciers has melted. In 2007, a scientific report stated that 80% of Europe's glaciers will vanish by the end of the 21st century because of global warming.

RUNNING WATER, ICE, AND WIND

In moist regions, rivers are effective in shaping the land. They transport material worn away by weathering and erode the land. They wear out V-shaped valleys in upland regions, while vigorous meanders widen their middle courses. The work of rivers is at its most spectacular when earth movements lift up flat areas and rejuvenate the rivers, giving them a new erosive power capable of wearing out such features as the Grand Canyon. Rivers also have a constructive role. Some of the world's most fertile regions are deltas and flood plains composed of sediments periodically dumped there by such rivers as the Ganges, Mississippi, and Nile.

▲ *Juneau Glacier, Alaska*

Like huge conveyor belts, glaciers transport weathered debris from mountain regions. Rocks frozen in the ice give the glaciers teeth, enabling them to wear out typical glaciated land features.

ANNUAL FLUCTUATIONS FOR SELECTED GLACIERS

Glacier name and location	Changes in the annual mass balance †		
	1970–1	1990–1	2000–2001
Alfotbreen, Norway	+940	+790	−50
Careser, Italy	−650	−1,730	−1,860
Djankuat, Russia	−230	−310	−1,760
Grasubreen, Norway	+470	−520	−30
Gries, Switzerland	−970	−1,480	−902
Hintereisferner, Austria	−600	−1,325	−806
Place, Canada	−343	−990	−690
Sarennes, France	−1,100	−,360	−1,160
Storglaciaren, Sweden	−190	+170	−115
Ürümqi, China	+102	−706	−1,170
Wolverine, USA	+770	−410	−480

† *The annual mass balance is defined as the difference between glacier accumulation and ablation (melting) averaged over the whole glacier. Balances are expressed as water equivalent in millimeters. A "plus" indicates an increase in the depth or length of the glacier; a "minus" indicates a reduction.*

Running water in the form of sea waves and currents shapes coastlines, wearing out caves, natural arches, and stacks. The sea also transports and deposits worn material to form such features as spits and bars.

Glaciers in cold mountain regions flow downhill, gradually deepening valleys and shaping dramatic landscapes. They erode steep-sided U-shaped valleys, into which rivers often plunge in large waterfalls. Other features include cirques, armchair-shaped basins bounded by knife-edged ridges called *arêtes*. When several glacial cirques erode to form radial *arêtes*, pyramidal peaks like the Matterhorn are created. Deposits of moraine, rock material dumped by the glacier, are further evidence that ice once covered large areas.

The work of glaciers, like other agents of erosion, varies with the climate. In recent years, global warming has been making glaciers retreat in many areas, while several of the ice shelves in Antarctica have been breaking up.

Many land features in deserts were formed by running water at a time when the climate was much rainier than it is today. Water erosion also occurs when flash floods are caused by rare thunderstorms. But the chief agent of erosion in dry areas is wind-blown sand, which can strip the paint from cars, and undercut boulders to create mushroom-shaped rocks.

OCEANS AND ICE

In 2005, Tim Barnett of the Scripps Institution of Oceanography presented a paper to the American Association for the Advancement of Science showing that the upper waters of the oceans had markedly warmed up in the last 65 years, dramatic evidence of global warming.

Oceanography is a major science, but, only about 50 years ago, little was known of the dark world beneath the waves. But through the use of modern technology, including echo-sounders, magnetometers, research ships equipped with huge drills, and satellites, many of the oceans' secrets have been unraveled. Scientists have visited the ocean ridges in submersibles. There, they found hot vents, or "black smokers" – chimney-like structures made up of minerals deposited from the hot water. Around them, are swarms of bacteria – the base of a food chain that includes strange creatures, many unknown to science, such as giant worms, eyeless shrimps, and white clams. These discoveries have led some to speculate that the first living organisms on Earth may have evolved in such conditions on ancient ocean floors.

The study of the ocean floor led to the discovery that the oceans are geologically young features – no more than 200 million years old. It also revealed evidence as to how oceans form and continents drift because of the action of plate tectonics.

THE BLUE PLANET

Water covers almost 71% of the Earth's surface, which makes it look blue when viewed from space. Oceanographers recognize five oceans: the Pacific, Atlantic, Indian, Southern (or Antarctic), and Arctic, but they are all interconnected. The average depth of the oceans is 12,238 ft [3,370 m], but they are divided into several zones.

Around most continents are gently sloping continental shelves, which are flooded parts of the continents. The shelves end at the continental slope, at a depth of about 656 ft [200 m]. This slope leads steeply down to the abyss. The deepest parts of the oceans are the trenches, which reach a maximum depth of 36,161 ft [11,022 m] in the Mariana Trench in the western Pacific.

Most marine life is found in the top 656 ft [200 m], where there is sufficient sunlight for plants, called phytoplankton, to grow. Below this zone, life becomes more and more scarce, though no part of the ocean, even at the bottom of the deepest trenches, is completely without living things.

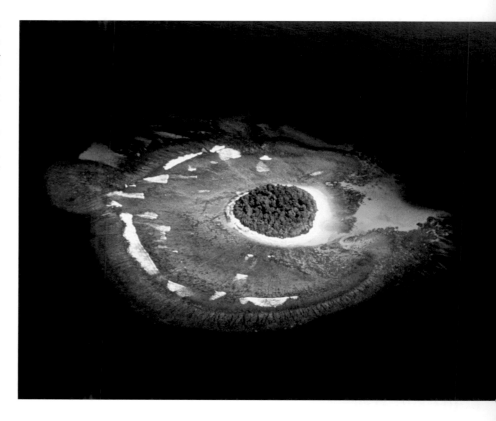

▲ *Vava'u Island, Tonga*
This small coral atoll in northern Tonga consists of a central island covered by rain forest. Low coral reefs washed by the waves surround a shallow central lagoon.

Continental islands, such as the British Isles, are high parts of the continental shelves. For example, until about 7,500 years ago, when the ice sheets formed during the Ice Ages were melting, raising the sea level and filling the North Sea and the Strait of Dover, Britain was linked to mainland Europe.

By contrast, oceanic islands, such as the Hawaiian chain in the North Pacific Ocean, rise from the ocean floor. All oceanic islands are of volcanic origin, although many of them in warm parts of the oceans have sunk and are capped by layers of coral to form ring- or horseshoe-shaped atolls and coral reefs.

OCEAN WATER

The oceans contain about 97% of the world's water. Seawater contains more than 70 dissolved elements, but chloride and sodium make up 85% of the total. Sodium chloride is common salt and it makes seawater salty. The salinity of the oceans is mostly between 3.3–3.7%. Ocean water fed by icebergs or large rivers is less saline than shallow seas in the tropics, where the evaporation rate is high. Seawater is a source of salt but the water is useless for agriculture or drinking unless it is desalinated. However, land areas get a regular

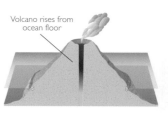
Volcano rises from ocean floor

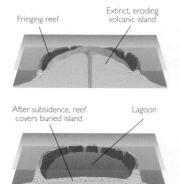
Fringing reef — Extinct, eroding volcanic island

After subsidence, reef covers buried island — Lagoon

▲ *Development of an atoll*
Some of the volcanoes that rise from the ocean floor reach the surface to form islands. Some of these islands subside and become submerged. As an island sinks, coral starts to grow around the rim of the volcano, building up layer upon layer of limestone deposits to form fringing reefs. Sometimes coral grows on the tip of a central cone to form an island in the middle of the atoll.

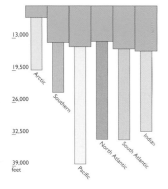

▲ The ocean depths
The diagram shows the average depths (in dark blue) and the greatest depths in the oceans. The Pacific Ocean contains the world's deepest trenches, including the Mariana Trench, where the deepest manned descent was made by the bathyscaphe Trieste in 1960. It reached a depth of 35,813 ft [10,916 m].

Relative sizes of the world's oceans:
PACIFIC 46.4%   ATLANTIC 22.9%
INDIAN 20.4%   SOUTHERN 6.1%
ARCTIC 4.2%

supply of fresh water through the hydrological cycle (see page 42).

The density of seawater depends on its salinity and temperature. Temperatures vary from 28°F [–2°C], the freezing point of seawater at the poles, to around 86°F [30°C] in parts of the tropics. Density differences help to maintain the circulation of the world's oceans, especially deep-sea currents. But the main cause of currents within 1,148 ft [350 m] of the surface is the wind. Because of the Earth's rotation, currents are deflected, creating huge circular motions of surface water – clockwise in the northern hemisphere and counterclockwise in the southern hemisphere.

Ocean currents transport heat from the tropics to the polar regions and thus form part of the heat engine that drives the Earth's climates. Ocean currents have an especially marked effect on coastal climates, such as northwestern Europe. Some scientists are concerned that global warming may radically alter climates by weakening currents, such as the Gulf Stream, which is responsible for the mild winters in northwestern Europe.

ICE SHEETS, ICE CAPS, AND GLACIERS
Of the world's two ice sheets, the largest, covering most of Antarctica, has maximum depths of 15,748 ft [4,800 m]. Its volume is about nine times greater than the Greenland ice sheet. The ice sheets, together with smaller ice caps and glaciers, account for about 2% of the world's water. However, in many parts

of the world, the ice is melting and many scientists think the cause is global warming. In 2008, the US National Ice and Snow Center reported that Arctic sea ice was melting so quickly that the ocean might be ice-free in summer within ten years. The governments of countries bordering the Arctic have already begun to stake competing claims on the ocean's resources.

Only about 11,000 years ago, during the final phase of the Pleistocene Ice Age, ice covered much of the northern hemisphere. The Ice Age, which began about 1.8 million years ago, was not a continuous period of cold. Instead, it consisted of glacial periods when the ice advanced and warmer interglacial periods when temperatures rose and the ice retreated.

Some scientists believe that we are now living in an interglacial period, and that glacial conditions will recur in the future. Others fear that global warming, caused mainly by pollution, may melt the world's ice, raising sea levels by up to 180 ft [55 m]. Many fertile and densely populated coastal plains, islands, and cities would vanish from the map.

▼ Icebergs float past the Antarctic Peninsula
The Antarctic peninsula overlooks the Weddell Sea. The Weddell Sea and the Ross Sea are largely covered by huge ice shelves, which are extensions of the continental ice sheet. Many scientists are concerned that warmer weather is melting the ice sheets. In 2002, parts of the Larsen Ice Shelf, which adjoins the Antarctic Peninsula, collapsed and split up into icebergs.

THE EARTH'S ATMOSPHERE

Since the discovery in 1985 of a thinning of the ozone layer, creating a so-called "ozone hole," over Antarctica, many governments have worked to reduce the emissions of ozone-eating substances, notably the chlorofluorocarbons (CFCs) used in aerosols, refrigeration, air-conditioning, and dry cleaning.

Following forecasts that the ozone layer would rapidly repair itself as a result of controls on these emissions, scientists were surprised in early 1996 when a marked thinning of the ozone layer over the northern hemisphere was recorded. In 2008, scientists reported that the ozone hole over Antarctica was one of the largest yet. Marked thinning has also occurred over the Arctic region. Scientists have predicted that it may take more than 50 years before the ozone layer makes a full recovery.

The ozone layer in the stratosphere blocks out most of the dangerous ultraviolet B radiation in the Sun's rays. This radiation causes skin cancer and cataracts, as well as harming plants on the land and plankton in the oceans. The ozone layer is only one way in which the atmosphere protects life on Earth. The atmosphere

▼ *Moonrise seen from orbit*

This photograph taken by an orbiting Shuttle shows the crescent of the Moon. Silhouetted at the horizon is a dense cloud layer. The reddish-brown band is the tropopause, which separates the blue-white stratosphere from the yellow troposphere.

also provides the air we breathe and the carbon dioxide required by plants. It is also a shield against meteors and it acts as a blanket to prevent heat radiated from the Earth escaping into space.

LAYERS OF AIR

The atmosphere is divided into four main layers. The troposphere at the bottom contains about 85% of the atmosphere's total mass, where most weather conditions occur. The troposphere is about 9 miles [15 km] thick over the equator and 5 miles [8 km] thick at the poles. Temperatures decrease with height by approximately 2°F [1°C] for every 328 ft [100 m]. At the top of the troposphere is a level called the tropopause where temperatures are stable at around −67°F [−55°C]. Above the tropopause is the stratosphere, which contains the ozone layer. Here, at about 30 miles [50 km] above the Earth's surface, temperatures rise to about 32°F [0°C].

The ionosphere extends from the stratopause to about 373 miles [600 km] above the surface. Here temperatures fall up to about 50 miles [80 km], but then rise. The aurorae, which occur in the ionosphere when charged particles

CIRCULATION OF AIR

HIGH PRESSURE

LOW PRESSURE

WARM AIR

COLD AIR

SURFACE WINDS

CLOUDS

▲ *The circulation of the atmosphere can be divided into three rotating but interconnected air systems. These systems, or cells, are responsible for redistributing heat from the warm regions to the cold, and back again.*

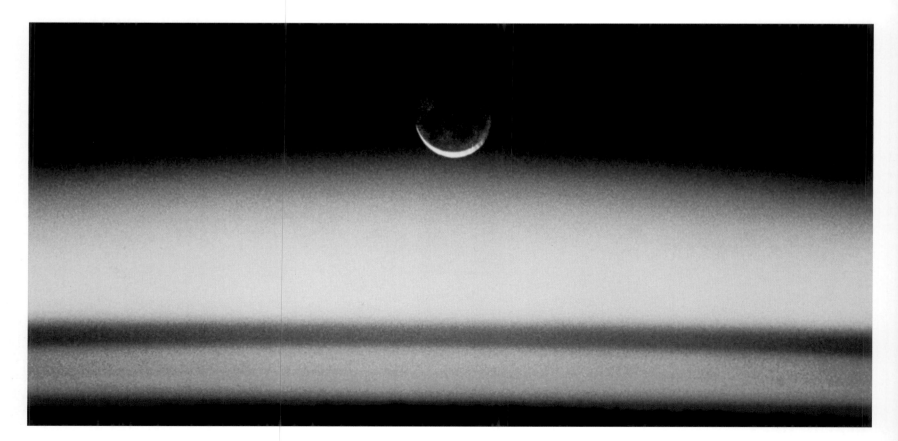

▶ *Classification of clouds*

Clouds are classified broadly into cumuliform, or "heap" clouds, and stratiform, or "layer" clouds. Both types occur at all levels. The highest clouds, composed of ice crystals, are cirrus, cirrostratus and cirrocumulus. Medium-height clouds include altostratus, a gray cloud that often indicates the approach of a depression, and altocumulus, a thicker and fluffier version of cirrocumulus. Low clouds include stratus, which forms dull, overcast skies; nimbostratus, a dark gray layer cloud which brings almost continuous rain and snow; cumulus, a brilliant white heap cloud; and stratocumulus, a layer cloud arranged in globular masses or rolls. Cumulonimbus, a cloud associated with thunderstorms, lightning, and heavy rain, often extends from low to medium altitudes. It has a flat base, a fluffy outline and often an anvil-shaped top.

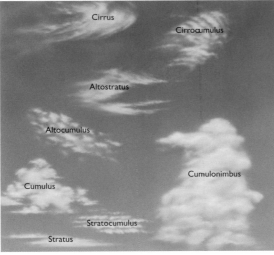

▲ *Jetstream from space*

Jetstreams are strong winds that normally blow near the tropopause. Cirrus clouds mark the route of the jet stream in this photograph, which shows the Red Sea, North Africa and the Nile valley, which appears as a dark band crossing the desert.

from the Sun interact with the Earth's magnetic field, are strongest near the poles. In the exosphere, the outermost layer, the atmosphere merges into space.

CIRCULATION OF THE ATMOSPHERE

The heating of the Earth is most intense around the equator where the Sun is high in the sky. Here warm, moist air rises in strong currents, creating a zone of low air pressure: the doldrums. The rising air eventually cools and spreads out north and south until it sinks downward around latitudes 30° North and 30° South. The zones of high air pressure caused

by the sinking air are called the "horse latitudes."

From the horse latitudes, trade winds blow back across the surface toward the equator, while westerly winds blow toward the poles. The warm westerlies finally meet the polar easterlies (cold dense air flowing from the poles). The line along which the warm and cold air streams meet is called the polar front. Depressions (or cyclones) are low-air-pressure frontal systems that form along the polar front.

COMPOSITION OF THE ATMOSPHERE

The air in the troposphere is made up mainly of nitrogen (78%) and oxygen (21%). Argon makes up more than 0.9% and there are also minute amounts of carbon dioxide, helium, hydrogen, krypton, methane, ozone, and xenon. The atmosphere also contains water vapor, the gaseous form of water, which, when it condenses around minute specks of dust and salt, forms tiny water droplets or ice crystals. Large masses of water droplets or ice crystals form clouds.

CLIMATE AND WEATHER

The year 2005 brought some phenomenal weather conditions. A record number of named tropical storms (26, of which 13 were classified as hurricanes) hit Central America and the United States. Hurricane Katrina devastated New Orleans in August. It was the most destructive hurricane ever to strike the United States, causing about 1,380 deaths. In 2007, the Intergovernmental Panel on Climate Change (IPCC) stated that extreme weather events resulting from global warming are caused at least in part by the greenhouse effect, whereby heat is trapped in the atmosphere by such gases as carbon dioxide. In 2008, carbon dioxide levels in the atmosphere reached 387 parts per million, as compared with about 280 parts per million in the late 1700s. The IPCC predicted a temperature rise of 7.2°F [4°C] by 2100. Sea levels would rise and flood coastal plains.

Climate is defined as the average weather of a place based on data obtained over a long period. By contrast, weather is the day-to-day condition of the atmosphere. In some areas, the weather is stable; in other areas, especially the middle latitudes, it is highly variable.

CLIMATIC FACTORS

Climate depends basically on the unequal heating of the Sun between the equator and the poles. But ocean currents and terrain also affect climate. For example, despite their northerly positions, Norway's ports remain ice-free in winter. This is because of the warming effect of the North Atlantic Drift, an extension of the Gulf Stream which flows across the Atlantic Ocean from the Gulf of Mexico.

▲ *Satellite image of Hurricane Floyd in 1999*
Hurricanes form over warm oceans north and south of the equator. Their movements are tracked by satellites, enabling forecasters to issue advance warnings. North American forecasters identify them with boys' and girls' names.

By contrast, the cold Benguela current which flows up the coast of southwestern Africa cools the coast and causes arid conditions. This is because the cold onshore winds are warmed as they pass over the land. The warm air can hold more water vapor than cold air, giving the winds a drying effect.

The terrain affects climate in several ways. Because temperatures fall with altitude, high-

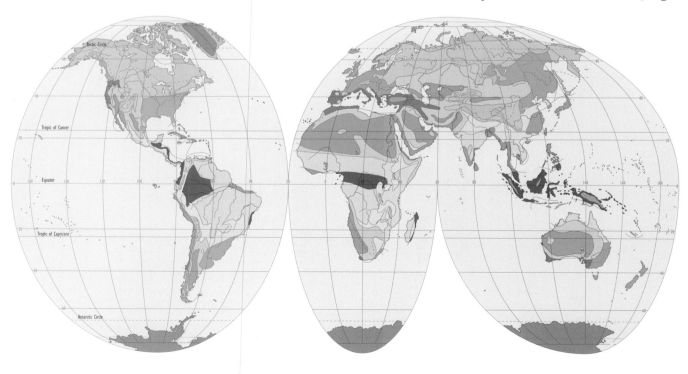

CLIMATIC REGIONS

Tropical rainy climates
All mean monthly temperatures above 64°F [18°C].

 RAIN FOREST CLIMATE

 MONSOON CLIMATE

 SAVANNA CLIMATE

Dry climates
Low rainfall combined with a wide range of temperatures.

 STEPPE CLIMATE

 DESERT CLIMATE

Warm temperate rainy climates
The mean temperature is below 64°F [18°C] but above 26°F [–3°C], and that of the warmest month is over 50°F [10°C].

 DRY WINTER CLIMATE

 DRY SUMMER CLIMATE

 CLIMATE WITH NO DRY SEASON

Cold temperate rainy climates
The mean temperature of the coldest month is below 37°F [3°C] but the warmest month is over 50°F [10°C].

 DRY WINTER CLIMATE

 CLIMATE WITH NO DRY SEASON

Polar climates
The temperature of the warmest month is below 50°F [10°C], giving permanently frozen subsoil.

 TUNDRA CLIMATE

 POLAR CLIMATE

▶ Floods in St Louis, USA

The satellite image, right, shows the extent of the floods at St Louis at the confluence of the Mississippi and the Missouri rivers in June and July 1993. The floods occurred when very heavy rainfall raised river levels by up to 46 ft [14 m]. The floods reached their greatest extent between Minneapolis in the north and a point approximately 93 miles [150 km] south of St Louis. In places, the width of the Mississippi increased to nearly 7 miles [11 km], while the Missouri reached widths of 20 miles [32 km]. In all, more than 10,800 sq miles [28,000 sq km] were inundated and hundreds of towns and cities were flooded. Damage to crops was estimated at $8 billion.

The US was hit again by flooding in early 1997, when heavy rainfall in North Dakota and Minnesota caused the Red River to flood. Many scientists believe that recent extreme weather events are probably linked to global warming.

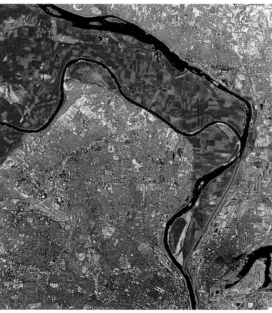

▲ Flood damage in the United States

In June and July 1993, the Mississippi River basin suffered record floods. The photograph shows a sunken church in Illinois. The flooding along the Mississippi, Missouri and other rivers caused great damage, amounting to about $12 billion. At least 48 people died in the floods.

CLIMATIC REGIONS

The two major factors that affect climate are temperature and precipitation, including rain and snow. In addition, seasonal variations and other climatic features are also taken into account. Climatic classifications vary because of the weighting given to various features. Yet most classifications are based on five main climatic types: tropical rainy climates; dry climates; warm temperate rainy climates; cold temperate rainy climates; and very cold polar climates. Some classifications also allow for the effect of altitude. The main climatic regions are subdivided according to seasonal variations and also to the kind of vegetation associated with the climate. With rain throughout the year, rain forest climates differ from monsoon and savanna climates, which have dry seasons, while desert climates differ from steppe climates, which have enough moisture for grasses to grow.

lands are cooler than lowlands at the same latitude. Terrain also affects rainfall. When moist onshore winds pass over mountain ranges, they are chilled as they are forced to rise and the water vapor they contain condenses to form clouds, which bring rain and snow. Beyond the mountains, the air descends and is warmed. These drying winds create rain-shadow (arid) regions on the lee side of mountains.

WATER AND LAND USE

All life on land depends on fresh water. Yet about 80 countries now face acute water shortages. The world demand for fresh water is increasing by about 2.3% a year and this demand will double every 21 years. About a billion people, mainly in developing countries, do not have access to clean drinking water and around 10 million die every year from drinking dirty water. This problem is made worse in many countries by the pollution of rivers and lakes.

UN experts predict that water is becoming the most pressing environmental and development issue facing the world. By 2003, heavily populated regions in 26 countries were suffering serious water shortages. In 20 years, this number

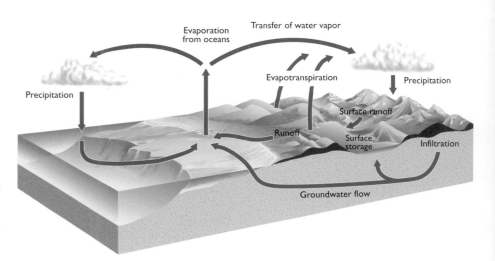

Evaporation from oceans
Transfer of water vapor
Precipitation
Evapotranspiration
Precipitation
Surface runoff
Runoff
Surface storage
Infiltration
Groundwater flow

▼ Hoover Dam, United States
The Hoover Dam in Arizona controls the Colorado River's flood waters. Its reservoir supplies domestic and irrigation water to the southwest, while a hydroelectric plant produces electricity.

will probably rise to 65. In 2006, the United Nations estimated that nearly 2 million children die every year due to lack of clean water and proper sanitation. Some 1.1 billion people do not have proper sanitation and 2.6 billion suffer from inadequate sewerage. In 2008, the UN predicted that, by 2025, two-thirds of the world's people will experience water shortages.

THE WORLD'S WATER SUPPLY

Of the world's total water supply, 99.4% is in the oceans or frozen in bodies of ice. Most of the rest circulates through the rocks beneath our feet as groundwater. Water in rivers and lakes, in the soil and in the atmosphere together make up only 0.013% of the world's water.

The freshwater supply on land is dependent on the hydrological, or water, cycle which is driven by the Sun's heat. Water is evaporated from the oceans and carried into the air as invisible water vapor. Although this vapor averages less than 2% of the total mass of the atmosphere, it is the chief component from the standpoint of weather.

When air rises, water vapor condenses into visible water droplets or ice crystals, which eventually fall to earth as rain, snow, sleet, hail, or frost. Some of the precipitation that reaches the ground returns directly to the atmosphere through evaporation or transpiration via plants. Much of the rest of the water flows into the rocks to become groundwater, or across the surface into rivers and, eventually, back to the oceans, so completing the hydrological cycle.

WATER AND AGRICULTURE

In 2005, a US study revealed that about 40% of the world's land is used to grow crops or to graze cattle. The biggest recent changes have occurred in the Amazon basin, where tropical forest is being felled to create land for growing soybeans.

▲ The hydrological cycle
The hydrological cycle is responsible for the continuous circulation of water around the planet. Water vapor contains and transports latent heat, or latent energy. When the water vapor condenses back into water (and falls as rain, hail or snow), the heat is released. When condensation takes place on cold nights, the cooling effect associated with nightfall is offset by the liberation of latent heat.

WATER DISTRIBUTION
The distribution of planetary water, by percentage.

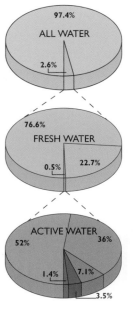

97.4%
ALL WATER
2.6%

76.6%
FRESH WATER
0.5%   22.7%

ACTIVE WATER
52%   36%
1.4%   7.1%
3.5%

ALL WATER	ACTIVE WATER
OCEANS	LAKES
FRESH WATER	SOIL
FRESH WATER	ATMOSPHERE
ICE CAPS	RIVERS
GROUNDWATER	LIVING THINGS
ACTIVE WATER	

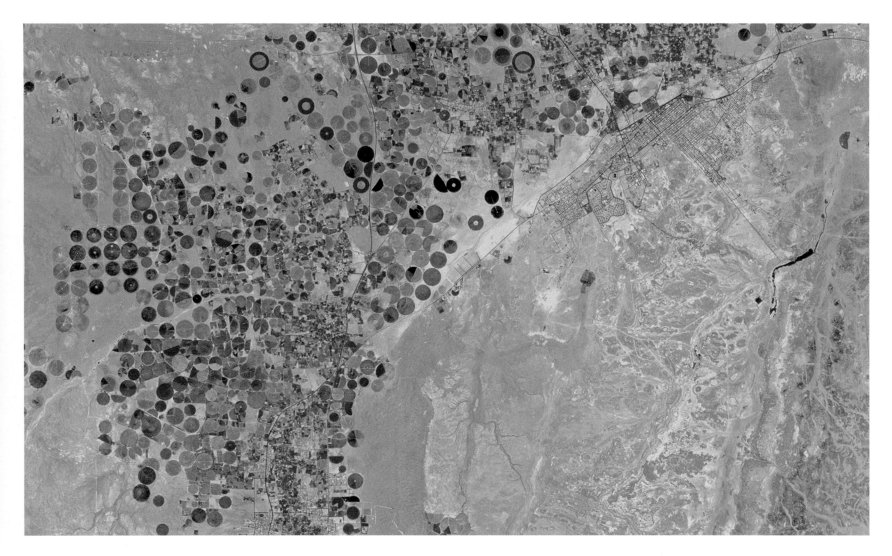

▲ *Irrigation in Saudi Arabia*

*Saudi Arabia is a desert country that gets its water from
oases, which tap groundwater supplies, and desalination
plants. The sale of oil has enabled the arid countries of
southwestern Asia to develop their agriculture. In the above
satellite image, vegetation appears as brown and red circles,
generated by center-pivot irrigation systems.*

The study pointed out that the world is running out of fertile land, because large areas are too dry, too cold or too mountainous for farming. Although the demand for food increases every year, problems arise when attempts are made to increase the area of farmland. The soils and climate of tropical forests or semiarid regions are not ideal for farming and often lead to the deterioration of fragile environments. To increase food supply, farmers must concentrate on making existing agriculture more productive.

To grow crops, farmers need fertile, workable land, an equable climate, and an adequate supply of fresh water. In some areas, the water supply comes directly from rain, but many other regions depend on irrigation.

Irrigation involves water conservation through the building of dams which hold back storage reservoirs. In some areas, irrigation water comes from underground aquifers, layers of permeable and porous rocks through which groundwater percolates. But in many cases, the water in the aquifers is not being renewed. About 270 major aquifers are shared by two or more countries. In 2008, UNESCO warned of possible conflict that might break out between countries as the water in the aquifers runs out.

Other sources of irrigation water are desalination plants, which remove salt from seawater and pump it to farms. This is a highly expensive process and is employed in areas where water supplies are extremely low, such as the island of Malta, or in the oil-rich desert countries around the Persian Gulf, which can afford to build huge desalination plants.

LAND USE BY CONTINENT (2006)

	Forest	Permanent pasture	Permanent crops	Arable	Non-productive
N. & C. America	26.0%	16.4%	0.7%	12.0%	45.0%
S. America	50.5%	26.4%	0.8%	6.1%	16.0%
Europe	46.0%	8.3%	0.8%	12.9%	32.0%
Africa	21.8%	31.1%	0.9%	6.7%	39.5%
Asia	17.8%	35.8%	2.1%	16.4%	28.0%
Oceania	23.3%	47.8%	0.4%	5.9%	23.0%

THE NATURAL WORLD

In 2007, the International Union for the Conservation of Nature published its Red List, stating that 16,306 animal and plant species were threatened with extinction, while, in 2008, the IUCN reported that at least a fifth of all mammal species were at risk of extinction, including 48% of primates. Around 75% of the world's assessed plants are also endangered, mainly because of human activities. This devastating reduction in our planet's biodiversity might lead to a loss of the unique combination of genes that could be vital in improving food production or in the manufacture of drugs used to combat disease.

Extinctions of species have occurred throughout Earth's history, but today the extinction rate is estimated to be about 10,000 times the natural average. Some scientists have even compared it with the mass extinction that wiped out the dinosaurs 65 million years ago. However, the main cause of today's high extinction rate is not some natural disaster, such as the impact of an asteroid a few miles across, but it is the result of human actions. In some areas, such

▼ *Rain forest in Rwanda*
Rain forests are the most threatened of the world's biomes. Effective conservation policies must demonstrate to poor local people that they can benefit from the survival of the forests.

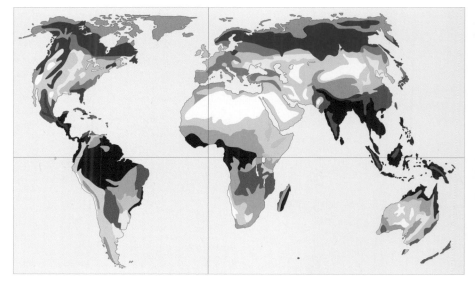

as Western Europe, the natural habitats were destroyed long ago. The greatest damage is now occurring in tropical rain forests, which contain more than half of the world's known species.

Modern technology has enabled people to live comfortably almost anywhere on Earth. But most plants and many animals are adapted to particular climatic conditions, and they live in association with and dependent on each other. Plant and animal communities that cover large areas are called biomes.

THE WORLD'S BIOMES

The world's biomes are defined mainly by climate and vegetation. They range from the tundra, in polar regions and high mountain regions, to the lush equatorial rain forests.

The Arctic tundra covers large areas in the polar regions of the northern hemisphere. Snow covers the land for more than half of the year and the subsoil, called permafrost, is permanently frozen. Comparatively few species can survive in this harsh, treeless environment. The main plants are hardy mosses, lichens, grasses, sedges, and low shrubs. However, in summer, the tundra plays an important part in world animal geography, when its growing plants and swarms of insects provide food for migrating animals and birds that arrive from the south.

The tundra of the northern hemisphere merges in the south into a vast region of needleleaf evergreen forest, called the boreal forest or taiga. Such trees as fir, larch, pine, and spruce are adapted to survive the long, bitterly cold winters of this region, but the number of plant and animal species is again small. South of the boreal forests is a zone of mixed needleleaf evergreens and broadleaf deciduous trees, which shed their leaves in winter. In warmer areas, this

NATURAL VEGETATION

- TUNDRA & MOUNTAIN VEGETATION
- NEEDLELEAF EVERGREEN FOREST
- MIXED NEEDLELEAF EVERGREEN & BROADLEAF DECIDUOUS TREES
- BROADLEAF DECIDUOUS WOODLAND
- MID-LATITUDE GRASSLAND
- EVERGREEN BROADLEAF & DECIDUOUS TREES & SHRUBS
- SEMIDESERT SCRUB
- DESERT
- TROPICAL GRASSLAND (SAVANNA)
- TROPICAL BROADLEAF RAIN FOREST & MONSOON FOREST
- SUBTROPICAL BROADLEAF & NEEDLELEAF FOREST

▲ *The map shows the world's main biomes. The classification is based on the natural "climax" vegetation of regions, a result of the climate and the terrain. But human activities have greatly modified this basic division. For example, the original deciduous forests of Western Europe and the eastern United States have largely disappeared. In recent times, human development of some semiarid areas has turned former dry grasslands into barren desert. Scientists predict that temperatures will rise by 7.2°F [4°C] by 2100, radically altering existing biomes. For example, many experts believe that global warming is currently threatening half of the Arctic tundra.*

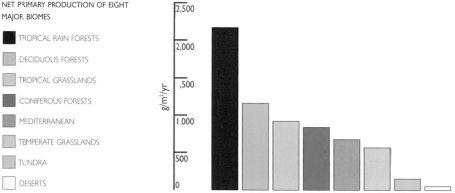

mixed forest merges into broadleaf deciduous forest, where the number and diversity of plant species is much greater.

Deciduous forests are adapted to temperate, humid regions. Evergreen broadleaf and deciduous trees grow in Mediterranean regions, with their hot, dry summers. But much of the original deciduous forest has been cut down and has given way to scrub and heathland. Grasslands occupy large areas in the middle latitudes, where the rainfall is insufficient to support forest growth. The moister grasslands are often called prairies, while drier areas are called steppe.

▲ *Tundra in subarctic Alaska, United States*
The Denali National Park, Alaska, contains magnificent mountain scenery and tundra vegetation that flourishes during the brief summer. The park is open between June 1 and September 15.

The tropics also contain vast dry areas of semidesert scrub that merges into desert, as well as large areas of tropical savanna, which is grassland, ranging from luxuriant to sparse, with scattered shrubs and trees, whose growth is limited by a marked dry season. Savanna regions support a wide range of animals.

Tropical and subtropical regions contain three types of forest biomes. The tropical rain forest, the world's richest biome measured by its plant and animal species, experiences rain and high temperatures throughout the year. Similar forests occur in monsoon regions, which have a season of very heavy rainfall. They, too, are rich in plant species, though less so than the tropical rain forest. A third type of forest is the subtropical broadleaf and needleleaf forest, found in such places as southeastern China, south-central Africa, and eastern Brazil.

▼ *The net primary production of eight major biomes is expressed in grams of dry organic matter per square meter per year. The tropical rain forests produce the greatest amount of organic material. The tundra and deserts produce the least.*

NET PRIMARY PRODUCTION OF EIGHT MAJOR BIOMES

■ TROPICAL RAIN FORESTS
▢ DECIDUOUS FORESTS
▢ TROPICAL GRASSLANDS
▢ CONIFEROUS FORESTS
▢ MEDITERRANEAN
▢ TEMPERATE GRASSLANDS
▢ TUNDRA
▢ DESERTS

THE HUMAN WORLD

In 2009, the UN calculated that the world's population was increasing by 152 every minute. Predictions of future growth vary. In 1999, UN demographers forecast that the world's population, which passed the 6 billion mark in October 1999, would reach 8.9 billion by 2050. It would level out after 2200, when it would peak at 11 billion. Another recent projection suggests that the world's population will peak at 9.22 billion in 2075, before declining slowly to reach 8.97 billion in 2300. Europe is expected to reach its lowest growth level in 2050. However, the populations of developing countries, those least able to afford the high costs arising from a population explosion, would continue to increase rapidly.

▼ *Quito, capital city of Ecuador*
In common with world trends, the annual growth rate in the population of Ecuador is declining, while urbanization is increasing rapidly.

Average world population growth rates are expected to decline from 1.6% per year in 1975–2001 to 1.1% in 2001–15. This is partly due to a decline in fertility rates – that is, the number of births to the number of women of child-bearing age – especially in developed countries where, as income has risen, the average size of families has fallen.

Declining fertility rates were also evident in many developing countries. Even Africa shows signs of such change, though its population is expected to triple before it begins to fall. Population growth is also dependent on death rates, which are affected by such factors as famine, disease, and the quality of medical care.

THE POPULATION EXPLOSION

The world's population has grown steadily throughout most of human history, though certain events triggered periods of population growth. The invention of agriculture, around 10,000 years ago, led to great changes in human society. Before then, most people had obtained food by hunting animals and gathering plants. Average life expectancies were probably no more than 20 years and life was hard. However, when farmers began to produce food surpluses, people began to live settled lives. This major milestone in human history led to the development of the first cities and early civilizations.

From an estimated 8 million in 8000 BC, the world population rose to about 300 million by AD 1000. Between 1000 and 1750, the rate of world population increase was around 0.1% per year, but another period of major economic and social change – the Industrial Revolution – began in the late 18th century. The Industrial Revolution led to improvements in farm technology and increases in food production. The world population began to increase quickly as industrialization spread across Europe and into North America. By 1850, it had reached 1.2 billion. The 2 billion mark was passed in the 1920s, and then the population rapidly doubled to 4 billion by the 1970s.

POPULATION FEATURES

Population growth affects the structure of societies. In developing countries with high annual rates of population increase, the large majority of the people are young and soon to become parents themselves. For example, in Kenya, which had until recently an annual rate of population growth of around 4%, about 43% of the population is under 15 years of age,

LARGEST CITIES

Within 10 years, for the first time ever, the majority of the world's population will live in urban areas. Almost all the urban growth will be in developing countries. Below is a list of cities with their estimated populations in the year 2015, in millions.

1	Tokyo	36.4
2	Mumbai (Bombay)	21.9
3	São Paulo	20.5
4	Mexico City	20.2
5	New York City	20.0
6	Delhi	18.7
7	Shanghai	17.2
8	Dhaka	17.0
9	Kolkata (Calcutta)	17.0
10	Karachi	14.9
11	Cairo	13.5
12	Buenos Aires	13.4
13	Los Angeles	13.2
14	Rio de Janiero	12.8
15	Metro Manila	12.8
16	Beijing	12.8
17	Lagos	12.4
18	Istanbul	11.1
19	Jakarta	10.8
20	Seoul	9.7

These city populations are based on figures for urban agglomerations rather than actual city limits.

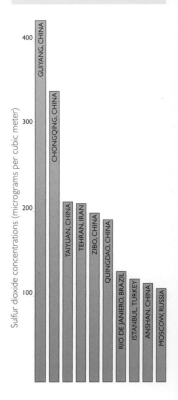

▲ *Urban air pollution*
This diagram shows the world's most polluted cities. Sulfur dioxide is an air pollutant which contributes to acid rain and can damage human health. The WHO threshold of sulfur dioxide concentrations is 150 micrograms per cubic meter.

as compared with 21% in the United States. Most developed countries have a fairly even spread across the age groups.

Such differences are reflected in average life expectancies. In a rich country, such as the USA, the average life expectancy in 2006 was 78 years (75 for men and 80 for women; women live longer, on average, than men). As a result, an increasing proportion of the people are elderly and retired. The reverse applies in many poor countries, where average life expectancies are below 60 years. In the early 21st century, life expectancies were falling in parts of southern Africa because of the spread of HIV and AIDS. However, overall, the world population is aging. In 2003, demographers predicted that the average age of the world's people will rise from 28 to 40 years.

Paralleling the population explosion has been a rapid growth in the number and size of cities. In 2008, for the first time in history, the number of people living in cities worldwide equaled the number living in rural areas.

Urbanization occurred first in areas under-

▲ Hong Kong's business district

By contrast with the picturesque old streets of Hong Kong, the business district of Hong Kong City, on the northern shore of Hong Kong Island, is a cluster of modern high-rise buildings. The glittering skyscrapers reflect the success of this tiny region, which has one of the strongest economies in Asia.

going the industrialization of their economies, but today it is also a feature of the developing world. In developing countries, people are leaving impoverished rural areas hoping to gain access to the education, health and other services available in cities. But many cities cannot provide the facilities necessitated by rapid population growth. By 2007, about a billion people lived in slums, where pollution, crime and disease are features of daily life.

The population explosion poses another problem for the entire world. No one knows how many people the world can support or how consumer demand will damage the fragile environments on our planet. The British economist Thomas Malthus argued in the late 18th century that overpopulation would lead to famine and war. But an increase in farm technology in the 19th and 20th centuries, combined with a green revolution, in which scientists developed high-yield crop varieties, has greatly increased food production since Malthus' time.

However, some modern scientists argue that overpopulation may become a problem in the 21st century. They argue that food and water shortages, caused at least in part by global warming, will lead to disastrous famines unless population growth can be halted. Some people favor birth-control programs. For example, in China, the world's most populous nation, the one-child family policy has slowed down the growth of its population.

POPULATION CHANGE

The projected population change for the years 2004–2050.

- OVER 125% POPULATION GAIN
- 100–125% POPULATION GAIN
- 50–100% POPULATION GAIN
- 25–50% POPULATION GAIN
- 0–25% POPULATION GAIN
- LOSS OR NO CHANGE
- NO DATA AVAILABLE

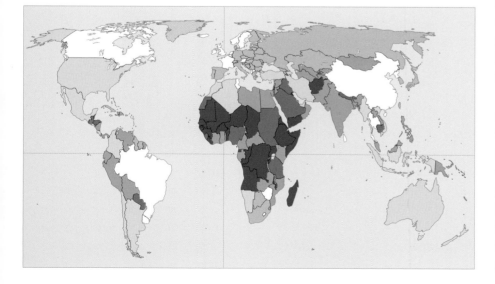

LANGUAGES AND RELIGIONS

In 2008, 89-year-old Marie Smith, the last person able to speak the Eyak language, died. Eyak became an extinct language, though before her death, she had compiled an Eyak dictionary and grammar guide. Eyak is one of about 20 native Alaskan languages, many of which are under threat of extinction. In 2009, UNESCO reported that about 2,500 languages were under risk, 500 "critically endangered" and 99 with fewer than 10 native speakers.

Improved transport and communications are partly to blame, because they bring people from various cultures into closer and closer contact. Many children no longer speak the language of their parents, preferring instead to learn the language used at their schools. The pressures on children to speak dominant rather than minority languages are often great. In the first part of the 20th century, Native American children were punished if they spoke their native language.

The disappearance of a language represents the extinction of a way of thinking, a unique expression of the experiences and knowledge of a group of people. Language and religion together give people an identity and a sense of belonging. However, there are others who argue that the disappearance of minority languages is a step toward international understanding and economic efficiency.

◄ The Kaaba, Makkah (Mecca), Saudi Arabia

Islam is a major world religion. It was first preached by the Prophet Muhammad who was born in Makkah (or Mecca) in Saudi Arabia in about AD 570. Its holiest shrine is the Kaaba, a black, square building in the Great Mosque in Makkah. Every adult Muslim must, if possible, make at least one pilgrimage (or hajj) to Makkah. More than a million Muslims make the pilgrimage every year. The pilgrims walk or run around the Kaaba seven times, praying or reciting verses from the Koran, the sacred book of the Muslims.

THE WORLD'S LANGUAGES

Definitions of what is a language or a dialect vary and, hence, estimates of the number of languages spoken around the world range from about 3,000 to 6,000. But whatever the figure, it is clear that the number of languages far exceeds the number of countries.

RELIGIOUS ADHERENTS

Number of adherents to the world's major religions, in millions (2006).

Christianity	2,100
Roman Catholic	1,050
Protestant	396
Orthodox	240
Anglican	73
Others	341
Islam	1,070
Sunni	940
Shi'ite	120
Others	10
Secular/Atheist/Agnostic/ Non-religious	1,100
Hinduism	900
Chinese folk	394
Buddhism	376
Ethnic religions	300
New religions	103
Sikhism	23
Spiritism	15
Judaism	14
Baha'i	7
Confucianism	6
Jainism	4
Shintoism	4

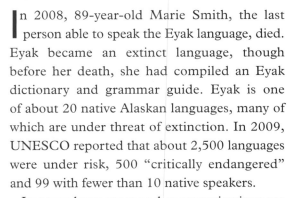

◄ Statues of the Buddha, Wat Yai Chai Mongkol, Thailand

Buddhism is a major religion in Southeast Asia, Sri Lanka, and Japan. The statues of the Buddha in the photograph are swathed in saffron robes. They surround the main chedi, or Golden Mount Pagoda, at Wat Yai Chai Mongkol, a World Heritage site near the ancient city of Ayutthaya, north of Bangkok.

Countries with only one language tend to be small. For example, in Liechtenstein, everyone speaks German. By contrast, more than 820 languages have been identified in Papua New Guinea, whose population is only about 5.9 million people. Hence, many of its languages are spoken by only small groups of people. In fact, scientists have estimated that about a third of the world's languages are now spoken by less than 1,000 people. By contrast, more than half of the world's population speak just seven languages.

The world's languages are grouped into families. The Indo-European family consists of languages spoken between Europe and the Indian subcontinent. The growth of European empires over the last 300 years led several Indo-European languages, most notably English, French, Portuguese, and Spanish, to spread throughout much of North and South America, Africa, Australia, and New Zealand.

English has become the official language in many countries which together contain more than a quarter of the world's population. It is now a major international language, surpassing in importance Mandarin Chinese, a member of the Sino-Tibetan family, which is the world's leading first language. Without a knowledge of English, businessmen face many problems when conducting international trade, especially with the United States or other English-speaking countries. But proposals that English, French, Russian or some other language should become a world language seem unlikely to be acceptable to a majority of the world's peoples.

WORLD RELIGIONS

Religion is another fundamental aspect of human culture. It has inspired much of the world's finest architecture, literature, music and art. It has also helped to shape human cultures since prehistoric times and is responsible for the codes of ethics by which most people live.

The world's major religions were all founded in Asia. Judaism, one of the first faiths to teach that there is only one god, is one of the world's oldest. Founded in southwestern Asia, it influenced the more recent Christianity and Islam, two other monotheistic religions which now have the great-

est number of followers. Hinduism, the third leading faith in terms of the numbers of followers, originated in the Indian subcontinent and most Hindus are now found in India. Another major religion, Buddhism, was founded in the subcontinent partly as a reaction to certain aspects of Hinduism. But unlike Hinduism, it has spread from India throughout much of eastern Asia.

Religion and language are powerful creative forces. They are also essential features of nationalism, which gives people a sense of belonging and pride. But nationalism is often also a cause of rivalry and tension. Cultural differences have led to racial hatred, the persecution of minorities, and to war between national groups.

▲ *The Church of San Giovanni, Dolomites, Italy*
Christianity has done much to shape Western civilization. Christian churches were built as places of worship, but many of them are among the finest achievements of world architecture.

MOTHER TONGUES
First-language speakers of the major languages, in millions.

■	MANDARIN CHINESE 873M
	HINDI 366M
	SPANISH 322M
	ENGLISH 309M
	PORTUGUESE 176M
	BENGALI 171M
	RUSSIAN 145M
	JAPANESE 122M
	GERMAN 95M
	WU CHINESE 77M

OFFICIAL LANGUAGES:
% OF WORLD POPULATION

English	27.0%
Chinese	19.0%
Hindi	13.5%
Spanish	5.4%
Russian	5.2%
French	4.2%
Arabic	3.3%
Portuguese	3.0%
Malay	3.0%
Bengali	2.9%
Japanese	2.3%

▶ *Polyglot nations*
The graph shows countries of the world with more than 200 languages. Although it has only about 5.9 million people, Papua New Guinea holds the record for the number of languages spoken.

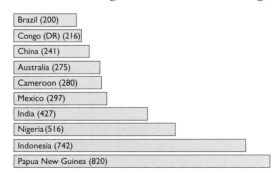

Brazil (200)
Congo (DR) (216)
China (241)
Australia (275)
Cameroon (280)
Mexico (297)
India (427)
Nigeria (516)
Indonesia (742)
Papua New Guinea (820)

AGRICULTURE

In 1798, the British economist Thomas Robert Malthus published his view that populations would outgrow food supply, leading to famine and war. His forecasts proved incorrect because intensive farming and new technology greatly increased production. Furthermore, while only 7% of the world's land was used for crops or grazing in 1700, a study based on satellite data in 2005 showed that currently around 40% of the land is used for some kind of agriculture. In rich countries, food is cheaper than ever, and obesity, not food shortages, has become a major health issue. However, malnutrition is still rife in Africa, where local farmers cannot compete with the flood of subsidized food from rich countries.

From the 1950s, the "green revolution" greatly increased food production. By using new crop varieties, irrigation, and the extensive use of

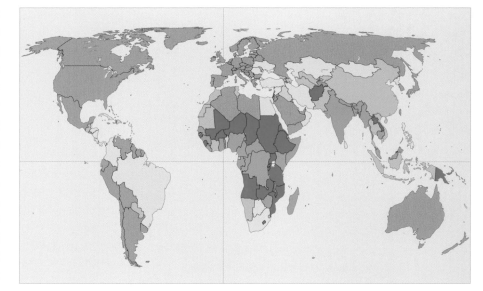

▼ *Rice harvest, Bali, Indonesia*
More than half of the world's people eat rice as their basic food. Rice grows well in tropical and subtropical regions, such as in Indonesia, India, and southeastern China.

fertilizers and pesticides, India, once a food importer, became self-sufficient in food. However, the increasing use of farmland to produce biofuels, which help to reduce global warming, may cause serious food shortages.

In the early 2000s, many people placed hopes in the use of genetically modified crops. Supporters argued that GM crops could be one of the greatest advances ever in farming. But critics of GM crops voiced serious environmental and health concerns.

FOOD PRODUCTION

Agriculture, which supplies most of our food, together with materials to make clothes and other products, is the world's most important economic activity. But its relative importance has declined in comparison with manufacturing and service industries. As a result, the end of the 20th century marked the first time for 10,000 years when the vast majority of the people no longer had to depend for their living on growing crops and herding animals.

However, agriculture remains the dominant economic activity in many developing countries in Africa and Asia. For example, in the early 21st century, 80% or more of the people of Burkina Faso, Laos, Mozambique, and Rwanda depended on farming for their living.

Many people in developing countries eke out the barest of livings by nomadic herding or shifting cultivation, combined with hunting, fishing, and gathering plant foods. A large proportion of farmers live at subsistence level, producing little more than they require to provide the basic needs of their families.

The world's largest food producer and exporter is the United States, although agriculture employs around 1.5% of its total work force.

IMPORTANCE OF AGRICULTURE
Agricultural work force as a percentage of the total work force (2006).

- OVER 80%
- 60–80%
- 40–60%
- 20–40%
- UNDER 20%
- NO DATA AVAILABLE

Food		Population
1.2%	AUSTRALASIA	0.4%
27.6%	EUROPE	15.5%
44.5%	ASIA	58.3%
6.5%	SOUTH AMERICA	6.7%
13.8%	NORTH AMERICA	7.1%
6.7%	AFRICA	12.0%

A comparison of world food production and population by continent.

The high production of the United States is explained by its use of scientific methods and mechanization, which are features of agriculture throughout the developed world.

INTENSIVE OR ORGANIC FARMING

In the early 21st century, some people were beginning to question the dependence of farmers on chemical fertilizers and pesticides. Many people became concerned that the widespread use of chemicals was seriously polluting and damaging the environment.

Others objected to the intensive farming of animals to raise production and lower prices. For example, the suggestion in Britain in 1996 that BSE, or "mad cow disease," might be passed on to people causing CJD (Creuzfeldt-Jakob Disease) caused widespread alarm. Such

▲ *Landsat image of the Nile delta, Egypt*

Most Egyptians live in the Nile valley and on its delta. Because much of the silt carried by the Nile now ends up on the floor of Lake Nasser, upstream of the Aswan Dam, the delta is now retreating and seawater is seeping inland. This eventuality was not foreseen when the Aswan High Dam was built in the 1960s.

factors, combined with the debate about the safety issues surrounding GM foods, have caused much concern.

Some farmers have returned to organic farming, which is based on animal-welfare principles and the banning of chemical fertilizers and pesticides. Organic foods are more expensive to produce than those produced by intensive farming, but an increasing number of consumers are demanding them.

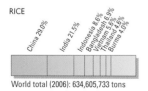

WHEAT

China 17.2% | India 11.4% | USA 9.5% | Russia 7.4% | France 5.6% | Canada 4.5% | Germany 3.7%

World total (2006): 605,945,825 tons

RICE

China 29.0% | India 21.5% | Indonesia 8.6% | Bangladesh 6.9% | Vietnam 5.6% | Thailand 4.6% | Burma 4.0%

World total (2006): 634,605,733 tons

CASSAVA

Nigeria 20.2% | Brazil 11.8% | Thailand 10.0% | Indonesia 8.8% | Congo (D.R.) 6.6% | Mozambique 5.1%

World total (2006): 226,337,396 tons

ENERGY AND MINERALS

In August 2004, a serious accident occurred when a pipe carrying superheated steam exploded at Mihama nuclear power plant, 50 miles [80 km] north of Kyoto, Japan. Four people were killed and seven injured. No nuclear contamination occurred, but the accident further weakened public confidence in the industry. Nuclear power provides about 17% of the world's electricity, though concerns about safety and high costs cloud its future. In the 1990s, some developed nations were proposing to phase out nuclear energy. But the threat of global warming caused by burning fossil fuels has led to a revival of interest in nuclear energy.

FOSSIL FUELS

Huge amounts of energy are needed for heating, generating electricity and for transport. In the early years of the Industrial Revolution, coal, formed from organic matter buried beneath the Earth's surface, was the leading source of energy. It remains important as a raw material in the manufacture of drugs and other products, and also as a fuel, despite the fact that burning coal causes air pollution and gives off carbon dioxide, an important greenhouse gas.

However, oil and natural gas, which came into wide use in the 20th century, are cheaper to produce and easier to handle than coal, while, kilogram for kilogram, they give out more heat. Oil is especially important in moving transport, supplying about 97% of the fuel required.

In the 1990s, proven reserves of oil were sufficient to supply the world, at current rates of production, for 43 years, while supplies of natural gas stood at about 66 years. Coal reserves are more abundant and known reserves would last 200 years at present rates of use. Although these figures must be regarded with caution, because they do not allow for future discoveries, it is clear that fossil fuel reserves will one day run out.

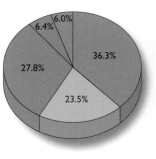

▼ Wind farms in California, United States

Wind farms using giant turbines can produce electricity at a lower cost than conventional power stations. But in many areas, winds are too light or too strong for wind farms to be effective.

6.0%
6.4%
36.3%
27.8%
23.5%

WORLD ENERGY CONSUMPTION

- OIL
- GAS
- COAL
- HYDRO
- NUCLEAR

▲ The diagram shows the proportion of world energy consumption in 2006 by form. Total energy consumption was 10,878 million tons of oil equivalent. Wood, peat, and animal wastes, plus renewable forms, such as wind power, are locally important but they comprise only 0.8% of the total.

SELECTED MINERAL PRODUCTION STATISTICS
(percentage of world total output, 2006)

Bauxite		Diamonds	
Australia	34.7%	Australia	29.4%
Brazil	11.9%	Congo (D.R.)	28.2%
China	11.3%	Russia	17.6%
Guinea	8.6%	S. Africa	10.6%
Jamaica	8.4%	Botswana	9.4%

Gold		Iron ore	
S. Africa	10.8%	China	30.8%
Australia	10.4%	Brazil	17.8%
USA	10.4%	Australia	16.0%
China	9.6%	India	8.9%
Peru	8.4%	Russia	6.2%

Manganese		Zinc	
S. Africa	20.0%	China	25.0%
Brazil	14.5%	Australia	14.0%
Gabon	14.1%	Peru	12.1%
Australia	13.6%	Canada	7.3%
China	10.9%	USA	7.3%

▼ MINERAL DISTRIBUTION

The map shows the richest sources of the most important minerals. Major mineral locations are named. Undersea deposits, most of which are considered inaccessible, are not shown.

▽ GOLD
⌂ SILVER
♦ DIAMONDS
▽ TUNGSTEN
● IRON ORE
■ NICKEL
▼ CHROME
▲ MANGANESE
⊏ COBALT
▲ MOLYBDENUM
■ COPPER
▲ LEAD
● BAUXITE
▽ TIN
♦ ZINC
▽ MERCURY

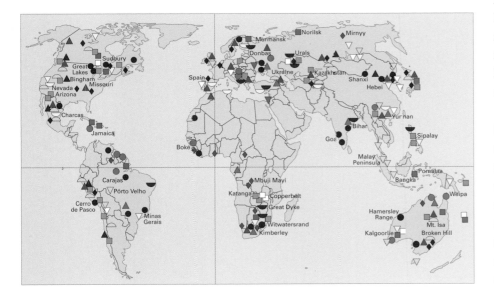

ALTERNATIVE ENERGY

Other sources of energy are therefore required. Besides nuclear energy, the main alternative to fossil fuels is water power. The costs of building dams and hydroelectric power stations are high, though hydroelectric production is comparatively cheap. But the creation of reservoirs uproots people and destroys natural habitats. Water power is also suitable only in areas with plenty of rivers and steep slopes, such as Norway.

In Brazil, alcohol made from sugar has been used to fuel cars. Initially, this government-backed policy met with success. However, it proved to be expensive and the production of ethanol-fueled cars was halted until Brazil struck a deal with Germany in the early 2000s.

▲ *Potash mines in Utah, United States*

Potash is a mineral used mainly to make fertilizers. Much of it comes from mines where deposits formed when ancient seas dried up are exploited. Potash is also extracted from salt lakes.

In 2006, President George W. Bush announced that ethanol production in the United States should increase in the next 10 years to reduce his country's dependency on imported oil.

Other forms of energy, which are renewable and cleaner than fossil fuels, are winds, sea waves, the rise and fall of tides, and geothermal power. While renewable energy sources are attractive, some experts doubt whether they can provide sufficient energy on their own.

MINERALS FOR INDUSTRY

In addition to energy, manufacturing industries need raw materials, including minerals, and these natural resources are also being used in such huge quantities that some experts have predicted shortages of some of them before long.

Manufacturers depend on supplies of about 80 minerals. Some, such as bauxite (aluminum ore) and iron, are abundant, but others are scarce or are found only in deposits that are uneconomical to mine. Many experts advocate a policy of recycling scrap metal, including aluminum, chromium, copper, lead, nickel, and zinc. This practice would reduce pollution and conserve the energy required for extracting and refining mineral ores.

WORLD ECONOMIES

In 2008, Liberia had a per capita GNI (Gross National Income) of US$300, as compared with Norway, whose per capita GNI was $58,500, according to the World Bank. These figures indicate the vast gap between the economies and standards of living of the two countries.

The GNI includes the GDP (Gross Domestic Product), which consists of the total output of goods and services in a country in a given year, plus net exports – that is, the value of goods and services sold abroad less the value of foreign goods and services used in the country in the same year. The GNI divided by the population gives a country's GNI per capita. In low-income developing countries, agriculture makes a high contribution to the GNI. For example, in Liberia, 44.5% of the country's GDP came from agriculture. On the other hand, industry was small-scale and contributed only 12.8% of the GDP. By comparison, in high-income economies, the percentage contribution of manufacturing far exceeds that of agriculture.

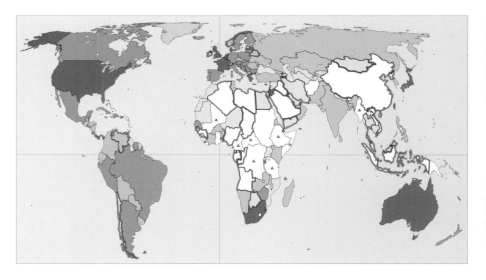

▼ *Hard-disk assembly factory*

The manufacture of computer equipment and computer software is a fairly new industrial phenomenon. In Asia, high-tech industries have developed quickly, helping relatively poor developing countries to achieve rapid economic growth.

INDUSTRIALIZATION

The Industrial Revolution began in Britain in the late 18th century. Before that time, most people worked on farms. But with the Industrial Revolution came factories, using machines that could manufacture goods much faster and more cheaply than those made by cottage industries that already existed.

The Industrial Revolution soon spread to several countries in mainland Europe and the United States and, by the late 19th century, it had reached Canada, Japan, and Russia. At first, industrial development was based on such areas as coalfields or ironfields. But in the 20th

IMPORTANCE OF THE SERVICE INDUSTRY
Percentage of total GDP from the service sector (2007).

- ■ OVER 70%
- ■ 60–70%
- ■ 50–60%
- ■ 40–50%
- □ UNDER 40%
- ■ NO DATA AVAILABLE
- □ OVER 40% OF TOTAL GDP FROM THE INDUSTRIAL SECTOR
- ▲ OVER 40% OF TOTAL GDP FROM THE AGRICULTURAL SECTOR

GROSS NATIONAL INCOME PER CAPITA IN US$ (2008)		
1	Luxembourg	$64,320
2	Norway	$58,500
3	Kuwait	$52,610
4	Brunei	$50,200
5	Singapore	$47,940
6	United States	$46,970
7	Switzerland	$46,460
8	Netherlands	$41,670
9	Sweden	$38,180
10	Austria	$37,680
11	Ireland	$37,350
12	Denmark	$37,280
13	Canada	$36,220
14	United Kingdom	$36,130
15	Germany	$35,940
16	Finland	$35,660
17	Japan	$35,220
18	Belgium	$34,760
19	France	$34,400
20	Australia	$34,040

century, the use of oil, which is easy to transport along pipelines, made it possible for industries to be set up anywhere.

Some nations, such as Switzerland, became industrialized even though they lacked natural resources. They depended instead on the specialized skills of their workers. This same pattern applies today. Some countries with rich natural resources, such as Mexico (with a per capita GNI in 2008 of US$14,270), lag far behind Japan ($35,220) and Malta ($22,460), which lack resources and have to import many of the materials they need to sustain their manufacturing industries.

SERVICE INDUSTRIES

Experts often refer to high-income countries as industrial economies. But manufacturing employs only one in six workers in the United States, one in five in Britain, and one in three in Germany and Japan.

THE WORK FORCE
Percentage of men and women over 15 years old in employment, selected countries.

■ MEN
■ WOMEN

▲ *New cars awaiting transportation, Los Angeles, USA*
Cars are the most important single manufactured item in world trade, followed by vehicle parts and engines. The world's leading car producers are Japan, the United States, Germany, and France.

In most developed economies, the percentage of manufacturing jobs has fallen in recent years, while jobs in service industries have risen. In Britain, between 1970 and the early 2000s, the proportion of jobs in manufacturing fell by about two-thirds, while jobs in the service sector rose by more than a half. Similar, if less rapid, changes have taken place in most industrial economies. Service industries now account for well over half of the jobs in the generally prosperous countries which make up the OECD (Organization for Economic Cooperation and Development). Instead of being called the "industrial" economies, these countries might be better named the "service" economies.

Service industries offer a wide range of jobs and many of them require high educational qualifications. These include finance, insurance, and high-tech industries, such as computer programing, entertainment, and telecommunications. Service industries also include marketing and advertising, which are essential if the cars and television sets made by manufacturers are to be sold. Another valuable service industry is tourism; in some countries, such as the Gambia, it is the major foreign-exchange earner. Trade in services plays a crucial part in world economies. Service industries now account for more than a fifth of world trade.

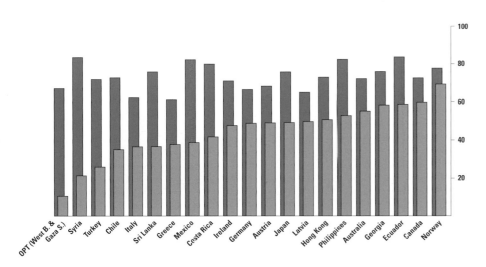

TRADE AND COMMERCE

The establishment of the WTO (World Trade Organization) on January 1, 1995, was the latest step in the long history of world trade. The WTO was set up by the eighth round of negotiations, popularly called the "Uruguay round," conducted by the General Agreement on Tariffs and Trade (GATT). This treaty was signed by representatives of 125 governments in April 1994. The membership reached 153 when Cape Verde joined in July 2008.

GATT was first established in 1948. Its initial aim was to produce a charter to create a body called the International Trade Organization. This body never came into being. Instead, GATT, acting as an *ad hoc* agency, pioneered a series of agreements aimed at liberalizing world trade by reducing tariffs on imports and other obstacles to free trade.

▼ *New York City Stock Exchange, United States*
Stock exchanges, where stocks and shares are sold and bought, are important in channeling savings and investments to companies and governments. The world's largest stock exchange is in Tokyo, Japan.

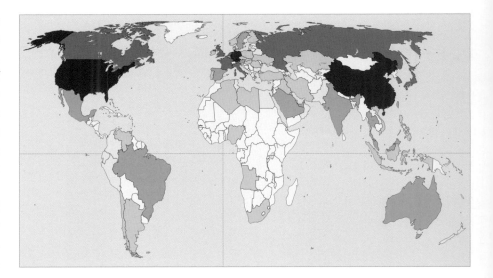

GATT's objectives were based on the belief that international trade creates wealth. Trade occurs because the world's resources are not distributed evenly between countries, and, in theory, free trade means that every country should concentrate on what it can do best and purchase from others goods and services that they can supply more cheaply. In practice, however, free trade may cause unemployment when imported goods are cheaper than those produced within the country.

Trade is sometimes an important factor in world politics, especially when trade sanctions are applied against countries whose actions incur the disapproval of the international community. For example, in the 1990s, world-wide trade sanctions were imposed on Serbia because of its involvement in the civil war in Bosnia-Herzegovina.

CHANGING TRADE PATTERNS

The early 16th century, when Europeans began to divide the world into huge empires, opened up a new era in international trade. By the 19th century, the colonial powers, who were among the first industrial powers, promoted trade with their colonies, from which they obtained unprocessed raw materials, such as food, natural fibers, minerals, and timber. In return, they shipped clothes, shoes, and other cheap items to the colonies.

From the late 19th century until the early 1950s, primary products dominated world trade, with oil becoming the leading item in the latter part of this period. Many developing countries still depend heavily on the export of one or two primary products, such as coffee or iron ore, but overall the proportion of primary products in world trade has fallen since the 1950s. Today the most important elements

WORLD TRADE
Percentage share of total world exports by value (2007).

■ OVER 5%
■ 2.5–5%
■ 1–2.5%
□ 0.25–1%
□ 0.1–0.25%
□ UNDER 0.1%

The world's leading trading nations, according to the combined value of their exports and imports, are the United States, Germany, Japan, France, and the United Kingdom.

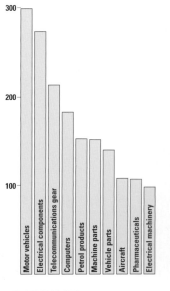

TRADED PRODUCTS
The diagram shows major manufactures traded by value in billions of US$. Manufactures in total comprise 74% of the world's total trade, the value of which was $13,870 billion in 2007.

in world trade are manufactures and semi-manufactures, exchanged mainly between the industrialized nations.

▲ *Melbourne, Australia*
World trade depends on transport. Containerization, introduced in the 1950s, reduced the risk of damage to cargo, and cut the time and cost of loading and unloading.

DEPENDENCE ON TRADE
Value of exports as a percentage of GDP (2007).

- OVER 50% GDP FROM EXPORTS
- 25–50% GDP FROM EXPORTS
- 10–25% GDP FROM EXPORTS
- 5–10% GDP FROM EXPORTS
- UNDER 5% GDP FROM EXPORTS
- NO DATA AVAILABLE

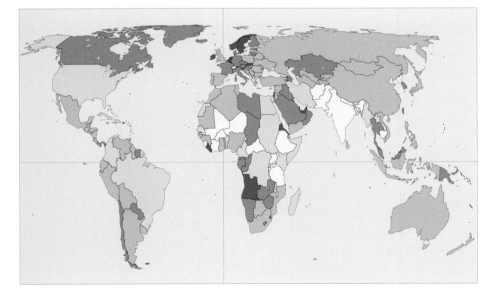

THE WORLD'S MARKETS

Private companies conduct most of world trade, but government policies affect it. Governments which believe that certain industries are strategic, or essential for the country's future, may impose tariffs on imports, or import quotas to limit the volume of imports, if they are thought to be undercutting the domestic industries.

For example, the United States has argued that Japan has greater access to its markets than the United States has to Japan's. This might have led the United States to resort to protectionism, but instead the United States remains committed to free trade despite occasional disputes.

Other problems in international trade occur when governments give subsidies to its producers, who can then export products at low prices. Another difficulty, called "dumping," occurs when products are sold at below the market price in order to gain a market share. One of the aims of the newly-created WTO is the phasing out of government subsidies for agricultural products, though the world's poorest countries will be exempt from many of the WTO's most severe regulations.

International trade suffered a setback in 2008–9, when the economies of several countries went into recession, caused by a collapse of major international banking systems. The ensuing global financial crisis led to a fall in demand for such major products as cars, leading to a decline in international trade and manufacturing output.

THE WORLD TODAY

The early years of the 20th century witnessed the exploration of Antarctica, the last uncharted continent. Today, less than 100 years later, tourists are able to take cruises to the icy southern continent, while almost no part of the globe is inaccessible to the determined traveler. Improved transport and images from space have made our world seem smaller.

A DIVIDED WORLD

Between the end of World War II in 1945 and the late 1980s, the world was divided, politically and economically, into three main groups: the developed countries or Western democracies, with their free enterprise or mixed economies; the centrally planned or Communist countries; and the developing countries or Third World.

This division became obsolete when the former Soviet Union and its old European allies, together with the "special economic zones" in eastern China, began the transition from centrally planned to free-enterprise economies. This left the world divided into two broad camps: the prosperous developed countries and the poorer developing countries. The simplest way of distinguishing between the groups is with reference to their per capita GNIs (Gross National Incomes).

The World Bank divides the developing countries into three main groups. At the bottom are the low-income economies, including India and most of sub-Saharan Africa. This group has a population of more than 2.3 billion. However, according to the World Bank, the average per

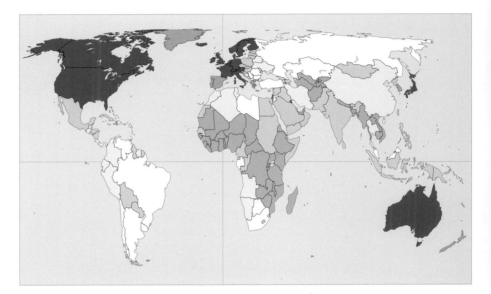

capita Gross National Income in 2007 was only US$574, with some countries as low as $280. Two other groups, with a combined population of around 3 billion people, are the lower-middle-income economies with an average per capita GNI of $1,905, and the upper-middle-income economies with an average per capita GNI of $7,107. The high-income economies, with around 1 billion people, had an average per capita GNI of $37,572.

ECONOMIC AND SOCIAL CONTRASTS

Other factors, such as rates of population growth, are also important. The low- and middle-income economies have a population growth of about 2%, while the average growth rate in the high-income economies is about 1%. While the populations of low- and middle-income economies are young, youths make up less than one-fifth of the populations of high-income economies, while over-65s make up one-seventh.

Stark contrasts exist in the quality of life around the world. In 2009, a UN report stated

GROSS NATIONAL INCOME PER CAPITA
The value of total income divided by the population (2006).

■	OVER 400% OF WORLD AVERAGE
▨	200–400% OF WORLD AVERAGE
▨	100–200% OF WORLD AVERAGE
□	50–100% OF WORLD AVERAGE
□	25–50% OF WORLD AVERAGE
□	10–25% OF WORLD AVERAGE
▨	UNDER 10% OF WORLD AVERAGE
□	NO DATA AVAILABLE

RICHEST COUNTRIES (GNI PER CAPITA, 2008)

Luxembourg	US$64,320
Norway	US$58,500
Kuwait	US$52,610
Brunei	US$50,200
Singapore	US$47,940

POOREST COUNTRIES (GNI PER CAPITA, 2008)

Congo (Dem. Rep.)	US$290
Liberia	US$300
Burundi	US$380
Guinea-Bissau	US$530
Eritrea	US$630

▼ *East African tourism*

Improved transport, including the use of four-wheel drive vehicles, has led to a boom in tourism in many developing regions, such as East Africa. But terrorist incidents may slow down the development of tourism in some areas.

that 1 billion people, mainly in the developing world, suffered from hunger. This record figure was caused partly by the global financial crisis.

In 2006, the World Health Organization stated that, due partly to AIDS and partly to poverty, average life expectancy at birth in Zimbabwe had fallen to 37 years for men and 34 years for women. By contrast, the average life expectancy in Japan was 82 years. Illiteracy rates in low-income economies are also substantially lower for women than for men, whereas, in high-income countries, illiteracy is rare for both sexes.

FUTURE DEVELOPMENT

In the last 50 years, despite all the aid supplied to developing countries, much of the world still suffers from poverty and economic backward-ness. Some countries are even poorer now than they were a generation ago.

However, several factors suggest that poor countries may find progress easier in the 21st century. For example, technology is now more readily transferable between countries, while improved transport and communications make it easier for countries to take part in the world economy. But industrial development could lead to an increase in global pollution. Hence, any strategy for global economic expansion must also take account of environmental factors.

▲ *Operation Enduring Freedom, Afghanistan*
A joint patrol of US Marines and Army soldiers is seen here patrolling through the village of Cem, Afghanistan, some 6 miles [10 km] from the airport near Kandahar, in January 2002.

A WORLD IN CONFLICT

The end of the Cold War held out hopes of a new world order. But ethnic, religious, and other rivalries have subsequently led to appalling violence in places as diverse as the Balkan peninsula, Israel and the Palestinian territories, and Rwanda–Burundi. Then, on September 11, 2001, the attack on those symbols of the economic and military might of the United States – the World Trade Center and the Pentagon Building – demonstrated that nowhere on Earth is safe from attack by extremists prepared to sacrifice their lives in pursuit of their aims.

The dangers posed by terrorist groups or rogue states has forced many countries into new alliances. International cooperation is also vital in combating global warming, which some experts believe is the greatest danger now threatening the world. Unless effective action is taken, they warn that the world faces such problems as falls in food production, the spread of diseases, increasing extreme weather phenomena, and the flooding of coastal plains.

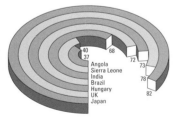

▲ *Years of life expectancy at birth, selected countries (2007).*
The chart shows the contrasting range of average life expectancies at birth for a range of countries, including both low-income and high-income economies. Generally, improved health services are raising life expectancies. On average, women live longer than men, even in the poorer developing countries.

Ngorongoro Crater, Tanzania
Situated within the Great Rift Valley in northern Tanzania, the crater is the largest complete collapsed volcanic cone, or caldera, in the world. The whole area was one of intense geological activity as can be seen from the surrounding craters, but currently only one, in the northeast, is active. Ngorongoro is the crater in the south of the image, with Lake Magadi within it. The steep sides of the crater limit normal animal migration and within it there is a unique ecosystem supporting a wide range of birds and animals. The two lakes in the south are Lake Eyasi (to the west) and Lake Manyara (to the east). [Map page 84]

WORLD MAPS

SETTLEMENTS

■ **PARIS**   ◉ **Rotterdam**   ◉ **Livorno**   ◉ **Brugge**   ◉ Exeter   ◦ *Torremolinos*   ◦ *Oberammergau*   ◦ *Thira*

Settlement symbols and type styles vary according to the scale of each map and indicate the importance of towns on the map rather than specific population figures

• *Vaduz*   Capital cities have red infills   ∴   Ruins or archaeological sites

⬠   Urban agglomerations   ⌣   Wells in desert

ADMINISTRATION

─────   International boundaries   ┄┄┄┄   Internal boundaries   **PERU**   Country names

─ ─ ─ ·   International boundaries (undefined or disputed)   ⬡   National parks   KENT   Administrative area names

International boundaries show the *de facto* situation where there are rival claims to territory

COMMUNICATIONS

═══   Motorways, freeways and expressways

────   Principal roads

───   Other roads

╾┄╼   Road tunnels

────   Principal railways

─ ─ ─   Railways under construction

────   Other railways

╾┄╼   Railway tunnels

LHR ✈   Principal airports

✈   Other airports

┄┄┄┄   Principal canals

⋈   Passes

PHYSICAL FEATURES

∽   Perennial streams

─ ─   Intermittent streams

⬭   Perennial lakes

░░   Sand deserts

◌   Intermittent lakes

⸖⸖   Swamps and marshes

❄❄   Permanent ice and glaciers

▲ 8850   Elevations in metres

▼ 8500   Sea depths in metres

1134   Height of lake surface above sea level in metres

ELEVATION AND DEPTH TINTS

Height of land above sea level

in metres	6000	4000	3000	2000	1500	1000	400	200	0
in feet	18 000	12 000	9000	6000	4500	3000	1200	600	

Land below sea level   Depth of sea

	6000	12 000	15 000	18 000	24 000	in feet
	0	200	2000	4000	5000	6000	8000	in metres

Some of the maps have different contours to highlight and clarify the principal relief features

Equatorial Scale 1:84 000 000

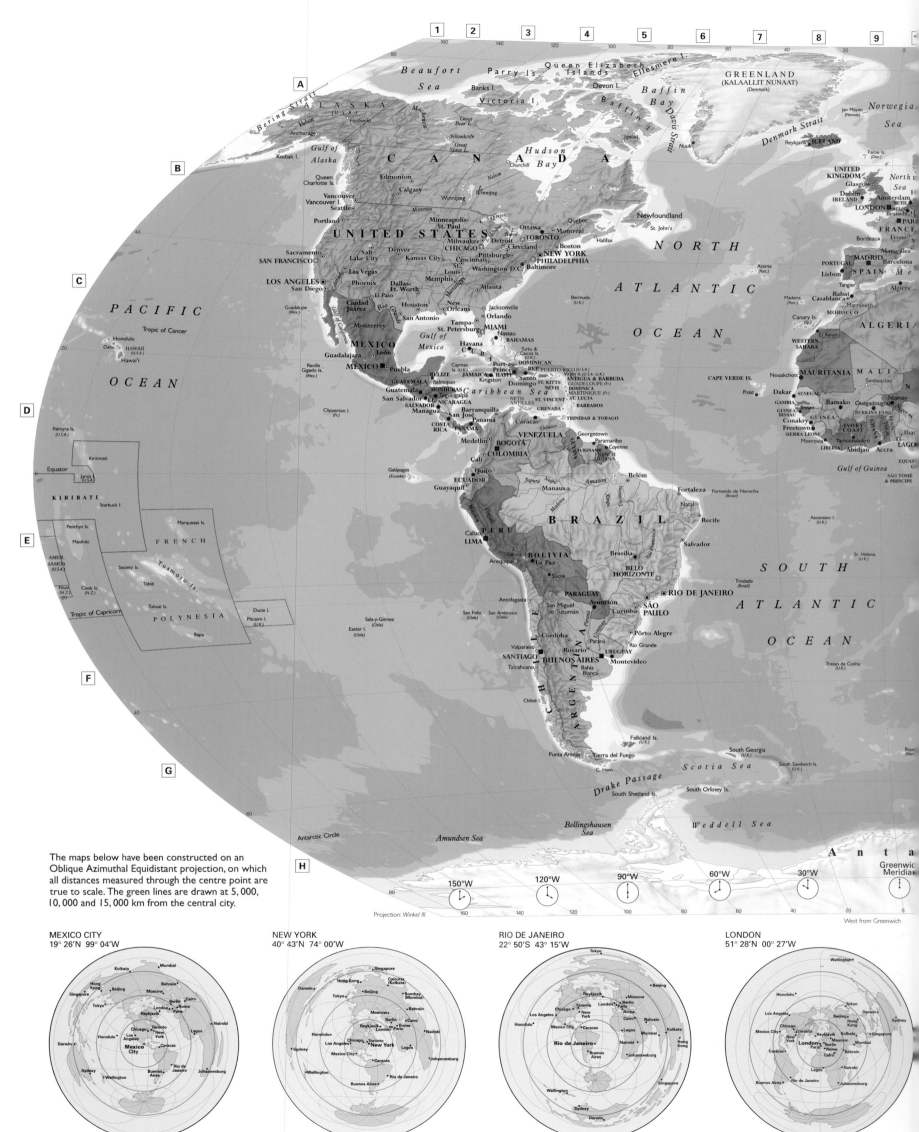

The maps below have been constructed on an Oblique Azimuthal Equidistant projection, on which all distances measured through the centre point are true to scale. The green lines are drawn at 5,000, 10,000 and 15,000 km from the central city.

Projection: Winkel III

West from Greenwich

MEXICO CITY
19° 26'N 99° 04'W

NEW YORK
40° 43'N 74° 00'W

RIO DE JANEIRO
22° 50'S 43° 15'W

LONDON
51° 28'N 00° 27'W

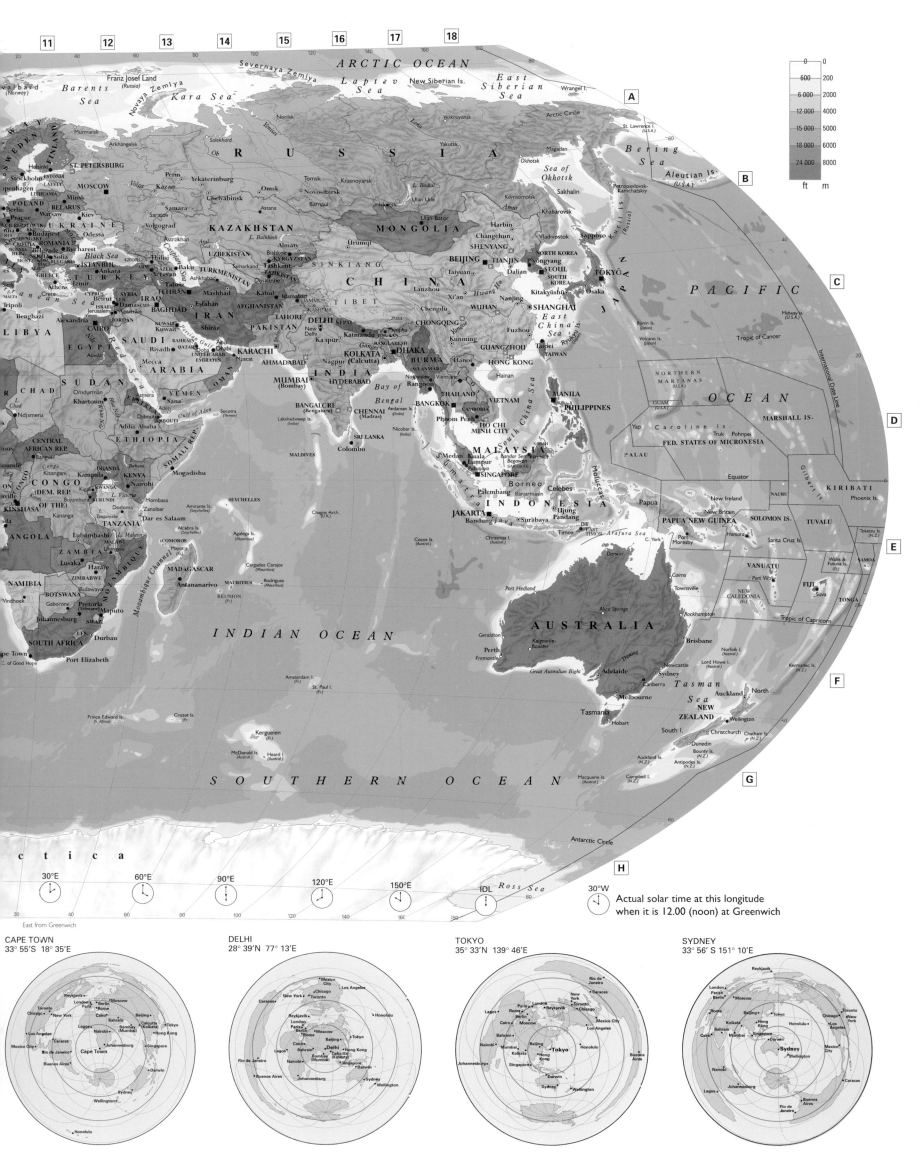

11   **12**   **13**   **14**   **15**   **16**   **17**   **18**

ARCTIC OCEAN

Severnaya Zemlya
Laptev Sea
New Siberian Is.
East Siberian Sea
Wrangel I.
Franz Josef Land (Russia)
Barents Sea
Novaya Zemlya
Kara Sea
Norilsk
Arctic Circle
St. Lawrence I. (U.S.A.)

A

Murmansk
Arkhangelsk
Salekhard
Lena
Verkhoyansk
Yakutsk
Magadan
Bering Sea
Aleutian Is. (U.S.A.)

SWEDEN FINLAND
Helsinki
St. PETERSBURG
MOSCOW
R U S S I A
Ob
Tomsk
Krasnoyarsk
Irkutsk
L. Baikal
Ulan Ude
Okhotsk
Sea of Okhotsk
Petropavlovsk-Kamchatskiy

B

Stockholm ESTONIA
Copenhagen LATVIA
POLAND LITHUANIA
Berlin BELARUS
Warsaw
Prague
Budapest
Minsk
Kiev
UKRAINE
KAZAKHSTAN
Perm
Yekaterinburg
Volga
Kazan
Chelyabinsk
Astana
Omsk
Novosibirsk
Barnaul
Ulan Bator
M O N G O L I A
Changchun
Harbin
Vladivostok
Khabarovsk
Amur
Komsomolsk
Sakhalin
Sapporo

ROMANIA
Odessa
Black Sea
GEORGIA
Samara
Saratov
Volgograd
Astrakhan
Aral Sea
L. Balkhash
Almaty
Bishkek
Ürümqi
Belgrade Bucharest
Sofia
ISTANBUL
Ankara
ARM. AZER. Baku
TURKMENISTAN
UZBEKISTAN
Samarkand
Tashkent
KYRGYZSTAN
SINKIANG
SHENYANG
NORTH KOREA
P'yongyang
TIANJIN
SEOUL
SOUTH KOREA
TŌKYŌ

C

Athens
CYPRUS
SYRIA
Beirut
ISRAEL
Damascus
IRAQ
BAGHDĀD
TEHRĀN
Mashhad
AFGHANISTAN
Kābul
Islamabad
TIBET
Lhasa
Chengdu
WUHAN
Xi'an
CHONGQING
Lanzhou
BEIJING
TAIYUAN
Dalian
Kitakyūshū
Osaka
PACIFIC
Bonin Is. (Japan)
Midway Is. (U.S.A.)

LIBYA
Alexandria
CAIRO
Jerusalem
Amman JORDAN
KUWAIT
Kuwait
BAHRAIN
QATAR
Abu Dhabi
UNITED ARAB EMIRATES
Shīrāz
PAKISTAN
LAHORE
New Delhi
DELHI
NEPAL
Katmandu
Thimphu
BANGLADESH
DHAKA
Hwang Ho
Nanjing
SHANGHAI
East China Sea
Fuzhou
GUANGZHOU
TAIPEI
TAIWAN
Tropic of Cancer
Volcano Is. (Japan)

EGYPT
Aswān
SAUDI
Riyadh
Mecca
Red Sea
ARABIA
Muscat
OMAN
KARACHI
AHMADABAD
MUMBAI (Bombay)
HYDERABAD
Nagpur
KOLKATA (Calcutta)
I N D I A
BURMA (MYANMAR)
Naypyidaw
Rangoon
Kunming
Hanoi
HONG KONG
Hainan
South China Sea
NORTHERN MARIANAS (U.S.A.)
GUAM (U.S.A.)

D

CHAD
L. Chad
Ndjamena
Omdurman
Khartoum
SUDAN
YEMEN
Sana'
Aden
Gulf of Aden
Socotra (Yemen)
ASMARA ERITREA DJIBOUTI
BANGALORE (Bengaluru)
CHENNAI (Madras)
Bay of Bengal
Andaman Is. (India)
THAILAND
BANGKOK
CAMBODIA
VIETNAM
Phnom Penh
HO CHI MINH CITY
MANILA
PHILIPPINES
Yap
Caroline Is.
Truk Pohnpei
FED. STATES OF MICRONESIA
MARSHALL IS.

CENTRAL AFRICAN REP.
Bangui
ETHIOPIA
Addis Ababa
SOMALI REP.
Mogadishu
SRI LANKA
Colombo
Lakshadweep (India)
MALDIVES
Nicobar Is. (India)
MALAYSIA
Medan
Kuala Lumpur
SINGAPORE
Bandar Seri Begawan
BRUNEI
SARAWAK
Celebes
PALAU
Equator
NAURU
KIRIBATI
Phoenix Is.

CAMEROON
CONGO
Kisangani
UGANDA
KENYA
Nairobi
Kampala
RWANDA
BURUNDI
Bujumbura
DODOMA
Dar es Salaam
Mombasa
SEYCHELLES
Amirante Is. (Seychelles)
Chagos Arch. (U.K.)
Sumatra
Palembang
Borneo
Banjarmasin
Ujung Pandang
I N D O N E S I A
JAKARTA
Bandung Java
Surabaya
Dili EAST TIMOR
Moluccas
Papua
New Ireland
New Britain
PAPUA NEW GUINEA
SOLOMON IS.
Honiara
Santa Cruz Is.
TUVALU

E

ANGOLA
CONGO (DEM. REP. OF THE)
KINSHASA
Kananga
Lubumbashi
TANZANIA
L. Tanganyika
L. Malawi
ZAMBIA
Lusaka
Harare
ZIMBABWE
Bulawayo
Mayotte
COMOROS
MADAGASCAR
Antananarivo
MAURITIUS
Cargados Carajos (Mauritius)
Agalega Is. (Mauritius)
Cocos Is. (Austral.)
Christmas I. (Austral.)
Timor
Arafura Sea
C. York
Darwin
Port Moresby
Cairns
NEW CALEDONIA (Fr.)
Port Vila
VANUATU
FIJI
Suva
Wallis & Futuna Is. (Fr.)
SAMOA

NAMIBIA
BOTSWANA
Gaborone
Pretoria
Johannesburg
SWAZ.
Maputo
MOZAMBIQUE
Mozambique Channel
Windhoek
Bulawayo
LES.
SOUTH AFRICA
Durban
Port Elizabeth
Cape of Good Hope
Port Hedland
AUSTRALIA
Alice Springs
Geraldton
Kalgoorlie-Boulder
Darling
Townsville
Rockhampton
Norfolk I. (Austral.)
Lord Howe I. (Austral.)
Tropic of Capricorn

Cape Town
Prince Edward Is. (S. Africa)
Crozet Is. (Fr.)
Amsterdam I. (Fr.)
St. Paul I. (Fr.)
I N D I A N   O C E A N
Perth
Fremantle
Great Australian Bight
Adelaide
Murray
Brisbane
Newcastle
Sydney
Canberra
Melbourne
Tasman Sea
Auckland
North I.
NEW ZEALAND
Wellington
Kermadec Is. (N.Z.)
TONGA

F

Kerguelen (Fr.)
McDonald Is. (Austral.)
Heard I. (Austral.)
Tasmania
Hobart
South I.
Christchurch
Dunedin
Chatham Is. (N.Z.)
Bounty Is. (N.Z.)
Antipodes Is. (N.Z.)
Auckland Is. (N.Z.)
Campbell I. (N.Z.)
Macquarie I. (Austral.)

G

S O U T H E R N   O C E A N

H

A n t a r c t i c a
Antarctic Circle
Ross Sea
IDL
30°W

30°E   60°E   90°E   120°E   150°E

East from Greenwich

Actual solar time at this longitude when it is 12.00 (noon) at Greenwich

Elevation legend (right side):
ft	m
0	0
600	200
6 000	2000
12 000	4000
15 000	5000
18 000	6000
24 000	8000

CAPE TOWN
33° 55'S 18° 35'E

DELHI
28° 39'N 77° 13'E

TOKYO
35° 33'N 139° 46'E

SYDNEY
33° 56'S 151° 10'E

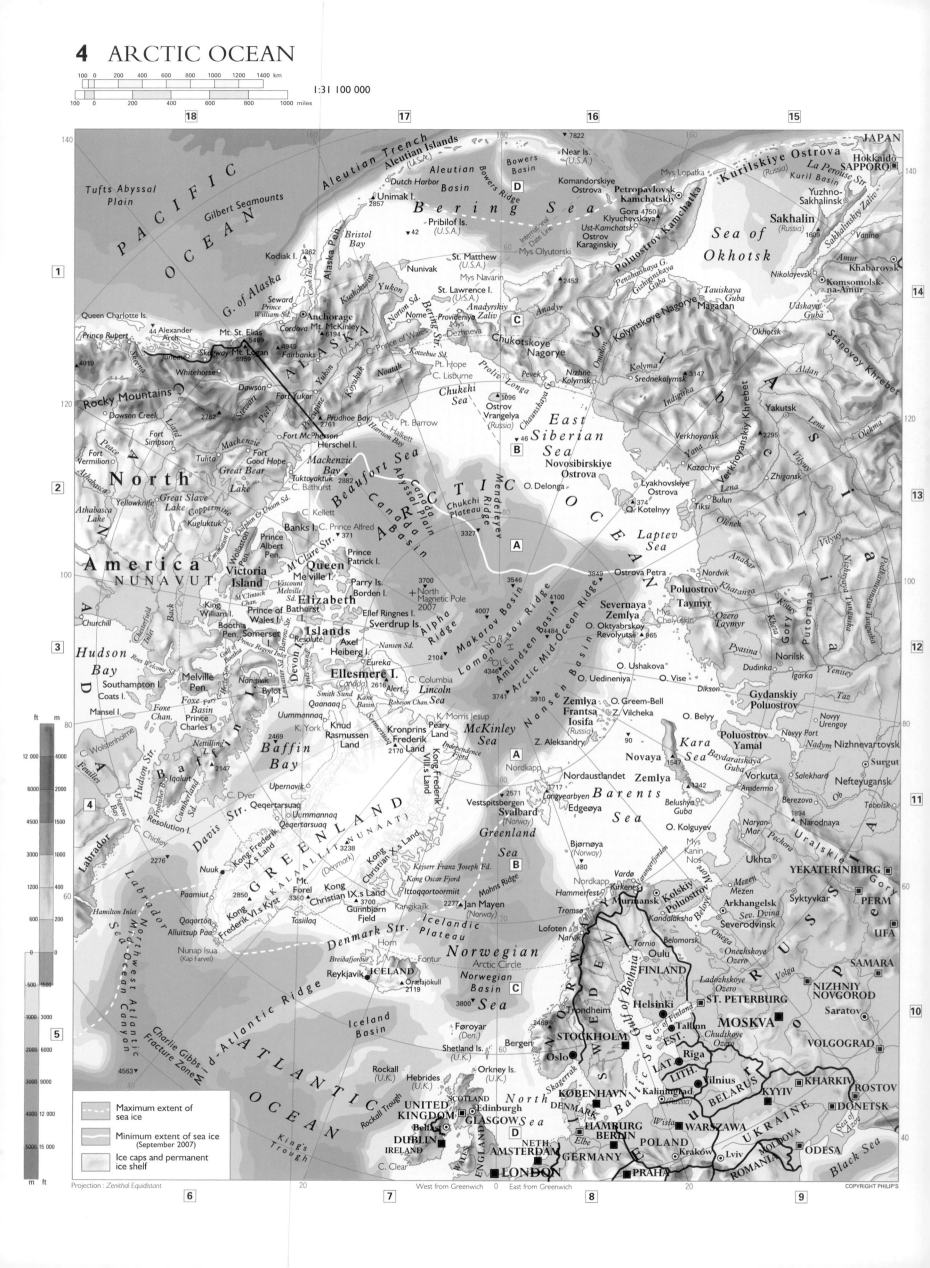

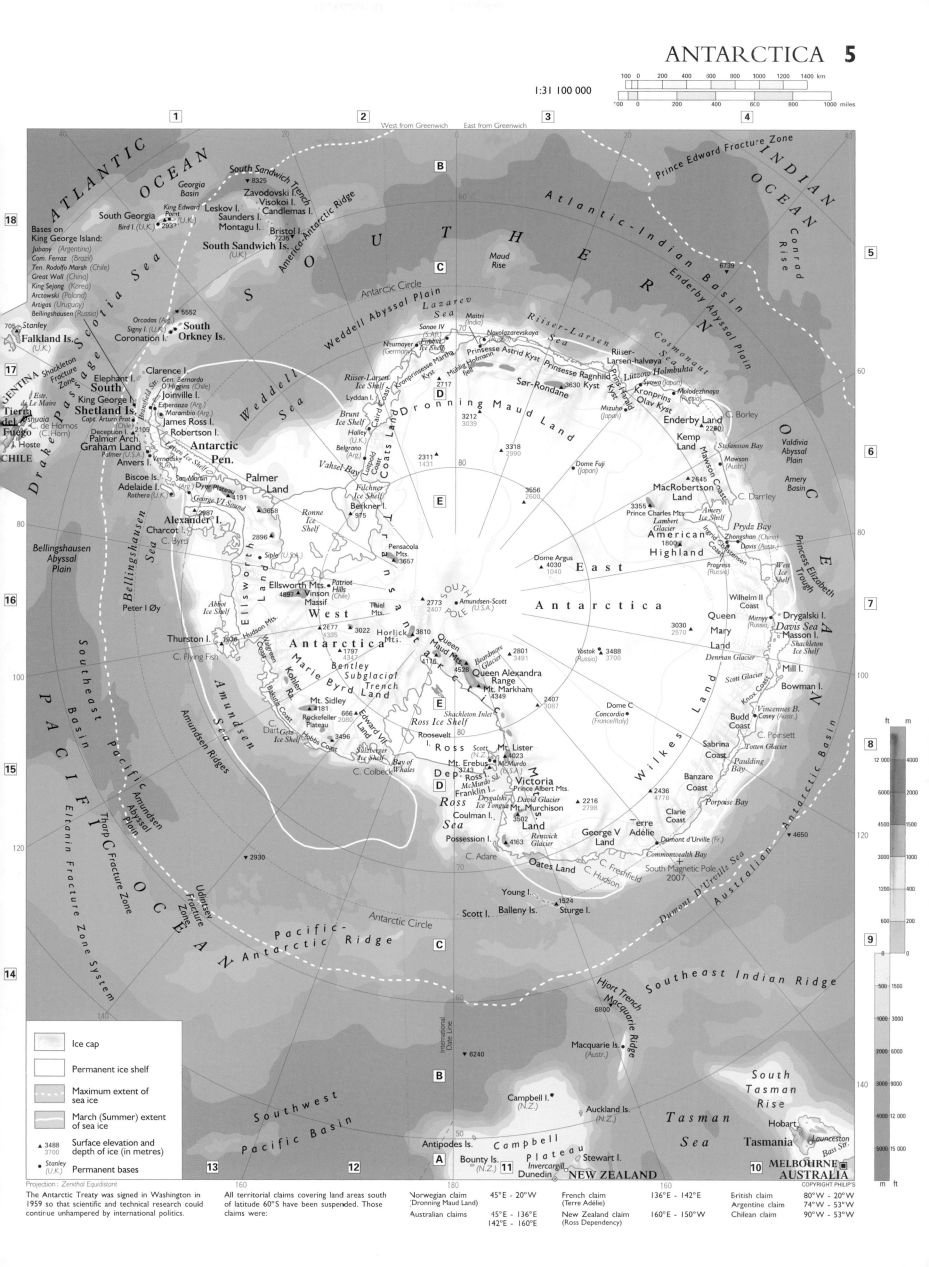

1:31 100 000

100 0 200 400 600 800 1000 1200 1400 km
100 0 200 400 600 800 1000 miles

West from Greenwich | East from Greenwich

Legend:

	Ice cap
	Permanent ice shelf
	Maximum extent of sea ice
	March (Summer) extent of sea ice
▲ 3488 ⁓ 3700	Surface elevation and depth of ice (in metres)
• Stanley (U.K.)	Permanent bases

Projection: *Zenithal Equidistant*

The Antarctic Treaty was signed in Washington in 1959 so that scientific and technical research could continue unhampered by international politics.

All territorial claims covering land areas south of latitude 60°S have been suspended. Those claims were:

Norwegian claim (Dronning Maud Land)	45°E – 20°W	French claim (Terre Adélie)	136°E – 142°E	British claim	80°W – 20°W
Australian claims	45°E – 136°E 142°E – 160°E	New Zealand claim (Ross Dependency)	160°E – 150°W	Argentine claim	74°W – 53°W
				Chilean claim	90°W – 53°W

Bases on King George Island:
Jubany (Argentina)
Com. Ferraz (Brazil)
Ten. Rodolfo Marsh (Chile)
Great Wall (China)
King Sejong (Korea)
Arctowski (Poland)
Artigas (Uruguay)
Bellingshausen (Russia)

COPYRIGHT PHILIP'S

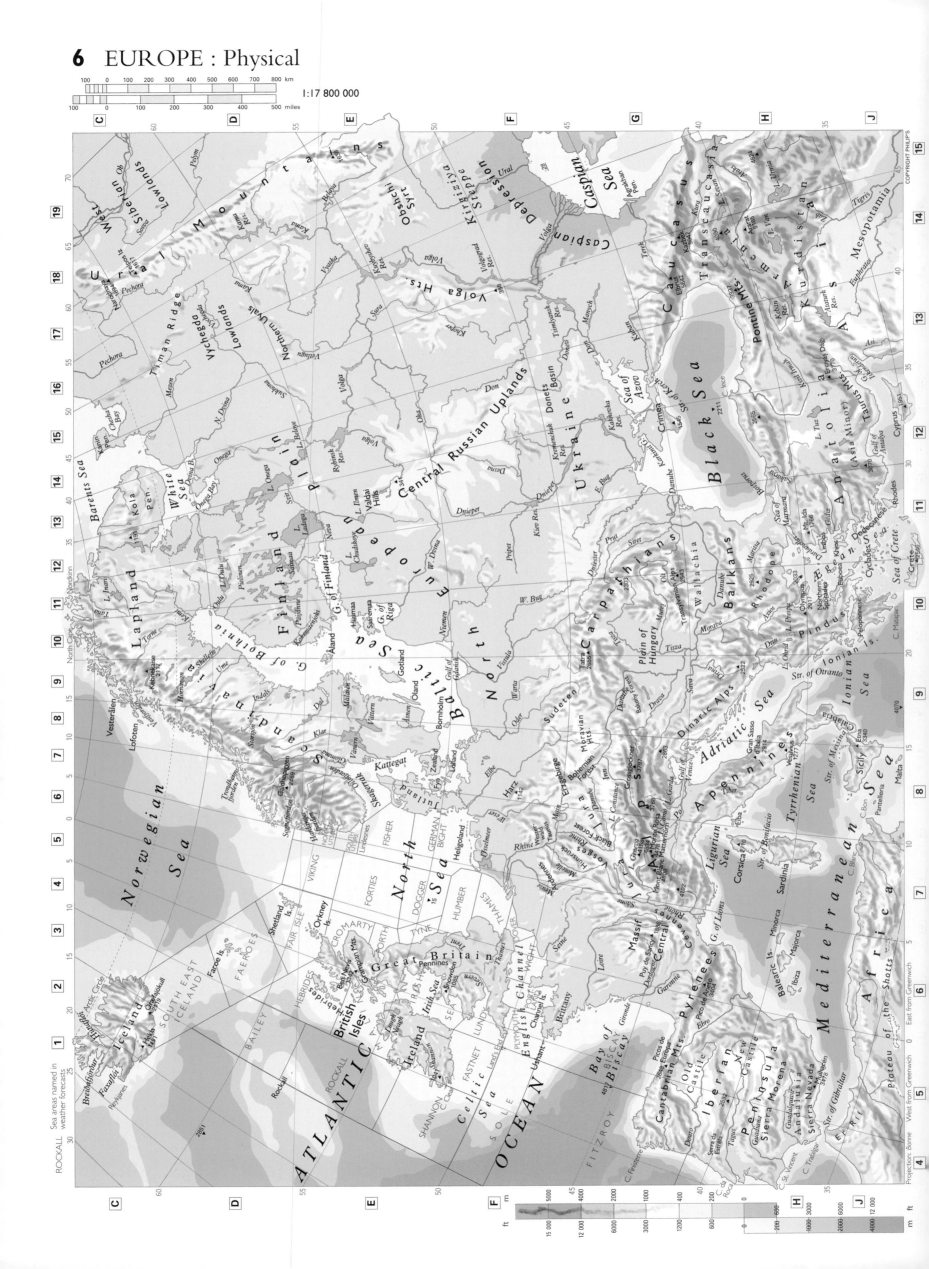

100   0   100   200   300   400   500   600   700   800 km

1:17 800 000

100   0   100   200   300   400   500 miles

1:17 800 000

100   0   100   200   300   400   500   600   700   800 km
100   0   100   200   300   400   500 miles

1:5 300 000

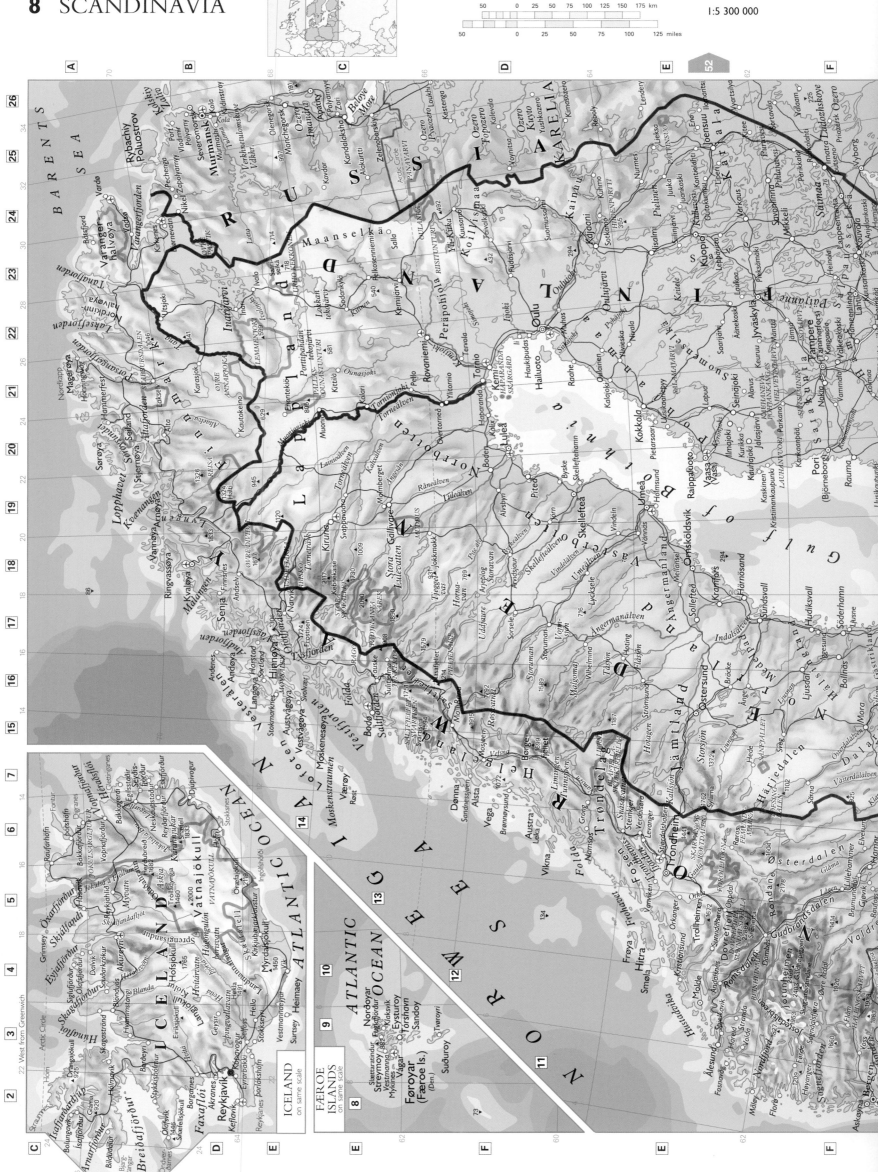

Projection: Conical with two standard parallels

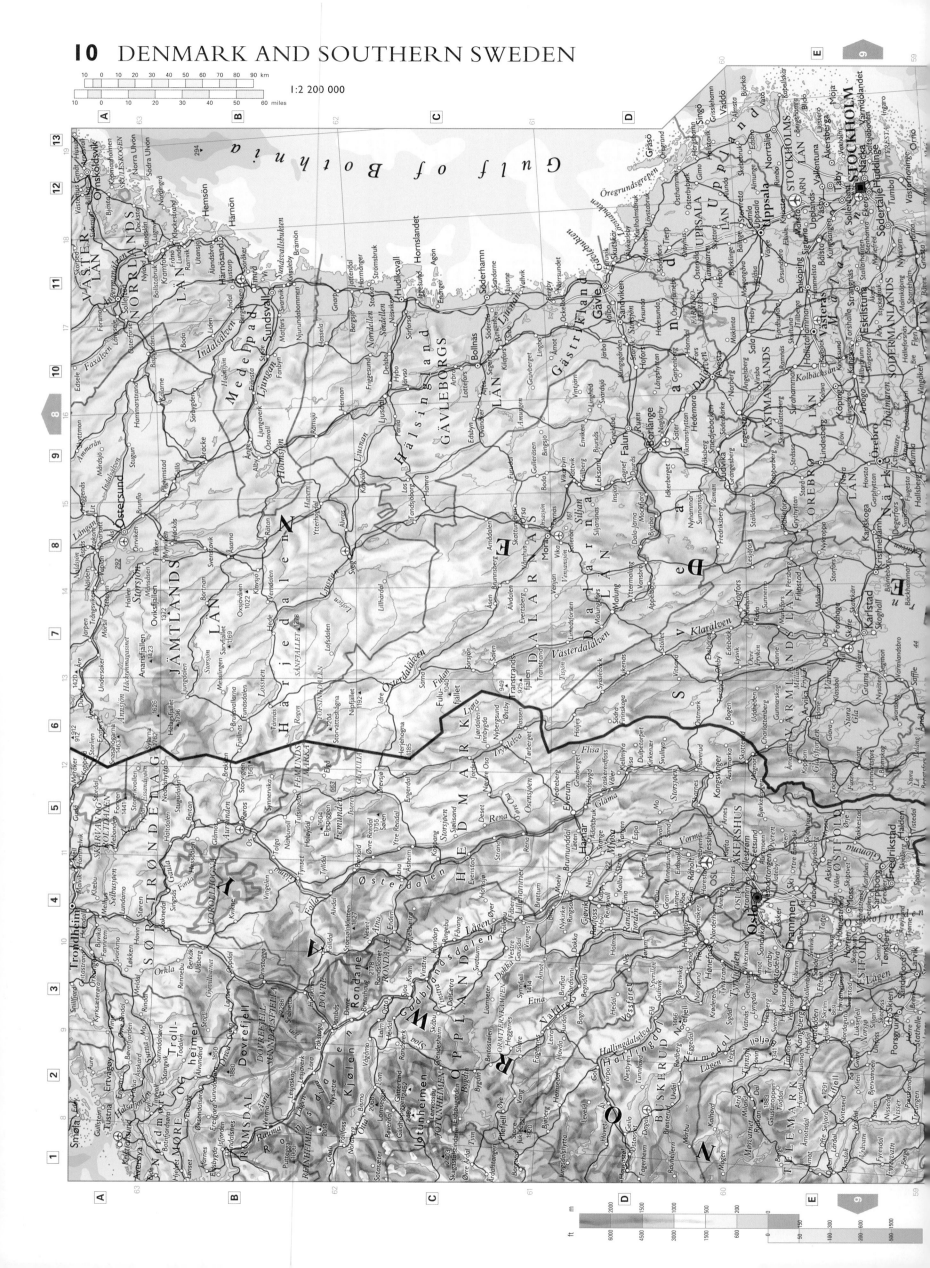

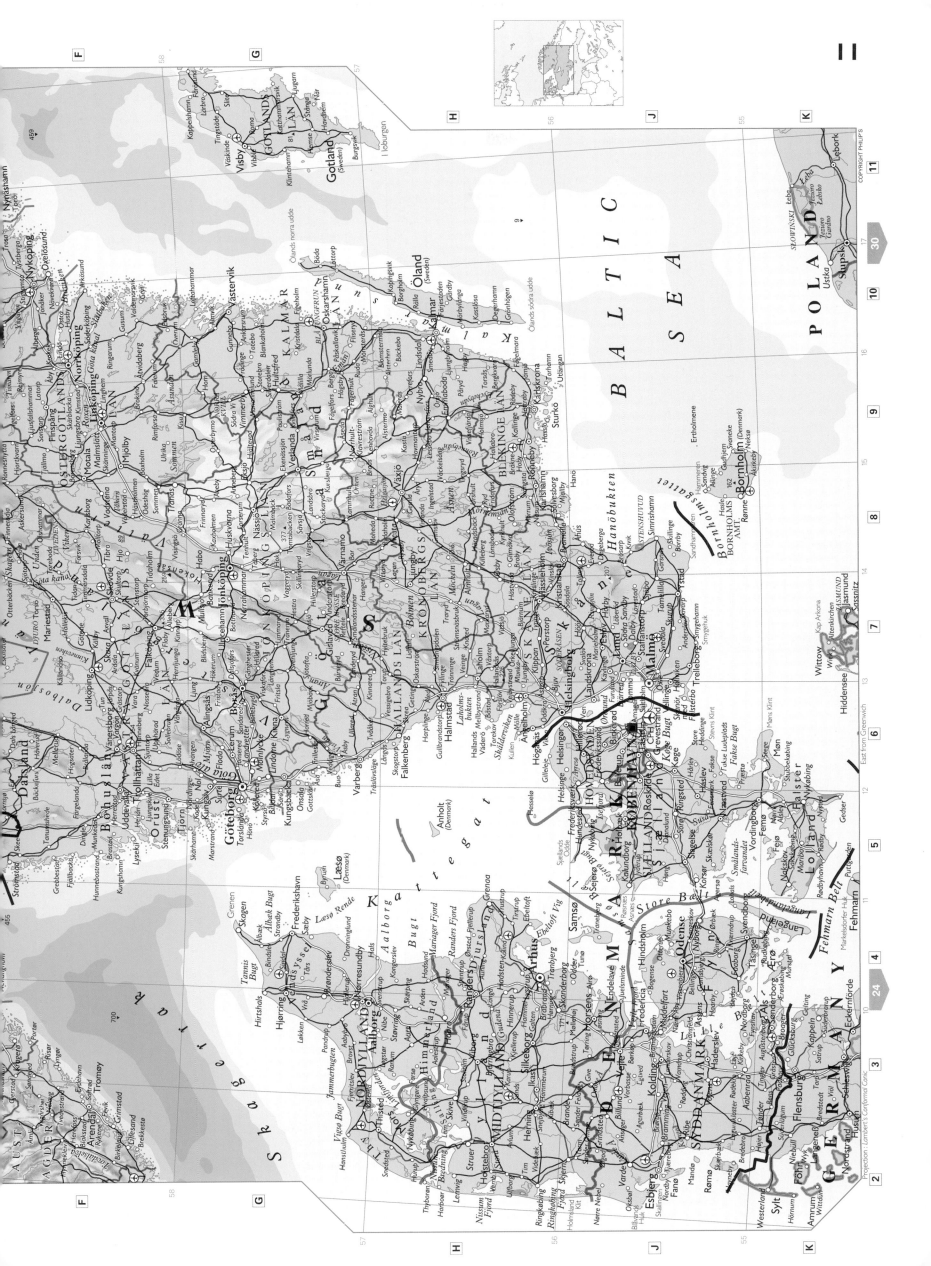

COPYRIGHT PHILIP'S

Projection : Lambert's Conformal Conic

East from Greenwich

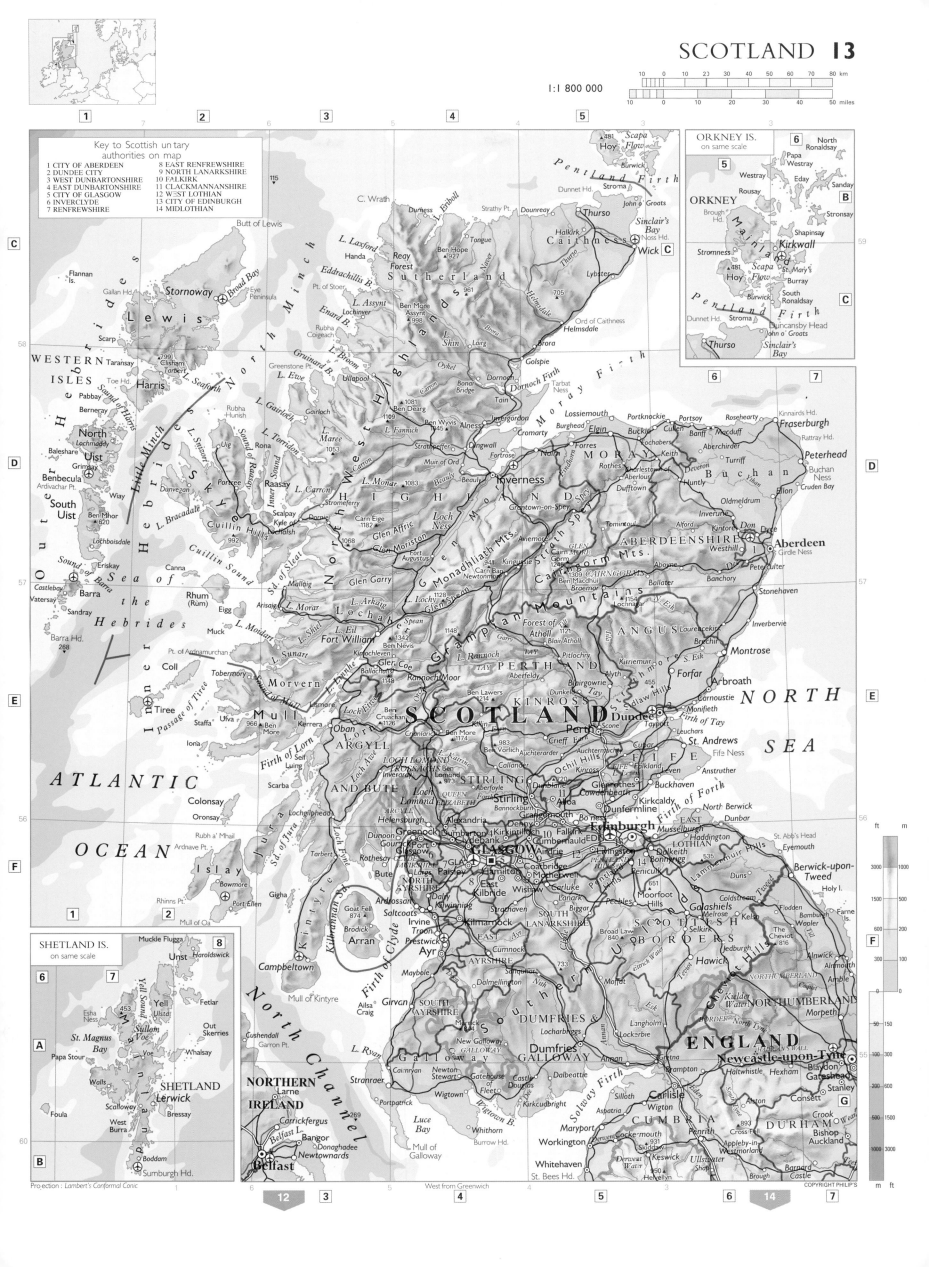

1:1 800 000

10 0 10 20 30 40 50 60 70 80 km
10 0 10 20 30 40 50 miles

Key to Scottish unitary
authorities on map
1 CITY OF ABERDEEN   8 EAST RENFREWSHIRE
2 DUNDEE CITY   9 NORTH LANARKSHIRE
3 WEST DUNBARTONSHIRE   10 FALKIRK
4 EAST DUNBARTONSHIRE   11 CLACKMANNANSHIRE
5 CITY OF GLASGOW   12 WEST LOTHIAN
6 INVERCLYDE   13 CITY OF EDINBURGH
7 RENFREWSHIRE   14 MIDLOTHIAN

ORKNEY IS.
on same scale

ORKNEY

SHETLAND IS.
on same scale

SHETLAND
Lerwick

Projection : Lambert's Conformal Conic

West from Greenwich

COPYRIGHT PHILIP'S

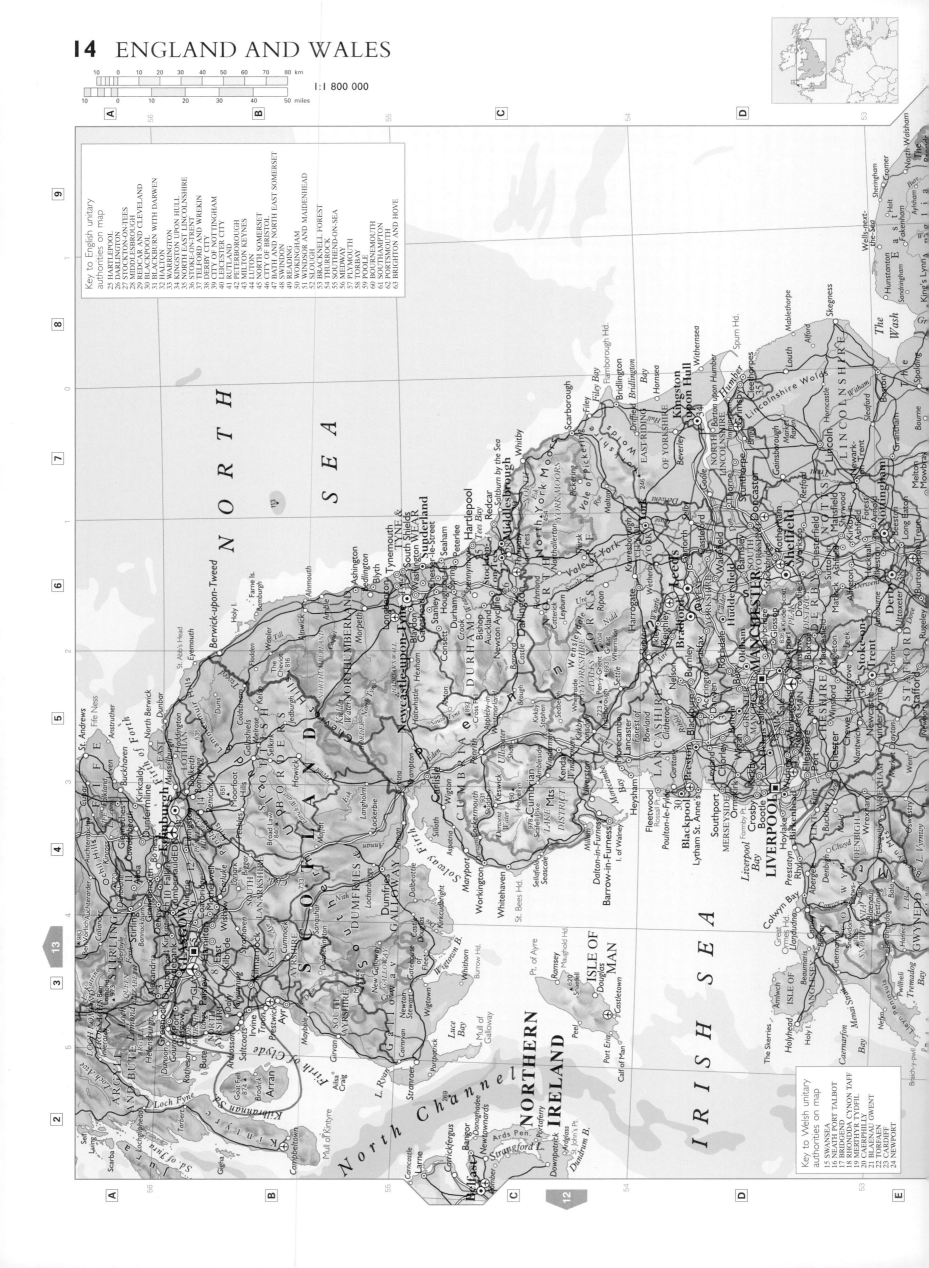

Projection : Lambert's Conformal Conic

FRANCE

HAUTE NORMANDIE

ENGLISH CHANNEL

LA MANCHE

Baie de la Seine

Le Havre

CHANNEL ISLANDS (U.K.)

Jersey

Guernsey

Alderney

ISLES OF SCILLY
on same scale

Isles of Scilly
St. Mary's

ENGLAND

WALES

Cardigan Bay

Bristol Channel

PEMBROKESHIRE COAST

POWYS

CEREDIGION

CARMARTHENSHIRE

GLAMORGAN

Cardiff

Swansea

BRECON BEACONS

DEVON

CORNWALL

DARTMOOR

EXMOOR

Plymouth

SOMERSET

DORSET

WILTSHIRE

HANTS

SUSSEX

WEST SUSSEX

EAST SUSSEX

KENT

SURREY

Strait of Dover

Calais

Dover

Folkestone

Hastings

Eastbourne

Brighton
Hove

Worthing

Portsmouth

Southampton

Bournemouth

ISLE OF WIGHT

LONDON

Oxford

BERKSHIRE

BUCKS

HERTS

ESSEX

SUFFOLK

NORFOLK

THE BROADS

Yarmouth
Lowestoft

Cambridge

CAMBRIDGESHIRE

Peterborough

NORTHAMPTON

BEDFORD

Leicester

Rutland

BIRMINGHAM

Coventry

WARWICKSHIRE

WORCESTER

HEREFORD

GLOUCS

SHROPSHIRE

Telford
Wolverhampton
Dudley

Gloucester

Bristol

Bath

SOMERSET

Taunton

Exeter

Torquay

NEWPORT

50 25 0 25 50 75 100 125 150 175 km
50   0 25   50   75   100   125 miles

1:4 400 000

1 **2** **3** **4** **5** **6** **7** **8** **9**

ATLANTIC OCEAN

Shetland Is. (U.K.)
Yell
Unst
Fetlar
Foula
Mainland
Lerwick

Fair Isle

NORWAY
Askøyna
Bergen
Osøyro
Stord
Bømlo
Leirvir
Hauge sund
Kopervik
Åkrahamn
Boknf
Stavanger
Sandnes
Bryne
Nærbø

Orkney Is.
Westray
Sanday
Stronsay
Mainland
Kirkwall
Hoy
South Ronaldsay
C. Wrath
Pentland Firth
Thurso
Wick

Lewis
Stornoway
North Minch
Harris
789
Ullapool
Lairg
Golspie
Helmsdale

St. Kilda (U.K.)
Outer Hebrides
North Uist
Benbecula
South Uist
Barra
Skye
Inner Hebrides
1182
North West Highlands
Tain
Invergordon
Dingwall
Nairn
Inverness
Elgin
Buckie
Banff
Fraserburgh
Peterhead
Huntly
Inverurie
Aberdeen

Rhum
Eigg
Coll
Mallaig
Fort William
1342
Ben Nevis
L. Ness
Glen More
Aviemore
CAIRNGORMS
Don
1311
Dee
SCOTLAND
Grampian Mts.
Ballater
Stonehaven

Tiree
Tobermory
Mull
Oban
1214
Tan
Forfar
Montrose
Arbroath

NORTH SEA

Colonsay
L. Awe
L. Lomond
LOMOND
TROSSACHS
973
Perth
Dundee
St. Andrews
238

Jura
Islay
L. Fyne
Dumbarton
Greenock
Stirling
Glenrothes
Kirkcaldy
Dunfermline
Dunbar

Campbeltown
Paisley
GLASGOW
Motherwell
Hamilton
East Kilbride
Edinburgh
Berwick-upon-Tweed
Arran
Kilmarnock
Galashiels
Irvine
Ayr
Southern Uplands
Jedburgh
Hawick
816
Cheviot Hills
Alnwick
840

Malin Hd.
Buncrana
Coleraine
Ballymena
Larne
Stranraer
Kirkcudbright
Dumfries
Annan
NORTHUMBERLAND
893
Newcastle-upon-Tyne
South Shields
Sunderland

Aran I.
Letterkenny
Lifford
Londonderry
GLENVEAGH
Donegal
Omagh
NORTHERN IRELAND
Lisburn
Lurgan
Portadown
Armagh
Newry
Carlisle
Pennines
Gateshead
Hexham
Durham
Hartlepool
Redcar
Darlington
Middlesbrough
Stockton-on-Tees
N. YORK MOORS
Scarborough

Bundoran
Sligo
Enniskillen
Lower L. Erne
Lough Neagh
Belfast
Bangor
Mull of Galloway
Workington
Whitehaven
978
Cumbrian Mts.
LAKE DISTRICT
Barrow-in-Furness
YORKSHIRE DALES
Bridlington

Ballina
X. Conn
Leitrim
Cavan
Clones
Castleblayney
Dundalk
Drogheda
Douglas
I. of Man
Lancaster
Harrogate
York
Beverley
Kingston upon Hull

Achill I.
Castlebar
Westport
Roscommon
Longford
Lough Ree
Athlone
Mullingar
Ceannanus Mor
Boyne
UNITED KINGDOM
Blackpool
Preston
Blackburn
Burnley
Keighley
Bradford
Leeds
Halifax
Huddersfield
Barnsley
Doncaster
Grimsby
Scunthorpe
Humber
Louth

Lough Mask
Connemara
Lough Corrib
Tuam
Lough Derg
Tullamore
IRISH SEA
Holyhead
Anglesey
Bangor
Colwyn Bay
Liverpool
MANCHESTER
Warrington
Stockport
Oldham
636
Sheffield
Rotherham
Chesterfield
Lincoln
Skegness

Galway B.
Galway
Ballinasloe
Port Laoise
Athy
Carlow
Bray
Wrexham
Chester
Crewe
Stoke-on-Trent
PEAK DISTRICT
Mansfield
Nottingham
Derby
Boston
The Wash
Cromer
THE BROADS

Aran Is.
BURREN
Ennis
Lough Derg
DUBLIN
Dun Laoghaire
Pwllheli
1085
Snowdon
SNOWDONIA
Shrewsbury
Telford
Stafford
Granthan
King's Lynn
Great Yarmouth
Lowestoft

Kilrush
Limerick
Nenagh
Thurles
Kilkenny
Arklow
Wexford
Cambrian Mts.
Cardigan
ENGLAND
Leicester
Corby
Peterborough
Thetford
Norwich
Haarlem

953
Shannon
Tipperary
Carrick-on-Suir
Rosslare
Aberystwyth
Cardigan Bay
886
Welshpool
Wolverhampton
BIRMINGHAM
Coventry
Nuneaton
Rugby
Northampton
Bedford
Ely
Cambridge
Bury St. Edmunds
Ipswich
NETHERLANDS
's-Gravenhage (Den Haag)

Dingle
1041
Carrantoohill
Mallow
Clonmel
Waterford
Dungarvan
Fishguard
WALES
Carmarthen
Merthyr Tydfil
Neath
Redditch
Royal Leamington Spa
Worcester
Hereford
Gloucester
Cheltenham
Cotswold Hills
Oxford
Milton Keynes
Hemel Hempstead
Stevenage
Luton
Harlow
Colchester
Harwich
Felixstowe
Chelmsford
Hoek van Holland
ROTTERDAM
Dordrecht

Valencia I.
MacGillycuddy's Reeks
Killarney
Blackwater
Haverfordwest
Milford Haven
Pembroke
PEMBROKESHIRE COAST
Llanelli
Swansea
Port Talbot
Rhondda
Brecon
BRECON BEACONS
Cwmbran
Newport
Cardiff
Bristol
Bath
Swindon
Newbury
Reading
Basingstoke
Guildford
High Wycombe
Slough
Watford
LONDON
Basildon
Southend-on-Sea
Chatham
Maidstone
Canterbury
Margate
Dover
Vlissingen
Zeebrugge
Oostende
Antwerp
Brugge
Gent
Mechelen

Kinsale
Cork
Bandon
Cobh
Youghal
Barry
Weston-super-Mare
Bristol Channel
EXMOOR
Barnstaple
Salisbury
Winchester
Southampton
Portsmouth
Worthing
Brighton
Eastbourne
Hastings
Folkestone
St.-Omer
Calais
Dunkerque
BELGIUM
BRUSSELS (Bruxelles)
LILLE
Tournai
Roubaix
Tourcoing

C. Clear
CELTIC SEA
Bude
NEW FOREST
Bournemouth
Poole
Weymouth
Newport
Isle of Wight
Portsmouth
Havant
Fareham
Taunton
Yeovil
Crawley
Gris Nez
Boulogne-sur-Mer
Béthune
Lens
Bruay-la-Buissière
Arras
Douai
Valenciennes
Cambrai

Newquay
Truro
818
DARTMOOR
Dartmoor
Exeter
Exmouth
Torbay
Le Touquet-Paris-Plage
Abbeville
Le Tréport
Dieppe
Picardie
St.-Quentin
Laon

Land's End
Penzance
St. Austell
Falmouth
Plymouth
ENGLISH CHANNEL
Fécamp
Le Havre
Rouen
FRANCE
Amiens
East from Greenwich
COPYRIGHT PHILIP'S

Îsles of Scilly
C. de la Hague
Pte. de Barfleur
Alderney
St. Peter Port
Guernsey
Sark
Cherbourg
Valognes
Bayeux
Caen
Lisieux
Elbeuf
Seine
Channel Is. (U.K.)
St. Helier
Jersey
Cotentin
Trouville-sur-Mer
West from Greenwich

Projection: Conical with two standard parallels

18 **19**

A B C D E F G

1:2 200 000

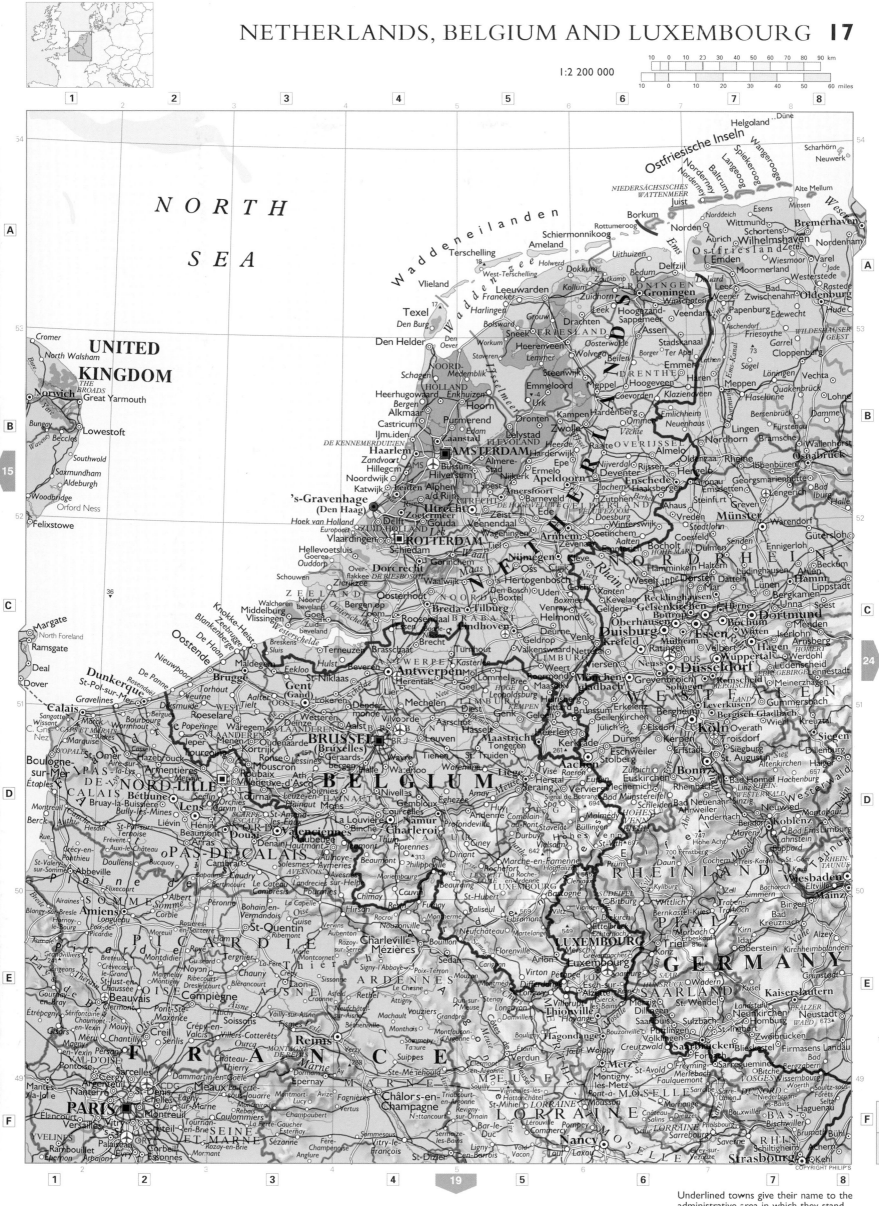

Underlined towns give their name to the administrative area in which they stand.

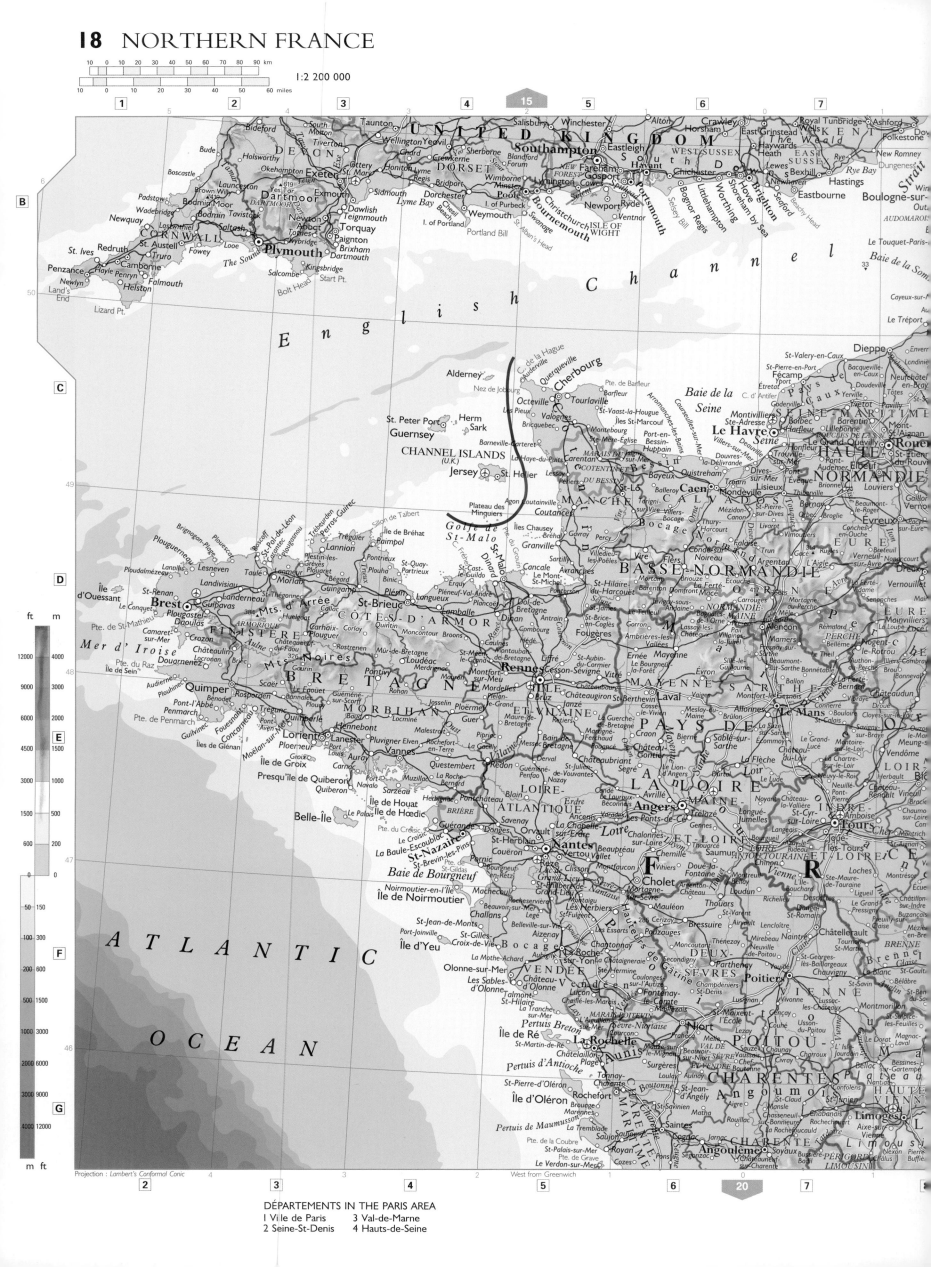

1:2 200 000

DÉPARTEMENTS IN THE PARIS AREA
1 Ville de Paris   3 Val-de-Marne
2 Seine-St-Denis   4 Hauts-de-Seine

Projection : Lambert's Conformal Conic

Underlined towns give their name to the
administrative area in which they stand.

1:2 200 000

Projection : Lambert's Conformal Conic

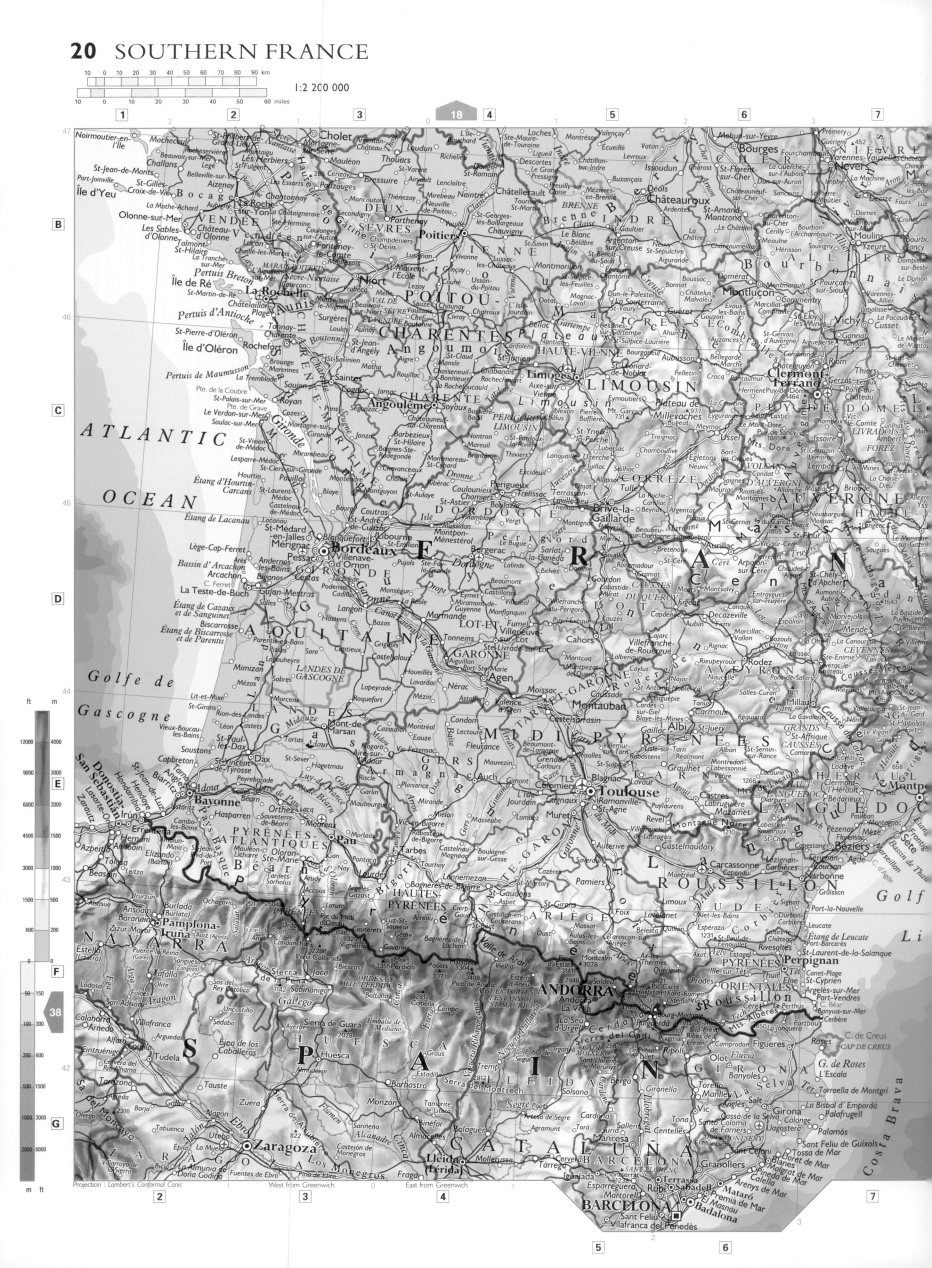

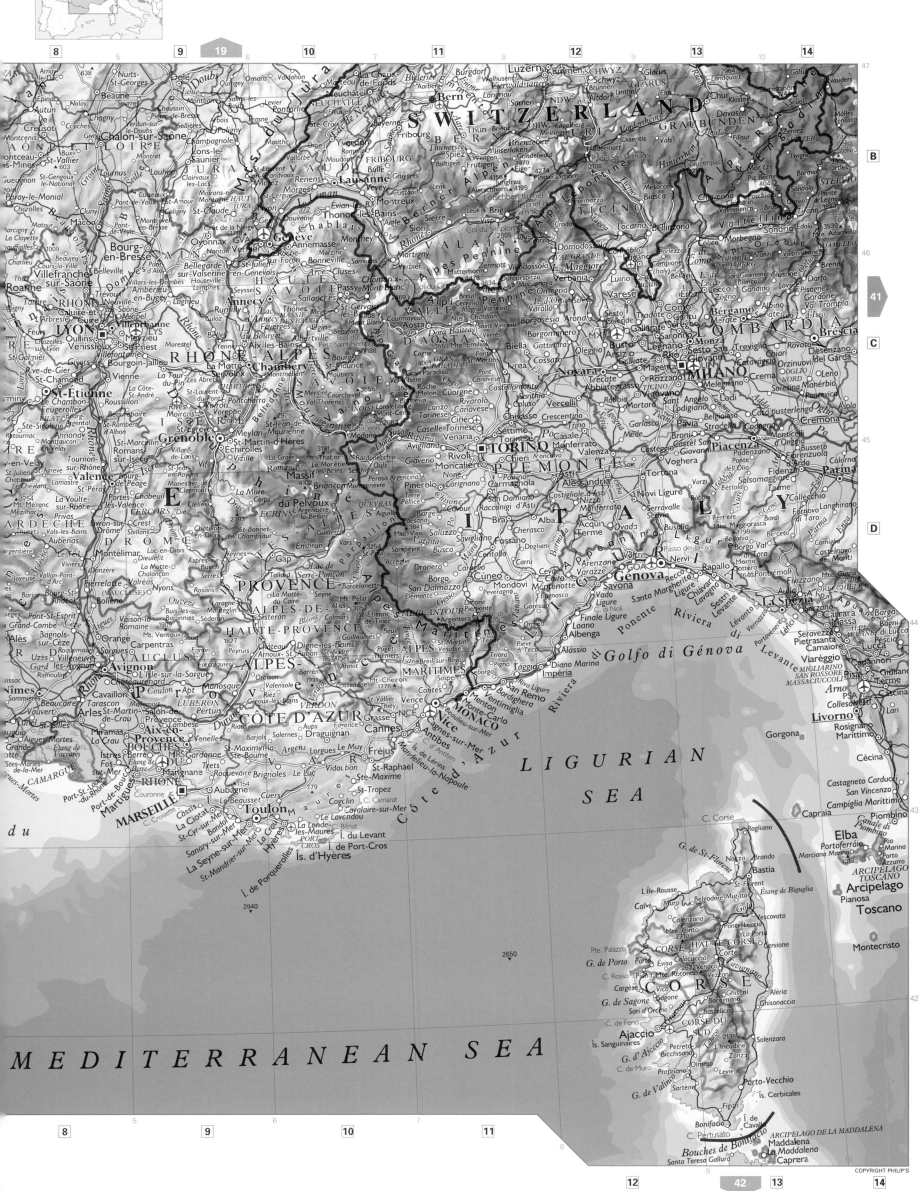

1:4 400 000

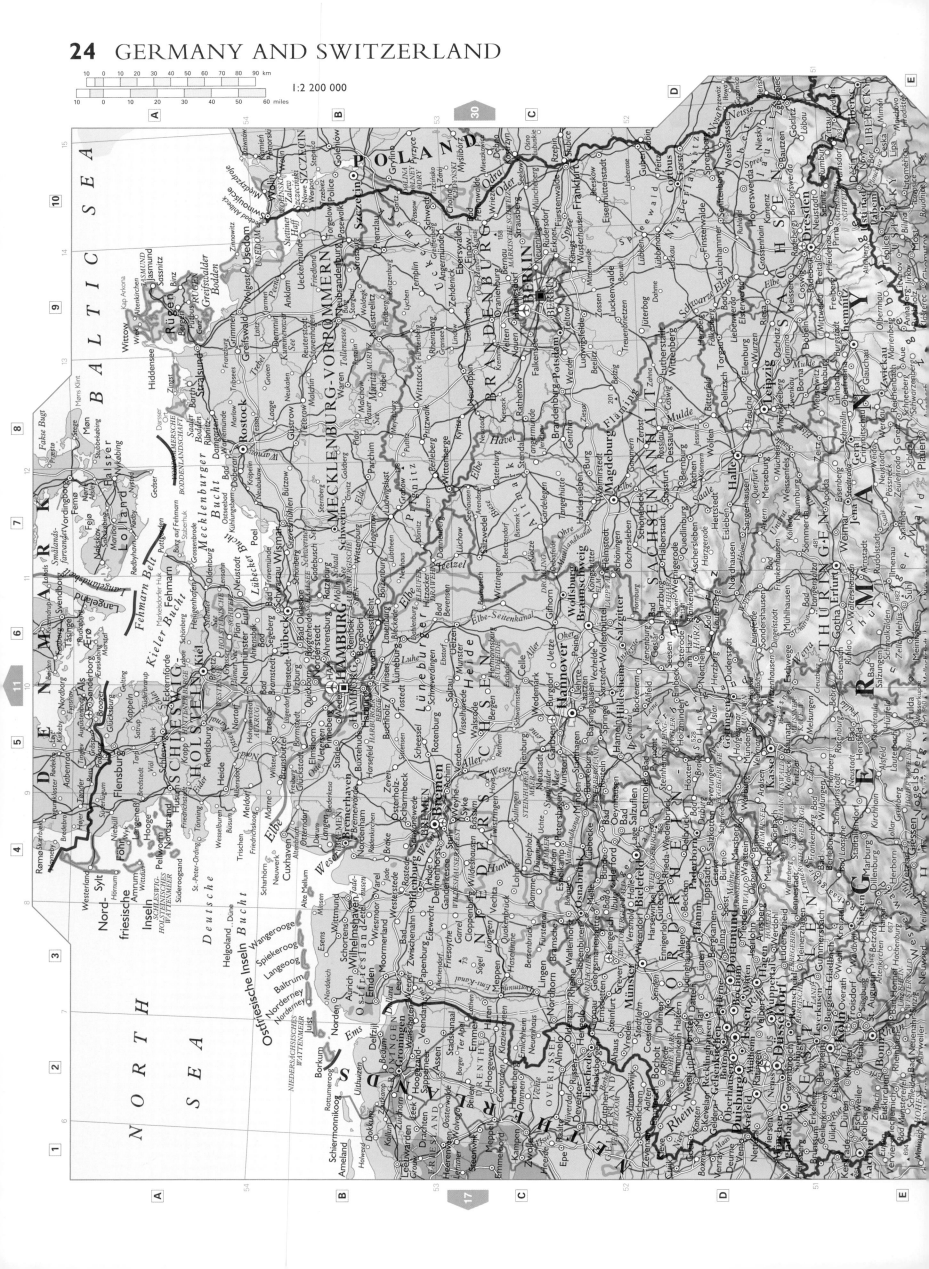

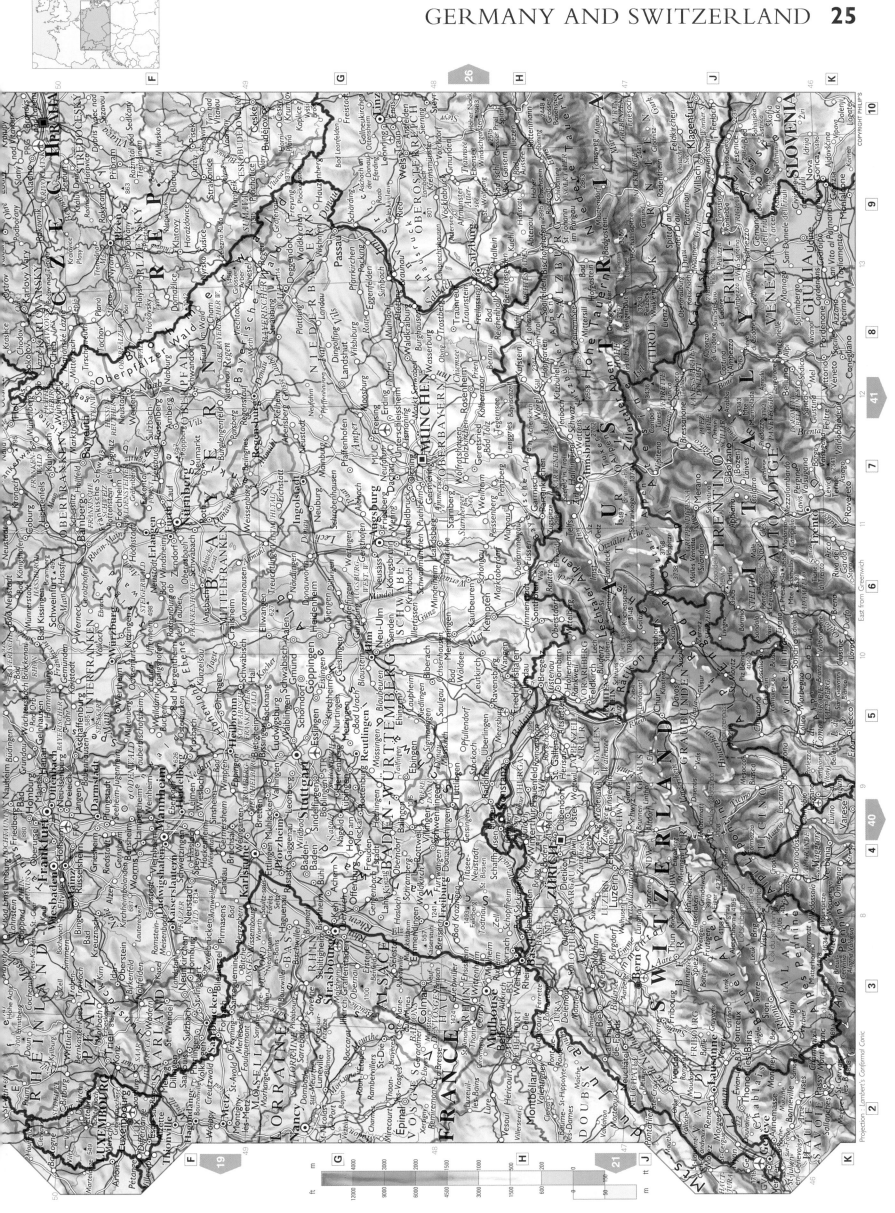

Underlined towns give their name to the administrative area in which they stand.

Underlined towns give their name to the
administrative area in which they stand.

1:2 200 000

Projection : Lambert's Conformal Conic

Administrative divisions in Croatia:
1 Brodsko-Posavska   5 Osječko-Baranjska   9 Vukovarsko-Srijemska
2 Koprivničko-Križevačka 6 Požeško-Slavonska
4 Medimurska   8 Virovitičko-Podravska

Underlined towns give their name to the
administrative area in which they stand.

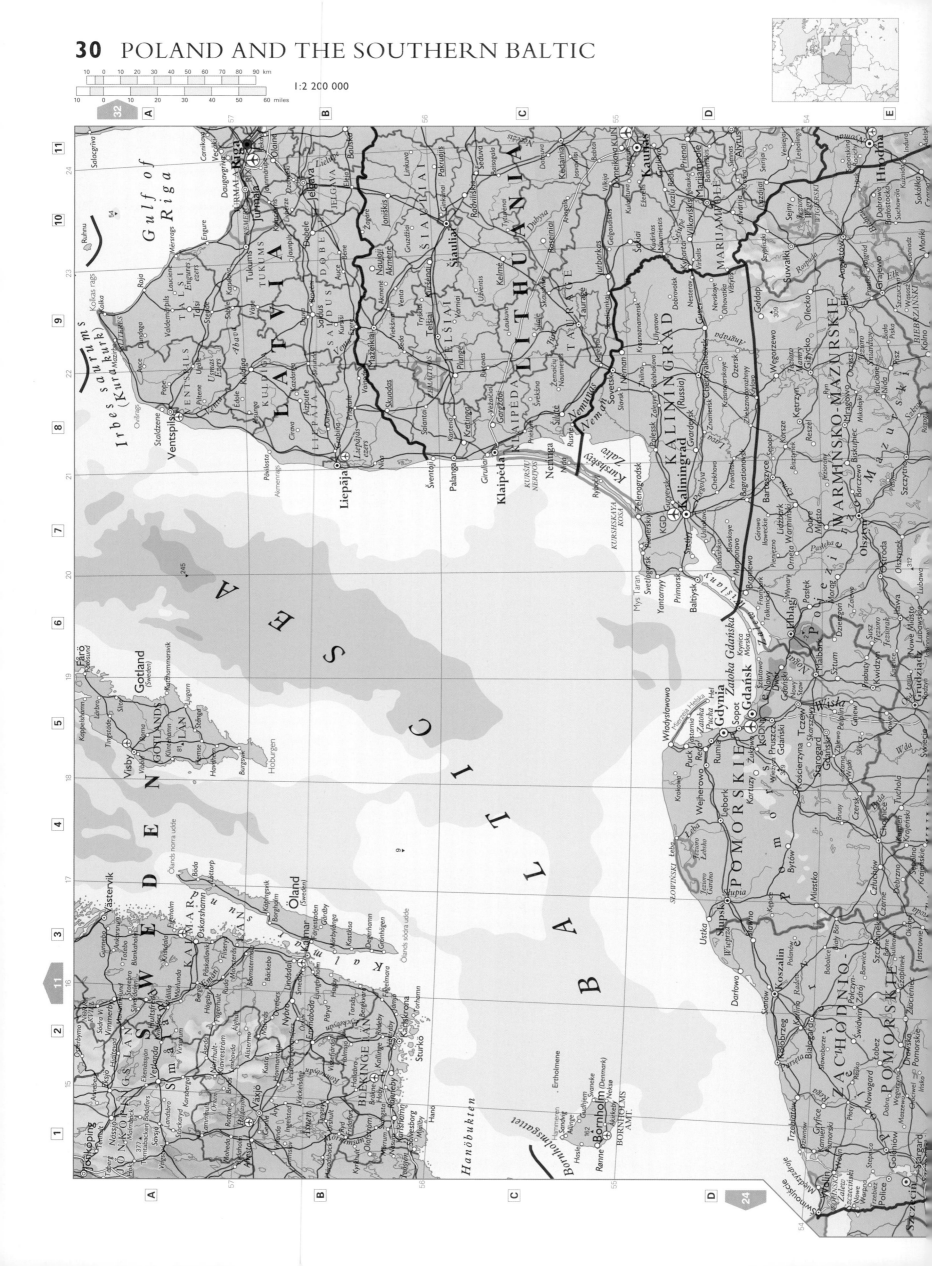

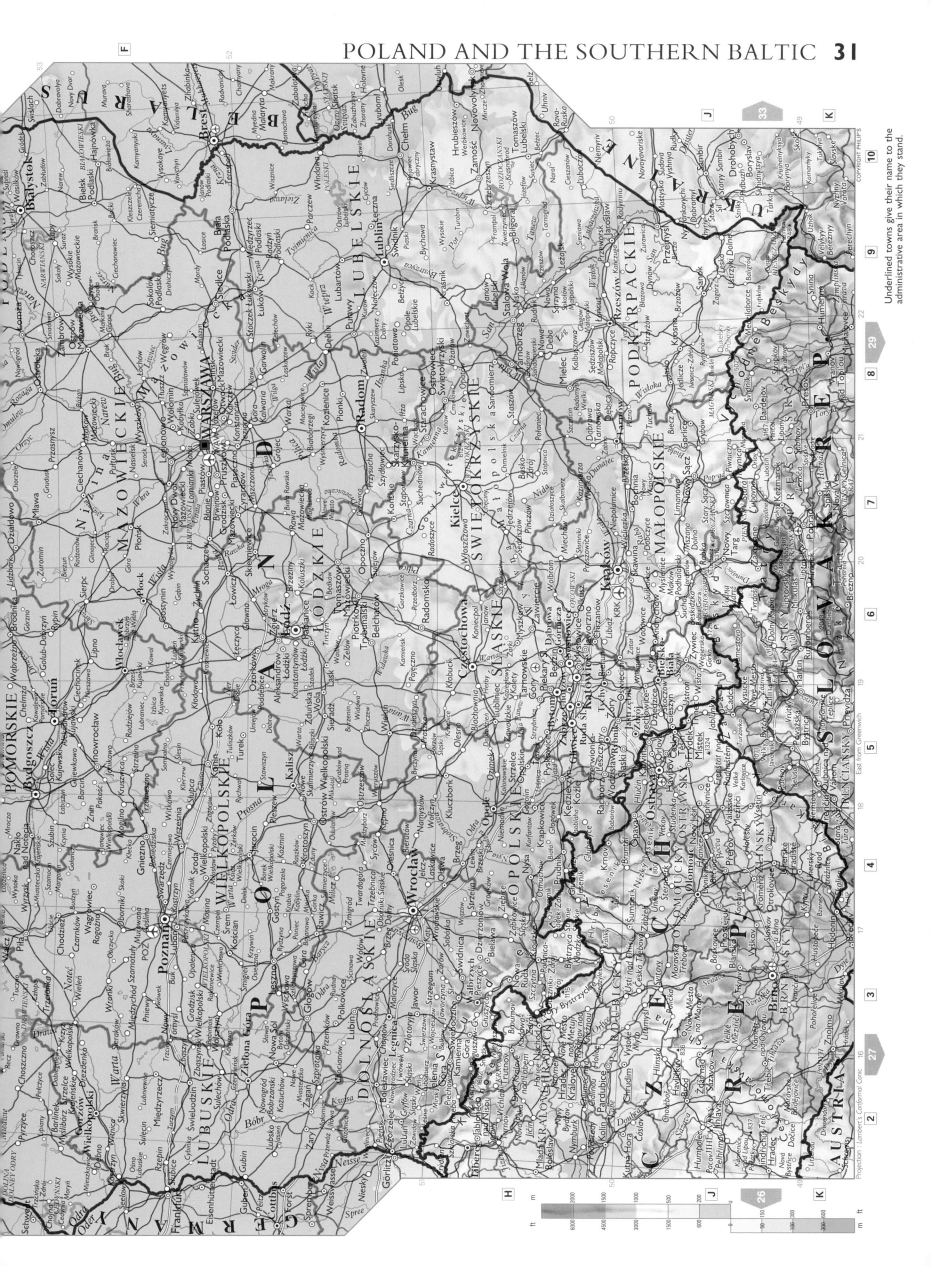

Underlined towns give their name to the administrative area in which they stand.

Projection: Lambert's Conformal Conic

East from Greenwich

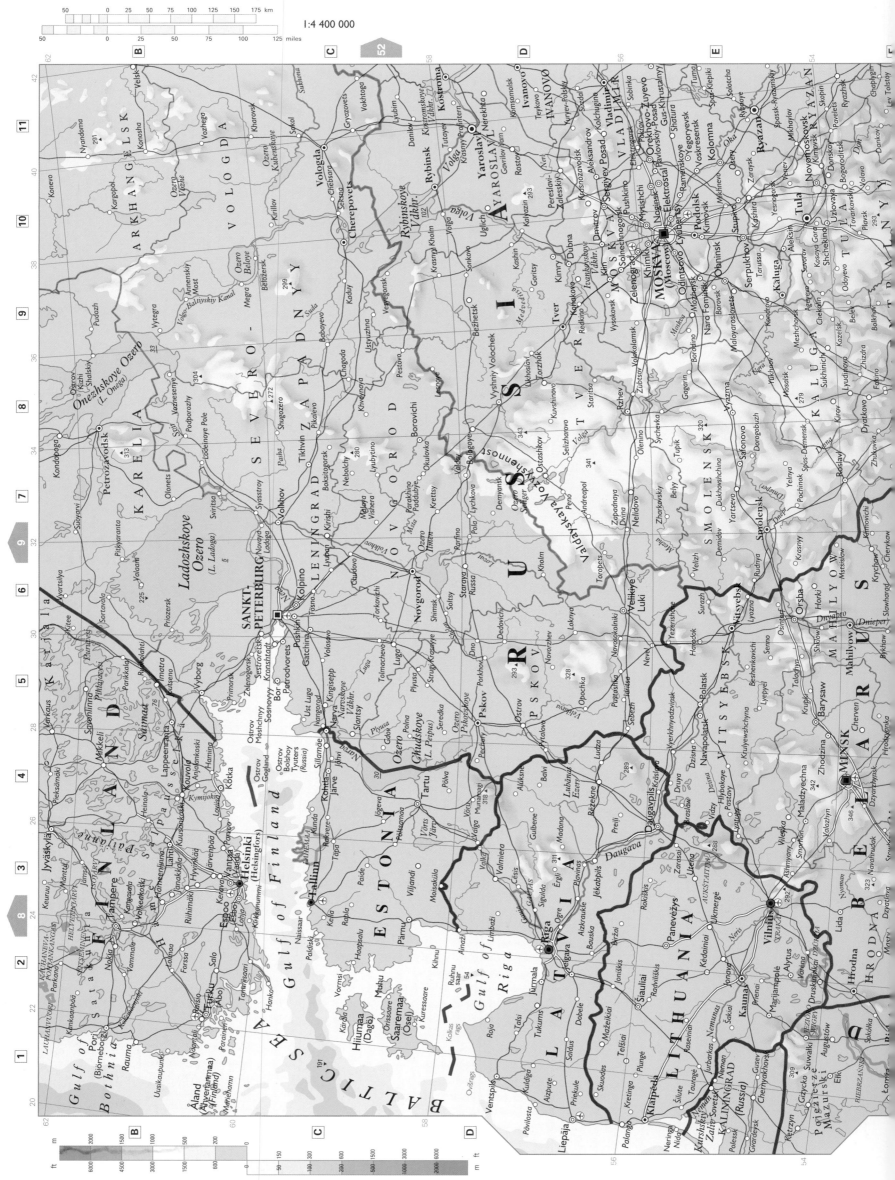

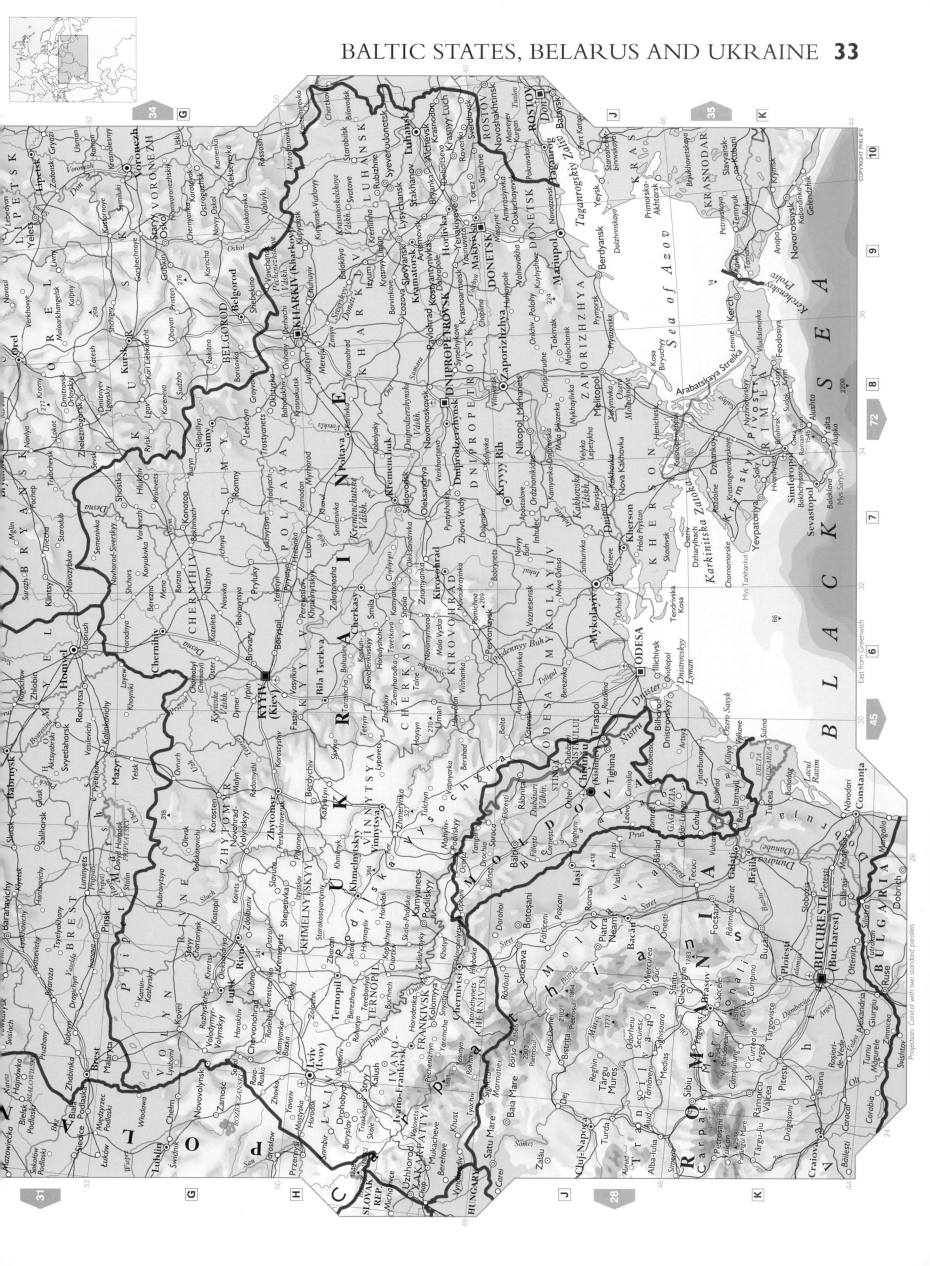

1:4 400 000

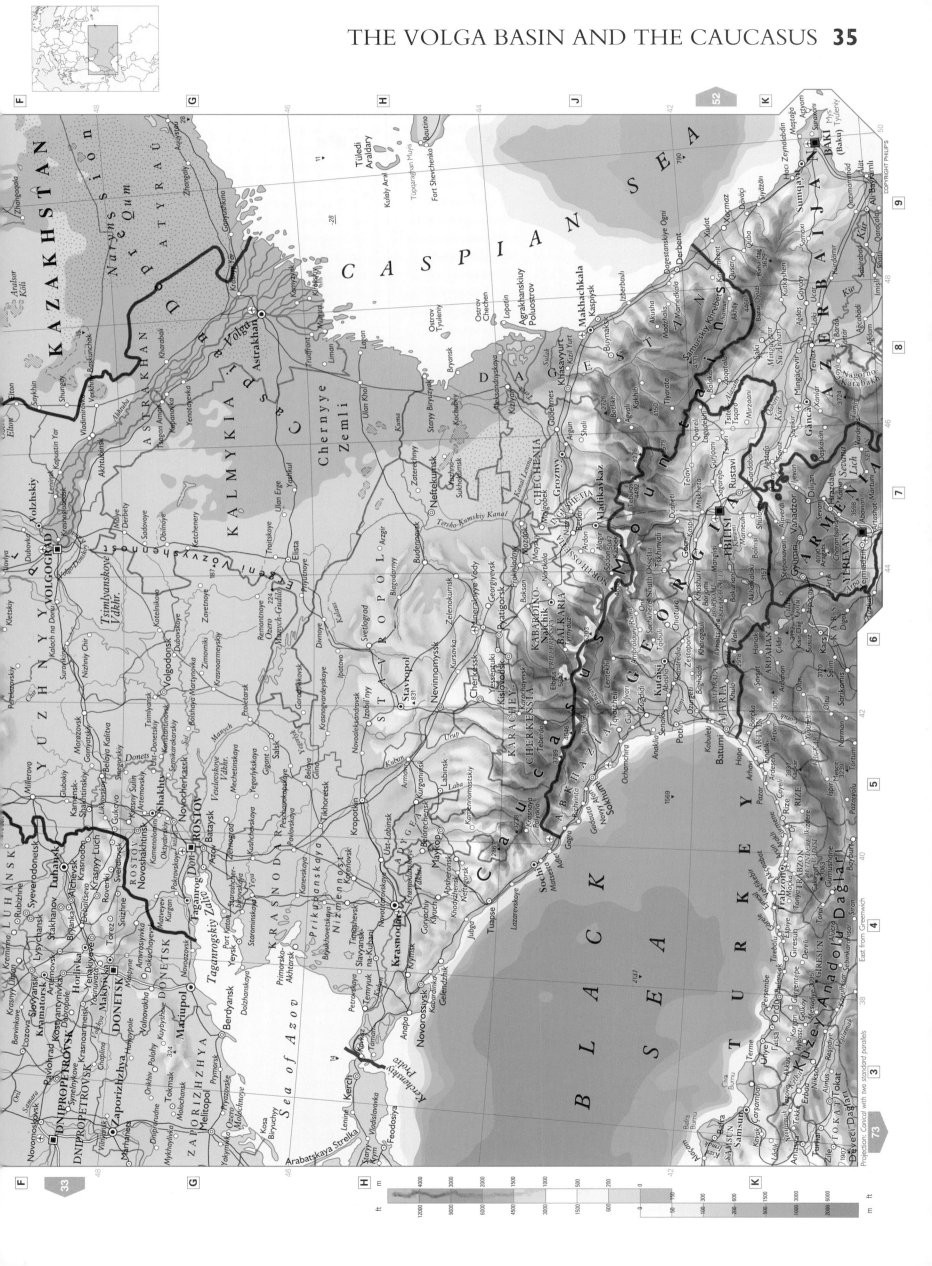

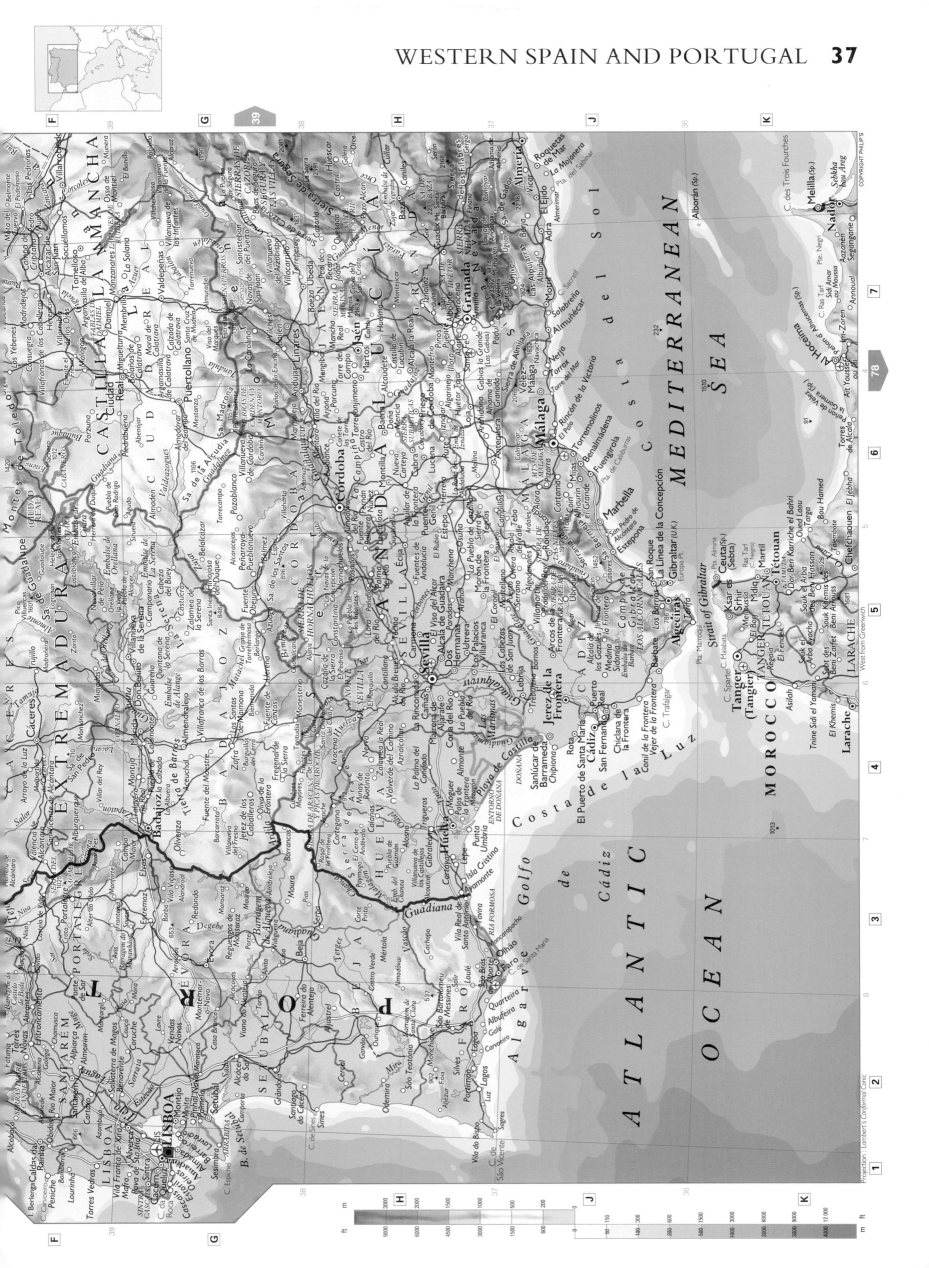

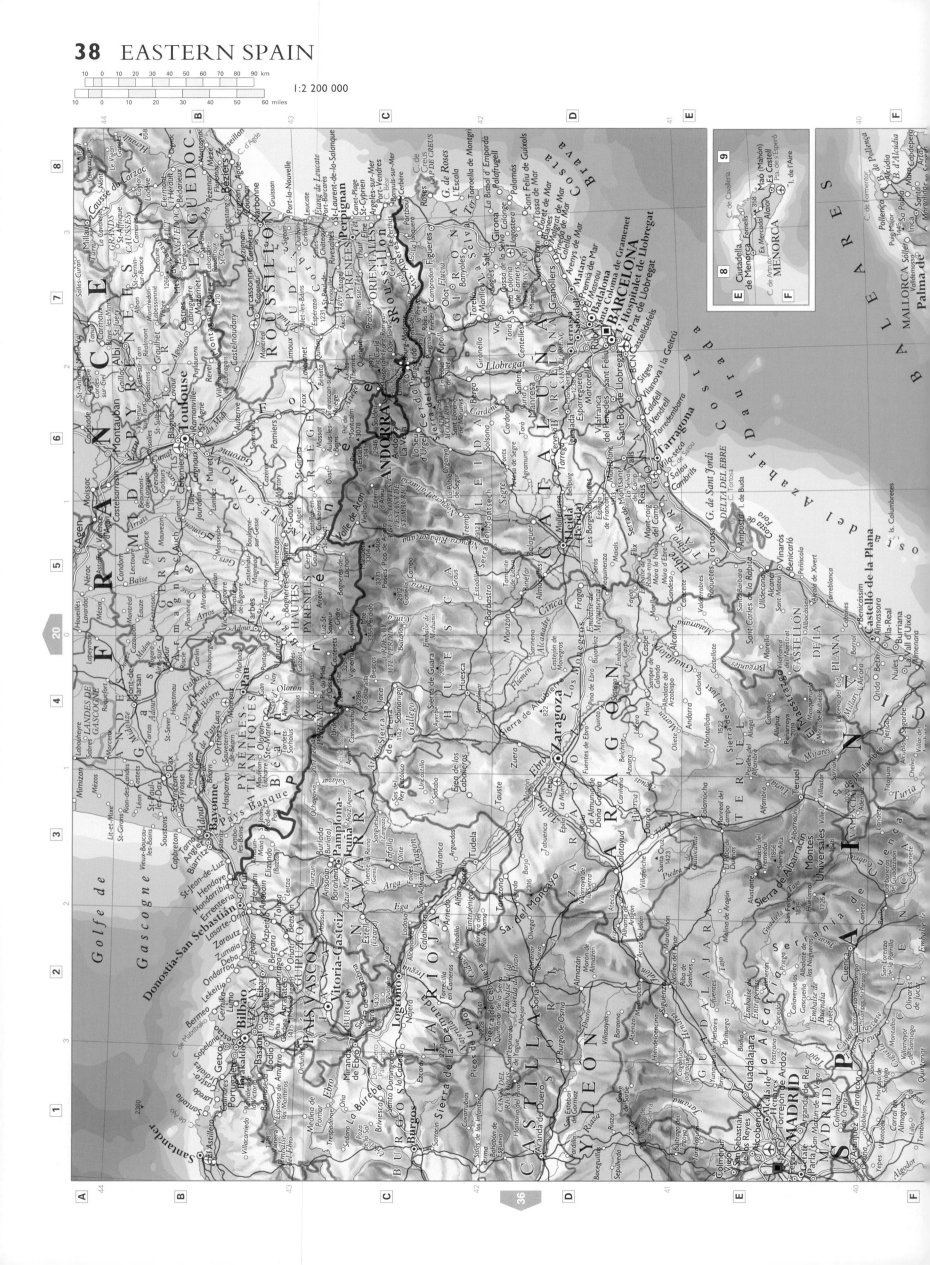

Projection : Lambert's Conformal Conic

1:2 200 000

Projection : Lambert's Conformal Conic

East from Greenwich

Underlined towns give their name to the
administrative area in which they stand.

COPYRIGHT PHILIP'S

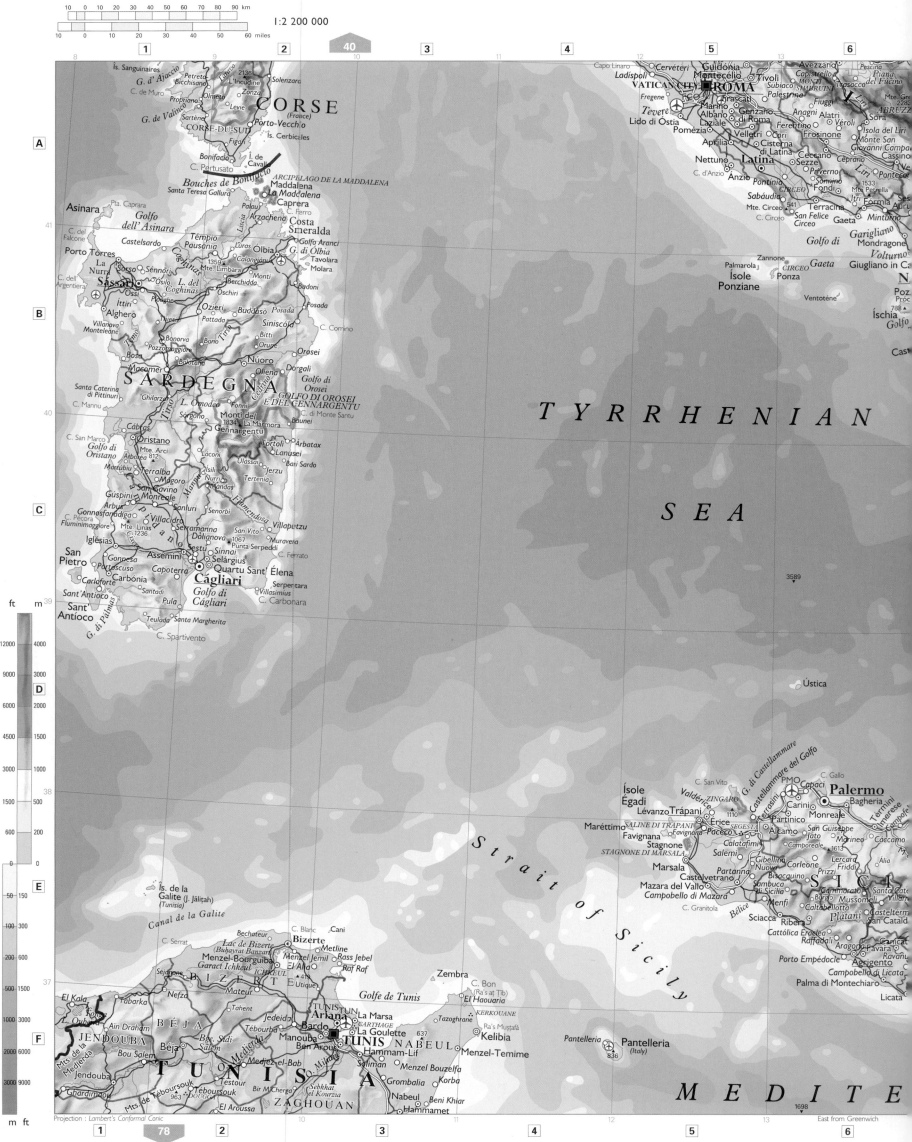

Underlined towns give their name to the
administrative area in which they stand.

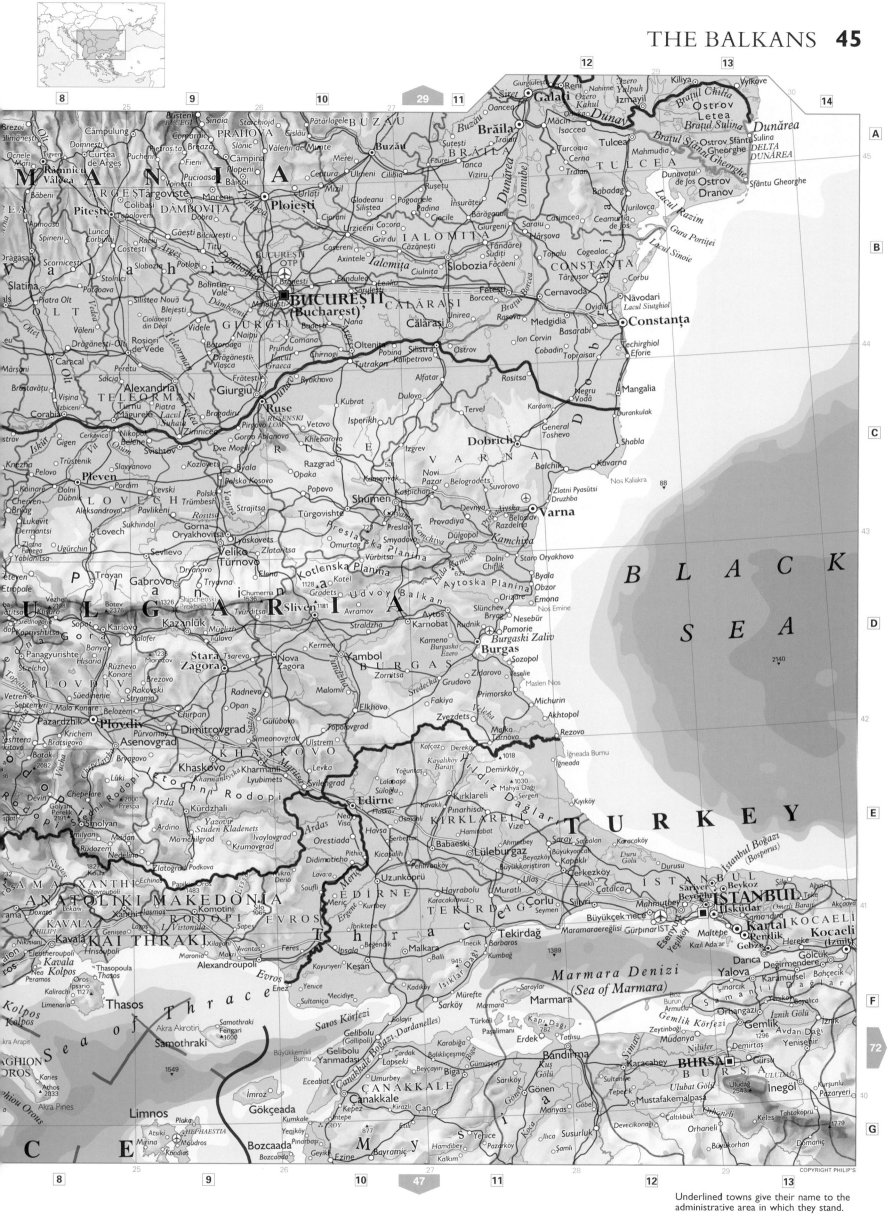

Underlined towns give their name to the
administrative area in which they stand.

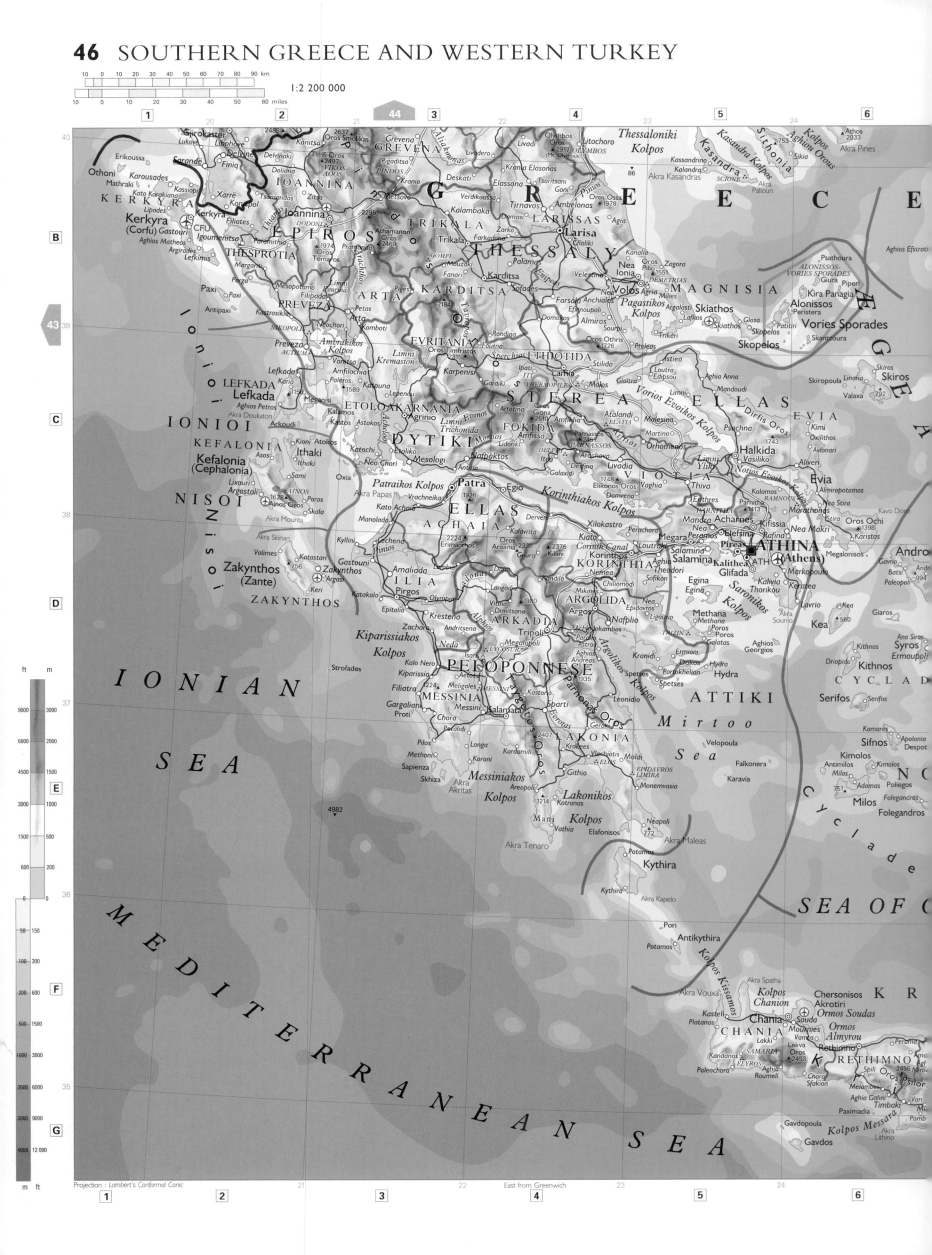

1:2 200 000

ft m

IONIAN

SEA

MEDITERRANEAN SEA

GREECE

IOANNINA
EPIROS
THESPROTIA
KERKYRA
Kerkyra (Corfu)

TRIKALA
THESSALY
Larisa
KARDITSA

GREVENA
PINDOS

LARISSAS

MAGNISIA
Volos
Pagastikos Kolpos
Skiathos
Skopelos

ALONISSOS-
VORIES SPORADES
Vories Sporades

ARTA
PREVEZA
Arta
Preveza
NIKOPOLI
ACTIUM
Amvrakikos Kolpos

EVRITANIA
STEREA
FOKIDA
DYTIKI
ELLAS
ACHAIA

FTHIOTIDA
Lamia
THERMOPILES
Sperchios

Vorios Evoikos Kolpos

ELLAS
EVIA
Halkida
Evia

LEFKADA
Lefkada

ETOLOAKARNANIA
Agrinio
Limni Trichonida

Mesologi
Nafpaktos

DELPHI
PARNASSOS
Livadia
VIOTIA
Thiva

Notios Evoikos Kolpos

IONIOI
KEFALONIA
Kefalonia (Cephalonia)

Ithaki

NISOI
AINOS
Ainos Oros

Patraikos Kolpos
Patra
Egio

Korinthiakos Kolpos
Korinthos
Corinth Canal

Megara
Elefsina
Pirea
Salamina
ATHINA (Athens)
Kalithea
Glifada
ATTIKI

Saronikos Kolpos

NISOI Zakynthos
Zakynthos (Zante)
ZAKYNTHOS

ILIA
Pirgos
Olympia

ARKADIA
Tripoli
Megalopoli

KORINTHIA
Nemea
Argos
ARGOLIDA
Nafplio

Argolikos Kolpos
Hydra

CYCLAD
Syros
Ermoupoli
Kithnos

Serifos

Sifnos
Kimolos
Milos

Folegandros

PELOPONNESE

MESSINIA
Kalamata

Kiparissiakos Kolpos
Kiparissia

Pilos
Methoni

Messiniakos Kolpos

LAKONIA
Sparti

Parnonas Oros

Lakonikos Kolpos

Mirtoo Sea

SEA OF C

Mani
Akra Tenaro

Kythira
Kythira

Antikythira

Kolpos Kissamos
Akra Spatha
Kolpos Chanion
Chania
CHANIA
SAMARIA
Ormos Soudas

KR

RETHIMNO

Kolpos Messara
Gavdos

IONIAN SEA

East from Greenwich

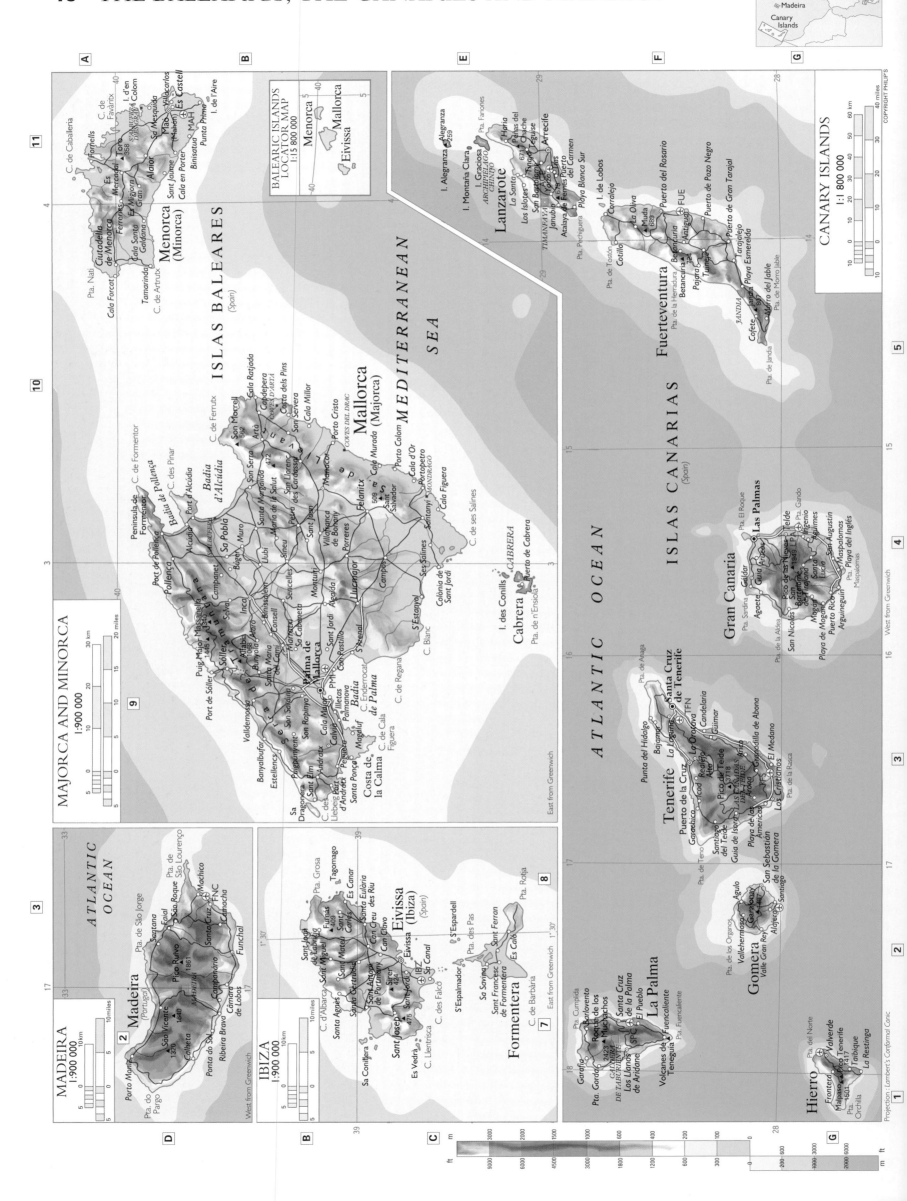

MEDITERRANEAN SEA

ISLAS BALEARES (Spain)

ATLANTIC OCEAN

ISLAS CANARIAS (Spain)

Menorca (Minorca)

Mallorca (Majorca)

CABRERA

Cabrera

Lanzarote

Fuerteventura

Gran Canaria

Tenerife

Gomera

La Palma

Hierro

Madeira (Portugal)

Eivissa (Ibiza) (Spain)

Formentera

BALEARIC ISLANDS LOCATOR MAP 1:15 800 000

Menorca
Mallorca
Eivissa

MAJORCA AND MINORCA 1:900 000

MADEIRA 1:900 000

IBIZA 1:900 000

CANARY ISLANDS 1:1 800 000

COPYRIGHT PHILIP'S

Projection: Lambert's Conformal Conic

West from Greenwich

East from Greenwich

Las Palmas

Santa Cruz de Tenerife

Funchal

Palma de Mallorca

Pico de Teide 3718

Arrecife

Puerto del Rosario

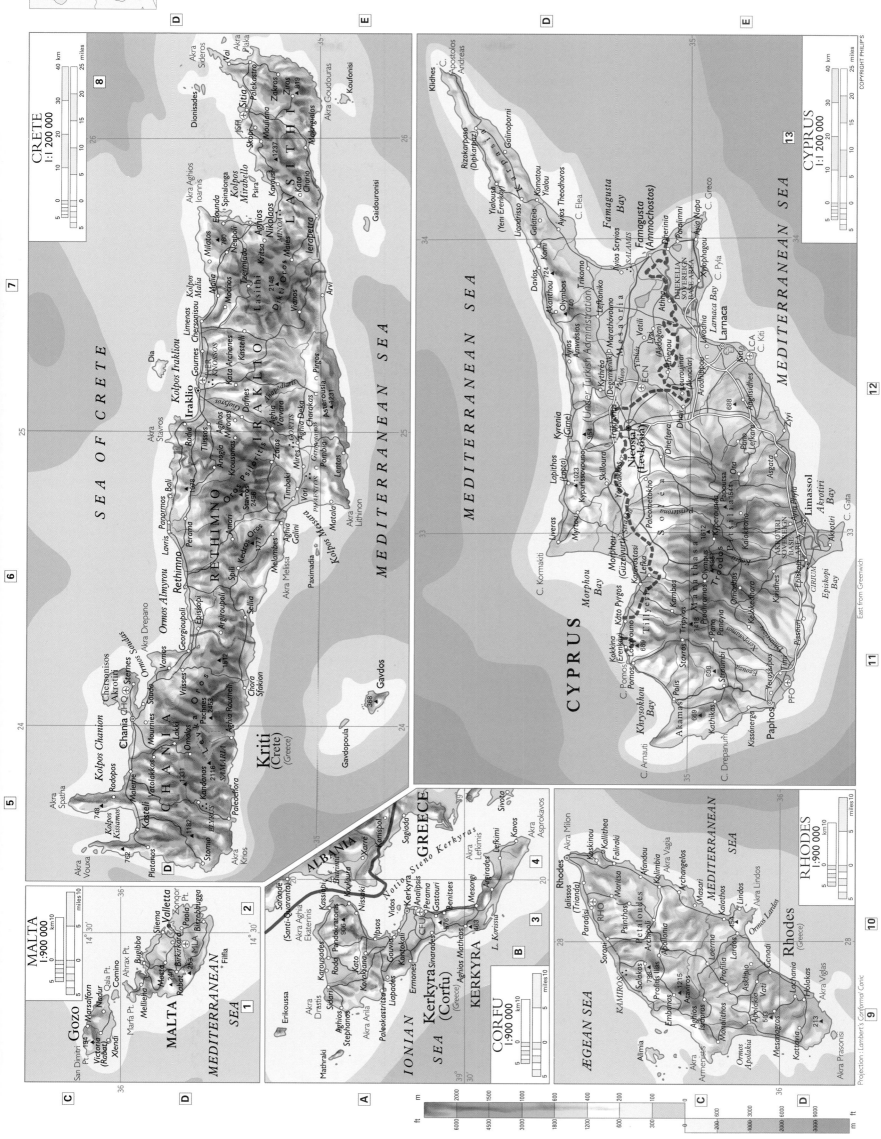

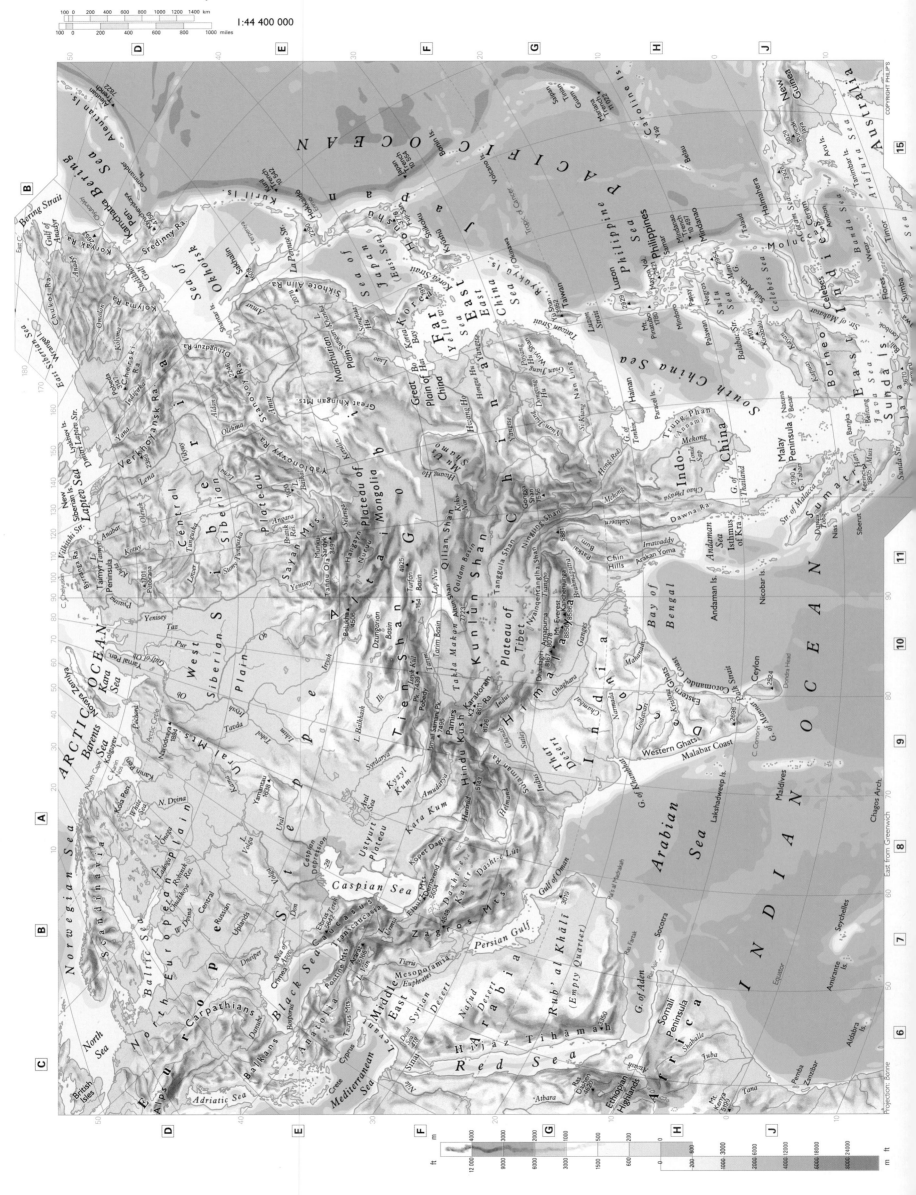

1:44 400 000

COPYRIGHT PHILIPS

Projection: Bonne

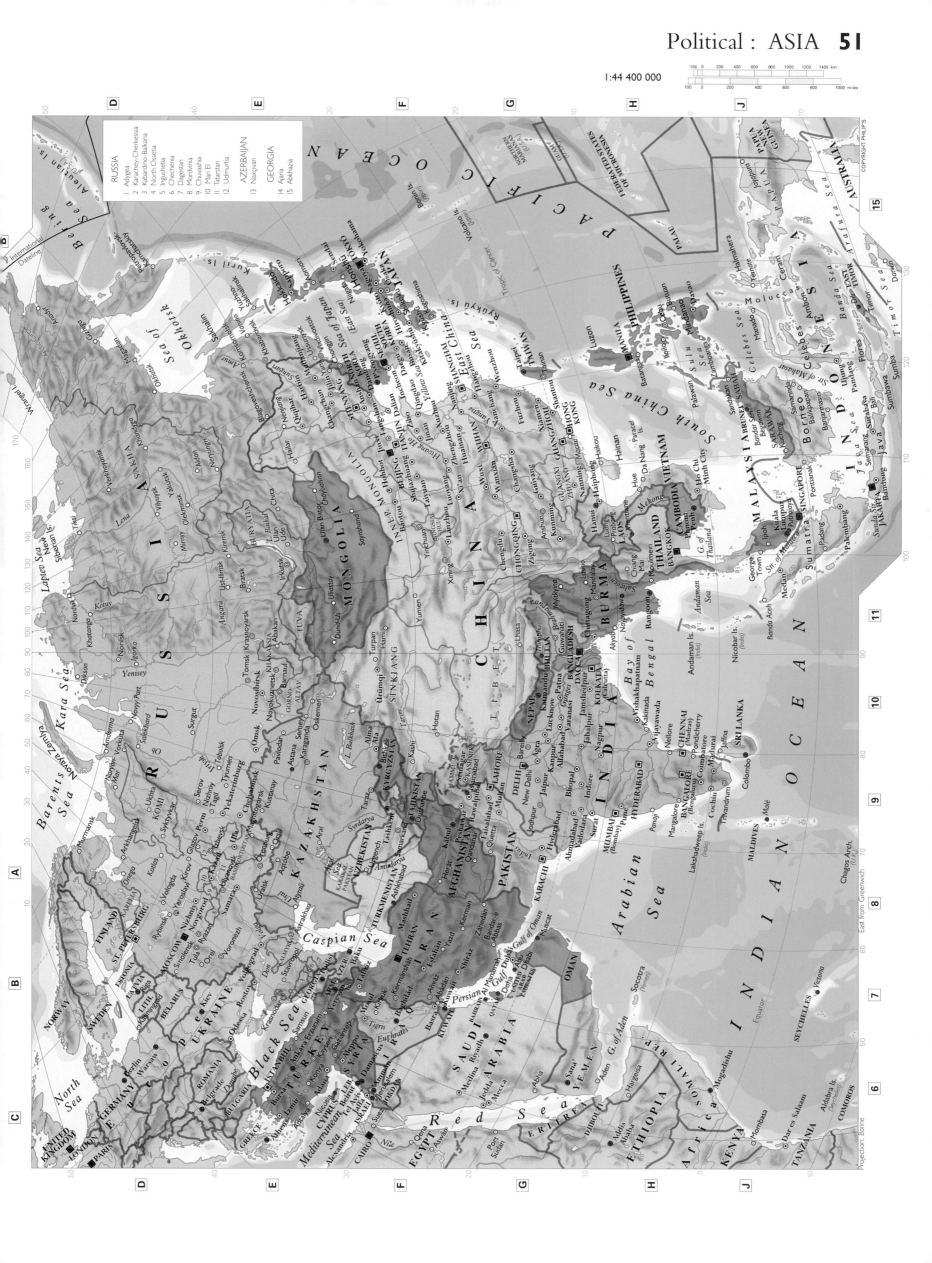

1:44 400 000

100 200 400 600 800 1000 1400 km
100 200 400 600 800 1000 miles

COPYRIGHT PHILIP'S

PACIFIC OCEAN

FEDERATED STATES OF MICRONESIA

PALAU

PAPUA NEW GUINEA

AUSTRALIA

RUSSIA
1 Adygea
2 Karachey-Cherkessia
3 Kabardino-Balkaria
4 North Ossetia
5 Ingushetia
6 Chechenia
7 Dagestan
8 Mordvinia
9 Chuvashia
10 Mari El
11 Tatarstan
12 Udmurtia
AZERBAIJAN
13 Naxçivan
GEORGIA
14 Ajaria
15 Abkhazia

Bering Sea

Aleutian Is.

International Dateline

Bering Strait

Sea of Okhotsk

JAPAN

NORTH KOREA

SOUTH KOREA

East China Sea

Ryukyu Is.

Tropic of Cancer

PHILIPPINES

MANILA

South China Sea

MALAYSIA

BRUNEI

SINGAPORE

INDONESIA

Celebes Sea

Borneo

Java Sea

Molucca Sea

Banda Sea

Arafura Sea

Timor Sea

EAST TIMOR

RUSSIA

MONGOLIA

Ulan Bator

INNER MONGOLIA

BEIJING

CHINA

SHANGHAI

HONG KONG

GUANGZHOU

TAIWAN

VIETNAM

LAOS

THAILAND

BANGKOK

CAMBODIA

Phnom Penh

BURMA

Rangoon

Bay of Bengal

Andaman Sea

Nicobar Is. (India)

Andaman Is. (India)

KAZAKHSTAN

UZBEKISTAN

TURKMENISTAN

KYRGYZSTAN

TAJIKISTAN

AFGHANISTAN

Kabul

PAKISTAN

KARACHI

SINKIANG

TIBET

NEPAL

BHUTAN

BANGLADESH

DACCA

INDIA

DELHI

New Delhi

MUMBAI (Bombay)

KOLKATA (Calcutta)

BANGALORE (Bengaluru)

CHENNAI (Madras)

HYDERABAD

SRI LANKA

Colombo

MALDIVES

Malé

Arabian Sea

INDIAN OCEAN

Chagos Arch. (UK)

IRAN

TEHRAN

IRAQ

BAGHDAD

SAUDI ARABIA

Riyadh

KUWAIT

OMAN

Persian Gulf

Gulf of Oman

QATAR

U.A.E.

Abu Dhabi

Muscat

YEMEN

Sana'

Gulf of Aden

Socotra (Yemen)

Caspian Sea

AZERBAIJAN

ARMENIA

GEORGIA

TURKEY

ANKARA

SYRIA

CYPRUS

LEBANON

ISRAEL

JORDAN

Mediterranean Sea

Black Sea

UKRAINE

ROMANIA

BULGARIA

GREECE

MOLDOVA

RUSSIA

MOSCOW

ST. PETERSBURG

FINLAND

ESTONIA

LATVIA

LITH.

BELARUS

POLAND

GERMANY

Berlin

Warsaw

UNITED KINGDOM

LONDON

PARIS

NORWAY

SWEDEN

North Sea

Barents Sea

Kara Sea

Laptev Sea

East Siberian Sea

Red Sea

EGYPT

CAIRO

ERITREA

ETHIOPIA

Addis Ababa

DJIBOUTI

SOMALI REP.

Mogadishu

KENYA

TANZANIA

COMOROS

SEYCHELLES

Aldabra Is. (Seychelles)

Equator

East from Greenwich

Projection: Bonne

1 : 17 800 000

	RUSSIA
1	Adygea
2	Karachey-Cherkessia
3	Kabardino-Balkaria
4	North Ossetia
5	Ingushetia
6	Chechenia
7	Dagestan
8	Mordvinia
9	Chuvashia
10	Mari El
11	Tatarstan
12	Udmurtia
13	Khakassia
	AZERBAIJAN
14	Naxçivan
	GEORGIA UKRAINE
15	Ajaria 17 Crimea
16	Abkhazia

Projection: Conical Orthomorphic with two standard parallels

East from Greenwich

71

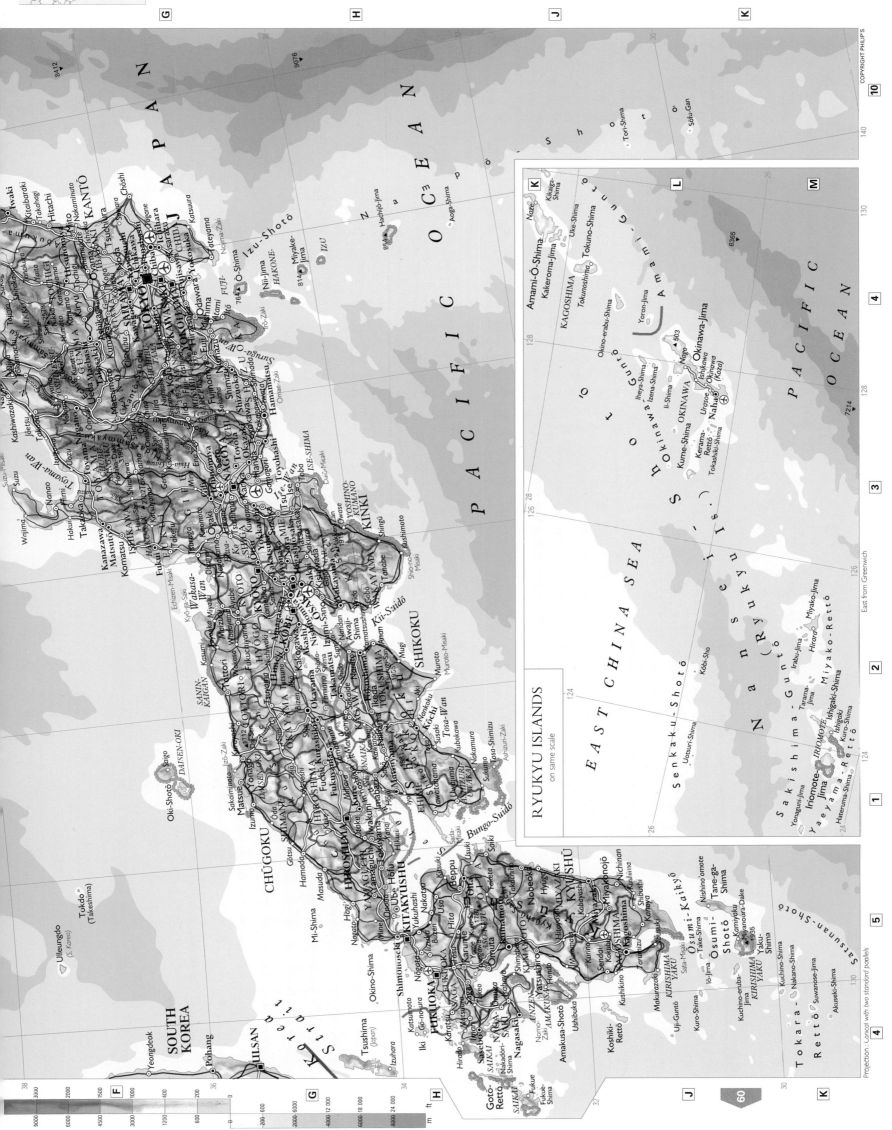

RYUKYU ISLANDS
on same scale

EAST CHINA SEA

PACIFIC OCEAN

PACIFIC OCEAN

SOUTH KOREA

Projection · Conical with two standard parallels

East from Greenwich

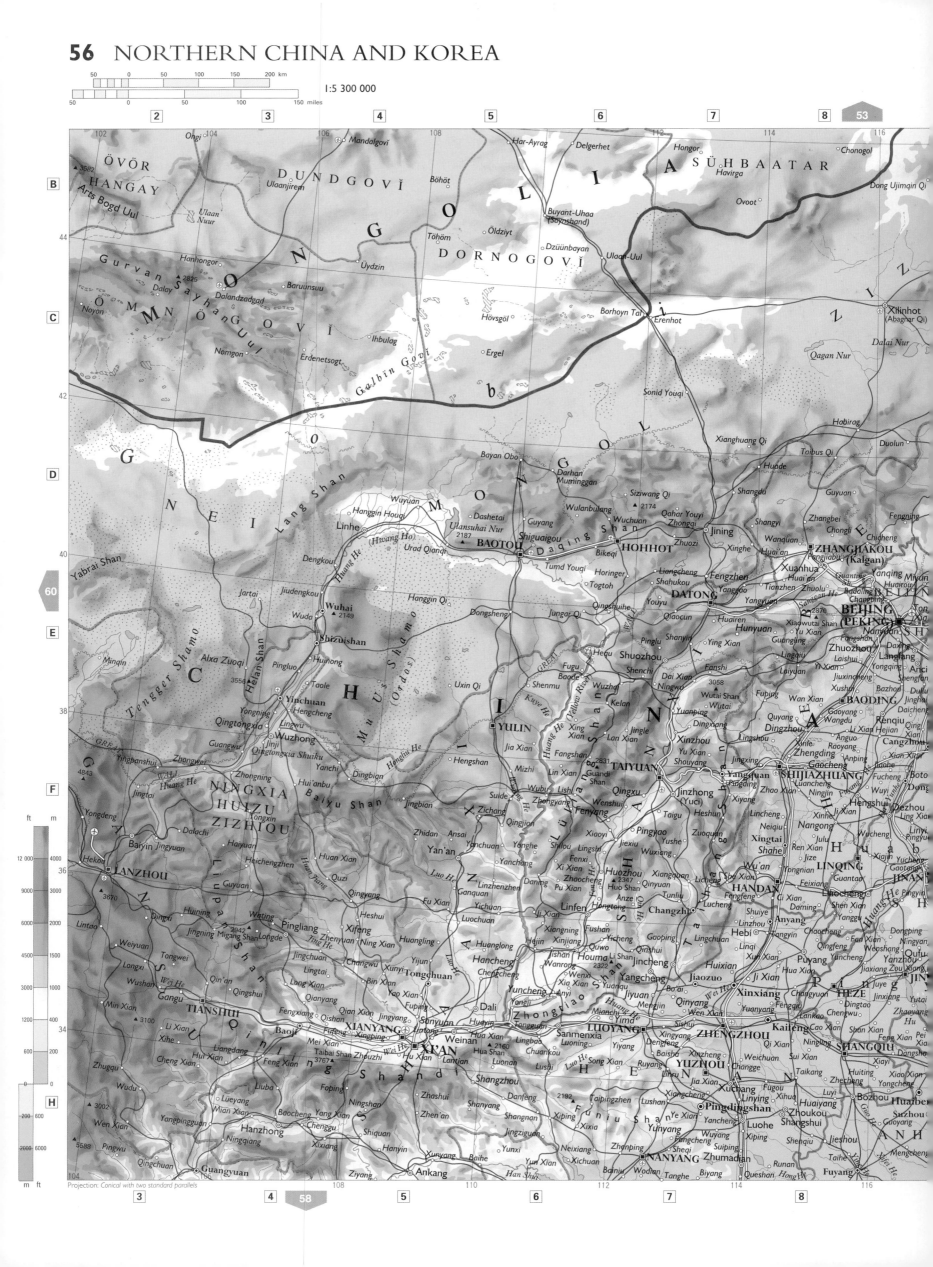

B

C

D

55

E

F

G

H

SEA OF JAPAN

JAPAN

(EAST SEA)

YELLOW SEA

(Huang Hai)

Horqin Youyi Qianqi
(Ulanhot)

Baicheng

HARBIN

Zhenlai

Bin Xian

Linkou   YIXI   Turiy Rog   Lake Khanka

RUSSIA

Maoxing   Shuangcheng   Acheng   Yanshou

Huolin Gol   Hulin He

Tuquan

Taonan

Qiqian Nur Qian   Gorlos   Sanchahe   Wuchang

Yimianpo

Hengdaohezi   1690   Maqiache

MUDANJIANG

Jixianzhen

Muling   Suifenhe

Ning'an

Pogranichnyy   Golenki

Huolin Gol

Da'an

Fulongquan   Shanhetun   Hailin

FUYU

Qagan

Nong'an   Dehui

Yushu   Shulan

Dongjingcheng   Jingpo Hu   Dongning

Ussuriysk

Zhanyu

Tongyu

Shenjingzi   Kaoshan

CHANGCHUN   JILIN   Jiaohe

Chunyang   Wangqing   Luozigou

Vladivostok

Jarud Qi

Beizhengzhen

Changling

Huaidezhen   Fanjiatun   Emu

Dunhua   Daxinggou

Mingyuegou   Shixian

Xinzhan

Artem

Bairin Zuoqi

Xinkai He

Horqin Zuoyi Zhongqi   Lishu   Shuangyang   Panshi   Huadian

Baihe

Wangqing   Tumen   Hunchun

Tairichanka

Kailu   Tongliao   Shuangliao   Gongzhuling   Yitong

Dongfeng

Huinan   Baishan

Quanyang   1677   Yanji

Namyang   Kino

Posyet

Xiliao He

Jorqalang

Bamiancheng   Siping   Liaoyuan   Hufa   Jingyu

Fusong   Songjianghe   Helong   Longjing   Aoji   Khasan

Xar Moron He

Liaoyuan   Xifeng

Meihekou   Jingyu

Changbai Shan   2744   Hoeryong   Musan   Unggi   Sosura

Wutonghaolai   WALL   Kaiyuan   Shanchengzhen

Shiren   Linjiang   Paektu-san

Hyesan   Nanam   Najin   Fugodong

Xiawa   Hure Qi   Tieling   Qingyuan   Hunjiang   Changbai   Puryong   Kyongsong

Chunggang-up

CHIFENG
(Ulanhad)

Faku   Tiefa   Xinbin   Tonghua

Huch'ang   Kasan-dong   Hapsu   Kilchu

Ch'ongjin

Fuxin   Xinlitun   Xinmin   Piao'ertun   Ji'an   Manp'o   Kapsan   Musudan

Ongniud Qi

Heishui

Beizhen

SHENYANG   FUSHUN   Huanren   1846   Kanggye   Puksubaek-san   P'ungsan   Odaejin

Bairin Youqi

Chaoyang   Heishan   Sujiatun

Yalu   Wiwon   Ch'osan   2522   Pujon-ho   Kimch'aek
(Songjin)

Beipiao   Qinghemen   Liaozhong   Qinghecheng   Pyokjong   Changjin-ho   Changhungni

Ningcheng   1885

Benxi   Tianshifu   Koin   Kwangdaeri   Iwon   Tanch'on

Chengde   Lingyuan   Liaoyang   Anting   Gongchangling   Sinhung   Sinp'o   Pukch'ong

Liugou   Jianchang   Panjin   ANSHAN   Lianshanguan   Kangye

Shangbancheng   Jinzhou   Niuzhuang   Haicheng   Kuandian   Pyoktong   Hamgyong   Hongwon

Pingquan   Kuancheng   JINXI   Tianzhuangtai   Dashiqiao   Fengcheng   Supung Shuiku   Taegwan   Kusong   Kujong   Hamju   Hamhung   Hungnam

Luanping   Jianchangying   Xingcheng   Huludao   Yingkou   Xiuyan   Kaksan   Sakchu   NORTH   Huichon   Oro

Xinglong   Suizhong   Xiongyuecheng   Gaizhou   Jiuliancheng   Dandong   Uiju   Taegwan

Xunhua   Fengrun   Qinhuangdao   Liaodong   Wanfu   1131   Buyun Shan   Langtou   Sinuiju   Yongamp'o   Chongju   Pakchon   KOREA

Luanxian   Liaodong Wan   Gushan   Donggou   Sonch'on   Tongjoson Man

Yatian   Funing   Changli   Wafangdian   Pulandian   Sinmi-do   Sukch'on   P'yongsong   Munch'on   Kowon   Wonsan

Qikou   Leting   Lulong   Changshan   Zhuanghe   Pikou   Sukch'on   Sunan   Anbyon   Kojo

TANGSHAN   Linxi   Qundao   P'yongyang   Chunghwa   Kangdong   Tongyang   Hoeyang   Kosong   1638   Cangdo-ri   Changdo-ri

TIANJIN SHI   Liaodong Bandao   Jinzhou   NAMPO   Sariwon   Songnim   Koksan   Sepo-ri   P'yonggang   Cangseong

TIANJIN   Hangu   Wuqing   Tanggu   Jingtanggang   Lushun   DALIAN   Cho-do   Chaeryong   Sinmak   Nam-ch'on   Sokcho   Yang-yang

Dagu   Tanggu   (Luda)   Changyon   Sinch'on   Kumch'on   Cheorwon   Hwacheon   Cheosuji   1708   Jumunjin

Oikou   Miaodao   Qundao   Haeju   Kaesong   Panmunjom   Chunchon   Gangneung

Huangnua   Korea Bay   Ongjin   Yonan   Munsan   Uijeongbu   Hongcheon   Donghae

Xincun   Baengnyeongdo
(S. Korea)   GOYANG   SEOUL   SEONGNAM   Hoengseong   Samcheok

Yanshan   Qingyun   Penglai   Longkou   Daxindian   YANTAI   Weihai   BUCHEON   Anyang   Wonju   Ulleungdo
(S. Korea)

Wudi   Zhanhua   Huang Xian   Fushan   Muping   INCHEON   Ansan   Icheon   Yeoju   Wonju   Yeongwol

Huimin   Longkou   Qixia   Chengshan Jiao   Suwon   Cheonan   Jecheon   Yeongju   Uljin

Yang'an   Dongying Wan   Zhaoyuan   923   Wendeng   Pyeongtaek   Osan   Chungju   Yecheon

Binzhou   Laizhou   Laiyang   Rushan   Rongcheng   SOUTH   Seosan   Cheongju   Yecheon   Andong   Yeongdeok

Dongying   Shandong Bandao   Shidao   KOREA   Hongseong   Goesan   Sangju   Seonsan   Uiseong

ZIBO   Hongshan   Fangzi   Pingdu   Laixi   Haiyang   Nanhuang   Anmyeondo   Gongju   Nonsan   Yeongdong   Gimcheon   Pohang

Zhoucun   WEIFANG   Gaomi   Jimo   DAEJEON   Heunghae

Yongcun   Hantia   Langcun   Jeonju   Simcheon   Gumi

Mashang   Linqu   Zhucheng   QINGDAO   Baryeong   Yeongam   Jeonju   Hamyang   Gyeongju

Boshan   Jiaozhou   Jiaozhou Wan   Gunsan   Gimje   Geochang   GYEONGJU

XINTAI   Mengyin   Huanghua   Iksan   Jeonju   Jinju   Waegwan   Cheongdo   ULSAN

Yishui   Wulian   Buan   Jeong-eup   Namwon   Hamyang   DAEGU   Miryang   Gimhae

Sishui   Pingyi   Ju Xian   Langcheng   Jeong-eup   1915   Jinju   Masan   Dongnae

LINYI   Yili   Rizhao   Shijiusuo   GWANGJU   Naju   Suncheon   Sacheon   Chang-won   BUSAN

Feixian   Teng Xian   Ganyu   Andongwei   Haizhou Wan   Mokpo   Boseong   Beolgyo   Yeosu   Tong-yeong

ZAOZHUANG   Hanzhuang   Lianyungang   Licnyungang   Heuksando
(S. Korea)   Jangheung   Haenam   Tsushima
(Japan)   Izuhara

XINYI   Xiangshui   Binhai   Jindo   Korea Strait

XUZHOU   Yaowan   Guannan   Sheyang   Iki

SUQIAN   Shuyang   Funing   Karatsu

Suining   Lianshui   Heuksando   Imari

HUAI'AN   Chuzhou   YANCHENG   JAPAN   Sasebo   Kashima

Huaiyin   Baoying   Liuzhuang   Jeju   Hallim   Hallasan   Omura   Isahaya

Hongze Hu   Gaoyou   Dongtai   Jeju-do
(S. Korea)   Nakadori-Shima   Nagasaki

Lingbi   Sixian   Wuhe   XINGHUA   Daejeong   Seogwipo   Namjeju   Fukue-Shima   Kuchinotsu

Bengbu   Fengyang   Dongtai

East from Greenwich   COPYRIGHT PHILIP'S

118   120   122   124   126   128

1:5 300 000

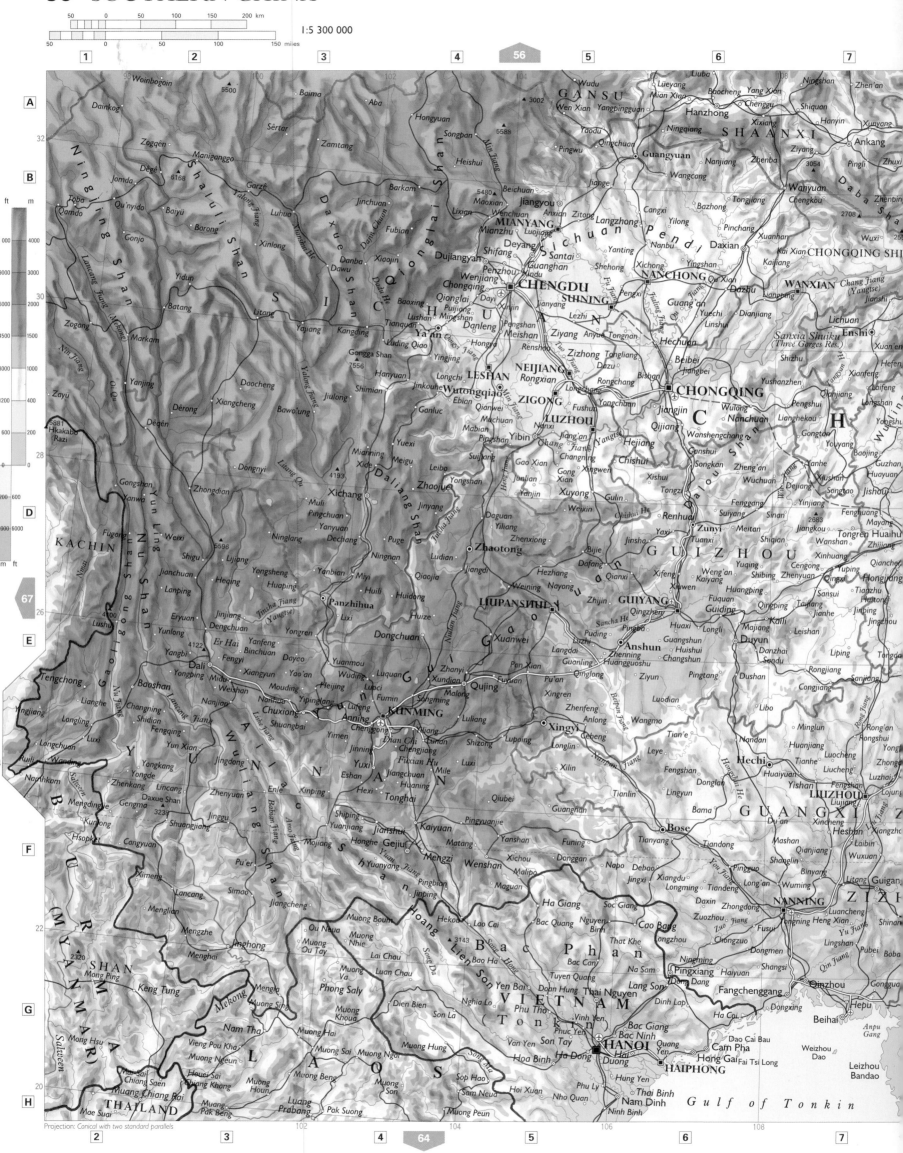

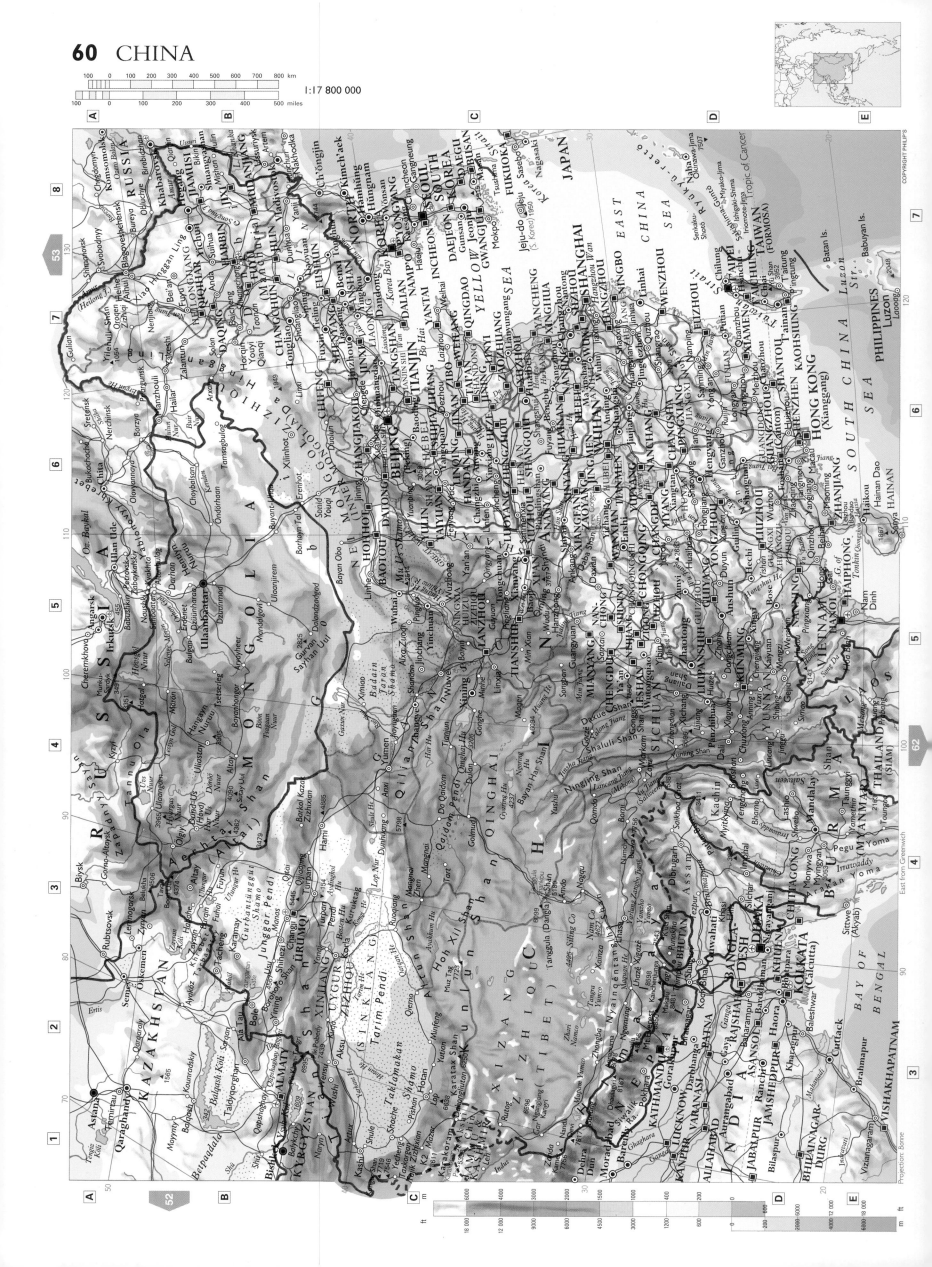

1:17 800 000

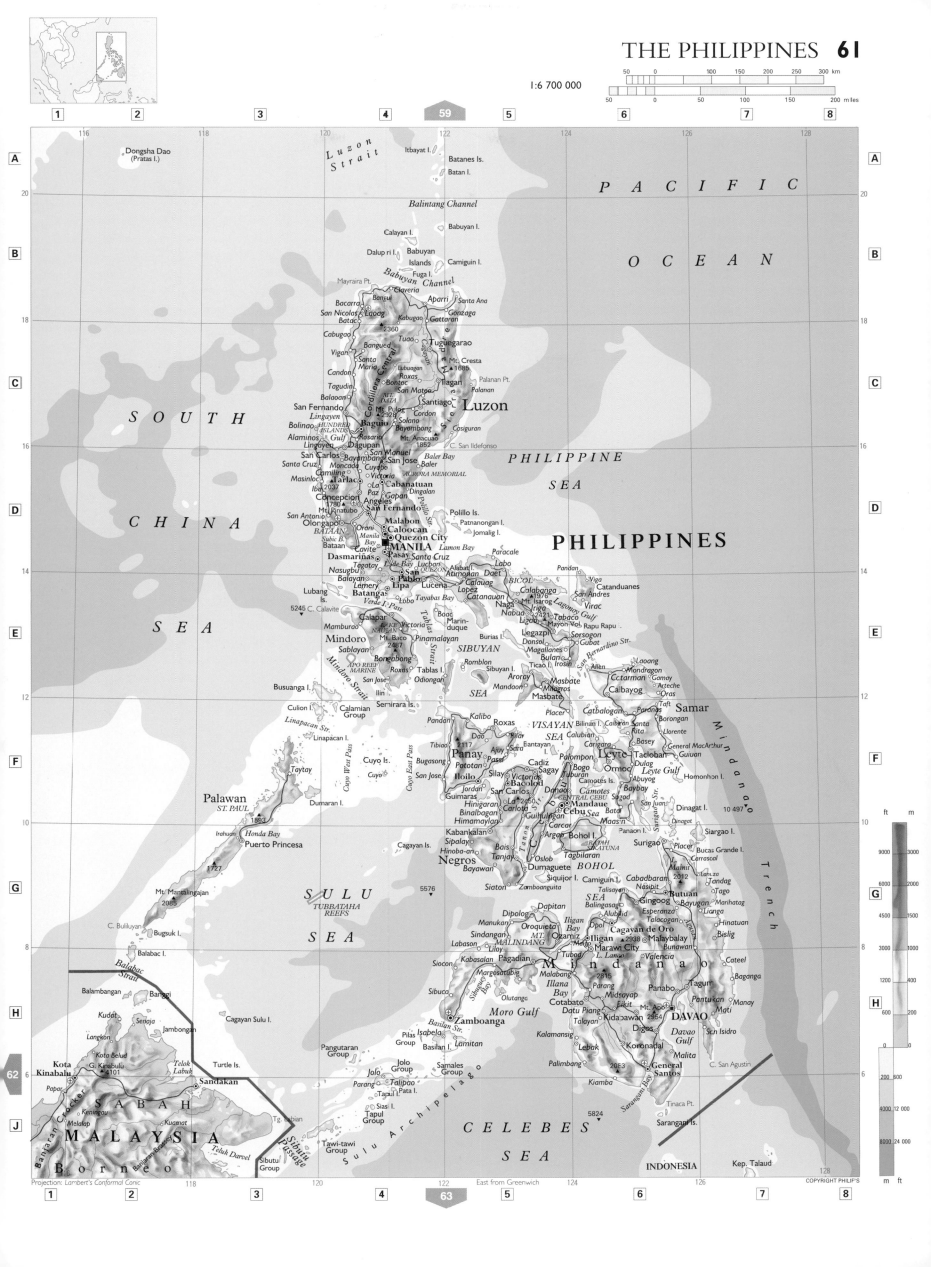

1:11 100 000

Projection: Mercator

East from Greenwich

1:5 300 000

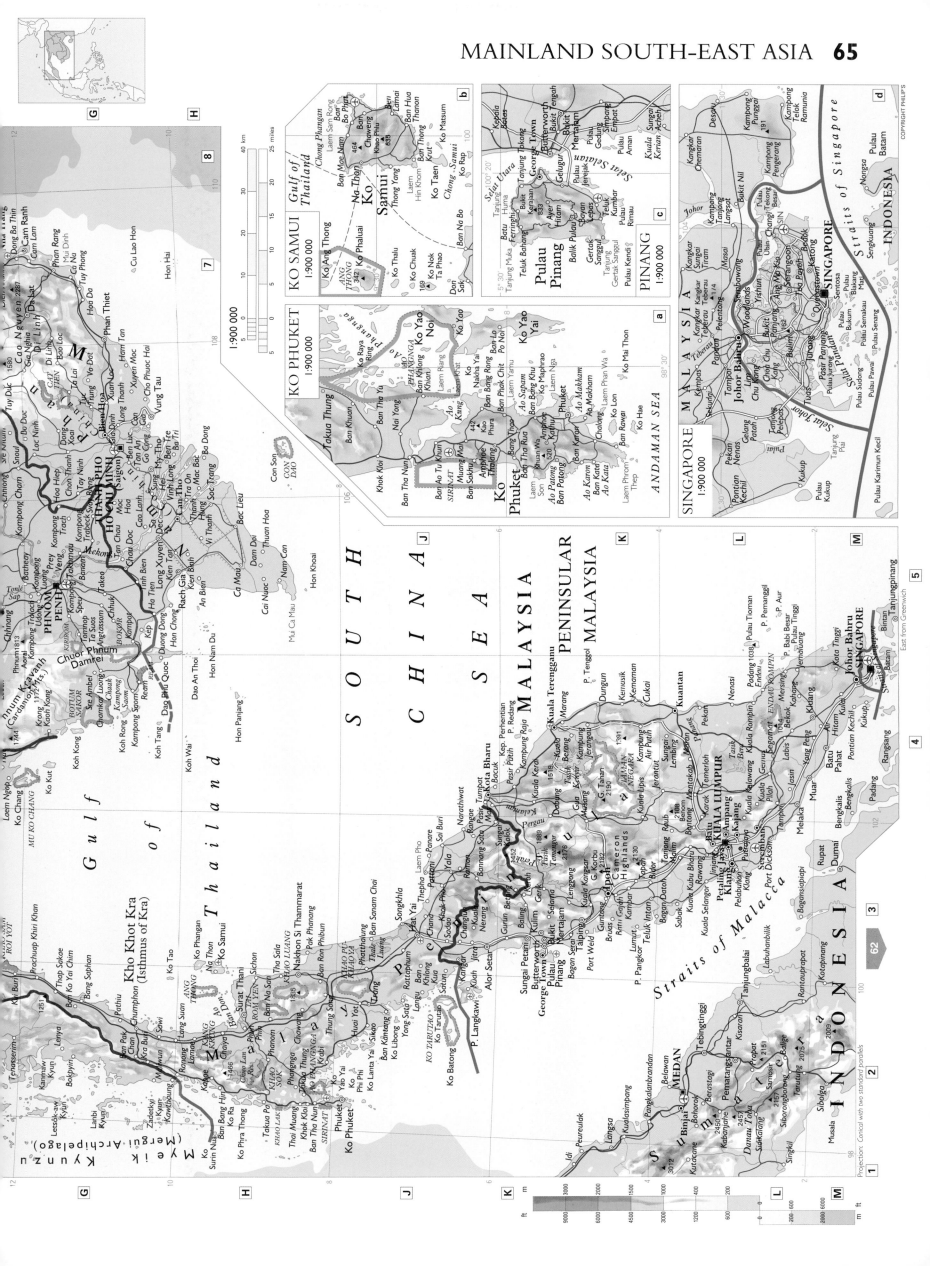

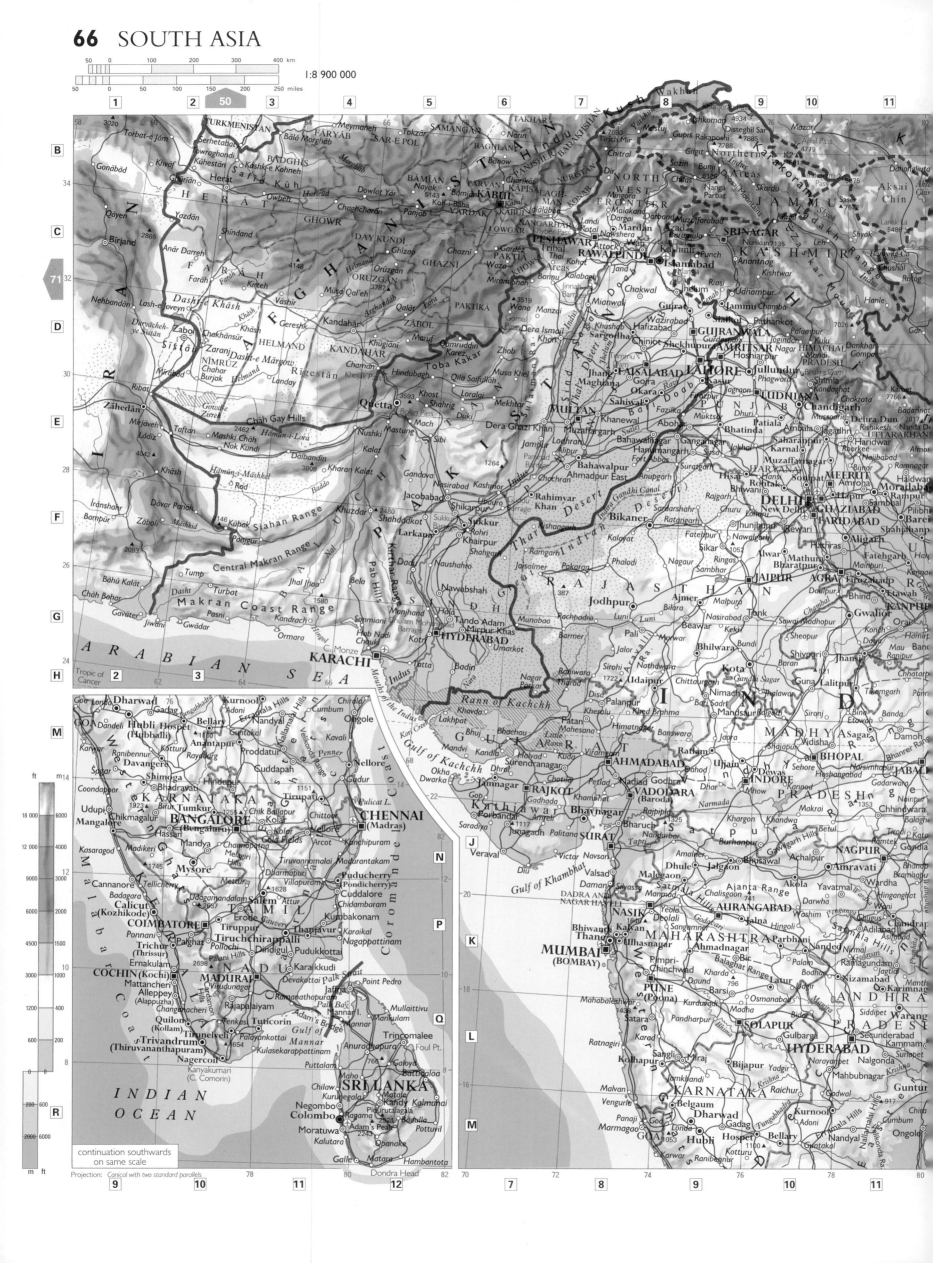

1:8 900 000

continuation southwards
on same scale

Projection: Conical with two standard parallels

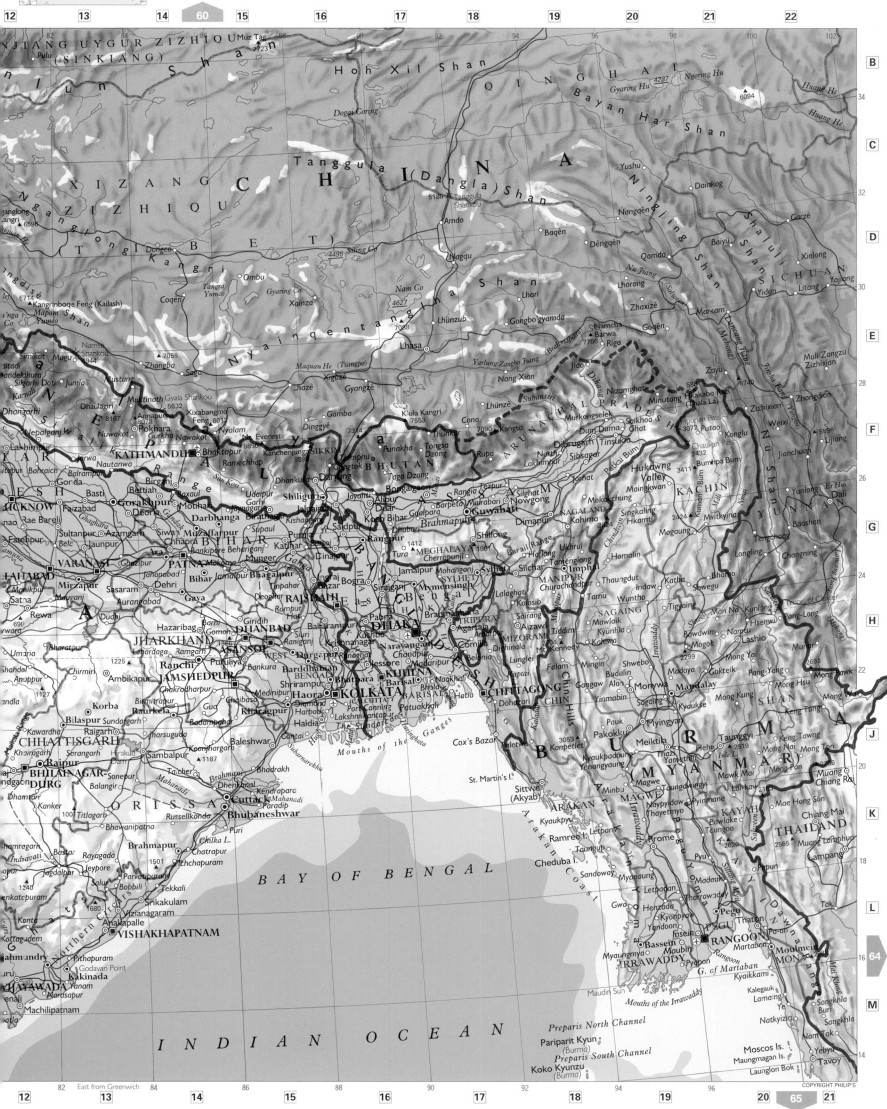

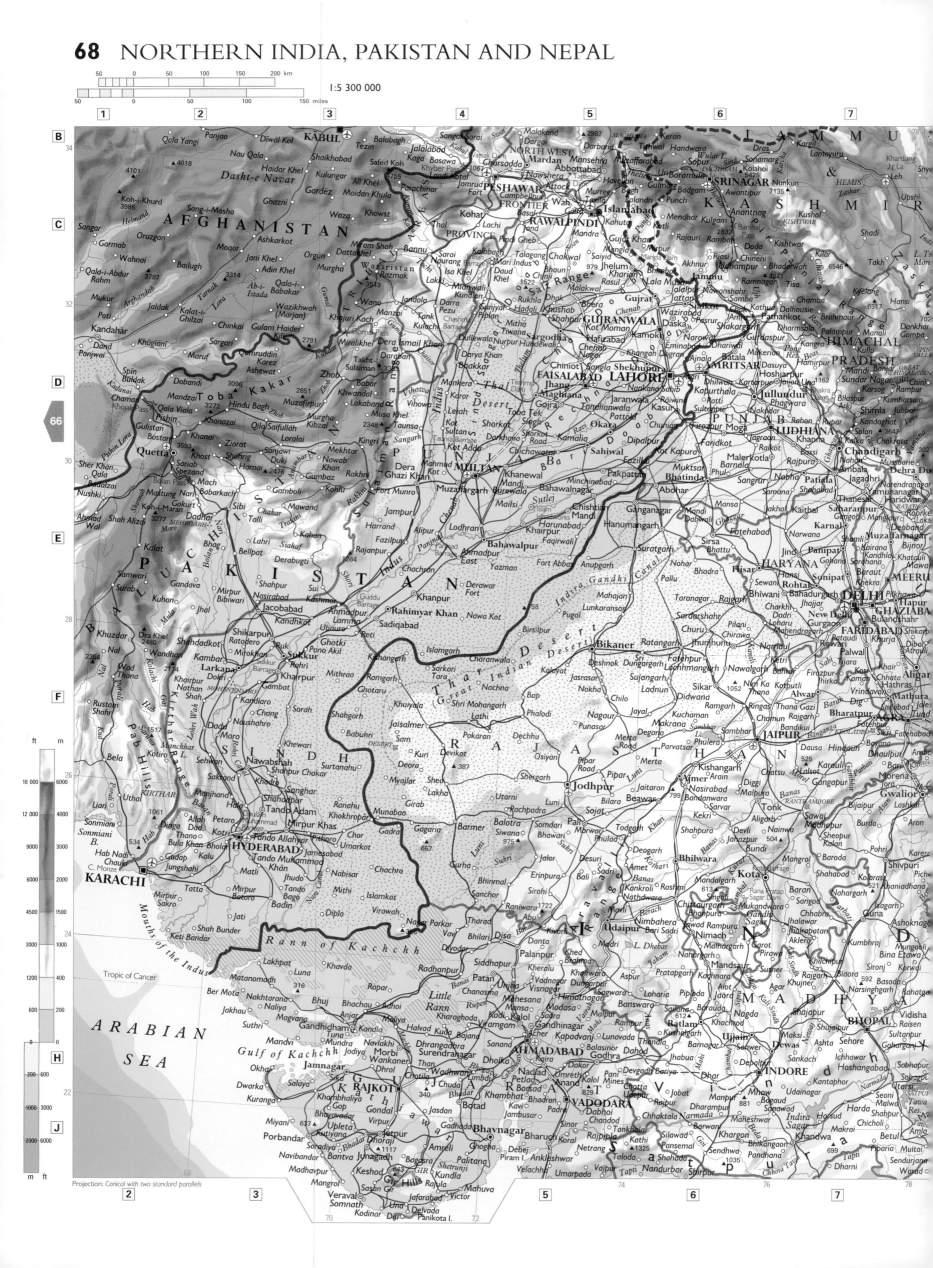

1:5 300 000

Projection: Conical with two standard parallels

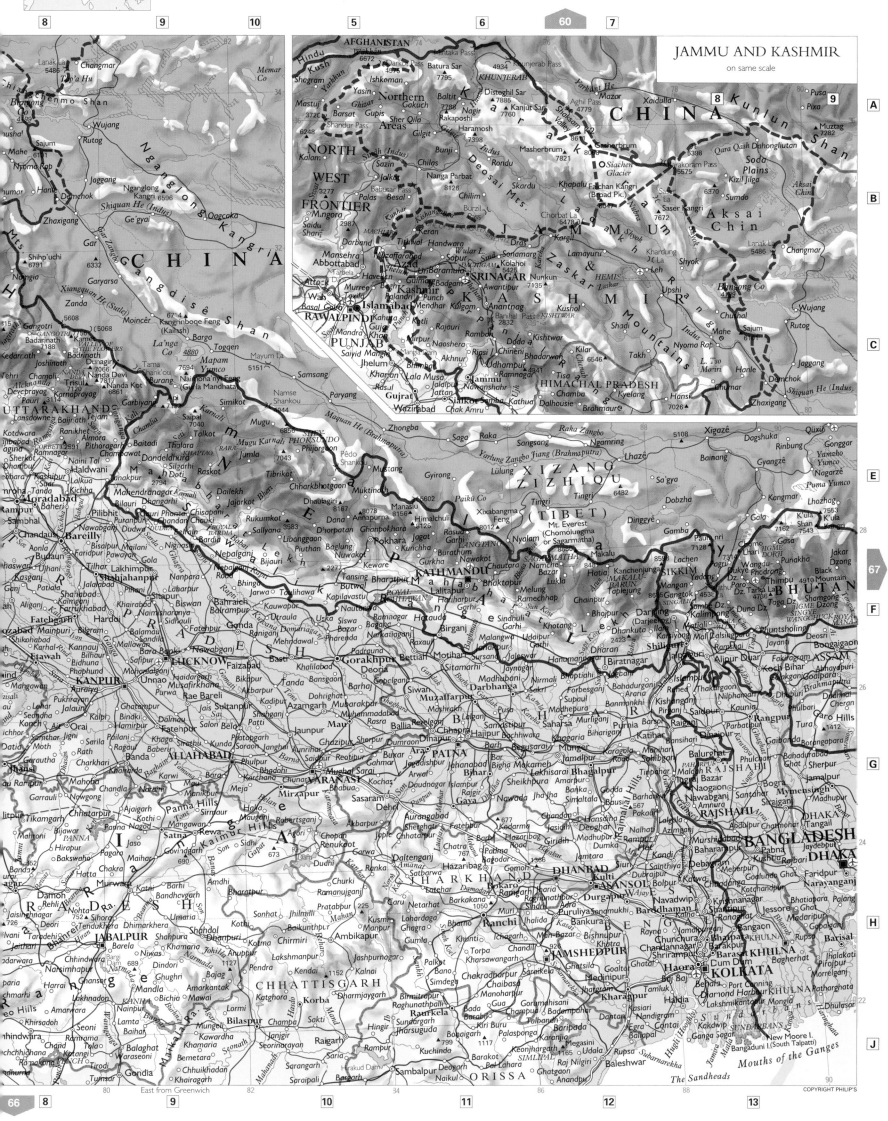

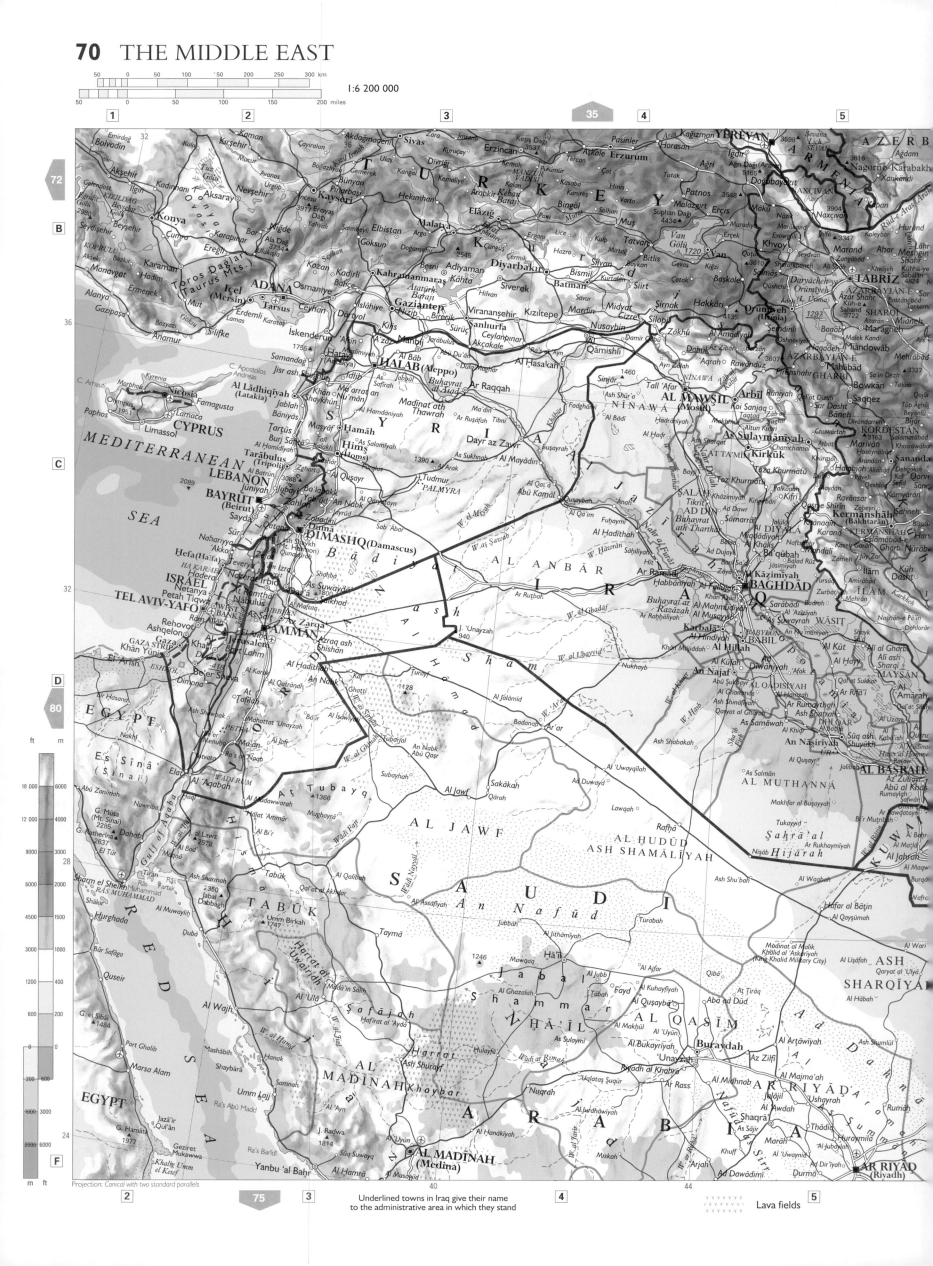

1:6 200 000

Projection: Conical with two standard parallels

Underlined towns in Iraq give their name
to the administrative area in which they stand

∨∨∨∨∨ Lava fields

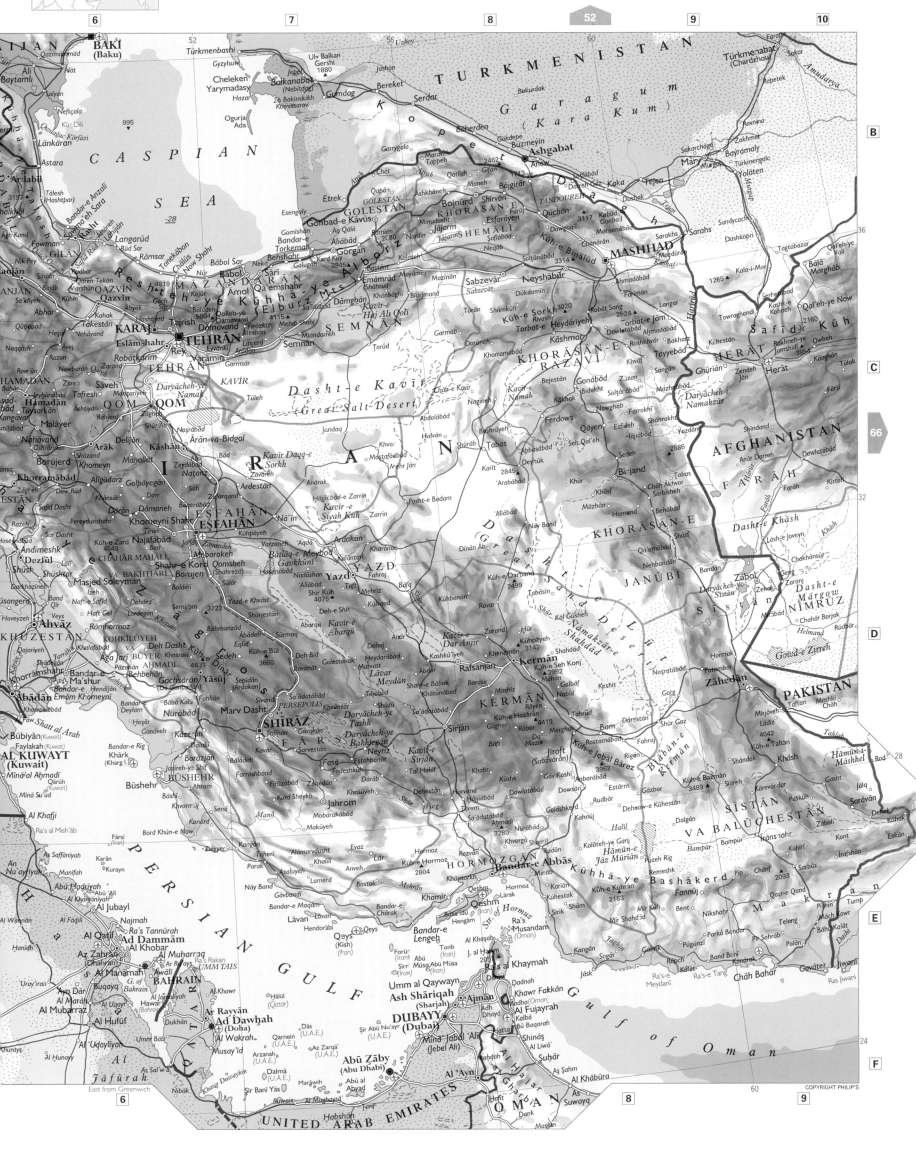

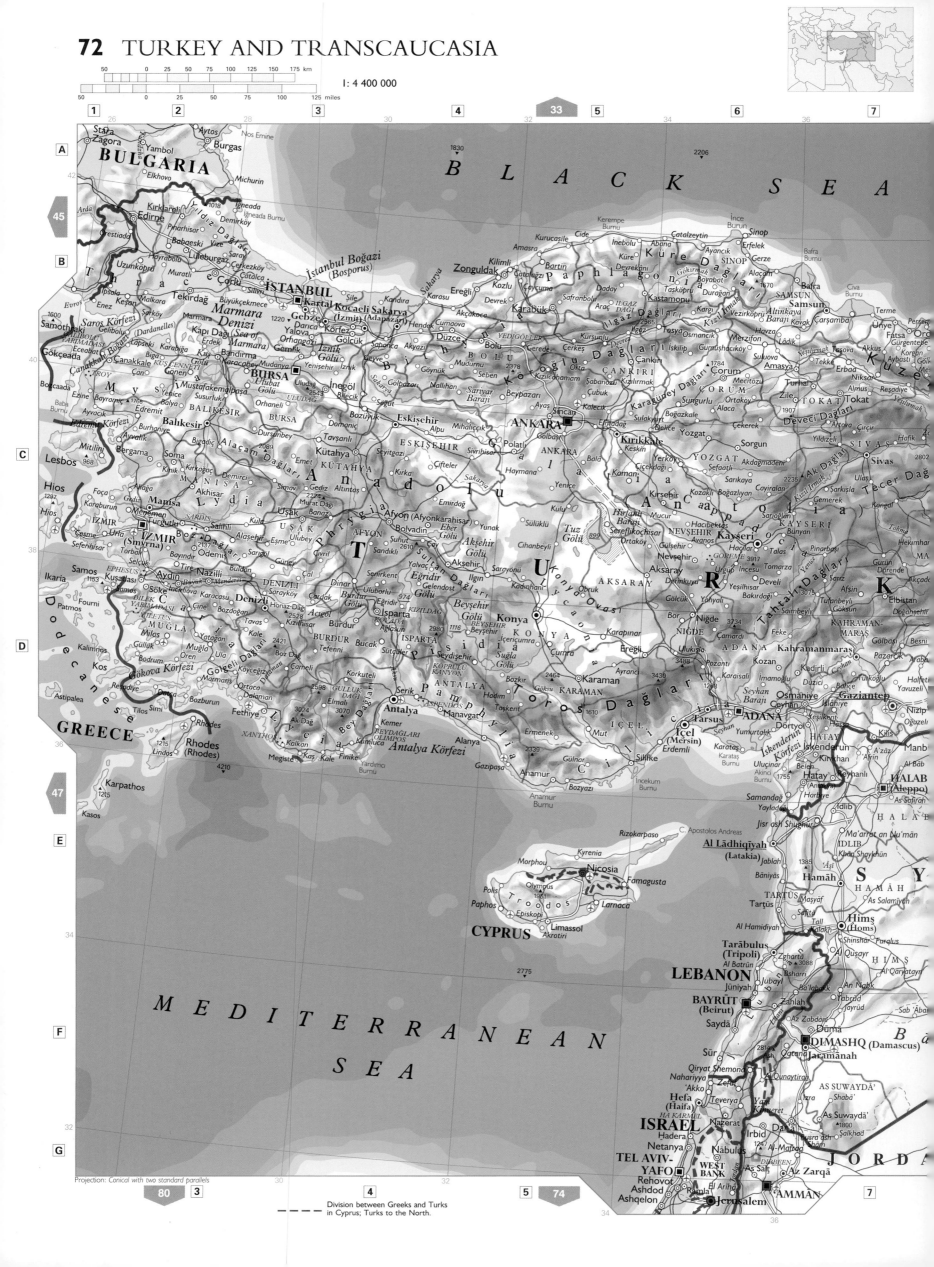

1: 4 400 000

50 0 25 50 75 100 125 150 175 km
50 0 25 50 75 100 125 miles

33

BLACK SEA

BULGARIA

Stara Zagora
Yambol
Aytos
Burgas
Nos Emine

Michurin

1830

2206

Kırklareli
Edirne
Yıldız Dağları
İğneada
İğneada Burnu
Demirköy
Pınarhisar
Babaeski
Vize
Çerkezköy
Çatalca
İstanbul
İstanbul Boğazı (Bosporus)
Kartal
Kocaeli
Sakarya (Adapazarı)
Şile
Zonguldak
Kilimli
Çaycuma
Ereğli
Akçakoca
Devrek
Karabük
Safranbolu
Amasra
İnebolu
Küre
Abana
Kerempe Burnu
İnce Burnu
Sinop
Erfelek
Çatalzeytin
Ayancık
SAMSUN
Bafra Burnu
Samsun
Terme
Civa Burnu

Lüleburgaz
Uzunköprü
Hayrabolu
Muratlı
Çorlu
Tekirdağ
Büyükçekmece
Gebze
Darıca
Körfez
İzmit
Hendek
Cumaova
Düzce
Bolu
Mudurnu
Gerede
Çerkeş
Kurşunlu
Ilgaz
Tosya
Osmancık
İskilip
Gümüşhacıköy
Merzifon
Havza
Kavak
Çarşamba
Ünye
Fatsa
Gürgentepe

Thrace
İpsala
Keşan
Malkara
Şarköy
Marmara Denizi (Sea of Marmara)
Kapı Dağı
Erdek
Bandırma
Mudanya
Gemlik
Orhangazi
Yalova
Gölcük
İznik Gölü
Geyve
Sapanca
Akyazı
Göynük
Göl pazarı
Nallıhan
Beypazarı
Ayaş
Sincan
ANKARA
Kalecik
Çubuk
Sabanözü
Çankırı
Kızılcahamam
Çorum
Sungurlu
Ortaköy
Alaca
Zile
Turhal
Amasya
Almus
Niksar
Reşadiye

Saros Körfezi
Gelibolu
Çanakkale Boğazı (Dardanelles)
Kapıdağ
Karabiga
Biga
Çan
Gönen
Karacabey
Mustafakemalpaşa
Bursa
İnegöl
Bilecik
Söğüt
Eskişehir
Mihalıççık
Alpu
Sivrihisar
Polatlı
Haymana
Yenice
Kulu
Kırıkkale
Keskin
Bala
Balâ
Yerköy
Kaman
Kırşehir
Çiçekdağı
Yozgat
Sorgun
Yıldızeli
Sivas
Hafik

Gökçeada
Bozcaada
Ezine
Ayvacık
Edremit
Burhaniye
Ayvalık
Balıkesir
Bigadiç
Dursunbey
Tavşanlı
Kütahya
Domaniç
Emet
Gediz
Simav
Murat Dağı
Banaz
Uşak
Afyon (Afyonkarahisar)
Bolvadin
Eber Gölü
Çay
Akşehir
Emirdağ
Yunak
Sülüklü
Tuz Gölü
Mucur
Hacıbektaş
Nevşehir
Gülşehir
Ürgüp
Avanos
Kayseri
Bünyan
Pınarbaşı
Gemerek
Kangal
Ulaş

Mitilini
Lesbos
Hios
Foça
Karaburun
Çeşme
Manisa
Akhisar
Soma
Kırkağaç
Demirci
Salihli
Alaşehir
Kula
Eşme
Ulubey
Sandıklı
Şuhut
Dinar
Senirkent
Yalvaç
Ilgın
Sarayönü
Cihanbeyli
Kulu
Obruk
Aksaray
Ortaköy
Gülağaç
Derinkuyu
Niğde
Bor
Çamardı
Tahtalı Dağları
Gürün
Darende
Sarız
Tufanbeyli

İzmir (Smyrna)
Urla
Seferihisar
Torbalı
Ödemiş
Tire
Nazilli
Aydın
Söke
Kuşadası
Samos
Ikaria
Fourni
Buldan
Denizli
Sarayköy
Çal
Honaz Dağı
Acıgöl
Eğirdir Gölü
Eğirdir
Gelendost
Isparta
Beyşehir Gölü
Beyşehir
Konya
Karapınar
Ereğli
Ulukışla
Pozantı
Kozan
Kadirli
Osmaniye
Gaziantep
Nizip

Samos
Kalymnos
Dodecanese
Patmos
Milas
Bodrum
Ören
Ula
Muğla
Yatağan
Köyceğiz
Dalaman
Fethiye
Kalkan
Kaş
Finike
Elmalı
Korkuteli
Bucak
Burdur
Tefenni
Ağlasun
Serik
Antalya
Kemer
Manavgat
Alanya
Gazipaşa
Anamur
Anamur Burnu
Bozyazı
Silifke
Erdemli
İçel (Mersin)
Tarsus
ADANA
Dörtyol
İskenderun
Kırıkhan
Kilis
Reyhanlı
Antakya (Antioch)
Harbiye

GREECE
Rhodes
Lindos
Karpathos
Kasos

MEDITERRANEAN SEA

CYPRUS
Morphou
Kyrenia
Rizokarpaso
C. Apostolos Andreas
Famagusta
Nicosia
Polis
Paphos
Troodos
Olympus
Episkopi
Limassol
Larnaca
Akrotiri

Al Lādhiqīyah (Latakia)
Jablah
Bāniyās
HAMĀH
Hamāh
Masyāf
Tartūs
TARTŪS
Al Hamidiyah
Ḥimṣ (Homs)
HIMS
Tarābulus (Tripoli)
LEBANON
BAYRŪT (Beirut)
Saydā
Sūr
DIMASHQ (Damascus)

SYRIA
HALAB (Aleppo)
HALAB
Idlib
IDLIB
Ma'arrat an Nu'mān
Jisr ash Shughūr

ISRAEL
Hefa (Haifa)
HA KARMEL
Nazerat
TEL AVIV-YAFO
Netanya
Hadera
Rehovot
Ashdod
Ashqelon
Qiryat Shemona
JERUSALEM
WEST BANK
Nābulus
El Arīha
Ramla

LEBANON
Zahlah

Nahariyya
'Akko
Teverya
Dar'ā
AS SUWAYDĀ'
As Suwaydā'
JORDAN
AMMĀN
Irbid
As Salt
Az Zarqā'

80

74

Projection: Conical with two standard parallels

Division between Greeks and Turks in Cyprus; Turks to the North.

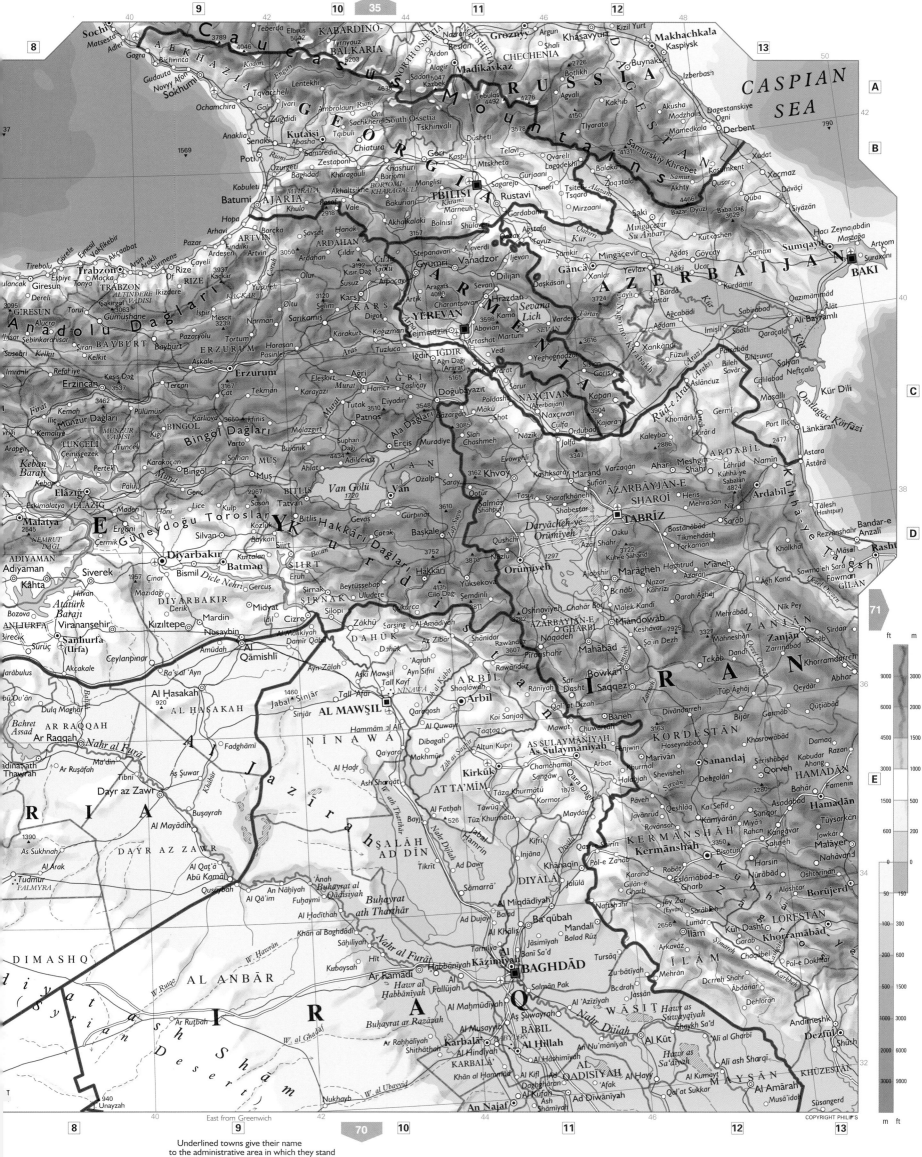

Underlined towns give their name
to the administrative area in which they stand

COPYRIGHT PHILIP'S

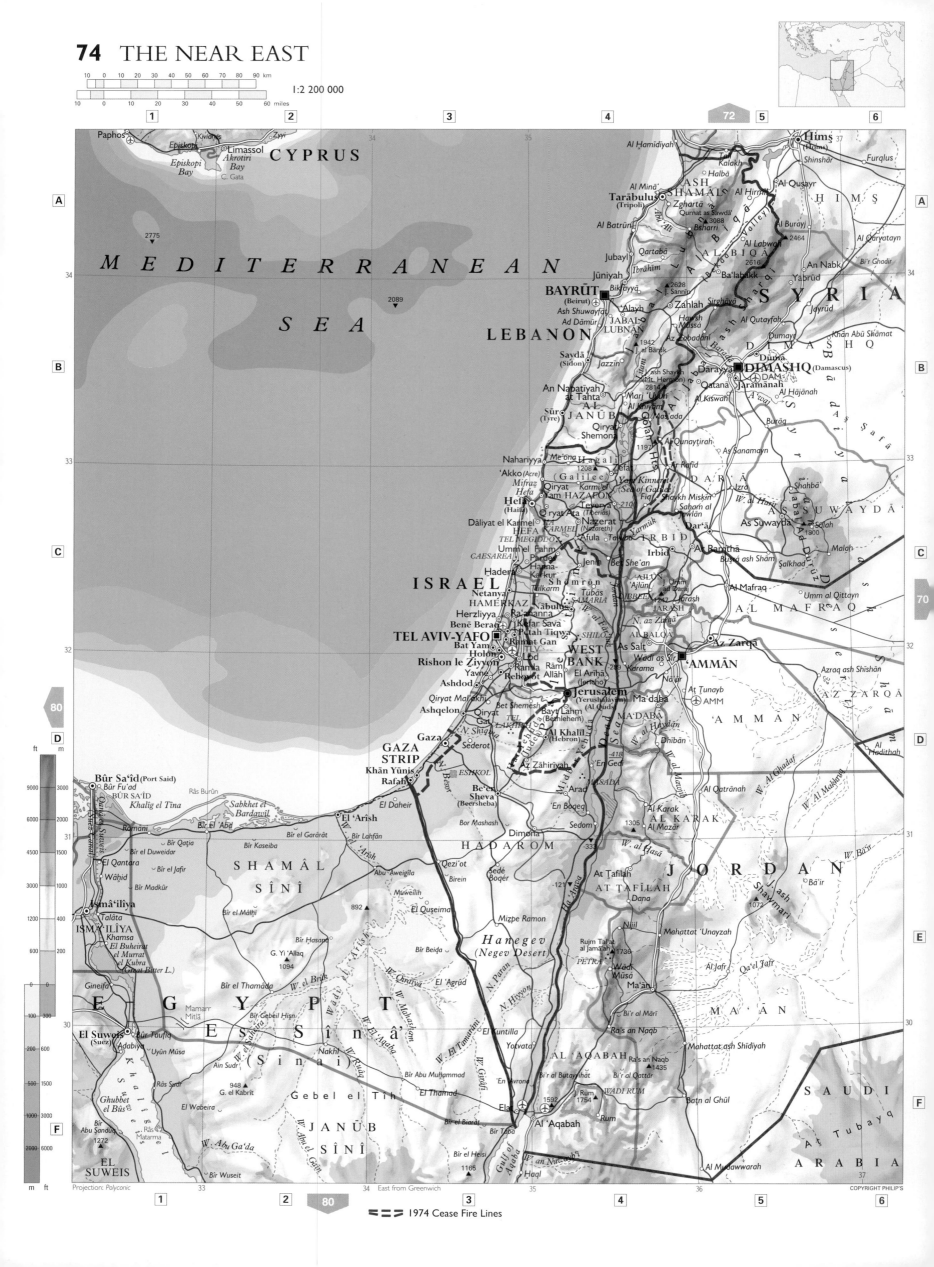

1:2 200 000

10 0 10 20 30 40 50 60 70 80 90 km

10 0 10 20 30 40 50 60 miles

72

CYPRUS

Paphos
Kividhes
Zyyi
Episkopi
Limassol
Akrotiri Bay
Episkopi Bay
C. Gata

M E D I T E R R A N E A N

2775

2089

S E A

LEBANON

Al Hamidiyah
Him̧ş (Hom̧ş)
Tall Kalakh
Shinshār
Furqlus
Al Qusayr

ASH SHAMĀL
Al Mīnā
Halbā
Al Hirmil
Tarābulus (Tripoli)
Zghartā
Qurnat as Sawdā'
3088
Al Burayj
Al Batrūn
Bsharrī
Al Qaryatayn
Bik̨fayyā
2464

Jubayl
Qartabā
Ibrāhīm
2616

An Nabk
Bī'r Ghadir

BAYRŪT (Beirut)
Jūniyah
2628
J. Sannīn
Ba'labakk
Yabrūd

Ash Shuwayfāt
'Alayh
Zahlah
Sirghāya
Khān Abū Shāmat

Ad Dāmūr
JABAL LUBNĀN
Az Zabadānī
Dumayr

SYRIA

DIMASHQ

Saydā (Sidon)
1942
J. al Bārak
Mt. Hermon
2814
Qatanā
Jaramānah
Al Hājānah

Jazzīn
AL JANŪB
An Nabatīyah at Tahta
'Ayn al 'Arab
'Arab
Burāq

Şūr (Tyre)
Qiryat Shemona
Marj 'Uyūn
Al Qunaytirah
As Sanamayn

Nahariyya
Me'ona Hagalil
1208
Zefat
Golan Hts.
1197
Ar Rafid

'Akko (Acre)
Karmi'el
Shaykh Miskin
AS SUWAYDĀ

Mifraz Hefa
Yam Kinneret (Sea of Galilee)
Saham al Jawlān
Shahbā

HEFA (Haifa)
Qiryat Ata
Teverya (Tiberias)
-210
Fiq
Izra'
As Suwaydā
1800

Oryat Ata
Nazerat (Nazareth)
Yarmūk
Malah

Dāliyat el Karmel
HEFA KARMEL
Afula
Taiybe
IRBID
Darā
Salah

TEL MEGIDDO
Umm el Fahm
Bet She'an
Darā'
Jabal ad Durūz

CAESAREA
Pardes
Jenin
'Ajlūn
Busrā ash Shām
Şalkhad

ISRAEL
Hadera
Hanna-Karkur
SHAMRŌN
J. Umm ad Daraj
1272
Jarash
Al Mafraq

HAMERKAZ
Netanya
Talkarm
SAMARIA
1247
JARASH
Umm al Qittayn

Herzliyya
Ra'ananna
Nabulus
N. az Zarqā
AL MAFRAQ

Kefar Sava
Benē Beraq
Petah Tiqwa
SHILOH
AL BALQĀ

TEL AVIV-YAFO
Ramat Gan
As Salt
Az Zarqā

Bat Yam
WEST BANK
Wadi as Sir
'AMMĀN

Holon
Lod
Ram Allah
Karama
Azraq ash Shīshān

Rishon le Ziyyon
Ramla
El Arīhā (Jericho)
289
Na'ūr
AZ ZARQĀ

Yavne
Rehovot
AMM

Ashdod
Jerusalem (Yerushalayim) (Al Quds)
Ma'daba

Qiryat Mal'akhi
Bet Shemesh
Bayt Lahm (Bethlehem)
MA'DĀBA
At Tunayb

Ashqelon
Qiryat Gat
TEL LAKHISH
Al Khalīl (Hebron)
'Amman

GAZA STRIP
Gaza
Sederot
N. Shiqma
Az Zāhiriyah
'En Gedi
Al Karak

Khān Yūnis
Be'er Sheva (Beersheba)
-418
AL KARAK

Rafah
ESHKOL
Arad
MASADA
Al Qatrānah

Bûr Sa'îd (Port Said)
Bûr Fu'ad
El Daheir
Bor Mashash
Sedom
Al Mazar

BÛR SA'ÎD
Râs Burûn
El 'Arîsh
Dimona
1305
Al Karak

Khalig el Tîna
Sabkhet el Bardawîl
W. al Qasā
W. Bâ'ir

Ramâni
Bîr el 'Abd
HADAROM
-335

Bîr Qatia
Bîr el Garârât
Bîr Lahfân
SHAMÂL SÎNÎ
At Tafilah
AT TAFÎLAH

El Qantara
Bîr el Duweidar
Bîr el Jafîr
Bîr Kaseiba
Qezi'ot
Abu Aweigila
Sedé Boqér
Dana
Bâ'ir

Wâhid
Bîr Madkûr
892
Muweilih
-121
Birein

EGYPT
Ismâ'ilîya
Bîr el Mâlhi
El Quseima
Mizpe Ramon
Nijil
Mahattat 'Unayzah

Talâta
El Agrûd
Ma'ān

ISMÂ'ILÎYA
Khamsa
G. Yi 'Allaq
1094
Bîr Hasana
Bîr Beida
Hanegev (Negev Desert)
Rujm Talat al Jamā'ah
1738
Al Jafr
Qa'el Jafr

El Buheirat el Murrat el Kubra (Great Bitter L.)
Bîr el Thamâda
W. el Bruk
El 'Agrûd
PETRA
Wādī Mūsā
MA'ĀN

Gineifa
Bîr el Thamâda
N. Hiyyon
N. Paran
Ma'ān

E G Y P T
Mamarr Mitla
Bîr Gebel Hisn
E S S Î N Â'
N. Paran
Bî'r al Mārī

El Suweis (Suez)
Bûr Taufîq
Adabiya
Uyûn Mûsa
Nakhl
(Sinai)
'En Yahav
Ra's an Naqb
1435
Mahattat ash Shīdīyah

Kharig el Bûs
Râs Sudr
Ain Sudr
AL 'AQABAH
Ra's an Naqb

Khalig es Suweis
948
G. el Kabrit
Gebel el Tih
El Thamad
J. Rum
1592
WADI RUM
Batn al Ghul

Ghubbet el Bûs
El Wabeira
Elat
1754
Rum

Bîr Abu Sandûq
1272
J A N Û B
S Î N Î
Bîr el Heisi
1165
Al 'Aqabah
Batn al Ghul

Râs Matarma
W. Abu Ga'da
Bîr el Biârât
Bîr Tūba
Haql
At Tubayq

EL SUWEIS
Bîr Wuseit
Gulf of Aqaba
W. an Nu'ayz
Al Mudawwarah
A R A B I A

SAUDI

JORDAN

Projection: Polyconic

East from Greenwich

COPYRIGHT PHILIP'S

▬▬▬ 1974 Cease Fire Lines

1:13 300 000

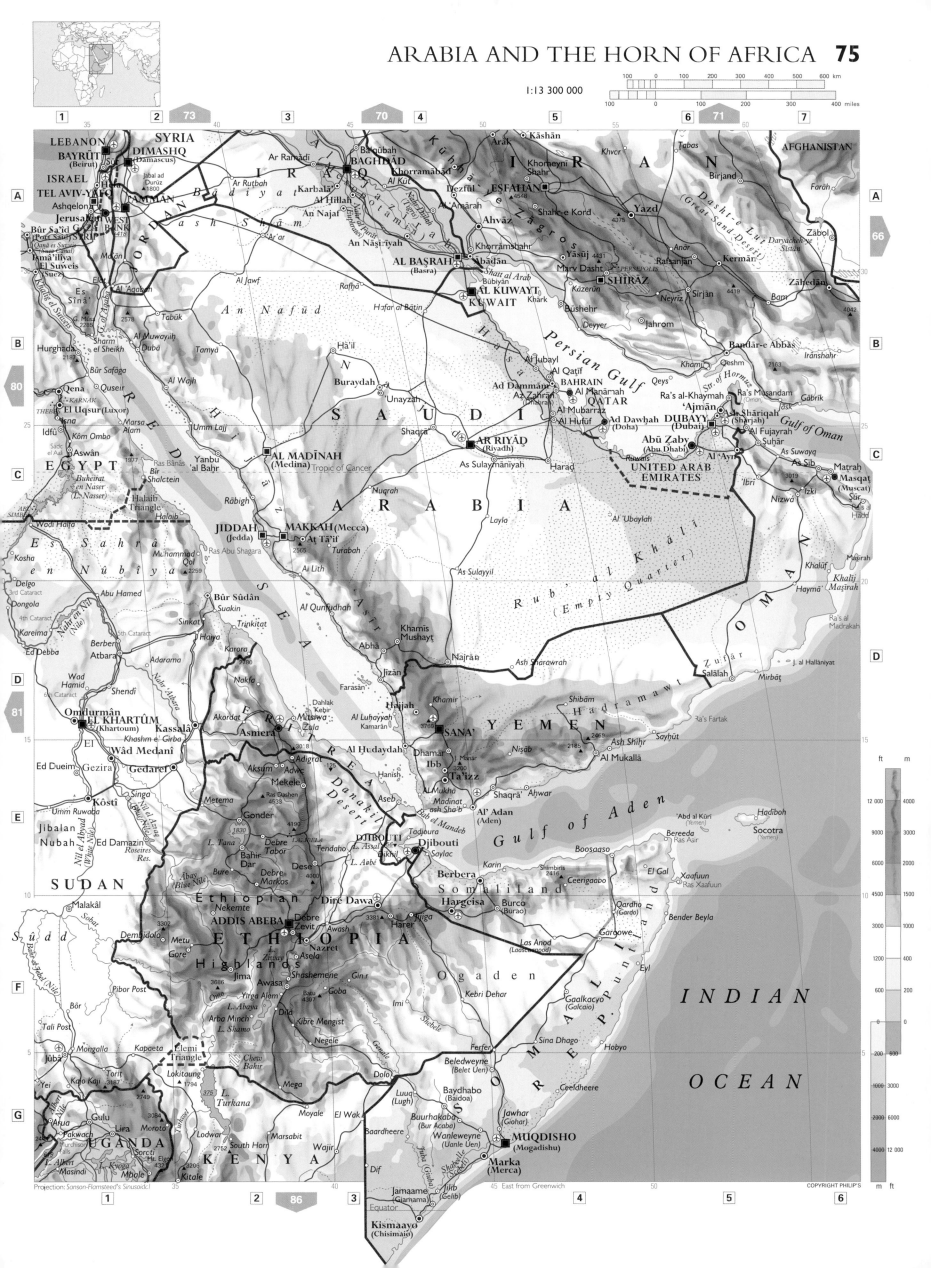

LEBANON
BAYRÛT
(Beirut)
SYRIA
DIMASHQ
(Damascus)
ISRAEL
TEL AVIV-YAFO
Ashqelon
JERUSALEM
WEST BANK
Bûr Sa'îd
(Port Said)
Qanâ es Suweis
Ismâ'îliya
El Suweis
Suez
Hurghada
Es Sînâ
Sharm el Sheikh
Bûr Safâga
Qena
KARNAK
THEBES
El Uqsur (Luxor)
Esna
Idfû
Kôm Ombo
Aswân
Sadd el Aâli
EGYPT

JORDAN
AMMAN
Ma'ân
El 'Aqaba
Al 'Aqabah
Tabûk
Al Muwayliḥ
Dubâ
Al Wajh
Umm Lajj
Yanbu 'al Bahr
Marsa Alam
Ras Bânâs
Bîr Shalctein
Halaib Triangle
Halaib
Muhammad Qol

Ar Ramâdî
IRAQ
BAGHDÂD
Ba'qûbah
Al Kût
Karbalâ'
An Najaf
Al Hillah
An Nâṣirīyah
Ar'ar
Rafḥâ'
Hafar al Bâtin
Ḥâ'il
Buraydah
Unayzah
Shaqra
SAUDI
ARABIA
AL MADĪNAH
(Medina)
Râbigh
JIDDAH
(Jedda)
MAKKAH (Mecca)
At Tâ'if
Al Lith
As Sulayyil

Khorramâbâd
Dezfûl
EṢFAHÂN
Al 'Amârah
Ahvâz
Khorramshahr
AL BAṢRAH
(Basra)
Âbâdân
Shatt al Arab
Bûbiyân
AL KUWAYT
KUWAIT
Khârk
Būshehr
Deyyer
Al Jubayl
Al Qaṭīf
Ad Dammâm
Az Zahrân
(Dhahran)
BAHRAIN
Al Manâmah
QATAR
Al Mubarraz
Al Hufûf
Ad Dawhah
(Doha)
AR RIYÂD
(Riyadh)
As Sulaymānīyah
Harad

IRAN
SHĪRÂZ
Kâzerûn
Neyrīz
Sirjân
Kermân
Jahrom
Bandar-e 'Abbâs
Qeshm
Ra's al-Khaymah
'Ajmân
Ra's Musandam (Oman)
DUBAYY
(Dubai)
Ash Shâriqah
(Sharjah)
Al Fujayrah
Gulf of Oman
Abû Zaby
(Abu Dhabi)
Al 'Ayn
Suḥâr
As Suwayq
As Sīb
Maṭraḥ
MASQAṬ
(Muscat)
Ṣûr
UNITED ARAB
EMIRATES
Nizwâ
'Ibri

AFGHANISTAN
Tabas
Birjand
Farâh
Zâbol
Daryâcheh-ye
Sīstân
Dasht-e Lut
(Great Sand Desert)
Zâhedân
Bam
Irânshahr
Gâbrīk
Jâsk

Persian Gulf
Str. of Hormuz

Buḥeirat en Naser
(L. Nasser)
Wadi Halfa
Es Saḥrâ' en Nûbîya
Kosha
Delgo
3rd Cataract
Dongola
4th Cataract
Kareima
Ed Debba
Wad Hamid
6th Cataract
Omdurmân
EL KHARTÛM
(Khartoum)
El Obeid
Wâd Medani
Ed Dueim
Kôstî
Umm Ruwaba
Jibalan
Nubah
SUDAN

Nahr el Nîl (Nile)
Abu Hamed
5th Cataract
Berber
Atbara
Adarama
Shendî
Nahr 'Atbara
Kashm e' Girba
Kassalâ
Gedaref
Gezira
Singa
Sennar
Ed Damazin
Roseires Res.
Âbay (Blue Nile)
Nil el Abyad White Nile
Malakâl

Suakin
Sinkat
Trinkitat
Haiya
Karora
Nakfa
Akordat
Aksum
Adwa
Adigrat
Metema
Mekele
Ras Dashen
4533
Gonder
Debre Tabor
L. Tana
Bahir Dar
Debre Markos
Bure
Nekemte
Metu
Gore
Demdidolo
Jima
Ethiopian Highlands
ADDIS ABEBA
Debre Zeyit
Nazret
Asela
Shashemene
Awasa
Yirga Alem
Arba Minch
L. Abaya
L. Shamo
Dila
Kibre Mengist
Negele
SUDAN

RED SEA
HIJÂZ
ASĪR
Al Qunfudhah
Abhâ
Khamis Mushayṭ
Jîzân
Najrân
Ash Sharawrah
Farasân
Dahlak Kebir
Mitsiwa
Zula
Aseb
ERITREA
Danakil Desert
Asmera
Ḥajjah
Khamir
SANA'
YEMEN
Dhamâr
Ibb
Ta'izz
Al Ḥudaydah
Al Luḥayyah
Kamarân
Hanish
Al Mukhâ
Madīnat ash Sha'b
Bâb el Mandeb
DJIBOUTI
Tadjoura
Djibouti
Zeila
Saylac

Rub' al Khâlī
(Empty Quarter)
Layla
Al 'Ubaylah
Harad
Ruwais

OMAN
Zufâr
Salâlah
Mirbâṭ
Shibâm
Ash Shiḥr
Al Mukallâ
Ḥaḍramawt
Sayḥut
Ra's Fartak
J. al Hallâniyat
Ra's al Madrakah
Maṣīrah
Khalūf
Haymâ'
Khalīj Maṣīrah

Gulf of Aden
'Abd al Kûrī
(Yemen)
Hadiboh
Socotra
(Yemen)
Bereeda
Ras Asir
Boosaaso
Karin
Ceerigaabo
El Gal
Shimbiris
2416
Berbera
Somaliland
Hargeisa
Burco (Burao)
Qardho (Gardo)
Gaalkacyo
(Galcaio)
Garoowe
Bender Beyla
Eyl

Dire Dawa
Harer
Jijiga
Awash
Gīnīr
Goba
Batu
4307
Imi
Shebele
Kebri Dehar
Ogaden
Ferfer
Dolo
Beledweyne
(Belet Uen)
Sina Dhago
Hobyo
Baydhabo
(Baidoa)
Buurhakaba
(Bur Acaba)
Jawhar
(Giohar)
Wanleweyne
(Uanle Uen)
MUQDISHO
(Mogadishu)
Marka
(Merca)
PUNTLAND
SOMALIA

INDIAN
OCEAN

ETHIOPIA

Elemi Triangle
Chew Bahir
Lokitaung
L. Turkana
Mega
Moyale
El Wak
Luuq
(Lugh)
Baardheere
Dif
Jamaame
(Giamama)
Kismaayo
(Chisimaio)
Equator

UGANDA
Gulu
Lira
Moroto
Kitale
Lodwar
South Horn
Wajir
Marsabit
KENYA

ft   m
12 000   4000
9000   3000
6000   2000
4500   1500
3000   1000
1200   400
600   200
0   0
200   600
1000   3000
2000   6000
4000   12000
m   ft

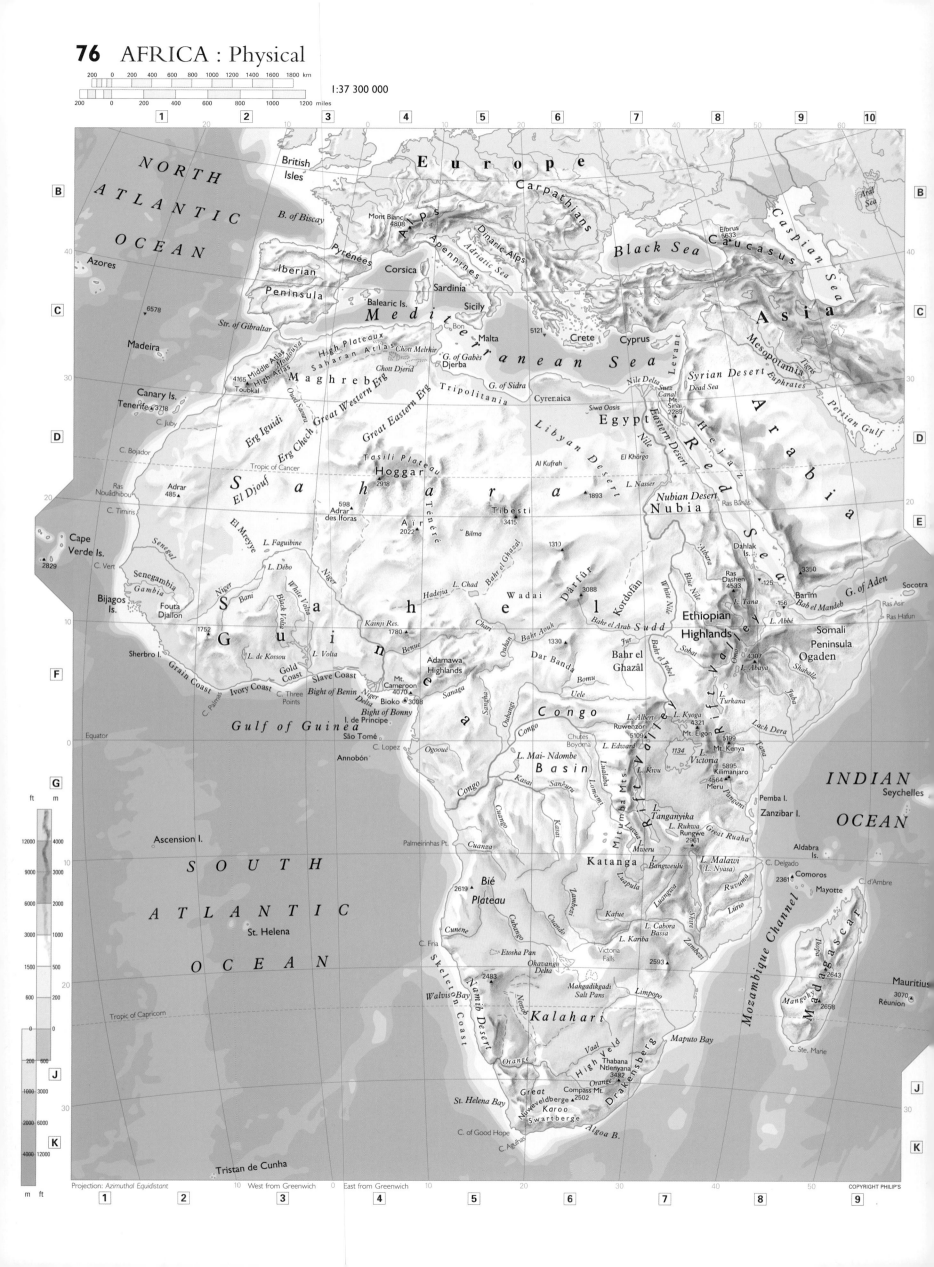

1:37 300 000

200 0 200 400 600 800 1000 1200 1400 1600 1800 km

200 0 200 400 600 800 1000 1200 miles

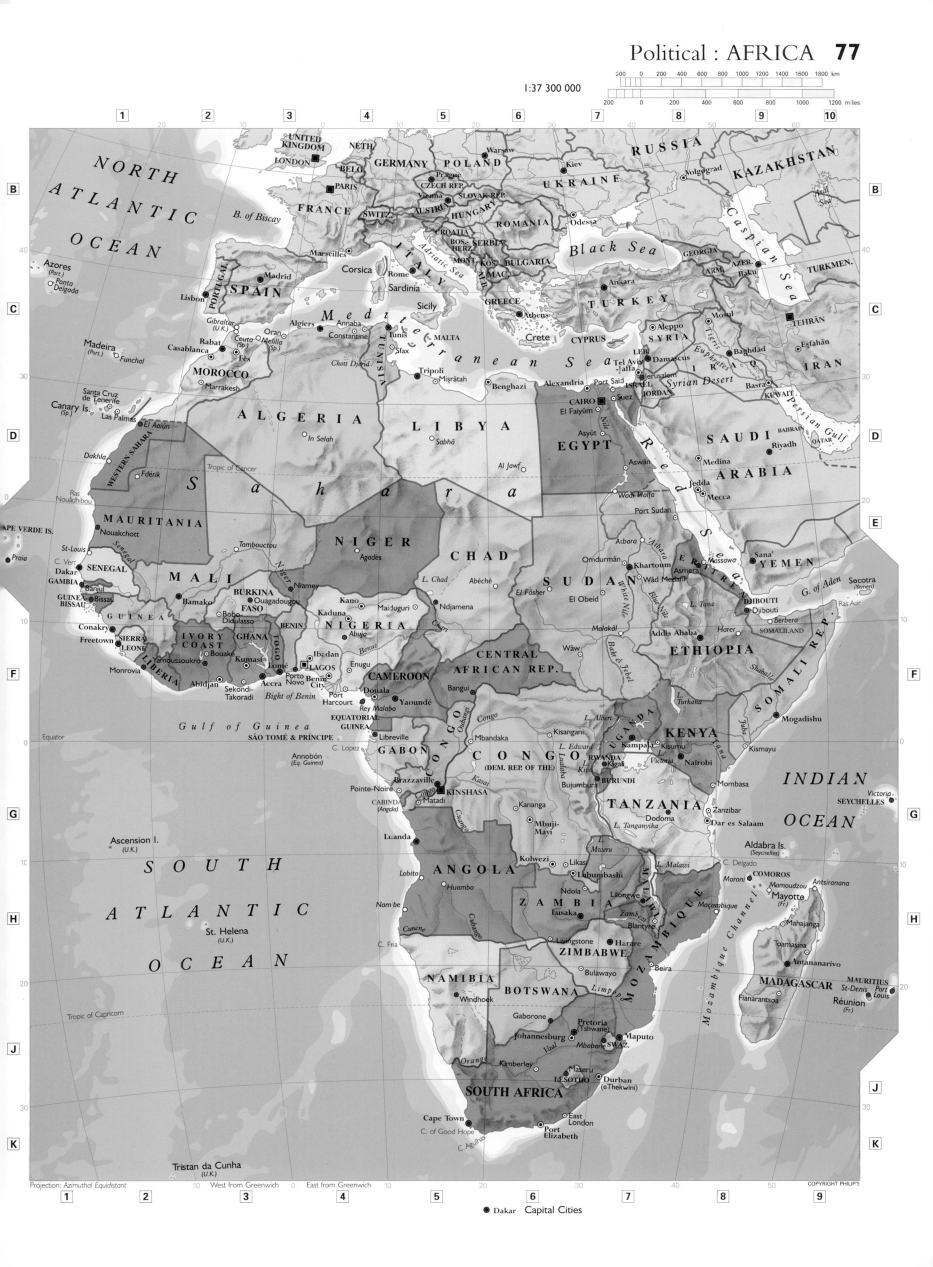

NORTH ATLANTIC OCEAN

Azores (Port.)
Ponta Delgada

Madeira (Port.)
Funchal

Canary Is. (Sp.)
Santa Cruz de Tenerife
Las Palmas

CAPE VERDE IS.
Praia
C. Verd.

SOUTH ATLANTIC OCEAN

Ascension I. (U.K.)

St. Helena (U.K.)

Tristan da Cunha (U.K.)

UNITED KINGDOM
LONDON
NETH.
BELG.
PARIS
FRANCE
B. of Biscay
Marseilles
PORTUGAL
Lisbon
SPAIN
Madrid
Gibraltar (U.K.)
Ceuta (Sp.)
Melilla (Sp.)
Oran
Algiers
Rabat
Casablanca
Fés
MOROCCO
Marrakesh
Dakhla
El Aaiún
WESTERN SAHARA
Fdérik
Ras Nouâdhibou
Nouâdhibou
MAURITANIA
Nouakchott
St-Louis
Dakar
SENEGAL
GAMBIA
Banjul
GUINEA-BISSAU
Bissau
GUINEA
Conakry
Freetown
SIERRA LEONE
LIBERIA
Monrovia
Yamoussoukro
IVORY COAST
Bouaké
Abidjan
Sekondi-Takoradi

GERMANY
POLAND
Warsaw
CZECH REP.
Prague
Vienna
SWITZ.
AUSTRIA
HUNGARY
SLOVAK REP.
CROATIA
BOS.-HERZ.
SERBIA
MONT.
KOS.
MAC.
ROMANIA
BULGARIA
Kiev
UKRAINE
Odessa
RUSSIA
Volgograd
KAZAKHSTAN
Aral Sea
Caspian Sea
GEORGIA
ARM.
AZER.
Baku
TURKMEN.
Black Sea
TURKEY
Ankara
GREECE
Athens
CYPRUS
Crete
Aleppo
SYRIA
LEB.
Tel Aviv-Jaffa
Damascus
Mosul
Baghdad
IRAQ
Esfahān
TEHRĀN
IRAN
MALTA
Sicily
Corsica
Rome
ITALY
Sardinia
Mediterranean Sea
Tunis
TUNISIA
Annaba
Constantine
Sfax
Tripoli
Mişrātah
Benghazi
Chott Djerid
ALGERIA
In Selah
LIBYA
Sabhā
Al Jawf
Tropic of Cancer
Sahara
EGYPT
Alexandria
Port Said
CAIRO
Suez
El Faiyûm
Asyût
El Aaiún
Jerusalem
ISRAEL
JORDAN
Red Sea
Aswân
Wadi Halfa
Port Sudan
SAUDI ARABIA
Riyadh
Medina
Jedda
Mecca
BAHRAIN
QATAR
KUWAIT
Basra
Persian Gulf

MALI
Tombouctou
Bamako
NIGER
Agadès
Niamey
BURKINA FASO
Ouagadougou
Bobo-Dioulasso
Kano
Kaduna
BENIN
NIGERIA
Abuja
Ibadan
Lagos
Porto Novo
GHANA
TOGO
Kumasi
Accra
Lomé
Benin City
Port Harcourt
Enugu
Benue
CAMEROON
Douala
Yaoundé
EQUATORIAL GUINEA
Rey Malabo
SÃO TOMÉ & PRÍNCIPE
Bight of Benin
Gulf of Guinea
C. Lopez
Annobón (Eq. Guinea)
Libreville
GABON
CONGO
Brazzaville
Pointe-Noire
CABINDA (Angola)
CONGO (DEM. REP. OF THE)
KINSHASA
Matadi
Mbandaka
Kananga
Mbuji-Mayi
Kisangani
Luanda
ANGOLA
Huambo
Lobito
Namibe
C. Fria
L. Chad
Ndjamena
CHAD
Abéché
Maiduguri
SUDAN
El Fâsher
El Obeid
Omdurman
Khartoum
Wâd Medani
Atbara
'Atbara
ERITREA
Massawa
Asmera
YEMEN
Sana'
Socotra (Yemen)
Ras Asir
DJIBOUTI
Djibouti
SOMALILAND
Berbera
G. of Aden
ETHIOPIA
Addis Ababa
Harer
SOMALI REP.
Mogadishu
Malakâl
Wâw
Bahr el Jebel
CENTRAL AFRICAN REP.
Bangui
Equator
Ubangi
Congo
L. Albert
L. Turkana
UGANDA
Kampala
Kisumu
KENYA
Nairobi
Kismayu
Juba
L. Edward
RWANDA
Kigali
L. Kivu
BURUNDI
Bujumbura
L. Victoria
Mombasa
TANZANIA
Dodoma
Dar es Salaam
Zanzibar
L. Tanganyika
INDIAN OCEAN
SEYCHELLES
Victoria
Aldabra Is. (Seychelles)
C. Delgado
COMOROS
Moroni
Mamoudzou
Mayotte (Fr.)
Antsiranana
MADAGASCAR
Mahajanga
Toamasina
Antananarivo
Fianarantsoa
MAURITIUS
St-Denis
Port Louis
Réunion (Fr.)
L. Mweru
Kolwezi
Likasi
Lubumbashi
Ndola
ZAMBIA
Lusaka
Lilongwe
MALAWI
L. Malawi
MOZAMBIQUE
Moçambique
Mozambique Channel
Blantyre
Beira
ZIMBABWE
Harare
Bulawayo
Livingstone
NAMIBIA
Windhoek
BOTSWANA
Gaborone
Pretoria (Tshwane)
Johannesburg
Kimberley
Maputo
Mbabane
SWAZ.
LESOTHO
Maseru
Durban (eThekwini)
SOUTH AFRICA
Cape Town
C. of Good Hope
C. Agulhas
East London
Port Elizabeth
Orange
Vaal
Limpopo
Zambezi
Cunene
Cubango
Okavango
Cuando
Kasai
Lualaba
Lomami
Kwango
Chari
Benue
Niger
Senegal

Projection: Azimuthal Equidistant
West from Greenwich
East from Greenwich
COPYRIGHT PHILIP'S

● Dakar Capital Cities

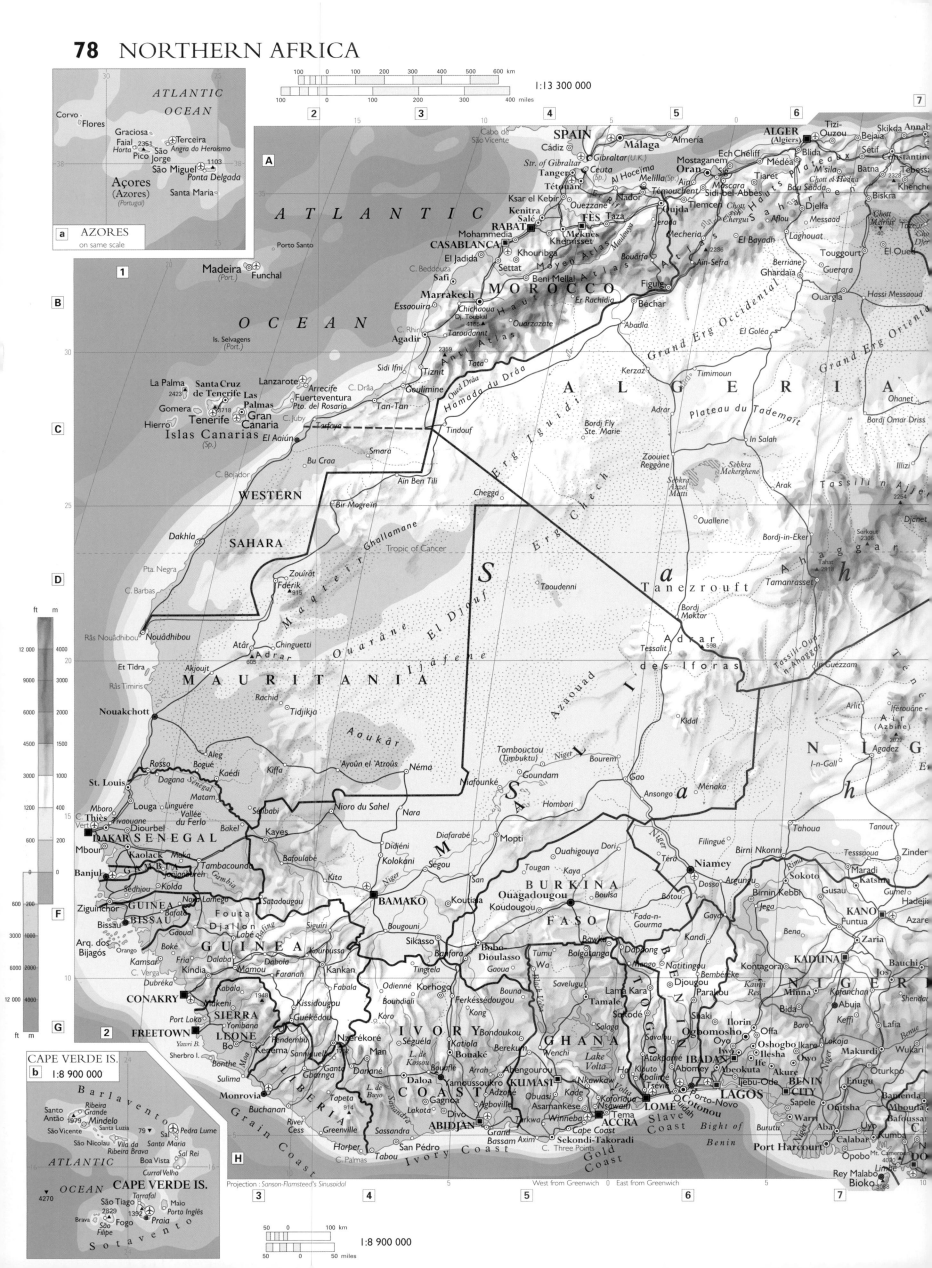

100 0 100 200 300 400 500 600 km
1:13 300 000
100 0 100 200 300 400 miles

AZORES
on same scale

ATLANTIC OCEAN
Corvo · Flores
Graciosa
Faial 2351 · Terceira · Angra do Heroísmo
Horta · Pico · São Jorge
1103
São Miguel · Ponta Delgada
Santa Maria
Açores
(Azores)
(Portugal)

a

CAPE VERDE IS.
b 1:8 900 000

Barlavento
Santo Antão 1979 · Ribeira Grande · Mindelo
São Vicente · Santa Luzia
São Nicolau · Sal · Pedra Lume
Ribeira Brava · Sal Rei
79 · Santa Maria
Boa Vista
Curral Velho
ATLANTIC OCEAN
4270
CAPE VERDE IS.
São Tiago · Tarrafal
2829 · Praia
Brava · 1392 · Porto Inglês
São Fogo · Maio
Filipe
Sotavento

Projection : Sanson-Flamsteed's Sinusoidal
West from Greenwich 0 East from Greenwich

50 0 100 km
1:8 900 000
50 0 50 miles

ATLANTIC OCEAN

SPAIN
Cádiz · Málaga · Almería
Str. of Gibraltar
Gibraltar (U.K.) · Tangier · Ceuta (Sp.) · Melilla (Sp.)
Tétouan · Al Hoceima
Ksar el Kebir
Kenitra · Salé
RABAT · Meknès · FES · Taza
Mohammedia
CASABLANCA · Khouriga
El Jadida · Settat · Beni Mellal
Safi · C. Beddouza
Marrakech · **MOROCCO**
Essaouira · Chichaoua · Dj. Toubkal 4165
Agadir · C. Rhir
2359
Sidi Ifni · Tiznit
Goulimine
Lanzarote · Arrecife
Fuerteventura · Pto. del Rosario
Gran Canaria · Las Palmas · C. Juby
La Palma · Santa Cruz de Tenerife
2423 · 3718
Gomera · Tenerife
Hierro · **Islas Canarias** (Sp.) · El Aaiún
C. Bojador
Smara
Bu Craa
WESTERN
Pta. Negra
Dakhla
C. Barbas
SAHARA

ALGERIA
Mostaganem · **ALGER** (Algiers) · Tizi-Ouzou · Skikda · Annaba
Oran · Mascara · Médéa · Blida · Sétif · Bejaia · Constantine
Sidi-bel-Abbès · Tiaret · M'sila · Batna · Tébessa
Tlemcen · Aflou · Djelfa · Biskra
Oujda · Bou Saâda · Messaad
Figuig · El Bayadh · Laghouat · Touggourt · El Oued
Béchar · Abadla · El Goléa · Ghardaia · Guerara · Ouargla
Grand Erg Occidental · Grand Erg Oriental
Timimoun · Adrar · Plateau du Tademaït · Ohanet
In Salah · Bordj Omar Driss
Kerzaz · Illizi
Bordj Fly Ste. Marie
Erg Chech
Chegga
Tanezrouft · Tassili n'Ajjer
2254
Bordj-in-Eker · Djanet
Serkout 2306
Arak
Ouallene
Ahaggar · Tamanrasset · Tahat 2910

MAURITANIA
Râs Nouâdhibou · Nouâdhibou
Atâr · Chinguetti
Adrar · 605
Et Tidra
Râs Timiris
Nouakchott
Rachid · Tidjikja
Aoukâr
Akjoujt
Zouîrât · Fdérik · 915
Tropic of Cancer
Mauteir
Ouarâne · El Djouf
Iguidi · Ijâfène
Taoudenni
Tessalit
Adrar des Iforas · 598
Bordj Moktar
Kidal
I-n-Gall · Arlit · Iférouâne · 2022
NIGER
Aïr (Azbine)
Agadez
Tahoua · Tanout · Zinder · Tessaoua · Maradi
Birni Nkonni · Katsina · KANO

SENEGAL
St. Louis · Dagana · Rosso · Bogué · Kaédi
Aleg · Kiffa · 'Ayoûn el 'Atroûs · Néma
Louga · Linguère
C. Vert · **DAKAR** · Thiès · Tivaouane · Diourbel
Mbour · Kaolack · Maka
GAMBIA · Banjul
Ziguinchor · Sédhiou · Kolda
GUINEA BISSAU · Bissau · Bafatá
Arq. dos Bijagós · Boké · Gaoual
C. Verga · Dubréka · Kindia
CONAKRY · Forécariah
SIERRA LEONE · Port Loko · Makeni
FREETOWN · Yonibana · Bo
Sherbro I. · Bonthe
LIBERIA · Sulima

MALI
Tombouctou (Timbuktu) · Goundam · Bourem · Gao · Ansongo
Niafounké · Ménaka
Diafarabé · Hombori
Mopti · Ouahigouya · Dori · Filingué · Tahoua
Nara · Nioro du Sahel · San · Téra · Niamey
Ségou · Koutiala · **BAMAKO** · Koulikoro
Kayes · Bafoulabé · Didiéni · Kolokani · Tougan · Kaya
Bakel · Kita · Tambacounda · Bougouni · Sikasso
Kédougou · Siguiri · Kankan

BURKINA FASO
Ouagadougou · Boulsa · Botou · Dosso · Gaya
Koudougou · Fada-n-Gourma · Kandi
Bobo Dioulasso · Banfora · Bawku · Dapaong · Kontagora
Tumu · Wa · Bolgatanga · Mango · Natitingou · Bembéréke · **NIGERIA**
Bawku · Minna · Abuja
Sokoto · Gusau · Zaria · **KADUNA** · Bauchi
Birnin Kebbi · Jega · Bena · Funtua · **KANO** · Azare · Hadejia
Gumel

GUINEA
Fouta Djallon · Dabola · Mamou · Labé · Dalaba
Kamsar · Fria · Kindia · Faranah · Kissidougou
Kabala · Kérouané · Beyla · Nzérékoré · Macenta

IVORY COAST
Odienné · Korhogo · Boundiali · Ferkéssédougou · Bouna
Séguéla · Katiola · Bondoukou · Kong
Man · Danané · Bouaké · Abengourou
Daloa · **Yamoussoukro** · Bouaflé · Agboville · Arrah
Gagnoa · Divo · Abidjan · Grand Bassam
San Pédro · Sassandra · Tabou · C. Palmas
Tapeta · Gbarnga · Buchanan · Greenville · Harper
Monrovia · River Cess
Grain Coast · Ivory Coast

GHANA
Salaga · Tamale · Savelugu · Yendi
Wenchi · Kumasi · Obuasi · Nkawkaw · Koforidua
Sekondi-Takoradi · Cape Coast · Winneba · **ACCRA** · Tema
Axim · C. Three Points · Gold Coast

TOGO · Lama Kara · Sokodé · Atakpamé · Kpalimé · **LOMÉ**
BENIN · Djougou · Parakou · Savalou · Abomey · Porto-Novo · Cotonou · Ouidah
Slave Coast

NIGERIA
Ilorin · Offa · Oshogbo · Ikare · Lokoja · Lafia · Makurdi · Wukari
Oyo · Ife · Ilesha · Akure · Owo · Otukpo · Enugu
Ogbomosho · Iwo · Ado · Abeokuta · **IBADAN** · **LAGOS** · **BENIN CITY** · Onitsha · Sapele · Aba · Calabar
Ijebu-Ode · Shaki · Warri · Burutu · Opobo · **Port Harcourt** · Kumba
Bight of Benin · Mt. Cameroon 4070 · Rey Malabo · Bioko 3008 · Limbe

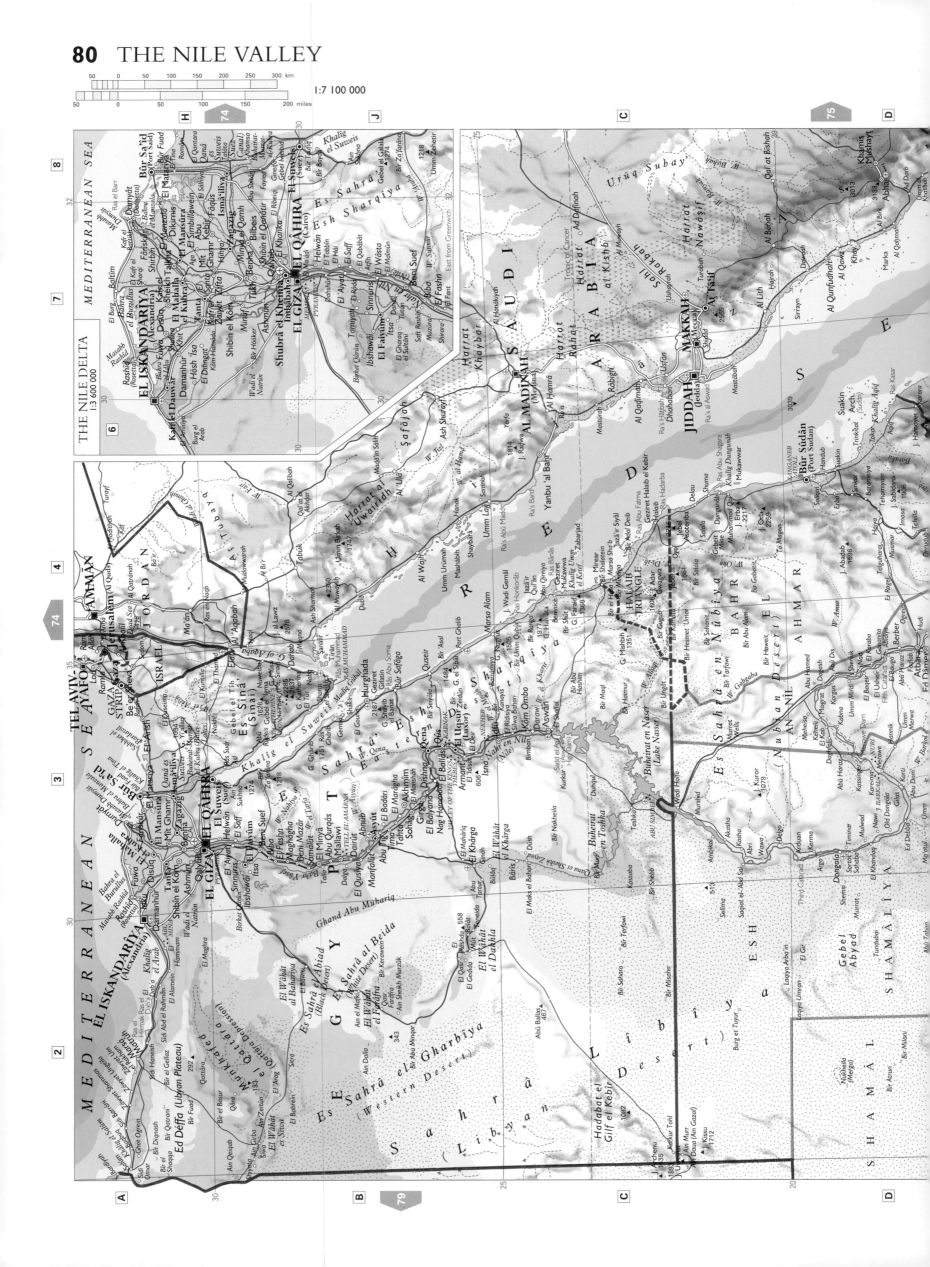

1:7 100 000

THE NILE DELTA
1:3 600 000

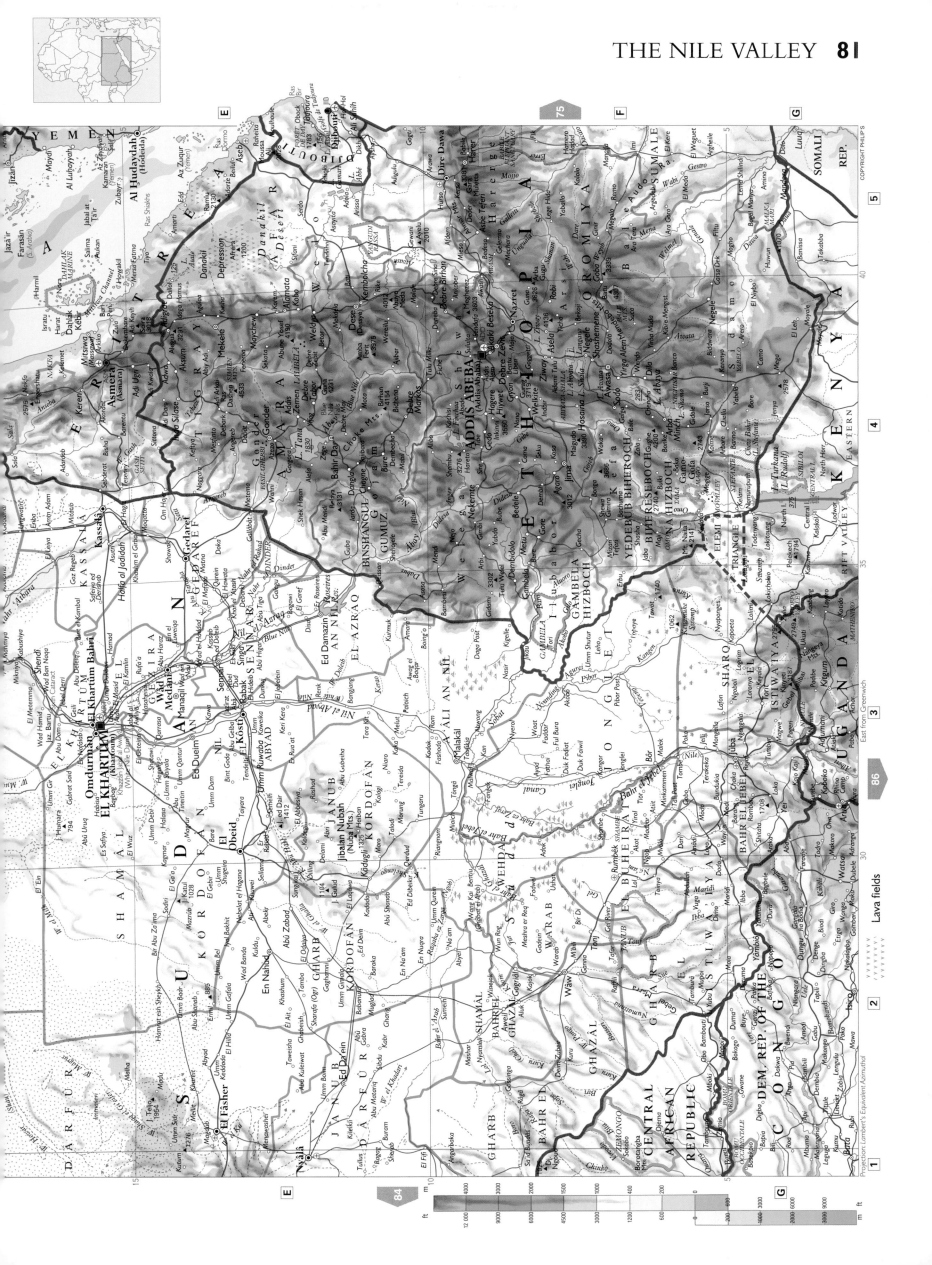

1:7 100 000

Projection: Lambert's Equivalent Azimuthal

Underlined towns give their name to the administrative area in which they stand.

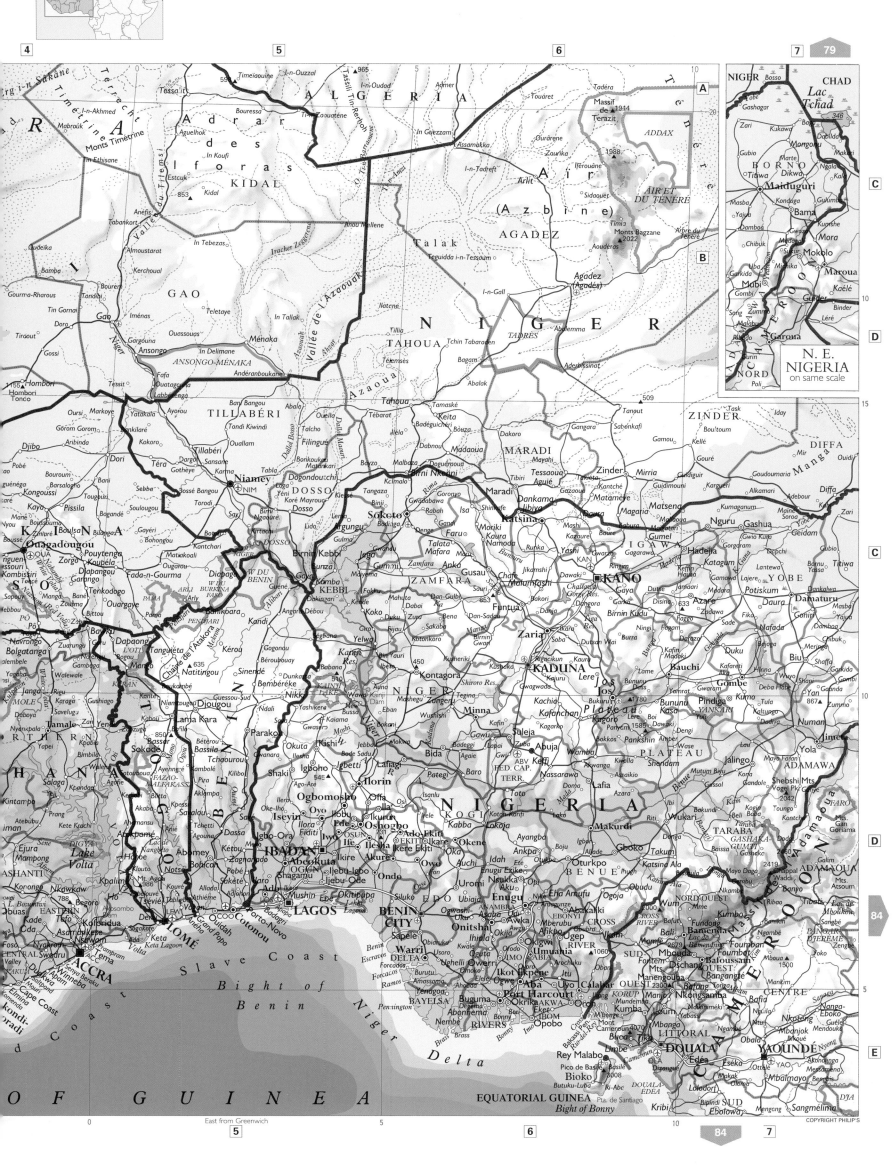

N. E.
NIGERIA
on same scale

84

COPYRIGHT PHILIP'S

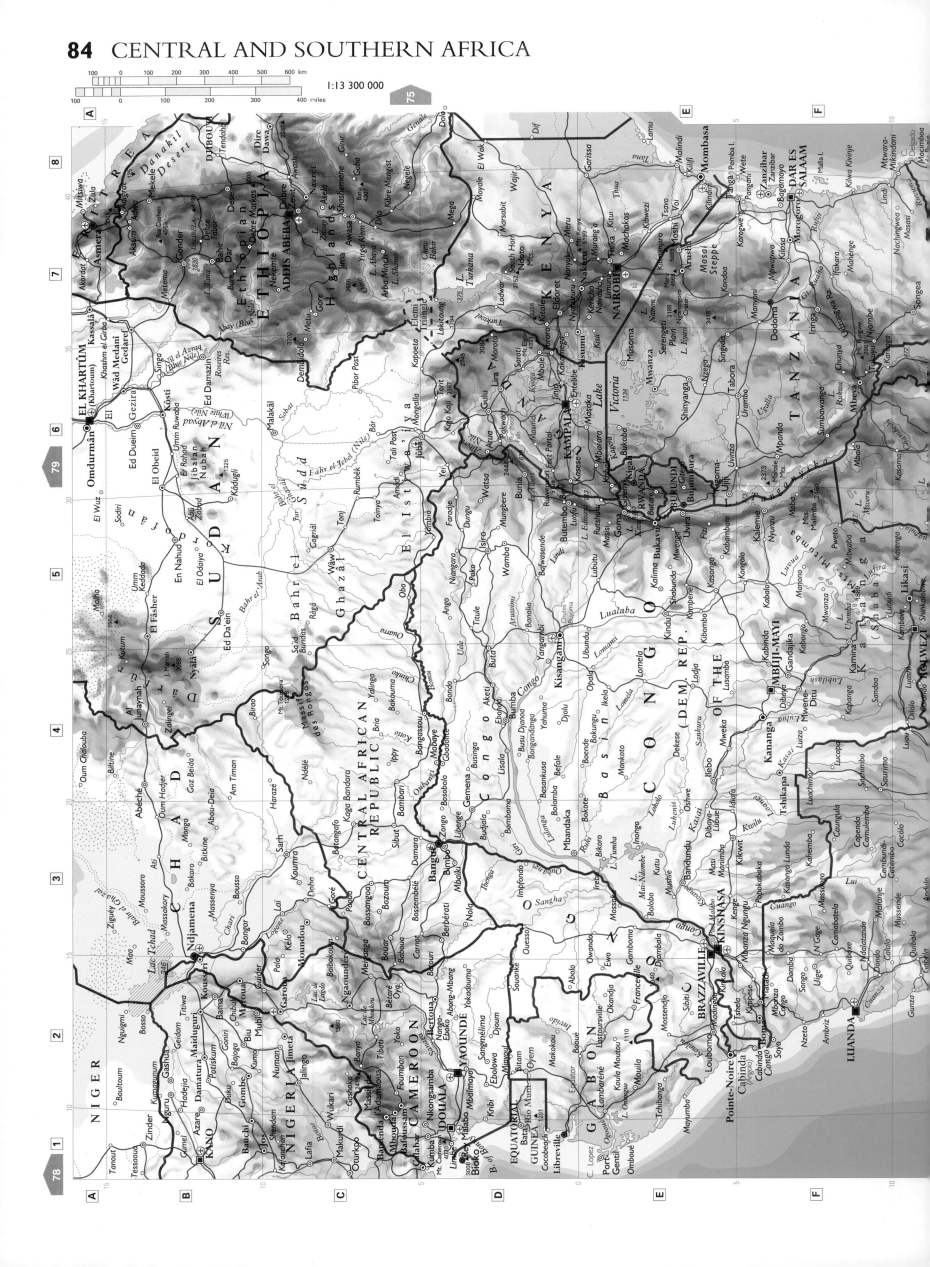

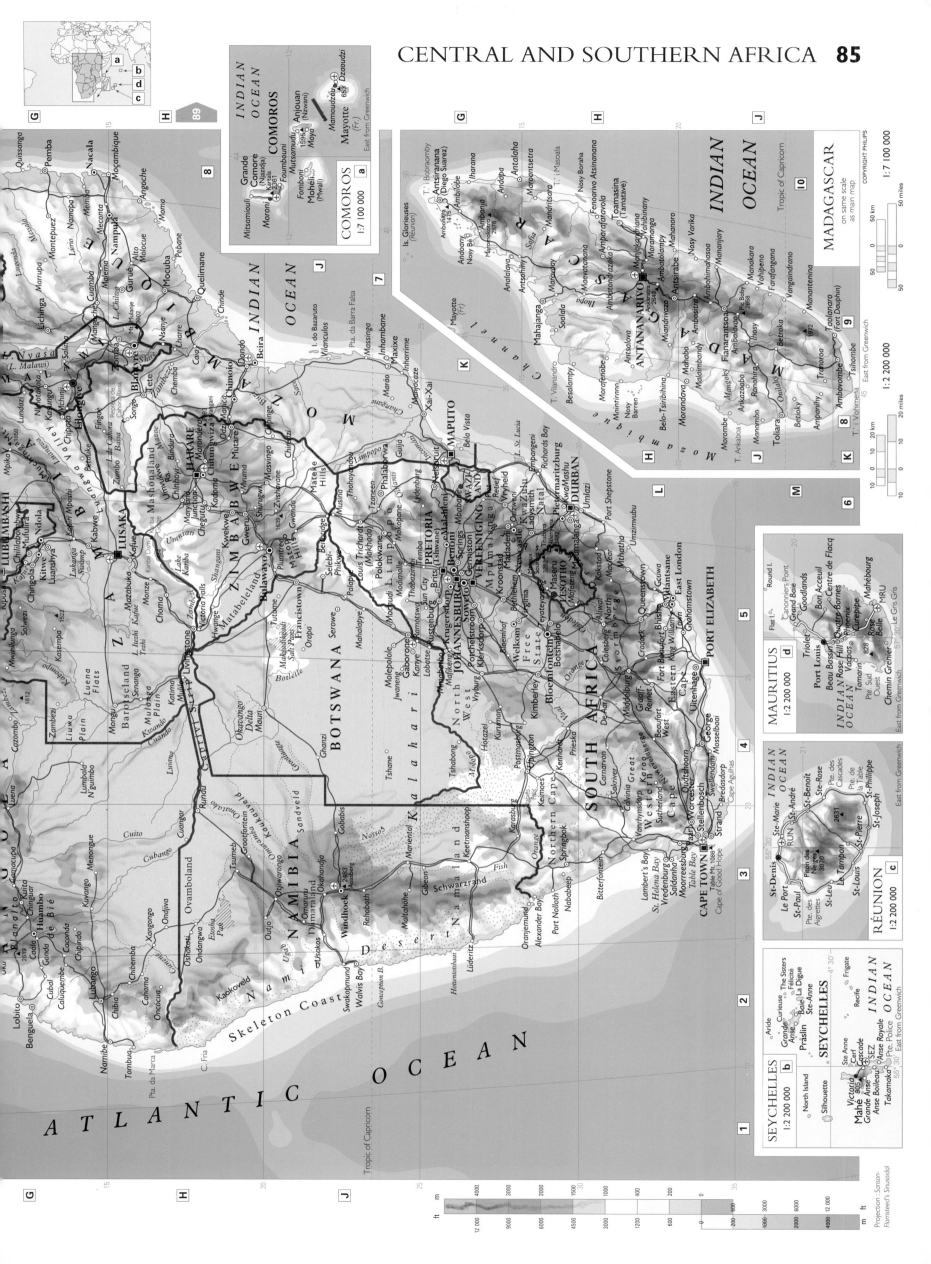

INDIAN OCEAN

COMOROS

Mitsamiouli
Moroni
Grande Comore (Njazidja)
2361
Fomboni Mohéli (Mwali)
Mutsamudu 1595
Moya Anjouan (Nzwani)
Mamoudzou 653
Dzaoudzi
Mayotte (Fr.)

COMOROS a
1:7 100 000
East from Greenwich

MADAGASCAR
on same scale
as main map
1:7 100 000

INDIAN OCEAN

Antananarivo

MADAGASCAR

1:2 200 000

COPYRIGHT PHILIPS

Tropic of Capricorn

MOZAMBIQUE

ZAMBIA

ZIMBABWE

Harare
Bulawayo

BOTSWANA

Gaborone

NAMIBIA

Windhoek

Lusaka

JOHANNESBURG
PRETORIA

SOUTH AFRICA

LESOTHO
Maseru

SWAZILAND
Mbabane

MAPUTO

DURBAN

PORT ELIZABETH

CAPE TOWN
Cape of Good Hope

ATLANTIC OCEAN

INDIAN OCEAN

Tropic of Capricorn

MAURITIUS d
1:2 200 000
Port Louis
East from Greenwich

RÉUNION c
1:2 200 000
St-Denis
East from Greenwich

SEYCHELLES b
1:2 200 000
Victoria
Mahé
East from Greenwich

Projection: Sanson-
Flamsteed's Sinusoidal

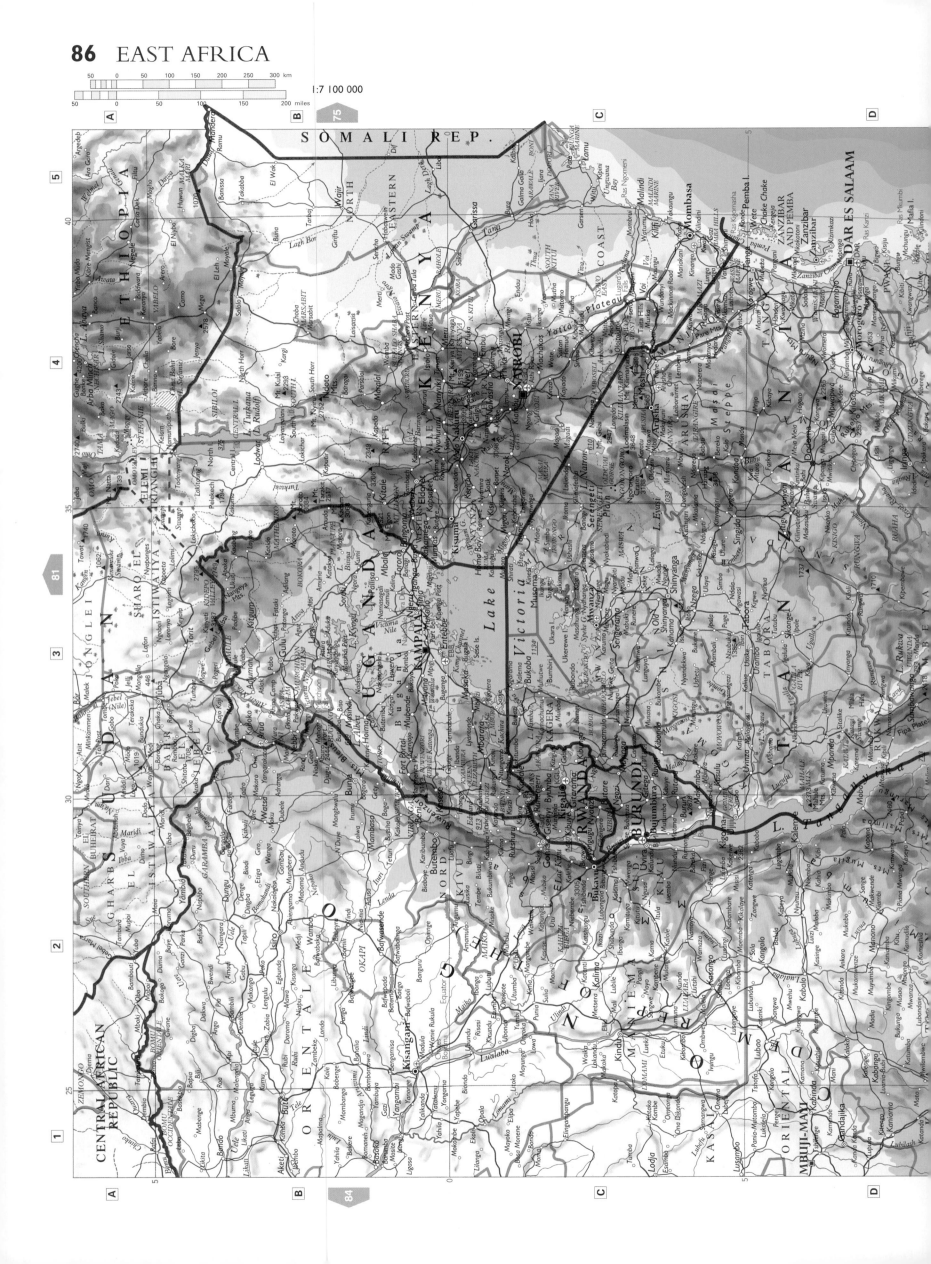

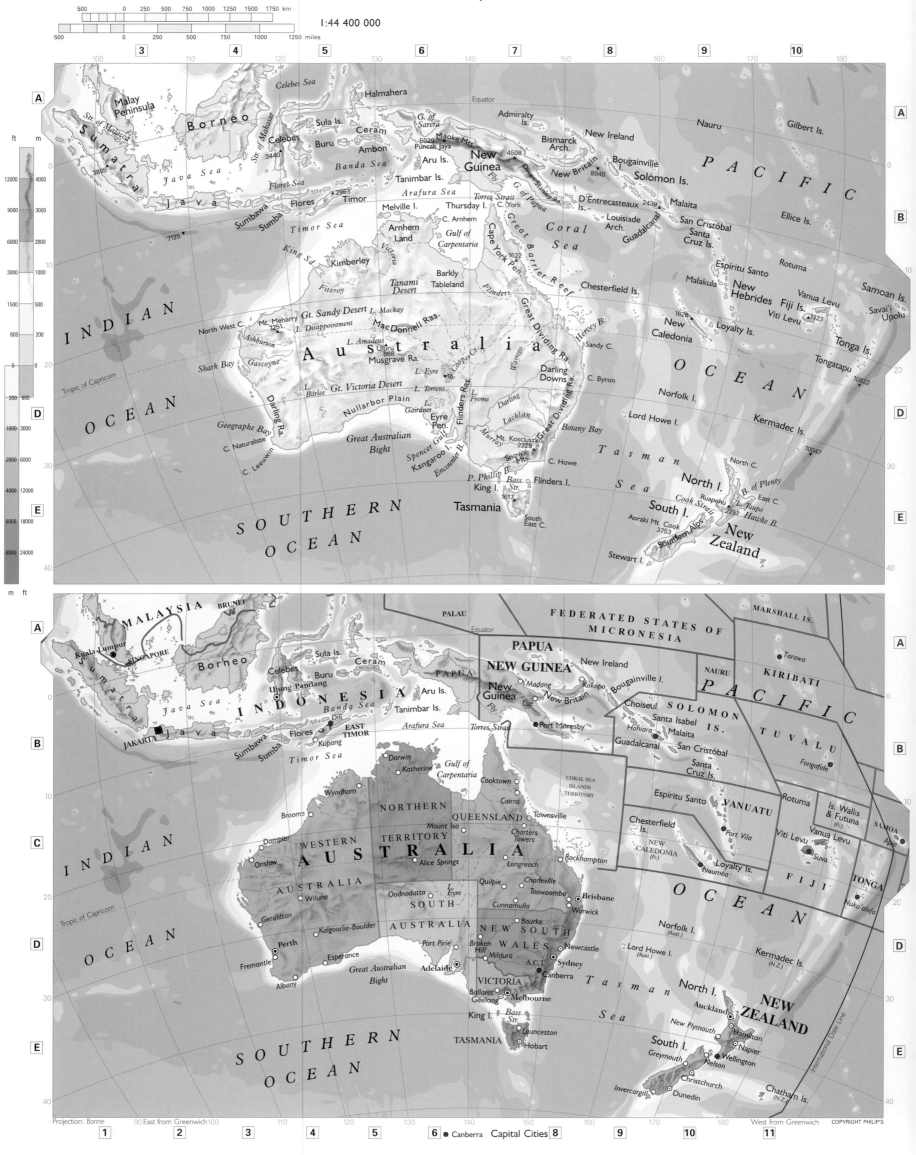

1:44 400 000

Physical map (top):

INDIAN OCEAN

Malay Peninsula
Str. of Malacca
Sumatra 3895
Borneo
Celebes Sea
Celebes 3440
Java Sea
Java
Sula Is.
Halmahera
Ceram
Buru
Ambon
Banda Sea
Aru Is.
G. of Sarera
Maoke Mts. 5029
Puncak Jaya
New Guinea
Fly
4508
Equator
Admiralty Is.
New Ireland
Bismarck Arch.
New Britain 8940
Owen Stanley Ra.
Bougainville
Solomon Is.
Malaita
D'Entrecasteaux 2439
San Cristóbal
Guadalcanal
Santa Cruz Is.
PACIFIC
Nauru
Gilbert Is.
Ellice Is.
Samoan Is.
Savai'i
Upolu
Espíritu Santo
Rotuma
Malakula
New Hebrides
Fiji Is.
Vanua Levu
1628
Viti Levu 1323
Loyalty Is.
New Caledonia
Tonga Is.
Tongatapu 10822

Timor Sea
Sumbawa
Sumba
Flores
Flores Sea
Timor 2963
Tanimbar Is.
Arafura Sea
Torres Strait
C. York
G. of Papua
Thursday I.
Melville I.
C. Arnhem
Arnhem Land
Gulf of Carpentaria
Cape York Pen.
1622
Great Barrier Reef
Coral Sea
Chesterfield Is.

7125
King Sd.
Kimberley
Fitzroy
Victoria
Barkly Tableland
Tanami Desert
Flinders
Great Dividing Ra.
Hervey B.
Sandy C.

North West C.
Ashburton
Mt. Meharry 1251
Gt. Sandy Desert
L. Disappointment
L. Mackay
MacDonnell Ras.
L. Amadeus
Ulúru 868
Musgrave Ra.
Australia
Cooper Cr.
Warrego
Darling Downs
Darling Ra.
C. Byron
New Caledonia
Norfolk I.

Shark Bay
Gascoyne
L. Barlee
Gt. Victoria Desert
L. Eyre
16
L. Torrens
L. Gairdner
L. Frome
Flinders Ras.
Darling
Lachlan
Botany Bay
Lord Howe I.

INDIAN OCEAN
Geographe Bay
C. Naturaliste
Darling Ra.
Nullarbor Plain
Eyre Pen.
Spencer Gulf
Murray
Mt. Kosciuszko 2228
Snowy Mts.
C. Howe
Tasman Sea
North C.

Great Australian Bight
Kangaroo I.
Encounter B.
P. Phillip B.
Bass Str.
King I.
1617
Flinders I.
South East C.
OCEAN
Ruapehu 2797
Lake Taupo
Hawke B.
B. of Plenty
East C.
North I.
Cook Strait
10047

SOUTHERN OCEAN
Tasmania
Stewart I.
Aoraki Mt. Cook 3753
Southern Alps
South I.
New Zealand

ft / m elevation scale:
12000 / 4000
9000 / 3000
6000 / 2000
3000 / 1000
1500 / 500
600 / 200
0 / 0
200 / 600
1000 / 3000
2000 / 6000
4000 / 12000
6000 / 18000
8000 / 24000

Political map (bottom):

MALAYSIA
BRUNEI
Kuala Lumpur
SINGAPORE
Sumatra
Borneo
Celebes
Ujung Pandang
Buru
Ceram
Sula Is.
PALAU
Equator
FEDERATED STATES OF MICRONESIA
MARSHALL IS.
PAPUA NEW GUINEA
New Ireland
Madang
Kokopo
New Britain
Bougainville I.
NAURU
Tarawa
KIRIBATI
PACIFIC

INDONESIA
JAKARTA
Java
Dili
EAST TIMOR
Kupang
Aru Is.
Tanimbar Is.
Banda Sea
PAPUA
New Guinea
Fly
Lae
Port Moresby
Choiseul
Santa Isabel
Hohiara
Malaita
San Cristóbal
SOLOMON IS.
TUVALU
Fongafale

Timor Sea
Sumbawa
Sumba
Flores
Arafura Sea
Torres Strait
Darwin
Katherine
Gulf of Carpentaria
Cooktown
Cairns
CORAL SEA ISLANDS TERRITORY
Santa Cruz Is.
Espíritu Santo
VANUATU
Rotuma
Is. Wallis & Futuna (Fr.)
SAMOA
Apia

INDIAN OCEAN
Wyndham
Broome
Dampier
Onslow
NORTHERN TERRITORY
Mount Isa
WESTERN AUSTRALIA
AUSTRALIA
Alice Springs
QUEENSLAND
Townsville
Charters Towers
Rockhampton
Longreach
Chesterfield Is.
Port Vila
NEW CALEDONIA (Fr.)
Loyalty Is.
Nouméa
Viti Levu
Suva
FIJI
Vanua Levu
TONGA
Nuku'alofa

Tropic of Capricorn
Geraldton
Wiluna
Kalgoorlie-Boulder
Oodnadatta
L. Eyre
SOUTH AUSTRALIA
Quilpie
Cunnamulla
Charleville
Toowoomba
Bourke
Warwick
Brisbane
NEW SOUTH WALES
Norfolk I. (Aust.)
Lord Howe I. (Aust.)
Kermadec Is. (N.Z.)

Perth
Fremantle
Esperance
Albany
Great Australian Bight
Port Pirie
Broken Hill
Mildura
Adelaide
A.C.T.
Canberra
Sydney
Newcastle
North I.
NEW ZEALAND

VICTORIA
Ballarat
Geelong
Melbourne
King I.
Bass Str.
Launceston
Hobart
TASMANIA
Tasman Sea
South I.
Auckland
New Plymouth
Hamilton
Napier
Wellington
Nelson
Greymouth
Christchurch
Dunedin
Invercargill
Chatham Is. (N.Z.)

SOUTHERN OCEAN

● Canberra Capital Cities

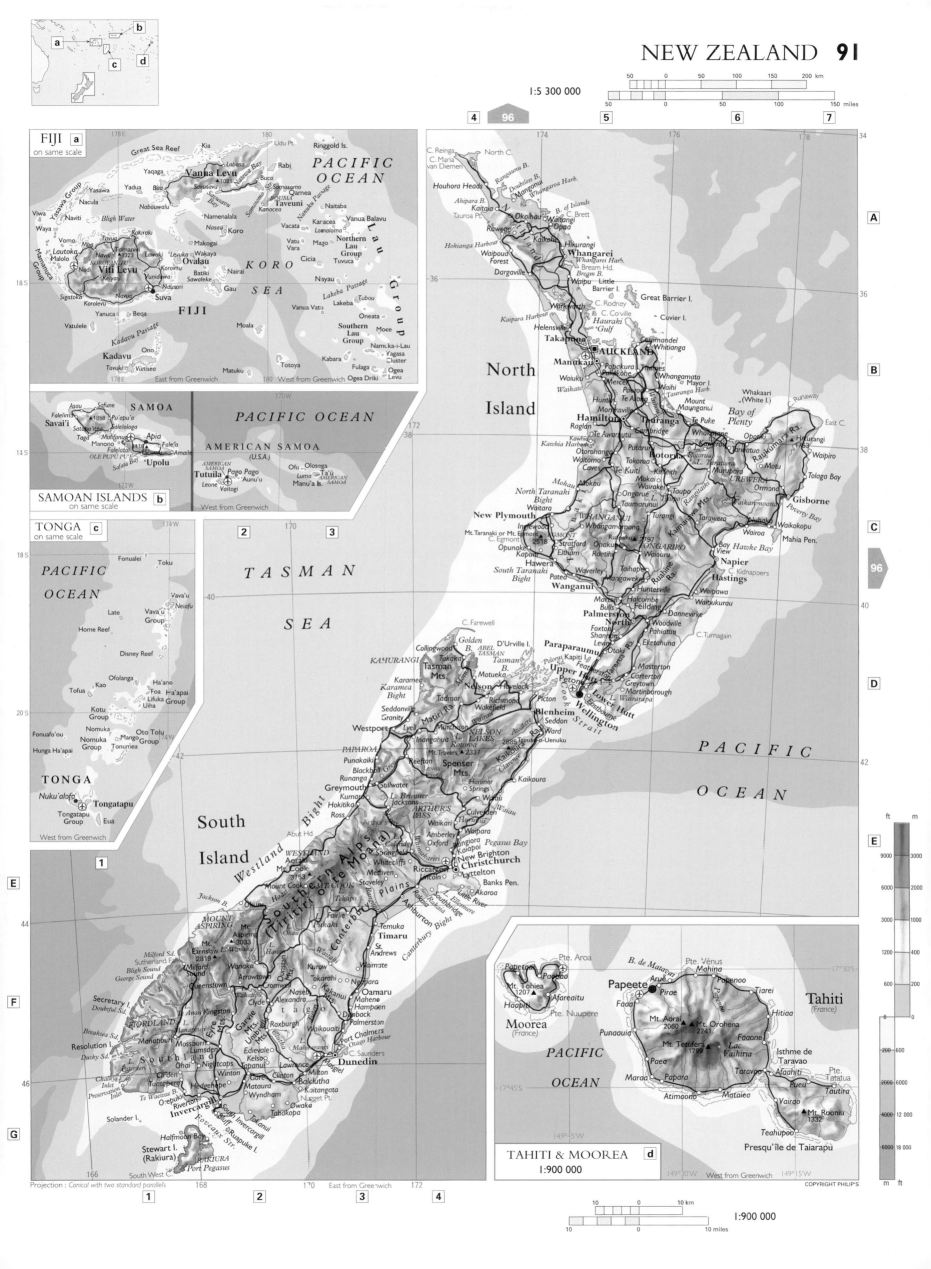

1:5 300 000

FIJI [a]
on same scale

SAMOAN ISLANDS [b]
on same scale

TONGA [c]
on same scale

NEW ZEALAND

North Island

South Island

TAHITI & MOOREA [d]
1:900 000

1:900 000

Projection : Conical with two standard parallels

COPYRIGHT PHILIP'S

INDIAN

OCEAN

SOUTHERN

OCEAN

WESTERN AUSTRALIA

SOUTH

AUSTRALIA

Great Victoria Desert

Nullarbor Plain

Great Australian Bight

PERTH

1. NGALIWURRU/NUNGALI
2. NYANGATU
3. WAMBARDI
4. LJALALIUMA
5. RODNA
6. NYANTJA
7. ROULPALAULPMA
8. URUNA

Aboriginal lands

Projection: Bonne

East from Greenwich

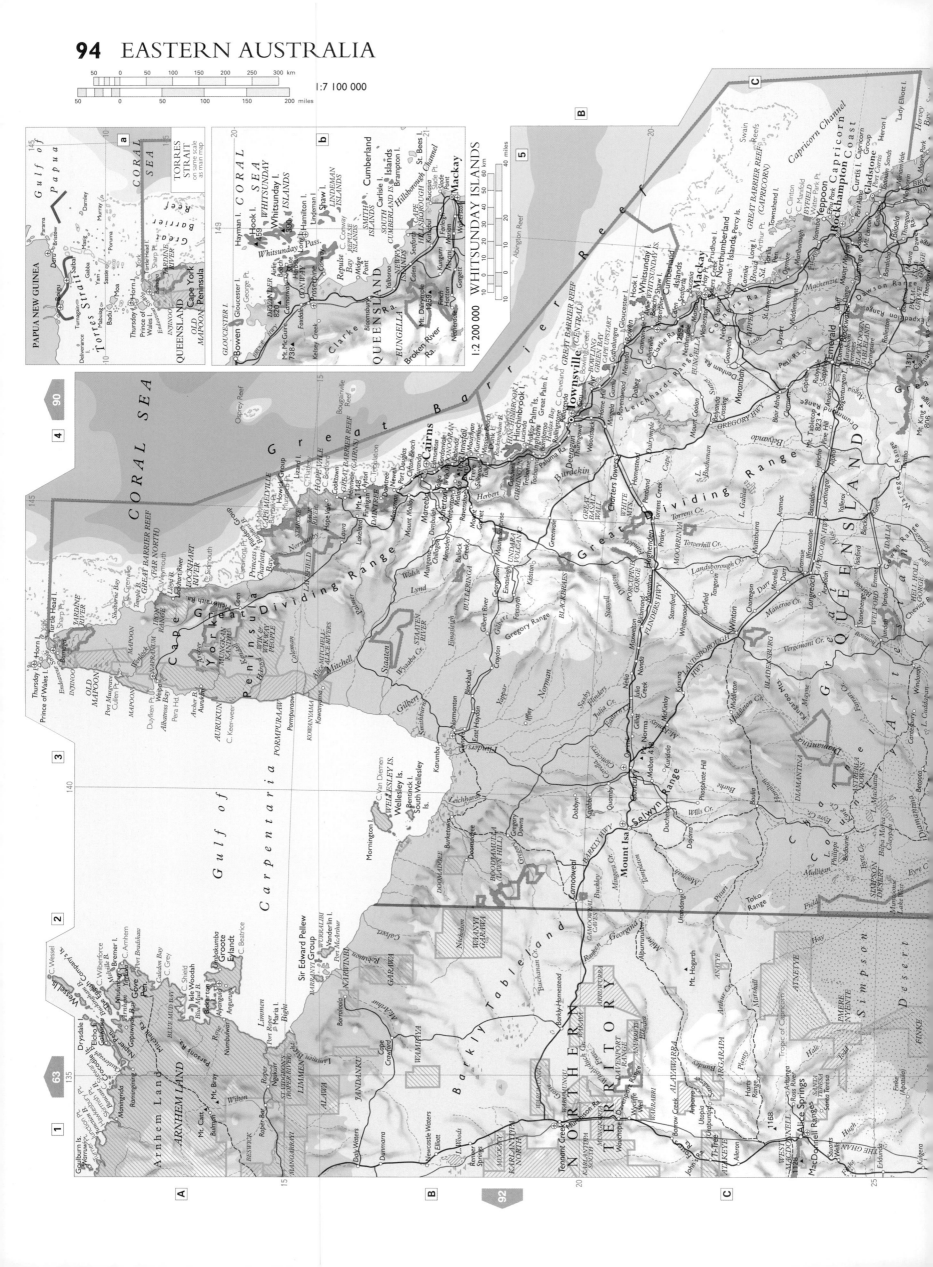

TASMAN

SEA

Aboriginal lands

on same scale

East from Greenwich

Projection: Bonne

Equatorial Scale 1:48 000 000

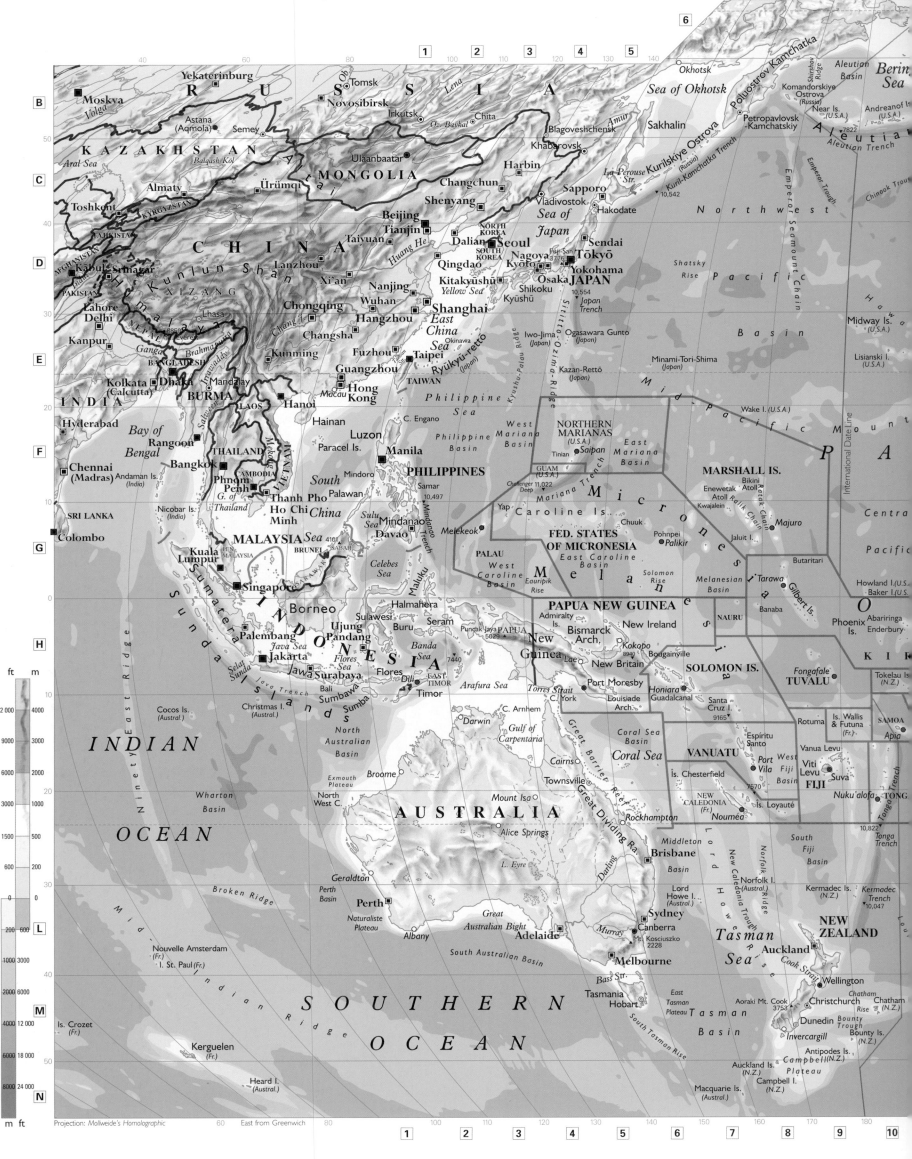

Top coordinates:
11 12 13 14 15 16 17 18 19 20
160 150 140 130 120 110 100 90 80 70 60 40 20

ALASKA
(U.S.A.)
Arctic Circle
Anchorage
Bristol Bay
Gulf of Alaska
Juneau
Is. (U.S.A.)
6959
Prince of Wales I.
(U.S.A.) Prince Rupert
Queen Charlotte Is.
(Canada)
ROCKY

CANADA
Edmonton
L. Winnipeg
Newfoundland
NORTH

Vancouver
Calgary
Regina
Winnipeg
St. Lawrence
Vancouver I.
Victoria
Seattle
Portland
Boise
L. Superior
Québec
Montréal
Ottawa
St. John's
Minneapolis
Toronto
L. Michigan L. Huron L. Ontario
Detroit
Buffalo
Boston
Northeast
Mendocino Fracture Zone C. Mendocino
Salt Lake City
L. Erie
Chicago
Pittsburgh
Cincinnati
New York
Philadelphia
Baltimore
Washington D.C.
ATLANTIC

Sacramento
6741
Murray Fracture Zone
4418
Denver
Kansas City
St. Louis
UNITED STATES
Oklahoma City
Memphis
Atlanta
C. Hatteras
Bermuda
(U.K.)

San Francisco
Pacific
Los Angeles
San Diego
Phoenix
Dallas
Houston
Mississippi
Jacksonville

Guadalupe
(Mex.)
Ciudad Juárez
New Orleans
Tampa
Sargasso Sea
OCEAN

Molokai Fracture Zone
Gulf of Mexico
Miami
BAHAMAS
West Indies

Tropic of Cancer
San Antonio
Monterrey
La Habana
CUBA

Basin
C. San Lucas
Guadalajara
Mexico
Mérida
Canal de Yucatán
HAITI
DOMINICAN REP.
9200

Honolulu
Maui
HAWAIIAN IS.
(U.S.A.)
Kauai
Oahu
4205
Hilo Hawaii
Clarion Fracture Zone
Is. Revilla Gigedo
(Mex.)
Puebla
Acapulco
7680
JAMAICA
Kingston
PUERTO RICO
(U.S.A.)
Leeward Is.

Johnston I.
(U.S.A.)
CIFIC
GUATEMALA
HONDURAS
Guatemala
BELIZE
Caribbean Sea
BARBADOS
Windward Is.

Palmyra Is.
(U.S.A.)
Middle America Trench
6662
San Salvador
EL SALVADOR
NICARAGUA
Managua
Barranquilla
Maracaibo

North West Christmas Ridge
Clipperton Fracture Zone
I. Clipperton
(Fr.)
Guatemala
Basin
San José
COSTA RICA
Colón
PANAMA
Panamá
Caracas
Orinoco
VENEZUELA

Teraina
Tabuaeran
Kiritimati
I. del Coco
(Costa Rica)
Cocos Ridge
Panama
Basin
Medellín
Bogotá
COLOMBIA

Cooper Ridge
Galápagos Fracture Zone
I. de Malpelo
(Colombia)
Cali

Jarvis I.
(U.S.A.)
Equator
Galápagos
(Ecuador)
Carnegie Ridge
Quito
ECUADOR

KIRIBATI
Line Islands
Malden I.
Starbuck I.
Guayaquil
Iquitos
Amazonas
BRAZIL

Penrhyn
(Tongareva)
Manihiki
Pukapuka
Manihiki
Plateau
Vostok I.
Caroline I.
(Millennium I.)
Flint I.
Îs. Marquises
Nuku Hiva Hiva Oa
Marquesas Fracture Zone
C. Pariñas
Trujillo

Suwarrow Is.
Yupanqui
Basin
6369
PERU
Lima
East Pacific Ridge

Rangiroa
Îs. de la Société
Bora Bora Huahine
Raiatea
Papeete Tahiti
Îs. Tuamotu
Galápagos Fracture Zone
Mendaña
Peru
Basin
Cuzco
L. Titicaca
Nevado Ancohuma
6550

Cook Is.
(N.Z.)
Aitutaki
Atiu
FRENCH POLYNESIA
Îs. Gambier
Mururoa
6866
Arequipa
Peru-
Arica
La Paz
BOLIVIA

Rarotonga
Mangaia
Îs. Tubuai
Austral Seamount Chain
Iquique
Chile
PARAGUAY

Oeno I.
Henderson I.
Pitcairn I.
(U.K.)
Ducie I.
Tropic of Capricorn
Easter Fracture Zone
Sala y Gómez Ridge
Antofagasta
8050
Chile
Trench
San Miguel de Tucumán

Rapa
Sala-y-Gómez
(Chile)
San Felix
(Chile)
San Ambrosio
(Chile)
ANDES
Porto Alegre

Roggeveen
Basin
I. de Pascua
(Chile)
Córdoba
Aconcagua
3982
Rosario
URUGUAY

Southwest
Arch. de
Juan Fernández
(Chile)
Valparaíso
Santiago
Buenos Aires
Montevideo
Río de la Plata

Pacific
Challenger Fracture Zone
Chile Rise
Concepción
ARGENTINA
SOUTH

Basin
Menard Fracture Zone
Patagonia
ATLANTIC
6212

Pacific-Antarctic Ridge
Punta Arenas
Est. de Magallanes
Falkland Is.
(U.K.)
South Georgia
(U.K.)
OCEAN

Southeast
Pacific Basin
C. de Hornos
Tierra del Fuego
Drake Passage
West from Greenwich

Bottom coordinates:
11 12 13 14 15 16 17 18 19 20
160 150 140 130 120 110 100 90 80 70 60 40

Right-side grid labels: B C D E F G H J K L M N

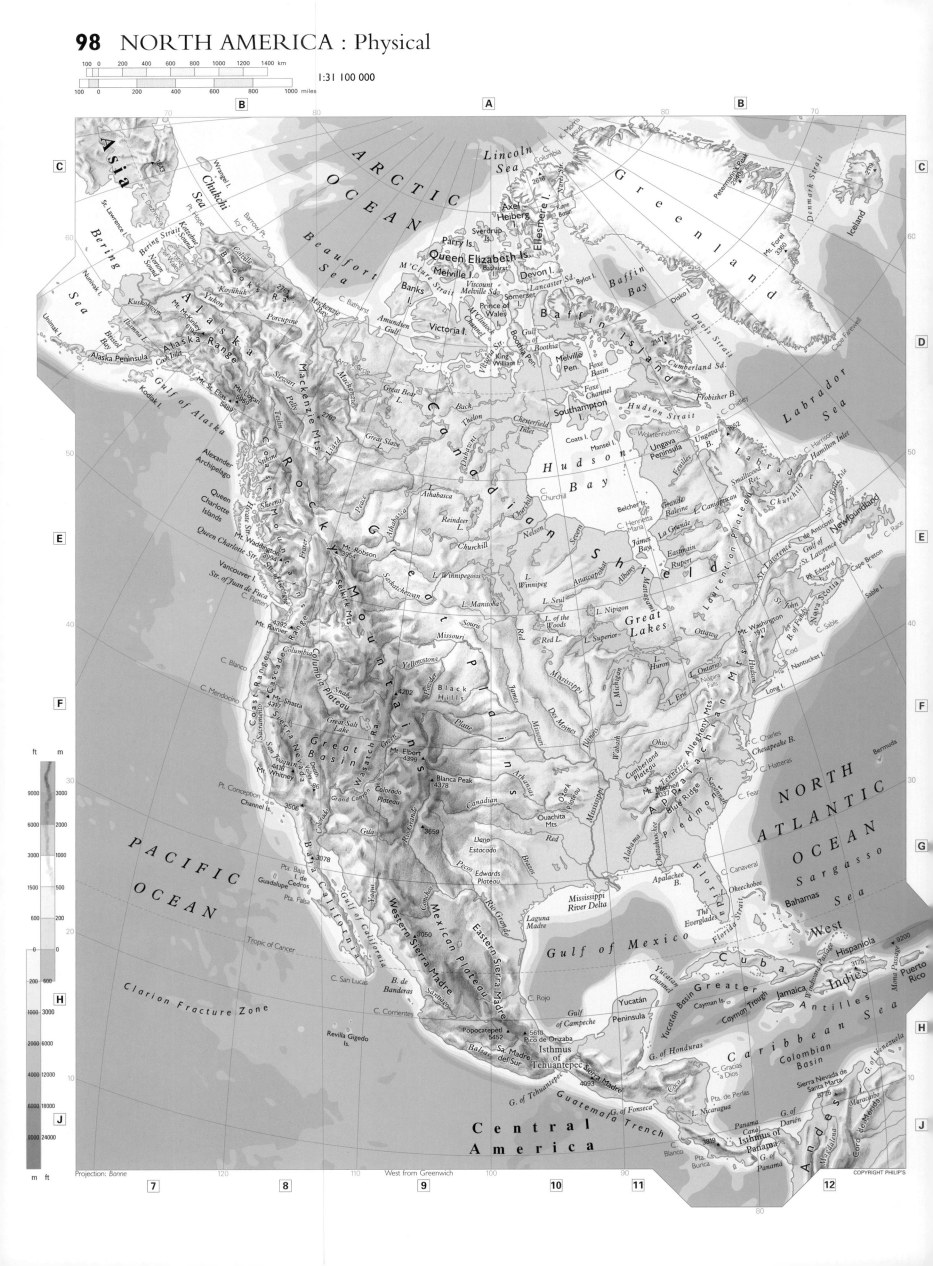

100 0 200 400 600 800 1000 1200 1400 km
100 0 200 400 600 800 1000 miles
1:31 100 000

ASIA

ARCTIC OCEAN

Lincoln Sea

Greenland

Iceland

Denmark Strait

Mt. Forel 3390

Cape Farewell

Chukchi Sea

Bering Sea

Beaufort Sea

Axel Heiberg I.

Ellesmere I.

Sverdrup Is.

Parry Is.

Queen Elizabeth Is.

Melville I.

Devon I.

Banks I.

Viscount Melville Sd.

Prince of Wales

Victoria I.

Boothia Pen.

Gulf of Boothia

Melville Pen.

Baffin Island

Baffin Bay

Davis Strait

Disko I.

Cumberland Sd.

Frobisher B.

ALASKA

Yukon

Alaska Range

Mt. McKinley 6194

Mackenzie Mts.

Mackenzie

Great Bear L.

Arctic Circle

Back

Thelon

Chesterfield Inlet

Southampton I.

Coats I.

Mansel I.

Ungava Peninsula

Hudson Bay

Labrador

Labrador Sea

Newfoundland

Gulf of Alaska

Mt. St. Elias 5489

Mt. Logan 5950

Great Slave L.

Dubawnt

Churchill

Alexander Archipelago

Queen Charlotte Islands

R o c k y   M o u n t a i n s

Mt. Robson 3954

L. Athabasca

Reindeer L.

Nelson

Churchill

L. Winnipeg

Belcher Is.

James Bay

C a n a d i a n   S h i e l d

L a u r e n t i a n   P l a t e a u

Gulf of St. Lawrence

Nova Scotia

Cape Breton I.

Vancouver I.

Mt. Waddington 3994

Mt. Rainier 4392

L. Winnipegosis

L. Manitoba

Saskatchewan

Souris

L. of the Woods

L. Seul

L. Nipigon

Great Lakes

Ottawa

St. Lawrence

C. Cod

C. Blanco

C. Mendocino

Columbia Plateau

Cascade Range

Mt. Shasta 4317

Snake

Yellowstone

4202

Black Hills

Missouri

Red

L. Superior

L. Michigan

L. Huron

L. Erie

L. Ontario

Niagara Falls

Mt. Washington 1917

Long I.

Great Salt Lake

Sierra Nevada

Wasatch Range

Mt. Elbert 4399

Platte

Green

Arkansas

Des Moines

Illinois

Ohio

Wabash

Cumberland Plateau

Allegheny Mts.

Appalachian Mts.

Mt. Mitchell 2037

Chesapeake B.

C. Hatteras

Pt. Conception

Mt. Whitney 4418

Death Valley –86

3506

Grand Canyon

Colorado Plateau

Blanca Peak 4378

Canadian

Red

Ozark Plateau

Ouachita Mts.

Blue Ridge

Piedmont

C. Fear

NORTH ATLANTIC OCEAN

Bermuda

PACIFIC OCEAN

Channel Is.

Pta. Baja I. de Cedros

3078

Pta. Falsa

Baja California

Gulf of California

Gila

Rio Grande 3659

Colorado

Pecos

Edwards Plateau

Llano Estacado

Brazos

Alabama

Chattahoochee

Mississippi

Apalachee B.

C. Canaveral

Florida

Okeechobee

The Everglades

Florida Strait

Sargasso Sea

Bahamas

West Indies

Tropic of Cancer

Guadalupe

C. San Lucas

B. de Banderas

Santiago

Mexican Plateau

Western Sierra Madre

Eastern Sierra Madre

8050

Yaqui

Conchos

Rio Grande

Laguna Madre

Gulf of Mexico

Mississippi River Delta

Gulf of Campeche

Yucatán

Yucatán Peninsula

Cuba

Yucatán Basin

Cayman Is.

Cayman Trough

Greater Antilles

Jamaica

Hispaniola

Windward Passage

Mona Passage

Puerto Rico

3175

9200

Clarion Fracture Zone

C. San Lucas

C. Corrientes

Revilla Gigedo Is.

Popocatepetl 5452

Pico de Orizaba 5610

Sa. Madre del Sur

Balsas

Isthmus of Tehuantepec

Sierra Madre

G. of Tehuantepec

Guatemala Trench

Gulf of Honduras

G. of Fonseca

Coco

L. Nicaragua

Pta. de Perlas

C. Gracias a Dios

Panamá Canal

Isthmus of Panamá

3819

G. of Panamá

Caribbean Sea

Colombian Basin

Sierra Nevada de Santa Marta 5775

Maracaibo

Magdalena

Cord. del Merida

G. of Venezuela

Andes

Pta. Burica

Pta. Panamá

C. Blanco

C e n t r a l   A m e r i c a

Projection: Bonne

West from Greenwich

COPYRIGHT PHILIP'S

ft m

9000 3000
6000 2000
3000 1000
1500 500
600 200
0 0
200 600
1000 3000
2000 6000
4000 12000
6000 18000
8000 24000

m ft

B   A   B

7   8   9   10   11   12

1:31 100 000

100 0 200 400 600 800 1000 1200 1400 km

100 0 200 400 600 800 1000 miles

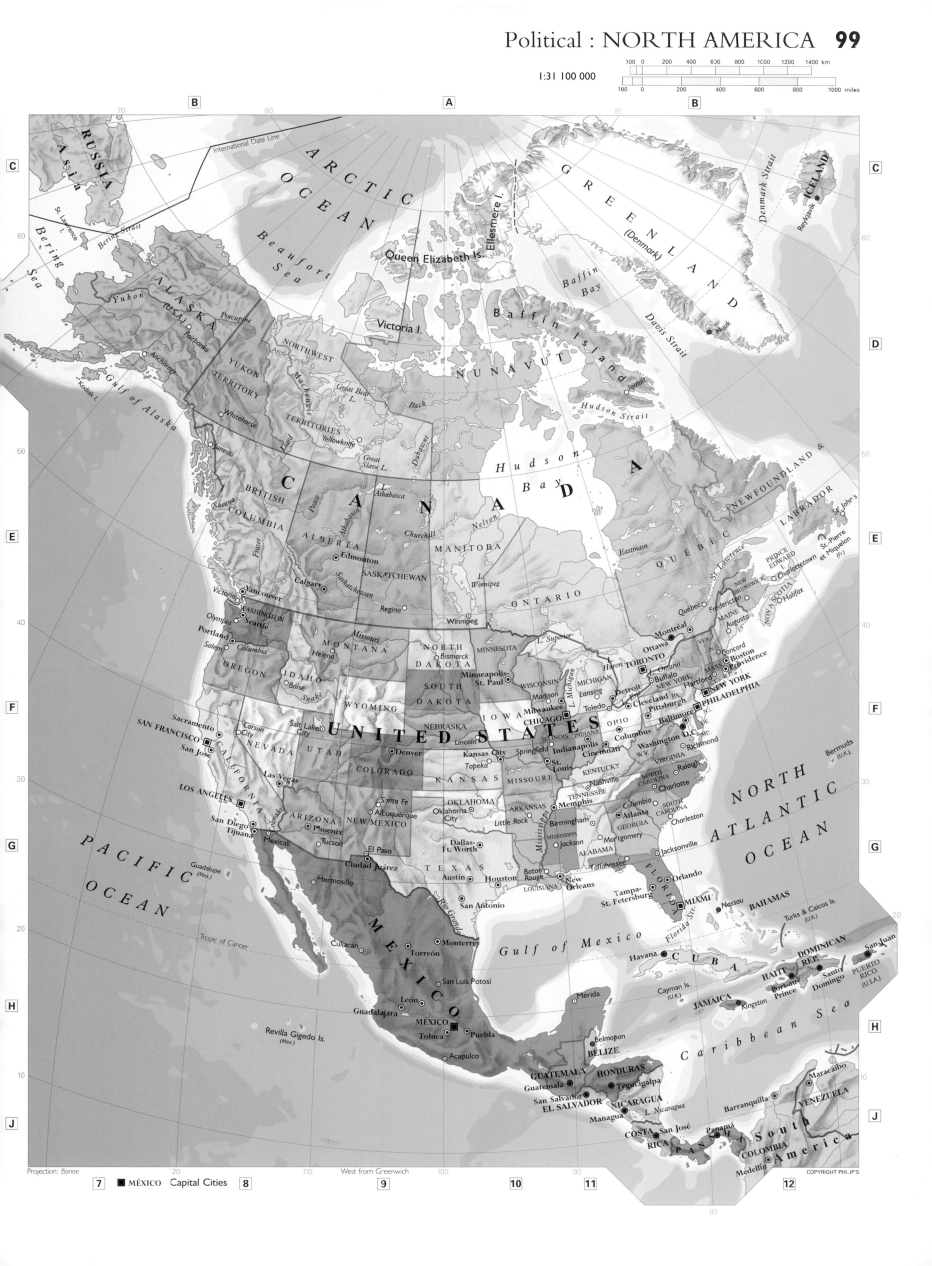

B **A** **B**

ARCTIC OCEAN

GREENLAND

RUSSIA

Asia

St. Lawrence

Bering Strait

Bering Sea

ICELAND

Reykjavik

Denmark Strait

Queen Elizabeth Is.

Ellesmere I.

International Date Line

Beaufort Sea

Baffin Bay

Nuuk

ALASKA (USA)

Yukon

Porcupine

Fairbanks

Anchorage

Kodiak I.

Gulf of Alaska

Victoria I.

NORTHWEST

Arctic Circle

Davis Strait

Baffin Island

YUKON TERRITORY

Whitehorse

Mackenzie

Great Bear L.

Back

TERRITORIES

NUNAVUT

Hudson Strait

Iqaluit

Juneau

Liard

Yellowknife

Great Slave L.

Dubawnt

Hudson

Skeena

BRITISH COLUMBIA

Fraser

CANADA

Prairie

Athabasca

L. Athabasca

Churchill

Nelson

Bay

NEWFOUNDLAND & LABRADOR

St. John's

Victoria

Vancouver

ALBERTA

Edmonton

Calgary

SASKATCHEWAN

Saskatchewan

Regina

MANITOBA

L. Winnipeg

Eastmain

QUÉBEC

St. Lawrence

PRINCE EDWARD I.

Charlottetown

St-Pierre et Miquelon (Fr.)

Olympia

Seattle

WASHINGTON

Portland

Salem

OREGON

Columbia

IDAHO

Boise

Helena

MONTANA

Missouri

Winnipeg

ONTARIO

L. Superior

Ottawa

TORONTO

Québec

Fredericton

NEW BRUNSWICK

MAINE

Augusta

NOVA SCOTIA

Halifax

Sacramento

San Francisco

San Jose

NEVADA

Carson City

Salt Lake City

UTAH

WYOMING

NORTH DAKOTA

Bismarck

SOUTH DAKOTA

MINNESOTA

Minneapolis-St. Paul

WISCONSIN

Madison

L. Michigan

Milwaukee

MICHIGAN

Lansing

L. Huron

Detroit

L. Ontario

Montréal

Buffalo

NEW YORK

VER.

N.H.

Concord

Boston

MASS.

Providence

Hartford

CONN.

Columbia

CALIFORNIA

Las Vegas

Denver

COLORADO

NEBRASKA

Lincoln

IOWA

CHICAGO

ILLINOIS

Springfield

INDIANA

Indianapolis

OHIO

Columbus

Cleveland

Toledo

PA.

Pittsburgh

Baltimore

PHILADELPHIA

NEW YORK

Los Angeles

San Diego

Tijuana

Mexicali

ARIZONA

Phoenix

Tucson

NEW MEXICO

Santa Fe

Albuquerque

OKLAHOMA

Oklahoma City

KANSAS

Topeka

Kansas City

MISSOURI

St. Louis

KENTUCKY

Nashville

TENNESSEE

Memphis

ARKANSAS

Little Rock

Cincinnati

Washington D.C.

W.V.

VIRGINIA

Richmond

Raleigh

NORTH CAROLINA

Charlotte

Columbia

SOUTH CAROLINA

Charleston

DE.

MD.

Bermuda (U.K.)

NORTH ATLANTIC OCEAN

PACIFIC OCEAN

Guadalupe (Mex.)

El Paso

Ciudad Juárez

TEXAS

Dallas-Ft. Worth

Austin

Houston

San Antonio

Baton Rouge

LOUISIANA

New Orleans

MISSISSIPPI

Jackson

ALABAMA

Montgomery

Birmingham

GEORGIA

Atlanta

Tallahassee

Jacksonville

FLORIDA

Orlando

Tampa-St. Petersburg

MIAMI

Nassau

BAHAMAS

Turks & Caicos Is. (U.K.)

Rio Grande

Tropic of Cancer

Hermosillo

Culiacán

Monterrey

Torreón

MEXICO

San Luis Potosí

Gulf of Mexico

Florida Str.

Havana

CUBA

Cayman Is. (U.K.)

JAMAICA

Kingston

HAITI

Port-au-Prince

DOMINICAN REP.

Santo Domingo

San Juan

PUERTO RICO (U.S.A.)

Revilla Gigedo Is. (Mex.)

León

Guadalajara

MÉXICO

Toluca

Puebla

Mérida

Acapulco

Belmopan

BELIZE

Caribbean Sea

GUATEMALA

Guatemala

HONDURAS

Tegucigalpa

San Salvador

EL SALVADOR

NICARAGUA

Managua

L. Nicaragua

Barranquilla

Maracaibo

VENEZUELA

COSTA RICA

San José

Panamá

PANAMA

COLOMBIA

Medellín

South America

Projection: Bonne

West from Greenwich

7 ■ MÉXICO Capital Cities **8** **9** **10** **11** **12**

COPYRIGHT PHILIP'S

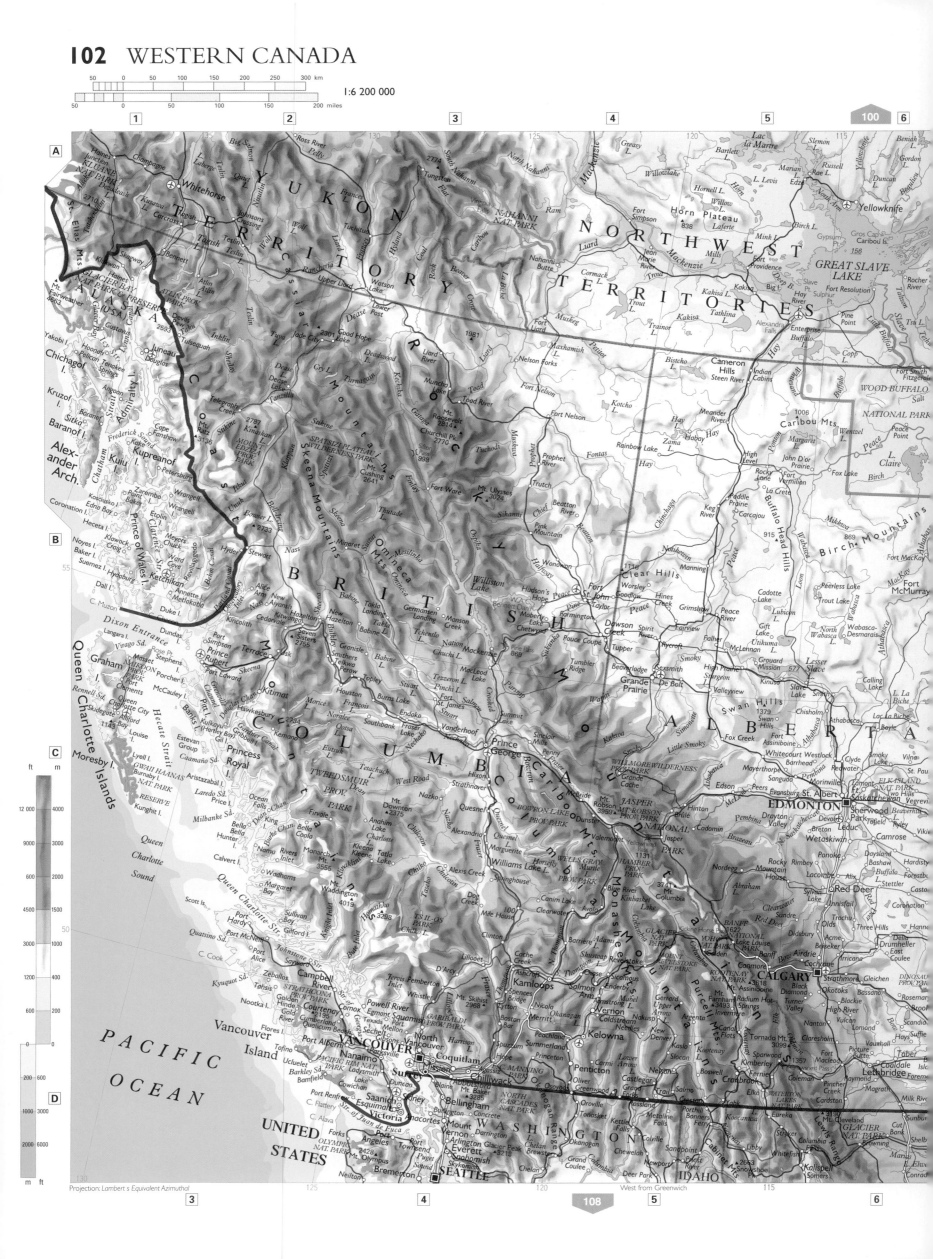

50 0 50 100 150 200 250 300 km
1:6 200 000
50 0 50 100 150 200 miles

| 1 | 2 | 3 | 4 | 5 | 100 | 6 |

PACIFIC OCEAN

UNITED STATES

YUKON TERRITORY

NORTHWEST TERRITORIES

GREAT SLAVE LAKE

ALASKA

Alexander Arch.

Queen Charlotte Islands

BRITISH COLUMBIA

ALBERTA

WASHINGTON

IDAHO

Vancouver Island

Whitehorse

Yellowknife

EDMONTON

CALGARY

VANCOUVER

Victoria

SEATTLE

WOOD BUFFALO NATIONAL PARK

KLUANE NAT. PARK

GLACIER BAY NAT. PARK & PRESERVE

NAHANNI NAT. PARK

Fort McMurray

Prince George

Kamloops

Kelowna

Projection: Lambert's Equivalent Azimuthal

West from Greenwich

| 3 | 4 | 120 | 108 | 5 | 6 |

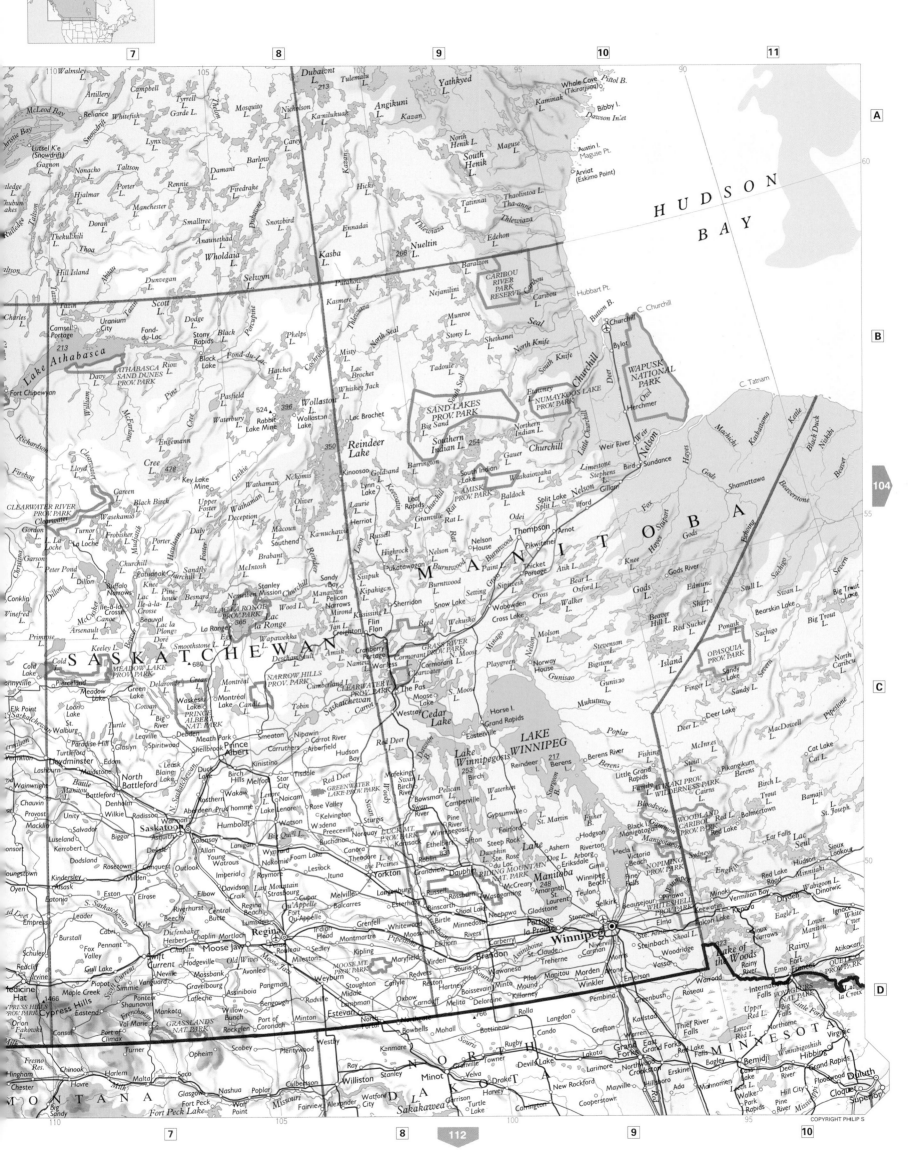

COPYRIGHT PHILIP'S

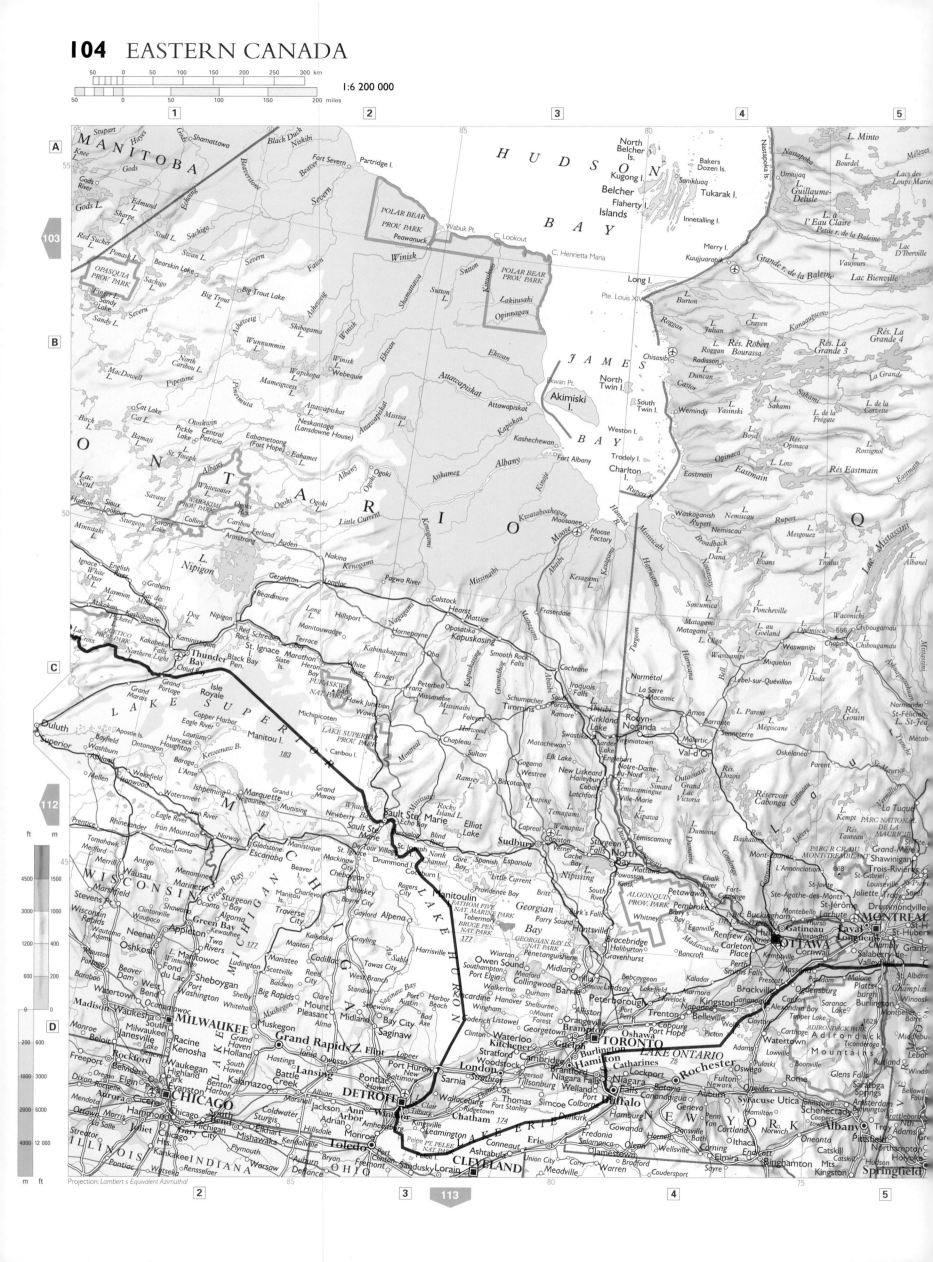

50 0 50 100 150 200 250 300 km
50 0 50 100 150 200 miles

1:6 200 000

Projection: Lambert's Equivalent Azimuthal

LABRADOR
SEA

NEWFOUNDLAND &

Labrador

LABRADOR

QUÉBEC

Newfoundland

Smallwood Reservoir

Happy Valley-
Goose Bay

Str. of Belle Isle

Long Range Mts.

Corner Brook

Gander

Île d'Anticosti

GULF OF

ST. LAWRENCE

Sept-Îles

St. John's

Pén. de la Gaspésie

Gaspé

NEW
BRUNSWICK

PRINCE EDWARD
ISLAND

Cape Breton
Island

ST-PIERRE-
ET-MIQUELON
(France)

St-Pierre

Cabot Strait

Québec

MAINE

NOVA
SCOTIA

Fredericton

Moncton

Charlottetown

Sydney

Saint
John

Halifax

Dartmouth

Fundy
Bay

ATLANTIC

Sable I.
(Nova Scotia)

UNITED

STATES

BOSTON

OCEAN

B

C

D

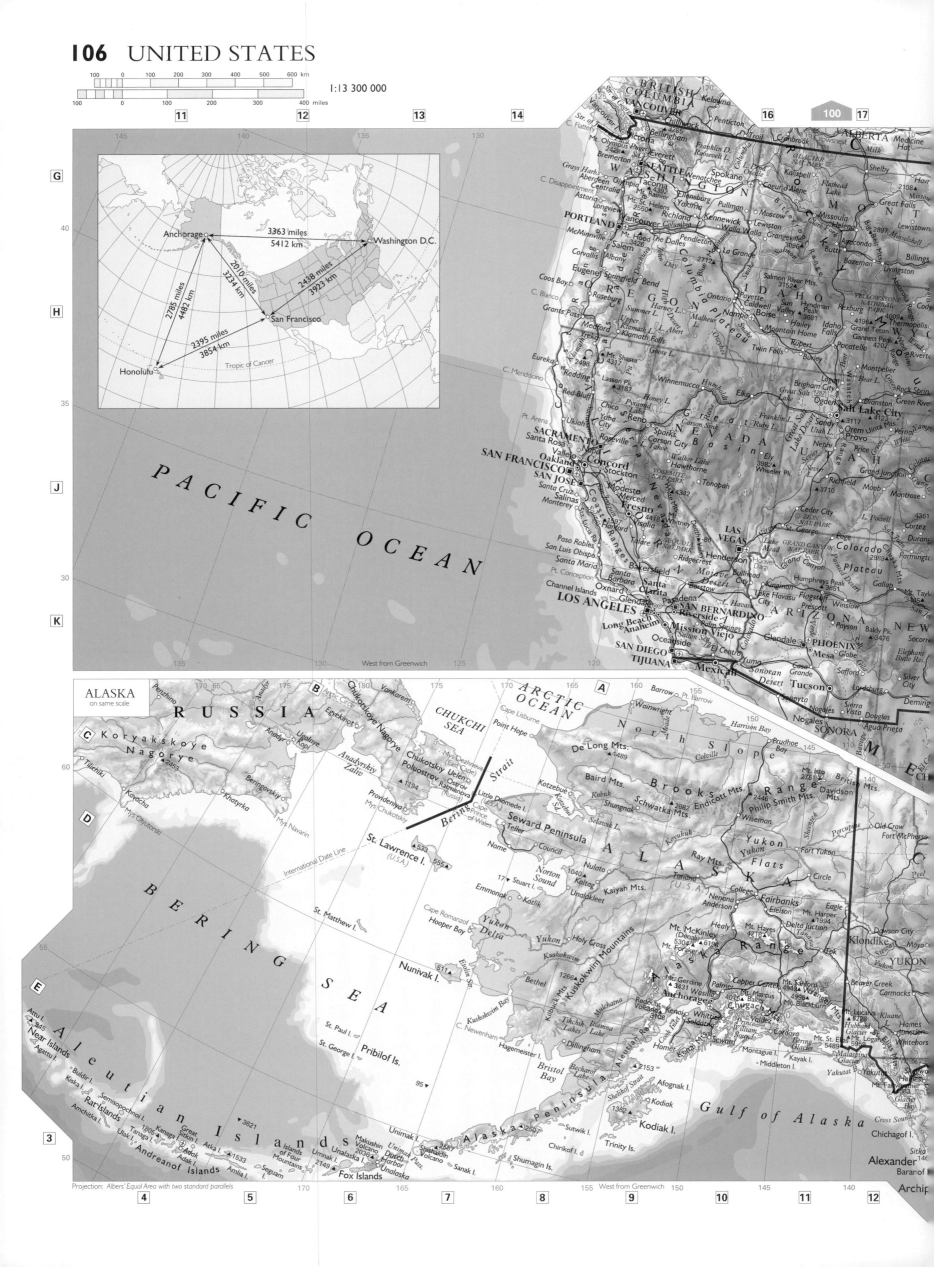

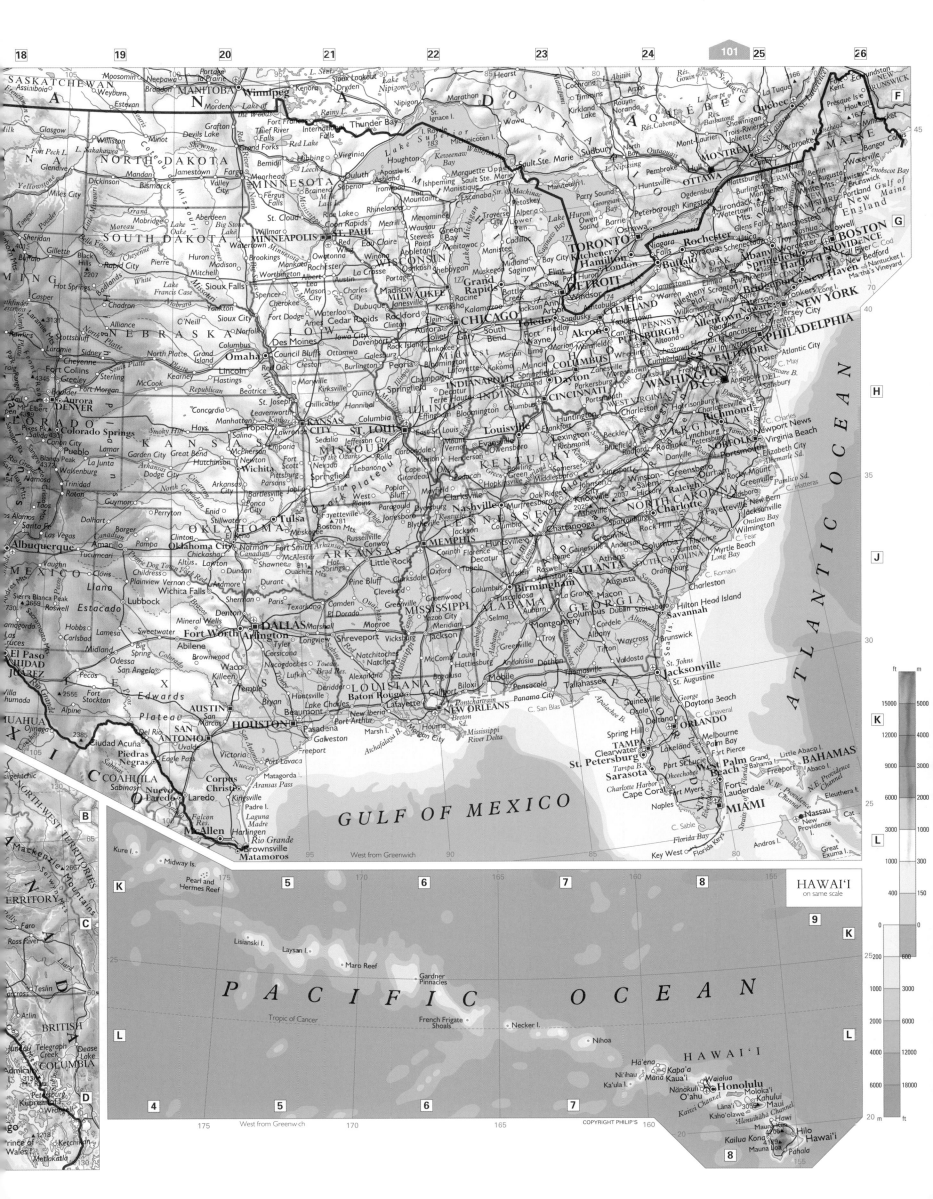

1:6 250 000

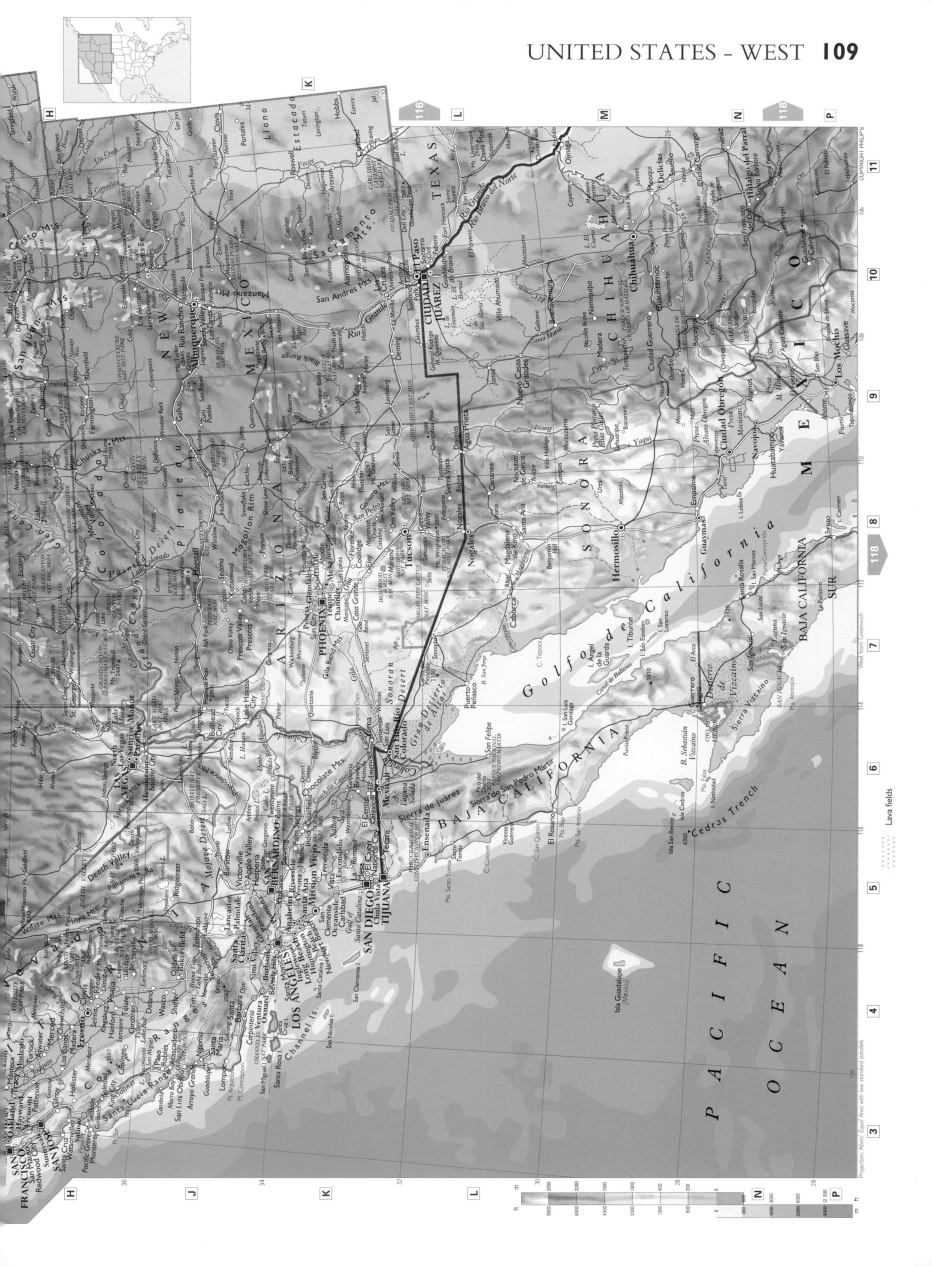

1:2 200 000

WESTERN WASHINGTON REGION
on same scale

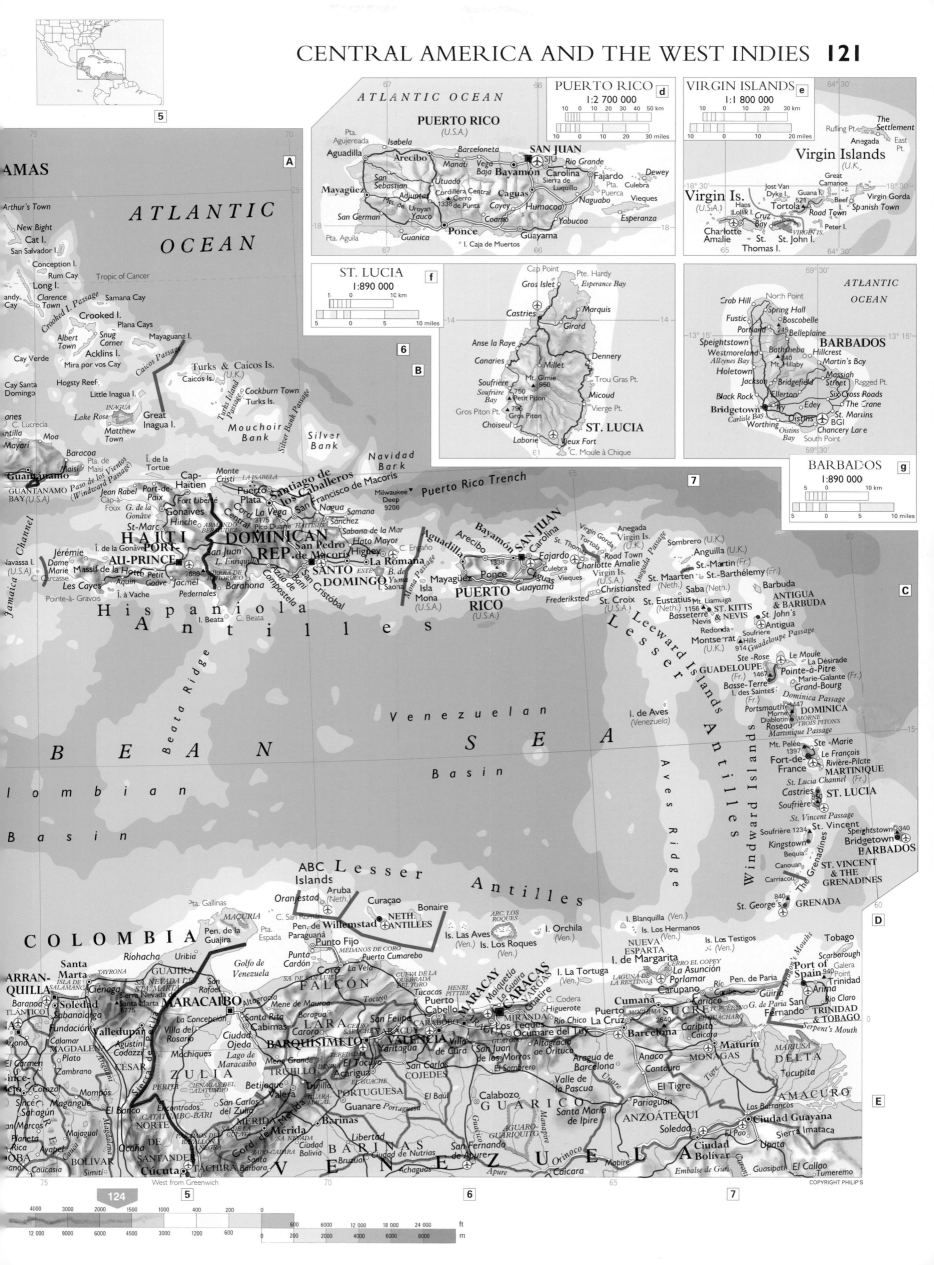

100 0 200 400 600 800 1000 1200 1400 km
100 0 200 400 600 800 1000 miles

1:31 100 000

1 **2** **3** **4** **5** **6** **7**

Tropic of Cancer

A

Bahamas
Cuba West
Greater Indies
Turks & Caicos Is.
Hispaniola
Yucatán Channel
Gulf of Campeche
Yucatán Peninsula
9200
▲3175 Puerto Rico
Leeward Islands
Jamaica Guadeloupe
Dominica
Martinique
Isthmus of Tehuantepec
G. de Honduras
Central America
4093▲
Antilles
C. Gracias a Dios
Caribbean Sea
St. Lucia
Barbados
St. Vincent
Grenada
Guatemala Trench
Coco
L. Nicaragua
Guajira Peninsula
G. of Venezuela
Lesser Antilles
Margarita Tobago
Trinidad

B

Panama Canal
3819▲ Isthmus of Panama
G. of Darién
▲5775
Sierra Nevada de Santa Marta
Curaçao
Paraguana Peninsula
L. Maracaibo
C. de la Aguja
C. de Mérida
Cordillera Occidental
Cordillera Central
Cordillera Oriental
Cauca
Magdalena
Apure
Meta
Llanos
Orinoco
Embalse de Guri
Angel Falls
Cuyuni
Guiana Highlands
Mt. Roraima ▲2772
Sierra Pacaraima
Casiquiare
Maroni
Oyapock
Serra Tumucumaque
Devil's I.
C. Orange
I. de Maracá

C

I. del Coco
I. de Malpelo
Buenaventura B.
C. de San Francisco
Gulf of Panama
Guaviare
Vaupés
Pico de Neblina 3014
Negro
Branco
Serra
Represa de Balbina
Marajó I.
Marajó B.
Equator
San Marcos B.

D

Galapagos Is.
1707▲
G. of Guayaquil
Pta. Pariñas
Pta. Negra
Cotopaxi ▲5897
Chimborazo 6267
Sechura Desert
Marañón
Napo
Ucayali
Putumayo
Caquetá
Japurá
Amazon
Basin
Juruá
Purus
Madeira
Amazon
Roosevelt
Aripuanã
Tapajós
Xingu
Madre de Dios
Sa. dos Parecis
Guaporé
Tocantins
Araguaia
Tocantins
Catinga
C. de São Roque
Plat. of Borborema
R. Branco
Huascarán ▲6768
Montaña
Perú-Chile Trench

E

PACIFIC
Nevado Coropuna ▲6425
Chincha Alta
L. Titicaca 3812
Nevado Ancohuma ▲6550
Altiplano (Bolivian Plateau)
L. de Poopó
Salar de Uyuni
Chaco Boreal
Plateau of Mato Grosso
Iauaretê
Paraguay
Araguaia
Paranaíba
Grande
São Francisco
Serra do Espinhaço
Brazilian Highlands
Serra Geral
Abrolhos Bank
B. de Todos os Santos
▲2890
Pico da Bandeira
Serra da Mantiqueira
C. de São Tomé

F

OCEAN
Tropic of Capricorn
San Félix
San Ambrosio
Pta. Tetas
8050▼
Atacama Desert
Cerro Ojos del Salado ▲6863
Monte Pissis ▲6779
Cerro Bonete ▲6872
Salinas Grandes
Cordillera de Catamarca
Dulce
Salado
Chaco Austral
Gran Chaco
Pilcomayo
Bermejo
Rep. de Itaipú
Iguaçu Falls
Iguaçu
Serra do Mar
Campos
Paraná
I. de São Sebastião
C. Frio
C. Santa Marta Grande

G

Arch. de Juan Fernández
Robinson Crusoe
Pta. Lengua da Vaca
Cerro Mercedario ▲6770
Mt. Aconcagua ▲6962
Sa. de Córdoba
L. Mar Chiquita
Pampas
Salado
Negro
Uruguay
Paraná
Entre Ríos
Río de la Plata
B. Samborombón
C. San Antonio
L. Mirim
L. dos Patos
SOUTH ATLANTIC

H

Chile Rise
Chiloé I.
Chonos Archipelago
Mte. San Valentín ▲4058
Taitao Peninsula
L. Buenos Aires
G. of Penas
Wellington I.
Madre de Dios I.
L. Argentino
Magellan's Str.
Riesco I.
Santa Inés I.
Cockburn Chan.
Beagle Chan.
C. Horn
Tierra del Fuego
Staten I.
West Falkland
East Falkland
Falkland Is.
6212▼
▼705
South Georgia
Mt. Paget ▲2937
Patagonia
Colorado
Bahía Blanca
San Matías G.
Valdés Peninsula
-40▼
Limay
Chubut
Chico
G. of San Jorge
C. Tres Puntas
L. del Carbón -105
L. Viedma
Argentine Abyssal Plain
NORTH ATLANTIC OCEAN
SOUTH ATLANTIC OCEAN

ft m
12000 4000
9000 3000
6000 2000
3000 1000
1500 500
600 200
0 0
200 600
1000 3000
2000 6000
4000 12000
6000 18000
8000 24000
m ft

1:31 100 000

100 0   200   400   600   800   1000 1200 1400 km

100 0   200   400   600   800   1000 miles

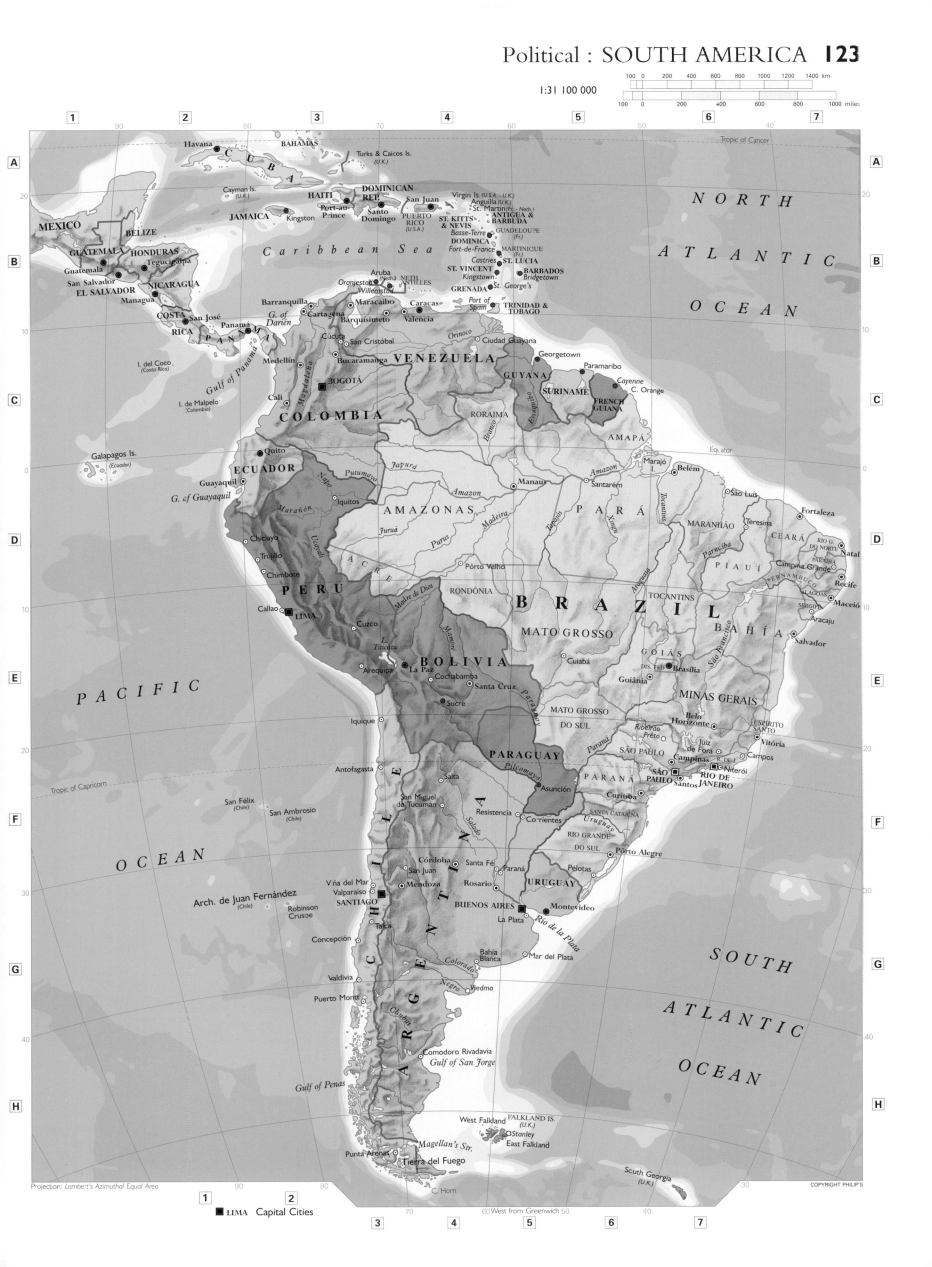

NORTH

ATLANTIC

OCEAN

Tropic of Cancer

Havana
BAHAMAS
CUBA
Turks & Caicos Is.
(U.K.)
Cayman Is.
(U.K.)
HAITI
DOMINICAN
REP.
San Juan
Virgin Is. (U.S.A.–U.K.)
Anguilla (U.K.)
St. Martin (Fr.– Neth.)
MEXICO
Kingston
Port-au-Prince
Santo
Domingo
PUERTO
RICO
(U.S.A.)
ST. KITTS
& NEVIS
ANTIGUA &
BARBUDA
GUADELOUPE
(Fr.)
JAMAICA
Basse-Terre
DOMINICA
BELIZE
Fort-de-France
MARTINIQUE
(Fr.)
GUATEMALA
HONDURAS
Caribbean Sea
Castries
ST. LUCIA
Guatemala
Tegucigalpa
ST. VINCENT
Kingstown
BARBADOS
Bridgetown
San Salvador
NICARAGUA
Aruba
(Neth.)
NETH.
ANTILLES
GRENADA
St. George's
EL SALVADOR
Oranjestad
Willemstad
Port of
Spain
TRINIDAD &
TOBAGO
Managua
COSTA
San José
Barranquilla
Maracaibo
Caracas
RICA
G. of
Darién
Cartagena
Valencia
Panamá
Barquisimeto
PANAMA
Cúcuta
San Cristóbal
Orinoco
Ciudad Guayana
I. del Coco
(Costa Rica)
Gulf of Panama
Medellín
Bucaramanga
VENEZUELA
Georgetown
Paramaribo
Cayenne
C. Orange
I. de Malpelo
(Colombia)
Cali
BOGOTÁ
GUYANA
SURINAME
FRENCH
GUIANA
COLOMBIA
RORAIMA
Esequibo
AMAPÁ
Galapagos Is.
(Ecuador)
Quito
Branco
Equator
ECUADOR
Japurá
Amazon
Marajó
I.
Belém
Guayaquil
Iquitos
Putumayo
Manaus
Santarém
São Luís
G. of Guayaquil
Napo
Marañón
Amazon
Fortaleza
Chiclayo
AMAZONAS
Madeira
PARÁ
MARANHÃO
CEARÁ
Juruá
Tapajós
Xingu
Teresina
RIO G.
DO NORTE
Natal
Trujillo
Ucayali
Purus
Tocantins
PIAUÍ
Campina Grande
Chimbote
ACRE
Pôrto Velho
PARAÍBA
Recife
PERU
RONDÔNIA
Araguaia
São Francisco
PERNAMBUCO
Callao
LIMA
Madre de Dios
B R A Z I L
TOCANTINS
ALAGOAS
Maceió
Cuzco
Mamoré
MATO GROSSO
BAHIA
SERGIPE
Aracaju
L.
Titicaca
Cuiabá
GOIÁS
DIS. FED.
Salvador
Arequipa
BOLIVIA
Brasília
La Paz
Cochabamba
Goiânia
MINAS GERAIS
Santa Cruz
Paraguay
ESPÍRITO
SANTO
Sucre
MATO GROSSO
DO SUL
Ribeirão
Prêto
Belo
Horizonte
Vitória
Iquique
Paraná
SÃO PAULO
Juiz
de Fora
Campos
Antofagasta
Salta
Campinas
R. DE J.
Niterói
PARAGUAY
Pilcomayo
SÃO
PAULO
RIO DE
JANEIRO
Tropic of Capricorn
San Félix
(Chile)
San Ambrosio
(Chile)
Asunción
PARANÁ
Santos
San Miguel
de Tucumán
Resistencia
Corrientes
SANTA CATARINA
Curitiba
Saladó
Uruguay
RIO GRANDE
DO SUL
Córdoba
Pôrto Alegre
Arch. de Juan Fernández
(Chile)
San Juan
Santa Fé
Paraná
Pelotas
Robinson
Crusoe
Viña del Mar
Mendoza
Rosario
URUGUAY
Valparaíso
SANTIAGO
Montevideo
BUENOS AIRES
Talca
La Plata
Río de la Plata
Concepción
Bahía
Blanca
Colorado
Mar del Plata
SOUTH
Valdivia
Negro
ATLANTIC
Puerto Montt
Viedma
OCEAN
Chubut
Comodoro Rivadavia
Gulf of San Jorge
Gulf of Penas
West Falkland
FALKLAND IS.
(U.K.)
Stanley
East Falkland
Magellan's Str.
Punta Arenas
Tierra del Fuego
South Georgia
(U.K.)
C. Horn

PACIFIC

OCEAN

CHILE

ARGENTINA

Projection: Lambert's Azimuthal Equal Area

COPYRIGHT PHILIP'S

■ LIMA Capital Cities

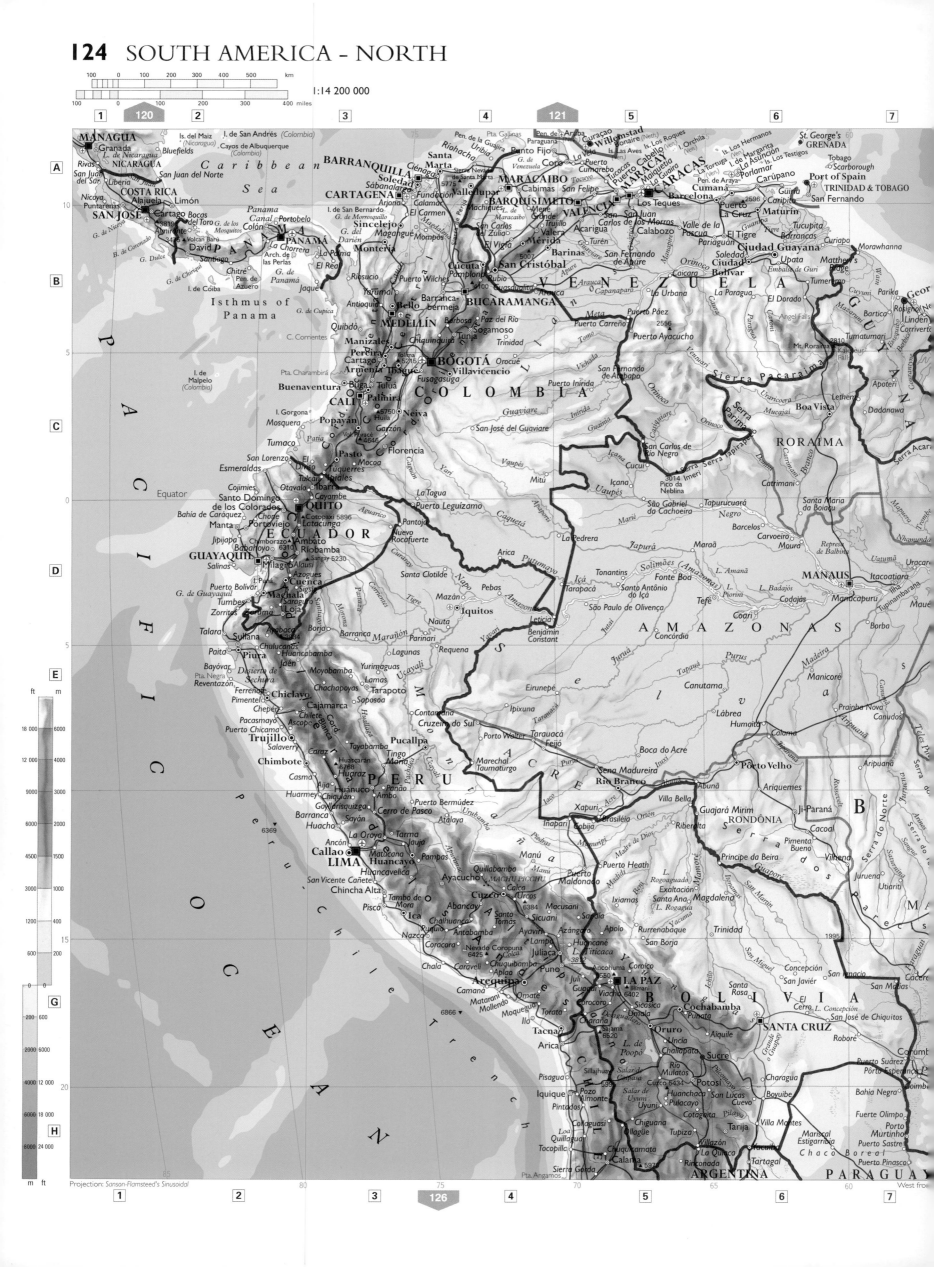

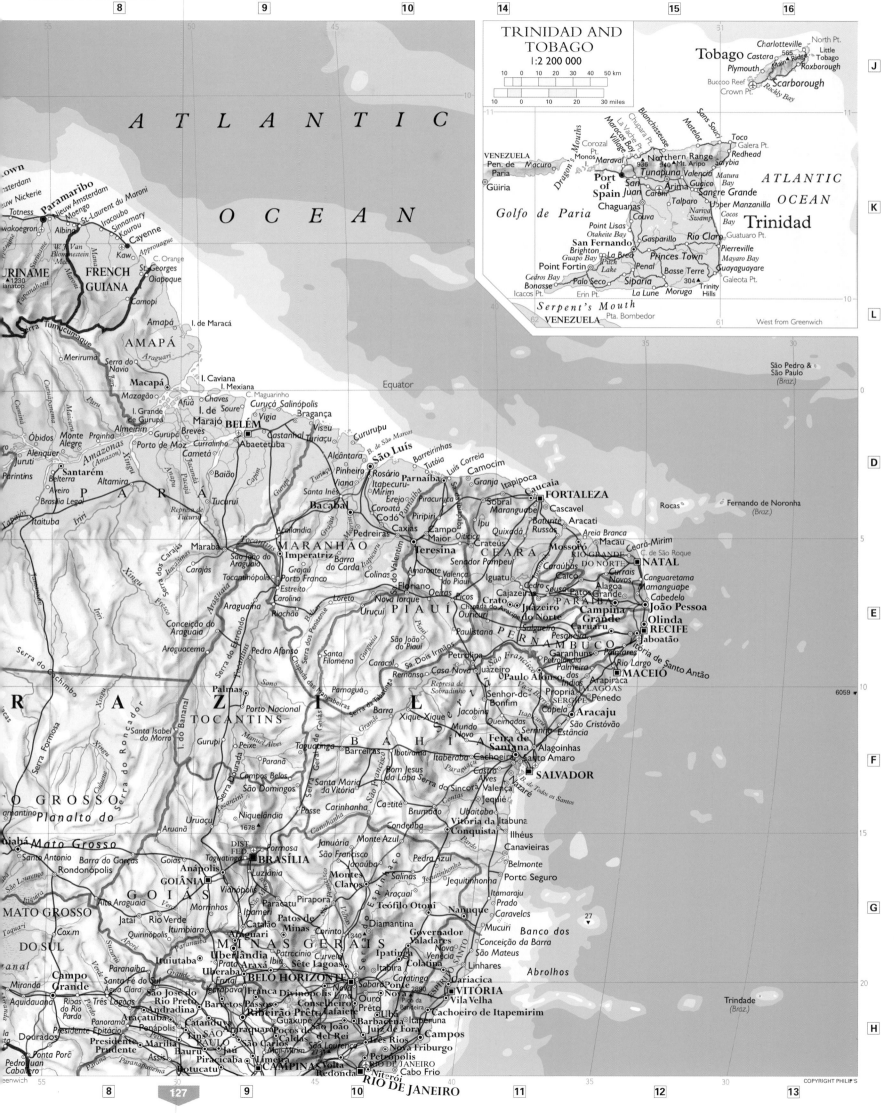

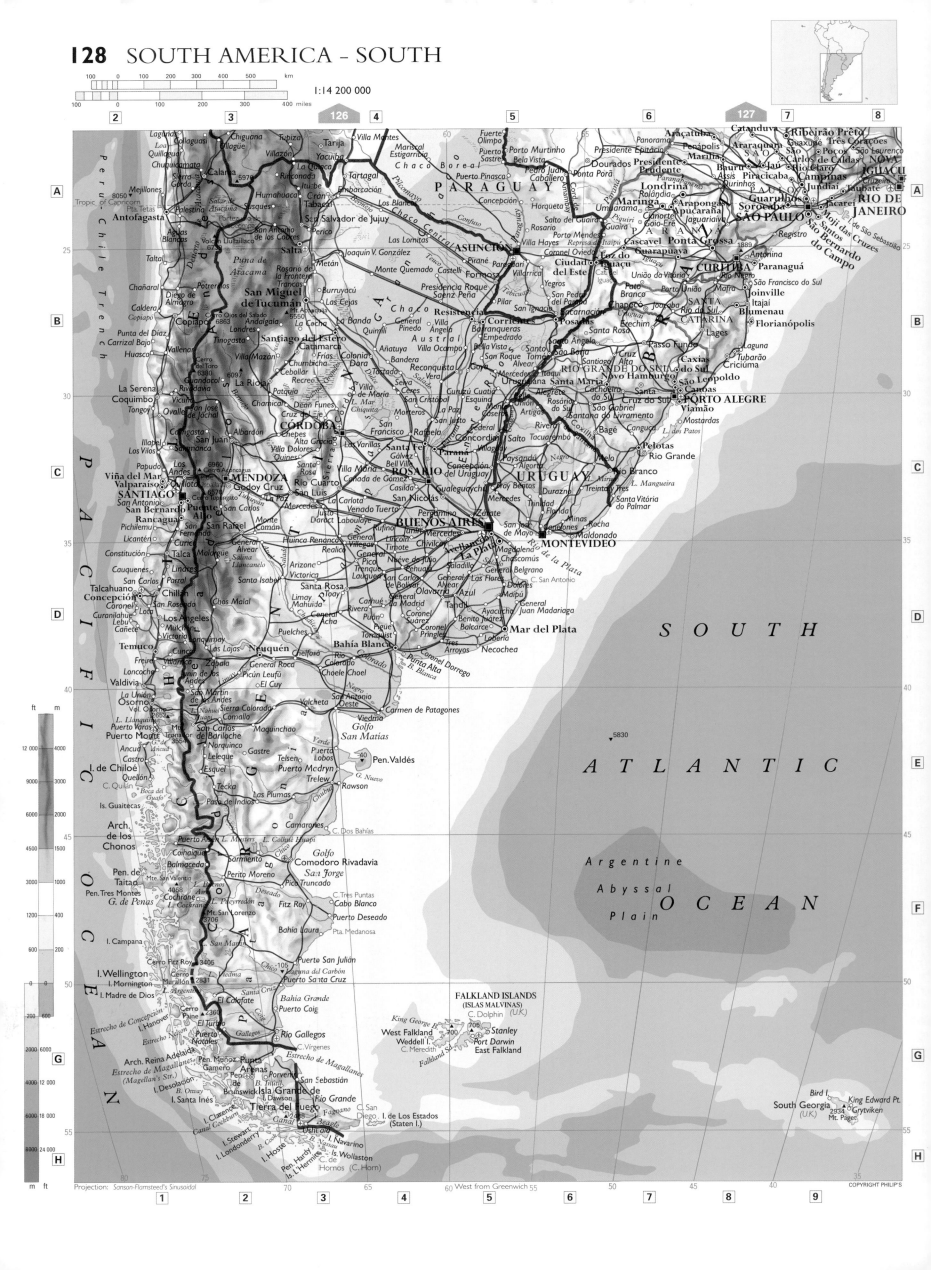

1:14 200 000

Projection: Sanson-Flamsteed's Sinusoidal

West from Greenwich

COPYRIGHT PHILIP'S

INDEX TO WORLD MAPS

How to use the index

The index contains the names of all the principal places and features shown on the World Maps. Each name is followed by an additional entry in italics giving the country or region within which it is located. The alphabetical order of names composed of two or more words is governed primarily by the first word and then by the second. This is an example of the rule:

Miquelon *St-P. & M.* **105 C8**
Mir *Niger* **83 C7**
Mīr Kūh *Iran* **71 E8**
Mīr Shahdād *Iran* **71 E8**
Mira *Italy* **41 C9**

Physical features composed of a proper name (Erie) and a description (Lake) are positioned alphabetically by the proper name. The description is positioned after the proper name and is usually abbreviated:

Erie, L. *N. Amer.* **114 D4**

Where a description forms part of a settlement or administrative name however, it is always written in full and put in its true alphabetic position:

Mount Morris *U.S.A.* **114 D7**

Names beginning with M' and Mc are indexed as if they were spelled Mac. Names beginning St. are alphabetised under Saint, but Sankt, Sint, Sant', Santa and San are all spelt in full and are alphabetised accordingly. If the same place name occurs two or more times in the index and all are in the same country, each is followed by the name of the administrative subdivision in which it is located. For example:

Jackson *Ky., U.S.A.* **113 G12**
Jackson *Mich., U.S.A.* **113 D11**
Jackson *Minn., U.S.A.* **112 D6**

The number in bold type which follows each name in the index refers to the number of the map page where that feature or place will be found. This is usually the largest scale at which the place or feature appears.

The letter and figure which are in bold type immediately after the page number give the grid square on the map page, within which the feature is situated. The letter represents the latitude and the figure the longitude. A lower case letter immediately after the page number refers to an inset map on that page.

In some cases the feature itself may fall within the specified square, while the name is outside. This is usually the case only with features which are larger than a grid square.

Rivers are indexed to their mouths or confluences, and carry the symbol → after their names. The following symbols are also used in the index: ■ country, ☑ overseas territory or dependency, ☐ first order administrative area, △ national park, ◠ other park (provincial park, nature reserve or game reserve), ✈ (LHR) principal airport (and location identifier), ◎ aboriginal land.

How to pronounce place names

English-speaking people usually have no difficulty in reading and pronouncing correctly English place names. However, foreign place name pronunciations may present many problems. Such problems can be minimised by following some simple rules. However, these rules cannot be applied to all situations, and there will be many exceptions.

1. In general, stress each syllable equally, unless your experience suggests otherwise.
2. Pronounce the letter 'a' as a broad 'a' as in 'arm'.
3. Pronounce the letter 'e' as a short 'e' as in 'elm'.
4. Pronounce the letter 'i' as a cross between a short 'i' and long 'e', as the two 'i's in 'California'.
5. Pronounce the letter 'o' as an intermediate 'o' as in 'soft'.
6. Pronounce the letter 'u' as an intermediate 'u' as in 'sure'.
7. Pronounce consonants hard, except in the Romance-language areas where 'g's are likely to be pronounced softly like 'j' in 'jam'. 'j' itself may be pronounced as 'y'; and 'x's may be pronounced as 'h'.
8. For names in mainland China, pronounce 'q' like the 'ch' in 'chin', 'x' like the 'sh' in 'she', 'zh' like the 'j' in 'jam', and 'z' as if it were spelled 'dz'. In general pronounce 'a' as in 'father', 'e' as in 'but', 'i' as in 'keep', 'o' as in 'or', and 'u' as in 'rule'.

Moreover, English has no diacritical marks (accent and pronunciation signs), although some languages do. The following is a brief and general guide to the pronunciation of those most frequently used in the principal Western European languages.

		Pronunciation as in
French	é	day and shows that the e is to be pronounced; e.g. Orléans.
	è	mare
	̂	used over any vowel and does not affect pronunciation; shows contraction of the name, usually omission of 's' following a vowel.
	ç	's' before 'a', 'o' and 'u'.
	ë, ï, ü	over 'e', 'i' and 'u' when they are used with another vowel and shows that each is to be pronounced.
German	ä	fate
	ö	fur
	ü	no English equivalent; like French 'tu'
Italian	à, é	over vowels and indicates stress.
Portuguese	ã, õ	vowels pronounced nasally.
	ç	boss
	á	shows stress
	ô	shows that a vowel has an 'i' or 'u' sound combined with it.
Spanish	ñ	canyon
	ü	pronounced as w and separately from adjoining vowels.
	á	usually indicates that this is a stressed vowel.

Abbreviations

A.C.T. – Australian Capital Territory
A.R. – Autonomous Region
Afghan. – Afghanistan
Afr. – Africa
Ala. – Alabama
Alta. – Alberta
Amer. – America(n)
Arch. – Archipelago
Ariz. – Arizona
Ark. – Arkansas
Atl. Oc. – Atlantic Ocean
B. – Baie, Bahía, Bay, Bucht, Bugt
B.C. – British Columbia
Bangla. – Bangladesh
Barr. – Barrage
Bos.-H. – Bosnia-Herzegovina
C. – Cabo, Cap, Cape, Coast
C.A.R. – Central African Republic
C. Prov. – Cape Province
Calif. – California
Cat. – Catarata
Cent. – Central
Chan. – Channel
Colo. – Colorado
Conn. – Connecticut
Cord. – Cordillera
Cr. – Creek
Czech. – Czech Republic
D.C. – District of Columbia
Del. – Delaware
Dem. – Democratic
Dep. – Dependency
Des. – Desert
Dét. – Détroit
Dist. – District
Dj. – Djebel
Domin. – Dominica
Dom. Rep. – Dominican Republic
E. – East

E. Salv. – El Salvador
Eq. Guin. – Equatorial Guinea
Est. – Estrecho
Falk. Is. – Falkland Is.
Fd. – Fjord
Fla. – Florida
Fr. – French
G. – Golfe, Golfo, Gulf, Guba, Gebel
Ga. – Georgia
Gt. – Great, Greater
Guinea-Biss. – Guinea-Bissau
H.K. – Hong Kong
H.P. – Himachal Pradesh
Hants. – Hampshire
Harb. – Harbor, Harbour
Hd. – Head
Hts. – Heights
I.(s). – Île, Ilha, Insel, Isla, Island, Isle
Ill. – Illinois
Ind. – Indiana
Ind. Oc. – Indian Ocean
Ivory C. – Ivory Coast
J. – Jabal, Jebel
Jaz. – Jazīrah
Junc. – Junction
K. – Kap, Kapp
Kans. – Kansas
Kep. – Kepulauan
Ky. – Kentucky
L. – Lac, Lacul, Lago, Lagoa, Lake, Limni, Loch, Lough
La. – Louisiana
Ld. – Land
Liech. – Liechtenstein
Lux. – Luxembourg
Mad. P. – Madhya Pradesh
Madag. – Madagascar
Man. – Manitoba

Mass. – Massachusetts
Md. – Maryland
Me. – Maine
Medit. S. – Mediterranean Sea
Mich. – Michigan
Minn. – Minnesota
Miss. – Mississippi
Mo. – Missouri
Mont. – Montana
Mozam. – Mozambique
Mt.(s) – Mont, Montaña, Mountain
Mte. – Monte
Mti. – Monti
N. – Nord, Norte, North, Northern, Nouveau
N.B. – New Brunswick
N.C. – North Carolina
N. Cal. – New Caledonia
N. Dak. – North Dakota
N.H. – New Hampshire
N.I. – North Island
N.J. – New Jersey
N. Mex. – New Mexico
N.S. – Nova Scotia
N.S.W. – New South Wales
N.W.T. – North West Territory
N.Y. – New York
N.Z. – New Zealand
Nac. – Nacional
Nat. – National
Nebr. – Nebraska
Neths. – Netherlands
Nev. – Nevada
Nfld. & L. – Newfoundland and Labrador
Nic. – Nicaragua
O. – Oued, Ouadi
Occ. – Occidentale
Okla. – Oklahoma

Ont. – Ontario
Or. – Orientale
Oreg. – Oregon
Os. – Ostrov
Oz. – Ozero
P. – Pass, Passo, Pasul, Pulau
P.E.I. – Prince Edward Island
Pa. – Pennsylvania
Pac. Oc. – Pacific Ocean
Papua N.G. – Papua New Guinea
Pass. – Passage
Peg. – Pegunungan
Pen. – Peninsula, Péninsule
Phil. – Philippines
Pk. – Peak
Plat. – Plateau
Prov. – Province, Provincial
Pt. – Point
Pta. – Ponta, Punta
Pte. – Pointe
Qué. – Québec
Queens. – Queensland
R. – Rio, River
R.I. – Rhode Island
Ra. – Range
Raj. – Rajasthan
Recr. – Recreational, Récréatif
Reg. – Region
Rep. – Republic
Res. – Reserve, Reservoir
Rhld-Pfz. – Rheinland-Pfalz
S. – South, Southern, Sur
Si. Arabia – Saudi Arabia
S.C. – South Carolina
S. Dak. – South Dakota
S.I. – South Island
S. Leone – Sierra Leone
Sa. – Serra, Sierra
Sask. – Saskatchewan

Scot. – Scotland
Sd. – Sound
Sev. – Severnaya
Sib. – Siberia
Sprs. – Springs
St. – Saint
Sta. – Santa
Ste. – Sainte
Sto. – Santo
Str. – Strait, Stretto
Switz. – Switzerland
Tas. – Tasmania
Tenn. – Tennessee
Terr. – Territory, Territoire
Tex. – Texas
Tg. – Tanjung
Trin. & Tob. – Trinidad & Tobago
U.A.E. – United Arab Emirates
U.K. – United Kingdom
U.S.A. – United States of America
Ut. P. – Uttar Pradesh
Va. – Virginia
Vdkhr. – Vodokhranilishche
Vdskh. – Vodoskhovyshche
Vf. – Vîrful
Vic. – Victoria
Vol. – Volcano
Vt. – Vermont
W. – Wadi, West
W. Va. – West Virginia
Wall. & F. Is. – Wallis and Futuna Is.
Wash. – Washington
Wis. – Wisconsin
Wlkp. – Wielkopolski
Wyo. – Wyoming
Yorks. – Yorkshire

A

A 'Âli an Nîl □ *Sudan* **81** F3
A Baña *Spain* **36** C2
A Cañiza *Spain* **36** C2
A Coruña *Spain* **36** B2
A Coruña □ *Spain* **36** B2
A Cruz do Incio *Spain* **36** C3
A Estrada *Spain* **36** C2
A Fonsagrada *Spain* **36** B3
A Guarda *Spain* **36** D2
A Gudiña *Spain* **36** C3
A Pobre *Spain* **36** C3
A Ramallosa *Spain* **36** C2
A Rúa *Spain* **36** C3
A Serra de Outes *Spain* **36** C2
Aabenraa *Denmark* **11** J3
Aabybro *Denmark* **11** G3
Aachen *Germany* **24** E2
Aalborg *Denmark* **11** G3
Aalborg Bugt *Denmark* **11** H4
Aalen *Germany* **25** G6
Aalestrup *Denmark* **11** H3
Aalst *Belgium* **17** D4
Aalten *Neths.* **17** C6
Aalter *Belgium* **17** C3
Äänekoski *Finland* **8** E21
Aarau *Switz.* **25** H4
Aarberg *Switz.* **25** H3
Aare → *Switz.* **25** H4
Aargau □ *Switz.* **25** H4
Aarhus = Århus *Denmark* **11** H4
Aars *Denmark* **11** H3
Aarschot *Belgium* **17** D4
Aba *China* **58** A3
Aba *Dem. Rep. of the Congo* **86** B3
Aba *Nigeria* **83** D6
Âbâ, Jazīrat *Sudan* **81** E3
Abaco I. *Bahamas* **120** A4
Abadab, J. *Sudan* **80** D4
Ābādān *Iran* **71** D6
Abade *Ethiopia* **81** F4
Ābādeh *Iran* **71** D7
Abadín *Spain* **36** B3
Abadla *Algeria* **78** B5
Abaetetuba *Brazil* **125** D9
Abagnar Qi = Xilinhot *China* **56** C9
Abah, Tanjung *Indonesia* **63** K18
Abai *Paraguay* **127** B4
Abak *Nigeria* **83** E6
Abakaliki *Nigeria* **83** D6
Abakan *Russia* **53** D10
Abala *Niger* **83** C5
Abalak *Niger* **83** B6
Abalemma *Niger* **83** B6
Abana *Turkey* **72** B6
Abancay *Peru* **124** F4
Abano Terme *Italy* **41** C8
Abarán *Spain* **39** G3
Abariringa *Kiribati* **96** H10
Abarqū *Iran* **71** D7
Abasha *Georgia* **35** J6
Abashiri *Japan* **54** B12
Abashiri-Wan *Japan* **54** C12
Abaújszántó *Hungary* **28** B6
Abava → *Latvia* **30** A8
Ābay = Nîl el Azraq → *Sudan* **81** D3
Abay *Kazakhstan* **52** E8
Abaya, L. *Ethiopia* **81** F4
Abaza *Russia* **52** D9
Abbadia di Fiastra △ *Italy* **41** E10
Abbadia San Salvatore *Italy* **41** F8
'Abbāsābād *Iran* **71** C8
Abbay = Nîl el Azraq → *Sudan* **81** D3
Abbaye, Pt. *U.S.A.* **112** B9
Abbé, L. *Ethiopia* **81** E5
Abbeville *France* **19** B8
Abbeville *Ala., U.S.A.* **117** F12
Abbeville *La., U.S.A.* **116** G8
Abbeville *S.C., U.S.A.* **117** D13
Abbeyfeale *Ireland* **12** D2
Abbiategrasso *Italy* **40** C5
Abbot Ice Shelf *Antarctica* **5** D16
Abbotsford *Canada* **102** D4
Abbottabad *Pakistan* **68** B5
ABC Islands = Netherlands Antilles ☑ *W. Indies* **124** A5
Abd al Kūrī *Yemen* **75** E5
Ābdānān *Iran* **73** F12
Ābdar *Iran* **71** D7
'Abdolābād *Iran* **71** C8
Abdulpur *Bangla.* **69** G13
Abéché *Chad* **79** F10
Abejar *Spain* **38** D2
Åbenrå = Aabenraa *Denmark* **11** J3
Abensberg *Germany* **25** G7
Abeokuta *Nigeria* **83** D5
Aberaeron *U.K.* **15** E3
Aberayron = Aberaeron *U.K.* **15** E3
Aberchirder *U.K.* **13** D6
Abercorn *Australia* **95** D5
Aberdare *U.K.* **15** F4

Aberdare △ *Kenya* **86** C4
Aberdare Ra. *Kenya* **86** C4
Aberdeen *Australia* **95** E5
Aberdeen *Canada* **103** C7
Aberdeen *S. Africa* **88** E3
Aberdeen *U.K.* **13** D6
Aberdeen *Idaho, U.S.A.* **108** E7
Aberdeen *Md., U.S.A.* **113** F15
Aberdeen *Miss., U.S.A.* **117** E10
Aberdeen *S. Dak., U.S.A.* **112** C4
Aberdeen *Wash., U.S.A.* **110** D3
Aberdeen, City of □ *U.K.* **13** D6
Aberdeen L. *Canada* **100** E12
Aberdeenshire □ *U.K.* **13** D6
Aberdovey = Aberdyfi *U.K.* **15** E3
Aberdyfi *U.K.* **15** E3
Aberfeldy *U.K.* **13** E5
Aberfoyle *U.K.* **13** E4
Abergavenny *U.K.* **15** F4
Abergele *U.K.* **14** D4
Abernathy *U.S.A.* **116** E4
Abert, L. *U.S.A.* **108** E3
Aberystwyth *U.K.* **15** E3
Abhā *Si. Arabia* **80** D5
Abhar *Iran* **73** D13
Abhayapuri *India* **69** F14
Abia □ *Nigeria* **83** D6
Abide *Turkey* **47** C11
Abidiya *Sudan* **80** D3
Abidjan *Ivory C.* **82** D4
Abilene *Kans., U.S.A.* **112** F5
Abilene *Tex., U.S.A.* **116** E5
Abingdon *U.K.* **15** F6
Abingdon *U.S.A.* **113** G13
Abington Reef *Australia* **94** B4
Abitau → *Canada* **103** B7
Abitibi → *Canada* **104** B3
Abitibi, L. *Canada* **104** C4
Abiy Adi *Ethiopia* **81** E4
Abiyata-Shala △ *Ethiopia* **81** F4
Abkhaz Republic = Abkhazia □ *Georgia* **35** J5
Abkhazia □ *Georgia* **35** J5
Abminga *Australia* **95** D1
Abnûb *Egypt* **80** B3
Åbo = Turku *Finland* **32** B2
Abohar *India* **68** D6
Aboisso *Ivory C.* **82** D4
Abomey *Benin* **83** D5
Abong-Mbang *Cameroon* **84** D2
Abonnema *Nigeria* **83** E6
Abony *Hungary* **28** C5
Aboso *Ghana* **82** D4
Abou-Deïa *Chad* **79** F9
Abovian *Armenia* **35** K7
Aboyne *U.K.* **13** D6
Abra Pampa *Argentina* **126** A2
Abraham L. *Canada* **102** C5
Abrantes *Portugal* **37** F2
Abreojos, Pta. *Mexico* **118** B2
Abri *Esh Shamâliya, Sudan* **80** C3
Abri *Janub Kordofân, Sudan* **80** D2
Abrolhos, Banco dos *Brazil* **125** F11
Abrud *Romania* **28** D8
Abruzzo □ *Italy* **41** F10
Absaroka Range *U.S.A.* **108** D9
Abtenau *Austria* **26** D6
Abu *India* **68** G5
Abū al Abyad *U.A.E.* **71** E7
Abū al Khaṣīb *Iraq* **70** D5
Abū 'Alī *Si. Arabia* **71** E6
Abū 'Alī → *Lebanon* **74** A4
Abu Ballas *Egypt* **80** C2
Abu Deleiq *Sudan* **81** D3
Abu Dhabi = Abū Ẓāby *U.A.E.* **71** E7
Abu Dis *Sudan* **80** D3
Abu Dom *Sudan* **81** D3
Abū Du'ān *Syria* **73** D8
Abu el Gaïn, W. → *Egypt* **74** F2
Abu Fatma, Ras *Sudan* **80** C4
Abū Gabra *Sudan* **81** E2
Abu Ga'da, W. → *Egypt* **74** F1
Abu Gelba *Sudan* **81** E3
Abu Gubeiha *Sudan* **81** E3
Abu Habl, Khawr → *Sudan* **81** E3
Abū Ḥadrīyah *Si. Arabia* **71** E6
Abu Hamed *Sudan* **80** D3
Abu Haraz *An Nîl el Azraq, Sudan* **81** E3
Abu Haraz *El Gezira, Sudan* **81** E3
Abu Haraz *Esh Shamâliya, Sudan* **80** D3
Abû Higar *Sudan* **81** E3
Abū Kamāl *Syria* **73** E9
Abu Kebir *Egypt* **80** H7
Abu Kuleiwat *Sudan* **81** E2
Abū Madd, Ra's *Si. Arabia* **70** E3
Abu Matariq *Sudan* **81** E2
Abu Mendi *Ethiopia* **81** E4
Abū Mūsā *U.A.E.* **71** E7
Abū Qaṣr *Si. Arabia* **70** D3
Abu Qireiya *Egypt* **80** C3
Abu Qurqâs *Egypt* **80** B3
Abu Shagara, Ras *Sudan* **80** C4
Abū Shanab *Sudan* **81** E2
Abu Simbel *Egypt* **80** C3
Abū Ṣukhayr *Iraq* **73** G11
Abu Sultân *Egypt* **80** H8
Abu Tabari *Sudan* **80** D2

Abu Tig *Egypt* **80** B3
Abu Tiga *Sudan* **81** E3
Abu Tineitin *Sudan* **81** E3
Abū Uruq *Sudan* **81** D3
Abū Zabad *Sudan* **81** E2
Abū Ẓāby *U.A.E.* **71** E7
Abū Zeydābād *Iran* **71** C6
Abuja *Nigeria* **83** D6
Abukuma-Gawa → *Japan* **54** E10
Abukuma-Sammyaku *Japan* **54** F10
Abunã *Brazil* **124** E5
Abunã → *Brazil* **124** E5
Abune Yosef *Ethiopia* **81** E4
Aburo *Dem. Rep. of the Congo* **86** B3
Abut Hd. *N.Z.* **91** E3
Abuye Meda *Ethiopia* **81** E4
Abwong *Sudan* **81** F3
Åby *Sweden* **11** F10
Aby, Lagune *Ivory C.* **82** D4
Abyad *Sudan* **81** E2
Abyei *Sudan* **81** F2
Ābyek *Iran* **71** B6
Acadia △ *U.S.A.* **113** C19
Açailândia *Brazil* **125** D9
Acajutla *El Salv.* **120** D2
Acámbaro *Mexico* **118** D4
Acanthus *Greece* **44** F7
Acaponeta *Mexico* **118** C3
Acapulco *Mexico* **119** D5
Acaraí, Serra *Brazil* **124** C7
Acarigua *Venezuela* **124** B5
Acatlán *Mexico* **119** D5
Acayucán *Mexico* **119** D6
Accéglio *Italy* **40** D4
Accomac *U.S.A.* **113** G16
Accous *France* **20** E3
Accra *Ghana* **83** D4
Accrington *U.K.* **14** D5
Acebal *Argentina* **126** C3
Aceh □ *Indonesia* **62** D1
Acerra *Italy* **43** B7
Achacachi *Bolivia* **124** G5
Achaguas *Venezuela* **124** B5
Achalpur *India* **66** J10
Acharnes *Greece* **46** C5
Acheloos → *Greece* **46** C3
Acheng *China* **57** B14
Achenkirch *Austria* **26** D4
Achensee *Austria* **26** D4
Achentrias *Greece* **47** G7
Acher *India* **68** H5
Achern *Germany* **25** G4
Achill Hd. *Ireland* **12** C1
Achill I. *Ireland* **12** C1
Achim *Germany* **24** B5
Achinsk *Russia* **53** D10
Achladokambos *Greece* **46** D4
Acıgöl *Turkey* **47** D11
Acıpayam *Turkey* **47** D11
Acireale *Italy* **43** E8
Acklins I. *Bahamas* **121** B5
Acme *Canada* **102** C6
Acme *U.S.A.* **114** F5
Aconcagua, Cerro *Argentina* **126** C2
Aconquija, Mt. *Argentina* **126** B2
Açores, Is. dos *Atl. Oc.* **78** a
Acornhoek *S. Africa* **89** C5
Acquapendente *Italy* **41** F8
Acquasanta Terme *Italy* **41** F10
Acquasparta *Italy* **41** F9
Acquaviva delle Fonti *Italy* **43** B9
Ácqui Terme *Italy* **40** D5
Acraman, L. *Australia* **95** E2
Acre = 'Akko *Israel* **74** C4
Acre □ *Brazil* **124** E4
Acre → *Brazil* **124** E5
Acri *Italy* **43** C9
Acs *Hungary* **28** C3
Actinolite *Canada* **114** B7
Actium *Greece* **46** C2
Acton *Canada* **114** C4
Ad Dafinah *Si. Arabia* **80** C5
Ad Daghgharah *Iraq* **73** G11
Ad Dammām *Si. Arabia* **71** E6
Ad Damūr *Lebanon* **74** B4
Ad Dawādimī *Si. Arabia* **70** E5
Ad Dawḥah *Qatar* **71** E6
Ad Dawr *Iraq* **73** E10
Ad Dir'īyah *Si. Arabia* **70** E5
Ad Dīwānīyah *Iraq* **73** F11
Ad Dujayl *Iraq* **73** F11
Ad Duwayd *Si. Arabia* **70** D4
Ada *Ghana* **83** D5
Ada *Serbia* **28** E5
Ada *Minn., U.S.A.* **112** B5
Ada *Okla., U.S.A.* **116** D6
Adabiya *Egypt* **74** F1
Adair, C. *Canada* **101** C17
Adaja → *Spain* **36** D6
Adak *U.S.A.* **106** E4
Adak I. *U.S.A.* **106** E4
Adamaoua □ *Cameroon* **83** D7
Adamaoua, Massif de l' *Cameroon* **83** D7
Adamawa □ *Nigeria* **83** D7
Adamawa Highlands = Adamaoua, Massif de l' *Cameroon* **83** D7

Adamello, Mte. *Italy* **40** B7
Adamello △ *Italy* **40** B7
Adami Tulu *Ethiopia* **81** F4
Adaminaby *Australia* **95** F4
Adams *Mass., U.S.A.* **115** D11
Adams *N.Y., U.S.A.* **115** C8
Adams *Wis., U.S.A.* **112** D9
Adams, Mt. *U.S.A.* **110** D5
Adam's Bridge *Sri Lanka* **66** Q11
Adams L. *Canada* **102** C5
Adam's Peak *Sri Lanka* **66** R12
Adamuz *Spain* **37** G6
Adana *Turkey* **72** D6
Adana □ *Turkey* **72** D6
Adanero *Spain* **36** E6
Adapazarı = Sakarya *Turkey* **72** B4
Adar Gwagwa, J. *Sudan* **80** C4
Adarama *Sudan* **81** D3
Adare, C. *Antarctica* **5** D11
Adarte *Eritrea* **81** E5
Adavale *Australia* **95** D3
Adda → *Italy* **40** C6
Addis Ababa = Addis Abeba *Ethiopia* **81** F4
Addis Abeba *Ethiopia* **81** F4
Addis Alem *Ethiopia* **81** F4
Addis Zemen *Ethiopia* **81** E4
Addison *U.S.A.* **114** D7
Addo *S. Africa* **88** E4
Addo △ *S. Africa* **88** E4
Adebour *Niger* **83** C7
Ādeh *Iran* **70** B5
Adel *U.S.A.* **117** F13
Adel Bagrou *Mauritania* **82** B3
Adelaide *Australia* **95** E2
Adelaide *S. Africa* **88** E4
Adelaide I. *Antarctica* **5** C17
Adelaide Pen. *Canada* **100** D12
Adelaide River *Australia* **92** B5
Adelaide Village *Bahamas* **120** A4
Adelanto *U.S.A.* **111** L9
Adele I. *Australia* **92** C3
Adélie, Terre *Antarctica* **5** C10
Adelie Land = Adélie, Terre *Antarctica* **5** C10
Adelsk *Belarus* **30** E10
Ademuz *Spain* **38** E3
Aden = Al 'Adan *Yemen* **75** E4
Aden, G. of *Ind. Oc.* **75** E4
Adendorp *S. Africa* **88** E3
Aderbissinat *Niger* **83** B6
Adh Dhayd *U.A.E.* **71** E7
Adhoi *India* **68** H4
Adi *Indonesia* **63** E8
Adi Arkai *Ethiopia* **81** E4
Adi Daro *Ethiopia* **81** E4
Adi Keyih *Eritrea* **81** E4
Adi Kwala *Eritrea* **81** E4
Adi Ugri *Eritrea* **81** E4
Adieu, C. *Australia* **93** F5
Adieu Pt. *Australia* **92** C3
Adigala *Ethiopia* **81** E5
Adige → *Italy* **41** C9
Adigrat *Ethiopia* **81** E4
Adigüzel Barajı *Turkey* **47** C11
Adilabad *India* **66** K11
Adilcevaz *Turkey* **73** C10
Adirondack △ *U.S.A.* **115** C10
Adirondack Mts. *U.S.A.* **115** C10
Adis Abeba = Addis Abeba *Ethiopia* **81** F4
Adıyaman *Turkey* **73** D8
Adıyaman □ *Turkey* **73** D8
Adjohon *Benin* **83** D5
Adjud *Romania* **29** D12
Adjumani *Uganda* **86** B3
Adjuntas *Puerto Rico* **121** d
Adlavik Is. *Canada* **105** B8
Adler *Russia* **35** J4
Admer *Algeria* **83** A6
Admiralty G. *Australia* **92** B4
Admiralty Gulf ⊙ *Australia* **92** B4
Admiralty I. *U.S.A.* **102** B2
Admiralty Inlet *Canada* **101** C14
Admiralty Is. *Papua N. G.* **90** B7
Adnan Menderes, İzmir ✈ (ADB) *Turkey* **47** C9
Ado *Nigeria* **83** D5
Ado-Ekiti *Nigeria* **83** D6
Adok *Sudan* **81** F3
Adola *Ethiopia* **81** E5
Adolfo González Chaves *Argentina* **126** D3
Adolfo Ruiz Cortines, Presa *Mexico* **118** B3
Adonara *Indonesia* **63** F6
Adoni *India* **66** M10
Adony *Hungary* **28** C3
Adour → *France* **20** E2
Adra *India* **69** H12
Adra *Spain* **37** J7
Adrano *Italy* **43** E7
Adrar *Algeria* **78** C6
Adrar *Mauritania* **78** D3
Adrar □ *Mauritania* **82** A3
Adrar des Iforas *Africa* **83** B5
Ádria *Italy* **41** C9
Adrian *Mich., U.S.A.* **113** E11

Adrian *Tex., U.S.A.* **116** D3
Adriatic Sea *Medit. S.* **6** G9
Adua *Indonesia* **63** E7
Adwa *Ethiopia* **81** E4
Adygea □ *Russia* **35** H5
Adzhar Republic = Ajaria □ *Georgia* **35** K6
Adzopé *Ivory C.* **82** D4
Ægean Sea *Medit. S.* **47** C7
Aerhtai Shan *Mongolia* **60** B4
Ærø *Denmark* **11** K4
Ærøskøbing *Denmark* **11** K4
Aetos *Greece* **46** D3
Afaahiti *Tahiti* **91** d
'Afak *Iraq* **73** F11
Afandou *Greece* **49** C10
Afar □ *Ethiopia* **81** E5
Afareaitu *Moorea* **91** d
Afdem *Ethiopia* **81** F5
Afghanistan ■ *Asia* **66** C4
Afikpo *Nigeria* **83** D6
Aflou *Algeria* **78** B6
Afognak I. *U.S.A.* **106** D9
Afragóla *Italy* **43** B7
Afram → *Ghana* **83** D4
Afrera *Ethiopia* **81** E5
Africa **76** E6
'Afrīn *Syria* **72** D7
Afşin *Turkey* **72** C7
Afton *N.Y., U.S.A.* **115** D9
Afton *Wyo., U.S.A.* **108** E8
Afuá *Brazil* **125** D8
'Afula *Israel* **74** C4
Afyon *Turkey* **47** C12
Afyon □ *Turkey* **47** C12
Afyonkarahisar = Afyon *Turkey* **47** C12
Aga *Egypt* **80** H7
Āgā Jarī *Iran* **71** D6
Agadès = Agadez *Niger* **83** B6
Agadez *Niger* **83** B6
Agadir *Morocco* **78** B4
Agaete *Canary Is.* **48** F4
Agaie *Nigeria* **83** D6
Agalega Is. *Mauritius* **3** E12
Agar *India* **68** H7
Agaro *Ethiopia* **81** F4
Agartala *India* **67** H17
Agaş *Romania* **29** D11
Agassiz *Canada* **102** D4
Agassiz Icecap *Canada* **101** A16
Agats *Indonesia* **63** F9
Agattu I. *U.S.A.* **106** E2
Agawam *U.S.A.* **115** D12
Agbélouvé *Togo* **83** D5
Agboville *Ivory C.* **82** D4
Ağcabādi *Azerbaijan* **35** K8
Ağdam *Azerbaijan* **35** L8
Ağdaş *Azerbaijan* **35** K8
Agde *France* **20** E7
Agde, C. d' *France* **20** E7
Agdzhabedi = Ağcabädi *Azerbaijan* **35** K8
Agen *France* **20** D4
Agerbæk *Denmark* **11** J2
Agersø *Denmark* **11** J5
Ageyevo *Russia* **32** E9
Aggteleki △ *Hungary* **28** B5
Āgh Kand *Iran* **73** D13
Aghathonisi *Greece* **47** D8
Aghia Anna *Greece* **46** C5
Aghia Deka *Greece* **49** D6
Aghia Ekaterini, Akra *Greece* **49** A3
Aghia Galini *Greece* **49** D6
Aghia Marina *Kasos, Greece* **47** F8
Aghia Marina *Leros, Greece* **47** D8
Aghia Paraskevi *Greece* **47** B8
Aghia Roumeli *Greece* **46** F5
Aghia Varvara *Greece* **49** D7
Aghiasos *Greece* **47** B8
Aghio Theodori *Greece* **46** D5
Aghion Oros □ *Greece* **45** F8
Aghios Andreas *Greece* **46** D4
Aghios Efstratios *Greece* **47** B6
Aghios Georgios *Greece* **46** D5
Aghios Ioannis, Akra *Greece* **49** D7
Aghios Isidoros *Greece* **49** C9
Aghios Kirikos *Greece* **47** D8
Aghios Matheos *Greece* **49** B3
Aghios Mironas *Greece* **49** D7
Aghios Nikolaos *Greece* **49** D7
Aghios Petros *Greece* **46** C2
Aghios Stephanos *Greece* **49** A3
Aghiou Orous, Kolpos *Greece* **44** F7
Aghireşu *Romania* **29** D8
Agia *Greece* **46** B4
Aginskoye *Russia* **53** D12
Agjert *Mauritania* **82** B3
Ağlasun *Turkey* **47** D12
Agly → *France* **20** F7
Agnew *Australia* **93** E3
Agnibilékrou *Ivory C.* **82** D4
Agnita *Romania* **29** E9
Agnone *Italy* **41** G11
Ago-Are *Nigeria* **83** D5
Agofie *Ghana* **83** D5
Agogna → *Italy* **40** C5

Agoitz = Aoiz *Spain* **38** C3
Agon Coutainville *France* **18** C5
Ágordo *Italy* **41** B9
Agori *India* **69** G10
Agouna *Benin* **83** D5
Agout → *France* **20** E5
Agra *India* **68** F7
Agrakhanskiuy Poluostrov *Russia* **35** J8
Agramunt *Spain* **38** D6
Ágreda *Spain* **38** D3
Ağri *Turkey* **73** C10
Ağrı □ *Turkey* **73** C10
Agri → *Italy* **43** B9
Ağri Dağı *Turkey* **73** C11
Ağri Karakose = Ağri *Turkey* **73** C10
Agria *Greece* **46** B5
Agrigento *Italy* **42** E6
Agrinio *Greece* **46** C3
Agrópoli *Italy* **43** B7
Ağstafa *Azerbaijan* **35** K7
Agua Caliente *Mexico* **111** N10
Agua Caliente Springs *U.S.A.* **111** N10
Água Clara *Brazil* **125** H8
Agua Fria △ *U.S.A.* **109** J8
Agua Hechicera *Mexico* **111** N10
Agua Prieta *Mexico* **118** A3
Aguadilla *Puerto Rico* **121** d
Aguadulce *Panama* **120** E3
Aguanga *U.S.A.* **111** M10
Aguanish *Canada* **105** B7
Aguanish → *Canada* **105** B7
Aguapey → *Argentina* **126** B4
Aguaray Guazú → *Paraguay* **126** A4
Aguarico → *Ecuador* **124** D3
Aguaro-Guariquito △ *Venezuela* **121** E6
Aguas → *Spain* **38** D4
Aguas Blancas *Chile* **126** A2
Aguas Calientes, Sierra de *Argentina* **126** B2
Aguascalientes *Mexico* **118** C4
Aguascalientes □ *Mexico* **118** C4
Agudo *Spain* **37** G6
Águeda *Portugal* **36** E2
Águeda → *Spain* **36** D4
Aguelhok *Mali* **83** B5
Aguié *Niger* **83** C6
Aguila, Punta *Puerto Rico* **121** d
Aguilafuente *Spain* **36** D6
Aguilar de Campóo *Spain* **36** C6
Aguilar de la Frontera *Spain* **37** H6
Aguilares *Argentina* **126** B2
Águilas *Spain* **39** H3
Agüimes *Canary Is.* **48** G4
Aguja, C. de la *Colombia* **122** B3
Agujereada, Pta. *Puerto Rico* **121** d
Agulaa *Ethiopia* **81** E4
Agulhas, C. *S. Africa* **88** E3
Agulo *Canary Is.* **48** F2
Agung, Gunung *Indonesia* **62** F5
Agur *Uganda* **86** B3
Agusan → *Phil.* **61** G6
Ağva *Turkey* **45** E13
Agvali *Russia* **35** J8
Aha Mts. *Botswana* **88** B3
Ahaggar *Algeria* **78** D7
Ahamansu *Ghana* **83** D5
Ahar *Iran* **73** C12
Ahat *Turkey* **47** C11
Ahaus *Germany* **24** C2
Ahipara B. *N.Z.* **91** A4
Ahir Dağı *Turkey* **47** C12
Ahiri *India* **66** K12
Ahlat *Turkey* **73** C10
Ahlen *Germany* **24** D3
Ahmad Wal *Pakistan* **68** E1
Ahmadabad *India* **68** H5
Aḥmadābād *Khorāsān, Iran* **71** C9
Aḥmadābād *Khorāsān, Iran* **71** C8
Aḥmadī *Iran* **71** E8
Ahmadnagar *India* **66** K9
Ahmadpur East *Pakistan* **68** E4
Ahmadpur Lamma *Pakistan* **68** E4
Ahmar, Mts. *Ethiopia* **81** F5
Ahmedabad = Ahmadabad *India* **68** H5
Ahmednagar = Ahmadnagar *India* **66** K9
Ahmetbey *Turkey* **45** E11
Ahmetler *Turkey* **47** C11
Ahmetli *Turkey* **47** C9
Ahoada *Nigeria* **83** D6
Ahome *Mexico* **118** B3
Ahoskie *U.S.A.* **117** C16
Ahr → *Germany* **24** E3
Ahram *Iran* **71** D6
Ahrax Pt. *Malta* **49** D1
Ahrensbök *Germany* **24** A6
Ahrensburg *Germany* **24** B6
Ahuachapán *El Salv.* **120** D2
Ahun *France* **19** F9
Åhus *Sweden* **11** J8
Ahvāz *Iran* **71** D6
Ahvenanmaa = Åland *Finland* **9** F19

Aḥwar *Yemen* 75 E4
Ahzar → *Mali* 83 B5
Ai → *India* 69 F14
Ai-Ais *Namibia* 88 D2
Ai-Ais and Fish River
    Canyon △ *Namibia* 88 C2
Aichach *Germany* 25 G7
Aichi □ *Japan* 55 G8
Aigle *Switz.* 25 J2
Aignay-le-Duc *France* 19 E11
Aigoual, Mt. *France* 20 D7
Aigre *France* 20 C4
Aigrettes, Pte. des *Réunion* 85 c
Aiguá *Uruguay* 127 C5
Aigueperse *France* 19 F10
Aigues → *France* 21 D8
Aigues-Mortes *France* 21 E8
Aigues-Mortes, G. d' *France* 21 E8
Aigües-Tortes i Estany de
    St. Maurici △ *Spain* 38 C4
Aiguilles *France* 21 D10
Aiguillon *France* 20 D4
Aigurande *France* 19 F8
Aihui = Heihe *China* 53 D13
Aija *Peru* 124 E3
Aikawa *Japan* 54 E9
Aiken *U.S.A.* 117 E14
Ailao Shan *China* 58 F3
Aileron *Australia* 94 C1
Aillant-sur-Tholon *France* 19 E10
Aillik *Canada* 105 A8
Ailsa Craig *Canada* 114 C3
Ailsa Craig *U.K.* 13 F3
Aim *Russia* 53 D14
Aimere *Indonesia* 63 F6
Aimogasta *Argentina* 126 B2
Ain □ *France* 19 F12
Ain → *France* 21 C9
Aïn Ben Tili *Mauritania* 78 C4
Ain Dalla *Egypt* 80 B2
Ain el Mafki *Egypt* 80 B2
Ain Girba *Egypt* 80 B2
Ain Murr *Sudan* 80 C2
Ain Qeiqab *Egypt* 80 B1
Ain Sudr *Egypt* 74 F2
Ain Sukhna *Egypt* 80 J8
Aïn Témouchent *Algeria* 78 A5
Ain Zeitûn *Egypt* 80 B2
Ainaži *Latvia* 32 D3
Ainos Oros *Greece* 46 C2
Ainsworth *U.S.A.* 112 D4
Aiquile *Bolivia* 124 G5
Aïr *Niger* 83 B6
Aïr et du Ténéré △ *Niger* 83 B6
Air Force I. *Canada* 101 D17
Air Hitam *Malaysia* 65 M4
Airaines *France* 19 C8
Airdrie *Canada* 102 C6
Airdrie *U.K.* 13 F5
Aire → *France* 19 C11
Aire → *U.K.* 14 D7
Aire, I. de l' *Spain* 48 B11
Aire-sur-la-Lys *France* 19 B9
Aire-sur-l'Adour *France* 20 E3
Airlie Beach *Australia* 94 b
Airvault *France* 18 F6
Aisch → *Germany* 25 F6
Aisne □ *France* 19 C10
Aisne → *France* 19 C9
Ait *India* 69 G8
Aitana, Sierra de *Spain* 39 G4
Aitkin *U.S.A.* 112 B7
Aitutaki *Cook Is.* 97 J12
Aiud *Romania* 29 D8
Aix-en-Provence *France* 21 E9
Aix-la-Chapelle = Aachen
    Germany 24 E2
Aix-les-Bains *France* 21 C9
Aixe-sur-Vienne *France* 20 C5
Aíyina = Egina *Greece* 46 D5
Aizawl *India* 67 H18
Aizenay *France* 18 F5
Aizkraukle *Latvia* 32 D3
Aizpute *Latvia* 30 B8
Aizuwakamatsu *Japan* 54 F9
Ajabshir *Iran* 73 D11
Ajaccio *France* 21 G12
Ajaccio, G. d' *France* 21 G12
Ajai → *Uganda* 86 B3
Ajaigarh *India* 69 G9
Ajalpan *Mexico* 119 D5
Ajanta Ra. *India* 66 J9
Ajari Rep. = Ajaria □ *Georgia* 35 K6
Ajaria □ *Georgia* 35 K6
Ajax *Canada* 114 C5
Ajdābiyā *Libya* 79 B10
Ajdovščina *Slovenia* 41 C10
Ajibar *Ethiopia* 81 E4
Ajka *Hungary* 28 C2
'Ajlūn *Jordan* 74 C4
'Ajlūn □ *Jordan* 74 C4
'Ajmān *U.A.E.* 71 E7
Ajmer *India* 68 F6
Ajnala *India* 68 D6
Ajo *U.S.A.* 109 K7
Ajo, C. de *Spain* 36 B7
Ajuy *Phil.* 61 F5

Ak Dağ *Turkey* 47 E11
Ak Dağlar *Turkey* 72 C7
Ak Dağları *Turkey* 47 E11
Akaba *Togo* 83 D5
Akabira *Japan* 54 C11
Akagera △ *Rwanda* 86 C3
Akaki Beseka *Ethiopia* 81 F4
Akamas *Cyprus* 49 D11
Akan △ *Japan* 54 C12
Akanthou *Cyprus* 49 D12
Akarca *Turkey* 47 C11
Akaroa *N.Z.* 91 E4
Akasha *Sudan* 80 C3
Akashi *Japan* 55 G7
Akbarpur *Bihar, India* 69 G10
Akbarpur *Ut. P., India* 69 F10
Akçaabat *Turkey* 73 B8
Akçadağ *Turkey* 72 C7
Akçakale *Turkey* 73 D8
Akçakoca *Turkey* 72 B4
Akçaova *Turkey* 45 E13
Akçay *Turkey* 47 E11
Akçay → *Turkey* 47 D10
Akdağ *Turkey* 47 C8
Akdağmadeni *Turkey* 72 C6
Akdoğan = Lysi *Cyprus* 49 D12
Akelamo *Indonesia* 63 D7
Åkers styckebruk *Sweden* 10 E11
Åkersberga *Sweden* 10 E12
Aketi *Dem. Rep. of the Congo* 84 D4
Akhalkalaki *Georgia* 35 K6
Akhaltsikhe *Georgia* 35 K6
Akhisar *Turkey* 47 C9
Akhmîm *Egypt* 80 B3
Akhnur *India* 69 C6
Akhtopol *Bulgaria* 45 D11
Akhtuba → *Russia* 35 G8
Akhtubinsk *Russia* 35 F8
Akhty *Russia* 35 K8
Akhtyrka = Okhtyrka
    Ukraine 33 G8
Aki *Japan* 55 H6
Akimiski I. *Canada* 104 B3
Akimovka *Ukraine* 33 J8
Akıncı Burnu *Turkey* 72 D6
Akincilar = Louroujina
    Cyprus 49 E12
Åkirkeby *Denmark* 11 J8
Akita *Japan* 54 E10
Akita □ *Japan* 54 E10
Akjoujt *Mauritania* 82 B2
Akka *Mali* 82 B4
Akkaya Tepesi *Turkey* 47 D11
Akkeshi *Japan* 54 C12
'Akko *Israel* 74 C4
Akköy *Turkey* 47 D9
Akkuş *Turkey* 72 B7
Aklampa *Benin* 83 D5
Aklavik *Canada* 100 D4
Aklera *India* 68 G7
Akmenė *Lithuania* 30 B9
Akmenrags *Latvia* 30 B8
Akmonte = Almonte *Spain* 37 H4
Akō *Japan* 55 G7
Ako *Nigeria* 83 C7
Akobô *Sudan* 81 F3
Akobo → *Ethiopia* 81 F3
Akola *India* 66 J10
Akonolinga *Cameroon* 83 E7
Akor *Mali* 82 C3
Akordat *Eritrea* 81 D4
Akosombo Dam *Ghana* 83 D5
Akot *Sudan* 81 F3
Akoupé *Ivory C.* 82 D4
Akpatok I. *Canada* 101 E18
Åkrahamn *Norway* 9 G11
Akranes *Iceland* 8 D2
Akreïjit *Mauritania* 82 B3
Akritas, Akra *Greece* 46 E3
Akron *Colo., U.S.A.* 108 F12
Akron *Ohio, U.S.A.* 114 E3
Akrotiri *Cyprus* 49 E11
Akrotiri, Akra *Greece* 45 F9
Akrotiri Bay *Cyprus* 49 E12
Aksai Chin *China* 69 B8
Aksaray *Turkey* 72 C6
Aksaray □ *Turkey* 72 C5
Aksay = Aqsay *Kazakhstan* 52 D6
Akşehir *Turkey* 72 C4
Akşehir Gölü *Turkey* 72 C4
Aksu *China* 60 B3
Aksu → *Turkey* 72 D4
Aksum *Ethiopia* 81 E4
Aktash *Russia* 34 C11
Aktsyabrski *Belarus* 23 B15
Aktyubinsk = Aqtöbe
    Kazakhstan 52 D6
Aku *Nigeria* 83 D6
Akure *Nigeria* 83 D6
Akureyri *Iceland* 8 D4
Akuseki-Shima *Japan* 55 K4
Akusha *Russia* 35 J8
Akwa-Ibom □ *Nigeria* 83 E6
Akwanga *Nigeria* 83 D6
Akyab = Sittwe *Burma* 67 J18
Akyazı *Turkey* 72 B4
Akyatan Gölü *Turkey* 72 D6
Al *Norway* 9 F13

Al Ajfar *Si. Arabia* 70 E4
Al Amādīyah *Iraq* 73 D10
Al 'Amārah *Iraq* 73 G12
Al Anbār □ *Iraq* 70 C4
Al 'Aqabah *Jordan* 74 F4
Al 'Aqabah □ *Jordan* 74 F4
Al Arak *Syria* 73 E8
Al 'Aramah *Si. Arabia* 70 E5
Al 'Arṭāwīyah *Si. Arabia* 70 E5
Al 'Āṣimah = 'Ammān □
    Jordan 74 D5
Al 'Assāfiyah *Si. Arab.a* 70 D3
Al 'Awdah *Si. Arabia* 70 E5
Al 'Ayn *Si. Arabia* 70 E3
Al 'Ayn *U.A.E.* 71 E7
Al 'Azīzīyah *Iraq* 73 F11
Al Bāb *Syria* 72 B7
Al Bad' *Si. Arabia* 70 D2
Al Bādī *Iraq* 70 C4
Al Bāḥah *Si. Arabia* 80 C5
Al Baḥrah *Kuwait* 70 D5
Al Baḥral Mayyit = Dead
    Sea *Asia* 74 D4
Al Balqā' □ *Jordan* 74 C4
Al Bārūk, J. *Lebanon* 74 B4
Al Bāşah *Si. Arabia* 80 C5
Al Başrah *Iraq* 70 D5
Al Baṭḥā *Iraq* 70 D5
Al Batrūn *Lebanon* 74 A4
Al Baydā *Syria* 79 B10
Al Biqā *Lebanon* 74 A5
Al Bi'r *Si. Arabia* 70 D3
Al Bukayrīyah *Si. Arabia* 70 E4
Al Burayj *Syria* 74 A5
Al Faḍilī *Si. Arabia* 71 E6
Al Fallūjah *Iraq* 73 F10
Al Fatḥah *Iraq* 73 E10
Al Fāw *Iraq* 71 D6
Al Fujayrah *U.A.E.* 71 E8
Al Ghadaf, W. → *Jordan* 74 D5
Al Ghammas *Iraq* 70 D5
Al Ghazālah *Si. Arabia* 70 E4
Al Ḥadīthah *Iraq* 73 E9
Al Ḥadīthah *Si. Ara^bia* 74 D6
Al Ḥaḍr *Iraq* 73 E10
Al Ḥājānah *Syria* 74 B5
Al Hajar al Gharbī *Oman* 71 E8
Al Ḥāmad *Si. Arabia* 70 D3
Al Ḥamdānīyah *Syria* 70 C3
Al Ḥamīdīyah *Syria* 74 A4
Al Ḥammār *Iraq* 70 D5
Al Ḥamrā' *Si. Arabia* 70 E3
Al Ḥamzah *Iraq* 70 D5
Al Ḥanākīyah *Si. Arabia* 70 E4
Al Harūj al Aswad *Libya* 79 C9
Al Ḥasakah *Syria* 73 D9
Al Ḥasakah □ *Syria* 73 D9
Al Hāshimīyah *Iraq* 73 G11
Al Ḥayy *Iraq* 73 F12
Al Ḥijārah *Asia* 70 D4
Al Ḥillah *Iraq* 73 F11
Al Ḥillah *Si. Arabia* 75 B4
Al Ḥindīyah *Iraq* 73 F11
Al Hirmil *Lebanon* 74 A5
Al Hoceïma *Morocco* 78 A5
Al Ḥudaydah *Yemen* 75 E3
Al Hudūd ash
    Shamālīyah □ *Si. Arabia* 70 D4
Al Hufūf *Si. Arabia* 71 E6
Al Ḥumaydah *Si. Arabia* 70 D2
Al Ḥunayy *Si. Arabia* 71 E6
Al Īsāwīyah *Si. Arabia* 70 D3
Al Jafr *Jordan* 74 E5
Al Jāfūrah *Si. Arabia* 71 E7
Al Jaghbūb *Libya* 79 C10
Al Jahrah *Kuwait* 70 D5
Al Jalāmīd *Si. Arabia* 70 D4
Al Jamalīyah *Qatar* 71 E6
Al Janūb □ *Lebanon* 74 B4
Al Jawf *Libya* 79 D10
Al Jawf *Si. Arabia* 70 D3
Al Jawf □ *Si. Arabia* 70 D3
Al Jazair = Algeria ■ *Africa* 78 C6
Al Jazirah *Iraq* 73 D10
Al Jithāmīyah *Si. Arabia* 70 E4
Al Jubayl *Si. Arabia* 71 E6
Al Jubaylah *Si. Arabia* 70 E5
Al Jubb *Si. Arabia* 70 E4
Al Junaynah *Sudan* 79 F10
Al Kabā'ish *Iraq* 70 D5
Al Karak *Jordan* 74 D4
Al Karak □ *Jordan* 74 E5
Al Kāzimīyah *Iraq* 73 F11
Al Khābūrah *Oman* 71 F8
Al Khafji *Si. Arabia* 71 E6
Al Khalīl *West Bank* 74 D4
Al Khāliş *Iraq* 73 F11
Al Kharsānīyah *Si. Arabia* 71 E6
Al Khaşab *Oman* 71 E8
Al Khawr *Qatar* 71 E6
Al Khiḍr *Iraq* 70 D5
Al Khiyām *Lebanon* 74 B4
Al Khobar *Si. Arabia* 71 E6
Al Khums *Libya* 79 B8
Al Kifl *Iraq* 73 G11
Al Kiswah *Syria* 74 B5
Al Kūfah *Iraq* 73 F11
Al Kufrah *Libya* 79 D10
Al Kuhayfiyah *Si. Arabia* 70 E4

Al Kumayt *Iraq* 73 G12
Al Kūt *Iraq* 73 F11
Al Kuwayt *Kuwait* 70 D5
Al Labwah *Lebanon* 74 A5
Al Lādhiqīyah *Syria* 72 E6
Al Lādhiqīyah □ *Syria* 72 E6
Al Līth *Si. Arabia* 80 C5
Al Liwā' *Oman* 71 E8
Al Luḩayyah *Yemen* 75 D3
Al Madīnah *Iraq* 70 D5
Al Madīnah *Si. Arabia* 70 E3
Al Mafraq *Jordan* 74 C5
Al Mafraq □ *Jordan* 74 C5
Al Maghreb = Morocco ■
    N. Afr. 78 B4
Al Maḥmūdīyah *Iraq* 73 F11
Al Majma'ah *Si. Arabia* 70 E5
Al Makhruq, W. → *Jordan* 74 D6
Al Makḥūl *Si. Arabia* 70 E4
Al Mālikīyah *Syria* 73 D10
Al Manāmah *Bahrain* 71 E6
Al Maqwa' *Kuwait* 70 D5
Al Marāḥ *Si. Arabia* 71 E6
Al Marj *Libya* 79 B10
Al Maṭlā *Kuwait* 70 D5
Al Mawṣil *Iraq* 73 D10
Al Mayādin *Syria* 73 E9
Al Mazār *Jordan* 74 D4
Al Midhnab *Si. Arabia* 70 E5
Al Mīnā' *Lebanon* 74 A4
Al Miqdādīyah *Iraq* 73 E11
Al Mubarraz *Si. Arabia* 71 E6
Al Mudawwarah *Jordan* 74 F5
Al Mughayrā' *U.A.E.* 71 E7
Al Muḩarraq *Bahrain* 71 E6
Al Mukallā *Yemen* 75 E4
Al Mukhā *Yemen* 75 E3
Al Musayjīd *Si. Arabia* 70 E3
Al Musayyib *Iraq* 73 F11
Al Muthanná □ *Iraq* 70 D5
Al Muwayh *Si. Arabia* 80 C5
Al Muwaylih *Si. Arabia* 70 E2
Al Owuho = Otukpa *Nigeria* 83 D6
Al Qā'im *Iraq* 73 E9
Al Qalībah *Si. Arabia* 70 D3
Al Qāmishlī *Syria* 73 D9
Al Qaryatayn *Syria* 74 A6
Al Qaşīm □ *Si. Arabia* 70 E4
Al Qaṭ'ā *Syria* 73 E9
Al Qaṭīf *Si. Arabia* 71 E6
Al Qaṭrānah *Jordan* 74 D5
Al Qaṭrūn *Libya* 79 D9
Al Qawz *Si. Arabia* 80 D5
Al Qayşūmah *Si. Arabia* 70 D5
Al Quds = Jerusalem
    Israel/West Bank 74 D4
Al Qunayṭirah *Syria* 74 C4
Al Qunfudhah *Si. Arabia* 80 D5
Al Qurnah *Iraq* 70 D5
Al Quşayr *Iraq* 70 D5
Al Quşayr *Syria* 74 A5
Al Qutayfah *Syria* 74 B5
Al Quwayr *Iraq* 73 D10
Al 'Ubaylah *Si. Arabia* 75 C5
Al 'Uḏaylīyah *Si. Arabia* 71 E6
Al 'Ulā *Si. Arabia* 70 E3
Al 'Uqayr *Si. Arabia* 71 E6
Al 'Uwaynid *Si. Arabia* 70 E5
Al 'Uwayqīlah *Si. Arabia* 70 D4
Al 'Uyūn *Ḥijāz, Si. Arabia* 70 E3
Al 'Uyūn *Najd, Si. Arabia* 70 E4
Al 'Uzayr *Iraq* 70 D5
Al Wajh *Si. Arabia* 70 E3
Al Wakrah *Qatar* 71 E6
Al Waqbah *Si. Arabia* 70 D5
Al Wari'āh *Si. Arabia* 70 E5
Al Yaman = Yemen ■ *Asia* 75 E3
Ala *Italy* 40 C8
Ala Dağ *Turkey* 70 B2
Ala Dağları *Turkey* 73 C10
Ala Tau *Asia* 52 E9
Alabama □ *U.S.A.* 117 E11
Alabama → *U.S.A.* 117 F11
Alabaster *U.S.A.* 117 E11
Alaca *Turkey* 72 B6
Alacaatlı *Turkey* 47 B10
Alaçam *Turkey* 72 B6
Alaçam Dağları *Turkey* 47 B10
Alacant = Alicante *Spain* 39 G4
Alaçatı *Turkey* 47 C8
Alachua *U.S.A.* 117 G13
Alaejos *Spain* 36 D5
Alagir *Russia* 35 J7
Alagna Valsésia *Italy* 40 C4
Alagoa Grande *Brazil* 125 E11
Alagoas □ *Brazil* 125 E11
Alagoinhas *Brazil* 125 F11
Alagón *Spain* 38 D3
Alagón → *Spain* 36 F4
Alaior *Spain* 48 B11
Alajero *Canary Is.* 48 F2
Alajuela *Costa Rica* 120 D3
Alakamisy *Madag.* 89 C8
Alaknanda → *India* 69 D8
Alaköl *Kazakhstan* 60 B3
Alakurtti *Russia* 8 C24
Alamarvdasht *Iran* 71 E7
Alamata *Ethiopia* 81 E4

Alameda *Calif., U.S.A.* 110 H4
Alameda *N. Mex., U.S.A.* 109 J10
Alaminos *Phil.* 61 C3
Alamo *U.S.A.* 111 H11
Alamogordo *U.S.A.* 109 K11
Alamos *Mexico* 118 B3
Alamosa *U.S.A.* 109 H11
Åland *Finland* 9 F19
Åland □ *Finland* 8 E20
Ålands hav *Europe* 9 G18
Alange, Embalse d' *Spain* 37 G4
Alania = North Ossetia □
    Russia 35 J7
Alanís *Spain* 37 G5
Alanya *Turkey* 72 D5
Alaotra, Farihin' *Madag.* 89 B8
Alapayevsk *Russia* 52 D7
Alappuzha = Alleppey *India* 66 Q10
Alar del Rey *Spain* 36 C6
Alaraz *Spain* 36 E5
Alarcón, Embalse de *Spain* 38 F2
Alaró *Spain* 48 B9
Alarobia-Vohiposa *Madag.* 89 C8
Alaşehir *Turkey* 47 C10
Alashtar *Iran* 73 F13
Alaska □ *U.S.A.* 106 C9
Alaska, G. of *Pac. Oc.* 100 F5
Alaska Peninsula *U.S.A.* 106 D8
Alaska Range *U.S.A.* 100 E1
Alássio *Italy* 40 E5
Ālāt *Azerbaijan* 35 L9
Alatau Shan = Ala Tau *Asia* 52 E9
Alatri *Italy* 41 G10
Alatyr *Russia* 34 C8
Alatyr → *Russia* 34 C8
Alausi *Ecuador* 124 D3
Álava □ *Spain* 38 C2
Alava, C. *U.S.A.* 108 B1
Alaverdi *Armenia* 35 K7
Alavo = Alavus *Finland* 8 E20
Alavus *Finland* 8 E20
Alawa ☼ *Australia* 94 B1
Alawoona *Australia* 95 E3
Alayawarra ☼ *Australia* 94 C1
'Alayh *Lebanon* 74 B4
Alazani → *Azerbaijan* 35 K8
Alba *Italy* 40 D5
Alba □ *Romania* 29 D8
Alba Adriática *Italy* 41 F10
Alba de Tormes *Spain* 36 E5
Alba-Iulia *Romania* 29 D8
Albac *Romania* 28 D7
Albacete *Spain* 39 F3
Albacete □ *Spain* 39 G3
Albacutya, L. *Australia* 95 F3
Alban *France* 20 E6
Albanel, L. *Canada* 104 B5
Albania ■ *Europe* 44 E4
Albano Laziale *Italy* 41 G9
Albany *Australia* 93 G2
Albany *Ga., U.S.A.* 117 F12
Albany *N.Y., U.S.A.* 115 D11
Albany *Oreg., U.S.A.* 108 D2
Albany *Tex., U.S.A.* 116 E5
Albany → *Canada* 104 B3
Albarca, C. d' *Spain* 48 B7
Albardón *Argentina* 126 C2
Albarracín *Spain* 38 E3
Albarracín, Sierra de *Spain* 38 E3
Albatera *Spain* 39 G4
Albatross B. *Australia* 94 A3
Albegna → *Italy* 41 F8
Albemarle *U.S.A.* 117 D14
Albemarle Sd. *U.S.A.* 117 C16
Albenga *Italy* 40 D5
Alberche → *Spain* 36 F6
Alberdi *Paraguay* 126 B4
Albères, Mts. *France* 20 F6
Albersdorf *Germany* 24 A5
Albert *France* 19 C9
Albert, L. *Africa* 86 B3
Albert, L. *Australia* 95 F2
Albert Edward Ra. *Australia* 92 C4
Albert Lea *U.S.A.* 112 D7
Albert Nile → *Uganda* 86 B3
Albert Town *Bahamas* 121 B5
Alberta □ *Canada* 102 C6
Alberti *Argentina* 126 C3
Albertinia *S. Africa* 88 E3
Albertirsa *Hungary* 28 C4
Alberton *Canada* 105 C7
Albertville *U.S.A.* 117 D11
Albi *France* 20 E6
Albia *U.S.A.* 112 E7
Albina *Suriname* 125 B8
Albina, Ponta *Angola* 88 B1
Albino *Italy* 40 C6
Albion *Mich., U.S.A.* 113 D11
Albion *Nebr., U.S.A.* 112 E4
Albion *Pa., U.S.A.* 114 E4

Albocàsser *Spain* 38 E5
Albolote *Spain* 37 H7
Alborán *Medit. S.* 37 K7
Ålborg = Aalborg *Denmark* 11 G3
Ålborg Bugt = Aalborg
    Bugt *Denmark* 11 H4
Alborz, Reshteh-ye
    Kūhhā-ye *Iran* 71 C7
Albox *Spain* 39 H2
Albufeira *Portugal* 37 H2
Albula → *Switz.* 25 J5
Albuñol *Spain* 37 J7
Albuquerque *U.S.A.* 109 J10
Albuquerque, Cayos de
    Caribbean 120 D3
Alburg *U.S.A.* 115 B11
Alburno, Mte. *Italy* 43 B8
Alburquerque *Spain* 37 F4
Albury *Australia* 95 F4
Alcácer do Sal *Portugal* 37 G2
Alcáçovas *Portugal* 37 G2
Alcalá de Guadaira *Spain* 37 H5
Alcalá de Henares *Spain* 36 E7
Alcalá de los Gazules *Spain* 37 J5
Alcalá de Xivert *Spain* 38 E5
Alcalá del Júcar *Spain* 39 F3
Alcalá del Río *Spain* 37 H5
Alcalá del Valle *Spain* 37 J5
Alcalá la Real *Spain* 37 H7
Álcamo *Italy* 42 E5
Alcanadre → *Spain* 38 C2
Alcanar *Spain* 38 E5
Alcanede *Portugal* 37 F2
Alcanena *Portugal* 37 F2
Alcañices *Spain* 36 D4
Alcañiz *Spain* 38 D4
Alcântara *Brazil* 125 D10
Alcántara *Spain* 37 F4
Alcántara, Embalse de *Spain* 36 F4
Alcantarilla *Spain* 39 H3
Alcaracejos *Spain* 37 G6
Alcaraz *Spain* 39 G2
Alcaraz, Sierra de *Spain* 39 G2
Alcaudete *Spain* 37 H6
Alcázar de San Juan *Spa.n* 37 F7
Alchevsk *Ukraine* 33 H10
Alcira = Alzira *Spain* 39 F4
Alcobaça *Portugal* 37 F2
Alcobendas *Spain* 36 E7
Alcolea del Pinar *Spain* 38 D2
Alcorcón *Spain* 36 E7
Alcoutim *Portugal* 37 H3
Alcova *U.S.A.* 108 E10
Alcoy *Spain* 39 G4
Alcubierre, Sierra de *Spain* 38 D4
Alcublas *Spain* 38 F4
Alcúdia *Spain* 48 B10
Alcúdia, B. d' *Spain* 48 B10
Alcúdia, Sierra de la *Spain* 37 G6
Aldabra Is. *Seychelles* 77 G8
Aldama *Mexico* 119 C5
Aldan *Russia* 53 D13
Aldan → *Russia* 53 C13
Aldea, Pta. de la *Canary Is.* 48 G4
Aldeburgh *U.K.* 15 E9
Alder Pk. *U.S.A.* 110 K5
Alderney *U.K.* 15 H5
Aldershot *U.K.* 15 F7
Åled *Sweden* 11 H6
Aledo *U.S.A.* 112 E8
Alefa *Ethiopia* 81 E4
Aleg *Mauritania* 82 B2
Alegranza *Canary Is.* 48 E6
Alegranza, I. *Canary Is.* 48 E6
Alegre *Brazil* 127 A7
Alegrete *Brazil* 127 B4
Aleksandriya =
    Oleksandriya *Kirovohrad,*
    Ukraine 33 H7
Aleksandriya =
    Oleksandriya *Rivne,*
    Ukraine 23 C14
Aleksandriyskaya *Russia* 35 J8
Aleksandrov *Russia* 32 D10
Aleksandrov Gay *Russia* 34 E9
Aleksandrovac *Serbia* 44 C5
Aleksandrovac *Serbia* 44 B5
Aleksandrovka =
    Oleksandrovka *Ukraine* 33 H7
Aleksandrovo *Bulgaria* 45 C8
Aleksandrovsk-
    Sakhalinskiy *Russia* 53 D15
Aleksandrów Kujawski
    Poland 31 F5
Aleksandrów Łódzki *Poland* 31 G6
Aleksandry, Zemlya *Russia* 52 A5
Alekseyevka *Samara, Russia* 34 D10
Alekseyevka *Voronezh,*
    Russia 33 G9
Aleksin *Russia* 32 E9
Aleksinac *Serbia* 44 C5
Além Paraíba *Brazil* 127 A7
Alemania *Argentina* 126 B2
Alemania *Chile* 126 B2
Alençon *France* 18 D7
Alenquer *Brazil* 125 D8
'Alenuihähä Channel
    U.S.A. 107 L8

Alépé Ivory C. 82 D4
Aleppo = Ḥalab Syria 72 D7
Aléria France 21 F13
Alert Canada 101 A20
Alès France 21 D8
Aleşd Romania 28 C7
Alessándria Italy 40 D5
Ålesund Norway 8 E12
Alet-les-Bains France 20 F6
Aletschhorn Switz. 25 J4
Aleutian Basin Pac. Oc. 96 B9
Aleutian Is. Pac. Oc. 106 E5
Aleutian Range U.S.A. 106 D9
Aleutian Trench Pac. Oc. 4 D17
Alexander U.S.A. 112 B2
Alexander, Mt. Australia 93 E3
Alexander Arch. U.S.A. 100 F4
Alexander Bay S. Africa 88 D2
Alexander City U.S.A. 117 E12
Alexander I. Antarctica 5 C17
Alexandra Australia 95 F4
Alexandra N.Z. 91 F2
Alexandra Falls Canada 102 A5
Alexandria = El Iskandarîya Egypt 80 H7
Alexandria B.C., Canada 102 C4
Alexandria Ont., Canada 115 A10
Alexandria Romania 29 G10
Alexandria S. Africa 88 E4
Alexandria U.K. 13 F4
Alexandria La., U.S.A. 116 F8
Alexandria Minn., U.S.A. 112 C6
Alexandria S. Dak., U.S.A. 112 D5
Alexandria Va., U.S.A. 113 F15
Alexandria Bay U.S.A. 115 B9
Alexandrina, L. Australia 95 F2
Alexandroupoli Greece 45 F9
Alexis → Canada 105 B8
Alexis Creek Canada 102 C4
Aleysk Russia 52 D9
Alfabia Spain 48 B9
Alfambra Spain 38 E3
Alfândega da Fé Portugal 36 D4
Alfaro Spain 38 C3
Alfatar Bulgaria 45 C11
Alfeld Germany 24 D5
Alfenas Brazil 127 A6
Alföld Hungary 28 D5
Alfonsine Italy 41 D9
Alford Aberds., U.K. 13 D6
Alford Lincs., U.K. 14 D8
Alfred Maine, U.S.A. 115 C14
Alfred N.Y., U.S.A. 114 D7
Alfreton U.K. 14 D6
Alfta Sweden 10 C10
Algaida Spain 48 B9
Algar Spain 37 J5
Ålgård Norway 9 G11
Algarinejo Spain 37 H6
Algarve Portugal 37 J2
Algeciras Spain 37 J5
Algemesí Spain 39 F4
Alger Algeria 78 A6
Alger □ Algeria 39 J8
Alger ✕ (ALG) Algeria 39 J8
Algeria ■ Africa 78 C6
Algha Kazakhstan 52 E6
Alghero Italy 42 B1
Älghult Sweden 11 G9
Algiers = Alger Algeria 78 A6
Algoa B. S. Africa 88 E4
Algodonales Spain 37 J5
Algodor → Spain 36 F7
Algoma U.S.A. 112 C10
Algona U.S.A. 112 D6
Algonac U.S.A. 114 D2
Algonquin ⌓ Canada 104 C4
Algorta Uruguay 128 C5
Alhama de Almería Spain 37 J8
Alhama de Aragón Spain 38 D3
Alhama de Granada Spain 37 H7
Alhama de Murcia Spain 39 H3
Alhambra U.S.A. 111 L8
Alhaurín el Grande Spain 37 J6
Alhucemas = Al Hoceïma Morocco 78 A5
'Alī al Gharbī Iraq 73 F12
'Alī ash Sharqī Iraq 73 F12
Äli Bayramlı Azerbaijan 35 L9
'Alī Khēl Afghan. 68 C3
Ali Sahîh Djibouti 81 E5
Alī Shāh Iran 70 B5
Ália Italy 42 E6
'Alīābād Golestān, Iran 71 B7
'Alīābād Khorāsān, Iran 71 C8
'Alīābād Kordestān, Iran 70 C5
'Alīābād Yazd, Iran 71 D7
Aliade Nigeria 83 D6
Aliaga Spain 38 E4
Aliağa Turkey 47 C8
Aliakmonas → Greece 44 F6
Alibo Ethiopia 81 F4
Alibori → Benin 83 C5
Alibunar Serbia 28 E5
Alicante Spain 39 G4
Alicante □ Spain 39 G4
Alicante ✕ (ALC) Spain 39 G4
Alice S. Africa 88 E4
Alice U.S.A. 116 H5
Alice → Queens., Australia 94 C3
Alice → Queens., Australia 94 B3
Alice, Punta Italy 43 C10
Alice Arm Canada 102 B3
Alice Springs Australia 94 C1
Alicedale S. Africa 88 E4
Aliceville U.S.A. 117 E10
Alicudi Italy 43 D7
Aliganj India 69 F8
Aligarh Raj., India 68 G7
Aligarh Ut. P., India 68 F8
Alīgūdarz Iran 71 C6
Alijó Portugal 36 D3
Alimia Greece 49 C9
Alingsås Sweden 11 G6
Alipur Pakistan 68 E4
Alipur Duar India 67 F16
Aliquippa U.S.A. 114 F4
Alishan Taiwan 59 F13
Aliste → Spain 36 D5
Alitus = Alytus Lithuania 32 E3
Aliveri Greece 46 C6
Aliwal North S. Africa 88 E4
Alix Canada 102 C6
Aljezur Portugal 37 H2
Aljustrel Portugal 37 H2
Alkamari Niger 83 C7
Alkmaar Neths. 17 B4
All American Canal U.S.A. 109 K6
Allada Benin 83 D5
Allagash → U.S.A. 113 B19
Allah Dad Pakistan 68 G2
Allahabad India 69 G9
Allan Canada 103 C7
Allanche France 20 C6
Allanridge S. Africa 88 D4
Allaqi, Wadi → Egypt 80 C3
Allariz Spain 36 C3
Allassac France 20 C5
Ålleberg Sweden 11 F7
Allegany U.S.A. 114 D6
Allegheny → U.S.A. 114 F5
Allegheny Mts. U.S.A. 113 F13
Allegheny Plateau U.S.A. 113 E14
Allegheny Res. U.S.A. 114 E6
Allègre France 20 C7
Allègre, Pte. Guadeloupe 120 b
Allen, Bog of Ireland 12 C5
Allen, L. Ireland 12 B3
Allendale U.S.A. 117 E14
Allende Mexico 118 B4
Allentown U.S.A. 115 F9
Allentsteig Austria 26 C8
Alleppey India 66 Q10
Allepuz Spain 38 E4
Aller → Germany 24 C5
Alleynes B. Barbados 121 g
Alliance Nebr., U.S.A. 112 D2
Alliance Ohio, U.S.A. 114 F3
Allier □ France 19 F9
Allier → France 19 F10
Alliford Bay Canada 102 C2
Alligator Pond Jamaica 120 a
Allinge Denmark 11 J8
Alliston Canada 114 B5
Alloa U.K. 13 E5
Allones France 18 D8
Allora Australia 95 D5
Allos France 21 D10
Alluitsup Paa Greenland 4 C5
Alma Canada 105 C5
Alma Ga., U.S.A. 117 F13
Alma Kans., U.S.A. 112 F5
Alma Mich., U.S.A. 113 D11
Alma Nebr., U.S.A. 112 E4
Alma Wis., U.S.A. 112 C8
Alma Ata = Almaty Kazakhstan 52 E8
Alma Hill U.S.A. 114 D7
Almacelles Spain 38 D5
Almada Portugal 37 G1
Almaden Australia 94 B3
Almadén Spain 37 G6
Almalyk = Olmaliq Uzbekistan 52 E7
Almanor, L. U.S.A. 108 F3
Almansa Spain 39 G3
Almanza Spain 36 C5
Almanzor, Pico Spain 36 E5
Almanzora → Spain 39 H3
Almaş, Munţii Romania 28 F7
Almassora Spain 38 F4
Almaty Kazakhstan 52 E8
Almazán Spain 38 D2
Almeirim Brazil 125 D8
Almeirim Portugal 37 F2
Almelo Neths. 17 B6
Almenar de Soria Spain 38 D2
Almenara Spain 38 F4
Almenara, Sierra de Spain 39 H3
Almendra, Embalse de Spain 36 D4
Almendralejo Spain 37 G4
Almere-Stad Neths. 17 B5
Almería Spain 37 J8
Almería □ Spain 39 H2
Almería, G. de Spain 39 J2
Almetyevsk Russia 34 C11
Älmhult Sweden 11 H8
Almirante Panama 120 E3
Almiropotamos Greece 46 C6
Almiros Greece 46 B4
Almodôvar Portugal 37 H2
Almodóvar del Campo Spain 37 G6
Almodóvar del Río Spain 37 H5
Almond U.S.A. 114 D7
Almont U.S.A. 114 D1
Almonte Canada 115 A8
Almonte Spain 37 H4
Almora India 69 E8
Almoradí Spain 39 G4
Almorox Spain 36 E6
Almoustarat Mali 83 B5
Älmsta Sweden 10 E12
Almudévar Spain 38 C4
Almuñécar Spain 37 J7
Almunge Sweden 10 E12
Almuradiel Spain 37 G7
Almus Turkey 72 B7
Almyrou, Ormos Greece 49 D6
Alness U.K. 13 D4
Alnmouth U.K. 14 B6
Alnwick U.K. 14 B6
Aloi Uganda 86 B3
Alon Burma 67 H19
Alonissos Greece 46 B5
Alonissos-Northern Sporades △ Greece 46 B6
Alor Indonesia 63 F6
Alor Setar Malaysia 65 J3
Álora Spain 37 J6
Alosno Spain 37 H3
Alot India 68 H6
Aloysius, Mt. Australia 93 E4
Alpaugh U.S.A. 110 K7
Alpe Apuane ⌓ Italy 40 D7
Alpedrinha Portugal 36 E3
Alpena U.S.A. 113 C12
Alpes-de-Haute-Provence □ France 21 D10
Alpes-Maritimes □ France 21 E11
Alpha Australia 94 C4
Alpha Ridge Arctic 4 A2
Alphen aan den Rijn Neths. 17 B4
Alphios → Greece 46 D3
Alpiarça Portugal 37 F2
Alpine Ariz., U.S.A. 109 K9
Alpine Calif., U.S.A. 111 N10
Alpine Tex., U.S.A. 116 F3
Alps Europe 22 E5
Alpu Turkey 72 C4
Alpurrurulam Australia 94 C2
Alqueta, Barragem do Portugal 37 G3
Alrø Denmark 11 J4
Als Denmark 11 K3
Alsace □ France 19 D14
Alsask Canada 103 C7
Alsasua Spain 38 C2
Alsek → U.S.A. 102 B1
Alsfeld Germany 24 E5
Alsta Norway 8 D15
Alstermo Sweden 11 H9
Alston U.K. 14 C5
Alta Norway 8 B20
Alta, Sierra Spain 38 E3
Alta Gracia Argentina 126 C3
Alta Sierra U.S.A. 111 K8
Altaelva → Norway 8 B20
Altafjorden Norway 8 A20
Altai = Aerhtai Shan Mongolia 60 B4
Altai = Gorno-Altay □ Russia 52 D9
Altamaha → U.S.A. 117 F14
Altamira Brazil 125 D8
Altamira Chile 126 B2
Altamira Mexico 119 C5
Altamira, Cuevas de Spain 36 B6
Altamont U.S.A. 115 D10
Altamura Italy 43 B9
Altanbulag Mongolia 60 A5
Altar Mexico 118 A2
Altar, Gran Desierto de Mexico 118 B2
Altata Mexico 118 C3
Altavista U.S.A. 113 G14
Altay China 60 B3
Altdorf Switz. 25 J4
Alte Mellum Germany 24 B4
Altea Spain 39 G4
Altenberg Germany 24 E9
Altenbruch Germany 24 B4
Altenburg Germany 24 E8
Altenkirchen Mecklenburg-Vorpommern, Germany 24 A9
Altenkirchen Rhld-Pfz., Germany 24 E3
Altenmarkt Austria 26 D7
Alter do Chão Portugal 37 F3
Altınkaya Barajı Turkey 72 B6
Altınoluk Turkey 47 B8
Altınova Turkey 47 B8
Altıntaş Turkey 47 B12
Altınyaka Turkey 47 E12
Altınyayla Turkey 47 D11
Altiplano Bolivia 124 G5
Altkirch France 19 E14
Altmark Germany 24 C7
Altmühl → Germany 25 G7
Altmühltal ⌓ Germany 25 G7
Alto Adige = Trentino-Alto Adige □ Italy 41 B8
Alto Araguaia Brazil 125 G8
Alto Cuchumatanes = Cuchumatanes, Sierra de los Guatemala 120 C1
Alto del Carmen Chile 126 B1
Alto Garda Bresciano ⌓ Italy 40 C7
Alto Ligonha Mozam. 87 F4
Alto Molocue Mozam. 87 F4
Alto Paraguay □ Paraguay 126 A4
Alto Paraná □ Paraguay 127 B5
Alton Canada 114 C4
Alton U.K. 15 F7
Alton Ill., U.S.A. 112 F8
Alton N.H., U.S.A. 115 C13
Altona Canada 103 D9
Altoona U.S.A. 114 F6
Altötting Germany 25 G8
Altstätten Switz. 25 H5
Altun Kupri Iraq 73 E11
Altun Shan China 60 C3
Alturas U.S.A. 108 F3
Altus U.S.A. 116 D5
Alubijid Phil. 61 G6
Alucra Turkey 73 B8
Aluk Sudan 81 F2
Alūksne Latvia 32 D4
Alunda Sweden 10 D12
Alunite U.S.A. 111 K12
Aluoro → Ethiopia 81 F3
Alupka Ukraine 33 K8
Alushta Ukraine 33 K8
Alusi Indonesia 63 F8
Alustante Spain 38 E3
Alva U.S.A. 116 C5
Alvaiázere Portugal 36 F2
Älvängen Sweden 11 G6
Alvão ⌓ Portugal 36 D3
Alvarado Mexico 119 D5
Alvarado U.S.A. 116 E6
Álvaro Obregón, Presa Mexico 118 B3
Älvdalen Sweden 10 C8
Alvear Argentina 126 B4
Alverca Portugal 37 G1
Alvesta Sweden 11 H8
Alvin U.S.A. 116 G7
Alvinston Canada 114 D3
Alvito Portugal 37 G3
Älvkarleby Sweden 10 D11
Alvord Desert U.S.A. 108 E4
Älvros Sweden 10 B8
Älvsbyn Sweden 8 D19
Alwar India 68 F7
Alxa Zuoqi China 56 E3
Alyangula Australia 94 A2
Alyata = Älät Azerbaijan 35 L9
Alyth U.K. 13 E5
Alytus Lithuania 32 E3
Alzada U.S.A. 108 D11
Alzamay Russia 53 D10
Alzey Germany 25 F4
Alzira Spain 39 F4
Am Timan Chad 79 F10
Amadeus, L. Australia 93 D5
Amadi Dem. Rep. of the Congo 86 B2
Amâdi Sudan 81 F3
Amadjuak L. Canada 101 E17
Amadora Portugal 37 G1
Amagansett U.S.A. 115 F12
Amagasaki Japan 55 G7
Amager Denmark 11 J6
Amagunze Nigeria 83 D6
Amahai Indonesia 63 E7
Amaile Samoa 91 b
Amaiun-Maia Spain 38 B3
Amakusa-Shotō Japan 55 H5
Åmål Sweden 10 E6
Amalfi Italy 43 B7
Amaliada Greece 46 D3
Amalner India 66 J9
Amamapare Indonesia 63 E9
Amambaí Brazil 127 A4
Amambaí → Brazil 127 A5
Amambay □ Paraguay 127 A4
Amambay, Cordillera de S. Amer. 127 A4
Amami-Guntō Japan 55 L4
Amami-Ō-Shima Japan 55 K4
Aman, Pulau Malaysia 65 c
Amaná, L. Brazil 124 D6
Amanat → India 69 G11
Amanda Park U.S.A. 110 C3
Amankeldi Kazakhstan 52 D7
Amantea Italy 43 C9
Amapá Brazil 125 C8
Amapá □ Brazil 125 C8
Amara Sudan 81 E3
Amara □ Ethiopia 81 E4
Amarante Brazil 125 E10
Amarante Portugal 36 D2
Amaranth Canada 103 C9
Amareleja Portugal 37 G3
Amargosa → U.S.A. 111 J10
Amargosa Desert U.S.A. 111 J10
Amargosa Range U.S.A. 111 J10
Amari Greece 49 D6
Amarillo U.S.A. 116 D4
Amarkantak India 69 H9
Amârna, Tell el' Egypt 80 B3
Amaro, Mte. Italy 41 F11
Amarpur India 69 G12
Amarti Eritrea 81 E5
Amarwara India 69 H8
Amasra Turkey 72 B5
Amassama Nigeria 83 D6
Amasya Turkey 72 B6
Amasya □ Turkey 72 B6
Amata Australia 93 E5
Amatikulu S. Africa 89 D5
Amatitlán Guatemala 120 D1
Amatrice Italy 41 F10
Amay Belgium 17 D5
Amazon = Amazonas → S. Amer. 125 D8
Amazonas □ Brazil 124 E6
Amazonas → S. Amer. 125 D8
Amba Ferit Ethiopia 81 E4
Ambah India 68 F8
Ambahakily Madag. 89 C7
Ambahita Madag. 89 C8
Ambala India 68 D7
Ambalavao Madag. 89 C8
Ambanja Madag. 89 A8
Ambararata Madag. 89 B8
Ambarchik Russia 53 C17
Ambarijeby Madag. 89 A8
Ambaro, Helodranon' Madag. 89 A8
Ambato Ecuador 124 D3
Ambato Madag. 89 A8
Ambato, Sierra de Argentina 126 B2
Ambato Boeny Madag. 89 B8
Ambatofinandrahana Madag. 89 C8
Ambatolampy Madag. 89 B8
Ambatomainty Madag. 89 B8
Ambatomanoina Madag. 89 B8
Ambatondrazaka Madag. 89 B8
Ambatosoratra Madag. 89 B8
Ambelonas Greece 46 B4
Ambenja Madag. 89 B8
Amberg Germany 25 F7
Ambergris Cay Belize 119 D7
Ambérieu-en-Bugey France 21 C9
Amberley Canada 114 B3
Amberley N.Z. 91 E4
Ambert France 20 C7
Ambidédi Mali 82 C2
Ambikapur India 69 H10
Ambikol Sudan 80 C3
Ambilobé Madag. 89 A8
Ambinanindrano Madag. 89 C8
Ambinanitelo Madag. 89 B8
Ambinda Madag. 89 B8
Amble U.K. 14 B6
Ambleside U.K. 14 C5
Ambo Peru 124 F3
Amboahangy Madag. 89 C8
Ambodifototra Madag. 89 B8
Ambodilazana Madag. 89 B8
Ambodiriana Madag. 89 B8
Ambohidratrimo Madag. 89 B8
Ambohidray Madag. 89 B8
Ambohimahamasina Madag. 89 C8
Ambohimahasoa Madag. 89 C8
Ambohimanga Madag. 89 C8
Ambohimitombo Madag. 89 C8
Ambohitra Madag. 89 A8
Amboise France 18 E8
Ambon Indonesia 63 E7
Ambondro Madag. 89 D8
Amboseli, L. Kenya 86 C4
Amboseli △ Kenya 86 C4
Ambositra Madag. 89 C8
Ambovombe Madag. 89 D8
Amboy U.S.A. 111 L11
Amboyna Cay S. China Sea 62 C4
Ambridge U.S.A. 114 F4
Ambriz Angola 84 F2
Ambrolauri Georgia 73 A10
Amchitka I. U.S.A. 106 E3
Amderma Russia 52 C7
Amdhi India 69 H9
Amdo China 67 C17
Ameca Mexico 118 C4
Ameca → Mexico 118 C3
Amecameca de Juárez Mexico 119 D5
Ameland Neths. 17 A5
Amélia Italy 41 F9
Amendolara Italy 43 C9
Amenia U.S.A. 115 E11
America-Antarctica Ridge S. Ocean 5 B2
American Falls U.S.A. 108 E7
American Falls Res. U.S.A. 108 E7
American Fork U.S.A. 108 F8
American Highland Antarctica 5 D6
American Samoa ☒ Pac. Oc. 91 b
American Samoa △ Amer. Samoa 91 b
Americana Brazil 127 A6
Americus U.S.A. 117 E12
Amerigo Vespucci, Firenze ✕ (FLR) Italy 41 E8
Amersfoort Neths. 17 B5
Amersfoort S. Africa 89 D4
Amery Basin S. Ocean 5 C6
Amery Ice Shelf Antarctica 5 C6
Ames = Bertamirans Spain 36 C2
Ames U.S.A. 112 D7
Amesbury U.S.A. 115 D14
Amet India 68 G5
Amfiklia Greece 46 C4
Amfilochia Greece 46 C3
Amfipoli Greece 44 F7
Amfissa Greece 46 C4
Amga Russia 53 C14
Amga → Russia 53 C14
Amgu Russia 54 B8
Amgun → Russia 53 D14
Amherst Canada 105 C7
Amherst Mass., U.S.A. 115 D12
Amherst N.Y., U.S.A. 114 D6
Amherst Ohio, U.S.A. 114 E2
Amherst I. Canada 115 B8
Amherstburg Canada 104 D3
Amiata, Mte. Italy 41 F8
Amidon U.S.A. 112 B2
Amiens France 19 C9
Amindeo Greece 44 F5
Åminne Sweden 11 G7
Amino Ethiopia 81 G5
Aminuis Namibia 88 C2
Amīrābād Iran 70 C5
Amirante Is. Seychelles 50 J7
Amisk ⌓ Canada 103 B9
Amisk L. Canada 103 C8
Amistad, Presa de la Mexico 118 B4
Amistad ⌓ U.S.A. 116 G4
Amite U.S.A. 117 F9
Amla India 68 J8
Amlapura = Karangasem Indonesia 63 J18
Amlia I. U.S.A. 106 E5
Amlwch U.K. 14 D3
Amm Adam Sudan 81 D4
'Ammān Jordan 74 D4
'Ammān □ Jordan 74 D5
'Ammān ✕ (AMM) Jordan 74 D5
Ammanford U.K. 15 F4
Ammassalik = Tasiilaq Greenland 4 C6
Ammerån → Sweden 10 A10
Ammersee Germany 25 G7
Ammochostos = Famagusta Cyprus 49 D12
Ammon U.S.A. 108 E8
Amnat Charoen Thailand 64 E5
Amnura Bangla. 69 G13
Amo Jiang → China 58 F3
Āmol Iran 71 B7
Amorgos Greece 47 E7
Amory U.S.A. 117 E10
Amos Canada 104 C4
Åmot Norway 9 G13
Åmotfors Sweden 10 E6
Amoy = Xiamen China 59 E12
Ampanavoana Madag. 89 B9
Ampang Malaysia 65 L3
Ampangalana, Lakandranon' Madag. 89 C8
Ampanihy Madag. 89 C7
Amparafaravola Madag. 89 B8
Ampasinambo Madag. 89 C8
Ampasindava, Helodranon' Madag. 89 A8
Ampasindava, Saikanosy Madag. 89 A8
Ampenan Indonesia 62 F5
Amper Nigeria 83 D6
Amper → Germany 25 G7
Ampezzo Italy 41 B9
Amphoe Kathu Thailand 65 a
Amphoe Thalang Thailand 65 a
Ampitsikinana Madag. 89 A8
Ampombiantambo Madag. 89 A8
Amposta Spain 38 E5
Ampotaka Madag. 89 D7
Ampoza Madag. 89 C7
Amqui Canada 105 C6
Amravati India 66 J10
Amreli India 68 J4
Amritsar India 68 D6
Amroha India 69 E8
Amrum Germany 24 A4
Amsterdam Neths. 17 B4
Amsterdam U.S.A. 115 D10
Amsterdam ✕ (AMS) Neths. 17 B4
Amsterdam, I. = Nouvelle Amsterdam, Î. Ind. Oc. 3 F13
Amstetten Austria 26 C7
'Amūdah Syria 73 D9
Amudarya → Uzbekistan 52 E6
Amund Ringnes I. Canada 101 B12
Amundsen Abyssal Plain S. Ocean 5 C14
Amundsen Basin Arctic 4 A
Amundsen Gulf Canada 100 C7
Amundsen Ridges S. Ocean 5 C14
Amundsen-Scott Antarctica 5 E

Amundsen Sea *Antarctica* 5 D15
Amungen *Sweden* 10 C9
Amuntai *Indonesia* 62 E5
Amur *Russia* 53 D15
Amur, W. → *Sudan* 80 D3
Amurang *Indonesia* 63 D6
Amurrio *Spain* 38 B1
Amursk *Russia* 53 D14
Amusco *Spain* 36 C6
Amvrakikos Kolpos *Greece* 46 C2
Amvrosiyivka *Ukraine* 33 J10
Amyderya = Amudarya →
  Uzbekistan 52 E6
An Bien *Vietnam* 65 H5
An Cabhán = Cavan *Ireland* 12 B4
An Cóbh = Cóbh *Ireland* 12 E3
An Daingean = Dingle
  Ireland 12 D1
An Hoa *Vietnam* 64 E7
An Longfort = Longford
  Ireland 12 C4
An Muileann gCearr =
  Mullingar *Ireland* 12 C4
An Nabaţīyah at Tahta
  Lebanon 74 B4
An Nabk *Si. Arabia* 70 D3
An Nabk *Syria* 74 A5
An Nafūd *Si. Arabia* 70 D4
An Nāḩīyah *Iraq* 73 E9
An Najaf *Iraq* 73 G11
An Nás = Naas *Ireland* 12 C5
An Nāşirīyah *Iraq* 70 D5
An Nhon *Vietnam* 64 F7
An Nîl □ *Sudan* 80 D3
An Nîl el Abyad □ *Sudan* 81 E3
An Nîl el Azraq □ *Sudan* 81 E3
An Nu'ayrīyah *Si. Arabia* 71 E6
An Nu'mānīyah *Iraq* 73 F11
An Ros = Rush *Ireland* 12 C5
An tAonach = Nenagh
  Ireland 12 D3
An Thoi, Dao *Vietnam* 65 H5
An tInbhear Mór = Arklow
  Ireland 12 D5
An Uaimh *Ireland* 12 C5
Anabar → *Russia* 53 B12
'Anabtā *West Bank* 74 C4
Anaconda *U.S.A.* 108 C7
Anacortes *U.S.A.* 110 B4
Anacuao, Mt. *Phil.* 61 C4
Anadarko *U.S.A.* 116 D5
Anadia *Portugal* 36 E2
Anadolu *Turkey* 72 C5
Anadyr *Russia* 53 C18
Anadyr → *Russia* 53 C18
Anadyrskiy Zaliv *Russia* 53 C19
Anafi *Greece* 47 E7
Anaga, Pta. de *Canary Is.* 48 F3
Anagni *Italy* 41 G10
'Ānah *Iraq* 73 E10
Anaheim *U.S.A.* 111 M9
Anahim Lake *Canada* 102 C3
Anakapalle *India* 67 L13
Anakie *Australia* 94 C4
Anaklia *Georgia* 35 J5
Analalava *Madag.* 89 A8
Analavoka *Madag.* 89 C8
Analipsis *Greece* 49 A3
Anambar → *Pakistan* 68 D3
Anambas, Kepulauan
  Indonesia 62 D3
Anambas Is. = Anambas,
  Kepulauan *Indonesia* 62 D3
Anambra □ *Nigeria* 83 D6
Anamosa *U.S.A.* 112 D4
Anamur *Turkey* 72 D5
Anamur Burnu *Turkey* 72 D5
Anan *Japan* 55 H7
Anand *India* 68 H5
Ananes *Greece* 46 E6
Anangu Pitjantjatjara ◎
  Australia 93 E5
Anantapur *India* 66 M10
Anantnag *India* 69 C6
Ananyiv *Ukraine* 29 C14
Anapa *Russia* 33 K9
Anapodiaris → *Greece* 49 E7
Anápolis *Brazil* 125 G9
Anapu → *Brazil* 125 D8
Anār *Iran* 71 D7
Anārak *Iran* 71 C7
Anarisfjällen *Sweden* 10 A7
Anas → *India* 68 H5
Anatolia = Anadolu *Turkey* 72 C5
Anatsogno *Madag.* 89 C7
Añatuya *Argentina* 126 B3
Anatye ◎ *Australia* 94 C2
Anauethad L. *Canada* 103 A8
Anbyŏn *N. Korea* 57 E14
Ancares, Sierra dos *Spain* 36 C4
Ancares △ *Spain* 36 C4
Ancaster *Canada* 114 C5
Ancenis *France* 18 E5
Anchor Bay *U.S.A.* 110 G3
Anchorage *U.S.A.* 100 E2
Anci *China* 56 E9
Ancohuma, Nevado *Bolivia* 124 G5
Ancón *Peru* 124 F3
Ancona *Italy* 41 E10

Ancud *Chile* 128 E2
Ancud, G. de *Chile* 128 E2
Ancy-le-Franc *France* 19 E11
Andacollo *Argentina* 126 D1
Andacollo *Chile* 126 C1
Andaingo *Madag.* 89 B8
Andalgalá *Argentina* 126 B2
Åndalsnes *Norway* 8 E12
Andalucía □ *Spain* 37 H6
Andalusia = Andalucía □
  Spain 37 H6
Andalusia *U.S.A.* 117 F11
Andaman Is. *Ind. Oc.* 51 G11
Andaman Sea *Ind. Oc.* 62 B1
Andamooka *Australia* 95 E2
Andapa *Madag.* 89 A8
Andara *Namibia* 88 B3
Andelot-Blancheville *France* 19 D12
Andenes *Norway* 8 B17
Andenne *Belgium* 17 D5
Andéranboukane *Mali* 83 B5
Andermatt *Switz.* 25 J4
Andernach *Germany* 24 E3
Andernos-les-Bains *France* 20 D2
Anderslöv *Sweden* 11 J7
Anderson *Alaska, U.S.A.* 106 C10
Anderson *Calif., U.S.A.* 108 F2
Anderson *Ind., U.S.A.* 113 E11
Anderson *Mo., U.S.A.* 112 G6
Anderson *S.C., U.S.A.* 117 D13
Anderson → *Canada* 100 D6
Anderstorp *Sweden* 11 G7
Andes *U.S.A.* 115 D10
Andes, Cord. de los *S. Amer.* 124 H5
Andfjorden *Norway* 8 B17
Andhra Pradesh □ *India* 66 L11
Andijon *Uzbekistan* 52 E8
Andikíthira = Antikythira
  Greece 46 F5
Andilamena *Madag.* 89 B8
Andīmeshk *Iran* 73 F13
Andímilos = Antimilos
  Greece 46 E6
Andíparos = Antiparos
  Greece 47 D7
Andípaxoi = Antipaxi *Greece* 46 B2
Andipsara *Greece* 47 C7
Andizhan = Andijon
  Uzbekistan 52 E8
Andoain *Spain* 38 B2
Andoany *Madag.* 89 A8
Andohahela △ *Madag.* 89 C8
Andong *S. Korea* 57 F15
Andongwei *China* 57 G10
Andorra ■ *Europe* 20 F5
Andorra La Vella *Andorra* 20 F5
Andover *U.K.* 15 F6
Andover *Maine, U.S.A.* 115 B14
Andover *Mass., U.S.A.* 115 D13
Andover *N.J., U.S.A.* 115 F10
Andover *N.Y., U.S.A.* 114 D7
Andover *Ohio, U.S.A.* 114 E4
Andøya *Norway* 8 B16
Andradina *Brazil* 125 H8
Andrahary *Madag.* 89 A8
Andramasina *Madag.* 89 C8
Andranopasy *Madag.* 89 C7
Andranovory *Madag.* 89 C7
Andratx *Spain* 48 B9
Andreanof Is. *U.S.A.* 106 E4
Andreapol *Russia* 32 D7
Andrews *S.C., U.S.A.* 117 E15
Andrews *Tex., U.S.A.* 116 E3
Andreyevka *Russia* 34 D10
Ándria *Italy* 43 A9
Andriamena *Madag.* 89 B8
Andriandampy *Madag.* 89 C8
Andriba *Madag.* 89 B8
Andrijevica *Montenegro* 44 D3
Andringitra △ *Madag.* 89 C8
Andritsena *Greece* 46 D3
Androka *Madag.* 89 C7
Andros *Greece* 46 D6
Andros I. *Bahamas* 120 B4
Andros Town *Bahamas* 120 B4
Androscoggin → *U.S.A.* 115 C14
Andrychów *Poland* 31 J6
Andselv *Norway* 8 B18
Andújar *Spain* 37 G6
Andulo *Angola* 84 G3
Aneby *Sweden* 11 G8
Anéfis *Mali* 83 B5
Anegada *Br. Virgin Is.* 121 e
Anegada Passage *W. Indies* 121 C7
Aného *Togo* 83 D5
Anenni-Noi *Moldova* 29 D14
Aneto, Pico de *Spain* 38 C5
Anfu *China* 59 D10
Ang Mo Kio *Singapore* 65 d
Ang Thong *Thailand* 64 E3
Ang Thong, Ko *Thailand* 65 b
Ang Thong △ *Thailand* 65 H2
Angamos, Punta *Chile* 126 A1
Angara → *Russia* 53 D10
Angara-Débou *Benin* 83 C5
Angarbaka *Sudan* 81 F1
Angarsk *Russia* 53 D11
Angas Hills *Australia* 92 D4

Angaston *Australia* 95 E2
Ånge *Sweden* 10 B9
Ángel, Salto = Angel Falls
  Venezuela 124 B6
Ángel de la Guarda, I.
  Mexico 118 B2
Angel Falls *Venezuela* 124 B6
Angeles *Phil.* 61 D4
Ängelholm *Sweden* 11 H6
Angels Camp *U.S.A.* 110 G6
Ängelsberg *Sweden* 10 E10
Anger → *Ethiopia* 81 F4
Angereb *Ethiopia* 81 E4
Angereb → *Ethiopia* 81 E4
Ångermanälven → *Sweden* 10 A11
Ångermanland *Sweden* 8 E17
Angermünde *Germany* 24 B9
Angers *Canada* 115 A9
Angers *France* 18 E6
Angerville *France* 19 D9
Ångesån → *Sweden* 8 C20
Angikuni L. *Canada* 103 A9
Angkor *Cambodia* 64 F4
Angledool *Australia* 95 D4
Anglès *Spain* 38 D7
Anglesey *U.K.* 14 D3
Anglesey, Isle of □ *U.K.* 14 D3
Anglet *France* 20 E2
Angleton *U.S.A.* 116 G7
Anglin → *France* 20 B4
Anglisidhes *Cyprus* 49 E12
Anglure *France* 19 D10
Angmagssalik = Tasiilaq
  Greenland 4 C6
Ango *Dem. Rep. of the Congo* 86 B2
Angoche *Mozam.* 87 F4
Angoche, I. *Mozam.* 87 F4
Angol *Chile* 126 D1
Angola *Ind., U.S.A.* 113 E11
Angola *N.Y., U.S.A.* 114 D5
Angola ■ *Africa* 85 G3
Angoulême *France* 20 C4
Angoumois *France* 20 C4
Angra do Heroísmo *Azores* 78 a
Angra dos Reis *Brazil* 127 A7
Angrapa → *Russia* 30 D8
Angtassom *Cambodia* 65 G5
Angu *Dem. Rep. of the Congo* 86 B1
Anguang *China* 57 B12
Anguilla ☑ *W. Indies* 121 C7
Anguo *China* 56 E8
Angurugu *Australia* 94 A2
Angus *Canada* 114 B5
Angus □ *U.K.* 13 E6
Angwa → *Zimbabwe* 89 B5
Anhanduí → *Brazil* 127 A5
Anholt *Denmark* 11 H5
Anhua *China* 59 C8
Anhui □ *China* 59 B11
Anhwei = Anhui □ *China* 59 B11
Anichab *Namibia* 88 C1
Anidros *Greece* 47 E7
Anié *Togo* 83 D5
Animas → *U.S.A.* 109 H9
Anina *Romania* 28 E6
Aninoasa *Romania* 29 F9
Anivorano *Madag.* 89 B8
Anjalankoski *Finland* 32 B4
Anjar *India* 68 H4
Anji *China* 59 B12
Anjou *France* 18 E6
Anjouan *Comoros Is.* 85 a
Anjozorobe *Madag.* 89 B8
Anju *N. Korea* 57 E13
Anka *Nigeria* 83 C6
Ankaboa, Tanjona *Madag.* 89 C7
Ankang *China* 56 H5
Ankara *Turkey* 72 C5
Ankara □ *Turkey* 72 C5
Ankarafantsika △ *Madag.* 89 B8
Ankaramena *Madag.* 89 C8
Ankaratra *Madag.* 85 H9
Ankarsrum *Sweden* 11 G10
Ankasakasa *Madag.* 89 B7
Ankavandra *Madag.* 89 B8
Ankazoabo *Madag.* 89 C7
Ankazobe *Madag.* 89 B8
Ankeny *U.S.A.* 112 E7
Ankilimalinika *Madag.* 89 C7
Ankilizato *Madag.* 89 C8
Ankisabe *Madag.* 89 B8
Anklam *Germany* 24 B9
Ankober *Ethiopia* 81 F4
Ankoro *Dem. Rep. of the Congo* 86 D2
Ankororoka *Madag.* 89 D8
Ankpa *Nigeria* 83 D6
Anlong *China* 58 E5
Anlong Veng *Cambodia* 64 E5
Anlu *China* 59 B9
Anmyeondo *S. Korea* 57 F14
Ånn *Sweden* 10 A6
Ann, C. *U.S.A.* 115 D14
Ann Arbor *U.S.A.* 113 D12
Anna *Russia* 34 E5
Anna *U.S.A.* 112 G9
Annaba *Algeria* 83 A7
Annaberg-Buchholz
  Germany 24 E9
Annalee → *Ireland* 12 B4

Annam *Vietnam* 64 E7
Annamitique, Chaîne *Asia* 64 D6
Annan *U.K.* 13 G5
Annan → *U.K.* 13 G5
Annapolis *U.S.A.* 113 F15
Annapolis Royal *Canada* 105 D6
Annapurna *Nepal* 69 E10
Annean, L. *Australia* 93 E2
Anneberg *Sweden* 11 G8
Annecy *France* 21 C10
Annecy, Lac d' *France* 21 C10
Annemasse *France* 19 F13
Annette I. *U.S.A.* 102 B2
Anning *China* 58 E4
Anniston *U.S.A.* 117 E12
Annobón *Atl. Oc.* 77 G4
Annonay *France* 21 C8
Annot *France* 21 E10
Annotto B. *Jamaica* 120 a
Annville *U.S.A.* 115 F8
Annweiler *Germany* 25 F3
Ano Poroia *Greece* 44 E7
Ano Siros *Greece* 46 D6
Anogia *Greece* 49 D6
Anorotsangana *Madag.* 89 A8
Anosibe *Madag.* 89 B8
Anou Mellene *Mali* 83 B5
Anoumaba *Ivory C.* 82 D4
Anping *Hebei, China* 56 E8
Anping *Liaoning, China* 57 D12
Anpu Gang *China* 58 G7
Anqing *China* 59 B11
Anqiu *China* 57 F10
Anren *China* 59 D9
Ansager *Denmark* 11 J2
Ansai *China* 56 F5
Ansan *S. Korea* 57 F14
Ansbach *Germany* 25 F6
Anse Boileau *Seychelles* 85 b
Anse Royale *Seychelles* 85 b
Anseba → *Eritrea* 81 D4
Ansfelden *Austria* 26 C7
Anshan *China* 57 D12
Anshun *China* 58 D5
Ansião *Portugal* 36 F2
Ansley *U.S.A.* 112 E4
Ansó *Spain* 38 C4
Ansoáin *Spain* 38 C3
Ansólo *Mali* 83 B5
Ansongo *Mali* 83 B5
Ansongo-Ménaka △ *Mali* 83 B5
Anson *U.S.A.* 116 E5
Anson B. *Australia* 92 B5
Ansonia *U.S.A.* 115 E11
Anstruther *U.K.* 13 E6
Ansudu *Indonesia* 63 E9
Antabamba *Peru* 124 F4
Antakya = Hatay *Turkey* 72 D7
Antalaha *Madag.* 89 A9
Antalya *Turkey* 72 D4
Antalya □ *Turkey* 47 E12
Antalya Körfezi *Turkey* 72 D4
Antambohobe *Madag.* 89 C8
Antanambao-Manampotsy
  Madag. 89 B8
Antanambe *Madag.* 89 B8
Antananarivo *Madag.* 89 B8
Antananarivo □ *Madag.* 89 B8
Antanifotsy *Madag.* 89 B8
Antanimbaribe *Madag.* 89 C7
Antanimora *Madag.* 89 C8
Antarctic Pen. *Antarctica* 5 C18
Antarctica 5 E3
Antelope *Zimbabwe* 87 G2
Antequera *Paraguay* 126 A4
Antequera *Spain* 37 H6
Antero, Mt. *U.S.A.* 108 G10
Antevamena *Madag.* 89 C7
Anthony *Kans., U.S.A.* 112 G4
Anthony *N. Mex., U.S.A.* 109 K10
Anti Atlas *Morocco* 78 C4
Anti-Lebanon = Sharqi, Al
  Jabal ash *Lebanon* 74 B5
Antibes *France* 21 E11
Antibes, C. d' *France* 21 E11
Anticosti, Î. d' *Canada* 105 C7
Antifer, C. d' *France* 18 C7
Antigo *U.S.A.* 112 C9
Antigonish *Canada* 105 C7
Antigua *Canary Is.* 48 F5
Antigua *Guatemala* 120 D1
Antigua *W. Indies* 121 C7
Antigua & Barbuda ■
  W. Indies 121 C7
Antikythira *Greece* 46 F5
Antilla *Cuba* 120 B4
Antilles = West Indies
  Cent. Amer. 121 D7
Antimilos *Greece* 46 E6
Antioch *U.S.A.* 110 G5
Antioche, Pertuis d' *France* 20 B2
Antioquia *Colombia* 124 B3
Antiparos *Greece* 47 D7
Antipaxi *Greece* 46 B2
Antipodes Is. *Pac. Oc.* 96 M9
Antirio *Greece* 46 C3
Antlers *U.S.A.* 116 D7
Antoetra *Madag.* 89 C8

Antofagasta *Chile* 126 A1
Antofagasta □ *Chile* 126 A2
Antofagasta de la Sierra
  Argentina 126 B2
Antofalla *Argentina* 126 B2
Antofalla, Salar de *Argentina* 126 B2
Anton *U.S.A.* 116 E3
Antongila, Helodrano
  Madag. 89 B8
Antonibé *Madag.* 89 B8
Antonibé, Presqu'île d'
  Madag. 89 A8
Antonina *Brazil* 127 B6
Antrain *France* 18 D5
Antrim *U.K.* 12 B5
Antrim *U.S.A.* 114 F3
Antrim □ *U.K.* 12 B5
Antrim, Mts. of *U.K.* 12 A5
Antrim Plateau *Australia* 92 C4
Antrodoco *Italy* 41 F10
Antropovo *Russia* 34 A6
Antsakabary *Madag.* 89 B8
Antsalova *Madag.* 89 B7
Antsenavolo *Madag.* 89 C8
Antsiafabositra *Madag.* 89 B8
Antsirabe *Antananarivo,*
  Madag. 89 B8
Antsirabe *Antsiranana, Madag.* 89 A8
Antsirabe *Mahajanga, Madag.* 89 B8
Antsiranana *Madag.* 89 A8
Antsiranana □ *Madag.* 89 A8
Antsohihy *Madag.* 89 A8
Antsohimbondrona
  Seranana *Madag.* 89 A8
Antu *China* 57 C15
Antwerp = Antwerpen
  Belgium 17 C4
Antwerp *U.S.A.* 115 B9
Antwerpen *Belgium* 17 C4
Antwerpen □ *Belgium* 17 C4
Anupgarh *India* 68 E5
Anuppur *India* 69 H9
Anuradhapura *Sri Lanka* 66 Q12
Anurrete ◎ *Australia* 94 C2
Anveh *Iran* 71 E7
Anvers = Antwerpen
  Belgium 17 C4
Anvers I. *Antarctica* 5 C17
Anwen *China* 59 C13
Anxi *Fujian, China* 59 E12
Anxi *Gansu, China* 60 B4
Anxian *China* 58 B5
Anxiang *China* 59 C9
Anxious B. *Australia* 95 E1
Anyama *Ivory C.* 82 D4
Anyang *China* 56 FE
Anyang *S. Korea* 57 F14
Anyer *Indonesia* 63 G11
Anyi *Jiangxi, China* 59 C10
Anyi *Shanxi, China* 56 G6
Anyuan *China* 59 E10
Anyue *China* 58 B5
Anza *U.S.A.* 111 M10
Anze *China* 56 F7
Anzhero-Sudzhensk *Russia* 52 D9
Ánzio *Italy* 42 A5
Ao Makham *Thailand* 65 a
Ao Phangnga △ *Thailand* 65 a
Aoga-Shima *Japan* 55 H9
Aoiz *Spain* 38 C3
Aoji *N. Korea* 57 C16
Aomen = Macau *China* 59 F9
Aomori *Japan* 54 D10
Aomori □ *Japan* 54 D10
Aonla *India* 69 E8
Aorai, Mt. *Tahiti* 91 d
Aoraki Mount Cook *N.Z.* 91 E3
Aoral, Phnum *Cambodia* 65 G5
Aosta *Italy* 40 C4
Aotearoa = New Zealand ■
  Oceania 91 D6
Aoudéras *Niger* 83 B6
Aoukâr *Mauritania* 82 B3
Aozou Strip *Chad* 79 D9
Apá → *S. Amer.* 126 A4
Apache *U.S.A.* 116 D5
Apache Junction *U.S.A.* 109 K8
Apalachee B. *U.S.A.* 117 G13
Apalachicola *U.S.A.* 117 G12
Apalachicola → *U.S.A.* 117 G12
Apam *Ghana* 83 D4
Apaporis → *Colombia* 124 D5
Aparados da Serra △ *Brazil* 127 B5
Aparri *Phil.* 61 B4
Apateu *Romania* 28 D6
Apatin *Serbia* 28 E4
Apatity *Russia* 8 C25
Apatula = Finke *Australia* 94 D1
Apatzingán *Mexico* 118 D4
Apeldoorn *Neths.* 17 B5
Apen *Germany* 24 B3
Apennines = Appennini
  Italy 40 D7
Aphrodisias *Turkey* 47 D10
Apia *Samoa* 91 b
Apiacás, Serra dos *Brazil* 124 E7
Apiazco *Mexico* 119 D5

Aplao *Peru* 124 G4
Apo, Mt. *Phil.* 63 C7
Apolakia *Greece* 49 C9
Apolakia, Ormos *Greece* 49 C9
Apolda *Germany* 24 D7
Apollonia = Sūsah *Libya* 79 B10
Apollonia *Greece* 49 C9
Apolo *Bolivia* 124 F5
Apolonia *Greece* 46 E6
Apopa *El Salv.* 120 D2
Aporé → *Brazil* 125 G8
Aporé *Brazil* 125 G8
Apostle Is. *U.S.A.* 112 B8
Apostle Islands △ *U.S.A.* 112 B8
Apóstoles *Argentina* 127 B4
Apostolos Andreas, C.
  Cyprus 49 D13
Apostolou *Ukraine* 33 J7
Apoteri *Guyana* 124 C7
Appalachian Mts. *U.S.A.* 113 G14
Äppelbo *Sweden* 10 D8
Appennini *Italy* 40 D7
Appennino Ligure *Italy* 40 D6
Appenzell-Ausser
  Rhoden □ *Switz.* 25 H5
Appenzell-Inner Rhoden □
  Switz. 25 H5
Appiano *Italy* 41 B8
Apple Hill *Canada* 115 A10
Apple Valley *U.S.A.* 111 L9
Appleby-in-Westmorland
  U.K. 14 C5
Appledore *U.K.* 15 F3
Appleton *U.S.A.* 112 C9
Approuague → *Fr. Guiana* 125 C8
Apricena *Italy* 41 G12
Aprília *Italy* 42 A5
Apsheronsk *Russia* 35 H4
Apsley *Canada* 114 B6
Apt *France* 21 E9
Apuane, Alpi *Italy* 40 D7
Apucarana *Brazil* 127 A5
Apulia = Púglia □ *Italy* 43 A9
Apure → *Venezuela* 124 B5
Apurímac → *Peru* 124 F4
Apuseni, Munţii *Romania* 28 D7
Āq Qālā *Iran* 71 B7
Aqaba = Al 'Aqabah *Jordan* 74 F4
Aqaba, G. of *Red Sea* 70 D2
'Aqabah, Khalīj al =
  Aqaba, G. of *Red Sea* 70 D2
'Aqdā *Iran* 71 C7
Aqiq *Sudan* 80 D4
Aqiq, Khalig *Sudan* 80 D4
'Aqrah *Iraq* 73 D10
Aqsay *Kazakhstan* 52 D6
Aqtaū *Kazakhstan* 52 E6
Aqtöbe *Kazakhstan* 52 D6
Aqtoghay *Kazakhstan* 52 E8
Aquidauana *Brazil* 125 H7
Aquila *Mexico* 118 D4
Aquiles Serdán *Mexico* 118 B3
Aquin *Haiti* 121 C5
Aquitaine □ *France* 20 D3
Ar Rafid *Syria* 74 C4
Ar Raḩḩālīyah *Iraq* 73 F10
Ar Ramādī *Iraq* 73 F10
Ar Ramthā *Jordan* 74 C5
Ar Raqqah *Syria* 73 E8
Ar Raqqah □ *Syria* 73 D8
Ar Rashidiya = Er Rachidia
  Morocco 78 B5
Ar Rass *Si. Arabia* 70 E4
Ar Rayyan *Qatar* 71 E6
Ar Rifā'ī *Iraq* 70 D5
Ar Riyāḍ *Si. Arabia* 70 E5
Ar Ru'ays *Qatar* 71 E6
Ar Rukhaymīyah *Iraq* 70 D5
Ar Rumaythah *Iraq* 70 D5
Ar Ruşāfah *Syria* 73 E8
Ar Ruţbah *Iraq* 73 F9
Ara *India* 69 G11
Ara Goro *Ethiopia* 81 F5
Ara Tera *Ethiopia* 81 F5
Arab *U.S.A.* 117 D11
'Arab, Bahr el → *Sudan* 81 F2
Arab, Khalîg el *Egypt* 80 A2
Arab, Shatt al → *Asia* 71 D6
'Araba, W. → *Egypt* 80 J8
'Arabābād *Iran* 71 C8
Araban *Turkey* 72 D7
Arabatskaya Strelka *Ukraine* 33 K8
Arabba *Italy* 41 B8
Arabia *Asia* 50 F5
Arabian Desert = Es Sahrâ'
  Esh Sharqîya *Egypt* 80 B3
Arabian Gulf = Persian
  Gulf *Asia* 71 E6
Arabian Sea *Ind. Oc.* 50 G8
Araç *Turkey* 72 B5
Aracaju *Brazil* 125 F11
Aracati *Brazil* 125 D11
Araçatuba *Brazil* 127 A5
Aracena *Spain* 37 H4
Aracena, Sierra de *Spain* 37 H4
Arachova *Greece* 46 C4
Arachthos → *Greece* 46 B3
Aračinovo *Macedonia* 44 D5
Araçuaí *Brazil* 125 G10
'Arad *Israel* 74 D4

Arad *Romania* **28** D6
Arad □ *Romania* **28** D6
Arādān *Iran* **71** C7
Aradhippou *Cyprus* **49** E12
Arafura Sea *E. Indies* **90** B6
Aragats *Armenia* **35** K7
Aragón □ *Spain* **38** D4
Aragón ➡ *Spain* **38** C3
Aragona *Italy* **42** E6
Araguacema *Brazil* **125** E9
Araguaia ➡ *Brazil* **125** E9
Araguaína *Brazil* **125** E9
Araguari *Brazil* **125** G9
Araguari ➡ *Brazil* **125** C9
Arahal *Spain* **37** H5
Arain *India* **68** F6
Arak *Algeria* **78** C6
Arāk *Iran* **71** C6
Araka *Sudan* **81** G3
Arakan Coast *Burma* **67** K19
Arakan Yoma *Burma* **67** K19
Araklı *Turkey* **73** B9
Araks = Aras, Rūd-e ➡ *Asia* **35** K9
Aral *Kazakhstan* **52** E7
Aral Sea *Asia* **52** E7
Aral Tengizi = Aral Sea *Asia* **52** E7
Aralık *Turkey* **73** C11
Aralsk = Aral *Kazakhstan* **52** E7
Aralskoye More = Aral Sea *Asia* **52** E7
Aralsor, Ozero = Aralsor Köli *Kazakhstan* **35** F9
Aralsor Köli *Kazakhstan* **35** F9
Aramac *Australia* **94** C4
Aran I. *Ireland* **12** B3
Aran Is. *Ireland* **12** C2
Aranda de Duero *Spain* **36** D7
Arandān *Iran* **70** C5
Aranđelovac *Serbia* **44** B4
Aranjuez *Spain* **36** E7
Aranos *Namibia* **88** C2
Aransas Pass *U.S.A.* **116** H6
Aranyaprathet *Thailand* **64** F4
Araouane *Mali* **82** B4
Arapahoe *U.S.A.* **112** E4
Arapey Grande ➡ *Uruguay* **126** C4
Arapgir *Turkey* **73** C8
Arapiraca *Brazil* **125** E11
Arapis, Akra *Greece* **45** F8
Arapongas *Brazil* **127** A5
Ar'ar *Si. Arabia* **70** D4
Araranguá *Brazil* **127** B6
Araraquara *Brazil* **125** H9
Ararás, Serra das *Brazil* **127** B5
Ararat *Armenia* **73** C11
Ararat *Australia* **95** F3
Ararat, Mt. = Ağrı Dağı *Turkey* **73** C11
Araria *India* **69** F12
Araripe, Chapada do *Brazil* **125** E11
Araruama, L. de *Brazil* **127** A7
Aras = Aras, Rūd-e ➡ *Asia* **35** K9
Aras, Rūd-e ➡ *Asia* **35** K9
Aratāne *Mauritania* **82** B3
Arauca *Colombia* **124** B4
Arauca ➡ *Venezuela* **124** B5
Arauco *Chile* **126** D1
Aravalli Range *India* **68** G5
Arawa *Ethiopia* **81** F5
Arawale ➡ *Kenya* **86** C5
Araxá *Brazil* **125** G9
Araxes = Aras, Rūd-e ➡ *Asia* **35** K9
Araya, Pen. de *Venezuela* **124** A6
Araz = Aras, Rūd-e ➡ *Asia* **35** K9
Arba Gugu *Ethiopia* **81** F5
Arba Minch *Ethiopia* **81** F4
Arbat *Iraq* **73** E11
Árbatax *Italy* **42** C2
Arbi *Ethiopia* **81** F4
Arbīl *Iraq* **73** D11
Arbīl □ *Iraq* **73** D11
Arboga *Sweden* **10** E9
Arbois *France* **19** F12
Arbore *Ethiopia* **81** F4
Arboréa *Italy* **42** C1
Arborfield *Canada* **103** C8
Arborg *Canada* **103** C9
Arbre du Ténéré *Niger* **83** B7
Arbroath *U.K.* **13** E6
Arbuckle *U.S.A.* **110** F4
Arbus *Italy* **42** C1
Arc ➡ *France* **21** C10
Arc-lès-Gray *France* **19** E12
Arcachon *France* **20** D2
Arcachon, Bassin d' *France* **20** D2
Arcade *U.S.A.* **114** D6
Arcadia *Fla., U.S.A.* **117** H14
Arcadia *La., U.S.A.* **116** E8
Arcadia *Pa., U.S.A.* **114** F6
Arcata *U.S.A.* **108** F1
Arcévia *Italy* **41** E9
Archanes *Greece* **47** F7
Archangel = Arkhangelsk *Russia* **52** C5
Archangelos *Greece* **49** C10
Archar *Bulgaria* **44** C6
Archbald *U.S.A.* **115** E9
Archena *Spain* **39** G3

Archer ➡ *Australia* **94** A3
Archer B. *Australia* **94** A3
Archer Bend = Mungkan Kandju △ *Australia* **94** A3
Archers Post *Kenya* **86** B4
Arches △ *U.S.A.* **108** G9
Archidona *Spain* **37** H6
Archipel-de-Mingan △ *Canada* **105** B7
Archipiélago Chinijo △ *Canary Is.* **48** E6
Archipiélago Los Roques △ *Venezuela* **121** D6
Arci, Mte. *Italy* **42** C1
Arcidosso *Italy* **41** F8
Arcipelago de la Maddalena △ *Italy* **42** A2
Arcipelago Toscano △ *Italy* **40** F7
Arcis-sur-Aube *France* **19** D11
Arckaringa Cr. ➡ *Australia* **95** D2
Arco *Italy* **40** C7
Arco *U.S.A.* **108** E7
Arcos de Jalón *Spain* **38** D2
Arcos de la Frontera *Spain* **37** J5
Arcos de Valdevez *Portugal* **36** D2
Arcot *India* **66** N11
Arcozelo *Portugal* **36** E3
Arctic Bay *Canada* **101** C14
Arctic Mid-Ocean Ridge *Arctic* **4** A
Arctic Ocean *Arctic* **4** B18
Arctic Red River = Tsiigehtchic *Canada* **100** D5
Arctowski *Antarctica* **5** C18
Arda ➡ *Bulgaria* **45** E10
Arda ➡ *Italy* **40** C6
Ardabīl *Iran* **73** C13
Ardabīl □ *Iran* **71** B6
Ardahan *Turkey* **73** B10
Ardahan □ *Turkey* **73** B10
Ardakān = Sepīdān *Iran* **71** D7
Ardakān *Iran* **71** C7
Ardala *Sweden* **11** F7
Ardales *Spain* **37** J6
Ardara *Ireland* **12** B3
Ardas ➡ *Greece* **45** E10
Ardèche □ *France* **21** D8
Ardèche ➡ *France* **21** D8
Ardee *Ireland* **12** C5
Arden *Canada* **114** B8
Arden *Denmark* **11** H3
Arden *Calif., U.S.A.* **110** G5
Arden *Nev., U.S.A.* **111** J11
Ardenne *Belgium* **17** E5
Ardennes = Ardenne *Belgium* **17** E5
Ardennes □ *France* **19** C11
Ardentes *France* **19** F8
Arderin *Ireland* **12** C4
Ardeşen *Turkey* **73** B9
Ardestān *Iran* **71** C7
Ardfert *Ireland* **12** D2
Ardglass *U.K.* **12** B6
Ardhéa = Aridea *Greece* **44** F6
Ardila ➡ *Portugal* **37** G3
Ardino *Bulgaria* **45** E9
Ardivachar Pt. *U.K.* **13** D1
Ardlethan *Australia* **95** E4
Ardmore *Okla., U.S.A.* **116** D6
Ardmore *Pa., U.S.A.* **115** F9
Ardmore Pt. *U.K.* **13** E2
Ardnamurchan, Pt. of *U.K.* **13** E2
Ardnave Pt. *U.K.* **13** F2
Ardon *Russia* **35** J7
Ardore *Italy* **43** D9
Ardres *France* **19** B8
Ardrossan *Australia* **95** E2
Ardrossan *U.K.* **13** F4
Ards Pen. □ *U.K.* **12** B6
Arduan *Sudan* **80** D3
Ardud *Romania* **28** C7
Åre *Sweden* **10** A7
Arecibo *Puerto Rico* **121** d
Areia Branca *Brazil* **125** E11
Arena, Pt. *U.S.A.* **110** G3
Arenal *Honduras* **120** C2
Arenas = Las Arenas *Spain* **36** B6
Arenas de San Pedro *Spain* **36** E5
Arendal *Norway* **9** G13
Arendsee *Germany* **24** C7
Arenys de Mar *Spain* **38** D7
Arenzano *Italy* **40** D5
Areópoli *Greece* **46** E4
Arequipa *Peru* **124** G4
Arero *Ethiopia* **81** G4
Arès *France* **20** D2
Arévalo *Spain* **36** D6
Arezzo *Italy* **41** E8
Arga *Turkey* **70** B3
Arga ➡ *Spain* **38** C3
Argalasti *Greece* **46** B5
Argamasilla de Alba *Spain* **37** F7
Argamasilla de Calatrava *Spain* **37** G6
Arganda del Rey *Spain* **36** E7
Arganil *Portugal* **36** E2
Argarapa ◎ *Australia* **94** C1
Argedeb *Ethiopia* **81** F5
Argelès-Gazost *France* **20** E3
Argelès-sur-Mer *France* **20** F7
Argens ➡ *France* **21** E10
Argent-sur-Sauldre *France* **19** E9

Argenta *Canada* **102** C5
Argenta *Italy* **41** D8
Argentan *France* **18** D6
Argentário, Mte. *Italy* **41** F8
Argentat *France* **20** C5
Argentera *Italy* **40** D4
Argenteuil *France* **19** D9
Argentia *Canada* **105** C9
Argentina ■ *S. Amer.* **128** D3
Argentine Basin *Atl. Oc.* **128** F6
Argentino, L. *Argentina* **128** G2
Argenton-Château *France* **18** F6
Argenton-sur-Creuse *France* **19** F8
Argeş □ *Romania* **29** F9
Argeş ➡ *Romania* **29** F11
Argheile *Ethiopia* **81** F5
Argirades *Greece* **49** B3
Argiroupoli *Greece* **49** D6
Argo *Sudan* **80** D3
Argolida □ *Greece* **46** D4
Argolikos Kolpos *Greece* **46** D4
Argonne *France* **19** C12
Argos *Greece* **46** D4
Argos Orestiko *Greece* **44** F5
Argostoli *Greece* **46** C2
Arguedas *Spain* **38** C3
Arguello, Pt. *U.S.A.* **111** L6
Argun *Russia* **35** J7
Argun ➡ *Russia* **53** D13
Argungu *Nigeria* **83** C5
Argus Pk. *U.S.A.* **111** K9
Argyle, L. *Australia* **92** C4
Argyll □ *U.K.* **13** E4
Argyll & Bute □ *U.K.* **13** E4
Arhavi *Turkey* **73** B9
Århus *Denmark* **11** H4
Ariadnoye *Russia* **54** B7
Ariamsvlei *Namibia* **88** D2
Ariana *Tunisia* **79** A8
Ariano Irpino *Italy* **43** A8
Aribinda *Burkina Faso* **83** C4
Arica *Chile* **124** G4
Arica *Colombia* **124** D4
Arico *Canary Is.* **48** F3
Arid, C. *Australia* **93** F3
Arida *Japan* **55** G7
Aride *Seychelles* **85** b
Aridea *Greece* **44** F6
Ariège □ *France* **20** F5
Ariège ➡ *France* **20** E5
Arieş ➡ *Romania* **29** D8
Arihā *Israel* **80** A4
Arila, Akra *Greece* **49** A3
Arilje *Serbia* **44** C4
Arima *Trin. & Tob.* **121** D7
Arinos ➡ *Brazil* **124** F7
Ario de Rosales *Mexico* **118** D4
Ariogala *Lithuania* **30** C10
Aripo, Mt. *Trin. & Tob.* **125** K15
Aripuanã *Brazil* **124** E6
Aripuanã ➡ *Brazil* **124** E6
Ariquemes *Brazil* **124** E6
Arisaig *U.K.* **13** E3
Arîsh, W. el ➡ *Egypt* **80** A3
Arissa *Ethiopia* **81** E5
Aristazabal I. *Canada* **102** C3
Arizaro, Salar de *Argentina* **126** A2
Arizona *Argentina* **126** D2
Arizona □ *U.S.A.* **109** J8
Arizpe *Mexico* **118** A2
'Arjah *Si. Arabia* **70** E5
Ärjäng *Sweden* **10** E6
Arjeplog *Sweden* **8** C17
Arjepluovve = Arjeplog *Sweden* **8** C17
Arjona *Colombia* **124** A3
Arjona *Spain* **37** H6
Arjuna *Indonesia* **63** G15
Arka *Russia* **53** C15
Arkadak *Russia* **34** E6
Arkadelphia *U.S.A.* **116** D8
Arkadia □ *Greece* **46** D4
Arkaig, L. *U.K.* **13** E3
Arkalyk = Arqalyk *Kazakhstan* **52** D7
Arkansas □ *U.S.A.* **116** D8
Arkansas ➡ *U.S.A.* **116** E9
Arkansas City *U.S.A.* **112** G5
Arkaroola *Australia* **95** E2
Arkavāz *Iran* **73** F12
Arkhangelsk *Russia* **52** C5
Arkhangelskoye *Russia* **34** E5
Arki *Greece* **47** D8
Arki *India* **68** D7
Arkiko *Eritrea* **81** D4
Arklow *Ireland* **12** D5
Arkona, Kap *Germany* **24** A9
Arkösund *Sweden* **11** F10
Arkoudi *Greece* **46** C2
Arkport *U.S.A.* **114** D7
Arkticheskiy, Mys *Russia* **53** A10
Arkul *Russia* **34** B10
Arkville *U.S.A.* **115** D10
Årla *Sweden* **10** E10

Arlanda, Stockholm ✈ (ARN) *Sweden* **10** E11
Arlanza ➡ *Spain* **36** C6
Arlanzón ➡ *Spain* **36** C6
Arlbergpass *Austria* **26** D3
Arlbergtunnel *Austria* **26** D3
Arles *France* **21** E8
Arli *Burkina Faso* **83** C5
Arli △ *Burkina Faso* **83** C5
Arlington *S. Africa* **89** D4
Arlington *N.Y., U.S.A.* **115** E11
Arlington *Oreg., U.S.A.* **108** D3
Arlington *S. Dak., U.S.A.* **112** C5
Arlington *Tex., U.S.A.* **116** E6
Arlington *Va., U.S.A.* **113** F15
Arlington *Vt., U.S.A.* **115** C11
Arlington *Wash., U.S.A.* **110** B4
Arlington Heights *U.S.A.* **112** D10
Arlit *Niger* **78** E7
Arlon *Belgium* **17** E5
Arlparra *Australia* **94** C1
Arltunga *Australia* **94** C1
Armadale *Australia* **93** F2
Armagh *U.K.* **12** B5
Armagh □ *U.K.* **12** B5
Armagnac *France* **20** E4
Armançon ➡ *France* **19** E10
Armando Bermudez △ *Dom. Rep.* **121** C5
Armant *Egypt* **80** B3
Armavir *Russia* **35** H5
Armenia *Colombia* **124** C3
Armenia ■ *Asia* **35** K7
Armeniş *Romania* **28** E7
Armenistis, Akra *Greece* **49** C9
Armentières *France* **19** B9
Armidale *Australia* **95** E5
Armilla *Spain* **37** H7
Armour *U.S.A.* **112** D4
Armstrong *B.C., Canada* **102** C5
Armstrong *Ont., Canada* **104** B2
Armutlu *Bursa, Turkey* **45** F12
Armutlu *İzmir, Turkey* **47** C9
Arnaud ➡ *Canada* **101** F18
Arnarfjörður *Iceland* **8** D2
Arnaud ➡ *Canada* **101** F18
Arnauti, C. *Cyprus* **49** D11
Arnay-le-Duc *France* **19** E11
Arnea *Greece* **44** F7
Arnedillo *Spain* **38** C2
Arnedo *Spain* **38** C2
Arnett *U.S.A.* **116** C5
Arnhem *Neths.* **17** C5
Arnhem, C. *Australia* **94** A2
Arnhem B. *Australia* **94** A2
Arnhem Land *Australia* **94** A1
Arnhem Land ◎ *Australia* **94** A1
Arnissa *Greece* **44** F6
Arno ➡ *Italy* **40** E7
Arno Bay *Australia* **95** E2
Arnold *U.K.* **14** D6
Arnold *U.S.A.* **110** G6
Arnoldstein *Austria* **26** E6
Arnon ➡ *France* **19** E9
Arnot *Canada* **103** B9
Arnøya *Norway* **8** A19
Arnprior *Canada* **115** A8
Arnsberg *Germany* **24** D4
Arnsberger Wald ○ *Germany* **24** D4
Arnstadt *Germany* **24** E6
Aroa, Pte. *Moorea* **91** d
Aroania Oros *Greece* **46** D4
Aroche *Spain* **37** H4
Arochuku *Nigeria* **83** D6
Aroab *Namibia* **88** D2
Aroma *Sudan* **80** D4
Aron *India* **68** G6
Aron ➡ *France* **19** F10
Arona *Italy* **40** C5
Aroroy *Phil.* **61** E5
Aros ➡ *Mexico* **118** B3
Arousa, Ría de ➡ *Spain* **36** C2
Arpa ➡ *Asia* **73** C11
Arpaçay *Turkey* **73** B10
Arpajon *France* **19** D9
Arpajon-sur-Cère *France* **20** D6
Arpaşu de Jos *Romania* **29** E9
Arqalyk *Kazakhstan* **52** D7
Arrah = Ara *India* **69** G11
Arrah *Ivory C.* **82** D4
Arraial do Cabo *Brazil* **127** A7
Arraiolos *Portugal* **37** G3
Arran *U.K.* **13** F3
Arras *France* **19** B9
Arrats ➡ *France* **20** D4
Arreau *France* **20** F4
Arrecife *Canary Is.* **48** F6
Arrecifes *Argentina* **126** C3
Arrée, Mts. d' *France* **18** D3
Arresø *Denmark* **11** J6
Arriaga *Mexico* **119** D6
Arribes del Duero ○ *Spain* **36** D4
Arrilalah *Australia* **94** C3
Arrino *Australia* **93** E2
Arriondas *Spain* **36** B5
Arromanches-les-Bains *France* **18** C6
Arronches *Portugal* **37** F3

Arros ➡ *France* **20** E3
Arrow, L. *Ireland* **12** B3
Arrowtown *N.Z.* **91** F2
Arroyo de la Luz *Spain* **37** F4
Arroyo Grande *U.S.A.* **111** K6
Ars *Iran* **70** B5
Ars-sur-Moselle *France* **19** C13
Arsenault L. *Canada* **103** B7
Arsenev *Russia* **54** B6
Arsi *Ethiopia* **81** F4
Arsiero *Italy* **41** C8
Arsin *Turkey* **73** B8
Arsk *Russia* **34** B9
Årsunda *Sweden* **10** D10
Arta *Greece* **46** B3
Artà *Spain* **48** B10
Arta □ *Greece* **46** B3
Artà, Coves d *Spain* **48** B10
Artashat *Armenia* **73** B11
Arteaga *Mexico* **118** D4
Arteche *Phil.* **61** E6
Arteijo = Arteixo *Spain* **36** B2
Arteixo *Spain* **36** B2
Artem = Artyom *Azerbaijan* **35** K10
Artem *Russia* **54** C6
Artemovsk *Russia* **53** D10
Artemovsk *Ukraine* **33** H9
Artemovskiy *Russia* **35** G5
Artenay *France* **19** D9
Artern *Germany* **24** D7
Artesa de Segre *Spain* **38** D6
Artesia = Mosomane *Botswana* **88** C4
Artesia *U.S.A.* **109** K11
Arthington *Liberia* **82** D2
Arthur *Canada* **114** C4
Arthur ➡ *Australia* **95** G3
Arthur Cr. ➡ *Australia* **94** C2
Arthur Pt. *Australia* **94** C5
Arthur River *Australia* **93** F2
Arthur's Pass *N.Z.* **91** E3
Arthur's Pass △ *N.Z.* **91** E3
Arthur's Town *Bahamas* **121** B4
Artigas *Antarctica* **5** C18
Artigas *Uruguay* **126** C4
Artik *Armenia* **35** K6
Artillery L. *Canada* **103** A7
Artois *France* **19** B9
Artotina *Greece* **46** C4
Artova *Turkey* **72** B7
Artrutx, C. de *Spain* **48** B10
Artsyz *Ukraine* **29** D14
Artvin *Turkey* **73** B9
Artvin □ *Turkey* **73** B9
Artyk *Russia* **53** C15
Artyom *Azerbaijan* **35** K10
Aru, Kepulauan *Indonesia* **63** F8
Aru Is. = Aru, Kepulauan *Indonesia* **63** F8
Arua *Uganda* **86** B3
Aruanã *Brazil* **125** F8
Aruba ☑ *W. Indies* **121** D6
Arucas *Canary Is.* **48** F4
Arudy *France* **20** E3
Arué *Tahiti* **91** d
Arun ➡ *Nepal* **69** F12
Arun ➡ *U.K.* **15** G7
Arunachal Pradesh □ *India* **67** F19
Arusha *Tanzania* **86** C4
Arusha □ *Tanzania* **86** C4
Arusha △ *Tanzania* **86** C4
Arusha Chini *Tanzania* **86** C4
Aruwimi ➡ *Dem. Rep. of the Congo* **86** B1
Arvada *Colo., U.S.A.* **108** G11
Arvada *Wyo., U.S.A.* **108** D10
Arvayheer *Mongolia* **53** E11
Arve ➡ *France* **19** F13
Arvi *Greece* **49** E7
Arviat *Canada* **103** A10
Arvidsjaur *Sweden* **8** D18
Arvika *Sweden* **10** E6
Arvin *U.S.A.* **111** K8
Arwal *India* **69** G11
Arxan *China* **60** B6
Aryd *Sweden* **11** H8
Arys *Kazakhstan* **52** E7
Arzachena *Italy* **42** A2
Arzamas *Russia* **34** C6
Arzanah *U.A.E.* **71** E7
Arzew *Algeria* **78** A5
Arzgir *Russia* **35** H7
Arzignano *Italy* **41** C8
Arzúa *Spain* **36** C2
Aš *Czech Rep.* **26** A5
Ås *Sweden* **10** A8
As Pontes de García Rodríguez *Spain* **36** B3
Aş Şafā *Syria* **74** B6
Aş Saffānīyah *Si. Arabia* **71** E6
Aş Şafirah *Syria* **72** D7
Aş Şahm *Oman* **71** E8
As Sājir *Si. Arabia* **70** E5
As Salamīyah *Syria* **72** E7
As Salmān *Iraq* **70** D5
As Salt *Jordan* **74** C4
As Sal'w'a *Qatar* **71** E6
As Samāwah *Iraq* **70** D5
As Sanamayn *Syria* **74** B5
As Sohar = Şuḩār *Oman* **71** E8

As Sukhnah *Syria* **73** E8
As Sulaymānīyah *Iraq* **73** E11
As Sulaymānīyah □ *Iraq* **73** E11
As Sulaymī *Si. Arabia* **70** E4
As Sulayyil *Si. Arabia* **75** C4
As Summān *Si. Arabia* **70** E5
Aş Şuwar *Syria* **73** E9
As Suwaydā' *Syria* **74** C5
As Suwaydā' □ *Syria* **74** C5
Aş Şuwayq *Oman* **71** F8
Aş Şuwayrah *Iraq* **73** F11
Āsa *Sweden* **11** G6
Asab *Namibia* **88** D2
Asaba *Nigeria* **83** D6
Asad, Buḩayrat al *Syria* **73** D8
Asadābād *Iran* **73** E13
Asafo *Ghana* **82** D4
Asahi-Gawa ➡ *Japan* **55** G6
Asahigawa *Japan* **54** C11
Asale, L. *Ethiopia* **81** E5
Asaluyeh *Iran* **71** E7
Asamankese *Ghana* **83** D4
Asan ➡ *India* **69** F8
Asansol *India* **69** H12
Åsarna *Sweden* **10** B8
Asau *Samoa* **91** b
Asayita *Ethiopia* **81** E5
Asbe Teferi *Ethiopia* **81** F5
Asbesberge *S. Africa* **88** D3
Asbestos *Canada* **105** C5
Asbury Park *U.S.A.* **115** F10
Ascea *Italy* **43** B8
Ascensión *Mexico* **118** A3
Ascensión, B. de la *Mexico* **119** D7
Ascension I. *Atl. Oc.* **77** G2
Aschach an der Donau *Austria* **26** C7
Aschaffenburg *Germany* **25** F5
Aschendorf *Germany* **24** B3
Aschersleben *Germany* **24** D7
Asciano *Italy* **41** E8
Áscoli Piceno *Italy* **41** F10
Áscoli Satriano *Italy* **43** A8
Ascope *Peru* **124** E3
Ascotán *Chile* **126** A2
Aseb *Eritrea* **81** E5
Åseda *Sweden* **11** G9
Asela *Ethiopia* **81** F4
Åsele *Sweden* **10** C7
Asen *Sweden* **10** C7
Asenovgrad *Bulgaria* **45** D8
Asfeld *France* **19** C11
Asfûn el Matâ'na *Egypt* **80** B3
Asgabat = Ashgabat *Turkmenistan* **71** B8
Asgata *Cyprus* **49** E12
Ash Fork *U.S.A.* **109** J7
Ash Grove *U.S.A.* **112** G7
Ash Shabakah *Iraq* **70** D4
Ash Shamāl □ *Lebanon* **74** A5
Ash Shāmīyah *Iraq* **73** D11
Ash Shāriqah *U.A.E.* **71** E7
Ash Sharmah *Si. Arabia* **70** D2
Ash Sharqāt *Iraq* **73** D10
Ash Shaṭrah *Iraq* **70** D5
Ash Shawbak *Jordan* **70** D2
Ash Shihr *Yemen* **75** E4
Ash Shināfīyah *Iraq* **70** D5
Ash Shu'bah *Si. Arabia* **70** D5
Ash Shumlūl *Si. Arabia* **70** E5
Ash Shūr'a *Iraq* **70** E3
Ash Shurayf *Si. Arabia* **70** E3
Ash Shuwayfāt *Lebanon* **74** B4
Ashanti □ *Ghana* **83** D4
Ashau *Vietnam* **64** D6
Ashbourne *U.K.* **14** D6
Ashburn *U.S.A.* **117** F13
Ashburton *N.Z.* **91** E3
Ashburton ➡ *Australia* **92** D1
Ashcroft *Canada* **102** C4
Ashdod *Israel* **74** D3
Ashdown *U.S.A.* **116** E7
Asheboro *U.S.A.* **117** D15
Ashern *Canada* **103** C9
Ashewat *Pakistan* **68** D3
Asheweig ➡ *Canada* **104** B2
Asheville *U.S.A.* **117** D13
Ashford *Australia* **95** D5
Ashford *U.K.* **15** F8
Ashgabat *Turkmenistan* **71** B8
Ashibetsu *Japan* **54** C11
Ashikaga *Japan* **55** F9
Ashington *U.K.* **14** B6
Ashizuri-Uwakai △ *Japan* **55** H6
Ashizuri-Zaki *Japan* **55** H6
Ashkarkot *Afghan.* **68** C2
Ashkhabad = Ashgabat *Turkmenistan* **71** B8
Āshkhāneh *Iran* **71** B8
Ashland *Kans., U.S.A.* **112** G4
Ashland *Ky., U.S.A.* **113** F12
Ashland *Maine, U.S.A.* **113** B11
Ashland *Mont., U.S.A.* **108** D10
Ashland *Ohio, U.S.A.* **114** F2
Ashland *Oreg., U.S.A.* **108** E2
Ashland *Pa., U.S.A.* **115** F8
Ashland *Va., U.S.A.* **113** G15
Ashland *Wis., U.S.A.* **112** B8
Ashley *N. Dak., U.S.A.* **112** B4

Ashley *Pa., U.S.A.* **115** E9
Ashmore and Cartier Is.
  Ind. Oc. **92** B3
Ashmore Reef *Australia* **92** B3
Ashmūn *Egypt* **80** H7
Ashmyany *Belarus* **23** A13
Ashokan Res. *U.S.A.* **115** E10
Ashoknagar *India* **68** G7
Ashta *India* **68** H7
Ashtabula *U.S.A.* **114** E4
Āshtiyān *Iran* **71** C6
Ashton *S. Africa* **88** E3
Ashton *U.S.A.* **108** D8
Ashuanipi, L. *Canada* **105** B6
Ashuapmushuan →
  Canada **104** C5
Ashville *U.S.A.* **114** F6
'Āṣī → *Asia* **72** D6
Asia **50** E9
Asia, Kepulauan *Indonesia* **63** D8
Asiago *Italy* **41** C3
Asifabad *India* **66** K11
Asinara *Italy* **42** A1
Asinara, G. dell' *Italy* **42** A1
Asino *Russia* **52** D9
Asipovichy *Belarus* **23** B15
'Asir *Si. Arabia* **80** D5
Aşkale *Turkey* **73** C9
Askersund *Sweden* **11** F8
Askham *S. Africa* **88** D3
Askī Mawṣil *Iraq* **73** D10
Askim *Norway* **9** G14
Askio, Oros *Greece* **44** F5
Askja *Iceland* **8** D5
Asklipio *Greece* **49** C9
Askøyna *Norway* **8** F11
Asl *Egypt* **80** B3
Aslan Burnu *Turkey* **47** C8
Aslanapa *Turkey* **47** B11
Aslānduz *Iran* **73** C12
Asmara = Asmera *Eritrea* **81** D4
Asmara *Eritrea* **81** D4
Asmera *Eritrea* **81** D4
Asnæs *Denmark* **11** J4
Åsnen *Sweden* **11** H8
Aso Kuju △ *Japan* **55** H5
Ásola *Italy* **40** C7
Asos *Greece* **46** C2
Asosa *Ethiopia* **81** E3
Asoteriba, Jebel *Sudan* **80** C4
Aspatria *U.K.* **14** C4
Aspe *Spain* **39** G4
Aspen *U.S.A.* **108** G10
Aspendos *Turkey* **72** D4
Aspermont *U.S.A.* **116** E4
Aspet *France* **20** E4
Aspiring, Mt. *N.Z.* **91** F2
Aspres-sur-Buëch *France* **21** D9
Asprokavos, Akra *Greece* **49** B4
Aspromonte △ *Italy* **43** D8
Aspur *India* **68** H6
Asquith *Canada* **103** C7
Assab = Aseb *Eritrea* **81** E5
Assâba *Mauritania* **82** B2
Assâba, Massif de l'
  Mauritania **82** B2
Assagny △ *Ivory C.* **82** D4
Assaikio *Nigeria* **83** D6
Assal, L. *Djibouti* **81** E5
Assam □ *India* **67** G18
Assamakka *Niger* **83** B6
Assateague Island △ *U.S.A.*
  113 F16
Asse *Belgium* **17** D4
Assémini *Italy* **42** C1
Assen *Neths.* **17** A6
Assens *Denmark* **11** J3
Assini *Ivory C.* **82** D4
Assiniboia *Canada* **103** D7
Assiniboine → *Canada* **103** D9
Assiniboine, Mt. *Canada* **102** C5
Assis *Brazil* **127** A5
Assisi *Italy* **41** E9
Assynt, L. *U.K.* **13** C3
Astaffort *France* **20** D4
Astakida *Greece* **47** F8
Astakos *Greece* **46** C3
Astana *Kazakhstan* **52** D8
Āstāneh *Iran* **71** B6
Astara *Azerbaijan* **73** C13
Āstārā *Iran* **73** C13
Astarabad = Gorgān *Iran* **71** B7
Asterousia *Greece* **49** E7
Asti *Italy* **40** D5
Astipalea *Greece* **47** E8
Astorga *Spain* **36** C4
Astoria *U.S.A.* **110** D3
Åstorp *Sweden* **11** H6
Astrakhan *Russia* **35** G9
Astrakhan □ *Russia* **35** G8
Astrebla Downs *Australia* **94** C3
Astudillo *Spain* **36** C6
Asturias □ *Spain* **36** B5
Asturias ✈ (OVD) *Spain* **36** B4
Asunción *Paraguay* **126** B4
Asunción Nochixtlán
  Mexico **119** D5
Åsunden *Sweden* **11** F9

Asutri *Sudan* **81** D4
Aswa → *Uganda* **86** B3
Aswa-Lolim △ *Uganda* **86** B3
Aswad, Ra's al *Si. Arabia* **80** C4
Aswân *Egypt* **80** C3
Aswan High Dam = Sadd
  el Aali *Egypt* **80** C3
Asyût *Egypt* **80** B3
Asyûti, Wadi → *Egypt* **80** B3
Aszód *Hungary* **28** C4
Aṭ Ṭafīlah *Jordan* **74** E4
Aṭ Ṭafīlah □ *Jordan* **74** E4
Aṭ Ṭā'if *Si. Arabia* **80** C5
Aṭ Ta'mīm □ *Iraq* **70** C5
Aṭ Ṭirāq *Si. Arabia* **70** E5
Aṭ Tubayq *Si. Arabia* **70** D3
Aṭ Ṭunayb *Jordan* **74** D4
Atabey *Turkey* **47** D12
Atacama □ *Chile* **126** B2
Atacama, Desierto de *Chile* **126** A2
Atacama, Salar de *Chile* **126** A2
Atakeye ☉ *Australia* **92** D5
Atakpamé *Togo* **83** D5
Atalandi *Greece* **46** C4
Atalaya *Peru* **124** F4
Atalaya de Femes *Canary Is.* **48** F6
Atami *Japan* **55** G9
Atamyrat *Turkmenistan* **52** F7
Atapupu *Indonesia* **63** F6
Atâr *Mauritania* **78** D3
Atarfe *Spain* **37** H7
Atari *Pakistan* **68** D6
Atascadero *U.S.A.* **110** K6
Atasū *Kazakhstan* **52** E8
Atatürk, İstanbul ✈ (IST)
  Turkey **45** F12
Atatürk Barajı *Turkey* **73** D8
Atauro *E. Timor* **63** F7
Ataviros *Greece* **49** C9
Atbara *Sudan* **80** D3
'Atbara, Nahr → *Sudan* **80** D3
Atbasar *Kazakhstan* **52** D7
Atça *Turkey* **47** D10
Atchafalaya B. *U.S.A.* **116** G9
Atchison *U.S.A.* **112** F6
Atebubu *Ghana* **83** D4
Ateca *Spain* **38** D3
Aterno → *Italy* **41** F10
Āteshān *Iran* **71** C7
Atesine, Alpi *Italy* **41** B8
Atessa *Italy* **41** F11
Atfih *Egypt* **80** J7
Ath *Belgium* **17** D3
Athabasca *Canada* **102** C6
Athabasca → *Canada* **103** B6
Athabasca, L. *Canada* **103** B7
Athabasca Sand Dunes △
  Canada **103** B7
Athamanon Oros *Greece* **46** B3
Athboy *Ireland* **12** C5
Athenry *Ireland* **12** C3
Athens = Athina *Greece* **46** D5
Athens *Ala., U.S.A.* **117** D11
Athens *Ga., U.S.A.* **117** E13
Athens *N.Y., U.S.A.* **115** D11
Athens *Ohio, U.S.A.* **113** F12
Athens *Pa., U.S.A.* **115** E8
Athens *Tenn., U.S.A.* **117** D12
Athens *Tex., U.S.A.* **116** E7
Atherley *Canada* **114** B5
Atherton *Australia* **94** B4
Athi River *Kenya* **86** C4
Athiéme *Benin* **83** D5
Athienou *Cyprus* **49** D12
Athina *Greece* **46** D5
Athina ✈ (ATH) *Greece* **46** D5
Athínai = Athina *Greece* **46** D5
Athlone *Ireland* **12** C4
Athna *Cyprus* **49** D12
Athol *U.S.A.* **115** D12
Atholl, Forest of *U.K.* **13** E5
Atholville *Canada* **105** C6
Athos *Greece* **45** F8
Athy *Ireland* **12** C5
Ati *Chad* **79** F9
Ati *Sudan* **81** E2
Atiak *Uganda* **86** B3
Atienza *Spain* **38** D2
Atiit *Sudan* **81** F3
Atik L. *Canada* **103** B9
Atikaki △ *Canada* **103** C9
Atikameg → *Canada* **104** B3
Atikokan *Canada* **104** B1
Atikonak L. *Canada* **105** B7
Atimaono *Tahiti* **91** d
Atimonan *Phil.* **61** E4
Atitlán △ *Cent. Amer.* **119** E6
Atiu *Cook Is.* **97** J12
Atka *Russia* **53** C16
Atka I. *U.S.A.* **106** E5
Atkarsk *Russia* **34** E7
Atkinson *U.S.A.* **112** D4
Atlanta *Ga., U.S.A.* **117** E12
Atlanta *Tex., U.S.A.* **116** E7
Atlantic *U.S.A.* **112** E6
Atlantic City *U.S.A.* **113** F16
Atlantic-Indian Basin
  Antarctica **5** B4
Atlantic Ocean **2** D8

Atlas Mts. = Haut Atlas
  Morocco **78** B4
Atlin *Canada* **102** B2
Atlin, L. *Canada* **102** B2
Atlin △ *Canada* **102** B2
Atmore *U.S.A.* **117** F11
Atoka *U.S.A.* **116** D6
Atokos *Greece* **46** C2
Atolia *U.S.A.* **111** K9
Atqasuk *U.S.A.* **106** A8
Atrai → *Bangla.* **69** G13
Atrak = Atrek →
  Turkmenistan **71** B8
Ätran *Sweden* **11** G6
Ätran → *Sweden* **11** H6
Atrauli *India* **68** E8
Atrek → *Turkmenistan* **71** B8
Atri *Italy* **41** F10
Atsiki *Greece* **47** B7
Atsuta *Japan* **54** C10
Attalla *U.S.A.* **117** D11
Attapu *Laos* **64** E6
Attawapiskat *Canada* **104** B3
Attawapiskat → *Canada* **104** B3
Attawapiskat L. *Canada* **104** B2
Attersee *Austria* **26** D6
Attica *Ind., U.S.A.* **112** E10
Attica *Ohio, U.S.A.* **114** E2
Attichy *France* **19** C1C
Attigny *France* **19** C11
Attika = Attiki □ *Greece* **46** D5
Attikamagen L. *Canada* **105** B6
Attiki □ *Greece* **46** D5
Attleboro *U.S.A.* **115** E13
Attock *Pakistan* **68** C5
Attopeu = Attapu *Laos* **64** E6
Attur *India* **66** P11
Attu I. *U.S.A.* **106** E2
Atuel → *Argentina* **126** D2
Atura *Uganda* **86** B3
Åtvidaberg *Sweden* **11** F10
Atwater *U.S.A.* **110** H6
Atwood *Canada* **114** C3
Atwood *U.S.A.* **112** F3
Atyraū *Kazakhstan* **52** E6
Au Sable *U.S.A.* **114** B1
Au Sable → *U.S.A.* **113** C12
Au Sable Forks *U.S.A.* **115** B11
Au Sable Pt. *U.S.A.* **114** B1
Auas Honduras **120** C3
Auasberg *Namibia* **88** C2
Aubagne *France* **21** E9
Aube □ *France* **19** D11
Aube → *France* **19** D10
Aubenas *France* **21** D8
Aubenton *France* **19** C11
Auberry *U.S.A.* **110** H7
Aubigny-sur-Nère *France* **19** E9
Aubin *France* **20** D6
Aubrac, Mts. d' *France* **20** D7
Auburn *Ala., U.S.A.* **117** E12
Auburn *Calif., U.S.A.* **110** G5
Auburn *Ind., U.S.A.* **113** E11
Auburn *Maine, U.S.A.* **113** C18
Auburn *N.Y., U.S.A.* **115** D8
Auburn *Nebr., U.S.A.* **112** E6
Auburn *Pa., U.S.A.* **115** F8
Auburn *Wash., U.S.A.* **110** C4
Auburn Ra. *Australia* **95** D5
Auburndale *U.S.A.* **117** G14
Auce *Latvia* **30** B9
Auch *France* **20** E4
Auchi *Nigeria* **83** D6
Auchterarder *U.K.* **13** E5
Auchtermuchty *U.K.* **13** E5
Auckland *N.Z.* **91** B5
Auckland Is. *Pac. Oc.* **96** N8
Aude □ *France* **20** E6
Aude → *France* **20** E7
Auden *Canada* **104** B2
Auderville *France* **18** C5
Audierne *France* **18** D2
Audincourt *France* **19** E13
Audo Ra. *Ethiopia* **81** F5
Audubon *U.S.A.* **112** E6
Aue *Germany* **24** E8
Auerbach *Germany* **24** E8
Augathella *Australia* **95** D4
Aughnacloy *U.K.* **12** B5
Aughrim *Ireland* **12** C3
Augrabies Falls *S. Africa* **88** D3
Augrabies Falls △ *S. Africa* **88** D3
Augsburg *Germany* **25** G6
Augsburg-Westliche
  Wälder △ *Germany* **25** G6
Augusta *Australia* **93** F2
Augusta *Italy* **43** E8
Augusta *Ark., U.S.A.* **116** D9
Augusta *Ga., U.S.A.* **117** E14
Augusta *Kans., U.S.A.* **112** G5
Augusta *Maine, U.S.A.* **113** C19
Augustenborg *Denmark* **11** K3
Augustów *Poland* **30** E9
Augustus, Mt. *Australia* **93** D2
Augustus I. *Australia* **92** C3
Aujuittuq = Grise Fiord
  Canada **101** B15

Aukan *Eritrea* **81** D5
Aukrug △ *Germany* **24** A5
Aukum *U.S.A.* **110** G6
Aulavik △ *Canada* **100** C8
Auld, L. *Australia* **92** D3
Aulifeltet *Norway* **10** D5
Aulla *Italy* **40** D6
Aulnay *France* **20** B3
Aulne → *France* **18** D2
Aulnoye-Aymeries *France* **19** B10
Ault *France* **18** B8
Ault *U.S.A.* **108** F11
Aulus-les-Bains *France* **20** F5
Aumale *France* **19** C8
Aumont-Aubrac *France* **20** D7
Auna *Nigeria* **83** C5
Auning *Denmark* **11** H4
Aunis *France* **20** B3
Aunu'u *Amer. Samoa* **91** b
Auponhia *Indonesia* **63** E7
Aups *France* **21** E10
Aur, Pulau *Malaysia* **65** L5
Auraiya *India* **69** F8
Aurangabad *Bihar, India* **69** G11
Aurangabad *Maharashtra,
  India* **66** K9
Auray *France* **18** E4
Aurich *Germany* **24** B3
Aurillac *France* **20** D6
Auronzo di Cadore *Italy* **41** B9
Aurora *Canada* **114** C5
Aurora *S. Africa* **88** E2
Aurora *Colo., U.S.A.* **108** G11
Aurora *Ill., U.S.A.* **112** E9
Aurora *Mo., U.S.A.* **112** G7
Aurora *N.Y., U.S.A.* **115** D8
Aurora *Nebr., U.S.A.* **112** E5
Aurora *Ohio, U.S.A.* **114** E3
Aurukun *Australia* **94** A3
Aurukun ☉ *Australia* **94** A3
Aus *Namibia* **88** D2
Ausable → *Canada* **114** C3
Auschwitz = Oświęcim
  Poland **31** H6
Auski Roadhouse *Australia* **92** D2
Austerlitz = Slavkov u
  Brna *Czech Rep.* **27** B9
Austin *Minn., U.S.A.* **112** D7
Austin *Nev., U.S.A.* **108** G5
Austin *Pa., U.S.A.* **114** E6
Austin *Tex., U.S.A.* **116** F6
Austin, L. *Australia* **93** E2
Austin I. *Canada* **103** A10
Austra *Norway* **8** D14
Austral Is. = Tubuaï, Îs.
  French Polynesia **97** K13
Austral Seamount Chain
  Pac. Oc. **97** K13
Australia ■ *Oceania* **90** D6
Australian-Antarctic Basin
  S. Ocean **5** C9
Australian Capital
  Territory □ *Australia* **95** F4
Australind *Australia* **93** F2
Austria ■ *Europe* **26** E7
Austvågøya *Norway* **8** B16
Auterive *France* **20** E5
Authie → *France* **19** B8
Authon-du-Perche *France* **18** D7
Autlán de Navarro *Mexico* **118** D4
Autun *France* **19** F11
Auvergne □ *France* **20** C7
Auvergne, Mts. d' *France* **20** C6
Auvézère → *France* **20** C4
Auxerre *France* **19** E10
Auxi-le-Château *France* **19** B9
Auxonne *France* **19** E12
Auyuittuq △ *Canada* **101** D18
Auzances *France* **19** F9
Av-Dovurak *Russia* **53** D10
Ava *U.S.A.* **112** G7
Avallon *France* **19** E10
Avalon *U.S.A.* **111** M8
Avalon Pen. *Canada* **105** C9
Avanos *Turkey* **72** C6
Avantas *Greece* **45** F9
Avaré *Brazil* **127** A6
Avawatz Mts. *U.S.A.* **111** K10
Avdan Dağı *Malaysia* **45** F13
Aveiro *Brazil* **125** D7
Aveiro *Portugal* **36** E2
Aveiro □ *Portugal* **36** E2
Āvej *Iran* **71** C6
Avellaneda *Argentina* **126** C4
Avellino *Italy* **43** B7
Avenal *U.S.A.* **110** K6
Avenue *U.S.A.* **110** K6
Aversa *Italy* **43** B7
Avery *U.S.A.* **108** C6
Aves, I. de *W. Indies* **121** C7
Aves, Is. las *Venezuela* **121** D6
Avesnes-sur-Helpe *France* **19** B10
Avesnois *France* **19** B10
Avesta *Sweden* **10** D10
Aveyron □ *France* **20** D6
Aveyron → *France* **20** D5
Avezzano *Italy* **41** F10
Avgo *Greece* **47** F7
Aviá Terai *Argentina* **126** B3

Aviano *Italy* **41** B9
Aviemore *U.K.* **13** D5
Avigliana *Italy* **40** C4
Avigliano *Italy* **43** B8
Avignon *France* **21** E8
Ávila *Spain* **36** E6
Ávila □ *Spain* **36** E6
Ávila, Sierra de *Spain* **36** E5
Avila Beach *U.S.A.* **111** K6
Avilés *Spain* **36** B5
Avintes *Portugal* **36** D2
Avis *Portugal* **37** F3
Avis *U.S.A.* **114** E7
Avisio → *Italy* **40** B8
Aviz = Avis *Portugal* **37** F3
Avize *France* **19** D11
Avlonari *Greece* **46** C6
Avlum *Denmark* **11** H2
Avoca *U.S.A.* **114** D7
Avoca → *Australia* **95** F3
Avoca → *Ireland* **12** D5
Avola *Canada* **102** C5
Avola *Italy* **43** F8
Avon *U.S.A.* **114** D7
Avon → *Australia* **93** F2
Avon → *Bristol, U.K.* **15** F5
Avon → *Dorset, U.K.* **15** G6
Avon → *Warks., U.K.* **15** E5
Avon Park *U.S.A.* **117** H14
Avondale *Zimbabwe* **87** F3
Avonlea *Canada* **103** D8
Avonmore *Canada* **115** A10
Avonmouth *U.K.* **15** F5
Avramov *Bulgaria* **45** D10
Avranches *France* **18** D5
Avre → *France* **18** E6
Avrig *Romania* **29** E9
Avrillé *France* **18** E6
Avtovac *Bos.-H.* **44** C2
Awa-Shima *Japan* **54** E9
Awag el Baqar *Sudan* **81** E3
Awaji-Shima *Japan* **55** G7
'Awālī *Bahrain* **71** E6
Awantipur *India* **69** C6
Awasa *Ethiopia* **81** F4
Awasa, L. *Ethiopia* **81** F4
Awash *Ethiopia* **81** F5
Awash → *Ethiopia* **81** E5
Awash △ *Ethiopia* **81** F5
Awaso *Ghana* **82** D4
Awatere → *N.Z.* **91** D5
Awbārī *Libya* **79** C8
Awbārī, Idehan *Libya* **79** C8
Awe, L. *U.K.* **13** E3
Aweil *Sudan* **81** F2
Awgu *Nigeria* **83** D6
Awjilah *Libya* **79** C10
Awka *Nigeria* **83** D6
Ax-les-Thermes *France* **20** F5
Axat *France* **20** F6
Axe → *U.K.* **15** F5
Axel Heiberg I. *Canada* **101** B14
Axim *Ghana* **82** E4
Axintele *Romania* **29** F11
Axios → *Greece* **44** F6
Axminster *U.K.* **15** G4
Axvall *Sweden* **11** F7
Ay *France* **19** C11
Ayabaca *Peru* **124** D3
Ayabe *Japan* **55** G7
Ayacucho *Argentina* **126** D4
Ayacucho *Peru* **124** F4
Ayaguz = Ayaköz *Kazakhstan* **52** E9
Ayaköz *Kazakhstan* **52** E9
Ayamé *Ivory C.* **82** D4
Ayamonte *Spain* **37** H3
Ayan *Russia* **53** D14
Ayancık *Turkey* **72** B6
Ayangba *Nigeria* **83** D6
Ayas *Turkey* **72** B5
Ayaviri *Peru* **124** F4
Aybastı *Turkey* **72** B7
Aydın *Turkey* **47** D9
Aydın □ *Turkey* **47** D9
Aydın Dağları *Turkey* **47** D10
Ayelu *Ethiopia* **81** E5
Ayenngré *Togo* **83** D5
Ayer *U.S.A.* **115** D13
Ayerbe *Spain* **38** C4
Ayer Hitam *Malaysia* **65** c
Ayer's Cliff *Canada* **115** A12
Ayers Rock = Uluru *Australia* **93** E5
Ayeyarwady =
  Irrawaddy → *Burma* **67** M19
Áyia Napa *Cyprus* **49** E13
Áyia Phyla *Cyprus* **49** E12
Áyios Amvrósios *Cyprus* **49** D12
Áyios Seryios *Cyprus* **49** D12
Áyios Theodhoros *Cyprus* **49** D13
Áyios Yeóryios = Aghios
  Georgios *Greece* **46** C2
Aykhal *Russia* **53** C12
Aykirikçi *Turkey* **47** B12
Aylesbury *U.K.* **15** F7
Aylmer *Canada* **114** D4
Aylmer, L. *Canada* **100** C9
'Ayn, Wādī al *Oman* **71** F7
Ayn Dār *Si. Arabia* **71** E7

Ayn Sifnī *Iraq* **73** D10
Ayn Zālah *Iraq* **73** D10
Ayna *Spain* **39** G2
Ayod *Sudan* **81** F3
Ayolas *Paraguay* **126** B4
Ayon, Ostrov *Russia* **53** C17
Ayora *Spain* **39** F3
Ayorou *Niger* **83** C5
'Ayoûn el 'Atroûs *Mauritania* **82** B3
Ayr *Australia* **94** B4
Ayr *Canada* **114** C4
Ayr *U.K.* **13** F4
Ayr → *U.K.* **13** F4
Ayrancı *Turkey* **72** D5
Ayrancılar *Turkey* **47** C9
Aysha *Ethiopia* **81** E5
Ayton *Australia* **94** B4
Aytos *Bulgaria* **45** D11
Aytoska Planina *Bulgaria* **45** D11
Ayu, Kepulauan *Indonesia* **63** D8
Ayutla *Guatemala* **120** D1
Ayutla de los Libres *Mexico* **119** D5
Ayvacık *Turkey* **72** C2
Ayvalık *Turkey* **47** B8
Az Zabadānī *Syria* **74** B5
Aẕ Ẕāhiriyah *West Bank* **74** D3
Aẕ Ẕahrān *Si. Arabia* **71** E6
Az Zarqā *Jordan* **74** C5
Az Zarqā □ *U.A.E.* **71** E7
Az Zarqā → *Jordan* **74** C5
Az Zāwiyah *Libya* **79** B8
Az Zībār *Iraq* **73** D11
Az Zilfī *Si. Arabia* **70** E5
Az Zubayr *Iraq* **70** D5
Az Zuqur *Yemen* **81** E3
Azad Kashmir □ *Pakistan* **69** C5
Azambuja *Portugal* **37** F2
Azamgarh *India* **69** F10
Azangaro *Peru* **124** F4
Azaouad *Mali* **82** B4
Azaouak → *Mali* **83** B5
Azaouak, Vallée de l' *Mali* **83** B5
Āzar Shahr *Iran* **73** D11
Azara *Nigeria* **83** D6
Azarān *Iran* **73** D12
Azärbayjan =
  Azerbaijan ■ *Asia* **35** K9
Āẕarbāyjān-e Gharbī □ *Iran* **70** B5
Āẕarbāyjān-e Sharqī □ *Iran* **70** B5
Azare *Nigeria* **83** C7
Azay-le-Rideau *France* **18** E7
A'zāz *Syria* **72** D7
Azbine = Aïr *Niger* **83** B6
Azerbaijan ■ *Asia* **35** K9
Azezo *Ethiopia* **81** E4
Azimganj *India* **69** G13
Aznalcóllar *Spain* **37** H4
Azogues *Ecuador* **124** D3
Azores = Açores, Is. dos
  Atl. Oc. **78** a
Azov *Russia* **35** G4
Azov, Sea of *Europe* **33** J9
Azovskoye More = Azov,
  Sea of *Europe* **33** J9
Azpeitia *Spain* **38** B2
Azraq ash Shīshān *Jordan* **74** D5
Aztec *U.S.A.* **109** H10
Azúa de Compostela
  Dom. Rep. **121** C5
Azuaga *Spain* **37** G5
Azuara *Spain* **38** D4
Azuer → *Spain* **37** G7
Azuero, Pen. de *Panama* **120** E3
Azuga *Romania* **29** E10
Azul *Argentina* **126** D4
Azusa *U.S.A.* **111** L9
Azzano Décimo *Italy* **41** C9
Azzel Matti, Sebkra *Algeria* **78** C6

B

Ba Be △ *Vietnam* **64** A5
Ba Don *Vietnam* **64** D6
Ba Dong *Vietnam* **65** H6
Ba Ngoi = Cam Lam *Vietnam* **65** G7
Ba Tri *Vietnam* **65** G6
Ba Vì △ *Vietnam* **64** B5
Ba Xian = Bazhou *China* **56** E9
Baa *Indonesia* **92** A3
Baamonde *Spain* **36** B3
Baardheere *Somali Rep.* **75** G3
Baarle-Nassau *Belgium* **17** C4
Bab el Mandeb *Red Sea* **75** E3
Baba *Bulgaria* **44** D7
Bābā, Koh-i- *Afghan.* **66** B5
Baba Burnu *Turkey* **47** B8
Baba dag *Azerbaijan* **35** K9
Bābā Kalū *Iran* **71** D6
Babadag *Romania* **29** F13
Babadağ *Turkey* **47** D10
Babaeski *Turkey* **45** E11
Babahoyo *Ecuador* **124** D3
Babai = Sarju → *India* **69** F9
Babana *Nigeria* **83** C5
Babanusa *Sudan* **81** E2
Babar *Indonesia* **63** F7
Babar *Pakistan* **68** D3

Babarkach *Pakistan* 68 E3
Babayevo *Russia* 32 C8
Babb *U.S.A.* 108 B7
Babenhausen *Germany* 25 F4
Baberu *India* 69 G9
Babi Besar, Pulau *Malaysia* 65 L4
Babia Gora *Europe* 31 J6
Babian Jiang → *China* 58 F3
Bābil □ *Iraq* 70 C5
Babile *Ethiopia* 81 F5
Babimost *Poland* 31 F2
Babinda *Australia* 94 B4
Babine *Canada* 102 B3
Babine → *Canada* 102 B3
Babine L. *Canada* 102 C3
Babiogórski △ *Poland* 31 J6
Babo *Indonesia* 63 E8
Babócsa *Hungary* 28 D2
Bābol *Iran* 71 B7
Bābol Sar *Iran* 71 B7
Baborów *Poland* 31 H5
Baboua *C.A.R.* 84 C2
Babruysk *Belarus* 23 B15
Babuhri *India* 68 F3
Babuna *Macedonia* 44 E5
Babura *Nigeria* 83 C6
Babusar Pass *Pakistan* 69 B5
Babušnica *Serbia* 44 C6
Babuyan Chan. *Phil.* 61 B4
Babylon *Iraq* 73 F11
Bač *Serbia* 28 E4
Bâc → *Moldova* 29 D14
Bac Can *Vietnam* 58 F5
Bac Giang *Vietnam* 58 G6
Bac Lieu *Vietnam* 65 H5
Bac Ninh *Vietnam* 58 G6
Bac Phan *Vietnam* 58 G5
Bac Quang *Vietnam* 58 F5
Bacabal *Brazil* 125 D10
Bacalar *Mexico* 119 D7
Bacan, Kepulauan *Indonesia* 63 E7
Bacarra *Phil.* 61 B4
Bacău *Romania* 29 D11
Bacău □ *Romania* 29 D11
Baccarat *France* 19 D13
Bacerac *Mexico* 118 A3
Băcești *Romania* 29 D12
Bach Long Vi, Dao *Vietnam* 64 B6
Bach Ma △ *Vietnam* 64 D6
Bacharach *Germany* 25 E3
Bachhwara *India* 69 G11
Bachuma *Ethiopia* 81 F4
Bačina *Serbia* 44 C5
Back → *Canada* 100 D11
Bačka Palanka *Serbia* 28 E4
Bačka Topola *Serbia* 28 E4
Bäckebo *Sweden* 11 H10
Bäckefors *Sweden* 11 F6
Bäckhammar *Sweden* 10 E8
Bački Petrovac *Serbia* 28 E4
Backnang *Germany* 25 G5
Baco, Mt. *Phil.* 61 E4
Bacolod *Phil.* 61 F5
Bacqueville-en-Caux *France* 18 C8
Bács-Kiskun □ *Hungary* 28 D4
Bácsalmás *Hungary* 28 D4
Bacuag = Placer *Phil.* 61 G6
Bacuk *Malaysia* 65 J4
Bácum *Mexico* 118 B2
Bād *Iran* 71 C7
Bad → *U.S.A.* 112 C3
Bad Aussee *Austria* 26 D6
Bad Axe *U.S.A.* 114 C2
Bad Bergzabern *Germany* 25 F3
Bad Berleburg *Germany* 24 D4
Bad Bevensen *Germany* 24 B6
Bad Bramstedt *Germany* 24 B5
Bad Brückenau *Germany* 25 E5
Bad Doberan *Germany* 24 A7
Bad Driburg *Germany* 24 D4
Bad Ems *Germany* 25 E3
Bad Frankenhausen
  Germany 24 D7
Bad Freienwalde *Germany* 24 C10
Bad Goisern *Austria* 26 D6
Bad Harzburg *Germany* 24 D6
Bad Hersfeld *Germany* 24 E5
Bad Hofgastein *Austria* 26 D6
Bad Homburg *Germany* 25 E4
Bad Honnef *Germany* 24 E3
Bad Iburg *Germany* 24 C4
Bad Ischl *Austria* 26 D6
Bad Kissingen *Germany* 25 E6
Bad Königshofen *Germany* 25 E6
Bad Kreuznach *Germany* 25 F3
Bad Krozingen *Germany* 25 H3
Bad Laasphe *Germany* 24 E4
Bad Langensalza *Germany* 24 D6
Bad Lauterberg *Germany* 24 D6
Bad Leonfelden *Austria* 26 C7
Bad Liebenwerda *Germany* 24 D9
Bad Mergentheim *Germany* 25 F5
Bad Münstereifel *Germany* 24 E2
Bad Nauheim *Germany* 25 E4
Bad Neuenahr-Ahrweiler
  Germany 24 E3
Bad Neustadt *Germany* 25 E6
Bad Oeynhausen *Germany* 24 C4

Bad Oldesloe *Germany* 24 B6
Bad Orb *Germany* 25 E5
Bad Pyrmont *Germany* 24 D5
Bad Reichenhall *Germany* 25 H8
Bad Säckingen *Germany* 25 H3
Bad St. Leonhard *Austria* 26 E7
Bad Salzuflen *Germany* 24 C4
Bad Salzungen *Germany* 24 E6
Bad Schwartau *Germany* 24 B6
Bad Segeberg *Germany* 24 B6
Bad Tölz *Germany* 25 H7
Bad Urach *Germany* 25 G5
Bad Vöslau *Austria* 27 D9
Bad Waldsee *Germany* 25 H5
Bad Wildungen *Germany* 24 D5
Bad Wimpfen *Germany* 25 F5
Bad Windsheim *Germany* 25 F6
Bad Zwischenahn *Germany* 24 B4
Bada Barabil *India* 69 H11
Badagara *India* 66 P9
Badagri *Nigeria* 83 D5
Badajós, L. *Brazil* 124 D6
Badajoz *Spain* 37 G4
Badajoz □ *Spain* 37 G4
Badakhshān □ *Afghan.* 66 A7
Badalona *Spain* 38 D7
Badalzai *Afghan.* 68 E1
Badampahar *India* 67 H15
Badanah *Si. Arabia* 70 D4
Badarinath *India* 69 D8
Badas, Kepulauan *Indonesia* 62 D3
Baddo → *Pakistan* 66 F4
Bade *Indonesia* 63 F9
Badeggi *Nigeria* 83 D6
Baden *Austria* 27 C9
Baden *Switz.* 25 H4
Baden *U.S.A.* 114 F4
Baden-Baden *Germany* 25 G4
Baden-Württemberg □
  Germany 25 G4
Badgam *India* 69 B6
Badgastein *Austria* 26 D6
Badger *Canada* 105 C8
Badger *U.S.A.* 110 J7
Bādghīs □ *Afghan.* 66 B3
Badgingarra △ *Australia* 93 F2
Badia Polésine *Italy* 41 C8
Badiar △ *Guinea* 82 C2
Badin *Pakistan* 68 G3
Badinka △ *Mali* 82 C3
Badlands *U.S.A.* 112 D2
Badlands △ *U.S.A.* 112 D2
Badogo *Mali* 82 C3
Badoumbé *Mali* 82 C2
Badrah *Iraq* 73 F11
Badrinath *India* 69 D8
Badu *Australia* 94 a
Badulla *Sri Lanka* 66 R12
Badung, Selat *Indonesia* 63 K18
Baena *Spain* 37 H6
Baengnyeongdo *S. Korea* 57 F13
Baeza *Spain* 37 H7
Bafang *Cameroon* 83 D7
Bafatá *Guinea-Biss.* 82 C2
Baffin B. *N. Amer.* 101 C19
Baffin I. *Canada* 101 D17
Bafia *Cameroon* 83 E7
Bafilo *Togo* 83 D5
Bafing → *Mali* 82 C2
Bafing △ *Mali* 82 C2
Bafliyūn *Syria* 70 B3
Bafoulabé *Mali* 82 C2
Bafoussam *Cameroon* 83 D7
Bâfq *Iran* 71 D7
Bafra *Turkey* 72 B6
Bafra Burnu *Turkey* 72 B7
Bâft *Iran* 71 D8
Bafut *Cameroon* 83 D7
Bafwasende
  Dem. Rep. of the Congo 86 B2
Bagaha *India* 69 F11
Bagam *Niger* 83 B6
Bagamoyo *Tanzania* 86 D4
Bagan Datoh *Malaysia* 65 L3
Bagan Serai *Malaysia* 65 K3
Baganga *Phil.* 61 H7
Bagani *Namibia* 88 B3
Bagansiapiapi *Indonesia* 62 D2
Bagasra *India* 68 J4
Bagaud *India* 68 H6
Bagawi *Sudan* 81 E3
Bagbag *Sudan* 81 D3
Bagdad *U.S.A.* 111 L11
Bagdarin *Russia* 53 D12
Bagé *Brazil* 127 C5
Bagenalstown = Muine
  Bheag *Ireland* 12 D5
Baggs *U.S.A.* 108 F10
Bagh *Pakistan* 69 C5
Baghain → *India* 69 G9
Baghdād *Iraq* 73 F11
Baghdadi *Georgia* 73 A10
Bagheria *Italy* 42 D6
Baghlān *Afghan.* 66 A6
Baghlān □ *Afghan.* 66 B6
Bagley *U.S.A.* 112 B6
Bagnara Cálabra *Italy* 43 D8
Bagnasco *Italy* 40 D5

Bagnères-de-Bigorre *France* 20 E4
Bagnères-de-Luchon *France* 20 F4
Bagni di Lucca *Italy* 40 D7
Bagno di Romagna *Italy* 41 E8
Bagnoles-de-l'Orne *France* 18 D6
Bagnols-sur-Cèze *France* 21 D8
Bagnorégio *Italy* 41 F9
Bago = Pegu *Burma* 67 L20
Bagodar *India* 69 G11
Baguio *Phil.* 61 C4
Bağyurdu *Turkey* 47 C9
Bagzane, Monts *Niger* 83 B6
Bah *India* 69 F8
Bahabón de Esgueva *Spain* 36 D7
Bahadurganj *India* 69 F12
Bahadurgarh *India* 68 E7
Bahama, Canal Viejo de
  W. Indies 120 B4
Bahamas ■ *N. Amer.* 121 B5
Bahār *Iran* 73 E13
Baharampur *India* 69 G13
Baharîya, El Wâhât al *Egypt* 80 B2
Baharu Pandan = Pandan
  Malaysia 65 d
Bahawalnagar *Pakistan* 68 E5
Bahawalpur *Pakistan* 68 E4
Bahçe *Turkey* 72 D7
Bahçecik *Turkey* 45 F13
Baheri *India* 69 E8
Bahgul → *India* 69 F8
Bahi *Tanzania* 86 D4
Bahi Swamp *Tanzania* 86 D4
Bahía = Salvador *Brazil* 125 F11
Bahía □ *Brazil* 125 F10
Bahía, Is. de la *Honduras* 120 C2
Bahía Blanca *Argentina* 126 D3
Bahía de Caráquez *Ecuador* 124 D2
Bahía Kino *Mexico* 118 B2
Bahía Laura *Argentina* 128 F3
Bahía Negra *Paraguay* 124 H7
Bahir Dar *Ethiopia* 81 E4
Bahmanzād *Iran* 71 D6
Bahr el Ahmar □ *Sudan* 80 D4
Bahr el Jabal □ *Sudan* 81 G3
Bahraich *India* 69 F9
Bahrain ■ *Asia* 71 E6
Bahror *India* 68 F7
Bāhū Kalāt *Iran* 71 E9
Bai *Mali* 82 C4
Bai Bung, Mui = Ca Mau,
  Mui *Vietnam* 65 H5
Bai Duc *Vietnam* 64 C5
Bai Thuong *Vietnam* 64 C5
Baia de Aramă *Romania* 28 E7
Baia Mare *Romania* 29 C8
Baia-Sprie *Romania* 29 C8
Baião *Brazil* 125 D9
Baïbokoum *Chad* 79 G9
Baicheng *China* 57 B12
Băicoi *Romania* 29 E10
Baidoa = Baardheere
  Somali Rep. 75 G3
Baidoa = Baydhabo
  Somali Rep. 75 G3
Baie-Comeau *Canada* 105 C6
Baie-St-Paul *Canada* 105 C5
Baie Ste-Anne *Seychelles* 85 b
Baie-Trinité *Canada* 105 C6
Baie Verte *Canada* 105 C8
Baignes-Ste-Radegonde
  France 20 C3
Baigneux-les-Juifs *France* 19 E11
Baihar *India* 69 H9
Baihe *China* 56 H6
Ba'ījī *Iraq* 73 E10
Baijnath *India* 69 E8
Baikal, L. = Baykal, Oz.
  Russia 53 D11
Baikonur = Bayqongyr
  Kazakhstan 52 E7
Baikunthpur *India* 69 H10
Baile Átha Cliath = Dublin
  Ireland 12 C5
Baile Átha Fhirdhia =
  Ardee *Ireland* 12 C5
Baile Átha I = Athy *Ireland* 12 C5
Baile Átha Luain =
  Athlone *Ireland* 12 C4
Baile Átha Troim = Trim
  Ireland 12 C5
Baile Brigín = Balbriggan
  Ireland 12 C5
Băile Govora *Romania* 29 E9
Băile Herculane *Romania* 28 F7
Băile Olănești *Romania* 29 E9
Băile Tușnad *Romania* 29 D10
Bailén *Spain* 37 G7
Băilești *Romania* 29 F8
Baima *China* 58 A3
Bain-de-Bretagne *France* 18 E5
Bainbridge *Ga., U.S.A.* 117 F12
Bainbridge *N.Y., U.S.A.* 115 D9
Bainbridge Island *U.S.A.* 110 C4
Baing *Indonesia* 63 F6
Bainiu *China* 56 H7
Baiona *Spain* 36 C2

Bā'ir *Jordan* 74 E5
Baird Mts. *U.S.A.* 106 B8
Bairiki = Tarawa *Kiribati* 96 G9
Bairin Youqi *China* 57 C10
Bairin Zuoqi *China* 57 C10
Bairnsdale *Australia* 95 F4
Bais *Phil.* 61 G5
Baisha *China* 56 G7
Baissa *Nigeria* 83 D7
Baitadi *Nepal* 69 E9
Baixa Limia-Sierra do
  Xurés △ *Spain* 36 D2
Baiyin *China* 56 F3
Baiyü *China* 58 B2
Baiyu Shan *China* 56 F4
Baiyuda *Sudan* 80 D3
Baj Baj *India* 69 H13
Baja *Hungary* 28 D3
Baja, Pta. *Mexico* 118 B1
Baja California *Mexico* 118 A1
Baja California □ *Mexico* 118 B2
Baja California Sur □
  Mexico 118 B2
Bajag *India* 69 H9
Bajamar *Canary Is.* 48 F3
Bajana *India* 68 H4
Bajatrejo *Indonesia* 63 J17
Bajera *Indonesia* 63 J18
Bäjgīrān *Iran* 71 B8
Bajimba, Mt. *Australia* 95 D5
Bajina Bašta *Serbia* 44 C3
Bajmok *Serbia* 28 E4
Bajo Boquete *Panama* 120 E3
Bajo Nuevo *Caribbean* 120 C4
Bajoga *Nigeria* 83 C7
Bajool *Australia* 94 C5
Bak *Hungary* 28 D1
Bakar *Croatia* 41 C11
Bakel *Senegal* 82 C2
Baker *Calif., U.S.A.* 111 K10
Baker *Mont., U.S.A.* 108 C11
Baker, L. *Canada* 100 E12
Baker, Mt. *U.S.A.* 108 B3
Baker City *U.S.A.* 108 D5
Baker I. *Pac. Oc.* 96 G10
Baker I. *U.S.A.* 102 B2
Baker L. *Australia* 93 E4
Baker Lake *Canada* 100 E12
Bakers Creek *Australia* 94 C4
Bakers Dozen Is. *Canada* 104 A4
Bakersfield *Calif., U.S.A.* 111 K8
Bakersfield *Vt., U.S.A.* 115 B12
Bakharden = Bäherden
  Turkmenistan 71 B8
Bakhchysaray *Ukraine* 33 K7
Bakhmach *Ukraine* 33 G7
Bäkhtarān = Kermänshäh
  Iran 73 E12
Bäkhtarān □ =
  Kermänshäh □ *Iran* 70 C5
Bakı *Azerbaijan* 35 K9
Bakır → *Turkey* 47 C9
Bakırdağı *Turkey* 72 C6
Bakkafjörður *Iceland* 8 C6
Baklan *Turkey* 47 C11
Bako *Ethiopia* 81 F4
Bako *Ivory C.* 82 D3
Bakony *Hungary* 28 C2
Bakony Forest = Bakony
  Hungary 28 C2
Bakori *Nigeria* 83 C6
Bakouma *C.A.R.* 84 C4
Baksan *Russia* 35 J6
Bakswaho *India* 69 G8
Baku = Bakı *Azerbaijan* 35 K9
Bakundi *Nigeria* 83 D7
Bakuriani *Georgia* 73 B10
Bakutis Coast *Antarctica* 5 D15
Baky = Bakı *Azerbaijan* 35 K9
Bala *Canada* 114 A5
Bala *Senegal* 82 C2
Bala *U.K.* 14 E4
Bala, L. *U.K.* 14 E4
Balabac *Phil.* 62 C5
Balabac Str. *E. Indies* 62 C5
Balabagh *Afghan.* 68 B4
Ba'labakk *Lebanon* 74 B5
Balabalangan, Kepulauan
  Indonesia 62 E5
Bălăcița *Romania* 29 F8
Balad *Iraq* 73 F11
Balad Rūz *Iraq* 73 F11
Bālādeh *Fārs, Iran* 71 D6
Bālādeh *Māzandaran, Iran* 71 B6
Balaghat *India* 66 J12
Balaghat Ra. *India* 66 K10
Balaguer *Spain* 38 D5
Balakän *Azerbaijan* 73 B12
Balakhna *Russia* 34 B6
Balaklava *Ukraine* 33 K7
Balakliya *Ukraine* 33 H9
Balakovo *Russia* 34 D8
Balamau *India* 69 F9
Bălan *Romania* 29 D10
Balancán *Mexico* 119 D6
Balanivka *Ukraine* 29 B14
Balashov *Russia* 34 E6

Balasinor *India* 68 H5
Balasore = Baleshwar *India* 67 J15
Balassagyarmat *Hungary* 28 B4
Balât *Egypt* 80 B2
Balaton *Hungary* 28 D2
Balaton-Felvidéki △ *Hungary* 28 D2
Balatonboglár *Hungary* 28 D2
Balatonfüred *Hungary* 28 D2
Balatonszentgyörgy *Hungary* 28 D2
Balayan *Phil.* 61 E4
Balazote *Spain* 39 G2
Balbieriškis *Lithuania* 30 D10
Balbigny *France* 21 C8
Balbina, Represa de *Brazil* 124 D7
Balboa *Panama* 120 E4
Balbriggan *Ireland* 12 C5
Balcarce *Argentina* 126 D4
Balcarres *Canada* 103 C8
Bălcești *Romania* 29 F8
Balchik *Bulgaria* 45 C12
Balclutha *N.Z.* 91 G2
Balcones Escarpment *U.S.A.* 116 G5
Balçova *Turkey* 47 C9
Bald I. *Australia* 93 F2
Bald Knob *U.S.A.* 116 D9
Baldock L. *Canada* 103 B9
Baldwin *Mich., U.S.A.* 113 D11
Baldwin *Pa., U.S.A.* 114 F5
Baldwinsville *U.S.A.* 115 C8
Baldy Peak *U.S.A.* 109 K9
Bale *Croatia* 41 C10
Bale *Oromiya, Ethiopia* 81 F5
Bale *Oromiya, Ethiopia* 81 F5
Bale Mts. △ *Ethiopia* 81 F4
Baleine → *Canada* 105 A6
Baleine, Petite R. de la →
  Canada 104 A4
Băleni *Romania* 29 E12
Baler *Phil.* 61 D4
Baler Bay *Phil.* 61 D4
Baleshare *U.K.* 13 D1
Baleshwar *India* 67 J15
Baley *Russia* 53 D12
Balezino *Russia* 34 B11
Balfate *Honduras* 120 C2
Balgo *Australia* 92 D4
Bali *Cameroon* 83 D7
Bali *Greece* 49 D6
Bali *India* 68 G5
Bali *Indonesia* 62 F4
Bali □ *Indonesia* 62 F5
Bali, Selat *Indonesia* 63 J17
Bali Sea *Indonesia* 63 J17
Balia *S. Leone* 82 D2
Baliapal *India* 69 J12
Balige *Indonesia* 65 L2
Baligród *Poland* 31 J9
Balik Pulau *Malaysia* 65 c
Balıkesir *Turkey* 47 B9
Balıkesir □ *Turkey* 47 B9
Balīkh → *Syria* 73 E8
Balıklıçeşme *Turkey* 45 F11
Balikpapan *Indonesia* 62 E5
Balimbing *Phil.* 63 C5
Baling *Malaysia* 65 K3
Balingen *Germany* 25 G4
Balint *Romania* 28 E6
Balintang Channel *Phil.* 61 B4
Balkan Mts. = Stara
  Planina *Bulgaria* 44 C7
Balkanabat *Turkmenistan* 71 B7
Balkhash = Balqash
  Kazakhstan 52 E8
Balkhash, Ozero = Balqash
  Köli *Kazakhstan* 52 E8
Ballachulish *U.K.* 13 E3
Balladonia *Australia* 93 F3
Ballaghaderreen *Ireland* 12 C3
Ballarat *Australia* 95 F3
Ballard, L. *Australia* 93 E3
Ballater *U.K.* 13 D5
Ballé *Mali* 82 B3
Ballenas, Canal de *Mexico* 118 B2
Balleny Is. *Antarctica* 5 C11
Balleroy *France* 18 C6
Ballerup *Denmark* 11 J6
Balli *Turkey* 45 F11
Ballia *India* 69 G11
Ballina *Australia* 95 D5
Ballina *Ireland* 12 B2
Ballinasloe *Ireland* 12 C3
Ballinger *U.S.A.* 116 F5
Ballinrobe *Ireland* 12 C2
Ballinskelligs B. *Ireland* 12 E1
Ballon *France* 18 D7
Ballons des Vosges △ *France* 19 E14
Ballsh *Albania* 44 F3
Ballston Spa *U.S.A.* 115 D11
Ballyboghil *Ireland* 12 C5
Ballybunion *Ireland* 12 D2
Ballycanew *Ireland* 12 D5
Ballycastle *U.K.* 12 A5
Ballyclare *U.K.* 12 B5
Ballydehob *Ireland* 12 E2
Ballygawley *U.K.* 12 B4
Ballyhaunis *Ireland* 12 C3

Ballyheige *Ireland* 12 D2
Ballymena *U.K.* 12 B5
Ballymoney *U.K.* 12 A5
Ballymote *Ireland* 12 B3
Ballynahinch *U.K.* 12 B6
Ballyquintin Pt. *U.K.* 12 B6
Ballyshannon *Ireland* 12 B3
Balmaceda *Chile* 128 F2
Balmaseda *Spain* 38 B1
Balmazújváros *Hungary* 28 C6
Balmertown *Canada* 103 C10
Balmoral *Australia* 95 F3
Balmorhea *U.S.A.* 116 F3
Balochistan =
  Baluchistan □ *Pakistan* 66 F4
Balonne → *Australia* 95 D4
Balotra *India* 68 G5
Balqash *Kazakhstan* 52 E8
Balqash Köli *Kazakhstan* 52 E8
Balrampur *India* 69 F10
Balranald *Australia* 95 E3
Balş *Romania* 29 F9
Balsas → *Brazil* 125 E9
Balsas *Mexico* 118 D4
Balsas → *Mexico* 118 D4
Balsas del Norte *Mexico* 119 D5
Bålsta *Sweden* 10 E11
Balta *Romania* 28 F7
Balta *Ukraine* 29 B14
Baltanás *Spain* 36 D6
Bălți *Moldova* 29 C12
Baltic Sea *Europe* 9 H18
Baltîm *Egypt* 80 H7
Baltimore *Ireland* 12 E2
Baltimore *Md., U.S.A.* 113 F15
Baltimore *Ohio, U.S.A.* 114 G2
Baltinglass *Ireland* 12 D5
Baltit *Pakistan* 69 A6
Baltiysk *Russia* 30 D6
Baltrum *Germany* 24 B3
Baluchistan □ *Pakistan* 66 F4
Baluqtybulaq *Kazakhstan* 34 E10
Balurghat *India* 69 G13
Balvi *Latvia* 32 D4
Balya *Turkey* 47 B9
Bam *Iran* 71 D8
Bama *China* 58 E6
Bama *Nigeria* 83 C7
Bamaga *Australia* 94 A3
Bamaji L. *Canada* 104 B1
Bamako *Mali* 82 C3
Bamba *Mali* 83 B4
Bambara Maoundé *Mali* 82 B4
Bambari *C.A.R.* 84 C4
Bambaroo *Australia* 94 B4
Bambaya *Guinea* 82 D2
Bamberg *Germany* 25 F6
Bamberg *U.S.A.* 117 E14
Bambesi *Ethiopia* 81 F3
Bambey *Senegal* 82 C1
Bambili *Dem. Rep. of the Congo* 86 B2
Bamboi *Ghana* 82 D4
Bamburgh *U.K.* 14 B6
Bamenda *Cameroon* 83 D7
Bamendjing, L. de *Cameroon* 83 D7
Bamfield *Canada* 102 D3
Bāmīān □ *Afghan.* 66 B5
Bamiancheng *China* 57 C13
Bamkin *Cameroon* 83 D7
Bampūr *Iran* 71 E9
Bampūr → *Iran* 71 E8
Ban *Burkina Faso* 82 C4
Ban Ao Tu Khun *Thailand* 65 a
Ban Ban *Laos* 64 C4
Ban Bang Hin *Thailand* 65 H2
Ban Bang Khu *Thailand* 65 a
Ban Bang Rong *Thailand* 65 a
Ban Bo Phut *Thailand* 65 b
Ban Chaweng *Thailand* 65 b
Ban Chiang Klang *Thailand* 64 C3
Ban Choho *Thailand* 64 E4
Ban Dan Lan Hoi *Thailand* 64 D2
Ban Don = Surat Thani
  Thailand 65 H2
Ban Don *Vietnam* 64 F6
Ban Don, Ao → *Thailand* 65 H2
Ban Dong *Thailand* 64 C3
Ban Hong *Thailand* 64 C2
Ban Hua Thanon *Thailand* 65 b
Ban Kantang *Thailand* 65 J2
Ban Karon *Thailand* 65 a
Ban Kata *Thailand* 65 a
Ban Keun *Laos* 64 C4
Ban Khai *Thailand* 64 F3
Ban Kheun *Laos* 64 B3
Ban Khlong Khian *Thailand* 65 a
Ban Khlong Kua *Thailand* 65 J3
Ban Khuan *Thailand* 65 a
Ban Khuan Mao *Thailand* 65 J2
Ban Ko Yai Chim *Thailand* 65 G2
Ban Laem *Thailand* 64 F2
Ban Lamai *Thailand* 65 b
Ban Lao Ngam *Laos* 64 E6
Ban Le Kathe *Thailand* 64 E2
Ban Lo Po Noi *Thailand* 65 a
Ban Mae Chedi *Thailand* 64 C2
Ban Mae Nam *Thailand* 65 b
Ban Mae Sariang *Thailand* 64 C1
Ban Mê Thuôt = Buon Ma
  Thuot *Vietnam* 64 F7

Ban Mi *Thailand* **64** E3
Ban Muong Mo *Laos* **64** C4
Ban Na Bo *Thailand* **65** b
Ban Na Mo *Laos* **64** D5
Ban Na San *Thailand* **65** H2
Ban Na Tong *Laos* **64** B3
Ban Nam Bac *Laos* **64** B4
Ban Nam Ma *Laos* **64** A3
Ban Ngang *Laos* **64** E6
Ban Nong Bok *Laos* **64** D5
Ban Nong Boua *Laos* **64** E6
Ban Nong Pling *Thailand* **64** E3
Ban Pak Chan *Thailand* **65** G2
Ban Patong *Thailand* **65** a
Ban Phai *Thailand* **64** D4
Ban Phak Chit *Thailand* **65** a
Ban Pong *Thailand* **64** F2
Ban Rawai *Thailand* **65** a
Ban Ron Phibun *Thailand* **65** H2
Ban Sakhu *Thailand* **65** a
Ban Sanam Chai *Thailand* **65** J3
Ban Sangkha *Thailand* **64** E4
Ban Tak *Thailand* **64** D2
Ban Tako *Thailand* **64** E4
Ban Tha Dua *Thailand* **64** D2
Ban Tha Nun *Thailand* **65** a
Ban Tha Rua *Thailand* **65** a
Ban Tha Yu *Thailand* **65** a
Ban Thahine *Laos* **64** E5
Ban Thong Krut *Thailand* **65** b
Ban Xien Kok *Laos* **64** B3
Ban Yen Nhan *Vietnam* **64** B6
Banaba *Kiribati* **96** H8
Banalia *Dem. Rep. of the Congo* **86** B2
Banam *Cambodia* **65** G5
Banamba *Mali* **82** C3
Banana Is. *S. Leone* **82** D2
Bananal, I. do *Brazil* **125** F8
Banaras = Varanasi *India* **69** G10
Banas → *Gujarat, India* **68** H4
Banas → *Mad. P., India* **69** G9
Bânâs, Ras *Egypt* **80** C4
Banaz *Turkey* **47** C11
Banaz → *Turkey* **47** C11
Banbridge *U.K.* **12** B5
Banbury *U.K.* **15** E6
Banchory *U.K.* **13** D6
Banco *Ethiopia* **81** F4
Bancroft *Canada* **114** A7
Band *Romania* **29** D9
Band Bonī *Iran* **71** E8
Band Qīr *Iran* **71** D6
Banda *Mad. P., India* **69** G8
Banda *Ut. P., India* **69** G9
Banda, Kepulauan *Indonesia* **63** E7
Banda Aceh *Indonesia* **62** C1
Banda Banda, Mt. *Australia* **95** E5
Banda Elat *Indonesia* **63** F8
Banda Is. = Banda,
  Kepulauan *Indonesia* **63** E7
Banda Sea *Indonesia* **63** F8
Bandai-Asahi △ *Japan* **54** F10
Bandai-San *Japan* **54** F10
Bandama → *Ivory C.* **82** D3
Bandama Blanc → *Ivory C.* **82** D4
Bandama Rouge → *Ivory C.* **82** D4
Bandān *Iran* **71** D9
Bandanaira *Indonesia* **63** E7
Bandanwara *India* **68** F6
Bandar = Machilipatnam
  India **67** L12
Bandar-e Abbās *Iran* **71** E8
Bandar-e Anzalī *Iran* **73** D13
Bandar-e Bushehr =
  Būshehr *Iran* **71** D6
Bandar-e Chārak *Iran* **71** E7
Bandar-e Deylam *Iran* **71** D6
Bandar-e Emām Khomeynī
  Iran **71** D6
Bandar-e Lengeh *Iran* **71** E7
Bandar-e Maqām *Iran* **71** E7
Bandar-e Ma'shur *Iran* **71** D6
Bandar-e Rīg *Iran* **71** D6
Bandar-e Torkeman *Iran* **71** B7
Bandar Lampung *Indonesia* **62** F3
Bandar Maharani = Muar
  Malaysia **65** L4
Bandar Penggaram = Batu
  Pahat *Malaysia* **65** M4
Bandar Seri Begawan *Brunei* **62** D5
Bandar Sri Aman = Sri
  Aman *Malaysia* **62** D4
Bandawe *Malawi* **87** E3
Bande *Spain* **36** C3
Bandeira, Pico da *Brazil* **127** A7
Bandera *Argentina* **126** B3
Banderas, B. de *Mexico* **118** C3
Bandhavgarh *India* **69** H9
Bandi → *India* **68** F6
Bandiagara *Mali* **82** C4
Bandikui *India* **68** F7
Bandırma *Turkey* **45** F11
Bandjarmasin =
  Banjarmasin *Indonesia* **62** E4
Bandol *France* **21** E9
Bandon *Ireland* **12** E3
Bandon → *Ireland* **12** E3
Bandula *Mozam.* **87** F3
Bandundu
  Dem. Rep. of the Congo **84** E3

Bandung *Indonesia* **62** F3
Bané *Burkina Faso* **83** C4
Băneasa *Romania* **29** E12
Băneh *Iran* **73** E11
Banes *Cuba* **121** B4
Banff *Canada* **102** C5
Banff *U.K.* **13** D6
Banff △ *Canada* **102** C5
Banfora *Burkina Faso* **82** C4
Bang Fai → *Laos* **64** D5
Bang Hieng → *Laos* **64** D5
Bang Krathum *Thailand* **64** D3
Bang Lamung *Thailand* **64** E3
Bang Mun Nak *Thailand* **64** D3
Bang Pa In *Thailand* **64** E3
Bang Rakam *Thailand* **64** D3
Bang Saphan *Thailand* **65** G2
Bang Thao *Thailand* **65** a
Banganduni I. *India* **69** J13
Bangala Dam *Zimbabwe* **87** G3
Bangalore *India* **66** N10
Banganga → *India* **68** F6
Bangangté *Cameroon* **83** D7
Bangaon *India* **69** H13
Bangassou *C.A.R.* **84** D4
Banggai *Indonesia* **63** E6
Banggai, Kepulauan
  Indonesia **63** E6
Banggai Arch. = Banggai,
  Kepulauan *Indonesia* **63** E6
Banggi, Pulau *Malaysia* **62** C5
Banghāzī *Libya* **79** B10
Bangjang *Sudan* **81** E3
Bangka *Sulawesi, Indonesia* **63** D7
Bangka *Sumatera, Indonesia* **62** E3
Bangka, Selat *Indonesia* **62** E3
Bangka-Belitung □ *Indonesia* **62** E3
Bangkalan *Indonesia* **63** G15
Bangkinang *Indonesia* **62** D2
Bangko *Indonesia* **62** E2
Bangkok *Thailand* **64** F3
Bangla = West Bengal □
  India **69** H13
Bangladesh ■ *Asia* **67** H17
Bangli *Indonesia* **63** J18
Bangolo *Ivory C.* **82** D3
Bangor Down, U.K. **12** B6
Bangor *Gwynedd, U.K.* **14** D3
Bangor *Maine, U.S.A.* **113** C19
Bangor *Pa., U.S.A.* **115** F9
Bangued *Phil.* **61** C4
Bangui *C.A.R.* **84** D3
Bangui *Phil.* **61** B4
Banguru
  Dem. Rep. of the Congo **86** B2
Bangweulu, L. *Zambia* **87** E3
Bangweulu Swamp *Zambia* **87** E3
Banhine △ *Mozam.* **89** C5
Bani *Burkina Faso* **83** C4
Baní *Dom. Rep.* **121** C5
Bani → *Mali* **82** C4
Bani Bangou *Niger* **83** B5
Banī Sa'd *Iraq* **73** F11
Bania *Ivory C.* **82** D4
Banihal Pass *India* **69** C6
Banikoara *Benin* **83** C5
Banissa *Kenya* **81** G5
Bāniyās *Syria* **72** E6
Banja Luka *Bos.-H.* **28** F2
Banjar *India* **68** D7
Banjar → *India* **69** H9
Banjarmasin *Indonesia* **62** E4
Banjul *Gambia* **82** C1
Banka *India* **69** G12
Bankas *Mali* **82** C4
Bankeryd *Sweden* **11** G8
Banket *Zimbabwe* **87** F3
Bankilaré *Niger* **83** C5
Bankipore *India* **67** G14
Banks I. = Moa *Australia* **94** a
Banks I. *B.C., Canada* **102** C3
Banks I. *N.W.T., Canada* **100** C7
Banks Pen. *N.Z.* **91** E4
Banks Str. *Australia* **95** G4
Bankura *India* **69** H12
Bankya *Bulgaria* **44** D7
Banmankhi *India* **69** G12
Bann → *Armagh, U.K.* **12** B5
Bann → *L'derry., U.K.* **12** A5
Bannalec *France* **18** E3
Banning *U.S.A.* **111** M10
Banno *Ethiopia* **81** G4
Bannockburn *Canada* **114** B7
Bannockburn *U.K.* **13** E5
Bannockburn *Zimbabwe* **87** G2
Bannu *Pakistan* **66** C7
Bano *India* **69** H11
Bañolas = Banyoles *Spain* **38** C7
Banon *France* **21** D9
Baños de la Encina *Spain* **37** G7
Baños de Molgas *Spain* **36** C3
Bánovce nad Bebravou
  Slovak Rep. **27** C11
Banovići *Bos.-H.* **28** F3
Bansgaon *India* **69** F10
Banská Bystrica *Slovak Rep.* **27** C12
Banská Štiavnica
  Slovak Rep. **27** C11

Bansko *Bulgaria* **44** E7
Banskobystrický □
  Slovak Rep. **27** C12
Banswara *India* **68** H6
Bantaeng *Indonesia* **63** F5
Bantaji *Nigeria* **83** D7
Bantayan *Phil.* **61** F5
Banten □ *Indonesia* **63** G11
Bantry *Ireland* **12** E2
Bantry B. *Ireland* **12** E2
Bantul *Indonesia* **63** G14
Bantva *India* **68** J4
Banya *Bulgaria* **45** D8
Banyak, Kepulauan
  Indonesia **62** D1
Banyalbufar *Spain* **48** B9
Banyeres de Mariola *Spain* **39** G4
Banyo *Cameroon* **83** D7
Banyoles *Spain* **38** C7
Banyuls-sur-Mer *France* **20** F7
Banyumas *Indonesia* **63** G13
Banyuwangi *Indonesia* **63** J17
Banzare Coast *Antarctica* **5** C9
Bao Ha *Vietnam* **58** F5
Bao Lac *Vietnam* **64** A5
Bao Loc *Vietnam* **65** G6
Bao'an = Shenzhen *China* **59** F10
Baocheng *China* **56** H4
Baode *China* **56** E6
Baodi *China* **57** E9
Baoding *China* **56** E8
Baoji *China* **56** G4
Baojing *China* **58** C7
Baokang *China* **59** B8
Baoshan *Shanghai, China* **59** B13
Baoshan *Yunnan, China* **58** E2
Baotou *China* **56** D6
Baoulé → *Mali* **82** C3
Baoxing *China* **58** B4
Baoying *China* **57** H10
Baoyou = Ledong *China* **64** C7
Bap *India* **68** F5
Bapatla *India* **67** M12
Bapaume *France* **19** B9
Bāqerābād *Iran* **71** C6
Ba'qūbah *Iraq* **73** F11
Baquedano *Chile* **126** A2
Bar *Montenegro* **44** D3
Bar *Ukraine* **23** D14
Bar Bigha *India* **69** G11
Bar Harbor *U.S.A.* **113** C19
Bar-le-Duc *France* **19** D12
Bar-sur-Aube *France* **19** D11
Bar-sur-Seine *France* **19** D11
Bara *India* **69** H9
Bâra *Romania* **29** C12
Bara Banki *India* **69** F9
Barabai *Indonesia* **62** E5
Baraboo *U.S.A.* **112** D9
Baracoa *Cuba* **121** B5
Baradā → *Syria* **74** B5
Baradero *Argentina* **126** C4
Baraga *U.S.A.* **112** B9
Barah → *India* **68** F6
Barahona *Dom. Rep.* **121** C5
Barail Range *India* **67** G18
Barajas, Madrid ✈ (MAD)
  Spain **36** E7
Baraka *Sudan* **81** E2
Baraka → *Sudan* **80** D4
Barakaldo *Spain* **38** B2
Barakar → *India* **69** G12
Barakot *India* **69** J11
Barakpur *India* **69** H13
Baralaba *Australia* **94** C4
Baralla *Spain* **36** C3
Baralzon L. *Canada* **103** B9
Barameiya *Sudan* **80** D4
Baramula *India* **69** B6
Baran *India* **68** G7
Baran → *Pakistan* **68** G3
Barañain *Spain* **38** C3
Baranavichy *Belarus* **23** B14
Barani *Burkina Faso* **82** C4
Baranof I. *U.S.A.* **100** F4
Baranów Sandomierski
  Poland **31** H8
Baranya □ *Hungary* **28** E3
Baraolt *Romania* **29** D10
Baraona *Spain* **38** D2
Barapasi *Indonesia* **63** E9
Barasat *India* **69** H13
Barat Daya, Kepulauan
  Indonesia **63** F7
Barataria B. *U.S.A.* **117** G10
Barauda *India* **68** H6
Baraut *India* **68** E7
Barbacena *Brazil* **127** A7
Barbados ■ *W. Indies* **121** g
Barban *Croatia* **41** C11
Barbària, C. de *Spain* **48** C7
Barbaros *Turkey* **45** F11
Barbas, C. *W. Sahara* **78** D2
Barbastro *Spain* **38** C5
Barbate *Spain* **37** J5
Barbeau Pk. *Canada* **101** A16

Barberino di Mugello *Italy* **41** E8
Barberton *S. Africa* **89** D5
Barberton *U.S.A.* **114** E3
Barbezieux-St-Hilaire *France* **20** C3
Barbosa *Colombia* **124** B4
Barbourville *U.S.A.* **113** G12
Barbuda *W. Indies* **121** C7
Bârca *Romania* **29** G8
Barcaldine *Australia* **94** C4
Barcarrota *Spain* **37** G4
Barcellona Pozzo di Gotto
  Italy **43** D8
Barcelona *Spain* **38** D7
Barcelona *Venezuela* **124** A6
Barcelona □ *Spain* **38** D7
Barcelona-Prat ✈ (BCN)
  Spain **38** D7
Barceloneta *Puerto Rico* **121** d
Barcelonette *France* **21** D10
Barcelos *Brazil* **124** D6
Barcin *Poland* **31** F4
Barclayville *Liberia* **82** E3
Barcoo → *Australia* **94** D3
Barcs *Hungary* **28** E2
Barczewo *Poland* **30** E7
Bärdä *Azerbaijan* **35** K8
Bardaï *Chad* **79** D9
Bardas Blancas *Argentina* **126** D2
Bardawîl, Sabkhet el *Egypt* **74** D2
Barddhaman *India* **69** H12
Bardejov *Slovak Rep.* **27** B14
Bardi *Italy* **40** D6
Bardīyah *Libya* **79** B10
Bardolino *Italy* **40** C7
Bardonécchia *Italy* **40** C3
Bardsey I. *U.K.* **14** E3
Bardstown *U.S.A.* **113** G11
Bareilly *India* **69** E8
Barela *India* **69** H9
Barentin *France* **18** C7
Barenton *France* **18** D6
Barents Sea *Arctic* **4** B9
Barentu *Eritrea* **81** D4
Barfleur *France* **18** C5
Barfleur, Pte. de *France* **18** C5
Barga *Italy* **40** D7
Bargara *Australia* **94** C5
Bargas *Spain* **36** F6
Bârgăului Bistrița *Romania* **29** C9
Barge *Italy* **40** D4
Bargi Dam *India* **69** H9
Bargteheide *Germany* **24** B6
Barguzin *Russia* **53** D11
Barh *India* **69** G11
Barhaj *India* **69** F10
Barharwa *India* **69** G12
Barhi *India* **69** G11
Bari *India* **68** F7
Bari *Italy* **43** A9
Bari Doab *Pakistan* **68** D5
Bari Sadri *India* **68** G6
Bari Sardo *Italy* **42** C2
Barīdī, Ra's *Si. Arabia* **70** E3
Barīm *Yemen* **76** E8
Barinas *Venezuela* **124** B4
Baring, C. *Canada* **100** D8
Baring, L. *Kenya* **86** B4
Bârîs *Egypt* **80** C3
Barisal *Bangla.* **67** H17
Barisal □ *Bangla.* **67** H17
Barisan, Pegunungan
  Indonesia **62** E2
Barito → *Indonesia* **62** E4
Baritú △ *Argentina* **126** A3
Barjac *France* **21** D8
Barjols *France* **21** E10
Barjūj, Wadi → *Libya* **79** C8
Bark L. *Canada* **114** A7
Barka = Baraka → *Sudan* **80** D4
Barkakana *India* **69** H11
Barkal, J. *Sudan* **80** D3
Barkam *China* **58** B4
Barker *U.S.A.* **114** C6
Barkley, L. *U.S.A.* **117** C10
Barkley Sound *Canada* **102** D3
Barkly East *S. Africa* **88** E4
Barkly Homestead *Australia* **94** B2
Barkly Tableland *Australia* **94** B2
Barkly West *S. Africa* **88** D3
Barkol, Wadi → *Sudan* **80** D3
Barla Dağı *Turkey* **47** C12
Bârlad *Romania* **29** D12
Bârlad → *Romania* **29** E12
Barlee, L. *Australia* **93** E2
Barlee, Mt. *Australia* **93** D4
Barletta *Italy* **43** A9
Barlinek *Poland* **31** F2
Barlovento *Canary Is.* **48** F2
Barlovento *C. Verde Is.* **78** b
Barlow L. *Canada* **103** A8
Barmedman *Australia* **95** E4
Barmer *India* **68** G4
Barmera *Australia* **95** E3
Barmouth *U.K.* **14** E3
Barmstedt *Germany* **24** B5
Barna → *India* **69** G10
Barnagar *India* **68** H6
Barnala *India* **68** D6

Barnaul *Russia* **52** D9
Barnesville *Ga., U.S.A.* **117** E12
Barnesville *Minn., U.S.A.* **112** B5
Barnet □ *U.K.* **15** F7
Barneveld *Neths.* **17** B5
Barneville-Carteret *France* **18** C5
Barnhart *U.S.A.* **116** F4
Barnsley *U.K.* **14** D6
Barnstable *U.S.A.* **113** E18
Barnstaple *U.K.* **15** F3
Barnstaple Bay = Bideford
  Bay *U.K.* **15** F3
Barnwell *U.S.A.* **117** E14
Baro *Nigeria* **83** D6
Baro → *Ethiopia* **81** F3
Baroda = Vadodara *India* **68** H5
Baroda *India* **68** G7
Baroe *S. Africa* **88** E3
Baron Ra. *Australia* **92** D4
Barong *China* **58** B2
Barotseland *Zambia* **85** H4
Barouéli *Mali* **82** C3
Barpeta *India* **67** F17
Barqa *Libya* **79** C10
Barques, Pt. Aux *U.S.A.* **114** B2
Barquísimeto *Venezuela* **124** A5
Barr *France* **19** D14
Barr, Ras el *Egypt* **80** H7
Barr Smith Range *Australia* **93** E3
Barra *Brazil* **125** F10
Barra *Gambia* **82** C1
Barra *U.K.* **13** E1
Barra, Sd. of *U.K.* **13** D1
Barra de Navidad *Mexico* **118** D4
Barra do Corda *Brazil* **125** E9
Barra do Garças *Brazil* **125** G8
Barra do Piraí *Brazil* **127** A7
Barra Falsa, Pta. da *Mozam.* **89** C6
Barra Hd. *U.K.* **13** E1
Barra Mansa *Brazil* **127** A7
Barraba *Australia* **95** E5
Barrackpur = Barakpur
  India **69** H13
Barrafranca *Italy* **43** E7
Barraigh = Barra *U.K.* **13** E1
Barrāmīya *Egypt* **80** B3
Barranca *Lima, Peru* **124** F3
Barranca *Loreto, Peru* **124** D3
Barranca del Cobre △
  Mexico **118** B3
Barrancabermeja *Colombia* **124** B4
Barrancas *Venezuela* **124** B6
Barrancos *Portugal* **37** G3
Barranqueras *Argentina* **126** B4
Barranquilla *Colombia* **124** A4
Barraute *Canada* **104** C4
Barre *Mass., U.S.A.* **115** D12
Barre *Vt., U.S.A.* **115** B12
Barreal *Argentina* **126** C2
Barreiras *Brazil* **125** F10
Barreirinhas *Brazil* **125** D10
Barreiro *Portugal* **37** G1
Barrême *France* **21** E10
Barretos *Brazil* **125** H9
Barrhead *Canada* **102** C6
Barrie *Canada* **114** B5
Barrier Ra. *Australia* **95** E3
Barrier Reef *Belize* **119** D7
Barrière *Canada* **102** C4
Barrington *U.S.A.* **115** E13
Barrington L. *Canada* **103** B8
Barrington Tops *Australia* **95** E5
Barringun *Australia* **95** D4
Barron *U.S.A.* **112** C8
Barrow *U.S.A.* **106** A8
Barrow → *Ireland* **12** D5
Barrow, Pt. *U.S.A.* **106** A8
Barrow Creek *Australia* **94** C1
Barrow I. *Australia* **92** D2
Barrow-in-Furness *U.K.* **14** C4
Barrow Pt. *Australia* **94** A3
Barrow Ra. *Australia* **93** E4
Barrow Str. *Canada* **4** B3
Barruecopardo *Spain* **36** D4
Barruelo de Santullán *Spain* **36** C6
Barry *U.K.* **15** F4
Barry's Bay *Canada* **114** A7
Barsalogho *Burkina Faso* **83** C4
Barsat *Pakistan* **69** A5
Barsham *Syria* **73** E9
Barsi *India* **66** K9
Barsinghausen *Germany* **24** C5
Barso *India* **67** G15
Barstow *U.S.A.* **111** L9
Barth *Germany* **24** A9
Barthélemy, Col *Vietnam* **64** C5
Bartica *Guyana* **124** B7
Bartın *Turkey* **72** B5
Bartle Frere *Australia* **94** B4
Bartlesville *U.S.A.* **116** C7
Bartlett *Calif., U.S.A.* **110** J8
Bartlett *Tenn., U.S.A.* **117** D10
Bartlett, L. *Canada* **102** A5
Bartolomeu Dias *Mozam.* **87** G4
Barton *U.S.A.* **115** B12
Barton upon Humber *U.K.* **14** D7
Bartoszyce *Poland* **30** D7
Bartow *U.S.A.* **117** H14
Barú, Volcan *Panama* **120** E3

Barumba
  Dem. Rep. of the Congo **86** B1
Baruth *Germany* **24** C9
Baruun Urt *Mongolia* **53** E12
Baruunsuu *Mongolia* **56** C3
Barwani *India* **68** H6
Barwice *Poland* **30** E3
Barycz → *Poland* **31** G3
Barysaw *Belarus* **23** A15
Barysh *Russia* **34** D8
Barzán *Iraq* **70** B5
Bârzava *Romania* **28** D6
Bas-Rhin □ *France* **19** D14
Başaid *Serbia* **28** E5
Bāsa'īdū *Iran* **71** E7
Basal *Pakistan* **68** C5
Basankusa
  Dem. Rep. of the Congo **84** D3
Basarabeasca *Moldova* **29** D13
Basarabi *Romania* **29** F13
Basarabia = Bessarabiya
  Moldova **23** E15
Basauri *Spain* **38** B2
Basawa *Afghan.* **68** B4
Bascuñán, C. *Chile* **126** B1
Basel *Switz.* **25** H3
Basel, Euroairport ✈ (BSL)
  Europe **19** E14
Basel-Landschaft □ *Switz.* **25** H3
Basento → *Italy* **43** B9
Bashākerd, Kūhhā-ye *Iran* **71** E8
Bashaw *Canada* **102** C6
Bāshī *Iran* **71** D6
Bashkir Republic =
  Bashkortostan □ *Russia* **52** D6
Bashkortostan □ *Russia* **52** D6
Bashtanivka *Ukraine* **29** E14
Basian *Phil.* **61** H5
Basilan Str. *Phil.* **61** H5
Basildon *U.K.* **15** F8
Basile *Eq. Guin.* **83** E6
Basilé, Pico de *Eq. Guin.* **83** E6
Basilicata □ *Italy* **43** B9
Basim = Washim *India* **66** J10
Basin *U.S.A.* **108** D9
Basingstoke *U.K.* **15** F6
Baška *Croatia* **41** D11
Başkale *Turkey* **73** C10
Baskatong, Rés. *Canada* **104** C4
Basle = Basel *Switz.* **25** H3
Başmakçı *Turkey* **47** D12
Basoda *India* **68** H7
Basoko *Dem. Rep. of the Congo* **86** B1
Basque, Pays *France* **20** E2
Basque Provinces = País
  Vasco □ *Spain* **38** C2
Basra = Al Başrah *Iraq* **70** D5
Bass Str. *Australia* **95** F4
Bassano *Canada* **102** C6
Bassano del Grappa *Italy* **41** C8
Bassar *Togo* **83** D5
Bassas da India *Ind. Oc.* **87** G4
Basse-Normandie □ *France* **18** D6
Basse-Pointe *Martinique* **120** c
Basse Santa-Su *Gambia* **82** C2
Basse-Terre *Guadeloupe* **120** b
Basse Terre *Trin. & Tob.* **125** K15
Bassein *Burma* **67** L19
Basses, Pte. des *Guadeloupe* **120** b
Basseterre *St. Kitts & Nevis* **121** C7
Bassett *U.S.A.* **112** D4
Bassi *India* **68** D7
Bassigny *France* **19** E12
Bassikounou *Mauritania* **82** B3
Bassila *Benin* **83** D5
Bassum *Germany* **24** C4
Båstad *Sweden* **11** H6
Bastak *Iran* **71** E7
Baştām *Iran* **71** B7
Bastar *India* **67** K12
Bastelica *France* **21** F13
Basti *India* **69** F10
Bastia *France* **21** F13
Bastogne *Belgium* **17** D5
Bastrop *La., U.S.A.* **116** E9
Bastrop *Tex., U.S.A.* **116** F6
Basuo = Dongfang *China* **64** C7
Bat Yam *Israel* **74** C3
Bata *Eq. Guin.* **84** D1
Bata *Romania* **28** D7
Bataan □ *Phil.* **61** D4
Batabanó *Cuba* **120** B3
Batabanó, G. de *Cuba* **120** B3
Batac *Phil.* **61** B4
Batagai *Russia* **53** C14
Batajnica *Serbia* **44** B4
Batak *Bulgaria* **45** E8
Batala *India* **68** D6
Batalha *Portugal* **36** F2
Batama *Dem. Rep. of the Congo* **86** B2
Batamay *Russia* **53** C13
Batang *China* **58** B2
Batang *Indonesia* **63** G13
Batangafo *C.A.R.* **84** C3
Batangas *Phil.* **61** E4
Batanta *Indonesia* **63** E8
Batatais *Brazil* **127** A6

Batavia U.S.A. **114** D6
Bataysk Russia **33** J10
Batchelor Australia **92** B5
Batdambang Cambodia **64** F4
Batemans B. Australia **95** F5
Batemans Bay Australia **95** F5
Batesburg-Leesville U.S.A. **117** E14
Batesville Ark., U.S.A. **116** D9
Batesville Miss., U.S.A. **117** D10
Batesville Tex., U.S.A. **116** G5
Bath Canada **115** B8
Bath U.K. **15** F5
Bath Maine, U.S.A. **113** D19
Bath N.Y., U.S.A. **114** D7
Bath & North East
    Somerset □ U.K. **15** F5
Batheay Cambodia **65** G5
Bathsheba Barbados **121** g
Bathurst Australia **95** E4
Bathurst Canada **105** C6
Bathurst S. Africa **88** E4
Bathurst, C. Canada **100** C6
Bathurst B. Australia **94** A3
Bathurst Harb. Australia **95** G4
Bathurst I. Australia **92** B5
Bathurst I. Canada **101** B11
Bathurst Inlet Canada **100** D10
Bati Ethiopia **81** E5
Batie Burkina Faso **82** D4
Batiki Fiji **91** a
Batlow Australia **95** F4
Batman Turkey **73** D9
Baṭn al Ghūl Jordan **74** F4
Batna Algeria **78** A7
Batobato = San Isidro Phil. **61** H7
Batočina Serbia **44** B5
Batoka Zambia **87** F2
Baton Rouge U.S.A. **116** F9
Batong, Ko Thailand **65** J2
Bátonyterenye Hungary **28** C4
Batopilas Mexico **118** B3
Batouri Cameroon **84** D2
Båtsfjord Norway **8** A23
Batsi Greece **46** D6
Battambang =
    Batdambang Cambodia **64** F4
Batticaloa Sri Lanka **66** R12
Battipáglia Italy **43** B7
Battle U.K. **15** G8
Battle → Canada **103** C7
Battle Creek U.S.A. **113** D11
Battle Ground U.S.A. **110** E4
Battle Harbour Canada **105** B8
Battle Lake U.S.A. **112** B6
Battle Mountain U.S.A. **108** F5
Battlefields Zimbabwe **87** F2
Battleford Canada **103** C7
Battonya Hungary **28** D6
Batu Ethiopia **81** F4
Batu Malaysia **65** L3
Batu, Kepulauan Indonesia **62** E1
Batu Ferringhi Malaysia **65** c
Batu Gajah Malaysia **65** K3
Batu Is. = Batu, Kepulauan
    Indonesia **62** E1
Batu Pahat Malaysia **65** M4
Batuata Indonesia **63** F6
Batugondang, Tanjung
    Indonesia **63** J17
Batukau, Gunung Indonesia **63** J18
Batumi Georgia **35** K5
Batur Indonesia **63** J18
Batur, Danau Indonesia **63** J18
Batur, Gunung Indonesia **63** J18
Batura Sar Pakistan **69** A6
Baturaja Indonesia **62** E2
Baturité Brazil **125** D11
Baturiti Indonesia **63** J18
Bau Malaysia **62** D4
Baubau Indonesia **63** F6
Baucau E. Timor **63** F7
Bauchi Nigeria **83** C6
Bauchi □ Nigeria **83** C7
Baud France **18** E3
Baudette U.S.A. **112** A6
Bauer, C. Australia **95** E1
Bauhinia Australia **94** C4
Bauld, C. Canada **101** G20
Baume-les-Dames France **19** E13
Baunei Italy **42** B2
Baure Nigeria **83** C6
Bauru Brazil **127** A6
Bausi India **69** G12
Bauska Latvia **30** B11
Bautino Kazakhstan **35** H10
Bautzen Germany **24** D10
Bauya S. Leone **82** D2
Bavānāt Iran **71** D7
Bavanište Serbia **28** F5
Bavaria = Bayern □
    Germany **25** G7
Båven Sweden **10** E10
Bavispe → Mexico **118** B3
Bawdwin Burma **67** H20
Bawean Indonesia **62** F4
Bawku Ghana **83** C4
Bawlake Burma **67** K20

Bawolung China **58** C3
Baxley U.S.A. **117** F13
Baxoi China **58** B1
Baxter U.S.A. **112** B6
Baxter Springs U.S.A. **112** G6
Baxter State △ U.S.A. **113** B19
Bay, L. de Phil. **61** D4
Bay City Mich., U.S.A. **113** D12
Bay City Tex., U.S.A. **116** G7
Bay Minette U.S.A. **117** F11
Bay Roberts Canada **105** C9
Bay St. Louis U.S.A. **117** F10
Bay Springs U.S.A. **117** F10
Bay View N.Z. **91** C6
Baya Dem. Rep. of the Congo **87** E2
Bayamo Cuba **120** B4
Bayamón Puerto Rico **121** d
Bayan Har Shan China **60** C4
Bayan Hot = Alxa Zuoqi
    China **56** E3
Bayan Lepas Malaysia **65** c
Bayan Obo China **56** D5
Bayan-Ovoo = Erdenetsogt
    Mongolia **56** C4
Bayana India **68** F7
Bayanaūyl Kazakhstan **52** D8
Bayandalay Mongolia **56** C2
Bayanhongor Mongolia **53** E11
Bayard N. Mex., U.S.A. **109** K9
Bayard Nebr., U.S.A. **112** E2
Bayawan Phil. **61** G5
Baybay Phil. **61** F6
Bayburt Turkey **73** B9
Bayburt □ Turkey **73** B8
Baydaratskaya Guba Russia **52** C7
Baydhabo Somali Rep. **75** G3
Bayelsa □ Nigeria **83** E6
Bayerische Alpen Germany **25** H7
Bayerische Rhön → Germany **25** E6
Bayerischer Spessart △
    Germany **25** F6
Bayerischer Wald Germany **25** G8
Bayern □ Germany **25** G7
Bayeux France **18** C6
Bayfield Canada **114** C3
Bayfield U.S.A. **112** B8
Bayındır Turkey **47** C9
Baykal, Oz. Russia **53** D11
Baykan Turkey **73** C9
Baynes Mts. Namibia **88** B1
Bayombong Phil. **61** C4
Bayon France **19** D13
Bayona = Baiona Spain **36** C2
Bayonne France **20** E2
Bayonne U.S.A. **115** F10
Bayovar Peru **124** E2
Bayqongyr Kazakhstan **52** E7
Bayram-Ali = Baýramaly
    Turkmenistan **71** B9
Baýramaly Turkmenistan **71** B9
Bayramiç Turkey **47** B8
Bayreuth Germany **25** F7
Bayrischzell Germany **25** H8
Bayrūt Lebanon **74** B4
Bays, L. of Canada **114** A5
Baysville Canada **114** A5
Bayt Lahm West Bank **74** D4
Baytown U.S.A. **116** G7
Bayun Indonesia **63** J18
Bayzo Niger **83** C5
Baza Spain **37** H8
Bazar Dyuzi Russia **35** K8
Bazardüzü = Bazar Dyuzi
    Russia **35** K8
Bāzargān Iran **73** C11
Bazarny Karabulak Russia **34** D8
Bazarnyy Syzgan Russia **34** D8
Bazaruto, I. do Mozam. **89** C6
Bazaruto △ Mozam. **89** C6
Bazas France **20** D3
Bazhong China **58** B6
Bazhou China **56** E9
Bazmān, Kūh-e Iran **71** D9
Baztan = Elizondo Spain **38** B3
Beach U.S.A. **112** B2
Beach City U.S.A. **114** F3
Beachport Australia **95** F3
Beachville Canada **114** C4
Beachy Hd. U.K. **15** G8
Beacon Australia **93** F2
Beacon U.S.A. **115** E11
Beaconsfield Australia **95** G4
Beagle, Canal S. Amer. **128** H3
Beagle Bay Australia **92** C3
Beagle Bay ◎ Australia **92** C3
Beagle G. Australia **92** B5
Béal an Átha = Ballina
    Ireland **12** B2
Béal Átha na Sluaighe =
    Ballinasloe Ireland **12** C3
Bealanana Madag. **89** A8
Beals Cr. → U.S.A. **116** E4
Beamsville Canada **114** C5
Bear → Calif., U.S.A. **110** G5
Bear → Utah, U.S.A. **106** G17
Béar, C. France **20** F7
Bear I. Ireland **12** E2
Bear L. Canada **103** B9
Bear L. U.S.A. **108** F8

Bear Lake Canada **114** A5
Beardmore Canada **104** C2
Beardmore Glacier Antarctica **5** E11
Beardstown U.S.A. **112** E8
Bearma → India **69** G8
Bearpaw Mts. U.S.A. **108** B9
Bearskin Lake Canada **104** B1
Beas → India **68** D6
Beas de Segura Spain **37** G8
Beasain Spain **38** B2
Beata, C. Dom. Rep. **121** C5
Beata, I. Dom. Rep. **121** C5
Beatrice U.S.A. **112** E5
Beatrice Zimbabwe **87** F3
Beatrice, C. Australia **94** A2
Beatton → Canada **102** B4
Beatton River Canada **102** B4
Beatty U.S.A. **110** J10
Beau Bassin Mauritius **85** d
Beaucaire France **21** E8
Beauce, Plaine de la France **19** D8
Beauceville Canada **105** C5
Beaudesert Australia **95** D5
Beaufort France **21** C10
Beaufort Malaysia **62** C5
Beaufort N.C., U.S.A. **117** D16
Beaufort S.C., U.S.A. **117** E14
Beaufort Sea Arctic **98** B5
Beaufort West S. Africa **88** E3
Beaugency France **19** E8
Beauharnois Canada **115** A11
Beaujeu France **19** F11
Beaujolais France **19** F11
Beaulieu → Canada **102** A6
Beaulieu-sur-Dordogne
    France **20** D5
Beaulieu-sur-Mer France **21** E11
Beauly U.K. **13** D4
Beauly → U.K. **13** D4
Beaumaris U.K. **14** D3
Beaumont Belgium **17** D4
Beaumont France **20** D4
Beaumont U.S.A. **116** F7
Beaumont-de-Lomagne
    France **20** E5
Beaumont-le-Roger France **18** C7
Beaumont-sur-Sarthe France **18** D7
Beaune France **19** E11
Beaune-la-Rolande France **19** D9
Beaupré Canada **105** C5
Beaupréau France **18** E6
Beauraing Belgium **17** D4
Beaurepaire France **21** C9
Beausejour Canada **103** C9
Beauvais France **19** C9
Beauval Canada **103** B7
Beauvoir-sur-Mer France **18** F4
Beauvoir-sur-Niort France **20** B3
Beaver Okla., U.S.A. **116** C4
Beaver Pa., U.S.A. **114** F4
Beaver Utah, U.S.A. **108** G7
Beaver → B.C., Canada **102** B4
Beaver → Ont., Canada **104** A2
Beaver → Sask., Canada **103** B7
Beaver → U.S.A. **116** C5
Beaver City U.S.A. **112** E4
Beaver Creek Canada **100** E3
Beaver Dam U.S.A. **112** D9
Beaver Falls U.S.A. **114** F4
Beaver Hill L. Canada **103** C10
Beaver I. U.S.A. **113** C11
Beavercreek U.S.A. **113** F11
Beaverhill L. Canada **102** C6
Beaverlodge Canada **102** B5
Beaverstone → Canada **104** B2
Beaverton Canada **114** B5
Beaverton U.S.A. **110** E4
Beawar India **68** F6
Bebedouro Brazil **127** A6
Bebera, Tanjung Indonesia **63** K18
Beboa Madag. **89** B7
Bebra Germany **24** C5
Becán Mexico **119** D7
Bécancour Canada **113** B17
Beccles U.K. **15** E9
Bečej Serbia **28** E5
Beceni Romania **29** E11
Becerreá Spain **36** C3
Béchar Algeria **78** B5
Becharof L. U.S.A. **106** D8
Bechyně Czech Rep. **26** B7
Beckley U.S.A. **113** G13
Beckum Germany **24** D4
Beclean Romania **29** C9
Bečov nad Teplou Czech Rep. **26** A5
Bečva → Czech Rep. **27** B10
Bédar Spain **39** H3
Bédarieux France **20** E7
Beddouza, C. Morocco **78** B4
Bedele Ethiopia **81** F4
Bederkesa Germany **24** B4
Bedeso Ethiopia **81** F5
Bedford Canada **115** A12
Bedford S. Africa **88** E4
Bedford U.K. **15** E7
Bedford Ind., U.S.A. **112** F10
Bedford Iowa, U.S.A. **112** E6
Bedford Ohio, U.S.A. **114** E3

Bedford Pa., U.S.A. **114** F6
Bedford Va., U.S.A. **113** G14
Bedford, C. Australia **94** B4
Bedfordshire □ U.K. **15** E7
Będków Poland **31** G8
Bednja → Croatia **41** B13
Bednodemyanovsk Russia **34** D6
Bedok Singapore **65** d
Bedónia Italy **40** D6
Bedourie Australia **94** C2
Bedum Neths. **17** A6
Będzin Poland **31** H6
Beebe Plain Canada **115** A12
Beech Creek U.S.A. **114** E7
Beechy Canada **103** C7
Beed = Bir India **66** K9
Beef I. Br. Virgin Is. **121** e
Beenleigh Australia **95** D5
Beeston U.K. **14** E6
Beeton Canada **114** B5
Beetzendorf Germany **24** C7
Beeville U.S.A. **116** G5
Befale Dem. Rep. of the Congo **84** D4
Befandriana Mahajanga,
    Madag. **89** B8
Befandriana Toliara, Madag. **89** C7
Befasy Madag. **89** C7
Befotaka Antsiranana, Madag. **89** A8
Befotaka Fianarantsoa, Madag. **89** C8
Bega Australia **95** F4
Bega, Canalul Romania **28** E5
Bégard France **18** D3
Beğendik Turkey **45** F10
Begoro Ghana **83** D4
Begusarai India **69** G12
Behābād Iran **71** C8
Behala India **69** H13
Behara Madag. **89** C8
Behbehān Iran **71** D6
Behm Canal U.S.A. **102** B2
Behshahr Iran **71** B7
Bei Jiang → China **59** F9
Bei'an China **60** B7
Beibei China **58** C6
Beichuan China **58** B5
Beihai China **58** G7
Beijing China **56** E9
Beijing □ China **56** E9
Beilen Neths. **17** B6
Beiliu China **59** F8
Beilngries Germany **25** F7
Beilpajah Australia **95** E3
Beilul Eritrea **81** E5
Beinn na Faoghla =
    Benbecula U.K. **13** D1
Beipan Jiang → China **58** E5
Beipiao China **57** D11
Beira Mozam. **87** F3
Beirut = Bayrūt Lebanon **74** B4
Beiseker Canada **102** C6
Beit Lekhem = Bayt Lahm
    West Bank **74** D4
Beitaolaizhao China **57** B13
Beitbridge Zimbabwe **87** G3
Beiuş Romania **28** D7
Beizhen = Binzhou China **57** F10
Beizhen China **57** D11
Beizhengzhen China **57** B12
Beja Portugal **37** H3
Béja Tunisia **79** A7
Beja □ Portugal **37** H3
Bejaïa Algeria **78** A7
Béjar Spain **36** E5
Bejestān Iran **71** C8
Bekçiler Turkey **47** E11
Békés Hungary **28** D6
Békés □ Hungary **28** D6
Békéscsaba Hungary **28** D6
Bekilli Turkey **47** C11
Bekily Madag. **89** C8
Bekisopa Madag. **89** C8
Bekitro Madag. **89** C8
Bekodoka Madag. **89** B8
Bekoji Ethiopia **81** F4
Bekok Malaysia **65** L4
Bekopaka Madag. **89** B7
Bekuli Indonesia **63** J17
Bekwai Ghana **83** D4
Bela India **69** G10
Bela Pakistan **68** F2
Bela Bela S. Africa **89** C4
Bela Crkva Serbia **28** E6
Bela Palanka Serbia **44** C6
Bela Vista Brazil **126** A4
Bela Vista Mozam. **89** D5
Bélabre France **20** B5
Belalcázar Spain **37** G5
Belan → India **69** G9
Belanovica Serbia **44** B4
Belarus ■ Europe **23** B14

Belau = Palau ■ Palau **90** A6
Belavenona Madag. **89** C8
Belawan Indonesia **62** D1
Belaya Ethiopia **81** E4
Belaya → Russia **34** D9
Belaya Glina Russia **35** G5
Belaya Kalitva Russia **35** F5
Belaya Tserkov = Bila
    Tserkva Ukraine **23** D16
Belaya Zemlya, Ostrova
    Russia **52** A7
Belceşti Romania **29** C12
Belchatów Poland **31** G6
Belcher Is. Canada **104** A3
Belchite Spain **38** D4
Belden U.S.A. **110** E5
Beledweyne Somali Rep. **75** G4
Belém Brazil **125** D9
Belén Argentina **126** B2
Belén Paraguay **126** A4
Belen Turkey **72** D7
Belen U.S.A. **109** J10
Belene Bulgaria **45** C9
Bélesta France **20** F5
Belet Uen = Beledweyne
    Somali Rep. **75** G4
Belev Russia **32** F9
Belevi Turkey **47** C9
Belfair U.S.A. **110** C4
Belfast S. Africa **89** D5
Belfast U.K. **12** B6
Belfast Maine, U.S.A. **113** C19
Belfast N.Y., U.S.A. **114** D6
Belfast L. U.K. **12** B6
Belfield U.S.A. **112** B2
Belfort France **19** E13
Belfort, Territoire de □
    France **19** E13
Belfry U.S.A. **108** D9
Belgaum India **66** M9
Belgavi = Belgaum India **66** M9
Belgioioso Italy **40** C6
Belgium ■ Europe **17** D4
Belgodère France **21** F13
Belgorod Russia **33** G9
Belgorod □ Russia **33** G9
Belgorod-Dnestrovskiy =
    Bilhorod-Dnistrovskyy
    Ukraine **33** K6
Belgrade = Beograd Serbia **44** B4
Belgrade U.S.A. **108** D8
Belgrano Antarctica **5** D1
Belhaven U.S.A. **117** D16
Béli Guinea-Biss. **82** C2
Beli Nigeria **83** D7
Beli Drim → Europe **44** D4
Beli Manastir Croatia **28** E3
Beli Timok → Serbia **44** C6
Bélice → Italy **42** E5
Belimbing Indonesia **63** J18
Belinskiy Russia **34** D6
Belinyu Indonesia **62** E3
Beliton Is. = Belitung
    Indonesia **62** E3
Belitung Indonesia **62** E3
Beliu Romania **28** D6
Belize ■ Cent. Amer. **119** D7
Belize City Belize **119** D7
Beljakovci Macedonia **44** D5
Beljanica Serbia **44** B5
Belkovskiy, Ostrov Russia **53** B14
Bell → Canada **104** C4
Bell I. Canada **105** B8
Bell-Irving → Canada **102** B3
Bell Peninsula Canada **101** E15
Bell Ville Argentina **126** C3
Bella Italy **43** B8
Bella Bella Canada **102** C3
Bella Coola Canada **102** C3
Bella Unión Uruguay **126** C4
Bella Vista Corrientes,
    Argentina **126** B4
Bella Vista Tucuman,
    Argentina **126** B3
Bellac France **20** B5
Bellágio Italy **40** C6
Bellaire U.S.A. **114** F4
Bellária Italy **41** D9
Bellary India **66** M10
Bellata Australia **95** D4
Belle Fourche U.S.A. **112** C2
Belle Fourche → U.S.A. **107** G19
Belle Glade U.S.A. **117** H14
Belle-Île France **18** E3
Belle Isle Canada **105** B8
Belle Isle, Str. of Canada **105** B8
Belle Plaine U.S.A. **112** E7
Belle River Canada **114** D2
Belle Yella Liberia **82** D3
Belledonne France **21** C10
Bellefontaine U.S.A. **113** E12
Bellefonte U.S.A. **114** F7
Bellegarde France **20** C6
Bellegarde-en-Marche
    France **19** F12
Bellegarde-sur-Valserine
    France **21** C9
Bellême France **18** D7
Belleoram Canada **105** C8
Belleplaine Barbados **121** g

Belleville Canada **114** B7
Belleville France **19** F11
Belleville Ill., U.S.A. **112** F9
Belleville Kans., U.S.A. **112** F5
Belleville N.J., U.S.A. **115** F10
Belleville N.Y., U.S.A. **115** C8
Belleville-sur-Vie France **18** F5
Bellevue Idaho, U.S.A. **108** E6
Bellevue Nebr., U.S.A. **112** E6
Bellevue Ohio, U.S.A. **114** E2
Bellevue Wash., U.S.A. **110** C4
Belley France **21** C9
Bellin = Kangirsuk Canada **101** F18
Bellinge Denmark **11** J4
Bellingen Australia **95** E5
Bellingham U.S.A. **110** B4
Bellingshausen Abyssal
    Plain S. Ocean **5** C16
Bellingshausen Sea
    Antarctica **5** C17
Bellinzona Switz. **25** J5
Bello Colombia **124** B3
Bellows Falls U.S.A. **115** C12
Bellpat Pakistan **68** E3
Bellpuig Spain **38** D6
Belluno Italy **41** B9
Bellwood U.S.A. **114** F6
Bélmez Spain **37** G5
Belmont Canada **114** D3
Belmont S. Africa **88** D3
Belmont U.S.A. **114** D6
Belmonte Brazil **125** G11
Belmonte Portugal **36** E3
Belmonte Spain **39** F2
Belmopan Belize **119** D7
Belmullet Ireland **12** B2
Belo Horizonte Brazil **125** G10
Belo-sur-Mer Madag. **89** C7
Belo-Tsiribihina Madag. **89** B7
Belogorsk = Bilohirsk
    Ukraine **33** K8
Belogorsk Russia **53** D13
Belogradchik Bulgaria **44** C6
Belogradets Bulgaria **45** C11
Beloha Madag. **89** D8
Beloit Kans., U.S.A. **112** F5
Beloit Wis., U.S.A. **112** D9
Belokorovichi Ukraine **23** C15
Belomorsk Russia **52** C4
Belonia India **67** H17
Belopolye = Bilopillya
    Ukraine **33** G8
Belorechensk Russia **35** H4
Belorussia = Belarus ■
    Europe **23** B14
Beloslav Bulgaria **45** C11
Belovo Bulgaria **45** D8
Belovo Russia **52** D9
Belovodsk Ukraine **33** H10
Beloyarskiy Russia **52** C7
Beloye, Ozero Russia **32** B9
Beloye More Russia **8** C25
Belozem Bulgaria **45** D9
Belozersk Russia **32** B9
Belpasso Italy **43** E7
Belpre U.S.A. **113** F13
Belrain India **69** E9
Belt U.S.A. **108** C8
Beltana Australia **95** E2
Belterra Brazil **125** D8
Beltinci Slovenia **41** B13
Belton U.S.A. **116** F6
Belton L. U.S.A. **116** F6
Beltsy = Bălți Moldova **29** C12
Belturbet Ireland **12** B4
Belukha Russia **52** E9
Beluran Malaysia **62** C5
Beluša Slovak Rep. **27** B11
Belushya Guba Russia **52** B6
Belušić Serbia **44** C5
Belvedere Maríttimo Italy **43** C8
Belvès France **20** D5
Belvidere Ill., U.S.A. **112** D9
Belvidere N.J., U.S.A. **115** F9
Belvís de la Jara Spain **36** F6
Belyando → Australia **94** C4
Belyando Crossing Australia **94** C4
Belyuen Australia **92** B5
Belyy Russia **32** E7
Belyy, Ostrov Russia **52** B8
Belyy Yar Russia **52** D9
Belz Ukraine **31** H11
Belzec Poland **31** H10
Belzig Germany **24** C8
Belzoni U.S.A. **117** D10
Bełżyce Poland **31** G9
Bemaraha, Lembalemban' i
    Madag. **89** B7
Bemarivo Madag. **89** C7
Bemarivo → Antsiranana,
    Madag. **89** A9
Bemarivo → Mahajanga,
    Madag. **89** B8
Bemavo Madag. **89** C8
Bemberéke Benin **83** C5
Bembesi Zimbabwe **87** G2
Bembesi → Zimbabwe **87** F2
Bembézar → Spain **37** H5
Bembibre Spain **36** C4

Bemetara *India* 69 J9
Bemidji *U.S.A.* 112 B6
Bemolanga *Madag.* 89 B8
Ben *Iran* 71 C6
Ben Cruachan *U.K.* 13 E3
Ben Dearg *U.K.* 13 D4
Ben En △ *Vietnam* 64 C5
Ben Gardane *Tunisia* 79 B8
Ben Hope *U.K.* 13 C4
Ben Lawers *U.K.* 13 E4
Ben Lomond *N.S.W., Australia* 95 E5
Ben Lomond *Tas., Australia* 95 G4
Ben Lomond *U.K.* 13 E4
Ben Lomond △ *Australia* 95 G4
Ben Luc *Vietnam* 65 G6
Ben Macdhui *U.K.* 13 D5
Ben Mhor *U.K.* 13 D1
Ben More *Argyll & Bute, U.K.* 13 E2
Ben More *Stirling, U.K.* 13 E4
Ben More Assynt *U.K.* 13 C4
Ben Nevis *U.K.* 13 E3
Ben Quang *Vietnam* 64 D6
Ben Tre *Vietnam* 65 G6
Ben Vorlich *U.K.* 13 E4
Ben Wyvis *U.K.* 13 D4
Bena *Nigeria* 83 C6
Benalla *Australia* 95 F4
Benalmádena *Spain* 37 J6
Benares = Varanasi *India* 69 G10
Bénat, C. *France* 21 E10
Benavente *Portugal* 37 G2
Benavente *Spain* 36 C5
Benavides *U.S.A.* 116 H5
Benavides de Órbigo *Spain* 36 C5
Benbecula *U.K.* 13 D1
Benbonyathe Hill *Australia* 95 E2
Bend *U.S.A.* 108 D3
Bender Beyla *Somali Rep.* 75 F5
Bendery = Tighina *Moldova* 29 D14
Bendigo *Australia* 95 F4
Bendorf *Germany* 24 E3
Bené Beraq *Israel* 74 C3
Bénéna *Mali* 82 C4
Benénitra *Madag.* 89 C8
Benešov *Czech Rep.* 26 B7
Benevento *Italy* 43 A7
Benfeld *France* 19 D14
Benga *Mozam.* 87 F3
Bengal, Bay of *Ind. Oc.* 67 M17
Bengaluru = Bangalore
  India 66 N10
Bengbis *Cameroon* 83 E7
Bengbu *China* 57 H9
Benghazi = Banghāzī *Libya* 79 B10
Bengkalis *Indonesia* 65 M4
Bengkulu *Indonesia* 62 E2
Bengkulu □ *Indonesia* 62 E2
Bengough *Canada* 103 D7
Bengtsfors *Sweden* 10 E6
Benguela *Angola* 85 G2
Benguérua, I. *Mozam.* 89 C6
Benha *Egypt* 80 H7
Beni *Dem. Rep. of the Congo* 86 B2
Beni ➤ *Bolivia* 124 F5
Beni Mazâr *Egypt* 80 B3
Beni Mellal *Morocco* 78 B4
Beni Suef *Egypt* 80 J7
Beniah L. *Canada* 102 A6
Benicarló *Spain* 38 E5
Benicàssim *Spain* 38 E5
Benidorm *Spain* 39 G4
Benin ■ *Africa* 83 D5
Benin ➤ *Nigeria* 83 D6
Benin, Bight of *W. Afr.* 83 E5
Benin City *Nigeria* 83 D6
Benissa *Spain* 39 G5
Benito Juárez *Argentina* 126 D4
Benitses *Greece* 49 A3
Benjamin Aceval *Paraguay* 126 A4
Benjamin Constant *Brazil* 124 D4
Benjamín Hill *Mexico* 118 A2
Benkelman *U.S.A.* 112 E3
Benkovac *Croatia* 41 D12
Bennett *Canada* 102 B2
Bennett, L. *Australia* 92 D5
Bennetta, Ostrov *Russia* 53 B15
Bennettsville *U.S.A.* 117 D15
Bennichchâb *Mauritania* 82 B1
Bennington *N.H., U.S.A.* 115 D11
Bennington *Vt., U.S.A.* 115 D11
Bénodet *France* 18 E2
Benom *Malaysia* 65 L4
Benoni *S. Africa* 89 D4
Benque Viejo *Belize* 119 D7
Bensheim *Germany* 25 F4
Benson *Ariz., U.S.A.* 109 L8
Benson *Minn., U.S.A.* 112 C6
Bent *Iran* 71 E8
Benteng *Indonesia* 63 F6
Bentinck I. *Australia* 94 B2
Bentiu *Sudan* 81 F2
Bentley Subglacial Trench
  Antarctica 5 E15
Bento Gonçalves *Brazil* 127 B5
Benton *Ark., U.S.A.* 116 D8
Benton *Calif., U.S.A.* 110 H8
Benton *Ill., U.S.A.* 112 F9
Benton *Pa., U.S.A.* 115 E8
Benton Harbor *U.S.A.* 112 D10

Bentong *Malaysia* 65 L3
Bentonville *U.S.A.* 116 C7
Bentu Liben *Ethiopia* 81 F4
Benue □ *Nigeria* 83 D6
Benue ➤ *Nigeria* 83 D6
Benxi *China* 57 D12
Beo *Indonesia* 63 D7
Beograd *Serbia* 44 B4
Beograd ✈ (BEG) *Serbia* 44 C4
Beolgyo *S. Korea* 57 G14
Beoumi *Ivory C.* 82 D3
Bepan Jiang ➤ *China* 58 E6
Beppu *Japan* 55 H5
Beqa *Fiji* 91 a
Beqaa Valley = Al Biqā
  Lebanon 74 A5
Ber Mota *India* 68 H3
Bera, Tasik *Malaysia* 65 L4
Berach ➤ *India* 68 G6
Beraketa *Madag.* 89 C7
Beral *Albania* 44 F3
Berastagi *Indonesia* 65 L2
Berau = Tanjungredeb
  Indonesia 62 D5
Berau, Teluk *Indonesia* 63 E8
Beravina *Madag.* 89 B8
Berber *Sudan* 80 D3
Berbera *Somali Rep.* 75 E4
Berbérati *C.A.R.* 84 D3
Berbice ➤ *Guyana* 124 B7
Berceto *Italy* 40 D6
Berchidda *Italy* 42 B2
Berchtesgaden *Germany* 25 H8
Berchtesgaden △ *Germany* 25 H8
Berck *France* 19 B8
Berdichev = Berdychiv
  Ukraine 23 D15
Berdsk *Russia* 52 D9
Berdyansk *Ukraine* 33 J9
Berdychiv *Ukraine* 23 D15
Berea *U.S.A.* 113 G11
Berebere *Indonesia* 63 D7
Bereeda *Somali Rep.* 75 E5
Berehomet *Ukraine* 29 B10
Berehove *Ukraine* 28 B7
Bereket *Turkmenistan* 71 B7
Berekum *Ghana* 82 D4
Berenice *Egypt* 80 C4
Berens ➤ *Canada* 103 C9
Berens I. *Canada* 103 C9
Berens River *Canada* 103 C9
Beresford *U.S.A.* 112 D5
Berestechko *Ukraine* 23 C13
Bereşti *Romania* 29 D12
Beretău ➤ *Romania* 28 C6
Berettyó ➤ *Hungary* 28 D6
Berettyóújfalu *Hungary* 28 D6
Berevo *Mahajanga, Madag.* 89 B7
Berevo *Toliara, Madag.* 89 B7
Bereza = Byaroza *Belarus* 23 F3
Berezhany *Ukraine* 23 D13
Berezina = Byarezina ➤
  Belarus 23 B16
Berezivka *Ukraine* 33 J6
Berezna *Ukraine* 33 G6
Bereznik *Russia* 52 C5
Berezniki *Russia* 52 D6
Berezovo *Russia* 52 C7
Berezyne *Ukraine* 29 D14
Berga *Spain* 38 C6
Berga *Sweden* 11 G10
Bergama *Turkey* 47 B9
Bérgamo *Italy* 40 C6
Bergara *Spain* 38 B2
Bergby *Sweden* 10 D11
Berge *Norway* 10 E2
Bergedorf *Germany* 24 B6
Bergeforsen *Sweden* 10 B11
Bergen
  *Mecklenburg-Vorpommern,
  Germany* 24 A9
Bergen *Niedersachsen,
  Germany* 24 C5
Bergen *Neths.* 17 B4
Bergen *Norway* 8 F11
Bergen *U.S.A.* 114 C7
Bergen op Zoom *Neths.* 17 C4
Bergerac *France* 20 D4
Bergheim *Germany* 24 E2
Bergholz *U.S.A.* 114 F4
Bergisch Gladbach *Germany* 17 D7
Bergisches Land △ *Germany* 24 E3
Bergkamen *Germany* 24 D3
Bergkvara *Sweden* 11 H10
Bergshamra *Sweden* 10 E12
Bergsjö *Sweden* 10 C11
Bergstrasse-Odenwald △
  Germany 25 F1
Bergues *France* 19 B9
Bergville *S. Africa* 89 D4
Bergviken *Sweden* 10 C10
Berhala, Selat *Indonesia* 62 E2
Berhampore =
  Baharampur *India* 69 G13
Berhampur = Brahmapur
  India 67 K14
Berheci ➤ *Romania* 29 E12
Bering Glacier *U.S.A.* 106 C11

Bering Sea *Pac. Oc.* 98 D1
Bering Strait *Pac. Oc.* 106 B6
Beringovskiy *Russia* 53 C18
Berisso *Argentina* 126 C4
Berja *Spain* 37 J8
Berkeley *U.S.A.* 110 H4
Berkner I. *Antarctica* 5 D18
Berkovitsa *Bulgaria* 44 C7
Berkshire *U.S.A.* 115 D8
Berkshire Downs *U.K.* 15 F6
Berlanga *Spain* 37 G5
Berlenga, I. *Portugal* 37 F1
Berlin *Germany* 24 C9
Berlin *Md., U.S.A.* 113 F16
Berlin *N.H., U.S.A.* 115 B13
Berlin *N.Y., U.S.A.* 115 D11
Berlin *Wis., U.S.A.* 112 D9
Berlin □ *Germany* 24 C9
Berlin L. *U.S.A.* 114 E4
Berlin Tegel ✈ (TXL)
  Germany 24 C9
Bermeja, Sierra *Spain* 37 J5
Bermejo =
  *Formosa,
  Argentina* 126 B4
Bermejo ➤ *San Juan,
  Argentina* 126 C2
Bermejo, Paso = Uspallata,
  P. de *Argentina* 126 C2
Bermen, L. *Canada* 105 B6
Bermeo *Spain* 38 B2
Bermillo de Sayago *Spain* 36 D4
Bermuda ☑ *Atl. Oc.* 99 F13
Bern *Switz.* 25 J3
Bern □ *Switz.* 25 J3
Bernalda *Italy* 43 B9
Bernalillo *U.S.A.* 109 J10
Bernardo de Irigoyen
  Argentina 127 B5
Bernasconi *Argentina* 126 D3
Bernau *Bayern, Germany* 25 H8
Bernau *Brandenburg, Germany* 24 C9
Bernay *France* 18 C7
Bernburg *Germany* 24 D7
Berndorf *Austria* 26 D9
Berne = Bern *Switz.* 25 J3
Berne = Bern □ *Switz.* 25 J3
Berner Alpen *Switz.* 25 J3
Berneray *U.K.* 13 D1
Bernier I. *Australia* 93 D1
Bernina, Piz *Switz.* 25 J5
Bernkastel-Kues *Germany* 25 F3
Beroroha *Madag.* 89 C8
Béroubouay *Benin* 83 C5
Beroun *Czech Rep.* 26 B7
Berounka ➤ *Czech Rep.* 26 B7
Berovo *Macedonia* 44 E6
Berre, Étang de *France* 21 E9
Berre-l'Étang *France* 21 E9
Berri *Australia* 95 E3
Berriane *Algeria* 78 B6
Berry *Australia* 95 E5
Berry *France* 19 F8
Berry Is. *Bahamas* 120 A4
Berryessa, L. *U.S.A.* 110 G4
Berryville *U.S.A.* 116 C8
Berseba *Namibia* 88 D2
Bersenbrück *Germany* 24 C3
Bershad *Ukraine* 29 B14
Bertamirans *Spain* 36 C2
Berthold *U.S.A.* 112 A3
Berthoud *U.S.A.* 108 F11
Bertincourt *France* 19 B9
Bertoua *Cameroon* 84 D2
Bertraghboy B. *Ireland* 12 C2
Berwick *U.S.A.* 115 E8
Berwick-upon-Tweed *U.K.* 14 B6
Berwyn Mts. *U.K.* 14 E4
Beryslav *Ukraine* 33 J7
Berzasca *Romania* 28 F6
Berzence *Hungary* 28 D2
Besal *Pakistan* 69 B5
Besalampy *Madag.* 89 B7
Besançon *France* 19 E13
Besar *Indonesia* 62 E5
Beshenkovichi *Belarus* 32 E5
Beška *Serbia* 44 B4
Beslan *Russia* 35 J7
Besna Kobila *Serbia* 44 D6
Besnard L. *Canada* 103 B7
Besni *Turkey* 72 D7
Besor, N. ➤ *Egypt* 74 D3
Bessarabiya = Moldova 23 E15
Bessarabka =
  Basarabeasca *Moldova* 29 D13
Bessèges *France* 21 D8
Bessemer *Ala., U.S.A.* 117 E11
Bessemer *Mich., U.S.A.* 112 B8
Bessemer *Pa., U.S.A.* 114 F4
Bessin *France* 18 C6
Bessines-sur-Gartempe
  France 20 B5
Beswick *Australia* 92 B5
Beswick ◎ *Australia* 92 B5
Bet She'an *Israel* 74 C4
Bet Shemesh *Israel* 74 D4
Betafo *Madag.* 89 B8
Betancuria *Canary Is.* 48 F5
Betanzos *Spain* 36 B2

Bétaré Oya *Cameroon* 84 C2
Betatao *Madag.* 89 B8
Bétera *Spain* 39 F4
Bétérou *Benin* 83 D5
Bethal *S. Africa* 89 D4
Bethanien *Namibia* 88 D2
Bethany *Canada* 114 B6
Bethany *Mo., U.S.A.* 112 E6
Bethany *Okla., U.S.A.* 116 D6
Bethel *Alaska, U.S.A.* 106 C7
Bethel *Conn., U.S.A.* 115 E11
Bethel *Maine, U.S.A.* 115 B14
Bethel *Vt., U.S.A.* 115 C12
Bethel Park *U.S.A.* 114 F4
Béthenville *France* 19 C11
Bethlehem = Bayt Lahm
  West Bank 74 D4
Bethlehem *S. Africa* 89 D4
Bethlehem *U.S.A.* 115 F9
Bethulie *S. Africa* 88 E4
Béthune *France* 19 B9
Béthune ➤ *France* 18 C8
Betioky *Madag.* 89 C7
Betong *Malaysia* 62 D4
Betong *Thailand* 65 K3
Betoota *Australia* 94 D3
Betor *Ethiopia* 81 E4
Betpaqdala *Kazakhstan* 52 E8
Betroka *Madag.* 89 C8
Betsiamites *Canada* 105 C6
Betsiamites ➤ *Canada* 105 C6
Betsiboka ➤ *Madag.* 89 B8
Bettendorf *U.S.A.* 112 E8
Bettiah *India* 69 F11
Bettna *Sweden* 11 F10
Béttola *Italy* 40 D6
Betul *India* 66 J10
Betws-y-Coed *U.K.* 14 D4
Betxi *Spain* 38 F4
Betzdorf *Germany* 24 E3
Beuil *France* 21 D10
Beulah *Mich., U.S.A.* 112 C10
Beulah *N. Dak., U.S.A.* 112 B3
Beuvron ➤ *France* 18 E8
Beveren *Belgium* 17 C4
Beverley *Australia* 93 F2
Beverley *U.K.* 14 D7
Beverly *U.S.A.* 115 D14
Beverly Hills *Calif., U.S.A.* 111 L8
Beverly Hills *Fla., U.S.A.* 117 G13
Beverungen *Germany* 24 D5
Bevoalavo *Madag.* 89 D7
Bewas ➤ *India* 69 H8
Bewdley *Canada* 114 B6
Bex *Switz.* 25 J3
Bexhill *U.K.* 15 G8
Bey Dağları *Turkey* 47 E12
Beyānlū *Iran* 70 C5
Beyazköy *Turkey* 45 E11
Beyçayırı *Turkey* 45 F10
Beydağ *Turkey* 47 C10
Beyeğaç *Turkey* 47 D10
Beyin *Ghana* 82 D4
Beykoz *Turkey* 45 E13
Beyla *Guinea* 82 D3
Beynat *France* 20 C5
Beyneu *Kazakhstan* 52 E6
Beyoba *Turkey* 47 C9
Beyoğlu *Turkey* 45 E12
Beypazarı *Turkey* 72 B4
Beyşehir *Turkey* 72 D4
Beyşehir Gölü *Turkey* 72 D4
Beytüşşebap *Turkey* 73 D10
Bezdan *Serbia* 28 E3
Bezhetsk *Russia* 32 D9
Béziers *France* 20 E7
Bezwada = Vijayawada
  India 67 L12
Bhabua *India* 69 G10
Bhachau *India* 66 H7
Bhadar ➤ *Gujarat, India* 68 H5
Bhadar ➤ *Gujarat, India* 68 J3
Bhadarwah *India* 69 C6
Bhadgaon = Bhaktapur
  Nepal 69 F11
Bhadohi *India* 69 G10
Bhadra *India* 68 E6
Bhadrakh *India* 67 J15
Bhadran *India* 68 H5
Bhadravati *India* 66 N9
Bhag *Pakistan* 68 E2
Bhagalpur *India* 69 G12
Bhagirathi ➤ *Uttarakhand,
  India* 69 D8
Bhagirathi ➤ *W. Bengal,
  India* 69 H13
Bhakkar *Pakistan* 68 D4
Bhakra Dam *India* 68 D7
Bhaktapur *Nepal* 69 F11
Bhamo *Burma* 67 G20
Bhandara *India* 66 J11
Bhanpura *India* 68 G6
Bhanrer Ra. *India* 69 H8
Bhaptiahi *India* 69 F12
Bharat = India ■ *Asia* 66 K11
Bharatpur *Chhattisgarh, India* 69 H9
Bharatpur *Raj., India* 68 F7
Bharatpur *Nepal* 69 F11
Bharno *India* 69 H11

Bharuch *India* 66 J8
Bhatinda *India* 68 D6
Bhatpara *India* 69 H13
Bhattu *India* 68 E6
Bhaun *Pakistan* 68 C5
Bhaunagar = Bhavnagar
  India 66 J8
Bhavnagar *India* 66 J8
Bhawari *India* 68 G5
Bhayavadar *India* 68 J4
Bhera *Pakistan* 68 C5
Bhikangaon *India* 68 J6
Bhilai = Bhilainagar-Durg
  India 67 J12
Bhilainagar-Durg *India* 67 J12
Bhilsa = Vidisha *India* 68 H7
Bhilwara *India* 68 G6
Bhima ➤ *India* 66 L10
Bhimbar *Pakistan* 69 C6
Bhind *India* 69 F8
Bhinga *India* 69 F9
Bhinmal *India* 68 G5
Bhisho *S. Africa* 89 E4
Bhiwandi *India* 66 K8
Bhiwani *India* 68 E7
Bhogava ➤ *India* 68 H5
Bhola *Bangla.* 67 H17
Bholari *Pakistan* 68 G3
Bhopal *India* 68 H7
Bhubaneshwar *India* 67 J14
Bhuj *India* 68 H3
Bhumiphol Res. *Thailand* 64 D2
Bhusawal *India* 66 J9
Bhutan ■ *Asia* 67 F17
Biafra, B. of = Bonny, Bight
  of *Africa* 83 E6
Biak *Indonesia* 63 E9
Biała *Poland* 31 H4
Biała ➤ *Poland* 31 H7
Biała Piska *Poland* 30 E9
Biała Podlaska *Poland* 31 F10
Biała Rawska *Poland* 31 G7
Białobrzegi *Poland* 31 G7
Białogard *Poland* 30 D2
Białowieski △ *Poland* 31 F10
Białowieża *Poland* 31 F10
Biały Bór *Poland* 30 E3
Białystok *Poland* 31 E10
Biancavilla *Italy* 43 E7
Bianco *Italy* 43 D9
Biankouma *Ivory C.* 82 D3
Biaora *India* 68 H7
Biārjmand *Iran* 71 B7
Biaro *Indonesia* 63 D7
Biarritz *France* 20 E2
Bias *Indonesia* 63 J18
Biasca *Switz.* 25 J4
Biba *Egypt* 80 J7
Bibai *Japan* 54 C10
Bibbiena *Italy* 41 E8
Bibby I. *Canada* 103 A10
Bibei ➤ *Spain* 36 C3
Biberach *Germany* 25 G5
Bibiani *Ghana* 82 D4
Bibungwa
  Dem. Rep. of the Congo 86 C2
Bicaj *Albania* 44 E4
Bicaz *Romania* 29 D11
Bicazu Ardelean *Romania* 29 D10
Bíccari *Italy* 43 A8
Bicester *U.K.* 15 F6
Bichena *Ethiopia* 81 E4
Bicheno *Australia* 95 G4
Bichia *India* 69 H9
Bichvinta *Georgia* 35 J5
Bickerton I. *Australia* 94 A2
Bicske *Hungary* 28 C3
Bid = Bir *India* 66 K9
Bida *Nigeria* 83 D6
Bidar *India* 66 L10
Biddeford *U.S.A.* 113 D18
Biddwara *Ethiopia* 81 F4
Bideford *U.K.* 15 F3
Bideford Bay *U.K.* 15 F3
Bidhuna *India* 69 F8
Bidokht *Iran* 71 C8
Bidor *Malaysia* 65 K3
Bidyadanga *Australia* 92 C3
Bie *Sweden* 11 F10
Bié, Planalto de *Angola* 85 G3
Bieber *U.S.A.* 108 F3
Biebrza ➤ *Poland* 31 E10
Biebrzański △ *Poland* 30 E9
Biecz *Poland* 31 J8
Biel *Switz.* 25 H3
Bielawa *Poland* 31 H3
Bielefeld *Germany* 24 C4
Bielersee *Switz.* 25 H3
Biella *Italy* 40 C5
Bielsk Podlaski *Poland* 31 F10
Bielsko-Biała *Poland* 31 J6
Bien Hoa *Vietnam* 65 G6
Bienne = Biel *Switz.* 25 H3
Bienvenida *Spain* 37 G4
Bienville, L. *Canada* 104 A5
Bierné *France* 18 E6
Bierun *Poland* 31 H6
Bierutów *Poland* 31 G4
Biescas *Spain* 38 C4

Biese ➤ *Germany* 24 C7
Biesiesfontein *S. Africa* 88 E2
Bieszczadzki △ *Poland* 31 J9
Bietigheim-Bissingen
  Germany 25 G5
Bieżuń *Poland* 31 F6
Biferno ➤ *Italy* 41 G12
Big ➤ *Canada* 105 B8
Big B. *Canada* 105 A7
Big Bear City *U.S.A.* 111 L10
Big Bear Lake *U.S.A.* 111 L10
Big Belt Mts. *U.S.A.* 108 C8
Big Bend *Swaziland* 89 D5
Big Bend △ *U.S.A.* 116 G3
Big Black ➤ *U.S.A.* 117 E9
Big Blue ➤ *U.S.A.* 112 F5
Big Creek *U.S.A.* 110 H7
Big Cypress △ *U.S.A.* 117 H14
Big Desert *Australia* 95 F3
Big Falls *U.S.A.* 112 A7
Big Fork ➤ *U.S.A.* 112 A7
Big Horn Mts. = Bighorn
  Mts. ➤ *U.S.A.* 108 D10
Big I. *Canada* 102 A5
Big Lake *U.S.A.* 116 F4
Big Moose *U.S.A.* 115 C10
Big Muddy Cr. ➤ *U.S.A.* 108 B11
Big Pine *U.S.A.* 110 H8
Big Piney *U.S.A.* 108 E8
Big Quill L. *Canada* 103 C8
Big Rapids *U.S.A.* 113 D11
Big Rideau L. *Canada* 115 B8
Big River *Canada* 103 C7
Big Run *U.S.A.* 114 F6
Big Sable Pt. *U.S.A.* 112 C10
Big Salmon ➤ *Canada* 102 A2
Big Sand L. *Canada* 103 B9
Big Sandy *U.S.A.* 108 B8
Big Sandy ➤ *U.S.A.* 113 F12
Big Sandy Cr. = Sandy
  Cr. ➤ *U.S.A.* 108 F9
Big Sandy Cr. ➤ *U.S.A.* 108 G12
Big Sioux ➤ *U.S.A.* 112 D5
Big South Fork △ *U.S.A.* 117 C12
Big Spring *U.S.A.* 116 E4
Big Stone City *U.S.A.* 112 C5
Big Stone Gap *U.S.A.* 113 G12
Big Stone L. *U.S.A.* 112 C5
Big Sur *U.S.A.* 110 J5
Big Timber *U.S.A.* 108 D9
Big Trout L. *Canada* 104 B2
Big Trout Lake *Canada* 104 B2
Biğa *Turkey* 45 F11
Biga ➤ *Turkey* 45 F11
Bigadiç *Turkey* 47 B10
Biganos *France* 20 D3
Biggar *Canada* 103 C7
Biggar *U.K.* 13 F5
Bigge I. *Australia* 92 B4
Biggenden *Australia* 95 D5
Biggleswade *U.K.* 15 E7
Biggs *U.S.A.* 110 F5
Bighorn *U.S.A.* 108 C10
Bighorn ➤ *U.S.A.* 108 C10
Bighorn Canyon △ *U.S.A.* 108 D10
Bighorn L. *U.S.A.* 108 D9
Bighorn Mts. *U.S.A.* 108 D10
Bignona *Senegal* 82 C1
Bigorre *France* 20 E4
Bigstone L. *Canada* 103 C9
Biguglia, Étang de *France* 21 F13
Bigwa *Tanzania* 86 D4
Bihać *Bos.-H.* 41 D12
Bihar *India* 69 G11
Bihar □ *India* 69 G12
Biharamulo *Tanzania* 86 C3
Biharamulo △ *Tanzania* 86 C3
Bihariganj *India* 69 G12
Biharkeresztes *Hungary* 28 C6
Bihor □ *Romania* 28 C6
Bihor, Munţii *Romania* 28 C6
Bijagós, Arquipélago dos
  Guinea-Biss. 82 C1
Bijaipur *India* 68 F7
Bijapur *Chhattisgarh, India* 67 K12
Bijapur *Karnataka, India* 66 L9
Bijār *Iran* 73 E12
Bijawar *India* 69 G8
Bijela *Montenegro* 44 D2
Bijeljina *Bos.-H.* 28 F4
Bijelo Polje *Montenegro* 44 C3
Bijie *China* 58 D5
Bijnor *India* 68 E8
Bikaner *India* 68 E5
Bikapur *India* 69 F10
Bikeqi *China* 56 D6
Bikfayyā *Lebanon* 74 B4
Bikin *Russia* 54 A7
Bikin ➤ *Russia* 54 A7
Bikini Atoll *Marshall Is.* 96 F8
Bikita *Zimbabwe* 89 C5
Bikkū Bīttī *Libya* 79 D9
Bikoué *Cameroon* 83 E7
Bila Tserkva *Ukraine* 23 D16
Bilanga *Burkina Faso* 83 C4
Bilara *India* 68 F5
Bilaspur *Chhattisgarh, India* 69 H10
Bilaspur *Punjab, India* 68 D7
Biläsuvar *Azerbaijan* 73 C13

Bilauk Taungdan *Thailand* 64 F2
Bilbao *Spain* 38 B2
Bilbao ✈ (BIO) *Spain* 38 B2
Bilbeis *Egypt* 80 H7
Bilbo = Bilbao *Spain* 38 B2
Bilbor *Romania* 29 C10
Bilche-Zolote *Ukraine* 29 B10
Bilciureşti *Romania* 29 F10
Bíldudalur *Iceland* 8 D2
Bílé Karpaty *Europe* 27 B11
Bileća *Bos.-H.* 44 D2
Bilecik *Turkey* 72 B4
Bilecik □ *Turkey* 72 B3
Bilećko Jezero *Bos.-H.* 44 D2
Bileh Savār *Iran* 73 C13
Biłgoraj *Poland* 31 H9
Bilgram *India* 69 F9
Bilhaur *India* 69 F9
Bilhorod-Dnistrovskyy
Ukraine 33 J6
Bilibino *Russia* 53 C17
Bililiza *Mozam.* 87 E5
Bilisht *Albania* 44 F5
Billdal *Sweden* 11 G5
Billiluna *Australia* 92 C4
Billings *U.S.A.* 108 D9
Billiton Is. = Belitung
Indonesia 62 E3
Billsta *Sweden* 10 A12
Billund *Denmark* 11 J3
Bilma *Niger* 79 E8
Bilo Gora *Croatia* 28 E2
Biloela *Australia* 94 C5
Bilohirsk *Ukraine* 33 K8
Bilopillya *Ukraine* 33 G8
Biloxi *U.S.A.* 117 F10
Bilpa Morea Claypan
Australia 94 D3
Biltine *Chad* 79 F10
Bilyarsk *Russia* 34 C10
Bima *Indonesia* 63 F5
Bimban *Egypt* 80 C3
Bimbila *Ghana* 83 D5
Bimbo *C.A.R.* 84 D3
Bimini Is. *Bahamas* 120 A4
Bin Xian *Heilongjiang, China* 57 B14
Bin Xian *Shaanxi, China* 56 G5
Bin Yauri *Nigeria* 83 C5
Bina-Etawah *India* 68 G8
Binalbagan *Phil.* 61 F5
Binalong *Australia* 95 E4
Bīnālūd, Kūh-e *Iran* 71 B8
Binatang = Bintangau
Malaysia 62 D4
Binche *Belgium* 17 D4
Binchuan *China* 58 E3
Binder *Chad* 83 D7
Bindki *India* 69 F9
Bindslev *Denmark* 11 G4
Bindura *Zimbabwe* 87 F3
Binéfar *Spain* 38 D5
Bingara *Australia* 95 D5
Bingen *Germany* 25 F3
Bingerville *Ivory C.* 82 D4
Bingham *U.S.A.* 113 C19
Binghamton *U.S.A.* 115 D9
Bingöl *Turkey* 73 C9
Bingöl □ *Turkey* 73 C9
Bingöl Dağları *Turkey* 73 C9
Bingsjö *Sweden* 10 C9
Binh Dinh = An Nhon
Vietnam 64 F7
Binh Khe *Vietnam* 64 F7
Binh Son *Vietnam* 64 E7
Binhai *China* 57 G10
Binic *France* 18 D4
Binisatua *Spain* 48 B11
Binissalem *Spain* 48 B9
Binjai *Indonesia* 62 D3
Binji *Nigeria* 83 C5
Binnaway *Australia* 95 E4
Binongko *Indonesia* 63 F6
Binscarth *Canada* 103 C8
Binshangul Gumuz □
Ethiopia 81 E4
Bint Goda *Sudan* 81 E3
Bintan *Indonesia* 62 D2
Bintangau *Malaysia* 62 D4
Bintulu *Malaysia* 62 D4
Bintuni *Indonesia* 63 E8
Binyang *China* 58 F7
Binz *Germany* 24 A9
Binzert = Bizerte *Tunisia* 79 A7
Binzhou *China* 57 F10
Bío Bío □ *Chile* 126 D1
Bíobío → *Chile* 126 D1
Biograd na Moru *Croatia* 41 E12
Biogradska Gora △
Montenegro 44 D3
Bioko *Eq. Guin.* 83 E6
Bipindi *Cameroon* 83 E7
Bir *India* 66 K9
Bir, Ras *Djibouti* 81 E5
Bîr Abu Hashim *Egypt* 80 C3
Bîr Abu Minqar *Egypt* 80 B2
Bîr Abu Muḥammad *Egypt* 74 F3
Bi'r ad Dabbāghāt *Jordan* 74 E4
Bîr Adal Deib *Sudan* 80 C4

Bi'r al Butayyihāt *Jordan* 74 F4
Bi'r al Mārī *Jordan* 74 E4
Bi'r al Qattār *Jordan* 74 F4
Bîr 'Asal *Egypt* 80 B3
Bîr Atrun *Sudan* 80 D2
Bîr Beiḍa *Egypt* 74 E3
Bîr Di *Sudan* 81 F2
Bîr Diqnash *Egypt* 80 A2
Bîr el 'Abd *Egypt* 74 D2
Bîr el Basur *Egypt* 80 B2
Bîr el Biarât *Egypt* 74 F3
Bîr el Duweidar *Egypt* 74 E1
Bîr el Garârât *Egypt* 74 D2
Bîr el Gellaz *Egypt* 80 A2
Bîr el Heisi *Egypt* 74 F3
Bîr el Jafir *Egypt* 74 E1
Bîr el Mâlhi *Egypt* 74 E2
Bîr el Shaqqa *Egypt* 80 A2
Bîr el Thamâda *Egypt* 74 E2
Bîr Fuad *Egypt* 80 A2
Bîr Gebeil Hisn *Egypt* 74 E2
Bi'r Ghaḍir *Syria* 74 A6
Bîr Haimur *Egypt* 80 C3
Bîr Ḥasana *Egypt* 74 E2
Bîr Hōōker *Egypt* 80 H7
Bîr Kanayis *Egypt* 80 C3
Bîr Kaseiba *Egypt* 74 E2
Bîr Kerawein *Egypt* 80 B2
Bîr Lahfan *Egypt* 74 E2
Bîr Madkûr *Egypt* 74 E1
Bîr Maql *Egypt* 80 C3
Bîr Mîneiga *Sudan* 80 C4
Bîr Misaha *Egypt* 80 C2
Bîr Mogreïn *Mauritania* 78 C3
Bîr Murr *Egypt* 80 C3
Bi'r Muṭribah *Kuwait* 70 D5
Bîr Nakheila *Egypt* 80 C3
Bîr Qaṭia *Egypt* 74 E1
Bîr Qatrani *Egypt* 80 A2
Bîr Ranga *Egypt* 80 C4
Bîr Sahara *Egypt* 80 C2
Bîr Seiyâla *Egypt* 80 B3
Bîr Shalatein *Egypt* 80 C4
Bîr Shebb *Egypt* 80 C2
Bîr Shût *Egypt* 80 C4
Bîr Terfawi *Egypt* 80 C2
Bîr Umm Qubûr *Egypt* 80 C3
Bîr Ungât *Egypt* 80 C3
Bîr Za'farâna *Egypt* 80 J8
Bîr Zeidûn *Egypt* 80 B3
Birāk *Libya* 79 C8
Biramféro *Guinea* 82 C3
Biratnagar *Nepal* 69 F12
Birawa *Dem. Rep. of the Congo* 86 C2
Birch → *Canada* 102 B6
Birch Hills *Canada* 103 C7
Birch I. *Canada* 103 C9
Birch L., N.W.T., *Canada* 102 A5
Birch L., Ont., *Canada* 104 B1
Birch Mts. *Canada* 102 B6
Birch River *Canada* 103 C8
Birchip *Australia* 95 F3
Birchiş *Romania* 28 E7
Bird *Canada* 103 B10
Bird I. = Aves, I. de *W. Indies* 121 C7
Bird I. *S. Georgia* 128 G9
Birds Creek *Canada* 114 A7
Birdsville *Australia* 94 D2
Birdum Cr. → *Australia* 92 C5
Birecik *Turkey* 73 D8
Birein *Israel* 74 E3
Bireuen *Indonesia* 62 C1
Birhan *Ethiopia* 81 E4
Biri → *Sudan* 81 F2
Birifo *Gambia* 82 C2
Birigüi *Brazil* 127 A5
Bīrjand *Iran* 71 C8
Birkenfeld *Germany* 25 F3
Birkenhead *U.K.* 14 D4
Birkerød *Denmark* 11 J6
Birket Qârûn *Egypt* 80 J7
Birkfeld *Austria* 26 D8
Bîrlad = Bârlad *Romania* 29 D12
Birmingham *U.K.* 15 E6
Birmingham *U.S.A.* 117 E11
Birmingham Int. ✈ (BHX)
U.K. 15 E6
Birmitrapur *India* 67 H14
Birni Ngaouré *Niger* 83 C5
Birni Nkonni *Niger* 83 C6
Birnin Gwari *Nigeria* 83 C6
Birnin Kebbi *Nigeria* 83 C5
Birnin Kudu *Nigeria* 83 C6
Birobidzhan *Russia* 53 E14
Birr *Ireland* 12 C4
Birrie → *Australia* 95 D4
Birsilpur *India* 68 E5
Birsk *Russia* 52 D6
Birštonas *Lithuania* 30 D11
Birtle *Canada* 103 C8
Birur *India* 66 N9
Biryuchiy *Ukraine* 33 J8
Biržai *Lithuania* 32 D3
Birzebbuga *Malta* 49 D2
Bisa *Indonesia* 63 E7
Bisáccia *Italy* 43 A8
Bisacquino *Italy* 42 E6
Bisalpur *India* 69 E8
Bisbee *U.S.A.* 109 L9

Biscarrosse *France* 20 D2
Biscarrosse et de Parentis,
Étang de *France* 20 D2
Biscay, B. of *Atl. Oc.* 6 F5
Biscayne B. *U.S.A.* 117 J14
Bisceglie *Italy* 43 A9
Bischheim *France* 19 D14
Bischofshofen *Austria* 26 D6
Bischofswerda *Germany* 24 D10
Bischwiller *France* 19 D14
Biscoe Is. *Antarctica* 5 C17
Biscotasing *Canada* 104 C3
Biševo *Croatia* 41 F13
Bisha *Eritrea* 81 D4
Bishah, W. → *Si. Arabia* 80 C5
Bishan *China* 58 C6
Bishkek *Kyrgyzstan* 52 E8
Bishnupur *India* 69 H12
Bisho = Bhisho *S. Africa* 89 E4
Bishop *Calif., U.S.A.* 110 H8
Bishop *Tex., U.S.A.* 116 H6
Bishop Auckland *U.K.* 14 C6
Bishop's Falls *Canada* 105 C8
Bishop's Stortford *U.K.* 15 F8
Bisignano *Italy* 43 C9
Bisina, L. *Uganda* 86 B3
Biskra *Algeria* 78 B7
Biskupiec *Poland* 30 E7
Bismarck *U.S.A.* 112 B4
Bismarck Arch. *Papua N. G.* 90 B7
Bismark *Germany* 24 C7
Bismil *Turkey* 73 D9
Biso *Uganda* 86 B3
Bison *U.S.A.* 112 C2
Bīsotūn *Iran* 73 E12
Bispgården *Sweden* 10 A10
Bissagos = Bijagós,
Arquipélago dos
Guinea-Biss. 82 C1
Bissau *Guinea-Biss.* 82 C1
Bissaula *Nigeria* 83 D7
Bissikrima *Guinea* 82 C2
Bissorã *Guinea-Biss.* 82 C1
Bistcho L. *Canada* 102 B5
Bistreţ *Romania* 29 G8
Bistrica = Ilirska-Bistrica
Slovenia 41 C11
Bistriţa *Romania* 29 C9
Bistriţa → *Romania* 29 D11
Bistriţa Năsăud □ *Romania* 29 C9
Bistriţei, Munţii *Romania* 29 C10
Biswan *India* 69 F9
Bisztynek *Poland* 30 D7
Bitam *Gabon* 84 D2
Bitburg *Germany* 25 F2
Bitche *France* 19 C14
Bithynia *Turkey* 72 B4
Bitkine *Chad* 79 F9
Bitlis *Turkey* 73 C10
Bitlis □ *Turkey* 73 C10
Bitola *Macedonia* 44 E5
Bitolj = Bitola *Macedonia* 44 E5
Bitonto *Italy* 43 A9
Bitter Creek *U.S.A.* 108 F9
Bitter L. = Buheirat-
Murrat-el-Kubra *Egypt* 80 H8
Bitterfontein *S. Africa* 88 E2
Bitterroot → *U.S.A.* 108 C6
Bitterroot Range *U.S.A.* 108 C6
Bitterwater *U.S.A.* 110 J6
Bitti *Italy* 42 B2
Bittou *Burkina Faso* 83 C4
Biu *Nigeria* 83 C7
Bivolari *Romania* 29 C12
Bivolu, Vf. *Romania* 29 C10
Biwa-Ko *Japan* 55 G8
Biwabik *U.S.A.* 112 B7
Bixad *Romania* 29 C8
Bixby *U.S.A.* 116 C7
Biyang *China* 56 H7
Biysk *Russia* 52 D9
Bizana *S. Africa* 89 E4
Bizen *Japan* 55 G7
Bizerte *Tunisia* 79 A7
Bjargtangar *Iceland* 8 D1
Bjärnum *Sweden* 11 H7
Bjästa *Sweden* 10 A12
Bjelasica *Montenegro* 44 D3
Bjelašnica *Bos.-H.* 28 G3
Bjelovar *Croatia* 41 C13
Bjerringbro *Denmark* 11 H3
Björbo *Sweden* 10 D8
Björklinge *Sweden* 10 D11
Björneborg = Pori *Finland* 32 B1
Björneborg *Sweden* 10 E8
Bjørnevatn *Norway* 8 B24
Bjørnøya *Arctic* 4 B8
Bjursås *Sweden* 10 D9
Bjuv *Sweden* 11 H6
Blå Jungfrun *Sweden* 11 G10
Blace *Serbia* 44 C5
Blachownia *Poland* 31 H5
Black → *Da* → *Vietnam* 58 G5
Black → *Canada* 114 B5
Black → *Ariz., U.S.A.* 109 K8
Black → *Ark., U.S.A.* 116 D9
Black → *La., U.S.A.* 116 F9

Black → *Mich., U.S.A.* 114 D2
Black → *N.Y., U.S.A.* 115 C8
Black → *Wis., U.S.A.* 112 D8
Black Bay Pen. *Canada* 104 C2
Black Birch L. *Canada* 103 B7
Black Canyon of the
Gunnison △ *U.S.A.* 108 G10
Black Diamond *Canada* 102 C6
Black Duck → *Canada* 104 A2
Black Forest =
Schwarzwald *Germany* 25 G4
Black Forest *U.S.A.* 108 G11
Black Hd. *Ireland* 12 C2
Black Hills *U.S.A.* 112 D2
Black I. *Canada* 103 C9
Black L. *Canada* 103 B7
Black L., *Mich., U.S.A.* 113 C11
Black L., *N.Y., U.S.A.* 115 C9
Black Lake *Canada* 103 B7
Black Mesa *U.S.A.* 116 C3
Black Mt. = Mynydd Du
U.K. 15 F4
Black Mts. *U.K.* 15 F4
Black Range *U.S.A.* 109 K10
Black River *Jamaica* 120 a
Black River *U.S.A.* 115 C9
Black River Falls *U.S.A.* 112 C8
Black Rock *Barbados* 121 g
Black Rock Desert *U.S.A.* 108 F4
Black Sea *Eurasia* 6 G12
Black Tickle *Canada* 105 B8
Black Volta → *Africa* 82 D4
Black Warrior → *U.S.A.* 117 E11
Blackall *Australia* 94 C4
Blackball *N.Z.* 91 E3
Blackbraes △ *Australia* 94 B3
Blackbull *Australia* 94 B3
Blackburn *U.K.* 14 D5
Blackburn, Mt. *U.S.A.* 106 C11
Blackburn with Darwen □
U.K. 14 D5
Blackdown Tableland △
Australia 94 C4
Blackfoot *U.S.A.* 108 E7
Blackfoot → *U.S.A.* 108 C7
Blackfoot Res. *U.S.A.* 108 E8
Blackpool *U.K.* 14 D4
Blackpool □ *U.K.* 14 D4
Blackriver *U.S.A.* 114 B1
Blacks Harbour *Canada* 105 C6
Blacksburg *U.S.A.* 113 G13
Blacksod B. *Ireland* 12 B1
Blackstairs Mt. *Ireland* 12 D5
Blackstone *U.S.A.* 113 G14
Blackstone Ra. *Australia* 93 E4
Blackwater = West
Road → *Canada* 102 C4
Blackwater *Australia* 94 C4
Blackwater → *Meath, Ireland* 12 C4
Blackwater → *Waterford,
Ireland* 12 D4
Blackwater → *U.K.* 12 B5
Blackwell *U.S.A.* 116 C6
Blackwells Corner *U.S.A.* 111 K7
Bladensburg △ *Australia* 94 C3
Blaenau Ffestiniog *U.K.* 14 E4
Blaenau Gwent □ *U.K.* 15 F4
Blagaj *Bos.-H.* 44 C1
Blagnac *France* 20 E5
Blagnac, Toulouse ✈ (TLS)
France 20 E5
Blagodarnoye =
Blagodarnyy *Russia* 35 H6
Blagodarnyy *Russia* 35 H6
Blagoevgrad *Bulgaria* 44 D7
Blagoveshchensk *Russia* 53 D13
Blahkiuh *Indonesia* 63 J18
Blain *France* 18 E5
Blain *U.S.A.* 114 F7
Blaine *Minn., U.S.A.* 112 C7
Blaine *Wash., U.S.A.* 110 B4
Blaine Lake *Canada* 103 C7
Blair *U.S.A.* 112 E5
Blair Athol *Australia* 94 C4
Blair Atholl *U.K.* 13 E5
Blairgowrie *U.K.* 13 E5
Blairsden *U.S.A.* 110 F6
Blairsville *U.S.A.* 114 F5
Blaj *Romania* 29 D8
Blakang Mati, Pulau *Singapore* 65 d
Blake Pt. *U.S.A.* 112 A9
Blakely *Ga., U.S.A.* 117 F12
Blakely *Pa., U.S.A.* 115 E9
Blâmont *France* 19 D13
Blanc, C. *Spain* 48 B9
Blanc, Mont *Europe* 21 C10
Blanca, B. *Argentina* 128 D4
Blanca, Cord. *Peru* 124 E3
Blanca Peak *U.S.A.* 109 H11
Blanche, C. *Australia* 95 E1
Blanche, L. *S. Austral.,
Australia* 95 D2
Blanche, L. *W. Austral.,
Australia* 92 D3
Blanchisseuse *Trin. & Tob.* 125 K15
Blanco *S. Africa* 88 E3
Blanco *U.S.A.* 116 F5
Blanco → *Argentina* 126 C2
Blanco, C. *Costa Rica* 120 E2

Blanco, C. *U.S.A.* 108 E1
Blanda → *Iceland* 8 D3
Blandford Forum *U.K.* 15 G5
Blanding *U.S.A.* 109 H9
Blanes *Spain* 38 D7
Blangy-sur-Bresle *France* 19 C8
Blanice → *Czech Rep.* 26 B7
Blankaholm *Sweden* 11 G10
Blankenberge *Belgium* 17 C3
Blankenburg *Germany* 24 D6
Blanquefort *France* 20 D3
Blanquilla *Venezuela* 121 D7
Blanquillo *Uruguay* 127 C4
Blansko *Czech Rep.* 27 B9
Blantyre *Malawi* 87 F4
Blarney *Ireland* 12 E3
Blasdell *U.S.A.* 114 D6
Blatná *Czech Rep.* 26 B6
Blato *Croatia* 41 F13
Blaubeuren *Germany* 25 G5
Blaustein *Germany* 25 G5
Blåvands Huk *Denmark* 11 J2
Blaydon *U.K.* 14 C6
Blaye *France* 20 C3
Blaye-les-Mines *France* 20 D6
Blayney *Australia* 95 E4
Blaze, Pt. *Australia* 92 B5
Bled *Slovenia* 41 B11
Bleiburg *Austria* 26 E7
Blejeşti *Romania* 29 F10
Blekinge *Sweden* 9 H16
Blekinge län □ *Sweden* 11 H9
Blenheim *Canada* 114 D3
Blenheim *N.Z.* 91 D4
Bléone → *France* 21 D10
Blérancourt *France* 19 C10
Bletchley *U.K.* 15 F7
Bleus, Monts
Dem. Rep. of the Congo 86 B3
Blida *Algeria* 78 A6
Blidö *Sweden* 10 E12
Blidsberg *Sweden* 11 G7
Blieskastel *Germany* 25 F3
Bligh Sound *N.Z.* 91 F1
Bligh Water *Fiji* 91 a
Blind River *Canada* 104 C3
Blinisht *Albania* 44 E3
Bliss *Idaho, U.S.A.* 108 E6
Bliss *N.Y., U.S.A.* 114 D6
Blissfield *U.S.A.* 114 F3
Blitar *Indonesia* 63 H15
Blitta *Togo* 83 D5
Block I. *U.S.A.* 115 E13
Block Island Sd. *U.S.A.* 115 E13
Bloemfontein *S. Africa* 88 D4
Bloemhof *S. Africa* 88 D4
Blois *France* 18 E8
Blomskog *Sweden* 10 E6
Blomstermåla *Sweden* 11 H10
Blönduós *Iceland* 8 D3
Blongas *Indonesia* 63 K19
Blonie *Poland* 31 F7
Bloodvein → *Canada* 103 C9
Bloody Foreland *Ireland* 12 A3
Bloomer *U.S.A.* 112 C8
Bloomfield *Canada* 114 C7
Bloomfield *Iowa, U.S.A.* 112 E8
Bloomfield *N. Mex., U.S.A.* 109 H10
Bloomfield *Nebr., U.S.A.* 112 D5
Bloomington *Ill., U.S.A.* 112 E9
Bloomington *Ind., U.S.A.* 112 F10
Bloomington *Minn., U.S.A.* 112 C7
Bloomsburg *U.S.A.* 115 F8
Bloomsbury *Australia* 94 b
Blora *Indonesia* 63 G14
Blossburg *U.S.A.* 114 E7
Blouberg *S. Africa* 89 C4
Blountstown *U.S.A.* 117 F12
Bludenz *Austria* 26 D2
Blue Earth *U.S.A.* 112 D7
Blue Hole △ *Belize* 120 C2
Blue Lagoon △ *Zambia* 87 F2
Blue Mesa Res. *U.S.A.* 108 G10
Blue Mountain Lake *U.S.A.*
115 C10
Blue Mountain Pk. *Jamaica* 120 a
Blue Mt. *U.S.A.* 115 F8
Blue Mts. *Jamaica* 120 a
Blue Mts. *Maine, U.S.A.* 115 B14
Blue Mts. *Oreg., U.S.A.* 108 D4
Blue Mud B. *Australia* 94 A2
Blue Nile = Nîl el Azraq →
Sudan 81 D3
Blue Nile Falls *Ethiopia* 81 E4
Blue Rapids *U.S.A.* 112 F6
Blue Ridge *U.S.A.* 113 G13
Blue River *Canada* 102 C5
Bluefield *U.S.A.* 113 G13
Bluefields *Nic.* 120 D3
Bluevale *Canada* 114 C3
Bluff *Australia* 94 C4
Bluff *N.Z.* 91 G2
Bluff *U.S.A.* 109 H9
Bluff Knoll *Australia* 93 F2
Bluff Pt. *Australia* 93 E1

Bluffton *U.S.A.* 113 E11
Blumenau *Brazil* 127 B6
Blunt *U.S.A.* 112 C4
Bly *U.S.A.* 108 E3
Blyde River Canyon △
S. Africa 89 C5
Blyth *Canada* 114 C3
Blyth *U.K.* 14 B6
Blythe *U.S.A.* 111 M12
Blytheville *U.S.A.* 117 D10
Bo *S. Leone* 82 D2
Bo Duc *Vietnam* 65 G6
Bo Hai *China* 57 E10
Bo Xian = Bozhou *China* 56 H8
Boa Vista *Brazil* 124 C6
Boa Vista *C. Verde Is.* 78 b
Boac *Phil.* 61 E4
Boaco *Nic.* 120 D2
Bo'ai *China* 56 G7
Boal *Spain* 36 B4
Boalsburg *U.S.A.* 114 F7
Boane *Mozam.* 89 D5
Boardman *U.S.A.* 114 E4
Bobadah *Australia* 95 E4
Bobai *China* 58 F7
Bobbili *India* 67 K13
Bóbbio *Italy* 40 D6
Bobcaygeon *Canada* 114 B6
Böblingen *Germany* 25 G5
Bobo-Dioulasso *Burkina Faso* 82 C4
Bobolice *Poland* 30 E3
Bobonong *Botswana* 87 G2
Boboshevo *Bulgaria* 44 D6
Bobov Dol *Bulgaria* 44 D6
Bóbr → *Poland* 31 F2
Bobraomby, Tanjon' i
Madag. 89 A8
Bobrinets *Ukraine* 33 H7
Bobrov *Russia* 34 E5
Bobrovitsa *Ukraine* 33 G6
Bobruysk = Babruysk
Belarus 23 B15
Boby, Pic *Madag.* 85 J9
Boca del Río *Mexico* 119 D5
Boca do Acre *Brazil* 124 E5
Boca Raton *U.S.A.* 117 H14
Bocanda *Ivory C.* 82 D4
Bocas del Dragón =
Dragon's Mouths
Venezuela 125 K15
Bocas del Toro *Panama* 120 E3
Boceguillas *Spain* 36 D7
Bochmanivka *Ukraine* 29 C14
Bochnia *Poland* 31 J7
Bocholt *Germany* 24 D2
Bochum *Germany* 24 D3
Bockenem *Germany* 24 C6
Boćki *Poland* 31 F10
Bocognano *France* 21 F13
Bocoyna *Mexico* 118 B3
Boda *Dalarna, Sweden* 10 C9
Böda *Kalmar, Sweden* 11 G11
Boda *Västernorrland, Sweden* 10 B10
Bodafors *Sweden* 11 G8
Bodaybo *Russia* 53 D12
Boddam *U.K.* 13 B7
Boddington *Australia* 93 F2
Bode Sadu *Nigeria* 83 D5
Bodega Bay *U.S.A.* 110 G3
Boden *Sweden* 8 D19
Bodensee *Europe* 25 H5
Bodenteich *Germany* 24 C6
Bodhan *India* 66 K10
Bodinga *Nigeria* 83 C6
Bodmin *U.K.* 15 G3
Bodmin Moor *U.K.* 15 G3
Bodø *Norway* 8 C16
Bodrog → *Hungary* 28 B6
Bodrum *Turkey* 47 D9
Bódva → *Hungary* 28 B5
Boën *France* 21 C8
Boende *Dem. Rep. of the Congo* 84 E4
Boerne *U.S.A.* 116 G5
Boesmans → *S. Africa* 88 E4
Boffa *Guinea* 82 C2
Bogalusa *U.S.A.* 117 F10
Bogan → *Australia* 95 D4
Bogan Gate *Australia* 95 E4
Bogandé *Burkina Faso* 83 C4
Bogantungan *Australia* 94 C4
Bogata *U.S.A.* 116 E7
Bogatić *Serbia* 44 B3
Boğazkale *Turkey* 72 B6
Boğazlıyan *Turkey* 72 C6
Bogen *Sweden* 10 E6
Bogense *Denmark* 11 J4
Bogetići *Montenegro* 44 D2
Boggabilla *Australia* 95 D5
Boggabri *Australia* 95 E5
Boggeragh Mts. *Ireland* 12 D3
Boğlan = Solhan *Turkey* 73 C9
Bognor Regis *U.K.* 15 G7
Bogo *Phil.* 61 F6
Bogodukhiv =
Bohodukhiv *Ukraine* 33 G8
Bogol Manya *Ethiopia* 81 G5
Bogong, Mt. *Australia* 95 F4
Bogor *Indonesia* 62 F3

Bogoroditsk *Russia* **32** F10
Bogorodsk *Russia* **34** B6
Bogoso *Ghana* **82** D4
Bogotá *Colombia* **124** C4
Bogotol *Russia* **52** D9
Bogou *Togo* **83** C5
Bogra *Bangla.* **67** G16
Boguchany *Russia* **53** D10
Boguchar *Russia* **34** F5
Bogué *Mauritania* **82** B2
Boguszów-Gorce *Poland* **31** H3
Bohain-en-Vermandois
  France **19** C10
Bohdan *Ukraine* **29** B9
Bohemian Forest =
  Böhmerwald *Germany* **25** F9
Bohinjska Bistrica *Slovenia* **41** B11
Böhmerwald *Germany* **25** F9
Bohmte *Germany* **24** C4
Bohodukhiv *Ukraine* **33** G8
Bohol □ *Phil.* **61** G6
Bohol Sea *Phil.* **63** C6
Bohongou *Burkina Faso* **83** C5
Böhönye *Hungary* **28** D2
Bohorodchany *Ukraine* **29** B9
Bohorok *Indonesia* **65** L2
Bohuslän *Sweden* **11** F5
Bohuslev *Ukraine* **33** H6
Boi *Nigeria* **83** D6
Boi, Pta. do *Brazil* **127** A6
Boiaçu *Brazil* **124** D6
Boigu *Australia* **94** a
Boileau, C. *Australia* **92** C3
Boing'o *Sudan* **81** F3
Boiro *Spain* **36** C2
Boise *U.S.A.* **108** E5
Boise City *U.S.A.* **116** C3
Boissevain *Canada* **103** D8
Bóite → *Italy* **41** B9
Boitzenburg *Germany* **24** B9
Boizenburg *Germany* **24** B6
Bojador, C. *W. Sahara* **78** C3
Bojana → *Albania* **44** E3
Bojano *Italy* **43** A7
Bojanowo *Poland* **31** G3
Bøjden *Denmark* **11** J4
Bojnūrd *Iran* **71** B8
Bojonegoro *Indonesia* **63** G14
Boju *Nigeria* **83** D6
Boka *Serbia* **28** E5
Boka Kotorska *Montenegro* **44** D2
Bokala *Ivory C.* **82** D4
Bokani *Nigeria* **83** D6
Bokaro *India* **69** H11
Boké *Guinea* **82** C2
Bokhara → *Australia* **95** D4
Bokkos *Nigeria* **83** D6
Boknafjorden *Norway* **9** G11
Bokor △ *Cambodia* **65** G5
Bokora △ *Uganda* **86** B3
Bokoro *Chad* **79** F9
Bokpyin *Burma* **65** G2
Boksitogorsk *Russia* **32** C7
Bokungu
  Dem. Rep. of the Congo **84** E4
Bol *Croatia* **41** E13
Bolama *Guinea-Biss.* **82** C1
Bolan → *Pakistan* **68** E2
Bolan Pass *Pakistan* **66** E5
Bolaños → *Mexico* **118** C4
Bolaños de Calatrava *Spain* **37** G7
Bolayır *Turkey* **45** F10
Bolbec *France* **18** C7
Boldājī *Iran* **71** D6
Boldești-Scăeni *Romania* **29** E11
Bole *China* **60** B3
Bole *Ethiopia* **81** F4
Bole *Ghana* **82** D4
Bolekhiv *Ukraine* **23** D12
Bolesławiec *Poland* **31** G2
Bolgatanga *Ghana* **83** C4
Bolgrad = Bolhrad *Ukraine* **29** E13
Bolhrad *Ukraine* **29** E13
Bolinao *Phil.* **61** C3
Bolintin-Vale *Romania* **29** F10
Bolivar *Mo., U.S.A.* **112** G7
Bolivar *N.Y., U.S.A.* **114** D6
Bolivar *Tenn., U.S.A.* **117** D10
Bolivia ■ *S. Amer.* **124** G6
Bolivian Plateau =
  Altiplano *Bolivia* **124** G5
Boljevac *Serbia* **44** C5
Bolkhov *Russia* **32** F9
Bolków *Poland* **31** H3
Bollebygd *Sweden* **11** G6
Bollène *France* **21** D8
Bollnäs *Sweden* **10** C10
Bollon *Australia* **95** D4
Bollstabruk *Sweden* **10** B11
Bolmen *Sweden* **11** H7
Bolnisi *Georgia* **35** K7
Bolobo *Dem. Rep. of the Congo* **84** E3
Bologna *Italy* **41** D8
Bologna ✈ (BLQ) *Italy* **41** D8
Bologoye *Russia* **32** D8
Bolomba
  Dem. Rep. of the Congo **84** D3
Bolon, Ozero *Russia* **60** B8
Bolonchén *Mexico* **119** D7

Bolótana *Italy* **42** B1
Boloven, Cao Nguyen *Laos* **64** E6
Bolpur *India* **69** H12
Bolsena *Italy* **41** F8
Bolsena, L. di *Italy* **41** F8
Bolshakovo *Russia* **30** D8
Bolshaya Chernigovka
  Russia **34** D10
Bolshaya Glushitsa *Russia* **34** D10
Bolshaya Martynovka
  Russia **35** G5
Bolshaya Vradiyevka *Ukraine* **33** J6
Bolshevik, Ostrov *Russia* **53** B11
Bolshoy Anyuy → *Russia* **53** C17
Bolshoy Begichev, Ostrov
  Russia **53** B12
Bolshoy Kamen *Russia* **54** C6
Bolshoy Kavkas =
  Caucasus Mountains
  Eurasia **35** J7
Bolshoy Lyakhovskiy,
  Ostrov *Russia* **53** B15
Bolshoy Tyuters, Ostrov
  Russia **32** C4
Bolsward *Neths.* **17** A5
Bolt Head *U.K.* **15** G4
Boltaña *Spain* **38** C5
Boltigen *Switz.* **25** J3
Bolton *Canada* **114** C5
Bolton *U.K.* **14** D5
Bolton Landing *U.S.A.* **115** C11
Bolu *Turkey* **72** B4
Bolu □ *Turkey* **72** B4
Bolungavík *Iceland* **8** C2
Bolvadin *Turkey* **72** C4
Bolzano *Italy* **41** B8
Bom Jesus da Lapa *Brazil* **125** F10
Boma *Dem. Rep. of the Congo* **84** F2
Bombala *Australia* **95** F4
Bombarral *Portugal* **37** F1
Bombay = Mumbai *India* **66** K8
Bombay *U.S.A.* **115** B10
Bombedor, Pta. *Venezuela* **125** L15
Bomboma
  Dem. Rep. of the Congo **84** D3
Bombombwa
  Dem. Rep. of the Congo **86** B2
Bomi Hills *Liberia* **82** D2
Bomili *Dem. Rep. of the Congo* **86** B2
Bomlo *Norway* **9** G11
Bomokandi →
  Dem. Rep. of the Congo **86** B2
Bomu → *C.A.R.* **84** D4
Bon, C. = Ra's aṭ Ṭīb *Tunisia* **76** C5
Bon Acceuil *Mauritius* **85** d
Bon Echo △ *Canada* **114** B7
Bon Sar Pa *Vietnam* **64** F6
Bonāb *Āzarbājān-e Sharqī,
  Iran* **73** D12
Bonāb *Zanjān, Iran* **73** D13
Bonaigarh *India* **69** J11
Bonaire *Neth. Ant.* **121** D6
Bonampak *Mexico* **119** D6
Bonang *Australia* **95** F4
Bonanza *Nic.* **120** D3
Bonaparte Arch. *Australia* **92** B3
Boñar *Spain* **36** C5
Bonar Bridge *U.K.* **13** D4
Bonasse *Trin. & Tob.* **125** K15
Bonaventure *Canada* **105** C6
Bonavista *Canada* **105** C9
Bonavista, C. *Canada* **105** C9
Bonavista B. *Canada* **105** C9
Bondeno *Italy* **41** D8
Bondo *Dem. Rep. of the Congo* **86** B1
Bondoukou *Ivory C.* **82** D4
Bondowoso *Indonesia* **63** G15
Bone, Teluk *Indonesia* **63** E6
Bonerate *Indonesia* **63** F6
Bonerate, Kepulauan
  Indonesia **63** F6
Bo'ness *U.K.* **13** E5
Bonete, Cerro *Argentina* **126** B2
Bong Son = Hoai Nhon
  Vietnam **64** E7
Bonga *Ethiopia* **81** F4
Bongabong *Phil.* **61** E4
Bongandanga
  Dem. Rep. of the Congo **84** D4
Bongor *Chad* **79** F9
Bongos, Massif des *C.A.R.* **84** C4
Bongouanou *Ivory C.* **82** D4
Bonham *U.S.A.* **116** E6
Boni *Mali* **82** B4
Boni △ *Kenya* **86** C5
Bonifacio *France* **21** G13
Bonifacio, Bouches de
  Medit. S. **42** A2
Bonin Is. = Ogasawara
  Gunto *Pac. Oc.* **51** F16
Bonke *Ethiopia* **81** F4
Bonkoukou *Niger* **83** C5
Bonn *Germany* **24** E4
Bonnat *France* **19** F8
Bonne Terre *U.S.A.* **112** G8
Bonners Ferry *U.S.A.* **108** B5
Bonnétable *France* **18** D7
Bonneval *France* **21** C11

Bonneval-sur-Arc *France* **18** D8
Bonneville *France* **19** F13
Bonney, L. *Australia* **95** F3
Bonnie Rock *Australia* **93** F2
Bonny *Nigeria* **83** E6
Bonny → *Nigeria* **83** E6
Bonny, Bight of *Africa* **83** E6
Bonny-sur-Loire *France* **19** E9
Bonnyrigg *U.K.* **13** F5
Bonnyville *Canada* **103** C6
Bono *Italy* **42** B2
Bonoi *Indonesia* **63** E9
Bonorva *Italy* **42** B1
Bonsall *U.S.A.* **111** M9
Bontang *Indonesia* **62** D5
Bontebok △ *S. Africa* **88** E3
Bonthe *S. Leone* **82** D2
Bontoc *Phil.* **61** C4
Bonyeri *Ghana* **82** D4
Bonyhád *Hungary* **28** D3
Bonython Ra. *Australia* **92** D4
Boodjamulla △ *Australia* **94** B2
Bookabie *Australia* **93** F5
Booker *U.S.A.* **116** C4
Boola *Guinea* **82** D3
Booligal *Australia* **95** E3
Boonah *Australia* **95** D5
Boone *Iowa, U.S.A.* **112** D7
Boone *N.C., U.S.A.* **117** C14
Booneville *Ark., U.S.A.* **116** D8
Booneville *Miss., U.S.A.* **117** D10
Boonville *Calif., U.S.A.* **110** F3
Boonville *Ind., U.S.A.* **112** F10
Boonville *Mo., U.S.A.* **112** F7
Boonville *N.Y., U.S.A.* **115** C9
Boorabbin △ *Australia* **93** F3
Boorindal *Australia* **95** E4
Boorowa *Australia* **95** E4
Boosaaso *Somali Rep.* **75** E4
Boothia, Gulf of *Canada* **100** C14
Boothia Pen. *Canada* **100** C13
Bootle *U.K.* **14** D4
Booué *Gabon* **84** E2
Boppard *Germany* **25** E3
Boquilla, Presa de la *Mexico* **118** B3
Boquillas del Carmen
  Mexico **118** B4
Bor *Czech Rep.* **26** B5
Bor *Russia* **34** B7
Bor *Serbia* **44** B6
Bôr *Sudan* **81** F3
Bor *Sweden* **11** G8
Bor *Turkey* **72** D6
Bor Mashash *Israel* **74** D3
Bora Bora *French Polynesia* **97** J12
Borah Peak *U.S.A.* **108** D7
Borang *Sudan* **81** G3
Borås *Sweden* **11** G6
Borāzjān *Iran* **71** D6
Borba *Brazil* **124** D7
Borba *Portugal* **37** G3
Borborema, Planalto da
  Brazil **122** D7
Borcea *Romania* **29** F12
Borçka *Turkey* **35** F7
Bord Khûn-e Now *Iran* **71** D6
Borda, C. *Australia* **95** F2
Bordeaux *France* **20** D3
Bordeaux ✈ (BOD) *France* **20** D3
Borden *Australia* **93** F2
Borden-Carleton *Canada* **105** C7
Borden I. *Canada* **101** B9
Borden Pen. *Canada* **101** C15
Border Ranges △ *Australia* **95** D5
Borders = Scottish
  Borders □ *U.K.* **13** F6
Bordertown *Australia* **95** F3
Borðeyri *Iceland* **8** D3
Bordighera *Italy* **40** E4
Bordj Fly Ste. Marie *Algeria* **78** C5
Bordj-in-Eker *Algeria* **78** D6
Bordj Mokhtar *Algeria* **78** D6
Bordj Omar Driss *Algeria* **78** C7
Bore *Ethiopia* **81** G4
Borehamwood *U.K.* **15** F7
Borek Wielkopolski *Poland* **31** G4
Borensberg *Sweden* **11** F9
Borgå = Porvoo *Finland* **32** B3
Borgarfjörður *Iceland* **8** D7
Borgarnes *Iceland* **8** D3
Børgefjellet *Norway* **8** D15
Borger *Neths.* **17** B6
Borger *U.S.A.* **116** D4
Borgholm *Sweden* **11** H10
Bórgia *Italy* **43** D9
Borgo San Dalmazzo *Italy* **40** D4
Borgo San Lorenzo *Italy* **41** E8
Borgo Val di Taro *Italy* **40** D6
Borgo Valsugana *Italy* **41** B8
Borgomanero *Italy* **40** C5
Borgorose *Italy* **41** F10
Borgosésia *Italy* **40** C5
Borḥan Tal *Mongolia* **56** C4
Bori *Nigeria* **83** D6
Borikhane *Laos* **64** C4
Borisoglebsk *Russia* **34** E6
Borisov = Barysaw *Belarus* **23** A15
Borisovka *Russia* **33** G9
Borja *Peru* **124** D3

Borja *Spain* **38** D3
Borjas Blancas = Les
  Borges Blanques *Spain* **38** D5
Borjomi *Georgia* **35** K6
Børkop *Denmark* **11** J3
Borkou *Chad* **79** E9
Borkum *Germany* **24** B2
Borlänge *Sweden* **10** D9
Borley, C. *Antarctica* **5** C5
Borlu *Turkey* **47** C10
Bormida → *Italy* **40** D5
Bórmio *Italy* **40** B7
Borna *Germany* **24** D8
Borne *Neths.* **17** B6
Borne Sulinowo *Poland* **30** E3
Borneo *E. Indies* **62** D5
Bornholm *Denmark* **11** J8
Bornholmsgattet *Europe* **11** J8
Borno □ *Nigeria* **83** C7
Bornos *Spain* **37** J5
Bornova *Turkey* **47** C9
Bornu Yassa *Nigeria* **83** C7
Boro → *Sudan* **81** F2
Borodino *Russia* **32** E8
Borodino *Ukraine* **29** D14
Borogontsy *Russia* **53** C14
Boromo *Burkina Faso* **82** C4
Boron *U.S.A.* **111** L9
Borongan *Phil.* **61** F6
Borotangba Mts. *C.A.R.* **81** F2
Borotou *Ivory C.* **82** D3
Borovan *Bulgaria* **44** C7
Borovichi *Russia* **32** C7
Borovsk *Russia* **32** E9
Borrby *Sweden* **11** J8
Borrego Springs *U.S.A.* **111** M10
Borriol *Spain* **38** E4
Borrisokane *Ireland* **12** D3
Borroloola *Australia* **94** B2
Borşa *Cluj, Romania* **29** D8
Borşa *Maramureş, Romania* **29** C9
Borsad *India* **68** H5
Borsec *Romania* **29** D10
Borshchiv *Ukraine* **29** B11
Borsod-Abaúj-Zemplén □
  Hungary **28** B6
Bort-les-Orgues *France* **20** C6
Borth *U.K.* **15** E3
Börtnan *Sweden* **10** B7
Borüjerd *Iran* **73** F13
Boryeong *S. Korea* **57** F14
Borynya *Ukraine* **31** J10
Boryslav *Ukraine* **31** J10
Boryspil *Ukraine* **33** G6
Borzhomi = Borjomi *Georgia* **35** K6
Borzna *Ukraine* **33** G7
Borzya *Russia* **53** D12
Bosa *Italy* **42** B1
Bosanska Dubica *Bos.-H.* **41** C13
Bosanska Gradiška *Bos.-H.* **28** E2
Bosanska Kostajnica
  Bos.-H. **41** C13
Bosanska Krupa *Bos.-H.* **41** D13
Bosanski Brod *Bos.-H.* **28** E2
Bosanski Novi *Bos.-H.* **41** C13
Bosanski Petrovac *Bos.-H.* **41** D13
Bosanski Šamac *Bos.-H.* **28** E3
Bosansko Grahovo *Bos.-H.* **41** D13
Boscastle *U.K.* **15** G3
Boscobelle *Barbados* **121** g
Bose *China* **58** F6
Boseong *S. Korea* **57** G14
Boshan *China* **57** F9
Boshof *S. Africa* **88** D4
Boshrūyeh *Iran* **71** C8
Bosilegrad *Serbia* **44** D6
Bosna → *Bos.-H.* **28** E3
Bosna i Hercegovina =
  Bosnia-Herzegovina ■
  Europe **28** G2
Bosnia-Herzegovina ■
  Europe **28** G2
Bosnik *Indonesia* **63** E9
Bosobolo
  Dem. Rep. of the Congo **84** D3
Bosporus = İstanbul Boğazı
  Turkey **45** E13
Bosque Farms *U.S.A.* **109** J10
Bossangoa *C.A.R.* **84** C3
Bossé Bangou *Niger* **83** C5
Bossier City *U.S.A.* **116** E8
Bosso *Niger* **83** C7
Bosso, Dallol → *Niger* **83** C5
Bostan *Pakistan* **68** D2
Bostānābād *Iran* **73** D12
Bosten Hu *China* **60** B3
Boston *U.K.* **14** E7
Boston *U.S.A.* **115** D13
Boston Bar *Canada* **102** D4
Boston Mts. *U.S.A.* **116** D8
Bosumtwi, L. *Ghana* **83** D4
Bosut → *Croatia* **28** E3
Boswell *Canada* **102** D5
Boswell *U.S.A.* **114** F5
Botad *India* **68** H4
Botan → *Turkey* **73** D10
Botany B. *Australia* **90** E8
Botev *Bulgaria* **45** D8

Botevgrad *Bulgaria* **44** D7
Bothaville *S. Africa* **88** D4
Bothnia, G. of *Europe* **8** F19
Bothwell *Australia* **95** G4
Bothwell *Canada* **114** D3
Boticas *Portugal* **36** D3
Botletle → *Botswana* **88** C3
Botlikh *Russia* **35** J8
Botna → *Moldova* **29** D14
Botoroaga *Romania* **29** F10
Botoşani *Romania* **29** C11
Botoşani □ *Romania* **29** C11
Botou *Burkina Faso* **83** C5
Botricello *Italy* **43** D9
Botro *Ivory C.* **82** D3
Botshabelo *S. Africa* **88** D4
Botswana ■ *Africa* **88** C3
Bottineau *U.S.A.* **112** A3
Bottnaryd *Sweden* **11** G7
Bottrop *Germany* **17** C6
Botucatu *Brazil* **127** A6
Botum Sakor △ *Cambodia* **65** G4
Botwood *Canada* **105** C8
Bou Djébéha *Mali* **82** B4
Boû Rjeïmât *Mauritania* **82** B1
Bou Saâda *Algeria* **78** A6
Bouaflé *Ivory C.* **82** D3
Bouaké *Ivory C.* **82** D3
Bouar *C.A.R.* **84** C3
Bouârfa *Morocco* **78** B5
Boucaut B. *Australia* **94** A1
Bouches-du-Rhône □ *France* **21** E9
Boucle de Baoulé △ *Mali* **82** C3
Boucles de la Seine
  Normande △ *France* **18** C7
Bouctouche *Canada* **105** C7
Bougainville, C. *Australia* **92** B4
Bougainville I. *Papua N. G.* **90** B8
Bougainville Reef *Australia* **94** B4
Bougie = Bejaïa *Algeria* **78** A7
Bougouni *Mali* **82** C3
Bouillon *Belgium* **17** E5
Boukombé *Benin* **83** C5
Boulal *Mali* **82** B3
Boulazac *France* **20** C4
Boulder *Colo., U.S.A.* **108** F11
Boulder *Mont., U.S.A.* **108** C7
Boulder City *U.S.A.* **111** K12
Boulder Creek *U.S.A.* **110** H4
Boulder Dam = Hoover
  Dam *U.S.A.* **111** K12
Bouli *Mauritania* **82** B2
Boulia *Australia* **94** C2
Bouligny *France* **19** C12
Boulogne → *France* **18** E5
Boulogne *France* **18** E7
Boulogne-sur-Gesse *France* **20** E4
Boulogne-sur-Mer *France* **19** B8
Bouloire *France* **18** E7
Boulouli *Mali* **82** B3
Boulsa *Burkina Faso* **83** C4
Boultoum *Niger* **83** C7
Bouma △ *Fiji* **91** a
Boûmdeïd *Mauritania* **82** B2
Boun Neua *Laos* **64** B3
Boun Tai *Laos* **64** B3
Bouna *Ivory C.* **82** D4
Boundary Peak *U.S.A.* **110** H8
Boundiali *Ivory C.* **82** D3
Bountiful *U.S.A.* **108** F8
Bounty Is. *Pac. Oc.* **96** M9
Bounty Trough *Pac. Oc.* **96** M9
Boura *Mali* **82** C4
Bourbon-Lancy *France* **19** F10
Bourbon-l'Archambault
  France **19** F10
Bourbonnais *France* **19** F10
Bourbonne-les-Bains *France* **19** E12
Bourbourg *France* **19** B9
Bourdel L. *Canada* **104** A5
Bourem *Mali* **83** B4
Bourg *France* **20** C3
Bourg-Argental *France* **21** C8
Bourg-de-Péage *France* **21** C9
Bourg-en-Bresse *France* **19** F12
Bourg-Lastic *France* **20** C6
Bourg-Madame *France* **20** F5
Bourg-St-Andéol *France* **21** D8
Bourg-St-Maurice *France* **21** C10
Bourganeuf *France* **20** C5
Bourgas = Burgas *Bulgaria* **45** D11
Bourges *France* **19** E9
Bourget *Canada* **115** A9
Bourget, Lac du *France* **21** C9
Bourgneuf, B. de *France* **18** E4
Bourgneuf-en-Retz *France* **18** E5
Bourgogne □ *France* **19** F11
Bourgoin-Jallieu *France* **21** C9
Bourgueil *France* **18** E7
Bourke *Australia* **95** E4
Bourne *U.K.* **14** E7
Bournemouth *U.K.* **15** G6
Bournemouth □ *U.K.* **15** G6
Bouroum *Burkina Faso* **83** C4
Bouse *U.S.A.* **111** M13
Boussac *France* **19** F9
Boussé *Burkina Faso* **83** C4
Bousso *Chad* **79** F9
Boussouma *Burkina Faso* **83** C4

Boutilimit *Mauritania* **82** B2
Boutonne → *France* **20** C3
Bouvet I. = Bouvetøya
  Antarctica **2** G10
Bouvetøya *Antarctica* **2** G10
Bouxwiller *France* **19** D14
Bouza *Niger* **83** C6
Bouzonville *France* **19** C13
Bova Marina *Italy* **43** E8
Bovalino Marina *Italy* **43** D9
Bovec *Slovenia* **41** B10
Bovill *U.S.A.* **108** C5
Bovino *Italy* **43** A8
Bovril *Argentina* **126** C4
Bow → *Canada* **102** C6
Bow Island *Canada* **108** B8
Bowbells *U.S.A.* **112** A2
Bowdle *U.S.A.* **112** C4
Bowelling *Australia* **93** F2
Bowen *Argentina* **126** D2
Bowen *Australia* **94** J6
Bowen Mts. *Australia* **95** F4
Bowers Basin *Pac. Oc.* **4** D-6
Bowers Ridge *Pac. Oc.* **4** D17
Bowie *Ariz., U.S.A.* **109** K9
Bowie *Tex., U.S.A.* **116** E6
Bowkān *Iran* **73** D12
Bowland, Forest of *U.K.* **14** D5
Bowling Green *Ky., U.S.A.* **112** G10
Bowling Green *Ohio, U.S.A.* **113** E12
Bowling Green, C. *Australia* **94** B4
Bowling Green Bay △
  Australia **94** B4
Bowman *U.S.A.* **112** B2
Bowman I. *Antarctica* **5** C8
Bowmanville = Clarington
  Canada **114** C6
Bowmore *U.K.* **13** F2
Bowral *Australia* **95** E5
Bowraville *Australia* **95** E5
Bowron → *Canada* **102** C4
Bowron Lake △ *Canada* **102** C4
Bowser L. *Canada* **102** B3
Bowsman *Canada* **103** C8
Bowwood *Zambia* **87** F2
Box Cr. → *Australia* **95** E3
Boxholm *Sweden* **11** F9
Boxmeer *Neths.* **17** C5
Boxtel *Neths.* **17** C5
Boyabat *Turkey* **72** B6
Boyalıca *Turkey* **45** F13
Boyang *China* **59** C11
Boyany *Ukraine* **29** B11
Boyce *U.S.A.* **116** F8
Boyd L. *Canada* **104** E4
Boyle *Canada* **102** C6
Boyle *Ireland* **12** C3
Boyne → *Ireland* **12** C5
Boyne City *U.S.A.* **113** C11
Boynitsa *Bulgaria* **44** C6
Boynton Beach *U.S.A.* **117** H14
Boyolali *Indonesia* **63** G14
Boyoma, Chutes
  Dem. Rep. of the Congo **86** B2
Boysen Res. *U.S.A.* **108** E9
Boyuibe *Bolivia* **124** G6
Boyup Brook *Australia* **93** F2
Boz Burun *Turkey* **45** F12
Boz Dağ *Turkey* **47** D11
Boz Dağları *Turkey* **47** C10
Bozburun *Turkey* **47** E10
Bozcaada *Turkey* **72** C2
Bozdoğan *Turkey* **47** D10
Bozeman *U.S.A.* **108** D8
Bozen = Bolzano *Italy* **41** B8
Boževac *Serbia* **44** B5
Bozhou *China* **56** H8
Bozkır *Turkey* **72** D5
Bozkurt *Turkey* **47** D11
Bozouls *France* **20** D6
Bozoum *C.A.R.* **84** C3
Bozova *Antalya, Turkey* **47** D12
Bozova *Şanlıurfa, Turkey* **73** D8
Bozovici *Romania* **28** F7
Bozüyük *Turkey* **47** B12
Bozyazı *Turkey* **70** B2
Bra *Italy* **40** D4
Braås *Sweden* **11** G9
Brabant □ *Belgium* **17** D4
Brabant L. *Canada* **103** B8
Brabrand *Denmark* **11** H4
Brač *Croatia* **41** E13
Bracadale, L. *U.K.* **13** D2
Bracciano *Italy* **41** F9
Bracciano, L di *Italy* **41** F9
Bracebridge *Canada* **114** A5
Bracieux *France* **19** E8
Bräcke *Sweden* **10** B9
Brackettville *U.S.A.* **116** G4
Bracki Kanal *Croatia* **41** E13
Bracknell *U.K.* **15** F7
Bracknell Forest □ *U.K.* **15** F7
Brad *Romania* **28** D7
Brádano → *Italy* **43** B9
Bradenton *U.S.A.* **117** H13
Bradford *Canada* **114** B5
Bradford *U.K.* **14** D6
Bradford *Pa., U.S.A.* **114** E6
Bradford *Vt., U.S.A.* **115** C12

Bradley *Ark., U.S.A.* **116** E8
Bradley *Calif., U.S.A.* **110** K6
Bradley Institute *Zimbabwe* **87** F3
Brady *U.S.A.* **116** F5
Brædstrup *Denmark* **11** J3
Braeside *Canada* **115** A8
Braga *Portugal* **36** D2
Braga □ *Portugal* **36** D2
Bragadiru *Romania* **29** G10
Bragado *Argentina* **126** D3
Bragança *Brazil* **125** D9
Bragança *Portugal* **36** D4
Bragança □ *Portugal* **36** D4
Bragança Paulista *Brazil* **127** A6
Brahestad = Raahe *Finland* **8** D21
Brahmanbaria *Bangla.* **67** H17
Brahmani ➤ *India* **67** J15
Brahmapur *India* **67** K14
Brahmaputra ➤ *Asia* **69** H13
Braich-y-pwll *U.K.* **14** E3
Braidwood *Australia* **95** F4
Brăila *Romania* **29** E12
Brăila □ *Romania* **29** E12
Brainerd *U.S.A.* **112** B6
Braintree *U.K.* **15** F8
Braintree *U.S.A.* **115** D14
Brak ➤ *S. Africa* **88** D3
Brake *Germany* **24** B4
Brakel *Germany* **24** D5
Brakna □ *Mauritania* **82** B2
Bräkne-Hoby *Sweden* **11** H9
Brakwater *Namibia* **88** C2
Brålanda *Sweden* **11** F6
Bramberg *Germany* **25** E6
Bramdrupdam *Denmark* **11** J3
Bramming *Denmark* **11** J2
Brämön *Sweden* **10** B11
Brampton *Canada* **114** C5
Brampton *U.K.* **14** C5
Brampton I. *Australia* **94** b
Bramsche *Germany* **24** C3
Branco ➤ *Brazil* **124** D6
Brandberg *Namibia* **88** C1
Brandberg △ *Namibia* **88** C1
Brande *Denmark* **11** J3
Brandenburg =
  Neubrandenburg *Germany* **24** B9
Brandenburg *Germany* **24** C8
Brandenburg □ *Germany* **24** C9
Brandfort *S. Africa* **88** D4
Brando *France* **21** F13
Brandon *Canada* **103** D9
Brandon *U.S.A.* **115** C11
Brandon B. *Ireland* **12** D1
Brandon Mt. *Ireland* **12** D1
Brandsen *Argentina* **126** D4
Brandvlei *S. Africa* **88** E3
Brandýs nad Labem
  Czech Rep. **26** A7
Brănești *Romania* **29** F11
Branford *U.S.A.* **115** E12
Braniewo *Poland* **30** D6
Bransfield Str. *Antarctica* **5** C18
Brańsk *Poland* **31** F9
Branson *U.S.A.* **112** G7
Brantford *Canada* **114** C4
Brantôme *France* **20** C4
Branzi *Italy* **40** B6
Bras d'Or L. *Canada* **105** C7
Brasher Falls *U.S.A.* **115** B10
Brasil = Brazil ■ *S. Amer.* **125** F9
Brasil, Planalto *Brazil* **122** E6
Brasiléia *Brazil* **124** F5
Brasília *Brazil* **125** G9
Brasília Legal *Brazil* **125** D7
Braslaw *Belarus* **32** E4
Braslovče *Slovenia* **41** B12
Brașov *Romania* **29** E10
Brașov □ *Romania* **29** E10
Brass *Nigeria* **83** E6
Brass ➤ *Nigeria* **83** E6
Brassac-les-Mines *France* **20** C7
Brasschaat *Belgium* **17** C4
Brassey, Banjaran *Malaysia* **62** D5
Brassey Ra. *Australia* **93** E3
Brasstown Bald *U.S.A.* **117** D13
Brastad *Sweden* **11** F5
Brastavățu *Romania* **29** G9
Bratan = Morozov *Bulgaria* **45** D9
Brateș *Romania* **29** E12
Bratislava *Slovak Rep.* **27** C10
Bratislava M.R. Štefánik ✈
  (BTS) *Slovak Rep.* **27** C10
Bratislavský □ *Slovak Rep.* **27** C10
Bratsigovo *Bulgaria* **45** D8
Bratsk *Russia* **53** D11
Brattleboro *U.S.A.* **115** D12
Bratunac *Bos.-H.* **28** F4
Braunau *Austria* **26** C6
Braunschweig *Germany* **24** C6
Braunton *U.K.* **15** F3
Brava *C. Verde Is.* **78** b
Bravicea *Moldova* **29** C13
Brǎviken *Sweden* **11** F10
Bravo del Norte, Rio =
  Grande, Rio ➤ *N. Amer.* **116** J6
Brawley *U.S.A.* **111** N11
Bray *Ireland* **12** C5
Bray, Mt. *Australia* **94** A1

Bray-sur-Seine *France* **19** D10
Brazeau ➤ *Canada* **102** C5
Brazil *U.S.A.* **112** F10
Brazil ■ *S. Amer.* **125** F9
Brazilian Highlands =
  Brasil, Planalto *Brazil* **122** E6
Brazo Sur ➤ *S. Amer.* **126** B4
Brazos ➤ *U.S.A.* **116** G7
Brazzaville *Congo* **84** E3
Brčko *Bos.-H.* **28** F3
Brda ➤ *Poland* **31** E5
Bré = Bray *Ireland* **12** C5
Breaden, L. *Australia* **93** E4
Breaksea Sd. *N.Z.* **91** F1
Bream B. *N.Z.* **91** A5
Bream Hd. *N.Z.* **91** A5
Breas *Chile* **126** B1
Breaza *Romania* **29** E10
Brebes *Indonesia* **63** G13
Brechin *Canada* **114** B5
Brechin *U.K.* **13** E6
Brecht *Belgium* **17** C4
Breckenridge *Colo., U.S.A.* **108** G10
Breckenridge *Minn., U.S.A.* **112** B5
Breckenridge *Tex., U.S.A.* **116** E5
Breckland *U.K.* **15** E8
Břeclav *Czech Rep.* **27** C9
Brecon *U.K.* **15** F4
Brecon Beacons *U.K.* **15** F4
Brecon Beacons △ *U.K.* **15** F4
Breda *Neths.* **17** C4
Bredaryd *Sweden* **11** G7
Bredasdorp *S. Africa* **88** E3
Bredebro *Denmark* **11** J2
Bredstedt *Germany* **24** A4
Bree *Belgium* **17** C5
Bregalnica ➤ *Macedonia* **44** E6
Bregenz *Austria* **26** D2
Bregovo *Bulgaria* **44** B6
Bréhal *France* **18** D5
Bréhat, Î. de *France* **18** D4
Breiðafjörður *Iceland* **8** D2
Breil-sur-Roya *France* **21** E11
Breisach *Germany* **25** G3
Brejo *Brazil* **125** D10
Bremen *Germany* **24** B4
Bremen □ *Germany* **24** B4
Bremer Bay *Australia* **93** F2
Bremer I. *Australia* **94** A2
Bremerhaven *Germany* **24** B4
Bremerton *U.S.A.* **110** C4
Bremervörde *Germany* **24** B5
Brenes *Spain* **37** H5
Brenham *U.S.A.* **116** F6
Brenne *France* **20** B5
Brenne △ *France* **20** B5
Brennerpass *Austria* **26** D4
Breno *Italy* **40** C7
Brent *U.S.A.* **117** E11
Brenta ➤ *Italy* **41** C9
Brentwood *U.K.* **15** F8
Brentwood *Calif., U.S.A.* **110** H5
Brentwood *N.Y., U.S.A.* **115** F11
Bréscia *Italy* **40** C7
Breskens *Neths.* **17** C3
Breslau = Wrocław *Poland* **31** G4
Bresle ➤ *France* **18** B8
Bressanone *Italy* **41** B8
Bressay *U.K.* **13** A7
Bresse *France* **19** F12
Bressuire *France* **18** F6
Brest *Belarus* **23** B12
Brest *France* **18** D2
Brest □ *Belarus* **33** F4
Brest-Litovsk = Brest
  Belarus **23** B12
Bretagne □ *France* **18** D3
Bretcu *Romania* **29** D11
Bretenoux *France* **20** D5
Breteuil *Eure, France* **18** D7
Breteuil *Oise, France* **19** C9
Breton *Canada* **102** C6
Breton, Pertuis *France* **20** B2
Breton Sd. *U.S.A.* **117** G10
Brett, C. *N.Z.* **91** A5
Bretten *Germany* **25** F4
Breuil-Cervínia *Italy* **40** C4
Brevard *U.S.A.* **117** D13
Breves *Brazil* **125** D8
Brewarrina *Australia* **95** E4
Brewer *U.S.A.* **113** C19
Brewer, Mt. *U.S.A.* **110** J8
Brewerville *Liberia* **82** D2
Brewster *N.Y., U.S.A.* **115** E11
Brewster *Ohio, U.S.A.* **114** F3
Brewster *Wash., U.S.A.* **108** B4
Brewster, Kap =
  Kangikajik *Greenland* **4** B6
Brewton *U.S.A.* **117** F11
Breyten *S. Africa* **89** D5
Breza *Bos.-H.* **28** F3
Brežice *Slovenia* **41** C12
Březnice *Czech Rep.* **26** B6
Breznik *Bulgaria* **44** D6
Brezno *Slovak Rep.* **27** C12
Brezoi *Romania* **29** E9
Brezovica *Kosovo* **44** D5
Brezovo *Bulgaria* **45** D9

Bria *C.A.R.* **84** C4
Briançon *France* **21** D10
Briare *France* **19** E9
Briático *Italy* **43** D9
Bribie I. *Australia* **95** D5
Bribri *Costa Rica* **120** E3
Briceni *Moldova* **29** B12
Bricquebec *France* **18** C5
Bridgefield *Barbados* **121** g
Bridgehampton *U.S.A.* **115** F12
Bridgend *U.K.* **15** F4
Bridgend *Sweden* **11** H8
Bridgend □ *U.K.* **15** F4
Bridgenorth *Canada* **114** B6
Bridgeport *Calif., U.S.A.* **110** G7
Bridgeport *Conn., U.S.A.* **115** E11
Bridgeport *N.Y., U.S.A.* **115** C9
Bridgeport *Nebr., U.S.A.* **112** E2
Bridgeport *Tex., U.S.A.* **116** E6
Bridger *U.S.A.* **108** D9
Bridgeton *U.S.A.* **113** F16
Bridgetown *Australia* **93** F2
Bridgetown *Barbados* **121** g
Bridgetown *Canada* **105** D6
Bridgewater *Australia* **95** G4
Bridgewater *Canada* **105** D7
Bridgewater *Mass., U.S.A.* **115** E14
Bridgewater *N.Y., U.S.A.* **115** D9
Bridgewater, C. *Australia* **95** F3
Bridgnorth *U.K.* **15** E5
Bridgton *U.S.A.* **115** B14
Bridgwater *U.K.* **15** F5
Bridgwater B. *U.K.* **15** F4
Bridlington *U.K.* **14** C7
Bridlington B. *U.K.* **14** C7
Bridport *Australia* **95** G4
Bridport *U.K.* **15** G5
Brie *France* **18** D2
Brie-Comte-Robert *France* **19** D9
Brielle *Neths.* **17** C4
Brienne-le-Château *France* **19** D11
Brienon-sur-Armançon
  France **19** E10
Brienz *Switz.* **25** J4
Brienzersee *Switz.* **25** J3
Brière △ *France* **18** E4
Brig *Switz.* **25** J3
Brigg *U.K.* **14** D7
Brigham City *U.S.A.* **108** F7
Bright *Australia* **95** F4
Brighton *Australia* **95** F2
Brighton *Canada* **114** B7
Brighton *Trin. & Tob.* **125** K15
Brighton *U.K.* **15** G7
Brighton *U.S.A.* **114** C7
Brightside *Canada* **115** A8
Brignogan-Plage *France* **18** D2
Brignoles *France* **21** E10
Brihuega *Spain* **38** E2
Brikama *Gambia* **82** C1
Brilliant *U.S.A.* **114** F4
Brilon *Germany* **24** D4
Bríndisi *Italy* **43** B10
Brinje *Croatia* **41** D12
Brinkley *U.S.A.* **116** D9
Brinnon *U.S.A.* **110** C4
Brion, Î. *Canada* **105** C7
Brionne *France* **18** C7
Brionski *Croatia* **41** D10
Brioude *France* **20** C7
Briouze *France* **18** D6
Brisay *Canada* **105** B5
Brisbane *Australia* **95** D5
Brisbane ➤ *Australia* **95** D5
Brisighella *Italy* **41** D8
Bristol *U.K.* **15** F5
Bristol *Conn., U.S.A.* **115** E12
Bristol *Pa., U.S.A.* **115** F10
Bristol *R.I., U.S.A.* **115** E13
Bristol *Tenn., U.S.A.* **117** C13
Bristol *Vt., U.S.A.* **115** B11
Bristol, City of □ *U.K.* **15** F5
Bristol B. *U.S.A.* **106** D6
Bristol Channel *U.K.* **15** F3
Bristol I. *Antarctica* **5** B1
Bristol L. *U.S.A.* **109** J6
Bristow *U.S.A.* **116** D6
Britain = Great Britain *Europe* **6** E5
British Columbia □ *Canada* **102** C3
British Indian Ocean Terr.
  = Chagos Arch. ☑ *Ind. Oc.* **50** J9
British Isles *Europe* **16** D5
British Mts. *N. Amer.* **106** B12
British Virgin Is. ☑ *W. Indies* **121** e
Brits *S. Africa* **89** D4
Britstown *S. Africa* **88** E3
Britt *Canada* **104** C3
Brittany = Bretagne □
  France **18** D3
Britton *U.S.A.* **112** C5
Brive-la-Gaillarde *France* **20** C5
Briviesca *Spain* **36** C7
Brixen = Bressanone *Italy* **41** B8
Brixham *U.K.* **15** G4
Brnaze *Croatia* **41** E13
Brněnský □ *Czech Rep.* **27** B9
Brno *Czech Rep.* **27** B9
Broach = Bharuch *India* **66** J8
Broad ➤ *U.S.A.* **117** D14
Broad Arrow *Australia* **93** F3
Broad B. *U.K.* **13** C2
Broad Haven *Ireland* **12** B2

Bria *C.A.R.* ...
Broad Law *U.K.* **13** F5
Broad Pk. = Faichan
  Kangri *India* **69** B7
Broad Sd. *Australia* **94** C4
Broadalbin *U.S.A.* **115** C10
Broadback ➤ *Canada* **104** B4
Broadhurst Ra. *Australia* **92** D3
Broads, The *U.K.* **14** E9
Broadus *U.S.A.* **108** D11
Broager *Denmark* **11** K3
Broby *Sweden* **11** H8
Brocēni *Latvia* **30** B9
Brochet *Canada* **103** B8
Brochet, L. *Canada* **103** B8
Brock I. *Canada* **101** B9
Brocken *Germany* **24** D6
Brockport *U.S.A.* **114** C7
Brockton *U.S.A.* **115** D13
Brockville *Canada* **115** B9
Brockway *Mont., U.S.A.* **108** C11
Brockway *Pa., U.S.A.* **114** E6
Brocton *U.S.A.* **114** D5
Brod *Macedonia* **44** E5
Brodarevo *Serbia* **44** C3
Brodeur Pen. *Canada* **101** C14
Brodick *U.K.* **13** F3
Brodnica *Poland* **31** E6
Brody *Ukraine* **23** C13
Brogan *U.S.A.* **108** D5
Broglie *France* **18** C7
Brok *Poland* **31** F8
Broken Arrow *U.S.A.* **116** C7
Broken Bow *Nebr., U.S.A.* **112** E4
Broken Bow *Okla., U.S.A.* **116** D7
Broken Bow Lake *U.S.A.* **116** D7
Broken Hill *Australia* **95** E3
Broken Ridge *Ind. Oc.* **96** L1
Broken River Ra. *Australia* **94** b
Brokind *Sweden* **11** F9
Bromley □ *U.K.* **15** F8
Bromo *Indonesia* **63** G15
Bromölla *Sweden* **11** H8
Bromsgrove *U.K.* **15** E5
Brønderslev *Denmark* **11** G3
Brong-Ahafo □ *Ghana* **82** D4
Broni *Italy* **40** C6
Bronkhorstspruit *S. Africa* **89** D4
Brønnøysund *Norway* **8** D15
Bronte *Italy* **43** E7
Brook Park *U.S.A.* **114** E4
Brookhaven *U.S.A.* **117** F9
Brookings *Oreg., U.S.A.* **108** E1
Brookings *S. Dak., U.S.A.* **112** C5
Brooklin *Canada* **114** C6
Brooklyn Park *U.S.A.* **112** C7
Brooks *Canada* **102** C6
Brooks Range *U.S.A.* **106** B9
Brooksville *U.S.A.* **117** G13
Brookton *Australia* **93** F2
Brookville *U.S.A.* **114** E5
Broom, L. *U.K.* **13** D3
Broome *Australia* **92** C3
Broons *France* **18** D4
Brora *U.K.* **13** C5
Brora ➤ *U.K.* **13** C5
Brørup *Denmark* **11** J2
Brösarp *Sweden* **11** J8
Brosna ➤ *Ireland* **12** C4
Broșteni *Mehedinți, Romania* **28** F7
Broșteni *Suceava, Romania* **29** C10
Brothers *U.S.A.* **108** E3
Brou *France* **18** D8
Brouage *France* **20** C2
Brough *U.K.* **14** C5
Brough Hd. *U.K.* **13** B5
Broughton Island =
  Qikiqtarjuaq *Canada* **101** D19
Broumov *Czech Rep.* **27** A9
Brovary *Ukraine* **33** G6
Brovst *Denmark* **11** G3
Brown, L. *Australia* **93** F2
Brown, Pt. *Australia* **95** E1
Brown City *U.S.A.* **114** C2
Brown Willy *U.K.* **15** G3
Brownfield *U.S.A.* **116** E3
Browning *U.S.A.* **108** B7
Brownsville *Oreg., U.S.A.* **108** D2
Brownsville *Pa., U.S.A.* **114** F5
Brownsville *Tenn., U.S.A.* **117** D10
Brownsville *Tex., U.S.A.* **116** J6
Brownville *U.S.A.* **115** C9
Brownwood *U.S.A.* **116** F5
Browse I. *Australia* **92** B3
Bruas *Malaysia* **65** K3
Bruay-la-Buissière *France* **19** B9
Bruce, Mt. *Australia* **92** D2
Bruce Pen. *Canada* **114** B3
Bruce Peninsula △ *Canada* **114** A3
Bruce Rock *Australia* **93** F2
Bruche ➤ *France* **19** D14
Bruchsal *Germany* **25** F4
Bruck an der Leitha *Austria* **27** C9
Bruck an der Mur *Austria* **26** D8
Brue ➤ *U.K.* **15** F5
Bruges = Brugge *Belgium* **17** C3
Brugg *Switz.* **25** H4
Brugge *Belgium* **17** C3
Bruin *U.S.A.* **114** E5
Brûk, W. el ➤ *Egypt* **74** E2

Brûlé *Canada* **102** C5
Brûlé, L. *Canada* **105** B7
Brûlon *France* **18** E6
Brumado *Brazil* **125** F10
Brumath *France* **19** D14
Brumunddal *Norway* **8** F14
Bruneau *U.S.A.* **108** E6
Bruneau ➤ *U.S.A.* **108** E6
Bruneck = Brunico *Italy* **41** B8
Brunei = Bandar Seri
  Begawan *Brunei* **62** D5
Brunei ■ *Asia* **62** D5
Brunflo *Sweden* **10** A8
Brunico *Italy* **41** B8
Brunna *Sweden* **10** E11
Brunnen *Switz.* **25** J4
Brunner, L. *N.Z.* **91** E3
Brunsbüttel *Germany* **24** B5
Brunssum *Neths.* **17** D5
Brunswick =
  Braunschweig *Germany* **24** C6
Brunswick *Ga., U.S.A.* **117** F14
Brunswick *Maine, U.S.A.* **113** D19
Brunswick *Md., U.S.A.* **113** F15
Brunswick *Mo., U.S.A.* **112** F7
Brunswick *Ohio, U.S.A.* **114** E3
Brunswick, Pen. de *Chile* **128** G2
Brunswick B. *Australia* **92** C3
Brunswick Junction *Australia* **93** F2
Brunt Ice Shelf *Antarctica* **5** D2
Bruntál *Czech Rep.* **27** B10
Brus Laguna *Honduras* **120** C3
Brusartsi *Bulgaria* **44** C7
Brush *U.S.A.* **108** F12
Brushton *U.S.A.* **115** B10
Brusio *Switz.* **25** J6
Brusque *Brazil* **127** B6
Brussel *Belgium* **17** D4
Brussel ✈ (BRU) *Belgium* **17** D5
Brussels = Brussel *Belgium* **17** D4
Brussels *Canada* **114** C3
Brusy *Poland* **30** E4
Bruthen *Australia* **95** F4
Bruxelles = Brussel *Belgium* **17** D4
Bruyères *France* **19** D13
Bruz *France* **18** D5
Brwinów *Poland* **31** F7
Bryagovo *Bulgaria* **45** E9
Bryan *Ohio, U.S.A.* **113** E11
Bryan *Tex., U.S.A.* **116** F6
Bryan, Mt. *Australia* **95** E2
Bryanka *Ukraine* **33** H10
Bryansk *Bryansk, Russia* **33** F8
Bryansk *Dagestan, Russia* **35** H8
Bryansk □ *Russia* **33** F7
Bryanskoye = Bryansk
  Russia **35** H8
Bryce Canyon △ *U.S.A.* **109** H7
Bryne *Norway* **9** G11
Bryson City *U.S.A.* **117** D13
Bryukhovetskaya *Russia* **33** K10
Brza Palanka *Serbia* **44** B6
Brzeg *Poland* **31** H4
Brzeg Dolny *Poland* **31** G3
Brześć Kujawski *Poland* **31** F5
Brzesko *Poland* **31** J7
Brzeziny *Poland* **31** G6
Brzozów *Poland* **31** J9
Bsharri *Lebanon* **74** A5
Bū Baqarah *U.A.E.* **71** E8
Bu Craa *W. Sahara* **78** C3
Bū Ḥasā *U.A.E.* **71** F7
Bua *Fiji* **91** a
Bua *Sweden* **11** G6
Bua ➤ *Malaysia* **87** E3
Bua Yai *Thailand* **64** E4
Buan *S. Korea* **57** G14
Buapinang *Indonesia* **63** E6
Buba *Guinea-Biss.* **82** C2
Bubanza *Burundi* **86** C2
Bubaque *Guinea-Biss.* **82** C1
Bube *Ethiopia* **81** F4
Bubi *Zimbabwe* **87** G3
Bubi ➤ *Zimbabwe* **89** B5
Bubiyan *Kuwait* **71** D6
Buca *Fiji* **91** a
Buca *Turkey* **47** C9
Bucak *Turkey* **47** D12
Bucaramanga *Colombia* **124** B4
Bucas Grande I. *Phil.* **61** G6
Bucasia *Australia* **94** b
Buccaneer Arch. *Australia* **92** C3
Buccino *Italy* **43** B8
Buccoo Reef *Trin. & Tob.* **125** J16
Bucecea *Romania* **29** C11
Bucegi △ *Romania* **29** E10
Buch an der Leitha = Bruck
  an der Leitha *Austria* **27** C9
Buchach *Ukraine* **23** D13
Buchan *U.K.* **13** D6
Buchan Ness *U.K.* **13** D7
Buchanan *Canada* **103** C8
Buchanan *Liberia* **82** D2
Buchanan, L. *Queens.,
  Australia* **94** C4
Buchanan, L. *W. Austral.,
  Australia* **93** E3
Buchanan, L. *U.S.A.* **116** F5
Buchanan Cr. ➤ *Australia* **94** B2
Buchans *Canada* **105** C8
Bucharest = București
  Romania **29** F11
Brûk, W. el ...
Buchen *Germany* **25** F5
Bucheon *S. Korea* **57** F14
Buchholz *Germany* **24** B5
Buchloe *Germany* **25** G6
Buchon, Pt. *U.S.A.* **110** K6
Buciumi *Romania* **28** C8
Buck Hill Falls *U.S.A.* **115** E9
Bückeburg *Germany* **24** C5
Buckeye Lake *U.S.A.* **114** G2
Buckhannon *U.S.A.* **113** F13
Buckhaven *U.K.* **13** E5
Buckhorn L. *Canada* **114** B6
Buckie *U.K.* **13** D6
Buckingham *Canada* **104** C4
Buckingham *U.K.* **15** F7
Buckingham B. *Australia* **94** A2
Buckinghamshire □ *U.K.* **15** F7
Buckle Hd. *Australia* **92** B4
Buckleboo *Australia* **95** E2
Buckley *U.K.* **14** D4
Buckley ➤ *Australia* **94** C2
Bucklin *U.S.A.* **112** G4
Bucks L. *U.S.A.* **110** F5
Bucquoy *France* **19** B9
București *Romania* **29** F11
București Otopeni ✈ (OTP)
  Romania **29** F11
Bucyrus *U.S.A.* **113** E12
Budacu, Vf. *Romania* **29** C10
Budalin *Burma* **67** H19
Budaörs *Hungary* **28** C3
Budapest *Hungary* **28** C4
Budapest ✈ (BUD) *Hungary* **28** C4
Budaun *India* **69** E8
Budd Coast *Antarctica* **5** C8
Buddusò *Italy* **42** B2
Bude *U.K.* **15** G3
Budennovsk *Russia* **35** H7
Budești *Romania* **29** F11
Budeyi *Ukraine* **29** B14
Budge Budge = Baj Baj
  India **69** H13
Budgewoi *Australia* **95** E5
Budia *Spain* **38** E2
Büdingen *Germany* **25** E5
Budjala *Dem. Rep. of the Congo* **84** D3
Budoni *Italy* **42** B2
Búdrio *Italy* **41** D8
Budva *Montenegro* **44** D2
Budzyń *Poland* **31** F3
Buea *Cameroon* **83** E6
Buellton *U.S.A.* **111** L6
Buena Esperanza *Argentina* **126** C2
Buena Park *U.S.A.* **111** M9
Buena Vista *Colo., U.S.A.* **108** G10
Buena Vista *Va., U.S.A.* **113** G14
Buena Vista Lake Bed
  U.S.A. **111** K7
Buenaventura *Colombia* **124** C3
Buenaventura *Mexico* **118** B3
Buendía, Embalse de *Spain* **38** E2
Buenos Aires *Argentina* **126** C4
Buenos Aires *Costa Rica* **120** E3
Buenos Aires □ *Argentina* **126** D4
Buenos Aires, L. *Argentina* **128** F2
Buffalo *Mo., U.S.A.* **112** G7
Buffalo *N.Y., U.S.A.* **114** D6
Buffalo *Okla., U.S.A.* **116** C5
Buffalo *S. Dak., U.S.A.* **112** C2
Buffalo *Wyo., U.S.A.* **108** D10
Buffalo ➤ *Canada* **102** A5
Buffalo ➤ *S. Africa* **89** D5
Buffalo ➤ *U.S.A.* **116** C8
Buffalo Head Hills *Canada* **102** B5
Buffalo L. *Alta., Canada* **102** C6
Buffalo L. *N.W.T., Canada* **102** A5
Buffalo Narrows *Canada* **103** B7
Buffalo Springs △ *Kenya* **86** B4
Buffels ➤ *S. Africa* **88** D2
Buford *U.S.A.* **117** D12
Bug = Buh ➤ *Ukraine* **33** J6
Bug ➤ *Poland* **31** F8
Buga *Colombia* **124** C3
Bugala I. *Uganda* **86** C3
Buganda *Uganda* **86** C3
Buganga *Uganda* **86** C3
Bugasong *Phil.* **61** F5
Bugeat *France* **20** C5
Bugel, Tanjung *Indonesia* **63** G14
Búger *Spain* **48** B9
Bugibba *Malta* **49** D1
Bugojno *Bos.-H.* **28** F2
Bugsuk I. *Phil.* **62** C5
Buguma *Nigeria* **83** E6
Bugun Shara *Mongolia* **60** B5
Bugungu △ *Uganda* **86** B3
Buguruslan *Russia* **52** D6
Buh ➤ *Ukraine* **33** J6
Buharkent *Turkey* **47** D10
Buheirat-Murrat-el-Kubra
  Egypt **80** H8
Buhera *Zimbabwe* **89** B5
Bühl *Germany* **25** G4
Buhl *U.S.A.* **108** E6
Buhuși *Romania* **29** D11
Bui △ *Ghana* **82** D4
Builth Wells *U.K.* **15** E4
Buinsk *Russia* **34** C9

Buir Nur *Mongolia* **60** B6
Buis-les-Baronnies *France* **21** D9
Buitrago del Lozoya *Spain* **36** E7
Bujalance *Spain* **37** H6
Bujanovac *Serbia* **44** D5
Bujaraloz *Spain* **38** D4
Buje *Croatia* **41** C10
Bujumbura *Burundi* **86** C2
Bük *Hungary* **28** C1
Buk *Poland* **31** F3
Bukachacha *Russia* **53** D12
Bukama
  Dem. Rep. of the Congo **87** D2
Bukavu *Dem. Rep. of the Congo* **86** C2
Bukene *Tanzania* **86** C3
Bukhara = Buxoro *Uzbekistan* **52** F7
Bukhoro = Buxoro *Uzbekistan* **52** F7
Bukima *Tanzania* **86** C3
Bukit Badung *Indonesia* **63** K18
Bukit Kerajaan *Malaysia* **65** c
Bukit Mertajam *Malaysia* **65** c
Bukit Ni *Malaysia* **65** c
Bukit Panjang *Singapore* **65** d
Bukit Tengah *Malaysia* **65** c
Bükk *Hungary* **28** B5
Bükki △ *Hungary* **28** 35
Bukoba *Tanzania* **86** C3
Bukum, Pulau *Singapore* **65** d
Bukuru *Nigeria* **83** D6
Bukuya *Uganda* **86** B3
Būl, Kuh-e *Iran* **71** D7
Bula *Guinea-Biss.* **82** C1
Bula *Indonesia* **63** E8
Bülach *Switz.* **25** H4
Bulahdelah *Australia* **95** E5
Bulan *Phil.* **61** E5
Bulancak *Turkey* **73** B8
Bulandshahr *India* **68** E7
Bulanık *Turkey* **73** C10
Būlâq *Egypt* **80** B3
Bulawayo *Zimbabwe* **87** G2
Buldan *Turkey* **47** C10
Buldir I. *U.S.A.* **106** E3
Bulenga *Ghana* **82** D4
Bulgar *Russia* **34** C9
Bulgaria ■ *Europe* **45** D9
Bulgheria, Monte *Italy* **43** B8
Bulgurca *Turkey* **47** C9
Buli, Teluk *Indonesia* **63** D7
Buliluyan, C. *Phil.* **61** G2
Bulim *Singapore* **65** d
Bulki *Ethiopia* **81** F4
Bulkley → *Canada* **102** B3
Bull Shoals L. *U.S.A.* **116** C8
Bullaque → *Spain* **37** G6
Bulle *Switz.* **25** J3
Bulleringa △ *Australia* **94** B3
Büllingen *Belgium* **17** D6
Bullock Creek *Australia* **94** B3
Bulloo → *Australia* **95** D3
Bulloo L. *Australia* **95** D3
Bulls *N.Z.* **91** D5
Bully-les-Mines *France* **19** B9
Bulman *Australia* **94** A1
Bulnes *Chile* **126** D1
Bulqizë *Albania* **44** E4
Bulsar = Valsad *India* **66** J8
Bultfontein *S. Africa* **88** D4
Bulukumba *Indonesia* **63** F6
Bulun *Russia* **53** B13
Bumba *Dem. Rep. of the Congo* **84** D4
Bumbah, Khalīj *Libya* **79** B10
Bumbeşti-Jiu *Romania* **29** E8
Bumbiri I. *Tanzania* **86** C3
Bumbuna *S. Leone* **82** D2
Bumhpa Bum *Burma* **67** F20
Bumi → *Zimbabwe* **87** F2
Buna *Kenya* **86** B4
Bunaken *Indonesia* **63** D6
Bunawan *Phil.* **61** G6
Bunazi *Tanzania* **86** C3
Bunbury *Australia* **93** F2
Bunclody *Ireland* **12** D5
Buncrana *Ireland* **12** A4
Bundaberg *Australia* **95** C5
Bünde *Germany* **24** C4
Bundey → *Australia* **94** C2
Bundi *India* **68** G6
Bundjalung △ *Australia* **95** D5
Bundoran *Ireland* **12** B3
Bundukia *Sudan* **81** F3
Bung Kan *Thailand* **64** C4
Bunga → *Nigeria* **83** C6
Bungay *U.K.* **15** E9
Bungil Cr. → *Australia* **95** D4
Bungle Bungle =
  Purnululu △ *Australia* **92** C4
Bungo-Suidō *Japan* **55** H6
Bungoma *Kenya* **86** B3
Bungotakada *Japan* **55** H5
Bungu *Tanzania* **86** D4
Bunia *Dem. Rep. of the Congo* **86** B3
Bunji *Pakistan* **69** B6
Bunkie *U.S.A.* **116** F8
Bunnell *U.S.A.* **117** G14
Buñol *Spain* **39** F4

Bunsuru → *Nigeria* **83** C5
Buntok *Indonesia* **62** E4
Bununu Dass *Nigeria* **83** C6
Bununu Kasa *Nigeria* **83** D6
Bunya Mts. △ *Australia* **95** D5
Bünyan *Turkey* **72** C6
Bunyola *Spain* **48** B9
Bunyu *Indonesia* **62** D5
Buol *Indonesia* **63** D6
Buon Brieng *Vietnam* **64** F7
Buon Ma Thuot *Vietnam* **64** F7
Buong Long *Cambodia* **64** F6
Buorkhaya, Mys *Russia* **53** B14
Buqayq *Si. Arabia* **71** E6
Buqbuq *Egypt* **80** A2
Bur Acaba = Buurhakaba
  Somali Rep. **75** G3
Bûr Fuad *Egypt* **80** H8
Bûr Safâga *Egypt* **70** E2
Bûr Sa'îd *Egypt* **80** H8
Bûr Sûdân *Sudan* **80** D4
Bûr Taufiq *Egypt* **80** J8
Bura *Kenya* **86** C4
Burakin *Australia* **93** F2
Buram *Sudan* **81** E2
Burao = Burco *Somali Rep.* **75** F4
Burāq *Syria* **74** B5
Buraydah *Si. Arabia* **70** E4
Burbank *U.S.A.* **111** L8
Burco *Somali Rep.* **75** F4
Burda *India* **68** G6
Burdekin → *Australia* **94** B4
Burdur *Turkey* **47** D12
Burdur → *Turkey* **47** D12
Burdur Gölü *Turkey* **47** D12
Burdwan = Barddhaman
  India **69** H12
Bure *Gojam, Ethiopia* **81** E4
Bure *Ilubabor, Ethiopia* **81** F4
Bure → *U.K.* **14** E9
Büren *Germany* **24** D4
Bureya → *Russia* **53** E13
Burford *Canada* **114** C4
Burg *Germany* **24** C7
Burg auf Fehmarn *Germany* **24** A7
Burg el Arab *Egypt* **80** H6
Burg et Tuyur *Sudan* **80** C2
Burg Stargard *Germany* **24** B9
Burgas *Bulgaria* **45** D11
Burgas □ *Bulgaria* **45** D10
Burgdorf *Germany* **24** C6
Burgdorf *Switz.* **25** H3
Burgenland □ *Austria* **27** D9
Burgeo *Canada* **105** C8
Burgersdorp *S. Africa* **88** E4
Burgess, Mt. *Australia* **93** F3
Burghausen *Germany* **25** G8
Burghead *U.K.* **13** D5
Búrgio *Italy* **42** F6
Burglengenfeld *Germany* **25** F8
Burgohondo *Spain* **36** E6
Burgos *Spain* **36** C7
Burgos □ *Spain* **36** C7
Burgstädt *Germany* **24** E8
Burgsvik *Sweden* **11** G12
Burguillos del Cerro *Spain* **37** G4
Burgundy = Bourgogne □
  France **19** F11
Burhaniye *Turkey* **47** B8
Burhanpur *India* **66** J10
Burhi Gandak → *India* **69** G12
Burhner → *India* **69** H9
Buri Pen. *Eritrea* **81** D4
Burias I. *Phil.* **61** E5
Burica, Pta. *Costa Rica* **120** E3
Burien *U.S.A.* **110** C4
Burigi, L. *Tanzania* **86** C3
Burigi △ *Tanzania* **86** C3
Burin *Canada* **105** C8
Buriram *Thailand* **64** E4
Burji *Ethiopia* **81** F4
Burkburnett *U.S.A.* **116** D5
Burke → *Australia* **94** C2
Burke Chan. *Canada* **102** C3
Burketown *Australia* **94** B2
Burkina Faso ■ *Africa* **82** C4
Burk's Falls *Canada* **104** C4
Burlada *Spain* **38** C3
Burleigh Falls *Canada* **114** B6
Burley *U.S.A.* **108** E7
Burlingame *U.S.A.* **110** H4
Burlington *Canada* **114** C5
Burlington *Colo., U.S.A.* **108** G12
Burlington *Iowa, U.S.A.* **112** E8
Burlington *Kans., U.S.A.* **112** F6
Burlington *N.C., U.S.A.* **117** C15
Burlington *N.J., U.S.A.* **115** F10
Burlington *Vt., U.S.A.* **115** B11
Burlington *Wash., U.S.A.* **110** B4
Burlington *Wis., U.S.A.* **112** D9
Burma ■ *Asia* **67** J20
Burnaby I. *Canada* **102** C2
Burnet *U.S.A.* **116** F5
Burney *U.S.A.* **108** F3
Burnham *U.S.A.* **114** F7
Burnham-on-Sea *U.K.* **15** F5
Burnie *Australia* **95** G4

Burnley *U.K.* **14** D5
Burns *U.S.A.* **108** E4
Burns Junction *U.S.A.* **108** E5
Burns Lake *Canada* **102** C3
Burnside → *Canada* **100** D10
Burnside, L. *Australia* **93** E3
Burnsville *U.S.A.* **112** C7
Burnt River *Canada* **114** B6
Burntwood → *Canada* **103** B9
Burntwood L. *Canada* **103** B8
Burqān *Kuwait* **70** D5
Burra *Australia* **95** E2
Burra *Nigeria* **83** C6
Burray *U.K.* **13** C6
Burrel *Albania* **44** E4
Burren *Ireland* **12** C2
Burren △ *Ireland* **12** C3
Burren Junction *Australia* **95** E4
Burriana *Spain* **38** F4
Burrinjuck, L. *Australia* **95** F4
Burro, Serranías del *Mexico* **118** B4
Burrow Hd. *U.K.* **13** G4
Burrum Coast △ *Australia* **95** D5
Burruyacú *Argentina* **126** B3
Burry Port *U.K.* **15** F3
Bursa *Turkey* **45** F13
Bursa □ *Turkey* **72** B3
Burseryd *Sweden* **11** G7
Burstall *Canada* **103** C7
Burton *Ohio, U.S.A.* **114** E3
Burton *S.C., U.S.A.* **117** E14
Burton, L. *Canada* **104** B4
Burton upon Trent *U.K.* **14** E6
Buru *Indonesia* **63** E7
Burullus, Bahra el *Egypt* **80** H7
Burûn, Râs *Egypt* **74** D2
Burundi ■ *Africa* **86** C3
Bururi *Burundi* **86** C2
Burutu *Nigeria* **83** D6
Burwell *U.S.A.* **112** E5
Burwick *U.K.* **13** C5
Bury *U.K.* **14** D5
Bury St. Edmunds *U.K.* **15** E8
Buryatia □ *Russia* **53** D12
Buryn *Ukraine* **33** G7
Burzenin *Poland* **31** G5
Busalla *Italy* **40** D5
Busan = Pusan *S. Korea* **57** G15
Busango Swamp *Zambia* **87** E2
Busaso = Boosaaso
  Somali Rep. **75** E4
Buşayrah *Syria* **73** E9
Busca *Italy* **40** D4
Bushat *Albania* **44** E3
Būshehr *Iran* **71** D6
Būshehr □ *Iran* **71** D6
Bushenyi *Uganda* **86** C3
Bushire = Būshehr *Iran* **71** D6
Bushtyna *Ukraine* **29** B8
Busie *Ghana* **82** C4
Businga *Dem. Rep. of the Congo* **84** D4
Büsingen *Germany* **25** H4
Busira → *Dem. Rep. of the Congo* **84** D4
Busko-Zdrój *Poland* **31** H7
Busovača Bos.-H *28* F2
Buşra ash Shām *Syria* **74** C5
Busselton *Australia* **93** F2
Bussière-Badil *France* **20** C4
Bussolengo *Italy* **40** C7
Bussum *Neths.* **17** B5
Busto, C. *Spain* **36** B4
Busto Arsízio *Italy* **40** C5
Busu Djanoa
  Dem. Rep. of the Congo **84** D4
Busuanga I. *Phil.* **61** E4
Büsum *Germany* **24** A4
Busungbiu *Indonesia* **63** J17
Buta *Dem. Rep. of the Congo* **86** B1
Butare *Rwanda* **86** C2
Butaritari *Kiribati* **96** G9
Bute △ *U.K.* **13** F3
Bute Inlet *Canada* **102** C4
Butemba *Uganda* **86** B3
Butembo
  Dem. Rep. of the Congo **86** B2
Buteni *Romania* **28** D7
Butera *Italy* **43** E7
Butere *Kenya* **86** B3
Butha Qi *China* **60** B7
Butiaba *Uganda* **86** B3
Butler *Mo., U.S.A.* **112** F6
Butler *Pa., U.S.A.* **114** F5
Buton *Indonesia* **63** F6
Butte *Mont., U.S.A.* **108** C7
Butte *Nebr., U.S.A.* **112** D4
Butte Creek → *U.S.A.* **110** F5
Butterworth = Gcuwa
  S. Africa **89** E4
Butterworth *Malaysia* **65** c
Buttevant *Ireland* **12** D3
Buttfield, Mt. *Australia* **93** D4
Button B. *Canada* **103** B10
Buttonwillow *U.S.A.* **111** K7
Butty Hd. *Australia* **93** F3
Butuan *Phil.* **61** G6
Butuku-Luba *Eq. Guin.* **83** E6
Butung = Buton *Indonesia* **63** F6

Buturlinovka *Russia* **34** E5
Butzbach *Germany* **25** E4
Bützow *Germany* **24** B7
Buurhakaba *Somali Rep.* **75** G3
Buxa Duar *India* **69** F13
Buxar *India* **69** G10
Buxoro *Uzbekistan* **52** F7
Buxtehude *Germany* **24** B5
Buxton *U.K.* **14** D6
Buxy *France* **19** F11
Buy *Russia* **34** A5
Buyant-Uhaa *Mongolia* **60** B6
Buynaksk *Russia* **35** J8
Buyo *Ivory C.* **82** D3
Buyo, L. de *Ivory C.* **82** D3
Büyük Menderes → *Turkey* **47** D9
Büyükçekmece *Turkey* **45** E12
Büyükkarıştıran *Turkey* **45** E11
Büyükkemikli Burnu
  Turkey **45** F10
Büyükorhan *Turkey* **47** B10
Büyükyoncalı *Turkey* **45** E11
Buzançais *France* **18** F8
Buzău *Romania* **29** E11
Buzău □ *Romania* **29** E11
Buzău → *Romania* **29** E12
Buzău, Pasul *Romania* **29** E11
Buzen *Japan* **55** H5
Buzet *Croatia* **41** C10
Buzi → *Mozam.* **87** F3
Buziaş *Romania* **28** E6
Büzmeyin *Turkmenistan* **71** B8
Buzuluk *Russia* **52** D6
Buzuluk → *Russia* **34** E6
Buzzards Bay *U.S.A.* **115** E14
Bwana Mkubwe
  Dem. Rep. of the Congo **87** E2
Bwindi △ *Uganda* **86** C2
Byala *Ruse, Bulgaria* **45** C9
Byala *Varna, Bulgaria* **45** D11
Byala Slatina *Bulgaria* **44** C7
Byam Martin I. *Canada* **101** B11
Byarezina → *Belarus* **23** B16
Byaroza *Belarus* **33** F3
Bychawa *Poland* **31** G9
Byczyna *Poland* **31** G5
Bydgoszcz *Poland* **31** E5
Byelorussia = Belarus ■
  Europe **23** B14
Byers *U.S.A.* **108** G11
Byesville *U.S.A.* **114** G3
Byfield △ *Australia* **94** C5
Bykhaw *Belarus* **23** B16
Bykhov = Bykhaw *Belarus* **23** B16
Bykovo *Russia* **34** F7
Bylas *U.S.A.* **109** K8
Bylot *Canada* **103** B10
Bylot I. *Canada* **101** C16
Byrd, C. *Antarctica* **5** C17
Byrock *Australia* **95** E4
Byron, C. *Australia* **95** D5
Byron Bay *Australia* **95** D5
Byrranga, Gory *Russia* **53** B11
Byrranga Mts. = Byrranga,
  Gory *Russia* **53** B11
Byrum *Denmark* **11** G5
Byske *Sweden* **8** D19
Byskeälven → *Sweden* **8** D19
Bystrytsya *Ukraine* **29** B9
Bystrzyca → *Dolnośląskie,*
  Poland **31** G3
Bystrzyca → *Lubelskie, Poland* **31** G9
Bystrzyca Kłodzka *Poland* **31** H3
Bytča *Slovak Rep.* **27** B11
Bytkiv *Ukraine* **29** B9
Bytom *Poland* **31** H5
Bytom Odrzański *Poland* **31** G2
Bytów *Poland* **30** D4
Byumba *Rwanda* **86** C3
Bzenec *Czech Rep.* **27** C10
Bzura → *Poland* **31** F7

C

C.W. McConaughy, L.
  U.S.A. **112** E3
Ca → *Vietnam* **64** C5
Ca Mau *Vietnam* **65** H5
Ca Mau, Mui *Vietnam* **65** H5
Ca Na *Vietnam* **65** G7
Caacupé *Paraguay* **126** B4
Caaguazú □ *Paraguay* **127** B4
Caála *Angola* **85** G3
Caamaño Sd. *Canada* **102** C3
Caazapá *Paraguay* **126** B4
Caazapá □ *Paraguay* **127** B4
Cabadbaran *Phil.* **61** G6
Cabalian = San Juan *Phil.* **61** F6
Caballeria, C. de *Spain* **48** A11
Cabana de Bergantiños *Spain* **36** B2
Cabañaquinta *Spain* **36** B5
Cabanatuan *Phil.* **61** D4
Cabañeros △ *Spain* **37** F6
Cabanes *Spain* **38** E5
Cabano *Canada* **105** C6
Čabar *Croatia* **41** C11
Cabazon *U.S.A.* **111** M10
Cabedelo *Brazil* **125** E12
Cabeza del Buey *Spain* **37** G5

Cabezón de la Sal *Spain* **36** B6
Cabildo *Chile* **126** C1
Cabimas *Venezuela* **124** A4
Cabinda *Angola* **84** F2
Cabinda □ *Angola* **84** F2
Cabinet Mts. *U.S.A.* **108** B6
Cabo Blanco *Argentina* **128** F3
Cabo Frio *Brazil* **127** A7
Cabo Pantoja *Peru* **124** D3
Cabo San Lucas *Mexico* **118** C3
Cabo Str. *Canada* **105** C8
Cabo Verde = Cape Verde
  Is. ■ *Atl. Oc.* **78** b
Cabonga, Réservoir *Canada* **104** C4
Cabool *U.S.A.* **112** G7
Caboolture *Australia* **95** D5
Cabora Bassa Dam =
  Cahora Bassa, Lago de
  Mozam. **87** F3
Caborca *Mexico* **118** A2
Cabot, Mt. *U.S.A.* **115** B13
Cabot Hd. *Canada* **114** A3
Cabot Str. *Canada* **105** C8
Cabra *Spain* **37** H6
Cabra del Santo Cristo *Spain* **37** H7
Cábras *Italy* **42** C1
Cabrera *Spain* **48** B9
Cabrera, Sierra *Spain* **36** C4
Cabrera △ *Spain* **39** F7
Cabri *Canada* **103** C7
Cabriel → *Spain* **39** F3
Cabugao *Phil.* **61** C4
Cacabelos *Spain* **36** C4
Caçador *Brazil* **127** B5
Čačak *Serbia* **44** C4
Caçapava do Sul *Brazil* **127** C5
Cáccamo *Italy* **42** E6
Cacém *Portugal* **37** G1
Cáceres *Brazil* **124** G7
Cáceres *Spain* **37** F4
Cáceres □ *Spain* **36** F5
Cache Bay *Canada* **104** C4
Cache Cr. → *U.S.A.* **110** G5
Cache Creek *Canada* **102** C4
Cacheu *Guinea-Biss.* **82** C1
Cachi *Argentina* **126** B2
Cachimbo, Serra do *Brazil* **125** E7
Cachinal de la Sierra *Chile* **126** A2
Cachoeira *Brazil* **125** F11
Cachoeira do Sul *Brazil* **127** C5
Cachoeiro de Itapemirim
  Brazil **127** A7
Cachopo *Portugal* **37** H3
Cacine *Guinea-Biss.* **82** C1
Cacoal *Brazil* **124** F6
Cacólo *Angola* **84** G3
Caconda *Angola* **85** G3
Čadca *Slovak Rep.* **27** B11
Caddo *U.S.A.* **116** D6
Cader Idris *U.K.* **15** E4
Cadereyta de Jiménez
  Mexico **118** B5
Cadí, Sierra del *Spain* **38** C6
Cadí-Moixeró △ *Spain* **38** C3
Cadibarrawirracanna, L.
  Australia **95** D2
Cadillac *France* **20** D3
Cadillac *U.S.A.* **113** C11
Cadiz *Phil.* **61** F5
Cádiz *Spain* **37** J4
Cadiz *Calif., U.S.A.* **111** L11
Cadiz *Ohio, U.S.A.* **114** F4
Cádiz □ *Spain* **37** J5
Cádiz, G. de *Spain* **37** J3
Cadiz L. *U.S.A.* **109** J6
Cadney Park *Australia* **95** D1
Cadomin *Canada* **102** C5
Cadotte Lake *Canada* **102** B5
Cadours *France* **20** E5
Cadoux *Australia* **93** F2
Caen *France* **18** C6
Caernarfon *U.K.* **14** D3
Caernarfon B. *U.K.* **14** D3
Caernarvon = Caernarfon
  U.K. **14** D3
Caerphilly *U.K.* **15** F4
Caerphilly □ *U.K.* **15** F4
Caesarea *Israel* **74** C3
Caetité *Brazil* **125** F10
Cafayate *Argentina* **126** B2
Cafu *Angola* **88** B2
Cagayan → *Phil.* **61** B4
Cagayan de Oro *Phil.* **61** G6
Cagayan Is. *Phil.* **61** G4
Cagayan Sulu I. *Phil.* **61** H3
Cagli *Italy* **41** E9
Cágliari *Italy* **42** C2
Cágliari, G. di *Italy* **42** C2
Cagnes-sur-Mer *France* **21** E11
Caguán → *Colombia* **124** D4
Caguas *Puerto Rico* **121** d
Caha Mts. *Ireland* **12** E2
Caher *Ireland* **12** D4
Cahersiveen *Ireland* **12** E1

Cahore Pt. *Ireland* **12** D5
Cahors *France* **20** D5
Cahul *Moldova* **29** E13
Cai Bau, Dao *Vietnam* **58** G6
Cai Nuoc *Vietnam* **65** H5
Caia *Mozam.* **87** F4
Caianda *Angola* **87** E1
Caibarién *Cuba* **120** B4
Caibiran *Phil.* **61** F6
Caicara *Venezuela* **124** B5
Caicó *Brazil* **125** E11
Caicos Is. *Turks & Caicos* **121** 35
Caicos Passage *W. Indies* **121** B5
Caidian *China* **59** B10
Caiguna *Australia* **93** F4
Căinari *Moldova* **29** D14
Caird Coast *Antarctica* **5** D1
Cairn Gorm *U.K.* **13** D5
Cairngorm Mts. *U.K.* **13** D5
Cairngorms △ *U.K.* **13** D5
Cairnryan *U.K.* **13** G3
Cairns *Australia* **94** B4
Cairns L. *Canada* **103** C10
Cairo = El Qâhira *Egypt* **80** H7
Cairo *Ga., U.S.A.* **117** F12
Cairo *Ill., U.S.A.* **112** G9
Cairo *N.Y., U.S.A.* **115** D10
Cairo Montenotte *Italy* **40** D5
Caiseal = Cashel *Ireland* **12** D4
Caisleán an Bharraigh =
  Castlebar *Ireland* **12** C2
Caithness *U.K.* **13** C5
Caithness, Ord of *U.K.* **13** C5
Caja de Muertos, I.
  Puerto Rico **121** d
Cajamarca *Peru* **124** E3
Cajarc *France* **20** D5
Cajazeiras *Brazil* **125** E11
Čajetina *Serbia* **44** C3
Çakırgol *Turkey* **73** B8
Çakırlar *Turkey* **47** E12
Čakovec *Croatia* **41** B13
Çal *Turkey* **47** C11
Cala *Spain* **37** H4
Cala → *Spain* **37** H4
Cala Cadolar, Punta de =
  Rotja, Pta. *Spain* **39** G6
Cala d'Or *Spain* **48** B10
Cala en Porter *Spain* **48** B11
Cala Figuera *Spain* **48** B10
Cala Figuera, C. de *Spain* **48** B10
Cala Forcat *Spain* **48** B10
Cala Major *Spain* **48** B9
Cala Mezquida = Sa
  Mesquida *Spain* **48** B11
Cala Millor *Spain* **48** B10
Cala Murada *Spain* **48** B10
Cala Ratjada *Spain* **48** B10
Cala Santa Galdana *Spain* **48** B10
Calabanga *Phil.* **61** E5
Calabar *Nigeria* **83** E6
Calabogie *Canada* **115** A8
Calabozo *Venezuela* **124** B5
Calábria □ *Italy* **43** C9
Calábria △ *Italy* **43** C9
Calaburras, Pta. de *Spain* **37** J6
Calaceite *Spain* **38** D5
Calacuccia *France* **21** F13
Calafat *Romania* **28** G7
Calafell *Spain* **38** D6
Calahorra *Spain* **38** C3
Calais *France* **19** B8
Calais *U.S.A.* **113** C20
Calakmul ≈ *Mexico* **119** D7
Calalaste, Cord. de *Argentina* **126** B2
Calama *Brazil* **124** E6
Calama *Chile* **126** A2
Calamar *Colombia* **124** A4
Calamian Group *Phil.* **61** F3
Calamocha *Spain* **38** E3
Calamonte *Spain* **37** G4
Călan *Romania* **28** E7
Cañas *Spain* **37** H4
Calanda *Spain* **38** E4
Calang *Indonesia* **62** D1
Calangiánus *Italy* **42** B2
Calanscio, Sarīr *Libya* **79** C10
Calapan *Phil.* **61** E4
Călăraşi *Moldova* **29** C13
Călăraşi *Romania* **29** F12
Călăraşi □ *Romania* **29** F12
Calasparra *Spain* **39** G3
Calatafimi *Italy* **42** E5
Calatayud *Spain* **38** D3
Călăţele *Romania* **28** D8
Calato = Kalathos *Greece* **47** E10
Calauag *Phil.* **61** E5
Calavà, C. *Italy* **43** D7
Calavite, C. *Phil.* **61** E4
Calayan *Phil.* **61** B4
Calbayog *Phil.* **61** E6
Calca *Peru* **124** F4
Calcasieu L. *U.S.A.* **116** G8
Calcium *U.S.A.* **115** B9
Calcutta = Kolkata *India* **69** H13
Caldaro *Italy* **41** B8
Caldas da Rainha *Portugal* **37** F1
Caldas de Reis *Spain* **36** C2

Calder → *U.K.* 14 D6
Caldera *Chile* 126 B1
Caldera de Taburiente △ *Canary Is.* 48 F2
Caldwell *Idaho, U.S.A.* 108 E5
Caldwell *Kans., U.S.A.* 112 G5
Caldwell *Tex., U.S.A.* 116 F6
Caledon *Canada* 114 C5
Caledon *S. Africa* 88 E2
Caledon → *S. Africa* 88 E4
Caledon B. *Australia* 94 A2
Caledonia *Canada* 114 C5
Caledonia *U.S.A.* 114 D7
Calella *Spain* 38 D7
Calemba *Angola* 88 B2
Calen *Australia* 94 b
Calenzana *France* 21 F12
Caletones *Chile* 126 C1
Calexico *U.S.A.* 111 N11
Calf of Man *I. of Man* 14 C3
Calgary *Canada* 102 C6
Calheta *Madeira* 48 D2
Calhoun *U.S.A.* 117 D12
Cali *Colombia* 124 C3
Calicut *India* 66 P9
Caliente *U.S.A.* 109 H6
California *Mo., U.S.A.* 112 F7
California *Pa., U.S.A.* 114 F5
California □ *U.S.A.* 110 H7
California, Baja, T.N. = Baja California □ *Mexico* 118 B2
California, Baja, T.S. = Baja California Sur □ *Mexico* 118 B2
California Sur □ *Mexico* 118 B2
California, G. de *Mexico* 118 B2
California City *U.S.A.* 111 K9
California Hot Springs *U.S.A.* 111 K8
Cälilabad *Azerbaijan* 73 C13
Calilegua △ *Argentina* 126 B3
Cälimănești *Romania* 29 E9
Cälimani, Munții *Romania* 29 C10
Calingasta *Argentina* 126 C2
Calipatria *U.S.A.* 111 M11
Calistoga *U.S.A.* 110 G4
Calitri *Italy* 43 B8
Calitzdorp *S. Africa* 88 E3
Callabonna, L. *Australia* 95 D3
Callac *France* 18 D3
Callan *Ireland* 12 D4
Callander *U.K.* 13 E4
Callao *Peru* 124 F3
Callicoon *U.S.A.* 115 E9
Calling Lake *Canada* 102 B6
Calliope *Australia* 94 C5
Callosa de Segura *Spain* 39 G4
Callosa d'En Sarrià *Spain* 39 G4
Calma, Costa de la *Spain* 48 B9
Calne *U.K.* 15 F6
Calola *Angola* 88 B2
Calonge *Spain* 38 D8
Caloocan *Phil.* 61 D4
Calore → *Italy* 43 A7
Caloundra *Australia* 95 D5
Calpe *Spain* 39 G5
Calpella *U.S.A.* 110 F3
Calpine *U.S.A.* 110 F6
Calstock *Canada* 104 C3
Caltabellotta *Italy* 42 E6
Caltagirone *Italy* 43 E7
Caltanissetta *Italy* 43 E7
Çaltılıbük *Turkey* 45 G12
Caluire-et-Cuire *France* 19 G11
Calulo *Angola* 84 G2
Caluso *Italy* 40 C4
Calvados □ *France* 18 C6
Calvert → *Australia* 94 B2
Calvert I. *Canada* 102 C3
Calvert Ra. *Australia* 92 D3
Calvi *France* 21 F12
Calvià *Spain* 48 B9
Calvillo *Mexico* 118 C4
Calvinia *S. Africa* 88 E2
Calvo, Mte. *Italy* 41 G12
Calwa *U.S.A.* 110 J7
Calzada Almuradiel = Almuradiel *Spain* 37 G7
Calzada de Calatrava *Spain* 37 G7
Cam → *U.K.* 15 E8
Cam Lam *Vietnam* 65 G7
Cam Pha *Vietnam* 58 G6
Cam Ranh *Vietnam* 65 G7
Cam Xuyen *Vietnam* 64 C6
Camabatela *Angola* 84 F3
Camacha *Madeira* 48 D3
Camacupa *Angola* 85 G3
Camagüey *Cuba* 120 B4
Camaiore *Italy* 40 E7
Camaná *Peru* 124 G4
Camanche Res. *U.S.A.* 110 G6
Camaquã *Brazil* 127 C5
Camaquã → *Brazil* 127 C5
Câmara de Lobos *Madeira* 48 D3
Camarat, C. *France* 21 E10
Çamardı *Turkey* 72 D6
Camarès *France* 20 E6
Camaret-sur-Mer *France* 18 D2
Camargo *Mexico* 119 B5
Camargue *France* 21 E8

Camargue △ *France* 21 E8
Camarillo *U.S.A.* 111 L7
Camariñas *Spain* 36 B1
Camarón, C. *Honduras* 120 C2
Camarones *Argentina* 128 E3
Camas *Spain* 37 H4
Camas *U.S.A.* 110 E4
Camas Valley *U.S.A.* 108 E2
Camballin *Australia* 92 C3
Cambará *Brazil* 127 A5
Cambay = Khambhat *India* 68 H5
Cambay, G. of = Khambhat, G. of *India* 66 J8
Cambil *Spain* 37 H7
Cambo-les-Bains *France* 20 E2
Cambodia ■ *Asia* 64 F5
Camborne *U.K.* 15 G2
Cambrai *France* 19 B10
Cambre *Spain* 36 B2
Cambria *U.S.A.* 110 K5
Cambrian Mts. *U.K.* 15 E4
Cambridge *Canada* 114 C4
Cambridge *Jamaica* 120 a
Cambridge *N.Z.* 91 B5
Cambridge *U.K.* 15 E8
Cambridge *Mass., U.S.A.* 115 D13
Cambridge *Minn., U.S.A.* 112 C7
Cambridge *N.Y., U.S.A.* 115 C11
Cambridge *Nebr., U.S.A.* 112 E3
Cambridge *Ohio, U.S.A.* 114 F3
Cambridge Bay *Canada* 100 D11
Cambridge G. *Australia* 92 B4
Cambridge Springs *U.S.A.* 114 E4
Cambridgeshire □ *U.K.* 15 E7
Cambrils *Spain* 38 D6
Cambuci *Brazil* 127 A7
Camden *Australia* 95 B5
Camden *Ala., U.S.A.* 117 F11
Camden *Ark., U.S.A.* 116 E8
Camden *Maine, U.S.A.* 113 C19
Camden *N.J., U.S.A.* 115 G9
Camden *N.Y., U.S.A.* 115 C9
Camden *S.C., U.S.A.* 117 D14
Camden Sd. *Australia* 92 C3
Camdenton *U.S.A.* 112 F7
Camelford *U.K.* 15 G3
Çameli *Turkey* 47 D11
Camenca *Moldova* 29 B13
Camerino *Italy* 41 E10
Cameron *Ariz., U.S.A.* 109 J8
Cameron *La., U.S.A.* 116 G8
Cameron *Mo., U.S.A.* 112 F6
Cameron *Tex., U.S.A.* 116 F6
Cameron Highlands *Malaysia* 65 K3
Cameron Hills *Canada* 102 B5
Cameroon ■ *Africa* 79 G7
Camerota *Italy* 43 B8
Cameroun → *Cameroon* 83 D6
Cameroun, Mt. *Cameroon* 83 E6
Cametá *Brazil* 125 D9
Çamiçi Gölü *Turkey* 47 D9
Camiguin □ *Phil.* 61 G6
Camiguin I. *Phil.* 61 B4
Camiling *Phil.* 61 D4
Camilla *U.S.A.* 117 F12
Caminha *Portugal* 36 D2
Camino *U.S.A.* 110 G6
Cammal *U.S.A.* 114 E7
Cammarata *Italy* 42 E6
Camocim *Brazil* 125 D10
Camooweal *Australia* 94 B2
Camooweal Caves △ *Australia* 94 C2
Camopi *Fr. Guiana* 125 C8
Camotes Is. *Phil.* 61 F6
Camotes Sea *Phil.* 61 F6
Camp Hill *U.S.A.* 114 F8
Camp Nelson *U.S.A.* 111 J8
Camp Pendleton *U.S.A.* 111 M9
Camp Verde *U.S.A.* 109 J8
Camp Wood *U.S.A.* 116 G4
Campagna *Italy* 43 B8
Campana *Argentina* 126 C4
Campana, I. *Chile* 128 F1
Campanário *Madeira* 48 D2
Campania □ *Italy* 43 B7
Campanet *Spain* 48 B9
Campbell *S. Africa* 88 D3
Campbell *Calif., U.S.A.* 110 H5
Campbell *Ohio, U.S.A.* 114 E4
Campbell I. *Pac. Oc.* 96 N8
Campbell L. *Canada* 103 A7
Campbell Plateau *S. Ocean* 5 A11
Campbell River *Canada* 102 C3
Campbellford *Canada* 114 B7
Campbellpur *Pakistan* 68 C5
Campbellsville *U.S.A.* 113 G11
Campbellton *Canada* 105 C6
Campbelltown *Australia* 95 E5
Campbeltown *U.K.* 13 F3
Campeche *Mexico* 119 D6
Campeche □ *Mexico* 119 D6
Campeche, Golfo de *Mexico* 119 D6
Câmpeni *Romania* 28 D8
Camperdown *Australia* 95 F3
Camperville *Canada* 103 C8
Campi Salentina *Italy* 43 B11
Campia Turzii *Romania* 29 D8

Câmpia Turzii *Romania* 29 D8
Campidano *Italy* 42 C1
Campíglia Maríttima *Italy* 40 E7
Campillo de Altobuey *Spain* 39 F3
Campillos *Spain* 37 H6
Câmpina *Romania* 29 E10
Campina Grande *Brazil* 125 E11
Campinas *Brazil* 127 A6
Campione *Italy* 21 C12
Campli *Italy* 41 F10
Campo *Spain* 38 C5
Campo de Criptana *Spain* 37 F7
Campo de Gibraltar *Spain* 37 J5
Campo Grande *Brazil* 125 H8
Campo Maior *Brazil* 125 D10
Campo Maior *Portugal* 37 F3
Campo Mourão *Brazil* 127 A5
Campo Túres *Italy* 41 B8
Campobasso *Italy* 43 A7
Campobello di Licata *Italy* 42 E6
Campobello di Mazara *Italy* 42 E5
Campofelice di Roccella *Italy* 42 E6
Campomarino *Italy* 41 G12
Camporeale *Italy* 42 E6
Camporrobles *Spain* 38 F3
Campos *Brazil* 127 A7
Campos *Spain* 48 B10
Campos Belos *Brazil* 125 F9
Campos del Paraíso = Carrascosa del Campo *Spain* 38 E2
Campos Novos *Brazil* 127 B5
Camprodon *Spain* 38 C7
Camptonville *U.S.A.* 110 F5
Camptown *U.S.A.* 115 E8
Câmpulung *Argeș, Romania* 29 E10
Câmpulung *Suceava, Romania* 29 C10
Câmpuri *Romania* 29 D11
Camrose *Canada* 102 C6
Camsell Portage *Canada* 103 B7
Çamyuva *Turkey* 47 E12
Can *Turkey* 45 F11
Can Clavo *Spain* 48 C7
Can Creu *Spain* 48 C7
Can Gio *Vietnam* 65 G6
Can Pastilla *Spain* 48 B9
Can Tho *Vietnam* 65 G5
Canaan *U.S.A.* 115 D11
Canada ■ *N. Amer.* 100 G11
Canada Abyssal Plain *Arctic* 4 B18
Canada Basin *Arctic* 4 B18
Cañada de Gómez *Argentina* 126 C3
Canadian *U.S.A.* 116 D4
Canadian → *U.S.A.* 116 D7
Canadian Shield *Canada* 98 D12
Canajoharie *U.S.A.* 115 D10
Çanakkale *Turkey* 45 F10
Çanakkale □ *Turkey* 45 F10
Çanakkale Boğazı *Turkey* 45 F10
Canal Flats *Canada* 102 C5
Canalejas *Argentina* 126 D2
Canals *Argentina* 126 C3
Canals *Spain* 39 G4
Canandaigua *U.S.A.* 114 D7
Canandaigua L. *U.S.A.* 114 D7
Cananea *Mexico* 118 A2
Canarias, Is. *Atl. Oc.* 48 F4
Canaries *St. Lucia* 121 f
Canarreos, Arch. de los *Cuba* 120 B3
Canary Is. = Canarias, Is. *Atl. Oc.* 48 F4
Canaseraga *U.S.A.* 114 D7
Canatlán *Mexico* 118 C4
Canaveral, C. *U.S.A.* 117 G14
Canaveral *U.S.A.* 117 G14
Cañaveruelas *Spain* 38 E2
Canavieiras *Brazil* 125 G11
Canberra *Australia* 95 F4
Canby *Calif., U.S.A.* 108 F3
Canby *Minn., U.S.A.* 112 C5
Canby *Oreg., U.S.A.* 110 E4
Cancale *France* 18 D5
Canche → *France* 19 B8
Canchungo *Guinea-Biss.* 82 C1
Cancún *Mexico* 119 C7
Candelaria *Argentina* 127 B4
Candelaria *Canary Is.* 48 F3
Candelario *U.S.A.* 109 G9
Cândeleda *Spain* 36 E5
Candelo *Australia* 95 F4
Candi Dasa *Indonesia* 63 J18
Candia = Iraklio *Greece* 49 D7
Candia, Sea of = Crete, Sea of *Greece* 47 E7
Candle L. *Canada* 103 C7
Candlemas I. *Antarctica* 5 B1
Cando *U.S.A.* 112 A4
Candon *Phil.* 61 C4
Canea = Chania *Greece* 49 D6
Canelli *Italy* 40 D5
Canelones *Uruguay* 127 C4

Canet-Plage *France* 20 F7
Cañete *Chile* 126 D1
Cañete *Spain* 38 E3
Cañete de las Torres *Spain* 37 H6
Cangas *Spain* 36 C2
Cangas de Onís *Spain* 36 B5
Cangas del Narcea *Spain* 36 B4
Cangnan *China* 59 D13
Canguaretama *Brazil* 125 E11
Canguçu *Brazil* 127 C5
Canguçu, Serra do *Brazil* 127 C5
Cangwu *China* 59 F8
Cangxi *China* 58 B5
Cangyuan *China* 58 F2
Cangzhou *China* 56 E9
Caniapiscau → *Canada* 105 A6
Caniapiscau, L. *Canada* 105 B6
Canicattì *Italy* 42 E6
Canicattini Bagni *Italy* 43 E8
Caniles *Spain* 37 H8
Canim Lake *Canada* 102 C4
Canindeyu □ *Paraguay* 127 A5
Canino *Italy* 41 F8
Canisteo *U.S.A.* 114 D7
Canisteo → *U.S.A.* 114 D7
Cañitas de Felipe Pescador *Mexico* 118 C4
Cañizal *Spain* 36 D5
Canjáyar *Spain* 37 H8
Çankırı *Turkey* 72 B5
Çankırı □ *Turkey* 72 B5
Cankuzo *Burundi* 86 C3
Canmore *Canada* 102 C5
Cann River *Australia* 95 F4
Canna *U.K.* 13 D2
Cannanore *India* 66 P9
Cannes *France* 21 E11
Canning Town = Port Canning *India* 69 H13
Cannington *Canada* 114 B5
Cannóbio *Italy* 40 B5
Cannock *U.K.* 15 E5
Cannonball → *U.S.A.* 112 B3
Cannondale Mt. *Australia* 94 D4
Cannonsville Res. *U.S.A.* 115 D9
Cannonvale *Australia* 94 b
Canoas *Brazil* 127 B5
Canoe L. *Canada* 103 B7
Cañon City *U.S.A.* 108 G11
Cañón de Río Blanco △ *Mexico* 119 D5
Cañón del Río Lobos △ *Spain* 36 D7
Cañón del Sumidero △ *Mexico* 119 D5
Canonniers Pt. *Mauritius* 85 d
Canora *Canada* 103 C8
Canosa di Púglia *Italy* 43 A9
Canowindra *Australia* 95 E4
Canso *Canada* 105 C7
Cantabria □ *Spain* 36 B7
Cantabria, Sierra de *Spain* 38 C2
Cantabrian Mts. = Cantábrica, Cordillera *Spain* 36 C5
Cantábrica, Cordillera *Spain* 36 C5
Cantal □ *France* 20 C6
Cantal, Plomb du *France* 20 C6
Cantanhede *Portugal* 36 E2
Cantavieja *Spain* 38 E4
Čantavir *Serbia* 28 E4
Cantemir *Moldova* 29 D13
Canterbury *Australia* 94 D3
Canterbury *U.K.* 15 F9
Canterbury Bight *N.Z.* 91 F3
Canterbury Plains *N.Z.* 91 E3
Cantil *U.S.A.* 111 K9
Cantillana *Spain* 37 H5
Canton = Guangzhou *China* 59 F9
Canton *Ga., U.S.A.* 117 D12
Canton *Ill., U.S.A.* 112 E8
Canton *Miss., U.S.A.* 117 E9
Canton *Mo., U.S.A.* 112 E8
Canton *N.Y., U.S.A.* 115 B9
Canton *Ohio, U.S.A.* 114 F3
Canton *Pa., U.S.A.* 114 E8
Canton *S. Dak., U.S.A.* 112 D5
Canton L. *U.S.A.* 116 C5
Cantù *Italy* 40 C6
Canudos *Brazil* 124 E7
Canumã → *Brazil* 124 D7
Canutama *Brazil* 124 E6
Canutillo *U.S.A.* 116 F1
Canvey *U.K.* 15 F8
Canyon *U.S.A.* 116 D4
Canyon De Chelly △ *U.S.A.* 109 H9
Canyonlands △ *U.S.A.* 109 G9
Canyons of the Ancients △ *U.S.A.* 109 H9
Canyonville *U.S.A.* 108 E2
Cao Bang *Vietnam* 58 F6
Cao He → *China* 57 D13
Cao Lanh *Vietnam* 65 G5
Cao Xian *China* 56 G8
Cáorle *Italy* 41 C9
Cap-aux-Meules *Canada* 105 C7
Cap-Chat *Canada* 105 C6
Cap-de-la-Madeleine *Canada* 104 C5
Cap-Haïtien *Haiti* 121 C5
Cap Pt. *St. Lucia* 121 f

Capac *U.S.A.* 114 C2
Capáccio *Italy* 43 B8
Capaci *Italy* 42 D6
Capanaparo → *Venezuela* 124 B5
Capánnori *Italy* 40 E7
Capbreton *France* 20 E2
Capdenac *France* 20 D6
Capdepera *Spain* 38 B10
Cape → *Australia* 94 C4
Cape Arid △ *Australia* 93 F3
Cape Barren I. *Australia* 95 G4
Cape Breton Highlands △ *Canada* 105 C7
Cape Breton I. *Canada* 105 C7
Cape Charles *U.S.A.* 113 G15
Cape Coast *Ghana* 83 D4
Cape Cod △ *U.S.A.* 113 E18
Cape Coral *U.S.A.* 117 H14
Cape Crawford *Australia* 94 B2
Cape Dorset = Kinngait *Canada* 101 E16
Cape Fear → *U.S.A.* 117 E15
Cape Girardeau *U.S.A.* 112 G9
Cape Hatteras △ *U.S.A.* 117 D17
Cape Hillsborough △ *Australia* 94 b
Cape Le Grand △ *Australia* 93 F3
Cape Lookout △ *U.S.A.* 117 D16
Cape May *U.S.A.* 113 F16
Cape May Point *U.S.A.* 113 F16
Cape Melville △ *Australia* 94 A3
Cape Mount △ *Liberia* 82 D2
Cape Range △ *Australia* 92 D1
Cape St. George *Canada* 105 C8
Cape Tormentine *Canada* 105 C7
Cape Town *S. Africa* 88 E2
Cape Upstart △ *Australia* 94 B4
Cape Verde Is. ■ *Atl. Oc.* 78 b
Cape Vincent *U.S.A.* 115 B8
Cape York Peninsula *Australia* 94 A3
Capela *Brazil* 125 F11
Capella *Australia* 94 C4
Capendu *France* 20 E6
Capestang *France* 20 E7
Capesterre-Belle-Eau *Guadeloupe* 120 b
Capesterre-de-Marie-Galante *Guadeloupe* 120 b
Capim → *Brazil* 125 D9
Capistrello *Italy* 41 G10
Capitan *U.S.A.* 109 K11
Capitán Arturo Prat *Antarctica* 5 C17
Capitol Reef △ *U.S.A.* 109 G8
Capitola *U.S.A.* 110 J5
Capizzi *Italy* 43 E7
Capoche → *Mozam.* 87 F3
Capodichino, Nápoli ✈ (NAP) *Italy* 43 B7
Capoterra *Italy* 42 C1
Cappadocia *Turkey* 72 C6
Capraia *Italy* 40 E6
Caprara, Pta. *Italy* 42 A1
Caprarola *Italy* 41 F9
Capreol *Canada* 104 C3
Caprera *Italy* 42 A2
Capri *Italy* 43 B7
Capricorn Coast *Australia* 94 C5
Capricorn Group *Australia* 94 C5
Capricorn Ra. *Australia* 92 D2
Caprino Veronese *Italy* 40 C7
Caprivi Game △ *Namibia* 88 B3
Caprivi Strip *Namibia* 88 B3
Caps et Marais d'Opale △ *France* 19 B9
Captains Flat *Australia* 95 F4
Captieux *France* 20 D3
Capulin Volcano △ *U.S.A.* 116 C3
Caquetá → *Colombia* 124 D5
Caracal *Romania* 29 F9
Caracas *Venezuela* 124 A5
Caracol *Belize* 120 C2
Caracol *Mato Grosso do Sul, Brazil* 125 A4
Caracol *Piauí, Brazil* 125 E10
Caráglio *Italy* 40 D4
Carajas *Brazil* 125 E8
Carajás, Serra dos *Brazil* 125 E8
Carangola *Brazil* 127 A7
Caransebeș *Romania* 28 E7
Carantec *France* 18 D3
Caraquet *Canada* 105 C6
Caraș Severin □ *Romania* 28 E7
Caraṣova *Romania* 28 E6
Caratasca, L. de *Honduras* 120 C3
Caratinga *Brazil* 125 G10
Caraúbas *Brazil* 125 E11
Caravaca de la Cruz *Spain* 39 G3
Caravaggio *Italy* 40 C6
Caravela *Guinea-Biss.* 82 C1
Caravelas *Brazil* 125 G11
Caraveli *Peru* 124 G4
Caravelle, Presqu'île de la *Martinique* 120 c
Caraz *Peru* 124 E3
Carazinho *Brazil* 127 B5
Carballino = O Carballiño *Spain* 36 C2
Carballo *Spain* 36 B2

Carberry *Canada* 103 D9
Carbó *Mexico* 118 B2
Carbón, L. del *Argentina* 122 G3
Carbonara, C. *Italy* 42 C2
Carbondale *Colo., U.S.A.* 108 G10
Carbondale *Ill., U.S.A.* 112 G9
Carbondale *Pa., U.S.A.* 115 E9
Carbonear *Canada* 105 C9
Carboneras *Spain* 39 J3
Carboneras de Guadazaón *Spain* 38 F3
Carbónia *Italy* 42 C1
Carcabuey *Spain* 37 H6
Carcagente = Carcaixent *Spain* 39 F4
Carcaixent *Spain* 39 F4
Carcajou *Canada* 102 B5
Carcar *Phil.* 61 F5
Carcarana → *Argentina* 126 C3
Carcasse, C. *Haiti* 121 C5
Carcassonne *France* 20 E6
Carcross *Canada* 102 A2
Çardak *Çanakkale, Turkey* 45 F10
Çardak *Denizli, Turkey* 47 D11
Cardamom Hills *India* 66 Q10
Cardamon Mts. = Kravanh, Chuor Phnum *Cambodia* 65 G4
Cardeña *Spain* 37 G6
Cárdenas *Cuba* 120 B3
Cárdenas *San Luis Potosí, Mexico* 119 C5
Cárdenas *Tabasco, Mexico* 119 D6
Cardener → *Spain* 38 D6
Cardenete *Spain* 38 F3
Cardiff *U.K.* 15 F4
Cardiff □ *U.K.* 15 F4
Cardiff-by-the-Sea *U.S.A.* 111 M9
Cardigan *U.K.* 15 E3
Cardigan B. *U.K.* 15 E3
Cardinal *Canada* 115 B9
Cardona *Spain* 38 D6
Cardona *Uruguay* 126 C4
Cardoso, Ilha do *Brazil* 127 B5
Cardston *Canada* 102 D6
Cardwell *Australia* 94 B4
Careen L. *Canada* 103 B7
Carei *Romania* 28 C7
Careme = Ciremay *Indonesia* 63 G13
Carentan *France* 18 C5
Carey *U.S.A.* 108 E7
Carey, L. *Australia* 93 E3
Carey L. *Canada* 103 A8
Careysburg *Liberia* 82 D2
Cargèse *France* 21 F12
Carhaix-Plouguer *France* 18 D3
Carhué *Argentina* 126 D3
Caria *Turkey* 47 D10
Cariacica *Brazil* 125 H10
Cariati *Italy* 43 C9
Caribbean Sea *W. Indies* 121 D5
Cariboo Mts. *Canada* 102 C4
Caribou *U.S.A.* 113 B19
Caribou → *Man., Canada* 103 B10
Caribou → *N.W.T., Canada* 102 A3
Caribou I. *Canada* 104 C2
Caribou Is. *Canada* 102 A6
Caribou L. *Man., Canada* 103 B9
Caribou L. *Ont., Canada* 104 B2
Caribou Mts. *Canada* 102 B5
Caribou River △ *Canada* 103 B9
Caribrod = Dimitrovgrad *Serbia* 44 C6
Carichíc *Mexico* 118 B3
Carigara *Phil.* 61 F6
Carignan *France* 19 C12
Carignano *Italy* 40 D4
Carinda *Australia* 95 E4
Cariñena *Spain* 38 D3
Carinhanha *Brazil* 125 F10
Carinhanha → *Brazil* 125 F10
Carini *Italy* 42 D6
Cariño *Spain* 36 B3
Carínola *Italy* 42 A6
Carinthia = Kärnten □ *Austria* 26 E6
Caripito *Venezuela* 124 A6
Carlet *Spain* 39 F4
Carleton, Mt. *Canada* 105 C6
Carleton Place *Canada* 115 A8
Carletonville *S. Africa* 88 D4
Cârlibaba *Romania* 29 C10
Carlin *U.S.A.* 108 F5
Carlingford L. *U.K.* 12 B5
Carlinville *U.S.A.* 112 F9
Carlisle *U.K.* 14 C5
Carlisle *U.S.A.* 114 F7
Carlisle B. *Barbados* 121 g
Carlisle I. *Australia* 94 b
Carlit, Pic *France* 20 F5
Carloforte *Italy* 42 C1
Carlos Casares *Argentina* 126 D3
Carlos Tejedor *Argentina* 126 D3
Carlow *Ireland* 12 D5
Carlow □ *Ireland* 12 D5
Carlsbad *Calif., U.S.A.* 111 M9
Carlsbad *N. Mex., U.S.A.* 109 J12
Carlsbad Caverns △ *U.S.A.* 109 K11
Carluke *U.K.* 13 F5

Carlyle *Canada* 103 D8
Carmacks *Canada* 100 E4
Carmagnola *Italy* 40 D4
Carman *Canada* 103 D9
Carmarthen *U.K.* 15 F3
Carmarthen B. *U.K.* 15 F3
Carmarthenshire □ *U.K.* 15 F3
Carmaux *France* 20 D6
Carmel *U.S.A.* 115 E11
Carmel-by-the-Sea *U.S.A.* 110 J5
Carmel Valley *U.S.A.* 110 J5
Carmelo *Uruguay* 126 C4
Carmen *Paraguay* 127 B4
Carmen ~ *Mexico* 118 A3
Carmen, I. *Mexico* 118 B2
Carmen de Patagones
  Argentina 128 E4
Cármenes *Spain* 36 C5
Carmensa *Argentina* 126 D2
Carmi *Canada* 102 D5
Carmi *U.S.A.* 112 F9
Carmichael *U.S.A.* 110 G5
Carmila *Australia* 94 C4
Carmona *Costa Rica* 120 E2
Carmona *Spain* 37 H5
Carn Ban *U.K.* 13 D4
Carn Eige *U.K.* 13 D3
Carnac *France* 18 E3
Carnamah *Australia* 93 E2
Carnarvon *Australia* 93 D1
Carnarvon *Canada* 114 A6
Carnarvon *S. Africa* 88 E3
Carnarvon △ *Australia* 94 C4
Carnarvon Ra. *Queens.,*
  Australia 94 D4
Carnarvon Ra. *W. Austral.,*
  Australia 93 E3
Carnation *U.S.A.* 110 C5
Carncastle *U.K.* 12 B6
Carndonagh *Ireland* 12 A4
Carnduff *Canada* 103 D8
Carnegie *U.S.A.* 114 F4
Carnegie, L. *Australia* 93 E3
Carnegie Ridge *Pac. Oc.* 97 H19
Carnic Alps = Karnische
  Alpen *Europe* 26 E6
Carniche Alpi = Karnische
  Alpen *Europe* 26 E6
Carnot *C.A.R.* 84 D3
Carnot, C. *Australia* 95 E2
Carnot B. *Australia* 92 C3
Carnoustie *U.K.* 13 E6
Carnsore Pt. *Ireland* 12 D5
Caro *U.S.A.* 113 D12
Caroga Lake *U.S.A.* 115 C10
Carol City *U.S.A.* 117 J14
Carolina *Brazil* 125 E9
Carolina *Puerto Rico* 121 d
Carolina *S. Africa* 89 D5
Caroline I. *Kiribati* 97 H12
Caroline Is. *Micronesia* 96 G6
Caroni *Trin. & Tob.* 125 K15
Caroní ~ *Venezuela* 124 B6
Caronie = Nébrodi, Monti
  Italy 43 E7
Caroona *Australia* 95 E5
Carpathians *Europe* 23 D11
Carpaţii Meridionali *Romania* 29 E9
Carpentaria, G. of *Australia* 94 A2
Carpentras *France* 21 D9
Carpi *Italy* 40 D7
Cărpineni *Moldova* 29 D13
Carpinteria *U.S.A.* 111 L7
Carpio *Spain* 36 D5
Carr Boyd Ra. *Australia* 92 C4
Carra, L. *Ireland* 12 C2
Carrabelle *U.S.A.* 117 G12
Carraig Mhachaire Rois =
  Carrickmacross *Ireland* 12 C5
Carraig na Siúire =
  Carrick-on-Suir *Ireland* 12 D4
Carral *Spain* 36 B2
Carranya ◎ *Australia* 92 C4
Carranza, Presa V. *Mexico* 118 B4
Carrara *Italy* 40 D7
Carrascal *Phil.* 61 G6
Carrascosa del Campo *Spain* 38 E2
Carrauntoohill *Ireland* 12 D2
Carrick-on-Shannon *Ireland* 12 C3
Carrick-on-Suir *Ireland* 12 D4
Carrickfergus *U.K.* 12 B6
Carrickmacross *Ireland* 12 C5
Carrieton *Australia* 95 E2
Carrillo *Mexico* 118 B4
Carrington *U.S.A.* 112 B4
Carrión ~ *Spain* 36 C6
Carrión de los Condes *Spain* 36 C6
Carrizal Bajo *Chile* 126 B1
Carrizalillo *Chile* 126 B1
Carrizo Cr. ~ *U.S.A.* 109 H12
Carrizo Plain ⌂ *U.S.A.* 110 K7
Carrizo Springs *U.S.A.* 116 G5
Carrizozo *U.S.A.* 109 K11
Carroll *U.S.A.* 112 D6
Carrollton Ga., *U.S.A.* 117 E12
Carrollton Ill., *U.S.A.* 112 F8
Carrollton Ky., *U.S.A.* 113 F11
Carrollton Mo., *U.S.A.* 112 F7
Carrollton Ohio, *U.S.A.* 114 F3

Carron ~ *U.K.* 13 D4
Carron, L. *U.K.* 13 D3
Carrot ~ *Canada* 103 C8
Carrot River *Canada* 103 C8
Carrouges *France* 18 D6
Carrù *Italy* 40 D4
Carruthers *Canada* 103 C7
Carsa Dek *Ethiopia* 81 F4
Çarşamba *Turkey* 72 B7
Carsóli *Italy* 41 F10
Carson *Calif., U.S.A.* 111 M8
Carson *N. Dak., U.S.A.* 112 B3
Carson ~ *U.S.A.* 110 F8
Carson City *U.S.A.* 110 F7
Carson Sink *U.S.A.* 108 G4
Cartagena *Colombia* 124 A3
Cartagena *Spain* 39 H4
Cartago *Colombia* 124 C3
Cartago *Costa Rica* 120 E3
Cártama *Spain* 37 J6
Cartaxo *Portugal* 37 F2
Cartaya *Spain* 37 H3
Cartersville *U.S.A.* 117 D12
Carterton *N.Z.* 91 D5
Carthage *Tunisia* 42 F3
Carthage *Ill., U.S.A.* 112 E8
Carthage *Mo., U.S.A.* 112 G6
Carthage *N.Y., U.S.A.* 113 D16
Carthage *Tex., U.S.A.* 116 E7
Cartier I. *Australia* 92 B3
Cartwright *Canada* 105 B8
Caruaru *Brazil* 125 E11
Carúpano *Venezuela* 124 A6
Caruthersville *U.S.A.* 112 G9
Carvin *France* 19 B9
Carvoeiro *Brazil* 124 D6
Carvoeiro, C. *Portugal* 37 F1
Cary *U.S.A.* 117 D15
Casa, Pas de la = Envalira,
  Port d' *Europe* 38 C6
Casa Branca *Portugal* 37 G2
Casa de Piedra *Argentina* 126 D2
Casa de Piedra, Embalse
  Argentina 126 D2
Casa Grande *U.S.A.* 109 K8
Casa Nova *Brazil* 125 E10
Casablanca *Chile* 126 C1
Casablanca *Morocco* 78 B4
Casacalenda *Italy* 41 G11
Casalbordino *Italy* 41 F11
Casale Monferrato *Italy* 40 C5
Casalmaggiore *Italy* 40 D7
Casalpusterlengo *Italy* 40 C6
Casamance ~ *Senegal* 82 C1
Casarano *Italy* 43 B11
Casares *Spain* 37 J5
Casas Ibáñez *Spain* 39 F3
Casasimarro *Spain* 39 F2
Casatejada *Spain* 36 F5
Casavieja *Spain* 36 E6
Cascada de Basaseachic △
  Mexico 118 B3
Cascade *Seychelles* 85 b
Cascade *Idaho, U.S.A.* 108 D5
Cascade *Mont., U.S.A.* 108 C8
Cascade Locks *U.S.A.* 110 E5
Cascade Ra. *U.S.A.* 110 D5
Cascade Res. *U.S.A.* 108 D5
Cascades, Pte. des *Réunion* 85 c
Cascais *Portugal* 37 G1
Cascavel *Brazil* 127 A5
Cáscina *Italy* 40 E7
Casco B. *U.S.A.* 113 D19
Caselle Torinese *Italy* 40 C4
Caserta *Italy* 43 A7
Casey *Antarctica* 5 C8
Caseyr, Raas = Asir, Ras
  Somali Rep. 75 E5
Cashel *Ireland* 12 D4
Casiguran *Phil.* 61 C5
Casilda *Argentina* 126 C3
Casimcea *Romania* 29 F13
Casino *Australia* 95 D5
Casiquiare ~ *Venezuela* 124 C5
Čáslav *Czech Rep.* 26 B8
Casma *Peru* 124 E3
Casmalia *U.S.A.* 111 L6
Cásola Valsénio *Italy* 41 D8
Cásoli *Italy* 41 F11
Caspe *Spain* 38 D4
Casper *U.S.A.* 108 E10
Caspian Depression *Eurasia* 35 G9
Caspian Sea *Eurasia* 52 E6
Cass City *U.S.A.* 114 C1
Cass Lake *U.S.A.* 112 B6
Cassà de la Selva *Spain* 38 D7
Cassadaga *U.S.A.* 114 D5
Cassano allo Iónio *Italy* 43 C9
Cassel *France* 19 B9
Casselman *Canada* 115 A9
Casselton *U.S.A.* 112 B5
Cassiar Mts. *Canada* 102 B2
Cassino *Italy* 42 A6
Cassis *France* 21 E9
Cassville *U.S.A.* 112 G7
Castagneto Carducci *Italy* 40 E7
Castaic *U.S.A.* 111 L8
Castalia *U.S.A.* 114 E2
Castanhal *Brazil* 125 D9

Castara *Trin. & Tob.* 125 J16
Castéggio *Italy* 40 C6
Castejón de Monegros *Spain* 38 D4
Castèl di Sangro *Italy* 41 G11
Castèl San Giovanni *Italy* 40 C6
Castèl San Pietro Terme *Italy* 41 D8
Castelbuono *Italy* 43 E7
Castelfidardo *Italy* 41 E10
Castelfiorentino *Italy* 40 E7
Castelfranco Emília *Italy* 41 D8
Castelfranco Véneto *Italy* 41 C9
Casteljaloux *France* 20 D4
Castellabate *Italy* 43 B7
Castellammare, G. di *Italy* 42 D5
Castellammare del Golfo
  Italy 42 D5
Castellammare di Stábia
  Italy 43 B7
Castellamonte *Italy* 40 C4
Castellane *France* 21 E10
Castellaneta *Italy* 43 B9
Castelli *Argentina* 126 D4
Castelló de la Plana *Spain* 38 F4
Castellón de la Plana □ *Spain* 38 E4
Castellote *Spain* 38 E4
Castelmáuro *Italy* 41 G11
Castelnau-de-Médoc *France* 20 C3
Castelnau-Magnoac *France* 20 E4
Castelnaudary *France* 20 E5
Castelnovo ne' Monti *Italy* 40 D7
Castelnuovo di Val di
  Cécina *Italy* 40 E7
Castelo *Brazil* 127 A7
Castelo Branco *Portugal* 36 F3
Castelo Branco □ *Portugal* 36 F3
Castelo de Paiva *Portugal* 36 D2
Castelo de Vide *Portugal* 37 F3
Castelsardo *Italy* 42 B1
Castelsarrasin *France* 20 D5
Casteltérmini *Italy* 42 E6
Castelvetrano *Italy* 42 E5
Castèn *France* 20 E2
Castéra *U.K.* 14 C3
Castlebar *Ireland* 12 C2
Castlebay *U.K.* 13 E1
Castleblaney *Ireland* 12 B5
Castlederg *U.K.* 12 B4
Castleford *U.K.* 14 D6
Castlegar *Canada* 102 D5
Castlemaine *Australia* 95 F3
Castlemaine *Ireland* 12 D2
Castlepollard *Ireland* 12 C4
Castlerea *Ireland* 12 C3
Castlereagh ~ *Australia* 95 E4
Castlereagh B. *Australia* 94 A2
Castleton *U.S.A.* 115 C11
Castleton-on-Hudson
  U.S.A. 115 D11
Castletown *I. of Man* 14 C3
Castletown Bearhaven
  Ireland 12 E2
Castor *Canada* 102 C6
Castor ~ *Canada* 104 B4
Castorland *U.S.A.* 115 C9
Castres *France* 20 E6
Castricum *Neths.* 17 B4
Castries *St. Lucia* 121 f
Castril *Spain* 37 H8
Castro *Brazil* 127 A6
Castro *Chile* 128 E2
Castro Alves *Brazil* 125 F11
Castro del Río *Spain* 37 H6
Castro-Urdiales *Spain* 36 B7
Castro Valley *U.S.A.* 110 H4
Castro Verde *Portugal* 37 H2
Castrojeriz *Spain* 36 C6
Castropol *Spain* 36 B4
Castroreale *Italy* 43 D8
Castrovillari *Italy* 43 C9
Castroville *U.S.A.* 110 J5
Castuera *Spain* 37 G5
Çat *Turkey* 73 C9
Cat Ba, Dao *Vietnam* 64 B6
Cat Ba △ *Vietnam* 64 B6
Cat I. *Bahamas* 121 B4
Cat L. *Canada* 104 B1
Cat Lake *Canada* 104 B1
Cat Tien △ *Vietnam* 65 G6
Čata *Slovak Rep.* 27 D11

Catacamas *Honduras* 120 D2
Cataguases *Brazil* 127 A7
Çatak *Turkey* 73 C10
Çatalağzı *Turkey* 72 B4
Catalão *Brazil* 125 G9
Catalca *Turkey* 45 E12
Catalina *Canada* 105 C9
Catalina *Chile* 126 B2
Catalina *U.S.A.* 109 K8
Cataluña = Cataluña □
  Spain 38 D6
Cataluña □ *Spain* 38 D6
Catamarca *Argentina* 126 B2
Catamarca □ *Argentina* 126 B2
Catanauan *Phil.* 61 E5
Catanduanes □ *Phil.* 61 E6
Catanduva *Brazil* 127 A6
Catánia *Italy* 43 E8
Catánia, G. di *Italy* 43 E8
Catanzaro *Italy* 43 D9
Catarman *Phil.* 61 E6
Catatumbo-Bari △ *Colombia* 121 E5
Catbalogan *Phil.* 61 F6
Cateel *Phil.* 61 H7
Catembe *Mozam.* 89 D5
Caterham *U.K.* 15 F7
Cathair na Mart =
  Westport *Ireland* 12 C2
Cathair Saidhbhín =
  Cahersiveen *Ireland* 12 E1
Cathcart *S. Africa* 88 E4
Cathedral City *U.S.A.* 111 M10
Cathlamet *U.S.A.* 110 D3
Catió *Guinea-Biss.* 82 C1
Catlettsburg *U.S.A.* 113 F12
Catlin *U.S.A.* 114 E2
Catoche, C. *Mexico* 119 C7
Cátria, Mte. *Italy* 41 E9
Catriló *Argentina* 126 D3
Catrimani *Brazil* 124 C6
Catrimani ~ *Brazil* 124 C6
Catskill *U.S.A.* 115 D11
Catskill Mts. *U.S.A.* 115 D10
Catt, Mt. *Australia* 94 A1
Cattaraugus *U.S.A.* 114 D6
Catterick *U.K.* 14 C6
Cattólica *Italy* 41 E9
Cattólica Eraclea *Italy* 42 E6
Catuala *Angola* 88 B2
Catuane *Mozam.* 89 D5
Catur *Mozam.* 87 E4
Caubvick, Mt. = Iberville,
  Mt. d' *Canada* 101 F19
Cauca ~ *Colombia* 124 B4
Caucaia *Brazil* 125 D11
Caucasus Mountains *Eurasia* 35 J7
Caucete *Argentina* 126 C2
Caudete *Spain* 39 G3
Caudry *France* 19 B10
Caulnes *France* 18 D4
Caulónia *Italy* 43 D9
Caungula *Angola* 84 F3
Cauquenes *Chile* 126 D1
Caura ~ *Venezuela* 124 B6
Cauresi ~ *Mozam.* 87 F3
Căuşani *Moldova* 29 D14
Causapscal *Canada* 105 C6
Caussade *France* 20 D5
Causse-Méjean *France* 20 D7
Causses du Quercy △ *France* 20 D5
Cauterets *France* 20 F4
Cauvery ~ *India* 66 P11
Caux, Pays de *France* 18 C7
Cava de' Tirreni *Italy* 43 B7
Cávado ~ *Portugal* 36 D2
Cavaillon *France* 21 E9
Cavalaire-sur-Mer *France* 21 E10
Cavalese *Italy* 41 B8
Cavalier *U.S.A.* 112 A5
Cavalla = Cavally ~ *Africa* 82 E3
Cavalla △ *Liberia* 82 D3
Cavallo, Î. de *France* 21 G13
Cavally ~ *Africa* 82 E3
Cavan *Ireland* 12 B4
Cavan □ *Ireland* 12 C4
Cavárzere *Italy* 41 C9
Çavdarhisar *Turkey* 47 B11
Çavdır *Turkey* 47 D11
Cave Creek *U.S.A.* 109 K8
Cavenagh Ra. *Australia* 93 E4
Cavendish *Australia* 95 F3
Caviana, I. *Brazil* 125 C8
Cavite *Phil.* 61 D4
Cavnic *Romania* 29 C8
Cavour *Italy* 40 D4
Cavtat *Croatia* 44 D2
Cawndilla L. *Australia* 95 E3
Cawnpore = Kanpur *India* 69 F9
Caxias *Brazil* 125 D10
Caxias do Sul *Brazil* 127 B5
Çay *Turkey* 72 C4
Cay Sal Bank *Bahamas* 120 B4
Cayambe *Ecuador* 124 C3

Çaycuma *Turkey* 72 B5
Çayeli *Turkey* 73 B9
Cayenne *Fr. Guiana* 125 B8
Caygören Barajı *Turkey* 47 B10
Çayıralan *Turkey* 72 C6
Çaylı *Azerbaijan* 73 B12
Caylus *France* 20 D5
Cayman Brac *Cayman Is.* 120 C4
Cayman Is. ☑ *W. Indies* 120 C3
Cayman Trough *Caribbean* 98 H11
Cayres *France* 20 D7
Cayuga *Canada* 114 D5
Cayuga *U.S.A.* 115 D8
Cayuga Heights *U.S.A.* 115 D8
Cayuga L. *U.S.A.* 115 D8
Cazalla de la Sierra *Spain* 37 H5
Căzăneşti *Romania* 29 F12
Cazaubon *France* 20 E3
Cazaux, G. de Sanguinet,
  Étang de *France* 20 D2
Cazenovia *U.S.A.* 115 D9
Cazères *France* 20 E4
Cazin *Bos.-H.* 41 D12
Čazma *Croatia* 41 C13
Cazombo *Angola* 85 G4
Cazorla *Spain* 37 H7
Cazorla, Sierra de *Spain* 37 G8
Cea ~ *Spain* 36 C5
Ceamurlia de Jos *Romania* 29 F13
Ceanannus Mor *Ireland* 12 C5
Ceará = Fortaleza *Brazil* 125 D11
Ceará □ *Brazil* 125 E11
Ceará-Mirim *Brazil* 125 E11
Ceatharlach = Carlow
  Ireland 12 D5
Ceauru, L. *Romania* 29 F8
Cébaco, I. de *Panama* 120 E3
Cebollar *Argentina* 126 B2
Cebollera, Sierra de *Spain* 38 D2
Cebreros *Spain* 36 E6
Cebu *Phil.* 61 F5
Cebu □ *Phil.* 61 F5
Čečava *Bos.-H.* 28 F2
Ceccano *Italy* 42 A6
Cece *Hungary* 28 D3
Cechi *Ivory C.* 82 D4
Cechy *Czech Rep.* 26 A7
Cecil Plains *Australia* 95 D5
Cécina *Italy* 40 E7
Cécina ~ *Italy* 40 E7
Ceclavín *Spain* 36 F4
Cedar ~ *U.S.A.* 112 E8
Cedar City *U.S.A.* 109 H7
Cedar Creek Res. *U.S.A.* 116 E6
Cedar Falls *Iowa, U.S.A.* 112 D7
Cedar Falls *Wash., U.S.A.* 110 C5
Cedar Key *U.S.A.* 117 G13
Cedar L. *Canada* 103 C9
Cedar Park *U.S.A.* 116 F6
Cedar Rapids *U.S.A.* 112 E8
Cedartown *U.S.A.* 117 D12
Cedarvale *Canada* 102 B3
Cedarville *S. Africa* 89 E4
Cedeira *Spain* 36 E2
Cedral *Mexico* 118 C4
Cedrino ~ *Italy* 42 B2
Cedro *Brazil* 125 E11
Cedros, I. *Mexico* 118 B1
Cedros B. *Trin. & Tob.* 125 K15
Ceduna *Australia* 95 E1
Cée *Spain* 36 C1
Ceel Gaal *Somali Rep.* 75 E5
Ceel Waaq *Kenya* 86 B5
Ceeldheere *Somali Rep.* 75 G4
Ceerigaabo *Somali Rep.* 75 E4
Cefalù *Italy* 43 D7
Cega ~ *Spain* 36 D6
Cegléd *Hungary* 28 C4
Céglie Messápico *Italy* 43 B10
Cehegín *Spain* 39 G3
Cehu-Silvaniei *Romania* 29 C8
Ceica *Romania* 28 D7
Ceira ~ *Portugal* 36 E2
Celano *Italy* 41 F10
Celanova *Spain* 36 D3
Celaque △ *Honduras* 120 D2
Celaya *Mexico* 118 C4
Celebes = Sulawesi *Indonesia* 63 E6
Celebes Sea *Indonesia* 63 D6
Celina *U.S.A.* 113 E11
Celinac *Bos.-H.* 41 D13
Celje *Slovenia* 41 B12
Celldömölk *Hungary* 28 C2
Celle *Germany* 24 C6
Celorico da Beira *Portugal* 36 E3
Celtic Sea *Atl. Oc.* 16 F2
Çeltikçi *Turkey* 47 D12
Çemişgezek *Turkey* 73 C8
Cenderawasih, Teluk *Indonesia* 63 E9
Cengong *China* 58 D7
Ceno ~ *Italy* 40 D7
Centallo *Italy* 40 D4
Centelles *Spain* 38 D7
Center *N. Dak., U.S.A.* 112 B3

Center *Tex., U.S.A.* 116 F7
Centerburg *U.S.A.* 114 F2
Centerville *Calif., U.S.A.* 110 J7
Centerville *Iowa, U.S.A.* 112 E7
Centerville *Pa., U.S.A.* 114 F5
Centerville *Tenn., U.S.A.* 117 D11
Centerville *Tex., U.S.A.* 116 F7
Cento *Italy* 41 D8
Central = Tsentralnyy □
  Russia 34 D4
Central □ *Ghana* 83 D4
Central □ *Kenya* 86 C4
Central □ *Malawi* 87 E3
Central □ *Zambia* 87 E2
Central, Cordillera *Colombia* 124 C4
Central, Cordillera
  Costa Rica 120 D3
Central, Cordillera
  Dom. Rep. 121 C5
Central, Cordillera *Phil.* 61 C4
Central, Cordillera
  Puerto Rico 121 d
Central African Rep. ■
  Africa 79 G9
Central America *America* 98 H11
Central Australia ◎ *Australia* 92 D4
Central Butte *Canada* 103 C7
Central City *Colo., U.S.A.* 108 G11
Central City *Ky., U.S.A.* 112 G10
Central City *Nebr., U.S.A.* 112 E5
Central Desert ◎ *Australia* 92 C5
Central I. *Kenya* 86 B4
Central Island □ *Kenya* 86 B4
Central Kalahari *Botswana* 88 C3
Central Makran Range
  Pakistan 66 F4
Central Pacific Basin
  Pac. Oc. 96 G10
Central Patricia *Canada* 104 B1
Central Point *U.S.A.* 108 E2
Central Russian Uplands
  Europe 6 E13
Central Siberian Plateau
  Russia 50 B12
Central Square *U.S.A.* 115 C8
Centralia *Canada* 114 C3
Centralia *Ill., U.S.A.* 112 F9
Centralia *Mo., U.S.A.* 112 F7
Centralia *Wash., U.S.A.* 110 D4
Centre □ *Cameroon* 83 D7
Centre de Flacq *Mauritius* 85 d
Centreville *N.Y., U.S.A.* 114 D6
Centreville *Pa., U.S.A.* 114 E5
Cenxi *China* 59 F8
Ceotina ~ *Bos.-H.* 44 C2
Cephalonia = Kefalonia
  Greece 46 C2
Čepin *Croatia* 28 E3
Ceprano *Italy* 42 A6
Ceptura *Romania* 29 E11
Cepu *Indonesia* 63 G14
Ceram = Seram *Indonesia* 63 E7
Ceram Sea = Seram Sea
  Indonesia 63 E7
Cerbère *France* 20 F7
Cerbicales, Îs. *France* 21 G13
Cercal *Portugal* 37 H2
Cerdanya *Spain* 38 C6
Cère ~ *France* 20 C5
Cerea *Italy* 41 C8
Ceres *Argentina* 126 B3
Ceres *S. Africa* 88 E2
Ceres *U.S.A.* 110 H6
Céret *France* 20 F6
Cerf *Seychelles* 85 b
Cergy *France* 19 C9
Cerignola *Italy* 43 A8
Cerigo = Kythira *Greece* 46 E5
Cérilly *France* 19 F9
Cerisiers *France* 19 D10
Cerizay *France* 18 F6
Çerkeş *Turkey* 72 B5
Çerkezköy *Turkey* 45 E12
Cerknica *Slovenia* 41 C11
Cerkovica *Bulgaria* 45 C8
Cermerno *Serbia* 44 C4
Çermik *Turkey* 73 C8
Cerna *Romania* 29 E13
Cerna ~ *Romania* 29 F9
Cernavodă *Romania* 29 F13
Cernay *France* 19 E14
Cernik *Croatia* 28 E2
Cerralvo, I. *Mexico* 118 C3
Cërrik *Albania* 44 E3
Cerritos *Mexico* 118 C4
Cerro Chato *Uruguay* 127 C4
Cerro Cofre de Perote △
  Mexico 119 D5
Cerro Corá △ *Paraguay* 127 A4
Cerro de Pasco *Peru* 124 F3
Cerro el Copey △ *Venezuela* 121 D7
Cerro Hoya △ *Panama* 120 E3
Cerro Saroche △ *Venezuela* 121 D6
Certaldo *Italy* 40 E8
Cervaro ~ *Italy* 43 A8
Cervati, Monte *Italy* 43 B8
Cervantes *Australia* 93 F2
Cervera *Spain* 38 D6

Cervera de Pisuerga *Spain* **36** C6
Cervera del Río Alhama
   Spain **38** C3
Cervéteri *Italy* **41** F9
Cérvia *Italy* **41** D9
Cervignano del Friuli *Italy* **41** C10
Cervinara *Italy* **43** A7
Cervione *France* **21** F13
Cervo *Spain* **36** B3
Cesaró *Italy* **43** E7
Cesena *Italy* **41** D9
Cesenático *Italy* **41** D9
Cēsis *Latvia* **32** D3
Česká Lípa *Czech Rep.* **26** A7
Česká Rep. = Czech Rep. ■
   Europe **26** B8
Česká Třebová *Czech Rep.* **27** B9
České Budějovice *Czech Rep.* **26** C7
České Velenice *Czech Rep.* **26** C7
Českobudějovický □
   Czech Rep. **26** B7
Českomoravská Vrchovina
   Czech Rep. **26** B8
Český Brod *Czech Rep.* **26** A7
Český Krumlov *Czech Rep.* **26** C7
Český Těšín *Czech Rep.* **27** B11
Česma → *Croatia* **41** C13
Çeşme *Turkey* **47** C8
Cessnock *Australia* **95** E5
Cesson-Sévigné *France* **18** D5
Cestas *France* **20** D3
Cestos → *Liberia* **82** D3
Cestos Sehnkwehn △ *Liberia* **82** D3
Cetate *Romania* **28** F8
Cetin Grad *Croatia* **41** C12
Cetina → *Croatia* **41** E13
Cetinje *Montenegro* **44** D2
Cetraro *Italy* **43** C8
Ceuta *N. Afr.* **78** A4
Ceva *Italy* **40** D5
Cévennes *France* **20** D7
Cévennes △ *France* **20** D7
Ceyhan *Turkey* **72** D6
Ceyhan → *Turkey* **72** D6
Ceylanpınar *Turkey* **73** D9
Ceylon = Sri Lanka ■ *Asia* **66** R12
Cèze → *France* **21** D8
Cha-am *Thailand* **64** F2
Chabanais *France* **20** C4
Chabeuil *France* **21** D9
Chablais *France* **19** F13
Chablis *France* **19** E10
Chacabuco *Argentina* **126** C3
Chachapoyas *Peru* **124** E3
Chachoengsao *Thailand* **64** F3
Chachran *Pakistan* **68** E4
Chachro *Pakistan* **68** G4
Chaco □ *Argentina* **126** B4
Chaco □ *Paraguay* **126** B4
Chaco → *U.S.A.* **109** H9
Chaco △ *Argentina* **126** B4
Chaco Austral *S. Amer.* **128** B4
Chaco Boreal *S. Amer.* **124** H6
Chaco Central *S. Amer.* **128** A4
Chaco Culture △ *U.S.A.* **109** H10
Chacon, C. *U.S.A.* **102** C2
Chad ■ *Africa* **79** F8
Chad, L. = Tchad, L. *Chad* **79** F8
Chadileuvú → *Argentina* **126** D2
Chadiza *Zambia* **87** E3
Chadron *U.S.A.* **112** D2
Chadyr-Lunga =
   Ciadâr-Lunga *Moldova* **29** D13
Chae Hom *Thailand* **64** C2
Chae Son △ *Thailand* **64** C2
Chaem → *Thailand* **64** C2
Chaeryŏng *N. Korea* **57** E13
Chafe *Nigeria* **83** C6
Chagai Hills = Chāh Gay
   Hills *Afghan.* **66** E3
Chagda *Russia* **53** D14
Chaghcharān *Afghan.* **66** B4
Chagne *Ethiopia* **81** E4
Chagny *France* **19** F11
Chagoda *Russia* **32** C8
Chagos Arch. ☑ *Ind. Oc.* **50** J9
Chagres △ *Panama* **120** E4
Chaguanas *Trin. & Tob.* **125** K15
Chāh Ākhvor *Iran* **71** C8
Chāh Bahar *Iran* **71** E9
Chāh-e Kavīr *Iran* **71** C8
Chāh Gay Hills *Afghan.* **66** E3
Chahār Borj *Iran* **73** D11
Chahār Borjak *Afghan.* **66** D3
Chahār Mahāll va
   Bakhtīārī □ *Iran* **71** C6
Chai Badan *Thailand* **64** E3
Chaibasa *India* **69** H11
Chaillé-les-Marais *France* **20** B2
Chainat *Thailand* **64** E3
Chaiya *Thailand* **65** H2
Chaiyaphum *Thailand* **64** E4
Chaj Doab *Pakistan* **68** C5
Chajari *Argentina* **126** C4
Chak Amru *Pakistan* **68** C6
Chaka *Sudan* **81** G3
Chakar → *Pakistan* **68** E3
Chakari *Zimbabwe* **89** B4
Chake Chake *Tanzania* **86** D4

Chakhānsūr *Afghan.* **66** D3
Chakonipau, L. *Canada* **105** A6
Chakradharpur *India* **69** H11
Chakrata *India* **68** D7
Chakwal *Pakistan* **68** C5
Chala *Peru* **124** G4
Chalais *France* **20** C4
Chalchihuites *Mexico* **118** C4
Chalcis = Halkida *Greece* **46** C5
Châlette-sur-Loing *France* **19** D9
Chaleur B. *Canada* **105** C6
Chalfant *U.S.A.* **110** H8
Chalhuanca *Peru* **124** F4
Chaliki *Greece* **46** B4
Chalindrey *France* **19** E12
Chaling *China* **59** D9
Chalisgaon *India* **66** J9
Chalk River *Canada* **104** C4
Chalkar, Ozero = Shalkar
   Köli *Kazakhstan* **34** E10
Chalky Inlet *N.Z.* **91** G1
Challans *France* **18** F5
Challapata *Bolivia* **124** G5
Challawa Gorge Res. *Nigeria* **83** C6
Challenger Deep *Pac. Oc.* **96** F6
Challenger Fracture Zone
   Pac. Oc. **97** L17
Challis *U.S.A.* **108** D6
Chalmette *U.S.A.* **117** G10
Chalon-sur-Saône *France* **19** F11
Chalong *Thailand* **65** a
Chalonnes-sur-Loire *France* **18** E6
Châlons-en-Champagne
   France **19** D11
Chálten, Cerro = Fitz Roy,
   Cerro *Argentina* **128** F2
Châlus *France* **20** C4
Chālūs *Iran* **71** B6
Cham *Germany* **25** F8
Cham, Cu Lao *Vietnam* **64** E7
Chama *U.S.A.* **109** H10
Chamaicó *Argentina* **126** D3
Chaman *Pakistan* **66** D5
Chamba *India* **68** C7
Chamba *Tanzania* **87** E4
Chambal → *India* **69** F8
Chamberlain *U.S.A.* **112** D4
Chamberlain → *Australia* **92** C4
Chamberlain L. *U.S.A.* **113** B19
Chambers *U.S.A.* **109** J9
Chambersburg *U.S.A.* **113** F15
Chambéry *France* **21** C9
Chambeshi → *Zambia* **84** G6
Chambly *Canada* **115** A11
Chambord *Canada* **105** C5
Chamboulive *France* **20** C5
Chamela *Mexico* **118** D3
Chamical *Argentina* **126** C2
Chamkar Luong *Cambodia* **65** G4
Chamoli *India* **69** D8
Chamonix-Mont Blanc
   France **21** C10
Chamouchouane =
   Ashuapmushuan →
   Canada **104** C5
Champa *India* **69** H10
Champagne *Canada* **102** A1
Champagne *France* **19** D11
Champagnole *France* **19** F12
Champaign *U.S.A.* **112** E9
Champassak *Laos* **64** E5
Champaubert *France* **19** D10
Champawat *India* **69** E9
Champdeniers-St-Denis
   France **20** B3
Champdoré, L. *Canada* **105** A6
Champeix *France* **20** C7
Champion *U.S.A.* **114** E4
Champlain *U.S.A.* **115** B11
Champlain, L. *U.S.A.* **115** B11
Champlitte *France* **19** E12
Champotón *Mexico* **119** D6
Champua *India* **69** H11
Chamusca *Portugal* **37** F2
Chana *Thailand* **65** J3
Chañaral *Chile* **126** B1
Chanārān *Iran* **71** B8
Chanasma *India* **68** H5
Chancery Lane *Barbados* **121** g
Chanco *Chile* **126** D1
Chand *India* **69** J12
Chandan *India* **69** G12
Chandan Chauki *India* **69** E9
Chandannagar *India* **69** H13
Chandausi *India* **69** E8
Chandeleur Is. *U.S.A.* **117** G10
Chandeleur Sd. *U.S.A.* **117** G10
Chandigarh *India* **68** D7
Chandil *India* **69** H12
Chandler *Australia* **95** D1
Chandler *Canada* **105** C7
Chandler *Ariz., U.S.A.* **109** K8
Chandler *Okla., U.S.A.* **116** D6
Chandod *India* **68** J5
Chandpur *Bangla.* **67** H17
Chandpur *India* **69** E8
Chandra *Greece* **47** F8
Chandrapur *India* **66** K11

Chang *Pakistan* **68** F3
Chang, Ko *Thailand* **65** G4
Ch'ang Chiang = Chang
   Jiang → *China* **59** B13
Chang Jiang → *China* **59** B13
Changa *India* **69** C7
Changanacheri *India* **66** Q10
Changanassery =
   Changanacheri *India* **66** Q10
Changane → *Mozam.* **89** C5
Changbai *China* **57** D15
Changbai Shan *China* **57** C15
Changchiak'ou =
   Zhangjiakou *China* **56** D8
Ch'angchou = Changzhou
   China **59** B12
Changchun *China* **57** C13
Changchunling *China* **57** B13
Changde *China* **59** C8
Changdo-ri *N. Korea* **57** E14
Changfeng *China* **59** A11
Changhai = Shanghai
   China **59** B13
Changhua *China* **59** B12
Changhua *Taiwan* **59** F12
Changhŭngni *N. Korea* **57** D15
Changi *Singapore* **65** d
Changi, Singapore ✈ (SIN)
   Singapore **65** M4
Changjiang *China* **64** C7
Changjin *N. Korea* **57** D14
Changjin-ho *N. Korea* **57** D14
Changle *China* **59** E12
Changli *China* **57** E10
Changling *China* **57** B12
Changlun *Malaysia* **65** J3
Changning *Hunan, China* **59** D9
Changning *Sichuan, China* **58** C5
Changning *Yunnan, China* **58** E2
Changping *China* **56** D9
Changsha *China* **59** C9
Changshan *China* **59** C12
Changshan Qundao *China* **57** E12
Changshu *China* **59** B13
Changshun *China* **58** D6
Changtai *China* **59** E11
Changting *China* **59** E11
Changuinola *Panama* **120** E3
Changwu *China* **56** G4
Changxing *China* **59** B12
Changyang *China* **59** B8
Changyi *China* **57** F10
Changyŏn *N. Korea* **57** E13
Changyuan *China* **56** G8
Changzhi *China* **56** F7
Changzhou *China* **59** B12
Chanhanga *Angola* **88** B1
Chania *Greece* **49** D6
Chania □ *Greece* **49** D6
Chanion, Kolpos *Greece* **49** D5
Chanlar = Xanlar *Azerbaijan* **35** K8
Channapatna *India* **66** N10
Channel Is. *U.K.* **15** H5
Channel Is. *U.S.A.* **111** M7
Channel Islands △ *U.S.A.* **111** L7
Channel-Port aux Basques
   Canada **105** C8
Channel Tunnel *Europe* **15** F9
Channing *U.S.A.* **116** D3
Chantada *Spain* **36** C3
Chanthaburi *Thailand* **64** F4
Chantilly *France* **19** C9
Chantonnay *France* **18** F5
Chantrey Inlet *Canada* **100** D12
Chanute *U.S.A.* **112** G6
Chanza → *Spain* **37** H3
Chao Hu *China* **59** B11
Chao Phraya → *Thailand* **64** F3
Chao Phraya Lowlands
   Thailand **64** E3
Chaocheng *China* **56** F8
Chaohu *China* **59** B11
Chaoyang *Guangdong, China* **59** F11
Chaoyang *Liaoning, China* **57** D11
Chaozhou *China* **59** F11
Chapaev *Kazakhstan* **34** E10
Chapais *Canada* **104** C5
Chapala *Mozam.* **87** F4
Chapala, L. de *Mexico* **118** C4
Chapayevsk *Russia* **34** D9
Chapecó *Brazil* **127** B5
Chapel Hill *U.S.A.* **117** D15
Chapleau *Canada* **104** C3
Chaplin *Canada* **103** C7
Chaplin L. *Canada* **103** C7
Chaplino *Ukraine* **33** H9
Chaplygin *Russia* **32** F11
Chappell *U.S.A.* **112** E2
Chapra = Chhapra *India* **69** G11
Chaqâbel *Iran* **73** F12
Chara *Russia* **53** D12
Charadai *Argentina* **126** B4
Charagua *Bolivia* **124** G6
Charaña *Bolivia* **124** G5
Charambirá, Punta
   Colombia **124** C3
Charaña *Bolivia* **124** G5
Charantsavan *Armenia* **35** K7

Charanwala *India* **68** F5
Charata *Argentina* **126** B3
Charcas *Mexico* **118** C4
Charcot I. *Antarctica* **5** C17
Chard *U.K.* **15** G5
Chardon *U.S.A.* **114** E3
Chardzhou =
   Türkmenabat
   Turkmenistan **71** B9
Charente □ *France* **20** C4
Charente → *France* **20** C2
Charente-Maritime □ *France* **20** C3
Charenton-du-Cher *France* **19** F9
Chari → *Chad* **79** F8
Chārīkār *Afghan.* **66** B6
Chariton *U.S.A.* **112** E7
Chariton → *U.S.A.* **112** F7
Chärjew = Türkmenabat
   Turkmenistan **71** B9
Charkhari *India* **69** G8
Charkhi Dadri *India* **68** E7
Charleroi *Belgium* **17** D4
Charleroi *U.S.A.* **114** F5
Charles, C. *U.S.A.* **113** G16
Charles, Peak *Australia* **93** F3
Charles City *U.S.A.* **112** D7
Charles de Gaulle, Paris ✈
   (CDG) *France* **19** D9
Charles L. *Canada* **101** E17
Charles L. *Canada* **103** B6
Charles Town *U.S.A.* **113** F15
Charlesbourg *Canada* **113** B18
Charleston *Ill., U.S.A.* **112** F9
Charleston *Miss., U.S.A.* **117** D9
Charleston *Mo., U.S.A.* **112** G9
Charleston *S.C., U.S.A.* **117** E15
Charleston *W. Va., U.S.A.* **113** F13
Charleston L. *Canada* **115** B9
Charleston Peak *U.S.A.* **111** J11
Charlestown *Ireland* **12** C3
Charlestown *S. Africa* **89** D4
Charlestown *Ind., U.S.A.* **113** F11
Charlestown *N.H., U.S.A.* **115** C12
Charlestown of Aberlour
   U.K. **13** D5
Charleville = Rath Luirc
   Ireland **12** D3
Charleville *Australia* **95** D4
Charleville-Mézières *France* **19** C11
Charlevoix *U.S.A.* **113** C11
Charlieu *France* **19** F11
Charlotte *Mich., U.S.A.* **113** D11
Charlotte *N.C., U.S.A.* **117** D14
Charlotte *Vt., U.S.A.* **115** B11
Charlotte Amalie
   U.S. Virgin Is. **121** e
Charlotte Harbor *U.S.A.* **117** H13
Charlotte L. *Canada* **102** C3
Charlottenberg *Sweden* **10** E6
Charlottesville *U.S.A.* **113** F14
Charlottetown *Nfld. & L.,
   Canada* **105** B8
Charlottetown *P.E.I., Canada* **105** C7
Charlotteville *Trin. & Tob.* **125** J16
Charlton *Australia* **95** F3
Charlton I. *Canada* **104** B4
Charmes *France* **19** D13
Charny *Canada* **105** C5
Charnyany *Belarus* **31** G11
Charolles *France* **19** F11
Chârost *France* **19** F9
Charre *Mozam.* **87** F4
Charroux *France* **20** B4
Charsadda *Pakistan* **68** B4
Charters Towers *Australia* **94** C4
Chartres *France* **18** D8
Chartreuse △ *France* **21** C9
Chascomús *Argentina* **126** D4
Chase *Canada* **102** C5
Chasefu *Zambia* **87** E3
Chashma Barrage *Pakistan* **68** C4
Chasseneuil-sur-Bonnieure
   France **20** C4
Chāt *Iran* **71** B7
Chatal Balkan = Udvoy
   Balkan *Bulgaria* **45** D10
Château-Arnoux-St-Auban
   France **21** D10
Château-Chinon *France* **19** E10
Château-d'Olonne *France* **20** B2
Château-du-Loir *France* **18** E7
Château-Gontier *France* **18** E6
Château-la-Vallière *France* **18** E7
Château-Landon *France* **19** D9
Château-Renard *France* **19** D9
Château-Renault *France* **18** E7
Château-Salins *France* **19** D13
Château-Thierry *France* **19** C10
Châteaubourg *France* **18** D5
Châteaubriant *France* **18** E5
Châteaudun *France* **18** D8
Chateaugay *U.S.A.* **115** B10
Châteaugiron *France* **18** D5
Châteauguay, L. *Canada* **105** A5
Châteaulin *France* **18** D2
Châteaumeillant *France* **19** F9
Châteauneuf-du-Faou *France* **18** D3
Châteauneuf-sur-Charente
   France **20** C3

Châteauneuf-sur-Cher
   France **19** F9
Châteauneuf-sur-Loire
   France **19** E9
Châteaurenard *France* **21** E8
Châteauroux *France* **19** F8
Châteauvillain *France* **19** D11
Châteaux, Pte. des *Guadeloupe* **120** b
Châtelaillon-Plage *France* **20** B2
Châtelguyon *France* **20** C7
Châtellerault *France* **18** F7
Châtelus-Malvaleix *France* **19** F9
Chatham = Miramichi
   Canada **105** C6
Chatham *Canada* **114** D2
Chatham *U.K.* **15** F8
Chatham *U.S.A.* **115** D11
Chatham Is. *Pac. Oc.* **96** M10
Chatham Rise *Pac. Oc.* **96** M10
Châtillon *Italy* **40** C4
Châtillon-Coligny *France* **19** E9
Châtillon-en-Diois *France* **21** D9
Châtillon-sur-Indre *France* **18** F8
Châtillon-sur-Loire *France* **19** E9
Châtillon-sur-Seine *France* **19** E11
Chatmohar *Bangla.* **69** G13
Chatra *India* **69** G11
Chatrapur *India* **67** K14
Chats, L. des *Canada* **115** A8
Chatsu *India* **68** F6
Chatsworth *Canada* **114** B4
Chatsworth *Zimbabwe* **87** F3
Châttagâm = Chittagong
   Bangla. **67** H17
Chattahoochee *U.S.A.* **117** F12
Chattahoochee → *U.S.A.* **117** F12
Chattanooga *U.S.A.* **117** D12
Chatteris *U.K.* **15** E8
Chatturat *Thailand* **64** E3
Chau Doc *Vietnam* **65** G5
Chaudes-Aigues *France* **20** D7
Chauffailles *France* **19** F11
Chaukan Pass *Burma* **67** F20
Chaumont *France* **19** D12
Chaumont *U.S.A.* **115** B8
Chaumont-en-Vexin *France* **19** C8
Chaumont-sur-Loire *France* **18** E8
Chaunay *France* **20** B4
Chaunskaya G. *Russia* **53** C17
Chauny *France* **19** C10
Chausey, Îs. *France* **18** D5
Chaussin *France* **19** F12
Chautauqua L. *U.S.A.* **114** D5
Chauvigny *France* **18** F7
Chauvin *Canada* **103** C6
Chavanges *France* **19** D11
Chaves *Brazil* **125** D9
Chaves *Portugal* **36** D3
Chazy *U.S.A.* **115** B11
Cheb *Czech Rep.* **26** A5
Cheboksarskoye Vdkhr.
   Russia **34** B8
Cheboksary *Russia* **34** B8
Cheboygan *U.S.A.* **113** C11
Chebsara *Russia* **32** C10
Chech, Erg *Africa* **78** D5
Chechelnyk *Ukraine* **29** B14
Chechen, Ostrov *Russia* **35** H8
Chechenia □ *Russia* **35** J7
Checheno-Ingush Republic
   = Chechenia □ *Russia* **35** J7
Chechnya = Chechenia □
   Russia **35** J7
Checotah *U.S.A.* **116** D7
Chedabucto B. *Canada* **105** C7
Cheduba I. *Burma* **67** K18
Cheektowaga *U.S.A.* **114** D6
Cheepie *Australia* **95** D4
Chef-Boutonne *France* **20** B3
Chegdomyn *Russia* **53** D14
Chegga *Mauritania* **78** C4
Chegutu *Zimbabwe* **87** F3
Chehalis *U.S.A.* **110** D4
Chehalis → *U.S.A.* **110** D3
Cheile Nerei-Beusnita △
   Romania **28** F6
Cheju = Jeju *S. Korea* **57** H14
Cheju-do = Jeju-do *S. Korea* **57** H14
Chekalin *Russia* **32** E9
Chekhov *Russia* **30** D7
Chekiang = Zhejiang □
   China **59** C13
Chel = Kuru, Bahr el →
   Sudan **81** F2
Chela, Sa. da *Angola* **88** B1
Chelan *U.S.A.* **108** C3
Chelan, L. *U.S.A.* **108** B3
Cheleken = Hazar
   Turkmenistan **52** F6
Cheleken Yarymadasy
   Turkmenistan **71** B7
Chelforó *Argentina* **128** D3
Chelkar = Shalqar
   Kazakhstan **52** E6
Chella *Ethiopia* **81** F4

Chelles *France* **19** D9
Chelm *Poland* **31** G10
Chelmno *Poland* **31** E5
Chelmsford *U.K.* **15** F8
Chełmża *Poland* **31** E5
Chelsea *Australia* **95** F4
Chelsea *U.S.A.* **115** C12
Cheltenham *U.K.* **15** F5
Chelva *Spain* **38** F4
Chelyabinsk *Russia* **52** D7
Chelyuskin, C. =
   Chelyuskin, Mys *Russia* **53** B11
Chelyuskin, Mys *Russia* **53** B11
Chemainus *Canada* **110** B3
Chemba *Mozam.* **85** H6
Chembar = Belinskiy *Russia* **34** D6
Chemillé *France* **18** E6
Chemin Grenier *Mauritius* **85** d
Chemnitz *Germany* **24** E8
Chemult *U.S.A.* **108** E3
Chen, Gora *Russia* **53** C15
Chenab → *Pakistan* **68** D4
Chenab Nagar *Pakistan* **68** D5
Chenango Forks *U.S.A.* **115** D9
Chencha *Ethiopia* **81** F4
Chenchiang = Zhenjiang
   China **59** A12
Cheney *U.S.A.* **108** C5
Cheng Xian *China* **56** H3
Chengbu *China* **59** D8
Chengcheng *China* **56** G5
Chengchou = Zhengzhou
   China **56** G7
Chengde *China* **57** D9
Chengdong Hu *China* **59** A11
Chengdu *China* **58** B5
Chenggong *China* **58** E4
Chenggu *China* **56** H4
Chenghai *China* **59** F11
Chengjiang *China* **58** E4
Chengkou *China* **58** B7
Chengmai *China* **64** C7
Ch'engtu = Chengdu *China* **58** B5
Chengwu *China* **56** G8
Chengxi Hu *China* **59** A11
Chengyang *China* **57** F11
Chenjiagang *China* **57** G10
Chennai *India* **66** N12
Chenôve *France* **19** E12
Chenxi *China* **59** C8
Chenzhou *China* **59** E9
Cheò, Eilean a' = Skye *U.K.* **13** D2
Cheom Ksan *Cambodia* **64** E5
Cheonan *S. Korea* **57** F14
Cheongdo *S. Korea* **57** G15
Cheongju *S. Korea* **57** F14
Cheorwon *S. Korea* **57** E14
Chepelare *Bulgaria* **45** E8
Chepén *Peru* **124** E3
Chepes *Argentina* **126** C2
Chepo *Panama* **120** E4
Chepstow *U.K.* **15** F5
Chequamegon B. *U.S.A.* **112** B9
Cher □ *France* **19** E9
Cher → *France* **18** E7
Chéradvi *Italy* **43** B10
Cherasco *Italy* **40** D4
Cheraw *U.S.A.* **117** D15
Cherbourg *France* **18** C5
Cherdakly *Russia* **34** C9
Cherdyn *Russia* **52** C6
Cheremkhovo *Russia* **53** D11
Cherepovets *Russia* **32** C9
Chergui, Chott ech *Algeria* **78** B6
Cherikov = Cherykaw
   Belarus **23** B16
Cherkasy *Ukraine* **33** H7
Cherkasy □ *Ukraine* **33** H6
Cherkessk *Russia* **35** H6
Cherlak *Russia* **52** D8
Chernaya *Russia* **53** B9
Chernelytsya *Ukraine* **29** B10
Cherni *Bulgaria* **44** D7
Chernigov = Chernihiv
   Ukraine **33** G6
Chernigovka *Russia* **54** B6
Chernihiv *Ukraine* **33** G6
Chernihiv □ *Ukraine* **33** G6
Chernivtsi *Chernivtsi, Ukraine* **29** B10
Chernivtsi *Vinnytsya,
   Ukraine* **29** B13
Chernivtsi □ *Ukraine* **29** B10
Chernobyl = Chornobyl
   Ukraine **23** C16
Chernogorsk *Russia* **53** D10
Chernomorskoye =
   Chornomorske *Ukraine* **33** K7
Chernovtsy = Chernivtsi
   Ukraine **29** B10
Chernyakhovsk *Russia* **30** D8
Chernyanka *Russia* **33** G9
Chernysheyskiy *Russia* **53** C12
Chernyye Zemli *Russia* **35** H8
Cherokee *Iowa, U.S.A.* **112** D6
Cherokee *Okla., U.S.A.* **116** C5
Cherokee Village *U.S.A.* **116** C9
Cherokees, Grand Lake O'
   The *U.S.A.* **116** C7
Cherrapunji *India* **67** G17

Cherry Valley *U.S.A.* **115** D10
Cherskiy *Russia* **53** C17
Cherskogo Khrebet *Russia* **53** C15
Chersonisos *Greece* **49** D7
Chersonisos Akrotiri *Greece* **49** D6
Chertkovo *Russia* **33** H11
Cherven *Belarus* **23** B15
Cherven-Bryag *Bulgaria* **45** C8
Chervonoarmiyske *Ukraine* **29** E13
Chervonohrad *Ukraine* **23** C13
Cherwell ➜ *U.K.* **15** F6
Cherykaw *Belarus* **23** B16
Chesapeake *U.S.A.* **113** G15
Chesapeake B. *U.S.A.* **113** F14
Cheshire □ *U.K.* **14** D5
Cheshskaya Guba *Russia* **52** C5
Cheshunt *U.K.* **15** F7
Chesil Beach *U.K.* **15** G5
Chesley *Canada* **114** B3
Cheste *Spain* **39** F4
Chester *U.K.* **14** D5
Chester *Calif., U.S.A.* **108** F3
Chester *Ill., U.S.A.* **112** G9
Chester *Mont., U.S.A.* **108** B8
Chester *Pa., U.S.A.* **113** F16
Chester *S.C., U.S.A.* **117** D14
Chester *Vt., U.S.A.* **115** C12
Chester *W. Va., U.S.A.* **114** F4
Chester-le-Street *U.K.* **14** C6
Chesterfield *U.K.* **14** D6
Chesterfield, Îs. *N. Cal.* **90** C8
Chesterfield Inlet *Canada* **100** E13
Chesterton Ra. *Australia* **95** D4
Chesterton Range △
  Australia **95** D4
Chestertown *U.S.A.* **115** C11
Chesterville *Canada* **115** A9
Chesuncook L. *U.S.A.* **113** C19
Chéticamp *Canada* **105** C7
Chetrosu *Moldova* **29** B12
Chetumal *Mexico* **119** D7
Chetumal, B. de *Cent. Amer.* **119** D7
Chetwynd *Canada* **102** B4
Chevanceaux *France* **20** C3
Cheviot, The *U.K.* **14** B5
Cheviot Hills *U.K.* **14** B5
Cheviot Ra. *Australia* **94** D3
Chew Bahir *Ethiopia* **81** G4
Chewelah *U.S.A.* **108** B5
Chewore △ *Zimbabwe* **87** F2
Cheyenne *Okla., U.S.A.* **116** D5
Cheyenne *Wyo., U.S.A.* **108** F11
Cheyenne ➜ *U.S.A.* **112** C3
Cheyenne Wells *U.S.A.* **108** G12
Cheyne B. *Austral.a* **93** F2
Chhabra *India* **68** G7
Chhaktala *India* **68** H6
Chhapra *India* **69** G11
Chhata *India* **68** F7
Chhatarpur *Jharkhand, India* **69** G11
Chhatarpur *Mad. P., India* **69** G8
Chhattisgarh □ *India* **69** J10
Chhep *Cambodia* **64** F5
Chhindwara *Mad. P., India* **69** H8
Chhindwara *Mad. P., India* **69** H8
Chhlong *Cambodia* **65** F5
Chhota Tawa ➜ *India* **68** H7
Chhoti Kali Sindh ➜ *India* **68** G6
Chhuikhadan *India* **69** J9
Chhuk *Cambodia* **65** G5
Chi ➜ *Thailand* **64** E5
Chiai *Taiwan* **59** F13
Chiali *Taiwan* **59** F13
Chiamboni *Somali Rep.* **84** E8
Chianciano Terme *Italy* **41** E8
Chiang Dao *Thailand* **64** C2
Chiang Kham *Thailand* **64** C3
Chiang Khan *Thailand* **64** D3
Chiang Khong *Thailand* **58** G3
Chiang Mai *Thailand* **64** C2
Chiang Rai *Thailand* **58** H2
Chiang Saen *Thailand* **58** G3
Chianti *Italy* **41** E8
Chiapa ➜ *Mexico* **119** D6
Chiapa de Corzo *Mexico* **119** D6
Chiapas □ *Mexico* **119** D6
Chiapas, Sa. Madre de
  Mexico **119** D6
Chiaramonte Gulfi *Italy* **43** E7
Chiaravalle *Italy* **41** E10
Chiaravalle Centrale *Italy* **43** D9
Chiari *Italy* **40** C6
Chiatura *Georgia* **35** J6
Chiautla de Tapia *Mexico* **119** D5
Chiávari *Italy* **40** D6
Chiavenna *Italy* **40** B6
Chiba *Japan* **55** G10
Chiba □ *Japan* **55** G10
Chibabava *Mozam.* **89** C5
Chibemba *Cunene, Angola* **85** H2
Chibemba *Huíla, Angola* **88** B2
Chibi *Zimbabwe* **89** C5
Chibia *Angola* **85** H2
Chibougamau *Canada* **104** C5
Chibougamau, L. *Canada* **104** C5
Chibuk *Nigeria* **83** C7
Chibuto *Mozam.* **89** C5
Chic-Chocs, Mts. *Canada* **105** C6
Chicacole = Srikakulam
  India **67** K13

Chicago *U.S.A.* **112** E10
Chicago Heights *U.S.A.* **112** E10
Chichagof I. *U.S.A.* **100** F4
Chichaoua *Morocco* **78** B4
Chichawatni *Pakistan* **68** D5
Chicheng *China* **56** D8
Chichester *U.K.* **15** G7
Chichester Ra. *Australia* **92** D2
Chichibu *Japan* **55** G9
Chichibu-Tama △ *Japan* **55** G9
Ch'ich'ihaerh = Qiqihar
  China **53** E13
Chicholi *India* **68** H8
Chickasaw △ *U.S.A.* **116** D6
Chickasha *U.S.A.* **116** D6
Chiclana de la Frontera *Spain* **37** J4
Chiclayo *Peru* **124** E3
Chico *U.S.A.* **110** F5
Chico ➜ *Chubut, Argentina* **128** E3
Chico ➜ *Santa Cruz,
  Argentina* **128** G3
Chicoa *Mozam.* **87** F3
Chicomo *Mozam.* **89** C5
Chicomostoc *Mexico* **118** C4
Chicontepec *Mexico* **119** C5
Chicopee *U.S.A.* **115** D12
Chicoutimi *Canada* **105** C5
Chicualacuala *Mozam.* **89** C5
Chidambaram *India* **66** P11
Chidenguele *Mozam.* **89** C5
Chidley, C. *Canada* **101** E19
Chiducuane *Mozam.* **89** C5
Chiede *Angola* **88** B2
Chiefs Pt. *Canada* **114** B3
Chiem Hoa *Vietnam* **64** A5
Chiemsee *Germany* **25** H8
Chiengi *Zambia* **87** D2
Chiengmai = Chiang Mai
  Thailand **64** C2
Chienti ➜ *Italy* **41** E10
Chieri *Italy* **40** C4
Chiers ➜ *France* **19** C11
Chiesa in Valmalenco *Italy* **40** B6
Chiese ➜ *Italy* **40** C7
Chieti *Italy* **41** F11
Chifeng *China* **57** C10
Chigirin *Ukraine* **33** H7
Chignecto B. *Canada* **105** C7
Chiguana *Bolivia* **126** A2
Chigwell *U.K.* **15** F8
Chihli, G. of = Bo Hai *China* **57** E10
Chihuahua *Mexico* **118** B3
Chihuahua □ *Mexico* **118** B3
Chiili = Shīeli *Kazakhstan* **52** E7
Chik Bollapur *India* **66** N10
Chikmagalur *India* **66** N9
Chikwawa *Malawi* **87** F3
Chilanga *Zambia* **87** F2
Chilapa *Mexico* **119** D5
Chilas *Pakistan* **69** B6
Chilaw *Sri Lanka* **66** R11
Chilcotin ➜ *Canada* **102** C4
Childers *Australia* **95** D5
Childress *U.S.A.* **116** D4
Chile ■ *S. Amer.* **128** D2
Chile Rise *Pac. Oc.* **97** L18
Chilecito *Argentina* **126** B2
Chilete *Peru* **124** E3
Chilia, Brațul ➜ *Romania* **29** E14
Chililabombwe *Zambia* **87** E2
Chilim *Pakistan* **69** B6
Chilin = Jilin *China* **57** C14
Chiliomodi *Greece* **46** D4
Chilka L. *India* **67** K14
Chilko ➜ *Canada* **102** C4
Chilko L. *Canada* **102** C4
Chillagoe *Australia* **94** B3
Chillán *Chile* **126** D1
Chillicothe *Ill., U.S.A.* **112** E9
Chillicothe *Mo., U.S.A.* **112** F7
Chillicothe *Ohio, U.S.A.* **113** F12
Chilliwack *Canada* **102** D4
Chilo *India* **68** F5
Chiloane, I. *Mozam.* **89** C5
Chiloé, I. de *Chile* **128** E2
Chilpancingo *Mexico* **119** D5
Chiltern Hills *U.K.* **15** F7
Chilton *U.S.A.* **112** C9
Chilubi *Zambia* **87** E2
Chilubula *Zambia* **87** E3
Chilumba *Malawi* **87** E3
Chilung *China* **57** E13
Chilwa, L. *Malawi* **87** F4
Chimaltitán *Mexico* **118** C4
Chimán *Panama* **120** E4
Chimanimani *Zimbabwe* **89** B5
Chimay *Belgium* **17** D4
Chimayo *U.S.A.* **109** J11
Chimba *Zambia* **87** D3
Chimbay *Uzbekistan* **52** E6
Chimborazo *Ecuador* **124** D3
Chimbote *Peru* **124** E3
Chimkent = Shymkent
  Kazakhstan **52** E7
Chimoio *Mozam.* **87** F3
Chimpembe *Zambia* **87** D2
Chin □ *Burma* **67** J18
Chin Hills *Burma* **67** H18

Chin Ling Shan = Qinling
  Shandi *China* **56** H5
China *Mexico* **119** B5
China ■ *Asia* **60** D6
China, Great Plain of *Asia* **50** E13
China Lake *U.S.A.* **111** K9
Chinan = Jinan *China* **56** F9
Chinandega *Nic.* **120** D2
Chinati Peak *U.S.A.* **116** G2
Chincha Alta *Peru* **124** F3
Chinchaga ➜ *Canada* **102** B5
Chinchilla *Australia* **95** D5
Chinchilla de Monte
  Aragón *Spain* **39** G3
Chinchorro, Banco *Mexico* **119** D7
Chinchou = Jinzhou *China* **57** D11
Chincoteague *U.S.A.* **113** G16
Chinde *Mozam.* **87** F4
Chindwin ➜ *Burma* **67** J19
Chineni *India* **69** C6
Chinga *Mozam.* **87** F4
Chingola *Zambia* **87** E2
Chingole *Malawi* **87** E3
Ch'ingtao = Qingdao *China* **57** F11
Chinguetti *Mauritania* **78** D3
Chingune *Mozam.* **89** C5
Chinhanguanine *Mozam.* **89** D5
Chinhoyi *Zimbabwe* **87** F3
Chini *India* **68** D8
Chiniot *Pakistan* **68** D5
Chínipas *Mexico* **118** B3
Chinji *Pakistan* **68** C5
Chinju = Jinju *S. Korea* **57** G15
Chinko ➜ *C.A.R.* **84** D4
Chinle *U.S.A.* **109** H9
Chinmen *Taiwan* **59** E13
Chinmen Tao *Taiwan* **59** E12
Chinnampo = Namp'o
  N. Korea **57** E13
Chino *Japan* **55** G9
Chino *U.S.A.* **111** L9
Chino Valley *U.S.A.* **109** J7
Chinon *France* **18** E7
Chinook *U.S.A.* **108** B9
Chinook Trough *Pac. Oc.* **96** C10
Chinsali *Zambia* **87** E3
Chinsura = Chunchura
  India **69** H13
Chióggia *Italy* **41** C9
Chíos = Hios *Greece* **47** C8
Chipata *Zambia* **87** E3
Chiperceni *Moldova* **29** C13
Chipindo *Angola* **85** G3
Chipinge *Zimbabwe* **87** G3
Chipinge △ *Zimbabwe* **87** G3
Chipiona *Spain* **37** J4
Chipley *U.S.A.* **117** F12
Chipman *Canada* **105** C6
Chipoka *Malawi* **87** E3
Chippenham *U.K.* **15** F5
Chippewa ➜ *U.S.A.* **112** C8
Chippewa Falls *U.S.A.* **112** C8
Chipping Norton *U.K.* **15** F6
Chiprovtsi *Bulgaria* **44** C6
Chiputneticook Lakes
  N. Amer. **113** C20
Chiquián *Peru* **124** F3
Chiquibul △ *Belize* **120** C2
Chiquimula *Guatemala* **120** D2
Chiquinquira *Colombia* **124** B4
Chir ➜ *Russia* **35** F6
Chirala *India* **66** M12
Chiramba *Mozam.* **87** F3
Chirawa *India* **68** E6
Chirchiq *Uzbekistan* **52** E7
Chiredzi *Zimbabwe* **89** C5
Chiricahua △ *U.S.A.* **109** K9
Chiricahua Peak *U.S.A.* **109** L9
Chirikof I. *U.S.A.* **106** D8
Chiriquí, G. de *Panama* **120** E3
Chiriquí, L. de *Panama* **120** E3
Chirisa △ *Zimbabwe* **87** F2
Chirivira Falls *Zimbabwe* **87** G3
Chirmiri *India* **69** H10
Chirnogi *Romania* **29** F11
Chirpan *Bulgaria* **45** D9
Chirripó Grande, Cerro
  Costa Rica **120** E3
Chirundu *Zimbabwe* **89** B4
Chisamba *Zambia* **87** E2
Chisapani *Nepal* **69** E9
Chisasibi *Canada* **104** B4
Ch'ishan *Taiwan* **59** F13
Chisholm *Canada* **102** C6
Chisholm *U.S.A.* **112** B7
Chishtian Mandi *Pakistan* **68** E5
Chishui *China* **58** C5
Chishui He ➜ *China* **58** C5
Chisimaio = Kismaayo
  Somali Rep. **75** H3
Chișinău *Moldova* **29** C13
Chișinău ✈ (KIV) *Moldova* **29** C13
Chișineu Criș *Romania* **28** D6
Chisone ➜ *Italy* **40** D4
Chisos Mts. *U.S.A.* **116** G3
Chistopol *Russia* **34** C10
Chita *Russia* **53** D12
Chitipa *Malawi* **87** D3

Chitose *Japan* **54** C10
Chitral *Pakistan* **66** B7
Chitré *Panama* **120** E3
Chittagong *Bangla.* **67** H17
Chittagong □ *Bangla.* **67** G17
Chittaurgarh *India* **68** G6
Chittoor *India* **66** N11
Chitungwiza *Zimbabwe* **87** F3
Chiusi *Italy* **41** E8
Chiva *Spain* **39** F4
Chivasso *Italy* **40** C4
Chivhu *Zimbabwe* **87** F3
Chivilcoy *Argentina* **126** C4
Chiwanda *Tanzania* **87** E3
Chixi *China* **59** G9
Chizarira *Zimbabwe* **87** F2
Chizarira △ *Zimbabwe* **87** F2
Chizela *Zambia* **87** E2
Chkalov = Orenburg *Russia* **52** D6
Chkolovsk *Russia* **34** B6
Chloride *U.S.A.* **111** K12
Chlumec nad Cidlinou
  Czech Rep. **26** A8
Chmielnik *Poland* **31** H7
Cho Bo *Vietnam* **58** 35
Cho-do *N. Korea* **57** E13
Cho Phuoc Hai *Vietnam* **65** G6
Choa Chu Kang *Singapore* **65** d
Choba *Kenya* **86** B4
Chobe △ *Botswana* **88** B4
Chobe ➜ *N. Korea* **66** N11
Chocianów *Poland* **31** G2
Chociwel *Poland* **30** E2
Chocolate Mts. *U.S.A.* **111** M11
Choctawhatchee ➜ *U.S.A.* **117** F11
Chodecz *Poland* **31** F6
Chodov *Czech Rep.* **26** A5
Chodzież *Poland* **31** F3
Choele Choel *Argentina* **128** D3
Choiseul *St. Lucia* **121** f
Choiseul *Solomon Is.* **90** B8
Choix *Mexico* **118** B3
Chojna *Poland* **31** F1
Chojnice *Poland* **30** E4
Chojnów *Poland* **31** G2
Chok Chai *Thailand* **64** E4
Chōkai-San *Japan* **54** E10
Choke Canyon Res. *U.S.A.* **116** G5
Choke Mts. *Ethiopia* **81** E4
Chokurdakh *Russia* **53** B15
Cholame *U.S.A.* **110** K6
Cholet *France* **18** E6
Cholguan *Chile* **126** D1
Choloma *Honduras* **120** C2
Choluteca *Honduras* **120** D2
Choluteca ➜ *Honduras* **120** D2
Chom Bung *Thailand* **64** F2
Chom Thong *Thailand* **64** C2
Choma *Zambia* **87** F2
Chomolungma = Everest,
  Mt. *Nepal* **69** E12
Chomun *India* **68** F6
Chomutov *Czech Rep.* **26** A6
Chon Buri *Thailand* **64** F3
Chon Thanh *Vietnam* **65** G6
Chone *Ecuador* **124** D2
Chong Kai *Cambodia* **64** F4
Chong Mek *Thailand* **64** E5
Chong Phangan *Thailand* **65** b
Chong Samui *Thailand* **65** b
Chongde *China* **59** B13
Ch'ŏngjin *N. Korea* **57** D15
Ch'ŏngju *N. Korea* **57** E13
Chongli *China* **56** D8
Chongming *China* **59** B13
Chongming Dao *China* **59** B13
Chongqing *Chongqing, China* **58** C6
Chongqing *Sichuan, China* **58** B4
Chongqing Shi □ *China* **58** C6
Chongren *China* **59** D11
Chonguene *Mozam.* **89** C5
Chongwe *Zambia* **87** F2
Chongyi *China* **59** E10
Chongzuo *China* **58** F6
Chonos, Arch. de los *Chile* **128** F2
Chop *Ukraine* **28** B7
Chopim ➜ *Brazil* **127** B5
Chor *Pakistan* **68** G3
Chora *Greece* **46** D3
Chora Sfakion *Greece* **49** D6
Chorbat La *India* **69** B7
Chorley *U.K.* **14** D5
Chorna *Ukraine* **29** C14
Chornobyl *Ukraine* **23** C16
Chornomorske *Ukraine* **33** K7
Chorolque, Cerro *Bolivia* **126** A2
Chorregon *Australia* **94** C3
Chorro el Indio △ *Venezuela* **121** E5
Chortkiv *Ukraine* **23** D13
Chorzele *Poland* **31** E7
Chorzów *Poland* **31** H5
Chos-Malal *Argentina* **126** D1
Ch'osan *N. Korea* **57** D13
Choszczno *Poland* **31** E2
Choteau *U.S.A.* **108** C7
Chotěboř *Czech Rep.* **26** B8
Chotila *India* **68** H4
Chotta Udepur *India* **68** H6
Chowchilla *U.S.A.* **110** H6

Choybalsan *Mongolia* **60** B6
Choyr *Mongolia* **53** E11
Christchurch *N.Z.* **91** E4
Christchurch *U.K.* **15** G6
Christian I. *Canada* **114** B4
Christian Sd. *U.S.A.* **107** D13
Christiana *S. Africa* **88** D4
Christiansfeld *Denmark* **11** J3
Christiansted *U.S. Virgin Is.* **121** C7
Christie B. *Canada* **103** A6
Christina ➜ *Canada* **103** B6
Christmas Cr. ➜ *Australia* **92** C4
Christmas I. = Kiritimati
  Kiribati **97** G12
Christmas I. *Ind. Oc.* **96** J2
Christopher, L. *Australia* **93** D4
Chrudim *Czech Rep.* **26** B8
Chrzanów *Poland* **31** H6
Chtimba *Malawi* **87** E3
Chū = Shū *Kazakhstan* **52** E8
Chu ➜ *Vietnam* **64** C5
Chu Lai *Vietnam* **64** E7
Chuadanga *Bangla.* **69** H13
Chuak, Ko *Thailand* **65** b
Chuankou *China* **56** G6
Chubbuck *U.S.A.* **108** E7
Chūbu □ *Japan* **55** F8
Chubu-Sangaku △ *Japan* **55** F8
Chubut □ *Argentina* **128** E3
Chuchi L. *Canada* **102** B4
Chuda *India* **68** H4
Chudovo *Russia* **32** C6
Chudskoye, Ozero *Russia* **32** C4
Chugach Mts. *U.S.A.* **106** C10
Chūgoku □ *Japan* **55** G6
Chūgoku-Sanchi *Japan* **55** 36
Chuguyiv = Chuhuyiv
  Ukraine **33** H9
Chugwater *U.S.A.* **108** F11
Chuhuyiv *Ukraine* **33** H9
Chuka *Kenya* **86** C4
Chukchi Plateau *Arctic* **4** 317
Chukchi Sea *Russia* **53** C19
Chukotskiy Mys *Russia* **106** C5
Chukotskiy Poluostrov
  Russia **106** B5
Chukotskoye Nagorye
  Russia **53** C18
Chula Vista *U.S.A.* **111** N9
Chulucanas *Peru* **124** E2
Chulym ➜ *Russia* **52** D9
Chum Phae *Thailand* **64** D4
Chum Saeng *Thailand* **64** E3
Chumar *India* **69** C8
Chumbicha *Argentina* **126** B2
Chumerna *Bulgaria* **45** D9
Chumikan *Russia* **53** D14
Chumphon *Thailand* **65** G2
Chumuare *Mozam.* **87** E3
Chuna ➜ *Russia* **53** D10
Chun'an *China* **59** C12
Chuncheon *S. Korea* **57** F14
Chunchura *India* **69** H13
Chunga *Zambia* **87** F2
Chunggang-ŭp *N. Korea* **57** D14
Chunghwa *N. Korea* **57** E13
Chungju *S. Korea* **57** F14
Chungking = Chongqing
  China **58** C6
Chungli *Taiwan* **59** E13
Chungt'iaoshan =
  Zhongtiao Shan *China* **56** G6
Chungyang Shanmo *Taiwan* **59** F13
Chunian *Pakistan* **68** D6
Chunya *Tanzania* **87** D3
Chunyang *China* **57** C15
Chupara Pt. *Trin. & Tob.* **125** K15
Chuquibamba *Peru* **124** G4
Chuquicamata *Chile* **126** A2
Chur *Switz.* **25** J5
Churachandpur *India* **67** G18
Church Stretton *U.K.* **15** E5
Churchill *Canada* **103** B10
Churchill ➜ *Man., Canada* **103** B10
Churchill ➜ *Nfld. & L.,
  Canada* **105** B7
Churchill, C. *Canada* **103** B10
Churchill Falls *Canada* **105** B7
Churchill L. *Canada* **103** B7
Churchill Pk. *Canada* **102** B3
Churki *India* **69** H10
Churu *India* **68** E6
Churún Merú = Angel
  Falls *Venezuela* **124** B6
Chushal *India* **69** C8
Chuska Mts. *U.S.A.* **109** H9
Chusovoy *Russia* **52** D6
Chute-aux-Outardes *Canada* **105** C6
Chuuk = Truk *Micronesia* **96** G7
Chuvash Republic =
  Chuvashia □ *Russia* **34** C8
Chuvashia □ *Russia* **34** C8
Chuwārtah *Iraq* **73** E11
Chuxiong *China* **58** E3
Chuy *Uruguay* **127** C5
Chuzhou *China* **59** A12

Ci Xian *China* **56** F8
Ciacova *Romania* **28** E6
Ciadâr-Lunga *Moldova* **29** D13
Ciamis *Indonesia* **63** G13
Cianjur *Indonesia* **63** G12
Cianorte *Brazil* **127** A5
Cibola *U.S.A.* **111** M12
Cicero *U.S.A.* **112** E10
Cicia *Fiji* **91** a
Cidacos ➜ *Spain* **38** C3
Cide *Turkey* **72** B5
Ciéagas del Cataumbo △
  Venezuela **121** D5
Ciechanów *Poland* **31** F7
Ciechanowiec *Poland* **31** F9
Ciechocinek *Poland* **31** F5
Ciego de Ávila *Cuba* **120** B4
Ciénaga *Colombia* **124** A4
Cienfuegos *Cuba* **120** B3
Cierp-Gaud *France* **20** F4
Cíes, Is. *Spain* **36** C2
Cieszanów *Poland* **31** H10
Cieszyn *Poland* **31** J5
Cieza *Spain* **39** G3
Çifteler *Turkey* **72** C4
Cifuentes *Spain* **38** E2
Cihanbeyli *Turkey* **72** C5
Cihuatlán *Mexico* **118** D4
Cijara, Embalse de *Spain* **37** F6
Cijara △ *Spain* **37** F6
Cijulang *Indonesia* **63** G13
Cilacap *Indonesia* **63** G13
Çıldır *Turkey* **73** B10
Çıldır Gölü *Turkey* **73** B10
Cilento e Vallo di Diano △
  Italy **43** B8
Cili *China* **59** C8
Cilibia *Romania* **29** E12
Cilicia *Turkey* **72** D5
Cill Airne = Killarney *Ireland* **12** D2
Cill Chainnigh = Kilkenny
  Ireland **12** D4
Cill Dara = Kildare *Ireland* **12** C5
Cill Mhantáin = Wicklow
  Ireland **12** D5
Cilo Dağı *Turkey* **73** D10
Cima *U.S.A.* **111** K11
Cimarron *Kans., U.S.A.* **112** G3
Cimarron *N. Mex., U.S.A.* **109** H11
Cimarron ➜ *U.S.A.* **116** C6
Cimișlia *Moldova* **29** D13
Cimone, Mte. *Italy* **40** D7
Çınar *Turkey* **73** D9
Çınarcık *Turkey* **45** F13
Cinca ➜ *Spain* **38** D5
Cincar *Bos.-H.* **28** G2
Cincinnati *U.S.A.* **113** F11
Cincinnatus *U.S.A.* **115** D9
Çine *Turkey* **47** D10
Ciney *Belgium* **17** D5
Cíngoli *Italy* **41** E10
Cinigiano *Italy* **41** F8
Cinto, Mte. *France* **21** F12
Cintruénigo *Spain* **38** C3
Ciocile *Romania* **29** F12
Ciorani *Romania* **29** F11
Čiovo *Croatia* **41** E13
Circeo, Mte. *Italy* **42** A6
Çırçır *Turkey* **72** C7
Circle *Alaska, U.S.A.* **106** B11
Circle *Mont., U.S.A.* **108** C11
Circleville *U.S.A.* **113** F12
Cirebon *Indonesia* **62** F3
Ciremay *Indonesia* **63** G13
Cirencester *U.K.* **15** F6
Cireșu *Romania* **28** F7
Cirey-sur-Vezouze *France* **19** D13
Ciriè *Italy* **40** C4
Cirium *Cyprus* **49** E11
Cirò *Italy* **43** C10
Cirò Marina *Italy* **43** C10
Ciron ➜ *France* **20** D3
Cisco *U.S.A.* **116** E5
Cislău *Romania* **29** E11
Cisna *Poland* **31** J9
Cisnădie *Romania* **29** E9
Cisterna di Latina *Italy* **42** A5
Cisternino *Italy* **43** B10
Cistierna *Spain* **36** C5
Citeli-Ckaro =
  Tsiteli-Tsqaro *Georgia* **35** K8
Citlaltépetl = Orizaba, Pico
  de *Mexico* **119** D5
Citrus Heights *U.S.A.* **110** G5
Citrusdal *S. Africa* **88** E2
Città del Vaticano =
  Vatican City ■ *Europe* **41** G9
Città della Pieve *Italy* **41** F9
Città di Castello *Italy* **41** E9
Città Sant' Angelo *Italy* **41** F11
Cittadella *Italy* **41** C8
Cittaducale *Italy* **41** F9
Cittanova *Italy* **43** D9
Ciuc, Munții *Romania* **29** D11
Ciucaș, Vf. *Romania* **29** E10
Ciucea *Romania* **28** D7
Ciuciulea *Moldova* **29** C12

Ciuciuleni *Moldova* **29 C13**
Ciudad Acuña *Mexico* **118 B4**
Ciudad Altamirano *Mexico* **118 D4**
Ciudad Anáhuac *Mexico* **118 B4**
Ciudad Bolívar *Venezuela* **124 B6**
Ciudad Camargo *Mexico* **118 B3**
Ciudad Cortés *Costa Rica* **120 E3**
Ciudad de México *Mexico* **119 D5**
Ciudad de Valles *Mexico* **119 C5**
Ciudad del Carmen *Mexico* **119 D6**
Ciudad del Este *Paraguay* **127 B5**
Ciudad Delicias = Delicias *Mexico* **118 B3**
Ciudad Frontera *Mexico* **118 B4**
Ciudad Guayana *Venezuela* **124 B6**
Ciudad Guerrero *Mexico* **118 B3**
Ciudad Guzmán *Mexico* **118 D4**
Ciudad Juárez *Mexico* **118 A3**
Ciudad Lerdo *Mexico* **118 B4**
Ciudad Madero *Mexico* **119 C5**
Ciudad Mante *Mexico* **119 C5**
Ciudad Obregón *Mexico* **118 B3**
Ciudad Real *Spain* **37 G7**
Ciudad Real □ *Spain* **37 G7**
Ciudad Rodrigo *Spain* **36 E4**
Ciudad Victoria *Mexico* **119 C5**
Ciudadela *Spain* **48 B10**
Ciulniţa *Romania* **29 F12**
Ciumeghiu *Romania* **28 D6**
Ciuperceni *Romania* **28 F8**
Civa Burnu *Turkey* **72 B7**
Cividale del Friuli *Italy* **41 B10**
Civita Castellana *Italy* **41 F9**
Civitanova Marche *Italy* **41 E10**
Civitavécchia *Italy* **41 F8**
Civray *France* **20 B4**
Çivril *Turkey* **47 C11**
Cixerri → *Italy* **42 C1**
Cixi *China* **59 B8**
Cizre *Turkey* **73 D10**
Clackmannanshire □ *U.K.* **13 E5**
Clacton-on-Sea *U.K.* **15 F9**
Clain → *France* **18 F7**
Clairton *U.S.A.* **114 F5**
Clairvaux-les-Lacs *France* **19 F12**
Claise → *France* **20 B5**
Clallam Bay *U.S.A.* **110 B2**
Clamecy *France* **19 E10**
Clanton *U.S.A.* **117 E11**
Clanwilliam *S. Africa* **88 E2**
Clara *Ireland* **12 C4**
Claraville *U.S.A.* **111 K8**
Clare *Australia* **95 E2**
Clare *U.S.A.* **113 D11**
Clare □ *Ireland* **12 D3**
Clare → *Ireland* **12 C2**
Clare I. *Ireland* **12 C1**
Claremont *Calif., U.S.A.* **111 L9**
Claremont *N.H., U.S.A.* **115 C12**
Claremont Pt. *Australia* **94 A3**
Claremore *U.S.A.* **116 C7**
Claremorris *Ireland* **12 C3**
Clarence → *Australia* **95 D5**
Clarence → *N.Z.* **91 E4**
Clarence, I. *Chile* **128 G2**
Clarence I. *Antarctica* **5 C18**
Clarence Str. *Australia* **92 B5**
Clarence Town *Bahamas* **121 B5**
Clarendon *Pa., U.S.A.* **114 E5**
Clarendon *Tex., U.S.A.* **116 D4**
Clarenville *Canada* **105 C9**
Claresholm *Canada* **102 D6**
Clarie Coast *Antarctica* **5 C9**
Clarinda *U.S.A.* **112 E6**
Clarington *Canada* **114 C6**
Clarion *Iowa, U.S.A.* **112 D7**
Clarion *Pa., U.S.A.* **114 E5**
Clarion → *U.S.A.* **114 E5**
Clarion Fracture Zone *Pac. Oc.* **98 H7**
Clark *U.S.A.* **112 C5**
Clark, Pt. *Canada* **114 B3**
Clark Fork *U.S.A.* **108 B5**
Clark Fork → *U.S.A.* **108 B5**
Clarkdale *U.S.A.* **109 J7**
Clarke City *Canada* **105 B6**
Clarke I. *Australia* **95 G4**
Clarke Ra. *Australia* **94 b**
Clarks Fork Yellowstone → *U.S.A.* **108 D9**
Clark's Harbour *Canada* **105 D6**
Clarks Hill L. = J. Strom Thurmond L. *U.S.A.* **117 E13**
Clarks Summit *U.S.A.* **115 E9**
Clarksburg *U.S.A.* **113 F13**
Clarksdale *U.S.A.* **117 D9**
Clarkston *U.S.A.* **108 C5**
Clarksville *Ark., U.S.A.* **116 D8**
Clarksville *Tenn., U.S.A.* **117 C11**
Clarksville *Tex., U.S.A.* **116 E7**
Clatskanie *U.S.A.* **110 D3**
Claude *U.S.A.* **116 D4**
Claveria *Phil.* **61 B4**
Clay *U.S.A.* **110 G5**
Clay Center *U.S.A.* **112 F5**
Claypool *U.S.A.* **109 K8**
Claysburg *U.S.A.* **114 F6**
Claysville *U.S.A.* **114 F4**

Clayton *Canada* **115 A8**
Clayton *N. Mex., U.S.A.* **109 H12**
Clayton *N.Y., U.S.A.* **115 B8**
Clear, C. *Ireland* **12 E2**
Clear, L. *Canada* **114 A7**
Clear Hills *Canada* **102 B5**
Clear I. *Ireland* **12 E2**
Clear L. *U.S.A.* **110 F4**
Clear Lake *Iowa, U.S.A.* **112 D7**
Clear Lake *S. Dak., U.S.A.* **112 C5**
Clear Lake Res. *U.S.A.* **108 F3**
Clearfield *Pa., U.S.A.* **114 E6**
Clearfield *Utah, U.S.A.* **108 F7**
Clearlake *U.S.A.* **110 G4**
Clearwater *Canada* **102 C4**
Clearwater *U.S.A.* **117 H13**
Clearwater → *Alta., Canada* **102 C6**
Clearwater → *Alta., Canada* **103 B6**
Clearwater L. *Canada* **103 C9**
Clearwater Lake *Canada* **103 C8**
Clearwater Mts. *U.S.A.* **108 C6**
Clearwater River △ *Canada* **103 B7**
Cleburne *U.S.A.* **116 E6**
Clee Hills *U.K.* **15 E5**
Cleethorpes *U.K.* **14 D7**
Cleeve Cloud *U.K.* **15 F6**
Clelles *France* **21 D9**
Clemson *U.S.A.* **117 D13**
Clerke Reef *Australia* **92 C2**
Clermont *Australia* **94 C4**
Clermont *France* **19 C9**
Clermont *U.S.A.* **117 G14**
Clermont-en-Argonne *France* **19 C12**
Clermont-Ferrand *France* **20 C7**
Clermont-l'Hérault *France* **20 E7**
Clerval *France* **19 E13**
Clervaux *Lux.* **17 D6**
Cles *Italy* **40 B8**
Clevedon *U.K.* **15 F5**
Cleveland *Miss., U.S.A.* **117 E9**
Cleveland *Ohio, U.S.A.* **114 E3**
Cleveland *Okla., U.S.A.* **116 C6**
Cleveland *Tex., U.S.A.* **116 F6**
Cleveland, C. *Australia* **94 B4**
Cleveland, Mt. *U.S.A.* **108 B7**
Cleveland Heights *U.S.A.* **114 E3**
Clevelândia *Brazil* **127 B5**
Clew B. *Ireland* **12 C2**
Clewiston *U.S.A.* **117 H14**
Clifden *Ireland* **12 C1**
Clifden *N.Z.* **91 G1**
Cliffdell *U.S.A.* **110 D5**
Cliffy Hd. *Australia* **93 G2**
Clifton *Australia* **95 D5**
Clifton *Ariz., U.S.A.* **109 K9**
Clifton *Colo., U.S.A.* **108 G9**
Clifton *Tex., U.S.A.* **116 F6**
Clifton Beach *Australia* **94 B4**
Clinch → *U.S.A.* **117 D12**
Clingmans Dome *U.S.A.* **117 D13**
Clint *U.S.A.* **116 F1**
Clinton *B.C., Canada* **102 C4**
Clinton *Ont., Canada* **114 C3**
Clinton *N.Z.* **91 G2**
Clinton *Ark., U.S.A.* **116 D8**
Clinton *Conn., U.S.A.* **115 E12**
Clinton *Ill., U.S.A.* **112 E9**
Clinton *Ind., U.S.A.* **112 F10**
Clinton *Iowa, U.S.A.* **112 E8**
Clinton *Mass., U.S.A.* **115 D13**
Clinton *Miss., U.S.A.* **117 E9**
Clinton *Mo., U.S.A.* **112 F7**
Clinton *N.C., U.S.A.* **117 D15**
Clinton *Okla., U.S.A.* **116 D5**
Clinton *S.C., U.S.A.* **117 D14**
Clinton *Tenn., U.S.A.* **117 C12**
Clinton *Wash., U.S.A.* **110 C4**
Clinton, C. *Australia* **94 C5**
Clinton Colden L. *Canada* **100 E10**
Clintonville *U.S.A.* **112 C9**
Clipperton, I. *Pac. Oc.* **97 F17**
Clipperton Fracture Zone *Pac. Oc.* **97 G16**
Clisham *U.K.* **13 D2**
Clisson *France* **18 E5**
Clitheroe *U.K.* **14 D5**
Clo-oose *Canada* **110 B2**
Cloates, Pt. *Australia* **92 D1**
Clocolan *S. Africa* **89 D4**
Clodomira *Argentina* **126 B3**
Clogher Hd. *Ireland* **12 C5**
Clonakilty *Ireland* **12 E3**
Clonakilty B. *Ireland* **12 E3**
Cloncurry *Australia* **94 C3**
Cloncurry *Ireland* **12 C5**
Cloncurry → *Australia* **94 B3**
Clondalkin *Ireland* **12 C5**
Clones *Ireland* **12 B4**
Clonmel *Ireland* **12 D4**
Cloppenburg *Germany* **24 C4**
Cloquet *U.S.A.* **112 B7**
Clorinda *Argentina* **126 B4**
Cloud Bay *Canada* **104 C2**
Cloud Peak *U.S.A.* **108 D10**
Cloudcroft *U.S.A.* **109 K11**
Cloverdale *U.S.A.* **110 G4**
Clovis *Calif., U.S.A.* **110 J7**

Clovis *N. Mex., U.S.A.* **109 J12**
Cloyes-sur-le-Loir *France* **18 E8**
Cloyne *Canada* **114 B7**
Cluain Meala = Clonmel *Ireland* **12 D4**
Cluj □ *Romania* **29 D8**
Cluj-Napoca *Romania* **29 D8**
Clunes *Australia* **95 F3**
Cluny *France* **19 F11**
Cluses *France* **19 F13**
Clusone *Italy* **40 C6**
Clutha → *N.Z.* **91 G2**
Clwyd → *U.K.* **14 D4**
Clyde *Canada* **102 C6**
Clyde *N.Z.* **91 F2**
Clyde *U.S.A.* **114 C8**
Clyde → *U.K.* **13 F4**
Clyde, Firth of *U.K.* **13 F3**
Clyde Muirshiel △ *U.K.* **13 F4**
Clyde River *Canada* **101 C18**
Clydebank *U.K.* **13 F4**
Clymer *N.Y., U.S.A.* **114 D5**
Clymer *Pa., U.S.A.* **114 D5**
Čmielów *Poland* **31 H8**
Côa → *Portugal* **36 D3**
Coachella *U.S.A.* **111 M10**
Coachella Canal *U.S.A.* **111 N12**
Coahoma *U.S.A.* **116 E4**
Coahuayana → *Mexico* **118 D4**
Coahuila □ *Mexico* **118 B4**
Coal → *Canada* **102 B3**
Coalane *Mozam.* **87 F4**
Coalcomán *Mexico* **118 D4**
Coaldale *Canada* **102 D6**
Coalgate *U.S.A.* **116 D6**
Coalinga *U.S.A.* **110 J6**
Coalisland *U.K.* **12 B5**
Coalville *U.K.* **14 E6**
Coalville *U.S.A.* **108 F8**
Coamo *Puerto Rico* **121 d**
Coari *Brazil* **124 D6**
Coast □ *Kenya* **86 C4**
Coast Mts. *Canada* **102 C3**
Coast Ranges *U.S.A.* **110 G4**
Coatbridge *U.K.* **13 F4**
Coatepec *Mexico* **119 D5**
Coatepeque *Guatemala* **120 D1**
Coatesville *U.S.A.* **113 F16**
Coaticook *Canada* **115 A13**
Coats I. *Canada* **101 E15**
Coats Land *Antarctica* **5 D1**
Coatzacoalcos *Mexico* **119 D6**
Cobá *Mexico* **119 C7**
Cobadin *Romania* **29 F13**
Cobalt *Canada* **104 C4**
Cobán *Guatemala* **120 C1**
Cobar *Australia* **95 E4**
Cóbh *Ireland* **12 E3**
Cobija *Bolivia* **124 F5**
Cobleskill *U.S.A.* **115 D10**
Coboconk *Canada* **114 B6**
Cobourg *Canada* **114 C6**
Cobourg Pen. *Australia* **92 B5**
Cobram *Australia* **95 F4**
Cóbué *Mozam.* **87 E3**
Coburg *Germany* **25 E6**
Coburg I. *Canada* **101 B16**
Coca *Spain* **36 D6**
Cocanada = Kakinada *India* **67 L13**
Cocentaina *Spain* **39 G4**
Cochabamba *Bolivia* **124 G5**
Cochem *Germany* **25 E3**
Cochemane *Mozam.* **87 F3**
Cochin *India* **66 Q10**
Cochin China = Nam-Phan *Vietnam* **65 G6**
Cochran *U.S.A.* **117 E13**
Cochrane *Alta., Canada* **102 C6**
Cochrane *Ont., Canada* **104 C3**
Cochrane *Chile* **128 F2**
Cochrane → *Canada* **103 B8**
Cochrane, L. *Chile* **128 F2**
Cochranton *U.S.A.* **114 E4**
Cockburn *Australia* **95 E3**
Cockburn, Canal *Chile* **128 G2**
Cockburn I. *Canada* **104 C3**
Cockburn Ra. *Australia* **92 C4**
Cockermouth *U.K.* **14 C4**
Cocklebiddy *Australia* **93 F4**
Cockpit Country, The *Jamaica* **120 a**
Coco → *Cent. Amer.* **120 D3**
Coco, I. del *Pac. Oc.* **97 G19**
Cocoa *U.S.A.* **117 G14**
Cocobeach *Gabon* **84 D1**
Cocora *Romania* **29 F12**
Cocos B. *Trin. & Tob.* **125 K15**
Cocos Is. *Ind. Oc.* **96 J1**
Cocos Ridge *Pac. Oc.* **97 G19**
Cod, C. *U.S.A.* **113 D18**
Codajás *Brazil* **124 D6**
Codigoro *Italy* **41 D9**
Codlea *Romania* **29 E10**
Codó *Brazil* **125 D10**
Codogno *Italy* **40 C6**
Codrói po *Italy* **41 C10**
Codru, Munţii *Romania* **28 D7**
Cody *U.S.A.* **108 D9**
Coe Hill *Canada* **114 B7**

Coelemu *Chile* **126 D1**
Coen *Australia* **94 A3**
Coesfeld *Germany* **24 D3**
Coeur d'Alene *U.S.A.* **108 C5**
Coeur d'Alene L. *U.S.A.* **108 C5**
Coevorden *Neths.* **17 B6**
Cofete *Canary Is.* **48 F5**
Coffeyville *U.S.A.* **112 G6**
Coffin B. *Australia* **95 E2**
Coffin Bay *Australia* **95 E2**
Coffin Bay △ *Australia* **95 E2**
Coffin Bay Peninsula *Australia* **95 E2**
Coffs Harbour *Australia* **95 E5**
Cofrentes *Spain* **39 F3**
Cogalnic → *Moldova* **29 E14**
Cogealac *Romania* **29 F13**
Coghinas → *Italy* **42 B1**
Coghinas, L. del *Italy* **42 B2**
Cognac *France* **20 C3**
Cogne *Italy* **40 C4**
Cogolin *France* **21 E10**
Cogolludo *Spain* **38 E1**
Cohocton *U.S.A.* **114 D7**
Cohocton → *U.S.A.* **114 D7**
Cohoes *U.S.A.* **115 D11**
Cohuna *Australia* **95 F3**
Coiba, I. de *Panama* **120 E3**
Coig → *Argentina* **128 G3**
Coigeach, Rubha *U.K.* **13 C3**
Coihaique *Chile* **128 F2**
Coimbatore *India* **66 P10**
Coimbra *Brazil* **124 G7**
Coimbra *Portugal* **36 E2**
Coimbra □ *Portugal* **36 E2**
Coín *Spain* **37 J6**
Coipasa, Salar de *Bolivia* **124 G5**
Cojimies *Ecuador* **124 C3**
Cojocna *Romania* **29 D8**
Cojutepequé *El Salv.* **120 D2**
Čoka *Serbia* **28 E5**
Cokeville *U.S.A.* **108 E8**
Colac *Australia* **95 F3**
Colatina *Brazil* **125 G10**
Colbeck, C. *Antarctica* **5 D13**
Colborne *Canada* **114 C7**
Colby *U.S.A.* **112 F3**
Colca → *Peru* **124 G4**
Colchester *U.K.* **15 F8**
Colchester *U.S.A.* **115 E12**
Cold L. *Canada* **103 C7**
Cold Lake *Alta., Canada* **100 G9**
Cold Lake *Alta., Canada* **103 C6**
Coldstream *Canada* **102 C5**
Coldstream *U.K.* **13 F6**
Coldwater *Canada* **114 B5**
Coldwater *Kans., U.S.A.* **112 G4**
Coldwater *Mich., U.S.A.* **113 E11**
Colebrook *U.S.A.* **115 B13**
Coleman *Canada* **102 D6**
Coleman *U.S.A.* **116 F5**
Coleman → *Australia* **94 B3**
Colenso *S. Africa* **89 D4**
Coleraine *Australia* **95 F3**
Coleraine *U.K.* **12 A5**
Coleridge, L. *N.Z.* **91 E3**
Colesberg *S. Africa* **88 E4**
Coleville *U.S.A.* **110 G7**
Colfax *Calif., U.S.A.* **110 F6**
Colfax *La., U.S.A.* **116 F8**
Colfax *Wash., U.S.A.* **108 C5**
Colhué Huapi, L. *Argentina* **128 F3**
Colibaşi *Moldova* **29 E13**
Colibaşi *Romania* **29 F9**
Cólico *Italy* **40 B6**
Coligny *France* **19 F12**
Coligny *S. Africa* **89 D4**
Colima *Mexico* **118 D4**
Colima □ *Mexico* **118 D4**
Colima, Nevado de *Mexico* **118 D4**
Colina *Chile* **126 C1**
Colina do Norte *Guinea-Biss.* **82 C2**
Colinas *Brazil* **125 E10**
Colindres *Spain* **36 B7**
Coll *U.K.* **13 E2**
Collaguasi *Chile* **126 A2**
Collarada, Peña *Spain* **38 C4**
Collarenebri *Australia* **95 D4**
Colle di Val d'Elsa *Italy* **40 E8**
Collécchio *Italy* **40 D7**
Colleen Bawn *Zimbabwe* **87 G2**
College *U.S.A.* **106 C10**
College Park *U.S.A.* **117 E12**
College Station *U.S.A.* **116 F6**
Collesalvetti *Italy* **40 E7**
Colli Euganei △ *Italy* **41 C8**
Collie *Australia* **93 F2**
Collier B. *Australia* **92 C3**
Collier Ra. *Australia* **93 D2**
Collier Range △ *Australia* **93 D2**
Collierville *U.S.A.* **117 D10**
Collina, Passo di *Italy* **40 D7**
Collingwood *Canada* **114 B4**
Collingwood *N.Z.* **91 D4**
Collins *Canada* **104 B2**
Collins Bay *Canada* **115 B8**
Collinson Pen. *Canada* **100 D11**
Collinsville *Australia* **94 C4**
Collipulli *Chile* **126 D1**

Collooney *Ireland* **12 B3**
Colmar *France* **19 D14**
Colmars *France* **21 D10**
Colmenar *Spain* **37 J6**
Colmenar de Oreja *Spain* **36 E7**
Colmenar Viejo *Spain* **36 E7**
Colo → *Australia* **95 E5**
Cologne = Köln *Germany* **24 E2**
Coloma *U.S.A.* **110 G6**
Colom, I. d'en *Spain* **48 B11**
Colomb-Béchar = Béchar *Algeria* **78 B5**
Colombey-les-Belles *France* **19 D12**
Colombey-les-Deux-Églises *France* **19 D11**
Colombia ■ *S. Amer.* **124 C4**
Colombian Basin *S. Amer.* **98 H12**
Colombo *Sri Lanka* **66 R11**
Colomiers *France* **20 E5**
Colón *B. Aires, Argentina* **126 C3**
Colón *Entre Ríos, Argentina* **126 C4**
Colón *Cuba* **120 B3**
Colón *Panama* **120 E4**
Colón, Arch. de *Ecuador* **122 D1**
Colònia de Sant Jordi *Spain* **48 B9**
Colonia del Sacramento *Uruguay* **126 C4**
Colonial Beach *U.S.A.* **113 F15**
Colonie *U.S.A.* **115 D11**
Colonna, C. *Italy* **43 C10**
Colonsay *Canada* **103 C7**
Colonsay *U.K.* **13 E2**
Colorado □ *U.S.A.* **108 G11**
Colorado → *Argentina* **128 D4**
Colorado → *N. Amer.* **109 L6**
Colorado → *U.S.A.* **116 G7**
Colorado City *U.S.A.* **116 E4**
Colorado Plateau *U.S.A.* **109 H8**
Colorado River Aqueduct *U.S.A.* **111 L12**
Colorado Springs *U.S.A.* **108 G11**
Colorno *Italy* **40 D7**
Colotlán *Mexico* **118 C4**
Colstrip *U.S.A.* **108 D10**
Colton *U.S.A.* **115 B10**
Columbia *Ky., U.S.A.* **113 G11**
Columbia *La., U.S.A.* **116 E8**
Columbia *Miss., U.S.A.* **117 F10**
Columbia *Mo., U.S.A.* **112 F7**
Columbia *Pa., U.S.A.* **115 F8**
Columbia *S.C., U.S.A.* **117 D14**
Columbia *Tenn., U.S.A.* **117 D11**
Columbia → *N. Amer.* **110 D2**
Columbia, C. *Canada* **101 A18**
Columbia, District of □ *U.S.A.* **113 F15**
Columbia Basin *U.S.A.* **108 C4**
Columbia Falls *U.S.A.* **108 B6**
Columbia Mts. *Canada* **102 C5**
Columbia Plateau *U.S.A.* **108 E5**
Columbiana *U.S.A.* **114 F4**
Columbretes, Is. *Spain* **38 F5**
Columbus *Ga., U.S.A.* **117 E12**
Columbus *Ind., U.S.A.* **113 F11**
Columbus *Kans., U.S.A.* **112 G6**
Columbus *Miss., U.S.A.* **117 E10**
Columbus *Mont., U.S.A.* **108 D9**
Columbus *N. Mex., U.S.A.* **109 L10**
Columbus *Nebr., U.S.A.* **112 E5**
Columbus *Ohio, U.S.A.* **113 F12**
Columbus *Tex., U.S.A.* **116 G6**
Colunga *Spain* **36 B5**
Colusa *U.S.A.* **110 F4**
Colville *U.S.A.* **108 B5**
Colville → *U.S.A.* **106 A9**
Colville, C. *N.Z.* **91 B5**
Colwood *Canada* **110 B3**
Colwyn Bay *U.K.* **14 D4**
Coma *Ethiopia* **81 F4**
Comácchio *Italy* **41 D9**
Comalcalco *Mexico* **119 D6**
Comallo *Argentina* **128 E2**
Comana *Romania* **29 F11**
Comanche *U.S.A.* **116 F5**
Comandante Ferraz *Antarctica* **5 C18**
Comăneşti *Romania* **29 D11**
Comarnic *Romania* **29 E10**
Comayagua *Honduras* **120 D2**
Combahee → *U.S.A.* **117 E14**
Combarbalá *Chile* **126 C1**
Combeaufontaine *France* **19 E12**
Comber *Canada* **114 D2**
Comber *U.K.* **12 B6**
Combermere *Canada* **114 A7**
Comblain-au-Pont *Belgium* **17 D5**
Combourg *France* **18 D5**
Combrailles *France* **19 F9**
Combronde *France* **20 C7**
Comeragh Mts. *Ireland* **12 D4**
Comet *Australia* **94 C4**
Comilla *Bangla.* **67 H17**
Comino *Malta* **49 C1**
Comino, C. *Italy* **42 B2**
Cómiso *Italy* **43 F7**
Comitán de Domínguez *Mexico* **119 D6**

Commentry *France* **19 F9**
Commerce *Ga., U.S.A.* **117 D13**
Commerce *Tex., U.S.A.* **116 E7**
Commercy *France* **19 D12**
Committee B. *Canada* **101 D14**
Commodore, C. *Canada* **114 B4**
Commonwealth B. *Antarctica* **5 C10**
Commoron Cr. → *Australia* **95 D5**
Communism Pk. = imeni Ismail Samani, Pik *Tajikistan* **52 F8**
Como *Italy* **40 C6**
Como, Lago di *Italy* **40 B6**
Comodoro Rivadavia *Argentina* **128 F3**
Comoé → *Ivory C.* **82 D4**
Comoé △ *Ivory C.* **82 D4**
Comorâşte *Romania* **28 E6**
Comorin, C. = Kannyakumari *India* **66 Q10**
Comoros ■ *Ind. Oc.* **85 a**
Comox *Canada* **102 D4**
Compiègne *France* **19 C9**
Comporta *Portugal* **37 G2**
Compostela *Mexico* **118 C4**
Comprida, I. *Brazil* **127 A6**
Compton *Canada* **115 A13**
Compton *U.S.A.* **111 M8**
Comrat *Moldova* **29 E13**
Con Cuong *Vietnam* **64 C5**
Con Dao △ *Vietnam* **65 H6**
Con Son *Vietnam* **65 H6**
Conakry *Guinea* **82 D2**
Conara *Australia* **95 G4**
Concarneau *France* **18 E3**
Conceição *Mozam.* **87 F4**
Conceição da Barra *Brazil* **125 G11**
Conceição do Araguaia *Brazil* **125 E9**
Concepción *Argentina* **126 B2**
Concepción *Bolivia* **124 G6**
Concepción *Chile* **126 D1**
Concepción *Mexico* **119 D6**
Concepción *Paraguay* **126 A4**
Concepción □ *Chile* **126 D1**
Concepción → *Mexico* **118 A2**
Concepción, Est. de *Chile* **128 G2**
Concepción, L. *Bolivia* **124 G6**
Concepción, Pta. *Mexico* **118 B2**
Concepción del Oro *Mexico* **118 C4**
Concepción del Uruguay *Argentina* **126 C4**
Conception, Pt. *U.S.A.* **111 L6**
Conception B. *Canada* **105 C9**
Conception B. *Namibia* **88 C1**
Conception I. *Bahamas* **121 B4**
Concession *Zimbabwe* **87 F3**
Conchas Dam *U.S.A.* **109 J11**
Conches-en-Ouche *France* **18 D7**
Concho *U.S.A.* **109 J9**
Concho → *U.S.A.* **116 F5**
Conchos → *Chihuahua, Mexico* **118 B4**
Conchos → *Chihuahua, Mexico* **118 B3**
Conchos → *Tamaulipas, Mexico* **119 B5**
Concord *Calif., U.S.A.* **110 H4**
Concord *N.C., U.S.A.* **117 D14**
Concord *N.H., U.S.A.* **115 C13**
Concordia *Antarctica* **5 D17**
Concordia *Argentina* **126 C4**
Concórdia *Amazonas, Brazil* **124 D5**
Concórdia *Sta. Catarina, Brazil* **127 B5**
Concordia *Mexico* **118 C3**
Concordia *U.S.A.* **112 F5**
Concrete *U.S.A.* **108 B3**
Condamine *Australia* **95 D5**
Condat *France* **20 C6**
Conde *U.S.A.* **112 C4**
Condé-sur-Noireau *France* **18 D6**
Condeúba *Brazil* **125 F10**
Condobolin *Australia* **95 E4**
Condom *France* **20 E4**
Condon *U.S.A.* **108 D3**
Conegliano *Italy* **41 C9**
Conejera, I. = Conills, I. des *Spain* **48 B9**
Conejos *Mexico* **118 B4**
Conemaugh → *U.S.A.* **114 F5**
Conero △ *Italy* **41 E10**
Confolens *France* **20 B4**
Confuso → *Paraguay* **126 B4**
Congaz *Moldova* **29 D13**
Conghua *China* **59 F9**
Congjiang *China* **58 E7**
Congleton *U.K.* **14 D5**
Congo (Brazzaville) = Congo ■ *Africa* **84 E3**
Congo (Kinshasa) = Congo, Dem. Rep. of the ■ *Africa* **84 E4**
Congo ■ *Africa* **84 E3**
Congo → *Africa* **84 F2**
Congo, Dem. Rep. of the ■ *Africa* **84 E4**
Congo Basin *Africa* **84 E4**
Congonhas *Brazil* **127 A7**
Congress *U.S.A.* **109 J7**

Conil de la Frontera *Spain* **37** J4
Conills, I. des *Spain* **48** B9
Coniston *Canada* **104** C3
Conjeeveram =
  Kanchipuram *India* **66** N11
Conklin *Canada* **103** B6
Conklin *U.S.A.* **115** D9
Conn, L. *Ireland* **12** B2
Connacht □ *Ireland* **12** C2
Conneaut *U.S.A.* **114** E4
Conneautville *U.S.A.* **114** E4
Connecticut □ *U.S.A.* **115** E12
Connecticut → *U.S.A.* **115** E12
Connell *U.S.A.* **108** C4
Connellsville *U.S.A.* **114** F5
Connemara *Ireland* **12** C2
Connemara △ *Ireland* **12** C2
Connerré *France* **18** D7
Connersville *U.S.A.* **113** F11
Connors Ra. *Australia* **94** C4
Conoename → *Suriname* **125** B7
Conques *France* **20** D6
Conquest *Canada* **103** C7
Conrad *U.S.A.* **108** B8
Conran, C. *Australia* **95** F4
Conroe *U.S.A.* **116** F7
Consecon *Canada* **114** C7
Conselheiro Lafaiete *Brazil* **127** A7
Consell *Spain* **48** B9
Conselve *Italy* **41** C8
Consett *U.K.* **14** C6
Consort *Canada* **103** C6
Constance = Konstanz
  Germany **25** H5
Constance, L. = Bodensee
  Europe **25** H5
Constanţa *Romania* **29** F13
Constanţa □ *Romania* **29** F13
Constantina *Spain* **37** H5
Constantine *Algeria* **78** A7
Constitución *Chile* **126** D1
Constitución *Uruguay* **126** C4
Constitución de 1857 △
  Mexico **118** A1
Consuegra *Spain* **37** F7
Consul *Canada* **103** D7
Contact *U.S.A.* **108** F6
Contai *India* **69** J12
Contamana *Peru* **124** E4
Contarina *Italy* **41** C9
Contas → *Brazil* **125** F11
Contes *France* **21** E11
Contoocook *U.S.A.* **115** C13
Contra Costa *Mozam.* **89** D5
Contres *France* **18** E8
Contrexéville *France* **19** D12
Contwoyto L. *Canada* **100** D9
Conversano *Italy* **43** B10
Conway = Conwy *U.K.* **14** D4
Conway = Conwy → *U.K.* **14** D4
Conway *Australia* **94** b
Conway *Canada* **114** B8
Conway Ark., *U.S.A.* **116** D8
Conway N.H., *U.S.A.* **115** C13
Conway S.C., *U.S.A.* **117** E15
Conway, C. *Australia* **94** b
Conway, L. *Australia* **95** D2
Conwy *U.K.* **14** D4
Conwy □ *U.K.* **14** D4
Conwy → *U.K.* **14** D4
Coober Pedy *Australia* **95** D1
Cooch Behar = Koch Bihar
  India **67** F16
Cooinda *Australia* **92** B5
Cook *Australia* **93** F5
Cook *U.S.A.* **112** E7
Cook, B. *Chile* **128** H3
Cook, C. *Canada* **102** C3
Cook, Mt. = Aoraki Mount
  Cook *N.Z.* **91** E3
Cook Inlet *U.S.A.* **100** F1
Cook Is. *Pac. Oc.* **97** J12
Cook Strait *N.Z.* **91** D5
Cookeville *U.S.A.* **117** C12
Cookhouse *S. Africa* **88** E4
Cooks Harbour *Canada* **105** B8
Cookshire *Canada* **115** A13
Cookstown *Canada* **114** B5
Cookstown *U.K.* **12** B5
Cooksville *Canada* **114** C5
Cooktown *Australia* **94** B4
Coolabah *Australia* **95** E4
Cooladdi *Australia* **95** D4
Coolah *Australia* **95** E4
Coolamon *Australia* **95** E4
Coolgardie *Australia* **93** F3
Coolidge *U.S.A.* **109** K8
Coolidge Dam *U.S.A.* **109** K8
Cooma *Australia* **95** F4
Coon Rapids *U.S.A.* **112** C7
Coonabarabran *Australia* **95** E4
Coonamble *Australia* **95** E4
Coonana ⊙ *Australia* **93** F3
Coondapoor *India* **66** N9
Cooninnie, L. *Australia* **95** D2
Cooper *U.S.A.* **116** E7
Cooper Cr. → *Australia* **95** D2

Cooper Ridge *Pac. Oc.* **97** G12
Cooperstown N. Dak., *U.S.A.* **112** B4
Cooperstown N.Y., *U.S.A.* **115** D10
Coorabie *Australia* **93** F5
Coorong, The *Australia* **95** F2
Coorow *Australia* **93** E2
Cooroy *Australia* **95** D5
Coos Bay *U.S.A.* **108** E1
Coosa → *U.S.A.* **117** E11
Cootamundra *Australia* **95** E4
Cootehill *Ireland* **12** B4
Copahue Paso *Argentina* **126** D1
Copainalá *Mexico* **119** D6
Copake *U.S.A.* **115** D11
Copalnic Mănăştur *Romania* **29** C8
Copán *Honduras* **120** D2
Cope *U.S.A.* **108** G12
Cope, C. *Spain* **39** H3
Copenhagen = København
  Denmark **11** J6
Copenhagen *U.S.A.* **115** C9
Copertino *Italy* **43** B11
Copiapó *Chile* **126** B1
Copiapó → *Chile* **126** B1
Coplay *U.S.A.* **115** F9
Copo △ *Argentina* **126** B3
Copp L. *Canada* **102** A6
Copparo *Italy* **41** D8
Copper Canyon = Barranca
  del Cobre △ *Mexico* **118** B3
Copper Center *U.S.A.* **106** C10
Copper Harbor *U.S.A.* **112** B10
Copper Queen *Zimbabwe* **87** F2
Copperas Cove *U.S.A.* **116** F6
Copperbelt □ *Zambia* **87** E2
Coppermine = Kugluktuk
  Canada **100** D8
Coppermine → *Canada* **100** D8
Copperopolis *U.S.A.* **110** H6
Copşa Mică *Romania* **29** D9
Coquet → *U.K.* **14** B6
Coquille *U.S.A.* **108** E1
Coquimbo *Chile* **126** C1
Coquimbo □ *Chile* **126** C1
Coquitlam *Canada* **102** D4
Corabia *Romania* **29** G9
Coracora *Peru* **124** G4
Coraki *Australia* **95** D5
Coral *U.S.A.* **114** F5
Coral Bay *Australia* **92** D1
Coral Gables *U.S.A.* **117** J14
Coral Harbour *Canada* **101** E15
Coral Sea *Pac. Oc.* **90** C8
Coral Sea Basin *Pac. Oc.* **96** J7
Coral Sea Islands Terr. □
  Australia **90** C8
Coral Springs *U.S.A.* **117** H14
Coraopolis *U.S.A.* **114** F4
Corato *Italy* **43** A9
Corbeil-Essonnes *France* **19** D9
Corbett △ *India* **69** E8
Corbie *France* **19** C9
Corbières *France* **20** F6
Corbigny *France* **19** E10
Corbin *U.S.A.* **113** G11
Corbones → *Spain* **37** H5
Corby *U.K.* **15** E7
Corcaigh = Cork *Ireland* **12** E3
Corcoran *U.S.A.* **110** J7
Corcovado △ *Costa Rica* **120** E3
Cordele *U.S.A.* **117** F13
Cordell *U.S.A.* **116** D5
Cordenòns *Italy* **41** C9
Cordes-sur-Ciel *France* **20** D5
Córdoba *Argentina* **126** C3
Córdoba *Mexico* **119** D5
Córdoba *Spain* **37** H6
Córdoba □ *Argentina* **126** C3
Córdoba □ *Spain* **37** G6
Córdoba, Sierra de *Argentina* **126** C3
Cordon *Phil.* **61** C4
Cordova *U.S.A.* **100** E2
Corella *Spain* **38** C3
Corella → *Australia* **94** B3
Corfield *Australia* **94** C3
Corfu = Kerkyra *Greece* **49** A3
Corfu *U.S.A.* **114** D6
Corfu ✈ (CFU) *Greece* **46** B1
Corfu, Str. of = Kerkyras,
  Notio Steno *Greece* **49** A4
Corgo = O Corgo *Spain* **36** C3
Cori *Italy* **42** A5
Coria *Spain* **36** F4
Coria del Río *Spain* **37** H4
Corigliano Cálabro *Italy* **43** C9
Coringa Is. *Australia* **94** B4
Corinth = Korinthos *Greece* **46** D4
Corinth Miss., *U.S.A.* **117** D10
Corinth N.Y., *U.S.A.* **115** C11
Corinth, G. of =
  Korinthiakos Kolpos
  Greece **46** C4
Corinth Canal *Greece* **46** D4
Corinto *Brazil* **125** G10
Corinto *Nic.* **120** D2
Cork *Ireland* **12** E3
Cork □ *Ireland* **12** E3
Cork Harbour *Ireland* **12** E3

Corlay *France* **18** D3
Corleone *Italy* **42** E6
Corleto Perticara *Italy* **43** B9
Çorlu *Turkey* **45** E11
Cormòns *Italy* **41** C10
Cormack L. *Canada* **102** A4
Cormorant *Canada* **103** C8
Cormorant L. *Canada* **103** C8
Corn Is. = Maíz, Is. del *Nic.* **120** D3
Cornalvo △ *Spain* **37** F4
Cornélio Procópio *Brazil* **127** A5
Corner Brook *Canada* **105** C8
Corneşti *Moldova* **29** C13
Corníglio *Italy* **40** D7
Corning Ark., *U.S.A.* **117** C9
Corning Calif., *U.S.A.* **108** G2
Corning Iowa, *U.S.A.* **112** E6
Corning N.Y., *U.S.A.* **114** D7
Corno Grande *Italy* **41** F10
Cornwall *Canada* **115** A10
Cornwall *U.S.A.* **115** F8
Cornwall □ *U.K.* **15** G3
Cornwall I. *Canada* **101** B13
Cornwallis I. *Canada* **101** B13
Corny Pt. *Australia* **95** E2
Coro *Venezuela* **124** A5
Coroatá *Brazil* **125** D10
Corocoro *Bolivia* **124** G5
Coroico *Bolivia* **124** G5
Coromandel *N.Z.* **91** B5
Coromandel Coast *India* **66** N12
Corona Calif., *U.S.A.* **111** M9
Corona N. Mex., *U.S.A.* **109** J11
Coronado *U.S.A.* **111** N9
Coronado, B. de *Costa Rica* **120** E3
Coronados, Is. Los *Mexico* **111** N9
Coronation *Canada* **102** C6
Coronation Gulf *Canada* **100** D10
Coronation I. *Antarctica* **5** C18
Coronation Is. *Australia* **92** B3
Coronda *Argentina* **126** C3
Coronel *Chile* **126** D1
Coronel Bogado *Paraguay* **126** B4
Coronel Dorrego *Argentina* **126** D3
Coronel Oviedo *Paraguay* **126** B4
Coronel Pringles *Argentina* **126** D3
Coronel Suárez *Argentina* **126** D3
Coronel Vidal *Argentina* **126** D4
Coropuna, Nevado *Peru* **124** G4
Çorovodë *Albania* **44** F4
Corowa *Australia* **95** F4
Corozal □ *Belize* **119** D7
Corozal Pt. *Trin. & Tob.* **125** K15
Corps *France* **21** D9
Corpus *Argentina* **127** B4
Corpus Christi *U.S.A.* **116** H6
Corpus Christi, L. *U.S.A.* **116** G6
Corral de Almaguer *Spain* **36** F7
Corralejo *Canary Is.* **48** F6
Corraun Pen. *Ireland* **12** C2
Corréggio *Italy* **40** D7
Correntes, C. das *Mozam.* **89** C6
Corrèze □ *France* **20** C5
Corrèze → *France* **20** C5
Corrib, L. *Ireland* **12** C2
Corridónia *Italy* **41** E10
Corrientes *Argentina* **126** B4
Corrientes □ *Argentina* **126** B4
Corrientes → *Argentina* **126** C4
Corrientes → *Peru* **124** D4
Corrientes, C. *Colombia* **124** B3
Corrientes, C. *Cuba* **120** B3
Corrientes, C. *Mexico* **118** C3
Corrigan *U.S.A.* **116** F7
Corrigin *Australia* **93** F2
Corry *U.S.A.* **114** E5
Corse □ *France* **21** G13
Corse, C. *France* **21** E13
Corse → *France* **21** F13
Corse-du-Sud □ *France* **21** G13
Corsica = Corse □ *France* **21** G13
Corsicana *U.S.A.* **116** E6
Corte *France* **21** F13
Corte Pinto *Portugal* **37** H3
Cortegana *Spain* **37** H4
Cortés, Mar de =
  California, G. de *Mexico* **118** B2
Cortez *U.S.A.* **109** H9
Cortina d'Ampezzo *Italy* **41** B9
Cortland N.Y., *U.S.A.* **115** D8
Cortland Ohio, *U.S.A.* **114** E4
Cortona *Italy* **41** E8
Corubal → *Guinea-Biss.* **82** C2
Coruche *Portugal* **37** G2
Çoruh → *Turkey* **73** K5
Çorum *Turkey* **72** B6
Çorum □ *Turkey* **72** B6
Corumbá *Brazil* **124** G7
Corund *Romania* **29** D10
Corunna = A Coruña *Spain* **36** B2
Corvallis *U.S.A.* **108** D2
Corvette, L. de la *Canada* **104** B5
Corvo *Azores* **78** a
Corydon *U.S.A.* **112** E7
Cosalá *Mexico* **118** C3
Cosamaloapan de Carpio
  Mexico **119** D5
Cosenza *Italy* **43** C9

Coşereni *Romania* **29** F11
Coshocton *U.S.A.* **114** F3
Cosmo Newberry *Australia* **93** E3
Cosmo Newberry ⊙ *Australia* **93** E3
Cosmonaut Sea *S. Ocean* **5** C5
Cosne-Cours-sur-Loire
  France **19** E9
Coso Junction *U.S.A.* **111** J9
Coso Pk. *U.S.A.* **111** J9
Cospeito *Spain* **36** B3
Cosquín *Argentina* **126** C3
Cossato *Italy* **40** C5
Cossé-le-Vivien *France* **18** E6
Cosson → *France* **18** E8
Costa Blanca *Spain* **39** G4
Costa Brava *Spain* **38** D8
Costa Cálida *Spain* **39** H3
Costa Daurada *Spain* **38** D6
Costa del Sol *Spain* **37** J6
Costa dels Pins *Spain* **48** B10
Costa Mesa *U.S.A.* **111** M9
Costa Rica ■ *Cent. Amer.* **120** E3
Costa Smeralda *Italy* **42** A2
Costeşti *Romania* **29** F9
Costigliole d'Asti *Italy* **40** D5
Cosumnes → *U.S.A.* **110** G5
Coswig *Sachsen*, *Germany* **24** D9
Coswig *Sachsen-Anhalt*,
  Germany **24** D8
Cotabato *Phil.* **61** H6
Cotagaita *Bolivia* **126** A2
Côte d'Azur *France* **21** E11
Côte-d'Ivoire = Ivory
  Coast ■ *Africa* **82** D4
Côte d'Or *France* **19** E11
Côte-d'Or □ *France* **19** E11
Coteau des Prairies *U.S.A.* **112** C5
Coteau du Missouri *U.S.A.* **112** B4
Cotentin *France* **18** C5
Côtes-d'Armor □ *France* **18** D4
Côtes de Meuse *France* **19** C12
Côtes-du-Nord =
  Côtes-d'Armor □ *France* **18** D4
Cotiella *Spain* **38** C5
Cotillo *Canary Is.* **48** F5
Cotiujeni *Moldova* **29** C13
Cotonou *Benin* **83** D5
Cotopaxi *Ecuador* **124** D3
Cotronei *Italy* **43** C9
Cotswold Hills *U.K.* **15** F5
Cottage Grove *U.S.A.* **108** E2
Cottam *Canada* **114** D2
Cottbus *Germany* **24** D10
Cottonwood *U.S.A.* **109** J7
Cotulla *U.S.A.* **116** G5
Coubre, Pte. de la *France* **20** C2
Couches *France* **19** F11
Coudersport *U.S.A.* **114** E6
Couedic, C. du *Australia* **95** F2
Couëron *France* **18** E5
Couesnon → *France* **18** D5
Couhé *France* **20** B4
Coulanges-sur-Yonne
  France **19** E10
Coulee City *U.S.A.* **108** C4
Coulee Dam Nat. Recr.
  Area = Lake Roosevelt △
  U.S.A. **108** B4
Coulman I. *Antarctica* **5** D11
Coulommiers *France* **19** D10
Coulon → *France* **21** E9
Coulonge → *Canada* **104** C4
Coulonges-sur-l'Autize
  France **20** B3
Coulounieix-Chamiers
  France **20** C4
Coulterville *U.S.A.* **110** H6
Council *Alaska, U.S.A.* **106** C7
Council *Idaho, U.S.A.* **108** D5
Council Bluffs *U.S.A.* **112** E6
Council Grove *U.S.A.* **112** F5
Coupeville *U.S.A.* **110** B4
Courantyne → *S. Amer.* **124** B7
Courcelles *Belgium* **17** D4
Courchevel *France* **21** C10
Courçon *France* **20** B3
Courmayeur *Italy* **40** C3
Couronne, C. *France* **21** E9
Cours-la-Ville *France* **19** F11
Coursan *France* **20** E7
Courseulles-sur-Mer *France* **18** C6
Courtenay *Canada* **102** D4
Courtenay *France* **19** D10
Courtland *Canada* **114** D4
Courtland *U.S.A.* **113** G13
Courtrai = Kortrijk *Belgium* **17** D3
Courtright *Canada* **114** D2
Coushatta *U.S.A.* **116** F8
Coutances *France* **18** C5
Couto Magalhães → *Brazil* **125** D9
Coutras *France* **20** C3
Coutts Crossing *Australia* **95** D5
Couva *Trin. & Tob.* **125** K15
Couvin *Belgium* **17** D4
Covarrubias *Spain* **36** C7
Covasna *Romania* **29** E11
Covasna □ *Romania* **29** E10
Cove I. *Canada* **114** A3
Coventry *U.K.* **15** E6

Covilhã *Portugal* **36** E3
Covington Ga., *U.S.A.* **117** E13
Covington Ky., *U.S.A.* **113** F11
Covington Tenn., *U.S.A.* **117** D10
Covington Va., *U.S.A.* **113** G14
Cowal, L. *Australia* **95** E4
Cowan *Canada* **103** C8
Cowan, L. *Australia* **93** F3
Cowan L. *Canada* **103** C7
Cowangie *Australia* **95** F3
Cowansville *Canada* **115** A12
Coward Springs *Australia* **95** D2
Cowcowing Lakes *Australia* **93** F2
Cowdenbeath *U.K.* **13** E5
Cowell *Australia* **95** E2
Cowes *U.K.* **15** G6
Cowichan L. *Canada* **110** B2
Cowlitz → *U.S.A.* **110** D4
Cowra *Australia* **95** E4
Cox *Spain* **39** G4
Cox's Bazar *Bangla.* **67** J17
Coxim *Brazil* **125** G8
Coxilha Grande *Brazil* **127** B5
Coyah *Guinea* **82** D2
Coyote Wells *U.S.A.* **111** N11
Coyuca de Benitez *Mexico* **119** D4
Coyuca de Catalán *Mexico* **118** D4
Cozad *U.S.A.* **112** E4
Cozes *France* **20** C3
Cozumel *Mexico* **119** C7
Cozumel, Isla *Mexico* **119** C7
Crab Hill *Barbados* **121** g
Cracow = Kraków *Poland* **31** H6
Cracow *Australia* **95** D5
Cradle Mt.-Lake St. Clair △
  Australia **95** G4
Cradock *Australia* **95** E2
Cradock *S. Africa* **88** E4
Craig *U.S.A.* **108** F10
Craigavon □ *U.K.* **12** B5
Craigmore *Zimbabwe* **87** G3
Craik *Canada* **103** C7
Crailsheim *Germany* **25** F6
Craiova *Romania* **29** F8
Cramsie *Australia* **94** C3
Cranberry L. *U.S.A.* **115** B10
Cranberry Portage *Canada* **103** C8
Cranbrook *Australia* **93** F2
Cranbrook *Canada* **102** D5
Crandon *U.S.A.* **112** C9
Crane Oreg., *U.S.A.* **108** E4
Crane Tex., *U.S.A.* **116** F3
Crane, The *Barbados* **121** g
Cranston *U.S.A.* **115** E13
Craon *France* **18** E6
Craonne *France* **19** C10
Craponne-sur-Arzon *France* **20** C7
Crasna *Romania* **29** D12
Crasna → *Romania* **28** D6
Crasnei, Munţii *Romania* **29** C8
Crater L. *U.S.A.* **108** E2
Crater Lake △ *U.S.A.* **108** E2
Craters of the Moon △
  U.S.A. **108** E7
Crateús *Brazil* **125** E10
Crati → *Italy* **43** C9
Crato *Brazil* **125** E11
Crato *Portugal* **37** F3
Craven *Canada* **103** C8
Crawford *U.S.A.* **112** D2
Crawfordsville *U.S.A.* **112** E10
Crawley *U.K.* **15** F7
Crazy Mts. *U.S.A.* **108** C8
Crean L. *Canada* **103** C7
Crécy-en-Ponthieu *France* **19** B8
Crediton *Canada* **114** C3
Crediton *U.K.* **15** G4
Cree → *Canada* **103** B7
Cree → *U.K.* **13** G4
Cree L. *Canada* **103** B7
Creede *U.S.A.* **109** H10
Creekside *U.S.A.* **114** F5
Creel *Mexico* **118** B3
Creemore *Canada* **114** B4
Creighton *Canada* **103** C8
Creighton *U.S.A.* **112** D5
Creil *France* **19** C9
Crema *Italy* **40** C6
Cremona *Italy* **40** C7
Crepaja *Serbia* **28** E5
Crépy *France* **19** C10
Crépy-en-Valois *France* **19** C9
Cres *Croatia* **41** D11
Crescent City *U.S.A.* **108** F1
Crescentino *Italy* **40** C5
Crespo *Argentina* **126** C3
Cresson *U.S.A.* **114** F6
Crest *France* **21** D9
Cresta, Mt. *Phil.* **61** C5
Crestline Calif., *U.S.A.* **111** L9
Crestline Ohio, *U.S.A.* **114** F2
Creston *Canada* **102** D5
Creston Iowa, *U.S.A.* **112** E6
Crestview Calif., *U.S.A.* **110** H8
Crestview Fla., *U.S.A.* **117** F11
Crêt de la Neige *France* **19** F12
Crete = Kriti *Greece* **49** D7
Crete *U.S.A.* **112** E5
Crete, Sea of *Greece* **47** E7

Créteil *France* **19** D9
Creus, C. de *Spain* **38** C8
Creuse □ *France* **19** F9
Creuse → *France* **20** B4
Creutzwald *France* **19** C13
Creuzburg *Germany* **24** D6
Crèvecœur-le-Grand *France* **19** C9
Crevillent *Spain* **39** G4
Crewe *U.K.* **14** D5
Crewkerne *U.K.* **15** G5
Crianlarich *U.K.* **13** E4
Criciúma *Brazil* **127** B6
Cricova *Moldova* **29** C13
Crieff *U.K.* **13** E5
Crikvenica *Croatia* **41** C11
Crimea □ *Ukraine* **33** K8
Crimean Pen. = Krymskyy
  Pivostriv *Ukraine* **33** K8
Crimmitschau *Germany* **24** E8
Cristuru Secuiesc *Romania* **29** D10
Crişul Alb → *Romania* **28** D6
Crişul Negru → *Romania* **28** D6
Crişul Repede → *Romania* **28** D5
Criuleni *Moldova* **29** C14
Crivitz *Germany* **24** B7
Crna → *Macedonia* **44** E5
Crna Gora =
  Montenegro ■ *Europe* **44** D3
Crna Gora *Macedonia* **44** D5
Crna Reka = Crna →
  Macedonia **44** E5
Crna Trava *Serbia* **44** D6
Crni Drim → *Macedonia* **44** E4
Crni Timok → *Serbia* **44** C6
Crnoljeva Planina *Kosovo* **44** D5
Črnomelj *Slovenia* **41** C12
Croagh Patrick *Ireland* **12** C2
Croatia ■ *Europe* **41** C13
Crocker, Banjaran *Malaysia* **62** C5
Crockett *U.S.A.* **116** F7
Crocodile = Umgwenya →
  Mozam. **89** D5
Crocodile Is. *Australia* **94** A1
Crocq *France* **20** C6
Crodo *Italy* **40** B5
Crohy Hd. *Ireland* **12** B3
Croisette, C. *France* **21** E9
Croisic, Pte. du *France* **18** E4
Croix, L. la *Canada* **104** C1
Croker, C. *Australia* **92** B5
Croker, C. *Canada* **114** B4
Croker I. *Australia* **92** B5
Croker Islands Seas ⊙
  Australia **92** B5
Cromarty *U.K.* **13** D4
Cromer *U.K.* **14** E9
Cromwell *N.Z.* **91** F2
Cromwell *U.S.A.* **115** E12
Cronat *France* **19** F10
Crook *U.K.* **14** C6
Crooked → *Canada* **102** C4
Crooked → *U.S.A.* **108** D3
Crooked I. *Bahamas* **121** B5
Crooked Island Passage
  Bahamas **121** B5
Crookston Minn., *U.S.A.* **112** B5
Crookston Nebr., *U.S.A.* **112** D3
Crookwell *Australia* **95** E4
Cropane-Micone △ *Italy* **43** D9
Crosby *U.K.* **14** D4
Crosby N. Dak., *U.S.A.* **112** A2
Crosby Pa., *U.S.A.* **114** E6
Crosia *Italy* **43** C9
Cross → *Nigeria* **83** E6
Cross City *U.S.A.* **117** G13
Cross Fell *U.K.* **14** C5
Cross L. *Canada* **103** C9
Cross Lake *Canada* **103** C9
Cross River □ *Nigeria* **83** D6
Cross River △ *Nigeria* **83** E6
Cross Sound *U.S.A.* **100** F4
Crossett *U.S.A.* **116** F9
Crosshaven *Ireland* **12** E3
Crossmaglen *U.K.* **12** B5
Crossmolina *Ireland* **12** B2
Crossville *U.S.A.* **117** D12
Croswell *U.S.A.* **114** C2
Croton-on-Hudson *U.S.A.* **115** E11
Crotone *Italy* **43** C10
Crow → *Canada* **102** B4
Crow Agency *U.S.A.* **108** D10
Crow Hd. *Ireland* **12** E1
Crowell *U.S.A.* **116** E5
Crowley *U.S.A.* **116** F8
Crowley, L. *U.S.A.* **110** H8
Crown Point Ind., *U.S.A.* **112** E10
Crown Point N.Y., *U.S.A.* **115** C11
Crown Pt. *Trin. & Tob.* **125** J16
Crownpoint *U.S.A.* **109** J9
Crows Landing *U.S.A.* **110** H5
Crows Nest *Australia* **95** D5
Crowsnest Pass *Canada* **102** D6
Croydon *Australia* **94** B3
Croydon □ *U.K.* **15** F7
Crozet, Is. *Ind. Oc.* **3** G12
Crozon *France* **18** D2
Crusheen *Ireland* **12** D3
Cruz, C. *Cuba* **120** C4

Cruz Alta *Brazil* **127** B5
Cruz Bay *U.S. Virgin Is.* **121** e
Cruz del Eje *Argentina* **126** C3
Cruzeiro *Brazil* **127** A7
Cruzeiro do Oeste *Brazil* **127** A5
Cruzeiro do Sul *Brazil* **124** E4
Cry L. *Canada* **102** B3
Crystal Bay *U.S.A.* **110** F7
Crystal Brook *Australia* **95** E2
Crystal City *U.S.A.* **116** G5
Crystal Falls *U.S.A.* **112** B9
Crystal River *U.S.A.* **117** G13
Crystal Springs *U.S.A.* **117** F9
Csenger *Hungary* **28** C7
Csongrád *Hungary* **28** D5
Csongrád □ *Hungary* **28** D5
Csorna *Hungary* **28** C2
Csurgo *Hungary* **28** D2
Cu Lao Hon *Vietnam* **65** G7
Cua Rao *Vietnam* **64** C5
Cuácua ➤ *Mozam.* **87** F4
Cuamato *Angola* **88** B2
Cuamba *Mozam.* **87** E4
Cuando ➤ *Angola* **85** H4
Cuando Cubango □ *Angola* **88** B3
Cuangar *Angola* **88** B2
Cuango = Kwango ➤
  Dem. Rep. of the Congo **84** E3
Cuanza ➤ *Angola* **84** F2
Cuarto ➤ *Argentina* **126** C3
Cuatrociénegas *Mexico* **118** B4
Cuauhtémoc *Mexico* **118** B3
Cuba *Portugal* **37** G3
Cuba *N. Mex., U.S.A.* **109** H10
Cuba *N.Y., U.S.A.* **114** D6
Cuba ■ *W. Indies* **120** B4
Cubango ➤ *Africa* **88** B3
Çubuk *Turkey* **72** B5
Cuc Phuong △ *Vietnam* **64** B5
Cuchumatanes, Sierra de
  los *Guatemala* **120** C1
Cuckfield *U.K.* **15** F7
Cucuí *Brazil* **124** C5
Cucurpé *Mexico* **118** A2
Cúcuta *Colombia* **124** B4
Cudalbi *Romania* **29** E12
Cuddalore *India* **66** P11
Cuddapah *India* **66** M11
Cuddapan, L. *Australia* **94** D3
Cudillero *Spain* **36** B4
Cue *Australia* **93** E2
Cuéllar *Spain* **36** D6
Cuenca *Ecuador* **124** D3
Cuenca *Spain* **38** E2
Cuenca □ *Spain* **38** F3
Cuenca, Serranía de *Spain* **38** F3
Cuenca Alta del
  Manzanares △ *Spain* **36** E7
Cuerda del Pozo, Embalse
  de la *Spain* **38** D2
Cuernavaca *Mexico* **119** D5
Cuero *U.S.A.* **116** G6
Cuers *France* **21** E10
Cueva de la Quebrada del
  Toro △ *Venezuela* **121** D6
Cuevas del Almanzora *Spain* **39** H3
Cuevo *Bolivia* **124** H6
Cugir *Romania* **29** E8
Cugnaux *France* **20** E5
Cuhai-Bakony ➤ *Hungary* **28** C2
Cuiabá *Brazil* **125** G7
Cuiabá ➤ *Brazil* **125** G7
Cuijk *Neths.* **17** C5
Cuilco *Guatemala* **120** C1
Cuillin Hills *U.K.* **13** D2
Cuillin Sd. *U.K.* **13** D2
Cuilo = Kwilu ➤
  Dem. Rep. of the Congo **84** E3
Cuiseaux *France* **19** F12
Cuito ➤ *Angola* **88** B3
Cuitzeo, L. de *Mexico* **118** D4
Cujmir *Romania* **28** F7
Cukai *Malaysia* **65** K4
Culbertson *U.S.A.* **108** B11
Culcairn *Australia* **95** F4
Culebra *Puerto Rico* **121** d
Culebra, Sierra de la *Spain* **36** D4
Culfa *Azerbaijan* **73** C11
Culgoa ➤ *Australia* **95** D4
Culgoa Flood Plain △
  Australia **95** D4
Culiacán *Mexico* **118** C3
Culiacán ➤ *Mexico* **118** C3
Culik *Indonesia* **63** J18
Culion *Phil.* **61** F4
Cúllar *Spain* **37** H8
Cullarin Ra. *Australia* **95** E4
Cullen *U.K.* **13** D6
Cullen Pt. *Australia* **94** A3
Cullera *Spain* **39** F4
Cullman *U.S.A.* **117** D11
Cullompton *U.K.* **15** G4
Culoz *France* **21** C9
Culpeper *U.S.A.* **113** F14
Culuene ➤ *Brazil* **125** F8
Culver, Pt. *Australia* **93** F3
Culverden *N.Z.* **91** E4
Cumaná *Venezuela* **124** A6

Cumaovası *Turkey* **47** C9
Cumberland *B.C., Canada* **102** D4
Cumberland *Ont., Canada* **115** A9
Cumberland *U.S.A.* **113** F14
Cumberland ➤ *U.S.A.* **112** G9
Cumberland, L. *U.S.A.* **113** G11
Cumberland Gap △ *U.S.A.* **113** G12
Cumberland I. *U.S.A.* **117** F14
Cumberland Is. *Australia* **94** b
Cumberland Island △
  U.S.A. **117** F14
Cumberland L. *Canada* **103** C8
Cumberland Pen. *Canada* **101** D19
Cumberland Plateau *U.S.A.*
  117 D12
Cumberland Sd. *Canada* **101** D18
Cumbernauld *U.K.* **13** F5
Cumborah *Australia* **95** D4
Cumbres de Majalca △
  Mexico **118** B3
Cumbres de Monterrey △
  Mexico **118** B4
Cumbres Mayores *Spain* **37** G4
Cumbria □ *U.K.* **14** C5
Cumbrian Mts. *U.K.* **14** C5
Cumbum *India* **66** M11
Cuminá ➤ *Brazil* **125** D7
Cummings Mt. *U.S.A.* **111** K8
Cummins *Australia* **95** E2
Cumnock *Australia* **95** E4
Cumnock *U.K.* **13** F4
Cumpas *Mexico* **118** B3
Cumplida, Pta. *Canary Is.* **48** F2
Çumra *Turkey* **72** D5
Cunco *Chile* **128** D2
Cuncumén *Chile* **126** C1
Cundeelee ☼ *Australia* **93** F3
Cunderdin *Australia* **93** F2
Cunene ➤ *Angola* **88** B1
Cúneo *Italy* **40** D4
Cunillera, I. = Sa Conillera
  Spain **48** C7
Cunlhat *France* **20** C7
Cunnamulla *Australia* **95** D4
Cuorgnè *Italy* **40** C4
Cupar *Canada* **103** C8
Cupar *U.K.* **13** E5
Cupcini *Moldova* **29** B12
Cupertino *U.S.A.* **110** H4
Cupica, G. de *Colombia* **124** B3
Čuprija *Serbia* **44** C5
Curanilahue *Chile* **126** D1
Curaray ➤ *Peru* **124** D4
Cure ➤ *France* **19** E10
Curepipe *Mauritius* **85** d
Curepto *Chile* **126** D1
Curiapo *Venezuela* **124** B6
Curicó *Chile* **126** C1
Curieuse *Seychelles* **85** b
Curinga *Italy* **43** D9
Curitiba *Brazil* **127** B6
Curitibanos *Brazil* **127** B5
Currabubula *Australia* **95** E5
Currais Novos *Brazil* **125** E11
Curral Velho *C. Verde Is.* **78** b
Curralinho *Brazil* **125** D9
Currant *U.S.A.* **108** G6
Currawinya △ *Australia* **95** D3
Current ➤ *U.S.A.* **116** C9
Currie *Australia* **95** F3
Currie *U.S.A.* **108** F6
Curtea de Argeş *Romania* **29** E9
Curtici *Romania* **28** D6
Curtin Springs *Australia* **93** E5
Curtis *U.S.A.* **112** E3
Curtis Group *Australia* **95** F4
Curtis I. *Australia* **94** C5
Curuápanema ➤ *Brazil* **125** D7
Curuçá *Brazil* **125** D9
Curuguaty *Paraguay* **127** A4
Curup *Indonesia* **62** E2
Cururupu *Brazil* **125** D10
Curuzú Cuatiá *Argentina* **126** B4
Curvelo *Brazil* **125** G10
Cusco = Cuzco *Peru* **124** F4
Cushendall *U.K.* **12** A5
Cushing *U.S.A.* **116** D6
Cushing, Mt. *Canada* **102** B3
Cusihuiríáchic *Mexico* **118** B3
Cusna, Mte. *Italy* **40** D7
Cusset *France* **19** F10
Custer *U.S.A.* **112** D2
Cut Bank *U.S.A.* **108** B7
Cutchogue *U.S.A.* **115** E12
Cuthbert *U.S.A.* **117** F12
Cutler *U.S.A.* **110** J7
Cutro *Italy* **43** C9
Cuttaburra ➤ *Australia* **95** D3
Cuttack *India* **67** J14
Cuvier, C. *Australia* **93** D1
Cuvier I. *N.Z.* **91** B5
Cuxhaven *Germany* **24** B4
Cuyahoga Falls *U.S.A.* **114** E3
Cuyahoga Valley △ *U.S.A.* **114** E3
Cuyapo *Phil.* **61** D4
Cuyo *Phil.* **61** F4

Cuyo East Pass *Phil.* **61** F4
Cuyo West Pass *Phil.* **61** F4
Cuyuni ➤ *Guyana* **124** B7
Cuzco *Bolivia* **124** H5
Cuzco *Peru* **124** F4
Čvrsnica *Bos.-H.* **28** G2
Cwmbran *U.K.* **15** F4
Cyangugu *Rwanda* **86** C2
Cybinka *Poland* **31** F1
Cyclades *Greece* **46** E6
Cyclades △ *Greece* **46** D6
Cygnet *Australia* **95** G4
Cynthiana *U.S.A.* **113** F11
Cypress Hills *Canada* **103** D7
Cypress Hills △ *Canada* **103** D7
Cyprus ■ *Asia* **49** E12
Cyrenaica = Barqa *Libya* **79** C10
Cyrene *Libya* **79** B10
Czaplinek *Poland* **30** E3
Czar *Canada* **103** C6
Czarna ➤ *Łódzkie, Poland* **31** G6
Czarna ➤ *Świętokrzyskie,
  Poland* **31** H8
Czarna Białostocka *Poland* **31** E10
Czarna Woda *Poland* **30** E5
Czarne *Poland* **30** E3
Czarnków *Poland* **31** F3
Czech Rep. ■ *Europe* **26** B8
Czechowice-Dziedzice *Poland* **31** J5
Czempiń *Poland* **31** F3
Czeremcha *Poland* **31** F10
Czerniejewo *Poland* **31** F4
Czersk *Poland* **30** E4
Czerwieńsk *Poland* **31** F2
Czerwionka-Leszczyny
  Poland **31** H5
Częstochowa *Poland* **31** H6
Człopa *Poland* **31** E3
Człuchów *Poland* **30** E4
Czyżew-Osada *Poland* **31** F9

D

Da ➤ *Vietnam* **58** G5
Da Hinggan Ling *China* **60** B7
Da Lat *Vietnam* **65** G7
Da Nang *Vietnam* **64** D7
Da Qaidam *China* **60** C4
Da Yunhe ➤ *Hopei, China* **57** E9
Da Yunhe ➤ *Jiangsu, China* **57** G11
Da'an *China* **57** B13
Daan Viljoen △ *Namibia* **88** C2
Dab'a, Ras el *Egypt* **80** H6
Daba Shan *China* **58** B7
Dabai *China* **57** B13
Dabakala *Ivory C.* **82** D4
Dabas *Hungary* **28** C4
Dabat *Ethiopia* **81** E4
Dabbagh, Jabal *Si. Arabia* **70** E2
Dabhoi *India* **68** H5
Dąbie *Poland* **31** F5
Dabie Shan *China* **59** B10
Dabilda *Cameroon* **83** C7
Dabnou *Niger* **83** C6
Dabo = Pasirkuning
  Indonesia **62** E2
Dabola *Guinea* **82** C2
Dabou *Ivory C.* **82** D4
Daboya *Ghana* **83** D4
Dabravolya *Belarus* **31** F10
Dąbrowa Białostocka
  Poland **31** E10
Dąbrowa Górnicza *Poland* **31** H6
Dąbrowa Tarnowska *Poland* **31** H7
Dabu *China* **59** E11
Dabung *Malaysia* **65** K4
Dabus ➤ *Ethiopia* **81** E4
Dacato ➤ *Ethiopia* **81** F5
Dacca = Dhaka *Bangla.* **69** H14
Dacca = Dhaka □ *Bangla.* **69** G14
Dachau *Germany* **25** G7
Dachigam △ *India* **68** B6
Dachstein, Hoher *Austria* **26** D6
Dačice *Czech Rep.* **26** B8
Dacre *Canada* **114** A8
Dadanawa *Guyana* **124** C7
Daday *Turkey* **72** B5
Dade City *U.S.A.* **117** G13
Dadhar *Pakistan* **68** E2
Dadiya *Nigeria* **83** D7
Dadnah *U.A.E.* **71** E8
Dadra & Nagar Haveli □
  India **66** J8
Dadri = Charkhi Dadri *India* **68** E7
Dadu *Pakistan* **68** F2
Dadu He ➤ *China* **58** C4
Daegu *S. Korea* **57** G15
Daejeon *S. Korea* **57** F14
Daejeong *S. Korea* **57** H14
Daet *Phil.* **61** D5
Dafang *China* **58** D5
Dafnes *Greece* **49** D7
Dafni *Greece* **46** D4
Dağ *Turkey* **47** D12
Dagana *Senegal* **82** B1
Dagash *Sudan* **80** D3
Dagestan □ *Russia* **35** J8
Dagestanskiye Ogni *Russia* **35** J9
Daggett *U.S.A.* **111** L10

Daghestan Republic =
  Dagestan □ *Russia* **35** J8
Daghfeli *Sudan* **80** D3
Dağlıq Qarabağ =
  Nagorno-Karabakh □
  Azerbaijan **73** C12
Dagö = Hiiumaa *Estonia* **32** C2
Dagu *China* **57** E9
Daguan *China* **58** D4
Dagupan *Phil.* **61** C4
Daguragu *Australia* **92** C5
Daguragu ☼ *Australia* **92** C5
Dahab *Egypt* **70** D2
Dahlak Kebir *Eritrea* **81** D5
Dahlak Marine △ *Eritrea* **81** D5
Dahlenburg *Germany* **24** B6
Dahlonega *U.S.A.* **117** D13
Dahme *Germany* **24** D9
Dahod *India* **68** H6
Dahong Shan *China* **59** B9
Dahongliutan *China* **69** B8
Dahra *Libya* **79** C9
Dahra *Senegal* **82** B1
Dahshûr *Egypt* **80** J7
Dahûk *Iraq* **73** D10
Dahûk □ *Iraq* **73** D10
Dai Hao *Vietnam* **64** C6
Dai-Sen *Japan* **55** G6
Dai Shan *China* **59** B14
Dai Xian *China* **56** E7
Daicheng *China* **56** E9
Daikondi = Day Kundī □
  Afghan. **66** C5
Daimiel *Spain* **37** F7
Daingean *Ireland* **12** C4
Dainkog *China* **58** A1
Daintree *Australia* **94** B4
Daintree △ *Australia* **94** B4
Daiō-Misaki *Japan* **55** G8
Dair, J. ed *Sudan* **81** E3
Dairût *Egypt* **80** B3
Daisen-Oki △ *Japan* **55** G6
Daisetsu-Zan *Japan* **54** C11
Daisetsu-Zan △ *Japan* **54** C11
Dajarra *Australia* **94** C2
Dajiawa *China* **57** F10
Dajin Chuan ➤ *China* **58** B3
Dak Dam *Cambodia* **64** F6
Dak Nhe *Vietnam* **64** E6
Dak Pek *Vietnam* **64** E6
Dak Song *Vietnam* **65** F6
Dak Sui *Vietnam* **64** E6
Dakar *Senegal* **82** C1
Dakar □ *Senegal* **82** C1
Dakhla *W. Sahara* **78** D2
Dakhla, El Wâhât el *Egypt* **80** B2
Dakingari *Nigeria* **83** C5
Dakor *India* **68** H5
Dakoro *Niger* **83** C6
Dakota City *U.S.A.* **112** D5
Ðakovica *Kosovo* **44** D4
Ðakovo *Croatia* **28** E3
Dalaba *Guinea* **82** C2
Dalachi *China* **56** F3
Dalai Nur *China* **56** C9
Dālakī *Iran* **71** D6
Dalälven ➤ *Sweden* **10** D10
Dalaman *Turkey* **47** E10
Dalaman ➤ *Turkey* **47** E10
Dalandzadgad *Mongolia* **56** C3
Dalap-Uliga-Darrit =
  Majuro *Marshall Is.* **96** G9
Dalarna *Sweden* **10** D8
Dalarnas län □ *Sweden* **10** C8
Dālbandīn *Pakistan* **66** E4
Dalbeattie *U.K.* **13** G5
Dalbeg *Australia* **94** C4
Dalbosjön *Sweden* **11** F6
Dalby *Australia* **95** D5
Dalby *Sweden* **11** J7
Dalby Söderskog △ *Sweden* **11** J7
Dale City *U.S.A.* **113** F15
Dale Hollow L. *U.S.A.* **117** C12
Dalga *Egypt* **80** B3
Dalgān *Iran* **71** E8
Dalhart *U.S.A.* **116** C3
Dalhousie *Canada* **105** C6
Dalhousie *India* **68** C6
Dali *Shaanxi, China* **56** G5
Dali *Yunnan, China* **58** E3
Dalian *China* **57** E11
Daliang Shan *China* **58** D4
Daling He ➤ *China* **57** D11
Dāliyat el Karmel *Israel* **74** C4
Dalj *Croatia* **28** E3
Dalkeith *U.K.* **13** F5
Dallas *Oreg., U.S.A.* **108** D2
Dallas *Tex., U.S.A.* **116** E6
Dalles, The *U.S.A.* **108** D3
Dallol *Ethiopia* **81** E5
Dalmã *U.A.E.* **71** E7
Dalmacija *Croatia* **41** E13
Dalmas, L. *Canada* **105** B5
Dalmatia = Dalmacija
  Croatia **41** E13
Dalmau *India* **69** F9
Dalmellington *U.K.* **13** F4
Dalnegorsk *Russia* **54** B7
Dalnerechensk *Russia* **54** B6

Dalnevostochnyy □ *Russia* **53** C14
Daloa *Ivory C.* **82** D3
Dalou Shan *China* **58** C6
Dalry *U.K.* **13** F4
Dalrymple, L. *Australia* **94** C4
Dalrymple, Mt. *Australia* **94** b
Dals Långed *Sweden* **11** F6
Dalsjöfors *Sweden* **11** G7
Dalsland *Sweden* **11** F6
Daltenganj *India* **69** H11
Dalton *Ga., Australia* **95** E4
Dalton *Mass., U.S.A.* **115** D11
Dalton *Nebr., U.S.A.* **112** E2
Dalton-in-Furness *U.K.* **14** C4
Dalupiri I. *Phil.* **61** B4
Dalvík *Iceland* **8** D4
Dálvvadis = Jokkmokk
  Sweden **8** C18
Dalwallinu *Australia* **93** F2
Daly ➤ *Australia* **92** B5
Daly City *U.S.A.* **110** H4
Daly River *Australia* **92** B5
Daly River-Port Keats ☼
  Australia **92** B4
Daly Waters *Australia* **94** B1
Dalyan *Turkey* **47** E10
Dam Doi *Vietnam* **65** H5
Dam Ha *Vietnam* **64** B6
Damachova *Belarus* **31** G10
Daman *India* **66** J8
Dāmaneh *Iran* **71** C6
Damanhûr *Egypt* **80** H7
Damant L. *Canada* **103** A7
Damanzhuang *China* **56** E9
Damaq *Iran* **73** E13
Damar *Indonesia* **63** F7
Damaraland *Namibia* **88** C2
Damas = Dimashq *Syria* **74** B5
Damasi *Greece* **46** B4
Damatura *Nigeria* **83** C7
Dāmāvand *Iran* **71** C7
Dāmāvand, Qolleh-ye *Iran* **71** C7
Damba *Angola* **84** F3
Damboa *Nigeria* **83** C7
Dâmbovița □ *Romania* **29** F10
Dâmbovița ➤ *Romania* **29** F11
Dâmbovnic ➤ *Romania* **29** F10
Dame Marie *Haiti* **121** C5
Dāmghān *Iran* **71** B7
Dāmienesti *Romania* **29** D11
Damietta = Dumyât *Egypt* **80** H7
Daming *China* **56** F8
Damīr Qābū *Syria* **70** B4
Dammam = Ad Dammām
  Si. Arabia **71** E6
Dammarie-les-Lys *France* **19** D9
Dammartin-en-Goële *France* **19** C9
Damme *Germany* **24** C4
Damodar ➤ *India* **69** H12
Damoh *India* **69** H8
Dampier *Australia* **92** D2
Dampier, Selat *Indonesia* **63** E8
Dampier Arch. *Australia* **92** D2
Damrei, Chuor Phnum
  Cambodia **65** G4
Damville *France* **19** C12
Damvillers *France* **19** C12
Damyang *S. Korea* **57** G14
Dan-Gulbi *Nigeria* **83** C6
Dan-Sadau *Nigeria* **83** C6
Dana *Indonesia* **63** F6
Dana *Jordan* **74** E4
Dana, L. *Canada* **104** B4
Dana, Mt. *U.S.A.* **110** H7
Danakil Desert *Ethiopia* **81** E5
Danané *Ivory C.* **82** D3
Danao *Phil.* **61** F6
Danau Poso *Indonesia* **63** E6
Danba *China* **58** B3
Danbury *U.S.A.* **115** E11
Danby L. *U.S.A.* **109** J6
Dand *Afghan.* **68** D1
Dande △ *Zimbabwe* **87** F3
Dandeldhura *Nepal* **69** E9
Dandeli *India* **66** M9
Dandenong *Australia* **95** F4
Dandī *Iran* **73** D12
Dandīl *Egypt* **80** J7
Dandong *China* **57** D13
Danfeng *China* **56** H6
Dangan Liedao *China* **59** F10
Dangé-St-Romain *France* **20** B4
Dângeni *Romania* **29** C11
Danger Is. = Pukapuka
  Cook Is. **97** J11
Danger Pt. *S. Africa* **88** E2
Danginpuri *Indonesia* **63** K18
Dangla *Ethiopia* **81** E4
Dangla Shan = Tanggula
  Shan *China* **60** C4
Dangora *Nigeria* **83** C6
Dangouadougou
  Burkina Faso **82** D4
Dangrek, Mts. = Dangrek,
  Phnom *Thailand* **64** E5
Dangrek, Phnom *Thailand* **64** E5
Dangriga *Belize* **119** D7
Dangshan *China* **56** G9

Dangtu *China* **59** B12
Dangyang *China* **59** B8
Daniel *U.S.A.* **108** E8
Daniel's Harbour *Canada* **105** B8
Danielskuil *S. Africa* **88** D3
Danielson *U.S.A.* **115** E13
Danilov *Russia* **32** C11
Danilovgrad *Montenegro* **44** D3
Danilovka *Russia* **34** E7
Daning *China* **56** F6
Danja *Nigeria* **83** C6
Danjiangkou *China* **59** A8
Danjiangkou Shuiku *China* **59** A8
Ðank *Oman* **71** F8
Dankalwa *Nigeria* **83** C7
Dankama *Nigeria* **83** C6
Dankhar Gompa *India* **68** C8
Dankov *Russia* **32** F10
Danleng *China* **58** B4
Danlí *Honduras* **120** D2
Danmark = Denmark ■
  Europe **11** J3
Dannemora *U.S.A.* **115** B11
Dannenberg *Germany* **24** B7
Dannevirke *N.Z.* **91** D6
Dannhauser *S. Africa* **89** D5
Dansville *U.S.A.* **114** D7
Danta *India* **68** G5
Dantan *India* **69** J12
Dante = Xaafuun *Somali Rep.* **75** B5
Danube = Dunărea ➤
  Europe **29** E14
Danvers *U.S.A.* **115** D14
Danville *Ill., U.S.A.* **112** E10
Danville *Ky., U.S.A.* **113** G11
Danville *Pa., U.S.A.* **115** F8
Danville *Va., U.S.A.* **113** G14
Danville *Vt., U.S.A.* **115** B12
Danyang *China* **59** B12
Danzhai *China* **58** D6
Danzhou *China* **64** C7
Danzig = Gdańsk *Poland* **30** D6
Dão ➤ *Portugal* **36** E2
Dao Xian *China* **59** E8
Daocheng *China* **58** C3
Daoukro *Ivory C.* **82** D4
Dapaong *Togo* **83** C5
Dapchi *Nigeria* **83** C7
Dapitan *Phil.* **61** G5
Daqing Shan *China* **56** D6
Daqq-e Sorkh, Kavīr *Iran* **71** C7
Daqu Shan *China* **59** B14
Dar Banda *Africa* **76** F6
Dar el Beida = Casablanca
  Morocco **78** B4
Dar es Salaam *Tanzania* **86** D4
Dar Mazār *Iran* **71** D8
Dar'ā *Syria* **74** C5
Dar'ā □ *Syria* **74** C5
Dārāb *Iran* **71** D7
Daraban *Pakistan* **68** D4
Darabani *Romania* **29** B11
Daraina *Madag.* **89** A8
Daraj *Libya* **79** B8
Dārān *Iran* **71** C6
Daravica *Kosovo* **44** D4
Daraw *Egypt* **80** C3
Dārayyā *Syria* **74** B5
Darazo *Nigeria* **83** C7
Darband *Pakistan* **68** B5
Darband, Kūh-e *Iran* **71** D8
Darbhanga *India* **69** F11
D'Arcy *Canada* **102** C4
Darda *Croatia* **28** E3
Dardanelle *Ark., U.S.A.* **116** D8
Dardanelle *Calif., U.S.A.* **110** G7
Dardanelles = Çanakkale
  Boğazı *Turkey* **45** F10
Dare ➤ *Ethiopia* **81** F5
Darende *Turkey* **72** C7
Dārestān *Iran* **71** D8
Darfo *Italy* **40** C7
Ðãrfūr *Sudan* **79** F10
Dargai *Pakistan* **68** B4
Dargaville *N.Z.* **91** A4
Dargol *Niger* **83** C5
Darhan *Mongolia* **60** B5
Darhan Muminggan
  Lianheqi *China* **56** D6
Dari *Sudan* **81** F3
Darıca *Turkey* **72** B3
Darién, G. del *Colombia* **124** B3
Darién ∩ *Panama* **120** E4
Dariganga = Ovoot *Mongolia* **56** B7
Darjeeling = Darjiling *India* **69** F13
Darjiling *India* **69** F13
Darkan *Australia* **93** F2
Darkhana *Pakistan* **68** D5
Darkhazineh *Iran* **71** D6
Darkot Pass *Pakistan* **69** A5
Darling ➤ *Australia* **95** E3
Darling Downs *Australia* **95** D5
Darling Ra. *Australia* **93** F2
Darlington *U.K.* **14** C6
Darlington *U.S.A.* **117** D15
Darlington □ *U.K.* **14** C6
Darlington, L. *S. Africa* **88** E4
Darlot, L. *Australia* **93** E3
Darłowo *Poland* **30** D3

Dărmăneşti *Bacău, Romania* **29** D11
Dărmăneşti *Suceava, Romania* **29** C11
Darmstadt *Germany* **25** F4
Darnah *Libya* **79** B10
Darney *France* **19** D13
Darnley *Australia* **94** a
Darnley, C. *Antarctica* **5** C6
Darnley B. *Canada* **100** D7
Daroca *Spain* **38** D3
Darou-Mousti *Senegal* **82** B1
Darr → *Australia* **94** C3
Darra Pezu *Pakistan* **68** C4
Darreh Shahr *Iran* **73** F12
Darrequeira *Argentina* **126** D3
Darrington *U.S.A.* **108** B3
Darsser Ort *Germany* **24** A8
Dart → *U.K.* **15** G4
Dart, C. *Antarctica* **5** D14
Dartford *U.K.* **15** F8
Dartmoor *U.K.* **15** G4
Dartmoor △ *U.K.* **15** G4
Dartmouth *Canada* **105** D7
Dartmouth *U.K.* **15** G4
Dartmouth Res. *Australia* **95** D4
Dartuch, C. = Artrutx, C. de *Spain* **48** B10
Daruvar *Croatia* **28** E2
Darvaza *Turkmenistan* **52** E6
Darvel, Teluk = Lahad Datu, Telok *Malaysia* **63** D5
Darwen *U.K.* **14** D5
Darwendale *Zimbabwe* **89** B5
Darwha *India* **66** J10
Darwin *Australia* **92** B5
Darwin *U.S.A.* **111** J9
Darya Khan *Pakistan* **68** D4
Daryācheh-ye Bakhtegān *Iran* **71** D7
Daryoi Amu = Amudarya → *Uzbekistan* **52** E6
Dās *U.A.E.* **71** E7
Dashen, Ras *Ethiopia* **81** E4
Dashetai *China* **56** D5
Dashkesan = Daşkäsän *Azerbaijan* **35** K7
Dashköpri *Turkmenistan* **71** B9
Dashoguz *Turkmenistan* **52** E6
Dasht → *Pakistan* **66** G2
Daska *Pakistan* **68** C5
Daşkäsän *Azerbaijan* **35** K7
Dassa *Benin* **83** D5
Dasuya *India* **68** D6
Datça *Turkey* **47** E9
Datia *India* **69** G8
Datian *China* **59** E11
Datong *Anhui, China* **59** B11
Datong *Shanxi, China* **56** D7
Dattakhel *Pakistan* **68** C3
Datteln *Germany* **24** D3
Datu, Tanjung *Indonesia* **62** D3
Datu Piang *Phil.* **61** H6
Datuk, Tanjung = Datu, Tanjung *Indonesia* **62** D3
Daua = Dawa → *Africa* **81** G5
Daud Khel *Pakistan* **68** C4
Daudnagar *India* **69** G11
Daugava → *Latvia* **32** D3
Daugavpils *Latvia* **32** E4
Daulpur *India* **68** F7
Daun *Germany* **25** E2
Dauphin *Canada* **103** C8
Dauphin *U.S.A.* **114** F8
Dauphin L. *Canada* **103** C9
Dauphiné *France* **21** C9
Daura *Borno, Nigeria* **83** C7
Daura *Katsina, Nigeria* **83** C6
Dausa *India* **68** F7
Dāväçi *Azerbaijan* **35** K9
Davangere *India* **66** M9
Davao *Phil.* **61** H6
Davao G. *Phil.* **61** H6
Dāvar Panāh = Sarāvān *Iran* **71** E9
Davenport *Calif., U.S.A.* **110** H4
Davenport *Iowa, U.S.A.* **112** E8
Davenport *Wash., U.S.A.* **108** C4
Davenport Ra. *Australia* **94** C1
Davenport Range △ *Australia* **94** C1
Daventry *U.K.* **15** E6
David *Panama* **120** E3
David City *U.S.A.* **112** E5
David Glacier *Antarctica* **5** D21
David Gorodok = Davyd Haradok *Belarus* **23** B14
Davidson *Canada* **103** C7
Davidson Mts. *U.S.A.* **106** B11
Davis *Antarctica* **5** C6
Davis *U.S.A.* **110** G5
Davis Dam *U.S.A.* **111** K12
Davis Inlet *Canada* **105** A7
Davis Mts. *U.S.A.* **116** F3
Davis Sea *Antarctica* **5** C7
Davis Str. *N. Amer.* **101** D19
Davlos *Cyprus* **49** D12
Davo → *Ivory C.* **82** D3
Davos *Switz.* **25** J5
Davutlar *Turkey* **47** D9

Davy L. *Canada* **103** B7
Davyd Haradok *Belarus* **23** B14
Dawa → *Africa* **81** G5
Dawaki *Bauchi, Nigeria* **83** D6
Dawaki *Kano, Nigeria* **83** C6
Dawei = Tavoy *Burma* **64** E2
Dawes Ra. *Australia* **94** C5
Dawlish *U.K.* **15** G4
Dawna Ra. *Burma* **64** D2
Dawros Hd. *Ireland* **12** B3
Dawson *U.S.A.* **117** F12
Dawson, I. *Chile* **128** G2
Dawson B. *Canada* **103** C8
Dawson City *Canada* **100** E4
Dawson Creek *Canada* **102** B4
Dawson Inlet *Canada* **103** A10
Dawson Ra. *Australia* **94** C4
Dawu *Hubei, China* **59** B9
Dawu *Sichuan, China* **58** B3
Daxian *China* **58** B6
Daxin *China* **58** F6
Daxindian *China* **57** F11
Daxinggou *China* **57** C15
Daxue Shan *Sichuan, China* **58** B3
Daxue Shan *Yunnan, China* **58** F2
Day Kundī □ *Afghan.* **66** C5
Dayao *China* **58** E3
Daye *China* **59** B10
Dayet en Naharat *Mali* **82** B4
Dayi *China* **58** B4
Daylesford *Australia* **95** F3
Dayong *China* **59** C8
Dayr az Zawr *Syria* **73** E9
Dayr az Zawr □ *Syria* **73** E9
Daysland *Canada* **102** C6
Dayton *Nev., U.S.A.* **110** F7
Dayton *Ohio, U.S.A.* **113** F11
Dayton *Pa., U.S.A.* **114** F5
Dayton *Tenn., U.S.A.* **117** D12
Dayton *Wash., U.S.A.* **108** C5
Dayton *Wyo., U.S.A.* **108** D10
Daytona Beach *U.S.A.* **117** G14
Dayu *China* **59** E10
Dayville *U.S.A.* **108** D4
Dazhu *China* **58** B6
Dazu *China* **58** C5
De Aar *S. Africa* **88** E3
De Biesbosch △ *Neths.* **17** C4
De Funiak Springs *U.S.A.* **117** F11
De Grey → *Australia* **92** D2
De Haan *Belgium* **17** C3
De Hoge Veluwe △ *Neths.* **17** B5
De Hoop △ *S. Africa* **88** E3
De Kalb Junction *U.S.A.* **115** B9
De Kennemerduinen △ *Neths.* **17** B4
De Land *U.S.A.* **117** G14
De Leon *U.S.A.* **116** E5
De Long Mts. *U.S.A.* **106** B7
De Panne *Belgium* **17** C2
De Pere *U.S.A.* **112** C9
De Queen *U.S.A.* **116** D7
De Quincy *U.S.A.* **116** F8
De Ruyters *U.S.A.* **115** D9
De Smet *U.S.A.* **112** C5
De Soto *U.S.A.* **112** F8
De Tour Village *U.S.A.* **113** B12
De Witt *U.S.A.* **116** D9
Dead Sea *Asia* **74** D4
Deadwood *U.S.A.* **112** C2
Deadwood L. *Canada* **102** B3
Deal *U.K.* **15** F9
Deal I. *Australia* **95** F4
Dealesville *S. Africa* **88** D4
De'an *China* **59** C10
Dean → *Canada* **102** C3
Dean, Forest of *U.K.* **15** F5
Dean Chan. *Canada* **102** C3
Deán Funes *Argentina* **126** C3
Dease → *Canada* **102** B3
Dease L. *Canada* **102** B2
Dease Lake *Canada* **102** B2
Death Valley *U.S.A.* **111** J10
Death Valley △ *U.S.A.* **111** J9
Death Valley Junction *U.S.A.* **111** J10
Deauville *France* **18** C7
Deba *Spain* **38** B2
Deba Habe *Nigeria* **83** C7
Debagram *India* **69** H14
Debaltsevo *Ukraine* **33** H10
Debao *China* **58** F6
Debar *Macedonia* **44** E4
Debark *Ethiopia* **81** E4
Debden *Canada* **103** C7
Debica *Poland* **31** H8
Deblin *Poland* **31** G8
Debno *Poland* **31** F1
Débo, L. *Mali* **82** B4
DeBolt *Canada* **102** B5
Deborah East, L. *Australia* **93** F2
Deborah West, L. *Australia* **93** F2
Debrc *Serbia* **44** B4
Debre Birhan *Ethiopia* **81** F4
Debre Markos *Ethiopia* **81** E4
Debre May *Ethiopia* **81** E4
Debre Sina *Ethiopia* **81** F4

Debre Tabor *Ethiopia* **81** E4
Debre Zebit *Ethiopia* **81** E4
Debre Zeyit *Ethiopia* **81** F4
Debrecen *Hungary* **28** C6
Debrzno *Poland* **30** E4
Dečani *Kosovo* **44** D4
Decatur *Ala., U.S.A.* **117** D11
Decatur *Ga., U.S.A.* **117** E12
Decatur *Ill., U.S.A.* **112** F9
Decatur *Ind., U.S.A.* **113** E11
Decatur *Tex., U.S.A.* **116** E6
Decazeville *France* **20** D6
Deccan *India* **66** L11
Deception Bay *Australia* **95** D5
Deception I. *Antarctica* **5** C17
Deception L. *Canada* **103** B8
Dechang *China* **58** D4
Dechhu *India* **68** F5
Děčín *Czech Rep.* **26** A7
Decize *France* **19** F10
Deckerville *U.S.A.* **114** C2
Decorah *U.S.A.* **112** D8
Deda *Romania* **29** D9
Dédéagach = Alexandroupoli *Greece* **45** F9
Deder *Ethiopia* **81** F5
Dedham *U.S.A.* **115** D13
Dedoplis Tskaro = Tsiteli-Tsqaro *Georgia* **35** K8
Dédougou *Burkina Faso* **82** C4
Dedovichi *Russia* **32** D5
Dedza *Malawi* **87** E3
Dee → *Aberds., U.K.* **13** D6
Dee → *Dumf. & Gall., U.K.* **13** G4
Dee → *Wales, U.K.* **14** D4
Deep B. *Canada* **102** A5
Deepwater *Australia* **95** D5
Deer → *Canada* **103** B10
Deer L. *Canada* **103** C10
Deer Lake *Nfld. & L., Canada* **105** C8
Deer Lake *Ont., Canada* **103** C10
Deer Lodge *U.S.A.* **108** C7
Deer Park *U.S.A.* **108** C5
Deer River *U.S.A.* **112** B7
Deeragun *Australia* **94** B4
Deerdepoort *S. Africa* **88** C4
Deeragun *Australia* **94** B4
Defiance *U.S.A.* **113** E11
Degana *India* **68** F6
Dêgê *China* **58** B2
Degebe → *Portugal* **37** G3
Degeberga *Sweden* **11** J8
Dégelis *Canada* **105** C6
Degema *Nigeria* **83** E6
Degerfors *Sweden* **10** E8
Degerhamn *Sweden* **11** H10
Deggendorf *Germany* **25** G8
Degh → *Pakistan* **68** D5
Değirmendere *Turkey* **45** F13
Degirmenlik = Kythréa *Cyprus* **49** D12
Deh Bīd *Iran* **71** D7
Deh Dasht *Iran* **71** D6
Deh-e Shīr *Iran* **71** D7
Dehaj *Iran* **71** D7
Dehak *Iran* **71** E9
Dehdez *Iran* **71** D6
Dehej *India* **68** J5
Dehestān *Iran* **71** D7
Dehgolān *Iran* **73** E12
Dehibat *Tunisia* **79** B8
Dehlorān *Iran* **73** F12
Dehnow-e Kūhestān *Iran* **71** E8
Dehra Dun *India* **68** D8
Dehri *India* **69** G11
Dehua *China* **59** E12
Dehui *China* **57** B13
Deim Zubeir *Sudan* **81** F2
Deinze *Belgium* **17** D3
Dej *Romania* **29** C8
Deje *Sweden* **10** E7
Dejiang *China* **58** C7
DeKalb *U.S.A.* **112** E9
Dekemhare *Eritrea* **81** D4
Dekese *Dem. Rep. of the Congo* **84** E4
Del Mar *U.S.A.* **111** N9
Del Norte *U.S.A.* **109** H10
Del Rio *U.S.A.* **116** G4
Delai *Sudan* **80** D4
Delambre I. *Australia* **92** D2
Delami *Sudan* **81** E3
Delano *U.S.A.* **111** K7
Delano Peak *U.S.A.* **108** G7
Delareyville *S. Africa* **88** D4
Delaronde L. *Canada* **103** C7
Delavan *U.S.A.* **112** D9
Delaware *U.S.A.* **113** E12
Delaware □ *U.S.A.* **113** F16
Delaware → *U.S.A.* **115** G9
Delaware B. *U.S.A.* **113** F16
Delaware Water Gap △ *U.S.A.* **115** E10
Delay → *Canada* **105** A5
Deleniquin *Australia* **95** E1
Delbrück *Germany* **24** D4
Delčevo *Macedonia* **44** E6
Delegate *Australia* **95** F4
Delémont *Switz.* **25** H3
Delevan *U.S.A.* **114** D6

Delft *Neths.* **17** B4
Delfzijl *Neths.* **17** A6
Delgado, C. *Mozam.* **87** E5
Delgerhet *Mongolia* **56** B6
Delgo *Sudan* **80** C3
Delhi *Canada* **114** D4
Delhi *India* **68** E7
Delhi *La., U.S.A.* **116** E9
Delhi *N.Y., U.S.A.* **115** D10
Deli Jovan *Serbia* **44** B6
Delia *Canada* **102** C6
Delice *Turkey* **72** C6
Delicias *Mexico* **118** B3
Delījān *Iran* **71** C6
Déline *Canada* **100** D7
Delisle *Canada* **103** C7
Delitzsch *Germany* **24** D8
Dell City *U.S.A.* **116** F2
Dell Rapids *U.S.A.* **112** D5
Delle *France* **19** E14
Dellys *Algeria*
Delmar *U.S.A.* **115** D11
Delmenhorst *Germany* **24** B4
Delnice *Croatia* **41** C11
Delonga, Ostrova *Russia* **53** B15
Deloraine *Australia* **95** G4
Deloraine *Canada* **103** D8
Delphi *Greece* **46** C4
Delphi *U.S.A.* **112** E10
Delphos *U.S.A.* **113** E11
Delportshoop *S. Africa* **88** D3
Delray Beach *U.S.A.* **117** H14
Delsbo *Sweden* **10** C10
Delta *Colo., U.S.A.* **108** G9
Delta *Utah, U.S.A.* **108** G7
Delta □ *Nigeria* **83** D6
Delta del Ebre △ *Spain* **38** E5
Delta del Po △ *Italy* **41** D9
Delta du Saloum △ *Senegal* **82** C1
Delta Dunărea △ *Romania* **29** E14
Delta Junction *U.S.A.* **100** E2
Deltona *U.S.A.* **117** G14
Delungra *Australia* **95** D5
Delvada *India* **68** J4
Delvinaki *Greece* **46** B2
Delvinë *Albania* **44** G4
Demak *Indonesia* **63** G14
Demanda, Sierra de la *Spain* **38** C2
Demavend = Damāvand, Qolleh-ye *Iran* **71** C7
Dembecha *Ethiopia* **81** E4
Dembi *Ethiopia* **81** F4
Dembia *C.A.R.* **86** B1
Dembia *Dem. Rep. of the Congo* **86** B2
Dembidolo *Ethiopia* **81** F3
Demchok *India* **69** C8
Demer → *Belgium* **17** D4
Demetrias *Greece* **46** B5
Demidov *Russia* **32** E6
Deming *N. Mex., U.S.A.* **109** K10
Deming *Wash., U.S.A.* **110** B4
Demini → *Brazil* **124** D6
Demirci *Turkey* **47** B10
Demirköprü Barajı *Turkey* **47** C10
Demirköy *Turkey* **45** E11
Demirtaş *Turkey* **72** D9
Demmin *Germany* **24** B9
Demonte *Italy* **40** D4
Demopolis *U.S.A.* **117** E11
Dempo *Indonesia* **62** E2
Demyansk *Russia* **32** D7
Den Bosch = 's-Hertogenbosch *Neths.* **17** C5
Den Burg *Neths.* **17** A4
Den Chai *Thailand* **64** D3
Den Haag = 's-Gravenhage *Neths.* **17** B4
Den Helder *Neths.* **17** B4
Den Oever *Neths.* **17** B5
Denain *France* **19** B10
Denair *U.S.A.* **110** H6
Denali = McKinley, Mt. *U.S.A.* **100** E1
Denau *Uzbekistan* **52** F7
Denbigh *Canada* **114** A7
Denbigh *U.K.* **14** D4
Denbighshire □ *U.K.* **14** D4
Dendang *Indonesia* **62** E3
Dendermonde *Belgium* **17** C4
Deneba *Ethiopia* **81** F4
Dengchuan *China* **58** E3
Denge *Nigeria* **83** C6
Dengfeng *China* **56** G7
Dengkou *China* **56** D4
Dengzhou *China* **59** A9
Denham *Australia* **93** E1
Denham, Mt. *Jamaica* **120** a
Denham Ra. *Australia* **94** C4
Denham Sd. *Australia* **93** E1
Denholm *Canada* **103** C7
Denia *Spain* **39** G5
Denial B. *Australia* **95** E1
Deniliquin *Australia* **95** E3
Denison *Iowa, U.S.A.* **112** D6
Denison *Tex., U.S.A.* **116** E6
Denison Plains *Australia* **92** C4
Denizli *Turkey* **47** D11
Denizli □ *Turkey* **47** D11

Denman Glacier *Antarctica* **5** C7
Denmark *Australia* **93** F2
Denmark ■ *Europe* **11** J3
Denmark Str. *Atl. Oc.* **98** C17
Dennery *St. Lucia* **121** f
Dennison *U.S.A.* **114** F3
Denny *U.K.* **13** E5
Denpasar *Indonesia* **62** F5
Denpasar ✈ (DPS) *Indonesia* **63** K18
Denton *Mont., U.S.A.* **108** C9
Denton *Tex., U.S.A.* **116** E6
D'Entrecasteaux, Pt. *Australia* **93** F2
D'Entrecasteaux △ *Australia* **93** F2
D'Entrecasteaux Is. *Papua N. G.* **90** B8
Denu *Ghana* **83** D5
Denver *Colo., U.S.A.* **108** G11
Denver *Pa., U.S.A.* **115** F8
Denver City *U.S.A.* **116** E3
Deoband *India* **68** E7
Deogarh *India* **68** G5
Deoghar *India* **69** G12
Deolali *India* **66** K8
Deoli = Devli *India* **68** G6
Dêols *France* **19** F8
Deora *India* **68** F4
Deoria *India* **69** F10
Deori *India* **69** H8
Deosai Mts. *Pakistan* **69** B6
Deosri *India* **69** F14
Deping *China* **57** D9
Deposit *U.S.A.* **115** D9
Depuch I. *Australia* **92** D2
Deputatskiy *Russia* **53** C14
Dêqên *China* **58** C2
Deqing *China* **59** F8
Dera Ghazi Khan *Pakistan* **68** D4
Dera Ismail Khan *Pakistan* **68** D4
Derabugti *Pakistan* **68** E3
Derawar Fort *Pakistan* **68** E4
Derbent *Russia* **35** J9
Derbent *Turkey* **47** C10
Derby *Australia* **92** C3
Derby *U.K.* **14** E6
Derby *Conn., U.S.A.* **115** E11
Derby *Kans., U.S.A.* **112** G5
Derby *N.Y., U.S.A.* **114** D6
Derby City □ *U.K.* **14** E6
Derby Line *U.S.A.* **115** B12
Derbyshire □ *U.K.* **14** D6
Derg → *U.K.* **12** B4
Derg, L. *Ireland* **12** D3
Dergachi = Derhaci *Ukraine* **33** G9
Derhaci *Ukraine* **33** G9
Deridder *U.S.A.* **116** F8
Derik *Turkey* **73** D9
Derinkuyu *Turkey* **72** C6
Dermantsi *Bulgaria* **45** C8
Dermott *U.S.A.* **116** E9
Derry = Londonderry *U.K.* **12** B4
Derry = Londonderry □ *U.K.* **12** B4
Derry *N.H., U.S.A.* **115** D13
Derry *Pa., U.S.A.* **114** F5
Derryveagh Mts. *Ireland* **12** B3
Derudub *Sudan* **80** D4
Derval *France* **18** E5
Derveni *Greece* **46** C4
Derventa *Bos.-H.* **28** F2
Derwent → *Cumb., U.K.* **14** C4
Derwent → *Derby, U.K.* **14** E6
Derwent → *N. Yorks., U.K.* **14** D7
Derwent Water *U.K.* **14** C4
Des Moines *Iowa, U.S.A.* **112** E7
Des Moines *N. Mex., U.S.A.* **109** H12
Des Moines *Wash., U.S.A.* **110** C4
Des Moines → *U.S.A.* **112** E8
Desa *Romania* **28** G8
Desaguadero → *Argentina* **126** C2
Desaguadero → *Bolivia* **124** G5
Desantne *Ukraine* **29** G8
Desar *Malaysia* **65** d
Descanso, Pta. *Mexico* **111** N9
Descartes *France* **20** B4
Deschaillons-sur-St-Laurent *Canada* **105** C5
Deschambault L. *Canada* **103** C8
Deschutes → *U.S.A.* **108** D3
Dese *Ethiopia* **81** E4
Deseado → *Argentina* **128** F3
Desenzano del Garda *Italy* **40** C7
Deseronto *Canada* **114** B7
Desert Center *U.S.A.* **111** M11
Desert Hot Springs *U.S.A.* **111** M10
Desfina *Greece* **46** C4
Deshnok *India* **68** F5
Desierto Central de Baja California △ *Mexico* **118** B2
Deskati *Greece* **44** G5
Desna → *Ukraine* **23** C16
Desnătui → *Romania* **29** G8

Desolación, I. *Chile* **128** G2
Despeñaperros, Paso *Spain* **37** G7
Despeñaperros △ *Spain* **37** G7
Despotiko *Greece* **46** E6
Despotovac *Serbia* **44** B5
Dessau *Germany* **24** D8
Dessye = Dese *Ethiopia* **81** E4
D'Estrees B. *Australia* **95** F2
Desuri *India* **68** G5
Desvres *France* **19** B8
Det Udom *Thailand* **64** E5
Deta *Romania* **28** E6
Dete *Zimbabwe* **88** B4
Detinja → *Serbia* **44** C4
Detmold *Germany* **24** D4
Detour, Pt. *U.S.A.* **112** C10
Detroit *U.S.A.* **114** D1
Detroit Lakes *U.S.A.* **112** B6
Detva *Slovak Rep.* **27** C12
Deua △ *Australia* **95** F4
Deurne *Neths.* **17** C5
Deutsch-Luxemburgischer △ *Germany* **25** F2
Deutsche Bucht *Germany* **24** A4
Deutschland = Germany ■ *Europe* **24** E6
Deutschlandsberg *Austria* **26** E8
Deux-Sèvres □ *France* **18** F6
Deva *Romania* **28** E7
Devakottai *India* **66** Q11
Devaprayag *India* **68** D8
Dévaványa *Hungary* **23** C5
Deveci Dağları *Turkey* **72** B7
Devecikonağı *Turkey* **45** G12
Devecser *Hungary* **28** C2
Develi *Turkey* **72** C6
Deventer *Neths.* **17** B6
Deveron → *U.K.* **13** D6
Devesel *Romania* **28** F7
Devgadh Bariya *India* **68** H5
Devikot *India* **68** F4
Devils Den *U.S.A.* **110** K7
Devils Hole = Death Valley △ *U.S.A.* **111** J9
Devils Lake *U.S.A.* **112** A4
Devils Paw *Canada* **102** B2
Devils Postpile △ *U.S.A.* **110** H7
Devils Tower *U.S.A.* **108** D11
Devils Tower △ *U.S.A.* **108** D11
Devin *Bulgaria* **45** E8
Devine *U.S.A.* **116** G5
Devizes *U.K.* **15** F6
Devli *India* **68** G6
Devnya *Bulgaria* **45** C11
Devoll → *Albania* **44** F4
Devon *Canada* **102** C6
Devon □ *U.K.* **15** G4
Devon I. *Canada* **101** B15
Devonport *Austral.a* **95** G4
Devonport *N.Z.* **91** B5
Devrek *Turkey* **72** B4
Devrekâni *Turkey* **72** B5
Devrez → *Turkey* **72** B6
Dewas *India* **68** H7
Dewetsdorp *S. Africa* **88** D4
Dewey *Puerto Rico* **121** d
Dexing *China* **59** C11
Dexter *Maine, U.S.A.* **113** C19
Dexter *Mo., U.S.A.* **112** G9
Dexter *N. Mex., U.S.A.* **109** K11
Dey-Dey, L. *Australia* **93** E5
Deyang *China* **58** B5
Deyhūk *Iran* **71** C8
Deyyer *Iran* **71** E6
Dez → *Iran* **73** F13
Dezadeash L. *Canada* **102** A1
Dezfūl *Iran* **73** F13
Dezhneva, Mys *Russia* **53** C19
Dezhou *China* **56** F9
Dhadhar → *India* **69** G11
Dhahaban *Si. Arabia* **80** C4
Dhahiriya = Az Zāhirīyah *West Bank* **74** D3
Dhahran = Az Zahrān *Si. Arabia* **71** E6
Dhak *Pakistan* **68** C5
Dhaka *Bangla.* **69** H14
Dhaka □ *Bangla.* **69** G14
Dhali *Cyprus* **49** D12
Dhamār *Yemen* **75** E3
Dhampur *India* **69** E8
Dhamtari *India* **67** J12
Dhanbad *India* **69** H12
Dhangarhi *Nepal* **69** E9
Dhankuta *Nepal* **69** F12
Dhanpuri *India* **69** H9
Dhar *India* **68** H6
Dharampur *India* **68** H6
Dharamsala = Dharmsala *India* **68** C7
Dharan *Nepal* **69** F12
Dhariwal *India* **68** D6
Dharla → *Bangla.* **69** G13
Dharmapuri *India* **66** N11
Dharmjaygarh *India* **69** H10
Dharmsala *India* **68** C7
Dharni *India* **68** J7
Dharwad *India* **66** M9

Dhasan → *India* 69 G8
Dhaulagiri *Nepal* 69 E10
Dhebar, L. *India* 68 G6
Dheftera *Cyprus* 49 D12
Dhenkanal *India* 67 J14
Dherinia *Cyprus* 49 D12
Dheskáti = Deskati *Greece* 44 G5
Dhí Qār □ *Iraq* 70 D5
Dhiarrizos → *Cyprus* 49 E11
Dhībān *Jordan* 74 D4
Dhilwan *India* 68 D6
Dhimarkhera *India* 69 H9
Dhodhekánisos =
    Dodecanese *Greece* 47 E8
Dholka *India* 68 H5
Dhomokós = Domokos
    Greece 46 B4
Dhoraji *India* 68 J4
Dhragonísi = Tragonhsi
    Greece 47 D7
Dhrangadhra *India* 68 H4
Dhrol *India* 68 H4
Dhuburi *India* 67 F16
Dhule *India* 66 J9
Di-ib, W. → *Sudan* 80 C4
Di Linh *Vietnam* 65 G7
Di Linh, Cao Nguyen
    Vietnam 65 G7
Dia *Greece* 49 D7
Diabakania *Guinea* 82 C2
Diablo Range *U.S.A.* 110 J5
Diafarabé *Mali* 82 C4
Diala *Mali* 82 C3
Dialakoro *Mali* 82 C3
Dialakoto *Senegal* 82 C2
Diallassagou *Mali* 82 C4
Diamante *Argentina* 126 C3
Diamante *Italy* 43 C8
Diamante → *Argentina* 126 C2
Diamantina *Brazil* 125 G10
Diamantina □ *Australia* 95 D2
Diamantina △ *Australia* 94 C3
Diamantino *Brazil* 125 F7
Diamond Bar *U.S.A.* 111 L9
Diamond Harbour *India* 69 H13
Diamond Is. *Australia* 94 B5
Diamond Mts. *U.S.A.* 108 G6
Diamond Springs *U.S.A.* 110 G6
Diamou *Mali* 82 C2
Dian Chi *China* 58 E4
Dianalund *Denmark* 11 J5
Dianbai *China* 59 G8
Diancheng *China* 59 G8
Dianjiang *China* 58 B6
Diano Marina *Italy* 40 E5
Dianra *Ivory C.* 82 D3
Diaoyu Tai = Senkaku-
    Shotō *E. China Sea* 55 M1
Diapaga *Burkina Faso* 83 C5
Diapangou *Burkina Faso* 83 C5
Diariguila *Guinea* 82 C2
Dibā *U.A.E.* 71 E8
Dibagah *Iraq* 73 E10
Dibai *India* 68 E8
Dibaya *Dem. Rep. of the Congo* 84 F4
Dibaya-Lubue
    Dem. Rep. of the Congo 84 E3
Dibbeen △ *Jordan* 74 C4
D'Iberville, Lac *Canada* 104 A5
Dibete *Botswana* 88 C4
Dibrugarh *India* 67 F19
Dickens *U.S.A.* 116 E4
Dickinson *U.S.A.* 112 B2
Dickson *U.S.A.* 117 C11
Dickson City *U.S.A.* 115 E9
Dicle Barajı *Turkey* 73 C9
Dicle Nehri → *Turkey* 73 D9
Dicomano *Italy* 41 E8
Didesa, W. → *Ethiopia* 81 E4
Didiéni *Mali* 82 C3
Didimoticho *Greece* 45 E10
Didsbury *Canada* 102 C6
Didwana *India* 68 F6
Die *France* 21 D9
Diébougou *Burkina Faso* 82 C4
Diecke *Guinea* 82 D3
Diefenbaker, L. *Canada* 103 C7
Diego de Almagro *Chile* 126 B1
Diego Suarez =
    Antsiranana *Madag.* 89 A8
Diekirch *Lux.* 17 E6
Diéma *Mali* 82 C3
Diembéring *Senegal* 82 C1
Diemelsee = *Germany* 24 D4
Dien Ban *Vietnam* 64 E7
Dien Bien *Vietnam* 58 G4
Diepholz *Germany* 24 C4
Dieppe *France* 18 C4
Dierks *U.S.A.* 116 D7
Diest *Belgium* 17 D5
Dietikon *Switz.* 25 H4
Dieulefit *France* 21 D9
Dieuze *France* 19 D13
Dif *Somali Rep.* 75 G3
Diffa *Niger* 83 C7
Diffa □ *Niger* 83 B7
Differdange *Lux.* 17 E5
Dig *India* 68 F7

Digba *Dem. Rep. of the Congo* 86 B2
Digby *Canada* 105 D6
Digges Is. *Canada* 101 E16
Diggi *India* 68 F6
Dighinala *Bangla.* 67 H18
Dighton *U.S.A.* 112 F3
Digna *Mali* 82 C3
Digne-les-Bains *France* 21 D10
Digoin *France* 19 F11
Digor *Turkey* 73 B10
Digos *Phil.* 61 H6
Digranes *Iceland* 8 C6
Digul → *Indonesia* 63 F9
Digya △ *Ghana* 83 D5
Dihang = Brahmaputra →
    Asia 69 H13
Dijlah, Nahr → *Asia* 70 D5
Dijon *France* 19 E12
Dikhil *Djibouti* 81 E5
Dikili *Turkey* 47 B8
Dikirnis *Egypt* 80 H7
Dikkil = Dikhil *Djibouti* 81 E5
Dikodougou *Ivory C.* 82 D3
Diksmuide *Belgium* 17 C2
Dikson *Russia* 53 B9
Dikti Oros *Greece* 49 D7
Dikwa *Nigeria* 83 C7
Dila *Ethiopia* 81 F4
Dilek Yarimadisi △ *Turkey* 47 D9
Dili *E. Timor* 63 F7
Dilijan *Armenia* 35 K7
Dilinata *Greece* 46 C2
Dilizhan = Dilijan *Armenia* 35 K7
Dilj *Croatia* 28 E3
Dillenburg *Germany* 24 E4
Dilley *U.S.A.* 116 G5
Dilli = Delhi *India* 68 E7
Dilli *Mali* 82 C4
Dilling *Sudan* 81 E2
Dillingen *Bayern, Germany* 25 G6
Dillingen *Saarland, Germany* 25 F2
Dillingham *U.S.A.* 106 D8
Dillon *Canada* 103 B7
Dillon *Mont., U.S.A.* 108 D7
Dillon *S.C., U.S.A.* 117 D15
Dillon → *Canada* 103 B7
Dillsburg *U.S.A.* 114 F7
Dilolo *Dem. Rep. of the Congo* 84 G4
Dilos *Greece* 47 D7
Dilove *Ukraine* 29 C9
Dimas *Mexico* 118 C3
Dimashq *Syria* 74 B5
Dimashq □ *Syria* 74 B5
Dimbaza *S. Africa* 89 E4
Dimbokro *Ivory C.* 82 D4
Dimboola *Australia* 95 F3
Dimboviţa →
    Dâmboviţa → *Romania* 29 F11
Dimbulah *Australia* 94 B4
Dimitrovgrad *Bulgaria* 45 D9
Dimitrovgrad *Russia* 34 C9
Dimitrovgrad *Serbia* 44 C6
Dimitrovo = Pernik *Bulgaria* 44 D7
Dimitsana *Greece* 46 D4
Dimmitt *U.S.A.* 116 D3
Dimo *Sudan* 81 F2
Dimona *Israel* 74 D4
Dimovo *Bulgaria* 44 C6
Dinagat *Phil.* 61 F6
Dinajpur *Bangla.* 67 G16
Dinan *France* 18 D4
Dīnān Āb *Iran* 71 C8
Dinant *Belgium* 17 D4
Dinapur *India* 69 G11
Dinar *Turkey* 47 C12
Dīnār, Kūh-e *Iran* 71 D6
Dinara Planina *Croatia* 41 D13
Dinard *France* 18 D4
Dinaric Alps = Dinara
    Planina *Croatia* 41 D13
Dindanko *Mali* 82 C3
Dinder, Nahr ed → *Sudan* 81 E3
Dinder △ *Sudan* 81 E4
Dindigul *India* 66 P11
Dindori *India* 69 H9
Ding Xian = Dingzhou *China* 56 E8
Dinga *Pakistan* 68 G2
Dingalan *Phil.* 61 D4
Ding'an *China* 64 C8
Dingbian *China* 56 F4
Dingelstädt *Germany* 24 D6
Dingle *Ireland* 12 D1
Dingle *Sweden* 11 F5
Dingle B. *Ireland* 12 D1
Dingmans Ferry *U.S.A.* 115 E10
Dingnan *China* 59 E10
Dingo *Australia* 94 C4
Dingolfing *Germany* 25 G8
Dingtao *China* 56 G8
Dinguiraye *Guinea* 82 C2
Dingwall *U.K.* 13 D4
Dingxi *China* 56 G3
Dingxiang *China* 56 E7
Dingyuan *China* 59 A11
Dingzhou *China* 56 E8
Dinh, Mui *Vietnam* 65 G7
Dinh Lap *Vietnam* 58 G6
Dinin → *Ireland* 12 D4
Dinira △ *Venezuela* 121 E6

Dinokwe *Botswana* 88 C4
Dinorwic *Canada* 103 D10
Dinosaur △ *Canada* 102 C6
Dinosaur *U.S.A.* 108 F9
Dinuba *U.S.A.* 110 J7
Diö *Sweden* 11 H8
Dioïla *Mali* 82 C3
Dioka *Mali* 82 C2
Diongoï *Mali* 82 C3
Dionisades *Greece* 49 D8
Diosig *Romania* 28 C7
Diougani *Mali* 82 C4
Dioura *Mali* 82 C3
Diourbel *Senegal* 82 C1
Diourbel □ *Senegal* 82 C1
Dipalpur *Pakistan* 68 D5
Dipkarpaz = Rizokarpaso
    Cyprus 49 D13
Diplo *Pakistan* 68 G3
Dipolog *Phil.* 61 G5
Dipperu △ *Australia* 94 C4
Dir *Pakistan* 66 B7
Diré *Mali* 82 B4
Dire Dawa *Ethiopia* 81 F5
Dirfis Oros *Greece* 46 C5
Diriamba *Nic.* 120 D2
Dirk Hartog I. *Australia* 93 E1
Dirranbandi *Australia* 95 D4
Disa *India* 68 G5
Disa *Sudan* 81 E3
Disappointment, C. *U.S.A.* 108 C1
Disappointment, L. *Australia* 92 D3
Disaster B. *Australia* 95 F4
Discovery B. *Australia* 95 F3
Disentis Muster *Switz.* 25 J4
Dishna *Egypt* 80 B3
Disina *Nigeria* 83 C6
Disko = Qeqertarsuaq
    Greenland 98 C14
Disna = Dzisna → *Belarus* 32 E5
Disney Reef *Tonga* 91 c
Diss *U.K.* 15 E9
Disteghil Sar *Pakistan* 69 A6
District of Columbia □
    U.S.A. 113 F15
Distrito Federal □ *Brazil* 125 G9
Distrito Federal □ *Mexico* 119 D5
Disûq *Egypt* 80 H7
Diu *India* 68 J4
Dīvāndarreh *Iran* 73 E12
Dives → *France* 18 C6
Dives-sur-Mer *France* 18 C6
Divichi = Däväçi *Azerbaijan* 35 K9
Divide *U.S.A.* 108 D7
Dividing Ra. *Australia* 93 E2
Divinópolis *Brazil* 125 H10
Divjake *Albania* 44 F3
Divnoye *Russia* 35 H6
Divo *Ivory C.* 82 D3
Diviği *Turkey* 73 C8
Diwāl Kol *Afghan.* 68 B2
Dixie Mt. *U.S.A.* 110 F6
Dixon *Calif., U.S.A.* 110 G5
Dixon *Ill., U.S.A.* 112 E9
Dixon Entrance *U.S.A.* 100 G5
Dixville *Canada* 115 A13
Diyadin *Turkey* 73 C10
Diyālā □ *Iraq* 70 C5
Diyālā → *Iraq* 73 F11
Diyarbakır *Turkey* 73 D9
Diyarbakır □ *Turkey* 73 D9
Diyodar *India* 68 G4
Dizangué *Cameroon* 83 E6
Djakarta = Jakarta *Indonesia* 62 F3
Djamba *Angola* 88 B1
Djambala *Congo* 84 E2
Djanet *Algeria* 78 D7
Djawa = Jawa *Indonesia* 62 F3
Djelfa *Algeria* 78 B6
Djema *C.A.R.* 86 A2
Djenné *Mali* 82 C4
Djerba, Î. de *Tunisia* 79 B8
Djerid, Chott *Tunisia* 78 B7
Djibo *Burkina Faso* 83 C4
Djibouti *Djibouti* 81 E5
Djibouti ■ *Africa* 81 E5
Djolu *Dem. Rep. of the Congo* 84 D4
Djougou *Benin* 83 D5
Djoum *Cameroon* 84 D2
Djourab, Erg du *Chad* 79 E9
Djugu *Dem. Rep. of the Congo* 86 B3
Djukbinj △ *Australia* 92 B5
Djúpivogur *Iceland* 8 D6
Djurás *Sweden* 10 D9
Djurö △ *Sweden* 11 F7
Djursland *Denmark* 11 H4
Dmitriya Lapteva, Proliv
    Russia 53 B15
Dmitriyev Lgovskiy *Russia* 33 F8
Dmitrov *Russia* 32 D9
Dmitrovsk-Orlovskiy *Russia* 33 F8
Dnepr = Dnipro → *Ukraine* 33 J7
Dneprodzerzhinsk =
    Dniprodzerzhynsk *Ukraine* 33 H8
Dneprodzerzhinskoye
    Vdkhr. =
    Dniprodzerzhynske
    Vdskh. *Ukraine* 33 H8

Dnepropetrovsk =
    Dnipropetrovsk *Ukraine* 33 H8
Dneprorudnoye =
    Dniprorudne *Ukraine* 33 J8
Dnestr = Dnister → *Europe* 23 E16
Dnieper = Dnipro → *Ukraine* 33 J7
Dniester = Dnister →
    Europe 23 E16
Dnipro → *Ukraine* 33 J7
Dniprodzerzhynsk *Ukraine* 33 H8
Dniprodzerzhynske Vdskh.
    Ukraine 33 H8
Dnipropetrovsk *Ukraine* 33 H8
Dnipropetrovsk □ *Ukraine* 33 H8
Dniprorudne *Ukraine* 33 J8
Dnister → *Europe* 23 E16
Dnistrovskyy Lyman *Ukraine* 33 J6
Dno *Russia* 32 D5
Dnyapro = Dnipro →
    Ukraine 33 J7
Do Gonbadān = Gachsārān
    Iran 71 D6
Doaktown *Canada* 105 C6
Doan Hung *Vietnam* 58 G5
Doany *Madag.* 89 A8
Doba *Chad* 79 G9
Dobandi *Pakistan* 68 D2
Dobbiaco *Italy* 41 B9
Dobbyn *Australia* 94 B3
Dobczyce *Poland* 31 J7
Dobele *Latvia* 30 B10
Dobele □ *Latvia* 30 B10
Döbeln *Germany* 24 D9
Doberai, Jazirah *Indonesia* 63 E8
Dobiegniew *Poland* 31 F2
Doblas *Argentina* 126 D3
Dobo *Indonesia* 63 F8
Doboj *Bos.-H.* 28 F3
Dobra *Wielkopolskie, Poland* 31 G5
Dobra *Zachodnio-Pomorskie,
    Poland* 30 E2
Dobra *Dâmbovita, Romania* 29 F10
Dobra *Hunedoara, Romania* 28 E7
Dobre Miasto *Poland* 30 E7
Dobrei *Romania* 28 D7
Dobrich *Bulgaria* 45 C11
Dobrinishta *Bulgaria* 44 E7
Dobříš *Czech Rep.* 26 B7
Dobrodzień *Poland* 31 H5
Dobromyl *Ukraine* 31 J9
Dobron *Ukraine* 28 B7
Dobropole *Ukraine* 33 H9
Dobrovolsk *Russia* 30 D9
Dobruja *Europe* 29 F13
Dobrush *Belarus* 23 B16
Dobrzany *Poland* 30 E2
Dobrzyń nad Wisłą *Poland* 31 F6
Doc, Mui *Vietnam* 64 D6
Docker River =
    Kaltukatjara *Australia* 93 E4
Docksta *Sweden* 10 A12
Doctor Arroyo *Mexico* 118 C4
Doctor Pedro P. Peña
    Paraguay 126 A3
Doda *India* 69 C6
Doda, L. *Canada* 104 C4
Dodecanese *Greece* 47 E8
Dodekanisa = Dodecanese
    Greece 47 E8
Dodekanisa □ *Greece* 47 E8
Dodge City *U.S.A.* 112 G3
Dodge L. *Canada* 103 B7
Dodgeville *U.S.A.* 112 D8
Dodo *Cameroon* 83 D7
Dodo *Sudan* 81 F2
Dodola *Ethiopia* 81 F4
Dodoma *Tanzania* 86 D4
Dodoma □ *Tanzania* 86 D4
Dodoni *Greece* 46 B2
Dodori △ *Kenya* 86 C5
Dodsland *Canada* 103 C7
Dodson *U.S.A.* 108 B9
Dodurga *Turkey* 47 B11
Doesburg *Neths.* 17 B6
Doetinchem *Neths.* 17 C6
Dog Creek *Canada* 102 C4
Dog L. *Man., Canada* 103 C9
Dog L. *Ont., Canada* 104 C2
Doğanşehir *Turkey* 72 C7
Dogliani *Italy* 40 D4
Dogondoutchi *Niger* 83 C5
Dogran *Pakistan* 68 D5
Doğubayazıt *Turkey* 73 C11
Doguéraoua *Niger* 83 C6
Doha = Ad Dawḩah *Qatar* 71 E6
Dohazari *Bangla.* 67 H18
Dohrighat *India* 69 F10
Doi *Indonesia* 63 D7
Doi Inthanon △ *Thailand* 64 C2
Doi Khuntan △ *Thailand* 64 C2
Doi Luang *Thailand* 64 C3
Doi Luang △ *Thailand* 64 C2
Doi Saket *Thailand* 64 C2
Doi Suthep △ *Thailand* 64 C2
Dois Irmãos, Sa. *Brazil* 125 E10
Dojransko Jezero *Macedonia* 44 E6
Doka *Sudan* 81 E4
Dokkum *Neths.* 17 A5
Dokos *Greece* 46 D5

Dokri *Pakistan* 68 F3
Dokuchayevsk *Ukraine* 33 J9
Dol-de-Bretagne *France* 18 D5
Dolac *Kosovo* 44 D4
Dolak, Pulau *Indonesia* 63 F9
Dole *France* 19 E12
Doleib, Wadi → *Sudan* 81 E3
Dolenji Logatec *Slovenia* 41 C11
Dolgellau *U.K.* 14 E4
Dolhasca *Romania* 29 C11
Doliana *Greece* 46 B2
Dolianova *Italy* 42 C2
Dolinsk *Russia* 53 E15
Dolinskaya = Dolynska
    Ukraine 33 H7
Dolj □ *Romania* 29 F8
Dollard *Neths.* 17 A7
Dolna Banya *Bulgaria* 44 D7
Dolni Chiflik *Bulgaria* 45 D11
Dolni Dŭbnik *Bulgaria* 45 C8
Dolnośląskie □ *Poland* 31 G3
Dolný Kubín *Slovak Rep.* 27 B12
Dolo *Ethiopia* 81 G5
Dolo *Italy* 41 C9
Dolomites = Dolomiti *Italy* 41 B8
Dolomiti *Italy* 41 B8
Dolomiti Bellunesi △ *Italy* 41 B9
Dolores *Argentina* 126 D4
Dolores *Uruguay* 126 C4
Dolores *U.S.A.* 109 H9
Dolores → *U.S.A.* 108 G9
Dolovo *Serbia* 28 F5
Dolphin, C. *Falk. Is.* 128 G5
Dolphin and Union Str.
    Canada 100 D9
Dolsk *Poland* 31 G4
Dolyna *Ukraine* 29 B9
Dolynska *Ukraine* 33 H7
Dolynske *Ukraine* 29 D14
Dolzhanskaya *Russia* 33 J9
Dom Pedrito *Brazil* 127 C5
Doma *Nigeria* 83 D6
Doma △ *Zimbabwe* 87 F3
Domaniç *Turkey* 47 B11
Domariaganj → *India* 69 F10
Domasi *Malawi* 87 F4
Domažlice *Czech Rep.* 26 B5
Dombarovskiy *Russia* 52 D6
Dombås *Norway* 8 E13
Dombasle-sur-Meurthe
    France 19 D13
Dombes *France* 21 C9
Dombóvár *Hungary* 28 D3
Dombrád *Hungary* 28 B6
Dome Argus *Antarctica* 5 E12
Dome C. *Antarctica* 5 D17
Dome Fuji *Antarctica* 5 D5
Domel I. = Letsôk-aw
    Kyun *Burma* 65 G2
Domérat *France* 19 F9
Domeyko *Chile* 126 B1
Domeyko, Cordillera *Chile* 126 A2
Domfront *France* 18 D6
Dominador *Chile* 126 A2
Dominica ■ *W. Indies* 121 C7
Dominica Passage *W. Indies* 121 C7
Dominican Rep. ■ *W. Indies* 121 C5
Dömitz *Germany* 24 B7
Domme *France* 20 D5
Dommel → *Neths.* 17 C5
Domneşti *Romania* 29 E9
Domodóssola *Italy* 40 B5
Domogled-Valea Cernei △
    Romania 28 F7
Domokos *Greece* 46 B4
Dompaire *France* 19 D13
Dompierre-sur-Besbre
    France 19 F10
Dompim *Ghana* 82 D4
Domrémy-la-Pucelle *France* 19 D12
Domvena *Greece* 46 C4
Domville, Mt. *Australia* 95 D5
Domžale *Slovenia* 41 B11
Don → *Russia* 33 J10
Don → *Aberds., U.K.* 13 D6
Don → *S. Yorks., U.K.* 14 D7
Don, C. *Australia* 92 B5
Don Benito *Spain* 37 G5
Don Figuero Mts. *Jamaica* 120 a
Don Sak *Thailand* 65 b
Dona Ana = Nhamaabué
    Mozam. 87 F4
Doña Mencía *Spain* 37 H6
Donaghadee *U.K.* 12 B6
Donaghmore *Ireland* 12 D4
Donald *Australia* 95 F3
Donaldsonville *U.S.A.* 116 F9
Donalsonville *U.S.A.* 117 F12
Doñana △ *Spain* 37 J4
Donau = Dunărea →
    Europe 29 E14
Donau → *Austria* 27 C10
Donau Auen △ *Austria* 27 C9
Donaueschingen *Germany* 25 H4
Donauwörth *Germany* 25 G6
Doncaster *U.K.* 14 D6
Dondo *Angola* 84 F2
Dondo *Mozam.* 87 F3

Dondo, Teluk *Indonesia* 63 D6
Dondra Head *Sri Lanka* 66 S12
Dondușeni *Moldova* 29 B12
Donegal *Ireland* 12 B3
Donegal □ *Ireland* 12 B4
Donegal B. *Ireland* 12 B3
Donets → *Russia* 35 G5
Donets Basin *Ukraine* 6 F13
Donetsk *Ukraine* 33 J9
Donetsk □ *Ukraine* 33 J9
Dong Ba Thin *Vietnam* 65 F7
Dong Dang *Vietnam* 58 G6
Dong Giam *Vietnam* 64 C5
Dong Ha *Vietnam* 64 D6
Dong Hene *Laos* 64 D5
Dong Hoi *Vietnam* 64 D6
Dong Jiang → *China* 59 F10
Dong Khe *Vietnam* 64 A6
Dong Ujimqin Qi *China* 56 B9
Dong Van *Vietnam* 58 G5
Dong Xoai *Vietnam* 65 G6
Donga *Nigeria* 83 D7
Donga → *Nigeria* 83 D7
Dong'an *China* 59 D8
Dongara *Australia* 93 E1
Dongbei *China* 54 A5
Dongchuan *China* 58 D4
Dongco *China* 67 C14
Donges *France* 18 E4
Dongfang *China* 64 C7
Dongfeng *China* 57 C13
Donggala *Indonesia* 63 E5
Donggan *China* 58 F5
Donggang *China* 57 E13
Dongguan *China* 59 F9
Dongguang *China* 56 F9
Donghae *S. Korea* 57 F15
Donghai Dao *China* 59 G8
Dongjingcheng *China* 57 B15
Dongkou *China* 59 D8
Donglan *China* 58 E7
Dongliu *China* 59 B11
Dongmen *China* 58 F6
Dongnae *S. Korea* 57 G15
Dongning *China* 57 B16
Dongnyi *China* 58 C3
Dongola *Sudan* 80 D3
Dongping *China* 56 G9
Dongsha Dao *S. China Sea* 59 G11
Dongshan *China* 59 F11
Dongsheng *China* 56 E6
Dongtai *China* 57 H11
Dongting Hu *China* 59 C9
Dongtou *China* 59 D13
Dongxiang *China* 59 C11
Dongxing *China* 58 G7
Dongyang *China* 59 C13
Dongzhi *China* 59 B11
Donington, C. *Australia* 95 E2
Doniphan *U.S.A.* 112 G8
Donja Stubica *Croatia* 41 C12
Donji Dušnik *Serbia* 44 C6
Donji Miholjac *Croatia* 28 E3
Donji Milanovac *Serbia* 44 B6
Donji Vakuf *Bos.-H.* 28 F2
Dønna *Norway* 8 C15
Donna *U.S.A.* 116 H5
Donnacona *Canada* 105 C5
Donnelly's Crossing *N.Z.* 91 A4
Donnybrook *Australia* 93 F2
Donnybrook *S. Africa* 89 D4
Donora *U.S.A.* 114 F5
Donostia = Donostia-San
    Sebastián *Spain* 38 B3
Donostia-San Sebastián
    Spain 38 B3
Donousa *Greece* 47 D7
Donskoy *Russia* 32 F10
Donsol *Phil.* 61 E5
Donwood *Canada* 114 B6
Donzère *France* 21 D8
Donzy *France* 19 E10
Doomadgee *Australia* 94 B2
Doomadgee ◎ *Australia* 94 B2
Doon → *U.K.* 13 F4
Doon Doon ◎ *Australia* 92 C4
Dora, L. *Australia* 92 D3
Dora Báltea → *Italy* 40 C5
Dora Ripária → *Italy* 40 C4
Doran L. *Canada* 103 A7
Dorchester *U.S.* 15 G5
Dorchester, C. *Canada* 101 D16
Dordabis *Namibia* 88 C2
Dordogne □ *France* 20 C4
Dordogne → *France* 20 C3
Dordrecht *Neths.* 17 C4
Dordrecht *S. Africa* 88 E4
Dore → *France* 20 C7
Dore, Mts. *France* 20 C6
Doré L. *Canada* 103 C7
Dorfen *Germany* 25 G8
Dorgali *Italy* 42 B2
Dori *Burkina Faso* 83 C4
Doring → *S. Africa* 88 E2
Doringbos *S. Africa* 88 E2
Dorking *U.K.* 15 F7
Dormaa-Ahenkro *Ghana* 82 D4
Dormans *France* 19 C10
Dormo, Ras *Eritrea* 81 E5

Dornbirn *Austria* **26** D2
Dornes *France* **19** F10
Dorneşti *Romania* **29** C11
Dornie *U.K.* **13** D3
Dornoch *Canada* **114** B4
Dornoch *U.K.* **13** D4
Dornoch Firth *U.K.* **13** D4
Dornogovĭ □ *Mongolia* **56** C6
Doro *Mali* **83** B4
Doro. Kavo *Greece* **46** C6
Dorog *Hungary* **28** C3
Dorogobuzh *Russia* **32** E7
Dorohoi *Romania* **29** C11
Dorr *Iran* **71** C6
Dorre I. *Australia* **93** E1
Dorrigo *Australia* **95** E5
Dorris *U.S.A.* **108** F3
Dorset *Canada* **114** A6
Dorset *Ohio, U.S.A.* **114** E4
Dorset *Vt., U.S.A.* **115** C11
Dorset □ *U.K.* **15** G5
Dorsten *Germany* **24** D2
Dortmund *Germany* **24** D3
Dortmund-Ems-Kanal ➔ *Germany* **24** D3
Dörtyol *Turkey* **72** D7
Dorum *Germany* **24** B4
Doruma *Dem. Rep. of the Congo* **86** B2
Dorûneh *Iran* **71** C8
Dos Bahías, C. *Argentina* **128** E3
Dos Hermanas *Spain* **37** H5
Dos Palos *U.S.A.* **110** J6
Döşemealtı *Turkey* **47** D12
Dosso *Niger* **83** C5
Dosso □ *Niger* **83** C5
Dosso △ *Niger* **83** C5
Dothan *U.S.A.* **117** F12
Doty *U.S.A.* **110** D3
Douai *France* **19** B10
Douako *Guinea* **82** D2
Douala *Cameroon* **83** E6
Douarnenez *France* **18** D2
Doubabougou *Mali* **82** C3
Double Island Pt. *Australia* **95** D5
Double Mountain Fork ➔ *U.S.A.* **116** E4
Doubrava ➔ *Czech Rep.* **26** A8
Doubs □ *France* **19** E13
Doubs ➔ *France* **19** F12
Doubtful Sd. *N.Z.* **91** F1
Doubtless B. *N.Z.* **91** A4
Doudeville *France* **18** C7
Doué-la-Fontaine *France* **18** E6
Douentza *Mali* **82** C4
Douentza △ *Mali* **82** B4
Douglas *Canada* **114** A8
Douglas *I. of Man* **14** C3
Douglas *S. Africa* **88** D3
Douglas *Ariz., U.S.A.* **109** L9
Douglas *Ga., U.S.A.* **117** F13
Douglas *Wyo., U.S.A.* **108** E11
Douglas Apsley △ *Australia* **95** G4
Douglas Chan. *Canada* **102** C3
Douglas Pt. *Canada* **114** B3
Douglasville *U.S.A.* **117** E12
Doukaton, Akra *Greece* **46** C2
Doulevant-le-Château *France* **19** D11
Doullens *France* **19** B9
Doumen *China* **59** F9
Dounreay *U.K.* **13** C5
Doura *Mali* **82** C3
Dourada, Serra *Brazil* **125** F9
Dourados *Brazil* **127** A5
Dourados ➔ *Brazil* **127** A5
Dourados, Serra dos *Brazil* **127** A5
Dourdan *France* **19** D9
Douro ➔ *Europe* **36** D2
Douvaine *France* **19** F13
Douvres-la-Délivrande *France* **18** C6
Douze ➔ *France* **20** E3
Dove ➔ *U.K.* **14** E6
Dove Creek *U.S.A.* **109** H9
Dover *Australia* **95** G4
Dover *U.K.* **15** F9
Dover *Del., U.S.A.* **113** F16
Dover *N.H., U.S.A.* **115** C14
Dover *N.J., U.S.A.* **115** F10
Dover *Ohio, U.S.A.* **114** F3
Dover, Pt. *Australia* **93** F4
Dover, Str. of *Europe* **15** G9
Dover-Foxcroft *U.S.A.* **113** C19
Dover Plains *U.S.A.* **115** E11
Dovey = Dyfi ➔ *U.K.* **15** E3
Dovhe *Ukraine* **29** B8
Dovrefjell *Norway* **8** E13
Dow Rūd *Iran* **71** C6
Dowa *Malawi* **87** E3
Dowagiac *U.S.A.* **112** E10
Dowerin *Australia* **93** F2
Dowgha'i *Iran* **71** B8
Dowlatābād *Kermān, Iran* **71** D8
Dowlatābād *Khorāsān, Iran* **71** C8
Down □ *U.K.* **12** B5
Downey *Calif., U.S.A.* **111** M8
Downey *Idaho, U.S.A.* **108** E7
Downham Market *U.K.* **15** E8

Downieville *U.S.A.* **110** F6
Downpatrick *U.K.* **12** B6
Downpatrick Hd. *Ireland* **12** B2
Downsville *U.S.A.* **115** D10
Downton, Mt. *Canada* **102** C4
Dowsārī *Iran* **71** D8
Doxato *Greece* **45** E8
Doyle *U.S.A.* **110** E6
Doylestown *U.S.A.* **115** F9
Dozois, Rés. *Canada* **104** C4
Dra Khel *Pakistan* **68** F2
Drâa, C. *Morocco* **78** C3
Drâa, Hamada du *Algeria* **78** C4
Drâa, Oued ➔ *Morocco* **78** C3
Drac ➔ *France* **21** C9
Drac, Coves del *Spain* **48** B10
Dračevo *Macedonia* **44** E5
Drachten *Neths.* **17** A6
Drăgăneşti *Moldova* **29** C13
Drăgăneşti-Olt *Romania* **29** F9
Drăgăneşti-Vlaşca *Romania* **29** F10
Dragaš *Kosovo* **44** D4
Drăgăşani *Romania* **29** F9
Dragocvet *Serbia* **44** C5
Dragon's Mouths *Venezuela* **125** K15
Dragovishtitsa *Bulgaria* **44** D6
Draguignan *France* **21** E10
Drahove *Ukraine* **29** B8
Drain *U.S.A.* **108** E2
Drake *U.S.A.* **112** B3
Drake Passage *S. Ocean* **5** B17
Drakensberg *S. Africa* **89** D4
Drama *Greece* **45** E8
Drama □ *Greece* **45** E8
Drammen *Norway* **9** G14
Drangajökull *Iceland* **8** C2
Dranov, Ostrov *Romania* **29** F14
Dras *India* **69** B6
Drastis, Akra *Greece* **49** A3
Drau = Drava ➔ *Croatia* **28** E3
Drava ➔ *Croatia* **28** E3
Dravograd *Slovenia* **41** B12
Drawa ➔ *Poland* **31** F2
Drawieński △ *Poland* **31** E2
Drawno *Poland* **31** E2
Drawsko Pomorskie *Poland* **30** E2
Drayton *Canada* **114** C4
Drayton Valley *Canada* **102** C6
Dreieich *Germany* **25** E4
Dren *Kosovo* **44** D4
Drenthe □ *Neths.* **17** B6
Drepano, Akra *Greece* **49** D6
Drepanum, C. *Cyprus* **49** E11
Dresden *Canada* **114** D2
Dresden *Germany* **24** D9
Dresden *U.S.A.* **114** D8
Dreux *France* **18** D8
Drezdenko *Poland* **31** F2
Driffield *U.K.* **14** C7
Driftwood *U.S.A.* **114** E6
Driggs *U.S.A.* **108** E8
Drin ➔ *Albania* **44** D3
Drin i Zi ➔ *Albania* **44** E4
Drina ➔ *Bos.-H.* **44** B3
Drincea ➔ *Romania* **28** F7
Drinjača ➔ *Bos.-H.* **28** F4
Driopida *Greece* **46** D6
Drissa = Vyerkhnyadzvinsk *Belarus* **32** E4
Drniš *Croatia* **41** E13
Drøbak *Norway* **9** G14
Drobeta-Turnu Severin *Romania* **28** F7
Drobin *Poland* **31** F6
Drochia *Moldova* **29** B12
Drogheda *Ireland* **12** C5
Drogichin = Dragichyn *Belarus* **23** B13
Drogobych = Drohobych *Ukraine* **31** J10
Drohiczyn *Poland* **31** F9
Drohobych *Ukraine* **31** J10
Droichead Atha = Drogheda *Ireland* **12** C5
Droichead na Bandan = Bandon *Ireland* **12** E3
Droichead Nua *Ireland* **12** C5
Droitwich *U.K.* **15** E5
Drôme □ *France* **21** D9
Drôme ➔ *France* **21** D8
Dromedary, C. *Australia* **95** F5
Drömling △ *Germany* **24** C7
Dromore *U.K.* **12** B4
Dromore West *Ireland* **12** B3
Dronero *Italy* **40** D4
Dronfield *U.K.* **14** D6
Dronne ➔ *France* **20** C3
Dronning Maud Land *Antarctica* **5** D3
Dronninglund *Denmark* **11** G3
Dronten *Neths.* **17** B5
Dropt ➔ *France* **20** D3
Drosendorf *Austria* **26** C8
Droué *France* **18** D8
Druk Yul = Bhutan ■ *Asia* **67** F17
Drumbo *Canada* **114** C4
Drumcliff *Ireland* **12** B3
Drumheller *Canada* **102** C6

Drummond *U.S.A.* **108** C7
Drummond I. *U.S.A.* **113** B12
Drummond Pt. *Australia* **95** E2
Drummond Ra. *Australia* **94** C4
Drummondville *Canada* **104** C5
Drumright *U.S.A.* **116** D6
Druskininkai *Lithuania* **32** E2
Drut ➔ *Belarus* **23** B16
Druya *Belarus* **32** E4
Druzhba *Bulgaria* **45** C12
Druzhina *Russia* **53** C15
Drvar *Bos.-H.* **41** D13
Drvenik *Croatia* **41** E13
Drwęca ➔ *Poland* **31** E5
Dry Harbour Mts. *Jamaica* **120** a
Dry Tortugas *U.S.A.* **117** F13
Dryander △ *Australia* **94** b
Dryden *Canada* **103** D10
Dryden *U.S.A.* **115** D8
Drygalski I. *Antarctica* **5** C7
Drygalski Ice Tongue *Antarctica* **5** C7
Drysdale ➔ *Australia* **92** B4
Drysdale I. *Australia* **94** A2
Drysdale River △ *Australia* **92** B4
Drzewica *Poland* **31** G7
Drzewiczka ➔ *Poland* **31** G7
Dschang *Cameroon* **83** D7
Du Gué ➔ *Canada* **104** A5
Du Quoin *U.S.A.* **112** F9
Du'an *China* **58** F7
Duanesburg *U.S.A.* **115** D10
Duaringa *Australia* **94** C4
Duarte, Pico *Dom. Rep.* **121** D5
Dubai = Dubayy *U.A.E.* **71** E7
Dubāsari *Moldova* **29** C14
Dubăsari Vdkhr. *Moldova* **29** C13
Dubawnt ➔ *Canada* **103** A8
Dubawnt L. *Canada* **103** A8
Dubayy *U.A.E.* **71** E7
Dubbo *Australia* **95** E4
Dube ➔ *Liberia* **82** D3
Dübele *Dem. Rep. of the Congo* **86** B2
Dübendorf *Switz.* **25** H4
Dubica *Croatia* **41** C13
Dublin *Ireland* **12** C5
Dublin *Ga., U.S.A.* **117** E13
Dublin *Tex., U.S.A.* **116** E5
Dublin □ *Ireland* **12** C5
Dublin ✈ (DUB) *Ireland* **12** C5
Dubna *Russia* **32** D9
Dubnica nad Váhom *Slovak Rep.* **27** C11
Dubno *Ukraine* **23** C13
Dubois *Idaho, U.S.A.* **108** D7
DuBois *Pa., U.S.A.* **114** E6
Dubossary = Dubăsari *Moldova* **29** C14
Dubossary Vdkhr. = Dubăsari Vdkhr. *Moldova* **29** C13
Dubove *Ukraine* **29** B8
Dubovka *Russia* **35** F7
Dubovskoye *Russia* **35** G6
Dubrajpur *India* **69** H12
Dubréka *Guinea* **82** D2
Dubrovitsa = Dubrovytsya *Ukraine* **23** C14
Dubrovnik *Croatia* **44** D2
Dubrovytsya *Ukraine* **23** C14
Dubuque *U.S.A.* **112** D8
Dubysa ➔ *Lithuania* **30** C10
Duchang *China* **59** C11
Duchesne *U.S.A.* **108** F8
Duchess *Australia* **94** C2
Ducie I. *Pac. Oc.* **97** K15
Duck ➔ *U.S.A.* **117** C11
Duck Cr. ➔ *Australia* **92** D2
Duck Lake *Canada* **103** C7
Duck Mountain △ *Canada* **103** C8
Duckwall, Mt. *U.S.A.* **110** H6
Duderstadt *Germany* **24** D6
Dudhi *India* **69** G10
Dudinka *Russia* **53** C9
Dudley *U.K.* **15** E5
Dudwa *India* **69** E9
Dudwa △ *India* **69** E9
Duékoué *Ivory C.* **82** D3
Dueñas *Spain* **36** D6
Duero = Douro ➔ *Europe* **36** D2
Dufftown *U.K.* **13** D5
Dufourspitz *Switz.* **25** K3
Dugi Otok *Croatia* **41** D11
Dugo Selo *Croatia* **41** C13
Duisburg *Germany* **24** D2
Duiwelskloof = Modjadjiskloof *S. Africa* **89** C5
Dujiangyan *China* **58** B4
Duk Fadiat *Sudan* **81** F3
Duk Faiwil *Sudan* **81** F3
Dukat *Albania* **44** F3
Dūkdamīn *Iran* **71** C8
Dukelský Průsmyk *Slovak Rep.* **27** B14
Dukhān *Qatar* **71** E6
Dukhovshchina *Russia* **32** E7
Duki *Pakistan* **66** D6
Dukla *Poland* **31** J8

Duku *Bauchi, Nigeria* **83** C7
Duku *Sokoto, Nigeria* **83** C5
Dulag *Phil.* **61** F6
Dulce *U.S.A.* **109** H10
Dulce ➔ *Argentina* **126** C3
Dulce, G. *Costa Rica* **120** E3
Dulf *Iraq* **70** C5
Dŭlgopol *Bulgaria* **45** C11
Duliu *China* **56** E9
Dullewala *Pakistan* **68** D4
Dullstroom *S. Africa* **89** D5
Dulq Maghār *Syria* **73** D8
Duluth *U.S.A.* **112** B7
Dum Dum *India* **69** H13
Dum Duma *India* **67** F19
Dūmā *Syria* **74** B5
Dumaguete *Phil.* **61** G5
Dumai *Indonesia* **62** D2
Dumaran *Phil.* **61** F3
Dumas *Ark., U.S.A.* **116** E9
Dumas *Tex., U.S.A.* **116** D4
Dumayr *Syria* **74** B5
Dumbarton *U.K.* **13** F4
Ďumbier *Slovak Rep.* **27** C12
Dumbleyung *Australia* **93** F2
Dumbrăveni *Romania* **29** D9
Dumfries *U.K.* **13** F5
Dumfries & Galloway □ *U.K.* **13** F5
Dumitreşti *Romania* **29** E11
Dumka *India* **69** G12
Dumlupınar *Turkey* **47** C12
Dümmer *Germany* **24** C4
Dümmer ○ *Germany* **24** C4
Dumoine ➔ *Canada* **104** C4
Dumoine, L. *Canada* **104** C4
Dumont d'Urville *Antarctica* **5** C10
Dumont d'Urville Sea *S. Ocean* **5** C9
Dumraon *India* **69** G11
Dumyât *Egypt* **80** H7
Dumyât, Masabb *Egypt* **80** H7
Dún Dealgan = Dundalk *Ireland* **12** B5
Dún Garbhán = Dungarvan *Ireland* **12** D4
Dún Laoghaire *Ireland* **12** C5
Dun-le-Palestel *France* **19** F8
Dun-sur-Auron *France* **19** F9
Dun-sur-Meuse *France* **19** C12
Duna = Dunărea ➔ *Europe* **29** E14
Duna-Drava △ *Hungary* **28** D3
Duna-völgyi-főcsatorna *Hungary* **28** D4
Dunaföldvár *Hungary* **28** D3
Dunagiri *India* **69** D8
Dunaj = Dunărea ➔ *Europe* **29** E14
Dunajec ➔ *Poland* **31** H7
Dunajská Streda *Slovak Rep.* **27** C10
Dunakeszi *Hungary* **28** C4
Dunapataj *Hungary* **28** D4
Dunărea ➔ *Europe* **29** E14
Dunaszekcső *Hungary* **28** D3
Dunaújváros *Hungary* **28** D3
Dunav = Dunărea ➔ *Europe* **29** E14
Dunavaţu de Jos *Romania* **29** F14
Dunavtsi *Bulgaria* **44** C6
Dunay *Russia* **54** C6
Dunayivtsi *Ukraine* **29** B11
Dunback *N.Z.* **91** F3
Dunbar *U.K.* **13** E6
Dunblane *U.K.* **13** E5
Duncan *Canada* **110** B3
Duncan *Ariz., U.S.A.* **109** K9
Duncan *Okla., U.S.A.* **116** D6
Duncan, L. *Canada* **104** B4
Duncan L. *Canada* **102** A6
Duncan Town *Bahamas* **120** B4
Duncannon *U.S.A.* **114** F7
Duncansby Head *U.K.* **13** C5
Duncansville *U.S.A.* **114** F6
Dundaga *Latvia* **30** A9
Dundalk *Canada* **114** B4
Dundalk *Ireland* **12** B5
Dundalk *U.S.A.* **113** F15
Dundalk Bay *Ireland* **12** C5
Dundas = Uummannaq *Greenland* **101** B18
Dundas *Canada* **114** C5
Dundas, L. *Australia* **93** F3
Dundas I. *Canada* **102** C2
Dundas Str. *Australia* **92** B5
Dundee *S. Africa* **89** D5
Dundee *U.K.* **13** E6
Dundee *U.S.A.* **114** D8
Dundee City □ *U.K.* **13** E6
Dundgovĭ □ *Mongolia* **56** B4
Dundrum *U.K.* **12** B6
Dundrum B. *U.K.* **12** B6
Dunedin *N.Z.* **91** F3
Dunedin *U.S.A.* **117** G13
Dunfanaghy *Ireland* **12** A4
Dunfermline *U.K.* **13** E5
Dungannon *Canada* **114** C3
Dungannon *U.K.* **12** B5
Dungarpur *India* **68** H5
Dungarvan *Ireland* **12** D4

Dungarvan Harbour *Ireland* **12** C4
Dungeness *U.K.* **15** G8
Dunglow *Ireland* **12** B3
Dungo, L. do *Angola* **88** B2
Dungog *Australia* **95** E5
Dungu *Dem. Rep. of the Congo* **86** B2
Dungun *Malaysia* **65** K4
Dungunâb *Sudan* **80** C4
Dungunâb, Khalîg *Sudan* **80** C4
Dunhua *China* **57** C15
Dunhuang *China* **60** B4
Dunk I. *Australia* **94** B4
Dunkassa *Benin* **83** C5
Dunkeld *Australia* **95** E4
Dunkeld *U.K.* **13** E5
Dunkerque *France* **19** A9
Dunkery Beacon *U.K.* **15** F4
Dunkirk = Dunkerque *France* **19** A9
Dunkirk *U.S.A.* **114** D5
Dunkuj *Sudan* **81** E3
Dunkwa *Central, Ghana* **82** D4
Dunkwa *Central, Ghana* **83** D4
Dúnleary = Dún Laoghaire *Ireland* **12** C5
Dunleer *Ireland* **12** C5
Dunmanus B. *Ireland* **12** E2
Dunmanway *Ireland* **12** E2
Dunmarra *Australia* **94** B1
Dunmore *U.S.A.* **115** E9
Dunmore East *Ireland* **12** D5
Dunmore Hd. *Ireland* **12** D1
Dunmore Town *Bahamas* **120** A4
Dunn *U.S.A.* **117** D15
Dunnellon *U.S.A.* **117** G13
Dunnet Hd. *U.K.* **13** C5
Dunning *U.S.A.* **112** E3
Dunnville *Canada* **114** D5
Dunolly *Australia* **95** F3
Dunoon *U.K.* **13** F4
Dunqul *Egypt* **80** C3
Duns *U.K.* **13** F6
Dunseith *U.S.A.* **112** A3
Dunshaughlin *Ireland* **12** C5
Dunsmuir *U.S.A.* **108** F2
Dunstable *U.K.* **15** F7
Dunstan Mts. *N.Z.* **91** F2
Dunster *Canada* **102** C5
Dunvegan *U.K.* **13** D2
Dunvegan L. *Canada* **103** A7
Duolun *China* **56** C9
Duong Dong *Vietnam* **65** G4
Dupree *U.S.A.* **112** C3
Dupuyer *U.S.A.* **108** B7
Duque de Caxias *Brazil* **127** A7
Durack ➔ *Australia* **92** C4
Durack Ra. *Australia* **92** C4
Durack River *Australia* **92** C4
Durağan *Turkey* **72** B6
Durak *Turkey* **47** B10
Ďurakovac *Kosovo* **44** D4
Durance ➔ *France* **21** E8
Durand *U.S.A.* **112** C8
Durango *Mexico* **118** C4
Durango *U.S.A.* **109** H10
Durango □ *Mexico* **118** C4
Durankulak *Bulgaria* **45** C12
Durant *Miss., U.S.A.* **117** E10
Durant *Okla., U.S.A.* **116** E6
Duratón ➔ *Spain* **36** D6
Đurđevac *Croatia* **28** D2
Düren *Germany* **24** E2
Durg = Bhilainagar-Durg *India* **67** J12
Durgapur *India* **69** H12
Durham *Canada* **114** B4
Durham *U.K.* **14** C6
Durham *Calif., U.S.A.* **110** F5
Durham *N.C., U.S.A.* **117** D15
Durham *N.H., U.S.A.* **115** C14
Durham □ *U.K.* **14** C6
Durlas = Thurles *Ireland* **12** D4
Durleşti *Moldova* **29** C13
Ḍurmā *Si. Arabia* **70** E5
Durmitor *Montenegro* **44** C2
Durmitor △ *Serbia* **44** C3
Durness *U.K.* **13** C4
Durrës *Albania* **44** E3
Durrow *Ireland* **12** D4
Dursey I. *Ireland* **12** E1
Dursley *U.K.* **15** F5
Dursunbey *Turkey* **47** B10
Durtal *France* **18** E6
Duru *Dem. Rep. of the Congo* **86** B2
Duru Gölü *Turkey* **45** E12
Durusu *Turkey* **45** E12
Durūz, Jabal ad *Jordan* **74** C5
D'Urville, Tanjung *Indonesia* **63** E9
D'Urville I. *N.Z.* **91** D4
Duryea *U.S.A.* **115** E9
Dūsh *Egypt* **80** C3
Dushak *Turkmenistan* **71** B9
Dushan *China* **58** E6

Dushanbe *Tajikistan* **52** F7
Dusheti *Georgia* **35** J7
Dushore *U.S.A.* **115** E8
Dusky Sd. *N.Z.* **91** F1
Dussejour, C. *Australia* **92** B4
Düsseldorf *Germany* **24** D2
Düsseldorf Rhein-Ruhr ✈ (DUS) *Germany* **24** D2
Duszniki-Zdrój *Poland* **31** H3
Dutch Harbor *U.S.A.* **106** E6
Dutlwe *Botswana* **88** C3
Dutse *Nigeria* **83** C6
Dutton *Canada* **114** D3
Dutton ➔ *Australia* **94** C3
Dutywa *S. Africa* **89** E4
Duved *Sweden* **10** A6
Düvertepe *Turkey* **47** B10
Duwayhin, Khawr *U.A.E.* **71** E6
Duyfken Pt. *Australia* **94** A3
Duyun *China* **58** D6
Düzağac *Turkey* **47** C12
Düzce *Turkey* **72** B4
Düzce □ *Turkey* **72** B4
Dve Mogili *Bulgaria* **45** C9
Dvina, Severnaya ➔ *Russia* **6** C14
Dvinsk = Daugavpils *Latvia* **32** E4
Dvor *Croatia* **41** C13
Dvůr Králové nad Labem *Czech Rep.* **26** A8
Dwarka *India* **68** H3
Dwellingup *Australia* **93** F2
Dwight *Canada* **114** A5
Dwight *U.S.A.* **112** E9
Dyakove *Ukraine* **28** B7
Dyatkovo *Russia* **32** F8
Dyatlovo = Dzyatlava *Belarus* **23** B13
Dyce *U.K.* **13** D6
Dyer, C. *Canada* **101** D19
Dyer Bay *Canada* **114** A3
Dyer Plateau *Antarctica* **5** D17
Dyersburg *U.S.A.* **117** C10
Dyfi ➔ *U.K.* **15** E3
Dyje ➔ *Czech Rep.* **27** C9
Dymer *Ukraine* **23** C16
Dynów *Poland* **31** J9
Dysart *Australia* **94** C4
Dyviziya *Ukraine* **29** E14
Dzaoudzi *Mayotte* **85** a
Dzerzhinsk *Russia* **34** B6
Dzhalinda *Russia* **53** D13
Dzhambul = Taraz *Kazakhstan* **52** E8
Dzhankoy *Ukraine* **33** K8
Dzhanybek = Zhänibek *Kazakhstan* **34** F8
Dzharylhach, Ostriv *Ukraine* **33** J7
Dzhezkazgan = Zhezqazghan *Kazakhstan* **52** E7
Dzhizak = Jizzax *Uzbekistan* **52** E7
Dzhugdzur, Khrebet *Russia* **53** D14
Dzhulynk *Ukraine* **29** B14
Dzhuryn *Ukraine* **29** B13
Dzhvari = Jvari *Georgia* **35** J6
Działdowo *Poland* **31** E7
Działoszyce *Poland* **31** H7
Działoszyn *Poland* **31** G5
Dzibilchaltún *Mexico* **119** C7
Dzierzgoń *Poland* **30** E6
Dzierżoniów *Poland* **31** H3
Dzilam de Bravo *Mexico* **119** C7
Dzisna *Belarus* **32** E5
Dzisna ➔ *Belarus* **32** E5
Dziwnów *Poland* **30** D1
Dzūkija △ *Lithuania* **9** J21
Dzungarian Basin = Junggar Pendi *China* **60** B3
Dzüünmod *Mongolia* **60** B5
Dzyarzhynsk *Belarus* **23** B14
Dzyatlava *Belarus* **23** B13

E

E.C. Manning △ *Canada* **102** D4
Eabamet L. *Canada* **104** B2
Eabametoong *Canada* **104** B2
Éadan Doire = Edenderry *Ireland* **12** C4
Eads *U.S.A.* **108** G12
Eagle *Alaska, U.S.A.* **100** E3
Eagle *Colo., U.S.A.* **108** G10
Eagle ➔ *Canada* **105** B8
Eagle Butte *U.S.A.* **112** C3
Eagle Grove *U.S.A.* **112** D7
Eagle L. *Canada* **103** D10
Eagle L. *Calif., U.S.A.* **108** F3
Eagle L. *Maine, U.S.A.* **113** B19
Eagle Lake *Canada* **114** A6
Eagle Lake *Maine, U.S.A.* **113** B19
Eagle Lake *Tex., U.S.A.* **116** G6
Eagle Mountain *U.S.A.* **111** M11
Eagle Nest *U.S.A.* **109** H11
Eagle Pass *U.S.A.* **116** G4
Eagle Pk. *U.S.A.* **110** G7
Eagle Pt. *Australia* **92** C4
Eagle River *Mich., U.S.A.* **112** B9
Eagle River *Wis., U.S.A.* **112** C9

Eaglehawk *Australia* **95** F3
Eagles Mere *U.S.A.* **115** E8
Ealing □ *U.K.* **15** F7
Ear Falls *Canada* **103** C10
Earle *U.S.A.* **117** D9
Earlimart *U.S.A.* **111** K7
Earlville *U.S.A.* **115** D9
Earn → *U.K.* **13** E5
Earn, L. *U.K.* **13** E4
Earnslaw, Mt. *N.Z.* **91** F2
Earth *U.S.A.* **116** D3
Easley *U.S.A.* **117** D13
East Anglia *U.K.* **14** E9
East Angus *Canada* **105** C5
East Antarctica *Antarctica* **5** D7
East Aurora *U.S.A.* **114** D6
East Ayrshire □ *U.K.* **13** F4
East Bengal *Bangla.* **67** G17
East Beskids = Vychodné
    Beskydy *Europe* **27** B15
East Brady *U.S.A.* **114** F5
East Branch Clarion River
    L. *U.S.A.* **114** E6
East C. = Dezhneva, Mys
    Russia **53** C19
East C. *N.Z.* **91** B7
East Caroline Basin *Pac. Oc.* **96** G6
East Chicago *U.S.A.* **112** E10
East China Sea *Asia* **60** C7
East Coulee *Canada* **102** C6
East Dereham = Dereham
    U.K. **15** E8
East Dunbartonshire □ *U.K.* **13** F4
East Falkland *Falk. Is.* **128** G5
East Grand Forks *U.S.A.* **112** B5
East Greenwich *U.S.A.* **115** E13
East Grinstead *U.K.* **15** F8
East Hartford *U.S.A.* **115** E12
East Haydon *Australia* **94** B3
East Helena *U.S.A.* **108** C8
East Indies *Asia* **50** J14
East Kilbride *U.K.* **13** F4
East Lansing *U.S.A.* **113** D11
East Liverpool *U.S.A.* **114** F4
East London *S. Africa* **89** E4
East Lothian □ *U.K.* **13** F6
East Main = Eastmain
    Canada **104** B4
East Mariana Basin *Pac. Oc.* **96** F7
East Northport *U.S.A.* **115** F11
East Orange *U.S.A.* **115** F10
East Pacific Rise *Pac. Oc.* **97** J17
East Palestine *U.S.A.* **114** F4
East Pine *Canada* **102** B4
East Point *U.S.A.* **117** E12
East Providence *U.S.A.* **115** E13
East Pt. *Br. Virgin Is.* **121** e
East Pt. *Canada* **105** C7
East Renfrewshire □ *U.K.* **13** F4
East Retford = Retford *U.K.* **14** D7
East Riding of Yorkshire □
    U.K. **14** D7
East Rochester *U.S.A.* **114** C7
East St. Louis *U.S.A.* **112** F8
East Schelde =
    Oosterschelde → *Neths.* **17** C4
East Sea = Japan, Sea of *Asia* **54** E7
East Siberian Sea *Russia* **53** B17
East Stroudsburg *U.S.A.* **115** E9
East Sussex □ *U.K.* **15** G8
East Tasman Plateau
    Pac. Oc. **96** M7
East Tawas *U.S.A.* **113** C12
East Timor ■ *Asia* **63** F7
East Toorale *Australia* **95** E4
East Walker → *U.S.A.* **110** G7
East Windsor *U.S.A.* **115** F10
Eastbourne *N.Z.* **91** D5
Eastbourne *U.K.* **15** G8
Eastend *Canada* **103** D7
Easter Fracture Zone
    Pac. Oc. **97** K16
Easter I. = Pascua, I. de
    Chile **97** K17
Eastern □ *Ghana* **83** D4
Eastern □ *Kenya* **86** C4
Eastern □ *S. Leone* **82** D2
Eastern Cape □ *S. Africa* **88** E4
Eastern Cr. → *Australia* **94** C3
Eastern Desert = Es Sahrâ'
    Esh Sharqîya *Egypt* **80** B3
Eastern Ghats *India* **66** N11
Eastern Group = Lau Group
    Fiji **91** a
Eastern Group *Australia* **93** F3
Eastern Guruma ○ *Australia* **92** D2
Eastern Transvaal =
    Mpumalanga □ *S. Africa* **89** D5
Easterville *Canada* **103** C9
Easthampton *U.S.A.* **115** D12
Eastlake *U.S.A.* **114** E3
Eastland *U.S.A.* **116** E5
Eastleigh *U.K.* **15** G6
Eastmain *Canada* **104** B4
Eastmain → *Canada* **104** B4
Eastman *Canada* **115** A12
Eastman *U.S.A.* **117** E13
Easton *Md., U.S.A.* **113** F15
Easton *Pa., U.S.A.* **115** F9

Easton *Wash., U.S.A.* **110** C5
Eastport *U.S.A.* **113** C20
Eastsound *U.S.A.* **110** B4
Eaton *U.S.A.* **108** F11
Eatonia *Canada* **103** C7
Eatonton *U.S.A.* **117** E13
Eatontown *U.S.A.* **115** F10
Eatonville *U.S.A.* **110** D4
Eau Claire *U.S.A.* **112** C8
Eau Claire, L. à l' *Canada* **104** A5
Eauripik Rise *Pac. Oc.* **96** G6
Eauze *France* **20** E4
Eban *Nigeria* **83** D5
Ebano *Mexico* **119** C5
Ebbegebirge ○ *Germany* **24** D3
Ebbw Vale *U.K.* **15** F4
Ebeltoft *Denmark* **11** H4
Ebeltoft Vig *Denmark* **11** H4
Ebensburg *U.S.A.* **114** F6
Ebensee *Austria* **26** D6
Eber Gölü *Turkey* **72** C4
Eberbach *Germany* **25** F4
Eberswalde-Finow *Germany* **24** C9
Ebetsu *Japan* **54** C10
Ebey's Landing ○ *U.S.A.* **110** B4
Ebian *China* **58** C4
Ebingen *Germany* **25** G5
Éboli *Italy* **43** B8
Ebolowa *Cameroon* **83** E7
Ebonda *Dem. Rep. of the Congo* **84** D4
Ebonyi □ *Nigeria* **83** D6
Ebrach *Germany* **25** F6
Ebre = Ebro → *Spain* **38** E5
Ébrié, Lagune *Ivory C.* **82** D4
Ebro → *Spain* **38** E5
Ebro, Embalse del *Spain* **36** C7
Ebstorf *Germany* **24** B6
Ecatepec de Morelos *Mexico* **119** D5
Ecbatana = Hamadān *Iran* **73** E13
Eceabat *Turkey* **45** F10
Ech Chéliff *Algeria* **78** A6
Echigo-Sammyaku *Japan* **55** F9
Echinos *Greece* **45** E9
Échirolles *France* **21** C9
Echizen-Misaki *Japan* **55** G7
Echmiadzin = Yejmiadzin
    Armenia **35** K7
Echo Bay *N.W.T., Canada* **100** D8
Echo Bay *Ont., Canada* **104** C3
Echoing → *Canada* **104** B1
Echterdingen, Stuttgart ✈
    (STR) *Germany* **25** G5
Echternach *Lux.* **17** E6
Echuca *Australia* **95** F3
Écija *Spain* **37** H5
Eckental *Germany* **25** F7
Eckernförde *Germany* **24** A5
Eclipse I. *Australia* **103** B7
Eclipse Is. *Australia* **92** B4
Eclipse Sd. *Canada* **101** C16
Écommoy *France* **18** E7
Écouché *France* **18** D6
Ecrins △ *France* **21** D10
Ecuador ■ *S. Amer.* **124** D3
Écueillé *France* **18** E8
Ed *Sweden* **11** F5
Ed Dabbura *Sudan* **80** D3
Ed Da'ein *Sudan* **81** E2
Ed Damazin *Sudan* **79** F12
Ed Dâmer *Sudan* **80** D3
Ed Dar el Beida =
    Casablanca *Morocco* **78** B4
Ed Debba *Sudan* **80** D3
Ed Déffa *Egypt* **80** A2
Ed Deim *Sudan* **81** E2
Ed Dueim *Sudan* **81** E3
Edam *Canada* **103** C7
Edam *Neths.* **17** B5
Edane *Sweden* **10** E6
Eday *U.K.* **13** B6
Edd *Eritrea* **81** E5
Eddrachillis B. *U.K.* **13** C3
Eddystone *U.K.* **15** G3
Eddystone Pt. *Australia* **95** G4
Ede *Neths.* **17** B5
Ede *Nigeria* **83** D5
Édéa *Cameroon* **83** E7
Edebäck *Sweden* **10** D7
Edehon L. *Canada* **103** A9
Edelény *Hungary* **28** B5
Eden *Australia* **95** F4
Eden *N.C., U.S.A.* **117** C15
Eden *N.Y., U.S.A.* **114** D6
Eden *Tex., U.S.A.* **116** F5
Eden → *U.K.* **14** C4
Edenburg *S. Africa* **88** D4
Edendale *S. Africa* **89** D5
Edenderry *Ireland* **12** C4
Edenton *U.S.A.* **117** C16
Edenville *S. Africa* **89** D4
Eder → *Germany* **24** D5
Eder-Stausee *Germany* **24** D4
Edessa *Greece* **44** F6
Edewecht *Germany* **24** B3
Edfu = Idfû *Egypt* **80** C3
Edgar *U.S.A.* **112** E5
Edgartown *U.S.A.* **115** E14
Edge Hill *U.K.* **15** E6
Edgefield *U.S.A.* **117** E14

Edgeley *U.S.A.* **112** B4
Edgemont *U.S.A.* **112** D2
Edgeøya *Svalbard* **4** B9
Édhessa = Edessa *Greece* **44** F6
Edievale *N.Z.* **91** F2
Edina *Liberia* **82** D2
Edina *U.S.A.* **112** E7
Edinboro *U.S.A.* **114** E4
Edinburg *U.S.A.* **116** H5
Edinburgh *U.K.* **13** F5
Edinburgh ✈ (EDI) *U.K.* **13** F5
Edinburgh, City of □ *U.K.* **13** F5
Edineţ *Moldova* **29** B12
Edirne *Turkey* **45** E10
Edirne □ *Turkey* **45** E10
Edison *U.S.A.* **110** B4
Edithburgh *Australia* **95** F2
Edmeston *U.S.A.* **115** D9
Edmond *U.S.A.* **116** D6
Edmonds *U.S.A.* **110** C4
Edmonton *Australia* **94** B4
Edmonton *Canada* **102** C6
Edmund L. *Canada* **104** B1
Edmundston *Canada* **105** C6
Edna *U.S.A.* **116** G6
Edo □ *Nigeria* **83** D6
Edolo *Italy* **40** B7
Edremit *Turkey* **47** B9
Edremit Körfezi *Turkey* **47** B8
Edsbro *Sweden* **10** E12
Edsbyn *Sweden* **10** D10
Edson *Canada* **102** C5
Eduardo Castex *Argentina* **126** D3
Edward → *Australia* **95** F3
Edward, L. *Africa* **86** C2
Edward VII Land *Antarctica* **5** E13
Edwards *Calif., U.S.A.* **111** L9
Edwards *N.Y., U.S.A.* **115** B9
Edwards Plateau *U.S.A.* **116** F4
Edwardsville *U.S.A.* **115** E9
Edzná *Mexico* **119** D6
Edzo *Canada* **102** A5
Eekloo *Belgium* **17** C3
Eesti = Estonia ■ *Europe* **32** C3
Eferding *Austria* **26** C7
Eforie *Romania* **29** F13
Efxinoupoli *Greece* **46** B4
Ega → *Spain* **38** C3
Égadi, Ísole *Italy* **42** E5
Egan Range *U.S.A.* **108** G6
Eganville *Canada* **114** A7
Eger = Cheb *Czech Rep.* **26** A5
Eger *Hungary* **28** C5
Eger → *Hungary* **28** C5
Egersund *Norway* **9** G12
Egg L. *Canada* **103** B7
Eggegebirge Südlicher
    Teutoburger Wald ○
    Germany **24** D4
Eggenburg *Austria* **26** C8
Eggenfelden *Germany* **25** G8
Éghezée *Belgium* **17** D4
Egina *Greece* **46** D5
Eginio *Greece* **44** F6
Egio *Greece* **46** C4
Égletons *France* **20** C6
Eglinton I. *Canada* **101** B8
Egmont *Canada* **102** D4
Egmont, C. *N.Z.* **91** C4
Egmont, Mt. = Taranaki,
    Mt. *N.Z.* **91** C5
Egmont → *N.Z.* **91** C5
Egra *India* **69** J12
Eğridir *Turkey* **72** D4
Eğridir Gölü *Turkey* **72** D4
Egtved *Denmark* **11** J3
Éguzon-Chantôme *France* **19** F8
Egvekinot *Russia* **53** C19
Egyek *Hungary* **28** C5
Egypt ■ *Africa* **80** B3
Eha Amufu *Nigeria* **83** D6
Ehime □ *Japan* **55** H6
Ehingen *Germany* **25** G5
Ehrenberg *U.S.A.* **111** M12
Ehrwald *Austria* **26** D3
Eibar *Spain* **38** B2
Eichstätt *Germany* **25** G7
Eider → *Germany* **24** A4
Eidsvold *Australia* **95** D5
Eidsvoll *Norway* **9** F14
Eifel *Germany* **25** E2
Eiffel Flats *Zimbabwe* **87** F3
Eiger △ *Switz.* **40** B5
Eigg *U.K.* **13** E2
Eighty Mile Beach *Australia* **92** C3
Eil, L. *U.K.* **13** E3
Eildon *Australia* **95** F4
Eildon, L. *Australia* **95** F4
Eilean Sar = Western
    Isles □ *U.K.* **13** D1
Eilenburg *Germany* **24** D8
Ein el Luweiqa *Sudan* **81** E3
Einasleigh *Australia* **94** B3
Einasleigh → *Australia* **94** B3
Einbeck *Germany* **24** D5
Eindhoven *Neths.* **17** C5
Einsiedeln *Switz.* **25** H4

Eire = Ireland ■ *Europe* **12** C4
Eiríksjökull *Iceland* **8** D3
Eirunepé *Brazil* **124** E5
Eiseb → *Namibia* **88** C2
Eisenach *Germany* **24** E6
Eisenberg *Germany* **24** E7
Eisenerz *Austria* **26** D7
Eisenhüttenstadt *Germany* **24** C10
Eisenkappel *Austria* **26** E7
Eisenstadt *Austria* **27** D9
Eisfeld *Germany* **25** E6
Eisleben *Germany* **24** D7
Eislingen *Germany* **25** G5
Eivissa *Spain* **48** C7
Eixe, Serra do *Spain* **36** C4
Ejea de los Caballeros *Spain* **38** C3
Ejeda *Madag.* **89** C7
Ejura *Ghana* **83** D4
Ejutla *Mexico* **119** D5
Ekalaka *U.S.A.* **108** D11
Ekaterinburg =
    Yekaterinburg *Russia* **52** D7
Ekenäs = Tammisaari
    Finland **32** B2
Ekenässjön *Sweden* **11** G9
Ekerö *Sweden* **10** E11
Eket *Nigeria* **83** E6
Eketahuna *N.Z.* **91** D5
Ekibastuz *Kazakhstan* **52** D8
Ekiti □ *Nigeria* **83** D6
Ekoli *Dem. Rep. of the Congo* **86** C1
Ekoln *Sweden* **10** E11
Ekshärad *Sweden* **10** D7
Eksjö *Sweden* **11** G8
Ekuma → *Namibia* **88** B2
Ekwan → *Canada* **104** B3
Ekwan Pt. *Canada* **104** B3
El Aaiún *W. Sahara* **78** C3
El Abanico *Chile* **126** D1
El Abbasiya *Sudan* **81** E3
El 'Agrûd *Egypt* **74** E3
El Ait *Sudan* **81** E3
El 'Aiyat *Egypt* **80** J7
El Alamein *Egypt* **80** A2
El 'Aqaba, W. → *Egypt* **74** E2
El 'Arag *Egypt* **80** B2
El Arîḥā *West Bank* **74** D4
El 'Arîsh *Egypt* **74** D2
El 'Arîsh, W. → *Egypt* **74** D2
El Asnam = Ech Chéliff
    Algeria **78** A6
El Astillero *Spain* **36** B7
El Badâri *Egypt* **80** B3
El Bahrein *Egypt* **80** B2
El Ballâs *Egypt* **80** B3
El Balyana *Egypt* **80** B3
El Baqeir *Sudan* **80** D3
El Barco de Ávila *Spain* **36** E5
El Barco de Valdeorras = O
    Barco *Spain* **36** C4
El Bauga *Sudan* **80** D3
El Bawiti *Egypt* **80** B2
El Bayadh *Algeria* **78** B6
El Bierzo *Spain* **36** C4
El Bluff *Nic.* **120** D3
El Bonillo *Spain* **39** G2
El Buheirat □ *Sudan* **81** F3
El Burgo de Osma *Spain* **38** D1
El Cajon *U.S.A.* **111** N10
El Calafate *Argentina* **128** G2
El Campello *Spain* **39** G4
El Campo *U.S.A.* **116** G6
El Capitan *U.S.A.* **110** H7
El Carbón *Honduras* **120** C2
El Carmen *Colombia* **124** B3
El Centro *U.S.A.* **111** N11
El Cerro *Bolivia* **124** G6
El Cerro de Andévalo *Spain* **37** H4
El Compadre *Mexico* **111** N10
El Coronil *Spain* **37** H5
El Cuy *Argentina* **128** D3
El Cuyo *Mexico* **119** C7
El Dab'a *Egypt* **80** H6
El Daheir *Egypt* **74** D3
El Deir *Egypt* **80** B3
El Descanso *Mexico* **111** N10
El Desemboque *Mexico* **118** A2
El Dilingat *Egypt* **80** H7
El Diviso *Colombia* **124** C3
El Djouf *Mauritania* **78** D4
El Dorado *Mexico* **118** C3
El Dorado *Ark., U.S.A.* **116** E8
El Dorado *Kans., U.S.A.* **116** D6
El Dorado *Venezuela* **124** B6
El Dorado Springs *U.S.A.* **112** G6
El 'Ein *Sudan* **81** D2
El Ejido *Spain* **37** J8
El Escorial *Spain* **36** E6
El Espinar *Spain* **36** E6
El Faiyûm *Egypt* **80** J7
El Fâsher *Sudan* **81** E2
El Fashn *Egypt* **80** J7
El Ferrol = Ferrol *Spain* **36** B2
El Fifi *Sudan* **81** E2
El Fuerte *Mexico* **118** B3
El Ga'a *Sudan* **81** E2
El Garef *Sudan* **81** E3
El Gebir *Sudan* **81** E2
El Gedida *Egypt* **80** B2

El Geneina = Al Junaynah
    Sudan **79** F10
El Geteina *Sudan* **81** E3
El Gezira □ *Sudan* **81** E3
El Gir *Sudan* **80** D2
El Gîza *Egypt* **80** J7
El Gogorrón △ *Mexico* **118** C4
El Goléa *Algeria* **78** B6
El Golfo de Santa Clara
    Mexico **118** A2
El Gouna *Egypt* **80** B3
El Grau *Spain* **39** G4
El Guácharo △ *Venezuela* **121** D7
El Guache △ *Venezuela* **121** E6
El Hagiz *Sudan* **81** D4
El Hâi *Egypt* **80** J7
El Hammam *Egypt* **80** A2
El Hawata *Sudan* **81** E3
El Heiz *Egypt* **80** B2
El Hideib *Sudan* **81** D3
El Hilla *Sudan* **81** E2
El 'Idisât *Egypt* **80** B3
El Iskandarîya *Egypt* **80** H7
El Istiwa'iya *Sudan* **79** G11
El Jadida *Morocco* **78** B4
El Jardal *Honduras* **120** D2
El Jebelein *Sudan* **81** E3
El Kab *Sudan* **80** D3
El Kafr el Sharqi *Egypt* **80** H7
El Kamlin *Sudan* **81** D3
El Karaba *Sudan* **80** D3
El Kef □ *Tunisia* **79** A7
El Kere *Ethiopia* **81** F5
El Khandaq *Sudan* **80** D3
El Khanka *Egypt* **80** H7
El Khârga *Egypt* **80** B3
El Khartûm *Sudan* **81** D3
El Khartûm □ *Sudan* **81** D3
El Khartûm Bahri *Sudan* **81** D3
El Kuntilla *Egypt* **74** E3
El Laqâwa *Sudan* **81** E2
El Leh *Ethiopia* **81** G4
El Leiya *Sudan* **81** D4
El Leoncito △ *Argentina* **126** C2
El Lucero *Mexico* **118** A3
El Maestrazgo *Spain* **38** E4
El Mafâza *Sudan* **81** E3
El Maghra *Egypt* **80** A2
El Mahalla el Kubra *Egypt* **80** H7
El Mahârîq *Egypt* **80** B3
El Maîmûn *Egypt* **80** J7
El Maks el Bahari *Egypt* **80** C3
El Malpais △ *U.S.A.* **109** J10
El Manshâh *Egypt* **80** B3
El Mansûra *Egypt* **80** H7
El Manzala *Egypt* **80** H7
El Marâgha *Egypt* **80** B3
El Masid *Sudan* **81** D3
El Masnou *Spain* **38** D7
El Matarîya *Egypt* **80** H8
El Meda *Ethiopia* **81** F5
El Medano *Canary Is.* **48** F3
El Ménia = El Goléa *Algeria* **78** B6
El Metemma *Sudan* **81** D3
El Milagro *Argentina* **126** C2
El Minyâ *Egypt* **80** B3
El Monte *U.S.A.* **111** L8
El Montseny *Spain* **38** D7
El Mreyye *Mauritania* **82** B3
El Niybo *Ethiopia* **81** G4
El Obeid *Sudan* **81** E3
El Odaiya *Sudan* **81** E2
El Oro *Mexico* **119** D4
El Oued *Algeria* **78** B7
El Palmar △ *Argentina* **126** C4
El Palmito, Presa *Mexico* **118** B3
El Paso *U.S.A.* **111** L10
El Pedernoso *Spain* **39** F2
El Pedroso *Spain* **37** H5
El Pinacate y Gran Desierto
    de Altar = Gran Desierto
    del Pinacate △ *Mexico* **118** A2
El Pobo de Dueñas *Spain* **38** E3
El Portal *U.S.A.* **110** H7
El Porvenir *Mexico* **118** A3
El Prat de Llobregat *Spain* **38** D7
El Progreso *Honduras* **120** C2
El Pueblito *Mexico* **118** B3
El Pueblo *Canary Is.* **48** F2
El Puente del Arzobispo *Spain* **36** F5
El Puerto de Santa María
    Spain **37** J4
El Qâhira *Egypt* **80** H7
El Qantara *Egypt* **74** E1
El Qasr *Egypt* **80** B2
El Qubâbât *Egypt* **80** J7
El Quseima *Egypt* **74** E3
El Qusîya *Egypt* **80** B3
El Râshda *Egypt* **80** B2
El Real de Santa María
    Panama **124** B3
El Reno *U.S.A.* **107** H20
El Rey △ *Argentina* **126** A3
El Rîdisiya *Egypt* **80** C3
El Río *U.S.A.* **111** L7
El Ronquillo *Spain* **37** H4
El Roque, Pta. *Canary Is.* **48** F4
El Rosarito *Mexico* **118** B2
El Rubio *Spain* **37** H5

El Saff *Egypt* **80** J7
El Salto *Mexico* **118** C3
El Salvador ■ *Cent. Amer.* **120** D2
El Sauce *Nic.* **120** D2
El Saucejo *Spain* **37** H5
El Shallal *Egypt* **80** C3
El Simbillawein *Egypt* **80** H7
El Sueco *Mexico* **118** B3
El Suweis *Egypt* **80** J8
El Tabbin *Egypt* **80** J7
El Tamarâni, W. → *Egypt* **74** E3
El Thamad *Egypt* **74** F3
El Tigre *Venezuela* **124** 36
El Tîh *Egypt* **74** F2
El Tîna *Egypt* **80** H8
El Tofo *Chile* **126** B1
El Tránsito *Chile* **126** B1
El Tûr *Egypt* **70** D2
El Turbio *Argentina* **128** G2
El Uqsur *Egypt* **80** B3
El Valle △ *Spain* **39** H3
El Vendrell *Spain* **38** D6
El Vergel *Mexico* **118** B3
El Vigía *Venezuela* **124** B4
El Viso del Alcor *Spain* **37** H5
El Wabeira *Egypt* **74** F2
El Waqf *Egypt* **80** B3
El Weguet *Ethiopia* **81** F5
El Wuz *Sudan* **81** D3
Elafonisos *Greece* **46** E4
Élancourt *France* **19** D8
Elasa *Greece* **47** F8
Elassona *Greece* **46** B4
Elat *Israel* **74** F3
Elatia *Greece* **46** C4
Elâzığ *Turkey* **73** C8
Elâzığ □ *Turkey* **73** C8
Elba *Italy* **40** F7
Elba *U.S.A.* **117** F11
Elbasan *Albania* **44** E4
Elbe *U.S.A.* **110** D4
Elbe → *Europe* **24** B4
Elbe-Seitenkanal *Germany* **24** C6
Elbert, Mt. *U.S.A.* **108** G10
Elberton *U.S.A.* **117** D13
Elbeuf *France* **18** C8
Elbing = Elbląg *Poland* **30** D6
Elbistan *Turkey* **72** C7
Elbląg *Poland* **30** D6
Elbow *Canada* **103** C7
Elbrus *Russia* **35** J6
Elbufer-Drawehn ○ *Germany* **24** B6
Elburz Mts. = Alborz,
    Reshteh-ye Kühhä-ye *Iran* **71** C7
Elche *Spain* **39** G4
Elche de la Sierra *Spain* **39** G2
Elcho I. *Australia* **94** A2
Elda *Spain* **39** G4
Eldama Ravine *Kenya* **86** B4
Elde → *Germany* **24** B7
Eldon *Mo., U.S.A.* **112** F7
Eldon *Wash., U.S.A.* **110** C3
Eldora *U.S.A.* **112** D7
Eldorado *Argentina* **127** B5
Eldorado *Canada* **114** B7
Eldorado *Ill., U.S.A.* **112** G9
Eldorado *Tex., U.S.A.* **116** F4
Eldoret *Kenya* **86** B4
Eldred *U.S.A.* **114** E6
Elea, C. *Cyprus* **49** D13
Eleanora, Pk. *Australia* **93** F3
Elefantes → *Africa* **89** C5
Elefsina *Greece* **46** C5
Eleftherios Venizelos ✈
    (ATH) *Greece* **46** D5
Elektrogorsk *Russia* **32** E10
Elektrostal *Russia* **32** E10
Elele *Nigeria* **83** D6
Elemi Triangle *Africa* **81** G4
Elena *Bulgaria* **45** D9
Elephant Butte Res. *U.S.A.* **109** K10
Elephant I. *Antarctica* **5** C18
Eleshnitsa *Bulgaria* **44** E7
Eleşkirt *Turkey* **73** C10
Eleuthera *Bahamas* **120** B4
Eleutheroupoli *Greece* **45** F8
Elgin *Canada* **115** B8
Elgin *U.K.* **13** D5
Elgin *Ill., U.S.A.* **112** D9
Elgin *N. Dak., U.S.A.* **112** B3
Elgin *Oreg., U.S.A.* **108** D5
Elgin *Tex., U.S.A.* **116** F6
Elgoibar *Spain* **38** B2
Elgon, Mt. *Africa* **86** B3
Eliase *Indonesia* **63** F8
Elikonos Oros *Greece* **46** C4
Elim *Namibia* **88** B2
Elim *S. Africa* **88** E2
Elin Pelin *Bulgaria* **44** D7
Elista *Russia* **35** G7
Elizabeth *Australia* **95** E2
Elizabeth *U.S.A.* **115** F10
Elizabeth City *U.S.A.* **117** C16
Elizabethton *U.S.A.* **117** C13
Elizabethtown *Ky., U.S.A.* **113** G11
Elizabethtown *N.Y., U.S.A.* **115** B11
Elizabethtown *Pa., U.S.A.* **115** F8
Elizondo *Spain* **38** B3
Elk *Poland* **30** E9

Elk → Canada 102 C5
Elk → Poland 30 E9
Elk → U.S.A. 117 D11
Elk City U.S.A. 116 D5
Elk Creek U.S.A. 110 F4
Elk Grove U.S.A. 110 G5
Elk Island △ Canada 102 C6
Elk Lake Canada 104 C3
Elk Point Canada 103 C6
Elk River Idaho, U.S.A. 108 C5
Elk River Minn., U.S.A. 112 C7
Elkedra → Australia 94 C2
Elkhart Ind., U.S.A. 113 E11
Elkhart Kans., U.S.A. 112 G3
Elkhorn Canada 103 D8
Elkhorn → U.S.A. 112 E5
Elkhovo Bulgaria 45 D10
Elkin U.S.A. 117 C14
Elkins U.S.A. 113 F14
Elkland U.S.A. 114 E7
Elko Canada 102 D5
Elko U.S.A. 108 F6
Elkton U.S.A. 114 C1
Ellas = Greece ■ Europe 46 B3
Ellef Ringnes I. Canada 101 B11
Ellen, Mt. U.S.A. 115 B12
Ellenburg U.S.A. 89 E4
Ellendale U.S.A. 112 B4
Ellensburg U.S.A. 108 C3
Ellenville U.S.A. 115 E10
Ellerton Barbados 121 g
Ellery, Mt. Australia 95 F4
Ellesmere, L. N.Z. 91 G4
Ellesmere I. Canada 101 B16
Ellesmere Island = Quttinirpaaq △ Canada 101 A17
Ellesmere Port U.K. 14 D5
Ellice Is. = Tuvalu ■ Pac. Oc. 90 B10
Ellicottville U.S.A. 114 D6
Ellington U.S.A. 114 D5
Elliot Australia 94 B1
Elliot S. Africa 89 E4
Elliot Lake Canada 104 C3
Elliotdale = Xhora S. Africa 89 E4
Ellis U.S.A. 112 F4
Elliston Australia 95 E1
Ellisville U.S.A. 117 F10
Ellon U.K. 13 D6
Ellore = Eluru India 67 L12
Ellsworth Kans., U.S.A. 112 F4
Ellsworth Maine, U.S.A. 113 C19
Ellsworth Land Antarctica 5 D16
Ellsworth Mts. Antarctica 5 D16
Ellwangen Germany 25 G6
Ellwood City U.S.A. 114 F4
Elm Switz. 25 J5
Elm-Lappwald △ Germany 24 C6
Elma Canada 103 D9
Elma U.S.A. 110 D3
Elmadağ Turkey 72 C5
Elmalı Turkey 47 E11
Elmhurst U.S.A. 112 E10
Elmina Ghana 83 D4
Elmira Canada 114 C4
Elmira U.S.A. 114 D8
Elmira Heights U.S.A. 114 D8
Elmore Australia 95 F3
Elmshorn Germany 24 B5
Elmvale Canada 114 B5
Elne France 20 F6
Elora Canada 114 C4
Elos Greece 46 E4
Elounda Greece 49 D7
Eloy U.S.A. 109 K8
Éloyes France 19 D13
Elphin Canada 115 B8
Elrose Canada 103 C7
Elsby △ Australia 92 B5
Elsdorf Germany 24 E2
Elsie U.S.A. 110 E3
Elsinore = Helsingør Denmark 11 H6
Elster → Germany 24 D7
Elsterwerda Germany 24 D9
Eltanin Fracture Zone System S. Ocean 5 B14
Eltham N.Z. 91 C5
Elton Russia 35 F8
Elton, Ozero Russia 35 F8
Eltville Germany 25 E4
Eluru India 67 L12
Elvas Portugal 37 G3
Elven France 18 E4
Elverum Norway 8 F14
Elvire → Australia 92 C4
Elvire, Mt. Australia 93 E2
Elvo → Italy 40 C5
Elwell, L. = Tiber Res. U.S.A. 108 B8
Elwood Ind., U.S.A. 113 E11
Elwood Nebr., U.S.A. 112 E4
Elx = Elche Spain 39 G4
Ely U.K. 15 E8
Ely Minn., U.S.A. 112 B8
Ely Nev., U.S.A. 108 G6
Elyria U.S.A. 114 E2
Elyros Greece 46 F5
Elz → Germany 25 G3

Emådalen Sweden 10 C8
eMalahleni S. Africa 89 D4
Emämrūd Iran 71 B7
Emån → Sweden 11 G10
Embarcación Argentina 126 A3
Embetsu Japan 54 B10
Embi Kazakhstan 52 E6
Embi → Kazakhstan 52 E6
Embonas Greece 49 C9
Embro Canada 114 C4
Embrun France 21 D10
Embu Kenya 86 C4
Emden Germany 24 B3
Emecik Turkey 47 E9
Emerald Australia 94 C4
Emerald I. Canada 101 B9
Emerson Canada 103 D9
Emet Turkey 47 B11
Emi Koussi Chad 79 E9
Emilia-Romagna □ Italy 40 D8
Emilius, Mte. Italy 40 C4
Eminabad Pakistan 68 C6
Emine, Nos Bulgaria 45 D11
Emirdağ Turkey 72 C4
Emissi, Tarso Chad 79 D9
Emlenton U.S.A. 114 E5
Emlichheim Germany 24 C2
Emmaboda Sweden 11 H9
Emmaus S. Africa 88 D4
Emmaus U.S.A. 115 F9
Emme → Switz. 25 H3
Emmeloord Neths. 17 B5
Emmen Neths. 17 B6
Emmen Switz. 25 H4
Emmendingen Germany 25 G3
Emmental Switz. 25 J3
Emmerich Germany 24 D2
Emmet Australia 94 C3
Emmetsburg U.S.A. 112 D6
Emmett Idaho, U.S.A. 108 E5
Emmett Mich., U.S.A. 114 D2
Emmonak U.S.A. 106 C7
Emo Canada 103 D10
Emőd Hungary 28 C5
Empalme Mexico 118 B2
Empangeni S. Africa 89 D5
Empedrado Argentina 126 B4
Emperor Seamount Chain Pac. Oc. 96 D9
Emperor Trough Pac. Oc. 96 C9
Empoli Italy 40 E7
Emporia Kans., U.S.A. 112 F5
Emporia Va., U.S.A. 113 G15
Emporium U.S.A. 114 E6
Empress Canada 103 C7
Empty Quarter = Rub' al Khālī Si. Arabia 75 D4
Ems → Germany 24 B3
Emsdale Canada 114 A5
Emsdetten Germany 24 C3
Emu China 57 C15
Emu Park Australia 94 C5
eMuziwezinto S. Africa 89 E5
'En 'Avrona Israel 74 F4
'En Boqeq Israel 71 D4
'En Gedi Israel 71 D4
En Nahud Sudan 81 E2
En Nofalab Sudan 81 D3
Ena Japan 55 G8
Enana Namibia 88 B2
Enånger Sweden 10 C11
Enard B. U.K. 13 C3
Enare = Inarijärvi Finland 8 B23
Enarotali Indonesia 63 E9
Encampment U.S.A. 108 F10
Encantadas, Serra Brazil 127 C5
Encarnación Paraguay 127 B4
Encarnación de Díaz Mexico 118 C4
Enchi Ghana 82 D4
Encinitas U.S.A. 111 M9
Encino U.S.A. 109 J11
Encounter B. Australia 95 F2
Encs Hungary 28 B6
Endako Canada 102 C3
Endau Kenya 86 C4
Endau Rompin △ Malaysia 65 L4
Ende Indonesia 63 F6
Endeavour Str. Australia 94 A3
Endelave Denmark 11 J4
Enderbury I. Kiribati 96 H10
Enderby Canada 102 C5
Enderby Abyssal Plain S. Ocean 5 C5
Enderby I. Australia 92 D2
Enderby Land Antarctica 5 C5
Enderlin U.S.A. 112 B5
Enderrocat, C. Spain 48 B9
Endicott U.S.A. 115 D8
Endicott Mts. U.S.A. 106 B9
Endwell U.S.A. 115 D8
Endyalgout I. Australia 92 B5
Eneabba Australia 93 E2
Enewetak Atoll Marshall Is. 96 F8
Enez Turkey 45 F10
Enfer, Pte. d' Martinique 120 c
Enfield Canada 105 D7
Enfield Conn., U.S.A. 115 E12
Enfield N.C., U.S.A. 117 C16

Enfield N.H., U.S.A. 115 C12
Engadin Switz. 25 J6
Engaño, C. Dom. Rep. 121 C6
Engaño, C. Phil. 63 A6
Engaru Japan 54 B11
Engcobo = Ngcobo S. Africa 89 E4
Engelberg Switz. 25 J4
Engels Russia 34 E8
Engemann L. Canada 103 B7
Engershatu Eritrea 81 D4
Enggano Indonesia 62 F2
England U.S.A. 116 D9
England □ U.K. 15 E5
Englee Canada 105 B8
Englehart Canada 104 C4
Englewood U.S.A. 108 G11
English → Canada 103 C10
English Bazar = Ingraj Bazar India 69 G13
English Channel Europe 15 G6
English Company's Is., The Australia 94 A2
English River Canada 104 C1
Engures ezers Latvia 30 A10
Enguri → Georgia 35 J5
Enid U.S.A. 116 C6
Enipeas → Greece 46 B4
Enkhuizen Neths. 17 B5
Enköping Sweden 10 E11
Enle China 58 F3
Enna Italy 43 E7
Ennadai L. Canada 103 A8
Ennedi Chad 79 E10
Enngonia Australia 95 D4
Ennigerloh Germany 24 D4
Ennis Ireland 12 D3
Ennis Mont., U.S.A. 108 D8
Ennis Tex., U.S.A. 116 E6
Enniscorthy Ireland 12 D5
Enniskillen U.K. 12 B4
Ennistimon Ireland 12 D2
Enns Austria 26 C7
Enns → Austria 26 C7
Eno Finland 8 E24
Enontekiö Finland 8 B20
Enosburg Falls U.S.A. 115 B12
Enping China 59 F9
Enriquillo, L. Dom. Rep. 121 C5
Enschede Neths. 17 B6
Ensenada Argentina 126 C4
Ensenada Mexico 118 A1
Ensenada de los Muertos Mexico 118 C2
Enshi China 58 B7
Ensiola, Pta. de n' Spain 48 B9
Ensisheim France 19 E14
Entebbe Uganda 86 B3
Enterprise Canada 102 A5
Enterprise Ala., U.S.A. 117 F12
Enterprise Oreg., U.S.A. 108 D5
Entorno de Doñana △ Spain 37 J4
Entraygues-sur-Truyère France 20 D6
Entre Ríos Bolivia 126 A3
Entre Ríos □ Argentina 126 C4
Entrepeñas, Embalse de Spain 38 E2
Entroncamento Portugal 37 F2
Enugu Nigeria 83 D6
Enugu □ Nigeria 83 D6
Enugu Ezike Nigeria 83 D6
Enumclaw U.S.A. 110 C5
Envalira, Port d' Europe 38 C6
Envermeu France 18 C8
Enviken Sweden 10 D9
Enying Hungary 28 D3
Enza → Italy 40 D7
Eochaill = Youghal Ireland 12 E4
Éólie, Ís. Italy 43 D7
Epanomi Greece 44 F6
Epe Neths. 17 B5
Epe Nigeria 83 D5
Épernay France 19 C10
Épernon France 19 D8
Ephesus Turkey 47 D9
Ephraim U.S.A. 108 G8
Ephrata Pa., U.S.A. 115 F8
Ephrata Wash., U.S.A. 108 C4
Epidavros Limira Greece 46 E5
Épila Spain 38 D3
Épinac France 19 F11
Épinal France 19 D13
Epiros □ Greece 46 B2
Episkopi Cyprus 49 E11
Episkopi Greece 49 D6
Episkopi Bay Cyprus 49 E11
Epitalio Greece 46 D3
Eppan = Appiano Italy 41 B8
Eppingen Germany 25 F4
Epsom U.K. 15 F7
Epukiro Namibia 88 C2
Equatoria = El Istiwa'iya Sudan 79 G11
Equatorial Guinea ■ Africa 84 D1
Er Hai China 58 E3
Er Rachidia Morocco 78 B5
Er Rahad Sudan 81 E3
Er Rif Morocco 78 A5
Er Rogel Sudan 80 D4
Er Roseires Sudan 81 E3

Er Rua'at Sudan 81 E3
Eraclea Italy 41 C9
Erāwadī Myit = Irrawaddy → Burma 67 M19
Erāwadī Myitwanya = Irrawaddy, Mouths of the Burma 67 M19
Erawan △ Thailand 64 E2
Erba Italy 40 C6
Erba Sudan 80 D4
Erba, J. Sudan 80 C4
Erbaa Turkey 72 B7
Erbeskopf Germany 25 F3
Erbil = Arbīl Iraq 73 D11
Erbu Ethiopia 81 E3
Erçek Turkey 70 B4
Erçiş Turkey 73 C10
Ercyaş Dağı Turkey 70 B2
Erdao Jiang → China 57 C14
Erdek Turkey 45 F11
Erdemli Turkey 72 D6
Erdene = Ulaan-Uul Mongolia 56 B6
Erdenetsogt Mongolia 56 C4
Erding Germany 25 G7
Erdre → France 18 E5
Erebus, Mt. Antarctica 5 D11
Erechim Brazil 127 B5
Ereğli Konya, Turkey 72 D6
Ereğli Zonguldak, Turkey 72 B4
Erei, Monti Italy 43 E7
Erenhot China 56 C7
Eresma → Spain 36 D6
Eresos Greece 47 B7
Erewan ← Yerevan Armenia
Erfelek Turkey 72 B6
Erfenisdam S. Africa 88 D4
Erfstadt Germany 24 E2
Erfurt Germany 24 E7
Ergani Turkey 73 C8
Ergel Mongolia 56 C5
Ergene → Turkey 45 E10
Ergeni Vozvyshennost Russia 35 G7
Ērgļi Latvia 32 D3
Erhlin Taiwan 59 F13
Eria → Spain 36 C5
Eriba Sudan 81 D4
Eribol, L. U.K. 13 C4
Érice Italy 42 D5
Erie U.S.A. 114 D4
Erie, L. N. Amer. 114 D4
Erie Canal U.S.A. 114 C7
Erieau Canada 114 D3
Erigavo = Ceerigaabo Somali Rep. 75 E4
Erikoussa Greece 49 A3
Eriksdale Canada 103 C9
Erimanthos Greece 46 D3
Erimo-misaki Japan 54 D11
Erin Canada 114 C4
Erin Pt. Trin. & Tob. 125 K15
Erinpura India 68 G5
Eriskay U.K. 13 D1
Erithres Greece 46 C5
Eritrea ■ Africa 81 E4
Erjas → Portugal 36 F3
Erkelenz Germany 24 D2
Erkner Germany 24 C9
Erlangen Germany 25 F6
Erldunda Australia 94 D1
Ermelo Neths. 17 B5
Ermelo S. Africa 89 D4
Ermenek Turkey 72 D5
Ermil Sudan 81 E2
Ermioni Greece 46 D5
Ermones Greece 49 A3
Ermoúpoli Greece 46 D6
Ernakulam India 66 Q10
Erne → Ireland 12 B3
Erne, Lower L. U.K. 12 B4
Erne, Upper L. U.K. 12 B4
Ernée France 18 D6
Ernest Giles Ra. Australia 93 E3
Ernstberg Germany 25 E2
Erode India 66 P10
Eromanga Australia 95 D3
Erongo Namibia 88 C2
Erquy France 18 D4
Erramala Hills India 66 M11
Errer → Ethiopia 81 F5
Erri-Nundra △ Australia 95 F4
Errigal Ireland 12 A3
Erris Hd. Ireland 12 B1
Erskine U.S.A. 112 B6
Erstein France 19 D14
Ertholmene Denmark 11 J9
Ertil Russia 34 E5
Ertis = Irtysh → Russia 52 C7
Eruh Turkey 73 D10
Eruwa Nigeria 83 D5
Ervy-le-Châtel France 19 D10
Erwin U.S.A. 117 C13
Eryuan China 58 D2
Erzgebirge Germany 24 E8
Erzin Russia 53 D10
Erzincan Turkey 73 C8
Erzincan □ Turkey 73 C8

Erzurum Turkey 73 C9
Erzurum □ Turkey 73 C9
Es Caló Spain 48 C8
Es Canar Spain 48 B8
Es Mercadal Spain 48 B11
Es Migjorn Gran Spain 48 B11
Es Safiya Sudan 81 D3
Es Sahrâ' el Beida Egypt 80 B2
Es Sahrâ' Esh Sharqîya Egypt 80 B3
Es Sînâ' Egypt 74 F3
Es Sûkî Sudan 81 E3
Es Vedrà Spain 48 C7
Esambo Dem. Rep. of the Congo 86 C1
Esan-Misaki Japan 54 D10
Esashi Hokkaidō, Japan 54 B11
Esashi Hokkaidō, Japan 54 D10
Esbjerg Denmark 11 J2
Esbo = Espoo Finland 32 B3
Escalante U.S.A. 109 H8
Escalante → U.S.A. 109 H8
Escalón Mexico 118 B4
Escambia → U.S.A. 117 F11
Escanaba U.S.A. 112 C10
Esch-sur-Alzette Lux. 17 E6
Eschede Germany 24 C6
Eschwege Germany 24 D6
Eschweiler Germany 24 E2
Escondido U.S.A. 111 M9
Escravos → Nigeria 83 D6
Escuinapa de Hidalgo Mexico 118 C3
Escuintla Guatemala 120 D1
Eséka Cameroon 83 E7
Esenguly Turkmenistan 52 F6
Esens Germany 24 B3
Esenyurt Turkey 45 E12
Esera → Spain 38 C5
Eşfahān Iran 71 C6
Eşfahān □ Iran 71 C6
Esfarāyen Iran 71 B8
Esfideh Iran 71 C8
Esgueva → Spain 36 D6
Esh Sham = Dimashq Syria 74 B5
Esh Shamâlîya □ Sudan 80 D2
Esha Ness U.K. 13 A7
Eshan China 58 E4
Esher U.K. 15 F7
Eshkol △ Israel 74 D3
Eshowe S. Africa 89 D5
Esiama Ghana 82 E4
Esigodini Zimbabwe 89 C4
Esil = Ishim → Russia 52 D8
Esino → Italy 41 E10
Esira Madag. 89 C8
Esk → Dumf. & Gall., U.K. 13 G5
Esk → N. Yorks., U.K. 14 C7
Eskān Iran 71 E9
Esker Canada 105 B6
Eskifjörður Iceland 8 D7
Eskilsäter Sweden 11 F7
Eskilstuna Sweden 10 E10
Eskimalatya Turkey 73 C8
Eskimo Point = Arviat Canada 103 A10
Eskişehir Turkey 47 B12
Eskişehir □ Turkey 47 B12
Esla → Spain 36 D4
Eslāmābād-e Gharb Iran 73 E12
Eslāmshahr Iran 71 C6
Eslöv Sweden 11 J7
Eşme Turkey 47 C10
Esmeraldas Ecuador 124 C3
Esna = Isna Egypt 80 B3
Esnagi L. Canada 104 C3
Espalion France 20 D6
España = Spain ■ Europe 7 H5
Espanola Canada 104 C3
Espanola U.S.A. 109 J10
Esparraguera Spain 38 D6
Esparza Costa Rica 120 E3
Espelkamp Germany 24 C4
Esperance Australia 93 F3
Esperance B. Australia 93 F3
Esperance Harbour St. Lucia 121 f
Esperanza Antarctica 5 C18
Esperanza Argentina 126 C3
Esperanza Phil. 61 G6
Esperanza Puerto Rico 121 d
Espéraza France 20 F6
Espichel, C. Portugal 37 G1
Espiel Spain 37 G5
Espigão, Serra do Brazil 127 B5
Espinazo, Sierra del = Espinhaço, Serra do Brazil 125 G10
Espinhaço, Serra do Brazil 125 G10
Espinho Portugal 36 D2
Espinilho, Serra do Brazil 127 B5
Espinosa de los Monteros Spain 36 B7
Espírito Santo □ Brazil 125 H10
Espírito Santo do Pinhal Brazil 127 A6
Espíritu Santo Vanuatu 90 C9
Espíritu Santo, B. del Mexico 119 D7
Espíritu Santo, I. Mexico 118 C2
Espita Mexico 119 C7
Espiye Turkey 73 B8

Espoo Finland 32 B3
Espuña, Sierra de Spain 39 H3
Espungabera Mozam. 89 C5
Esquel Argentina 128 E2
Esquimalt Canada 110 B3
Esquina Argentina 126 C4
Essaouira Morocco 78 B4
Essebie Dem. Rep. of the Congo 86 B3
Essen Belgium 17 C4
Essen Germany 24 D3
Essendon, Mt. Australia 93 E3
Essequibo → Guyana 124 B7
Essex Canada 114 D2
Essex Calif., U.S.A. 111 L11
Essex N.Y., U.S.A. 115 B11
Essex □ U.K. 15 F8
Essex Junction U.S.A. 115 B11
Esslingen Germany 25 G5
Essonne □ France 19 D9
Estaca de Bares, C. de Spain 36 B3
Estación Camacho Mexico 118 C4
Estación Simón Mexico 118 C4
Estadilla Spain 38 C5
Estados, I. de Los Argentina 128 G4
Estagel France 20 F6
Eştahbānāt Iran 71 D7
Estância Brazil 125 F11
Estancia U.S.A. 109 J10
Estārm Iran 71 D8
Estarreja Portugal 36 E2
Estats, Pic d' Spain 38 C6
Estcourt S. Africa 89 D4
Este Italy 41 C8
Este △ Dom. Rep. 121 C6
Estelí Nic. 120 D2
Estella Spain 38 C2
Estellencs Spain 48 B9
Estena → Spain 37 F6
Estepa Spain 37 H6
Estepona Spain 37 J5
Esterhazy Canada 103 C8
Esternay France 19 D10
Esterri d'Àneu Spain 38 C6
Estevan Canada 103 D8
Estevan Group Canada 102 C3
Estherville U.S.A. 112 D6
Estissac France 19 D10
Eston Canada 103 C7
Estonia ■ Europe 32 C3
Estoril Portugal 37 G1
Estouk Mali 83 B5
Estreito Brazil 125 E9
Estrela, Serra da Portugal 36 E3
Estrella Spain 37 G7
Estremoz Portugal 37 G3
Estrondo, Serra do Brazil 125 E9
Esztergom Hungary 28 C3
Et Tidra Mauritania 82 B1
Etah India 69 F8
Étain France 19 C12
Étampes France 19 D9
Etanga Namibia 88 B1
Étaples France 19 B8
Etawah India 69 F8
Etawney L. Canada 103 B9
Etchojoa Mexico 118 B3
Ete Nigeria 83 D6
eThekwini = Durban S. Africa 89 D5
Ethel U.S.A. 110 D4
Ethelbert Canada 103 C8
Ethiopia ■ Africa 75 F3
Ethiopian Highlands Ethiopia 75 F2
Etili Turkey 45 G10
Etive, L. U.K. 13 E3
Etna Italy 43 E7
Etoile Dem. Rep. of the Congo 87 E2
Etoliko Greece 46 C3
Etolin Strait U.S.A. 106 C6
Etoloakarnania □ Greece 46 C3
Etosha △ Namibia 88 B2
Etosha Pan Namibia 88 B2
Etowah U.S.A. 117 D12
Étréchy France 19 D9
Etrek Turkmenistan 71 B7
Étrépagny France 19 C8
Étretat France 18 C7
Etropole Bulgaria 45 D8
Ettelbruck Lux. 17 E6
Ettlingen Germany 25 G4
Ettrick Water → U.K. 13 F6
Etuku Dem. Rep. of the Congo 86 C2
Etulia Moldova 29 E13
Etzná-Tixmucuy = Edzná Mexico 119 D6
Eu France 19 B8
Eua Tonga 91 c
Euboea = Evia Greece 46 C6
Eucla Australia 93 F4
Euclid U.S.A. 114 E3
Eucumbene, L. Australia 95 F4
Eudora U.S.A. 116 E9
Eufaula Ala., U.S.A. 117 F12
Eufaula Okla., U.S.A. 116 D7
Eufaula L. U.S.A. 116 D7
Eugene U.S.A. 108 D2
Eugowra Australia 95 E4
Eulo Australia 95 D4
Eungella △ Australia 94 b

Eunice *La., U.S.A.* **116** F8
Eunice *N. Mex., U.S.A.* **109** K12
Eupen *Belgium* **17** D6
Euphrates = Furāt, Nahr
  al ➤ *Asia* **70** D5
Eure □ *France* **18** C8
Eure ➤ *France* **18** C8
Eure-et-Loir □ *France* **18** D8
Eureka *Canada* **101** B14
Eureka *Calif., U.S.A.* **108** F1
Eureka *Kans., U.S.A.* **112** G5
Eureka *Mont., U.S.A.* **108** B6
Eureka *Nev., U.S.A.* **108** G6
Eureka *S. Dak., U.S.A.* **112** C4
Eureka, Mt. *Australia* **93** E3
Eureka Sd. *Canada* **101** B15
Euroa *Australia* **95** F4
Europa, Île *Ind. Oc.* **85** J8
Europa, Picos de *Spain* **36** B6
Europa, Pt. *Gib.* **37** J5
Europe **6** E10
Europoort *Neths.* **17** C4
Euskirchen *Germany* **24** E2
Eustis *U.S.A.* **117** G14
Eutin *Germany* **24** A6
Eutsuk L. *Canada* **102** C3
Evale *Angola* **88** B2
Evans *U.S.A.* **108** F11
Evans, L. *Canada* **104** B4
Evans City *U.S.A.* **114** F4
Evans Head *Australia* **95** D5
Evansburg *Canada* **102** C5
Evanston *Ill., U.S.A.* **112** D10
Evanston *Wyo., U.S.A.* **108** F8
Evansville *U.S.A.* **112** G10
Évaux-les-Bains *France* **19** F9
Evaz *Iran* **71** E7
Evciler *Afyon, Turkey* **47** C11
Evciler *Çanakkale, Turkey* **47** B8
Eveleth *U.S.A.* **112** B7
Evensk *Russia* **53** C16
Everard, L. *Australia* **95** E2
Everard Ranges *Australia* **93** E5
Everest, Mt. *Nepal* **69** E12
Everett *Pa., U.S.A.* **114** F6
Everett *Wash., U.S.A.* **110** C4
Everglades, The *U.S.A.* **117** J14
Everglades △ *U.S.A.* **117** J14
Everglades City *U.S.A.* **117** J14
Evergreen *Ala., U.S.A.* **117** F11
Evergreen *Mont., U.S.A.* **108** B6
Everöd *Sweden* **11** J8
Evertsberg *Sweden* **10** C7
Evesham *U.K.* **15** E6
Evia *Greece* **46** C6
Evia ➤ *Greece* **46** C5
Évian-les-Bains *France* **19** F13
Evinos ➤ *Greece* **46** C3
Évisa *France* **21** F12
Evje *Norway* **9** G12
Évora *Portugal* **37** G3
Évora □ *Portugal* **37** G3
Evowghlī *Iran* **73** C11
Évreux *France* **18** C8
Evritania □ *Greece* **46** B3
Évron *France* **18** D6
Evros □ *Greece* **45** E10
Evros ➤ *Greece* **72** B2
Evrotas ➤ *Greece* **46** E4
Évry *France* **19** D9
Évvoia = Evia *Greece* **46** C6
Ewe, L. *U.K.* **13** D3
Ewing *U.S.A.* **112** D4
Ewo *Congo* **84** E2
Exaltación *Bolivia* **124** F5
Excelsior Springs *U.S.A.* **112** F6
Excideuil *France* **20** C5
Exe ➤ *U.K.* **15** G4
Exeter *Canada* **114** C3
Exeter *U.K.* **15** G4
Exeter *Calif., U.S.A.* **110** J7
Exeter *N.H., U.S.A.* **115** D14
Exmoor *U.K.* **15** F4
Exmoor △ *U.K.* **15** F4
Exmouth *Australia* **92** D1
Exmouth *U.K.* **15** G4
Exmouth G. *Australia* **92** D1
Exmouth Plateau *Ind. Oc.* **96** J3
Expedition △ *Australia* **95** D4
Expedition Ra. *Australia* **94** C4
Extremadura □ *Spain* **37** F4
Exuma Sound *Bahamas* **120** B4
Eyasi, L. *Tanzania* **86** C4
Eye Pen. *U.K.* **13** C2
Eyemouth *U.K.* **13** F6
Eygues = Aigues ➤ *France* **21** D8
Eygurande *France* **19** G9
Eyjafjörður *Iceland* **8** C4
Eyl *Somali Rep.* **75** F4
Eymet *France* **20** D4
Eymoutiers *France* **20** C5
Eynesil *Turkey* **73** B8
Évora *Portugal* **37** G3
Eyre (North), L. *Australia* **95** D2
Eyre (South), L. *Australia* **95** D2
Eyre, L. *Australia* **90** D6
Eyre Mts. *N.Z.* **91** F2
Eyre Pen. *Australia* **95** E2
Eysturoy *Færoe Is.* **8** E9
Eyvān = Jūy Zar *Iran* **73** F12

Eyvänkī *Iran* **71** C6
Ez Zeidab *Sudan* **80** D3
Ezcaray *Spain* **38** C1
Ežerėlis *Lithuania* **30** D10
Ezhou *China* **59** B10
Ezine *Turkey* **47** B8
Ezouza ➤ *Cyprus* **49** E11

F

F.Y.R.O.M. = Macedonia ■
  Europe **44** E5
Faaa *Tahiti* **91** d
Faaborg *Denmark* **11** J4
Faaone *Tahiti* **91** d
Fabala *Guinea* **82** D3
Fabens *U.S.A.* **116** F1
Fabero *Spain* **36** C4
Fabius *U.S.A.* **115** D9
Fabriano *Italy* **41** E9
Făcăeni *Romania* **29** F12
Fachi *Niger* **79** E8
Fada *Chad* **79** E10
Fada-n-Gourma *Burkina Faso* **83** C5
Fadd *Hungary* **28** D3
Faddeyevskiy, Ostrov
  Russia **53** B15
Faddor *Sudan* **81** F3
Fadghāmī *Syria* **73** E9
Fadlab *Sudan* **80** D3
Faenza *Italy* **41** D8
Færoe Is. = Føroyar ☑ *Atl. Oc.* **8** F9
Fafa *Mali* **83** B5
Fafe *Portugal* **36** D2
Fagam *Nigeria* **83** C7
Făgăras *Romania* **29** E9
Făgăras, Munţii *Romania* **29** E9
Fågelfors *Sweden* **11** G9
Fagelmara *Sweden* **11** H9
Fagerhult *Sweden* **11** G9
Fagersta *Sweden* **10** D9
Făget *Romania* **28** E7
Făget, Munţii *Romania* **29** C8
Faggo *Nigeria* **83** C6
Fagnano, L. *Argentina* **128** G3
Fagnières *France* **19** D11
Faguibine, L. *Mali* **82** B4
Fahlīān *Iran* **71** D6
Fahraj *Kermān, Iran* **71** D8
Fahraj *Yazd, Iran* **71** D7
Fai Tsi Long *Vietnam* **58** G6
Faial *Azores* **78** a
Faial *Madeira* **48** D3
Faichan Kangri *India* **69** B7
Fair Haven *N.Y., U.S.A.* **114** C4
Fair Haven *Vt., U.S.A.* **113** D17
Fair Hd. *U.K.* **12** A5
Fair Isle *U.K.* **16** B6
Fair Oaks *U.S.A.* **110** G5
Fairbanks *U.S.A.* **100** E2
Fairbury *U.S.A.* **112** E5
Fairfax *U.S.A.* **115** B11
Fairfield *Ala., U.S.A.* **117** E11
Fairfield *Calif., U.S.A.* **110** G4
Fairfield *Conn., U.S.A.* **115** E11
Fairfield *Idaho, U.S.A.* **108** E6
Fairfield *Ill., U.S.A.* **112** F9
Fairfield *Iowa, U.S.A.* **112** E8
Fairfield *Tex., U.S.A.* **116** F6
Fairford *Canada* **103** C9
Fairhope *U.S.A.* **117** F11
Fairlie *N.Z.* **91** F3
Fairmead *U.S.A.* **110** H6
Fairmont *Minn., U.S.A.* **112** D6
Fairmont *W. Va., U.S.A.* **113** F13
Fairmount *Calif., U.S.A.* **111** L8
Fairmount *N.Y., U.S.A.* **115** C8
Fairplay *U.S.A.* **108** G10
Fairport *U.S.A.* **114** C7
Fairport Harbor *U.S.A.* **114** E3
Fairview *Canada* **102** B5
Fairview *Mont., U.S.A.* **108** C11
Fairview *Okla., U.S.A.* **116** C5
Fairweather, Mt. *U.S.A.* **102** B1
Faisalabad *Pakistan* **68** D5
Faith *U.S.A.* **112** C2
Faizabad *India* **69** F10
Fajardo *Puerto Rico* **121** d
Fajr, W. ➤ *Si. Arabia* **70** D3
Fakenham *U.K.* **14** E8
Fåker *Sweden* **10** A8
Fakfak *Indonesia* **63** E8
Fakiya *Bulgaria* **45** D11
Fakobli *Ivory C.* **82** D3
Fakse *Denmark* **11** J6
Fakse Bugt *Denmark* **11** J6
Fakse Ladeplads *Denmark* **11** J6
Faku *China* **57** C12
Falaba *S. Leone* **82** D2
Falaise *France* **18** D6
Falaise, Mui *Vietnam* **64** C5
Falakrón Oros *Greece* **44** E7
Falam *Burma* **67** H18
Falces *Spain* **38** C3
Fălciu *Romania* **29** D13
Falcó, C. des *Spain* **48** C7
Falcón, Presa *Mexico* **119** B5
Falcon Lake *Canada* **103** D9
Falcon Res. *U.S.A.* **116** H5

Falconara Maríttima *Italy* **41** E10
Falcone, C. del *Italy* **42** B1
Falconer *U.S.A.* **114** D5
Faléa *Mali* **82** C2
Falefa *Samoa* **91** b
Falelatai *Samoa* **91** b
Falelima *Samoa* **91** b
Falémé ➤ *Senegal* **82** C2
Falerum *Sweden* **11** F10
Faleshty = Fălesti *Moldova* **29** C12
Fălesti *Moldova* **29** C12
Falfurrias *U.S.A.* **116** H5
Falher *Canada* **102** B5
Faliraki *Greece* **49** C10
Falkenberg *Germany* **24** D9
Falkenberg *Sweden* **11** H6
Falkensee *Germany* **24** C9
Falkirk *U.K.* **13** F5
Falkirk □ *U.K.* **13** F5
Falkland *U.K.* **13** E5
Falkland Is. ☑ *Atl. Oc.* **128** G5
Falkland Sd. *Falk. Is.* **128** G5
Falkonera *Greece* **46** D5
Falköping *Sweden* **11** F7
Fall River *U.S.A.* **115** E13
Fall Creek *U.S.A.* **114** E6
Fallbrook *U.S.A.* **111** M9
Fallon *U.S.A.* **108** G4
Falls City *U.S.A.* **112** E6
Falls Creek *U.S.A.* **114** E6
Falmouth *Jamaica* **120** a
Falmouth *U.K.* **15** G2
Falmouth *U.S.A.* **115** E14
Falsa, Pta. *Mexico* **118** B1
False B. *S. Africa* **88** E2
False, C. *Honduras* **120** C3
Falster *Denmark* **11** K5
Falsterbo *Sweden* **9** J15
Fălticeni *Romania* **29** C11
Falun *Sweden* **10** D9
Famagusta *Cyprus* **49** D12
Famagusta Bay *Cyprus* **49** D13
Famatina, Sierra de
  Argentina **126** B2
Famenin *Iran* **73** E13
Family L. *Canada* **103** C9
Famoso *U.S.A.* **111** K7
Fan Xian *China* **56** G8
Fana *Mali* **82** C3
Fanad Hd. *Ireland* **12** A4
Fanari *Greece* **46** B3
Fandriana *Madag.* **89** C8
Fánes-Sénnes e Braies △
  Italy **41** B9
Fang *Thailand* **58** H2
Fang Xian *China* **59** A8
Fangaga *Sudan* **80** D4
Fangak *Sudan* **81** F3
Fangcheng *China* **59** B12
Fangcheng *China* **56** H7
Fangchenggang *China* **58** G7
Fangliao *Taiwan* **59** F13
Fangshan *China* **56** E6
Fangzi *China* **57** F10
Fani i Madh ➤ *Albania* **44** E4
Fanjakana *Madag.* **89** C8
Fanjiatun *China* **57** C13
Fannich, L. *U.K.* **13** D4
Fannūj *Iran* **71** E8
Fanø *Denmark* **11** J2
Fano *Italy* **41** E10
Fanshi *China* **56** E7
Fao = Al Fāw *Iraq* **71** D6
Faqirwali *Pakistan* **68** E5
Fâqûs *Egypt* **80** H7
Far East =
  Dalnevostochnyy □
  Russia **53** C14
Far East *Asia* **50** E14
Fara in Sabina *Italy* **41** F9
Faradje *Dem. Rep. of the Congo* **86** B2
Farafangana *Madag.* **89** C8
Farafenni *Gambia* **82** C1
Farâfra, El Wâhât el *Egypt* **80** B2
Farāh *Afghan.* **66** C3
Farāh □ *Afghan.* **66** C3
Farahalana *Madag.* **89** A9
Faraid, Gebel *Egypt* **80** C4
Farako *Ivory C.* **82** D4
Faramana *Burkina Faso* **82** C4
Faranah *Guinea* **82** C2
Farasān, Jazā'ir *Si. Arabia* **75** D3
Farasan Is. = Farasān,
  Jazā'ir *Si. Arabia* **75** D3
Faratsiho *Madag.* **89** B8
Fardes ➤ *Spain* **37** H7
Fareham *U.K.* **15** G6
Farewell, C. *N.Z.* **91** D4
Farewell C. = Nunap Isua
  Greenland **98** D15
Färgelanda *Sweden* **11** F5
Farghona *Uzbekistan* **52** E8
Fargo *U.S.A.* **112** B6
Fār'iah, W. al ➤ *West Bank* **74** C4
Faribault *U.S.A.* **112** C7
Faridabad *India* **68** E7
Faridkot *India* **68** D6
Faridpur *Bangla.* **69** H13
Faridpur *India* **69** E8
Färila *Sweden* **10** C9

Farim *Guinea-Biss.* **82** C1
Farīmān *Iran* **71** C8
Fariones, Pta. *Canary Is.* **48** E6
Fâriskûr *Egypt* **80** H7
Farkadona *Greece* **46** B4
Farleigh *Australia* **94** B3
Farmakonisi *Greece* **47** D9
Farmerville *U.S.A.* **116** E8
Farmingdale *U.S.A.* **115** F10
Farmington *Canada* **102** B4
Farmington *Calif., U.S.A.* **110** H6
Farmington *Maine, U.S.A.* **113** C18
Farmington *Mo., U.S.A.* **112** G8
Farmington *N.H., U.S.A.* **115** C13
Farmington *N. Mex., U.S.A.* **109** H9
Farmington *Utah, U.S.A.* **108** F8
Farmington ➤ *U.S.A.* **115** E12
Farmville *U.S.A.* **113** G14
Färnäs *Sweden* **10** D8
Farne Is. *U.K.* **14** B6
Farnham *U.S.A.* **115** A12
Farnham, Mt. *Canada* **102** C5
Faro *Brazil* **125** D7
Faro *Canada* **100** E5
Faro *Portugal* **37** H3
Fårö *Sweden* **9** H18
Faro □ *Portugal* **37** H2
Faro ✕ (FAO) *Portugal* **37** H3
Fårösund *Sweden* **11** G13
Farquhar, C. *Australia* **93** D1
Farrars Cr. ➤ *Australia* **94** D3
Farrell *U.S.A.* **114** E4
Farrāshband *Iran* **71** D7
Farrokhī *Iran* **71** C8
Farruch, C. = Ferrutx, C. de
  Spain **48** B10
Farrukhabad *India* **69** F8
Fārs □ *Iran* **71** D7
Fársala *Greece* **46** B4
Fārsī *Iran* **71** E6
Farson *U.S.A.* **108** E9
Farsund *Norway* **9** G12
Fartak, Râs *Si. Arabia* **70** D2
Fartak, Ra's *Yemen* **75** D5
Fârtānesti *Romania* **29** E12
Fartura, Serra da *Brazil* **127** B5
Faru *Nigeria* **83** C6
Fārūj *Iran* **71** B8
Fārup *Denmark* **11** H3
Farvel, Kap = Nunap Isua
  Greenland **98** D15
Farwell *U.S.A.* **116** D3
Färyāb □ *Afghan.* **66** B4
Fasā *Iran* **71** D7
Fasano *Italy* **43** B10
Fashoda *Sudan* **81** F3
Fasil Ghebbi *Ethiopia* **81** E4
Fassa *Mali* **82** C3
Fastiv *Ukraine* **23** C15
Fastnet Rock *Ireland* **12** E2
Fastov = Fastiv *Ukraine* **23** C15
Fatagar, Tanjung *Indonesia* **63** E8
Fatehabad *Haryana, India* **68** E6
Fatehabad *Ut. P., India* **68** F8
Fatehgarh *India* **69** F8
Fatehpur *Bihar, India* **69** G11
Fatehpur *Raj., India* **68** F6
Fatehpur *Ut. P., India* **69** G9
Fatehpur *Ut. P., India* **69** F9
Fatehpur Sikri *India* **68** F6
Fatesh *Russia* **33** F8
Fathai *Sudan* **81** F3
Fathom Five △ *Canada* **114** A3
Fatick *Senegal* **82** C1
Fatick □ *Senegal* **82** C1
Fatima *Canada* **105** C7
Fátima *Portugal* **37** F2
Fatoya *Guinea* **82** C3
Fatsa *Turkey* **72** B7
Faucille, Col de la *France* **19** F13
Faulkton *U.S.A.* **112** C4
Faulquemont *France* **19** C13
Faure I. *Australia* **93** E1
Făurei *Romania* **29** E12
Fauresmith *S. Africa* **88** D4
Fauske *Norway* **8** C16
Favara *Italy* **42** E6
Faváritx, C. de *Spain* **48** B11
Faverges *France* **21** C10
Favignana *Italy* **42** E5
Favignana, I. *Italy* **42** E5
Fawcett, Pt. *Australia* **92** B5
Fawn ➤ *Canada* **104** A2
Fawnskin *U.S.A.* **111** L10
Faxaflói *Iceland* **8** D2
Faxälven ➤ *Sweden* **10** A10
Faya-Largeau *Chad* **79** E9
Fayd *Si. Arabia* **70** E4
Fayence *France* **21** E10
Fayette *Ala., U.S.A.* **117** E11
Fayette *Mo., U.S.A.* **112** F7
Fayette, W., U.S.A. **115** D8
Fayetteville *Ark., U.S.A.* **116** C7
Fayetteville *N.C., U.S.A.* **117** D15
Fayetteville *N.Y., U.S.A.* **115** C9
Fayetteville *Tenn., U.S.A.* **117** D11

Fayied *Egypt* **80** H8
Faylakah *Kuwait* **71** D6
Fayón *Spain* **38** D5
Fazao-Malfakassa △ *Togo* **83** D5
Fazilka *India* **68** D6
Fazilpur *Pakistan* **68** E4
Fdérik *Mauritania* **78** D3
Feakle *Ireland* **12** D3
Feale ➤ *Ireland* **12** D2
Fear, C. *U.S.A.* **117** E16
Feather ➤ *U.S.A.* **108** G3
Feather Falls *U.S.A.* **110** F5
Featherston *N.Z.* **91** D5
Featherstone *Zimbabwe* **87** F3
Fécamp *France* **18** C7
Fedala = Mohammedia
  Morocco **78** B4
Fedeshküh *Iran* **71** D7
Fehérgyarmat *Hungary* **28** C7
Fehmarn *Germany* **24** A7
Fehmarn Bælt *Europe* **11** K5
Fehmarn Belt = Fehmarn
  Bælt *Europe* **11** K5
Fei Xian *China* **57** G9
Feijó *Brazil* **124** E4
Feilding *N.Z.* **91** D5
Feira de Santana *Brazil* **125** F11
Feixi *China* **59** B11
Feixiang *China* **56** F8
Fejér □ *Hungary* **28** C3
Fejø *Denmark* **11** K5
Feke *Turkey* **72** D6
Fekete ➤ *Hungary* **28** E3
Felanitx *Spain* **48** B10
Feldbach *Austria* **26** E8
Feldberg *Baden-W., Germany* **25** H3
Feldberg
  *Mecklenburg-Vorpommern,
  Germany* **24** B9
Feldkirch *Austria* **26** E3
Feldkirchen *Austria* **26** E7
Félicité *Seychelles* **85** b
Felipe Carrillo Puerto
  Mexico **119** D7
Felixburg *Zimbabwe* **89** B5
Felixstowe *U.K.* **15** F9
Felletin *France* **20** C6
Fellingsbro *Sweden* **10** E9
Felton *U.S.A.* **110** H4
Feltre *Italy* **41** B8
Femer Bælt = Fehmarn
  Bælt *Europe* **11** K5
Femø *Denmark* **11** K5
Femunden *Norway* **8** E14
Fen He ➤ *China* **56** G6
Fene *Spain* **36** B2
Fenelon Falls *Canada* **114** B6
Fener Burnu *Turkey* **47** E9
Feneroa *Ethiopia* **81** E4
Feng Xian *Jiangsu, China* **56** G9
Feng Xian *Shaanxi, China* **56** H4
Fengari *Greece* **45** F9
Fengcheng *Jiangxi, China* **59** C10
Fengcheng *Liaoning, China* **57** D13
Fengfeng *China* **56** F8
Fenggang *China* **58** D6
Fenghua *China* **59** C13
Fenghuang *China* **58** D7
Fengjie *China* **58** B7
Fengkang *Taiwan* **59** F13
Fengle *China* **59** B9
Fenglin *Taiwan* **59** F13
Fengning *China* **56** D9
Fengqing *China* **58** E2
Fengqiu *China* **56** G8
Fengrun *China* **57** E10
Fengshan *Guangxi Zhuangzu,
  China* **58** E7
Fengshan *Guangxi Zhuangzu,
  China* **58** E6
Fengshan *Taiwan* **59** F13
Fengshun *China* **59** F11
Fengtai *Anhui, China* **59** A11
Fengtai *Beijing, China* **56** E9
Fengxian *China* **59** B13
Fengxiang *China* **56** G4
Fengxin *China* **59** C10
Fengyang *China* **57** H9
Fengyi *China* **58** E3
Fengyüan *Taiwan* **59** E13
Fengzhen *China* **56** D7
Feno, C. de *France* **21** G12
Fens, The *U.K.* **14** E7
Fensmark *Denmark* **11** J5
Fenton *U.S.A.* **113** D12
Fenxi *China* **56** F6
Fenyang *China* **56** F6

Fenyi *China* **59** D10
Feodosiya *Ukraine* **33** K8
Ferbane *Ireland* **12** C4
Ferdows *Iran* **71** C8
Fère-Champenoise *France* **19** D10
Fère-en-Tardenois *France* **19** C10
Ferentino *Italy* **41** G10
Feres *Greece* **45** F10
Ferfer *Somali Rep.* **75** F4
Fergana = Farghona
  Uzbekistan **52** E8
Fergus *Canada* **114** C4
Fergus Falls *U.S.A.* **112** B5
Feričanci *Croatia* **28** E2
Feriheky, Budapest ✕
  (BUD) *Hungary* **28** C3
Ferlach *Austria* **26** E7
Ferland *Canada* **104** B2
Ferlo ➤ *Senegal* **82** B2
Ferlo-Nord △ *Senegal* **82** B2
Ferlo-Sud △ *Senegal* **82** B2
Fermanagh □ *U.K.* **12** B4
Fermo *Italy* **41** E10
Fermont *Canada* **105** B6
Fermoselle *Spain* **36** D4
Fermoy *Ireland* **12** D3
Fernán Núñez *Spain* **37** H6
Fernández *Argentina* **126** B3
Fernandina Beach *U.S.A.* **117** F14
Fernando de Noronha
  Brazil **125** D12
Fernando Póo = Bioko
  Eq. Guin. **83** E6
Ferndale *Canada* **114** B3
Ferndale *U.S.A.* **110** B4
Fernie *Canada* **102** D5
Fernlees *Australia* **94** C4
Fernley *U.S.A.* **108** G4
Fernwood *U.S.A.* **115** C11
Ferozepore = Firozpur *India* **68** D6
Ferrandina *Italy* **43** B9
Ferrara *Italy* **41** D8
Ferrato, C. *Italy* **42** C2
Ferreira do Alentejo *Portugal* **37** G2
Ferreñafe *Peru* **124** E3
Ferrerías *Spain* **48** B11
Ferret, C. *France* **20** D2
Ferrette *France* **19** E14
Ferriday *U.S.A.* **116** F9
Ferriere *Italy* **40** D6
Ferrières *France* **19** D9
Ferro, Capo *Italy* **42** A2
Ferron *U.S.A.* **108** G8
Ferrutx, C. de *Spain* **48** B10
Ferryland *Canada* **105** C9
Fertile *U.S.A.* **112** B5
Fertő-Hanság △ *Hungary* **28** C2
Fertőszentmiklós *Hungary* **28** C1
Fès *Morocco* **78** B5
Fessenden *U.S.A.* **112** B4
Festus *U.S.A.* **112** F8
Feté Bowé *Senegal* **82** C2
Fetesti *Romania* **29** F12
Fethiye *Turkey* **47** E11
Fethiye Körfezi *Turkey* **47** E10
Fetlar *U.K.* **13** A8
Feuilles ➤ *Canada* **101** F17
Feurs *France* **21** C8
Fez = Fès *Morocco* **78** B5
Fezzan *Libya* **79** C8
Fiambalá *Argentina* **126** B2
Fianarantsoa *Madag.* **89** C8
Fianarantsoa □ *Madag.* **89** B8
Fiche *Ethiopia* **81** F4
Fichtelgebirge *Germany* **25** E7
Fichtelgebirge △ *Germany* **25** E7
Ficksburg *S. Africa* **89** D4
Fidenza *Italy* **40** D7
Fiditi *Nigeria* **83** D5
Field ➤ *Australia* **94** C2
Field I. *Australia* **92** B5
Fieni *Romania* **29** E10
Fier *Albania* **44** F3
Fierzë *Albania* **44** D4
Fife □ *U.K.* **13** E5
Fife △ *U.K.* **13** E5
Fife Ness *U.K.* **13** E6
Fifth Cataract *Sudan* **80** D3
Figari *France* **21** G13
Figeac *France* **20** D5
Figeholm *Sweden* **11** G10
Figline Valdarno *Italy* **41** E8
Figtree *Zimbabwe* **87** G2
Figueira Castelo Rodrigo
  Portugal **36** E4
Figueira da Foz *Portugal* **36** E2
Figueiró dos Vinhos *Portugal* **36** F2
Figueres *Spain* **38** C7
Figuig *Morocco* **78** B5
Fihaonana *Madag.* **89** B8
Fiherenana *Madag.* **89** B8
Fiherenana ➤ *Madag.* **89** C7
Fiji ■ *Pac. Oc.* **91** a
Fik *Ethiopia* **81** F5
Fika *Nigeria* **83** C7
Filabres, Sierra de los *Spain* **37** H8
Filabusi *Zimbabwe* **89** C4

Filadélfia *Italy* **43** D9
Filadélfia *Paraguay* **126** A3
Fil'akovo *Slovak Rep.* **27** C12
Filchner Ice Shelf *Antarctica* **5** D1
Filey *U.K.* **14** C7
Filey B. *U.K.* **14** C7
Filfla *Malta* **49** D1
Filiaşi *Romania* **29** F8
Filiates *Greece* **46** B2
Filiatra *Greece* **46** D3
Filicudi *Italy* **43** D7
Filingué *Niger* **83** C5
Filiourí = Lissos → *Greece* **45** E9
Filipada *Greece* **46** B2
Filipstad *Sweden* **10** E8
Filisur *Switz.* **25** J5
Fillmore *Calif., U.S.A.* **111** L8
Fillmore *Utah, U.S.A.* **108** G7
Filotio *Greece* **47** D7
Filottrano *Italy* **41** E10
Filtu *Ethiopia* **81** F5
Fimbul Ice Shelf *S. Ocean* **5** C2
Fina → *Mali* **82** C3
Finale Emília *Italy* **41** D8
Finale Lígure *Italy* **40** D5
Fiñana *Spain* **37** H8
Finch *Canada* **115** A9
Finch Hatton *Australia* **94** b
Finchaa, L. *Ethiopia* **81** F4
Findhorn → *U.K.* **13** D5
Fındıklı *Turkey* **73** B9
Findlay *U.S.A.* **113** E12
Fine *U.S.A.* **115** B9
Finger L. *Canada* **104** B1
Finger Lakes *U.S.A.* **115** D8
Fíngoè *Mozam.* **87** E3
Finike *Turkey* **47** E12
Finike Körfezi *Turkey* **47** E12
Finiq *Albania* **44** G4
Finistère □ *France* **18** D3
Finisterre = Fisterra *Spain* **36** C1
Finisterre, C. = Fisterra, C.
  Spain **36** C1
Finke *Australia* **94** D1
Finke Gorge △ *Australia* **92** D5
Finland ■ *Europe* **8** E22
Finland, G. of *Europe* **32** C3
Finlay → *Canada* **102** B3
Finley *Australia* **95** F4
Finley *U.S.A.* **112** B5
Finn → *Ireland* **12** B4
Finnerödja *Sweden* **11** F8
Finnigan, Mt. *Australia* **94** B4
Finniss, C. *Australia* **95** E1
Finnmark *Norway* **8** B20
Finnsnes *Norway* **8** B18
Finspång *Sweden* **11** F9
Finsteraarhorn *Switz.* **25** J4
Finsterwalde *Germany* **24** D9
Fiora → *Italy* **41** F8
Fiordland △ *N.Z.* **91** F1
Fiorenzuola d'Arda *Italy* **40** D6
Fīq *Syria* **74** C4
Firat = Furāt, Nahr al →
  Asia **70** D5
Fire Island △ *U.S.A.* **115** F11
Firebag → *Canada* **103** B6
Firebaugh *U.S.A.* **110** J6
Firedrake L. *Canada* **103** A8
Firenze *Italy* **41** E8
Firenze Amerigo
  Vespucci ✈ (FLR) *Italy* **41** E8
Firenze Pisa ✈ (PSA) *Italy* **40** E7
Firenzuola *Italy* **41** D8
Firk, Sha'ib → *Iraq* **70** D5
Firmi *France* **20** D6
Firminy *France* **21** C8
Firozabad *India* **69** F8
Firozpur *India* **68** D6
Firozpur-Jhirka *India* **68** F7
Fīrūzābād *Iran* **71** D7
Fīrūzkūh *Iran* **71** C7
Firvale *Canada* **102** C3
Fish → *Namibia* **88** D2
Fish → *S. Africa* **88** E3
Fish River Canyon *Namibia* **88** D2
Fisher B. *Canada* **103** C9
Fisher I. *U.S.A.* **115** E13
Fishguard *U.K.* **15** E3
Fishing L. *Canada* **103** C9
Fishkill *U.S.A.* **115** E11
Fismes *France* **19** C10
Fisterra *Spain* **36** C1
Fisterra, C. *Spain* **36** C1
Fitchburg *Mass., U.S.A.* **115** D13
Fitchburg *Wis., U.S.A.* **112** D9
Fitz Roy *Argentina* **128** F3
Fitz Roy, Cerro *Argentina* **128** F2
Fitzgerald *Canada* **102** B6
Fitzgerald *U.S.A.* **117** F13
Fitzgerald River △ *Australia* **93** F3
Fitzmaurice → *Australia* **92** B5
Fitzroy → *Queens., Australia* **94** C5
Fitzroy → *W. Austral.,
  Australia* **92** C3
Fitzroy Crossing *Australia* **92** C4
Fitzwilliam I. *Canada* **114** A3
Fiuggi *Italy* **41** G10
Fiume = Rijeka *Croatia* **41** C11

Fiumicino, Roma ✈ (FCO)
  Italy **41** G9
Five Points *U.S.A.* **110** J6
Fivizzano *Italy* **40** D7
Fizi *Dem. Rep. of the Congo* **86** C2
Fjällbacka *Sweden* **11** F5
Fjärdhundra *Sweden* **10** E10
Fjellerup *Denmark* **11** H4
Fjerritslev *Denmark* **11** G3
Fjugesta *Sweden* **10** E8
Flagstaff *U.S.A.* **109** J8
Flagstaff L. *U.S.A.* **115** A14
Flaherty I. *Canada* **104** A4
Flåm *Norway* **8** F12
Flambeau → *U.S.A.* **112** C8
Flamborough Hd. *U.K.* **14** C7
Fläming *Germany* **24** C8
Flaming Gorge △ *U.S.A.* **108** F9
Flaming Gorge Res. *U.S.A.* **108** F9
Flamingo, Teluk *Indonesia* **63** F9
Flanders = Flandre *Europe* **19** B9
Flandre *Europe* **19** B9
Flandre-Occidentale =
  West-Vlaanderen □
  Belgium **17** D2
Flandre-Orientale = Oost-
  Vlaanderen □ *Belgium* **17** C3
Flandreau *U.S.A.* **112** C5
Flanigan *U.S.A.* **110** E7
Flannan Is. *U.K.* **13** C1
Flåsjön *Sweden* **8** D16
Flat → *Canada* **102** A3
Flat I. *Mauritius* **85** d
Flathead L. *U.S.A.* **108** C6
Flattery, C. *Australia* **94** A4
Flattery, C. *U.S.A.* **110** B2
Flatwoods *U.S.A.* **113** F12
Fleetwood *U.K.* **14** D4
Fleetwood *U.S.A.* **115** F9
Flekkefjord *Norway* **9** G12
Flemington *U.S.A.* **114** E7
Flen *Sweden* **10** E10
Flensburg *Germany* **24** A5
Flers *France* **18** D6
Flesherton *Canada* **114** B4
Flesko, Tanjung *Indonesia* **63** D6
Fleurance *France* **20** E4
Fleurieu Pen. *Australia* **95** F2
Fleurier *Switz.* **25** J2
Flevoland □ *Neths.* **17** B5
Flin Flon *Canada* **103** C8
Flinders → *Australia* **94** B3
Flinders B. *Australia* **93** F2
Flinders Group *Australia* **94** A3
Flinders I. *S. Austral., Australia* **95** E1
Flinders I. *Tas., Australia* **95** G4
Flinders Ranges *Australia* **95** E2
Flinders Reefs *Australia* **94** B4
Flint *U.K.* **14** D4
Flint *U.S.A.* **113** D12
Flint → *U.S.A.* **117** F12
Flint I. *Kiribati* **97** J12
Flintshire □ *U.K.* **14** D4
Fliseryd *Sweden* **11** G10
Flix *Spain* **38** D5
Flixecourt *France* **19** B9
Floby *Sweden* **11** F7
Floda *Sweden* **11** G6
Flodden *U.K.* **14** B5
Flogny-la-Chapelle *France* **19** E10
Floodwood *U.S.A.* **112** B7
Flora *U.S.A.* **112** F9
Florac *France* **20** D7
Florala *U.S.A.* **117** F11
Florence = Firenze *Italy* **41** E8
Florence *Ala., U.S.A.* **117** D11
Florence *Ariz., U.S.A.* **109** K8
Florence *Colo., U.S.A.* **108** G11
Florence *Oreg., U.S.A.* **108** D1
Florence *S.C., U.S.A.* **117** D15
Florence, L. *Australia* **95** D2
Florencia *Colombia* **124** C3
Florennes *Belgium* **17** D4
Florensac *France* **20** E7
Florenville *Belgium* **17** E5
Flores *Azores* **78** a
Flores *Guatemala* **120** C2
Flores *Indonesia* **63** F6
Flores I. *Canada* **102** D3
Flores Sea *Indonesia* **63** F6
Floreşti *Moldova* **29** C13
Floresville *U.S.A.* **116** G5
Floriano *Brazil* **125** E10
Florianópolis *Brazil* **127** B6
Florida *Cuba* **120** B4
Florida *Uruguay* **127** C4
Florida □ *U.S.A.* **117** G14
Florida, Straits of *U.S.A.* **120** B4
Florida B. *U.S.A.* **120** B3
Florida Keys *U.S.A.* **117** J14
Florídia *Italy* **43** E8
Florin *U.S.A.* **110** G5
Florina *Greece* **44** F5
Florina □ *Greece* **44** F5
Florissant *U.S.A.* **112** F8
Florø *Norway* **8** F11
Flower Station *Canada* **115** A8
Flowerpot I. *Canada* **114** A3
Floydada *U.S.A.* **116** E4

Fluk *Indonesia* **63** E7
Flúmen → *Spain* **38** D4
Flumendosa → *Italy* **42** C2
Fluminimaggiore *Italy* **42** C1
Flushing = Vlissingen *Neths.* **17** C3
Fluvià → *Spain* **38** C8
Fly → *Papua N. G.* **90** B7
Flying Fish, C. *Antarctica* **5** D15
Foa *Tonga* **91** c
Foam Lake *Canada* **103** C8
Foča *Bos.-H.* **44** C2
Foça *Turkey* **47** C8
Fochabers *U.K.* **13** D5
Focşani *Romania* **29** E12
Fodécontéa *Guinea* **82** C2
Fogang *China* **59** F9
Fóggia *Italy* **43** A8
Fogo *Canada* **105** C9
Fogo C. Verde Is. *78* b
Fogo I. *Canada* **105** C9
Fohnsdorf *Austria* **26** D7
Föhr *Germany* **24** A4
Foia *Portugal* **37** H2
Foix *France* **20** E5
Fojnica *Bos.-H.* **28** C2
Fokida □ *Greece* **46** C4
Fokino *Russia* **32** E3
Fokku *Nigeria* **83** C5
Folda *Nord-Trøndelag, Norway* **8** D14
Folda *Nordland, Norway* **8** C16
Földeák *Hungary* **28** D5
Folegandros *Greece* **46** E6
Foley *Botswana* **88** C4
Foley *U.S.A.* **117** F11
Foleyet *Canada* **104** C3
Folgefonna *Norway* **9** F12
Foligno *Italy* **41** F9
Folkestone *U.K.* **15** F9
Folkston *U.S.A.* **117** F13
Follansbee *U.S.A.* **114** F4
Follónica *Italy* **40** F7
Follónica, G. di *Italy* **40** F7
Folsom L. *U.S.A.* **110** G5
Folteşti *Romania* **29** E13
Fomboni *Comoros Is.* **85** a
Fond-du-Lac *Canada* **103** B7
Fond du Lac *U.S.A.* **112** D9
Fond-du-Lac → *Canada* **103** B7
Fonda *U.S.A.* **115** D10
Fondi *Italy* **42** A6
Fonfría *Spain* **36** D4
Fongafale *Tuvalu* **90** B10
Fonni *Italy* **42** B2
Fonsagrada = A
  Fonsagrada *Spain* **36** B3
Fonseca, G. de *Cent. Amer.* **120** D2
Font-Romeu-Odeillo-Via
  France **20** F5
Fontaine-Française *France* **19** E12
Fontainebleau *France* **19** D9
Fontana *U.S.A.* **111** L9
Fontas → *Canada* **102** B4
Fonte Boa *Brazil* **124** D5
Fontem *Cameroon* **83** D6
Fontenay-le-Comte *France* **20** B3
Fontenelle Res. *U.S.A.* **108** E8
Fontur *Iceland* **8** C6
Fonuafo'ou *Tonga* **91** c
Fonualei *Tonga* **91** c
Fonyód *Hungary* **28** D2
Foochow = Fuzhou *China* **59** D12
Foping *China* **56** H5
Foraker, Mt. *U.S.A.* **106** C9
Forbach *France* **19** C13
Forbes *Australia* **95** E4
Forbesganj *India* **69** F12
Forcados *Nigeria* **83** D6
Forcados → *Nigeria* **83** D6
Forcalquier *France* **21** E9
Forchheim *Germany* **25** F7
Ford City *Calif., U.S.A.* **111** K7
Ford City *Pa., U.S.A.* **114** F5
Førde *Norway* **8** F11
Fords Bridge *Australia* **95** D4
Fordyce *U.S.A.* **116** E8
Forécariah *Guinea* **82** D2
Forel, Mt. *Greenland* **98** C16
Foremost *Canada* **102** D6
Forest *Canada* **114** C3
Forest *U.S.A.* **117** E10
Forest City *Iowa, U.S.A.* **112** D7
Forest City *N.C., U.S.A.* **117** D14
Forest City *Pa., U.S.A.* **115** E9
Forest Grove *U.S.A.* **110** E3
Forestburg *Canada* **102** C6
Foreste Casentinesi-Monte
  Falterona-Campigna △
  Italy **41** E8
Foresthill *U.S.A.* **110** F6
Forestier Pen. *Australia* **95** G4
Forestville *Canada* **105** C6
Forestville *Calif., U.S.A.* **110** G4
Forestville *N.Y., U.S.A.* **114** D5
Forêt d'Orient △ *France* **19** D11
Forez, Mts. du *France* **20** C7
Forfar *U.K.* **13** E6
Forillon △ *Canada* **105** C7
Forks *U.S.A.* **110** C2

Forksville *U.S.A.* **115** E8
Forlì *Italy* **41** D9
Forman *U.S.A.* **112** B5
Formazza *Italy* **40** B5
Formby Pt. *U.K.* **14** D4
Formentera *Spain* **48** C7
Formentor, C. de *Spain* **48** B10
Formentor, Pen. de *Spain* **48** B10
Former Yugoslav Republic
  of Macedonia =
  Macedonia ■ *Europe* **44** E5
Fórmia *Italy* **42** A6
Formígine *Italy* **40** D7
Formosa = Taiwan ■ *Asia* **59** F13
Formosa *Argentina* **126** B4
Formosa *Brazil* **125** G9
Formosa □ *Argentina* **126** B4
Formosa, Serra *Brazil* **125** F8
Formosa B. = Ungwana B.
  Kenya **86** C5
Fornells *Spain* **48** A11
Fornos de Algodres *Portugal* **36** E3
Fornovo di Taro *Italy* **40** D7
Føroyar ☑ *Atl. Oc.* **8** F9
Forres *U.K.* **13** D5
Forrest *Australia* **93** F4
Forrest, Mt. *Australia* **93** D4
Forrest City *U.S.A.* **117** D9
Fors *Sweden* **10** D10
Forsayth *Australia* **94** B3
Forshaga *Sweden* **10** E7
Forsmo *Sweden* **10** A11
Forssa *Finland* **32** B2
Forst *Germany* **24** D10
Forster *Australia* **95** E5
Forsvik *Sweden* **11** F8
Forsyth *U.S.A.* **108** C10
Fort Abbas *Pakistan* **68** E5
Fort Albany *Canada* **104** B3
Fort Assiniboine *Canada* **102** C6
Fort Augustus *U.K.* **13** D4
Fort Beaufort *S. Africa* **88** E4
Fort Benton *U.S.A.* **108** C8
Fort Bragg *U.S.A.* **108** G2
Fort Bridger *U.S.A.* **108** F8
Fort Chipewyan *Canada* **103** B6
Fort Clatsop = Lewis and
  Clark △ *U.S.A.* **110** D3
Fort Collins *U.S.A.* **108** F11
Fort-Coulonge *Canada* **104** C4
Fort Covington *U.S.A.* **115** B10
Fort Dauphin = Taolanaro
  Madag. **89** D8
Fort Davis *U.S.A.* **116** F3
Fort Defiance *U.S.A.* **109** J9
Fort Dodge *U.S.A.* **112** D6
Fort Edward *U.S.A.* **115** C11
Fort Erie *Canada* **114** D6
Fort Fairfield *U.S.A.* **113** B20
Fort Frances *Canada* **103** D10
Fort Franklin = Déline
  Canada **100** D7
Fort Garland *U.S.A.* **109** H11
Fort George = Chisasibi
  Canada **104** B4
Fort Good Hope *Canada* **100** D6
Fort Hancock *U.S.A.* **116** F2
Fort Hope = Eabametoong
  Canada **104** B2
Fort Irwin *U.S.A.* **111** K10
Fort Kent *U.S.A.* **113** B19
Fort Klamath *U.S.A.* **108** D3
Fort Laramie *U.S.A.* **108** E11
Fort Lauderdale *U.S.A.* **117** H14
Fort Liard *Canada* **102** A4
Fort Liberté *Haiti* **121** C5
Fort Lupton *U.S.A.* **108** F11
Fort MacKay *Canada* **102** B6
Fort Macleod *Canada* **102** D6
Fort McMurray *Canada* **102** B6
Fort McPherson *Canada* **100** D5
Fort Madison *U.S.A.* **112** E8
Fort Meade *U.S.A.* **117** H14
Fort Morgan *U.S.A.* **108** F12
Fort Myers *U.S.A.* **117** H14
Fort Nelson *Canada* **102** B4
Fort Nelson → *Canada* **102** B4
Fort Norman = Tulita
  Canada **100** E6
Fort Payne *U.S.A.* **117** D12
Fort Peck *U.S.A.* **108** B10
Fort Peck Dam *U.S.A.* **108** C10
Fort Peck L. *U.S.A.* **108** C10
Fort Pierce *U.S.A.* **117** H14
Fort Pierre *U.S.A.* **112** C3
Fort Plain *U.S.A.* **115** D10
Fort Portal *Uganda* **86** B3
Fort Providence *Canada* **102** A5
Fort Qu'Appelle *Canada* **103** C8
Fort Resolution *Canada* **102** A6
Fort Rixon *Zimbabwe* **87** G2
Fort Ross *U.S.A.* **110** G3
Fort Rupert =
  Waskaganish *Canada* **104** B4
Fort St. James *Canada* **102** C4
Fort St. John *Canada* **102** B4
Fort Saskatchewan *Canada* **102** C6

Fort Scott *U.S.A.* **112** G6
Fort Severn *Canada* **104** A2
Fort Shevchenko *Kazakhstan* **35** H10
Fort Simpson *Canada* **102** A4
Fort Smith *Canada* **102** B6
Fort Smith *U.S.A.* **116** D7
Fort Stockton *U.S.A.* **116** F3
Fort Sumner *U.S.A.* **109** J11
Fort Thompson *U.S.A.* **112** C4
Fort Union △ *U.S.A.* **109** J11
Fort Valley *U.S.A.* **117** E13
Fort Vermilion *Canada* **102** B5
Fort Walton Beach *U.S.A.* **117** F11
Fort Ware *Canada* **102** B3
Fort Wayne *U.S.A.* **113** E11
Fort William *U.K.* **13** E3
Fort Worth *U.S.A.* **116** E6
Fort Yates *U.S.A.* **112** B3
Fort Yukon *U.S.A.* **100** D2
Fortaleza *Brazil* **125** D11
Forteau *Canada* **105** B8
Fortescue → *Australia* **92** D2
Fortescue River Roadhouse
  Australia **92** D2
Forth → *U.K.* **13** E5
Forth, Firth of *U.K.* **13** E6
Fortore → *Italy* **41** G12
Fortrose *U.K.* **13** D4
Fortuna *Spain* **39** G3
Fortuna *Calif., U.S.A.* **108** F1
Fortuna *N. Dak., U.S.A.* **112** A2
Fortune *Canada* **105** C8
Fortune B. *Canada* **105** C8
Forür *Iran* **71** E7
Fos-sur-Mer *France* **21** E8
Fosen *Norway* **8** E14
Foshan *China* **59** F9
Fossil *U.S.A.* **108** D3
Fossano *Italy* **40** D4
Fossil *U.S.A.* **108** D3
Fossil Butte △ *U.S.A.* **108** F8
Fossombrone *Italy* **41** E9
Foster *Australia* **95** A12
Foster → *Canada* **103** B7
Fosters Ra. *Australia* **94** C1
Fostoria *U.S.A.* **113** E12
Fotadrevo *Madag.* **89** C8
Fouesnant *France* **18** E2
Fougères *France* **18** D5
Foul Pt. *Sri Lanka* **66** Q12
Foula *U.K.* **13** A6
Foulness I. *U.K.* **15** F8
Foulpointe *Madag.* **89** B8
Fouman *Cameroon* **83** D7
Foumban *Cameroon* **83** D7
Foumbot *Cameroon* **83** D7
Foumbouni *Comoros Is.* **85** a
Foundiougne *Senegal* **82** C1
Fountain *U.S.A.* **108** G11
Fountain Hills *U.S.A.* **109** K8
Fountain Springs *U.S.A.* **111** K8
Four Mountains, Is. of
  U.S.A. **106** E5
Fourchambault *France* **19** E10
Fouriesburg *S. Africa* **88** D4
Fourmies *France* **19** B11
Fourna *Greece* **46** B3
Fourni *Greece* **47** D8
Fours *France* **19** F10
Fourth Cataract *Sudan* **79** E12
Fouta Djallon *Guinea* **82** C2
Foux, Cap-à- *Haiti* **121** C5
Foveaux Str. *N.Z.* **91** G2
Fowey *U.K.* **15** G3
Fowler *Calif., U.S.A.* **110** J7
Fowler *Colo., U.S.A.* **108** G11
Fowler, Pt. *Australia* **93** F5
Fowlers B. *Australia* **93** F5
Fowman *Iran* **73** D13
Fox → *Canada* **103** B10
Fox Creek *Canada* **102** C5
Fox Is. *U.S.A.* **106** E6
Fox Lake *Canada* **102** B6
Fox Valley *Canada* **103** C7
Foxboro *Canada* **114** B7
Foxboro *U.S.A.* **115** D13
Foxdale *Australia* **94** b
Foxe Basin *Canada* **101** D16
Foxe Chan. *Canada* **101** E16
Foxe Pen. *Canada* **101** E16
Foxen *Sweden* **10** E5
Foxford *Ireland* **12** C2
Foxton *N.Z.* **91** D5
Foyle, Lough *U.K.* **12** A4
Foynes *Ireland* **12** D2
Foz *Spain* **36** B3
Foz do Cunene *Angola* **88** B1
Foz do Iguaçu *Brazil* **127** B5
Frackville *U.S.A.* **115** F8
Fraga *Spain* **38** D5
Fraile Muerto *Uruguay* **127** C5
Framingham *U.S.A.* **115** D13
Frampol *Poland* **31** H9
Franca *Brazil* **125** H9
Francavilla al Mare *Italy* **41** F11
Francavilla Fontana *Italy* **43** B10
France ■ *Europe* **7** F6
Frances *Australia* **95** F3

Frances → *Canada* **102** A3
Frances L. *Canada* **102** A3
Franceville *Gabon* **84** E2
Franche-Comté □ *France* **19** F12
Francis Case, L. *U.S.A.* **112** D4
Francisco Beltrão *Brazil* **127** B5
Francisco Ignacio Madero
  Coahuila, Mexico **118** B4
Francisco Ignacio Madero
  Durango, Mexico **118** C4
Francisco Ignacio Madero,
  Presa *Mexico* **118** B3
Francistown *Botswana* **89** C4
Francofonte *Italy* **43** E7
François *Canada* **105** C8
François L. *Canada* **102** C3
Francois Peron △ *Australia* **93** E1
Francs Pk. *U.S.A.* **108** E9
Franeker *Neths.* **17** A5
Frank Hann △ *Australia* **93** F3
Frankenberg *Germany* **24** D4
Frankenhöhe △ *Germany* **25** F6
Frankenwald *Germany* **25** E7
Frankenwald △ *Germany* **25** E7
Frankford *Canada* **114** B7
Frankfort *S. Africa* **89** D4
Frankfort *Ind., U.S.A.* **112** E10
Frankfort *Kans., U.S.A.* **112** F5
Frankfort *Ky., U.S.A.* **113** F11
Frankfort *N.Y., U.S.A.* **115** C9
Frankfurt *Brandenburg,
  Germany* **24** C10
Frankfurt *Hessen, Germany* **25** E4
Frankfurt ✈ (FRA) *Germany* **25** E4
Fränkische Alb *Germany* **25** F7
Fränkische Rezat →
  Germany **25** F7
Fränkische Saale →
  Germany **25** E5
Fränkische Schweiz *Germany* **25** F7
Fränkische
  Schweiz-Veldensteiner
  Forst △ *Germany* **25** F7
Frankland → *Australia* **93** G2
Franklin *Ky., U.S.A.* **112** G10
Franklin *La., U.S.A.* **116** G9
Franklin *Mass., U.S.A.* **115** D13
Franklin *N.H., U.S.A.* **115** C13
Franklin *N.Y., U.S.A.* **115** D9
Franklin *Nebr., U.S.A.* **112** E4
Franklin *Pa., U.S.A.* **114** E5
Franklin *Va., U.S.A.* **113** G15
Franklin *W. Va., U.S.A.* **113** F14
Franklin B. *Canada* **100** D6
Franklin D. Roosevelt L.
  U.S.A. **108** B4
Franklin-Gordon Wild
  Rivers △ *Australia* **95** G4
Franklin I. *Antarctica* **5** D11
Franklin I. *Canada* **114** A4
Franklin L. *U.S.A.* **108** F6
Franklin Mts. *Canada* **100** D6
Franklin Str. *Canada* **100** C12
Franklinton *U.S.A.* **117** F9
Franklinville *U.S.A.* **114** D6
Frankston *Australia* **95** F4
Frånö *Sweden* **10** B11
Fransfontein *Namibia* **88** C2
Fränsta *Sweden* **10** B10
Frantsa Iosifa, Zemlya *Russia* **52** A6
Franz *Canada* **104** C3
Franz Josef Land = Frantsa
  Iosifa, Zemlya *Russia* **52** A6
Franz Josef Strauss ✈
  (MUC) *Germany* **25** G7
Franzburg *Germany* **24** A8
Frascati *Italy* **41** G9
Fraser *U.S.A.* **114** D2
Fraser → *B.C., Canada* **110** A3
Fraser → *Nfld. & L., Canada* **105** A7
Fraser, Mt. *Australia* **93** E2
Fraser I. *Australia* **95** D5
Fraser Lake *Canada* **102** C4
Fraserburg *S. Africa* **88** E3
Fraserburgh *U.K.* **13** D6
Fraserdale *Canada* **104** C3
Frashër *Albania* **44** F4
Frasne *France* **19** F13
Frătești *Romania* **29** G10
Frauenfeld *Switz.* **25** H4
Fray Bentos *Uruguay* **126** C4
Fray Jorge △ *Chile* **126** C1
Frechilla *Spain* **36** C6
Fredericia *Denmark* **11** J3
Frederick *Md., U.S.A.* **113** F15
Frederick *Okla., U.S.A.* **116** D5
Frederick *S. Dak., U.S.A.* **112** C4
Fredericksburg *Pa., U.S.A.* **115** F8
Fredericksburg *Tex., U.S.A.* **116** F5
Fredericksburg *Va., U.S.A.* **113** F15
Fredericktown *Mo., U.S.A.* **112** G8
Fredericktown *Ohio, U.S.A.* **114** F2
Frederico Westphalen *Brazil* **127** B5
Fredericton *Canada* **105** C6
Fredericton Junction *Canada* **105** C6
Frederikshåb = Paamiut
  Greenland **4** C5
Frederikshamn = Hamina
  Finland **32** B4

Frederikshavn *Denmark* 11 G4
Frederikssund *Denmark* 11 J6
Frederiksted *U.S. Virgin Is.* 121 C7
Frederiksværk *Denmark* 11 J6
Fredonia *Ariz., U.S.A.* 109 H7
Fredonia *Kans., U.S.A.* 112 G6
Fredonia *N.Y., U.S.A.* 114 D5
Fredriksberg *Sweden* 10 D8
Fredrikstad *Norway* 9 G14
Free State □ *S. Africa* 88 D4
Freehold *U.S.A.* 115 F10
Freeland *U.S.A.* 115 E9
Freels, C. *Nfld. & L., Canada* 105 C9
Freels, C. *Nfld. & L., Canada* 105 C9
Freeman *Calif., U.S.A.* 111 K9
Freeman *S. Dak., U.S.A.* 112 D5
Freeport *Bahamas* 120 A4
Freeport *Ill., U.S.A.* 112 D9
Freeport *N.Y., U.S.A.* 115 F11
Freeport *Ohio, U.S.A.* 114 F3
Freeport *Pa., U.S.A.* 114 F5
Freeport *Tex., U.S.A.* 116 G7
Freetown *S. Leone* 82 D2
Freeville *U.S.A.* 115 D8
Frégate, L. de la *Canada* 104 B5
Fregenal de la Sierra *Spain* 37 G4
Fregene *Italy* 41 G9
Fréhel, C. *France* 18 D4
Freiberg *Germany* 24 E9
Freibourg = Fribourg *Switz.* 25 J3
Freiburg *Baden-W., Germany* 25 H3
Freiburg *Niedersachsen,
  Germany* 24 B5
Freilassing *Germany* 25 H8
Freire *Chile* 128 D2
Freirina *Chile* 126 B1
Freising *Germany* 25 G7
Freistadt *Austria* 26 C7
Freital *Germany* 24 D9
Fréjus *France* 21 E10
Fremantle *Australia* 93 F2
Fremont *Calif., U.S.A.* 110 H4
Fremont *Mich., U.S.A.* 113 D11
Fremont *Nebr., U.S.A.* 112 E6
Fremont *Ohio, U.S.A.* 113 E12
Fremont → *U.S.A.* 108 G8
French Camp *U.S.A.* 110 H5
French Cays = Plana Cays
  Bahamas 121 B5
French Creek → *U.S.A.* 114 E5
French Frigate Shoals
  U.S.A. 107 L6
French Guiana ☑ *S. Amer.* 125 C8
French Polynesia ☑ *Pac. Oc.* 97 J13
Frenchman Cr. → *N. Amer.*
  108 B10
Frenchman Cr. → *U.S.A.* 112 E3
Frenštát pod Radhoštěm
  Czech Rep. 27 B11
Fresco *Ivory C.* 82 D3
Fresco → *Brazil* 125 E8
Freshfield, C. *Antarctica* 5 C10
Fresnay-sur-Sarthe *France* 18 D7
Fresnillo *Mexico* 118 C4
Fresno *U.S.A.* 110 J7
Fresno Alhándiga *Spain* 36 E5
Fresno Res. *U.S.A.* 108 B9
Freudenstadt *Germany* 25 G4
Frévent *France* 19 B9
Frew → *Australia* 94 C2
Frewsburg *U.S.A.* 114 D5
Freycinet △ *Australia* 95 G4
Freycinet Pen. *Australia* 95 G4
Freyming-Merlebach *France* 19 C13
Freyung *Germany* 25 G9
Fria *Guinea* 82 C2
Fria, C. *Namibia* 88 B1
Friant *U.S.A.* 110 J7
Frías *Argentina* 126 B2
Fribourg *Switz.* 25 J3
Fribourg □ *Switz.* 25 J3
Fridafors *Sweden* 11 H8
Friday Harbor *U.S.A.* 110 B3
Friedberg *Bayern, Germany* 25 G6
Friedberg *Hessen, Germany* 25 E4
Friedens *U.S.A.* 114 F6
Friedland *Germany* 24 B9
Friedrichshafen *Germany* 25 H5
Friedrichskoog *Germany* 24 A4
Friedrichstadt *Germany* 24 A5
Friendship *U.S.A.* 114 D6
Friesach *Austria* 26 E7
Friesack *Germany* 24 C8
Friesland □ *Neths.* 17 A5
Friesoythe *Germany* 24 B3
Frigate *Seychelles* 85 b
Friggesund *Sweden* 10 C10
Frillesås *Sweden* 11 G6
Frinnaryd *Sweden* 11 G8
Frio → *U.S.A.* 116 G5
Frio, C. *Brazil* 122 F6
Friol *Spain* 36 B3
Friona *U.S.A.* 116 D3
Fristad *Sweden* 11 G6
Fritch *U.S.A.* 116 D4
Fritsla *Sweden* 11 G6
Fritzlar *Germany* 24 D5
Friuli-Venézia Giulia □ *Italy* 41 B9

Frobisher B. *Canada* 101 E18
Frobisher Bay = Iqaluit
  Canada 101 E18
Frobisher L. *Canada* 103 B7
Frohavet *Norway* 8 E13
Frohnleiten *Austria* 26 D8
Frolovo *Russia* 34 F6
Frombork *Poland* 30 D6
Frome *U.K.* 15 F5
Frome → *U.K.* 15 G5
Frome, L. *Australia* 95 E2
Frómista *Spain* 36 C6
Front Range *U.S.A.* 107 G18
Front Royal *U.S.A.* 113 F14
Frontenac △ *Canada* 115 B8
Frontera *Canary Is.* 48 G2
Frontera *Mexico* 119 D6
Fronteras *Mexico* 118 A3
Frontignan *France* 20 E7
Frosinone *Italy* 42 A6
Frostburg *U.S.A.* 113 F14
Frostisen *Norway* 8 B17
Frouard *France* 19 D13
Frövi *Sweden* 10 E9
Frøya *Norway* 8 E13
Frumoasa *Romania* 29 D10
Frunze = Bishkek *Kyrgyzstan* 52 E8
Frunzivka *Ukraine* 29 C14
Fruška Gora *Serbia* 28 E4
Fruška Gora △ *Serbia* 44 A3
Frutal *Brazil* 125 H9
Frutigen *Switz.* 25 J3
Frýdek-Místek *Czech Rep.* 27 B11
Frýdlant *Czech Rep.* 26 A8
Fryeburg *U.S.A.* 115 B14
Fryvaldov = Jeseník
  Czech Rep. 27 A10
Fthiótida □ *Greece* 46 C4
Fu Jiang → *China* 58 C6
Fu Xian = Wafangdian
  China 57 E11
Fu Xian *China* 56 G5
Fu'an *China* 59 D12
Fubian *China* 58 B4
Fucécchio *Italy* 40 E7
Fucheng *China* 56 F9
Fuchou = Fuzhou *China* 59 D12
Fuchū *Japan* 55 G6
Fuchuan *China* 59 E8
Fuchun Jiang → *China* 59 B13
Fúcino, Piana del *Italy* 41 F10
Fuding *China* 59 D13
Fuencaliente *Canary Is.* 48 F2
Fuencaliente *Spain* 37 G6
Fuencaliente, Pta. *Canary Is.* 48 F2
Fuengirola *Spain* 37 J6
Fuenlabrada *Spain* 36 E7
Fuensalida *Spain* 36 E6
Fuente-Álamo *Spain* 39 G3
Fuente Álamo de Murcia
  Spain 39 H3
Fuente de Cantos *Spain* 37 G4
Fuente del Maestre *Spain* 37 G4
Fuente el Fresno *Spain* 37 F7
Fuente Obejuna *Spain* 37 G5
Fuente Palmera *Spain* 37 H5
Fuentes de Andalucía *Spain* 37 H5
Fuentes de Ebro *Spain* 38 D4
Fuentes de León *Spain* 37 G4
Fuentes de Oñoro *Spain* 36 E4
Fuentesaúco *Spain* 36 D5
Fuerte → *Mexico* 118 B3
Fuerte Olimpo *Paraguay* 126 A4
Fuerteventura *Canary Is.* 48 F6
Fuerteventura ✈ (FUE)
  Canary Is. 48 F6
Fufeng *China* 56 G5
Fuga I. *Phil.* 61 B4
Fugong *China* 58 D2
Fugou *China* 56 G8
Fugu *China* 56 E6
Fuhai *China* 60 B3
Fuḥaymī *Iraq* 73 E10
Fuhlsbüttel, Hamburg ✈
  (HAM) *Germany* 24 B5
Fuji *Japan* 55 G9
Fuji-Hakone-Izu △ *Japan* 55 G9
Fuji-San *Japan* 55 G9
Fuji-Yoshida *Japan* 55 G9
Fujian □ *China* 59 E12
Fujinomiya *Japan* 55 G9
Fujisawa *Japan* 55 G9
Fujiyama, Mt. = Fuji-San
  Japan 55 G9
Fukagawa *Japan* 54 C11
Fukien = Fujian □ *China* 59 E12
Fukuchiyama *Japan* 55 G7
Fukue-Shima *Japan* 55 H4
Fukui *Japan* 55 F8
Fukui □ *Japan* 55 G8
Fukuoka *Japan* 55 H5
Fukuoka □ *Japan* 55 H5
Fukushima *Japan* 54 F10
Fukushima □ *Japan* 54 F10
Fukuyama *Japan* 55 G6
Fulacunda *Guinea-Biss.* 82 C1
Fulaga *Fiji* 91 a
Fulda *Germany* 24 E5

Fulda → *Germany* 24 D5
Fulford Harbour *Canada* 110 B3
Fuliang *China* 59 C11
Fullerton *Calif., U.S.A.* 111 M9
Fullerton *Nebr., U.S.A.* 112 E5
Fullongquan *China* 57 B13
Fulöpszállás *Hungary* 28 D4
Fulton *Mo., U.S.A.* 112 F8
Fulton *N.Y., U.S.A.* 115 C8
Fulufjället *Sweden* 10 C6
Fulun → *Sweden* 10 C7
Fumay *France* 19 C11
Fumel *France* 20 D4
Fumin *China* 58 E4
Funabashi *Japan* 55 G10
Funafuti = Fongafale *Tuvalu* 90 B10
Funäsdalen *Sweden* 10 B6
Funchal *Madeira* 48 D3
Funchal ✈ (FNC) *Madeira* 48 D3
Fundación *Colombia* 124 A4
Fundão *Portugal* 36 E3
Fundong *Cameroon* 83 D7
Fundu Moldovei *Romania* 29 C10
Fundulea *Romania* 29 F11
Fundy, B. of *Canada* 105 D6
Fundy △ *Canada* 105 C6
Funhalouro *Mozam.* 89 C5
Funing *Hebei, China* 57 E10
Funing *Jiangsu, China* 57 H10
Funing *Yunnan, China* 58 F5
Funiu Shan *China* 56 H7
Funsi *Ghana* 82 C4
Funtua *Nigeria* 83 C6
Fuping *Hebei, China* 56 E8
Fuping *Shaanxi, China* 56 G5
Fuqing *China* 59 E12
Fuquan *China* 58 D6
Furano *Japan* 54 C11
Furat, Nahr al → *Asia* 70 D5
Fürg *Iran* 71 D7
Furmanov *Russia* 34 B5
Furnás *Spain* 48 B8
Furnas, Represa de *Brazil* 127 A6
Furneaux Group *Australia* 95 G4
Furqlus *Syria* 74 A6
Fürstenau *Germany* 24 C3
Fürstenberg *Germany* 24 B9
Fürstenfeld *Austria* 26 D9
Fürstenfeldbruck *Germany* 25 G7
Fürstenwalde *Germany* 24 C10
Fürth *Germany* 25 F6
Fürth im Wald *Germany* 25 F8
Furtwangen *Germany* 25 G4
Furudal *Sweden* 10 C9
Furukawa *Japan* 54 E10
Furulund *Sweden* 11 J7
Fusagasugá *Colombia* 124 C4
Fuscaldo *Italy* 43 C9
Fushan *Shandong, China* 57 F11
Fushan *Shanxi, China* 56 G6
Fushë Arrëz *Albania* 44 D4
Fushë Krujë *Albania* 44 E3
Fushun *Liaoning, China* 57 D12
Fushun *Sichuan, China* 58 C5
Fusong *China* 57 C14
Füssen *Germany* 25 H6
Fustic *Barbados* 121 g
Fusui *China* 58 F6
Futog *Serbia* 28 E4
Futuna *Wall. & F. Is.* 90 —
Fuwa *Egypt* 80 H7
Fuxian Hu *China* 58 E4
Fuxin *China* 57 C11
Fuyang *Anhui, China* 56 H8
Fuyang *Zhejiang, China* 59 B12
Fuyang He → *China* 56 E9
Fuying Dao *China* 59 D13
Fuyu *Heilongjiang, China* 53 E13
Fuyu *Jilin, China* 57 B13
Fuyuan *China* 58 E5
Füzesgyarmat *Hungary* 28 C6
Fuzhou = Linchuan *China* 59 D11
Fuzhou *China* 59 D12
Füzuli *Azerbaijan* 73 C12
Fylde *U.K.* 14 D5
Fyn *Denmark* 11 J4
Fyne, L. *U.K.* 13 F3
Fynshav *Denmark* 11 K3

G

Ga *Ghana* 82 D4
Gaalkacyo *Somali Rep.* 75 F4
Gaanda *Nigeria* 83 C7
Gabas → *France* 20 E3
Gabba *Australia* 94 a
Gabela *Angola* 84 G2
Gabès *Tunisia* 79 B8
Gabès, G. de *Tunisia* 79 B8
Gabgaba, W. → *Egypt* 80 C3
Gabia la Grande *Spain* 37 H7
Gabin *Poland* 31 F6
Gabon ■ *Africa* 84 E2
Gaborone *Botswana* 88 C4
Gabriels *U.S.A.* 115 B10
Gäbrik *Iran* 71 E8
Gabrovo *Bulgaria* 45 D9
Gacé *France* 18 D7
Gäch Sär *Iran* 71 B6

Gachsārān *Iran* 71 D6
Gacko *Bos.-H.* 44 C2
Gadag *India* 66 M9
Gadamai *Sudan* 81 D4
Gadap *Pakistan* 68 G2
Gadarwara *India* 69 H8
Gadebusch *Germany* 24 B7
Gadein *Sudan* 81 F2
Gadhada *India* 68 J4
Gádor, Sierra de *Spain* 37 J8
Gadra *Pakistan* 68 G4
Gadsden *U.S.A.* 117 D11
Gadwal *India* 66 L10
Gadyach = Hadyach *Ukraine* 33 G8
Găeşti *Romania* 29 F10
Gaeta *Italy* 42 A6
Gaeta, G. di *Italy* 42 A6
Gaffney *U.S.A.* 117 D14
Gafsa *Tunisia* 78 B7
Gagarawa *Nigeria* 83 C6
Gagaria *India* 68 G4
Gagarin *Russia* 32 E8
Găgăuzia □ *Moldova* 29 D13
Gaggenau *Germany* 25 G4
Gaghamni *Sudan* 81 E2
Gagino *Russia* 34 B7
Gagliano del Capo *Italy* 43 C11
Gagnef *Sweden* 10 D9
Gagnoa *Ivory C.* 82 D3
Gagnon *Canada* 105 B6
Gagnon, L. *Canada* 103 A6
Gagra *Georgia* 35 J5
Gahini *Rwanda* 86 C3
Gahmar *India* 69 G10
Gai Xian = Gaizhou *China* 57 D12
Gaidouronisi *Greece* 49 E7
Gail → *U.S.A.* 116 E4
Gail → *Austria* 26 E6
Gaillac *France* 20 E5
Gaillimh = Galway *Ireland* 12 C2
Gaillon *France* 18 C8
Gaines *U.S.A.* 114 E7
Gainesville *Fla., U.S.A.* 117 G13
Gainesville *Ga., U.S.A.* 117 D13
Gainesville *Mo., U.S.A.* 112 G7
Gainesville *Tex., U.S.A.* 116 E6
Gainsborough *U.K.* 14 D7
Gairdner, L. *Australia* 95 E2
Gairloch *U.K.* 13 D3
Gairloch, L. *U.K.* 13 D3
Gaizhou *China* 57 D12
Gaj *Croatia* 28 E2
Gaj → *Pakistan* 68 F2
Gakuch *Pakistan* 69 A5
Galâla, Gebel el *Egypt* 80 J8
Galán, Cerro *Argentina* 126 B2
Galana → *Kenya* 86 C5
Galanta *Slovak Rep.* 27 C10
Galápagar *Spain* 36 E7
Galápagos = Colón, Arch.
  de *Ecuador* 122 D1
Galapagos Fracture Zone
  Pac. Oc. 97 G17
Galapagos Rise *Pac. Oc.* 97 J18
Galashiels *U.K.* 13 F6
Galatas *Greece* 46 D5
Galateia *Cyprus* 49 D13
Galați *Romania* 29 E13
Galați □ *Romania* 29 E12
Galatia *Turkey* 72 C5
Galatina *Italy* 43 B11
Galátone *Italy* 43 B11
Galax *U.S.A.* 113 G13
Galaxidi *Greece* 46 C4
Galcaio = Gaalkacyo
  Somali Rep. 75 F4
Galdhøpiggen *Norway* 8 F13
Galeana *Chihuahua, Mexico* 118 A3
Galeana *Nuevo León, Mexico* 118 A3
Galegu *Sudan* 81 E4
Galela *Indonesia* 63 D7
Galeota Pt. *Trin. & Tob.* 125 K16
Galera *Spain* 39 H2
Galera Pt. *Trin. & Tob.* 121 D7
Galesburg *U.S.A.* 112 E9
Galestan △ *Iran* 71 B8
Galeton *U.S.A.* 114 E7
Galga → *Ethiopia* 81 F4
Gali *Georgia* 35 J5
Galicea Mare *Romania* 29 F8
Galich *Russia* 34 A6
Galiche *Bulgaria* 44 C7
Galicia □ *Spain* 36 C3
Galičica △ *Macedonia* 44 E4
Galilee = Hagalil *Israel* 74 C4
Galilee, L. *Australia* 94 C4
Galilee, Sea of = Yam
  Kinneret *Israel* 74 C4
Galim *Cameroon* 83 D7
Galina Pt. *Jamaica* 120 a
Galinoporni *Cyprus* 49 D13
Galion *U.S.A.* 114 F2
Galiuro Mts. *U.S.A.* 109 K8
Galiwinku *Australia* 94 A2
Gallâbât *Sudan* 81 E4
Gallan Hd. *U.K.* 13 C1
Gallarate *Italy* 40 C5
Gallatin *U.S.A.* 117 C11
Galle *Sri Lanka* 66 R12

Gállego → *Spain* 38 D4
Gallegos → *Argentina* 128 G3
Galletti *Italy* 81 F5
Galley Hd. *Ireland* 12 E3
Gallinas, Pta. *Colombia* 124 A4
Gallipoli = Gelibolu *Turkey* 45 F10
Gallípoli *Italy* 43 B10
Gallipolis *U.S.A.* 113 F12
Gällivare *Sweden* 8 C19
Gallneukirchen *Austria* 26 C7
Gällö *Sweden* 10 B9
Gallo, C. *Italy* 42 D6
Gallocanta, L. de *Spain* 38 E3
Galloo I. *U.S.A.* 115 C8
Galloway *U.K.* 13 G4
Galloway, Mull of *U.K.* 13 G4
Galloway △ *U.K.* 13 F4
Gallup *U.S.A.* 109 J9
Gallur *Spain* 38 D3
Galoya *Sri Lanka* 66 Q12
Galt *U.S.A.* 110 G5
Galten *Denmark* 11 H3
Galtür *Austria* 26 E3
Galty Mts. *Ireland* 12 D3
Galtymore *Ireland* 12 D3
Galugāh *Iran* 71 B7
Galva *U.S.A.* 112 E8
Galve de Sorbe *Spain* 38 D1
Gálvez *Argentina* 126 C3
Galveston *U.S.A.* 116 G7
Galveston B. *U.S.A.* 116 G7
Galway *Ireland* 12 C2
Galway □ *Ireland* 12 C2
Galway B. *Ireland* 12 C2
Gam → *Vietnam* 64 B5
Gamagōri *Japan* 55 G8
Gamari, L. *Ethiopia* 81 E5
Gamawa *Nigeria* 83 C7
Gamay *Phil.* 61 E6
Gambaga *Ghana* 83 C4
Gambat *Pakistan* 68 F3
Gambela *Ethiopia* 81 F3
Gambela △ *Ethiopia* 81 F3
Gambela Hizboch □ *Ethiopia* 81 F3
Gambhir → *India* 68 F6
Gambia ■ *W. Afr.* 82 C1
Gambia → *W. Afr.* 82 C1
Gambier, C. *Australia* 92 B5
Gambier, Îs. *French Polynesia* 97 K14
Gambier Is. *Australia* 95 F2
Gambo *Canada* 105 C9
Gamboli *Pakistan* 68 E3
Gamboma *Congo* 84 E3
Gamka → *S. Africa* 88 E3
Gamkab → *Namibia* 88 D2
Gamla Uppsala *Sweden* 10 E11
Gamlakarleby = Kokkola
  Finland 8 E20
Gamleby *Sweden* 11 G10
Gammon → *Canada* 103 C9
Gammon Ranges △ *Australia* 95 E2
Gamo-Gofa *Ethiopia* 81 F4
Gamou *Niger* 83 C6
Gamtoos → *S. Africa* 88 E4
Gan *France* 20 E3
Gan Goriama, Mts. *Cameroon* 83 D7
Gan Jiang → *China* 59 C11
Ganado *U.S.A.* 109 J9
Gananita *Sudan* 80 D3
Gananoque *Canada* 115 B8
Ganāveh *Iran* 71 D6
Gäncä *Azerbaijan* 35 K8
Gancheng *China* 64 C7
Gand = Gent *Belgium* 17 C3
Ganda *Angola* 85 G2
Gandajika
  Dem. Rep. of the Congo 84 F4
Gandak → *India* 69 G11
Gandava *Pakistan* 68 E2
Gander *Canada* 105 C9
Gander L. *Canada* 105 C9
Ganderkesee *Germany* 24 B4
Ganderowe Falls *Zimbabwe* 87 F2
Gandesa *Spain* 38 D5
Gandhi Sagar *India* 68 G6
Gandhinagar *India* 68 H5
Gandi *Nigeria* 83 C6
Gandia *Spain* 39 G4
Gandino *Italy* 40 C7
Gando, Pta. *Canary Is.* 48 G4
Gandole *Nigeria* 83 D7
Ganedidalem = Gani
  Indonesia 63 E7
Ganga → *India* 69 H14
Ganga Sagar *India* 69 J13
Gangafani *Mali* 82 C4
Gangan → *India* 69 E8
Ganganagar *India* 68 E5
Gangapur *India* 68 F7
Gangara *Niger* 83 C6
Gangaw *Burma* 67 H19
Gangdisê Shan *China* 69 D9
Ganges = Ganga → *India* 69 H14
Ganges *France* 20 E7
Ganges, Mouths of the *India* 69 J14

Ganggyeong *S. Korea* 57 F14
Gånghester *Sweden* 11 G7
Ganghwa *S. Korea* 57 F14
Gangi *Italy* 43 E7
Gângiova *Romania* 29 G8
Gangneung *S. Korea* 57 F15
Gangoh *India* 68 E7
Gangotri *India* 69 D8
Gangotri △ *India* 69 D8
Gangseong *S. Korea* 57 E15
Gangtok *India* 67 F16
Gangu *China* 56 G3
Gangyao *China* 57 B14
Ganluc *China* 58 C4
Gannat *France* 19 F10
Gannett Peak *U.S.A.* 108 E9
Ganquan *China* 56 F5
Gänserdorf *Austria* 27 C9
Ganshui *China* 58 C6
Gansu □ *China* 56 G3
Ganta *Liberia* 82 D3
Gantheaume, C. *Australia* 95 F2
Gantheaume B. *Australia* 93 E1
Gantsevichi = Hantsavichy
  Belarus 23 B14
Ganye *Nigeria* 83 D7
Ganyem = Genyem
  Indonesia 63 E10
Ganyu *China* 57 G10
Ganyushkino *Kazakhstan* 35 G9
Ganzhou *China* 59 E10
Gao *Mali* 83 B5
Gao Xian *China* 58 C5
Gao'an *China* 59 C10
Gaochun *China* 59 B12
Gaohe *China* 59 F9
Gaohebu *China* 59 B11
Gaolan Dao *China* 59 G9
Gaoligong Shan *China* 58 E2
Gaomi *China* 57 F10
Gaoping *China* 56 G7
Gaotang *China* 56 F9
Gaoua *Burkina Faso* 82 C4
Gaoual *Guinea* 82 C2
Gaoxiong = Kaohsiung
  Taiwan 59 F13
Gaoyang *China* 56 E8
Gaoyao *China* 59 F9
Gaoyou *China* 59 A12
Gaoyuan *China* 57 F10
Gaozhou *China* 59 G8
Gap *France* 21 D10
Gapan *Phil.* 61 D4
Gapat → *India* 69 G10
Gapuwiyak *Australia* 94 A2
Gar *China* 60 C2
Gara, L. *Ireland* 12 C3
Garáb *Iran* 73 F12
Garabogazköl Aylagy
  Turkmenistan 52 E6
Garachico *Canary Is.* 48 F3
Garachiné *Panama* 120 E4
Garafia *Canary Is.* 48 F2
Garagum *Turkmenistan* 71 B8
Garah *Australia* 95 D4
Garajonay *Canary Is.* 48 F2
Garamba △
  Dem. Rep. of the Congo 86 B2
Garango *Burkina Faso* 83 C4
Garanhuns *Brazil* 125 E11
Garautha *India* 69 G8
Garawa ☼ *Australia* 94 B2
Garawe *Liberia* 82 E3
Garba Tula *Kenya* 86 B4
Garberville *U.S.A.* 108 F2
Garbiyang *India* 69 D9
Garbsen *Germany* 24 C5
Gard □ *France* 21 D8
Gard → *France* 21 E8
Garda, L. di *Italy* 40 C7
Gardabani *Georgia* 35 K7
Gardanne *France* 21 E9
Gårdby *Sweden* 11 H10
Garde, L. *Canada* 103 A7
Gardelegen *Germany* 24 C7
Garden City *Ga., U.S.A.* 117 E14
Garden City *Kans., U.S.A.* 112 G3
Garden City *Tex., U.S.A.* 116 F4
Garden Grove *U.S.A.* 111 M9
Gardēz *Afghan.* 68 C3
Gardiki *Greece* 46 C3
Gardiner *Maine, U.S.A.* 113 C19
Gardiner *Mont., U.S.A.* 108 D8
Gardiners I. *U.S.A.* 115 E13
Gardner *U.S.A.* 115 D13
Gardner Canal *Canada* 102 C3
Gardner Pinnacles *U.S.A.* 107 L6
Gardnerville *U.S.A.* 110 G7
Gardno, Jezioro *Poland* 30 D4
Gardo = Qardho *Somali Rep.* 75 F4
Gardone Val Trómpia *Italy* 40 C7
Gárdony *Hungary* 28 C3
Gares = Puente la Reina
  Spain 38 C3
Garešnica *Croatia* 41 C13

Garéssio *Italy* **40** D5
Garey *U.S.A.* **111** L6
Garfield *U.S.A.* **108** C5
Garforth *U.K.* **14** D6
Gargaliani *Greece* **46** D3
Gargan, Mt. *France* **20** C5
Gargano △ *Italy* **41** G12
Gargantua, C. *Canada* **113** B11
Gargett *Australia* **94** b
Gargouna *Mali* **83** B5
Gargždai *Lithuania* **30** C8
Garibaldi △ *Canada* **102** D4
Gariep, L. *S. Africa* **88** E4
Garies *S. Africa* **88** E2
Garig Gunak Barlu △
    Australia **92** B5
Garigliano → *Italy* **42** A6
Garissa *Kenya* **86** C4
Garkida *Nigeria* **83** C7
Garko *Nigeria* **83** C6
Garland *Tex., U.S.A.* **116** E6
Garland *Utah, U.S.A.* **108** F7
Garlasco *Italy* **40** C5
Garliava *Lithuania* **30** D10
Garlin *France* **20** E3
Garmāb *Semnān, Iran* **71** C8
Garmāb *Zanjān, Iran* **73** E13
Garmisch-Partenkirchen
    Germany **25** H7
Garmsār *Iran* **71** C7
Garner *U.S.A.* **112** D7
Garnett *U.S.A.* **112** F6
Garo Hills *India* **69** G14
Garoe = Garoowe *Somali Rep.* **75** F4
Garonne → *France* **20** C3
Garonne, Canal Latéral à la
    France **20** D4
Garoowe *Somali Rep.* **75** F4
Garot *India* **68** G6
Garou, L. *Mali* **82** B4
Garoua *Cameroon* **83** D7
Garpenberg *Sweden* **10** D10
Garphyttan *Sweden* **10** E8
Garrauli *India* **69** G8
Garrel *Germany* **24** C4
Garrigues *France* **20** E7
Garrison *Mont., U.S.A.* **108** C7
Garrison *N. Dak. U.S.A.* **112** B3
Garrison Res. =
    Sakakawea, L. *U.S.A.* **112** B3
Garron Pt. *U.K.* **12** A6
Garrovillas de Alconétar
    Spain **37** F4
Garrucha *Spain* **39** H3
Garry → *U.K.* **13** E5
Garry, L. *Canada* **100** D11
Garrygala *Turkmenistan* **71** B8
Garsen *Kenya* **86** C5
Gärsnäs *Sweden* **11** J8
Garson L. *Canada* **103** B6
Garstang *U.K.* **14** D5
Gartempe → *France* **20** B4
Gartz *Germany* **24** B10
Garu *Ghana* **83** C4
Garu *India* **69** H11
Garub *Namibia* **88** D2
Garut *Indonesia* **63** G12
Garvão *Portugal* **37** H2
Garvie Mts. *N.Z.* **91** F2
Garwa = Garoua *Cameroon* **83** D7
Garwa *India* **69** G10
Garwolin *Poland* **31** G8
Gary *U.S.A.* **112** E10
Garzê *China* **58** B3
Garzón *Colombia* **124** C3
Gas-San *Japan* **54** E10
Gasan Kuli = Esenguly
    Turkmenistan **52** F6
Gascogne *France* **20** E4
Gascogne, G. de *Europe* **20** E2
Gascony = Gascogne *France* **20** E4
Gascoyne → *Australia* **93** D1
Gascoyne Junction *Australia* **93** E2
Gascueña *Spain* **38** E2
Gash, Wadi → *Africa* **81** D4
Gash Setit △ *Eritrea* **81** D4
Gashagar *Nigeria* **83** C7
Gashaka *Nigeria* **83** D7
Gashaka-Gumti △ *Nigeria* **83** D7
Gasherbrum *Pakistan* **69** B7
Gashua *Nigeria* **83** C7
Gasparillo *Trin. & Tob.* **125** K15
Gaspé *Canada* **105** C7
Gaspé, C. de *Canada* **105** C7
Gaspé Pen. = Gaspésie,
    Pén. de la *Canada* **105** C6
Gaspésie, Pén. de la *Canada* **105** C6
Gaspésie △ *Canada* **105** C6
Gassan *Burkina Faso* **82** C4
Gassol *Nigeria* **83** D7
Gasteiz = Vitoria-Gasteiz
    Spain **38** C2
Gastonia *U.S.A.* **117** D14
Gastouni *Greece* **46** D3
Gastouri *Greece* **46** B1
Gastre *Argentina* **128** E3
Gästrikland *Sweden* **10** D10
Gata, C. *Cyprus* **49** E12

Gata, C. de *Spain* **39** J2
Gata, Sierra de *Spain* **36** E4
Gataga → *Canada* **102** B3
Gătaia *Romania* **28** E6
Gatchina *Russia* **32** C6
Gatehouse of Fleet *U.K.* **13** G4
Gates *U.S.A.* **114** C7
Gateshead *U.K.* **14** C6
Gateshead I. *Canada* **100** C11
Gatesville *U.S.A.* **116** F6
Gateway △ *U.S.A.* **115** F11
Gaths *Zimbabwe* **87** G3
Gâtinais *France* **19** D9
Gatineau *Canada* **115** A9
Gatineau → *Canada* **104** C4
Gatineau △ *Canada* **104** C4
Gattaran *Phil.* **61** B4
Gattinara *Italy* **40** C5
Gatton *Australia* **95** D5
Gatún, L. *Panama* **120** E4
Gatwick, London ✈ (LGW)
    U.K. **15** F7
Gatyana *S. Africa* **89** E4
Gau *Fiji* **91** a
Gaucín *Spain* **37** J5
Gauer L. *Canada* **103** B9
Gauhati = Guwahati *India* **67** F17
Gauja → *Latvia* **30** A11
Gaujas △ *Latvia* **9** H21
Gaula → *Norway* **8** E14
Gauri Phanta *India* **69** E9
Gaustatoppen *Norway* **9** G13
Gauteng □ *S. Africa* **89** D4
Gāv Koshī *Iran* **71** D8
Gāvakān *Iran* **71** D7
Gavarnie *France* **20** F3
Gavāter *Iran* **71** E9
Gāvbandī *Iran* **71** E7
Gavdopoula *Greece* **49** E6
Gavdos *Greece* **49** E6
Gavi *Italy* **40** D5
Gaviota *U.S.A.* **111** L6
Gävkhūnī, Bāṭlāq-e *Iran* **71** C7
Gävle *Sweden* **10** D11
Gävleborgs län □ *Sweden* **10** C10
Gävlebukten *Sweden* **10** D11
Gavorrano *Italy* **40** F7
Gavray *France* **18** D5
Gavrilov Yam *Russia* **32** D10
Gavrio *Greece* **46** D6
Gawachab *Namibia* **88** D2
Gawilgarh Hills *India* **66** J10
Gawler *Australia* **95** E2
Gawler Ranges *Australia* **95** E2
Gawu *Nigeria* **83** D6
Gaxun Nur *China* **60** B5
Gaya *India* **69** G11
Gaya *Niger* **83** C5
Gaya *India* **83** C6
Gayéri *Burkina Faso* **83** C5
Gaylord *U.S.A.* **113** C11
Gayndah *Australia* **95** D5
Gaysin = Haysyn *Ukraine* **29** B14
Gayvoron = Hayvoron
    Ukraine **29** B14
Gaza *Gaza Strip* **74** D3
Gaza □ *Mozam.* **89** C5
Gaza Strip ■ *Asia* **74** D3
Gazanjyk = Bereket
    Turkmenistan **71** B7
Gazaoua *Niger* **83** C6
Gäzbor *Iran* **71** D8
Gazi *Dem. Rep. of the Congo* **86** B1
Gaziantep *Turkey* **72** D7
Gaziantep □ *Turkey* **72** D7
Gazimağusa = Famagusta
    Cyprus **49** D12
Gazipaşa *Turkey* **72** D5
Gbadolite
    Dem. Rep. of the Congo **84** D4
Gbarnga *Liberia* **82** D3
Gboko *Nigeria* **83** D6
Gbongan *Nigeria* **83** D5
Gcoverega *Botswana* **88** B3
Gcuwa *S. Africa* **89** E4
Gdańsk *Poland* **30** D5
Gdańsk ✈ (GDN) *Poland* **30** D5
Gdańska, Zatoka *Poland* **30** D6
Gdov *Russia* **32** C4
Gdynia *Poland* **30** D5
Geba → *Guinea-Biss.* **82** C1
Gebe *Indonesia* **63** D7
Gebeciler *Turkey* **47** C12
Gebeit Mine *Sudan* **80** C4
Gebel Abyad *Sudan* **80** D2
Gebel Iweibid *Egypt* **80** H8
Gebze *Turkey* **45** F13
Gecha *Ethiopia* **81** F4
Gedaref *Sudan* **81** E4
Gedaref □ *Sudan* **81** E4
Gediz *Turkey* **47** B11
Gediz → *Turkey* **47** C8
Gedo *Ethiopia* **81** F4
Gèdre *France* **20** F4
Gedser *Denmark* **11** K5
Gedung, Pulau *Malaysia* **65** c
Geegully Cr. → *Australia* **92** C3

Geel *Belgium* **17** C4
Geelong *Australia* **95** F3
Geelvink B. =
    Cenderwasih, Teluk
    Indonesia **63** E9
Geelvink Chan. *Australia* **93** E1
Geesthacht *Germany* **24** B6
Geidam *Nigeria* **83** C7
Geikie → *Canada* **103** B8
Geikie Gorge △ *Australia* **92** C4
Geilenkirchen *Germany* **24** E2
Geili *Sudan* **81** D3
Geisingen *Germany* **25** H4
Geislingen *Germany* **25** G5
Geistown *U.S.A.* **114** F6
Geita *Tanzania* **86** C3
Gejiu *China* **58** F4
Gel → *Sudan* **81** F2
Gel, Meydān-e *Iran* **71** D7
Gel River *Sudan* **81** F2
Gela *Italy* **43** E7
Gela, G. di *Italy* **43** F7
Gelahun *Liberia* **82** D2
Gelang Patah *Malaysia* **65** d
Gelderland □ *Neths.* **17** B6
Geldern *Germany* **24** D2
Geldrop *Neths.* **17** C5
Geleen *Neths.* **17** D5
Gelehun *S. Leone* **82** D2
Gelembe *Turkey* **47** B9
Gelemso *Ethiopia* **81** F5
Gelendost *Turkey* **72** C4
Gelendzhik *Russia* **33** K10
Gelib = Jilib *Somali Rep.* **75** G3
Gelibolu *Turkey* **45** F10
Gelibolu Yarımadası *Turkey* **45** F10
Gelidonya Burnu *Turkey* **72** D4
Gelnhausen *Germany* **25** E5
Gelnica *Slovak Rep.* **27** C13
Gelsenkirchen *Germany* **24** D3
Gelting *Germany* **24** A5
Geltügur *Malaysia* **65** c
Gemas *Malaysia* **65** L4
Gembloux *Belgium* **17** D4
Gembu *Nigeria* **83** D7
Gemena *Dem. Rep. of the Congo* **84** D3
Gemerek *Turkey* **72** C7
Gemla *Sweden* **11** H8
Gemlik *Turkey* **45** F13
Gemlik Körfezi *Turkey* **45** F12
Gemona del Friuli *Italy* **41** B10
Gemsa *Egypt* **80** B3
Gemsbok △ *Botswana* **88** D3
Gemünden *Germany* **25** E5
Genadi *Greece* **49** C9
Genale → *Ethiopia* **81** F4
Genç *Turkey* **73** C9
Gençay *France* **20** B4
Geneina, Gebel *Egypt* **80** B3
General Acha *Argentina* **126** D3
General Alvear *B. Aires,
    Argentina* **126** D4
General Alvear *Mendoza,
    Argentina* **126** D2
General Artigas *Paraguay* **126** B4
General Belgrano *Argentina* **126** D4
General Bernardo
    O'Higgins *Antarctica* **5** C18
General Cabrera *Argentina* **126** C3
General Cepeda *Mexico* **118** B4
General Guido *Argentina* **126** D4
General Juan Madariaga
    Argentina **126** D4
General La Madrid
    Argentina **126** D3
General MacArthur *Phil.* **61** F6
General Martin Miguel de
    Güemes *Argentina* **126** A3
General Pico *Argentina* **126** D3
General Pinedo *Argentina* **126** B3
General Pinto *Argentina* **126** C3
General Roca *Argentina* **128** D3
General Santos *Phil.* **61** H6
General Toshevo *Bulgaria* **45** C12
General Treviño *Mexico* **119** B5
General Trías *Mexico* **118** B3
General Viamonte *Argentina* **126** D3
General Villegas *Argentina* **126** D3
Genesee *Idaho, U.S.A.* **108** C5
Genesee *Pa., U.S.A.* **114** E7
Genesee → *U.S.A.* **114** C7
Geneseo *Ill., U.S.A.* **112** E8
Geneseo *N.Y., U.S.A.* **114** D7
Geneva = Genève *Switz.* **25** J2
Geneva *Ala., U.S.A.* **117** F12
Geneva *N.Y., U.S.A.* **114** D8
Geneva *Nebr., U.S.A.* **112** E5
Geneva *Ohio, U.S.A.* **114** E4
Geneva, L. = Léman, L.
    Europe **19** F13
Genève *Switz.* **25** J2
Gengenbach *Germany* **25** G4
Gengma *China* **58** F2
Genichesk = Henichesk
    Ukraine **33** J8
Genil → *Spain* **37** H5
Genisea *Greece* **45** E8
Genk *Belgium* **17** D5
Genlis *France* **19** E12

Gerokgak *Indonesia* **63** J17
Gennargentu, Mti. del *Italy* **42** B2
Gennes *France* **18** E6
Genoa = Génova *Italy* **40** D5
Genoa *Australia* **95** F4
Genoa N.Y., *U.S.A.* **115** D8
Genoa Nebr., *U.S.A.* **112** E5
Genoa Nev., *U.S.A.* **110** F7
Génova *Italy* **40** D5
Génova ✈ (GOA) *Italy* **40** D5
Génova, Gorge di *Italy* **40** D5
Genriyetty, Ostrov *Russia* **53** B16
Gent *Belgium* **17** C3
Genteng *Bali, Indonesia* **63** J17
Genteng *Jawa Barat,
    Indonesia* **63** G12
Genthin *Germany* **24** C8
Genyem *Indonesia* **63** E10
Genzano di Lucánia *Italy* **43** B9
Genzano di Roma *Italy* **41** G9
Geoagiu *Romania* **29** E8
Geochang *S. Korea* **57** G14
Geographe B. *Australia* **93** F2
Geographe Chan. *Australia* **93** D1
Geokchay = Göyçay
    Azerbaijan **35** K8
Georga, Zemlya *Russia* **52** A5
George → *S. Africa* **88** E3
George → *Canada* **105** A6
George, L. *N.S.W., Australia* **95** F4
George, L. *S. Austral., Australia* **95** F3
George, L. *W. Austral.,
    Australia* **92** D3
George, L. *Uganda* **86** B3
George, L. *Fla., U.S.A.* **117** G14
George, L. *N.Y., U.S.A.* **115** C11
George Gill Ra. *Australia* **92** D5
George Pt. *Australia* **94** b
George River =
    Kangiqsualujjuaq *Canada*
    101 F18
George Sound *N.Z.* **91** F1
George Town *Australia* **95** G4
George Town *Bahamas* **120** B4
George Town *Cayman Is.* **120** C3
George Town *Malaysia* **65** c
George V Land *Antarctica* **5** C10
George VI Sound *Antarctica* **5** D17
George West *U.S.A.* **116** G5
Georgetown = Janjanbureh
    Gambia **82** C2
Georgetown *Australia* **94** B3
Georgetown *Ont., Canada* **114** C5
Georgetown *P.E.I. Canada* **105** C7
Georgetown *Guyana* **124** B7
Georgetown *Calif., U.S.A.* **110** G6
Georgetown *Colo., U.S.A.* **108** G11
Georgetown *Ky., U.S.A.* **113** F11
Georgetown *N.Y., U.S.A.* **115** D9
Georgetown *Ohio, U.S.A.* **113** F12
Georgetown *S.C., U.S.A.* **117** E15
Georgetown *Tex., U.S.A.* **116** F6
Georgia □ *U.S.A.* **117** E13
Georgia ■ *Asia* **35** J6
Georgia, Str. of *N. Amer.* **110** A3
Georgia Basin *S. Amer.* **5** B4
Georgian B. *Canada* **114** A4
Georgian Bay Islands △
    Canada **114** B5
Georgíevka *Kazakhstan* **52** E9
Georgina → *Australia* **94** C2
Georgina I. *Canada* **114** B5
Georgioupoli *Greece* **49** D6
Georgiyevsk *Russia* **35** H6
Georgsmarienhütte *Germany* **24** C4
Gera *Germany* **24** E8
Geraardsbergen *Belgium* **17** D3
Geraki *Greece* **46** E4
Geral, Serra *Brazil* **127** B6
Geral de Goiás, Serra *Brazil* **125** F9
Geraldine *U.S.A.* **108** C8
Geraldton *Australia* **93** E1
Geraldton *Canada* **104** C2
Gérardmer *France* **19** D13
Gercüş *Turkey* **73** D9
Gerede *Turkey* **72** B5
Gerês, Sierra do *Portugal* **36** D3
Gereshk *Afghan.* **66** D4
Geretsried *Germany* **25** H7
Gérgal *Spain* **39** H2
Gerik *Malaysia* **65** K3
Gering *U.S.A.* **112** E2
Gerlach *U.S.A.* **108** F4
Gerlachovský štít
    Slovak Rep. **27** B13
German Bight = Deutsche
    Bucht *Germany* **24** A4
German Planina *Macedonia* **44** D6
Germansen Landing *Canada* **102** B4
Germantown *U.S.A.* **117** D10
Germany ■ *Europe* **24** E6
Germencik *Turkey* **47** D9
Germering *Germany* **25** G7
Germersheim *Germany* **25** F4
Germī *Iran* **73** C13
Germiston *S. Africa* **89** D4
Gernika-Lumo *Spain* **38** B2
Gernsheim *Germany* **25** F4
Gero *Japan* **55** G8

Giant Forest *U.S.A.* **110** J8
Giant Mts. = Krkonoše
    Czech Rep. **26** A8
Giant Sequoia △ *U.S.A.* **110** K3
Giants Causeway *U.K.* **12** A5
Gianyar *Indonesia* **63** K18
Giarabub = Al Jaghbūb
    Libya **79** C10
Giaros *Greece* **46** D6
Giarre *Italy* **43** E8
Giaveno *Italy* **40** C4
Gibara *Cuba* **120** B4
Gibbon *U.S.A.* **112** E4
Gibe → *Ethiopia* **81** F4
Gibellina Nuova *Italy* **42** E5
Gibeon *Namibia* **88** D2
Gibraleón *Spain* **37** H4
Gibraltar ☑ *Europe* **37** J5
Gibraltar, Str. of *Medit. S.* **37** K5
Gibraltar Range △ *Australia* **95** D5
Gibson Desert *Australia* **92** D4
Gibsons *Canada* **102** D4
Gibsonville *U.S.A.* **110** F6
Giddings *U.S.A.* **116** F6
Gidole *Ethiopia* **81** F4
Giebnegáisi = Kebnekaise
    Sweden **8** C18
Gien *France* **19** E9
Giengen *Germany* **25** G6
Giessen *Germany* **24** E4
Gīfān *Iran* **71** B8
Gifatin, Geziret *Egypt* **80** B3
Gifhorn *Germany* **24** C6
Gift Lake *Canada* **102** B5
Gifu *Japan* **55** G8
Gifu □ *Japan* **55** G8
Gigant *Russia* **35** G5
Giganta, Sa. de la *Mexico* **118** B2
Gigen *Bulgaria* **45** C8
Gigha *U.K.* **13** F3
Gíglio *Italy* **40** F7
Gignac *France* **20** E7
Güela → *Spain* **37** F7
Gijón *Spain* **36** B5
Gikongoro *Rwanda* **86** C2
Gil I. *Canada* **102** C3
Gila → *U.S.A.* **109** K6
Gila Bend *U.S.A.* **109** K7
Gila Bend Mts. *U.S.A.* **109** K7
Gila Cliff Dwellings △
    U.S.A. **109** K9
Gīlān □ *Iran* **71** B6
Gīlān-e Gharb *Iran* **73** E11
Gilău *Romania* **29** D8
Gilbert → *Australia* **94** B3
Gilbert Is. *Kiribati* **90** A10
Gilbert River *Australia* **94** B3
Gilbert Seamounts *Pac. Oc.* **4** D18
Gilead *U.S.A.* **115** B14
Gilf el Kebir, Hadabat el
    Egypt **80** C2
Gilford I. *Canada* **102** C3
Gilgandra *Australia* **95** E4
Gilgil *Kenya* **86** C4
Gilgit *India* **69** B6
Gilgit → *Pakistan* **69** B6
Gili △ *Mozam.* **87** F4
Gilima *Dem. Rep. of the Congo* **63** J-7
Giljeva Planina *Europe* **44** C3
Gillam *Canada* **103** B10
Gilleleje *Denmark* **11** H6
Gillen, L. *Australia* **93** E3
Gilles, L. *Australia* **95** E2
Gillette *U.S.A.* **108** D11
Gilliat *Australia* **94** C3
Gillingham *U.K.* **15** F8
Gilmer *U.S.A.* **116** E7
Gilmore, L. *Australia* **93** F3
Gilmour *Canada* **114** B7
Gilo → *Ethiopia* **81** F3
Gilort → *Romania* **29** F8
Gilroy *U.S.A.* **110** H5
Gimbi *Ethiopia* **81** F4
Gimcheon *S. Korea* **57** F15
Gimhae *S. Korea* **57** G15
Gimhwa *S. Korea* **57** E14
Gimie, Mt *St. Lucia* **121** f
Gimje *S. Korea* **57** G14
Gimli *Canada* **103** C9
Gimo *Sweden* **10** D12
Gimone → *France* **20** E4
Gimont *France* **20** E4
Gin Gin *Australia* **95** D5
Gināh *Egypt* **80** B3
Gingin *Australia* **93** F2
Gingindlovu *S. Africa* **89** D5
Ginir *Ethiopia* **81** F5
Ginosa *Italy* **43** B9
Ginzo de Limia = Xinzo de
    Limia *Spain* **36** C3
Giofyros → *Greece* **49** E7
Giohar = Jawhar *Somali Rep.* **75** G4
Gióia, G. di *Italy* **43** D8
Gióia del Colle *Italy* **43** B9
Gióia Táuro *Italy* **43** DE
Gioiosa Iónica *Italy* **43** D9
Gioiosa Marea *Italy* **43** D7

Giona, Oros *Greece* 46 C4
Giovi, Passo dei *Italy* 40 D5
Giovinazzo *Italy* 43 A9
Gir △ *India* 68 J4
Gir Hills *India* 68 J4
Girab *India* 68 F4
Girâfi, W. → *Egypt* 74 F3
Giraltovce *Slovak Rep.* 27 B14
Girard *St. Lucia* 121 D7
Girard *Kans., U.S.A.* 112 G6
Girard *Ohio, U.S.A.* 114 E4
Girard *Pa., U.S.A.* 114 E4
Girdle Ness *U.K.* 13 D6
Giresun *Turkey* 73 B8
Giresun □ *Turkey* 73 B8
Girga *Egypt* 80 B3
Giri → *India* 68 D7
Giridih *India* 69 G12
Girifalco *Italy* 43 D9
Giriftu *Kenya* 86 B4
Giriyondo *S. Africa* 89 C5
Girne = Kyrenia *Cyprus* 49 D12
Giro *Nigeria* 83 C5
Giromagny *France* 19 E13
Giron = Kiruna *Sweden* 8 C19
Girona *Spain* 38 D7
Girona □ *Spain* 38 D7
Gironde □ *France* 20 D3
Gironde → *France* 20 C2
Gironella *Spain* 38 C6
Girraween △ *Australia* 95 D5
Girringun △ *Australia* 94 B4
Giru *Australia* 94 B4
Girvan *U.K.* 13 F4
Gisborne *N.Z.* 91 C7
Gisenyi *Rwanda* 86 C2
Gislaved *Sweden* 11 G7
Gisors *France* 19 C8
Gitarama *Rwanda* 86 C2
Gitega *Burundi* 86 C2
Githio *Greece* 46 E4
Giuba = Juba → *Somali Rep.* 75 G3
Giugliano in Campania *Italy* 43 B7
Giulianova *Italy* 41 F10
Giura *Greece* 46 B6
Giurgeni *Romania* 29 F12
Giurgiu *Romania* 29 G10
Giurgiu □ *Romania* 29 F10
Giurgiuleşti *Moldova* 29 E13
Give *Denmark* 11 J3
Givet *France* 19 B11
Givors *France* 21 C8
Givry *France* 19 F11
Giyon *Ethiopia* 81 F4
Giza = El Gîza *Egypt* 80 J7
Giza Pyramids *Egypt* 80 J7
Gizab *Afghan.* 68 C1
Gizhiga *Russia* 53 C17
Gizhiginskaya Guba *Russia* 53 C16
Giżycko *Poland* 30 D8
Gizzeria *Italy* 43 D9
Gjalicë e Lumës, Mal. *Albania* 44 D4
Gjegjan *Albania* 44 E4
Gjirokastër *Albania* 44 F4
Gjoa Haven *Canada* 100 D12
Gjøvik *Norway* 8 F14
Gjuhës, Kep i *Albania* 44 F3
Glace Bay *Canada* 105 C8
Glacier △ *Canada* 102 C5
Glacier △ *U.S.A.* 108 B7
Glacier Bay *U.S.A.* 100 F4
Glacier Bay △ *U.S.A.* 102 B1
Glacier Peak *U.S.A.* 108 B3
Gladewater *U.S.A.* 116 E7
Gladstone *Queens., Australia* 94 C5
Gladstone *S. Austral., Australia* 95 E2
Gladstone *Canada* 103 C9
Gladstone *U.S.A.* 112 C10
Gladwin *U.S.A.* 113 D11
Glafsfjorden *Sweden* 10 E6
Glagah *Indonesia* 63 J17
Głogów Małopolski *Poland* 31 H8
Glåma = Glomma → *Norway* 9 G14
Gláma *Iceland* 8 D2
Glamis *U.S.A.* 111 N11
Glamoč *Bos.-H.* 41 D13
Glamorgan, Vale of □ *U.K.* 15 F4
Glamsbjerg *Denmark* 11 J4
Glarus *Switz.* 25 H5
Glarus □ *Switz.* 25 J5
Glasco *Kans., U.S.A.* 112 F5
Glasco *N.Y., U.S.A.* 115 D11
Glasgow *U.K.* 13 F4
Glasgow *Ky., U.S.A.* 113 G11
Glasgow *Mont., U.S.A.* 108 B10
Glasgow, City of □ *U.K.* 13 F4
Glasgow Int. ✈ (GLA) *U.K.* 13 F4
Glaslyn *Canada* 103 C7
Glastonbury *U.K.* 15 F5
Glastonbury *U.S.A.* 115 E12
Glauchau *Germany* 24 E8
Glava *Sweden* 10 E6
Glavice *Croatia* 41 E13
Glazov *Russia* 34 A11
Gleichen *Canada* 102 C6
Gleisdorf *Austria* 26 D8
Gleiwitz = Gliwice *Poland* 31 H5
Glen *U.S.A.* 115 B13

Glen Affric *U.K.* 13 D3
Glen Canyon *U.S.A.* 109 H8
Glen Canyon △ *U.S.A.* 109 H8
Glen Canyon Dam *U.S.A.* 109 H8
Glen Coe *U.K.* 13 E3
Glen Cove *U.S.A.* 115 F11
Glen Garry *U.K.* 13 D3
Glen Innes *Australia* 95 D5
Glen Lyon *U.S.A.* 115 E8
Glen Mor *U.K.* 13 D4
Glen More → *U.K.* 13 D5
Glen Moriston *U.K.* 13 D4
Glen Robertson *Canada* 115 A10
Glen Spean *U.K.* 13 E4
Glen Ullin *U.S.A.* 112 B3
Glénan, Îs. de *France* 18 E3
Glenariff *Ireland* 12 A5
Glenbeigh *Ireland* 12 D2
Glencoe *Canada* 114 D3
Glencoe *S. Africa* 89 D5
Glencoe *U.S.A.* 112 C6
Glencolumbkille *Ireland* 12 B3
Glendale *Ariz., U.S.A.* 109 K7
Glendale *Calif., U.S.A.* 111 L8
Glendale *Zimbabwe* 87 F3
Glendive *U.S.A.* 108 C11
Glendo *U.S.A.* 108 E11
Glenelg → *Australia* 95 F3
Glenfield *U.S.A.* 115 C9
Glengad Hd. *Ireland* 12 A4
Glengarriff *Ireland* 12 E2
Glenmont *U.S.A.* 114 F2
Glenmorgan *Australia* 95 D4
Glenn *U.S.A.* 110 F4
Glennallen *U.S.A.* 100 E2
Glennamaddy *Ireland* 12 C3
Glenns Ferry *U.S.A.* 108 E6
Glenora *Canada* 114 B7
Glenorchy *Australia* 95 G4
Glenore *Australia* 94 B3
Glenreagh *Australia* 95 E5
Glenrock *U.S.A.* 108 E11
Glenrothes *U.K.* 13 E5
Glens Falls *U.S.A.* 115 C11
Glenside *U.S.A.* 115 F9
Glenties *Ireland* 12 B3
Glenveagh △ *Ireland* 12 A3
Glenville *U.S.A.* 113 F13
Glenwood *Canada* 105 C9
Glenwood *Ark., U.S.A.* 116 D8
Glenwood *Iowa, U.S.A.* 112 E6
Glenwood *Minn., U.S.A.* 112 C6
Glenwood *Wash., U.S.A.* 110 D5
Glenwood Springs *U.S.A.* 108 G10
Glettinganes *Iceland* 8 D7
Glifada *Greece* 46 D5
Glimåkra *Sweden* 11 H8
Glin *Ireland* 12 D2
Glina *Croatia* 41 C13
Glinojeck *Poland* 31 F7
Gliwice *Poland* 31 H5
Globe *U.S.A.* 109 K8
Glodeanu Sililştea *Romania* 29 F11
Glodeni *Moldova* 29 C12
Glödnitz *Austria* 26 E7
Gloggnitz *Austria* 26 D8
Głogów *Poland* 31 G3
Głogówek *Poland* 31 H4
Glomma → *Norway* 9 G14
Glorieuses, Îs. *Ind. Oc.* 89 A8
Glosa *Greece* 46 B5
Glossop *U.K.* 14 D6
Gloucester *Australia* 95 E5
Gloucester *U.K.* 15 F5
Gloucester *U.S.A.* 115 D14
Gloucester I. *Australia* 94 b
Gloucester Island △ *Australia* 94 b
Gloucester Point *U.S.A.* 113 G15
Gloucestershire □ *U.K.* 15 F5
Gloversville *U.S.A.* 115 C10
Glovertown *Canada* 105 C9
Głowno *Poland* 31 G6
Glubczyce *Poland* 31 H4
Glubokiy *Russia* 35 F5
Glubokoye = Hlybokaye *Belarus* 32 E4
Głuchołazy *Poland* 31 H4
Glücksburg *Germany* 24 A5
Glückstadt *Germany* 24 B5
Glukhov = Hlukhiv *Ukraine* 33 G7
Glusk *Belarus* 23 B15
Głuszyca *Poland* 31 H3
Glyngøre *Denmark* 11 H2
Gmünd *Kärnten, Austria* 26 E6
Gmünd *Niederösterreich, Austria* 26 C8
Gmunden *Austria* 26 D6
Gnarp *Sweden* 10 B11
Gnesta *Sweden* 10 E11
Gniew *Poland* 30 E5
Gniewkowo *Poland* 31 F5
Gniezno *Poland* 31 F4
Gnjilane *Kosovo* 44 D5
Gnoien *Germany* 24 B8
Gnosjö *Sweden* 11 G7
Gnowangerup *Australia* 93 F2
Go Cong *Vietnam* 65 G6
Gô-no-ura *Japan* 55 H4
Goa *India* 66 M8

Goa □ *India* 66 M8
Goalen Hd. *Australia* 95 F5
Goalpara *India* 67 F17
Goaltor *India* 69 H12
Goalundo Ghat *Bangla.* 69 H13
Goaso *Ghana* 82 D4
Goat Fell *U.K.* 13 F3
Goba *Ethiopia* 81 F4
Goba *Mozam.* 89 D5
Gobabis *Namibia* 88 C2
Göbel *Turkey* 45 F12
Gobi *Asia* 56 C6
Gobō *Japan* 55 H7
Gobo *Sudan* 81 F3
Göçbeyli *Turkey* 47 B9
Goch *Germany* 24 D2
Gochas *Namibia* 88 C2
Godalming *U.K.* 15 F7
Godavari → *India* 67 L13
Godavari Pt. *India* 67 L13
Godbout *Canada* 105 C6
Godda *India* 69 G12
Godech *Bulgaria* 44 C7
Goderich *Canada* 114 C3
Goderville *France* 18 C7
Godfrey Ra. *Australia* 93 D2
Godhavn = Qeqertarsuaq *Greenland* 99 C14
Godhra *India* 68 H5
Gödöllő *Hungary* 28 C4
Godoy Cruz *Argentina* 126 C2
Gods → *Canada* 104 A1
Gods L. *Canada* 104 B1
Gods River *Canada* 103 C10
Godthåb = Nuuk *Greenland* 99 C14
Goeie Hoop, Kaap die = Good Hope, C. of *S. Africa* 88 E2
Goéland, L. au *Canada* 104 C4
Goélands, L. aux *Canada* 105 A7
Goeree *Neths.* 17 C3
Goes *Neths.* 17 C3
Goffstown *U.S.A.* 115 C13
Gogama *Canada* 104 C3
Gogebic, L. *U.S.A.* 112 B9
Goggetti *Ethiopia* 81 F4
Gogolin *Poland* 31 H5
Gogonou *Benin* 83 C5
Gogra = Ghaghara → *India* 69 G11
Gogriâl *Sudan* 81 F11
Gogti *Ethiopia* 81 E5
Gohana *India* 68 E7
Goharganj *India* 68 H7
Goi → *India* 68 H6
Goiânia *Brazil* 125 G9
Goiás *Brazil* 125 G8
Goiás □ *Brazil* 125 F9
Goio-Erê *Brazil* 127 A5
Góis *Portugal* 36 E2
Gojam *Ethiopia* 81 E4
Gojeb, Wabi → *Ethiopia* 81 F4
Gojō *Japan* 55 H7
Gojra *Pakistan* 68 D5
Gökçeada *Turkey* 45 F9
Gökçedağ *Turkey* 47 B10
Gökçen *Turkey* 47 C9
Gökçeören *Turkey* 47 C10
Gökçeyazı *Turkey* 47 B9
Gökırmak → *Turkey* 72 B6
Gökova *Turkey* 47 D10
Gökova Körfezi *Turkey* 47 E9
Göksu → *Turkey* 72 D6
Göksun *Turkey* 72 C7
Gokteik *Burma* 67 H20
Göktepe *Turkey* 47 D10
Gokurt *Pakistan* 68 E2
Gokwe *Zimbabwe* 89 B4
Gola *India* 69 E9
Golakganj *India* 69 F13
Golan Heights = Hagolan *Syria* 74 C4
Gołańcz *Poland* 31 F4
Goläshkerd *Iran* 71 E8
Golaya Pristen = Hola Pristan *Ukraine* 33 J7
Gölbaşı *Adıyaman, Turkey* 72 D7
Gölbaşı *Ankara, Turkey* 72 C5
Golchikha *Russia* 4 B12
Golconda *U.S.A.* 108 F5
Gölcük *Kocaeli, Turkey* 45 F13
Gölcük *Niğde, Turkey* 72 C6
Gold *U.S.A.* 114 E7
Gold Beach *U.S.A.* 108 E1
Gold Coast *W. Afr.* 83 E4
Gold Hill *U.S.A.* 108 E2
Gold River *Canada* 102 D3
Goldap *Poland* 30 D9
Goldberg *Germany* 24 B8
Golden *Canada* 102 C5
Golden B., N.Z. *N.Z.* 91 D4
Golden Gate *U.S.A.* 109 H2
Golden Gate Highlands △ *S. Africa* 89 D4
Golden Hinde *Canada* 102 D3
Golden Lake *Canada* 114 A7
Golden Spike △ *U.S.A.* 108 F7
Golden Vale *Ireland* 12 D3
Goldendale *U.S.A.* 108 D3
Goldfield *U.S.A.* 109 H5
Goldsand L. *Canada* 103 B8

Goldsboro *U.S.A.* 117 D16
Goldsmith *U.S.A.* 116 F3
Goldthwaite *U.S.A.* 116 F5
Golega *Portugal* 37 F2
Goleniów *Poland* 30 E1
Golestān □ *Iran* 71 B7
Golestānak *Iran* 71 D7
Goleta *U.S.A.* 111 L7
Golfito *Costa Rica* 120 E3
Golfo Aranci *Italy* 42 B2
Golfo di Orosei e del Gennargentu △ *Italy* 42 B2
Gölgeli Dağları *Turkey* 47 D10
Gölhisar *Turkey* 47 D11
Goliad *U.S.A.* 116 G6
Golija *Montenegro* 44 C2
Golija *Serbia* 44 C4
Golina *Poland* 31 F5
Gölköy *Turkey* 72 B7
Gölova *Turkey* 47 E12
Golpāyegān *Iran* 71 C6
Gölpazarı *Turkey* 72 B4
Golra *Pakistan* 68 C5
Golspie *U.K.* 13 D5
Golub-Dobrzyń *Poland* 31 E6
Golubac *Serbia* 44 B5
Golyam Perelik *Bulgaria* 45 E8
Golyama Kamchiya → *Bulgaria* 45 C11
Goma *Dem. Rep. of the Congo* 86 C2
Gomal Pass *Pakistan* 68 D3
Gomati → *India* 69 G10
Gombari *Dem. Rep. of the Congo* 86 B2
Gombe *Nigeria* 83 C7
Gombe → *Tanzania* 86 C3
Gombe □ *Nigeria* 83 C7
Gombe → *Tanzania* 86 C3
Gombe Stream △ *Tanzania* 86 C2
Gombi *Nigeria* 83 C7
Gomel = Homyel *Belarus* 23 B16
Gomera *Canary Is.* 48 F2
Gómez Palacio *Mexico* 118 B4
Gomfi *Greece* 46 B3
Gomīshān *Iran* 71 B7
Gommern *Germany* 24 C7
Gomogomo *Indonesia* 63 F8
Gomoh *India* 69 H12
Gomotartsi *Bulgaria* 44 B6
Gompa = Ganta *Liberia* 82 D3
Gonābād *Iran* 71 C8
Gonaïves *Haiti* 121 C5
Gonarezhou △ *Zimbabwe* 87 G3
Gonâve, G. de la *Haiti* 121 C5
Gonâve, Île de la *Haiti* 121 C5
Gonbad-e Kāvūs *Iran* 71 B7
Gönc *Hungary* 28 B6
Gonda *India* 69 F9
Gondal *India* 68 J4
Gonder *Ethiopia* 81 E4
Gondia *India* 66 J12
Gondola *Mozam.* 87 F3
Gondomar *Portugal* 36 D2
Gondrecourt-le-Château *France* 19 D12
Gönen *Balıkesir, Turkey* 45 F11
Gönen *Isparta, Turkey* 47 D12
Gönen → *Turkey* 45 F11
Gong Xian *China* 58 C5
Gong'an *China* 59 B9
Gongcheng *China* 59 E8
Gongga Shan *China* 58 C3
Gongguan *China* 58 G7
Gonghe *China* 60 C5
Gongju *S. Korea* 57 F14
Gongola → *Nigeria* 83 D7
Gongolgon *Australia* 95 E4
Gongshan *China* 58 D2
Gongtan *China* 58 C7
Gongzhuling *China* 57 C13
Goni *Greece* 46 B4
Goniadz *Poland* 30 E9
Goniri *Nigeria* 83 C7
Gonjo *China* 58 B2
Gonnesa *Italy* 42 C1
Gonnosfanádiga *Italy* 42 C1
Gonzaga *Phil.* 61 B5
Gonzales *Calif., U.S.A.* 110 J5
Gonzales *Tex., U.S.A.* 116 G6
González Mexico 119 C5
Good Hope, C. of *S. Africa* 88 E2
Good Hope Lake *Canada* 102 B3
Gooderham *Canada* 114 B6
Goodhouse *S. Africa* 88 D2
Gooding *U.S.A.* 108 E6
Goodland *U.S.A.* 112 F3
Goodlands *Mauritius* 85 d
Goodlow *Canada* 102 B4
Goodooga *Australia* 95 D4
Goodsprings *U.S.A.* 111 K11
Goole *U.K.* 14 D7
Goolgowi *Australia* 95 E4
Goomalling *Australia* 93 F2
Goomeri *Australia* 95 D5
Goonda *Mozam.* 87 F3
Goondiwindi *Australia* 95 D5

Goongarrie, L. *Australia* 93 F3
Goongarrie △ *Australia* 93 F3
Goonyella *Australia* 94 C4
Goose → *Canada* 105 B7
Goose Creek *U.S.A.* 117 E14
Goose L. *U.S.A.* 108 F3
Gop *India* 68 H3
Gopalganj *India* 69 F11
Göppingen *Germany* 25 G5
Gor *Spain* 37 H8
Góra *Dolnośląskie, Poland* 31 G3
Góra *Mazowieckie, Poland* 31 F7
Góra Kalwaria *Poland* 31 G8
Gorakhpur *India* 69 F10
Goražde *Bos.-H.* 28 G3
Gorbatov *Russia* 34 B6
Gorbea, Peña *Spain* 38 B2
Gorczański △ *Poland* 31 J7
Gorda, Pta. *Canary Is.* 48 F2
Gorda, Pta. *Nic.* 120 D3
Gordan B. *Australia* 92 B5
Gördes *Turkey* 47 C10
Gordon *U.S.A.* 112 D2
Gordon → *Australia* 95 G4
Gordon Bay *Canada* 114 A5
Gordon L. *Alta., Canada* 103 B6
Gordon L. *N.W.T., Canada* 102 A6
Gordonvale *Australia* 94 B4
Goré *Chad* 79 G9
Gore *Ethiopia* 81 F4
Gore *N.Z.* 91 G2
Gore Bay *Canada* 104 C3
Gorée, Île de *Senegal* 82 C1
Görele *Turkey* 73 B8
Goreme *Turkey* 72 C6
Gorey *Ireland* 12 D5
Gorg *Iran* 71 D8
Gorgān *Iran* 71 B7
Gorgol □ *Mauritania* 82 B2
Gorgona *Italy* 40 E6
Gorgona, I. *Colombia* 124 C3
Gorgora *Ethiopia* 81 E4
Gorgoram *Nigeria* 83 C7
Gorham *U.S.A.* 115 B13
Gori *Georgia* 35 J7
Goriganga → *India* 69 E9
Gorinchem *Neths.* 17 C4
Goris *Armenia* 73 C12
Goritsy *Russia* 32 D9
Gorízia *Italy* 41 C10
Gorj □ *Romania* 29 E8
Gorki = Horki *Belarus* 32 E6
Gorkiy = Nizhniy Novgorod *Russia* 34 B7
Gorkovskoye Vdkhr. *Russia* 34 B6
Gorleston *U.K.* 15 E9
Gorlice *Poland* 31 J8
Görlitz *Germany* 24 D10
Gorlovka = Horlivka *Ukraine* 33 H10
Gorman *U.S.A.* 111 L8
Gorna Dzhumayo = Blagoevgrad *Bulgaria* 44 D7
Gorna Oryakhovitsa *Bulgaria* 45 C9
Gornja Radgona *Slovenia* 41 B13
Gornja Tuzla *Bos.-H.* 28 F3
Gornji Grad *Slovenia* 41 B11
Gornji Milanovac *Serbia* 44 B4
Gornji Vakuf *Bos.-H.* 28 G2
Gorno Ablanovo *Bulgaria* 45 C9
Gorno-Altay □ *Russia* 52 D9
Gorno-Altaysk *Russia* 52 D9
Gornozavodsk *Russia* 53 E15
Gornyatskiy *Russia* 35 F5
Gornyy *Primorsk, Russia* 54 B6
Gornyy *Saratov, Russia* 34 E9
Gorodenka = Horodenka *Ukraine* 29 B10
Gorodets *Russia* 34 B6
Gorodishche = Horodyshche *Ukraine* 33 H6
Gorodishche *Russia* 34 D7
Gorodnya = Horodnya *Ukraine* 33 G6
Gorodok = Haradok *Belarus* 32 E6
Gorodok = Horodok *Ukraine* 23 D12
Gorodovikovsk *Russia* 35 G5
Gorokhov = Horokhiv *Ukraine* 23 C13
Gorokhovets *Russia* 34 B6
Gorom Gorom *Burkina Faso* 83 C4
Goromonzi *Zimbabwe* 87 F3
Gorong, Kepulauan *Indonesia* 63 E8
Gorongosa △ *Mozam.* 89 B5
Gorongose → *Mozam.* 89 C5
Gorongoza *Mozam.* 87 F3
Gorongoza, Sa. da *Mozam.* 87 F3
Gorontalo *Indonesia* 63 D6
Gorontalo □ *Indonesia* 63 D6
Goronyo *Nigeria* 83 C6
Gorron *France* 18 D6
Gorshechnoye *Russia* 33 G10
Gort *Ireland* 12 C3
Gortis *Greece* 49 D7
Góry Bystrzyckie *Poland* 31 H3
Goryachiy Klyuch *Russia* 35 H4
Goryeong *S. Korea* 57 G15

Gorzkowice *Poland* 31 G6
Górzno *Poland* 31 E6
Gorzów Śląski *Poland* 31 G5
Gorzów Wielkopolski *Poland* 31 F2
Gosford *Australia* 95 E5
Goshen *Calif., U.S.A.* 110 J7
Goshen *Ind., U.S.A.* 113 E11
Goshen *N.Y., U.S.A.* 115 E10
Goshogawara *Japan* 54 D10
Goslar *Germany* 24 D6
Gospić *Croatia* 41 D12
Gosport *U.K.* 15 G6
Gossas *Senegal* 82 C1
Gosse → *Australia* 94 B1
Gossi *Mali* 83 B4
Gossinga *Sudan* 81 F2
Gostivar *Macedonia* 44 E4
Gostyń *Poland* 31 G4
Gostynin *Poland* 31 F6
Göta älv → *Sweden* 11 G5
Göta kanal *Sweden* 11 F9
Götaland *Sweden* 11 G6
Göteborg *Sweden* 11 G5
Götene *Sweden* 11 F7
Gotești *Moldova* 29 D13
Gotha *Germany* 24 E6
Gothenburg = Göteborg *Sweden* 11 G5
Gothenburg *U.S.A.* 112 E3
Gothèye *Niger* 83 C5
Gotland *Sweden* 11 G12
Gotlands län □ *Sweden* 11 G12
Gotō-Rettō *Japan* 55 H4
Gotse Delchev *Bulgaria* 44 E7
Gotska Sandön *Sweden* 9 G18
Gõtsu *Japan* 55 G6
Góttero, Monte *Italy* 40 D6
Göttingen *Germany* 24 D5
Gottwald = Zmiyev *Ukraine* 33 H9
Gottwaldov = Zlín *Czech Rep.* 27 B10
Goubangzi *China* 57 D11
Gouda *Neths.* 17 B4
Goudiri *Senegal* 82 C2
Goudoumaria *Niger* 83 C7
Gouéké *Guinea* 82 D3
Gouin, Rés. *Canada* 104 C5
Gouitafla *Ivory C.* 82 D3
Goulburn *Australia* 95 E4
Goulburn Is. *Australia* 94 A1
Goulia *Ivory C.* 82 D3
Goulimine *Morocco* 78 C4
Goumbou *Mali* 82 C3
Goumenissa *Greece* 44 F6
Goundam *Mali* 82 B4
Goura *Greece* 46 D4
Gourbassi *Mali* 82 C2
Gourdon *France* 20 D5
Gouré *Niger* 83 C7
Gourin *France* 18 D3
Gourits → *S. Africa* 88 E3
Gourma-Rharous *Mali* 83 B4
Gournay-en-Bray *France* 19 C8
Gournes *Greece* 49 D7
Gourock *U.K.* 13 F4
Goursi *Burkina Faso* 82 C4
Gouverneur *U.S.A.* 115 B9
Gouvia *Greece* 49 A3
Gouzon *France* 19 F9
Gove Peninsula *Australia* 94 A2
Governador Valadares *Brazil* 125 G10
Governor's Harbour *Bahamas* 120 A4
Govindgarh *India* 69 G9
Gowan Ra. *Australia* 94 D4
Gowanda *U.S.A.* 114 D6
Gower *U.K.* 15 F3
Gowna, L. *Ireland* 12 C4
Goya *Argentina* 126 B4
Göyçay *Azerbaijan* 35 K8
Goyder Lagoon *Australia* 95 D2
Goyllarisquizga *Peru* 124 F3
Göynük *Antalya, Turkey* 47 E12
Göynük *Bolu, Turkey* 72 B4
Goz Beïda *Chad* 79 F10
Goz Regeb *Sudan* 81 D4
Gozdnica *Poland* 31 G2
Gozo *Malta* 49 C1
Graaff-Reinet *S. Africa* 88 E3
Grabo *Ivory C.* 82 D3
Grabow *Germany* 24 B7
Grabów nad Prosną *Poland* 31 G5
Gračac *Croatia* 41 D12
Gračanica *Bos.-H.* 28 F3
Graçay *France* 19 E8
Gracias a Dios, C. *Honduras* 120 D3
Graciosa *Azores* 78 a
Graciosa, I. *Canary Is.* 48 E6
Grad Sofiya □ *Bulgaria* 44 D7
Gradac *Montenegro* 44 C3
Gradačac *Bos.-H.* 28 F3
Gradeška Planina *Macedonia* 44 E6
Gradets *Bulgaria* 45 D10
Gradišče *Slovenia* 41 B12
Grădiştea de Munte *Romania* 29 E8
Grado *Italy* 41 C10
Grado *Spain* 36 B4

Grady *U.S.A.* **109** J12
Graeca, Lacul *Romania* **29** F11
Grafenau *Germany* **25** G9
Gräfenberg *Germany* **25** F7
Grafham Water *U.K.* **15** E7
Grafton *Australia* **95** D5
Grafton *N. Dak., U.S.A.* **112** A5
Grafton *W. Va., U.S.A.* **113** F13
Graham *Canada* **104** C1
Graham *U.S.A.* **116** E5
Graham, Mt. *U.S.A.* **109** K9
Graham Bell, Ostrov =
  Greem-Bell, Ostrov *Russia* **52** A7
Graham I. *B.C., Canada* **102** C2
Graham I. *Nunavut, Canada* **101** B13
Grahamstown *S. Africa* **88** E4
Grahamsville *U.S.A.* **115** E10
Grahovo *Montenegro* **44** D2
Graie, Alpi *Europe* **21** C11
Grain Coast *W. Afr.* **82** E3
Grajagan *Indonesia* **63** K17
Grajagan, Teluk *Indonesia* **63** K17
Grajaú *Brazil* **125** E9
Grajaú → *Brazil* **125** D10
Grajewo *Poland* **30** E9
Gramada *Bulgaria* **44** C6
Gramat *France* **20** D5
Grammichele *Italy* **43** E7
Grampian *U.S.A.* **114** F6
Grampian Highlands =
  Grampian Mts. *U.K.* **13** E5
Grampian Mts. *U.K.* **13** E5
Grampians, The *Australia* **95** F3
Gramsh *Albania* **44** F4
Gran Canaria *Canary Is.* **48** G4
Gran Chaco *S. Amer.* **126** B3
Gran Desierto del
  Pinacate △ *Mexico* **118** A2
Gran Paradiso *Italy* **40** C4
Gran Sasso d'Itália *Italy* **41** F10
Gran Sasso e Monti Della
  Laga △ *Italy* **41** F10
Granada *Nic.* **120** D2
Granada *Spain* **37** H7
Granada *U.S.A.* **108** G12
Granada □ *Spain* **37** H7
Granadilla de Abona
  Canary Is. **48** F3
Granard *Ireland* **12** C4
Granbury *U.S.A.* **116** E6
Granby *Canada* **115** A12
Granby *U.S.A.* **108** F11
Grand → *Canada* **114** D5
Grand → *Mo., U.S.A.* **112** F7
Grand → *S. Dak., U.S.A.* **112** C3
Grand Bahama I. *Bahamas* **120** A4
Grand Baie *Mauritius* **85** d
Grand Bank *Canada* **105** C8
Grand Bassam *Ivory C.* **82** D4
Grand Bend *Canada* **114** C3
Grand Béréby *Ivory C.* **82** E3
Grand-Bourg *Guadeloupe* **120** b
Grand Canal = Da
  Yunhe → *China* **57** E9
Grand Canyon *U.S.A.* **109** H7
Grand Canyon △ *U.S.A.* **109** H7
Grand Canyon-
  Parashant △ *U.S.A.* **109** H7
Grand Cayman *Cayman Is.* **120** C3
Grand Cess *Liberia* **82** E3
Grand Coulee *U.S.A.* **108** C4
Grand Coulee Dam *U.S.A.* **108** C4
Grand Erg de Bilma *Niger* **79** E8
Grand Falls *Canada* **105** C8
Grand Falls-Windsor *Canada* **105** C8
Grand Forks *Canada* **102** D5
Grand Forks *U.S.A.* **112** B5
Grand Gorge *U.S.A.* **115** D10
Grand Haven *U.S.A.* **112** D10
Grand I. *Mich., U.S.A.* **112** B10
Grand I. *N.Y., U.S.A.* **114** D6
Grand Island *U.S.A.* **112** E4
Grand Isle *La., U.S.A.* **117** G9
Grand Isle *Vt., U.S.A.* **115** B11
Grand Junction *U.S.A.* **108** G9
Grand L. *N.B., Canada* **105** C6
Grand L. *Nfld. & L., Canada* **105** C8
Grand L. *Nfld. & L., Canada* **105** B7
Grand L. *U.S.A.* **116** G8
Grand Lahou *Ivory C.* **82** D3
Grand Lake *U.S.A.* **108** F11
Grand-Lieu, L. de *France* **18** E5
Grand Manan I. *Canada* **105** D6
Grand Marais *Mich., U.S.A.* **113** B11
Grand Marais *Minn., U.S.A.* **104** C1
Grand-Mère *Canada* **104** C5
Grand Popo *Benin* **83** D5
Grand Portage *U.S.A.* **112** B9
Grand Prairie *U.S.A.* **116** E6
Grand Rapids *Canada* **103** C9
Grand Rapids *Mich., U.S.A.* **113** D11
Grand Rapids *Minn., U.S.A.* **112** B7
Grand St-Bernard, Col du
  Europe **25** K3
Grand Staircase-
  Escalante △ *U.S.A.* **109** H8
Grand Teton *U.S.A.* **108** E8

Grand Teton △ *U.S.A.* **108** E8
Grand Union Canal *U.K.* **15** E7
Grandas de Salime *Spain* **36** B4
Grande → *Jujuy, Argentina* **126** A2
Grande → *Mendoza,
  Argentina* **126** D2
Grande → *Bolivia* **124** G6
Grande → *Bahia, Brazil* **125** F10
Grande → *Minas Gerais,
  Brazil* **125** H8
Grande, B. *Argentina* **128** G3
Grande, Rio → *N. Amer.* **116** J6
Grande Anse *Seychelles* **85** b
Grande Baleine → *Canada* **104** A4
Grande Cache *Canada* **102** C5
Grande Casse, Pte. de la
  France **21** C10
Grande Comore *Comoros Is.* **85** a
Grande-Entrée *Canada* **105** C7
Grande Prairie *Canada* **102** B5
Grande-Rivière *Canada* **105** C7
Grande-Terre *Guadeloupe* **120** b
Grande-Vallée *Canada* **105** C6
Grande Vigie, Pte. de la
  Guadeloupe **120** b
Grandfalls *U.S.A.* **116** F3
Grândola *Portugal* **37** G2
Grandpré *France* **19** C11
Grands Causses △ *France* **20** D6
Grands-Jardins △ *Canada* **105** C5
Grandview *Canada* **103** C8
Grandview *U.S.A.* **108** C4
Grandvilliers *France* **19** C8
Graneros *Chile* **126** C1
Grangemouth *U.K.* **13** E5
Grangeville *U.S.A.* **108** D5
Granisle *Canada* **102** C3
Granite City *U.S.A.* **112** F8
Granite Falls *U.S.A.* **112** C6
Granite L. *Canada* **105** C8
Granite Mt. *U.S.A.* **111** M10
Granite Pk. *U.S.A.* **108** D9
Graniteville *U.S.A.* **115** B12
Granitola, C. *Italy* **42** E5
Granity *N.Z.* **91** D3
Granja *Brazil* **125** D10
Granja de Moreruela *Spain* **36** D5
Granja de Torrehermosa
  Spain **37** G5
Gränna *Sweden* **11** F8
Granollers *Spain* **38** D7
Gransee *Germany* **24** B9
Grant *U.S.A.* **112** E3
Grant, Mt. *U.S.A.* **108** G4
Grant City *U.S.A.* **112** E6
Grant I. *Australia* **92** B5
Grant Range *U.S.A.* **108** G6
Grantham *U.K.* **14** E7
Grantown-on-Spey *U.K.* **13** D5
Grants *U.S.A.* **109** J10
Grants Pass *U.S.A.* **108** E2
Grantsville *U.S.A.* **108** F7
Granville *France* **18** D5
Granville *N. Dak., U.S.A.* **112** A3
Granville *N.Y., U.S.A.* **115** C11
Granville *Ohio, U.S.A.* **114** F2
Granville L. *Canada* **103** B8
Graskop *S. Africa* **89** C5
Gräsö *Sweden* **10** D12
Grass → *Canada* **103** B9
Grass Range *U.S.A.* **108** C9
Grass River △ *Canada* **103** C8
Grass Valley *Calif., U.S.A.* **110** F6
Grass Valley *Oreg., U.S.A.* **108** D3
Grassano *Italy* **43** B9
Grasse *France* **21** E10
Grassflat *U.S.A.* **114** E6
Grasslands △ *Canada* **103** D7
Grassy *Australia* **95** G3
Gråsten *Denmark* **11** K3
Grästorp *Sweden* **11** F6
Gratkorn *Austria* **26** D8
Graubünden □ *Switz.* **25** J5
Graulhet *France* **20** E5
Graus *Spain* **38** C5
Grave, Pte. de *France* **20** C2
Gravelbourg *Canada* **103** D7
Gravelines *France* **19** A9
Gravenhurst *Canada* **114** B5
Gravesend *Australia* **95** D5
Gravesend *U.K.* **15** F8
Gravina in Púglia *Italy* **43** B9
Gravois, Pointe-à- *Haiti* **121** C5
Gravone → *France* **21** G12
Gray *France* **19** E12
Grayling *U.S.A.* **113** C11
Grays *U.K.* **15** F8
Grays Harbor *U.S.A.* **108** C1
Grays L. *U.S.A.* **108** E8
Grays River *U.S.A.* **110** D3
Grayvoron *Russia* **33** G8

Great Artesian Basin
  Australia **94** C3
Great Australian Bight
  Australia **93** F5
Great Bahama Bank
  Bahamas **120** B4
Great Barrier I. *N.Z.* **91** B5
Great Barrier Reef *Australia* **94** B4
Great Barrier Reef ○
  Australia **94** B4
Great Barrington *U.S.A.* **115** D11
Great Basalt Wall △ *Australia* **94** B4
Great Basin *U.S.A.* **108** G5
Great Basin △ *U.S.A.* **108** G6
Great Bear → *Canada* **100** E7
Great Bear L. *Canada* **100** D8
Great Belt = Store Bælt
  Denmark **11** J4
Great Bend *Kans., U.S.A.* **112** F4
Great Bend *Pa., U.S.A.* **115** E9
Great Blasket I. *Ireland* **12** D1
Great Britain *Europe* **6** E5
Great Camanoe *Br. Virgin Is.* **121** e
Great Codroy *Canada* **105** C8
Great Divide, The = Great
  Dividing Ra. *Australia* **94** C4
Great Divide Basin *U.S.A.* **108** E9
Great Dividing Ra. *Australia* **94** C4
Great Driffield = Driffield
  U.K. **14** C7
Great Exuma I. *Bahamas* **120** B4
Great Falls *U.S.A.* **108** C8
Great Fish = Groot-Vis →
  S. Africa **88** E4
Great Guana Cay *Bahamas* **120** B4
Great Himalayan △ *India* **68** D7
Great Inagua I. *Bahamas* **121** B5
Great Indian Desert = Thar
  Desert *India* **68** F5
Great Karoo *S. Africa* **88** E3
Great Khingan Mts. = Da
  Hinggan Ling *China* **60** B7
Great Lake *Australia* **95** G4
Great Lakes *N. Amer.* **98** E11
Great Limpopo
  Transfrontier △ *Africa* **89** C5
Great Malvern *U.K.* **15** E5
Great Miami → *U.S.A.* **113** F11
Great Ormes Head *U.K.* **14** D4
Great Ouse → *U.K.* **14** E8
Great Palm I. *Australia* **94** B4
Great Pedro Bluff *Jamaica* **120** a
Great Pee Dee → *U.S.A.* **117** E15
Great Plains *N. Amer.* **98** E9
Great Ruaha → *Tanzania* **86** D4
Great Sacandaga L. *U.S.A.* **115** C10
Great Saint Bernard Pass =
  Grand St-Bernard, Col du
  Europe **25** K3
Great Salt Desert = Kavīr,
  Dasht-e *Iran* **71** C7
Great Salt Desert = Lūt,
  Dasht-e *Iran* **71** D8
Great Salt L. *U.S.A.* **108** F7
Great Salt Lake Desert
  U.S.A. **108** F7
Great Salt Plains L. *U.S.A.* **116** C5
Great Sand Dunes △ *U.S.A.*
  109 H11
Great Sandy △ *Australia* **95** D5
Great Sandy Desert *Australia* **92** D3
Great Sangi = Sangihe,
  Pulau *Indonesia* **63** D7
Great Scarcies → *S. Leone* **82** D2
Great Sea Reef *Fiji* **91** a
Great Sitkin I. *U.S.A.* **106** E4
Great Skellig *Ireland* **12** E1
Great Slave L. *Canada* **102** A5
Great Smoky Mts. △ *U.S.A.*
  117 D13
Great Stour = Stour → *U.K.* **15** F9
Great Victoria Desert
  Australia **93** E4
Great Wall *Antarctica* **5** C18
Great Wall *China* **56** E5
Great Whernside *U.K.* **14** C6
Great Yarmouth *U.K.* **15** E9
Great Zab = Zāb al
  Kabīr → *Iraq* **73** D10
Great Zimbabwe *Zimbabwe* **87** G3
Greater Antilles *W. Indies* **121** C5
Greater London □ *U.K.* **15** F7
Greater Manchester □ *U.K.* **14** D5
Greater St. Lucia
  Wetlands △ *S. Africa* **89** D5
Greater Sudbury =
  Sudbury *Canada* **104** C3
Greater Sunda Is. *Indonesia* **62** F4
Grebbestad *Sweden* **11** F5
Grebenka = Hrebenka
  Ukraine **33** G7
Greco, C. *Cyprus* **49** E13
Greco, Mte. *Italy* **41** G10
Gredos, Sierra de *Spain* **36** E6
Greece □ *U.S.A.* **114** C7
Greece ■ *Europe* **46** B3
Greeley *Colo., U.S.A.* **108** F11
Greeley *Nebr., U.S.A.* **112** E4
Greely Fd. *Canada* **101** A15

Greem-Bell, Ostrov *Russia* **52** A7
Green → *Ky., U.S.A.* **112** G10
Green → *Utah, U.S.A.* **108** G9
Green B. *U.S.A.* **112** C10
Green Bay *U.S.A.* **112** C9
Green C. *Australia* **95** F5
Green Cove Springs *U.S.A.* **117** G14
Green I. = Lü Tao *Taiwan* **59** F13
Green Lake *Canada* **103** C7
Green Mts. *U.S.A.* **115** C12
Green River *Utah, U.S.A.* **108** G8
Green River *Wyo., U.S.A.* **108** F9
Green Valley *U.S.A.* **109** L8
Greenbank *U.S.A.* **110** B4
Greenbush *Mich., U.S.A.* **114** B1
Greenbush *Minn., U.S.A.* **112** A5
Greencastle *U.S.A.* **112** F10
Greene *U.S.A.* **115** D9
Greeneville *U.S.A.* **117** C13
Greenfield *Calif., U.S.A.* **110** J5
Greenfield *Calif., U.S.A.* **111** K8
Greenfield *Ind., U.S.A.* **113** F11
Greenfield *Iowa, U.S.A.* **112** E6
Greenfield *Mass., U.S.A.* **115** D12
Greenfield *Mo., U.S.A.* **112** G7
Greenfield Park *Canada* **115** A11
Greenland ☑ *N. Amer.* **99** C15
Greenland Sea *Arctic* **4** B7
Greenock *U.K.* **13** F4
Greenore *Ireland* **12** B5
Greenore Pt. *Ireland* **12** D5
Greenough → *Australia* **93** E1
Greenough Pt. *Canada* **114** B3
Greenport *U.S.A.* **115** E12
Greensboro *Ga., U.S.A.* **117** E13
Greensboro *N.C., U.S.A.* **117** C15
Greensburg *Ind., U.S.A.* **113** F11
Greensburg *Kans., U.S.A.* **112** G4
Greensburg *Pa., U.S.A.* **114** F5
Greenstone Pt. *U.K.* **13** D3
Greenvale *Australia* **94** B4
Greenville *Liberia* **82** D3
Greenville *Ala., U.S.A.* **117** F11
Greenville *Calif., U.S.A.* **110** E6
Greenville *Maine, U.S.A.* **113** C19
Greenville *Mich., U.S.A.* **113** D11
Greenville *Miss., U.S.A.* **117** E9
Greenville *Mo., U.S.A.* **112** G8
Greenville *N.C., U.S.A.* **117** D16
Greenville *N.H., U.S.A.* **115** D13
Greenville *N.Y., U.S.A.* **115** D10
Greenville *Ohio, U.S.A.* **113** E11
Greenville *Pa., U.S.A.* **114** E4
Greenville *S.C., U.S.A.* **117** D13
Greenville *Tex., U.S.A.* **116** E6
Greenwater Lake △ *Canada* **103** C8
Greenwich *Conn., U.S.A.* **115** E11
Greenwich *N.Y., U.S.A.* **115** C11
Greenwich *Ohio, U.S.A.* **114** E2
Greenwich □ *U.K.* **15** F8
Greenwood *Canada* **102** D5
Greenwood *Ark., U.S.A.* **116** D7
Greenwood *Ind., U.S.A.* **112** F10
Greenwood *Miss., U.S.A.* **117** E9
Greenwood *S.C., U.S.A.* **117** D13
Greenwood, Mt. *Australia* **92** B5
Gregbe *Ivory C.* **82** D3
Gregory *U.S.A.* **112** D4
Gregory → *Australia* **94** B2
Gregory, L. *S. Austral.,
  Australia* **95** D2
Gregory, L. *W. Austral.,
  Australia* **92** D4
Gregory, L. *W. Austral.,
  Australia* **93** E2
Gregory △ *Australia* **92** C5
Gregory Downs *Australia* **94** B2
Gregory Ra. *Queens., Australia* **94** B3
Gregory Ra. *W. Austral.,
  Australia* **92** D3
Greiffenberg *Germany* **24** B9
Greifswald *Germany* **24** A9
Greifswalder Bodden
  Germany **24** A9
Grein *Austria* **26** C7
Greiz *Germany* **24** E8
Gremikha *Russia* **52** C4
Grenaa *Denmark* **11** H4
Grenada *U.S.A.* **117** E10
Grenada ■ *W. Indies* **121** D7
Grenade *France* **20** E5
Grenadier I. *U.S.A.* **115** B8
Grenadines *W. Indies* **121** D7
Grenchen *Switz.* **25** H3
Grenen *Denmark* **11** G4
Grenfell *Australia* **95** E4
Grenfell *Canada* **103** C8
Grenoble *France* **21** C9
Grenville, C. *Australia* **94** A3
Grenville Chan. *Canada* **102** C3
Gresham *U.S.A.* **110** E4
Gresik *Indonesia* **63** G15
Gretna *U.K.* **13** F5
Gretna *U.S.A.* **117** G9
Greve Strand *Denmark* **11** J6
Greven *Germany* **24** C3

Grevena *Greece* **44** F5
Grevena □ *Greece* **44** F5
Grevenbroich *Germany* **24** D2
Grevenmacher *Lux.* **17** E6
Grevesmühlen *Germany* **24** B7
Grey → *Canada* **105** C8
Grey → *N.Z.* **91** E3
Grey, C. *Australia* **94** A2
Grey Is. *Canada* **101** G20
Grey Ra. *Australia* **95** D3
Greybull *U.S.A.* **108** D9
Greymouth *N.Z.* **91** E3
Greystones *Ireland* **12** C5
Greytown *N.Z.* **91** D5
Greytown *S. Africa* **89** D5
Gribanovskiy *Russia* **34** E5
Gribbell I. *Canada* **102** C3
Gribës, Mal i *Albania* **44** F3
Gridley *U.S.A.* **110** F5
Griekwastad *S. Africa* **88** D3
Griesheim *Germany* **25** F4
Grieskirchen *Austria* **26** C6
Griffin *U.S.A.* **117** E12
Griffith *Australia* **95** E4
Griffith *Canada* **114** A7
Griffith I. *Canada* **114** B4
Grignols *France* **20** D3
Grigoriopol *Moldova* **29** C14
Grimaylov = Hrymayliv
  Ukraine **23** D14
Grimes *U.S.A.* **110** F5
Grimma *Germany* **24** D8
Grimmen *Germany* **24** A9
Grimsay *U.K.* **13** D1
Grimsby *Canada* **114** D5
Grimsby *U.K.* **14** D7
Grímsey *Iceland* **8** C5
Grimshaw *Canada* **102** B5
Grimslöv *Sweden* **11** H8
Grimstad *Norway* **9** G13
Grindelwald *Switz.* **25** J4
Grindsted *Denmark* **11** J2
Grindu *Romania* **29** F11
Grinnell *U.S.A.* **112** E7
Grinnell Pen. *Canada* **101** E13
Grintavec *Slovenia* **41** B11
Gris-Nez, C. *France* **19** B8
Grise Fiord *Canada* **101** B15
Grisolles *France* **20** E5
Grisons = Graubünden □
  Switz. **25** J5
Grisslehamn *Sweden* **10** D12
Grmeč Planina *Bos.-H.* **41** D13
Groais I. *Canada* **105** B8
Grobina *Latvia* **30** B8
Groblersdal *S. Africa* **89** D4
Grobming *Austria* **26** D6
Grocka *Serbia* **44** B4
Gródek *Poland* **31** E10
Grodków *Poland* **31** G7
Grodno = Hrodna *Belarus* **30** E10
Grodzisk Mazowiecki *Poland* **31** F7
Grodzisk Wielkopolski
  Poland **31** F3
Grodzyanka = Hrodzyanka
  Belarus **23** B15
Groesbeck *U.S.A.* **116** F6
Groix *France* **18** E3
Groix, Î. de *France* **18** E3
Grójec *Poland* **31** G7
Gronau *Niedersachsen,
  Germany* **24** C5
Gronau *Nordrhein-Westfalen,
  Germany* **24** C3
Grong *Norway* **8** D15
Grönhögen *Sweden* **11** H10
Groningen *Neths.* **17** A6
Groningen □ *Neths.* **17** A6
Groom *U.S.A.* **116** D4
Groot → *S. Africa* **88** E3
Groot-Berg → *S. Africa* **88** E2
Groot-Brakrivier *S. Africa* **88** E3
Groot Karasberge *Namibia* **88** D2
Groot-Kei → *S. Africa* **89** E4
Groot-Vis → *S. Africa* **88** E4
Grootdrink *S. Africa* **88** D3
Groote Eylandt *Australia* **94** A2
Grootfontein *Namibia* **88** B2
Grootlaagte → *Africa* **88** C3
Grootvloer → *S. Africa* **88** E3
Gros C. *Canada* **102** A6
Gros Islet *St. Lucia* **121** f
Gros Morne △ *Canada* **105** C8
Gros Piton *St. Lucia* **121** f
Gros Piton Pt. *St. Lucia* **121** f
Grósio *Italy* **40** B7
Grosne → *France* **19** F11
Grossa, Pta. *Spain* **48** B8
Grosse Point *U.S.A.* **114** D2
Grossenbrode *Germany* **24** A7
Grossenhain *Germany* **24** D9
Grosser Arber *Germany* **25** F9
Grosser Plöner See *Germany* **24** A6
Grosseto *Italy* **41** F8
Grossgerungs *Austria* **26** C7
Grossglockner *Austria* **26** D5
Groswater B. *Canada* **105** B8
Groton *Conn., U.S.A.* **115** E12
Groton *N.Y., U.S.A.* **115** D8

Groton *S. Dak., U.S.A.* **112** C4
Grottáglie *Italy* **43** B10
Grottaminarda *Italy* **43** A8
Grottammare *Italy* **41** F10
Grouard Mission *Canada* **102** B5
Grouin, Pte. du *France* **18** D5
Groundhog → *Canada* **104** C3
Grouw *Neths.* **17** A5
Grove City *U.S.A.* **114** E4
Grove Hill *U.S.A.* **117** F11
Groveland *U.S.A.* **110** H6
Grover Beach *U.S.A.* **111** K6
Groves *U.S.A.* **116** G8
Groveton *U.S.A.* **115** B13
Grožnjan *Croatia* **41** C10
Groznyy *Russia* **35** J7
Grubišno Polje *Croatia* **28** E2
Grudovo *Bulgaria* **45** D11
Grudusk *Poland* **31** E7
Grudziądz *Poland* **30** E5
Gruinard B. *U.K.* **13** D3
Gruissan *France* **20** E7
Grumo Áppula *Italy* **43** A9
Grums *Sweden* **10** E7
Grünberg *Germany* **24** E4
Gründau *Germany* **25** E5
Grundy Center *U.S.A.* **112** D7
Grünstadt *Germany* **25** F4
Gruppo di Tessa △ *Italy* **40** B8
Gruver *U.S.A.* **116** C4
Gruyères *Switz.* **25** J3
Gruža *Serbia* **44** C4
Gryazi *Russia* **33** F10
Gryazovets *Russia* **32** C11
Grybów *Poland* **31** J7
Grycksbo *Sweden* **10** D9
Gryfice *Poland* **30** E2
Gryfino *Poland* **31** E1
Gryfów Śląski *Poland* **31** G2
Grythyttan *Sweden* **10** E8
Grytviken *S. Georgia* **128** G9
Gstaad *Switz.* **25** J3
Gua *India* **69** H11
Gua Musang *Malaysia* **65** K3
Guacanayabo, G. de *Cuba* **120** B4
Guachipas → *Argentina* **126** B2
Guadajoz → *Spain* **37** H6
Guadalajara *Mexico* **118** C4
Guadalajara *Spain* **38** E1
Guadalajara □ *Spain* **38** E2
Guadalcanal *Solomon Is.* **90** B9
Guadalcanal *Spain* **37** G5
Guadalén → *Spain* **37** G7
Guadales *Argentina* **126** C2
Guadalete → *Spain* **37** J4
Guadalimar → *Spain* **37** G7
Guadalmena → *Spain* **37** G8
Guadalmez → *Spain* **37** G5
Guadalope → *Spain* **38** D4
Guadalquivir → *Spain* **37** J4
Guadalupe =
  Guadeloupe ☑ *W. Indies* **120** b
Guadalupe *Mexico* **118** C4
Guadalupe *Spain* **37** F5
Guadalupe *U.S.A.* **111** L6
Guadalupe → *U.S.A.* **116** G6
Guadalupe, Sierra de *Spain* **37** F5
Guadalupe Bravos *Mexico* **118** A3
Guadalupe I. *Pac. Oc.* **98** G8
Guadalupe Mts. △ *U.S.A.* **116** F2
Guadalupe Peak *U.S.A.* **116** F2
Guadalupe y Calvo *Mexico* **118** B3
Guadarrama, Sierra de *Spain* **36** E7
Guadeloupe ☑ *W. Indies* **120** b
Guadeloupe △ *Guadeloupe* **120** b
Guadeloupe Passage
  W. Indies **121** C7
Guadiamar → *Spain* **37** J4
Guadiana → *Portugal* **37** H3
Guadiana Menor → *Spain* **37** H7
Guadiaro → *Spain* **37** J5
Guadiato → *Spain* **37** H5
Guadiela → *Spain* **38** E2
Guadix *Spain* **37** H7
Guafo, Boca del *Chile* **128** E2
Guaico *Trin. & Tob.* **125** K15
Guainía → *Colombia* **124** C5
Guaíra *Brazil* **127** A5
Guaíra □ *Paraguay* **126** B4
Guaire = Gorey *Ireland* **12** D5
Guaitecas, Is. *Chile* **128** E2
Guajará-Mirim *Brazil* **124** F5
Guajira, Pen. de la *Colombia* **124** A4
Gualán *Guatemala* **120** C2
Gualdo Tadino *Italy* **41** E9
Gualeguay *Argentina* **126** C4
Gualeguay → *Argentina* **126** C4
Gualeguaychú *Argentina* **126** C4
Gualequay → *Argentina* **126** C4
Guam ☑ *Pac. Oc.* **96** F6
Guamini *Argentina* **126** D3
Guamúchil *Mexico* **118** B3
Guana I. *Br. Virgin Is.* **121** e
Guanabacoa *Cuba* **120** B3
Guanacaste, Cordillera de
  Costa Rica **120** D2
Guanacaste △ *Costa Rica* **120** D2
Guanaceví *Mexico* **118** B3
Guanahani = San Salvador
  I. *Bahamas* **121** B5

Guanaja *Honduras* **120 C2**
Guanajay *Cuba* **120 B3**
Guanajuato *Mexico* **118 C4**
Guanajuato □ *Mexico* **118 C4**
Guandacol *Argentina* **126 B2**
Guane *Cuba* **120 B3**
Guang'an *China* **58 B6**
Guangchang *China* **59 D11**
Guangde *China* **59 B12**
Guangdong □ *China* **59 F9**
Guangfeng *China* **59 C12**
Guanghan *China* **58 B5**
Guangling *China* **56 E8**
Guangnan *China* **58 E5**
Guangning *China* **59 F9**
Guangrao *China* **57 F10**
Guangshui *China* **59 B9**
Guangshun *China* **58 D6**
Guangwu *China* **56 F3**
Guangxi Zhuangzu
    Zizhiqu □ *China* **58 F7**
Guangyuan *China* **58 A5**
Guangze *China* **59 D11**
Guangzhou *China* **59 F9**
Guanica *Puerto Rico* **121 d**
Guanipa → *Venezuela* **124 B6**
Guanling *China* **58 E5**
Guannan *China* **57 G10**
Guantánamo *Cuba* **121 B4**
Guantánamo B. *Cuba* **121 C4**
Guantao *China* **56 F8**
Guanyang *China* **59 E8**
Guanyun *China* **57 G10**
Guapay = Grande →
    Bolivia **124 G6**
Guápiles *Costa Rica* **120 D3**
Guapo B. *Trin. & Tob.* **125 K15**
Guaporé *Brazil* **127 B5**
Guaporé → *Brazil* **124 F5**
Guaqui *Bolivia* **124 G5**
Guara, Sierra de *Spain* **38 C4**
Guaramacal △ *Venezuela* **121 E5**
Guarapari *Brazil* **127 A7**
Guarapuava *Brazil* **127 B5**
Guaratinguetá *Brazil* **127 A6**
Guaratuba *Brazil* **127 B6**
Guarda *Portugal* **36 E3**
Guarda □ *Portugal* **36 E3**
Guardafui, C. = Asir, Ras
    Somali Rep. **75 E5**
Guardamar del Segura *Spain* **39 G4**
Guardavalle *Italy* **43 D9**
Guárdia Sanframondi *Italy* **43 A7**
Guardo *Spain* **36 C6**
Guareña *Spain* **37 G4**
Guareña → *Spain* **36 D5**
Guárico □ *Venezuela* **124 B5**
Guarujá *Brazil* **127 A6**
Guarulhos *Brazil* **127 A6**
Guasave *Mexico* **118 B3**
Guasdualito *Venezuela* **124 B4**
Guastalla *Italy* **40 D7**
Guatemala *Guatemala* **120 D1**
Guatemala ■ *Cent. Amer.* **120 C1**
Guatemala Basin *Pac. Oc.* **97 F18**
Guatemala Trench *Pac. Oc.* **98 H10**
Guatopo △ *Venezuela* **121 D6**
Guatuaro Pt. *Trin. & Tob.* **125 K16**
Guaviare → *Colombia* **124 C5**
Guaxupé *Brazil* **127 A6**
Guayaguayare *Trin. & Tob.* **125 K15**
Guayama *Puerto Rico* **121 d**
Guayaquil *Ecuador* **124 D2**
Guayaquil *Mexico* **118 B1**
Guayaquil, G. de *Ecuador* **124 D2**
Guaymas *Mexico* **118 B2**
Guba *Dem. Rep. of the Congo* **87 E2**
Guba *Ethiopia* **81 E4**
Gûbâl, Madîq *Egypt* **80 B3**
Gubat *Phil.* **61 E6**
Gúbbio *Italy* **41 E9**
Guben *Germany* **24 D10**
Gubin *Poland* **31 G1**
Gubio *Nigeria* **83 C7**
Gubkin *Russia* **33 G9**
Gubkinskiy *Russia* **52 C8**
Guča *Serbia* **44 C4**
Gucheng *China* **59 A8**
Gudauta *Georgia* **35 J5**
Gudbrandsdalen *Norway* **8 F14**
Guddu Barrage *Pakistan* **68 E3**
Gudená → *Denmark* **11 H4**
Gudermes *Russia* **35 J8**
Gudhjem *Denmark* **11 J8**
Gudur *India* **66 M11**
Guebwiller *France* **19 E14**
Guecho = Getxo *Spain* **38 B2**
Guékédou *Guinea* **82 D2**
Guéle Mendouka *Cameroon* **83 E7**
Guelmine = Goulimine
    Morocco **78 C3**
Guelph *Canada* **114 C4**
Guémené-Penfao *France* **18 E5**
Guémené-sur-Scorff *France* **18 D3**
Guéné *Benin* **83 C5**
Guer *France* **18 E4**
Guérande *France* **18 E4**
Guérara *Algeria* **78 B6**

Guéret *France* **19 F8**
Guérigny *France* **19 E10**
Guerneville *U.S.A.* **110 G4**
Guernica = Gernika-Lumo
    Spain **38 B2**
Guernsey *U.K.* **15 H5**
Guernsey *U.S.A.* **108 E11**
Guerrero □ *Mexico* **119 D5**
Guessou-Sud *Benin* **83 C5**
Gueugnon *France* **19 F11**
Guéyo *Ivory C.* **82 D3**
Gughe *Ethiopia* **81 F4**
Gügher *Iran* **71 D8**
Guglionesi *Italy* **41 G11**
Guhakolak, Tanjung
    Indonesia **63 G11**
Gui Jiang → *China* **59 F8**
Guia *Canary Is.* **48 F4**
Guia de Isora *Canary Is.* **48 F3**
Guia Lopes da Laguna
    Brazil **127 A4**
Guiana Highlands *S. Amer.* **122 C4**
Guibéroua *Ivory C.* **82 D3**
Guichi *China* **59 B11**
Guider *Cameroon* **83 D7**
Guidiguir *Niger* **83 C6**
Guidimaka □ *Mauritania* **82 B2**
Guidimouni *Niger* **83 C6**
Guiding *China* **58 D6**
Guidong *China* **59 D9**
Guidónia-Montecélio *Italy* **41 F9**
Guiers, L. de *Senegal* **82 B1**
Guigang *China* **58 F7**
Guiglo *Ivory C.* **82 D3**
Guihulñgan *Phil.* **61 F5**
Guijá *Mozam.* **89 C5**
Guijuelo *Spain* **36 E5**
Guildford *U.K.* **15 F7**
Guilford *U.S.A.* **115 E12**
Guilin *China* **59 E8**
Guillaume-Delisle, L.
    Canada **104 A4**
Guillaumes *France* **21 D10**
Guillestre *France* **21 D10**
Guilvinec *France* **18 E2**
Güimar *Canary Is.* **48 F3**
Guimarães *Portugal* **36 D2**
Guimaras □ *Phil.* **61 F5**
Guinda *U.S.A.* **110 G4**
Guinea *Africa* **76 F4**
Guinea ■ *W. Afr.* **82 C2**
Guinea, Gulf of *Atl. Oc.* **83 E5**
Guinea-Bissau ■ *Africa* **82 C2**
Güines *Cuba* **120 B3**
Guingamp *France* **18 D3**
Guinguinéo *Senegal* **82 C1**
Guipavas *France* **18 D2**
Guiping *China* **59 F8**
Guipúzcoa □ *Spain* **38 B2**
Guir *Mali* **82 B4**
Guirel *Mauritania* **82 B3**
Güiria *Venezuela* **124 A6**
Guiscard *France* **19 C10**
Guise *France* **19 C10**
Guitiriz *Spain* **36 B3**
Guitri *Ivory C.* **82 D3**
Guiuan *Phil.* **61 F6**
Guixi *China* **59 C11**
Guiyang *Guizhou, China* **58 D6**
Guiyang *Hunan, China* **59 E9**
Guizhou □ *China* **58 D6**
Gujan-Mestras *France* **20 D2**
Gujar Khan *Pakistan* **68 C5**
Gujarat □ *India* **68 H4**
Gujiang *China* **59 D10**
Gujranwala *Pakistan* **68 C6**
Gujrat *Pakistan* **68 C6**
Gukovo *Russia* **35 F5**
Gulbarga *India* **66 L10**
Gulbene *Latvia* **32 D4**
Gulf, The = Persian Gulf *Asia* **71 E6**
Gulf Islands △ *U.S.A.* **117 F11**
Gulfport *U.S.A.* **117 F10**
Gulgong *Australia* **95 E4**
Gulin *China* **58 C5**
Gulistan *Pakistan* **68 D2**
Gulja = Yining *China* **52 E9**
Gull Lake *Canada* **103 C7**
Gullbrandstorp *Sweden* **11 H6**
Gullspång *Sweden* **11 F8**
Güllük *Turkey* **47 D9**
Güllük Dağı △ *Turkey* **47 E12**
Güllük Körfezi *Turkey* **47 D9**
Gulma *Nigeria* **83 C5**
Gulmarg *India* **69 B6**
Gülnar *Turkey* **72 D5**
Gülpınar *Turkey* **47 B8**
Gülşehir *Turkey* **72 C6**
Gülshat *Kazakhstan* **52 C8**
Gulu *Uganda* **86 B3**
Gülübovo *Bulgaria* **45 D9**
Gulud □ *Sudan* **81 F2**
Gulwe *Tanzania* **86 D4**
Gulyaypole = Hulyaypole
    Ukraine **33 J9**
Gumal → *Pakistan* **68 D4**
Gumbaz *Pakistan* **68 D3**
Gumel *Nigeria* **83 C6**
Gumi *S. Korea* **57 F15**

Gumiel de Hizán *Spain* **36 D7**
Gumla *India* **69 H11**
Gumlu *Australia* **94 B4**
Gumma □ *Japan* **55 F9**
Gummersbach *Germany* **24 D3**
Gummi *Nigeria* **83 C6**
Gümüldür *Turkey* **47 C9**
Gümüşçay *Turkey* **45 F11**
Gümüşhacıköy *Turkey* **72 B6**
Gümüşhane *Turkey* **73 B8**
Gümüşsu *Turkey* **47 C11**
Gumzai *Indonesia* **63 F8**
Guna *Ethiopia* **81 F4**
Guna *India* **68 G7**
Gunbalanya *Australia* **92 B5**
Gundabooka △ *Australia* **95 E4**
Gundelfingen *Germany* **25 G6**
Güney *Burdur, Turkey* **47 D11**
Güney *Denizli, Turkey* **47 C11**
Güneydoğu Toroslar *Turkey* **73 C9**
Gunisao → *Canada* **103 C9**
Gunisao L. *Canada* **103 C9**
Gunjur *Gambia* **82 C1**
Gunjyal *Pakistan* **68 C4**
Günlüce *Turkey* **47 E10**
Gunnarskog *Sweden* **10 E6**
Gunnbjørn Fjeld *Greenland* **4 C6**
Gunnedah *Australia* **95 E5**
Gunnewin *Australia* **95 D4**
Gunningbar Cr. → *Australia* **95 E4**
Gunnison *Colo., U.S.A.* **108 G10**
Gunnison *Utah, U.S.A.* **108 G8**
Gunnison → *U.S.A.* **108 G9**
Gunsan *S. Korea* **57 G14**
Guntakal *India* **66 M10**
Gunter *Canada* **114 B7**
Guntersville *U.S.A.* **117 D11**
Guntong *Malaysia* **65 K3**
Guntur *India* **67 L12**
Gunungapi *Indonesia* **63 F7**
Gunungsitoli *Indonesia* **62 D1**
Günz → *Germany* **25 G6**
Gunza *Angola* **84 G2**
Günzburg *Germany* **25 G6**
Gunzenhausen *Germany* **25 F6**
Guo He → *China* **57 H9**
Guoyang *China* **56 H9**
Gupis *Pakistan* **69 A5**
Gura Humorului *Romania* **29 C10**
Gura-Teghii *Romania* **29 E11**
Gurag *Ethiopia* **81 F4**
Gurahonț *Romania* **28 D7**
Gurbantünggüt Shamo
    China **52 E3**
Gurdaspur *India* **68 C6**
Gurdon *U.S.A.* **116 E8**
Güre *Balıkesir, Turkey* **47 B8**
Güre *Uşak, Turkey* **47 C11**
Gurgaon *India* **68 E7**
Gürgentepe *Turkey* **72 B7**
Gurghiu, Munții *Romania* **29 D10**
Gurgueia → *Brazil* **125 E10**
Gurha *India* **68 G4**
Guri, Embalse de *Venezuela* **124 B6**
Gurin *Nigeria* **83 D7**
Gurjaani *Georgia* **35 K7**
Gurk → *Austria* **26 E7**
Gurkha *Nepal* **69 E11**
Gurla Mandhata =
    Naimona'nyi Feng *Nepal* **69 D9**
Gurley *Australia* **95 D4**
Gurnet Point *U.S.A.* **115 D14**
Guro *Mozam.* **87 F3**
Gürpınar *İstanbul, Turkey* **45 F12**
Gürpınar *Van, Turkey* **73 C10**
Gürsu *Turkey* **45 F13**
Gurué *Mozam.* **87 F4**
Gurun *Malaysia* **65 K3**
Gürün *Turkey* **72 C7**
Gurupá *Brazil* **125 D8**
Gurupá, I. Grande de *Brazil* **125 D8**
Gurupi *Brazil* **125 F9**
Gurupi → *Brazil* **125 D9**
Guruwe *Zimbabwe* **89 B5**
Guryev = Atyraū *Kazakhstan* **52 E6**
Guryevsk *Russia* **30 D7**
Gus-Khrustalnyy *Russia* **34 C5**
Gusau *Nigeria* **83 C6**
Gusev *Russia* **30 D9**
Gushan *China* **57 E12**
Gushgy = Serhetabat
    Turkmenistan **71 C9**
Gushi *China* **59 A10**
Gushiago *Ghana* **83 D4**
Gusinje *Montenegro* **44 D3**
Gusinoozersk *Russia* **53 D11**
Gúspini *Italy* **42 C1**
Güssing *Austria* **27 D9**
Gustavsberg *Sweden* **10 E12**
Gustavus *U.S.A.* **102 B1**
Gustine *U.S.A.* **110 H6**
Güstrow *Germany* **24 B8**
Gusum *Sweden* **11 F10**
Guta = Kolárovo *Slovak Rep.* **27 D10**
Gütersloh *Germany* **24 D4**
Gutha *Australia* **93 E2**
Guthalungra *Australia* **94 B4**
Guthrie *Canada* **114 B5**

Guthrie *Okla., U.S.A.* **116 D6**
Guthrie *Tex., U.S.A.* **116 E4**
Gutian *China* **59 D12**
Guttenberg *U.S.A.* **112 D8**
Gutu *Zimbabwe* **89 B5**
Guwahati *India* **67 F17**
Guy Fawkes River △
    Australia **95 D5**
Guyana ■ *S. Amer.* **124 C7**
Guyane française = French
    Guiana ☑ *S. Amer.* **125 C7**
Guyang *China* **56 D6**
Guyenne *France* **20 D4**
Guymon *U.S.A.* **116 C4**
Guyra *Australia* **95 E5**
Guyuan *Hebei, China* **56 D8**
Guyuan *Ningxia Huizu, China* **56 F4**
Güzelbahçe *Turkey* **47 C8**
Güzelyurt = Morphou
    Cyprus **49 D11**
Guzhang *China* **58 C7**
Guzhen *China* **57 H9**
Guzmán, L. de *Mexico* **118 A3**
Gvardeysk *Russia* **30 D8**
Gvardeyskoye *Ukraine* **33 K8**
Gwa *Burma* **67 L19**
Gwaai *Zimbabwe* **87 F2**
Gwaai → *Zimbabwe* **87 F2**
Gwabegar *Australia* **95 E4**
Gwadabawa *Nigeria* **83 C6**
Gwädar *Pakistan* **66 G3**
Gwagwada *Nigeria* **83 C6**
Gwaii Haanas △ *Canada* **102 C2**
Gwalior *India* **68 F8**
Gwanara *Nigeria* **83 D5**
Gwanda *Zimbabwe* **87 G2**
Gwandu *Nigeria* **83 C5**
Gwane *Dem. Rep. of the Congo* **86 B2**
Gwangju *S. Korea* **57 G14**
Gwanju = Gwangju *S. Korea* **57 G14**
Gwaram *Nigeria* **83 C7**
Gwarzo *Nigeria* **83 C6**
Gwasero *Nigeria* **83 D5**
Gwda → *Poland* **31 E3**
Gweebarra B. *Ireland* **12 B3**
Gweedore *Ireland* **12 A3**
Gweru *Zimbabwe* **87 F2**
Gwi *Nigeria* **83 D6**
Gwinn *U.S.A.* **112 B10**
Gwio Kura *Nigeria* **83 C7**
Gwoza *Nigeria* **83 C7**
Gwydir → *Australia* **95 D4**
Gwynedd □ *U.K.* **14 E3**
Gyandzha = Gäncä
    Azerbaijan **35 K8**
Gyaring Hu *China* **60 C4**
Gydanskiy Poluostrov *Russia* **52 C8**
Gyeongju *S. Korea* **57 G15**
Gympie *Australia* **95 D5**
Gyomaendrőd *Hungary* **28 D5**
Gyöngyös *Hungary* **28 C4**
Győr *Hungary* **28 C2**
Győr-Moson-Sopron □
    Hungary **28 C2**
Gypsum Pt. *Canada* **102 A6**
Gypsumville *Canada* **103 C9**
Gyueshevo *Bulgaria* **44 D6**
Gyula *Hungary* **28 D6**
Gyumri *Armenia* **35 K6**
Gyzylarbat = Serdar
    Turkmenistan **71 B8**
Gyzyletrek = Etrek
    Turkmenistan **71 B7**
Gzhatsk = Gagarin *Russia* **32 E8**

H

Ha 'Arava → *Israel* **74 E4**
Ha Coi *Vietnam* **58 G6**
Ha Dong *Vietnam* **58 G5**
Ha Giang *Vietnam* **58 F5**
Ha Karmel △ *Israel* **74 C4**
Ha Long, Vinh *Vietnam* **64 B6**
Ha Tien *Vietnam* **65 G5**
Ha Tinh *Vietnam* **64 C5**
Ha Trung *Vietnam* **64 C5**
Haaksbergen *Neths.* **17 B6**
Ha'ano *Tonga* **91 c**
Ha'apai Group *Tonga* **91 c**
Haapiti *Moorea* **91 d**
Haapsalu *Estonia* **32 C2**
Haarby *Denmark* **11 J4**
Haarlem *Neths.* **17 B4**
Haast → *N.Z.* **91 E2**
Haasts Bluff *Australia* **92 D5**
Haasts Bluff ☺ *Australia* **92 D5**
Hab → *Pakistan* **68 G3**
Hab Nadi Chauki *Pakistan* **68 G2**
Habahe *China* **60 B3**
Habaswein *Kenya* **86 B4**
Habay *Canada* **102 B5**
Ḥabbānīyah *Iraq* **73 F10**
Habibas, Îles *Algeria* **39 K3**
Habichtswald ☺ *Germany* **24 D5**
Habo *Sweden* **11 G8**
Haboro *Japan* **54 B10**
Habshān *U.A.E.* **71 F7**
Hachenburg *Germany* **24 E3**
Hachijō-Jima *Japan* **55 H9**

Hachijō-Jima *Japan* **55 H9**
Hachinohe *Japan* **54 D10**
Hachiōji *Japan* **55 G9**
Hacı Zeynalabdin *Azerbaijan* **73 B13**
Hacıbektaş *Turkey* **72 C6**
Hacılar *Turkey* **72 C6**
Hackås *Sweden* **10 B8**
Hackensack *U.S.A.* **115 F10**
Hackettstown *U.S.A.* **115 F10**
Hadali *Pakistan* **68 C5**
Hadarba, Ras *Sudan* **80 C4**
Hadarom □ *Israel* **74 E4**
Hadd, Ra's al *Oman* **75 C6**
Haddington *U.K.* **13 F6**
Hadejia *Nigeria* **83 C7**
Hadejia → *Nigeria* **83 C7**
Hadera *Israel* **74 C3**
Hadera, N. → *Israel* **74 C3**
Haderslev *Denmark* **11 J3**
Hadhramaut =
    Ḥaḍramawt *Yemen* **75 D4**
Hadiboh *Yemen* **75 E5**
Hadım *Turkey* **72 D5**
Hadley B. *Canada* **100 C10**
Hadong *S. Korea* **57 G14**
Ḥaḍramawt *Yemen* **75 D4**
Ḥaḍrānīyah *Iraq* **70 C4**
Hadrian's Wall *U.K.* **14 B5**
Hadsten *Denmark* **11 H4**
Hadsund *Denmark* **11 H4**
Hadyach *Ukraine* **33 G8**
Hae, Ko *Thailand* **65 a**
Haeju *N. Korea* **57 E13**
Haenam *S. Korea* **57 G14**
Haenertsburg *S. Africa* **89 C4**
Haerhpin = Harbin *China* **57 B14**
Hafar al Bāṭin *Si. Arabia* **70 D5**
Hafik *Turkey* **72 C7**
Ḥafirat al 'Aydā *Si. Arabia* **70 E3**
Hafit *Oman* **71 F7**
Hafizabad *Pakistan* **68 C5**
Haflong *India* **67 G18**
Haft Gel *Iran* **71 D6**
Hagalil *Israel* **74 C4**
Hagby *Sweden* **11 H10**
Hagemeister I. *U.S.A.* **106 D7**
Hagen *Germany* **24 D3**
Hagenow *Germany* **24 B7**
Hagere Hiywet *Ethiopia* **81 F4**
Hagerman *U.S.A.* **109 K11**
Hagerman Fossil Beds △
    U.S.A. **108 E6**
Hagerstown *U.S.A.* **113 F15**
Hagersville *Canada* **114 D4**
Hagetmau *France* **20 E3**
Hagfors *Sweden* **10 D7**
Hagi *Japan* **55 G5**
Hagolan *Syria* **74 C4**
Hagondange *France* **19 C13**
Hags Hd. *Ireland* **12 D2**
Hague, C. de la *France* **18 C5**
Hague, The =
    's-Gravenhage *Neths.* **17 B4**
Haguenau *France* **19 D14**
Hai Duong *Vietnam* **58 G6**
Hai'an *Guangdong, China* **59 G8**
Hai'an *Jiangsu, China* **59 A13**
Haicheng *Fujian, China* **59 E11**
Haicheng *Liaoning, China* **57 D12**
Haidar Khel *Afghan.* **68 C3**
Haidarâbâd = Hyderabad
    India **66 L11**
Haidargarh *India* **69 F9**
Haifa = Ḥefa *Israel* **74 C4**
Haifeng *China* **59 F10**
Haiger *Germany* **24 E4**
Haikou *China* **64 B8**
Ḥā'il □ *Si. Arabia* **70 E4**
Hailar *China* **60 B6**
Hailey *U.S.A.* **108 E6**
Haileybury *Canada* **104 C4**
Hailin *China* **57 B15**
Hailing Dao *China* **59 G8**
Hailun *Guangdong, China* **59 F11**
Haimen *Jiangsu, China* **59 B13**
Hainan □ *China* **64 C7**
Hainan Dao *China* **64 C7**
Hainan Str. = Qiongzhou
    Haixia *China* **64 B8**
Hainaut □ *Belgium* **17 D4**
Hainburg *Austria* **27 C9**
Haines *Alaska, U.S.A.* **102 B1**
Haines City *U.S.A.* **117 G14**
Haines Junction *Canada* **102 A1**
Hainfeld *Austria* **26 C8**
Haining *China* **59 B13**
Haiphong *Vietnam* **58 G6**
Haitan Dao *China* **59 E12**
Haiti ■ *W. Indies* **121 C5**
Haiya *Sudan* **80 D4**
Haiyan *China* **59 B13**
Haiyang *China* **57 F11**
Haiyuan *Guangxi Zhuangzu,
    China* **58 F6**
Haiyuan *Ningxia Huizu, China* **56 F3**
Haizhou *China* **57 G10**

Haizhou Wan *China* **57 G10**
Haj Ali Qoli, Kavīr *Iran* **71 C7**
Hajdú-Bihar □ *Hungary* **28 C6**
Hajdúböszörmény *Hungary* **28 C6**
Hajdúdorog *Hungary* **28 C6**
Hajdúhadház *Hungary* **28 C6**
Hajdúnánás *Hungary* **28 C6**
Hajdúsámson *Hungary* **28 C6**
Hajdúszoboszló *Hungary* **28 C6**
Haji Ibrahim *Iraq* **73 D11**
Hājjīābād *Iran* **71 C9**
Hajipur *India* **69 G11**
Hajjah *Yemen* **75 D3**
Ḥājjīābād *Iran* **71 D7**
Ḥājjīābād-e Zarrīn *Iran* **71 C7**
Hajnówka *Poland* **31 F10**
Hakansson, Mts.
    Dem. Rep. of the Congo **87 D2**
Hakkâri *Turkey* **73 D10**
Hakkâri □ *Turkey* **73 D10**
Hakkâri Dağları *Turkey* **73 C10**
Hakken-Zan *Japan* **55 G7**
Hakodate *Japan* **54 D10**
Hakos *Namibia* **88 C2**
Håksberg *Sweden* **10 D9**
Haku-San *Japan* **55 F8**
Haku-San △ *Japan* **55 F8**
Hakui *Japan* **55 F8**
Hala *Pakistan* **66 G6**
Ḥalab *Syria* **72 D7**
Ḥalab □ *Syria* **72 D7**
Ḥalabjah *Iraq* **73 E11**
Halaib *Sudan* **80 C4**
Halaib Triangle *Africa* **80 C4**
Halasa *Sudan* **81 E3**
Hālat 'Ammār *Si. Arabia* **70 D3**
Halbâ *Lebanon* **74 A5**
Halberstadt *Germany* **24 D7**
Halcombe *N.Z.* **91 D5**
Halcon *Phil.* **63 B6**
Halde Fjäll = Haltiatunturi
    Finland **8 B19**
Halden *Norway* **9 G14**
Haldensleben *Germany* **24 C7**
Haldia *Bangla.* **69 H13**
Haldwani *India* **69 E8**
Hale → *Australia* **94 C2**
Halesowen *U.K.* **15 E5**
Halesworth *U.K.* **15 E9**
Haleyville *U.S.A.* **117 D11**
Half Assini *Ghana* **82 D4**
Half Dome *U.S.A.* **110 H7**
Halfa al Jadidah *Sudan* **81 D4**
Halfeti *Turkey* **72 D7**
Halfmoon Bay *N.Z.* **91 G2**
Halfway → *Canada* **102 B4**
Halia *India* **69 G10**
Haliburton *Canada* **114 A6**
Halifax *Australia* **94 B4**
Halifax *Canada* **105 D7**
Halifax *U.K.* **14 D6**
Halifax *U.S.A.* **114 F8**
Halifax B. *Australia* **94 B4**
Halifax I. *Namibia* **88 D2**
Halīl → *Iran* **71 E8**
Halki *Greece* **47 E9**
Halkida *Greece* **46 C5**
Halkidiki □ *Greece* **44 F7**
Halkirk *U.K.* **13 C5**
Hall Beach *Canada* **101 D15**
Hall in Tirol *Austria* **26 D4**
Hall Pen. *Canada* **101 E18**
Hall Pt. *Australia* **92 C3**
Hallabro *Sweden* **11 H9**
Halland *Sweden* **9 H15**
Hallands län □ *Sweden* **11 H6**
Hallands Väderö *Sweden* **11 H6**
Hallandsås *Sweden* **11 H7**
Hallāniyat, Jazā'ir al *Oman* **75 D6**
Hallasan *S. Korea* **57 H14**
Hällbybrunn *Sweden* **10 E10**
Halle *Belgium* **17 D4**
Halle *Nordrhein-Westfalen,
    Germany* **24 C4**
Halle *Sachsen-Anhalt, Germany* **24 D7**
Hällefors *Sweden* **10 E8**
Hälleforsnäs *Sweden* **10 E10**
Hallein *Austria* **26 D6**
Hällekis *Sweden* **11 F7**
Hallen *Sweden* **10 A8**
Hallett *Australia* **95 E2**
Halley *Antarctica* **5 D1**
Hallim *S. Korea* **57 H14**
Hallingdalselva → *Norway* **8 F13**
Hallock *U.S.A.* **103 D9**
Halls Creek *Australia* **92 C4**
Halls Gap *Australia* **95 F3**
Halls Lake *Canada* **114 A6**
Hallsberg *Sweden* **10 E9**
Hallstahammar *Sweden* **10 E10**
Hallstatt *Austria* **26 D6**
Hallstavik *Sweden* **10 D12**
Hallstead *U.S.A.* **115 E9**
Halmahera *Indonesia* **63 D7**
Halmeu *Romania* **28 C8**
Halmstad *Sweden* **11 H6**
Hals *Denmark* **11 H4**
Hälsingborg = Helsingborg
    Sweden **11 H6**

Hälsingland *Sweden* **10** C10
Halstead *U.K.* **15** F8
Haltern *Germany* **24** D3
Haltiatunturi *Finland* **8** B19
Halton □ *U.K.* **14** D5
Haltwhistle *U.K.* **14** C5
Ḩālūl *Qatar* **71** E7
Halvad *India* **68** H4
Halvān *Iran* **71** C3
Ham *France* **19** C10
Ham Tan *Vietnam* **65** G6
Ham Yen *Vietnam* **64** A5
Hamab *Namibia* **88** D2
Hamad *Sudan* **81** D3
Hamada *Japan* **55** G6
Hamadān *Iran* **73** E13
Hamadān □ *Iran* **71** C6
Ḩamāh *Syria* **72** E7
Ḩamāh □ *Syria* **72** E7
Hamamatsu *Japan* **55** G8
Hamar *Norway* **8** F14
Hamâta, Gebel *Egypt* **70** E2
Hambantota *Sri Lanka* **66** R12
Hamber △ *Canada* **102** C5
Hamburg *Germany* **24** B5
Hamburg *Ark., U.S.A.* **116** E9
Hamburg *N.Y., U.S.A.* **114** D6
Hamburg *Pa., U.S.A.* **115** F9
Hamburg □ *Germany* **24** B5
Hamburg Fuhlsbüttel ✈
  (HAM) *Germany* **24** B5
Ḩamd, W. al ➤ *Si. Arabia* **70** E3
Hamden *U.S.A.* **115** E12
Hamdibey *Turkey* **47** B9
Hāme *Finland* **32** B2
Hämeenlinna *Finland* **32** B3
Hamélé *Ghana* **82** C4
Hamelin Pool *Australia* **93** E1
Hameln *Germany* **24** C5
Hamerkaz □ *Israel* **74** C3
Hamero Hadad *Ethiopia* **81** F5
Hamersley Ra. *Australia* **92** D2
Hamhŭng *N. Korea* **57** E14
Hami *China* **60** B4
Hamili *Greece* **47** F8
Hamilton *Australia* **95** F3
Hamilton *Canada* **114** C5
Hamilton *N.Z.* **91** B5
Hamilton *U.K.* **13** F4
Hamilton *Ala., U.S.A.* **117** D11
Hamilton *Mont., U.S.A.* **108** C6
Hamilton *N.Y., U.S.A.* **115** D9
Hamilton *Ohio, U.S.A.* **113** F11
Hamilton *Tex., U.S.A.* **116** F5
Hamilton ➤ *Queens.,*
  Australia **94** C2
Hamilton ➤ *S. Austral.,*
  Australia **95** D2
Hamilton City *U.S.A.* **110** F4
Hamilton I. *Australia* **94** b
Hamilton Inlet *Canada* **105** B8
Hamilton Mt. *U.S.A.* **115** C10
Hamina *Finland* **32** B4
Hamirpur *H.P., India* **68** D7
Hamirpur *Ut. P., India* **69** G9
Hamitabat *Turkey* **45** E11
Hamju *N. Korea* **57** E14
Hamlet *U.S.A.* **117** D15
Hamley Bridge *Australia* **95** E2
Hamlin = Hameln *Germany* **24** C5
Hamlin *N.Y., U.S.A.* **114** C7
Hamlin *Tex., U.S.A.* **116** E4
Hamm *Germany* **24** D3
Ḩammām al 'Alīl *Iraq* **73** D10
Ḩammār, Hawr al *Iraq* **70** D5
Hammarstrand *Sweden* **10** A10
Hammelburg *Germany* **25** E5
Hammeren *Denmark* **11** J8
Hammerfest *Norway* **8** A20
Hammerum *Denmark* **11** H3
Hamminkeln *Germany* **24** D2
Hammond *Ind., U.S.A.* **112** E10
Hammond *La., U.S.A.* **117** F9
Hammond *N.Y., U.S.A.* **115** B9
Hammondsport *U.S.A.* **114** D7
Hammonton *U.S.A.* **113** F16
Hamneda *Sweden* **11** H7
Hampden *N.Z.* **91** F3
Hampshire □ *U.K.* **15** F6
Hampshire Downs *U.K.* **15** F6
Hampton *N.B., Canada* **105** C6
Hampton *Ont., Canada* **114** C6
Hampton *Ark., U.S.A.* **116** E8
Hampton *Iowa, U.S.A.* **112** D7
Hampton *N.H., U.S.A.* **115** D14
Hampton *S.C., U.S.A.* **117** E14
Hampton *Va., U.S.A.* **113** G15
Hampton Bays *U.S.A.* **115** F12
Hampton Tableland *Australia* **93** F4
Hamra *Sweden* **10** C8
Hamrat esh Sheykh *Sudan* **81** E2
Ḩamrin, Jabal *Iraq* **73** E11
Hamur *Turkey* **73** C10
Hamyang *S. Korea* **57** G14
Han i Hotit *Albania* **44** D3
Han Jiang ➤ *China* **59** F11
Han Shui ➤ *China* **59** B10
Hanak *Si. Arabia* **70** E3

Hanak *Turkey* **73** B10
Hanamaki *Japan* **54** E10
Hanang *Tanzania* **86** C4
Hanau *Germany* **25** E4
Hanbogd = Ihbulag *Mongolia* **56** C4
Hançalar *Turkey* **47** C11
Hânceşti *Moldova* **29** D13
Hancheng *China* **56** G6
Hanchuan *China* **59** B9
Hancock *Mich., U.S.A.* **112** B9
Hancock *N.Y., U.S.A.* **115** E9
Hancock *Vt., U.S.A.* **115** C12
Handa *Japan* **55** G8
Handa I. *U.K.* **13** C3
Handan *China* **56** F8
Handeni *Tanzania* **86** D4
Handlová *Slovak Rep.* **27** C11
Handub *Sudan* **80** D4
Handwara *India* **69** B6
Hanegev *Israel* **74** E4
Hanford *U.S.A.* **110** J7
Hanford Reach △ *U.S.A.* **108** C4
Hang Chat *Thailand* **64** C2
Hang Dong *Thailand* **64** C2
Hangang ➤ *S. Korea* **57** F14
Hangayn Nuruu *Mongolia* **60** B4
Hangchou = Hangzhou
  China **59** B13
Hanggin Houqi *China* **56** D4
Hanggin Qi *China* **56** E5
Hangu *China* **57** E9
Hangzhou *China* **59** B13
Hangzhou Wan *China* **59** B13
Hanh *Mongolia* **53** D11
Hanhongor *Mongolia* **56** C3
Hani *Turkey* **73** C9
Hania = Chania *Greece* **49** D6
Haniska *Slovak Rep.* **27** C14
Hanjiang *China* **59** E12
Hankinson *U.S.A.* **112** B5
Hankö *Finland* **32** C2
Hankou *China* **59** B10
Hanksville *U.S.A.* **108** G8
Hanle *India* **69** C8
Hanmer Springs *N.Z.* **91** E4
Hann ➤ *Australia* **92** C4
Hann, Mt. *Australia* **92** C4
Hanna *Canada* **102** C6
Hanna *U.S.A.* **108** F10
Hannah B. *Canada* **104** B4
Hannibal *Mo., U.S.A.* **112** F8
Hannibal *N.Y., U.S.A.* **115** C8
Hannik *Sudan* **80** D3
Hannover *Germany* **24** C5
Hanö *Sweden* **11** H8
Hanöbukten *Sweden* **11** J8
Hanoi *Vietnam* **58** G5
Hanover = Hannover
  Germany **24** C5
Hanover *Canada* **114** B3
Hanover *S. Africa* **88** E3
Hanover *N.H., U.S.A.* **115** C12
Hanover *Ohio, U.S.A.* **114** F2
Hanover *Pa., U.S.A.* **113** F15
Hanover, I. *Chile* **128** G2
Hans Lollik I. *U.S. Virgin Is.* **121** e
Hansdiha *India* **69** G12
Hanshou *China* **59** C8
Hansi *H.P., India* **68** C7
Hansi *Haryana, India* **68** E6
Hanson, L. *Australia* **95** E2
Hanstholm *Denmark* **11** G2
Hantsavichy *Belarus* **23** B14
Hanyin *China* **58** A7
Hanyuan *China* **58** C4
Hanzhong *China* **56** H4
Hanzhuang *China* **57** G9
Haora *India* **69** H13
Haoxue *China* **59** B9
Haparanda *Sweden* **8** D21
Happy *U.S.A.* **116** D4
Happy Camp *U.S.A.* **108** F2
Happy Valley-Goose Bay
  Canada **105** B7
Hapsu *N. Korea* **57** D15
Hapur *India* **68** E7
Ḩaql *Si. Arabia* **74** F3
Har *Indonesia* **63** F8
Har-Ayrag *Mongolia* **56** B5
Har Hu *China* **60** C4
Har Us Nuur *Mongolia* **60** B4
Har Yehuda *Israel* **74** D3
Ḩarad *Si. Arabia* **75** H6
Haradok *Belarus* **32** E6
Härädsbäck *Sweden* **11** H8
Haramosh *Pakistan* **69** B6
Haranomachi *Japan* **54** F10
Harare *Zimbabwe* **87** F3
Harat *Eritrea* **81** D4
Harazé *Chad* **79** G10
Harbel *Liberia* **82** D2
Harbin *China* **57** B14
Harbıye *Turkey* **72** D7
Harbo *Sweden* **10** D11
Harbøøre *Denmark* **11** H2
Harbor Beach *U.S.A.* **114** C2

Harborcreek *U.S.A.* **114** D5
Harbour Breton *Canada* **105** C8
Harbour Deep *Canada* **105** B8
Harburg *Germany* **24** B5
Harburger Berge △ *Germany* **24** B5
Harda *India* **68** H7
Hardangerfjorden *Norway* **9** F12
Hardangervidda *Norway* **8** F12
Hardap □ *Namibia* **88** C2
Hardap Dam *Namibia* **88** C2
Hardenberg *Neths.* **17** B6
Harderwijk *Neths.* **17** B5
Hardey ➤ *Australia* **92** D2
Hardin *U.S.A.* **108** D10
Harding *S. Africa* **89** E4
Harding Ra. *Australia* **92** C3
Hardisty *Canada* **102** C6
Hardoi *India* **69** F9
Hardwar = Haridwar *India* **68** E8
Hardwick *U.S.A.* **115** B12
Hardwood Lake *Canada* **114** A7
Hardy, Pen. *Chile* **128** H3
Hardy, Pte. *St. Lucia* **121** f
Hare B. *Canada* **105** B8
Hareid *Norway* **8** E12
Haren *Germany* **24** C3
Harer *Ethiopia* **81** F5
Harerge *Ethiopia* **81** F5
Hareto *Ethiopia* **81** F4
Harfleur *France* **18** C7
Hargeisa *Somali Rep.* **75** F3
Harghita □ *Romania* **29** D10
Harghita, Munţii *Romania* **29** D10
Hargshamn *Sweden* **10** D12
Hari ➤ *Indonesia* **62** E2
Haria *Canary Is.* **48** E6
Haridwar *India* **68** E8
Harim, Jabal al *Oman* **71** E8
Haringhata ➤ *Bangla.* **67** J16
Harīr, W. al ➤ *Syria* **74** C4
Harirūd ➤ *Asia* **71** B9
Härjedalen *Sweden* **10** B7
Harlan *Iowa, U.S.A.* **112** E6
Harlan *Ky., U.S.A.* **113** G12
Hârlău *Romania* **29** C11
Harlech *U.K.* **14** E3
Harlem *U.S.A.* **108** B9
Hårlev *Denmark* **11** J6
Harlingen *Neths.* **17** A5
Harlingen *U.S.A.* **116** H6
Harlow *U.K.* **15** F8
Harlowton *U.S.A.* **108** C9
Harmancık *Turkey* **47** B11
Harmånger *Sweden* **10** C11
Harmil *Eritrea* **81** D5
Harnai *Pakistan* **68** D2
Harney Basin *U.S.A.* **108** E4
Harney L. *U.S.A.* **108** E4
Harney Peak *U.S.A.* **112** D2
Härnön *Sweden* **10** B12
Härnösand *Sweden* **10** B11
Haro *Spain* **38** C2
Haroldswick *U.K.* **13** A8
Harp L. *Canada* **105** A7
Harper *Liberia* **82** E3
Harper, Mt. *U.S.A.* **106** C11
Harplinge *Sweden* **11** H6
Harrai *India* **69** H8
Harrand *Pakistan* **68** E4
Harriman *U.S.A.* **117** D12
Harrington Harbour *Canada* **105** B8
Harris *U.K.* **13** D2
Harris, L. *Australia* **95** E2
Harris, Sd. of *U.K.* **13** D1
Harris Pt. *Canada* **114** C2
Harrisburg *Ill., U.S.A.* **112** G9
Harrisburg *Nebr., U.S.A.* **112** E2
Harrisburg *Pa., U.S.A.* **114** F8
Harrismith *S. Africa* **89** D4
Harrison *Ark., U.S.A.* **116** C8
Harrison *Maine, U.S.A.* **115** B14
Harrison *Nebr., U.S.A.* **112** D2
Harrison, C. *Canada* **105** B8
Harrison Bay *U.S.A.* **106** A9
Harrison L. *Canada* **102** D4
Harrisonburg *U.S.A.* **113** F14
Harrisonville *U.S.A.* **112** F6
Harriston *Canada* **114** C4
Harrisville *Mich., U.S.A.* **114** B1
Harrisville *N.Y., U.S.A.* **115** B9
Harrisville *Pa., U.S.A.* **114** E5
Harrodsburg *U.S.A.* **113** G11
Harrogate *U.K.* **14** C6
Harrow *Canada* **114** D2
Harrow □ *U.K.* **15** F7
Harrowsmith *Canada* **115** B8
Harry S. Truman Res.
  U.S.A. **112** F7
Harsefeld *Germany* **24** B5
Harsewinkel *Germany* **24** D4
Harsın *Iran* **73** E12
Hârşova *Romania* **29** F12
Harstad *Norway* **8** B17
Harsud *India* **68** H7
Hart *U.S.A.* **112** D10
Hart, L. *Australia* **95** E2

Hartbees ➤ *S. Africa* **88** D3
Hartberg *Austria* **26** D8
Hartford *Conn., U.S.A.* **115** E12
Hartford *Ky., U.S.A.* **112** G10
Hartford *S. Dak., U.S.A.* **112** D5
Hartford *Vt., U.S.A.* **115** C12
Hartford *Wis., U.S.A.* **112** D9
Hartford City *U.S.A.* **113** E11
Hartland *Canada* **105** C6
Hartland Pt. *U.K.* **15** F3
Hartlepool *U.K.* **14** C6
Hartlepool □ *U.K.* **14** C6
Hartley Bay *Canada* **102** C3
Hartmannberge *Namibia* **88** B1
Hartney *Canada* **103** D8
Hârtop *Moldova* **29** D13
Harts ➤ *S. Africa* **88** D3
Harts Range *Australia* **94** C1
Hartselle *U.S.A.* **117** D11
Hartshorne *U.S.A.* **116** D7
Hartstown *U.S.A.* **114** E4
Hartsville *U.S.A.* **117** D14
Hartswater *S. Africa* **88** D3
Hartwell *U.S.A.* **117** D13
Harunabad *Pakistan* **68** E5
Harvand *Iran* **71** D7
Harvey *Australia* **93** F2
Harvey *Ill., U.S.A.* **112** E10
Harvey *N. Dak., U.S.A.* **112** B4
Harwich *U.K.* **15** F9
Haryana □ *India* **68** E7
Haryn ➤ *Belarus* **23** B14
Harz *Germany* **24** D6
Harz △ *Germany* **24** D6
Harzgerode *Germany* **24** D7
Hasa *Si. Arabia* **71** E6
Hasaheisa *Sudan* **81** E3
Ḩasan ➤ *Iran* **71** D7
Ḩasanābād *Iran* **71** C7
Hasankeyf *Turkey* **73** D9
Hasb, W. ➤ *Iraq* **70** D5
Hasdo ➤ *India* **69** J10
Haselünne *Germany* **24** C3
Hashimoto *Japan* **55** G7
Hashtjerd *Iran* **71** C6
Hashtpar = Tālesh *Iran* **73** D13
Hashtrud *Iran* **73** D12
Haskell *U.S.A.* **116** E5
Haskovo = Khaskovo
  Bulgaria **45** E9
Hasköy *Turkey* **45** E10
Haslach *Germany* **25** G4
Hasle *Denmark* **11** J8
Haslemere *U.K.* **15** F7
Haslev *Denmark* **11** J5
Hasparren *France* **20** E2
Hassa *Turkey* **72** D7
Hassberge △ *Germany* **25** E6
Hassela *Sweden* **10** B10
Hasselt *Belgium* **17** D5
Hassfurt *Germany* **25** E6
Hassi Messaoud *Algeria* **78** B7
Hässleholm *Sweden* **11** H7
Hassloch *Germany* **25** F4
Hästholmen *Sweden* **11** F8
Hastings *N.Z.* **91** C6
Hastings *U.K.* **15** G8
Hastings *Mich., U.S.A.* **113** D11
Hastings *Minn., U.S.A.* **112** C7
Hastings *Nebr., U.S.A.* **112** E4
Hastings Ra. *Australia* **95** E5
Hästveda *Sweden* **11** H7
Hat Ukraine **28** B7
Hat Yai *Thailand* **65** J3
Hatanbulag = Ergel *Mongolia* **56** C5
Hatay *Turkey* **72** D7
Hatay □ *Turkey* **72** D7
Hatch *U.S.A.* **109** K10
Hatchet L. *Canada* **103** B8
Ḩateg *Romania* **28** E7
Hateruma-Shima *Japan* **55** M1
Hatfield *Australia* **95** E3
Hatgal *Mongolia* **60** A5
Hathras *India* **68** F8
Hatia *Bangla.* **67** H17
Ḩātibah, Ra's *Si. Arabia* **80** C4
Hato Mayor *Dom. Rep.* **121** C6
Hatta *India* **69** G8
Hatta *U.A.E.* **71** E8
Hattah *Australia* **95** E3
Hattah Kulkyne △ *Australia* **95** E3
Hatteras, C. *U.S.A.* **117** D17
Hattiesburg *U.S.A.* **117** F10
Hatvan *Hungary* **28** C4
Hau Duc *Vietnam* **64** E7
Haugesund *Norway* **9** G11
Haukipudas *Finland* **8** D21
Haultain ➤ *Canada* **103** B7
Hauraki G. *N.Z.* **91** B5
Hausruck *Austria* **26** C6
Haut Atlas *Morocco* **78** B4
Haut-Jura △ *France* **19** F9
Haut-Languedoc △ *France* **20** E6
Haut-Niger △ *Guinea* **82** C2
Haut-Rhin □ *France* **19** E14
Haute-Corse □ *France* **21** F13
Haute-Garonne □ *France* **20** E5
Haute-Loire □ *France* **20** C7
Haute-Marne □ *France* **19** D12

Haute-Normandie □ *France* **18** C7
Haute-Saône □ *France* **19** E13
Haute-Savoie □ *France* **21** C10
Haute-Vienne □ *France* **20** C5
Hautes-Alpes □ *France* **21** D10
Hautes Fagnes = Hohes
  Venn *Belgium* **17** D6
Hautes-Pyrénées □ *France* **20** F4
Hauteville-Lompnès *France* **21** C9
Hautmont *France* **19** B10
Hauts-de-Seine □ *France* **19** D9
Hauts Plateaux *Algeria* **78** B6
Hauzenberg *Germany* **25** G9
Havana = La Habana *Cuba* **120** B3
Havana *U.S.A.* **112** E8
Havant *U.K.* **15** G7
Havârna *Romania* **29** B11
Havasor = Kızgı *Turkey* **70** B4
Havasu, L. *U.S.A.* **111** L12
Havdhem *Sweden* **11** G12
Havel ➤ *Germany* **24** C8
Havelian *Pakistan* **68** B5
Havelock *Canada* **114** B7
Havelock *N.Z.* **91** D4
Havelock *U.S.A.* **117** D16
Haverfordwest *U.K.* **15** F3
Haverhill *U.K.* **15** E8
Haverhill *U.S.A.* **115** D13
Haverstraw *U.S.A.* **115** E11
Håverud *Sweden* **11** F6
Havirga *Mongolia* **56** B7
Havířov *Czech Rep.* **27** B11
Havlíčkův Brod *Czech Rep.* **26** B8
Havneby *Denmark* **11** J2
Havran *Turkey* **47** B9
Havre *France* **18** C7
Havre-Aubert *Canada* **105** C7
Havre-St.-Pierre *Canada* **105** B7
Havsa *Turkey* **45** E10
Havza *Turkey* **72** B6
Haw ➤ *U.S.A.* **117** D15
Hawai'i *U.S.A.* **107** M8
Hawai'i □ *U.S.A.* **107** M8
Hawaiian Is. *Pac. Oc.* **97** E12
Hawaiian Ridge *Pac. Oc.* **97** E11
Hawarden *U.S.A.* **112** D5
Hawea, L. *N.Z.* **91** F2
Hawera *N.Z.* **91** C5
Hawi *U.S.A.* **107** L8
Hawick *U.K.* **13** F6
Hawk Junction *Canada* **104** C3
Hawke B. *N.Z.* **91** C6
Hawker *Australia* **95** E2
Hawke's Bay *Canada* **105** B8
Hawkesbury *Canada* **104** C5
Hawkesbury I. *Canada* **102** C3
Hawkesbury Pt. *Australia* **94** A1
Hawkinsville *U.S.A.* **117** E13
Hawley *Minn., U.S.A.* **112** B5
Hawley *Pa., U.S.A.* **115** E9
Ḩawrān, W. ➤ *Iraq* **73** F10
Hawsh Mūssá *Lebanon* **74** B4
Hawthorne *U.S.A.* **108** G4
Hay *Australia* **95** E3
Hay ➤ *Australia* **94** C2
Hay ➤ *Canada* **102** A5
Hay, C. *Australia* **92** B4
Hay I. *Canada* **114** B4
Hay L. *Canada* **102** B5
Hay-on-Wye *U.K.* **15** E4
Hay Point *Australia* **94** C4
Hay River *Canada* **102** A5
Hay Springs *U.S.A.* **112** D2
Haya = Tehoru *Indonesia* **63** E7
Hayachine-San *Japan* **54** E10
Hayange *France* **19** C13
Hayastan = Armenia ■ *Asia* **35** K7
Haydān, W. al ➤ *Jordan* **74** D4
Haydarlı *Turkey* **47** C12
Hayden *U.S.A.* **108** F10
Hayes *U.S.A.* **112** C3
Hayes ➤ *Canada* **104** A1
Hayes, Mt. *U.S.A.* **106** C10
Hayes Creek *Australia* **92** B5
Hayle *U.K.* **15** G2
Hayling I. *U.K.* **15** G7
Hayman I. *Australia* **94** b
Haymana *Turkey* **72** C5
Hayrabolu *Turkey* **45** E11
Hays *U.S.A.* **112** C6
Hays *U.S.A.* **112** F4
Haysyn *Ukraine* **29** B14
Hayvoron *Ukraine* **29** B14
Hayward *Calif., U.S.A.* **110** H4
Hayward *Wis., U.S.A.* **112** B8
Haywards Heath *U.K.* **15** G7
Hazafon □ *Israel* **74** C4
Hazar *Turkmenistan* **52** F6
Hazārān, Kūh-e *Iran* **71** D8
Hazard *U.S.A.* **113** G12
Hazaribag *India* **69** H11
Hazaribag Road *India* **69** G11
Hazebrouck *France* **19** B9
Hazelton *Canada* **102** B3
Hazelton *U.S.A.* **112** B3
Hazen *U.S.A.* **112** B3
Hazen, L. *Canada* **101** A17
Hazenmore *Canada* **103** D7
Hazlehurst *Ga., U.S.A.* **117** F13
Hazlehurst *Miss., U.S.A.* **117** F9

Hazlet *U.S.A.* **115** F10
Hazleton *U.S.A.* **115** F9
Hazlett, L. *Australia* **92** D4
Hazro *Turkey* **70** B4
He Xian *Anhui, China* **59** B12
He Xian *Guangxi Zhuangzu,*
  China **59** E8
Head of Bight *Australia* **93** F5
Headlands *Zimbabwe* **87** F3
Healdsburg *U.S.A.* **110** G4
Healdton *U.S.A.* **116** D6
Healesville *Australia* **95** F4
Healy *U.S.A.* **106** C10
Heany Junction *Zimbabwe* **89** C4
Heard I. *Ind. Oc.* **3** G13
Hearne *U.S.A.* **116** F6
Hearst *Canada* **104** C3
Heart ➤ *U.S.A.* **112** B3
Heart's Content *Canada* **105** C9
Heath, Pte. *Canada* **105** C7
Heathrow, London ✈
  (LHR) *U.K.* **15** F7
Heavener *U.S.A.* **116** D7
Hebbronville *U.S.A.* **116** H5
Hebei □ *China* **56** E9
Hebel *Australia* **95** D4
Heber *U.S.A.* **111** N11
Heber Springs *U.S.A.* **116** D8
Hebgen L. *U.S.A.* **108** D8
Hebi *China* **56** G8
Hebrides *U.K.* **6** D4
Hebrides, Sea of the *U.K.* **13** D2
Hebron = Al Khalīl
  West Bank **74** D4
Hebron *Canada* **101** F19
Hebron *N. Dak., U.S.A.* **112** B2
Hebron *Nebr., U.S.A.* **112** E5
Heby *Sweden* **10** E10
Hecate Str. *Canada* **102** C2
Heceta I. *U.S.A.* **102** B2
Hechi *China* **58** E7
Hechingen *Germany* **25** G4
Hechuan *China* **58** B6
Hecla *U.S.A.* **112** C4
Hecla I. *Canada* **103** C9
Hedal *Norway* **10** D3
Hédé *France* **18** D5
Hede *Sweden* **10** B7
Hedemora *Sweden* **10** D9
Hedensted *Denmark* **11** J3
Hedesunda *Sweden* **10** D10
Heerde *Neths.* **17** B6
Heerenveen *Neths.* **17** B5
Heerhugowaard *Neths.* **17** B4
Heerlen *Neths.* **17** D5
Hefa *Israel* **74** C4
Hefa □ *Israel* **74** C4
Hefei *China* **59** B11
Hefeng *China* **59** C8
Hegalig *Sudan* **81** E3
Hegang *China* **60** B8
Heiban *Sudan* **81** E3
Heichengzhen *China* **56** F4
Heide *Germany* **24** A5
Heidelberg *Germany* **25** F4
Heidelberg *S. Africa* **88** E3
Heidenau *Germany* **24** E9
Heidenheim *Germany* **25** G6
Heihe *China* **53** D13
Heijing *China* **58** E3
Heilbad Heiligenstadt
  Germany **24** D6
Heilbron *S. Africa* **89** D4
Heilbronn *Germany* **25** F5
Heiligenblut *Austria* **26** D5
Heiligenhafen *Germany* **24** A6
Heilongjiang □ *China* **60** B7
Heilunkiang =
  Heilongjiang □ *China* **60** B7
Heimaey *Iceland* **8** E3
Heinola *Finland* **32** B4
Heinsberg *Germany* **24** D2
Heinze Kyun *Burma* **64** E1
Heishan *China* **57** D12
Heishui *Liaoning, China* **57** C10
Heishui *Sichuan, China* **58** A4
Hejaz = Ḩijāz *Si. Arabia* **70** E3
Hejian *China* **56** E9
Hejiang *China* **58** C5
Hejin *China* **56** G6
Hekimhan *Turkey* **72** C7
Hekla *Iceland* **8** E4
Hekou *Guangdong, China* **59** F9
Hekou *Yunnan, China* **58** F4
Hel *Poland* **30** D5
Helagsfjället *Sweden* **10** B6
Helan Shan *China* **56** E3
Helechosa de los Montes
  Spain **37** F6
Helen Atoll *Pac. Oc.* **63** D8
Helena *Ark., U.S.A.* **117** D9
Helena *Mont., U.S.A.* **108** C7
Helendale *U.S.A.* **111** L9
Helensburgh *U.K.* **13** E4
Helensville *N.Z.* **91** B5
Helgeland *Norway* **8** C15
Helgasjön *Sweden* **11** H8
Helgoland *Germany* **24** A3

Heligoland = Helgoland *Germany* **24** A3
Heligoland B. = Deutsche Bucht *Germany* **24** A4
Heliopolis = Masr el Gedida *Egypt* **80** H7
Hell Hole Gorge △ *Australia* **94** D3
Hella *Iceland* **8** E3
Hellas = Greece ■ *Europe* **46** B3
Hellertown *U.S.A.* **115** F9
Hellespont = Çanakkale Boğazı *Turkey* **45** F10
Hellevoetsluis *Neths.* **17** C4
Hellín *Spain* **39** G3
Hells Canyon △ *U.S.A.* **108** D5
Hell's Gate △ *Kenya* **86** C4
Helmand □ *Afghan.* **66** D2
Helmand ➡ *Afghan.* **66** D2
Helme ➡ *Germany* **24** D7
Helmeringhausen *Namibia* **88** D2
Helmond *Neths.* **17** C5
Helmsdale *U.K.* **13** C5
Helmsdale ➡ *U.K.* **13** C5
Helmstedt *Germany* **24** C7
Helong *China* **57** C15
Helper *U.S.A.* **108** G8
Helsingborg *Sweden* **11** H6
Helsinge *Denmark* **11** H6
Helsingfors = Helsinki *Finland* **32** B3
Helsingør *Denmark* **11** H6
Helsinki *Finland* **32** B3
Helska, Mierzeja *Poland* **30** D5
Helston *U.K.* **15** G2
Helvellyn *U.K.* **14** C4
Helwân *Egypt* **80** J7
Hemel Hempstead *U.K.* **15** F7
Hemet *U.S.A.* **111** M10
Hemingford *U.S.A.* **112** D2
Hemis △ *India* **68** B7
Hemmingford *Canada* **115** A11
Hempstead *N.Y., U.S.A.* **115** F11
Hempstead *Tex., U.S.A.* **116** F6
Hemse *Sweden* **11** G12
Hemsön *Sweden* **10** B12
Henån *Sweden* **11** F5
Henan □ *China* **56** H8
Henares ➡ *Spain* **36** E7
Henashi-Misaki *Japan* **54** D9
Hendaye *France* **20** E2
Hendek *Turkey* **72** B4
Henderson *Argentina* **126** D3
Henderson *Ky., U.S.A.* **112** G10
Henderson *N.C., U.S.A.* **117** C15
Henderson *N.Y., U.S.A.* **115** C8
Henderson *Nev., U.S.A.* **111** J12
Henderson *Tenn., U.S.A.* **117** D10
Henderson *Tex., U.S.A.* **116** E7
Henderson I. *Pac. Oc.* **97** K15
Hendersonville *N.C., U.S.A.* **117** D13
Hendersonville *Tenn., U.S.A.* **117** C11
Hendījān *Iran* **71** D6
Hendorābī *Iran* **71** E7
Heng Jiang *China* **58** C5
Heng Xian *China* **58** F7
Hengcheng *China* **56** E4
Hèngch'un *Taiwan* **59** F13
Hengdaohezi *China* **57** B15
Hengelo *Neths.* **17** B6
Hengfeng *China* **59** C10
Hengshan *Hunan, China* **59** D9
Hengshan *Shaanxi, China* **56** F5
Hengshui *China* **56** F8
Hengyang *China* **59** D9
Henichesk *Ukraine* **33** J8
Hénin-Beaumont *France* **19** B9
Henley-on-Thames *U.K.* **15** F7
Henlopen, C. *U.S.A.* **113** F16
Hennan *Sweden* **10** B9
Hennebont *France* **18** E3
Hennenman *S. Africa* **88** D4
Hennessey *U.S.A.* **116** C6
Hennigsdorf *Germany* **24** C9
Henri Pittier △ *Venezuela* **121** D6
Henrietta *N.Y., U.S.A.* **114** C7
Henrietta *Tex., U.S.A.* **116** E5
Henrietta, Ostrov = Genriyetty, Ostrov *Russia* **53** B16
Henrietta Maria, C. *Canada* **104** A3
Henry *U.S.A.* **112** E9
Henryetta *U.S.A.* **116** D7
Henryville *Canada* **115** A11
Hensall *Canada* **114** C3
Henstedt-Ulzburg *Germany* **24** B6
Hentiesbaai *Namibia* **88** C1
Hentiyn Nuruu *Mongolia* **60** B5
Henty *Australia* **95** F4
Henzada *Burma* **67** L19
Hephaestia *Greece* **47** B7
Heping *China* **59** E10
Heppner *U.S.A.* **108** D4
Hepu *China* **58** G7
Hepworth *Canada* **114** B3
Heqing *China* **58** D3
Hequ *China* **56** E6
Héraðsflói *Iceland* **8** D6
Héraðsvötn ➡ *Iceland* **8** D4
Heraklion = Iraklio *Greece* **49** D7

Herald Cays *Australia* **94** B4
Herāt *Afghan.* **66** B3
Herāt □ *Afghan.* **66** B3
Hérault □ *France* **20** E7
Hérault ➡ *France* **20** E7
Herbault *France* **18** E8
Herbert *Canada* **103** C7
Herbert ➡ *Australia* **94** B4
Herberton *Australia* **94** B4
Herbertsdale *S. Africa* **88** E3
Herbignac *France* **18** E4
Herborn *Germany* **24** E4
Herby *Poland* **31** H5
Herceg-Novi *Montenegro* **44** D2
Herchmer *Canada* **103** B10
Herðubreið *Iceland* **8** D5
Hereford *U.K.* **15** E5
Hereford *U.S.A.* **116** D3
Herefordshire □ *U.K.* **15** E5
Hereke *Turkey* **45** F13
Herencia *Spain* **37** F7
Herentals *Belgium* **17** C4
Herford *Germany* **24** C4
Héricourt *France* **19** E13
Herington *U.S.A.* **112** F5
Herisau *Switz.* **25** H5
Hérisson *France* **19** F9
Herkimer *U.S.A.* **115** D10
Herlong *U.S.A.* **110** E6
Herm *U.K.* **15** H5
Hermakivka *Ukraine* **29** B11
Hermann *U.S.A.* **112** F8
Hermannsburg *Australia* **92** D5
Hermannsburg *Germany* **24** C6
Hermanus *S. Africa* **88** E2
Herment *France* **20** C6
Hermidale *Australia* **95** E4
Hermiston *U.S.A.* **108** D4
Hermon *Canada* **114** A7
Hermon *U.S.A.* **115** B9
Hermon, Mt. = Shaykh, J. ash *Lebanon* **74** B4
Hermosillo *Mexico* **118** B2
Hernád ➡ *Hungary* **28** D5
Hernandarias *Paraguay* **127** B5
Hernandez *U.S.A.* **110** J6
Hernando *Argentina* **126** C3
Hernando *U.S.A.* **117** D10
Hernani *Spain* **38** B3
Herndon *U.S.A.* **114** F8
Herne *Germany* **17** C7
Herne Bay *U.K.* **15** F9
Herning *Denmark* **11** H2
Heroica Caborca = Caborca *Mexico* **118** A2
Heroica Nogales = Nogales *Mexico* **118** A2
Heron Bay *Canada* **104** C2
Heron I. *Australia* **94** C5
Herradura, Pta. de la *Canary Is.* **48** F5
Herreid *U.S.A.* **112** C3
Herrenberg *Germany* **25** G4
Herrera *Spain* **37** H6
Herrera de Alcántara *Spain* **37** F3
Herrera de Pisuerga *Spain* **36** C6
Herrera del Duque *Spain* **37** F5
Herrestad *Sweden* **11** F5
Herrin *U.S.A.* **112** G9
Herriot *Canada* **103** B8
Herrljunga *Sweden* **11** F7
Herschel I. *Canada* **4** C1
Hershey *U.S.A.* **115** F8
Herso *Greece* **44** E6
Herstal *Belgium* **17** D5
Hertford *U.K.* **15** F7
Hertfordshire □ *U.K.* **15** F7
's-Hertogenbosch *Neths.* **17** C5
Hertsa *Ukraine* **29** B11
Hertzogville *S. Africa* **88** D4
Hervás *Spain* **36** E5
Hervey B. *Australia* **94** C5
Herzberg *Brandenburg, Germany* **24** D9
Herzberg *Niedersachsen, Germany* **24** D6
Herzliyya *Israel* **74** C3
Herzogenburg *Austria* **26** C8
Heşar *Fārs, Iran* **71** D6
Heşār *Markazī, Iran* **71** C6
Hesdin *France* **19** B9
Heshan *China* **58** F7
Heshui *China* **56** G5
Heshun *China* **56** F7
Hesperia *U.S.A.* **111** L9
Hesse = Hessen □ *Germany* **24** E4
Hessen □ *Germany* **24** E4
Hessenreuther und Manteler Wald △ *Germany* **25** F8
Hestra *Sweden* **11** G7
Hetauda *Nepal* **69** F11
Hetch Hetchy Aqueduct *U.S.A.* **110** H5
Hettinger *U.S.A.* **112** B2
Hettstedt *Germany* **24** D7
Heuksando *S. Korea* **57** G13
Heunghae *S. Korea* **57** F15

Heuvelton *U.S.A.* **115** B9
Heves *Hungary* **28** C5
Heves □ *Hungary* **28** C5
Hewitt *Australia* **94** B4
Hexham *U.K.* **14** C5
Hexi *Yunnan, China* **58** E4
Hexi *Zhejiang, China* **59** D12
Hexigten Qi *China* **57** C9
Heydarābād *Iran* **71** D7
Heysham *U.K.* **14** C5
Heyuan *China* **59** F10
Heywood *Australia* **95** F3
Heze *China* **56** G8
Hezhang *China* **58** D5
Hi Vista *U.S.A.* **111** L9
Hialeah *U.S.A.* **117** J14
Hiawatha *U.S.A.* **112** F6
Hibbing *U.S.A.* **112** B7
Hibernia Reef *Australia* **92** B3
Hickman *U.S.A.* **112** G9
Hickory *U.S.A.* **117** D14
Hicks, Pt. *Australia* **95** F4
Hicks L. *Canada* **103** A9
Hicksville *U.S.A.* **115** F11
Hida *Romania* **29** C8
Hida-Gawa ➡ *Japan* **55** G8
Hida-Sammyaku *Japan* **55** F8
Hidaka-Sammyaku *Japan* **54** C11
Hidalgo □ *Mexico* **119** C5
Hidalgo, Presa M. *Mexico* **118** B3
Hidalgo del Parral *Mexico* **118** B3
Hiddensee *Germany* **24** A9
Hieflau *Austria* **26** D7
Hiendelaencina *Spain* **38** D2
Hierro *Canary Is.* **48** G1
Higashiajima-San *Japan* **54** F10
Higashiōsaka *Japan* **55** G7
Higgins *U.S.A.* **116** C4
Higgins Corner *U.S.A.* **110** F5
High Bridge *U.S.A.* **115** F10
High Desert *U.S.A.* **106** G15
High Level *Canada* **102** B5
High Point *U.S.A.* **117** D15
High Prairie *Canada* **102** B5
High River *Canada* **102** C6
High Tatra = Tatry *Slovak Rep.* **27** B13
High Veld *Africa* **76** J6
High Wycombe *U.K.* **15** F7
Highland □ *U.K.* **13** D4
Highland Park *U.S.A.* **112** D10
Highmore *U.S.A.* **112** C4
Highrock L. *Canada* **103** B8
Higüey *Dom. Rep.* **121** C6
Hihya *Egypt* **80** H7
Hiiumaa *Estonia* **32** C2
Híjar *Spain* **38** D4
Hijāz □ *Si. Arabia* **70** E3
Hijo = Tagum *Phil.* **61** H6
Hikari *Japan* **55** H5
Hikmak, Ras el *Egypt* **80** A2
Hiko *U.S.A.* **110** H11
Hikone *Japan* **55** G8
Hikurangi *Gisborne, N.Z.* **91** C6
Hikurangi *Northland, N.Z.* **91** A5
Hildburghausen *Germany* **24** E6
Hildesheim *Germany* **24** C5
Hill ➡ *Australia* **93** F2
Hill City *Idaho, U.S.A.* **108** E6
Hill City *Kans., U.S.A.* **112** F4
Hill City *Minn., U.S.A.* **112** B7
Hill City *S. Dak., U.S.A.* **112** D2
Hill Island L. *Canada* **103** A7
Hillaby, Mt. *Barbados* **121** g
Hillared *Sweden* **11** G7
Hillcrest *Barbados* **121** g
Hillcrest Center *U.S.A.* **111** K8
Hillegom *Neths.* **17** B4
Hillerød *Denmark* **11** J6
Hillerstorp *Sweden* **11** G7
Hillsboro *Kans., U.S.A.* **112** F5
Hillsboro *N. Dak., U.S.A.* **112** B5
Hillsboro *Ohio, U.S.A.* **113** F12
Hillsboro *Oreg., U.S.A.* **110** E4
Hillsboro *Tex., U.S.A.* **116** E6
Hillsborough *Grenada* **121** D7
Hillsborough *U.S.A.* **115** C13
Hillsborough Channel *Australia* **94** b
Hillsdale *Mich., U.S.A.* **113** E11
Hillsdale *N.Y., U.S.A.* **115** D11
Hillsport *Canada* **104** C2
Hillston *Australia* **95** E4
Hilo *U.S.A.* **107** M8
Hilton *U.S.A.* **114** C7
Hilton Head Island *U.S.A.* **117** E14
Hilvan *Turkey* **73** D8
Hilversum *Neths.* **17** B5
Himachal Pradesh □ *India* **68** D7
Himalaya *Asia* **69** E11
Himalchuli *Nepal* **69** E11
Himamaylan *Phil.* **61** F5
Himarë *Albania* **44** F3
Himatnagar *India* **68** H5
Himeji *Japan* **55** G7
Himi *Japan* **55** F8
Himmerland *Denmark* **11** H3
Ḥimṣ *Syria* **74** A5
Ḥimṣ □ *Syria* **74** A6

Hinche *Haiti* **121** C5
Hinchinbrook I. *Australia* **94** B4
Hinchinbrook Island △ *Australia* **94** B4
Hinckley *U.K.* **15** E6
Hinckley *U.S.A.* **112** B7
Hindaun *India* **68** F7
Hindmarsh, L. *Australia* **95** F3
Hindsholm *Denmark* **11** J4
Hindu Bagh *Pakistan* **68** D2
Hindu Kush *Asia* **66** B7
Hindupur *India* **66** N10
Hines Creek *Canada* **102** B5
Hinesville *U.S.A.* **117** F14
Hinganghat *India* **66** J11
Hingham *U.S.A.* **108** B8
Hingir *India* **69** J10
Hingoli *India* **66** K10
Hinigaran *Phil.* **61** F5
Hinis *Turkey* **73** C9
Hinna = Imi *Ethiopia* **81** F5
Hinna *Nigeria* **83** C7
Hinnerup *Denmark* **11** H4
Hinnøya *Norway* **8** B16
Hinojosa del Duque *Spain* **37** G5
Hinsdale *U.S.A.* **115** D12
Hinterrhein ➡ *Switz.* **25** J5
Hinthada = Henzada *Burma* **67** L19
Hinton *Canada* **102** C5
Hinton *U.S.A.* **113** G13
Hios *Greece* **47** C8
Hios □ *Greece* **47** C8
Hirado *Japan* **55** H4
Hirakud Dam *India* **67** J13
Hiran ➡ *India* **69** H8
Hirapur *India* **69** G8
Hirara *Japan* **55** M2
Hiratsuka *Japan* **55** G9
Hirfanlı Barajı *Turkey* **72** C5
Hiroo *Japan* **54** C11
Hirosaki *Japan* **54** D10
Hiroshima *Japan* **55** G6
Hiroshima □ *Japan* **55** G6
Hirson *France* **19** C11
Hirtshals *Denmark* **11** G3
Hisar *India* **68** E6
Hisarcık *Turkey* **47** B11
Hisaria *Bulgaria* **45** D8
Ḥisb, Sha'ib = Ḥasb, W. ➡ *Iraq* **70** D5
Ḥismá *Si. Arabia* **70** D3
Hispaniola *W. Indies* **121** C5
Ḥīt *Iraq* **73** F10
Hita *Japan* **55** H5
Hitachi *Japan* **55** F10
Hitchin *U.K.* **15** F7
Hitiaa *Tahiti* **91** d
Hitoyoshi *Japan* **55** H5
Hitra *Norway* **8** E13
Hitzacker *Germany* **24** B7
Hiva Oa *French Polynesia* **97** H14
Hixon *Canada* **102** C4
Ḥiyyon, N. ➡ *Israel* **74** E4
Hjalmar L. *Canada* **103** A7
Hjälmaren *Sweden* **10** E9
Hjältevad *Sweden* **11** G9
Hjo *Sweden* **11** F8
Hjørring *Denmark* **11** G3
Hjort Trench *S. Ocean* **5** B10
Hjortkvarn *Sweden* **11** F9
Hkakabo Razi *Burma* **67** E20
Hkamti = Singkaling Hkamti *Burma* **67** G19
Hlinsko *Czech Rep.* **26** B8
Hlobane *S. Africa* **89** D5
Hlohovec *Slovak Rep.* **27** C10
Hlučín *Czech Rep.* **27** B11
Hluhluwe *S. Africa* **89** D5
Hluhluwe △ *S. Africa* **89** C5
Hlukhiv *Ukraine* **33** G7
Hlyboka *Ukraine* **29** B10
Hlybokaye *Belarus* **32** E4
Hnúšťa *Slovak Rep.* **27** C12
Ho *Ghana* **83** D5
Ho Chi Minh City = Thanh Pho Ho Chi Minh *Vietnam* **65** G6
Ho Thuong *Vietnam* **64** G5
Hoa Binh *Vietnam* **58** G5
Hoa Da *Vietnam* **65** G7
Hoa Hiep *Vietnam* **65** G5
Hoai Nhon *Vietnam* **64** E7
Hoang Lien Son *Vietnam* **58** F4
Hoanib ➡ *Namibia* **88** B2
Hoare B. *Canada* **101** D19
Hoarusib ➡ *Namibia* **88** B2
Hobart *Australia* **95** G4
Hobart *U.S.A.* **116** D5
Hobbs *U.S.A.* **109** K12
Hobbs Coast *Antarctica* **5** D14
Hobe Sound *U.S.A.* **117** H14
Hoboken *U.S.A.* **115** F10
Hobro *Denmark* **11** H3
Hoburgen *Sweden* **11** H12
Hobyo *Somali Rep.* **75** F4
Hocalar *Turkey* **47** C11
Hochfeld *Namibia* **88** C2
Hochharz △ *Germany* **24** D6
Hochschwab *Austria* **26** D8
Höchstadt *Germany* **25** F6

Hochtaunus △ *Germany* **25** E4
Hockenheim *Germany* **25** F4
Hodaka-Dake *Japan* **55** F8
Hodeida = Al Ḥudaydah *Yemen* **75** E3
Hodgeville *Canada* **103** C7
Hodgson *Canada* **103** C9
Hodh El Gharbi □ *Mauritania* **82** B3
Hódmezővásárhely *Hungary* **28** D5
Hodna, Chott el *Algeria* **78** A6
Hodonín *Czech Rep.* **27** C10
Hœdic, Î. de *France* **18** E4
Hoek van Holland *Neths.* **17** C4
Hoengseong *S. Korea* **57** F14
Hoeryong *N. Korea* **57** C15
Hoeyang *N. Korea* **57** E14
Hof *Germany* **25** E7
Hofgeismar *Germany* **24** D5
Hofheim *Germany* **25** E4
Hofmeyr *S. Africa* **88** E4
Höfn *Iceland* **8** D6
Hofors *Sweden* **10** D10
Hofsjökull *Iceland* **8** D4
Hōfu *Japan* **55** G5
Hogan Group *Australia* **95** F4
Höganäs *Sweden* **11** H6
Hogarth, Mt. *Australia* **94** C2
Hoge Kempen △ *Belgium* **17** C5
Hoggar = Ahaggar *Algeria* **78** D7
Högsäter *Sweden* **11** F6
Högsby *Sweden* **11** G10
Högsjö *Sweden* **10** E9
Hogsty Reef *Bahamas* **121** B5
Hoh ➡ *U.S.A.* **110** C2
Hohd ech Chargui □ *Mauritania* **82** B3
Hohe Acht *Germany* **25** E3
Hohe Tauern *Austria* **26** D5
Hohe Tauern △ *Austria* **26** D5
Hohenau *Austria* **27** C9
Hohenems *Austria* **26** D2
Hohenloher Ebene *Germany* **25** F5
Hohenwald *U.S.A.* **117** D11
Hohenwestedt *Germany* **24** A5
Hoher Rhön = Rhön *Germany* **24** E5
Hoher Vogelsberg △ *Germany* **24** E5
Hohes Venn *Belgium* **17** D6
Hohes Venn-Eifel △ *Europe* **24** E2
Hohhot *China* **56** D6
Hohoe *Ghana* **83** D5
Hoi An *Vietnam* **64** E7
Hoi Xuan *Vietnam* **58** G5
Hoisington *U.S.A.* **112** F4
Højer *Denmark* **11** K2
Hōjō *Japan* **55** G6
Hok *Sweden* **11** G8
Hökensås *Sweden* **11** F8
Hökerum *Sweden* **11** G7
Hokianga Harbour *N.Z.* **91** A4
Hokitika *N.Z.* **91** E3
Hokkaidō □ *Japan* **54** C11
Hol-Hol *Djibouti* **81** E5
Hola *Kenya* **86** B4
Hola Pristan *Ukraine* **33** J7
Holakas *Greece* **49** D9
Holbæk *Denmark* **11** J5
Holbrook *Australia* **95** F4
Holbrook *U.S.A.* **109** J8
Holcomb *U.S.A.* **114** D7
Holden *U.S.A.* **108** G7
Holdenville *U.S.A.* **116** D6
Holdrege *U.S.A.* **112** E4
Holešov *Czech Rep.* **27** B10
HolETown *Barbados* **121** g
Holguín *Cuba* **120** B4
Holíč *Slovak Rep.* **27** C10
Holice *Czech Rep.* **26** A8
Höljes *Sweden* **10** D6
Hollabrunn *Austria* **26** C9
Hollams Bird I. *Namibia* **88** C1
Holland = Netherlands ■ *Europe* **17** C5
Holland *Mich., U.S.A.* **112** D10
Holland *N.Y., U.S.A.* **114** D6
Holland Centre *Canada* **114** B4
Holland Patent *U.S.A.* **115** C9
Hollandale *U.S.A.* **117** E9
Holley *U.S.A.* **114** C6
Hollfeld *Germany* **25** F7
Hollidaysburg *U.S.A.* **114** F6
Hollis *U.S.A.* **116** D5
Hollister *Calif., U.S.A.* **110** J5
Hollister *Idaho, U.S.A.* **108** E6
Höllviken = Höllviksnäs *Sweden* **11** J6
Höllviksnäs *Sweden* **11** J6
Holly Hill *U.S.A.* **117** G14
Holly Springs *U.S.A.* **117** D10
Hollywood *U.S.A.* **117** J14
Holman *Canada* **100** C8
Hólmavík *Iceland* **8** D3
Holmen *U.S.A.* **112** D8
Holmes Reefs *Australia* **94** B4
Holmsjö *Sweden* **11** H9
Holmsjön *Västernorrland, Sweden* **10** B10
Holmsjön *Västernorrland, Sweden* **10** B9

Holmsland Klit *Denmark* **11** J2
Holmsund *Sweden* **8** E19
Holod *Romania* **28** D7
Holovne *Ukraine* **31** G11
Holroyd ➡ *Australia* **94** A3
Holstebro *Denmark* **11** H2
Holsteinische Schweiz △ *Germany* **24** A6
Holsworthy *U.K.* **15** G3
Holton *Canada* **105** B8
Holton *U.S.A.* **112** F6
Holtville *U.S.A.* **111** N11
Holwerd *Neths.* **17** A5
Holy Cross *U.S.A.* **106** C8
Holy I. *Anglesey, U.K.* **14** D3
Holy I. *Northumberland, U.K.* **14** B6
Holyhead *U.K.* **14** D3
Holyoke *Colo., U.S.A.* **108** F12
Holyoke *Mass., U.S.A.* **115** D12
Holyrood *Canada* **105** C9
Holzkirchen *Germany* **25** H7
Holzminden *Germany* **24** D5
Homa Bay *Kenya* **86** C3
Homalin *Burma* **67** G19
Homand *Iran* **71** C8
Homathko ➡ *Canada* **102** C4
Homberg *Germany* **24** D5
Hombori *Mali* **83** B4
Hombori Tondo *Mali* **83** B4
Homburg *Germany* **25** F3
Home B. *Canada* **101** D18
Home Hill *Australia* **94** B4
Home Reef *Tonga* **91** c
Homedale *U.S.A.* **108** E5
Homer *Alaska, U.S.A.* **100** F1
Homer *La., U.S.A.* **116** E8
Homer *N.Y., U.S.A.* **115** D8
Homer City *U.S.A.* **114** F5
Homert △ *Germany* **24** D4
Homestead *Australia* **94** C4
Homestead *U.S.A.* **117** J14
Homestead △ *U.S.A.* **112** E5
Homoine *Mozam.* **89** C6
Homoljske Planina *Serbia* **44** B5
Homorod *Romania* **29** D10
Homs = Ḥimṣ *Syria* **74** A5
Homyel *Belarus* **23** B16
Homyel □ *Belarus* **33** F6
Hon Chong *Vietnam* **65** G5
Hon Hai *Vietnam* **65** H7
Hon Me *Vietnam* **64** C5
Honan = Henan □ *China* **56** H8
Honaz *Turkey* **47** D11
Honbetsu *Japan* **54** C11
Honcut *U.S.A.* **110** F5
Honda, Bahía *Cuba* **120** B3
Honda Bay *Phil.* **61** G3
Hondarribia *Spain* **38** B3
Hondeklipbaai *S. Africa* **88** E2
Hondo *Japan* **55** H5
Hondo *U.S.A.* **116** G5
Hondo, Río ➡ *Belize* **119** D7
Honduras ■ *Cent. Amer.* **120** D2
Honduras, G. de *Caribbean* **120** C2
Hønefoss *Norway* **9** F14
Honesdale *U.S.A.* **115** E9
Honey Harbour *Canada* **114** B5
Honey L. *U.S.A.* **110** E6
Honfleur *France* **18** C7
Høng *Denmark* **11** J5
Hong Gai *Vietnam* **58** G6
Hong He ➡ *China* **56** H8
Hong Hu *China* **59** C9
Hong Kong □ *China* **59** F10
Hong'an *China* **59** B10
Hongcheon *S. Korea* **57** F14
Honghai Wan *China* **59** F10
Honghe *China* **58** F4
Honghu *China* **59** C9
Hongjiang *China* **59** D8
Hongliu He ➡ *China* **56** F5
Hongor *Mongolia* **56** B7
Hongsa *Laos* **64** C3
Hongseong *S. Korea* **57** F14
Hongshui He ➡ *China* **58** F7
Hongtong *China* **56** F6
Honguedo, Détroit d' *Canada* **105** C7
Hongwon *N. Korea* **57** E14
Hongya *China* **58** C4
Hongyuan *China* **58** A4
Hongze Hu *China* **57** H10
Honiara *Solomon Is.* **90** B8
Honiton *U.K.* **15** G4
Honjō *Japan* **54** E10
Honkorâb, Ras *Egypt* **80** C4
Honningsvåg *Norway* **8** A21
Hönö *Sweden* **11** G5
Honolulu *U.S.A.* **107** L8
Honshū *Japan* **54** F10
Hontoria del Pinar *Spain* **38** D1
Hood, Mt. *U.S.A.* **108** D3
Hood, Pt. *Australia* **93** F2
Hood River *U.S.A.* **108** D3
Hoodsport *U.S.A.* **110** C3
Hooge *Germany* **24** A4
Hoogeveen *Neths.* **17** B6
Hoogezand-Sappemeer *Neths.* **17** A6

Hooghly = Hugli ⇢ *India* **69** J13
Hooghly-Chinsura =
   Chunchura *India* **69** H13
Hook Hd. *Ireland* **12** D5
Hook I. *Australia* **94** b
Hook of Holland = Hoek
   van Holland *Neths.* **17** C4
Hooker *U.S.A.* **116** C4
Hooker Creek = Lajamanu
   Australia **92** C5
Hooker Creek ⓧ *Australia* **92** C5
Hoonah *U.S.A.* **102** B1
Hooper Bay *U.S.A.* **106** C6
Hoopeston *U.S.A.* **112** E10
Hoopstad *S. Africa* **88** D4
Höör *Sweden* **11** J7
Hoorn *Neths.* **17** B5
Hoover *U.S.A.* **117** E11
Hoover Dam *U.S.A.* **111** K12
Hooversville *U.S.A.* **114** F6
Hop Bottom *U.S.A.* **115** E9
Hopa *Turkey* **73** B9
Hope *Canada* **102** D4
Hope *Ariz., U.S.A.* **111** M13
Hope *Ark., U.S.A.* **116** E8
Hope, L. *S. Austral., Australia* **95** D2
Hope, L. *W. Austral., Australia* **93** F3
Hope, Pt. *U.S.A.* **98** C3
Hope I. *Canada* **114** B4
Hope Town *Bahamas* **120** A4
Hope Vale *Australia* **94** B4
Hope Vale ⓧ *Australia* **94** B4
Hopedale *Canada* **105** A7
Hopedale *U.S.A.* **115** D13
Hopefield *S. Africa* **88** E2
Hopei = Hebei □ *China* **56** E9
Hopelchén *Mexico* **119** D7
Hopetoun *Vic., Australia* **95** F3
Hopetoun *W. Austral.,
   Australia* **93** F3
Hopetown *S. Africa* **88** D3
Hopewell *U.S.A.* **113** G15
Hopfgarten *Austria* **26** D5
Hopkins, L. *Australia* **92** D4
Hopkinsville *U.S.A.* **112** G10
Hopland *U.S.A.* **110** G3
Hoquiam *U.S.A.* **110** D3
Hora Hoverla *Ukraine* **29** B9
Horasan *Turkey* **73** B10
Horaždovice *Czech Rep.* **26** B6
Horb *Germany* **25** G4
Hörby *Sweden* **11** J7
Horcajo de Santiago *Spain* **38** F1
Hordern Hills *Australia* **92** D5
Horezu *Romania* **29** E8
Horgen *Switz.* **25** H4
Horgoš *Serbia* **28** D4
Hořice *Czech Rep.* **26** A8
Horinchove *Ukraine* **29** B8
Horinger *China* **56** D6
Horizontina *Brazil* **127** B5
Horki *Belarus* **32** E6
Horlick Mts. *Antarctica* **5** E15
Horlivka *Ukraine* **33** H10
Hormak *Iran* **71** D9
Hormoz *Iran* **71** E7
Hormoz, Jaz.-ye *Iran* **71** E8
Hormozgān □ *Iran* **71** E8
Hormuz, Kūh-e *Iran* **71** E7
Hormuz, Str. of *The Gulf* **71** E8
Horn *Austria* **26** C8
Horn *Sweden* **11** G9
Horn ⇢ *Canada* **102** A5
Horn, Cape = Hornos, C. de
   Chile **128** H3
Horn Head *Ireland* **12** A3
Horn I. *Australia* **94** A3
Horn Plateau *Canada* **102** A5
Hornachuelos *Spain* **37** H5
Hornavan *Sweden* **8** C17
Hornbeck *U.S.A.* **116** F8
Hornbrook *U.S.A.* **108** F2
Hornburg *Germany* **24** C6
Horncastle *U.K.* **14** D7
Horndal *Sweden* **10** D10
Hornell *U.S.A.* **114** D7
Hornell L. *Canada* **102** A5
Hornepayne *Canada* **104** C3
Horní Planá *Czech Rep.* **26** C7
Hornings Mills *Canada* **114** B4
Hornitos *U.S.A.* **110** H6
Hornos, C. de *Chile* **128** H3
Hornoy-le-Bourg *France* **19** C8
Hornsby *Australia* **95** B5
Hornsea *U.K.* **14** D7
Hornslandet *Sweden* **10** C11
Hörnum *Germany* **24** A4
Horobetsu = Noboribetsu
   Japan **54** C10
Horodenka *Ukraine* **29** B10
Horodnya *Ukraine* **33** G6
Horodok *Khmelnytskyy,
   Ukraine* **23** D14
Horodok *Lviv, Ukraine* **23** D12
Horodyshche *Ukraine* **33** H6
Horokhiv *Ukraine* **23** C13
Horovice *Czech Rep.* **26** B6
Horqin Youyi Qianqi *China* **57** A12
Horqueta *Paraguay* **126** A4

Horred *Sweden* **11** G6
Horse Cr. ⇢ *U.S.A.* **108** F12
Horse I. *Canada* **103** C9
Horse Is. *Canada* **105** B8
Horsefly L. *Canada* **102** C4
Horseheads *U.S.A.* **114** D8
Horsens *Denmark* **11** J3
Horseshoe Lake *Canada* **114** A5
Horsham *Australia* **95** F3
Horsham *U.K.* **15** F7
Horšovský Týn *Czech Rep.* **26** B5
Horta *Azores* **78** a
Horten *Norway* **9** G14
Hortobágy ⇢ *Hungary* **28** C6
Hortobágyi △ *Hungary* **28** C6
Horton *U.S.A.* **112** F6
Horton ⇢ *Canada* **100** D6
Horwood L. *Canada* **104** C3
Hosaina *Ethiopia* **81** F4
Hosapete = Hospet *India* **66** M10
Hoseynābād *Khuzestān, Iran* **71** C6
Hoseynābād *Kordestān, Iran* **73** E12
Hōsh 'Īsa *Egypt* **80** H7
Hoshangabad *India* **68** H7
Hoshiarpur *India* **68** D6
Hospet *India* **66** M10
Hoste, I. *Chile* **128** H3
Hostens *France* **20** D3
Hot *Thailand* **64** C2
Hot Creek Range *U.S.A.* **108** G5
Hot Springs *Ark., U.S.A.* **116** D8
Hot Springs *S. Dak., U.S.A.* **112** D2
Hot Springs △ *U.S.A.* **116** D8
Hotagen *Sweden* **8** E16
Hotan *China* **60** C2
Hotazel *S. Africa* **88** D3
Hotchkiss *U.S.A.* **108** G10
Hoting *Sweden* **8** D17
Hotolisht *Albania* **44** E4
Hotte, Massif de la *Haiti* **121** C5
Hottentotsbaai *Namibia* **88** D1
Houat, Î. de *France* **18** E4
Houdan *France* **19** D8
Houei Sai *Laos* **58** G3
Houeillès *France* **20** D4
Houffalize *Belgium* **17** D5
Houghton *Mich., U.S.A.* **112** B9
Houghton *N.Y., U.S.A.* **114** D6
Houghton L. *Canada* **113** C11
Houghton-le-Spring *U.K.* **14** C6
Houhora Heads *N.Z.* **91** A4
Houlton *U.S.A.* **113** B20
Houma *U.S.A.* **117** G9
Houndé *Burkina Faso* **82** C4
Hourtin *France* **20** C2
Hourtin-Carcans, Étang d'
   France **20** C2
Housatonic ⇢ *U.S.A.* **115** E11
Houston *Canada* **102** C3
Houston *Mo., U.S.A.* **112** G8
Houston *Tex., U.S.A.* **116** G7
Hout = Mogwadi ⇢ *S. Africa* **89** C4
Houtkraal *S. Africa* **88** E3
Houtman Abrolhos *Australia* **93** E1
Hovd □ *Mongolia* **60** B4
Hove *U.K.* **15** G7
Hovedstaden □ *Denmark* **11** J6
Hovenweep △ *U.S.A.* **109** H9
Hoveyzeh *Iran* **71** D6
Hovmantorp *Sweden* **11** H9
Hövsgöl *Mongolia* **56** C5
Hövsgöl Nuur *Mongolia* **60** A5
Hovsta *Sweden* **10** E9
Howakil *Eritrea* **81** D5
Howar, Wadi ⇢ *Sudan* **81** D2
Howard *Australia* **95** D5
Howard *Pa., U.S.A.* **114** F7
Howard *S. Dak., U.S.A.* **112** C5
Howe *U.S.A.* **108** E7
Howe, C. *Australia* **95** F5
Howe, West Cape *Australia* **93** G2
Howe I. *Canada* **115** B8
Howell *U.S.A.* **113** D12
Howick *Canada* **115** A11
Howick *S. Africa* **89** D5
Howick Group *Australia* **94** A4
Howitt, L. *Australia* **95** D2
Howland I. *Pac. Oc.* **96** G10
Howrah = Haora *India* **69** H13
Howth *Ireland* **12** C5
Howth Hd. *Ireland* **12** C5
Hoy *U.K.* **13** C5
Hoya *Germany* **24** C5
Høyanger *Norway* **8** F12
Hoyerswerda *Germany* **24** D10
Hoylake *U.K.* **14** D4
Hoyos *Spain* **36** E4
Hpa-an = Pa-an *Burma* **67** L20
Hpunan Pass *Burma* **67** F20
Hradec Králové *Czech Rep.* **26** A8
Hrádek *Czech Rep.* **27** C9
Hranice *Czech Rep.* **27** B10
Hrazdan *Armenia* **35** K7
Hrebenka *Ukraine* **33** G7
Hrisoupoli *Greece* **45** F8
Hristiana *Greece* **47** E7
Hrodna *Belarus* **30** E10

Hrodna □ *Belarus* **32** F3
Hrodzyanka *Belarus* **23** B15
Hron ⇢ *Slovak Rep.* **27** D11
Hrubieszów *Poland* **31** H10
Hrubý Jeseník *Czech Rep.* **27** A10
Hrvatska = Croatia ∎
   Europe **41** C13
Hrymayliv *Ukraine* **23** D14
Hrynyava *Ukraine* **29** C9
Hsenwi *Burma* **67** H20
Hsiamen = Xiamen *China* **59** E12
Hsian = Xi'an *China* **56** G5
Hsinchu *Taiwan* **59** E13
Hsinhailien =
   Lianyungang *China* **57** G10
Hsinying *Taiwan* **59** F13
Hsüchou = Xuzhou *China* **57** G9
Htapodia *Greece* **47** D7
Hu Xian *China* **56** G5
Hua Hin *Thailand* **64** F2
Hua Xian *Henan, China* **56** G8
Hua Xian *Shaanxi, China* **56** G5
Hua'an *China* **59** E11
Huab ⇢ *Namibia* **88** B2
Huacheng *China* **59** E10
Huachinera *Mexico* **118** A3
Huacho *Peru* **124** F3
Huade *China* **56** D7
Huadian *China* **57** C14
Huadu *China* **59** F9
Huahine, Î. *French Polynesia* **97** J12
Huai Hat ⇢ *Thailand* **64** D5
Huai He ⇢ *China* **59** A12
Huai Nam Dang △ *Thailand* **64** C2
Huai Yot *Thailand* **65** J2
Huai'an *Hebei, China* **56** D8
Huai'an *Jiangsu, China* **57** H10
Huaibei *China* **56** G9
Huaibin *China* **59** A10
Huaide = Gongzhuling
   China **57** C13
Huaidezhen *China* **57** C13
Huaihua *China* **58** D7
Huaiji *China* **59** F9
Huainan *China* **59** A11
Huaining *China* **59** B11
Huairen *China* **56** E7
Huairou *China* **56** D9
Huaiyang *China* **56** H8
Huaiyin *China* **57** H10
Huaiyuan *Anhui, China* **57** H9
Huaiyuan *Guangxi Zhuangzu,
   China* **58** E7
Huajuapán de León *Mexico* **119** D5
Hualapai Peak *U.S.A.* **109** J7
Hualien *Taiwan* **59** E13
Huallaga ⇢ *Peru* **124** E3
Huambo *Angola* **85** G3
Huan Jiang ⇢ *China* **56** G5
Huan Xian *China* **56** G4
Huancabamba *Peru* **124** E3
Huancane *Peru* **124** G5
Huancavelica *Peru* **124** F3
Huancayo *Peru* **124** F3
Huanchaca *Bolivia* **124** H5
Huang Hai = Yellow Sea
   China **57** G12
Huang He ⇢ *China* **57** F10
Huang Xian *China* **57** F11
Huangchuan *China* **59** A10
Huanggang *China* **59** B10
Huangguoshu *China* **58** E5
Huangling *China* **56** G5
Huanglong *China* **56** G5
Huanglongtan *China* **59** A8
Huangmei *China* **59** B10
Huangpi *China* **59** B10
Huangping *China* **58** D6
Huangshan *Anhui, China* **59** B12
Huangshan *Anhui, China* **59** C12
Huangshi *China* **59** B10
Huangsongdian *China* **57** C14
Huangyan *China* **59** C13
Huaning *China* **58** E4
Huanjiang *China* **58** E7
Huanren *China* **57** D13
Huantai *China* **57** F9
Huánuco *Peru* **124** E3
Huaping *China* **58** D3
Huaraz *Peru* **124** E3
Huarmey *Peru* **124** F3
Huarong *China* **59** C9
Huascarán, Nevado *Peru* **124** E3
Huasco *Chile* **126** B1
Huasco ⇢ *Chile* **126** B1
Huasna *U.S.A.* **111** K6
Huatabampo *Mexico* **118** B3
Huauchinango *Mexico* **119** C5
Huautla de Jiménez *Mexico* **119** D5
Huaxi *China* **58** D6
Huayin *China* **56** G6
Huayuan *China* **58** C7
Huayun *China* **58** B6
Huazhou *China* **59** G8
Hubballi = Hubli *India* **66** M9
Hubbard *Ohio, U.S.A.* **114** E4
Hubbard *Tex., U.S.A.* **116** F6

Hubbard Glacier *Canada* **100** E4
Hubbart Pt. *Canada* **103** B10
Hubei □ *China* **59** B9
Hubli *India* **66** M9
Huch'ang *N. Korea* **57** D14
Hucknall *U.K.* **14** D6
Huddersfield *U.K.* **14** D6
Hude *Germany* **24** B4
Hudi *Sudan* **80** D3
Hudiksvall *Sweden* **10** C11
Hudson *Canada* **104** B1
Hudson *Mass., U.S.A.* **115** D13
Hudson *N.Y., U.S.A.* **115** D11
Hudson *Wis., U.S.A.* **112** C7
Hudson *Wyo., U.S.A.* **108** E9
Hudson ⇢ *U.S.A.* **115** F10
Hudson, C. *Antarctica* **5** C20
Hudson Bay *Nunavut, Canada* **101** F14
Hudson Bay *Sask., Canada* **103** C8
Hudson Falls *U.S.A.* **115** C11
Hudson Mts. *Antarctica* **5** D16
Hudson Str. *Canada* **101** E18
Hudson's Hope *Canada* **102** B4
Hue *Vietnam* **64** D6
Huebra ⇢ *Spain* **36** D3
Huedin *Romania* **28** D8
Huehuetenango *Guatemala* **120** C1
Huejúcar *Mexico* **118** C4
Huélamo *Spain* **38** E3
Huelgoat *France* **18** D3
Huelma *Spain* **37** H7
Huelva *Spain* **37** H4
Huelva □ *Spain* **37** H4
Huelva ⇢ *Spain* **37** H5
Huentelauquén *Chile* **126** C1
Huércal-Overa *Spain* **39** H3
Huerta, Sa. de la *Argentina* **126** C2
Huertas, C. de las *Spain* **39** G4
Huerva ⇢ *Spain* **38** D4
Huesca *Spain* **38** C4
Huesca □ *Spain* **38** C4
Huéscar *Spain* **39** H2
Huetamo *Mexico* **118** D4
Huete *Spain* **38** E2
Hugh ⇢ *Australia* **94** D1
Hughenden *Australia* **94** C3
Hughesville *U.S.A.* **115** E8
Hugli ⇢ *India* **69** J13
Hugo *Colo., U.S.A.* **108** G12
Hugo *Okla., U.S.A.* **116** D7
Hugoton *U.S.A.* **112** G3
Hui Xian = Huixian *China* **56** G7
Hui Xian *China* **56** H4
Hui'an *China* **59** E12
Hui'anbu *China* **56** F4
Huichang *China* **59** E10
Huichapan *Mexico* **119** C5
Huichon *N. Korea* **57** D14
Huidong *Guangdong, China* **59** F10
Huidong *Sichuan, China* **58** D4
Huifa He ⇢ *China* **57** C14
Huila, Nevado del *Colombia* **124** C3
Huilai *China* **59** F11
Huili *China* **58** D4
Huimin *China* **57** F9
Huinan *China* **57** C14
Huinca Renancó *Argentina* **126** C3
Huining *China* **56** G3
Huinong *China* **56** E4
Huishui *China* **58** D6
Huisne ⇢ *France* **18** E7
Huiting *China* **56** G9
Huitong *China* **58** D7
Huixian *China* **56** G7
Huixtla *Mexico* **119** D6
Huize *China* **58** D4
Huizhou *China* **59** F10
Hukawng Valley *Burma* **67** F20
Hukou *China* **59** C11
Hukuntsi *Botswana* **88** C3
Hulayfā' *Si. Arabia* **70** E4
Hulin *China* **57** B12
Hull = Kingston upon Hull
   U.K. **14** D7
Hull *Canada* **115** A9
Hull ⇢ *U.K.* **14** D7
Hulst *Neths.* **17** C4
Hultsfred *Sweden* **11** G9
Hulun Nur *China* **60** B6
Hulyaypole *Ukraine* **33** J9
Huma, Tanjung *Malaysia* **65** c
Humacao *Puerto Rico* **121** d
Humahuaca *Argentina* **126** A2
Humaitá *Brazil* **124** E6
Humaitá *Paraguay* **126** B4
Humansdorp *S. Africa* **88** E3
Humara, J. *Sudan* **81** D3
Humbe *Angola* **88** B1
Humber ⇢ *U.K.* **14** D7
Humboldt *Canada* **103** C7
Humboldt *Iowa, U.S.A.* **112** D6
Humboldt *Tenn., U.S.A.* **117** D10
Humboldt ⇢ *U.S.A.* **108** G4
Humboldt Gletscher =
   Sermersuaq *Greenland* **101** B19
Hume *U.S.A.* **110** J8
Hume, L. *Australia* **95** F4
Humenné *Slovak Rep.* **27** C14

Hummelsta *Sweden* **10** E10
Humphreys, Mt. *U.S.A.* **110** H3
Humphreys Peak *U.S.A.* **109** J8
Humpolec *Czech Rep.* **26** B8
Humptulips *U.S.A.* **110** C3
Hūn *Libya* **79** C9
Hun Jiang ⇢ *China* **57** D13
Húnaflói *Iceland* **8** D3
Hunan □ *China* **59** D9
Hunchun *China* **57** C16
Hundested *Denmark* **11** J5
Hundewali *Pakistan* **68** D5
Hundred Mile House *Canada* **102** C4
Hunedoara *Romania* **28** E7
Hunedoara □ *Romania* **28** E7
Hünfeld *Germany* **24** E5
Hung Yen *Vietnam* **58** G6
Hunga Ha'apai *Tonga* **91** c
Hungary ∎ *Europe* **27** D12
Hungary, Plain of *Europe* **6** F10
Hungerford *Australia* **95** D3
Hüngnam *N. Korea* **57** E14
Huni Valley *Ghana* **82** D4
Hunjiang *China* **57** D14
Hunneberg *Sweden* **11** F6
Hunnebostrand *Sweden* **11** F5
Hunsberge *Namibia* **88** D2
Hunsrück *Germany* **25** F3
Hunstanton *U.K.* **14** E8
Hunte ⇢ *Germany* **24** B4
Hunter ⇢ *U.S.A.* **115** D10
Hunter I. *Australia* **95** G3
Hunter I. *Canada* **102** C3
Hunter Ra. *Australia* **95** E5
Hunters Road *Zimbabwe* **87** F2
Hunterville *N.Z.* **91** C5
Huntingburg *U.S.A.* **112** F10
Huntingdon *U.S.A.* **114** F6
Huntington *Ind., U.S.A.* **113** E11
Huntington *N.Y., U.S.A.* **115** F11
Huntington *Oreg., U.S.A.* **108** D5
Huntington *Utah, U.S.A.* **108** G8
Huntington *W. Va., U.S.A.* **113** F12
Huntington Beach *U.S.A.* **111** M9
Huntly *N.Z.* **91** B5
Huntly *U.K.* **13** D6
Huntsville *Canada* **114** A5
Huntsville *Ala., U.S.A.* **117** D11
Huntsville *Tex., U.S.A.* **116** F7
Hunyani ⇢ *Zimbabwe* **87** F3
Hunyuan *China* **56** E7
Hunza ⇢ *India* **69** B6
Huo Xian = Huozhou *China* **56** F6
Huong Khe *Vietnam* **64** C5
Huonville *Australia* **95** G4
Huoqiu *China* **59** A11
Huoshan *Anhui, China* **59** A12
Huoshan *Anhui, China* **59** B11
Huoshao Dao = Lü Tao
   Taiwan **59** F13
Huozhou *China* **56** F6
Hupeh = Hubei □ *China* **59** B9
Hūr *Iran* **71** D8
Huránd *Iran* **73** C12
Huraymīla *Si. Arabia* **70** E5
Hurbanovo *Slovak Rep.* **27** D11
Hurd, C. *Canada* **114** A3
Hure Qi *China* **57** C11
Hurezani *Romania* **29** F8
Hurghada *Egypt* **80** B3
Hurley *N. Mex., U.S.A.* **109** K9
Hurley *Wis., U.S.A.* **112** B8
Huron *Calif., U.S.A.* **110** J6
Huron *Ohio, U.S.A.* **114** E2
Huron *S. Dak., U.S.A.* **112** C4
Huron, L. *U.S.A.* **114** B2
Huron East *Canada* **114** C3
Hurricane *U.S.A.* **109** H7
Hurso *Ethiopia* **81** F5
Hurungwe △ *Zimbabwe* **87** F2
Hurunui ⇢ *N.Z.* **91** E4
Hurup *Denmark* **11** H2
Húsavík *Iceland* **8** C5
Huşi *Romania* **29** D13
Huskvarna *Sweden* **11** G8
Hustadvika *Norway* **8** E12
Hustontown *U.S.A.* **114** F6
Hustopeče *Czech Rep.* **27** C9
Husum *Germany* **24** A5
Husum *Sweden* **10** A13
Hutchinson *Kans., U.S.A.* **112** F5
Hutchinson *Minn., U.S.A.* **112** C7
Hutte Sauvage, L. de la
   Canada **105** A7
Hüttenberg *Austria* **26** E7
Hüttener Berge △ *Germany* **24** A5
Hutton, Mt. *Australia* **95** D4
Huwun *Ethiopia* **81** G5
Huy *Belgium* **17** D5
Huzhou *China* **59** B13

Hwacheon-Cheosuji
   S. Korea **57** E14
Hwang Ho = Huang He ⇢
   China **57** F10
Hwange *Zimbabwe* **87** F2
Hwange △ *Zimbabwe* **88** B4
Hyannis *Mass., U.S.A.* **113** E13
Hyannis *Nebr., U.S.A.* **112** E3
Hyargas Nuur *Mongolia* **60** B4
Hybo *Sweden* **10** C10
Hydaburg *U.S.A.* **102** B2
Hyde Park *U.S.A.* **115** E11
Hyden *Australia* **93** F2
Hyder *U.S.A.* **102** B2
Hyderabad *India* **66** L11
Hyderabad *Pakistan* **68** G3
Hydra *Greece* **46** D5
Hyères *France* **21** E10
Hyères, Îs. d' *France* **21** F10
Hyesan *N. Korea* **57** D15
Hyland ⇢ *Canada* **102** B3
Hyltebruk *Sweden* **11** H7
Hymia *India* **69** C8
Hyndman Peak *U.S.A.* **108** E6
Hyōgo □ *Japan* **55** G7
Hyrum *U.S.A.* **108** F8
Hysham *U.S.A.* **108** C10
Hythe *U.K.* **15** F9
Hyūga *Japan* **55** H5
Hyvinge = Hyvinkää *Finland* **32** B3
Hyvinkää *Finland* **32** B3

I

I-n-Akhmed *Mali* **83** B4
I-n-Gall *Niger* **83** B6
I-n-Oudad *Algeria* **83** A5
I-n-Ouzzal *Algeria* **83** A5
I-n-Tadreft *Niger* **83** B6
Iablaniţa *Romania* **28** F7
Iaco ⇢ *Brazil* **124** E5
Iacobeni *Romania* **29** C10
Iakora *Madag.* **89** C8
Ialissos *Greece* **49** C10
Ialomiţa □ *Romania* **29** F12
Ialomiţa ⇢ *Romania* **29** F12
Ialoveni *Moldova* **29** D13
Ialpug ⇢ *Moldova* **29** E13
Ianca *Romania* **29** E12
Iara *Romania* **29** D8
Iarda *Ethiopia* **81** E4
Iargara *Moldova* **29** D13
Iaşi *Romania* **29** C12
Iaşi □ *Romania* **29** C12
Iasmos *Greece* **45** E9
Ib ⇢ *India* **69** J10
Iba *Phil.* **61** D4
Ibadan *Nigeria* **83** D5
Ibagué *Colombia* **124** C3
Iballë *Albania* **44** D4
Ibăneşti *Botoşani, Romania* **29** B11
Ibăneşti *Mureş, Romania* **29** D9
Ibar ⇢ *Serbia* **44** C4
Ibaraki □ *Japan* **55** F10
Ibarra *Ecuador* **124** C3
Ibb *Yemen* **75** E3
Ibba *Sudan* **81** G2
Ibba, Bahr el ⇢ *Sudan* **81** F2
Ibbenbüren *Germany* **24** C3
Ibembo *Dem. Rep. of the Congo* **86** D1
Ibenga ⇢ *Congo* **84** D3
Ibera, L. *Argentina* **125** B4
Iberian Peninsula *Europe* **6** H5
Iberville *Canada* **115** A11
Iberville, Mt. d' *Canada* **101** F19
Ibeto *Nigeria* **83** C6
Ibi *Nigeria* **83** D6
Ibi *Spain* **39** G4
Ibiá *Brazil* **125** G9
Ibiapaba, Sa. da *Brazil* **125** D10
Ibicuí ⇢ *Brazil* **127** B4
Ibicuy *Argentina* **126** C4
Ibiza = Eivissa *Spain* **48** C7
Ibiza ✈ (IBZ) *Spain* **48** C7
Íblei, Monti *Italy* **43** E7
Ibo *Mozam.* **87** E5
Ibonma *Indonesia* **63** E8
Ibotirama *Brazil* **125** F10
Ibrāhīm ⇢ *Lebanon* **74** A4
'Ibrī *Oman* **71** F8
İbriktepe *Turkey* **45** E10
Ibshawâi *Egypt* **80** J7
Ibu *Indonesia* **63** D7
Ibusuki *Japan* **55** J5
Ica *Peru* **124** F3
Içá ⇢ *Brazil* **124** D5
Icacos Pt. *Trin. & Tob.* **125** K15
Içana *Brazil* **124** C5
Içana ⇢ *Brazil* **124** C5
İçel *Turkey* **72** D6
İçel □ *Turkey* **72** D5
Iceland ∎ *Europe* **8** D4
Iceland Basin *Atl. Oc.* **4** C7
Icelandic Plateau *Arctic* **4** C7
Içeriçumra *Turkey* **72** D5
Ich'ang = Yichang *China* **59** B8
Ichchapuram *India* **67** K14
Icheon *S. Korea* **57** F14
Ichhawar *India* **68** H7

Ichihara *Japan* **55** G10
Ichikawa *Japan* **55** G9
Ichilo → *Bolivia* **124** G6
Ichinohe *Japan* **54** D10
Ichinomiya *Japan* **55** G8
Ichinoseki *Japan* **54** E10
Ichnya *Ukraine* **33** G7
Icod *Canary Is.* **48** F3
Icy C. *U.S.A.* **98** B3
Ida Grove *U.S.A.* **112** D6
Idabel *U.S.A.* **116** E7
Idaga Hamus *Ethiopia* **81** E4
Idah *Nigeria* **83** D6
Idaho □ *U.S.A.* **108** D6
Idaho City *U.S.A.* **108** E6
Idaho Falls *U.S.A.* **108** E7
Idalia △ *Australia* **94** C3
Idanha-a-Nova *Portugal* **36** F3
Idar-Oberstein *Germany* **25** F3
Idensalmi = Iisalmi *Finland* **8** E22
Idfû *Egypt* **80** C3
Ídhra = Hydra *Greece* **46** D5
Idi *Indonesia* **62** C1
Idi, Oros = Psiloritis, Oros *Greece* **49** D6
İdil *Turkey* **73** D9
Idiofa *Dem. Rep. of the Congo* **84** E3
Idkerberget *Sweden* **10** D9
Idku *Egypt* **80** H7
Idku, Bahra el *Egypt* **80** H7
Idlib *Syria* **72** E7
Idlib □ *Syria* **72** E7
Idre *Sweden* **10** C6
Idria *U.S.A.* **110** J6
Idrija *Slovenia* **41** C11
Idritsa *Russia* **32** D5
Idutywa = Dutywa *S. Africa* **89** E4
Ieper *Belgium* **17** D2
Ierapetra *Greece* **49** E7
Ierissos *Greece* **44** F7
Ierissos Kolpos *Greece* **44** F7
Iernut *Romania* **29** D9
Iesi *Italy* **41** E10
Iésolo *Italy* **41** C9
Ifac, Penyal d' *Spain* **39** G5
Ifakara *Tanzania* **84** F7
'Ifal, W. al *Si. Arabia* **70** D2
Ifanadiana *Madag.* **89** C8
Ife *Nigeria* **83** D5
Iférouâne *Niger* **83** B6
Iffley *Australia* **94** B3
Ifon *Nigeria* **83** D6
Iforas, Adrar des *Africa* **83** B5
Ifould, L. *Australia* **93** F5
Igalo *Montenegro* **44** D2
Iganga *Uganda* **86** B3
Igarapava *Brazil* **125** H9
Igarka *Russia* **52** C9
Igbetti *Nigeria* **83** D5
Igboho *Nigeria* **83** D5
Igbor *Nigeria* **83** D6
Iğdır *Turkey* **73** C11
Igelfors *Sweden* **11** F9
Iggesund *Sweden* **10** C11
Iglésias *Italy* **42** C1
Igloolik = Iglulik *Canada* **101** D15
Igluligaarjuk = Chesterfield Inlet *Canada* **100** E13
Iglulik *Canada* **101** D15
'Igma, Gebel el *Egypt* **80** B3
Ignace *Canada* **104** C1
İğneada *Turkey* **45** E11
İğneada Burnu *Turkey* **45** E12
Igoumenitsa *Greece* **46** B2
Igrim *Russia* **52** C7
Iguaçu → *Brazil* **127** B5
Iguaçu, Cat. del *Brazil* **127** B5
Iguaçu △ *Brazil* **127** B5
Iguaçu Falls = Iguaçu, Cat. del *Brazil* **127** B5
Iguala *Mexico* **119** D5
Igualada *Spain* **38** D6
Iguassu = Iguaçu → *Brazil* **127** B5
Iguatu *Brazil* **125** E11
Iguazú △ *Argentina* **127** B5
Iguidi, Erg *Africa* **78** C4
Iharana *Madag.* **89** A9
Ihbulag *Mongolia* **56** C4
Iheya-Shima *Japan* **55** L3
Ihiala *Nigeria* **83** D6
Ihosy *Madag.* **89** C8
Ihotry, Farihy *Madag.* **89** C7
Ihugh *Nigeria* **83** D6
Ii *Finland* **8** D21
Ii-Shima *Japan* **55** L3
Iida *Japan* **55** G8
Iijoki → *Finland* **8** D21
Iisalmi *Finland* **8** E22
Iiyama *Japan* **55** F9
Iizuka *Japan* **55** H5
Ijâfene *Mauritania* **78** D4
Ijebu-Igbo *Nigeria* **83** D5
Ijebu-Ode *Nigeria* **83** D5
Ijevan *Armenia* **73** B11
IJmuiden *Neths.* **17** B4
IJo älv = Iijoki → *Finland* **8** D21
IJssel → *Neths.* **17** B5
IJsselmeer *Neths.* **17** B5

Ijuí *Brazil* **127** B5
Ijuí → *Brazil* **127** B4
Ikalamavony *Madag.* **89** C8
Ikale *Nigeria* **83** D6
Ikaluktutiak = Cambridge Bay *Canada* **100** D11
Ikang *Nigeria* **83** E6
Ikanga *Kenya* **86** C4
Ikara *Nigeria* **83** C6
Ikare *Nigeria* **83** D6
Ikaria *Greece* **47** D8
Ikast *Denmark* **11** H3
Ikeda *Japan* **55** G6
Ikeja *Nigeria* **83** D5
Ikela *Dem. Rep. of the Congo* **84** E4
Ikere *Nigeria* **83** D6
İkizdere *Turkey* **73** B9
Ikom *Nigeria* **83** D6
Ikongo *Madag.* **89** C8
Ikopa → *Madag.* **89** B8
Ikorongo △ *Tanzania* **86** C3
Ikot Ekpene *Nigeria* **83** D6
Ikparjuk = Arctic Bay *Canada* **101** C14
Iksan *S. Korea* **57** G14
Ikungu *Tanzania* **86** C3
Ikuntji = Haasts Bluff *Australia* **92** D5
Ikurun *Nigeria* **83** D5
Ila *Nigeria* **83** D5
Ilagan *Phil.* **61** C4
Ilaka *Madag.* **89** B8
Ilām *Iran* **73** F12
Ilam *Nepal* **69** F12
Ilām □ *Iran* **70** C5
Ilan *Taiwan* **59** E13
Ilanskiy *Russia* **53** D10
Ilaro *Nigeria* **83** D5
Ilatane *Niger* **83** B5
Iława *Poland* **30** E6
Ile → *Kazakhstan* **52** E8
Île-à-la-Crosse *Canada* **103** B7
Île-à-la-Crosse, Lac *Canada* **103** B7
Île-de-France □ *France* **19** D9
Ileanda *Romania* **29** C8
Ilebo *Dem. Rep. of the Congo* **84** E4
Ilek *Russia* **52** D6
Ilero *Nigeria* **83** D5
Ilesha *Kwara, Nigeria* **83** D5
Ilesha *Oyo, Nigeria* **83** D5
Ilford *Canada* **103** B9
Ilfracombe *Australia* **94** C3
Ilfracombe *U.K.* **15** F3
Ilgaz *Turkey* **72** B5
Ilgaz Dağları *Turkey* **72** B5
Ilgın *Turkey* **72** C4
Ilha Grande, Represa *Brazil* **127** A5
Ilha Grande △ *Brazil* **127** A5
Ílhavo *Portugal* **36** E2
Ilhéus *Brazil* **125** F11
Ili = Ile → *Kazakhstan* **52** E8
Ilia *Romania* **28** E7
Ilia □ *Greece* **46** D3
Iliamna L. *U.S.A.* **106** D8
Ilias, Profitis *Greece* **49** C9
Iliç *Turkey* **73** C8
Ilıca *Turkey* **47** B9
Iligan *Phil.* **61** G6
Iligan Bay *Phil.* **61** G6
Ilin I. *Phil.* **61** E4
Ilion *U.S.A.* **115** D9
Ilirska-Bistrica *Slovenia* **41** C11
Ilkeston *U.K.* **14** E6
Ilkley *U.K.* **14** D6
Illampu = Ancohuma, Nevado *Bolivia* **124** G5
Illana B. *Phil.* **61** H5
Illapel *Chile* **126** C1
Ille-et-Vilaine □ *France* **18** D5
Ille-sur-Têt *France* **20** F6
Illéla *Niger* **83** C6
Iller → *Germany* **25** G5
Illertissen *Germany* **25** G6
Illescas *Spain* **36** E7
Illetas *Spain* **48** B9
Illichivsk *Ukraine* **33** J6
Illiers-Combray *France* **18** D8
Illimani, Nevado *Bolivia* **124** G5
Illinois □ *U.S.A.* **112** E9
Illinois → *U.S.A.* **112** F8
Illizi *Algeria* **78** C7
Illkirch-Graffenstaden *France* **19** D14
Íllora *Spain* **37** H7
Ilm → *Germany* **24** D7
Ilma, L. *Australia* **93** E4
Ilmajoki *Finland* **8** E20
Ilmen, Ozero *Russia* **32** C6
Ilmenau *Germany* **24** E6
Ilnytsya *Ukraine* **28** B8
Ilo *Peru* **124** G4
Ilobu *Nigeria* **83** D5
Iloilo *Phil.* **61** F5
Ilomantsi *Finland* **8** E24
Ilora *Nigeria* **83** D5

Ilorin *Nigeria* **83** D5
Ilovatka *Russia* **34** E7
Ilovlya *Russia* **35** F7
Ilovlya → *Russia* **35** F7
Iłowa *Poland* **31** G2
Ilubabor □ *Ethiopia* **81** F4
Ilva Mică *Romania* **29** C9
Ilwaco *U.S.A.* **110** D2
Ilwaki *Indonesia* **63** F7
Ilyichevsk = Illichivsk *Ukraine* **33** J6
Iłża *Poland* **31** G8
Iłżanka → *Poland* **31** G8
Imabari *Japan* **55** G6
Imaloto → *Madag.* **89** C8
İmamoğlu *Turkey* **72** D6
Imandra, Ozero *Russia* **8** C25
Imanombo *Madag.* **89** C8
Imari *Japan* **55** H4
Imasa *Sudan* **80** D4
Imathia □ *Greece* **44** F6
Imatra *Finland* **32** B5
Iménas *Mali* **83** B5
imeni 26 Bakinskikh Komissarov = Neftçala *Azerbaijan* **73** C13
imeni 26 Bakinskikh Komissarov *Turkmenistan* **71** B7
imeni Ismail Samani, Pik *Tajikistan* **52** F8
Imeri, Serra *Brazil* **124** C5
Imerimandroso *Madag.* **89** B8
Imfolozi △ *S. Africa* **89** D5
Imi *Ethiopia* **81** F5
Imishly = Imişli *Azerbaijan* **35** L9
Imişli *Azerbaijan* **35** L9
Imlay *U.S.A.* **108** F4
Imlay City *U.S.A.* **114** D1
Immaseri *Sudan* **81** D2
Immenstadt *Germany* **25** H6
Immingham *U.K.* **14** D7
Immokalee *U.S.A.* **117** H14
Imo □ *Nigeria* **83** D6
Imo → *Nigeria* **83** E6
Ímola *Italy* **41** D8
Imotski *Croatia* **41** E14
Imperatriz *Brazil* **125** E9
Impéria *Italy* **40** E5
Imperial *Canada* **103** C7
Imperial *Calif., U.S.A.* **111** N11
Imperial *Nebr., U.S.A.* **112** E3
Imperial Beach *U.S.A.* **111** N9
Imperial Dam *U.S.A.* **111** N12
Imperial Res. *U.S.A.* **111** N12
Imperial Valley *U.S.A.* **111** N11
Imperieuse Reef *Australia* **92** C2
Impfondo *Congo* **84** D3
Imphal *India* **67** G18
Imphy *France* **19** F10
İmranlı *Turkey* **73** C8
İmroz = Gökçeada *Turkey* **45** F9
İmroz *Turkey* **45** F9
Imst *Austria* **26** D3
Imuris *Mexico* **118** A2
Imuruan B. *Phil.* **63** B5
In Alef *Mali* **82** B4
In Delimane *Mali* **83** B5
In Guezzam *Algeria* **83** B6
In Koufi *Mali* **83** B5
In Salah *Algeria* **78** C6
In Tallak *Mali* **83** B5
In Tebezas *Mali* **83** B5
Ina *Japan* **55** G8
Inagua □ *Bahamas* **121** B5
Inangahua *N.Z.* **91** D3
Inanwatan *Indonesia* **63** E8
Iñapari *Peru* **124** F5
Inari *Finland* **8** B22
Inarijärvi *Finland* **8** B23
Inawashiro-Ko *Japan* **54** F10
Inca *Spain* **48** B9
Inca de Oro *Chile* **126** B2
Incahuasi *Argentina* **126** B2
Incahuasi *Chile* **126** B1
İnce Burun *Turkey* **72** A6
İncekum Burnu *Turkey* **72** D5
İncesu *Turkey* **72** C6
Incheon *S. Korea* **57** F14
Inchiri □ *Mauritania* **82** B2
Incio = A Cruz do Incio *Spain* **36** C3
İncirliova *Turkey* **47** D9
Incline Village *U.S.A.* **108** G4
Incomáti → *Mozam.* **89** D5
Incudine, Mte. *France* **21** G13
Inda Silase *Ethiopia* **81** E4
Indal *Sweden* **10** B11
Indalsälven → *Sweden* **10** B11
Indaw *Burma* **67** G20
Indbir *Ethiopia* **81** F4
Independence *Calif., U.S.A.* **110** J8
Independence *Iowa, U.S.A.* **112** D8
Independence *Kans., U.S.A.* **113** G11
Independence *Ky., U.S.A.* **112** F6
Independence *Mo., U.S.A.* **112** F6
Independence Fjord *Greenland* **4** A6
Independence Mts. *U.S.A.* **108** F5
Independența *Romania* **29** E12
Index *U.S.A.* **110** C5
India ■ *Asia* **66** K11

Indian → *U.S.A.* **117** H14
Indian Cabins *Canada* **102** B5
Indian Harbour *Canada* **105** B8
Indian Head *Canada* **103** C8
Indian L. *U.S.A.* **115** C10
Indian Lake *U.S.A.* **115** C10
Indian Springs *U.S.A.* **111** J11
Indiana *U.S.A.* **114** F5
Indiana □ *U.S.A.* **113** F11
Indianapolis *U.S.A.* **112** F10
Indianola *Iowa, U.S.A.* **112** E7
Indianola *Miss., U.S.A.* **117** E9
Indigirka → *Russia* **53** B15
Indija *Serbia* **28** E5
Indio *U.S.A.* **111** M10
Indira Gandhi Canal *India* **68** F5
Indira Sagar *India* **68** H7
Indo-China *Asia* **50** G12
Indonesia ■ *Asia* **62** F5
Indore *India* **68** H6
Indramayu *Indonesia* **63** G13
Indravati → *India* **67** K12
Indre □ *France* **19** F8
Indre → *France* **18** E7
Indre-et-Loire □ *France* **18** E7
Indulkana *Australia* **95** D1
Indura *Belarus* **31** E10
Indus → *Pakistan* **68** G2
Indus, Mouths of the *Pakistan* **68** H3
İnebolu *Turkey* **72** B5
İnecik *Turkey* **45** F11
İnegöl *Turkey* **45** F13
Ineu *Romania* **28** D6
Infantes = Villanueva de los Infantes *Spain* **37** G7
Infiernillo, Presa del *Mexico* **118** D4
Infiesto *Spain* **36** B5
Ingelstad *Sweden* **11** H8
Ingenio *Canary Is.* **48** G4
Ingenio Santa Ana *Argentina* **126** B2
Ingersoll *Canada* **114** C4
Ingham *Australia* **94** B4
Ingleborough *U.K.* **14** C5
Inglewood *Queens., Australia* **95** D5
Inglewood *Vic., Australia* **95** F3
Inglewood *N.Z.* **91** C5
Inglewood *U.S.A.* **111** M8
Ingólfshöfði *Iceland* **8** E5
Ingolstadt *Germany* **25** G7
Ingomar *U.S.A.* **108** C10
Ingonish *Canada* **105** C7
Ingore *Guinea-Biss.* **82** C1
Ingraj Bazar *India* **69** G13
Ingrid Christensen Coast *Antarctica* **5** C6
Ingul = Inhul → *Ukraine* **33** J7
Ingulec = Inhulec *Ukraine* **33** J7
Ingulets = Inhulets → *Ukraine* **33** J7
Inguri = Enguri → *Georgia* **35** J5
Ingushetia □ *Russia* **35** J7
Ingwavuma *S. Africa* **89** D5
Inhaca *Mozam.* **89** D5
Inhafenga *Mozam.* **89** C5
Inhambane *Mozam.* **89** C6
Inhambane □ *Mozam.* **89** C5
Inhaminga *Mozam.* **87** F4
Inharrime *Mozam.* **89** C6
Inharrime → *Mozam.* **89** C6
Inhisar *Turkey* **47** A12
Inhul → *Ukraine* **33** J7
Inhulec *Ukraine* **33** J7
Inhulets → *Ukraine* **33** J7
Iniesta *Spain* **39** F3
Ining = Yining *China* **52** E9
Inírida → *Colombia* **124** C5
Inis = Ennis *Ireland* **12** D3
Inis Córthaidh = Enniscorthy *Ireland* **12** D5
Inishbofin *Ireland* **12** C1
Inisheer *Ireland* **12** D2
Inishfree B. *Ireland* **12** A3
Inishkea North *Ireland* **12** B1
Inishkea South *Ireland* **12** B1
Inishmaan *Ireland* **12** C2
Inishmore *Ireland* **12** C2
Inishmurray I. *Ireland* **12** B3
Inishowen Pen. *Ireland* **12** A4
Inishshark *Ireland* **12** C1
Inishturk *Ireland* **12** C1
Inishvickillane *Ireland* **12** D1
Injāna *Iraq* **73** E11
Injibara *Ethiopia* **81** E4
Injinoo ○ *Australia* **94** A3
Injune *Australia* **95** D4
Inklin → *N. Amer.* **102** B2
Inland Kaikoura Ra. *N.Z.* **91** D4
Inland Sea = Setonaikai *Japan* **55** G6
Inle L. *Burma* **67** J20
Inlet *U.S.A.* **115** C10
Inn → *Austria* **26** C6
Innamincka *Australia* **95** D3
Inner Hebrides *U.K.* **13** E2
Inner Mongolia = Nei Monggol Zizhiqu □ *China* **56** D7
Inner Sound *U.K.* **13** D3

Innerkip *Canada* **114** C4
Innetalling I. *Canada* **104** A4
Innisfail *Australia* **94** B4
Innisfail *Canada* **102** C6
In'noshima *Japan* **55** G6
Innsbruck *Austria* **26** D4
Innviertel *Austria* **26** C6
Inny → *Ireland* **12** C4
Inongo *Dem. Rep. of the Congo* **84** E3
İnönü *Turkey* **47** B12
Inoucdjouac = Inukjuak *Canada* **101** F16
Inowrocław *Poland* **31** F5
Inscription, C. *Australia* **93** E1
Insein *Burma* **67** L20
Insjön *Sweden* **10** D9
Ińsko *Poland* **30** E2
Inta *Russia* **52** C6
Intendente Alvear *Argentina* **126** D3
İntepe *Turkey* **47** A8
Interlaken *Switz.* **25** J3
Interlaken *U.S.A.* **115** D8
International Falls *U.S.A.* **112** A7
Intiyaco *Argentina* **126** B3
Întorsura Buzăului *Romania* **29** E11
Inukjuak *Canada* **101** F16
Inútil, B. *Chile* **128** G2
Inuvik *Canada* **100** D5
Inveraray *U.K.* **13** E3
Inverbervie *U.K.* **13** E6
Invercargill *N.Z.* **91** G2
Inverclyde □ *U.K.* **13** F4
Inverell *Australia* **95** D5
Invergordon *U.K.* **13** D4
Inverloch *Australia* **95** F4
Invermere *Canada* **102** C5
Inverness *Canada* **105** C7
Inverness *U.K.* **13** D4
Inverness *U.S.A.* **117** G13
Inverurie *U.K.* **13** D6
Investigator Group *Australia* **95** E1
Investigator Str. *Australia* **95** F2
Inya *Russia* **52** D9
Inyanga *Zimbabwe* **87** F3
Inyangani *Zimbabwe* **87** F3
Inyantue *Zimbabwe* **88** B4
Inyo Mts. *U.S.A.* **110** J9
Inyokern *U.S.A.* **111** K9
Inyonga *Tanzania* **86** D3
Inza *Russia* **34** D8
Inzhavino *Russia* **34** D6
Iō-Jima *Japan* **55** J5
Ioannina *Greece* **46** B2
Ioannina □ *Greece* **46** B2
Iola *U.S.A.* **112** G6
Ion Corvin *Romania* **29** F12
Ione *U.S.A.* **110** G6
Ionia *U.S.A.* **113** D11
Ionian Is. = Ionioi Nisoi *Greece* **46** C2
Ionian Sea *Medit. S.* **6** H9
Ionioi Nisoi *Greece* **46** C2
Ionioi Nisoi □ *Greece* **46** C2
Ios *Greece* **47** E7
Iowa □ *U.S.A.* **112** D7
Iowa → *U.S.A.* **112** E8
Iowa City *U.S.A.* **112** E8
Iowa Falls *U.S.A.* **112** D7
Iowa Park *U.S.A.* **116** E5
Ipala *Tanzania* **86** C3
Ipameri *Brazil* **125** G9
Ipati *Greece* **46** C4
Ipatinga *Brazil* **125** G10
Ipatovo *Russia* **35** H6
Ipel' → *Europe* **27** D11
Ipiales *Colombia* **124** C3
Ipin = Yibin *China* **58** C5
Ipixuna *Brazil* **124** E4
Ipoh *Malaysia* **65** K3
Ippy *C.A.R.* **84** C4
İpsala *Turkey* **45** F10
Ipsario, Oros *Greece* **45** F8
Ipswich *Australia* **95** D5
Ipswich *U.K.* **15** E9
Ipswich *Mass., U.S.A.* **115** D14
Ipswich *S. Dak., U.S.A.* **112** C4
Ipu *Brazil* **125** D10
Iqaluit *Canada* **101** E18
Iquique *Chile* **124** H4
Iquitos *Peru* **124** D4
Irabu-Jima *Japan* **55** M2
Iracoubo *Fr. Guiana* **125** B8
Iráklia *Cyclades, Greece* **47** E7
Iráklia *Serres, Greece* **44** E7
Iráklio *Greece* **49** D7
Iráklio □ *Greece* **49** D7
Iráklion = Iráklio *Greece* **49** D7
Irákliou, Kolpos *Greece* **49** D7
Irala *Paraguay* **127** B5
Iran ■ *Asia* **71** D7
Iran, Pegunungan *Malaysia* **62** D4
Iran Ra. = Iran, Pegunungan *Malaysia* **62** D4
Īrānshahr *Iran* **71** E9

Irapuato *Mexico* **118** C4
Iraq ■ *Asia* **73** F10
Irati *Brazil* **127** B5
Irbes saurums *Latvia* **30** A9
Irbid *Jordan* **74** C4
Irbid □ *Jordan* **74** C5
Irebu *Dem. Rep. of the Congo* **84** E3
Iregua → *Spain* **38** C2
Ireland ■ *Europe* **12** C4
Irele *Nigeria* **83** D6
Irgiz, Bolshaya → *Russia* **34** D9
Iri = Iksan *S. Korea* **57** G14
Irian Jaya = Papua □ *Indonesia* **63** E9
Irian Jaya Barat □ *Indonesia* **63** E8
Irié *Guinea* **82** D3
Iriga *Phil.* **61** E5
Iringa *Tanzania* **86** D4
Iringa □ *Tanzania* **86** D4
Iriomote △ *Japan* **55** M1
Iriomote-Jima *Japan* **55** M1
Iriona *Honduras* **120** C2
Iriri → *Brazil* **125** D8
Irish Republic ■ *Europe* **12** C4
Irish Sea *Europe* **14** D3
Irkutsk *Russia* **53** D11
Irlğanlı *Turkey* **47** D11
Irma *Canada* **103** C6
Irō-Zaki *Japan* **55** G9
Iroise, Mer d' *France* **18** D2
Iron Baron *Australia* **95** E2
Iron Gate = Portile de Fier *Europe* **28** F7
Iron Knob *Australia* **95** E2
Iron Mountain *U.S.A.* **112** C9
Iron Range △ *Australia* **94** A3
Iron River *U.S.A.* **112** B9
Irondequoit *U.S.A.* **114** C7
Ironton *Mo., U.S.A.* **112** G8
Ironton *Ohio, U.S.A.* **113** F12
Ironwood *U.S.A.* **112** B8
Ironwood Forest △ *U.S.A.* **109** K8
Iroquois *Canada* **115** B9
Iroquois Falls *Canada* **104** C3
Irosin *Phil.* **61** E6
Irpin *Ukraine* **23** C16
Irrara Cr. → *Australia* **95** D4
Irrawaddy □ *Burma* **67** L19
Irrawaddy → *Burma* **67** M19
Irrawaddy, Mouths of the *Burma* **67** M19
Irricana *Canada* **102** C6
Irrunytju *Australia* **93** E4
Irshava *Ukraine* **28** B8
Irsina *Italy* **43** B9
Irtysh → *Russia* **52** C7
Irumu *Dem. Rep. of the Congo* **86** B2
Irún *Spain* **38** B3
Irunea = Pamplona-Iruña *Spain* **38** C3
Irurzun *Spain* **38** C3
Irvine *Canada* **103** D6
Irvine *U.K.* **13** F4
Irvine *Calif., U.S.A.* **111** M9
Irvine *Ky., U.S.A.* **113** G12
Irvinestown *U.K.* **12** B4
Irving *U.S.A.* **116** E6
Irvona *U.S.A.* **114** F6
Irwin → *Australia* **93** E1
Irymple *Australia* **95** E3
Is, Jebel *Sudan* **80** C4
Is-sur-Tille *France* **19** E12
Isa *Nigeria* **83** C6
Isa Khel *Pakistan* **68** C4
Isaac → *Australia* **94** C4
Isabel *U.S.A.* **112** C4
Isabel, I. *Mexico* **118** C3
Isabela *Phil.* **61** H5
Isabela *Puerto Rico* **121** d
Isabela, Cord. *Nic.* **120** D2
Isabella Ra. *Australia* **92** D3
Isaccea *Romania* **29** E13
Isachsen, C. *Canada* **101** B10
İsafjarðardjúp *Iceland* **8** C2
İsafjörður *Iceland* **8** C2
Isagarh *India* **68** G7
Isahaya *Japan* **55** H5
Isaka *Tanzania* **86** C3
İşalnița *Romania* **29** F8
Isalo △ *Madag.* **89** C8
Isan → *India* **69** F9
Isana = Içana → *Brazil* **124** C5
Isangano □ *Zambia* **87** E3
Isanlu Makutu *Nigeria* **83** D6
Isar → *Germany* **25** G8
Isarco → *Italy* **41** B8
Isaris *Greece* **46** D3
Íscar *Spain* **36** D6
İscehisar *Turkey* **47** C12
Íschia *Italy* **42** B6
Isdell → *Australia* **92** C3
Ise *Japan* **55** G8
Ise-Shima △ *Japan* **55** G8
Ise-Wan *Japan* **55** G8
Isefjord *Denmark* **11** J5
Isel → *Austria* **26** E5
Iseo *Italy* **40** C7
Iseo, L. d' *Italy* **40** C7
Iseramagazi *Tanzania* **86** C3

Isère □ *France* **21** C9
Isère ➤ *France* **21** D8
Iserlohn *Germany* **24** D3
Isérnia *Italy* **43** A7
Iseyin *Nigeria* **83** D5
Isfahan = Eşfahān *Iran* **71** C6
Ishëm *Albania* **44** E3
Ishigaki *Japan* **55** M2
Ishigaki-Shima *Japan* **55** M2
Ishikari-Gawa ➤ *Japan* **54** C10
Ishikari-Sammyaku *Japan* **54** C11
Ishikari-Wan *Japan* **54** C10
Ishikawa *Japan* **55** L3
Ishikawa □ *Japan* **55** F8
Ishim *Russia* **52** D7
Ishim ➤ *Russia* **52** D8
Ishinomaki *Japan* **54** E10
Ishioka *Japan* **55** F10
Ishkoman *Pakistan* **69** A5
Ishpeming *U.S.A.* **112** B10
Isigny-sur-Mer *France* **18** C5
Işıklar Dağı *Turkey* **45** F11
Işıklı *Turkey* **47** C11
Ísil Kul *Russia* **52** D8
Ísili *Italy* **42** C2
Isiolo *Kenya* **86** B4
Isiro *Dem. Rep. of the Congo* **86** B2
Isisford *Australia* **94** C3
Iskenderun *Turkey* **72** D7
İskenderun Körfezi *Turkey* **72** D6
İskilip *Turkey* **72** B6
Iskŭr ➤ *Bulgaria* **45** C8
Iskŭr, Yazovir *Bulgaria* **44** D7
Iskut ➤ *Canada* **102** B2
Isla ➤ *U.K.* **13** E5
Isla Coiba △ *Panama* **120** E3
Isla Cristina *Spain* **37** H3
Isla de Salamanca △
　　Colombia **121** D5
Isla Gorge △ *Australia* **94** D4
Isla Isabel △ *Mexico* **118** C3
Isla Tiburón y San
　　Estebán △ *Mexico* **118** B2
Isla Vista *U.S.A.* **111** L7
İslâhiye *Turkey* **72** D7
Islam Headworks *Pakistan* **68** E5
Islamabad *Pakistan* **68** C5
Islamgarh *Pakistan* **68** F4
Islamkot *Pakistan* **68** G4
Islampur *Bihar, India* **69** G11
Islampur *W. Bengal, India* **69** F13
Island = Iceland ■ *Europe* **8** D4
Island L. *Canada* **103** C10
Island Lagoon *Australia* **95** E2
Island Pond *U.S.A.* **115** B13
Islands, B. of *Canada* **105** C8
Islands, B. of N.Z. **91** B5
Islay *U.K.* **13** F2
Isle ➤ *France* **20** D3
Isle aux Morts *Canada* **105** C8
Isle of Wight □ *U.K.* **15** G6
Isle Royale △ *U.S.A.* **112** B9
Isleton *U.S.A.* **110** G5
Ismail = Izmayil *Ukraine* **29** E13
Ismâ'ilîya *Egypt* **80** H8
Ismaning *Germany* **25** G7
Isna *Egypt* **80** B3
Isoanala *Madag.* **89** C8
Isogstalo *India* **69** B8
Ísola del Liri *Italy* **41** G10
Ísola della Scala *Italy* **40** C7
Ísola di Capo Rizzuto *Italy* **43** D10
Ísparta *Turkey* **47** D12
Isparta □ *Turkey* **72** D4
Isperikh *Bulgaria* **45** C10
Íspica *Italy* **43** F7
İspir *Turkey* **73** B9
Israel ■ *Asia* **74** D3
Isratu *Eritrea* **81** D4
Issakly *Russia* **34** C10
Issia *Ivory C.* **82** D3
Issoire *France* **20** C7
Issoudun *France* **19** F8
Issyk-Kul, Ozero =
　　Ysyk-Köl *Kyrgyzstan* **52** E8
Ist *Croatia* **41** D11
Istállós-kő *Hungary* **28** B5
İstanbul *Turkey* **45** E12
İstanbul □ *Turkey* **45** E12
İstanbul ✈ (IST) *Turkey* **45** F12
İstanbul Boğazı *Turkey* **45** E13
Istiea *Greece* **46** C5
Isto, Mt. *U.S.A.* **106** B11
Istok *Kosovo* **44** D4
Istokpoga, L. *U.S.A.* **117** H14
Istra *Croatia* **41** C10
Istres *France* **21** E8
Istria = Istra *Croatia* **41** C10
Itá *Paraguay* **126** B4
Itaberaba *Brazil* **125** F10
Itabira *Brazil* **125** G10
Itabirito *Brazil* **127** A7
Itabuna *Brazil* **125** F11
Itacaúnas ➤ *Brazil* **125** E9
Itacoatiara *Brazil* **124** D7
Itaipú, Represa de *Brazil* **127** B5
Itaituba *Brazil* **125** D7
Itajaí *Brazil* **127** B6
Itajubá *Brazil* **127** A6

Itaka *Tanzania* **87** D3
Itala △ *S. Africa* **89** D5
Italy ■ *Europe* **7** G8
Itamaraju *Brazil* **125** G11
Itampolo *Madag.* **89** C7
Itandrano *Madag.* **89** C8
Itapecuru Mirim *Brazil* **125** D10
Itaperuna *Brazil* **127** A7
Itapetininga *Brazil* **127** A6
Itapeva *Brazil* **127** A6
Itapicuru *Bahia, Brazil* **125** F11
Itapicuru ➤ *Maranhão,*
　　Brazil **125** D10
Itapipoca *Brazil* **125** D11
Itapuá □ *Paraguay* **127** B4
Itaquí *Brazil* **126** B4
Itararé *Brazil* **127** A6
Itarsi *India* **68** H7
Itatí *Argentina* **126** B4
Itatiaia △ *Brazil* **127** A7
Itbayat *Phil.* **61** A4
Itchen ➤ *U.K.* **15** G6
Itea *Greece* **46** C4
Itezhi Tezhi, L. *Zambia* **87** F2
Ithaca = Ithaki *Greece* **46** C2
Ithaca *U.S.A.* **115** D8
Ithaki *Greece* **46** C2
Iti △ *Greece* **46** C4
Itiquira ➤ *Brazil* **125** G7
Itiyuro ➤ *Argentina* **126** A3
Itō *Japan* **55** G9
Itoigawa *Japan* **55** F8
Iton ➤ *France* **18** C8
Itonamas ➤ *Bolivia* **124** F6
Ittoqqortoormiit *Greenland* **4** B6
Itu *Brazil* **127** A6
Itu *Nigeria* **83** D6
Itu Aba I. *S. China Sea* **62** B4
Ituiutaba *Brazil* **125** G9
Itumbiara *Brazil* **125** G9
Ituna *Canada* **103** C8
Itunge Port *Tanzania* **87** D3
Iturbe *Argentina* **126** A2
Ituri ➤ *Dem. Rep. of the Congo* **86** B2
Iturup, Ostrov *Russia* **53** E15
Ituxi ➤ *Brazil* **124** E6
Itzehoe *Germany* **24** B5
Ivahona *Madag.* **89** C8
Ivaí ➤ *Brazil* **127** A5
Ivalo *Finland* **8** B22
Ivalojoki ➤ *Finland* **8** B22
Ivanava *Belarus* **23** B13
Ivančice *Czech Rep.* **27** B9
Ivane-Puste *Ukraine* **29** B11
Ivangorod *Russia* **32** C5
Ivanhoe *Australia* **95** E3
Ivanhoe *Canada* **114** B7
Ivanhoe *Calif., U.S.A.* **110** J7
Ivanhoe *Minn., U.S.A.* **112** C5
Ivanhorod *Ukraine* **29** B14
Ivanić Grad *Croatia* **41** C13
Ivanjica *Serbia* **44** C4
Ivanjska *Bos.-H.* **28** F2
Ivankoyskoye Vdkhr. *Russia* **32** D9
Ivano-Frankivsk *Ukraine* **29** B9
Ivano-Frankivsk □ *Ukraine* **29** B9
Ivanovo = Ivanava *Belarus* **23** B13
Ivanovo *Russia* **32** D11
Ivanovo □ *Russia* **34** B5
Ivanščica *Croatia* **41** B13
Ivato *Madag.* **89** C8
Ivatsevichy *Belarus* **23** B13
Ivaylovgrad *Bulgaria* **45** E10
Ivinheima *Brazil* **127** A5
Ivinhema ➤ *Brazil* **127** A5
Ivohibe *Madag.* **89** C8
Ivory Coast *W. Afr.* **82** D4
Ivory Coast ■ *Africa* **82** D4
Ivösjön *Sweden* **11** H8
Ivrea *Italy* **40** C4
İvrindi *Turkey* **47** B9
Ivujivik *Canada* **101** E16
Ivvavik △ *Canada* **100** D4
Ivybridge *U.K.* **15** G4
Iwaizumi *Japan* **54** E10
Iwaki *Japan* **55** F10
Iwakuni *Japan* **55** G6
Iwamizawa *Japan* **54** C10
Iwanai *Japan* **54** C10
Iwata *Japan* **55** G8
Iwate □ *Japan* **54** E10
Iwate-San *Japan* **54** E10
Iwo *Nigeria* **83** D5
Iwŏn *N. Korea* **57** D15
Iwonicz-Zdrój *Poland* **31** J8
Ixiamas *Bolivia* **124** F5
Ixopo *S. Africa* **89** E5
Ixtepec *Mexico* **119** D5
Ixtlán del Río *Mexico* **118** C4
Iyal Bakhit *Sudan* **81** E2
Iyo *Japan* **55** H6
Izabal, L. de *Guatemala* **120** C2
Izamal *Mexico* **119** C7
Izberbash *Russia* **35** J8
Izbica *Poland* **31** H10

Izbica Kujawska *Poland* **31** F5
Izbiceni *Romania* **29** G9
Izena-Shima *Japan* **55** L3
Izgrev *Bulgaria* **45** C10
Izhevsk *Russia* **52** D6
Izmayil *Ukraine* **29** E13
İzmir *Turkey* **47** C9
İzmir □ *Turkey* **47** C9
İzmir Adnan Menderes ✈
　　(ADB) *Turkey* **47** C9
İzmit = Kocaeli *Turkey* **45** F13
İznájar *Spain* **37** H6
İznalloz *Spain* **37** H7
İznik *Turkey* **72** B3
İznik Gölü *Turkey* **45** F13
Izobil'nyy *Russia* **35** H5
Izola *Slovenia* **41** C10
Izra *Syria* **74** C5
Iztochni Rodopi *Bulgaria* **45** E9
Izu-Shotō *Japan* **55** G10
Izúcar de Matamoros
　　Mexico **119** D5
Izumi-Sano *Japan* **55** G7
Izumo *Japan* **55** G6
Izyaslav *Ukraine* **23** C14
Izyum *Ukraine* **33** H9

J

J.F.K. Int. ✈ (JFK) *U.S.A.* **115** F11
J. Strom Thurmond L.
　　U.S.A. **117** E13
Jaba *Ethiopia* **81** F4
Jabal at Ţā'ir *Red Sea* **81** D5
Jabalón ➤ *Spain* **37** G6
Jabalpur *India* **69** H8
Jabbūl *Syria* **70** B3
Jablah *Syria* **70** B3
Jablanac *Croatia* **41** D11
Jablanica *Bos.-H.* **28** G2
Jablonec nad Nisou
　　Czech Rep. **26** A8
Jablonica *Slovak Rep.* **27** C10
Jabłonowo Pomorskie *Poland* **30** E6
Jablunkov *Czech Rep.* **27** B11
Jaboatão *Brazil* **125** E11
Jaboticabal *Brazil* **127** A6
Jabukovac *Serbia* **44** B6
Jaca *Spain* **38** C4
Jacareí *Brazil* **127** A6
Jacarèzinho *Brazil* **127** A6
Jack River △ *Australia* **94** A3
Jackman *U.S.A.* **113** C18
Jacksboro *U.S.A.* **116** E5
Jackson *Barbados* **121** g
Jackson *Ala., U.S.A.* **117** F11
Jackson *Calif., U.S.A.* **110** G6
Jackson *Ky., U.S.A.* **113** G12
Jackson *Mich., U.S.A.* **113** D11
Jackson *Minn., U.S.A.* **112** D6
Jackson *Miss., U.S.A.* **117** E9
Jackson *Mo., U.S.A.* **112** G9
Jackson *N.H., U.S.A.* **115** B13
Jackson *Ohio, U.S.A.* **113** F12
Jackson *Tenn., U.S.A.* **117** D10
Jackson *Wyo., U.S.A.* **108** E8
Jackson B. *N.Z.* **91** E2
Jackson L. *U.S.A.* **108** E8
Jacksons *N.Z.* **91** E3
Jackson's Arm *Canada* **105** C8
Jacksonville *Ala., U.S.A.* **117** E12
Jacksonville *Ark., U.S.A.* **116** D8
Jacksonville *Calif., U.S.A.* **110** H6
Jacksonville *Fla., U.S.A.* **117** F14
Jacksonville *Ill., U.S.A.* **112** F8
Jacksonville *N.C., U.S.A.* **117** D16
Jacksonville *Tex., U.S.A.* **116** F7
Jacksonville Beach *U.S.A.* **117** F14
Jacmel *Haiti* **121** C5
Jacob Lake *U.S.A.* **109** H7
Jacobabad *Pakistan* **68** E3
Jacobina *Brazil* **125** F10
Jacques-Cartier, Dét. de
　　Canada **105** C7
Jacques-Cartier, Mt. *Canada* **105** C6
Jacques-Cartier △ *Canada* **105** C5
Jacqueville *Ivory C.* **82** D4
Jacuí ➤ *Brazil* **127** C5
Jacumba *U.S.A.* **111** N10
Jacundá ➤ *Brazil* **125** D8
Jade *Germany* **24** B4
Jade City *Canada* **102** B3
Jade Mt. = Yü Shan *Taiwan* **59** F13
Jadebusen *Germany* **24** B4
Jadovnik *Serbia* **44** C3
Jadraque *Spain* **38** E2
Jaén *Peru* **124** E3
Jaén *Spain* **37** H7
Jaén □ *Spain* **37** H7
Jafarabad *India* **68** J4
Jaffa = Tel Aviv-Yafo *Israel* **74** C3
Jaffa, C. *Australia* **95** F2
Jaffna *Sri Lanka* **66** Q12
Jaffrey *U.S.A.* **115** D12
Jagadhri *India* **68** D7
Jagadishpur *India* **69** G11
Jagdalpur *India* **67** K13

Jagersfontein *S. Africa* **88** D4
Jaghīn ➤ *Iran* **71** E8
Jagodina *Serbia* **44** B5
Jagraon *India* **68** D6
Jagst ➤ *Germany* **25** F5
Jagtial *India* **66** K11
Jaguariaíva *Brazil* **127** A6
Jaguaribe ➤ *Brazil* **125** D11
Jagüey Grande *Cuba* **120** B3
Jahanabad *India* **69** G11
Jahazpur *India* **68** G6
Jahrom *Iran* **71** D7
Jaijon *India* **68** D7
Jailolo *Indonesia* **63** D7
Jailolo, Selat *Indonesia* **63** D7
Jaipur *India* **68** F6
Jais *India* **69** F9
Jaisalmer *India* **68** F4
Jaisinghnagar *India* **69** H8
Jaitaran *India* **68** F5
Jaithari *India* **69** H8
Jājarm *Iran* **71** B8
Jajce *Bos.-H.* **28** F2
Jakam ➤ *India* **68** H6
Jakarta *Indonesia* **62** F3
Jakhal *India* **68** E6
Jakhau *India* **68** H3
Jakobstad = Pietarsaari
　　Finland **8** E20
Jakupica *Macedonia* **44** E5
Jal *U.S.A.* **109** K12
Jalājil *Si. Arabia* **70** E5
Jalālābād *Afghan.* **68** B4
Jalalabad *India* **69** F8
Jalalpur Jattan *Pakistan* **68** C6
Jalama *U.S.A.* **111** L6
Jalandhar = Jullundur *India* **68** D6
Jalapa *Guatemala* **120** D2
Jalapa Enríquez = Xalapa
　　Mexico **119** D5
Jalasjärvi *Finland* **8** E20
Jalaun *India* **69** F8
Jaldhaka ➤ *Bangla.* **69** F13
Jalesar *India* **68** F8
Jaleswar *Nepal* **69** F11
Jalgaon *India* **66** J9
Jalībah *Iraq* **70** D5
Jalingo *Nigeria* **83** D7
Jalisco □ *Mexico* **118** D4
Jalkot *Pakistan* **69** B5
Jalna *India* **66** K9
Jalón ➤ *Spain* **38** D3
Jalor *India* **68** G5
Jalpa *Mexico* **118** C4
Jalpaiguri *India* **67** F16
Jalpan *Mexico* **119** C5
Jaluit I. *Marshall Is.* **96** G8
Jalūlā *Iraq* **73** E11
Jamaame *Somali Rep.* **75** G3
Jamaari *Nigeria* **83** C6
Jamaica ■ *W. Indies* **120** a
Jamalpur *Bangla.* **67** G16
Jamalpur *India* **69** G12
Jamalpurganj *India* **69** H13
Jamanxim ➤ *Brazil* **125** D7
Jambewangi *Indonesia* **63** J17
Jambi *Indonesia* **62** E2
Jambi □ *Indonesia* **62** E2
Jambongan, Pulau *Malaysia* **62** C5
Jambongon *Phil.* **61** H2
Jambusar *India* **68** H5
James ➤ *S. Dak., U.S.A.* **112** D5
James ➤ *Va., U.S.A.* **113** G15
James B. *Canada* **104** B3
James I. *Canada* **82** C1
James Ranges *Australia* **92** D5
James Ross I. *Antarctica* **5** C18
Jamesabad *Pakistan* **68** G3
Jamestown *Australia* **95** E2
Jamestown *S. Africa* **88** E4
Jamestown *N. Dak., U.S.A.* **112** B4
Jamestown *N.Y., U.S.A.* **114** D5
Jamestown *Pa., U.S.A.* **114** E4
Jamīlābād *Iran* **71** C6
Jamira ➤ *India* **69** J13
Jämjö *Sweden* **11** H9
Jamkhandi *India* **66** L9
Jamkhed *India* **66** K9
Jamm *India* **68** F4
Jammalamadugu *India* **66** M11
Jammu *India* **68** C6
Jammu & Kashmir □ *India* **69** B7
Jamnagar *India* **68** H4
Jamni ➤ *India* **69** G8
Jampur *Pakistan* **68** E4
Jamrud *Pakistan* **68** C4
Jämsä *Finland* **32** B3
Jamshedpur *India* **69** H12
Jamtara *India* **69** H12
Jämtland *Sweden* **8** E16
Jämtlands län □ *Sweden* **10** B7
Jan L. *Canada* **103** C8
Jan Mayen *Arctic* **4** B7
Janakkala *Finland* **32** B3
Janaúba *Brazil* **125** G10
Janaucu, I. *Brazil* **125** D8
Jand *Pakistan* **68** C5
Jandaq *Iran* **71** C7
Jandía *Canary Is.* **48** F5
Jandía, Pta. de *Canary Is.* **48** F5

Jandía △ *Canary Is.* **48** F5
Jandola *Pakistan* **68** C4
Jandowae *Australia* **95** D5
Jándula ➤ *Spain* **37** G6
Janesville *U.S.A.* **112** D9
Janga *Ghana* **83** C4
Jangamo *Mozam.* **89** C6
Janghai *India* **69** G10
Jangheung *S. Korea* **57** G14
Janikowo *Poland* **31** F5
Janin = Ioánnina □ *Greece* **46** B2
Janja *Bos.-H.* **28** F4
Janjanbureh *Gambia* **82** C2
Janjevo *Kosovo* **44** D5
Janjgir *India* **69** J10
Janjina *Croatia* **41** F14
Janjina *Bos.-H.* **28** G3
Janos *Mexico* **118** A3
Jánoshalma *Hungary* **28** D4
Jánosháza *Hungary* **28** C2
Jánossomorja *Hungary* **28** C2
Janów *Poland* **31** H6
Janów Lubelski *Poland* **31** H9
Janów Podlaski *Poland* **31** F10
Janowiec Wielkopolski
　　Poland **31** F4
Januária *Brazil* **125** G10
Janub △ *Sudan* **81** F2
Janub Dârfûr □ *Sudan* **81** E2
Janub Kordofân □ *Sudan* **81** E3
Janûb Sînî □ *Egypt* **74** F2
Janubio *Canary Is.* **48** F6
Janville *France* **19** D8
Janzé *France* **18** E5
Jaora *India* **68** H6
Japan ■ *Asia* **54** E7
Japan, Sea of *Asia* **54** E7
Japan Trench *Pac. Oc.* **96** D6
Japen = Yapen *Indonesia* **63** E9
Japla *India* **69** G11
Japurá ➤ *Brazil* **124** D5
Jaqué *Panama* **120** E4
Jaquarão *Brazil* **127** C5
Jaraicejo *Spain* **37** F5
Jaraíz de la Vera *Spain* **36** E5
Jarama ➤ *Spain* **36** E7
Jaramānah *Syria* **72** E6
Jarandilla de la Vera *Spain* **36** E5
Jaranwala *Pakistan* **68** D5
Jarash *Jordan* **74** C4
Jarash □ *Jordan* **74** C4
Järbo *Sweden* **10** D10
Jardim *Brazil* **126** A4
Jardín ➤ *Spain* **39** G2
Jardín América *Argentina* **127** B4
Jardine River △ *Australia* **94** A3
Jardines de la Reina, Arch.
　　de los *Cuba* **120** B4
Jargalang *China* **57** C12
Jari ➤ *Brazil* **125** D8
Jarīr, W. al ➤ *Si. Arabia* **70** E4
Järlåsa *Sweden* **10** E11
Jarmen *Germany* **24** B9
Järna *Dalarna, Sweden* **10** D8
Järna *Stockholm, Sweden* **10** E11
Jarnac *France* **20** C3
Jarny *France* **19** C12
Jarocin *Poland* **31** G4
Jaroměř *Czech Rep.* **26** A8
Jarosław *Poland* **31** H9
Järpås *Sweden* **11** F6
Järpen *Sweden* **10** A7
Jarrahdale *Australia* **93** F2
Jarrahi ➤ *Iran* **71** D6
Jarres, Plaine des *Laos* **64** C4
Jarso *Ethiopia* **81** F4
Jartai *China* **56** E3
Jarud Qi *China* **57** B11
Järvenpää *Finland* **32** B3
Jarvis *Canada* **114** D4
Jarvis I. *Pac. Oc.* **97** H12
Jarvorník *Czech Rep.* **27** A10
Jarwa *India* **69** F10
Jaša Tomić *Serbia* **28** E5
Jasdan *India* **68** H4
Jashpurnagar *India* **69** H11
Jasidih *India* **69** G12
Jāsimīyah *Iraq* **73** F11
Jasień *Poland* **31** G2
Jasin *Malaysia* **65** L4
Jāsk *Iran* **71** E8
Jasło *Poland* **31** J8
Jasmund *Germany* **24** A9
Jasmund □ *Germany* **24** A9
Jaso *India* **69** G9
Jasper *Alta., Canada* **102** C5
Jasper *Ont., Canada* **115** B9
Jasper *Ala., U.S.A.* **117** E11
Jasper *Fla., U.S.A.* **117** F13
Jasper *Ind., U.S.A.* **112** F10
Jasper *Tex., U.S.A.* **116** F7
Jasper △ *Canada* **102** C5
Jasrasar *India* **68** F5
Jassān *Iraq* **73** G11
Jastarnia *Poland* **30** D5
Jastrebarsko *Croatia* **41** C12
Jastrowie *Poland* **30** E3

Jastrzębie Zdrój *Poland* **31** J5
Jász-Nagykun-Szolnok □
　　Hungary **28** C5
Jászapáti *Hungary* **28** C5
Jászárokszállás *Hungary* **28** C4
Jászberény *Hungary* **28** C4
Jászkisér *Hungary* **28** C5
Jászladány *Hungary* **28** C5
Jataí *Brazil* **125** G8
Jati *Pakistan* **68** G3
Jatibarang *Indonesia* **63** G13
Jatiluwih *Indonesia* **63** J18
Jatinegara *Indonesia* **63** G12
Játiva = Xátiva *Spain* **39** G4
Jättendal *Sweden* **10** C11
Jaú *Brazil* **127** A6
Jauja *Peru* **124** F3
Jaunpur *India* **69** G10
Java = Jawa *Indonesia* **62** F3
Java Sea *Indonesia* **62** F3
Java Trench *Ind. Oc.* **62** F3
Javalambre, Sa. de *Spain* **38** E4
Javānrūd *Iran* **73** E12
Jávea *Spain* **39** G5
Jawa *Indonesia* **62** F3
Jawa Barat □ *Indonesia* **63** G12
Jawa Tengah □ *Indonesia* **63** G14
Jawa Timur □ *Indonesia* **63** G15
Jawad *India* **68** G6
Jawhar *Somali Rep.* **75** G4
Jawor *Poland* **31** G3
Jaworzno *Poland* **31** H6
Jaworzyna Śląska *Poland* **31** H3
Jawoyn ◊ *Australia* **92** B5
Jay Peak *U.S.A.* **115** B12
Jaya, Puncak *Indonesia* **63** E9
Jayanti *India* **67** F16
Jayapura *Indonesia* **63** E10
Jayawijaya, Pegunungan
　　Indonesia **63** E9
Jaynagar *India* **69** F12
Jaypur = Jeypore *India* **67** K13
Jayrūd *Syria* **72** F7
Jayton *U.S.A.* **116** E4
Jāz Mūrīān, Hāmūn-e *Iran* **71** E8
Jazīreh-ye Shīf *Iran* **71** D6
Jazminal *Mexico* **118** C4
Jazzīn *Lebanon* **74** B4
Jean *U.S.A.* **111** K11
Jean Marie River *Canada* **102** A4
Jean-Rabel *Haiti* **121** C5
Jeanerette *U.S.A.* **116** G9
Jeanette, Ostrov =
　　Zhannetty, Ostrov *Russia* **53** B16
Jeannette *U.S.A.* **114** F5
Jebāl Bārez, Kūh-e *Iran* **71** D8
Jebba *Nigeria* **83** D5
Jebel, Bahr el ➤ *Sudan* **81** F3
Jebel Ali = Minā' Jabal 'Alī
　　U.A.E. **71** E7
Jebel Dud *Sudan* **81** E3
Jebel Qerri *Sudan* **81** D3
Jecheon *S. Korea* **57** F15
Jedburgh *U.K.* **13** F6
Jedda = Jiddah *Si. Arabia* **75** C2
Jeddore L. *Canada* **105** C8
Jedlicze *Poland* **31** J8
Jędrzejów *Poland* **31** H7
Jedwabne *Poland* **31** E9
Jeetzel ➤ *Germany* **24** B7
Jefferson *Iowa, U.S.A.* **112** D6
Jefferson *Ohio, U.S.A.* **114** E4
Jefferson *Tex., U.S.A.* **116** E7
Jefferson, Mt. *Nev., U.S.A.* **108** G5
Jefferson, Mt. *Oreg., U.S.A.* **108** D3
Jefferson City *Mo., U.S.A.* **112** F7
Jefferson City *Tenn., U.S.A.* **117** C13
Jeffersontown *U.S.A.* **113** F11
Jeffersonville *U.S.A.* **113** F11
Jeffrey City *U.S.A.* **108** E10
Jega *Nigeria* **83** C5
Jeju *S. Korea* **57** H14
Jeju-do *S. Korea* **57** H14
Jēkabpils *Latvia* **32** D3
Jekyll I. *U.S.A.* **117** F14
Jelcz-Laskowice *Poland* **31** G4
Jelenia Góra *Poland* **31** H2
Jelgava *Latvia* **30** B10
Jelgava □ *Latvia* **30** B10
Jelica *Serbia* **44** C4
Jelli *Sudan* **81** F3
Jelšava *Slovak Rep.* **27** C13
Jemaja *Indonesia* **65** L5
Jemaluang *Malaysia* **65** L4
Jember *Indonesia* **63** H15
Jena *Germany* **24** E7
Jena *U.S.A.* **116** F8
Jenbach *Austria* **26** D4
Jenīn *West Bank* **74** C4
Jenkins *U.S.A.* **113** G12
Jenner *U.S.A.* **110** G3
Jennings *U.S.A.* **116** F8
Jeonag-eup *S. Korea* **57** G14
Jeonju *S. Korea* **57** G14
Jepara *Indonesia* **63** G14
Jeparit *Australia* **95** F3
Jequié *Brazil* **125** F10
Jequitinhonha *Brazil* **125** G10
Jequitinhonha ➤ *Brazil* **125** G11

Jerada *Morocco* **78** B5
Jerantut *Malaysia* **65** L4
Jerejak, Pulau *Malaysia* **65** c
Jérémie *Haiti* **121** C5
Jerez, Pta. *Mexico* **119** C5
Jerez de García Salinas
   Mexico **118** C4
Jerez de la Frontera *Spain* **37** J4
Jerez de los Caballeros *Spain* **37** G4
Jericho = El Arīḥā *West Bank* **74** D4
Jericho *Australia* **94** C4
Jerichow *Germany* **24** C8
Jerid, Chott el = Djerid,
   Chott *Tunisia* **78** B7
Jerilderie *Australia* **95** F4
Jermyn *U.S.A.* **115** E9
Jerome *U.S.A.* **108** E6
Jerramungup *Australia* **93** F2
Jersey *U.K.* **15** H5
Jersey City *U.S.A.* **115** F10
Jersey Shore *U.S.A.* **114** E7
Jerseyville *U.S.A.* **112** F8
Jerusalem *Israel/West Bank* **74** D4
Jervis B. *Australia* **95** F5
Jervis Inlet *Canada* **102** C4
Jerzu *Italy* **42** C2
Jesenice *Slovenia* **41** B11
Jeseník *Czech Rep.* **27** A10
Jesenké *Slovak Rep.* **27** C13
Jesi = Iesi *Italy* **41** E10
Jessore *Bangla.* **67** H16
Jesup *U.S.A.* **117** F14
Jesús Carranza *Mexico* **119** D5
Jesús María *Argentina* **126** C3
Jetmore *U.S.A.* **112** F4
Jetpur *India* **68** J4
Jeumont *France* **19** B11
Jevnaker *Norway* **9** F14
Jewett *U.S.A.* **114** F3
Jewett City *U.S.A.* **115** E13
Jeyḥūnābād *Iran* **71** C6
Jeypore *India* **67** K13
Jeziorak, Jezioro *Poland* **30** E6
Jeziorany *Poland* **30** E7
Jeziorka ➤ *Poland* **31** F8
Jha Jha *India* **69** G12
Jhaarkand = Jharkhand □
   India **69** H11
Jhabua *India* **68** H6
Jhajjar *India* **68** E7
Jhal *Pakistan* **68** E2
Jhal Jhao *Pakistan* **66** F4
Jhalawar *India* **68** G7
Jhalida *India* **69** H12
Jhalrapatan *India* **68** G7
Jhang Maghiana *Pakistan* **68** D5
Jhansi *India* **69** G8
Jhargram *India* **69** H12
Jharia *India* **69** H12
Jharkhand □ *India* **69** H11
Jharsuguda *India* **67** J14
Jhelum *Pakistan* **68** C5
Jhelum ➤ *Pakistan* **68** D5
Jhilmilli *India* **69** H10
Jhudo *Pakistan* **68** G3
Jhunjhunu *India* **68** E6
Ji-Paraná *Brazil* **124** F6
Ji Xian *Hebei, China* **56** F8
Ji Xian *Henan, China* **56** G8
Ji Xian *Shanxi, China* **56** F6
Jia Xian *Henan, China* **56** H7
Jia Xian *Shaanxi, China* **56** E6
Jiading *China* **59** B13
Jiahe *China* **59** E9
Jiaji = Qionghai *China* **64** C8
Jialing Jiang ➤ *China* **58** C6
Jiamusi *China* **60** B8
Ji'an *Jiangxi, China* **59** D10
Ji'an *Jilin, China* **57** D14
Jianchang *China* **57** D11
Jianchangying *China* **57** D10
Jianchuan *China* **58** D2
Jiande *China* **59** C12
Jiang'an *China* **58** C5
Jiangbei *China* **58** C6
Jiangcheng *China* **58** F3
Jiangchuan *China* **58** E4
Jiangdi *China* **58** D4
Jiangdu *China* **59** A12
Jiange *China* **58** A5
Jianghua *China* **59** E8
Jiangjin *China* **58** C6
Jiangkou *China* **58** D7
Jiangle *China* **59** D11
Jiangling *China* **59** B9
Jiangmen *China* **59** F9
Jiangning *China* **59** A12
Jiangshan *China* **59** C12
Jiangsu □ *China* **57** H11
Jiangxi □ *China* **59** D11
Jiangyan *China* **59** A13
Jiangyin *China* **59** B13
Jiangyong *China* **59** E8
Jiangyou *China* **58** B5
Jianhe *China* **58** D7
Jianli *China* **59** C9
Jianning *China* **59** D11
Jian'ou *China* **59** D12

Jianshi *China* **58** B7
Jianshui *China* **58** F4
Jianyang *Fujian, China* **59** D12
Jianyang *Sichuan, China* **58** B5
Jiao Xian = Jiaozhou *China* **57** F11
Jiaohe *Hebei, China* **56** E9
Jiaohe *Jilin, China* **57** C14
Jiaojiang *China* **59** C13
Jiaoling *China* **59** E11
Jiaozhou *China* **57** F11
Jiaozhou Wan *China* **57** F11
Jiaozuo *China* **56** G7
Jiashan *China* **59** B13
Jiawang *China* **57** G9
Jiaxiang *China* **56** G9
Jiaxing *China* **59** B13
Jiayi = Chiai *Taiwan* **59** F13
Jiayu *China* **59** C9
Jibiya *Nigeria* **83** C6
Jibou *Romania* **29** C8
Jibuti = Djibouti ■ *Africa* **81** E5
Jicarón, I. *Panama* **120** E3
Jičín *Czech Rep.* **26** A8
Jiddah *Si. Arabia* **75** C2
Jido *India* **67** E19
Jieshou *China* **56** H8
Jiexiu *China* **56** F6
Jieyang *China* **59** F11
Jigalong *Australia* **92** D3
Jigalong ☉ *Australia* **92** D3
Jigawa □ *Nigeria* **83** C6
Jigni *India* **69** G8
Jihlava *Czech Rep.* **26** B8
Jihlava ➤ *Czech Rep.* **27** C9
Jihlavský □ *Czech Rep.* **26** B8
Jihočeský □ *Czech Rep.* **26** B7
Jihomoravský □ *Czech Rep.* **27** B9
Jijiga *Ethiopia* **75** F3
Jikamshi *Nigeria* **83** C6
Jikau *Sudan* **81** F3
Jilib *Somali Rep.* **75** G3
Jilin *China* **57** C14
Jilin □ *China* **57** C14
Jiloca ➤ *Spain* **38** D3
Jilong = Chilung *Taiwan* **59** E13
Jim Thorpe *U.S.A.* **115** F9
Jima *Ethiopia* **81** F4
Jimbaran, Teluk *Indonesia* **63** K18
Jimbolia *Romania* **28** E5
Jimena de la Frontera *Spain* **37** J5
Jiménez *Mexico* **118** B4
Jimeta *Nigeria* **83** D7
Jimo *China* **57** F11
Jin Jiang ➤ *China* **59** C10
Jin Xian = Jinzhou *Hebei,*
   China **56** E8
Jin Xian = Jinzhou *Liaoning,*
   China **57** E11
Jinan *China* **56** F9
Jinchang *China* **60** C5
Jincheng *China* **56** G7
Jinchuan *China* **58** B4
Jind *India* **68** E7
Jindabyne *Australia* **95** F4
Jindo *S. Korea* **57** G14
Jindřichův Hradec *Czech Rep.* **26** B8
Jing He ➤ *China* **56** G5
Jing Shan *China* **59** B8
Jing Xian *China* **59** B12
Jing'an *China* **59** C10
Jingbian *China* **56** F5
Jingchuan *China* **56** G4
Jingde *China* **59** B12
Jingdezhen *China* **59** C11
Jingdong *China* **58** E3
Jinggangshan *China* **59** D10
Jinggu *China* **58** F3
Jinghai *China* **56** E9
Jinghong *China* **58** G3
Jingjiang *China* **59** A13
Jingle *China* **56** E6
Jingmen *China* **59** B9
Jingning *China* **56** G3
Jingpo Hu *China* **57** C15
Jingshan *China* **59** B9
Jingtai *China* **56** F3
Jingxi *China* **58** F6
Jingxing *China* **56** E8
Jingyang *China* **56** G5
Jingyu *China* **57** C14
Jingyuan *China* **56** F3
Jingzhou *China* **58** D7
Jingziguan *China* **56** H6
Jinhua *China* **59** C12
Jining *Nei Monggol Zizhiqu,*
   China **56** D7
Jining *Shandong, China* **56** G9
Jinja *Uganda* **86** B3
Jinjang *Malaysia* **65** L3
Jinji *China* **56** F4
Jinjiang *Fujian, China* **59** E12
Jinjiang *Yunnan, China* **58** D3
Jinjini *Ghana* **82** D4
Jinju *S. Korea* **57** G15
Jinkou *China* **59** B10
Jinkouhe *China* **58** C4
Jinmen Dao *China* **59** E12
Jinnah Barrage *Pakistan* **68** C4

Jinotega *Nic.* **120** D2
Jinotepe *Nic.* **120** D2
Jinping *Guizhou, China* **58** D7
Jinping *Yunnan, China* **58** F4
Jinsha *China* **58** D6
Jinsha Jiang ➤ *China* **58** C5
Jinshan *China* **59** B13
Jinshi *China* **59** C8
Jintan *China* **59** B12
Jinxi *Jiangxi, China* **59** D11
Jinxi *Liaoning, China* **57** D11
Jinxian *China* **59** C11
Jinxiang *China* **56** G9
Jinyang *China* **58** D4
Jinyun *China* **59** C13
Jinzhai *China* **59** B10
Jinzhong *China* **56** F7
Jinzhou *Hebei, China* **56** E8
Jinzhou *Liaoning, China* **57** E11
Jinzhou *Liaoning, China* **57** D11
Jiparaná ➤ *Brazil* **124** E6
Jipijapa *Ecuador* **124** D2
Jiquilpan *Mexico* **118** D4
Jirisan *S. Korea* **57** G14
Jiroft *Iran* **71** D8
Jishan *China* **56** G6
Jishou *China* **58** C7
Jishui *China* **59** D10
Jisr ash Shughūr *Syria* **72** E7
Jitarning *Australia* **93** F2
Jitra *Malaysia* **65** J3
Jiu ➤ *Romania* **29** G8
Jiudengkou *China* **56** E4
Jiujiang *Guangdong, China* **59** F9
Jiujiang *Jiangxi, China* **59** C10
Jiuling Shan *China* **59** C10
Jiulong = Kowloon *China* **59** F10
Jiulong *China* **58** C3
Jiutai *China* **57** B13
Jiuxincheng *China* **56** E8
Jiuyuhang *China* **59** B12
Jiwani *Pakistan* **66** G2
Jixi *Anhui, China* **59** B12
Jixi *Heilongjiang, China* **57** B16
Jiyang *China* **57** F9
Jiyuan *China* **56** G7
Jīzān *Si. Arabia* **75** D3
Jize *China* **56** F7
Jizera ➤ *Czech Rep.* **26** A7
Jizl, Wādī al ➤ *Si. Arabia* **70** E3
Jizō-Zaki *Japan* **55** G6
Jizzax *Uzbekistan* **52** E7
Joaçaba *Brazil* **127** B5
Joal Fadiout *Senegal* **82** C1
João Pessoa *Brazil* **125** E12
Joaquín V. González
   Argentina **126** B3
Jobat *India* **68** H6
Jobourg, Nez de *France* **18** C5
Jódar *Spain* **37** H7
Jodhpur *India* **68** F5
Jodiya *India* **68** H4
Joensuu *Finland* **8** E23
Jõetsu *Japan* **55** F9
Jœuf *France* **19** C12
Jofane *Mozam.* **89** C5
Jogbani *India* **69** F12
Jōgeva *Estonia* **32** C4
Jogjakarta = Yogyakarta
   Indonesia **62** F4
Johannesburg *S. Africa* **89** D4
Johannesburg *U.S.A.* **111** K9
Johansfors *Sweden* **11** H9
Johilla ➤ *India* **69** H9
John Crow Mts. *Jamaica* **120** a
John Day *U.S.A.* **108** D4
John Day ➤ *U.S.A.* **108** D3
John Day Fossil Beds ◠
   U.S.A. **108** D4
John D'or Prairie *Canada* **102** B5
John H. Kerr Res. *U.S.A.* **117** C15
John o' Groats *U.K.* **13** C5
Johnnie *U.S.A.* **111** J10
John's Ra. *Australia* **94** C1
Johnson *U.S.A.* **115** B12
Johnson City *Kans., U.S.A.* **112** G3
Johnson City *N.Y., U.S.A.* **115** D9
Johnson City *Tenn., U.S.A.* **117** C13
Johnson City *Tex., U.S.A.* **116** F5
Johnsonburg *U.S.A.* **114** E6
Johnsondale *U.S.A.* **111** K8
Johnsons Crossing *Canada* **102** A2
Johnston, L. *Australia* **93** F3
Johnston Falls =
   Mambilima Falls *Zambia* **87** E2
Johnston I. *Pac. Oc.* **97** F11
Johnstone Str. *Canada* **102** C3
Johnstown *Ireland* **12** D4
Johnstown *N.Y., U.S.A.* **115** C10
Johnstown *Ohio, U.S.A.* **114** F2
Johnstown *Pa., U.S.A.* **114** F6
Johor, Selat *Asia* **65** d
Johor Bahru *Malaysia* **65** d
Jōhvi *Estonia* **32** C4
Joigny *France* **19** E10
Joinville *Brazil* **127** B6
Joinville *France* **19** D12
Joinville I. *Antarctica* **5** C18
Jojutla *Mexico* **119** D5

Jokkmokk *Sweden* **8** C18
Jökulsá á Bru ➤ *Iceland* **8** D6
Jökulsá á Fjöllum ➤ *Iceland* **8** C5
Jolfā *Āzarbājān-e Sharqī, Iran* **73** C11
Jolfā *Eṣfahan, Iran* **71** C6
Joliet *U.S.A.* **112** E9
Joliette *Canada* **104** C5
Jolo *Phil.* **61** J4
Jolon *U.S.A.* **110** K5
Jomalig I. *Phil.* **61** D5
Jombang *Indonesia* **63** G15
Jomda *China* **58** B2
Jonava *Lithuania* **32** E3
Jones Sound *Canada* **101** B15
Jonesboro *Ark., U.S.A.* **117** D9
Jonesboro *La., U.S.A.* **116** E8
Jong ➤ *S. Leone* **82** D2
Jonglei *Sudan* **81** F3
Jonglei □ *Sudan* **81** F3
Joniškis *Lithuania* **30** B10
Jönköping *Sweden* **11** G8
Jönköpings län □ *Sweden* **11** G8
Jonquière *Canada* **105** C5
Jonsered *Sweden* **11** G6
Jonzac *France* **20** C3
Joplin *U.S.A.* **112** G6
Jora *India* **68** F6
Jordan *Mont., U.S.A.* **108** C10
Jordan *N.Y., U.S.A.* **115** C8
Jordan ■ *Asia* **74** E5
Jordan ➤ *Asia* **74** D4
Jordan Valley *U.S.A.* **108** E5
Jordanów *Poland* **31** J6
Jorhat *India* **67** F19
Jori ➤ *Norway* **10** B3
Jörn *Sweden* **8** D19
Jorong *Indonesia* **62** E4
Jørpeland *Norway* **9** G12
Jorquera ➤ *Chile* **126** B2
Joru *S. Leone* **82** D2
Jos *Nigeria* **83** D6
Jos Plateau *Nigeria* **83** D6
Jošanička Banja *Serbia* **44** C4
José Batlle y Ordóñez
   Uruguay **127** C4
Joseni *Romania* **29** D10
Joseph, L. *Canada* **114** A5
Joseph Bonaparte G.
   Australia **92** B4
Joseph L. *Canada* **105** B6
Joshinath *India* **69** D8
Joshinetsu-Kōgen △ *Japan* **55** F9
Joshua Tree *U.S.A.* **111** L10
Joshua Tree △ *U.S.A.* **111** M10
Josselin *France* **18** E4
Jost Van Dyke I. *Br. Virgin Is.* **121** e
Jostedalsbreen *Norway* **8** F12
Jotunheimen *Norway* **8** F13
Joubertberge *Namibia* **88** B1
Joué-lès-Tours *France* **18** E7
Jourdanton *U.S.A.* **116** G5
Joutseno *Finland* **32** B5
Jovellanos *Cuba* **120** B3
Jowkār *Iran* **73** E13
Joyeuse *France* **21** D8
Józefów *Lubelskie, Poland* **31** H10
Józefów *Mazowieckie, Poland* **31** F8
Ju Xian *China* **57** F10
Juan Aldama *Mexico* **118** C4
Juan Bautista Alberdi
   Argentina **126** C3
Juan de Fuca, Str of.
   N. Amer. **110** B3
Juán de Nova *Ind. Oc.* **89** B7
Juan Fernández, Arch. de
   Pac. Oc. **122** G2
Juan José Castelli *Argentina* **126** B3
Juan L. Lacaze *Uruguay* **126** C4
Juankoski *Finland* **8** E23
Juárez *Mexico* **118** B4
Juárez, Sierra de *Mexico* **118** A1
Juàzeiro *Brazil* **125** E10
Juàzeiro do Norte *Brazil* **125** E11
Juazohn *Liberia* **82** D3
Jûbâ *Sudan* **81** G3
Juba ➤ *Somali Rep.* **75** G3
Jubany *Antarctica* **5** C18
Jubayl *Lebanon* **74** A4
Jubbah *Si. Arabia* **70** D4
Jubbal *India* **68** D7
Jubbulpore = Jabalpur *India* **69** H8
Jübek *Germany* **24** A5
Jubga *Russia* **35** H4
Jubilee L. *Australia* **93** E4
Juby, C. *Morocco* **78** C3
Júcar = Xúquer ➤ *Spain* **39** F4
Júcaro *Cuba* **120** B4
Juchitán de Zaragoza
   Mexico **119** D5
Judea = Har Yehuda *Israel* **74** D3
Judenburg *Austria* **26** D7
Judith ➤ *U.S.A.* **108** C9
Judith, Pt. *U.S.A.* **115** E13
Judith Gap *U.S.A.* **108** C9
Juelsminde *Denmark* **11** J4
Juigalpa *Nic.* **120** D2
Juillac *France* **20** C5
Juist *Germany* **24** B2
Juiz de Fora *Brazil* **127** A7

Jujuy □ *Argentina* **126** A2
Julesburg *U.S.A.* **108** F12
Juli *Peru* **124** G5
Julia Cr. ➤ *Australia* **94** C3
Julia Creek *Australia* **94** C3
Juliaca *Peru* **124** G4
Julian *U.S.A.* **111** M10
Julian, L. *Canada* **104** B4
Julian Alps = Julijske Alpe
   Slovenia **41** B11
Julianatop *Suriname* **125** C7
Julianehåb = Qaqortoq
   Greenland **4** C5
Jülich *Germany* **24** E2
Julijske Alpe *Slovenia* **41** B11
Julimes *Mexico* **118** B3
Jullundur *India* **68** D6
Julu *China* **56** F8
Jumbo *Zimbabwe* **87** F3
Jumbo Pk. *U.S.A.* **111** J12
Jumentos Cays *Bahamas* **120** B4
Jumilla *Spain* **39** G3
Jumla *Nepal* **69** E10
Jumna = Yamuna ➤ *India* **69** G9
Junagadh *India* **68** J4
Junction *Tex., U.S.A.* **116** F5
Junction *Utah, U.S.A.* **109** G7
Junction B. *Australia* **94** A1
Junction City *Kans., U.S.A.* **112** F5
Junction City *Oreg., U.S.A.* **108** D2
Junction Pt. *Australia* **94** A1
Jundah *Australia* **94** C3
Jundiaí *Brazil* **127** A6
Juneau *U.S.A.* **102** B2
Junee *Australia* **95** E4
Jungfrau *Switz.* **25** J3
Junggar Pendi *China* **60** B3
Jungshahi *Pakistan* **68** G2
Juniata ➤ *U.S.A.* **114** F7
Junín *Argentina* **126** C3
Junín de los Andes *Argentina* **128** D2
Jūniyah *Lebanon* **74** B4
Junlian *China* **58** C5
Juntas *Chile* **126** B2
Juntura *U.S.A.* **108** E4
Jur, Nahr el ➤ *Sudan* **81** F2
Jura = Jura, Mts. du *Europe* **19** F13
Jura = Schwäbische Alb
   Germany **25** G5
Jura *U.K.* **13** F3
Jura □ *France* **19** F12
Jura □ *Switz.* **25** H3
Jūra ➤ *Lithuania* **30** C9
Jura, Mts. du *Europe* **19** F13
Jura, Sd. of *U.K.* **13** F3
Jurbarkas *Lithuania* **30** C9
Jurien Bay *Australia* **93** F2
Jurilovca *Romania* **29** F13
Jūrmala *Latvia* **30** B10
Jurong *China* **59** B12
Jurong *Singapore* **65** d
Juruá ➤ *Brazil* **124** D5
Juruena *Brazil* **124** F7
Juruena ➤ *Brazil* **124** E7
Juruti *Brazil* **125** D7
Jussey *France* **19** E12
Justo Daract *Argentina* **126** C2
Jutaí ➤ *Brazil* **124** D5
Jüterbog *Germany* **24** D9
Juticalpa *Honduras* **120** D2
Jutland = Jylland *Denmark* **11** H3
Juuka *Finland* **8** E23
Juventud, I. de la *Cuba* **120** B3
Juvigny-sous-Andaine
   France **18** D6
Jüy Zar *Iran* **73** F12
Juye *China* **56** G9
Juzennecourt *France* **19** D11
Jvari *Georgia* **35** J6
Jwaneng *Botswana* **85** J4
Jyderup *Denmark* **11** J5
Jylland *Denmark* **11** H3
Jyväskylä *Finland* **32** A3

K

K2 *Pakistan* **69** B7
Ka ➤ *Nigeria* **83** C5
Kaakha = Kaka *Turkmenistan* **71** B8
Kaap Plateau *S. Africa* **88** D3
Kaapkruis *Namibia* **88** C1
Kaapstad = Cape Town
   S. Africa **88** E2
Kaba *Guinea* **82** C2
Kabaena *Indonesia* **63** F6
Kabala *S. Leone* **82** D2
Kabale *Uganda* **86** C3
Kabalo *Dem. Rep. of the Congo* **86** D2
Kabambare
   Dem. Rep. of the Congo **86** C2
Kabango
   Dem. Rep. of the Congo **87** D2
Kabanjahe *Indonesia* **62** D1
Kabankalan *Phil.* **61** G5
Kabara *Fiji* **91** a
Kabara *Mali* **82** B4
Kabardinka *Russia* **33** K10
Kabardino-Balkaria □
   Russia **35** J6

Kabarega Falls =
   Murchison Falls *Uganda* **86** B3
Kabarnet *Kenya* **86** B4
Kabasalan *Phil.* **61** H5
Kabat *Indonesia* **63** J17
Kabba *Nigeria* **83** D6
Kabi *Niger* **83** C7
Kabin Buri *Thailand* **64** F3
Kabinakagami L. *Canada* **104** C3
Kabinda *Dem. Rep. of the Congo* **84** F4
Kabna *Sudan* **80** D3
Kabompo *Zambia* **87** E1
Kabompo ➤ *Zambia* **85** G4
Kabondo
   Dem. Rep. of the Congo **87** D2
Kabongo
   Dem. Rep. of the Congo **86** D2
Kabot *Guinea* **82** C2
Kabou *Togo* **83** D5
Kabr *Sudan* **81** E2
Kabrousse *Senegal* **82** C1
Kabūd Gonbad *Iran* **71** B8
Kabudar Ahang *Iran* **73** E13
Kabugao *Phil.* **61** B4
Kābul *Afghan.* **68** B3
Kābul □ *Afghan.* **66** B6
Kābul ➤ *Pakistan* **68** C5
Kabunga
   Dem. Rep. of the Congo **86** C2
Kaburuang *Indonesia* **63** D7
Kabushiya *Sudan* **81** D3
Kabwe *Zambia* **87** E2
Kačanik *Kosovo* **44** D5
Kačerginė *Lithuania* **30** D10
Kachchh, Gulf of *India* **68** H3
Kachchh, Rann of *India* **68** H4
Kachchhidhana *India* **69** J8
Kachebera *Zambia* **87** E3
Kachia *Nigeria* **83** D6
Kachikau *Botswana* **88** B3
Kachin □ *Burma* **58** F1
Kachira, L. *Uganda* **86** C3
Kachīry *Kazakhstan* **52** D8
Kachisi *Ethiopia* **81** F4
Kachnara *India* **68** H6
Kachot *Cambodia* **65** G4
Kaçkar *Turkey* **73** B9
Kadam, Mt. *Uganda* **86** B3
Kadan *Czech Rep.* **26** A6
Kadan Kyun *Burma* **64** F2
Kadanai ➤ *Afghan.* **68** D1
Kadarkút *Hungary* **28** D2
Kadavu *Fiji* **91** a
Kadavu Passage *Fiji* **91** a
Kade *Ghana* **83** D4
Kadhimain = Al
   Kāẓimīyah *Iraq* **73** F11
Kadi *India* **68** H5
Kadiana *Mali* **82** C3
Kadina *Australia* **95** E2
Kadınhanı *Turkey* **72** C5
Kadiolo *Mali* **82** C3
Kadipur *India* **69** F10
Kadirli *Turkey* **72** D7
Kadiyevka = Stakhanov
   Ukraine **33** H10
Kadodo *Sudan* **81** E2
Kadoka *U.S.A.* **112** D3
Kadom *Russia* **34** C6
Kadoma *Zimbabwe* **87** F2
Kâdugli *Sudan* **81** E2
Kaduna *Nigeria* **83** C6
Kaduna □ *Nigeria* **83** C6
Kaduna ➤ *Nigeria* **83** D6
Kaduy *Russia* **32** C9
Kaédi *Mauritania* **82** B2
Kaélé *Cameroon* **83** C7
Kaeng Khoï *Thailand* **64** E3
Kaeng Krachan △ *Thailand* **64** F2
Kaeng Tana △ *Thailand* **64** E5
Kaesŏng *N. Korea* **57** F14
Kāf *Si. Arabia* **70** D3
Kafan = Kapan *Armenia* **73** C12
Kafanchan *Nigeria* **83** D6
Kafareti *Nigeria* **83** C7
Kaffrine *Senegal* **82** C1
Kafin *Nigeria* **83** D6
Kafin Madaki *Nigeria* **83** C6
Kafinda *Zambia* **87** E3
Kafr el Battikh *Egypt* **80** H7
Kafr el Dauwâr *Egypt* **80** H7
Kafr el Sheikh *Egypt* **80** H7
Kafr el Zaiyât *Egypt* **80** H7
Kafue *Zambia* **87** F2
Kafue ➤ *Zambia* **85** H5
Kafue △ *Zambia* **87** F2
Kafue Flats *Zambia* **87** F2
Kafulwe *Zambia* **87** D2
Kaga *Afghan.* **68** B4
Kaga Bandoro *C.A.R.* **84** C3
Kagarko *Nigeria* **83** D6
Kagawa □ *Japan* **55** G7
Kagera □ *Tanzania* **86** C3
Kagera ➤ *Uganda* **86** C3
Kağızman *Turkey* **73** B10
Kagmar *Sudan* **81** E3
Kagoro *Nigeria* **83** D6
Kagoshima *Japan* **55** J5

Kagoshima ☐ *Japan* 55 J5
Kagul = Cahul *Moldova* 29 E13
Kahak *Iran* 71 B6
Kahama *Tanzania* 86 C3
Kahan *Pakistan* 68 E3
Kahang *Malaysia* 65 L4
Kahayan → *Indonesia* 62 E4
Kahe *Tanzania* 86 C4
Kahemba
　Dem. Rep. of the Congo 84 F3
Kahnūj *Iran* 71 E8
Kahoka *U.S.A.* 112 E8
Kaho'olawe *U.S.A.* 107 L8
Kahramanmaras *Turkey* 72 D7
Kahramanmaras ☐ *Turkey* 72 D7
Kâhta *Turkey* 73 D8
Kahul, Ozero *Ukraine* 29 E13
Kahului *U.S.A.* 107 L8
Kahurangi △ *N.Z.* 91 D4
Kahuta *Pakistan* 68 C5
Kahuzi-Biega △
　Dem. Rep. of the Congo 86 C2
Kai, Kepulauan *Indonesia* 63 F8
Kai Besar *Indonesia* 63 F8
Kai Is. = Kai, Kepulauan
　Indonesia 63 F8
Kai Kecil *Indonesia* 63 F8
Kai Xian *China* 58 B7
Kaiama *Nigeria* 83 D5
Kaiapoi *N.Z.* 91 E4
Kaieteur Falls *Guyana* 124 B7
Kaifeng *China* 56 G8
Kaihua *China* 59 C12
Kaijiang *China* 58 B6
Kaikohe *N.Z.* 91 A4
Kaikoura *N.Z.* 91 E4
Kailahun *S. Leone* 82 D2
Kailash = Kangrinboqe
　Feng *China* 69 D9
Kaili *China* 58 D6
Kailu *China* 57 C11
Kailua Kona *U.S.A.* 107 M8
Kaimaktsalan Oros =
　Voras Oros *Greece* 44 F5
Kaimana *Indonesia* 63 E8
Kaimanawa Mts. *N.Z.* 91 C5
Kaimganj *India* 69 F8
Kaimur Hills *India* 69 G10
Kainab → *Namibia* 88 D2
Kainji Dam *Nigeria* 83 D5
Kainji Lake △ *Nigeria* 83 C5
Kainji Res. *Nigeria* 83 C5
Kainuu *Finland* 8 D23
Kaipara Harbour *N.Z.* 91 B5
Kaiping *China* 59 F9
Kaipokok B. *Canada* 105 B8
Kaira *India* 68 H5
Kairana *India* 68 E7
Kaironi *Indonesia* 63 E8
Kairouan *Tunisia* 79 A8
Kaiserslautern *Germany* 25 F3
Kaiserstuhl *Germany* 25 G3
Kaitaia *N.Z.* 91 A4
Kaitangata *N.Z.* 91 G2
Kaithal *India* 68 E7
Kaitu → *Pakistan* 68 C4
Kaiwi Channel *U.S.A.* 107 L8
Kaiyang *China* 58 D6
Kaiyuan *Liaoning, China* 57 C13
Kaiyuan *Yunnan, China* 58 F4
Kaiyuh Mts. *U.S.A.* 106 C8
Kajaani *Finland* 8 D22
Kajabbi *Australia* 94 C3
Kajana = Kajaani *Finland* 8 D22
Kajang *Malaysia* 65 L3
Kajaran *Armenia* 73 C12
Kajiado *Kenya* 86 C4
Kajo Kaji *Sudan* 81 G3
Kajok *Sudan* 81 F2
Kajuru *Nigeria* 83 C6
Kaka *Sudan* 81 E3
Kaka *Turkmenistan* 71 B8
Kakabeka Falls *Canada* 104 C2
Kakadu △ *Australia* 92 B5
Kakamas *S. Africa* 88 D3
Kakamega *Kenya* 86 B3
Kakanj *Bos.-H.* 28 F3
Kakanui Mts. *N.Z.* 91 F3
Kakata *Liberia* 82 D2
Kakdwip *India* 69 J13
Kake *Japan* 55 G6
Kake *U.S.A.* 102 B2
Kakegawa *Japan* 55 G9
Kakeroma-Jima *Japan* 55 K4
Kâkhak *Iran* 71 C8
Kakhib *Russia* 35 J8
Kakhovka *Ukraine* 33 J7
Kakhovske Vdskh. *Ukraine* 33 J7
Kakinada *India* 67 L13
Kakisa *Canada* 102 A5
Kakisa → *Canada* 102 A5
Kakisa L. *Canada* 102 A5
Kakogawa *Japan* 55 G7
Kakum △ *Ghana* 83 D4
Kakuma *Kenya* 86 B3
Kakwa → *Canada* 102 C5
Kal Gūsheh *Iran* 71 D8
Kal Sefid *Iran* 73 E12
Kala *Nigeria* 83 C7

Kalaallit Nunaat =
　Greenland ☑ *N. Amer.* 99 C15
Kalabagh *Pakistan* 68 C4
Kalabahi *Indonesia* 63 F6
Kalabana *Mali* 82 C3
Kalach *Russia* 34 E5
Kalach na Donu *Russia* 35 F6
Kaladan → *Burma* 67 J18
Kaladar *Canada* 114 B7
Kalahari *Africa* 88 C3
Kalahari Gemsbok △
　S. Africa 88 D3
Kalajoki *Finland* 8 D21
Kalakamati *Botswana* 89 C4
Kalakan *Russia* 53 D12
K'alak'unlun Shank'ou =
　Karakoram Pass *Asia* 69 B7
Kalam *Pakistan* 69 B5
Kalama *Dem. Rep. of the Congo* 86 C2
Kalama *U.S.A.* 110 E4
Kalamaria *Greece* 44 F6
Kalamata *Greece* 46 D4
Kalamazoo *U.S.A.* 113 D11
Kalamazoo → *U.S.A.* 112 D10
Kalambaka *Greece* 46 B3
Kalambo Falls *Tanzania* 87 D3
Kalamos *Attiki, Greece* 46 C5
Kalamos *Lefkada, Greece* 46 C2
Kalan *Turkey* 70 B3
Kalankalan *Guinea* 82 C3
Kalannie *Australia* 93 F2
Kalao *Indonesia* 63 F6
Kalaotoa *Indonesia* 63 F6
Kälarne *Sweden* 10 B10
Kalasin *Thailand* 64 D4
Kālat *Iran* 71 E8
Kalat *Pakistan* 66 E5
Kalāteh *Iran* 71 B7
Kalāteh-ye Ganj *Iran* 71 E8
Kalathos *Greece* 47 E10
Kalaus → *Russia* 35 H7
Kalavrita *Greece* 46 C4
Kalbā *U.A.E.* 71 E8
Kalbarri *Australia* 93 E1
Kalbarri △ *Australia* 93 E1
Kalce *Slovenia* 22 F8
Kale *Antalya, Turkey* 47 E12
Kale *Denizli, Turkey* 47 D10
Kalecik *Turkey* 72 B5
Kalegauk Kyun *Burma* 64 E1
Kalehe *Dem. Rep. of the Congo* 86 C2
Kalema *Tanzania* 86 C3
Kalemie *Dem. Rep. of the Congo* 86 D2
Kalety *Poland* 31 H5
Kalewa *Burma* 67 H19
Kaleybar *Iran* 73 C12
Kalgoorlie-Boulder *Australia* 93 F3
Kali → *India* 69 F8
Kali Sindh → *India* 68 G6
Kaliakra, Nos *Bulgaria* 45 C12
Kalianda *Indonesia* 62 F3
Kalibo *Phil.* 61 F5
Kalima *Dem. Rep. of the Congo* 86 C2
Kalimantan *Indonesia* 62 E4
Kalimantan Barat ☐
　Indonesia 62 E4
Kalimantan Selatan ☐
　Indonesia 62 E5
Kalimantan Tengah ☐
　Indonesia 62 E4
Kalimantan Timur ☐
　Indonesia 62 D5
Kálimnos *Greece* 47 D8
Kalimpong *India* 69 F13
Kaliningrad *Russia* 30 D6
Kaliningrad ✈ (KGD) *Russia* 30 D7
Kalininsk *Russia* 34 E7
Kalinkavichy *Belarus* 23 B15
Kalinkovichi =
　Kalinkavichy *Belarus* 23 B15
Kalinovik *Bos.-H.* 44 C2
Kalipetrovo *Bulgaria* 45 B11
Kalirachi *Greece* 45 F8
Kaliro *Uganda* 86 B3
Kalispell *U.S.A.* 108 B6
Kalisz *Poland* 31 G5
Kalisz Pomorski *Poland* 31 E2
Kalithea *Greece* 46 D5
Kaliua *Tanzania* 86 D3
Kalivia Thorikou *Greece* 46 D5
Kalix = Kalixälven →
　Sweden 8 D20
Kalix *Sweden* 8 D20
Kalixälven → *Sweden* 8 D20
Kalka *India* 68 D7
Kalkan *Turkey* 47 E11
Kalkarindji *Australia* 92 C5
Kalkaska *U.S.A.* 113 C11
Kalkfeld *Namibia* 88 C2
Kalkfontein *Botswana* 88 C3
Kalkrand *Namibia* 88 C2
Kållandsö *Sweden* 11 F7
Kallavesi *Finland* 8 E22
Källby *Sweden* 11 F7
Kållered *Sweden* 11 G6
Kallimasia *Greece* 47 C8

Kallinge *Sweden* 11 H9
Kallmet *Albania* 44 E3
Kallsjön *Sweden* 8 E15
Kalmalo *Nigeria* 83 C6
Kalmar *Sweden* 11 H10
Kalmar län ☐ *Sweden* 11 G10
Kalmar sund *Sweden* 11 H10
Kalmykia ☐ *Russia* 35 G8
Kalna *India* 69 H13
Kalnai *India* 69 H10
Kalo Nero *Greece* 46 D3
Kalocsa *Hungary* 28 D4
Kalofer *Bulgaria* 45 D8
Kalokhorio *Cyprus* 49 E12
Kaloko *Dem. Rep. of the Congo* 86 D2
Kalol *Gujarat, India* 68 H5
Kalol *Gujarat, India* 83 C6
Kalolimnos *Greece* 47 D9
Kalomo *Zambia* 87 F2
Kaloni *Greece* 47 B8
Kaloni, Kolpos *Greece* 47 B8
Kalookan = Caloocan *Phil.* 61 D4
Kalpi *India* 69 F8
Kaltag *U.S.A.* 106 C8
Kaltern = Caldaro *Italy* 41 B8
Kaltukatjara *Australia* 93 D4
Kaltungo *Nigeria* 83 D7
Kalu *Pakistan* 68 G2
Kaluga *Russia* 32 E9
Kaluga ☐ *Russia* 32 E8
Kalulushi *Zambia* 87 E2
Kalumburu *Australia* 92 B4
Kalumburu ✫ *Australia* 92 B4
Kalundborg *Denmark* 11 J5
Kalush *Ukraine* 23 D13
Kałuszyn *Poland* 31 F8
Kalutara *Sri Lanka* 66 R12
Kalvarija *Lithuania* 30 D10
Kalyan *India* 66 K8
Kalyazin *Russia* 32 D9
Kam *Albania* 44 D4
Kam → *Nigeria* 83 D7
Kama *Dem. Rep. of the Congo* 86 C2
Kama → *Russia* 6 D16
Kamachumu *Tanzania* 86 C3
Kamaishi *Japan* 54 E10
Kamalia *Pakistan* 68 D5
Kaman *India* 68 F6
Kaman *Turkey* 72 C5
Kamanjab *Namibia* 88 B2
Kamara *Mali* 82 C3
Kamaran *Yemen* 75 D3
Kamativi *Zimbabwe* 88 B4
Kamba *Nigeria* 83 C5
Kambalda West *Australia* 93 F3
Kambar *Pakistan* 68 F3
Kambia *S. Leone* 82 D2
Kambolé *Togo* 83 D5
Kambolé *Zambia* 87 D3
Kambos *Cyprus* 49 D11
Kambove
　Dem. Rep. of the Congo 87 E2
Kamchatka, Poluostrov
　Russia 53 D17
Kamchatka Pen. =
　Kamchatka, Poluostrov
　Russia 53 D17
Kamchiya → *Bulgaria* 45 C11
Kame Ruins *Zimbabwe* 87 G2
Kamen *Russia* 52 D9
Kamen-Rybolov *Russia* 54 B6
Kamenica *Serbia* 44 C6
Kamenica *Serbia* 44 B3
Kamenice nad Lipou
　Czech Rep. 26 B8
Kamenjak, Rt *Croatia* 41 D10
Kamenka = Kaminka
　Ukraine 33 H7
Kamenka *Kazakhstan* 34 E10
Kamenka *Penza, Russia* 34 D6
Kamenka *Voronezh, Russia* 33 G10
Kamenka Bugskaya =
　Kamyanka-Buzka
　Ukraine 23 C13
Kamenka Dneprovskaya =
　Kamyanka-Dniprovska
　Ukraine 33 J8
Kamennomostskiy *Russia* 35 H5
Kameno *Bulgaria* 45 D11
Kamenolomni *Russia* 35 G5
Kamensk-Shakhtinskiy
　Russia 35 F5
Kamensk Uralskiy *Russia* 52 D7
Kamenskiy *Russia* 34 E7
Kamenskoye *Russia* 53 C17
Kamenyak *Bulgaria* 45 C10
Kamenz *Germany* 24 D10
Kameoka *Japan* 55 G7
Kamet *India* 69 D8
Kamiah *U.S.A.* 108 C5
Kamień Krajeński *Poland* 30 E4
Kamień Pomorski *Poland* 30 E1
Kamienna → *Poland* 31 G8
Kamienna Góra *Poland* 31 H3
Kamieńsk *Poland* 31 G6
Kamieskroon *S. Africa* 88 E2
Kamilukuak L. *Canada* 103 A8
Kamin-Kashyrskyy *Ukraine* 23 C13

Kamina *Dem. Rep. of the Congo* 87 D2
Kaminak L. *Canada* 103 A10
Kaministiquia *Canada* 104 C1
Kaminka *Ukraine* 33 H7
Kaminoyama *Japan* 54 E10
Kamiros *Greece* 49 C9
Kamituga
　Dem. Rep. of the Congo 86 C2
Kamla → *India* 69 G12
Kamloops *Canada* 102 C4
Kamnik *Slovenia* 41 B11
Kamo *Armenia* 35 K7
Kamo *Japan* 54 F9
Kamoke *Pakistan* 68 C6
Kamp → *Austria* 26 C8
Kampala *Uganda* 86 B3
Kampar → *Malaysia* 65 K3
Kampar → *Indonesia* 62 D2
Kampen *Neths.* 17 B5
Kampene
　Dem. Rep. of the Congo 84 E5
Kamphaeng Phet *Thailand* 64 D2
Kampinoski △ *Poland* 31 F7
Kampolombo, L. *Zambia* 87 E2
Kampong Chhnang *Cambodia* 65 F5
Kampong Pengerang
　Malaysia 65 d
Kampong Punggai *Malaysia* 65 d
Kampong Saom *Cambodia* 65 G4
Kampong Saom, Chaak
　Cambodia 65 G4
Kampong Tanjong Langsat
　Malaysia 65 d
Kampong Telok Ramunia
　Malaysia 65 d
Kampot *Cambodia* 65 G5
Kampti *Burkina Faso* 82 C4
Kampuchea = Cambodia ■
　Asia 64 F5
Kampung Air Putih *Malaysia* 65 K4
Kampung Jerangau *Malaysia* 65 K4
Kampung Raja *Malaysia* 65 K4
Kampungbaru = Tolitoli
　Indonesia 63 D6
Kamrau, Teluk *Indonesia* 63 E8
Kamsack *Canada* 103 C8
Kamsar *Guinea* 82 C2
Kamskoye Ustye *Russia* 34 C9
Kamuchawie L. *Canada* 103 B8
Kamui-Misaki *Japan* 54 C10
Kamyanets-Podilskyy
　Ukraine 29 B11
Kamyanka-Buzka *Ukraine* 23 C13
Kamyanka-Dniprovska
　Ukraine 33 J8
Kamyanets *Belarus* 31 F10
Kamyanyuki *Belarus* 31 F10
Kâmyārān *Iran* 73 E12
Kamyshin *Russia* 34 E7
Kamyzyak *Russia* 35 G9
Kan *Sudan* 81 F3
Kanaaupscow → *Canada* 104 B4
Kanab *U.S.A.* 109 H7
Kanab Cr. → *U.S.A.* 109 H7
Kanacea *Lau Group, Fiji* 91 a
Kanacea *Taveuni, Fiji* 91 a
Kanaga I. *U.S.A.* 106 E4
Kanagi *Japan* 54 D10
Kanairiktok → *Canada* 105 A7
Kanalia *Greece* 46 B4
Kananga
　Dem. Rep. of the Congo 84 F4
Kanash *Russia* 34 C8
Kanaskat *U.S.A.* 110 C5
Kanastraíon, Ákra =
　Paliouri, Akra *Greece* 44 G7
Kanawha → *U.S.A.* 113 F12
Kanazawa *Japan* 55 F8
Kanchanaburi *Thailand* 64 E2
Kanchenjunga *Nepal* 69 F13
Kanchipuram *India* 66 N11
Kańczuga *Poland* 31 J9
Kandaghat *India* 68 D7
Kandahar = Qandahār
　Afghan. 66 D4
Kandahār ☐ *Afghan.* 66 D4
Kandalaksha *Russia* 8 C25
Kandangan *Indonesia* 62 E5
Kandanghaur *Indonesia* 63 G13
Kandanos *Greece* 49 D5
Kandava *Latvia* 30 B9
Kandavu = Kadavu *Fiji* 91 a
Kandavu Passage =
　Kadavu Passage *Fiji* 91 a
Kandhkot *Pakistan* 68 E3
Kandhla *India* 68 E7
Kandi *Benin* 83 C5
Kandi *India* 69 H13
Kandiaro *Pakistan* 68 F3
Kandila *Greece* 46 D3
Kandira *Turkey* 72 B4
Kandla *India* 68 H4
Kandos *Australia* 95 E4
Kandreho *Madag.* 89 B8
Kandy *Sri Lanka* 66 R12
Kane *U.S.A.* 114 E6
Kane Basin *Greenland* 101 B18
Kanel *Senegal* 82 B2
Kanevskaya *Russia* 35 G4
Kanfanar *Croatia* 41 C10

Kang *Botswana* 88 C3
Kang Krung △ *Thailand* 65 H2
Kangaba *Mali* 82 C3
Kangal *Turkey* 72 C7
Kangān *Fārs, Iran* 71 E7
Kangān *Hormozgān, Iran* 71 E8
Kangar *Malaysia* 65 J3
Kangaré *Mali* 82 C3
Kangaroo I. *Australia* 95 F2
Kangaroo Mts. *Australia* 94 C3
Kangasala *Finland* 32 B3
Kangāvar *Iran* 73 E12
Kangding *China* 58 B3
Kangdong *N. Korea* 57 E14
Kangean, Kepulauan
　Indonesia 62 F5
Kangean Is. = Kangean,
　Kepulauan *Indonesia* 62 F5
Kangen → *Sudan* 81 F3
Kanggye *N. Korea* 57 D14
Kangikajik *Greenland* 4 B6
Kangiqliniq = Rankin Inlet
　Canada 100 E13
Kangiqsualujjuaq *Canada* 101 F18
Kangiqsujuaq *Canada* 101 E17
Kangiqtugaapik = Clyde
　River *Canada* 101 C18
Kangirsuk *Canada* 101 F18
Kangkar Chemaran *Malaysia* 65 d
Kangkar Sungai Tiram
　Malaysia 65 d
Kangkar Teberau *Malaysia* 65 d
Kangping *China* 57 C12
Kangra *India* 68 C7
Kangrinboqe Feng *China* 69 D9
Kangto *China* 67 F18
Kanha △ *India* 69 H9
Kanhar → *India* 69 G10
Kani *Ivory C.* 82 D3
Kaniama
　Dem. Rep. of the Congo 86 D1
Kaniapiskau =
　Caniapiscau → *Canada* 105 A6
Kaniapiskau, L. =
　Caniapiscau, L. *Canada* 105 B6
Kanin, Poluostrov *Russia* 6 B14
Kanin Nos, Mys *Russia* 52 C5
Kanin Pen. = Kanin,
　Poluostrov *Russia* 6 B14
Kaninë *Albania* 44 F3
Kaniva *Australia* 95 F3
Kanjiža *Serbia* 28 D5
Kanjut Sar *Pakistan* 69 A6
Kankaanpää *Finland* 32 B2
Kankakee *U.S.A.* 112 E10
Kankakee → *U.S.A.* 112 E9
Kankan *Guinea* 82 C3
Kankendy = Xankändi
　Azerbaijan 73 C12
Kanker *India* 67 J12
Kankossa *Mauritania* 82 B2
Kankroli *India* 68 G5
Kannapolis *U.S.A.* 117 D14
Kannauj *India* 69 F8
Kannod *India* 66 H10
Kannur = Cannanore *India* 66 P9
Kannyakumari *India* 66 Q10
Kano *Nigeria* 83 C6
Kano ☐ *Nigeria* 83 C6
Kan'onji *Japan* 55 G6
Kanoroba *Ivory C.* 82 D3
Kanowit *Malaysia* 62 D4
Kanoya *Japan* 55 J5
Kanpetlet *Burma* 67 J18
Kanpur *India* 69 F9
Kansas ☐ *U.S.A.* 112 F4
Kansas → *U.S.A.* 112 F6
Kansas City *Kans., U.S.A.* 112 F6
Kansas City *Mo., U.S.A.* 112 F6
Kansenia
　Dem. Rep. of the Congo 87 E2
Kansk *Russia* 53 D10
Kansu = Gansu ☐ *China* 56 G3
Kantaphor *India* 68 H7
Kantchari *Burkina Faso* 83 C5
Kantché *Niger* 83 C6
Kanté *Togo* 83 D5
Kantemirovka *Russia* 33 H10
Kantharalak *Thailand* 64 E5
Kanthi = Contai *India* 69 J12
Kantli → *India* 68 E6
Kantō ☐ *Japan* 55 F9
Kantō-Sanchi *Japan* 55 F9
Kanturk *Ireland* 12 D3
Kanus *Namibia* 88 D2
Kanye *Botswana* 88 C4
Kanzenze
　Dem. Rep. of the Congo 87 E2
Kanzi, Ras *Tanzania* 86 D4
Kao *Tonga* 91 c
Kao Phara *Thailand* 65 a
Kaohsiung *Taiwan* 59 F13
Kaokoveld *Namibia* 88 B1
Kaolack *Senegal* 82 C1
Kaolack ☐ *Senegal* 82 C1
Kaoshan *China* 57 B13
Kapa'a *U.S.A.* 107 L8
Kapadvanj *India* 68 H5

Kapaklı *Turkey* 45 E11
Kapan *Armenia* 73 C12
Kapanga
　Dem. Rep. of the Congo 84 F4
Kapchagai = Qapshaghay
　Kazakhstan 52 E8
Kapedo *Kenya* 86 B4
Kapela = Velika Kapela
　Croatia 41 C12
Kapelo, Akra *Greece* 46 E5
Kapema *Dem. Rep. of the Congo* 87 E2
Kapenguria *Kenya* 86 B4
Kapfenberg *Austria* 26 D8
Kapı Dağı *Turkey* 45 F11
Kapiri Mposhi *Zambia* 87 E2
Kāpīsā ☐ *Afghan.* 66 B6
Kapiskau → *Canada* 104 B3
Kapit *Malaysia* 62 D4
Kapiti I. *N.Z.* 91 D5
Kaplan *U.S.A.* 116 F8
Kaplice *Czech Rep.* 26 C7
Kapoe *Thailand* 65 H2
Kapoeta *Sudan* 81 G3
Kápolnásnyék *Hungary* 28 C3
Kapos → *Hungary* 28 D3
Kaposvár *Hungary* 28 D2
Kapowsin *U.S.A.* 110 D4
Kappeln *Germany* 24 A5
Kappelshamn *Sweden* 11 G12
Kapps *Namibia* 88 C2
Kaprije *Croatia* 41 E13
Kapsabet *Kenya* 86 B4
Kapsan *N. Korea* 57 D15
Kapsukas = Marijampolė
　Lithuania 30 D10
Kaptai L. *Bangla.* 67 H18
Kapuas → *Indonesia* 62 E3
Kapuas Hulu, Pegunungan
　Malaysia 62 D4
Kapuas Hulu Ra. = Kapuas
　Hulu, Pegunungan
　Malaysia 62 D4
Kapulo *Dem. Rep. of the Congo* 87 D2
Kapunda *Australia* 95 E2
Kapuni *N.Z.* 91 C5
Kapurthala *India* 68 D6
Kapuskasing *Canada* 104 C3
Kapuskasing → *Canada* 104 C3
Kapustin Yar *Russia* 35 F7
Kaputar, Mt. *Australia* 95 E5
Kaputir *Kenya* 86 B4
Kapuvár *Hungary* 28 C2
Kara *Russia* 52 C7
Karā, W. → *Si. Arabia* 80 C5
Kara Ada *Turkey* 47 E9
Kara Bogaz Gol, Zaliv =
　Garabogazköl Aylagy
　Turkmenistan 52 E6
Kara Burun *Turkey* 47 E9
Kara-Kala = Garrygala
　Turkmenistan 71 B8
Kara Kalpak Republic =
　Qoraqalpoghistan ☐
　Uzbekistan 52 E6
Kara Kum = Garagum
　Turkmenistan 52 E7
Kara Sea *Russia* 52 B8
Karaadilli *Turkey* 47 C12
Karabiğa *Turkey* 45 F11
Karabük *Turkey* 72 B5
Karabük ☐ *Turkey* 72 B5
Karaburun *Albania* 44 F3
Karaburun *Turkey* 47 C8
Karabutak = Qarabutaq
　Kazakhstan 52 E7
Karacabey *Turkey* 45 F12
Karacakılavuz *Turkey* 45 E11
Karacaköy *Turkey* 45 E12
Karacasu *Turkey* 47 D10
Karachala = Qaraçala
　Azerbaijan 35 L9
Karachayevsk *Russia* 35 J5
Karachev *Russia* 33 F8
Karachey-Cherkessia ☐
　Russia 35 J5
Karachi *Pakistan* 68 G2
Karad *India* 66 L9
Karadirek *Turkey* 47 C12
Karaga *Ghana* 83 D4
Karaganda = Qaraghandy
　Kazakhstan 52 E8
Karagayly = Qaraghayly
　Kazakhstan 52 E8
Karaginskiy, Ostrov *Russia* 53 D17
Karagola Road *India* 69 G12
Karagüney Dağları *Turkey* 72 B6
Karahallı *Turkey* 47 C11
Karaikal *India* 66 P11
Karaikkudi *India* 66 P11
Karaisali *Turkey* 72 D6
Karaj *Iran* 71 C6
Karajarin ✫ *Australia* 92 C3
Karak *Malaysia* 65 L4
Karakalpakstan =
　Qoraqalpoghistan ☐
　Uzbekistan 52 E6
Karakaya Baraji *Turkey* 73 C8
Karakelong *Indonesia* 63 D7
Karakitang *Indonesia* 63 D7

Karakoçan *Turkey* **73** C9
Karakol *Kyrgyzstan* **52** E8
Karakoram Pass *Asia* **69** B7
Karakoram Ra. *Pakistan* **69** B7
Karakurt *Turkey* **73** B10
Karakuwisa *Namibia* **88** B2
Karalon *Russia* **53** D12
Karama *Jordan* **74** D4
Karaman *Balıkesir, Turkey* **47** B9
Karaman *Konya, Turkey* **72** D5
Karamanlı *Turkey* **47** D11
Karamay *China* **60** B3
Karambu *Indonesia* **62** E5
Karamea Bight *N.Z.* **91** D3
Karamnasa → *India* **69** G10
Karamürsel *Turkey* **45** F13
Karān *Si. Arabia* **71** E6
Karand *Iran* **73** E12
Karangana *Mali* **82** C3
Karanganyar *Indonesia* **63** G13
Karangasem *Indonesia* **63** J18
Karanjia *India* **69** J11
Karankasso *Burkina Faso* **82** C4
Karaova *Turkey* **47** D9
Karapınar *Turkey* **72** D5
Karasburg *Namibia* **88** D2
Karasino *Russia* **52** C9
Karasjok *Norway* **8** B21
Karasu *Turkey* **72** B4
Karasu → *Turkey* **47** E12
Karasuk *Russia* **52** D8
Karasuyama *Japan* **55** F10
Karataş *Adana, Turkey* **73** D7
Karataş *Manisa, Turkey* **47** C10
Karataş Burnu *Turkey* **72** D6
Karatau, Khrebet =
  Qarataū *Kazakhstan* **52** E7
Karatoprak *Turkey* **47** D9
Karatsu *Japan* **55** H5
Karaul *Russia* **52** B9
Karauli *India* **68** F7
Karavastasë, L. e *Albania* **44** F3
Karavia *Greece* **46** C5
Karavostasi *Cyprus* **49** D11
Karawang *Indonesia* **63** G12
Karawanken *Europe* **26** E7
Karayazı *Turkey* **73** C10
Karazhal = Qarazhal
  Kazakhstan **52** E7
Karbalā' *Iraq* **73** F11
Karbalā' □ *Iraq* **73** F10
Kårböle *Sweden* **10** C9
Karcag *Hungary* **28** C5
Karcha → *Pakistan* **69** B7
Karchana *India* **69** G9
Karczew *Poland* **31** F8
Kardam *Bulgaria* **45** C12
Kardamila *Greece* **47** C8
Kardamili *Greece* **46** E4
Kardeljovo = Ploče *Croatia* **41** E14
Karditsa *Greece* **46** B3
Karditsa □ *Greece* **46** B3
Kärdla *Estonia* **32** C2
Kareeberge *S. Africa* **88** E3
Kareha → *India* **69** G12
Kareima *Sudan* **80** D3
Karelia □ *Russia* **8** D25
Karelian Republic =
  Karelia □ *Russia* **8** D25
Karera *India* **68** G8
Kārevāndar *Iran* **71** E9
Kargasok *Russia* **52** D9
Kargat *Russia* **52** D9
Kargi *Kenya* **86** B4
Kargı *Turkey* **72** B6
Kargil *India* **69** B7
Kargopol *Russia* **32** B10
Kargowa *Poland* **31** F2
Karhal *India* **69** F8
Karia *Greece* **46** C2
Kariān *Iran* **71** E8
Karianga *Madag.* **89** C8
Kariba *Zimbabwe* **87** F2
Kariba, L. *Zimbabwe* **87** F2
Kariba Dam *Zimbabwe* **87** F2
Kariba Gorge *Zambia* **87** F2
Karibib *Namibia* **88** C2
Karies *Greece* **45** F8
Karijini △ *Australia* **92** D2
Karimata, Kepulauan
  Indonesia **62** E3
Karimata, Selat *Indonesia* **62** E3
Karimata Is. = Karimata,
  Kepulauan *Indonesia* **62** E3
Karimnagar *India* **66** K11
Karimunjawa, Kepulauan
  Indonesia **62** F4
Karimun Kecil, Pulau
  Indonesia **65** d
Karin *Somali Rep.* **75** E4
Karistos *Greece* **46** C6
Karīt *Iran* **71** C8
Kariya *Japan* **55** G8
Kariyangwe *Zimbabwe* **89** B4
Karjala *Finland* **8** E23
Karkaralinsk = Qarqaraly
  Kazakhstan **52** E8
Karkheh → *Iran* **70** D5

Karkinitska Zatoka *Ukraine* **33** K7
Karkinitskiy Zaliv =
  Karkinitska Zatoka
  Ukraine **33** K7
Karkuk = Kirkūk *Iraq* **73** E11
Karkur Tohl *Egypt* **80** C2
Karl Liebknecht *Russia* **33** G8
Karla, L. = Volvi, L. *Greece* **44** F7
Karlantijpa North ☼
  Australia **92** C5
Karlantijpa South ☼
  Australia **92** D5
Karleby = Kokkola *Finland* **8** E20
Karlholmsbruk *Sweden* **10** D11
Karlino *Poland* **30** D2
Karlıova *Turkey* **73** C9
Karlivka *Ukraine* **33** H8
Karlobag *Croatia* **41** D12
Karlovac *Croatia* **41** C12
Karlovarský □ *Czech Rep.* **26** A5
Karlovasi *Greece* **47** D8
Karlovka = Karlivka *Ukraine* **33** H8
Karlovo *Bulgaria* **45** D8
Karlovy Vary *Czech Rep.* **26** A5
Karlsbad = Karlovy Vary
  Czech Rep. **26** A5
Karlsborg *Sweden* **11** F8
Karlsena, Mys *Russia* **52** B7
Karlshamn *Sweden* **11** H8
Karlskoga *Sweden* **10** E8
Karlskrona *Sweden* **11** H9
Karlsruhe *Germany* **25** F4
Karlstad *Sweden* **10** E7
Karlstad *U.S.A.* **112** A5
Karlstadt *Germany* **25** F5
Karma *Egypt* **80** B5
Karmélava *Lithuania* **30** D11
Karmi'el *Israel* **74** C4
Karnak *Egypt* **80** B3
Karnal *India* **68** E7
Karnali → *Nepal* **69** E9
Karnaphuli Res. = Kaptai
  L. *Bangla.* **67** H18
Karnaprayag *India* **69** D8
Karnataka □ *India* **66** N10
Karnes City *U.S.A.* **116** G6
Karnische Alpen *Europe* **26** E6
Kärnten □ *Austria* **26** E6
Karo *Mali* **82** C4
Karoi *Zimbabwe* **87** F2
Karon, Ao *Thailand* **65** a
Karonga *Malawi* **87** D3
Karoo △ *S. Africa* **88** E3
Karoonda *Australia* **95** F2
Karor *Pakistan* **68** D4
Karora *Sudan* **80** D4
Karounga *Mali* **82** B3
Karousades *Greece* **46** B1
Karpacz *Poland* **31** H2
Karpasia *Cyprus* **49** D13
Karpathos *Greece* **47** F9
Karpathos, Stenon *Greece* **47** F9
Karpatsky △ *Ukraine* **29** B9
Karpenisi *Greece* **46** C3
Karpuz Burnu = Apostolos
  Andreas, C. *Cyprus* **49** D13
Karpuzlu *Turkey* **47** D9
Karratha *Australia* **92** D2
Kars *Turkey* **73** B10
Kars □ *Turkey* **73** B10
Karsakpay *Kazakhstan* **52** E7
Karsha *Kazakhstan* **34** F10
Karshi = Qarshi *Uzbekistan* **52** F7
Karsiyang *India* **69** F13
Karsog *India* **68** D7
Karst = Kras *Croatia* **41** C10
Kartal *Turkey* **45** F13
Kartaly *Russia* **52** D7
Kartapur *India* **68** D6
Karthaus *U.S.A.* **114** E6
Kartuzy *Poland* **30** D5
Karufa *Indonesia* **63** E8
Karuma △ *Uganda* **86** B3
Karumba *Australia* **94** B3
Karumo *Tanzania* **86** C3
Karumwa *Tanzania* **86** C3
Kārūn → *Iran* **71** D6
Karungu *Kenya* **86** C3
Karup *Denmark* **11** H3
Karviná *Czech Rep.* **27** B11
Karwan → *India* **68** F8
Karwar *India* **66** M9
Karwendel △ *Austria* **26** D4
Karwi *India* **69** G9
Karymskoye *Russia* **53** D12
Kaş *Turkey* **47** E11
Kasaba *Turkey* **47** E11
Kasache *Malawi* **87** E3
Kasai →
  Dem. Rep. of the Congo **84** E3
Kasai-Oriental □
  Dem. Rep. of the Congo **86** D1
Kasaji *Dem. Rep. of the Congo* **87** E1
Kasama *Zambia* **87** E3
Kasan N. *Korea* **57** D14
Kasandra *Greece* **44** F7
Kasandra Kolpos *Greece* **44** F7

Kasandras, Akra *Greece* **44** G7
Kasane *Namibia* **88** B3
Kasanga *Tanzania* **87** D3
Kasanka △ *Zambia* **87** E3
Kasar, Ras *Sudan* **80** D4
Kasaragod *India* **66** N9
Kasba L. *Canada* **103** A8
Käseh Garān *Iran* **70** C5
Kasempa *Zambia* **87** E2
Kasenga
  Dem. Rep. of the Congo **87** E2
Kasese *Uganda* **86** B3
Kasewa *Zambia* **87** E2
Kasganj *India* **69** F8
Kashabowie *Canada* **104** C1
Kashaf *Iran* **71** C9
Kāshān *Iran* **71** C6
Kashechewan *Canada* **104** B3
Kashgān → *Iran* **73** F12
Kashgar = Kashi *China* **60** C2
Kashi *China* **60** C2
Kashimbo
  Dem. Rep. of the Congo **87** E2
Kashin *Russia* **32** D9
Kashipur *India* **69** E8
Kashira *Russia* **32** E10
Kashiwazaki *Japan* **55** F9
Kashk-e Kohneh *Afghan.* **66** B3
Kashksaray *Iran* **73** C11
Kashkū'īyeh *Iran* **71** D7
Kāshmar *Iran* **71** C8
Kashmir *Asia* **69** C7
Kashmor *Pakistan* **68** E3
Kashpirovka *Russia* **34** D9
Kashun Noerh = Gaxun
  Nur *China* **60** B5
Kasiari *India* **69** H12
Kasimov *Russia* **34** C5
Kasinge *Dem. Rep. of the Congo* **86** D2
Kasiruta *Indonesia* **63** E7
Kaskaskia → *U.S.A.* **112** G9
Kaskattama → *Canada* **103** B10
Kaskinen *Finland* **8** E19
Kaskö = Kaskinen *Finland* **8** E19
Kaslo *Canada* **102** D5
Kasmere L. *Canada* **103** B8
Kasongo
  Dem. Rep. of the Congo **86** C2
Kasongo Lunda
  Dem. Rep. of the Congo **84** F3
Kasos *Greece* **47** F8
Kasos, Stenon *Greece* **47** F8
Kaspi *Georgia* **35** K7
Kaspichan *Bulgaria* **45** C11
Kaspiysk *Russia* **35** J8
Kaspiyskiy *Russia* **35** H8
Kassab ed Doleib *Sudan* **81** E3
Kassaba *Egypt* **80** C2
Kassalâ *Sudan* **81** D4
Kassalâ □ *Sudan* **81** D4
Kassandrino *Greece* **44** F7
Kassel *Germany* **24** D5
Kassinger *Sudan* **80** D3
Kassiopi *Greece* **49** A3
Kasson *U.S.A.* **112** C7
Kastamonu *Turkey* **72** B5
Kastamonu □ *Turkey* **72** B5
Kastav *Croatia* **41** C11
Kasteli *Greece* **49** D5
Kastelli *Greece* **49** D7
Kastellórizon = Megisti
  Greece **47** E11
Kastelo, Akra *Greece* **47** F9
Kasterlee *Belgium* **17** C4
Kastlösa *Sweden* **11** H10
Kastoria *Greece* **44** F5
Kastoria □ *Greece* **44** F5
Kastorias, L. *Greece* **44** F5
Kastorio *Greece* **46** D4
Kastornoye *Russia* **33** G10
Kastos *Greece* **46** C2
Kastrosikia *Greece* **46** B2
Kastrup = København ✈
  (CPH) *Denmark* **11** J6
Kastsyukovichy *Belarus* **32** F7
Kasulu *Tanzania* **86** C3
Kasumi *Japan* **55** G7
Kasumkent *Russia* **35** K9
Kasungu *Malawi* **87** E3
Kasungu △ *Malawi* **87** E3
Kasur *Pakistan* **68** D6
Kata, Ao *Thailand* **65** J2
Kata Archanes *Greece* **49** D7
Kata Tjuta *Australia* **93** E5
Kataba *Zambia* **87** F2
Katagum *Nigeria* **83** C7
Katahdin, Mt. *U.S.A.* **113** C19
Kataka = Cuttack *India* **67** J14
Katako Kombe
  Dem. Rep. of the Congo **86** C1
Katakolo *Greece* **46** D3
Katale *Tanzania* **86** C3
Katanda *Katanga,*
  Dem. Rep. of the Congo **86** D1
Katanda *Nord-Kivu,*
  Dem. Rep. of the Congo **86** C2
Katanga □
  Dem. Rep. of the Congo **86** D2
Katangi *India* **66** J11

Katanning *Australia* **93** F2
Katastari *Greece* **46** D2
Katavi △ *Tanzania* **86** D3
Katavi Swamp *Tanzania* **86** D3
Katerini *Greece* **44** F6
Katghora *India* **69** H10
Katha *Burma* **67** G20
Katherîna, Gebel *Egypt* **70** D2
Katherine *Australia* **92** B5
Katherine Gorge =
  Nitmiluk △ *Australia* **92** B5
Kathi *India* **68** J6
Kathiawar *India* **68** H4
Kathikas *Cyprus* **49** E11
Kathmandu *Nepal* **69** F11
Kathua *India* **68** C6
Kati *Mali* **82** C3
Katihar *India* **69** G12
Katima Mulilo *Namibia* **88** B3
Katimbira *Malawi* **87** E3
Katingan = Mendawai →
  Indonesia **62** E4
Katiola *Ivory C.* **82** D3
Katiti ☼ *Australia* **93** E5
Katlabukh, Ozero *Ukraine* **29** E14
Katlanovo *Macedonia* **44** E5
Katmandu = Kathmandu
  Nepal **69** F11
Katni = Murwara *India* **69** H9
Katni *India* **69** H9
Kato Achaia *Greece* **46** C3
Kato Chorio *Greece* **49** D7
Kato Korakiana *Greece* **49** A3
Káto Pyrgos *Cyprus* **49** D11
Katochi *Greece* **46** C3
Katompe
  Dem. Rep. of the Congo **86** D2
Katong *Singapore* **65** d
Katonga → *Uganda* **86** B3
Katoomba *Australia* **95** E5
Katouna *Greece* **46** C3
Katowice *Poland* **31** H6
Katrancı Dağı *Turkey* **47** D12
Katrine, L. *U.K.* **13** E4
Katrineholm *Sweden* **10** E10
Katsepe *Madag.* **89** B8
Katsina *Nigeria* **83** C6
Katsina □ *Nigeria* **83** C6
Katsina Ala *Nigeria* **83** D6
Katsina Ala → *Nigeria* **83** D6
Katsumoto *Japan* **55** H4
Katsuura *Japan* **55** G10
Katsuyama *Japan* **55** F8
Kattavia *Greece* **49** D9
Kattegat *Denmark* **11** H5
Katthammarsvik *Sweden* **11** G12
Katul, J. *Sudan* **81** E2
Katumba
  Dem. Rep. of the Congo **86** D2
Katwa *India* **69** H13
Katwijk *Neths.* **17** B4
Kąty Wrocławskie *Poland* **31** G3
Kaua'i *U.S.A.* **107** L8
Kaub *Germany* **25** E3
Kaudom △ *Namibia* **88** B3
Kaufbeuren *Germany* **25** H6
Kaufman *U.S.A.* **116** E6
Kauhajoki *Finland* **8** E20
Kaukauna *U.S.A.* **112** C9
Kaukauveld *Namibia* **88** C3
Ka'ula I. *U.S.A.* **107** L7
Kaunas *Lithuania* **30** D10
Kaunas ✈ (KUN) *Lithuania* **30** D11
Kaunia *Bangla.* **69** G13
Kaunos *Turkey* **47** E10
Kaura Namoda *Nigeria* **83** C6
Kauru *Nigeria* **83** C6
Kautokeino *Norway* **8** B20
Kauwapur *India* **69** F10
Kavacha *Russia* **53** C17
Kavadarci *Macedonia* **44** E6
Kavajë *Albania* **44** E3
Kavak *Turkey* **72** B7
Kavak Dağı *Turkey* **47** D10
Kavaklı *Turkey* **45** E11
Kavaklıdere *Turkey* **47** D10
Kavala *Greece* **45** F8
Kavala □ *Greece* **45** E8
Kavala Kolpos *Greece* **45** F8
Kavalerovo *Russia* **54** B7
Kavali *India* **66** M12
Kavār *Iran* **71** D7
Kavarna *Bulgaria* **45** C12
Kavi *India* **68** H5
Kavimba *Botswana* **88** B3
Kavīr, Dasht-e *Iran* **71** C7
Kavīr △ *Iran* **71** C7
Kävlinge *Sweden* **11** J7
Kavos *Greece* **49** B4
Kavousi *Greece* **47** F7
Kaw *Fr. Guiana* **125** C8
Kawa *Sudan* **81** E3
Kawagama L. *Canada* **114** A6
Kawagoe *Japan* **55** G9
Kawaguchi *Japan* **55** G9
Kawambwa *Zambia* **87** D2
Kawanoe *Japan* **55** G6
Kawardha *India* **69** J9

Kawasaki *Japan* **55** G9
Kawasi *Indonesia* **63** E7
Kawawachikamach *Canada* **105** B6
Kawerau *N.Z.* **91** C6
Kawhia *N.Z.* **91** C5
Kawhia Harbour *N.Z.* **91** C5
Kawio, Kepulauan *Indonesia* **63** D7
Kawthaung *Burma* **65** H2
Kawthoolei = Kayin □
  Burma **67** L20
Kawthule = Kayin □
  Burma **67** L20
Kaxholmen *Sweden* **11** G8
Kaya *Burkina Faso* **83** C4
Kayah □ *Burma* **67** K20
Kayak I. *U.S.A.* **106** D11
Kayan → *Indonesia* **62** D5
Kaycee *U.S.A.* **108** E10
Kayeli *Indonesia* **63** E7
Kayenta *U.S.A.* **109** H8
Kayes *Mali* **82** C2
Kayes □ *Mali* **82** C2
Kayı *Turkey* **47** B12
Kayima *S. Leone* **82** D2
Kayin □ *Burma* **67** L20
Kaymakçı *Turkey* **47** C10
Kayoa *Indonesia* **63** D7
Kayomba *Zambia* **87** E1
Kaysatskoye *Russia* **34** F8
Kayseri *Turkey* **72** C7
Kayseri □ *Turkey* **72** C7
Kaysville *U.S.A.* **108** F8
Kaz Dağı *Turkey* **47** B9
Kazachye *Russia* **53** B14
Kazakhstan ■ *Asia* **52** E8
Kazan *Russia* **34** C9
Kazan → *Canada* **103** A9
Kazan-Rettō *Pac. Oc.* **96** E6
Kazanlŭk *Bulgaria* **45** D9
Kazanskaya *Russia* **34** F5
Kazatin = Kozyatyn *Ukraine* **23** D15
Kazaure *Nigeria* **83** C6
Kazbek *Russia* **35** J7
Kāzerūn *Iran* **71** D6
Kazi Magomed =
  Qazımämmäd *Azerbaijan* **35** K9
Kazimierz Dolny *Poland* **31** G8
Kazimierza Wielka *Poland* **31** H7
Kazincbarcika *Hungary* **28** B5
Kazlų Rūda *Lithuania* **30** D10
Kaztalovka *Kazakhstan* **34** F9
Kazuma Pan △ *Zimbabwe* **87** F2
Kazuno *Japan* **54** D10
Kazym → *Russia* **52** C7
Kcynia *Poland* **31** F4
Ké-Macina *Mali* **82** C3
Kea *Greece* **46** D6
Keady *U.K.* **12** B5
Kearney *U.S.A.* **112** E4
Kearney ☼ *Australia* **92** D4
Kearny *U.S.A.* **109** K8
Kearsarge, Mt. *U.S.A.* **115** C13
Keban *Turkey* **73** C8
Keban Baraji *Turkey* **73** C8
Kebbi □ *Nigeria* **83** C5
Kébémèr *Senegal* **82** B1
Kébi *Ivory C.* **82** D3
Kebnekaise *Sweden* **8** C18
Kebri Dehar *Ethiopia* **75** F3
Kebumen *Indonesia* **63** G13
Kecel *Hungary* **28** D4
Kechika → *Canada* **102** B3
Keçiborlu *Turkey* **47** D12
Kecskemét *Hungary* **28** D4
Kedada *Ethiopia* **81** F4
Kédainiai *Lithuania* **30** C11
Kedarnath *India* **69** D8
Kedgwick *Canada* **105** C6
Kediri *Indonesia* **63** G15
Kedjebi *Ghana* **83** D5
Kédougou *Senegal* **82** C2
Kędzierzyn-Koźle *Poland* **31** H5
Keeler *U.S.A.* **110** J9
Keeley L. *Canada* **103** C7
Keeling Is. = Cocos Is.
  Ind. Oc. **96** J1
Keelung = Chilung *Taiwan* **59** E13
Keene *Canada* **114** B6
Keene *Calif., U.S.A.* **111** K8
Keene *N.H., U.S.A.* **115** D12
Keene *N.Y., U.S.A.* **115** B11
Keep River △ *Australia* **92** C4
Keeper Hill *Ireland* **12** D3
Keerweer, C. *Australia* **94** A3
Keeseville *U.S.A.* **115** B11
Keetmanshoop *Namibia* **88** D2
Keewatin *U.S.A.* **112** B7
Keewatin → *Canada* **103** B8
Kefa *Ethiopia* **81** F4
Kefalonia = Kefallinia
  Greece **46** C2
Kefallinia *Greece* **46** C2
Kefallonia □ *Greece* **46** C2
Kefalos *Greece* **47** E8
Kefamenanu *Indonesia* **63** F6
Kefar Sava *Israel* **74** C3
Keffi *Nigeria* **83** D6
Keffin Hausa *Nigeria* **83** C6
Keflavík *Iceland* **8** D2

Keftya *Ethiopia* **81** E4
Keg River *Canada* **102** B5
Kegaska *Canada* **105** B7
Kehancha *Kenya* **86** C3
Keheili *Sudan* **80** D3
Kehl *Germany* **25** G3
Keighley *U.K.* **14** D6
Keila *Estonia* **32** C3
Keimoes *S. Africa* **88** D3
Keita *Niger* **83** C6
Keitele *Finland* **8** E22
Keith *Australia* **95** F3
Keith *U.K.* **13** D6
Keiyasi *Fiji* **91** a
Keizer *U.S.A.* **108** D2
Kejimkujik △ *Canada* **105** D6
Kejserr Franz Joseph Fd.
  Greenland **4** B6
Kekri *India* **68** G6
Kelam *Ethiopia* **81** G4
Kelamet *Eritrea* **81** D4
Kelan *China* **56** E6
Kelang = Klang *Malaysia* **65** L3
Kelantan → *Malaysia* **65** J4
Këlcyrë *Albania* **44** F4
Kelekçi *Turkey* **47** D11
Keles *Turkey* **45** G13
Keleti-főcsatorna *Hungary* **28** C5
Kelheim *Germany* **25** G7
Kelkit *Turkey* **73** B8
Kelkit → *Turkey* **72** B7
Kellé *Niger* **83** C7
Kellerberrin *Australia* **93** F2
Kellett, C. *Canada* **4** B1
Kelleys I. *U.S.A.* **114** E2
Kellogg *U.S.A.* **108** C5
Kells = Ceanannus Mor
  Ireland **12** C5
Kelmë *Lithuania* **30** C9
Kelmentsi *Ukraine* **29** B11
Kélo *Chad* **79** G9
Kelokedhara *Cyprus* **49** E11
Kelowna *Canada* **102** D5
Kelsey Creek *Australia* **94** b
Kelseyville *U.S.A.* **110** G4
Kelso *N.Z.* **91** F2
Kelso *U.K.* **13** F6
Kelso *U.S.A.* **110** D4
Keluang = Kluang *Malaysia* **65** L4
Kelvington *Canada* **103** C8
Kem *Russia* **52** C4
Kema *Indonesia* **63** D7
Kemah *Turkey* **73** C8
Kemaliye *Erzincan, Turkey* **73** C8
Kemaliye *Manisa, Turkey* **47** C10
Kemalpaşa *Turkey* **47** C9
Kemaman *Malaysia* **65** K4
Kemano *Canada* **102** C3
Kemasik *Malaysia* **65** K4
Kembolcha *Ethiopia* **81** E4
Kemer *Antalya, Turkey* **47** E12
Kemer *Burdur, Turkey* **47** D12
Kemer *Muğla, Turkey* **47** E11
Kemer Baraji *Turkey* **47** D10
Kemerovo *Russia* **52** D9
Kemeru △ *Latvia* **30** B10
Kemi *Finland* **8** D21
Kemi älv = Kemijoki →
  Finland **8** D21
Kemi träsk = Kemijärvi
  Finland **8** C22
Kemijärvi *Finland* **8** C22
Kemijoki → *Finland* **8** D21
Kemmerer *U.S.A.* **108** F8
Kemmuna = Comino *Malta* **49** C1
Kemp, L. *U.S.A.* **116** E5
Kemp Land *Antarctica* **5** C5
Kempas *Malaysia* **65** d
Kempsey *Australia* **95** E5
Kempt, L. *Canada* **104** C5
Kempten *Germany* **25** H6
Kempton *Australia* **95** G4
Kemptville *Canada* **115** B9
Ken → *India* **69** G9
Kenai *U.S.A.* **100** E1
Kenai Mts. *U.S.A.* **106** D9
Kenamuke Swamp *Sudan* **81** F3
Kendai *India* **69** H10
Kendal *Indonesia* **63** G14
Kendal *U.K.* **14** C5
Kendall *Australia* **95** E5
Kendall *U.S.A.* **117** J14
Kendall → *Australia* **94** A3
Kendallville *U.S.A.* **113** E11
Kendari *Indonesia* **63** E6
Kendawangan *Indonesia* **62** E4
Kende *Nigeria* **83** C5
Kendi, Pulau *Malaysia* **65** c
Kendrapara *India* **67** J15
Kendrew *S. Africa* **88** E3
Kene Thao *Laos* **64** D3
Kenedy *U.S.A.* **116** G6
Kenema *S. Leone* **82** D2
Keng Kok *Laos* **64** D5
Keng Tawng *Burma* **67** J21
Keng Tung *Burma* **58** G2
Kengeja *Tanzania* **86** D4
Kenhardt *S. Africa* **88** D3

Kéniéba *Mali* **82** C2
Kenitra *Morocco* **78** B4
Kenli *China* **57** F10
Kenmare *Ireland* **12** E2
Kenmare *U.S.A.* **112** A2
Kenmare River *Ireland* **12** E2
Kennebago Lake *U.S.A.* **115** A14
Kennebec *U.S.A.* **112** D4
Kennebec → *U.S.A.* **113** D19
Kennebunk *U.S.A.* **115** C14
Kennedy *Zimbabwe* **88** B4
Kennedy Kanal *Arctic* **101** A18
Kennedy Ra. *Australia* **93** D2
Kennedy Range △ *Australia* **93** D2
Kenner *U.S.A.* **117** G9
Kenneth Ra. *Australia* **93** D2
Kennett *U.S.A.* **112** G8
Kennewick *U.S.A.* **108** C4
Kennisis Lake *Canada* **114** A6
Kenogami → *Canada* **104** B3
Kenora *Canada* **103** D10
Kenosha *U.S.A.* **112** D10
Kensington *Canada* **105** C7
Kent *Ohio, U.S.A.* **114** E3
Kent *Tex., U.S.A.* **116** F2
Kent *Wash., U.S.A.* **110** C4
Kent □ *U.K.* **15** F8
Kent Group *Australia* **95** F4
Kent Pen. *Canada* **100** D10
Kentaū *Kazakhstan* **52** E7
Kentland *U.S.A.* **112** E10
Kenton *U.S.A.* **113** E12
Kentucky □ *U.S.A.* **113** G11
Kentucky → *U.S.A.* **113** F11
Kentucky L. *U.S.A.* **112** G9
Kentville *Canada* **105** C7
Kentwood *U.S.A.* **117** F9
Kenya ■ *Africa* **86** B4
Kenya, Mt. *Kenya* **86** C4
Kenyir, Tasik *Malaysia* **65** K4
Keo Neua, Deo *Vietnam* **64** C5
Keokuk *U.S.A.* **112** E8
Keoladeo △ *India* **68** F7
Keonjhargarh *India* **69** J11
Kep *Cambodia* **65** G5
Kep *Vietnam* **64** B6
Kepala Batas *Malaysia* **65** c
Kepez *Turkey* **45** F10
Kepi *Indonesia* **63** F9
Kepice *Poland* **30** D3
Kępno *Poland* **31** G4
Kepsut *Turkey* **47** B10
Kerala □ *India* **66** P10
Kerama-Rettō *Japan* **55** L3
Keran *Pakistan* **69** B5
Keran △ *Togo* **83** C5
Kerang *Australia* **95** F3
Keranyo *Ethiopia* **81** F4
Kerao → *Sudan* **81** E3
Keratea *Greece* **46** D5
Keraudren, C. *Australia* **92** C2
Kerava *Finland* **32** B3
Kerch *Ukraine* **33** K9
Kerchenskiy Proliv *Black Sea* **33** K9
Kerchoual *Mali* **83** B5
Kerempe Burnu *Turkey* **72** A5
Keren *Eritrea* **81** D4
Kerewan *Gambia* **82** C1
Kerguelen *Ind. Oc.* **3** G13
Keri *Greece* **46** D2
Keri Kera *Sudan* **81** E3
Kericho *Kenya* **86** C4
Kerinci *Indonesia* **62** E2
Kerki = Atamyrat
  Turkmenistan **52** F7
Kerkini, L. *Greece* **44** E7
Kerkouane *Tunisia* **42** F4
Kerkrade *Neths.* **17** D6
Kerkyra *Greece* **49** A3
Kerkyra □ *Greece* **46** B1
Kerkyra ✈ (CFU) *Greece* **46** B1
Kerkyras, Notio Steno *Greece* **49** A4
Kerma *Sudan* **80** D3
Kermadec Is. *Pac. Oc.* **90** E11
Kermadec Trench *Pac. Oc.* **96** L10
Kermān *Iran* **71** D8
Kerman *U.S.A.* **110** J6
Kermān □ *Iran* **71** D8
Kermān, Bīābān-e *Iran* **71** D8
Kermānshāh *Iran* **73** E12
Kermānshāh □ *Iran* **70** C5
Kermen *Bulgaria* **45** D10
Kermit *U.S.A.* **116** F3
Kern → *U.S.A.* **111** K7
Kernhof *Austria* **26** D8
Kernow = Cornwall □ *U.K.* **15** G3
Kernville *U.S.A.* **111** K8
Keroh *Malaysia* **65** K3
Keros *Greece* **47** E7
Kérou *Benin* **83** C5
Kérouane *Guinea* **82** D3
Kerpen *Germany* **24** E2
Kerrera *U.K.* **13** E3
Kerrobert *Canada* **103** C7
Kerrville *U.S.A.* **116** F5
Kerry □ *Ireland* **12** D2
Kerry Hd. *Ireland* **12** D2
Kersa *Ethiopia* **81** F5

Kerulen → *Asia* **60** B6
Kervo = Kerava *Finland* **32** B3
Kerzaz *Algeria* **78** C5
Kesagami → *Canada* **104** B4
Kesagami L. *Canada* **104** B3
Keşan *Turkey* **45** F10
Kesennuma *Japan* **54** E10
Keshāvar *Iran* **73** D12
Keshit *Iran* **71** D8
Keşiş Dağ *Turkey* **73** C8
Keskin *Turkey* **72** C5
Kestell *S. Africa* **89** D4
Kestenga *Russia* **8** D24
Keswick *U.K.* **14** C4
Keszthely *Hungary* **28** D2
Ket → *Russia* **52** D9
Keta *Ghana* **83** D5
Keta Lagoon *Ghana* **83** D5
Ketapang *Bali, Indonesia* **63** J17
Ketapang *Kalimantan,*
  Indonesia **62** E4
Ketchenery *Russia* **35** G7
Ketchikan *U.S.A.* **102** B2
Ketchum *U.S.A.* **108** E6
Kete Krachi *Ghana* **83** D4
Ketef, Khalig Umm el *Egypt* **70** F2
Keti Bandar *Pakistan* **68** G2
Kétou *Benin* **83** D5
Ketri *India* **68** E6
Kętrzyn *Poland* **30** D8
Kettering *U.K.* **15** E7
Kettering *U.S.A.* **113** F11
Kettle → *Canada* **103** B11
Kettle Falls *U.S.A.* **108** B4
Kettle Point *Canada* **114** C2
Kettle Pt. *Canada* **114** C2
Kettleman City *U.S.A.* **110** J7
Kęty *Poland* **31** J6
Keuka L. *U.S.A.* **114** D7
Keuruu *Finland* **32** A3
Kevelaer *Germany* **24** D2
Kewanee *U.S.A.* **112** E9
Kewaunee *U.S.A.* **112** C10
Keweenaw B. *U.S.A.* **112** B9
Keweenaw Pen. *U.S.A.* **112** B9
Keweenaw Pt. *U.S.A.* **112** B10
Key, L. *Ireland* **12** C3
Key Lake Mine *Canada* **103** B7
Key Largo *U.S.A.* **117** J14
Key West *U.S.A.* **120** F5
Keyala *Sudan* **81** G3
Keynsham *U.K.* **15** F5
Keyser *U.S.A.* **113** F14
Kezhma *Russia* **53** D11
Kezi *Zimbabwe* **87** G2
Kežmarok *Slovak Rep.* **27** B13
Kgalagadi Transfrontier △
  Africa **88** D3
Khabarovsk *Russia* **53** E14
Khabr *Iran* **71** D8
Khābūr → *Syria* **73** E9
Khachmas = Xaçmaz
  Azerbaijan **35** K9
Khachrod *India* **68** H6
Khadari, W. el → *Sudan* **81** E2
Khadro *Pakistan* **68** F3
Khadzhilyangar =
  Dahongliutan *China* **69** B8
Khaga *India* **69** G9
Khagaria *India* **69** G12
Khaipur *Pakistan* **68** E5
Khair *India* **68** F7
Khairabad *India* **69** F9
Khairagarh *India* **69** J9
Khairpur *Pakistan* **68** F3
Khairpur Nathan Shah
  Pakistan **68** F2
Khairwara *India* **68** H5
Khaisor → *Pakistan* **68** D3
Khajuri Kach *Pakistan* **68** C3
Khakassia □ *Russia* **52** D9
Khakhea *Botswana* **88** C3
Khalafābād *Iran* **71** D6
Khalīlī *Iran* **71** E7
Khalilabad *India* **69** F10
Khalkhāl *Iran* **73** D13
Khalkís = Halkida *Greece* **46** C5
Khalmer Yu *Russia* **52** C7
Khalūf *Oman* **75** C6
Kham Keut *Laos* **64** C5
Khamaria *India* **69** H9
Khambhaliya *India* **68** H3
Khambhat *India* **68** H5
Khambhat, G. of *India* **66** J8
Khamir *Iran* **71** E7
Khamir *Yemen* **75** D3
Khamīs Mushayt *Si. Arabia* **75** D3
Khamsa *Egypt* **74** E1
Khān → *Namibia* **88** C2
Khān Abū Shāmat *Syria* **74** B5
Khān al Baghdādī *Iraq* **73** F10
Khān al Ḥammād *Iraq* **73** G11
Khān Āzād *Iraq* **70** C5
Khān Mujiddah *Iraq* **70** C4
Khān Shaykhūn *Syria* **72** E7
Khān Yūnis *Gaza Strip* **74** D3
Khanai *Pakistan* **68** D2
Khānaqīn *Iraq* **73** E11

Khānbāghī *Iran* **71** B7
Khandwa *India* **66** J10
Khandyga *Russia* **53** C14
Khanewal *Pakistan* **68** D4
Khangah Dogran *Pakistan* **68** D5
Khanh Duong *Vietnam* **64** F7
Khania = Chania *Greece* **49** D6
Khaniadhana *India* **68** G8
Khanka, L. *Asia* **54** B6
Khankendy = Xankändi
  Azerbaijan **73** C12
Khanna *India* **68** D7
Khanpur *Pakistan* **68** E4
Khanty-Mansiysk *Russia* **52** C7
Khao Laem △ *Thailand* **64** E2
Khao Laem Res. *Thailand* **64** E2
Khao Lak △ *Malaysia* **65** H2
Khao Luang △ *Thailand* **65** H2
Khao Phlu *Thailand* **65** b
Khao Pu-Khao Ya △ *Thailand* **65** J2
Khao Sam Roi Yot △
  Thailand **65** F2
Khao Sok △ *Thailand* **65** H2
Khao Yai △ *Thailand* **64** E3
Khaoen Si Nakarin △
  Thailand **64** E2
Khapalu *Pakistan* **69** B7
Khapcheranga *Russia* **53** E12
Khaptao △ *Nepal* **69** D8
Kharabali *Russia* **35** G8
Kharagauli *Georgia* **35** J6
Kharaghoda *India* **68** H4
Kharagpur *India* **69** H12
Kharan Kalat *Pakistan* **66** E4
Khārānaq *Iran* **71** C7
Kharda *India* **66** K9
Khardung La *India* **69** B7
Kharg = Khārk, Jazīreh-ye
  Iran **71** D6
Khargon *India* **66** J9
Khari → *India* **68** G6
Kharian *Pakistan* **68** C5
Kharit, Wadi el → *Egypt* **80** C3
Khārk, Jazīreh-ye *Iran* **71** D6
Kharkiv *Ukraine* **33** H9
Kharkiv □ *Ukraine* **33** H9
Kharkov = Kharkiv *Ukraine* **33** H9
Kharmanli *Bulgaria* **45** E9
Kharovsk *Russia* **32** C11
Kharsawangarh *India* **69** H11
Kharta *Turkey* **72** B3
Khartoum = El Khartûm
  Sudan **81** D3
Khartum *Canada* **114** A7
Khasan *Russia* **54** C5
Khasavyurt *Russia* **35** J8
Khāsh *Iran* **71** D9
Khashm el Girba *Sudan* **81** E4
Khashum *Sudan* **81** E2
Khashuri *Georgia* **35** J6
Khaskovo *Bulgaria* **45** E9
Khaskovo □ *Bulgaria* **45** E9
Khatanga *Russia* **53** B11
Khatanga → *Russia* **53** B11
Khatauli *India* **68** E7
Khatra *India* **69** H12
Khātūnābād *Iran* **71** D7
Khatyrka *Russia* **53** C18
Khavda *India* **68** H3
Khawr Fakkān *U.A.E.* **71** E8
Khay' *Si. Arabia* **80** D5
Khaybar, Ḥarrat *Si. Arabia* **70** E4
Khāzimiyah *Iraq* **70** C4
Khazzān Jabal al Awliyā
  Sudan **81** D3
Khe Bo *Vietnam* **64** C5
Khe Long *Vietnam* **64** B5
Khe Sanh *Vietnam* **64** D6
Khed Brahma *India* **68** G5
Khekra *India* **68** E7
Khemarak Phouminville =
  Krong Kaoh Kong
  Cambodia **65** G4
Khemisset *Morocco* **78** B4
Khemmarat *Thailand* **64** D5
Khenāmān *Iran* **71** D8
Khenchela *Algeria* **78** A7
Khersān → *Iran* **71** D6
Kherson *Ukraine* **33** J7
Kherson □ *Ukraine* **33** J7
Kheta → *Russia* **53** B11
Khewari *Pakistan* **68** F3
Khilchipur *India* **68** G7
Khilok *Russia* **53** D12
Khimki *Russia* **32** E9
Khíos = Hios *Greece* **47** C8
Khirsadoh *India* **69** H8
Khiuma = Hiiumaa *Estonia* **32** C2
Khiva *Uzbekistan* **52** E7
Khlebarovo *Bulgaria* **45** C10
Khlong Khlung *Thailand* **64** D2
Khmelnik *Ukraine* **23** D14
Khmelnytskyy *Ukraine* **23** D14
Khmelnytskyy □ *Ukraine* **33** H4
Khmer Rep. = Cambodia ■
  Asia **64** F5
Khoai, Hon *Vietnam* **65** H5

Khodoriv *Ukraine* **23** D13
Khodzent = Khŭjand
  Tajikistan **52** E7
Khojak Pass *Afghan.* **68** D2
Khok Kloi *Thailand* **65** a
Khok Pho *Thailand* **65** J3
Khok Samrong *Thailand* **64** E3
Kholm *Russia* **32** D6
Kholmsk *Russia* **53** E15
Khomārlū *Iran* **73** C12
Khomas Hochland *Namibia* **88** C2
Khombole *Senegal* **82** C1
Khomeyn *Iran* **71** C6
Khomeynī Shahr *Iran* **71** C6
Khomodino *Botswana* **88** C3
Khon Kaen *Thailand* **64** D4
Khong → *Cambodia* **64** F5
Khong Sedone *Laos* **64** E5
Khonuu *Russia* **53** C15
Khoper → *Russia* **34** F6
Khor el 'Atash *Sudan* **81** E3
Khorāsān □ *Iran* **71** C8
Khorat = Nakhon
  Ratchasima *Thailand* **64** E4
Khorat, Cao Nguyen *Thailand* **64** E4
Khorixas *Namibia* **88** C1
Khorol *Ukraine* **33** H7
Khorramābād *Khorāsān, Iran* **71** C8
Khorramābād *Lorestān, Iran* **73** F13
Khorramdarreh *Iran* **73** D13
Khorrāmshahr *Iran* **71** D6
Khorugh *Tajikistan* **52** F8
Khosravī *Iran* **71** D6
Khosrowābād *Khuzestān, Iran* **71** D6
Khosrowābād *Kordestān,*
  Iran **73** E12
Khost *Pakistan* **68** D2
Khosūyeh *Iran* **71** D7
Khotyn *Ukraine* **29** B11
Khouribga *Morocco* **78** B4
Khowst *Afghan.* **68** C3
Khowst □ *Afghan.* **66** C6
Khoyniki *Belarus* **23** C15
Khrami → *Georgia* **35** K7
Khrenovoye *Russia* **34** E5
Khrysokhou B. *Cyprus* **49** D11
Khu Khan *Thailand* **64** E5
Khuan Wa *Thailand* **65** a
Khudzhand = Khŭjand
  Tajikistan **52** E7
Khuff *Si. Arabia* **70** E5
Khūgīānī *Afghan.* **68** D2
Khuis *Botswana* **88** D3
Khuiyala *India* **68** F4
Khŭjand *Tajikistan* **52** E7
Khujner *India* **68** H7
Khulna *Bangla.* **67** H16
Khulna □ *Bangla.* **67** H16
Khulo *Georgia* **35** K6
Khumago *Botswana* **88** C3
Khunjerab △ *Pakistan* **69** A6
Khunjerab Pass = Kinjirap
  Daban *Asia* **66** A9
Khūnsorkh *Iran* **71** E8
Khunti *India* **69** H11
Khūr *Iran* **71** C8
Khurai *India* **68** G8
Khuraysān *Si. Arabia* **71** E6
Khureit *Sudan* **81** E2
Khurja *India* **68** E7
Khūrmāl *Iraq* **73** E12
Khurr, Wādī al *Iraq* **70** C4
Khūsf *Iran* **71** C8
Khushab *Pakistan* **68** C5
Khust *Ukraine* **29** B8
Khutse △ *Botswana* **88** C3
Khuwei *Sudan* **81** E2
Khuzdar *Pakistan* **68** F2
Khūzestān □ *Iran* **71** D6
Khvāf *Iran* **71** C9
Khvājeh *Iran* **70** B5
Khvalynsk *Russia* **34** D9
Khvānsār *Iran* **71** D7
Khvatovka *Russia* **34** D8
Khvor *Iran* **71** C7
Khvorgū *Iran* **71** E8
Khvormūj *Iran* **71** D6
Khvoy *Iran* **73** C11
Khvoynaya *Russia* **32** C8
Khyber Pass *Afghan.* **68** B4
Khyriv *Ukraine* **31** J9
Kia *Fiji* **91** a
Kiabukwa
  Dem. Rep. of the Congo **87** D1
Kiama *Australia* **95** E5
Kiamba *Phil.* **61** J6
Kiambi *Dem. Rep. of the Congo* **86** D2
Kiambu *Kenya* **86** C4
Kiang West △ *Gambia* **82** C1
Kiangara *Madag.* **89** B8
Kiangsi = Jiangxi □ *China* **59** D11
Kiangsu = Jiangsu □ *China* **57** H11
Kiato *Greece* **46** C4
Kibæk *Denmark* **11** H2
Kibale △ *Uganda* **86** B3
Kibanga Port *Uganda* **86** B3
Kibara *Tanzania* **86** C3
Kibare, Mts.
  Dem. Rep. of the Congo **86** D2

Kibira △ *Burundi* **86** C3
Kiboga *Uganda* **86** B3
Kibombo
  Dem. Rep. of the Congo **86** C2
Kibondo *Tanzania* **86** C3
Kibre Mengist *Ethiopia* **81** F4
Kibris = Cyprus ■ *Asia* **49** E12
Kibumbu *Burundi* **86** C2
Kibungo *Rwanda* **86** C3
Kibuye *Burundi* **86** C2
Kibuye *Rwanda* **86** C2
Kibwesa *Tanzania* **86** D2
Kibwezi *Kenya* **86** C4
Kicasalih *Turkey* **45** E10
Kičevo *Macedonia* **44** E4
Kichha *India* **69** E8
Kichha → *India* **69** E8
Kicking Horse Pass *Canada* **102** C5
Kidal *Mali* **83** B5
Kidal □ *Mali* **83** B5
Kidamang *Phil.* **61** H6
Kidderminster *U.K.* **15** E5
Kidepo Valley △ *Uganda* **86** B3
Kidete *Tanzania* **86** D4
Kidira *Senegal* **82** C2
Kidnappers, C. *N.Z.* **91** C6
Kidsgrove *U.K.* **14** D5
Kidston *Australia* **94** B3
Kidugallo *Tanzania* **86** D4
Kiel *Germany* **24** A6
Kiel Canal = Nord-Ostsee-
  Kanal *Germany* **24** A5
Kielce *Poland* **31** H7
Kielder Water *U.K.* **14** B5
Kieler Bucht *Germany* **24** A6
Kiembara *Burkina Faso* **82** C4
Kien Binh *Vietnam* **65** H5
Kien Tan *Vietnam* **65** G5
Kienge *Dem. Rep. of the Congo* **87** E2
Kiessé *Niger* **83** C5
Kiev = Kyyiv *Ukraine* **23** C16
Kifaya *Guinea* **82** C2
Kiffa *Mauritania* **82** B2
Kifisos → *Greece* **46** C5
Kifissia *Greece* **46** C5
Kifrī *Iraq* **73** E11
Kigali *Rwanda* **86** C3
Kigarama *Tanzania* **86** C3
Kigelle *Sudan* **81** F3
Kigezi △ *Uganda* **86** C3
Kiği *Turkey* **73** C9
Kigoma *Tanzania* **86** D3
Kigoma-Ujiji *Tanzania* **86** C2
Kigomasha, Ras *Tanzania* **86** C4
Kigosi △ *Tanzania* **86** C3
Kihnu *Estonia* **32** C3
Kii-Sanchi *Japan* **55** G8
Kii-Suidō *Japan* **55** H7
Kiira Dam *Uganda* **86** B3
Kikaiga-Shima *Japan* **55** K4
Kikinda *Serbia* **28** E5
Kikládhes = Cyclades *Greece* **46** E6
Kikwit *Dem. Rep. of the Congo* **84** F3
Kil *Sweden* **10** E7
Kilafors *Sweden* **10** C10
Kilar *India* **68** C7
Kilbeggan *Ireland* **12** C4
Kilbirnie *Ireland* **12** C4
Kilbrannan Sd. *U.K.* **13** F3
Kilbuck Mts. *U.S.A.* **106** C8
Kilchu *N. Korea* **57** D15
Kilcoy *Australia* **95** D5
Kildare *Ireland* **12** C5
Kildare □ *Ireland* **12** C5
Kildinstroy *Russia* **8** B25
Kileikli *Sudan* **81** E2
Kilfinnane *Ireland* **12** D3
Kilgarvan *Ireland* **12** E2
Kilgore *U.S.A.* **116** E7
Kilgoris *Kenya* **86** C3
Kilibo *Benin* **83** D5
Kilifi *Kenya* **86** C4
Kilimanjaro *Tanzania* **86** C4
Kilimanjaro □ *Tanzania* **86** C4
Kilimanjaro △ *Tanzania* **86** C4
Kilimli *Turkey* **72** B4
Kilindini *Kenya* **86** C4
Kilis *Turkey* **72** D7
Kilis □ *Turkey* **72** D7
Kiliya *Ukraine* **29** E14
Kilkee *Ireland* **12** D2
Kilkeel *U.K.* **12** B5
Kilkenny *Ireland* **12** D4
Kilkenny □ *Ireland* **12** D4
Kilkieran B. *Ireland* **12** C2
Kilkis *Greece* **44** F6
Kilkis □ *Greece* **44** E6
Killala *Ireland* **12** B2
Killala B. *Ireland* **12** B2
Killaloe *Canada* **114** A7
Killaloe *Ireland* **12** D3
Killarney *Australia* **95** D5
Killarney *Canada* **103** D9
Killarney *Ireland* **12** D2
Killarney □ *Ireland* **12** D2
Killary Harbour *Ireland* **12** C2
Killdeer *U.S.A.* **112** B2
Killeberg *Sweden* **11** H8
Killeen *U.S.A.* **116** F6

Killin *U.K.* **13** E4
Killiney *Ireland* **12** C5
Killington Pk. *U.S.A.* **115** C12
Killini = Kyllini *Greece* **46** D3
Killini *Greece* **46** D3
Killorglin *Ireland* **12** D2
Killybegs *Ireland* **12** B3
Kilmarnock *U.K.* **13** F4
Kilmez *Russia* **34** B10
Kilmez → *Russia* **34** B10
Kilmore *Australia* **95** F3
Kilmore Quay *Ireland* **12** D5
Kilondo *Tanzania* **87** D3
Kilosa *Tanzania* **86** D4
Kilrush *Ireland* **12** D2
Kilwa Kisiwani *Tanzania* **87** D4
Kilwa Kivinje *Tanzania* **87** D4
Kilwa Masoko *Tanzania* **87** D4
Kilwinning *U.K.* **13** F4
Kim *U.S.A.* **109** H12
Kim → *Cameroon* **83** D7
Kimaam *Indonesia* **63** F9
Kimamba *Tanzania* **86** D4
Kimba *Australia* **95** E2
Kimball *Nebr., U.S.A.* **112** E2
Kimball *S. Dak., U.S.A.* **112** D4
Kimberley *Australia* **92** C4
Kimberley *B.C., Canada* **102** D5
Kimberley *Ont., Canada* **114** B4
Kimberley *S. Africa* **88** D3
Kimberly *U.S.A.* **108** E6
Kimch'aek *N. Korea* **57** D15
Kimhae = Gimhae *S. Korea* **57** G15
Kimi *Greece* **46** C6
Kimmirut *Canada* **101** E18
Kimolos *Greece* **46** E6
Kimovsk *Moskva, Russia* **32** E9
Kimovsk *Tula, Russia* **32** E10
Kimparana *Mali* **82** C4
Kimpese *Dem. Rep. of the Congo* **84** F2
Kimry *Russia* **32** D9
Kimstad *Sweden* **11** F9
Kinabalu, Gunung *Malaysia* **62** C5
Kinango *Kenya* **86** C4
Kinaros *Greece* **47** E8
Kinaskan L. *Canada* **102** B2
Kinbasket L. *Canada* **102** C5
Kincardine *Canada* **114** B3
Kincolith *Canada* **102** C3
Kinda *Dem. Rep. of the Congo* **87** D2
Kindberg *Austria* **26** D8
Kinde *U.S.A.* **114** C2
Kinder Scout *U.K.* **14** D6
Kindersley *Canada* **103** C7
Kindia *Guinea* **82** D2
Kindu *Dem. Rep. of the Congo* **86** C2
Kinel *Russia* **34** D10
Kineshma *Russia* **34** B6
Kinesi *Tanzania* **86** C3
King, L. *Australia* **93** F2
King, Mt. *Australia* **94** D4
King Christian I. *Canada* **101** B11
King City *U.S.A.* **110** J5
King Cr. → *Australia* **94** C2
King Edward → *Australia* **92** B4
King Edward Point
  S. Georgia **128** G9
King Frederick VI Land =
  Kong Frederik VI Kyst
  Greenland **4** C5
King George I. *Antarctica* **5** C18
King George Is. *Canada* **101** F15
King George Sd. *Australia* **93** G2
King I. = Kadan Kyun
  Burma **64** F2
King I. *Australia* **95** F3
King I. *Canada* **102** C3
King Khalid Military City =
  Madinat al Malik Khālid
  al Askarīyah *Si. Arabia* **70** E5
King Leopold Ranges
  Australia **92** C4
King of Prussia *U.S.A.* **115** F9
King Sd. *Australia* **92** C3
King Sejong *Antarctica* **5** C18
King William I. *Canada* **100** D12
King William's Town
  S. Africa **88** E4
Kingaok = Bathurst Inlet
  Canada **100** D10
Kingaroy *Australia* **95** D5
Kingfisher *U.S.A.* **116** D6
Kingirbān *Iraq* **70** C5
Kingisepp = Kuressaare
  Estonia **32** C2
Kingisepp *Russia* **32** C5
Kingman *Ariz., U.S.A.* **111** K12
Kingman *Kans., U.S.A.* **112** G4
Kingoonya *Australia* **95** E2
Kingri *Pakistan* **68** D3
Kings → *U.S.A.* **110** J7
Kings Canyon *Australia* **92** D5
Kings Canyon △ *U.S.A.* **110** J8
King's Lynn *U.K.* **15** E8
Kings Park *U.S.A.* **115** F11
Kings Peak *U.S.A.* **108** F8
Kingsbridge *U.K.* **15** G4
Kingsburg *U.S.A.* **110** J7

Kingscote *Australia* **95** F2
Kingscourt *Ireland* **12** C5
Kingsford *U.S.A.* **112** C9
Kingsland *U.S.A.* **117** F14
Kingsport *U.S.A.* **117** C13
Kingston *Canada* **115** B8
Kingston *Jamaica* **120** a
Kingston *N.Z.* **91** F2
Kingston *N.H., U.S.A.* **115** D13
Kingston *N.Y., U.S.A.* **115** E11
Kingston *Pa., U.S.A.* **115** E9
Kingston *R.I., U.S.A.* **115** E13
Kingston Pk. *U.S.A.* **111** K11
Kingston South East
  Australia **95** F2
Kingston upon Hull *U.K.* **14** D7
Kingston upon Hull □ *U.K.* **14** D7
Kingston-upon-Thames □
  U.K. **15** F7
Kingstown *St. Vincent* **121** D7
Kingstree *U.S.A.* **117** E15
Kingsville *Canada* **114** D2
Kingsville *U.S.A.* **116** H6
Kingussie *U.K.* **13** D4
Kingwood *U.S.A.* **116** F7
Kınık *Antalya, Turkey* **47** E11
Kınık *İzmir, Turkey* **47** B9
Kinistino *Canada* **103** C7
Kinjirap Daban *Asia* **66** A9
Kinkala *Congo* **84** E2
Kinki □ *Japan* **55** H8
Kinleith *N.Z.* **91** C5
Kinlochleven *U.K.* **13** E4
Kinmount *Canada* **114** B6
Kinna *Sweden* **11** G6
Kinnairds Hd. *U.K.* **13** D6
Kinnared *Sweden* **11** G7
Kinnarp *Sweden* **11** F7
Kinneviken *Sweden* **11** F7
Kinngait *Canada* **101** E16
Kino Nuevo *Mexico* **118** B2
Kinoje → *Canada* **104** B3
Kinomoto *Japan* **55** G8
Kinoni *Uganda* **86** C3
Kinoosao *Canada* **103** B8
Kinross *U.K.* **13** E5
Kinsale *Ireland* **12** E3
Kinsale, Old Hd. of *Ireland* **12** E3
Kinsha = Chang Jiang →
  China **59** B13
Kinshasa
  Dem. Rep. of the Congo **84** E3
Kinsley *U.S.A.* **112** G4
Kinsman *U.S.A.* **114** E4
Kinston *U.S.A.* **117** D16
Kintamani *Indonesia* **63** J18
Kintampo *Ghana* **83** D4
Kintore *U.K.* **13** D6
Kintore Ra. *Australia* **92** D4
Kintyre *U.K.* **13** F3
Kintyre, Mull of *U.K.* **13** F3
Kinushseo → *Canada* **104** A3
Kinuso *Canada* **102** B5
Kinvarra *Ireland* **12** C3
Kinyangiri *Tanzania* **86** C3
Kinyeti *Sudan* **81** G3
Kinzig → *Germany* **25** G3
Kinzua *U.S.A.* **114** E6
Kioni *Greece* **46** C2
Kiosk *Canada* **104** C4
Kiowa *Kans., U.S.A.* **112** G4
Kiowa *Okla., U.S.A.* **116** D7
Kipahigan L. *Canada* **103** B8
Kipanga *Tanzania* **86** D4
Kiparissia *Greece* **46** D3
Kiparissiakos Kolpos *Greece* **46** D3
Kipawa, L. *Canada* **104** C4
Kipembawe *Tanzania* **86** D3
Kipengere Ra. *Tanzania* **87** D3
Kipili *Tanzania* **86** D3
Kipini *Kenya* **86** C5
Kipling *Canada* **103** C8
Kippure *Ireland* **12** C5
Kipushi *Dem. Rep. of the Congo* **87** E2
Kira Panagia *Greece* **46** B6
Kirane *Mali* **82** B2
Kiranomena *Madag.* **89** B8
Kiraz *Turkey* **47** C10
Kirazlı *Turkey* **45** F10
Kirchhain *Germany* **24** E4
Kirchheim *Germany* **25** G5
Kirchheimbolanden *Germany* **25** F3
Kirchschlag *Austria* **27** D9
Kireç *Turkey* **47** B10
Kirensk *Russia* **53** D11
Kirghizia = Kyrgyzstan ■
  Asia **52** E8
Kiribati ■ *Pac. Oc.* **90** B10
Kırıkhan *Turkey* **72** D7
Kırıkkale *Turkey* **72** C5
Kirillov *Russia* **32** C10
Kirin = Jilin *China* **57** C14
Kirinyaga = Kenya, Mt.
  Kenya **86** C4
Kirirom △ *Cambodia* **65** G5
Kirishi *Russia* **32** C7
Kirishima Yaku △ *Japan* **55** J5
Kiritimati *Kiribati* **97** G12
Kırka *Turkey* **47** B12

Kırkağaç *Turkey* **47** B9
Kirkby *U.K.* **14** D5
Kirkby-in-Ashfield *U.K.* **14** D6
Kirkby Lonsdale *U.K.* **14** C5
Kirkby Stephen *U.K.* **14** C5
Kirkcaldy *U.K.* **13** E5
Kirkcudbright *U.K.* **13** G4
Kirkenes *Norway* **8** B24
Kirkfield *Canada* **114** B6
Kirkintilloch *U.K.* **13** F4
Kirkjubæjarklaustur *Iceland* **8** E4
Kirkkonummi *Finland* **32** B3
Kirkland *U.S.A.* **110** C4
Kirkland Lake *Canada* **104** C3
Kırklareli *Turkey* **45** E11
Kırklareli □ *Turkey* **45** E11
Kirksville *U.S.A.* **112** E7
Kirkūk *Iraq* **73** E11
Kirkwall *U.K.* **13** C6
Kirkwood *S. Africa* **88** E4
Kirn *Germany* **25** F3
Kirov *Kaluga, Russia* **32** E8
Kirov *Kirov, Russia* **52** D5
Kirovabad = Gäncä
  Azerbaijan **35** K8
Kirovograd = Kirovohrad
  Ukraine **33** H7
Kirovohrad *Ukraine* **33** H7
Kirovohrad □ *Ukraine* **33** H6
Kirovskiy *Astrakhan, Russia* **35** H9
Kirovskiy *Kamchatka, Russia* **53** D16
Kirovskiy *Primorsk, Russia* **54** B6
Kirriemuir *U.K.* **13** E5
Kirsanov *Russia* **34** D6
Kırşehir *Turkey* **72** C6
Kirtachi *Niger* **83** C5
Kirthar △ *Pakistan* **68** F2
Kirthar Range *Pakistan* **68** F2
Kirtland *U.S.A.* **109** H9
Kiruna *Sweden* **8** C19
Kirundu
  Dem. Rep. of the Congo **86** C2
Kirya *Russia* **34** C8
Kiryū *Japan* **55** F9
Kisa *Sweden* **11** G9
Kisaga *Tanzania* **86** C3
Kisalföld *Hungary* **28** C2
Kisanga *Dem. Rep. of the Congo* **86** B2
Kisangani
  Dem. Rep. of the Congo **86** B2
Kisar *Indonesia* **63** F7
Kisarawe *Tanzania* **86** D4
Kisarazu *Japan* **55** G9
Kisbér *Hungary* **28** C3
Kiselevsk *Russia* **52** D9
Kish = Qeys *Iran* **71** E7
Kishanganga → *Pakistan* **69** B5
Kishanganj *India* **69** F13
Kishangarh *Raj., India* **68** F6
Kishangarh *Raj., India* **68** F4
Kishi *Nigeria* **83** D5
Kishinev = Chişinău
  Moldova **29** C13
Kishiwada *Japan* **55** G7
Kishtwar *India* **68** C6
Kisielice *Poland* **30** E6
Kisigo → *Tanzania* **86** D3
Kisii *Kenya* **86** C3
Kisiju *Tanzania* **86** D4
Kisir *Turkey* **73** B10
Kisizi *Uganda* **86** C2
Kiska I. *U.S.A.* **106** E3
Kiskomárom = Zalakomár
  Hungary **28** D2
Kisköre-víztároló *Hungary* **28** C5
Kiskőrös *Hungary* **28** D4
Kiskundorozsma *Hungary* **28** D5
Kiskunfélegyháza *Hungary* **28** D4
Kiskunhalas *Hungary* **28** D4
Kiskunmajsa *Hungary* **28** D4
Kiskunsági △ *Hungary* **28** D4
Kislovodsk *Russia* **35** J6
Kismaayo *Somali Rep.* **75** H3
Kiso-Gawa → *Japan* **55** G8
Kiso-Sammyaku *Japan* **55** G8
Kisofukushima *Japan* **55** G8
Kisoro *Uganda* **86** C2
Kissamos = Kasteli *Greece* **49** D5
Kissamos, Kolpos *Greece* **49** D5
Kissidougou *Guinea* **82** D2
Kissimmee *U.S.A.* **117** G14
Kissimmee → *U.S.A.* **117** H14
Kississing L. *Canada* **103** B8
Kissónerga *Cyprus* **49** E11
Kissu, J. *Sudan* **80** C2
Kistanje *Croatia* **41** E12
Kisújszállás *Hungary* **28** C5
Kisumu *Kenya* **86** C3
Kisvárda *Hungary* **28** B7
Kiswani *Tanzania* **86** C4
Kiswere *Tanzania* **87** D4
Kit Carson *U.S.A.* **108** G12
Kita *Mali* **82** C3
Kitaibaraki *Japan* **55** F10
Kitakami *Japan* **54** E10
Kitakami-Gawa → *Japan* **54** E10
Kitakami-Sammyaku *Japan* **54** E10
Kitakata *Japan* **54** F9
Kitakyūshū *Japan* **55** H5

Kitale *Kenya* **86** B4
Kitami *Japan* **54** C11
Kitami-Sammyaku *Japan* **54** B11
Kitangiri, L. *Tanzania* **86** C3
Kitaya *Tanzania* **87** E5
Kitchener *Canada* **114** C4
Kitee *Finland* **32** A6
Kitega = Gitega *Burundi* **86** C2
Kitengo *Dem. Rep. of the Congo* **86** D1
Kitgum *Uganda* **86** B3
Kíthira = Kythira *Greece* **46** E5
Kithnos *Greece* **46** D6
Kiti *Cyprus* **49** E12
Kiti, C. *Cyprus* **49** E12
Kitiyab *Sudan* **81** D3
Kitros *Greece* **44** F6
Kitsman *Ukraine* **29** B10
Kitsuki *Japan* **55** H5
Kittakittaooloo, L. *Australia* **95** D2
Kittanning *U.S.A.* **114** F5
Kittatinny Mt. *U.S.A.* **115** F10
Kittery *U.S.A.* **115** C14
Kittilä *Finland* **8** C21
Kitui *Kenya* **86** C4
Kitwanga *Canada* **102** B3
Kitwe *Zambia* **87** E2
Kitzbühel *Austria* **26** D5
Kitzbühler Alpen *Austria* **26** D5
Kitzingen *Germany* **25** F6
Kiunga Marine △ *Kenya* **86** C5
Kivarli *India* **68** G5
Kivertsi *Ukraine* **23** C13
Kividhes *Cyprus* **49** E11
Kivik *Sweden* **11** J8
Kivotos *Greece* **44** F5
Kivu, L. *Dem. Rep. of the Congo* **86** C2
Kiwirrkurra *Australia* **92** D4
Kiwirrkurra ⊙ *Australia* **92** D4
Kiyev = Kyyiv *Ukraine* **23** C16
Kiyevskoye Vdkhr. =
  Kyyivske Vdskh. *Ukraine* **23** C16
Kıyıköy *Turkey* **45** E12
Kızıl Adalar *Turkey* **45** F13
Kızıl Irmak → *Turkey* **72** B6
Kizil Jilga *China* **69** B8
Kizil Yurt *Russia* **35** J8
Kızılcabölük *Turkey* **47** D11
Kızılcadağ *Turkey* **47** D11
Kızılcahamam *Turkey* **72** B5
Kızıldağ △ *Turkey* **70** B1
Kızılhisar *Turkey* **72** D3
Kızılırmak *Turkey* **72** B5
Kızılkaya *Turkey* **47** D12
Kızılören *Turkey* **47** C12
Kızıltepe *Turkey* **73** D9
Kizimkazi *Tanzania* **86** D4
Kizlyar *Russia* **35** J8
Kizyl-Arvat = Serdar
  Turkmenistan **71** B8
Kjellerup *Denmark* **11** H3
Kjölur *Iceland* **8** D4
Kladanj *Bos.-H.* **28** F3
Kladnica *Serbia* **44** C4
Kladno *Czech Rep.* **26** A7
Kladovo *Serbia* **44** B6
Klaeng *Thailand* **64** F3
Klagenfurt *Austria* **26** E7
Klaipėda *Lithuania* **30** C8
Klaipėda □ *Lithuania* **30** C8
Klaksvík *Færoe Is.* **8** E9
Klamath → *U.S.A.* **108** F1
Klamath Falls *U.S.A.* **108** E3
Klamath Mts. *U.S.A.* **108** F2
Klamono *Indonesia* **63** E8
Klang *Malaysia* **65** L3
Klanjec *Croatia* **41** B12
Klappan → *Canada* **102** B3
Klarälven → *Sweden* **10** E7
Klässbol *Sweden* **10** E6
Klatovy *Czech Rep.* **26** B6
Klawer *S. Africa* **88** E2
Klazienaveen *Neths.* **17** B6
Klé *Mali* **82** C3
Klecko *Poland* **31** F4
Kleczew *Poland* **31** F5
Kleena Kleene *Canada* **102** C4
Klein-Karas *Namibia* **88** D2
Klekovača *Bos.-H.* **41** D13
Klembivka *Ukraine* **29** B13
Klenoec *Macedonia* **44** E4
Klenovec *Slovak Rep.* **27** C12
Klerksdorp *S. Africa* **88** D4
Kleszczele *Poland* **31** F10
Kletna *Russia* **32** F7
Kletsk = Klyetsk *Belarus* **23** B14
Kletskiy *Russia* **35** F6
Kleve *Germany* **24** D2
Klickitat *U.S.A.* **108** D3
Klickitat → *U.S.A.* **110** E5
Klidhes *Cyprus* **49** D13
Klin *Russia* **32** D9
Klinaklini → *Canada* **102** C3
Klintehamn *Sweden* **11** G12

Klintsy *Russia* **33** F7
Klip → *S. Africa* **89** D4
Klipdale *S. Africa* **88** E2
Klippan *Sweden* **11** H7
Klipplaat *S. Africa* **88** E3
Klishkivtsi *Ukraine* **29** B11
Klisura *Bulgaria* **45** D8
Kljajićevo *Serbia* **28** E4
Ključ *Bos.-H.* **41** D13
Klobuck *Poland* **31** H5
Klockestrand *Sweden* **10** B11
Kłodawa *Poland* **31** F5
Kłodzko *Poland* **31** H3
Klondike *Canada* **100** E4
Klong Wang Chao △
  Thailand **64** D2
Klos *Albania* **44** E4
Klosterneuburg *Austria* **27** C9
Klosters *Switz.* **25** J5
Klötze *Germany* **24** C7
Klouto *Togo* **83** D5
Kluane △ *Canada* **102** A1
Kluane L. *Canada* **100** E4
Kluang *Malaysia* **65** L4
Kluczbork *Poland* **31** H5
Klukwan *U.S.A.* **102** B1
Klungkung *Indonesia* **63** K18
Klyetsk *Belarus* **23** B14
Klyuchevskaya, Gora
  Russia **53** D17
Klyuchi *Russia* **53** D17
Knäred *Sweden* **11** H7
Knaresborough *U.K.* **14** C6
Knee L. *Man., Canada* **104** A1
Knee L. *Sask., Canada* **103** B7
Knezha *Bulgaria* **45** C8
Knight Inlet *Canada* **102** C3
Knighton *U.K.* **15** E4
Knights Ferry *U.S.A.* **110** H6
Knights Landing *U.S.A.* **110** G5
Knin *Croatia* **41** D13
Knislinge *Sweden* **11** H8
Knittelfeld *Austria* **26** D7
Knivsta *Sweden* **10** E11
Knjaževac *Serbia* **44** C6
Knob, C. *Australia* **93** F2
Knock *Ireland* **12** C3
Knockmealdown Mts.
  Ireland **12** D4
Knokke-Heist *Belgium* **17** C3
Knossos *Greece* **49** D7
Knowlton *Canada* **115** A12
Knox *U.S.A.* **112** E10
Knox Coast *Antarctica* **5** C8
Knoxville *Iowa, U.S.A.* **112** E7
Knoxville *Pa., U.S.A.* **114** E7
Knoxville *Tenn., U.S.A.* **117** D13
Knud Rasmussen Land
  Greenland **101** B20
Knysna *S. Africa* **88** E3
Knyszyn *Poland* **30** E9
Ko Kha *Thailand* **64** C2
Ko Tarutao △ *Thailand* **65** J2
Ko Yao *Thailand* **65** a
Koartac = Quaqtaq *Canada* **101** E18
Koba *Indonesia* **63** E8
Kobarid *Slovenia* **41** B10
Kobayashi *Japan* **55** J5
Kōbe *Japan* **55** G7
Kobelyaky *Ukraine* **33** H8
København *Denmark* **11** J6
København ✈ (CPH)
  Denmark **11** J6
Kobenni *Mauritania* **82** B3
Kōbi-Sho *Japan* **55** M1
Koblenz *Germany* **25** E3
Kobo *Ethiopia* **81** E4
Kobroör *Indonesia* **63** E8
Kobryn *Belarus* **23** B13
Kobuk → *U.S.A.* **106** B7
Kobuleti *Georgia* **35** K5
Kobyletska Polyana *Ukraine* **29** B9
Kobylin *Poland* **31** G4
Kobyłka *Poland* **31** F8
Kobylkino *Russia* **34** C6
Koca → *Turkey* **45** F11
Kocabaş *Turkey* **47** D11
Kocaeli *Turkey* **45** F13
Kocaeli □ *Turkey* **45** F13
Kočane *Serbia* **44** C5
Kočani *Macedonia* **44** E6
Koçarlı *Turkey* **47** D9
Koceljevo *Serbia* **44** B3
Kočevje *Slovenia* **41** C11
Koch Bihar *India* **67** F16
Kochas *India* **69** G10
Kocher → *Germany* **25** F5
Kochi *India = Cochin* **66** Q10
Kōchi *Japan* **55** H6
Kōchi □ *Japan* **55** H6
Kochiu = Gejiu *China* **58** F4
Kochubey *Russia* **35** H8
Kock *Poland* **31** G9
Kodarma *India* **69** G11
Kode *Sweden* **11** G5
Kodi *Indonesia* **92** A2
Kodiak *U.S.A.* **106** D9
Kodiak I. *U.S.A.* **106** D9
Kodinar *India* **68** J4
Kodinsk *Russia* **53** D10

Kodok *Sudan* **81** F3
Kodori → *Georgia* **35** J5
Kodyma *Ukraine* **29** B14
Koedoesberge *S. Africa* **88** E3
Koes *Namibia* **88** D2
Kofçaz *Turkey* **45** E11
Koffiefontein *S. Africa* **88** D4
Kofiau *Indonesia* **63** E7
Köflach *Austria* **26** D8
Koforidua *Ghana* **83** D4
Kōfu *Japan* **55** G9
Koga *Japan* **55** F9
Kogaluc → *Canada* **105** A7
Kogi □ *Nigeria* **83** D6
Kogin Baba *Nigeria* **83** D7
Kogon *Uzbekistan* **52** F7
Koh-i-Khurd *Afghan.* **68** C1
Koh-i-Maran *Pakistan* **68** E2
Kohat *Pakistan* **68** C4
Kohima *India* **67** G19
Kohkīlūyeh va Būyer
  Aḥmadi □ *Iran* **71** D6
Kohler Ra. *Antarctica* **5** D15
Kohlu *Pakistan* **68** E3
Kohtla-Järve *Estonia* **32** C4
Kohylnyk → *Ukraine* **29** E14
Koi Sanjaq *Iraq* **73** D11
Koidu *S. Leone* **82** D2
Koillismaa *Finland* **8** D23
Koin *N. Korea* **57** D14
Koinare *Bulgaria* **45** C8
Koindu *S. Leone* **82** D2
Kojetín *Czech Rep.* **27** B10
Kojŏ *N. Korea* **57** E14
Kojŭr *Iran* **71** B6
Kokand = Qŭqon *Uzbekistan* **52** E8
Kokas *Indonesia* **63** E8
Kokava *Slovak Rep.* **27** C12
Kokchetav = Kökshetaŭ
  Kazakhstan **52** D7
Kokemäenjoki → *Finland* **32** B1
Kokhma *Russia* **34** B5
Koki *Senegal* **82** B1
Kokkola *Finland* **8** E20
Koko *Nigeria* **83** C5
Koko Kyunzu *Burma* **67** M18
Kokologo *Burkina Faso* **82** C4
Kokolopozo *Ivory C.* **82** D3
Kokomo *U.S.A.* **112** E10
Kokoro *Niger* **83** C5
Koksan *N. Korea* **57** E14
Kökshetaŭ *Kazakhstan* **52** D7
Koksoak → *Canada* **101** F18
Kokstad *S. Africa* **89** E4
Kokubu *Japan* **55** J5
Kola *Indonesia* **63** F8
Kola *Russia* **8** B25
Kola Pen. = Kolskiy
  Poluostrov *Russia* **6** B13
Kolachi → *Pakistan* **68** F2
Kolahoi *India* **69** B6
Kolaka *Indonesia* **63** E6
Kolar *India* **66** N11
Kolar Gold Fields *India* **66** N11
Kolaras *India* **68** G6
Kolari *Finland* **8** C20
Kolárovo *Slovak Rep.* **27** D10
Kolašin *Montenegro* **44** D3
Kolayat *India* **68** F5
Kolbäck *Sweden* **10** E10
Kolbäcksån → *Sweden* **10** E10
Kolব uszowa *Poland* **31** H8
Kolchugino *Russia* **32** D10
Kolda *Senegal* **82** C2
Kolda □ *Senegal* **82** C2
Koldegi *Sudan* **81** E3
Kolding *Denmark* **11** J3
Kolepom = Dolak, Pulau
  Indonesia **63** F9
Kolguyev, Ostrov *Russia* **52** C5
Kolhapur *India* **66** L9
Kolia *Ivory C.* **82** D3
Kolimbia *Greece* **49** C10
Kolín *Czech Rep.* **26** A8
Kolind *Denmark* **11** H4
Kolkas rags *Latvia* **30** A9
Kolkata *India* **69** H13
Kollam = Quilon *India* **66** Q10
Kölleda *Germany* **24** D7
Kollum *Neths.* **17** A6
Kolmanskop *Namibia* **88** D2
Köln *Germany* **24** E2
Kolno *Poland* **30** E8
Koło *Poland* **31** F5
Kołobrzeg *Poland* **30** D2
Kolochava *Ukraine* **29** B8
Kologi *Sudan* **81** E3
Kolokani *Mali* **82** C3
Koloko *Burkina Faso* **82** C4
Kololo *Ethiopia* **81** F5
Kolomna *Russia* **32** E10
Kolomyya *Ukraine* **29** B9
Kolondiéba *Mali* **82** C3
Kolonedale *Indonesia* **63** E6

Kolonowskie *Poland* **31** H5
Kolosib *India* **67** G18
Kolpashevo *Russia* **52** D9
Kolpino *Russia* **32** C6
Kolpny *Russia* **33** G9
Kolskiy Poluostrov *Russia* **6** B13
Kolskiy Zaliv *Russia* **8** B26
Kolsva *Sweden* **10** E9
Kolubara → *Serbia* **44** B4
Koluszki *Poland* **31** G6
Kolwezi *Dem. Rep. of the Congo* **87** E2
Kolyma → *Russia* **53** C17
Kolymskoye Nagorye
  Russia **53** C16
Kôm Hamâda *Egypt* **80** H7
Kôm Ombo *Egypt* **80** C3
Komadugu Gana → *Nigeria* **83** C7
Komandorskiye Is. =
  Komandorskiye Ostrova
  Russia **53** D17
Komandorskiye Ostrova
  Russia **53** D17
Komárno *Slovak Rep.* **27** D11
Komarnyky *Ukraine* **28** B8
Komárom *Hungary* **28** C3
Komárom-Esztergom □
  Hungary **28** C3
Komatipoort *S. Africa* **89** D5
Komatou Yialou *Cyprus* **49** D13
Komatsu *Japan* **55** F8
Komatsushima *Japan* **55** H7
Kombissiri *Burkina Faso* **83** C4
Kombori *Burkina Faso* **82** C4
Komboti *Greece* **46** B3
Kome Channel *Uganda* **86** C3
Komen *Slovenia* **41** C10
Komenda *Ghana* **83** D4
Komi *Cyprus* **49** D13
Komi □ *Russia* **52** C6
Komiža *Croatia* **41** E13
Komló *Hungary* **28** D3
Kommunarsk = Alchevsk
  Ukraine **33** H10
Kommunizma, Pik = imeni
  Ismail Samani, Pik
  Tajikistan **52** F8
Komodo *Indonesia* **63** F5
Komoran, Pulau *Indonesia* **63** F9
Komoro *Japan* **55** F9
Komotini *Greece* **45** E9
Komovi *Montenegro* **44** D3
Kompasberg *S. Africa* **88** E3
Kompong Cham *Cambodia* **65** G5
Kompong Chhnang =
  Kampong Chhnang =
  Cambodia **65** F5
Kompong Chikreng *Cambodia* **64** F5
Kompong Kleang *Cambodia* **64** F5
Kompong Luong *Cambodia* **65** G5
Kompong Pranak *Cambodia* **64** F5
Kompong Som = Kampong
  Saom *Cambodia* **65** G4
Kompong Som, Chhung =
  Kampong Saom, Chaak
  Cambodia **65** G4
Kompong Speu *Cambodia* **65** G5
Kompong Sralau *Cambodia* **64** E5
Kompong Thom *Cambodia* **64** F5
Kompong Trabeck *Cambodia* **64** F5
Kompong Trabeck *Cambodia* **65** G5
Kompong Trach *Cambodia* **65** G5
Kompong Tralach *Cambodia* **65** G5
Komrat = Comrat *Moldova* **29** D13
Komsberg *S. Africa* **88** E3
Komsomolets, Ostrov
  Russia **53** A10
Komsomolsk *Russia* **32** D11
Komsomolsk-na-Amur
  Russia **53** D14
Komsomolskiy *Russia* **34** C7
Kömür Burnu *Turkey* **47** C8
Kon Tum *Vietnam* **64** E7
Kon Tum, Plateau du
  Vietnam **64** E7
Kona *Mali* **82** C4
Kona *Nigeria* **83** D7
Konakovo *Russia* **32** D9
Konar □ *Afghan.* **66** B7
Konārī *Iran* **71** D6
Konch *India* **69** G8
Konde *Tanzania* **86** C4
Kondias *Greece* **47** B7
Kondinin *Australia* **93** F2
Kondoa *Tanzania* **86** C4
Kondopoga *Russia* **32** A8
Kondratyevo *Russia* **53** D10
Kondrovo *Russia* **32** E8
Konduga *Nigeria* **83** C7
Köneürgench *Turkmenistan* **52** E6
Konevo *Russia* **32** A10
Kong = Khong → *Cambodia* **64** F5
Kong *Ivory C.* **82** D4
Kong, Koh *Cambodia* **65** G4
Kong Christian IX Land
  Greenland **4** C5
Kong Christian X Land
  Greenland **4** B6
Kong Frederik IX Land
  Greenland **4** C5

Kong Frederik VI Kyst *Greenland* **4** C5
Kong Frederik VIII Land *Greenland* **4** B5
Kong Oscar Fjord *Greenland* **4** B6
Kongeå ➤ *Denmark* **11** J2
Kongerslev *Denmark* **11** H4
Konglu *Burma* **67** F20
Kongola *Namibia* **88** B3
Kongolo *Kasai-Or.,* *Dem. Rep. of the Congo* **86** D1
Kongolo *Katanga,* *Dem. Rep. of the Congo* **86** D2
Kongor *Sudan* **81** F3
Kongossambougou △ *Mali* **82** C3
Kongoussi *Burkina Faso* **83** C4
Kongsberg *Norway* **9** G13
Kongsvinger *Norway* **9** F15
Kongwa *Tanzania* **86** D4
Koni *Dem. Rep. of the Congo* **87** E2
Koni, Mts. *Dem. Rep. of the Congo* **87** E2
Koniakari *Mali* **82** C2
Koniecpol *Poland* **31** H6
Konin *Poland* **31** F5
Konispol *Albania* **44** G4
Konitsa *Greece* **46** A2
Konjic *Bos.-H.* **28** C7
Konkiep ➤ *Namibia* **88** D2
Konkouré ➤ *Guinea* **82** D2
Könnern *Germany* **24** D7
Kono *S. Leone* **82** D2
Konongo *Ghana* **83** D4
Konosha *Russia* **32** B11
Kōnosu *Japan* **55** F9
Konotop *Ukraine* **33** G7
Konsankoro *Guinea* **82** D3
Końskie *Poland* **31** G7
Konstancin-Jeziorna *Poland* **31** F8
Konstantinovka = Kostyantynivka *Ukraine* **33** H9
Konstantinovsk *Russia* **35** G5
Konstantynów Łódzki *Poland* **31** G6
Konstanz *Germany* **25** H5
Kont *Iran* **71** E9
Kontagora *Nigeria* **83** C6
Kontcha *Cameroon* **83** D7
Kontiolahti *Finland* **8** E23
Kontokali *Greece* **49** A3
Konya *Turkey* **72** D5
Konya □ *Turkey* **72** D5
Konya Ovası *Turkey* **72** C5
Konz *Germany* **25** F2
Konza *Kenya* **86** C4
Koocanusa, L. *Canada* **108** B6
Kookynie *Australia* **93** E3
Koolyanobbing *Australia* **93** F2
Koonibba *Australia* **95** E1
Koorawatha *Australia* **95** E4
Koorda *Australia* **93** F2
Kooskia *U.S.A.* **108** C6
Kootenay ➤ *U.S.A.* **102** D5
Kootenay △ *Canada* **102** C5
Kootenay L. *Canada* **108** B5
Kootjieskolk *S. Africa* **88** E3
Kopanovka *Russia* **35** G8
Kopaonik *Serbia* **44** C4
Kopaonik △ *Serbia* **44** C4
Kópavogur *Iceland* **8** D3
Kopayhorod *Ukraine* **29** B12
Koper *Slovenia* **41** C10
Kopervik *Norway* **9** G11
Kopet Dagh *Asia* **71** B8
Kopi *Australia* **95** E2
Köping *Sweden* **10** E10
Köpingsvik *Sweden* **11** H10
Kopište *Croatia* **41** F13
Koplik *Albania* **44** D3
Köpmanholmen *Sweden* **10** A12
Kopparberg *Sweden* **10** E9
Koppeh Dāgh = Kopet Dagh *Asia* **71** B8
Koppies *S. Africa* **89** D4
Koppom *Sweden* **10** E6
Koprivlen *Bulgaria* **44** E7
Koprivnica *Croatia* **41** B13
Kopřivnice *Czech Rep.* **27** B11
Koprivshtitsa *Bulgaria* **45** D8
Köprübaşı *Turkey* **47** C10
Köprülü △ *Turkey* **70** B1
Kopychyntsi *Ukraine* **23** D13
Kora △ *Kenya* **86** C4
Korab *Macedonia* **44** E4
Koral *India* **68** J5
Korarou, L. *Mali* **82** B4
Korba *India* **69** H10
Korbu, G. *Malaysia* **65** K3
Korça *Albania* **44** F4
Korčula *Croatia* **41** F13
Korčulanski Kanal *Croatia* **41** E13
Kord Kūy *Iran* **71** B7
Kord Sheykh *Iran* **71** D7
Kordestān = Kurdistan *Asia* **73** D10

Kordestān □ *Iran* **70** C5
Kordié *Burkina Faso* **82** C4
Kordofân *Sudan* **79** F11
Koré Mayroua *Niger* **83** C5
Korea, North ■ *Asia* **57** E14
Korea, South ■ *Asia* **57** G15
Korea Bay *Korea* **57** E13
Korea Strait *Asia* **57** H15
Korem *Ethiopia* **81** E4
Korenevo *Russia* **33** G8
Korenovsk *Russia* **35** H4
Korets *Ukraine* **23** C14
Korfantów *Poland* **31** H4
Korgan *Turkey* **72** B7
Korgus *Sudan* **80** D3
Korhogo *Ivory C.* **82** D3
Koribundu *S. Leone* **82** D2
Korienzé *Mali* **82** B4
Korinthia □ *Greece* **46** D4
Korinthiakos Kolpos *Greece* **46** C4
Korinthos *Greece* **46** D4
Korioumé *Mali* **82** B4
Korissia, L. *Greece* **49** B3
Kōriyama *Japan* **54** F10
Korkuteli *Turkey* **47** D12
Kormakiti, C. *Cyprus* **49** D11
Körmend *Hungary* **28** C1
Kormor *Iraq* **73** E11
Kornat *Croatia* **41** E12
Kornat △ *Croatia* **41** E12
Korneshty = Corneşti *Moldova* **29** C13
Korneuburg *Austria* **27** C9
Kórnik *Poland* **31** F4
Koro *Fiji* **91** a
Koro *Ivory C.* **82** D3
Koro *Mali* **82** C4
Koro Sea *Fiji* **91** a
Korocha *Russia* **33** G9
Köroğlu Dağları *Turkey* **72** B5
Korogwe *Tanzania* **86** D4
Korolevo *Ukraine* **29** B8
Korolevu *Fiji* **91** a
Koronadal *Phil.* **61** H6
Koroni *Greece* **46** E3
Koronia, L. *Greece* **44** F7
Koronos *Greece* **47** D7
Koronowo *Poland* **31** E4
Koropets *Ukraine* **29** B10
Koror *Palau* **96** G5
Körös ➤ *Hungary* **28** D5
Körös Maros △ *Hungary* **28** C5
Köröstarcsa *Hungary* **28** D6
Korosten *Ukraine* **23** C15
Korostyshev *Ukraine* **23** C15
Korotoyak *Russia* **33** G10
Korovou *Fiji* **91** a
Koroyanitu △ *Fiji* **91** a
Korraraika, Helodranon' i *Madag.* **89** B7
Korsakov *Russia* **53** E15
Korsberga *Sweden* **11** G9
Korshiv *Ukraine* **29** B10
Korshunovo *Russia* **53** D12
Korsør *Denmark* **11** J5
Korsun Shevchenkovskiy *Ukraine* **33** H6
Korsze *Poland* **30** D8
Korti *Sudan* **80** D3
Kortrijk *Belgium* **17** D3
Korucu *Turkey* **47** B9
Korwai *India* **68** G8
Koryakskoye Nagorye *Russia* **53** C18
Koryukovka *Ukraine* **33** G7
Kos *Greece* **47** E9
Kosa *Ethiopia* **81** F4
Kosan *N. Korea* **57** E14
Kosaya Gora *Russia* **32** E9
Kościan *Poland* **31** F3
Kościerzyna *Poland* **30** D4
Kosciusko *U.S.A.* **117** E10
Kosciuszko, Mt. *Australia* **95** F4
Kösély ➤ *Hungary* **28** C6
Kosha *Sudan* **80** C3
Koshava *Bulgaria* **44** B7
K'oshih = Kashi *China* **60** C2
Koshiki-Rettō *Japan* **55** J4
Koshim ➤ *Kazakhstan* **34** F10
Kosi *India* **68** F7
Kosi ➤ *India* **69** E8
Košice *Slovak Rep.* **27** C14
Košický □ *Slovak Rep.* **27** C14
Kosiv *Ukraine* **29** B10
Kosjerić *Serbia* **44** B3
Köşk *Turkey* **47** D10
Koskinou *Greece* **49** C10
Koslan *Russia* **52** C5
Kosmach *Ukraine* **29** B9
Kosŏng *N. Korea* **57** E15
Kosovo ■ *Europe* **44** D4
Kosovo Polje *Kosovo* **44** D5
Kosovska Kamenica *Kosovo* **44** D5
Kosovska Mitrovica *Kosovo* **44** D4
Kossou, L. de *Ivory C.* **82** D3
Kosta *Sweden* **11** H9
Kostajnica *Croatia* **41** C13
Kostanjevica *Slovenia* **41** C12
Kostenets *Bulgaria* **44** D7

Koster *S. Africa* **88** D4
Kôstî *Sudan* **81** E3
Kostinbrod *Bulgaria* **44** D7
Kostolac *Serbia* **44** B5
Kostopil *Ukraine* **23** C14
Kostroma *Russia* **32** D11
Kostromo ➤ *Russia* **34** A6
Kostromskoye Vdkhr. *Russia* **32** D11
Kostryzhivka *Ukraine* **29** B10
Kostrzyn *Lubuskie, Poland* **31** F1
Kostrzyn *Wielkopolskie, Poland* **31** F4
Kostyantynivka *Ukraine* **33** H9
Kostyukovichi = Kastsyukovichy *Belarus* **32** F7
Koszalin *Poland* **30** D3
Kőszeg *Hungary* **28** C1
Kot Addu *Pakistan* **68** D4
Kot Kapura *India* **68** D6
Kot Moman *Pakistan* **68** C5
Kot Sultan *Pakistan* **68** D4
Kota *India* **68** G6
Kota Barrage *India* **68** G6
Kota Belud *Malaysia* **62** C5
Kota Bharu *Malaysia* **65** J4
Kota Kinabalu *Malaysia* **62** C5
Kota Tinggi *Malaysia* **65** M4
Kotaagung *Indonesia* **62** F2
Kotabaru *Indonesia* **62** E5
Kotabumi *Indonesia* **62** E2
Kotamobagu *Indonesia* **63** D6
Kotapinang *Indonesia* **65** M3
Kotcho L. *Canada* **102** B4
Kotdwara *India* **69** E8
Kotel *Bulgaria* **45** D10
Kotelnich *Russia* **34** A9
Kotelnikovo *Russia* **35** G6
Kotelnyy, Ostrov *Russia* **53** B14
Kothari ➤ *India* **68** G6
Köthen *Germany* **24** D7
Kothi *Chhattisgarh, India* **69** H10
Kothi *Mad. P., India* **69** G9
Kotiro *Pakistan* **68** F2
Kotka *Finland* **32** B4
Kotlas *Russia* **52** C5
Kotlenska Planina *Bulgaria* **45** D10
Kotli *Pakistan* **68** C5
Kotlik *U.S.A.* **106** C7
Kotma *India* **69** H9
Koton-Karifi *Nigeria* **83** D6
Kotonkoro *Nigeria* **83** C6
Kotor *Montenegro* **44** D3
Kotor Varoš *Bos.-H.* **28** F2
Kotoriba *Croatia* **41** B13
Kotovo *Russia* **34** E7
Kotovsk *Russia* **34** E6
Kotovsk *Ukraine* **23** E15
Kotputli *India* **68** F7
Kotri *Pakistan* **68** G3
Kotronas *Greece* **46** E4
Kötschach-Mauthen *Austria* **26** E6
Kotto ➤ *C.A.R.* **84** D4
Kotturu *India* **66** M10
Kotu Group *Tonga* **91** c
Kotuy ➤ *Russia* **53** B11
Kotyuzhany *Ukraine* **29** B12
Kotzebue *U.S.A.* **106** B7
Kotzebue Sound *U.S.A.* **106** B7
Kouchibouguac △ *Canada* **105** C6
Koudougou *Burkina Faso* **82** C4
Koufonisi *Iraklio, Greece* **49** E8
Koufonisi *Notio Aigaio, Greece* **47** E7
Kougaberge *S. Africa* **88** E3
Kouibli *Ivory C.* **82** D3
Kouilou ➤ *Congo* **84** E2
Koukdjuak ➤ *Canada* **101** D17
Koula *Greece* **45** E8
Koula Moutou *Gabon* **84** E2
Koulen = Kulen *Cambodia* **64** F5
Koulikoro *Mali* **82** C3
Koulikoro □ *Mali* **82** C3
Kouloura *Greece* **49** A3
Koumala *Australia* **94** C4
Koumankou *Mali* **82** C3
Koumbia *Burkina Faso* **82** C4
Koumbia *Guinea* **82** C2
Koumboum *Guinea* **82** C2
Koumenntoum *Senegal* **82** C2
Koumra *Chad* **79** G9
Koun-Fao *Ivory C.* **82** D4
Koundara *Guinea* **82** C2
Koundian *Guinea* **82** C3
Koungheul *Senegal* **82** C2
Kountze *U.S.A.* **116** F7
Kouroumé *Mali* **82** C2
Kouris ➤ *Cyprus* **49** E11
Kourou *Fr. Guiana* **125** B8
Kourouba *Mali* **82** C2
Koûroudjél *Mauritania* **82** B2
Kouroukoto *Mali* **82** C2
Kouroussa *Burkina Faso* **82** C4
Kourouninkoto *Mali* **82** C3
Kouroussa *Guinea* **82** C3
Koussané *Mali* **82** C2
Koussane *Senegal* **82** C2
Kousséri *Cameroon* **79** F8
Koutiala *Mali* **82** C3

Kouto *Ivory C.* **82** D3
Kouvé *Togo* **83** D5
Kouvola *Finland* **32** B4
Kovačica *Serbia* **28** E5
Kovdor *Russia* **8** C24
Kovel *Ukraine* **23** C13
Kovin *Serbia* **28** F5
Kovrov *Russia* **34** B5
Kowal *Poland* **31** F6
Kowalewo Pomorskie *Poland* **31** E5
Kowanyama *Australia* **94** B3
Kowanyama ✪ *Australia* **94** B3
Kowloon *China* **59** F10
Kowŏn *N. Korea* **57** E14
Koyampattur = Coimbatore *India* **66** P10
Köyceğiz *Turkey* **47** E10
Köyceğiz Gölü *Turkey* **47** E10
Koyukuk ➤ *U.S.A.* **106** C8
Koyulhisar *Turkey* **72** B7
Koyunyeri *Turkey* **45** F10
Koza = Okinawa *Japan* **55** L3
Kozak *Turkey* **47** B9
Kozaklı *Turkey* **72** C6
Kozan *Turkey* **72** D6
Kozani *Greece* **44** F5
Kozani □ *Greece* **44** F5
Kozara *Bos.-H.* **28** D14
Kozara △ *Bos.-H.* **28** F2
Kozarac *Bos.-H.* **41** D13
Kozelets *Ukraine* **33** G6
Kozelsk *Russia* **32** E8
Kozhikode = Calicut *India* **66** P9
Kozieglowy *Poland* **31** H6
Kozienice *Poland* **31** G8
Kozje *Slovenia* **41** C12
Kozloduy *Bulgaria* **44** C7
Kozlovets *Bulgaria* **45** C9
Kozlovka *Russia* **34** B8
Kozlu *Turkey* **72** B4
Kozluk *Turkey* **73** C9
Koźmin *Poland* **31** G4
Kozmodemyansk *Russia* **34** B8
Kożuchów *Poland* **31** G2
Kozyatyn *Ukraine* **23** D15
Kozyrevsk *Russia* **53** D16
Kpabia *Ghana* **83** D4
Kpalimé *Togo* **83** D5
Kpandae *Ghana* **83** D4
Kpessi *Togo* **83** D5
Kra, Isthmus of = Kra, Kho Khot *Thailand* **65** G2
Kra, Kho Khot *Thailand* **65** G2
Kra Buri *Thailand* **65** G2
Kraai ➤ *S. Africa* **88** E4
Krabi *Thailand* **65** H2
Kracheh *Cambodia* **64** F6
Kragan *Indonesia* **63** G14
Kragerø *Norway* **9** G13
Kragujevac *Serbia* **44** B4
Krajenka *Poland* **31** E3
Krakatau = Rakata, Pulau *Indonesia* **62** F3
Krakatoa = Rakata, Pulau *Indonesia* **62** F3
Krakor *Cambodia* **64** F5
Kraków *Poland* **31** H6
Kraków ✈ (KRK) *Poland* **31** H6
Kralanh *Cambodia* **64** F4
Králíky *Czech Rep.* **27** A9
Kraljevo *Serbia* **44** C4
Kralovéhradecký □ *Czech Rep.* **26** A8
Kráľovský Chlmec *Slovak Rep.* **27** C14
Kralupy nad Vltavou *Czech Rep.* **26** A7
Kramatorsk *Ukraine* **33** H9
Kramfors *Sweden* **10** B11
Krania *Greece* **44** F4
Krania Elasonas *Greece* **44** B4
Kranidi *Greece* **46** D5
Kranj *Slovenia* **41** B11
Kranjska Gora *Slovenia* **41** B10
Krankskop *S. Africa* **89** D5
Krapina *Croatia* **41** B12
Krapina ➤ *Croatia* **41** C12
Krapkowice *Poland* **31** H4
Kras *Croatia* **41** C10
Kraskino *Russia* **54** C5
Krāslava *Latvia* **32** E2
Kraslice *Czech Rep.* **26** A5
Krasnaya Gorbatka *Russia* **34** C5
Krasnaya Polyana *Russia* **35** J5
Krasne *Ukraine* **29** D14
Krasni Okny *Ukraine* **29** C14
Kraśnik *Poland* **31** H9
Krasnoarmeisk *Ukraine* **33** H9
Krasnoarmensk *Russia* **34** E7
Krasnoarmeyskiy *Russia* **35** G6
Krasnobrod *Poland* **31** H10
Krasnodar *Russia* **30** D5
Krasnodar □ *Russia* **35** G4
Krasnodarskoye Vdkhr. *Russia* **35** H4
Krasnodon *Ukraine* **33** H10
Krasnogorskiy *Russia* **34** B9
Krasnograd = Krasnohrad *Ukraine* **33** H8

Krasnogvardeysk *Ukraine* **33** K8
Krasnogvardeyskoye *Russia* **35** H5
Krasnohrad *Ukraine* **33** D12
Krasnokamensk *Russia* **53** E12
Krasnokutsk *Ukraine* **33** G8
Krasnolesnyy *Russia* **33** G10
Krasnoperekopsk *Ukraine* **33** J7
Krasnorechenskiy *Russia* **54** B7
Krasnoselkup *Russia* **52** C9
Krasnoslobodsk *Mordvinia, Russia* **34** C6
Krasnoslobodsk *Volgograd, Russia* **35** F7
Krasnoturinsk *Russia* **52** D7
Krasnoyarsk *Russia* **53** D10
Krasnoyarskoye *Russia* **30** D8
Krasnoye = Krasnyy *Russia* **32** E6
Krasnoyilsk *Ukraine* **29** C10
Krasnozavodsk *Russia* **32** D10
Krasnoznamensk *Russia* **30** D9
Krasny Sulin *Russia* **33** J11
Krasnystaw *Poland* **31** H10
Krasnyy *Russia* **32** E6
Krasnyy Kholm *Russia* **32** C9
Krasnyy Kut *Russia* **34** E8
Krasnyy Liman *Ukraine* **33** H9
Krasnyy Luch *Ukraine* **33** H10
Krasnyy Profintern *Russia* **32** D11
Krasnyy Yar *Astrakhan, Russia* **35** G9
Krasnyy Yar *Samara, Russia* **34** D10
Krasnyy Yar *Volgograd, Russia* **34** E7
Krasnyyoskolske Vdkh. *Ukraine* **33** H9
Kraszna ➤ *Hungary* **28** B7
Kratie = Kracheh *Cambodia* **64** F6
Kratovo *Macedonia* **44** D6
Krau *Indonesia* **63** E10
Kravanh, Chuor Phnum *Cambodia* **65** G4
Krefeld *Germany* **24** D2
Kremaston, L. *Greece* **46** C3
Kremen *Croatia* **41** D12
Kremenchuk *Ukraine* **33** H7
Kremenchuksk Vdkh. *Ukraine* **33** H7
Kremenets *Ukraine* **23** C13
Kremennaya *Ukraine* **33** H10
Kremges = Svitlovodsk *Ukraine* **33** H7
Kremmen *Germany* **24** C9
Kremmling *U.S.A.* **108** F10
Kremnica *Slovak Rep.* **27** C11
Krems *Austria* **26** C8
Kremsmünster *Austria* **26** C7
Krestena *Greece* **46** D3
Kretinga *Lithuania* **30** C8
Krettsy *Russia* **32** C7
Kreuzberg *Germany* **25** E5
Kreuztal *Germany* **24** E4
Kria Vrisi *Greece* **44** F6
Kribi *Cameroon* **83** E6
Krichem *Bulgaria* **45** D8
Krichev = Krychaw *Belarus* **23** B16
Kril'on, Mys *Russia* **54** B11
Krim *Slovenia* **41** C11
Krios, Akra *Greece* **49** D5
Krishna ➤ *India* **67** M12
Krishnanagar *India* **69** H13
Kristdala *Sweden* **11** H10
Kristiansand *Norway* **9** G13
Kristianstad *Sweden* **11** H8
Kristiansund *Norway* **8** E12
Kristiinankaupunki *Finland* **8** E19
Kristinehamn *Sweden* **10** E8
Kristinestad = Kristiinankaupunki *Finland* **8** E19
Kriti *Greece* **49** D7
Kritsa *Greece* **49** D7
Kriva ➤ *Macedonia* **44** D5
Kriva Palanka *Macedonia* **44** D6
Krivaja ➤ *Bos.-H.* **28** F3
Krivelj *Serbia* **44** B6
Krivoy Rog = Kryvyy Rih *Ukraine* **33** J7
Križevci *Croatia* **41** B13
Krk *Croatia* **41** C11
Krk △ *Croatia* **41** E12
Krka ➤ *Slovenia* **41** C12
Krka △ *Croatia* **41** E12
Krkonoše *Czech Rep.* **26** A8
Krkonoše △ *Czech Rep.* **26** A8
Krnov *Czech Rep.* **27** A10
Krobia *Poland* **31** G3
Krokees *Greece* **46** E4
Krokek *Sweden* **11** F10
Krokodil = Umgwenya ➤ *Mozam.* **89** D5
Krokom *Sweden* **10** A8
Krokowa *Poland* **30** D5
Krolevets *Ukraine* **33** G7
Kroměříž *Czech Rep.* **27** B10
Krompachy *Slovak Rep.* **27** C13
Kromy *Russia* **33** F8
Kronach *Germany* **25** E7
Krong Kaoh Kong *Cambodia* **65** G4
Kronobergs län □ *Sweden* **11** H8

Kronprins Christian Land *Greenland* **101**
Kronprins Frederik Land *Greenland* **4** B5
Kronprins Olav Kyst *Antarctica* **5** C5
Kronprinsesse Märtha Kyst *Antarctica* **5** D2
Kronshtadt *Russia* **32** C5
Kroonstad *S. Africa* **88** D4
Kröpelin *Germany* **24** A7
Kropotkin *Russia* **35** H5
Kropp *Germany* **24** A5
Krosna *Lithuania* **30** D10
Krośniewice *Poland* **31** F6
Krosno *Poland* **31** J8
Krosno Odrzańskie *Poland* **31** F2
Krotoszyn *Poland* **31** G4
Krotovka *Russia* **34** D10
Krousonas *Greece* **49** D6
Krrabë *Albania* **44** E3
Krško *Slovenia* **41** C12
Krstača *Serbia* **44** D4
Kruger △ *S. Africa* **89** C5
Krugersdorp *S. Africa* **89** D4
Kruisfontein *S. Africa* **88** E3
Krujë *Albania* **44** E3
Krulevshchina = Krulyewshchyna *Belarus* **32** E4
Krulyewshchyna *Belarus* **32** E4
Krumbach *Germany* **25** G6
Krumë *Albania* **44** D4
Krumovgrad *Bulgaria* **45** E9
Krung Thep = Bangkok *Thailand* **64** F3
Krupanj *Serbia* **44** B3
Krupina *Slovak Rep.* **27** C12
Krupinica ➤ *Slovak Rep.* **27** C11
Krupki *Belarus* **23** A15
Kruševac *Serbia* **44** C5
Krushelnyksya *Ukraine* **31** J10
Kruszwica *Poland* **31** F5
Kruševo *Macedonia* **44** E5
Krychaw *Belarus* **23** B16
Krymsk *Russia* **33** K10
Krymskiy Poluostrov = Krymskyy Pivostriv *Ukraine* **33** K8
Krymskyy Pivostriv *Ukraine* **33** K8
Krynica *Poland* **31** J7
Krynica Morska *Poland* **30** D6
Krynki *Poland* **31** E10
Krynychne *Ukraine* **29** E13
Kryvyy Rih *Ukraine* **33** J7
Kryzhopil *Ukraine* **29** B13
Krzepice *Poland* **31** H5
Krzeszów *Poland* **31** H9
Krzna ➤ *Poland* **31** F10
Krzywiń *Poland* **31** G3
Krzyż Wielkopolski *Poland* **31** F2
Ksar el Kebir *Morocco* **78** B4
Ksar es Souk = Er Rachidia *Morocco* **78** B5
Książ Wielkopolski *Poland* **31** F4
Ku, W. el ➤ *Sudan* **81** E2
Kuah *Malaysia* **65** J2
Kuala Berang *Malaysia* **62** D4
Kuala Berang *Malaysia* **65** K4
Kuala Dungun = Dungun *Malaysia* **65** K4
Kuala Kangsar *Malaysia* **65** K3
Kuala Kelawang *Malaysia* **65** L4
Kuala Kerian *Malaysia* **65** c
Kuala Kubu Bharu *Malaysia* **65** L3
Kuala Lipis *Malaysia* **65** K4
Kuala Lumpur *Malaysia* **65** L4
Kuala Nerang *Malaysia* **65** J3
Kuala Pilah *Malaysia* **65** L4
Kuala Rompin *Malaysia* **65** L4
Kuala Selangor *Malaysia* **65** L3
Kuala Sepetang *Malaysia* **65** K3
Kuala Terengganu *Malaysia* **65** K4
Kualajelai *Indonesia* **62** E4
Kualakapuas *Indonesia* **62** E4
Kualakurun *Indonesia* **62** E4
Kualapembuang *Indonesia* **62** E4
Kualasimpang *Indonesia* **62** D1
Kuancheng *China* **57** D10
Kuandang *Indonesia* **63** D6
Kuandian *China* **57** D13
Kuangchou = Guangzhou *China* **59** F9
Kuanshan *Taiwan* **59** F13
Kuantan *Malaysia* **65** L4
Kuba = Quba *Azerbaijan* **35** K9
Kuban ➤ *Russia* **33** K9
Kuban Depression = Prikubanskaya Nizmennost *Russia* **35** H4
Kubaysah *Iraq* **73** G10
Kubenskoye, Ozero *Russia* **32** C10
Kubokawa *Japan* **55** H6
Kubrat *Bulgaria* **45** C10
Kubu *Indonesia* **63** J18
Kubutambahan *Indonesia* **63** J18
Kucar, Tanjung *Indonesia* **63** K18
Kučevo *Serbia* **44** B5

Kuchaman *India* 68 F6
Kuchenspitze *Austria* 26 D3
Kuchinda *India* 69 J11
Kuching *Malaysia* 62 D4
Kuchino-eruba-Jima *Japan* 55 J5
Kuchinotsu *Japan* 55 H5
Kuchl *Austria* 26 D6
Kuchurhan ➤ *Ukraine* 29 D14
Kucing = Kuching *Malaysia* 62 D4
Kuçovë *Albania* 44 F3
Küçükbahçe *Turkey* 47 C8
Küçükköy *Turkey* 47 B8
Küçükkuyu *Turkey* 47 B8
Küçükmenderes ➤ *Turkey* 47 D9
Kud ➤ *Pakistan* 68 F2
Kuda *India* 68 H4
Kudat *Malaysia* 62 C5
Kudirkos Naumiestis
   Lithuania 30 D9
Kudowa-Zdrój *Poland* 31 H3
Kudus *Indonesia* 63 G14
Kudymkar *Russia* 52 D6
Kueiyang = Guiyang *China* 58 D6
Kufra Oasis = Al Kufrah
   Libya 101 D14
Kufstein *Austria* 26 D5
Kugaaruk = Pelly Bay
   Canada 101 D14
Kugluktuk *Canada* 100 D8
Kugong I. *Canada* 104 A4
Kūh Dasht *Iran* 73 F12
Kūh-e-Jebāl Bārez *Iran* 71 D8
Kūhak *Iran* 71 E9
Kuhan *Pakistan* 68 E2
Kūhbonān *Iran* 71 D8
Kūhestak *Iran* 71 E8
Kuhin *Iran* 71 B6
Kūhīrī *Iran* 71 E9
Kuhmo *Finland* 8 D23
Kuhnsdorf *Austria* 26 E7
Kūhpāyeh *Esfahan, Iran* 71 C7
Kūhpāyeh *Kermān, Iran* 71 D8
Kūhrān, Kūh-e *Iran* 71 E8
Kui Buri *Thailand* 65 F2
Kuiseb ➤ *Namibia* 88 C1
Kuito *Angola* 85 G3
Kuiu I. *U.S.A.* 102 B2
Kujang *N. Korea* 57 E14
Kujawsko-Pomorskie □
   Poland 30 E5
Kuji *Japan* 54 D10
Kujū-San *Japan* 55 H5
Kukava *Ukraine* 29 B12
Kukavica *Serbia* 44 D5
Kukawa *Nigeria* 83 C7
Kukës *Albania* 44 D4
Kukmor *Russia* 34 B10
Kukup *Malaysia* 65 d
Kukup, Pulau *Malaysia* 65 d
Kukvidze *Russia* 34 E6
Kula *Bulgaria* 44 C6
Kula *Serbia* 28 E4
Kula *Turkey* 47 C10
Kulachi *Pakistan* 68 D4
Kulai *Malaysia* 65 M4
Kulaly, Ostrov = Kulaly
   Aral *Kazakhstan* 35 H10
Kulaly Aral *Kazakhstan* 35 H10
Kulasekarappattinam *India* 66 Q11
Kulautuva *Lithuania* 30 D10
Kuldīga *Latvia* 30 B8
Kuldīga □ *Latvia* 30 B8
Kuldu *Sudan* 81 E2
Kulebaki *Russia* 34 C6
Kulen *Cambodia* 64 F5
Kulen Vakuf *Bos.-H.* 41 D13
Kulgam *India* 69 C6
Kulgera *Australia* 94 D1
Kulim *Malaysia* 65 K3
Kulin *Australia* 93 F2
Kulkayu = Hartley Bay
   Canada 102 C3
Kullen *Sweden* 11 H6
Kullu *India* 68 D7
Kulmbach *Germany* 25 E7
Kŭlob *Tajikistan* 52 F7
Kulp *Turkey* 73 C9
Kulpawn ➤ *Ghana* 83 D4
Kulsary = Qulsary
   Kazakhstan 52 E6
Kulti *India* 69 H12
Kulu *Turkey* 72 C5
Kulunda *Russia* 52 D8
Kulungar *Afghan.* 68 C3
Kŭlvand *Iran* 71 D7
Kulwin *Australia* 95 F3
Kulyab = Kŭlob *Tajikistan* 52 F7
Kuma ➤ *Russia* 35 H8
Kumafşarı *Turkey* 47 D11
Kumaganum *Nigeria* 83 C7
Kumagaya *Japan* 55 F9
Kumai *Indonesia* 62 E4
Kumalar Dağı *Turkey* 47 C12
Kumamba, Kepulauan
   Indonesia 63 E9
Kumamoto *Japan* 55 H5
Kumamoto □ *Japan* 55 H5
Kumanovo *Macedonia* 44 D5

Kumara *N.Z.* 91 E3
Kumarina Roadhouse
   Australia 93 D2
Kumasi *Ghana* 82 D4
Kumba *Cameroon* 83 E6
Kumbağ *Turkey* 45 F11
Kumbakonam *India* 66 P11
Kumbarilla *Australia* 95 D5
Kumbhraj *India* 68 G7
Kumbia *Australia* 95 D5
Kumbo *Cameroon* 83 D7
Kŭmch'ŏn *N. Korea* 57 E14
Kumdok *India* 69 C8
Kume-Shima *Japan* 55 L3
Kumeny *Russia* 34 A9
Kumharsain *India* 68 D7
Kumi *Uganda* 86 B3
Kumkale *Turkey* 45 G10
Kumla *Sweden* 10 E9
Kumluca *Turkey* 47 E12
Kummerower See *Germany* 24 B8
Kumo *Nigeria* 83 C7
Kumo älv =
   Kokemäenjoki ➤ *Finland* 32 B1
Kumon Bum *Burma* 67 F20
Kumylzhenskaya *Russia* 34 F6
Kunágota *Hungary* 28 D6
Kunashir, Ostrov *Russia* 53 E15
Kunda *Estonia* 32 C4
Kunda *India* 69 G9
Kundar ➤ *Pakistan* 68 D3
Kundelungu △
   Dem. Rep. of the Congo 87 E2
Kundelungu Ouest △
   Dem. Rep. of the Congo 87 D2
Kundian *Pakistan* 68 C4
Kundla *India* 68 J4
Kung, Ao *Thailand* 65 a
Kunga ➤ *Bangla.* 69 J13
Kunga ➤ *S. Africa* 88 D3
Kungälv *Sweden* 11 G5
Kunghit I. *Canada* 102 C2
Kungrad = Qŭnghirot
   Uzbekistan 52 E6
Kungsängen *Sweden* 10 E11
Kungsbacka *Sweden* 11 G6
Kungsgården *Sweden* 10 D10
Kungshamn *Sweden* 11 F5
Kungsör *Sweden* 10 E10
Kungur *Russia* 52 D6
Kungurri *Australia* 94 b
Kunhegyes *Hungary* 28 C5
Kunhar ➤ *Pakistan* 69 B5
Kuningan *Indonesia* 63 G13
Kunlong *Burma* 58 F2
Kunlun Shan *Asia* 60 C3
Kunmadaras *Hungary* 28 C5
Kunming *China* 58 E4
Kunmunya ☺ *Australia* 92 C3
Kunów *Poland* 31 H8
Kunshan *China* 59 B13
Kunszentmárton *Hungary* 28 D5
Kunszentmiklós *Hungary* 28 C4
Kuntaur *Senegal* 82 C2
Kununurra *Australia* 92 C4
Kunwari ➤ *India* 69 F8
Kunya-Urgench =
   Köneürgench *Turkmenistan* 52 E6
Künzelsau *Germany* 25 F5
Kuopio *Finland* 8 E22
Kupa ➤ *Croatia* 41 C13
Kupang *Indonesia* 63 F6
Kupreanof I. *U.S.A.* 102 B2
Kupres *Bos.-H.* 28 G2
Kupyansk *Ukraine* 33 H9
Kupyansk-Uzlovoi *Ukraine* 33 H9
Kuqa *China* 60 B3
Kür ➤ *Azerbaijan* 73 C13
Kür Dili *Azerbaijan* 73 C13
Kura = Kür ➤ *Azerbaijan* 73 C13
Kuranda *Australia* 94 B4
Kuranga *India* 68 H3
Kurashiki *Japan* 55 G6
Kurayn *Si. Arabia* 71 E6
Kurayoshi *Japan* 55 G6
Kŭrchatov *Kazakhstan* 52 D8
Kürdämir *Azerbaijan* 35 K9
Kurdistan *Asia* 73 D10
Kürdzhali *Bulgaria* 45 E9
Kure *Japan* 55 G6
Küre *Turkey* 72 B5
Küre Dağları *Turkey* 72 B6
Kure I. *U.S.A.* 107 K4
Kuressaare *Estonia* 32 C2
Kurgan *Russia* 52 D7
Kurgannaya =
   Kurganinsk *Russia* 35 H5
Kuri *India* 68 F4
Kuria Maria Is. =
   Hallāniyat, Jazā'ir al *Oman* 75 D6
Kuridala *Australia* 94 C3
Kurigram *Bangla.* 67 G16
Kurikka *Finland* 8 E20
Kuril Basin *Pac. Oc.* 4 E15
Kuril Is. = Kurilskiye
   Ostrova *Russia* 53 E16
Kuril-Kamchatka Trench
   Pac. Oc. 96 C7
Kurilsk *Russia* 53 E15

Kurilskiye Ostrova *Russia* 53 E16
Kurino *Japan* 55 J5
Kurinskaya Kosa = Kür
   Dili *Azerbaijan* 73 C13
Kurkur *Egypt* 80 C3
Kurlkuta ☺ *Australia* 92 D4
Kurlovsky *Russia* 34 C5
Kurmuk *Sudan* 81 E3
Kurnool *India* 66 M11
Kuro-Shima *Kagoshima, Japan* 55 J4
Kuro-Shima *Okinawa, Japan* 55 M2
Kuror, J. *Sudan* 80 C3
Kurow *N.Z.* 91 F3
Kurów *Poland* 31 G9
Kurram ➤ *Pakistan* 68 C4
Kurri Kurri *Australia* 95 E5
Kurrimine *Australia* 94 B4
Kursavka *Russia* 35 H6
Kurseong = Karsiyang *India* 69 F13
Kurshskaya Kosa △ *Russia* 30 C7
Kuršhskiy Zaliv *Russia* 30 C8
Kuršių Nerijos △ *Lithuania* 30 C8
Kursk *Russia* 33 G9
Kursk □ *Russia* 33 G9
Kuršumlija *Serbia* 44 C5
Kuršumlijska Banja *Serbia* 44 C5
Kurşunlu *Bursa, Turkey* 45 F13
Kurşunlu *Çankırı, Turkey* 72 B5
Kurtalan *Turkey* 73 D9
Kurtbey *Turkey* 45 E10
Kuruçay *Turkey* 70 B3
Kurukshetra = Thanesar
   India 68 D7
Kuruktag *China* 60 B3
Kuruman *S. Africa* 88 D3
Kuruman ➤ *S. Africa* 88 D3
Kurume *Japan* 55 H5
Kurun ➤ *Sudan* 81 F3
Kurunegala *Sri Lanka* 66 R12
Kurya *Russia* 52 C6
Kus Gölü *Turkey* 45 F11
Kuşadası *Turkey* 47 D8
Kuşadası Körfezi *Turkey* 47 D8
Kusamba *Indonesia* 63 K18
Kusatsu *Japan* 55 F9
Kusawa L. *Canada* 102 A1
Kusel *Germany* 25 F3
Kushaka *Nigeria* 83 C6
Kushalgarh *India* 68 H6
Kusheriki *Nigeria* 83 C6
Kushikino *Japan* 55 J5
Kushima *Japan* 55 J5
Kushimoto *Japan* 55 H7
Kushiro *Japan* 54 C12
Kushiro-Gawa ➤ *Japan* 54 C12
Kushiro Shitsugen △ *Japan* 54 C12
Kŭshk *Iran* 71 D8
Kushka = Serhetabat
   Turkmenistan 71 C9
Kushnytsya *Ukraine* 29 B8
Kushol *India* 69 C7
Kushtia *Bangla.* 67 H16
Kuskokwim ➤ *U.S.A.* 106 C7
Kuskokwim B. *U.S.A.* 106 D7
Kuskokwim Mts. *U.S.A.* 106 C8
Kusmi *India* 69 H10
Kusŏng *N. Korea* 57 E13
Kussharo-Ko *Japan* 54 C12
Kustanay = Qostanay
   Kazakhstan 52 D7
Kut, Ko *Thailand* 65 G4
Kuta *Indonesia* 63 K18
Kütahya *Turkey* 47 B12
Kütahya □ *Turkey* 47 B11
Kutaisi *Georgia* 35 J6
Kutaraja = Banda Aceh
   Indonesia 62 C1
Kutch, Gulf of = Kachchh,
   Gulf of *India* 68 H3
Kutch, Rann of =
   Kachchh, Rann of *India* 68 H4
Kutina *Croatia* 41 C13
Kutiyana *India* 68 J4
Kutjevo *Croatia* 28 E2
Kutkashen *Azerbaijan* 35 K8
Kutná Hora *Czech Rep.* 26 B8
Kutno *Poland* 31 F6
Kutse *Botswana* 88 C3
Kuttabul *Australia* 94 b
Kutu *Dem. Rep. of the Congo* 84 E3
Kutum *Sudan* 81 E1
Kúty *Slovak Rep.* 27 C10
Kuty *Ukraine* 29 B10
Kuujjuaq *Canada* 101 F18
Kuujjuarapik *Canada* 104 A4
Kuusamo *Finland* 8 D23
Kuusankoski *Finland* 32 B4
Kuvshinovo *Russia* 32 D8
Kuwait = Al Kuwayt *Kuwait* 70 D5
Kuwait ■ *Asia* 70 D5
Kuwana *Japan* 55 G8
Kuwana ➤ *India* 69 F10
Kuybyshev = Samara
   Russia 34 D10
Kuybyshev *Russia* 52 D8

Kuybyshevo *Ukraine* 33 J9
Kuybyshevskoye Vdkhr.
   Russia 34 C9
Kuye He ➤ *China* 56 E6
Kūyeh *Iran* 70 B5
Kuyto, Ozero *Russia* 8 D24
Kuyucak *Turkey* 47 D10
Kuyumba *Russia* 53 C10
Kuzey Anadolu Dağları
   Turkey 72 B7
Kuzmin *Serbia* 28 E4
Kuznetsk *Russia* 34 D8
Kuzomen *Russia* 8 C10
Kvænangen *Norway* 8 A19
Kværndrup *Denmark* 11 J4
Kvaløya *Norway* 8 B18
Kvänum *Sweden* 11 F7
Kvareli = Qvareli *Georgia* 35 K7
Kvarner *Croatia* 41 D11
Kvarnerič *Croatia* 41 D11
Kvicksund *Sweden* 10 E10
Kvillsfors *Sweden* 11 G9
Kvismare kanal *Sweden* 10 E9
Kvissleby *Sweden* 10 B11
Kwabhaca *S. Africa* 89 E4
Kwajalein *Marshall Is.* 96 G8
Kwakhanai *Botswana* 88 C3
Kwakoegron *Suriname* 125 B7
Kwale *Kenya* 86 C4
Kwale *Nigeria* 83 D6
KwaMashu *S. Africa* 89 D5
Kwando ➤ *Africa* 88 B3
Kwangchow = Guangzhou
   China 59 F9
Kwango ➤
   Dem. Rep. of the Congo 84 E3
Kwangsi-Chuang =
   Guangxi Zhuangzu
   Zizhiqu □ *China* 58 F7
Kwangtung =
   Guangdong □ *China* 59 F9
Kwara □ *Nigeria* 83 D6
Kwataboahegan ➤ *Canada* 104 B3
Kwatisore *Indonesia* 63 E8
KwaZulu Natal □ *S. Africa* 89 D5
Kweichow = Guizhou □
   China 58 D6
Kwekwe *Zimbabwe* 87 F2
Kwidzyn *Poland* 30 E5
Kwiha *Ethiopia* 81 E4
Kwilu ➤
   Dem. Rep. of the Congo 84 E3
Kwinana *Australia* 93 F2
Kwisa ➤ *Poland* 31 G2
Kwoka *Indonesia* 63 E8
Kwolla *Nigeria* 83 D6
Kyabra Cr. ➤ *Australia* 95 D3
Kyabram *Australia* 95 F4
Kyaikto *Burma* 64 D1
Kyakhta *Russia* 53 D11
Kyambura ➤ *Uganda* 86 C3
Kyancutta *Australia* 95 E2
Kyaukpadaung *Burma* 67 J19
Kyaukpyu *Burma* 67 K18
Kyaukse *Burma* 67 J20
Kyburz *U.S.A.* 110 G6
Kyelang *India* 68 C7
Kyenjojo *Uganda* 86 B3
Kyjov *Czech Rep.* 27 B10
Kyle *Canada* 103 C7
Kyle Dam *Zimbabwe* 87 G3
Kyle of Lochalsh *U.K.* 13 D3
Kyll ➤ *Germany* 25 E7
Kyllburg *Germany* 25 E2
Kyllini *Greece* 46 D3
Kymijoki ➤ *Finland* 32 B4
Kymmene älv =
   Kymijoki ➤ *Finland* 32 B4
Kyneton *Australia* 95 F3
Kynuna *Australia* 94 C3
Kyō-ga-Saki *Japan* 55 G7
Kyoga, L. *Uganda* 86 B3
Kyogle *Australia* 95 D5
Kyom ➤ *Sudan* 81 F2
Kyŏngju = Gyeongju
   S. Korea 57 G15
Kyŏngsŏng *N. Korea* 57 D15
Kyonpyaw *Burma* 67 L19
Kyōto *Japan* 55 G7
Kyōto □ *Japan* 55 G7
Kyparissovouno *Cyprus* 49 D12
Kyperounda *Cyprus* 49 E11
Kypros = Cyprus ■ *Asia* 49 E12
Kyrenia *Cyprus* 49 D12
Kyrgyzstan ■ *Asia* 52 E8
Kyritz *Germany* 24 C8
Kyrkhult *Sweden* 11 H8
Kyrnasivka *Ukraine* 29 B13
Kyrnychky *Ukraine* 29 E14
Kyro älv = Kyrönjoki ➤
   Finland 8 E19
Kyrönjoki ➤ *Finland* 8 E19
Kystatyam *Russia* 53 C13
Kysucké Nové Mesto
   Slovak Rep. 27 B11
Kytay, Ozero *Ukraine* 29 E14
Kythira *Greece* 46 E5
Kythréa *Cyprus* 49 D12

Kyunhla *Burma* 67 H19
Kyuquot Sound *Canada* 102 D3
Kyurdamir = Kürdämir
   Azerbaijan 35 K9
Kyūshū *Japan* 55 H5
Kyūshū □ *Japan* 55 H5
Kyushu-Palau Ridge *Pac. Oc.* 96 E5
Kyūshū-Sanchi *Japan* 55 H5
Kyustendil *Bulgaria* 44 D6
Kyusyur *Russia* 53 B13
Kyyiv *Ukraine* 23 C16
Kyyiv □ *Ukraine* 33 G6
Kyyivske Vdskh. *Ukraine* 23 C16
Kyzyl *Russia* 53 D10
Kyzyl Kum *Uzbekistan* 52 E7
Kyzyl Kyya *Kyrgyzstan* 52 E8
Kyzyl Orda = Qyzylorda
   Kazakhstan 52 E7

L

La Albuera *Spain* 37 G4
La Alcarria *Spain* 38 E2
La Almarcha *Spain* 38 D2
La Almunia de Doña
   Godina *Spain* 38 D3
La Amistad △ *Cent. Amer.* 120 E3
La Asunción *Venezuela* 124 A6
La Baie *Canada* 105 C5
La Banda *Argentina* 126 B3
La Bañeza *Spain* 36 C5
La Barca *Mexico* 118 C4
La Barge *U.S.A.* 108 E8
La Barra *Nic.* 120 D3
La Bastide-Puylaurent
   France 20 D7
La Baule *France* 18 E4
La Belle *U.S.A.* 117 H14
La Biche *Canada* 102 B4
La Biche, L. *Canada* 102 C6
La Bisbal d'Empordà *Spain* 38 D8
La Brea *Trin. & Tob.* 125 K15
La Brède *France* 20 D3
La Bresse *France* 19 D13
La Bureba *Spain* 36 C7
La Calera *Chile* 126 C1
La Campana △ *Chile* 126 C1
La Campiña *Spain* 37 H6
La Canal = Sa Canal *Spain* 48 C7
La Cañiza = A Cañiza *Spain* 36 C2
La Canourgue *France* 20 D7
La Capelle *France* 19 C10
La Carlota *Argentina* 126 C3
La Carlota *Phil.* 61 F5
La Carlota *Spain* 37 H6
La Carolina *Spain* 37 G7
La Cavalerie *France* 20 D7
La Ceiba *Honduras* 120 C2
La Chaise-Dieu *France* 20 C7
La Chapelle d'Angillon
   France 19 E9
La Chapelle-St-Luc *France* 19 D11
La Chapelle-sur-Erdre *France* 18 E5
La Charité-sur-Loire *France* 19 E10
La Chartre-sur-le-Loir *France* 18 E7
La Châtaigneraie *France* 20 B3
La Châtre *France* 19 F9
La Chaux-de-Fonds *Switz.* 25 H2
La Chorrera *Panama* 120 E4
La Ciotat *France* 21 E9
La Clayette *France* 19 F11
La Cocha *Argentina* 126 B2
La Concepción *Panama* 120 E3
La Concordia *Mexico* 119 D6
La Coruña = A Coruña *Spain* 36 B2
La Côte-St-André *France* 21 C9
La Courtine *France* 20 C6
La Crau *Bouches-du-Rhône,
   France* 21 E8
La Crau *Var, France* 21 E10
La Crescent *U.S.A.* 112 D8
La Crete *Canada* 102 B5
La Crosse *Kans., U.S.A.* 112 F4
La Crosse *Wis., U.S.A.* 112 D8
La Cruz *Costa Rica* 120 D2
La Cruz *Mexico* 118 C3
La Désirade *Guadeloupe* 120 b
La Digue *Seychelles* 85 b
La Esperanza *Cuba* 120 B3
La Esperanza *Honduras* 120 D2
La Estrada = A Estrada *Spain* 36 C2
La Faouët *France* 18 D3
La Fayette *U.S.A.* 117 D12
La Fé *Cuba* 120 B3
La Fère *France* 19 C10
La Ferté-Bernard *France* 18 D7
La Ferté-Gaucher *France* 19 D10
La Ferté-Macé *France* 18 D6
La Ferté-St-Aubin *France* 19 E8
La Ferté-sous-Jouarre
   France 19 D10
La Ferté-Vidame *France* 18 D7
La Flèche *France* 18 E6
La Follette *U.S.A.* 117 C12
La Fregeneda *Spain* 36 E4
La Fuente de San Esteban
   Spain 36 E4
La Gacilly *France* 18 E4
La Gineta *Spain* 39 F2

La Grand'Combe *France* 21 D8
La Grande *U.S.A.* 108 D4
La Grande ➤ *Canada* 104 B5
La Grande 3, Rés. *Canada* 104 B5
La Grande 4, Rés. *Canada* 104 B5
La Grande-Motte *France* 21 E8
La Grange *Calif., U.S.A.* 110 H6
La Grange *Ga., U.S.A.* 117 E12
La Grange *Ky., U.S.A.* 113 F11
La Grange *Tex., U.S.A.* 116 G6
La Grave *France* 21 C10
La Guaira *Venezuela* 124 A5
La Guardia = A Guarda
   Spain 36 D2
La Gudiña = A Gudiña *Spain* 36 C3
La Guerche-de-Bretagne
   France 18 E5
La Guerche-sur-l'Aubois
   France 19 F9
La Habana *Cuba* 120 B3
La Haute Vallée de
   Chevreuse △ *France* 19 D8
La Haye-du-Puits *France* 18 C5
La Horra *Spain* 36 D7
La Independencia *Mexico* 119 D6
La Isabela *Dom. Rep.* 121 C5
La Jonquera *Spain* 38 C7
La Junta *U.S.A.* 108 H12
La Laguna *Canary Is.* 48 F3
La Libertad = Puerto
   Libertad *Mexico* 118 B2
La Libertad *Guatemala* 120 C1
La Ligua *Chile* 126 C1
La Línea de la Concepción
   Spain 37 J5
La Loche *Canada* 103 B7
La Londe-les-Maures *France* 21 E10
La Lora *Spain* 36 C7
La Loupe *France* 18 D8
La Louvière *Belgium* 17 D4
La Lune *Trin. & Tob.* 125 K15
La Machine *France* 19 F10
La Maddalena *Italy* 42 A2
La Malbaie *Canada* 105 C5
La Malinche ☺ *Mexico* 119 D5
La Mancha *Spain* 39 F2
La Mariña *Spain* 36 B3
La Martre, L. *Canada* 102 A5
La Mesa *Mexico* 111 N10
La Mesa *U.S.A.* 111 N9
La Mesilla *U.S.A.* 109 K10
La Misión *Mexico* 118 A1
La Mothe-Achard *France* 18 F5
La Motte-Chalançon *France* 21 D9
La Motte-du-Caire *France* 21 D10
La Motte-Servolex *France* 21 C9
La Moure *U.S.A.* 112 B4
La Muela *Spain* 38 D3
La Mure *France* 21 D9
La Negra *Chile* 126 A1
La Oliva *Canary Is.* 48 F6
La Orotava *Canary Is.* 48 F3
La Oroya *Peru* 124 F3
La Pacaudière *France* 19 F10
La Palma *Canary Is.* 48 F2
La Palma *Panama* 120 E4
La Palma del Condado *Spain* 37 H4
La Paloma *Chile* 126 C1
La Pampa □ *Argentina* 126 D2
La Paragua *Venezuela* 124 B6
La Paz *Entre Ríos, Argentina* 126 C4
La Paz *San Luis, Argentina* 126 C2
La Paz *Bolivia* 124 G5
La Paz *Honduras* 120 D2
La Paz *Mexico* 118 C2
La Paz *Phil.* 61 D4
La Paz Centro *Nic.* 120 D2
La Pedrera *Colombia* 124 D5
La Pérade *Canada* 105 C5
La Perla *Mexico* 118 B4
La Perouse Str. *Asia* 54 B11
La Pesca *Mexico* 119 C5
La Piedad *Mexico* 118 C4
La Pine *U.S.A.* 108 E3
La Plata *Argentina* 126 C4
La Pobla de Lillet *Spain* 38 C6
La Pobla de Segur *Spain* 38 C5
La Pocatière *Canada* 105 C5
La Pola de Gordón *Spain* 36 C5
La Porta *France* 21 F13
La Porte *U.S.A.* 116 G7
La Presanella *Italy* 40 B7
La Puebla = Sa Pobla *Spain* 38 F8
La Puebla de Cazalla *Spain* 37 H5
La Puebla de los Infantes
   Spain 37 H5
La Puebla de Montalbán
   Spain 36 F6
La Puebla del Río *Spain* 37 H4
La Puerta de Segura *Spain* 37 G8
La Purísima *Mexico* 118 B2
La Push *U.S.A.* 110 C2
La Quiaca *Argentina* 126 A2
La Réole *France* 20 D3
La Restinga *Canary Is.* 48 G2
La Rioja *Argentina* 126 B2
La Rioja □ *Argentina* 126 B2
La Rioja □ *Spain* 38 C2
La Robla *Spain* 36 C5

La Roche-Bernard *France* **18** E4
La Roche-Canillac *France* **20** C5
La Roche-en-Ardenne
  Belgium **17** D5
La Roche-sur-Foron *France* **19** F13
La Roche-sur-Yon *France* **18** F5
La Rochefoucauld *France* **20** C4
La Rochelle *France* **20** B2
La Roda *Spain* **39** F2
La Roda de Andalucía *Spain* **37** H6
La Romaine *Canada* **105** B7
La Romana *Dom. Rep.* **121** C6
La Ronge *Canada* **103** B7
La Rumorosa *Mexico* **111** N10
La Sabina = Sa Savina *Spain* **48** C7
La Sagra *Spain* **39** H2
La Salle *U.S.A.* **112** E9
La Sanabria *Spain* **36** C4
La Santa *Canary Is.* **48** E6
La Sarre *Canada* **104** C4
La Scie *Canada* **105** C8
La Selva *Spain* **38** C7
La Selva Beach *U.S.A.* **110** J5
La Selva del Camp *Spain* **38** D6
La Serena *Chile* **126** B1
La Serena *Spain* **37** G5
La Seu d'Urgell *Spain* **38** C6
La Seyne-sur-Mer *France* **21** E9
La Sila *Italy* **43** C9
La Solana *Spain* **37** G7
La Soufrière *St. Vincent* **121** D7
La Souterraine *France* **19** F8
La Spézia *Italy* **40** D6
La Suze-sur-Sarthe *France* **18** E7
La Tagua *Colombia* **124** C3
La Teste-de-Buch *France* **20** D2
La Tortuga *Venezuela* **121** D6
La Tour-du-Pin *France* **21** C9
La Tranche-sur-Mer *France* **18** F5
La Tremblade *France* **20** C2
La Trinité *Martinique* **120** c
La Tuque *Canada* **104** C5
La Unión *Chile* **128** E2
La Unión *El Salv.* **120** D2
La Unión *Mexico* **118** D4
La Unión *Spain* **39** H4
La Urbana *Venezuela* **124** B5
La Vache Pt. *Trin. & Tob.* **125** K15
La Vall d'Uixó *Spain* **38** F4
La Vecilla *Spain* **36** C5
La Vega *Dom. Rep.* **121** C5
La Vela de Coro *Venezuela* **124** A5
La Veleta *Spain* **37** H7
La Venta *Mexico* **119** D6
La Vergne *U.S.A.* **117** C11
La Villa Joiosa =
  Villajoyosa *Spain* **39** G4
La Voulte-sur-Rhône *France* **21** D8
Laa an der Thaya *Austria* **27** C9
Laaber, Grosse → *Germany* **25** G8
Laage *Germany* **24** B8
Laascaanood = Las Anod
  Somali Rep. **75** F4
Laatzen *Germany* **24** C5
Laba → *Russia* **35** H4
Labasa *Fiji* **91** a
Labason *Phil.* **61** G5
Labastide-Murat *France* **20** D5
Labastide-Rouairoux *France* **20** E6
Labbézenga *Mali* **83** B5
Labdah = Leptis Magna
  Libya **79** B8
Labe = Elbe → *Europe* **24** B4
Labé *Guinea* **82** C2
Laberge, L. *Canada* **102** A1
Labin *Croatia* **41** C11
Labinsk *Russia* **35** H5
Labis *Malaysia* **65** L4
Łabiszyn *Poland* **31** F4
Labo *Phil.* **61** D5
Laboe *Germany* **24** A6
Laborec → *Slovak Rep.* **27** C14
Laborie *St. Lucia* **121** f
Labouheyre *France* **20** D3
Laboulaye *Argentina* **126** C3
Labrador *Canada* **105** B7
Labrador City *Canada* **105** B6
Labrador Sea *Atl. Oc.* **101** F21
Lábrea *Brazil* **124** E6
Labruguière *France* **20** E6
Labuan *Malaysia* **62** C5
Labuan, Pulau *Malaysia* **62** C5
Labuha *Indonesia* **63** E7
Labuhan *Indonesia* **63** G11
Labuhanbajo *Indonesia* **63** F6
Labuhanbilik *Indonesia* **65** L3
Labuk, Telok *Malaysia* **62** C5
Labyrinth, L. *Australia* **95** E2
Labytnangi *Russia* **52** C7
Laç *Albania* **44** E3
Lac-Bouchette *Canada* **105** C5
Lac Édouard *Canada* **104** C5
Lac La Biche *Canada* **102** C6
Lac la Martre = Wha Ti
  Canada **100** E8
Lac La Ronge △ *Canada* **103** B7
Lac-Mégantic *Canada* **105** C5
Lac Thien *Vietnam* **64** F7
Lacanau *France* **20** D2

Lacanau, Étang de *France* **20** D2
Lacantún → *Mexico* **119** D6
Lácara → *Spain* **37** G4
Lacaune *France* **20** E6
Lacaune, Mts. de *France* **20** E6
Laccadive Is. =
  Lakshadweep Is. *India* **3** D13
Lacepede B. *Australia* **95** F2
Lacepede Is. *Australia* **92** C3
Lacerdónia *Mozam.* **87** F4
Lacey *U.S.A.* **110** C4
Lachania *Greece* **49** D9
Lachhmangarh *India* **68** F6
Lachi *Pakistan* **68** C4
Lachine *Canada* **104** C5
Lachlan → *Australia* **95** E3
Lachute *Canada* **104** C5
Lackagh Hills *Ireland* **12** B3
Lackawanna *U.S.A.* **114** D6
Lackawaxen *U.S.A.* **115** E10
Lacolle *Canada* **115** A11
Lacombe *Canada* **102** C6
Lacona *U.S.A.* **115** C8
Láconi *Italy* **42** C2
Laconia *U.S.A.* **115** C13
Lacq *France* **20** E3
Ladakh Ra. *India* **69** C8
Lądek-Zdrój *Poland* **31** H3
Ládik *Turkey* **72** B6
Ladismith *S. Africa* **88** E3
Ladíspoli *Italy* **41** G9
Lādīz *Iran* **71** D9
Ladnun *India* **68** F6
Ladoga, L. = Ladozhskoye
  Ozero *Russia* **32** B6
Ladonas → *Greece* **46** D3
Ladozhskoye Ozero *Russia* **32** B6
Ladushkin *Russia* **30** D7
Lady Elliott I. *Australia* **94** C5
Lady Grey *S. Africa* **88** E4
Ladybrand *S. Africa* **88** D4
Ladysmith *Canada* **110** D3
Ladysmith *S. Africa* **89** D4
Ladysmith *U.S.A.* **112** C8
Ladyzhyn *Ukraine* **29** B14
Lae *Papua N. G.* **90** B7
Laem Hin Khom *Thailand* **65** b
Laem Khat *Thailand* **65** a
Laem Nga *Thailand* **65** a
Laem Ngop *Thailand* **65** F4
Laem Phan Wa *Thailand* **65** a
Laem Pho *Thailand* **65** J3
Laem Phrom Thep *Thailand* **65** a
Laem Riang *Thailand* **65** a
Laem Sam Rong *Thailand* **65** b
Laem Son *Thailand* **65** a
Laem Yamu *Thailand* **65** a
Laerma *Greece* **49** C9
Læsø *Denmark* **11** G5
Læsø Rende *Denmark* **11** G4
Lafayette *Ind., U.S.A.* **112** E10
Lafayette *La., U.S.A.* **116** F8
Lafayette *Tenn., U.S.A.* **117** C11
Laferte → *Canada* **102** A5
Lafia *Nigeria* **83** D6
Lafiagi *Nigeria* **83** D6
Lafkos *Greece* **46** B5
Laflèche *Canada* **103** D7
Lafon *Sudan* **81** F3
Lagan *Sweden* **11** H7
Lagan → *Sweden* **11** H6
Lagan → *U.K.* **12** B6
Lagarfljót → *Iceland* **8** D6
Lagdo, L. de *Cameroon* **79** D7
Lage *Germany* **24** D4
Lågen → *Oppland, Norway* **8** F14
Lågen → *Vestfold, Norway* **9** G14
Lägerdorf *Germany* **24** B5
Lages *Brazil* **127** B5
Laghouat *Algeria* **78** B6
Lagnieu *France* **21** C9
Lagny-sur-Marne *France* **19** D9
Lago *Italy* **43** C9
Lago de Sanabria y
  Entorno △ *Spain* **36** C4
Lagôa *Portugal* **37** H2
Lagoa do Peixe △ *Brazil* **127** C5
Lagoa Vermelha *Brazil* **127** B5
Lagoaça *Portugal* **36** D4
Lagodekhi *Georgia* **35** K8
Lagónegro *Italy* **43** B8
Lagonoy G. *Phil.* **61** E5
Lagos *Greece* **45** E9
Lagos *Nigeria* **83** D5
Lagos *Portugal* **37** H2
Lagos □ *Nigeria* **83** D5
Lagos de Moreno *Mexico* **118** C4
Lagrange = Bidyadanga
  Australia **92** C3
Lagrange B. *Australia* **92** C3
Laguardia *Spain* **38** C2
Laguépie *France* **20** D5
Laguna *Brazil* **127** B6
Laguna *U.S.A.* **109** J10
Laguna, Sa. de la *Mexico* **118** C3
Laguna Beach *U.S.A.* **111** M9
Laguna de Duera *Spain* **36** D6
Laguna de la Restinga △
  Venezuela **121** D6

Laguna de Lachuá △
  Guatemala **120** C1
Laguna del Laja △ *Chile* **126** D1
Laguna del Tigre △
  Guatemala **120** C1
Laguna Limpia *Argentina* **126** B4
Lagunas *Chile* **126** A2
Lagunas *Peru* **124** E3
Lagunas de Chacahua △
  Mexico **119** D5
Lagunas de Montebello △
  Mexico **119** D6
Lagunas de Ruidera △ *Spain* **39** G2
Lahad Datu *Malaysia* **63** D5
Lahad Datu, Telok *Malaysia* **63** D5
Lahan Sai *Thailand* **64** E4
Lahanam *Laos* **64** D5
Lahar *India* **69** F8
Laharpur *India* **69** F9
Lahat *Indonesia* **62** E2
Lahewa *Indonesia* **62** D1
Lāhījān *Iran* **71** B6
Lahn → *Germany* **25** E3
Lahnstein *Germany* **25** E3
Laholm *Sweden* **11** H7
Laholmsbukten *Sweden* **11** H6
Lahore *Pakistan* **68** D6
Lahr *Germany* **25** G3
Lahri *Pakistan* **68** E3
Lāhrūd *Iran* **73** C12
Lahti *Finland* **32** B3
Lahtis = Lahti *Finland* **32** B3
Laï *Chad* **79** G9
Lai Chau *Vietnam* **58** F4
Lai'an *China* **59** A12
Laibin *China* **58** F7
Laifeng *China* **58** C7
L'Aigle *France* **18** D7
Laignes *France* **19** E11
L'Aiguillon-sur-Mer *France* **20** B2
Laila = Layla *Si. Arabia* **75** C4
Lainioälven → *Sweden* **8** C20
Lairg *U.K.* **13** C4
Laisamis *Kenya* **86** B4
Laishui *China* **56** E8
Laissac *France* **20** D6
Láives *Italy* **41** B8
Laiwu *China* **57** F9
Laixi *China* **57** F11
Laiyang *China* **57** F11
Laiyuan *China* **56** E8
Laizhou *China* **57** F10
Laizhou Wan *China* **57** F10
Laja → *Mexico* **118** C4
Lajamanu *Australia* **92** C5
Lajere *Nigeria* **83** C7
Lajkovac *Serbia* **44** B4
Lajosmizse *Hungary* **28** C4
Lak Sao *Laos* **64** C5
Lakaband *Pakistan* **68** D3
Lakamané *Mali* **82** C3
Lake *U.S.A.* **108** D8
Lake Alpine *U.S.A.* **110** G7
Lake Andes *U.S.A.* **112** D4
Lake Arthur *U.S.A.* **116** F8
Lake Bindegolly △ *Australia* **95** D3
Lake Cargelligo *Australia* **95** E4
Lake Charles *U.S.A.* **116** F8
Lake City *Colo., U.S.A.* **108** G10
Lake City *Fla., U.S.A.* **117** F13
Lake City *Mich., U.S.A.* **113** C11
Lake City *Minn., U.S.A.* **112** C8
Lake City *Pa., U.S.A.* **114** D4
Lake City *S.C., U.S.A.* **117** E15
Lake Cowichan *Canada* **102** D4
Lake District △ *U.K.* **14** C4
Lake Elsinore *U.S.A.* **111** M9
Lake Eyre △ *Australia* **95** D2
Lake Gairdner △ *Australia* **95** E2
Lake George *U.S.A.* **115** C11
Lake Grace *Australia* **93** F2
Lake Gregory ☉ *Australia* **92** D4
Lake Harbour = Kimmirut
  Canada **101** E18
Lake Havasu City *U.S.A.* **111** L12
Lake Hughes *U.S.A.* **111** L8
Lake Isabella *U.S.A.* **111** K8
Lake Jackson *U.S.A.* **116** G7
Lake King *Australia* **93** F2
Lake Lenore *Canada* **103** C8
Lake Louise *Canada* **102** C5
Lake Mackay ☉ *Australia* **92** D4
Lake Mburo △ *Uganda* **86** C3
Lake Mead △ *U.S.A.* **111** K12
Lake Meredith △ *U.S.A.* **116** D4
Lake Mills *U.S.A.* **112** D7
Lake Nakuru △ *Kenya* **86** C4
Lake Placid *U.S.A.* **115** B11
Lake Pleasant *U.S.A.* **115** C10
Lake Providence *U.S.A.* **116** E9
Lake Roosevelt △ *U.S.A.* **108** B4
Lake St. Peter *Canada* **114** A6
Lake Superior △ *Canada* **104** C3
Lake Torrens △ *Australia* **95** E2
Lake Village *U.S.A.* **116** E9
Lake Wales *U.S.A.* **117** H14
Lake Worth *U.S.A.* **117** H14
Lakeba *Fiji* **91** a

Lakeba Passage *Fiji* **91** a
Lakefield *Canada* **114** B6
Lakefield △ *Australia* **94** B3
Lakehurst *U.S.A.* **115** F10
Lakeland *Australia* **94** B3
Lakeland *U.S.A.* **117** G14
Lakemba = Lakeba *Fiji* **91** a
Lakeport *Calif., U.S.A.* **110** F4
Lakeport *Mich., U.S.A.* **114** C2
Lakes Entrance *Australia* **95** F4
Lakeside *Calif., U.S.A.* **111** N10
Lakeside *Nebr., U.S.A.* **112** D2
Lakeview *U.S.A.* **108** E3
Lakeville *U.S.A.* **112** C7
Lakewood *Colo., U.S.A.* **108** G11
Lakewood *N.J., U.S.A.* **115** F10
Lakewood *N.Y., U.S.A.* **114** D5
Lakewood *Ohio, U.S.A.* **114** E3
Lakewood *Wash., U.S.A.* **110** C4
Lakha *India* **68** F4
Lakhimpur *India* **69** F9
Lakhisarai *India* **69** G12
Lakhnadon *India* **69** H8
Lakhnau = Lucknow *India* **69** F9
Lakhonpheng *Laos* **64** E5
Lakhpat *India* **68** H3
Laki *Azerbaijan* **35** K8
Lakin *U.S.A.* **112** G3
Lakitusaki → *Canada* **104** B3
Lakki *Greece* **49** D5
Lakki *Pakistan* **68** C4
Lakonia □ *Greece* **46** E4
Lakonikos Kolpos *Greece* **46** E4
Lakor *Indonesia* **63** F7
Lakota *Ivory C.* **82** D4
Lakota *U.S.A.* **112** A4
Laksar *India* **68** E8
Laksefjorden *Norway* **8** A22
Lakselv *Norway* **8** A21
Lakshadweep Is. *India* **3** D13
Lakshmanpur *India* **69** H10
Lakshmikantapur *India* **69** H13
Lala Musa *Pakistan* **68** C5
Lalaghat *India* **67** G18
Lalago *Tanzania* **86** C3
Lalapanzi *Zimbabwe* **87** F3
Lalapaşa *Turkey* **45** E10
Lalbenque *France* **20** D5
L'Albufera *Spain* **39** F4
L'Alcora *Spain* **38** E4
L'Alfàs del Pi *Spain* **39** G4
Lalganj *India* **69** G11
Lalgola *India* **69** G13
Lālī *Iran* **71** C6
Lalibela *Ethiopia* **81** E4
Lalín *China* **57** B14
Lalín *Spain* **36** C2
Lalin He → *China* **57** B13
Lalinde *France* **20** D4
Lalitapur *Nepal* **69** F11
Lalitpur *India* **69** G8
Lalkua *India* **69** E8
Lalsot *India* **68** F7
Lam Pao Res. *Thailand* **64** D4
Lama Kara *Togo* **83** D5
Lamae *Thailand* **65** H2
Lamaing *Burma* **64** E1
Lamar *Colo., U.S.A.* **108** G12
Lamar *Mo., U.S.A.* **112** G6
Lamas *Peru* **124** E3
Lamastre *France* **21** D8
Lamayuru *India* **69** B7
Lambach *Austria* **26** C6
Lamballe *France* **18** D4
Lambaréné *Gabon* **84** E2
Lambasa = Labasa *Fiji* **91** a
Lambay I. *Ireland* **12** C5
Lambert's Bay *S. Africa* **88** E2
Lambesc *France* **21** E9
Lambeth *Canada* **114** D3
Lambia *Greece* **46** D3
Lambomakondro *Madag.* **89** C7
Lambton Shores *Canada* **114** C3
Lame *Nigeria* **83** C6
Lame Deer *U.S.A.* **108** D10
Lamego *Portugal* **36** D3
Lamèque *Canada* **105** C7
Lameroo *Australia* **95** F3
Lamesa *U.S.A.* **116** E4
Lamia *Greece* **46** C4
Lamington △ *Australia* **95** D5
Lamitan *Phil.* **61** H5
Lammermuir Hills *U.K.* **13** F6
Lammhult *Sweden* **11** G8
Lamoille → *U.S.A.* **115** B11
Lamon B. *Phil.* **61** D5
Lamont *Canada* **102** C6
Lamont *Calif., U.S.A.* **111** K8
Lamont *Wyo., U.S.A.* **108** E10
Lampa *Peru* **124** G4
Lampang *Thailand* **64** C2
Lampasas *U.S.A.* **116** F5
Lampazos de Naranjo
  Mexico **118** B4
Lampedusa *Italy* **43** H6
Lampertheim *Germany* **25** F4
Lampeter *U.K.* **15** E3
Lampman *Canada* **103** D8

Lamprechtshausen *Austria* **26** D5
Lampung □ *Indonesia* **62** F2
Lamta *India* **69** H9
Lamu *Kenya* **86** C5
Lamy *U.S.A.* **109** J11
Lan Xian *China* **56** E6
Lan Yü *Taiwan* **59** F13
Lanak La *China* **69** B8
Lanak'o Shank'ou =
  Lanak La *China* **69** B8
Lanao, L. *Phil.* **61** H6
Lanark *Canada* **115** A8
Lanark *U.K.* **13** F5
Lancang *China* **58** F2
Lancang Jiang → *China* **58** 63
Lancashire □ *U.K.* **14** D5
Lancaster *Canada* **115** A10
Lancaster *U.K.* **14** C5
Lancaster *Calif., U.S.A.* **111** L8
Lancaster *Ky., U.S.A.* **113** G11
Lancaster *N.H., U.S.A.* **115** B13
Lancaster *Ohio, U.S.A.* **113** F12
Lancaster *Pa., U.S.A.* **115** F8
Lancaster *S.C., U.S.A.* **117** D14
Lancaster *Wis., U.S.A.* **112** D8
Lancaster Sd. *Canada* **101** C5
Lancelin *Australia* **93** F2
Lanciano *Italy* **41** F11
Lancun *China* **57** F11
Lańcut *Poland* **31** H9
Land Between the Lakes △
  U.S.A. **117** C11
Landau *Bayern, Germany* **25** G8
Landau *Rhld-Pfz., Germany* **25** F4
Landeck *Austria* **26** D3
Lander *U.S.A.* **108** E9
Lander → *Australia* **92** D5
Landerneau *France* **18** D2
Landeryd *Sweden* **11** G7
Landes *France* **20** D2
Landes □ *France* **20** D3
Landes de Gascogne △
  France **20** D3
Landete *Spain* **38** F3
Landi Kotal *Pakistan* **68** B4
Landisburg *U.S.A.* **114** F7
Landivisiau *France* **18** D2
Landmannalaugar *Iceland* **8** D4
Landquart *Switz.* **25** J5
Landrecies *France* **19** B10
Land's End *U.K.* **15** G2
Landsberg *Germany* **25** G3
Landsborough Cr. →
  Australia **94** C3
Landsbro *Sweden* **11** G8
Landshut *Germany* **25** G8
Landskrona *Sweden* **11** J6
Landstuhl *Germany* **25** F3
Landvetter *Sweden* **11** G6
Lanesboro *U.S.A.* **115** E9
Lanester *France* **18** E3
Lanett *U.S.A.* **117** E12
Lang Shan *China* **56** D4
Lang Son *Vietnam* **58** G6
Lang Suan *Thailand* **65** H2
Langå *Denmark* **11** H3
La'nga Co *China* **69** D9
Langar *Iran* **71** C9
Langara I. *Canada* **102** C2
Langas *Greece* **44** F7
Langadia *Greece* **46** D4
Lángan → *Sweden* **10** A8
Langano, L. *Ethiopia* **81** F4
Langar *Iran* **71** C9
Langara I. *Canada* **102** C2
Langarūd *Iran* **71** B6
Lángås *Sweden* **11** H6
Langdai *China* **58** D5
Langdon *U.S.A.* **112** A4
Lange Jan = Ölands södra
  udde *Sweden* **11** H10
Langeac *France* **20** C7
Langeais *France* **18** E7
Langeb Baraka → *Sudan* **80** D4
Langeberg *S. Africa* **88** E3
Langeberge *S. Africa* **88** D3
Langeland *Denmark* **11** K4
Langelands Bælt *Denmark* **11** K4
Langen *Hessen, Germany* **25** F4
Langen *Niedersachsen,
  Germany* **24** B4
Langenburg *Canada* **103** C8
Langeneß *Germany* **24** A4
Langenlois *Austria* **26** C8
Langeoog *Germany* **24** B3
Langeskov *Denmark* **11** J4
Länghem *Sweden* **11** G7
Langhirano *Italy* **40** D7
Langholm *U.K.* **13** F5
Langjökull *Iceland* **8** D3
Langkawi, Pulau *Malaysia* **65** J2
Langklip *S. Africa* **88** D3
Langkon *Malaysia* **62** C5
Langley *Canada* **110** A4
Langnau *Switz.* **25** J3
Langogne *France* **20** D7
Langon *France* **20** D3

Langøya *Norway* **8** B16
Langreo *Spain* **36** B5
Langres *France* **19** E12
Langres, Plateau de *France* **19** E12
Langsa *Indonesia* **62** D1
Långsele *Sweden* **10** A11
Långshyttan *Sweden* **10** D10
Langtang △ *Nepal* **69** E11
Langtry *U.S.A.* **116** G4
Langu *Thailand* **65** J2
Langue de Barbarie △
  Senegal **82** C1
Languedoc *France* **20** E7
Languedoc-Roussillon □
  France **20** E6
Langxi *China* **59** B12
Langxiangzhen *China* **56** E9
Langzhong *China* **58** B5
Lanigan *Canada* **103** C7
Lankao *China* **56** G8
Länkäran *Azerbaijan* **73** C13
Lanmeur *France* **18** D3
Lannemezan *France* **20** E4
Lannilis *France* **18** D2
Lannion *France* **18** D3
L'Annonciation *Canada* **104** C5
Lanouaille *France* **20** C5
Lanping *China* **58** D2
Lansdale *U.S.A.* **115** F9
Lansdowne *Australia* **95** E5
Lansdowne *Canada* **115** B8
Lansdowne *India* **69** E8
Lansdowne House =
  Neskantaga *Canada* **104** B2
L'Anse *U.S.A.* **112** B9
L'Anse au Loup *Canada* **105** B8
L'Anse aux Meadows
  Canada **105** B8
L'Anse la Raye *St. Lucia* **121** f
Lansford *U.S.A.* **115** F9
Lanshan *China* **59** E9
Lansing *U.S.A.* **113** D11
Lanslebourg-Mont-Cenis
  France **21** C10
Lanta Yai, Ko *Thailand* **65** J2
Lantewa *Nigeria* **83** C7
Lantian *China* **56** G5
Lanus *Argentina* **126** C4
Lanusei *Italy* **42** C2
Lanuza *Phil.* **61** G7
Lanxi *China* **59** C12
Lanzarote *Canary Is.* **48** F6
Lanzarote ✈ (ACE) *Canary Is.* **48** F6
Lanzhou *China* **56** F2
Lanzo Torinese *Italy* **40** C4
Lao → *Italy* **43** C8
Lao Bao *Laos* **64** D6
Lao Cai *Vietnam* **58** F4
Laoag *Phil.* **61** B4
Laoang *Phil.* **61** E6
Laoha He → *China* **57** C11
Laohekou *China* **59** A8
Laois □ *Ireland* **12** D4
Laon *France* **19** C10
Laona *U.S.A.* **112** C9
Laos ■ *Asia* **64** D5
Lapa *Brazil* **127** B6
Lapai *Nigeria* **83** D6
Lapalisse *France* **19** F10
Lapeer *U.S.A.* **113** D12
Lapeyrade *France* **20** D3
Lapithos *Cyprus* **49** D12
Lapland = Lappland *Europe* **8** B21
LaPorte *Ind., U.S.A.* **112** E10
Laporte *Pa., U.S.A.* **115** E8
Lapovo *Serbia* **44** B5
Lappeenranta *Finland* **32** B5
Lappland *Europe* **8** B21
Lappo = Lapua *Finland* **8** E20
Laprida *Argentina* **126** D3
Lâpseki *Turkey* **45** F10
Laptev Sea *Russia* **53** B13
Lapua *Finland* **8** E20
Lãpuş → *Romania* **29** C8
Lãpuş, Munţii *Romania* **29** C8
Lãpuşna *Moldova* **29** D13
Lapy *Poland* **31** F9
Laqiya Arba'in *Sudan* **80** C2
Laqiya Umran *Sudan* **80** D2
L'Áquila *Italy* **41** F10
Lãr *Iran* **71** E7
Larabanga *Ghana* **82** D4
Laragne-Montéglin *France* **21** D9
Laramie *U.S.A.* **108** F11
Laramie Mts. *U.S.A.* **108** F11
Laranjeiras do Sul *Brazil* **127** B5
Larantuka *Indonesia* **63** F6
Larat *Indonesia* **63** F8
L'Arbresle *France* **21** C8
Lärbro *Sweden* **11** G12
Larde *Mozam.* **87** F4
Larder Lake *Canada* **104** C4
Lardos *Greece* **49** C10
Lardos, Akra = Lindos,
  Akra *Greece* **49** C10
Lardos, Ormos *Greece* **49** C10
Lare *Kenya* **86** C4
Laredo *Spain* **36** B7
Laredo *U.S.A.* **116** H5

Laredo Sd. *Canada* **102** C3
Largentière *France* **21** D8
L'Argentière-la-Bessée *France* **21** D10
Largo *U.S.A.* **117** H13
Largs *U.K.* **13** F4
Lari *Italy* **40** E7
Lariang *Indonesia* **63** E5
Larimore *U.S.A.* **112** B5
Larino *Italy* **41** G11
Larisa *Greece* **46** B4
Larissas □ *Greece* **46** B4
Larkana *Pakistan* **68** F3
Larnaca *Cyprus* **49** E12
Larnaca Bay *Cyprus* **49** E12
Larne *U.K.* **12** B6
Larned *U.S.A.* **112** F4
Laroquebrou *France* **20** D6
Larose *U.S.A.* **117** G9
Larrimah *Australia* **92** C5
Laruns *France* **20** F3
Larvik *Norway* **9** G14
Larzac, Causse du *France* **20** E7
Las Alpujarras *Spain* **39** J1
Las Animas *U.S.A.* **108** G12
Las Anod *Somali Rep.* **75** F4
Las Arenas *Spain* **36** B6
Las Batuecas △ *Spain* **36** E4
Las Brenas *Argentina* **126** B3
Las Cabezas de San Juan *Spain* **37** J5
Las Cañadas del Teide △ *Canary Is.* **48** F3
Las Cejas *Argentina* **128** B4
Las Chimeneas *Mexico* **111** N10
Las Cruces *U.S.A.* **109** K10
Las Flores *Argentina* **126** D4
Las Gabias = Gabia la Grande *Spain* **37** H7
Las Heras *Argentina* **126** C2
Las Lajas *Argentina* **128** D2
Las Lomitas *Argentina* **126** A3
Las Marismas *Spain* **37** H4
Las Minas *Spain* **39** G3
Las Navas de la Concepción *Spain* **37** H5
Las Navas del Marqués *Spain* **36** E6
Las Palmas *Argentina* **126** B4
Las Palmas *Canary Is.* **48** F4
Las Palmas → *Mexico* **111** N10
Las Palmas ✈ (LPA) *Canary Is.* **48** G4
Las Pedroñas *Spain* **39** F2
Las Piedras *Uruguay* **127** C4
Las Pipinas *Argentina* **126** D4
Las Plumas *Argentina* **128** E3
Las Rosas *Argentina* **126** C3
Las Rozas *Spain* **36** E7
Las Tablas *Panama* **120** E3
Las Toscas *Argentina* **126** B4
Las Truchas *Mexico* **118** D4
Las Tunas *Cuba* **120** B4
Las Varillas *Argentina* **126** C3
Las Vegas *N. Mex., U.S.A.* **109** J11
Las Vegas *Nev., U.S.A.* **111** J11
Las Vegas McCarran Int. ✈ (LAS) *U.S.A.* **111** J11
Lasarte-Oria *Spain* **38** B2
Lascano *Uruguay* **127** C4
Lash-e Joveyn *Afghan.* **66** D2
Lashburn *Canada* **103** C7
Lashio *Burma* **67** H20
Lashkar *India* **68** F8
Lasin *Poland* **30** E6
Lasithi *Greece* **49** D7
Lasithi □ *Greece* **49** D7
Läsjerd *Iran* **71** C7
Lask *Poland* **31** G6
Laskarzew *Poland* **31** G8
Lasko *Slovenia* **41** B12
Lassay-les-Châteaux *France* **18** D6
Lassen Pk. *U.S.A.* **108** F3
Last Mountain L. *Canada* **103** C8
Lassen Volcanic △ *U.S.A.* **108** F3
Lastchance Cr. → *U.S.A.* **110** E5
Lastoursville *Gabon* **84** E2
Lastovo *Croatia* **41** F13
Lastovski Kanal *Croatia* **41** F14
Lat Yao *Thailand* **64** E2
Latacunga *Ecuador* **124** D3
Latakia = Al Lādhiqīyah *Syria* **72** E6
Latchford *Canada* **104** C4
Late *Tonga* **91** c
Latehar *India* **69** H11
Laterza *Italy* **43** B9
Latham *Australia* **93** E2
Lathen *Germany* **24** C3
Lathi *India* **68** H4
Lathrop Wells *U.S.A.* **111** J10
Latiano *Italy* **43** B10
Latina *Italy* **42** A5
Latisana *Italy* **41** C10
Latium = Lazio □ *Italy* **41** F9
Laton *U.S.A.* **110** J7
Latorytsya → *Slovak Rep.* **27** C14
Latouche Treville, C. *Australia* **92** C3

Latrobe *Australia* **95** G4
Latrobe *U.S.A.* **114** F5
Latrónico *Italy* **43** B9
Latvia ■ *Europe* **32** D2
Lau *Nigeria* **83** D7
Lau Group *Fiji* **91** a
Lauchhammer *Germany* **24** D9
Lauda-Königshofen *Germany* **25** F5
Lauenburg *Germany* **24** B6
Lauenburgische Seen △ *Germany* **24** B6
Lauf *Germany* **25** F7
Lauge Koch Kyst *Greenland* **101** B20
Laughlin *U.S.A.* **109** J6
Laujar de Andarax *Spain* **39** H2
Laukaa *Finland* **8** E21
Launceston *Australia* **95** G4
Launceston *U.K.* **15** G3
Laune → *Ireland* **12** D2
Launglon Bok *Burma* **64** F1
Laupheim *Germany* **25** G5
Laura *Australia* **94** B3
Laureana di Borrello *Italy* **43** D9
Laurel *Miss., U.S.A.* **117** F10
Laurel *Mont., U.S.A.* **108** D9
Laurel Hill *U.S.A.* **114** F5
Laurencekirk *U.K.* **13** E6
Laurens *U.S.A.* **117** D13
Laurentian Plateau *Canada* **105** B6
Lauria *Italy* **43** B8
Laurie L. *Canada* **103** B8
Laurinburg *U.S.A.* **117** D15
Laurium *U.S.A.* **112** B9
Lausanne *Switz.* **25** J2
Laut *Indonesia* **62** D3
Laut, Pulau *Indonesia* **62** E5
Laut Kecil, Kepulauan *Indonesia* **62** E5
Lauterbach *Germany* **24** E5
Lauterecken *Germany* **25** F3
Lautoka *Fiji* **91** a
Lauzès *France* **20** D5
Lava → *Russia* **30** D8
Lava Beds △ *U.S.A.* **108** F3
Lavagh More *Ireland* **12** B3
Lavagna *Italy* **40** D6
Laval *France* **18** D6
Laval-des-Rapides *Canada* **104** C5
Lavalle *Argentina* **126** B2
Lävän *Iran* **71** E7
Lavant *Canada* **115** A8
Lävar Meydän *Iran* **71** D7
Lavara *Greece* **45** E10
Lavardac *France* **20** D4
Lavaur *France* **20** E5
Lavelanet *France* **20** F5
Lavello *Italy* **43** A8
Laverton *Australia* **93** E3
Lavis *Italy* **40** B8
Lavos *Portugal* **36** E2
Lavradio *Portugal* **37** G1
Lavras *Brazil* **127** A7
Lavre *Portugal* **37** G2
Lavrio *Greece* **46** D6
Lavris *Greece* **49** D6
Lavumisa *Swaziland* **89** D5
Lavushi Manda △ *Zambia* **87** E3
Lawaki *Fiji* **91** a
Lawas *Malaysia* **62** D5
Lawele *Indonesia* **63** F6
Lawn Hill = Boodjamulla △ *Australia* **94** B2
Lawqah *Si. Arabia* **70** D4
Lawra *Ghana* **82** C4
Lawrence *N.Z.* **91** F2
Lawrence *Ind., U.S.A.* **112** F10
Lawrence *Kans., U.S.A.* **112** F6
Lawrence *Mass., U.S.A.* **115** D13
Lawrenceburg *Ind., U.S.A.* **113** F11
Lawrenceburg *Tenn., U.S.A.* **117** D11
Lawrenceville *Ga., U.S.A.* **117** E13
Lawrenceville *Pa., U.S.A.* **114** E7
Laws *U.S.A.* **110** H8
Lawton *U.S.A.* **116** D5
Lawu *Indonesia* **63** G14
Lawz, J. al *Si. Arabia* **80** B4
Laxå *Sweden* **11** F8
Laxford, L. *U.K.* **13** C3
Laxou *France* **19** D13
Lay → *France* **18** B3
Layla *Si. Arabia* **75** C4
Laylän *Iraq* **70** C5
Layon → *France* **18** E6
Laysan I. *U.S.A.* **107** K5
Layton *U.S.A.* **108** F8
Laytonville *U.S.A.* **108** G2
Lazarev *Russia* **53** D15
Lazarev Sea *S. Ocean* **5** C2
Lazarevac *Serbia* **44** B4
Lazarevskoye *Russia* **35** J4
Lazarivo *Madag.* **89** C8
Lázaro Cárdenas *Mexico* **118** D4
Lazdijai *Lithuania* **30** D10
Lazio □ *Italy* **41** F9
Lazo *Moldova* **29** C13
Lazo *Russia* **54** C6
Le Beausset *France* **21** E9
Le Bic *Canada* **105** C6

Le Blanc *France* **20** B5
Le Bleymard *France* **20** D7
Le Bourgneuf-la-Fôret *France* **18** D6
Le Bugue *France* **20** D4
Le Cateau Cambrésis *France* **19** B10
Le Caylar *France* **20** E7
Le Chambon-Feugerolles *France* **21** C8
Le Châtelet *France* **19** F9
Le Chesne *France* **19** C11
Le Cheylard *France* **21** D8
Le Conquet *France* **18** D2
Le Creusot *France* **19** F11
Le Croisic *France* **18** E4
Le Donjon *France* **19** F10
Le Dorat *France* **20** B5
Le François *Martinique* **120** c
Le Gosier *Guadeloupe* **120** b
Le Grand-Lucé *France* **18** E7
Le Grand-Pressigny *France* **18** F7
Le Grand-Quevilly *France* **18** C8
Le Gris Gris *Mauritius* **85** d
Le Havre *France* **18** C7
Le Lamentin *Martinique* **120** c
Le Lavandou *France* **21** E10
Le Lion-d'Angers *France* **18** E6
Le Louroux-Béconnais *France* **18** E6
Le Luc *France* **21** E10
Le Lude *France* **18** E7
Le Mans *France* **18** E7
Le Marin *Martinique* **120** c
Le Mars *U.S.A.* **112** D5
Le Mayet-de-Montagne *France* **19** F10
Le Mêle-sur-Sarthe *France* **18** D7
Le Monastier-sur-Gazeille *France* **20** D7
Le Monêtier-les-Bains *France* **21** D10
Le Mont-Dore *France* **20** C6
Le Mont-St-Michel *France* **18** D5
Le Moule *Guadeloupe* **120** b
Le Moyne, L. *Canada* **105** A6
Le Muy *France* **21** E10
Le Palais *France* **18** E3
Le Perthus *France* **20** F6
Le Port *Réunion* **85** c
Le Prêcheur *Martinique* **120** c
Le Puy-en-Velay *France* **20** C7
Le Raysville *U.S.A.* **115** E8
Le Robert *Martinique* **120** c
Le Roy *U.S.A.* **114** D7
Le St-Esprit *Martinique* **120** c
Le Sueur *U.S.A.* **112** C7
Le Tampon *Réunion* **85** c
Le Teil *France* **21** D8
Le Teilleul *France* **18** D6
Le Theil *France* **18** D7
Le Thillot *France* **19** E13
Le Thuy *Vietnam* **64** D6
Le Touquet-Paris-Plage *France* **19** B8
Le Tréport *France* **18** B8
Le Val-d'Ajol *France* **19** E13
Le Verdon-sur-Mer *France* **20** C2
Le Vigan *France* **20** D7
Lea → *U.K.* **15** F8
Leach *Cambodia* **65** F4
Lead *U.S.A.* **112** C2
Leader *Canada* **103** C7
Leadville *U.S.A.* **108** G10
Leaf → *U.S.A.* **117** F10
Leaf Rapids *Canada* **103** B9
Leamington *Canada* **114** D2
Leamington *U.S.A.* **108** G7
Leamington Spa = Royal Leamington Spa *U.K.* **15** E6
Le'an *China* **59** D10
Leandro Norte Alem *Argentina* **127** B4
Leane, L. *Ireland* **12** D2
Learmonth *Australia* **92** D1
Leask *Canada* **103** C7
Leatherhead *U.K.* **15** F7
Leavenworth *Kans., U.S.A.* **112** F6
Leavenworth *Wash., U.S.A.* **108** C3
Leawood *U.S.A.* **112** F6
Leba *Poland* **30** D4
Łeba → *Poland* **30** D4
Lebach *Germany* **25** F2
Lebak *Phil.* **61** H6
Lebam *U.S.A.* **110** D3
Lebane *Serbia* **44** D5
Lebanon *Ind., U.S.A.* **112** E10
Lebanon *Kans., U.S.A.* **112** F4
Lebanon *Ky., U.S.A.* **113** G11
Lebanon *Mo., U.S.A.* **112** G7
Lebanon *N.H., U.S.A.* **115** C12
Lebanon *Oreg., U.S.A.* **108** D2
Lebanon *Pa., U.S.A.* **115** F8
Lebanon *Tenn., U.S.A.* **117** C11
Lebanon ■ *Asia* **74** B5
Lebec *U.S.A.* **111** L8
Lebedyan *Russia* **33** F10
Lebedyn *Ukraine* **33** G8
Lebel-sur-Quévillon *Canada* **104** C4
Lebomboberge *S. Africa* **89** C5
Lebork *Poland* **30** D4

Lebrija *Spain* **37** J4
Lebsko, Jezioro *Poland* **30** D4
Lebu *Chile* **126** D1
Leca da Palmeira *Portugal* **36** D2
Lecce *Italy* **43** B11
Lecco *Italy* **40** C6
Lecco, L. di *Italy* **40** C6
Lécera *Spain* **38** D4
Lech *Austria* **26** D3
Lech → *Germany* **25** G6
Lechang *China* **59** E9
Lechtaler Alpen *Austria* **26** D3
Lecontes Mills *U.S.A.* **114** E6
Lectoure *France* **20** E4
Łęczna *Poland* **31** G9
Łęczyca *Poland* **31** F6
Ledesma *Spain* **36** D5
Ledong *China* **64** C7
Leduc *Canada* **102** C6
Lee *U.S.A.* **115** D11
Lee → *Ireland* **12** E3
Lee Vining *U.S.A.* **110** H7
Leech L. *U.S.A.* **112** B6
Leechburg *U.S.A.* **114** F5
Leeds *U.K.* **14** D6
Leeds *U.S.A.* **117** E11
Leek *Neths.* **17** A6
Leek *U.K.* **14** D5
Leeman *Australia* **93** E1
Leeper *U.S.A.* **114** E5
Leer *Germany* **24** B3
Leesburg *U.S.A.* **117** G14
Leeton *Australia* **95** E4
Leetonia *U.S.A.* **114** F4
Leeu Gamka *S. Africa* **88** E3
Leeuwarden *Neths.* **17** A5
Leeuwin, C. *Australia* **93** F2
Leeuwin Naturaliste △ *Australia* **93** F2
Leeward Is. *Atl. Oc.* **121** C7
Lefka *Cyprus* **49** D11
Lefkada *Greece* **46** C2
Lefkimi *Greece* **49** B4
Lefkimis, Akra *Greece* **49** B4
Lefkoniko *Cyprus* **49** D12
Lefroy *Canada* **114** B5
Lefroy, L. *Australia* **93** F3
Łeg → *Poland* **31** H8
Legazpi *Phil.* **61** E5
Lège-Cap-Ferret *France* **20** D2
Lege Hida *Ethiopia* **81** F5
Legendre I. *Australia* **92** D2
Leghorn = Livorno *Italy* **40** E7
Legionowo *Poland* **31** F7
Legnago *Italy* **41** C8
Legnano *Italy* **40** C5
Legnica *Poland* **31** G3
Legrad *Croatia* **41** B13
Leh *India* **69** B7
Lehigh Acres *U.S.A.* **117** H14
Lehighton *U.S.A.* **115** F9
Lehliu *Romania* **29** F11
Leho *Sudan* **81** F3
Lehrte *Germany* **24** C5
Lehututu *Botswana* **88** C3
Lei Shui → *China* **59** D9
Leiah *Pakistan* **68** D4
Leibnitz *Austria* **26** E8
Leibo *China* **58** C4
Leicester *U.K.* **15** E6
Leicester City □ *U.K.* **15** E6
Leicestershire □ *U.K.* **15** E6
Leichhardt → *Australia* **94** B2
Leichhardt Ra. *Australia* **94** C4
Leiden *Neths.* **17** B4
Leie → *Belgium* **17** C3
Leifers = Láives *Italy* **41** B8
Leimen *Germany* **25** F4
Leimus *Nic.* **120** D3
Leine → *Germany* **24** C5
Leinefelde *Germany* **24** D6
Leinster *Australia* **93** E3
Leinster □ *Ireland* **12** C4
Leinster, Mt. *Ireland* **12** D5
Leipalingis *Lithuania* **30** D10
Leipzig *Germany* **24** D8
Leiria *Portugal* **36** F2
Leiria □ *Portugal* **36** F2
Leirvik *Norway* **9** G11
Leishan *China* **58** D7
Leisler, Mt. *Australia* **92** D4
Leith *U.K.* **13** F5
Leith Hill *U.K.* **15** F7
Leitha → *Europe* **27** D10
Leitir Ceanainn = Letterkenny *Ireland* **12** B4
Leitrim *Ireland* **12** B4
Leitrim □ *Ireland* **12** B4
Leitza *Spain* **38** B3
Leiyang *China* **59** D9
Leizhou *China* **59** G8
Leizhou Bandao *China* **58** G7
Leizhou Wan *China* **59** G8
Lek → *Neths.* **17** C4
Leka *Norway* **8** D14
Lekani *Greece* **45** E8

Lekbibaj *Albania* **44** D3
Lekeitio *Spain* **38** B2
Lekki Lagoon *Nigeria* **83** D5
Leksand *Sweden* **10** D9
Leland *Mich., U.S.A.* **113** C11
Leland *Miss., U.S.A.* **117** E9
Lelång *Sweden* **10** E6
Leleque *Argentina* **128** E2
Lélouma *Guinea* **82** C2
Lelystad *Neths.* **17** B5
Lem *Denmark* **11** H2
Lema *Nigeria* **83** C5
Lema Shilindi *Ethiopia* **81** G5
Lemera *Dem. Rep. of the Congo* **86** C2
Lemery *Phil.* **61** E4
Lemhi Ra. *U.S.A.* **108** D7
Lemmer *Neths.* **17** B5
Lemmon *U.S.A.* **112** C2
Lemon Grove *U.S.A.* **111** N9
Lemoore *U.S.A.* **110** J7
Lempdes *France* **20** C7
Lemvig *Denmark* **11** H2
Lena → *Russia* **53** B13
Lenadoon Pt. *Ireland* **12** B2
Lenart *Slovenia* **41** B12
Lenartovce *Slovak Rep.* **27** C13
Lencloître *France* **18** F7
Lendava *Slovenia* **41** B13
Lendinara *Italy* **41** C8
Lengerich *Germany* **24** C3
Lenggong *Malaysia* **65** K3
Lenggries *Germany* **25** H7
Lengshuijiang *China* **59** D8
Lengshuitan *China* **59** D8
Lengua de Vaca, Pta. *Chile* **126** C1
Lengwe △ *Malawi* **87** F3
Lengyeltóti *Hungary* **28** D2
Lenhovda *Sweden* **11** G9
Lenina, Kanal → *Russia* **35** J7
Leningrad □ *Russia* **32** C7
Leningorsk *Kazakhstan* **52** D9
Lenino *Ukraine* **33** K8
Leninsk *Russia* **35** F7
Leninsk-Kuznetskiy *Russia* **52** D9
Leninskoye *Russia* **34** A8
Lenk *Switz.* **25** J3
Lenkoran = Länkäran *Azerbaijan* **73** C13
Lenmalu *Indonesia* **63** E8
Lenne → *Germany* **24** D3
Lennestadt *Germany* **24** D4
Lennox *U.S.A.* **112** D5
Lennoxville *Canada* **115** A13
Leno *Italy* **40** C7
Lenoir *U.S.A.* **117** D14
Lenoir City *U.S.A.* **117** D12
Lenore L. *Canada* **103** C8
Lenox *U.S.A.* **115** D11
Lens *France* **19** B9
Lensahn *Germany* **24** A6
Lensk *Russia* **53** C12
Lentas *Greece* **49** E6
Lentekhi *Georgia* **35** J6
Lenti *Hungary* **28** D1
Lentini *Italy* **43** E8
Lenwood *U.S.A.* **111** L9
Lenya *Burma* **65** G2
Lenzen *Germany* **24** B7
Léo *Burkina Faso* **82** C4
Leoben *Austria* **26** D8
Leodhas = Lewis *U.K.* **13** C2
Leola *U.S.A.* **112** C4
Leominster *U.K.* **15** E5
Leominster *U.S.A.* **115** D13
Léon *France* **20** E2
León *Mexico* **118** C4
León *Nic.* **120** D2
León *Spain* **36** C5
León □ *Spain* **36** C5
León → *U.S.A.* **116** F6
León, Montes de *Spain* **36** C4
Leonardo da Vinci, Roma ✈ (FCO) *Italy* **41** G9
Leonardtown *U.S.A.* **113** F15
Leonardville *Namibia* **88** C2
Leonberg *Germany* **25** G5
Leonding *Austria* **26** C7
Leone, *Amer. Samoa* **91** b
Leonessa *Italy* **41** F9
Leonforte *Italy* **43** E7
Leonidio *Greece* **46** D4
Leonora *Australia* **93** E3
Leopoldina *Brazil* **127** A7
Leopoldsburg *Belgium* **17** C5
Leoti *U.S.A.* **112** F3
Leova *Moldova* **29** D13
Leoville *Canada* **103** C7
Lepe *Spain* **37** H3
Lepel = Lyepyel *Belarus* **32** E5
Lepenou *Greece* **46** C3
Leping *China* **59** C11
Lépo, L. do *Angola* **88** B2

Lepontine, Alpi *Italy* **40** B5
Leposavić *Kosovo* **44** C4
Leppävirta *Finland* **8** E22
Lepsény *Hungary* **28** D3
Leptis Magna *Libya* **79** B8
Lequeitio = Lekeitio *Spain* **38** B2
Lercara Friddi *Italy* **42** E6
Léré *Chad* **83** D7
Léré *Mali* **82** B4
Lere *Bauchi, Nigeria* **83** D6
Lere *Kaduna, Nigeria* **83** C6
Leribe *Lesotho* **89** D4
Lérici *Italy* **40** D6
Lérida = Lleida *Spain* **38** D5
Lérins, Îs. de *France* **21** E11
Lerma *Spain* **36** C7
Leros *Greece* **47** D8
Lérouville *France* **19** D12
Lerum *Sweden* **11** G6
Lerwick *U.K.* **13** A7
Leş *Romania* **28** D6
Les Abrets *France* **21** C9
Les Andelys *France* **18** C8
Les Borges Blanques *Spain* **38** D5
Les Cayes *Haiti* **121** C5
Les Coteaux *Canada* **115** A10
Les Escoumins *Canada* **105** C6
Les Essarts *France* **18** F5
Les Herbiers *France* **18** F5
Les Minquiers, Plateau des *Chan. Is.* **18** D4
Les Pieux *France* **18** C5
Les Ponts-de-Cé *France* **18** E6
Les Riceys *France* **19** E11
Les Sables-d'Olonne *France* **20** B2
Les Vans *France* **21** D8
Lesbos *Greece* **47** B8
L'Escala *Spain* **38** C8
Leshan *China* **58** C4
Leshwe △ *Dem. Rep. of the Congo* **87** E2
Lésina *Italy* **41** G12
Lésina, L. di *Italy* **41** G12
Lesjöfors *Sweden* **10** E8
Lesko *Poland* **31** J9
Leskov I. *Antarctica* **5** B1
Leskovac *Serbia* **44** C5
Leskovik *Albania* **44** F4
Leśna *Poland* **31** G2
Lesneven *France* **18** D2
Leśnica *Poland* **31** H5
Lesnoye *Russia* **32** C8
Lesopilnoye *Russia* **54** A7
Lesotho ■ *Africa* **89** D4
Lesozavodsk *Russia* **54** B6
Lesparre-Médoc *France* **20** C3
L'Espluga de Francolí *Spain* **38** D6
Lessay *France* **18** C5
Lesse → *Belgium* **17** D4
Lesse et Lomme △ *Belgium* **17** D5
Lessebo *Sweden* **11** H9
Lesser Antilles *W. Indies* **121** C7
Lesser Slave L. *Canada* **102** B5
Lesser Sunda Is. *Indonesia* **63** F6
Lessines *Belgium* **17** D3
Lester B. Pearson Int., Toronto ✈ (YYZ) *Canada* **114** C5
Lestock *Canada* **103** C8
Lesuer I. *Australia* **92** B4
Lesueur △ *Australia* **93** F2
Lésvos = Lesbos *Greece* **47** B8
Leszno *Poland* **31** G3
Letaba *S. Africa* **89** C5
Letälven → *Sweden* **10** E8
Letävértes *Hungary* **28** C6
Letchworth *U.K.* **15** F7
Letea, Ostrov *Romania* **29** E14
Lethbridge *Canada* **102** D6
Lethem *Guyana* **124** C7
Leti, Kepulauan *Indonesia* **63** F7
Leti Is. = Leti, Kepulauan *Indonesia* **63** F7
Letiahau → *Botswana* **88** C3
Leticia *Colombia* **124** D5
Leting *China* **57** E10
Letjiesbos *S. Africa* **88** E3
Letlhakane *Botswana* **88** C4
Letlhakeng *Botswana* **88** C3
Letpadan *Burma* **67** L19
Letpan *Burma* **67** K19
Letsôk-aw Kyun *Burma* **65** G2
Letterkenny *Ireland* **12** B4
Leu *Romania* **29** F9
Leucadia *U.S.A.* **111** M9
Leucate *France* **20** F7
Leucate, Étang de *France* **20** F7
Leuchars *U.K.* **13** E6
Leuk *Switz.* **25** J3
Leuşeni *Moldova* **29** D13
Leuser, G. *Indonesia* **62** D1
Leutkirch *Germany* **25** H6
Leuven *Belgium* **17** D4
Leuze-en-Hainaut *Belgium* **17** D3
Lev Tolstoy *Russia* **32** F10
Levan *Albania* **44** F3
Levanger *Norway* **8** E14
Levant, Î. du *France* **21** E10
Levanto *Italy* **40** D6

Lévanzo *Italy* **42** D5
Levelland *U.S.A.* **116** E3
Leven *U.K.* **13** E6
Leven, L. *U.K.* **13** E5
Leven, Toraka *Madag.* **89** A8
Leveque C. *Australia* **92** C3
Leverano *Italy* **43** B10
Leverkusen *Germany* **24** D3
Levice *Slovak Rep.* **27** C11
Lévico Terme *Italy* **41** C8
Levie *France* **21** G13
Levier *France* **19** F13
Levin *N.Z.* **91** D5
Lévis *Canada* **105** C5
Levis, L. *Canada* **102** A5
Levitha *Greece* **47** D8
Levittown *N.Y., U.S.A.* **115** F11
Levittown *Pa., U.S.A.* **115** F10
Levka *Bulgaria* **45** E10
Levka Oros *Greece* **49** D6
Levkada □ *Greece* **46** C2
Levkás = Lefkada *Greece* **46** C2
Levkôsia = Nicosia *Cyprus* **49** D12
Levoča *Slovak Rep.* **27** B13
Levroux *France* **19** F8
Levski *Bulgaria* **45** C9
Levskigrad = Karlovo
   Bulgaria **45** D8
Levuka *Fiji* **91** a
Lewes *U.K.* **15** G8
Lewes *U.S.A.* **113** F16
Lewin Brzeski *Poland* **31** H4
Lewis *U.K.* **13** C2
Lewis → *U.S.A.* **110** E4
Lewis, Butt of *U.K.* **13** C2
Lewis and Clark △ *U.S.A.* **110** D3
Lewis Ra. *Australia* **92** D4
Lewis Range *U.S.A.* **108** B7
Lewis Run *U.S.A.* **114** E6
Lewisburg *Pa., U.S.A.* **114** F8
Lewisburg *Tenn., U.S.A.* **117** D11
Lewisburg *W. Va., U.S.A.* **113** G13
Lewisporte *Canada* **105** C8
Lewiston *Idaho, U.S.A.* **108** C5
Lewiston *Maine, U.S.A.* **113** C18
Lewiston *N.Y., U.S.A.* **114** C5
Lewistown *Mont., U.S.A.* **108** C9
Lewistown *Pa., U.S.A.* **114** F7
Lexington *Ill., U.S.A.* **112** E9
Lexington *Ky., U.S.A.* **113** F11
Lexington *Mich., U.S.A.* **114** C2
Lexington *Mo., U.S.A.* **112** F7
Lexington *N.C., U.S.A.* **117** D14
Lexington *N.Y., U.S.A.* **115** D10
Lexington *Nebr., U.S.A.* **112** E4
Lexington *Ohio, U.S.A.* **114** F2
Lexington *Tenn., U.S.A.* **117** D10
Lexington *Va., U.S.A.* **113** G14
Lexington Park *U.S.A.* **113** F15
Leyburn *U.K.* **14** C6
Leye *China* **58** E6
Leyland *U.K.* **14** D5
Leyre → *France* **20** D2
Leyte □ *Phil.* **61** F6
Leyte Gulf *Phil.* **61** F6
Leżajsk *Poland* **31** H9
Lezay *France* **20** B3
Lezhë *Albania* **44** E3
Lezhi *China* **58** B5
Lézignan-Corbières *France* **20** E6
Lezoux *France* **20** C7
Lgov *Russia* **33** G8
Lhasa *China* **60** D4
Lhazê *China* **60** D3
L'Hermite, I. *Chile* **128** H3
Lhokkruet *Indonesia* **62** C1
Lhokseumawe *Indonesia* **62** C1
L'Hospitalet de Llobregat
   Spain **38** D7
Li *Thailand* **64** D2
Li Jiang → *China* **59** E8
Li Shui → *China* **59** C9
Li Xian *Gansu, China* **56** G3
Li Xian *Hebei, China* **56** E8
Li Xian *Hunan, China* **59** C8
Liadi *Greece* **47** E8
Liancheng *China* **59** E11
Liancourt Rocks = Tokdo
   Asia **55** F5
Lianga *Phil.* **61** G7
Liangcheng
   Nei Monggol Zizhiqu, China **56** D7
Liangcheng *Shandong, China* **57** G10
Liangdang *China* **56** H4
Lianghe *China* **58** E2
Lianghekou *China* **58** C7
Liangping *China* **58** B6
Liangpran *Indonesia* **62** D4
Lianhua *China* **59** D9
Lianjiang *Fujian, China* **59** D12
Lianjiang *Guangdong, China* **59** G8
Lianping *China* **59** E10
Lianshan *China* **59** E9
Lianshanguan *China* **57** D12
Lianshui *China* **57** H10
Lianyuan *China* **59** D8
Lianyungang *China* **57** G10
Lianzhou *China* **59** E9
Liao He → *China* **57** D11

Liaocheng *China* **56** F8
Liaodong Bandao *China* **57** E12
Liaodong Wan *China* **57** D11
Liaoning □ *China* **57** D12
Liaotung, G. of = Liaodong
   Wan *China* **57** D11
Liaoyang *China* **57** D12
Liaoyuan *China* **57** C13
Liaozhong *China* **57** D12
Liapades *Greece* **49** A3
Liard → *Canada* **102** A4
Liard River *Canada* **102** B3
Liari *Pakistan* **68** G2
Libau = Liepāja *Latvia* **30** B8
Libby *U.S.A.* **108** B6
Libenge *Dem. Rep. of the Congo* **84** D3
Liberal *U.S.A.* **112** G3
Liberec *Czech Rep.* **26** A8
Liberecký □ *Czech Rep.* **26** A8
Liberia *Costa Rica* **120** D2
Liberia ■ *W. Afr.* **82** D3
Libertador □ *Chile* **126** C1
Liberty *Mo., U.S.A.* **112** F6
Liberty *N.Y., U.S.A.* **115** E10
Liberty *Pa., U.S.A.* **114** E7
Liberty *Tex., U.S.A.* **116** F7
Liberty-Newark Int. ✈
   (EWR) *U.S.A.* **115** F10
Libiąż *Poland* **31** H6
Libîya, Sahrâ' *Africa* **79** C10
Libo *China* **58** E6
Libobo, Tanjung *Indonesia* **63** E7
Libode *S. Africa* **89** E4
Libong, Ko *Thailand* **65** J2
Libourne *France* **20** D3
Libramont *Belgium* **17** E5
Librazhd *Albania* **44** E4
Libreville *Gabon* **84** D1
Libya ■ *N. Afr.* **79** C9
Libyan Desert = Libîya,
   Sahrâ' *Africa* **79** C10
Libyan Plateau = Ed Déffa
   Egypt **80** A2
Licantén *Chile* **126** D1
Licata *Italy* **42** E6
Lice *Turkey* **73** C9
Licheng *China* **56** F7
Lichfield *U.K.* **15** E6
Lichinga *Mozam.* **87** E4
Lichtenburg *S. Africa* **88** D4
Lichtenfels *Germany* **25** E7
Lichuan *Hubei, China* **58** B7
Lichuan *Jiangxi, China* **59** D11
Licking → *U.S.A.* **113** F11
Licosa, Punta *Italy* **43** B7
Licungo → *Mozam.* **87** F4
Lida *Belarus* **23** B13
Liden *Sweden* **10** B10
Lidhult *Sweden* **11** H7
Lidköping *Sweden* **11** F7
Lido *Italy* **41** C9
Lido *Niger* **83** C5
Lido di Roma = Óstia, Lido
   di *Italy* **41** G9
Lidoriki *Greece* **46** C4
Lidzbark *Poland* **31** E6
Lidzbark Warmiński *Poland* **30** D7
Liebenwalde *Germany* **24** C9
Lieberose *Germany* **24** D10
Liebig, Mt. *Australia* **92** D5
Liebling *Romania* **28** E6
Liechtenstein ■ *Europe* **25** H5
Liège *Belgium* **17** D5
Liège □ *Belgium* **17** D5
Liegnitz = Legnica *Poland* **31** G3
Lieksa *Finland* **8** E24
Lienart *Dem. Rep. of the Congo* **86** B2
Lienyünchiangshih =
   Lianyungang *China* **57** G10
Lienz *Austria* **26** E5
Liepāja *Latvia* **30** B8
Liepāja □ *Latvia* **30** B8
Liepājas ezers *Latvia* **30** B8
Lier *Belgium* **17** C4
Liernais *France* **19** E11
Liești *Romania* **29** E12
Lietuva = Lithuania ■
   Europe **32** E2
Liévin *France* **19** B9
Lièvre → *Canada* **104** C4
Liezen *Austria* **26** D7
Liffey → *Ireland* **12** C5
Lifford *Ireland* **12** B4
Liffré *France* **18** D5
Ligao *Phil.* **61** E5
Lightning Ridge *Australia* **95** D4
Lignano Sabbiadoro *Italy* **41** C10
Ligny-en-Barrois *France* **19** D12
Ligonha → *Mozam.* **87** F4
Ligonier *U.S.A.* **114** F5
Ligourio *Greece* **46** D5
Liguell *France* **18** E7
Liguria □ *Italy* **40** D5
Ligurian Sea *Medit. S.* **40** E5
Lihou Reefs and Cays
   Australia **94** B5
Lihué Calel △ *Argentina* **126** D2

Lijiang *China* **58** D3
Likasi *Dem. Rep. of the Congo* **87** E2
Likenäs *Sweden* **10** D7
Likhoslavl *Russia* **32** D8
Likhovskoy *Russia* **33** H11
Likoma I. *Malawi* **87** E3
Likumburu *Tanzania* **87** D4
L'Île-Bouchard *France* **18** E7
L'Île-Rousse *France* **21** F12
Liling *China* **59** D9
Lilla Edet *Sweden* **11** F6
Lille *France* **19** B10
Lille Bælt *Denmark* **11** J3
Lillebonne *France* **18** C7
Lillehammer *Norway* **8** F14
Lillesand *Norway* **9** G13
Lillhärdal *Sweden* **10** C8
Lillian Pt. *Australia* **93** E4
Lillo *Spain* **36** F7
Lillooet *Canada* **102** C4
Lillooet → *Canada* **102** D4
Lilongwe *Malawi* **87** E3
Liloy *Phil.* **63** C6
Lim → *Europe* **44** C3
Lim Chu Kang *Singapore* **65** d
Lima *Indonesia* **63** E7
Lima *Peru* **124** F3
Lima *Mont., U.S.A.* **108** D7
Lima *N.Y., U.S.A.* **114** D7
Lima *Ohio, U.S.A.* **113** E11
Lima → *Portugal* **36** D2
Liman *Indonesia* **63** G14
Liman *Russia* **35** H8
Limanowa *Poland* **31** J7
Limassol = Lemesós *Cyprus* **49** E12
Limavady *U.K.* **12** A5
Limay → *Argentina* **128** D3
Limay Mahuida *Argentina* **126** D2
Limbach-Oberfrohna
   Germany **24** E8
Limbang *Brunei* **62** D5
Limbara, Mte. *Italy* **42** B2
Limbaži *Latvia* **32** C3
Limbdi *India* **68** H4
Limbe *Cameroon* **83** E6
Limburg *Germany* **25** E4
Limburg □ *Belgium* **17** C5
Limburg □ *Neths.* **17** C5
Limedsforsen *Sweden* **10** D7
Limeira *Brazil* **127** A6
Limenaria *Greece* **45** F8
Limenas Chersonisou *Greece* **47** F7
Limeira = Lima → *Portugal* **36** D2
Limerick *Ireland* **12** D3
Limerick *U.S.A.* **115** C14
Limerick □ *Ireland* **12** D3
Limestone *U.S.A.* **114** D6
Limestone → *Canada* **103** B10
Limfjorden *Denmark* **11** H3
Limia = Lima → *Portugal* **36** D2
Limingen *Norway* **8** D15
Limmared *Sweden* **11** G7
Limmen Bight *Australia* **94** A2
Limmen Bight → *Australia* **94** B2
Limmen ۞ *Australia* **94** B2
Limni *Greece* **46** C5
Limnos *Greece* **47** B7
Limoges *Canada* **115** A9
Limoges *France* **20** C5
Limón *Costa Rica* **120** E3
Limon *U.S.A.* **108** G12
Limone Piemonte *Italy* **40** D4
Limousin □ *France* **20** C5
Limousin, Plateaux du
   France **20** C5
Limoux *France* **20** E6
Limpopo → *S. Africa* **89** C4
Limpopo □ *Africa* **89** D5
Limuru *Kenya* **86** C4
Lin Xian *China* **56** F6
Lin'an *China* **59** B12
Linapacan I. *Phil.* **61** F3
Linapacan Str. *Phil.* **61** F3
Linares *Chile* **126** D1
Linares *Mexico* **119** C5
Linares *Spain* **37** G7
Linaria *Greece* **46** C6
Linaro, Capo *Italy* **41** F8
Lincang *China* **58** F3
Lincheng *China* **56** F8
Linchuan *China* **59** D11
Lincoln = Beamsville
   Canada **114** C5
Lincoln *N.Z.* **91** E4
Lincoln *U.K.* **14** D7
Lincoln *Calif., U.S.A.* **110** G5
Lincoln *Ill., U.S.A.* **112** E9
Lincoln *Kans., U.S.A.* **112** F4
Lincoln *Maine, U.S.A.* **113** C19
Lincoln *N.H., U.S.A.* **115** B13
Lincoln *N. Mex., U.S.A.* **109** K11
Lincoln *Nebr., U.S.A.* **112** E6
Lincoln City *U.S.A.* **108** D1
Lincoln Hav = Lincoln Sea
   Arctic **101** A21
Lincoln Sea *Arctic* **101** A21
Lincolnshire □ *U.K.* **14** D7

Lincolnshire Wolds *U.K.* **14** D7
Lincolnton *U.S.A.* **117** D14
Lind *U.S.A.* **108** C4
Linda *U.S.A.* **110** F5
Lindau *Germany* **25** H5
Lindeman I. *Australia* **94** b
Lindeman Islands △ *Australia* **94** b
Linden *Guyana* **124** B7
Linden *Ala., U.S.A.* **117** E11
Linden *Calif., U.S.A.* **110** G5
Linden *Tex., U.S.A.* **116** E7
Lindenhurst *U.S.A.* **115** F11
Lindesberg *Sweden* **10** E9
Lindesnes *Norway* **9** H12
Lindi *Tanzania* **87** D4
Lindi □ *Tanzania* **87** D4
Lindi → *Dem. Rep. of the Congo* **86** B2
Lindley *U.S.A.* **114** D7
Lindö *Sweden* **11** F10
Lindome *Sweden* **11** G6
Lindos *Greece* **49** C10
Lindoso, Akra *Greece* **49** C10
Lindoso *Portugal* **36** D2
Lindow *Germany* **24** C8
Lindsay *Canada* **114** B6
Lindsay *Calif., U.S.A.* **110** J7
Lindsay *Okla., U.S.A.* **116** D6
Lindsborg *U.S.A.* **112** F5
Lindsdal *Sweden* **11** H10
Line Islands *Pac. Oc.* **97** H12
Linesville *U.S.A.* **114** E4
Linfen *China* **56** F6
Ling Xian *Hunan, China* **59** D9
Ling Xian *Shandong, China* **56** F9
Lingao *China* **64** C7
Lingayen *Phil.* **63** A6
Lingayen G. *Phil.* **61** C4
Lingbi *China* **57** H9
Lingbo *Sweden* **10** C10
Lingchuan
   Guangxi Zhuangzu, China **59** E8
Lingchuan *Shanxi, China* **56** G7
Lingen *Germany* **24** C3
Lingga *Indonesia* **62** E2
Lingga, Kepulauan *Indonesia* **62** E2
Lingga Arch. = Lingga,
   Kepulauan *Indonesia* **62** E2
Linghem *Sweden* **11** F9
Lingle *U.S.A.* **108** E11
Lingling *China* **59** D8
Lingqiu *China* **56** E8
Lingshan *China* **58** F7
Lingshi *China* **56** F6
Lingshou *China* **56** E8
Lingshui *China* **64** C8
Lingtai *China* **56** G4
Linguère *Senegal* **82** B1
Lingui *China* **59** E8
Lingwu *China* **56** E4
Lingyuan *China* **57** D10
Lingyun *China* **58** E6
Linhai *China* **59** C13
Linhares *Brazil* **125** G10
Linhe *China* **56** D4
Linjiang *China* **57** D14
Linköping *Sweden* **11** F9
Linkou *China* **57** B16
Linli *China* **59** C8
Linnhe, L. *U.K.* **13** E3
Linqi *China* **56** G7
Linqing *China* **56** F8
Linqu *China* **57** F10
Linru *China* **56** G7
Lins *Brazil* **127** A6
Linshui *China* **58** B6
Linstead *Jamaica* **120** a
Linta → *Madag.* **89** D7
Linth → *Switz.* **25** H5
Linthal *Switz.* **25** J5
Linton *Ind., U.S.A.* **112** F10
Linton *N. Dak., U.S.A.* **112** B3
Lintong *China* **56** G5
Linwood *Canada* **114** C4
Linwu *China* **59** E9
Linxi *China* **57** C10
Linxia *China* **60** C5
Linxiang *China* **59** C9
Linyanti → *Africa* **88** B4
Linyi *China* **57** G10
Linz *Austria* **26** C7
Linz *Germany* **24** E3
Linzhenzhen *China* **56** F5
Linzi *China* **57** F10
Lion, G. du *France* **20** E7
Lionárisso *Cyprus* **49** D13
Lioni *Italy* **43** B8
Lions, G. of = Lion, G. du
   France **20** E7
Lion's Den *Zimbabwe* **87** F3
Lion's Head *Canada* **114** B3
Liozno = Lyozna *Belarus* **32** E6
Lipa *Phil.* **61** E4
Lipali *Mozam.* **87** F4
Lípari *Italy* **43** D7
Lípari, I. *Italy* **43** D7
Lípari, Is. = Eólie, Ís. *Italy* **43** D7
Lipcani *Moldova* **29** B11
Liperi *Finland* **8** E23
Lipetsk *Russia* **33** F10

Lipetsk □ *Russia* **34** D4
Lipiany *Poland* **31** E1
Liping *China* **58** D7
Lipisi *Greece* **47** D8
Lipkany = Lipcani *Moldova* **29** B11
Lipljan *Kosovo* **44** D5
Lipník nad Bečvou
   Czech Rep. **27** B10
Lipno *Poland* **31** F6
Lipova *Romania* **28** D6
Lipovets *Ukraine* **23** D15
Lippe → *Germany* **24** D2
Lippstadt *Germany* **24** D4
Lipscomb *U.S.A.* **116** C4
Lipsk *Poland* **30** E10
Liptovský Hrádok
   Slovak Rep. **27** B12
Liptovský Mikuláš
   Slovak Rep. **27** B12
Liptrap, C. *Australia* **95** F4
Lipu *China* **59** E8
Lira *Uganda* **86** B3
Liri → *Italy* **42** A6
Liria = Lliria *Spain* **39** F4
Lisala *Dem. Rep. of the Congo* **84** D4
Lisboa *Portugal* **37** G1
Lisboa □ *Portugal* **37** F1
Lisboa ✈ (LIS) *Portugal* **37** G1
Lisbon = Lisboa *Portugal* **37** G1
Lisbon *N. Dak., U.S.A.* **112** B5
Lisbon *N.H., U.S.A.* **115** B13
Lisbon *N.Y., U.S.A.* **115** B9
Lisbon *Ohio, U.S.A.* **114** F4
Lisbon Falls *U.S.A.* **113** D18
Lisburn *U.K.* **12** B5
Lisburne, C. *U.S.A.* **106** B6
Liscannor B. *Ireland* **12** D2
Liscia → *Italy* **42** A2
Lisdoonvarna *Ireland* **12** C2
Lishe Jiang → *China* **58** E3
Lishi *China* **56** F6
Lishu *China* **57** C13
Lishui *Jiangsu, China* **59** B12
Lishui *Zhejiang, China* **59** C12
Lisianski I. *U.S.A.* **107** K5
Lisichansk = Lysychansk
   Ukraine **33** H10
Lisieux *France* **18** C7
Liski *Russia* **33** G10
L'Isle-Jourdain *Gers, France* **20** E5
L'Isle-Jourdain *Vienne, France* **20** B4
L'Isle-sur-la-Sorgue *France* **21** E9
Lisle-sur-Tarn *France* **20** E5
Lismore *Australia* **95** D5
Lismore *Ireland* **12** D4
Lissos → *Greece* **45** E9
Lista *Norway* **9** G12
Lister, Mt. *Antarctica* **5** D11
Liston *Australia* **95** D5
Listowel *Canada* **114** C4
Listowel *Ireland* **12** D2
Lit *Sweden* **10** A8
Lit-et-Mixe *France* **20** D2
Litang *Guangxi Zhuangzu,
   China* **58** F7
Litang *Sichuan, China* **58** B3
Litang Qu → *China* **58** C3
Litani → *Lebanon* **74** B4
Litchfield *Calif., U.S.A.* **110** E6
Litchfield *Conn., U.S.A.* **115** E11
Litchfield *Ill., U.S.A.* **112** F9
Litchfield *Minn., U.S.A.* **112** C6
Litchfield △ *Australia* **92** B5
Liteni *Romania* **29** C11
Lithgow *Australia* **95** E5
Lithino, Akra *Greece* **49** E6
Lithuania ■ *Europe* **32** E2
Litija *Slovenia* **41** B11
Lititz *U.S.A.* **115** F8
Litochoro *Greece* **44** F6
Litoměřice *Czech Rep.* **26** A7
Litomyšl *Czech Rep.* **27** B9
Litschau *Austria* **26** C8
Little Abaco *Bahamas* **120** A4
Little Barrier I. *N.Z.* **91** B5
Little Belt Mts. *U.S.A.* **108** C8
Little Bighorn Battlefield △
   U.S.A. **108** D10
Little Blue → *U.S.A.* **112** F5
Little Buffalo → *Canada* **102** A6
Little Cayman *Cayman Is.* **120** C3
Little Churchill → *Canada* **103** B9
Little Colorado → *U.S.A.* **109** H8
Little Current *Canada* **104** C3
Little Current → *Canada* **104** B3
Little Diomede I. *U.S.A.* **106** B6
Little Falls *Minn., U.S.A.* **112** C6
Little Falls *N.Y., U.S.A.* **115** C10
Little Fork → *U.S.A.* **112** A7
Little Grand Rapids *Canada* **103** C9
Little Humboldt → *U.S.A.* **108** F5
Little Inagua I. *Bahamas* **121** B5
Little Karoo *S. Africa* **88** E3
Little Khingan Mts. = Xiao
   Hinggan Ling *China* **60** B7
Little Lake *U.S.A.* **111** K9
Little Laut Is. = Laut Kecil,
   Kepulauan *Indonesia* **62** E5

Little Mecatina =
   Petit-Mécatina → *Canada* **105** B8
Little Minch *U.K.* **13** D2
Little Missouri → *U.S.A.* **112** B2
Little Ouse → *U.K.* **15** E9
Little Rann *India* **68** H4
Little Red → *U.S.A.* **116** D9
Little River *N.Z.* **91** E4
Little Rock *U.S.A.* **116** D8
Little Ruaha → *Tanzania* **86** D4
Little Sable Pt. *U.S.A.* **112** D10
Little Scarcies → *S. Leone* **82** D2
Little Sioux → *U.S.A.* **112** E5
Little Smoky → *Canada* **102** C5
Little Snake → *U.S.A.* **108** F9
Little Tobago *Trin. & Tob.* **125** J16
Little Valley *U.S.A.* **114** D6
Little Wabash → *U.S.A.* **112** G9
Little White → *U.S.A.* **112** D3
Little Zab = Zâb aş
   Şaghîr → *Iraq* **73** E10
Littlefield *U.S.A.* **116** E3
Littlehampton *U.K.* **15** G7
Littleton *U.S.A.* **115** B13
Littoral □ *Cameroon* **83** E7
Litvínov *Czech Rep.* **26** A6
Liu He → *China* **57** D11
Liu Jiang → *China* **58** F7
Liuba *China* **56** H4
Liucheng *China* **58** E7
Liugou *China* **57** D10
Liuhe *China* **57** C13
Liuheng Dao *China* **59** C14
Liujiang *China* **58** E7
Liukang Tenggaja =
   Sabalana, Kepulauan
   Indonesia **63** F5
Liuli *Tanzania* **87** E3
Liupanshui *China* **58** D5
Liuwa Plain *Zambia* **85** G4
Liuyang *China* **59** C9
Liuzhou *China* **58** E7
Liuzhuang *China* **57** H11
Livada *Romania* **28** C8
Livadero *Greece* **44** F5
Livadhia *Cyprus* **49** E12
Livadi *Greece* **46** A4
Livadia *Greece* **46** C4
Livarot *France* **18** D7
Live Oak *Calif., U.S.A.* **110** F5
Live Oak *Fla., U.S.A.* **117** F13
Lively *Canada* **113** B13
Liveras *Cyprus* **49** D11
Livermore *U.S.A.* **110** H5
Livermore, Mt. *U.S.A.* **116** F2
Livermore Falls *U.S.A.* **113** C18
Liverpool *Australia* **95** E5
Liverpool *Canada* **105** D7
Liverpool *U.K.* **14** D4
Liverpool *U.S.A.* **115** C8
Liverpool Bay *U.K.* **14** D4
Liverpool Ra. *Australia* **95** E5
Livigno *Italy* **40** B7
Livingston *Guatemala* **120** C2
Livingston *U.K.* **13** F5
Livingston *Ala., U.S.A.* **117** E10
Livingston *Calif., U.S.A.* **110** H6
Livingston *Mont., U.S.A.* **108** D8
Livingston *S.C., U.S.A.* **117** E14
Livingston *Tenn., U.S.A.* **117** C12
Livingston *Tex., U.S.A.* **116** F7
Livingston Manor *U.S.A.* **115** E10
Livingston, L. *U.S.A.* **116** F7
Livingstone *Zambia* **87** F2
Livingstone Mts. *Tanzania* **87** D3
Livingstonia *Malawi* **87** E3
Livno *Bos.-H.* **28** G2
Livny *Russia* **33** F9
Livonia *Mich., U.S.A.* **113** D12
Livonia *N.Y., U.S.A.* **114** D7
Livorno *Italy* **40** E7
Livradois-Forez □ *France* **20** C7
Livramento *Brazil* **127** C4
Livyntsi *Ukraine* **29** B11
Liwale *Tanzania* **87** D4
Liwiec → *Poland* **31** F8
Liwonde *Malawi* **87** F4
Liwonde △ *Malawi* **87** E4
Lixi *China* **58** D3
Lixian *China* **58** B4
Lixouri *Greece* **46** C2
Liyang *China* **59** B12
Lizard I. *Australia* **94** A4
Lizard Pt. *U.K.* **15** H2
Lizarra = Estella *Spain* **38** C2
Lizzano *Italy* **43** B10
Ljig *Serbia* **44** B4
Ljubija *Bos.-H.* **41** D13
Ljubinje *Bos.-H.* **44** D2
Ljubišnja *Europe* **44** C3
Ljubljana *Slovenia* **41** B11
Ljubljana ✈ (LJU) *Slovenia* **41** B11
Ljubno *Slovenia* **41** B11
Ljubovija *Serbia* **44** B3
Ljugarn *Sweden* **11** G12
Ljung *Sweden* **11** G7
Ljungan → *Sweden* **10** B11
Ljungaverk *Sweden* **10** B10

Ljungby *Sweden* **11** H7
Ljungbyholm *Sweden* **11** H10
Ljungdalen *Sweden* **10** B6
Ljungsbro *Sweden* **11** F9
Ljungskile *Sweden* **11** F5
Ljusdal *Sweden* **10** C10
Ljusfallshammar *Sweden* **11** F9
Ljusnan ➣ *Sweden* **10** C11
Ljusne *Sweden* **10** C11
Ljutomer *Slovenia* **41** B13
Llagostera *Spain* **38** D7
Llancanelo, Salina *Argentina* **126** D2
Llandeilo *U.K.* **15** F4
Llandovery *U.K.* **15** F4
Llandudno *U.K.* **14** D4
Llanelli *U.K.* **15** F3
Llanes *Spain* **36** B6
Llangollen *U.K.* **14** E4
Llanidloes *U.K.* **15** E4
Llano *U.S.A.* **116** F5
Llano ➣ *U.S.A.* **116** F5
Llano Estacado *U.S.A.* **116** E3
Llanos *S. Amer.* **124** C4
Llanos de Challe △ *Chile* **126** B1
Llanquihue, L. *Chile* **128** E1
Llanwrtyd Wells *U.K.* **15** E4
Llebeig, C. des *Spain* **48** B9
Lleida *Spain* **38** D5
Lleida □ *Spain* **38** C6
Llentrisca, C. *Spain* **48** C7
Llera de Canales *Mexico* **119** C5
Llerena *Spain* **37** G5
Lleyn Peninsula *U.K.* **14** E3
Llico *Chile* **126** C1
Lliria *Spain* **39** F4
Llívia *Spain* **20** F5
Llobregat ➣ *Spain* **38** D7
Llodio *Spain* **38** B2
Lloret de Mar *Spain* **38** D7
Lloseta *Spain* **48** B9
Lloyd B. *Australia* **94** A3
Lloyd L. *Canada* **103** B7
Lloydminster *Canada* **103** C7
Llubí *Spain* **48** B10
Llucena del Cid *Spain* **38** E4
Llucmajor *Spain* **48** B9
Llullaillaco, Volcán △ *S. Amer.* **126** A2
Llullaillaco △ *Chile* **126** A2
Lo ➣ *Vietnam* **64** B5
Loa *U.S.A.* **108** G8
Loa ➣ *Chile* **126** A1
Loaita I. *S. China Sea* **62** B4
Loange ➣
  Dem. Rep. of the Congo **84** E4
Loano *Italy* **40** D5
Lobatse *Botswana* **88** D4
Löbau *Germany* **24** D10
Lobenstein *Germany* **24** E7
Lobería *Argentina* **126** D4
Löberöd *Sweden* **11** J7
Łobez *Poland* **30** E2
Lobito *Angola* **85** G2
Lobo ➣ *Ivory C.* **82** D3
Lobos *Argentina* **126** D4
Lobos, I. *Mexico* **118** B3
Lobos, I. de *Canary Is.* **48** F6
Łobżenica *Poland* **31** E4
Loc Binh *Vietnam* **64** B6
Loc Ninh *Vietnam* **65** G6
Locarno *Switz.* **25** J4
Loch Baghasdail =
  Lochboisdale *U.K.* **13** D1
Loch Garman = Wexford
  Ireland **12** D5
Loch Lomond and the
  Trossachs △ *U.K.* **13** E4
Loch Nam Madadh =
  Lochmaddy *U.K.* **13** D1
Lochaber *U.K.* **13** E3
Locharbriggs *U.K.* **13** F5
Lochboisdale *U.K.* **13** D1
Loche, L. La *Canada* **103** B7
Lochem *Neths.* **17** B6
Loches *France* **18** E7
Lochgilphead *U.K.* **13** E3
Lochinvar △ *Zambia* **87** F2
Lochinver *U.K.* **13** C3
Lochmaddy *U.K.* **13** D1
Lochnagar *Australia* **94** C4
Lochnagar *U.K.* **13** E5
Łochów *Poland* **31** F8
Lochy, L. *U.K.* **13** E4
Lock *Australia* **95** E2
Lock Haven *U.S.A.* **114** E7
Lockeford *U.S.A.* **110** G5
Lockeport *Canada* **105** D6
Lockerbie *U.K.* **13** F5
Lockhart *U.S.A.* **116** G6
Lockhart, L. *Australia* **93** F2
Lockhart River *Australia* **94** A3
Lockhart River ◎ *Australia* **94** A3
Lockney *U.S.A.* **116** D4
Lockport *U.S.A.* **114** C6
Locminé *France* **18** E4
Locri *Italy* **43** D9
Locronan *France* **18** D2
Lod *Israel* **74** D3
Lodeinoye Pole *Russia* **32** B7

Lodève *France* **20** E7
Lodge Bay *Canada* **105** B8
Lodge Grass *U.S.A.* **108** D10
Lodhran *Pakistan* **68** E4
Lodi *Italy* **40** C6
Lodi *Calif., U.S.A.* **110** G5
Lodi *Ohio, U.S.A.* **114** E3
Lodja *Dem. Rep. of the Congo* **86** Cʳ
Lodosa *Spain* **38** C2
Lödöse *Sweden* **11** F6
Lodwar *Kenya* **86** B4
Łódź *Poland* **31** G6
Łódzkie □ *Poland* **31** G6
Loei *Thailand* **64** D3
Loengo *Dem. Rep. of the Congo* **86** C2
Loeriesfontein *S. Africa* **88** E2
Lofa ➣ *Liberia* **83** D2
Lofa Mano △ *Liberia* **82** D2
Lofer *Austria* **26** D5
Lofoten *Norway* **8** B16
Lofsdalen *Sweden* **10** B7
Lofsen ➣ *Sweden* **10** B7
Loftahammar *Sweden* **11** G10
Loga *Niger* **83** C5
Logan *Iowa, U.S.A.* **112** E6
Logan *Ohio, U.S.A.* **113** F12
Logan *Utah, U.S.A.* **108** F8
Logan *W. Va., U.S.A.* **113** G13
Logan, Mt. *Canada* **100** E1
Logandale *U.S.A.* **111** J12
Logansport *Ind., U.S.A.* **112** E10
Logansport *La., U.S.A.* **116** F8
Logirim *Sudan* **81** G3
Logo *Sudan* **81** F3
Logone ➣ *Chad* **79** F9
Logroño *Spain* **38** C2
Logrosán *Spain* **37** F5
Løgstør *Denmark* **11** H3
Løgumkloster *Denmark* **11** J2
Lohals *Denmark* **11** J4
Lohardaga *India* **69** H11
Loharia *India* **68** H6
Loharu *India* **68** E6
Lohja *Finland* **32** B3
Löhne *Germany* **24** C4
Lohr *Germany* **25** F5
Lohri Wah ➣ *Pakistan* **68** F2
Loi-kaw *Burma* **67** K20
Loimaa *Finland* **32** B2
Loir ➣ *France* **18** E6
Loir-et-Cher □ *France* **18** E8
Loire □ *France* **21** C8
Loire ➣ *France* **18** E4
Loire Anjou Touraine △
  France **18** E6
Loire-Atlantique □ *France* **18** E5
Loiret □ *France* **19** E9
Loitz *Germany* **24** B9
Loja *Ecuador* **124** D3
Loja *Spain* **37** H6
Loji = Kawasi *Indonesia* **63** E7
Lojo = Lohja *Finland* **32** B3
Løjt Kirkeby *Denmark* **11** J3
Lojung *China* **58** E7
Loka *Sudan* **81** G3
Lokandu
  Dem. Rep. of the Congo **86** C2
Lokeren *Belgium* **17** C3
Lokgwabe *Botswana* **88** C3
Lokhvitsa *Ukraine* **33** G7
Lokichar *Kenya* **86** B4
Lokichokio *Kenya* **86** B3
Lokitaung *Kenya* **86** B4
Løkken tekojärvi *Finland* **8** C22
Løkken *Denmark* **11** G3
Loknya *Russia* **32** D6
Loko *Nigeria* **83** D6
Lokoja *Nigeria* **83** D6
Lokolo ➣
  Dem. Rep. of the Congo **84** E3
Lokot *Russia* **33** F8
Lol *Sudan* **81** F2
Lol ➣ *Sudan* **81** F2
Lola *Guinea* **82** D3
Lola, Mt. *U.S.A.* **110** F6
Lolgorien *Kenya* **86** C3
Lolibai, Gebel *Sudan* **81** G3
Lolimi *Sudan* **81** G3
Loliondo *Tanzania* **86** C4
Lolland *Denmark* **11** K5
Lollar *Germany* **24** E4
Lolo *Tanzania* **86** C4
Lolodorf *Cameroon* **83** E7
Lom *Bulgaria* **44** C7
Lom ➣ *Bulgaria* **44** C7
Lom Kao *Thailand* **64** D3
Lom Sak *Thailand* **64** D3
Loma *U.S.A.* **108** C8
Loma Linda *U.S.A.* **111** L9
Loma Mansa *S. Leone* **82** D2
Loma Nts. *S. Leone* **82** D2
Lomaloma *Fiji* **91** a
Lomami ➣
  Dem. Rep. of the Congo **86** B1
Lomas de Zamora *Argentina* **126** C4
Lombadina *Australia* **92** C3
Lombárdia □ *Italy* **40** C6
Lombardy = Lombárdia □
  Italy **40** C6

Lombez *France* **20** E4
Lomblen *Indonesia* **63** F6
Lombok *Indonesia* **62** F5
Lombok, Selat *Indonesia* **63** K18
Lomé *Togo* **83** D5
Lomela *Dem. Rep. of the Congo* **84** E4
Lomela ➣
  Dem. Rep. of the Congo **84** E4
Lomianki *Poland* **31** F7
Lomma *Sweden* **11** J7
Lommel *Belgium* **17** C5
Lomond *Canada* **102** C6
Lomond, L. *U.K.* **13** E4
Lomonosov Ridge *Arctic* **4** A
Lomphat *Cambodia* **64** F6
Lompobatang *Indonesia* **63** F5
Lompoc *U.S.A.* **111** L6
Łomża *Poland* **31** E9
Lon, Ko *Thailand* **65** a
Loncoche *Chile* **128** D2
Londa *India* **66** M9
Londiani *Kenya* **86** C4
Londinières *France* **18** C8
London *Canada* **114** D3
London *U.K.* **15** F7
London *Ky., U.S.A.* **113** G11
London *Ohio, U.S.A.* **113** F12
London, Greater □ *U.K.* **15** F7
London Gatwick ✈ (LGW)
  U.K. **15** F7
London Heathrow ✈ (LHR)
  U.K. **15** F7
London Stansted ✈ (STN)
  U.K. **15** F8
Londonderry *U.K.* **12** B4
Londonderry □ *U.K.* **12** B4
Londonderry, C. *Australia* **92** B4
Londonderry, I. *Chile* **128** H2
Londres *Argentina* **128** B3
Londrina *Brazil* **127** A5
Lone Pine *U.S.A.* **110** J8
Lonely Mine *Zimbabwe* **89** B4
Long B. *U.S.A.* **117** E15
Long Beach *Calif., U.S.A.* **111** M8
Long Beach *N.Y., U.S.A.* **115** F11
Long Beach *Wash., U.S.A.* **110** D2
Long Branch *U.S.A.* **115** F11
Long Creek *U.S.A.* **108** D4
Long Eaton *U.K.* **14** E6
Long I. *Australia* **94** b
Long I. *Bahamas* **121** B4
Long I. *Canada* **104** B4
Long I. *Ireland* **12** E2
Long I. *U.S.A.* **115** F11
Long Island Sd. *U.S.A.* **115** E12
Long L. *Canada* **104** C2
Long L. *U.S.A.* **115** C10
Long Lake *U.S.A.* **115** C10
Long Point *Canada* **114** D4
Long Point B. *Canada* **114** D4
Long Prairie *U.S.A.* **112** C6
Long Prairie ➣ *U.S.A.* **112** B6
Long Pt. *Ont., Canada* **104** C5
Long Pt. *Ont., Canada* **115** C8
Long Range Mts. *Canada* **105** C8
Long Reef *Australia* **92** B4
Long Sault *Canada* **115** A10
Long Str. = Longa, Proliv
  Russia **53** C18
Long Thanh *Vietnam* **65** G6
Long Xian *China* **56** G4
Long Xuyen *Vietnam* **65** G5
Longa *Greece* **46** E3
Longa, Proliv *Russia* **53** C18
Long'an *China* **58** F6
Longarone *Italy* **41** B9
Longbenton *U.K.* **14** B6
Longboat Key *U.S.A.* **117** H13
Longchang *China* **58** C5
Longchi *China* **58** C4
Longchuan *Guangdong, China* **59** E10
Longchuan *Yunnan, China* **58** E1
Longde *China* **56** G4
Longeau *France* **19** E12
Longford *Australia* **95** G4
Longford *Ireland* **12** C4
Longford □ *Ireland* **12** C4
Longhai *China* **59** E11
Longhua *China* **57** D9
Longhui *China* **59** D8
Longido *Tanzania* **86** C4
Longiram *Indonesia* **62** E5
Longkou *Jiangxi, China* **59** D10
Longkou *Shandong, China* **57** F11
Longlac *Canada* **104** C2
Longli *China* **58** D6
Longlin *China* **58** E5
Longling *China* **58** E2
Longmeadow *U.S.A.* **115** D12
Longmen *China* **59** F10
Longming *China* **58** F5
Longmont *U.S.A.* **108** F11
Longnan *China* **59** E10
Longnawan *Indonesia* **62** D4
Longobucco *Italy* **43** C9
Longquan *China* **59** C12
Longreach *Australia* **94** C3
Longshan *China* **58** C7
Longsheng *China* **59** E8

Longué-Jumelles *France* **18** E6
Longueau *France* **19** C9
Longueuil *Canada* **115** A11
Longuyon *France* **19** C12
Longvic *France* **19** E12
Longview *Tex., U.S.A.* **116** E7
Longview *Wash., U.S.A.* **110** D4
Longwy *France* **19** C12
Longxi *China* **56** G3
Longyan *China* **59** E11
Longyearbyen *Svalbard* **4** B8
Longyou *China* **59** C12
Longzhou *China* **58** F6
Lonigo *Italy* **41** C8
Löningen *Germany* **24** C3
Lonja ➣ *Croatia* **41** C13
Lonoke *U.S.A.* **116** D9
Lonquimay *Chile* **128** D2
Lons-le-Saunier *France* **19** F12
Lönsboda *Sweden* **11** H8
Looe *U.K.* **15** G3
Lookout, C. *Canada* **104** A3
Lookout, C. *U.S.A.* **117** D16
Loolmalasin *Tanzania* **86** C4
Loon ➣ *Alta., Canada* **102** B5
Loon ➣ *Man., Canada* **103** B8
Loon Lake *Canada* **103** C7
Loongana *Australia* **93** F4
Loop Hd. *Ireland* **12** D2
Lop Buri *Thailand* **64** E3
Lop Nor = Lop Nur *China* **60** B4
Lop Nur *China* **60** B4
Lopare *Bos.-H.* **28** F3
Lopatin *Russia* **35** J8
Lopatina, Gora *Russia* **53** D15
Lopatka, Mys *Russia* **53** D16
Lopaye *Sudan* **81** F3
Lopez *Phil.* **61** E5
Lopez *U.S.A.* **115** E8
Lopez, C. *Gabon* **84** E1
Lopphavet *Norway* **8** A19
Lora ➣ *Afghan.* **66** D2
Lora Cr. ➣ *Australia* **95** D2
Lora del Río *Spain* **37** H5
Lora, Hāmūn-i- *Pakistan* **66** E4
Lorain *U.S.A.* **114** E2
Loralai *Pakistan* **68** D3
Lorca *Spain* **39** H3
Lord Howe I. *Pac. Oc.* **90** E8
Lord Howe Rise *Pac. Oc.* **96** L8
Lordsburg *U.S.A.* **109** K9
Lorestān □ *Iran* **71** C6
Loreto *Brazil* **125** E9
Loreto *Italy* **41** E10
Loreto *Mexico* **118** B2
Lorgues *France* **21** E10
Lorhosso *Burkina Faso* **82** C4
Lorient *France* **18** E3
Lorn, Firth of *U.K.* **13** E3
Lorne *Australia* **95** F3
Loronyo *Sudan* **81** G3
Lorovouno *Cyprus* **49** D11
Lörrach *Germany* **25** H3
Lorraine □ *France* **19** D13
Lorraine △ *France* **19** D12
Los *Sweden* **10** C9
Los, Îles de *Guinea* **82** D2
Los Alamos *Calif., U.S.A.* **111** L6
Los Alamos *N. Mex., U.S.A.* **109** J10
Los Alcornocales △ *Spain* **37** J5
Los Altos *U.S.A.* **110** H4
Los Andes *Chile* **126** C1
Los Angeles *Chile* **126** D1
Los Angeles *U.S.A.* **111** M8
Los Angeles, Bahía de
  Mexico **118** B2
Los Angeles Aqueduct
  U.S.A. **111** K9
Los Angeles Int. ✈ (LAX)
  U.S.A. **111** M8
Los Banos *U.S.A.* **110** H6
Los Barrios *Spain* **37** J5
Los Blancos *Argentina* **126** A3
Los Cardones △ *Argentina* **126** B2
Los Chiles *Costa Rica* **120** D3
Los Cristianos *Canary Is.* **48** F3
Los Corrales de Buelna *Spain* **36** B6
Los Gallardos *Spain* **39** H3
Los Gatos *U.S.A.* **110** H5
Los Haïtises △ *Dom. Rep.* **121** C6
Los Hermanos Is. *Venezuela* **121** D7
Los Islotes *Canary Is.* **48** E6
Los Llanos de Aridane
  Canary Is. **48** F2
Los Loros *Chile* **126** B1
Los Lunas *U.S.A.* **109** J10
Los Mochis *Mexico* **118** B3
Los Monegros *Spain* **38** D4
Los Nietos *Spain* **39** H4
Los Olivos *U.S.A.* **111** L6
Los Palacios *Cuba* **120** B3
Los Palacios y Villafranca
  Spain **37** H5
Los Queñes *Chile* **126** D1
Los Reyes de Salgado
  Mexico **118** D4

Los Roques Is. *Venezuela* **121** D6
Los Santos de Maimona
  Spain **37** G4
Los Teques *Venezuela* **124** A5
Los Testigos, Is. *Venezuela* **124** A6
Los Vilos *Chile* **126** C1
Los Yébenes *Spain* **37** F7
Łosice *Poland* **31** F9
Lošinj *Croatia* **41** D11
Loskop Dam *S. Africa* **89** D4
Løsning *Denmark* **11** J3
Lossiemouth *U.K.* **13** D5
Lossen △ *Sweden* **10** B6
Lostwithiel *U.K.* **15** G3
Lot □ *France* **20** D5
Lot ➣ *France* **20** D4
Lot-et-Garonne □ *France* **20** D4
Lota *Chile* **126** D1
Lotagipi Swamp *Sudan* **81** G3
Lotfābād *Iran* **71** B8
Lothair *S. Africa* **89** D5
Lotorp *Sweden* **11** F9
Lötschbergtunnel *Switz.* **25** J3
Lotta ➣ *Europe* **8** B24
Löttorp *Sweden* **11** G11
Lotung *Taiwan* **59** E13
Loubomo *Congo* **84** E2
Loudéac *France* **18** D4
Loudi *China* **59** D8
Loudon *U.S.A.* **117** D12
Loudonville *U.S.A.* **114** F2
Loudun *France* **18** E7
Loue ➣ *France* **19** E12
Louga *Senegal* **82** B1
Louga □ *Senegal* **82** B1
Loughborough *U.K.* **14** E6
Lougheed I. *Canada* **101** B10
Loughrea *Ireland* **12** C3
Loughros More B. *Ireland* **12** B3
Louhans *France* **19** F12
Louis Trichardt *S. Africa* **89** C4
Louis XIV, Pte. *Canada* **104** B4
Louisa *U.S.A.* **113** F12
Louisbourg *Canada* **105** C8
Louisburgh *Ireland* **12** C2
Louise I. *Canada* **102** C2
Louisiade Arch. *Papua N. G.* **90** C8
Louisiana *U.S.A.* **112** F8
Louisiana □ *U.S.A.* **116** F9
Louisville *Ky., U.S.A.* **113** F11
Louisville *Miss., U.S.A.* **117** E10
Louisville *Ohio, U.S.A.* **114** F3
Louisville Ridge *Pac. Oc.* **96** L10
Loulay *France* **20** B3
Loulé *Portugal* **37** H3
Loulouni *Mali* **82** C3
Loum *Cameroon* **83** E6
Louny *Czech Rep.* **26** A6
Loup City *U.S.A.* **112** E4
Loups Marins, Lacs des
  Canada **104** A5
Lourdes *France* **20** E3
Lourdes-de-Blanc-Sablon
  Canada **105** B8
Lourinhã *Portugal* **37** F1
Louroujina *Cyprus* **49** E12
Lousã *Portugal* **36** E2
Louta *Burkina Faso* **82** C4
Louth *Australia* **95** E4
Louth *Ireland* **12** C5
Louth □ *Ireland* **12** C5
Louth *U.K.* **14** D7
Loutra Edipsou *Greece* **46** C5
Loutraki *Greece* **46** D4
Loutropoli Thermis *Greece* **47** B8
Louvain = Leuven *Belgium* **17** D4
Louviers *France* **18** C8
Louwsburg *S. Africa* **89** D5
Lovat ➣ *Russia* **32** C6
Lovćen *Montenegro* **44** D2
Lovćen △ *Montenegro* **44** D2
Lovech *Bulgaria* **45** C8
Lovech □ *Bulgaria* **45** C8
Loveland *U.S.A.* **108** F11
Lovell *U.S.A.* **108** D9
Lovelock *U.S.A.* **108** F4
Lóvere *Italy* **40** C7
Lövestad *Sweden* **11** J7
Loviisa *Finland* **32** B4
Loving *U.S.A.* **109** K11
Lovington *U.S.A.* **109** K12
Lovisa = Loviisa *Finland* **32** B4
Lovran *Croatia* **41** C11
Lovrin *Romania* **28** E5
Lovisice *Czech Rep.* **26** A7
Lowa *Dem. Rep. of the Congo* **86** C2
Lowa ➣
  Dem. Rep. of the Congo **86** C2
Lowell *U.S.A.* **115** D13
Lowellville *U.S.A.* **114** E4
Löwen ➣ *Namibia* **88** D2
Lower Alkali L. *U.S.A.* **108** F3
Lower Arrow L. *Canada* **102** D5

Lower Austria =
  Niederösterreich □ *Austria* **26** C8
Lower California = Baja
  California *Mexico* **118** A1
Lower Hutt *N.Z.* **91** D5
Lower Lake *U.S.A.* **110** G4
Lower Manitou L. *Canada* **103** D10
Lower Post *Canada* **102** B3
Lower Red L. *U.S.A.* **112** B6
Lower Saxony =
  Niedersachsen □ *Germany* **24** C4
Lower Tunguska =
  Tunguska,
  Nizhnyaya ➣ *Russia* **53** C9
Lower Zambezi △ *Zambia* **87** F2
Lowestoft *U.K.* **15** E9
Lowgar □ *Afghan.* **66** B6
Łowicz *Poland* **31** F6
Lowther I. *Canada* **101** C12
Lowville *U.S.A.* **115** C9
Loxton *Australia* **95** E3
Loxton *S. Africa* **88** E3
Loyalton *U.S.A.* **110** F6
Loyalty Is. = Loyauté, Îs.
  N. Cal. **90** D9
Loyang = Luoyang *China* **56** G7
Loyauté, Îs. *N. Cal.* **90** D9
Loyev = Loyew *Belarus* **23** C16
Loyew *Belarus* **23** C16
Loyoro *Uganda* **86** B3
Lož *Slovenia* **41** C11
Lozère □ *France* **20** D7
Loznica *Serbia* **44** B3
Lozova *Ukraine* **33** H9
Ltalaltuma ◎ *Australia* **92** D5
Lü Shan *China* **59** C11
Lü Tao *Taiwan* **59** F13
Luachimo *Angola* **84** F4
Luajan ➣ *India* **69** G11
Lualaba ➣
  Dem. Rep. of the Congo **86** B2
Luambe △ *Zambia* **87** E3
Luampa *Zambia* **87** F1
Lu'an *China* **59** B11
Luan Chau *Vietnam* **58** G4
Luan He ➣ *China* **57** E10
Luan Xian *China* **57** E10
Luancheng
  Guangxi Zhuangzu, China **58** F7
Luancheng *Hebei, China* **56** F8
Luanco *Spain* **36** B5
Luanda *Angola* **84** F2
Luang, Thale *Thailand* **65** J3
Luang Prabang *Laos* **58** H4
Luangwa *Zambia* **87** F3
Luangwa ➣ *Zambia* **87** E3
Luangwa Valley *Zambia* **87** E3
Luangwe = Loange ➣
  Dem. Rep. of the Congo **84** E4
Luanne *China* **57** D9
Luanping *China* **57** D9
Luanshya *Zambia* **87** E2
Luapula □ *Zambia* **87** E2
Luapula ➣ *Africa* **87** D2
Luarca *Spain* **36** B4
Luashi *Dem. Rep. of the Congo* **87** E1
Luau *Angola* **84** G4
Lubaczów *Poland* **31** H10
Lubań *Poland* **31** G2
Lubana, Ozero = Lubānas
  Ezers *Latvia* **32** D4
Lubānas Ezers *Latvia* **32** D4
Lubang *Phil.* **61** E4
Lubang Is. *Phil.* **63** B6
Lubango *Angola* **85** G2
Lubao *Dem. Rep. of the Congo* **86** D2
Lubartów *Poland* **31** G9
Lubawa *Poland* **30** E6
Lübbecke *Germany* **24** C4
Lübben *Germany* **24** D9
Lübbenau *Germany* **24** D9
Lubbock *U.S.A.* **116** E4
Lübeck *Germany* **24** B6
Lübecker Bucht *Germany* **24** A6
Lubefu *Dem. Rep. of the Congo* **86** C1
Lubefu ➣
  Dem. Rep. of the Congo **86** C1
Lubelskie □ *Poland* **31** G9
Lubero = Luofu
  Dem. Rep. of the Congo **86** C2
Luberon △ *France* **21** E9
Lubersac *France* **20** C5
Lubicon L. *Canada* **102** B5
Lubień Kujawski *Poland* **31** F6
Lubilash ➣
  Dem. Rep. of the Congo **84** F4
Lubin *Poland* **31** G3
Lublin *Poland* **31** G9
Lubliniec *Poland* **31** H5
Lubnān = Lebanon ■ *Asia* **74** B5
Lubnān, Jabal *Lebanon* **74** B4
Lubniewice *Poland* **31** F2
Lubny *Ukraine* **33** G7
Lubomierz *Poland* **31** G2
Luboń *Poland* **31** F3
Lubongola
  Dem. Rep. of the Congo **86** C2
L'ubotín *Slovak Rep.* **27** B13
Lubraniec *Poland* **31** F5

Lubsko *Poland* **31** G1
Lübtheen *Germany* **24** B7
Lubuagan *Phil.* **61** C4
Lubudi *Dem. Rep. of the Congo* **84** F5
Lubudi ➔
  Dem. Rep. of the Congo **87** D2
Lubuklinggau *Indonesia* **62** E2
Lubuksikaping *Indonesia* **62** D2
Lubumbashi
  Dem. Rep. of the Congo **87** E2
Lubunda
  Dem. Rep. of the Congo **86** D2
Lubungu *Zambia* **87** E2
Lubuskie □ *Poland* **31** F2
Lubutu *Dem. Rep. of the Congo* **86** C2
Luc An Chau *Vietnam* **64** A5
Luc-en-Diois *France* **21** D9
Lucan *Canada* **114** C3
Lucania, Mt. *Canada* **100** E3
Lucas Channel = Main
  Channel *Canada* **114** A3
Lucban *Phil.* **61** D4
Lucca *Italy* **40** E7
Lucé *France* **18** D8
Luce Bay *U.K.* **13** G4
Lucea *Jamaica* **120** a
Lucedale *U.S.A.* **117** F10
Lucena *Phil.* **61** E4
Lucena *Spain* **37** H6
Lučenec *Slovak Rep.* **27** C12
Lucera *Italy* **43** A8
Lucerne = Luzern *Switz.* **25** H4
Lucerne *U.S.A.* **110** F4
Lucerne Valley *U.S.A.* **111** L10
Lucero *Mexico* **118** A3
Luchena ➔ *Spain* **39** H3
Lucheng *China* **56** F7
Lucheringo ➔ *Mozam.* **87** E4
Lüchow *Germany* **24** C7
Luchuan *China* **59** F8
Lucia *U.S.A.* **110** J5
Lucinda *Australia* **94** B4
Luckau *Germany* **24** D9
Luckenwalde *Germany* **24** C9
Luckhoff *S. Africa* **88** D3
Lucknow *Canada* **114** C3
Lucknow *India* **69** F9
Luçon *France* **20** B2
Lüda = Dalian *China* **57** E11
Luda Kamchiya ➔ *Bulgaria* **45** C11
Ludbreg *Croatia* **41** B13
Lüdenscheid *Germany* **24** D3
Lüderitz *Namibia* **88** D2
Lüderitzbaai *Namibia* **88** D2
Ludhiana *India* **68** D6
Ludian *China* **58** D4
Luding Qiao *China* **58** C4
Lüdinghausen *Germany* **24** D3
Ludington *U.S.A.* **112** D10
Ludlow *U.K.* **15** E5
Ludlow *Calif., U.S.A.* **111** L10
Ludlow *Pa., U.S.A.* **114** E6
Ludlow *Vt., U.S.A.* **115** C12
Ludus *Romania* **29** D9
Ludvika *Sweden* **10** D9
Ludwigsburg *Germany* **25** G5
Ludwigsfelde *Germany* **24** C9
Ludwigshafen *Germany* **25** F4
Ludwigslust *Germany* **24** B7
Ludza *Latvia* **32** D4
Lueki *Dem. Rep. of the Congo* **86** C2
Luena *Dem. Rep. of the Congo* **87** D2
Luena *Zambia* **87** E2
Luena Flats *Zambia* **85** G4
Luenha = Ruenya ➔ *Africa* **87** F3
Lüeyang *China* **56** H4
Lufeng *Guangdong, China* **59** F10
Lufeng *Yunnan, China* **58** E4
Lufira ➔
  Dem. Rep. of the Congo **87** D2
Lufkin *U.S.A.* **116** F7
Lufupa *Dem. Rep. of the Congo* **87** E1
Luga *Russia* **32** C5
Luga ➔ *Russia* **32** C5
Lugano *Switz.* **25** J4
Lugano, L. di *Switz.* **40** C6
Lugansk = Luhansk
  Ukraine **33** H10
Lugard's Falls *Kenya* **86** C4
Lugela *Mozam.* **87** F4
Lugenda ➔ *Mozam.* **87** E4
Lugh Ganana = Luuq
  Somali Rep. **75** G3
Lugnaquillia *Ireland* **12** D5
Lugo *Italy* **41** D8
Lugo *Spain* **36** B3
Lugo □ *Spain* **36** C3
Lugoj *Romania* **28** E5
Lugovoy = Qulan *Kazakhstan* **52** E8
Luhansk *Ukraine* **33** H10
Luhansk □ *Ukraine* **33** H10
Luhe *China* **59** A12
Luhe ➔ *Germany* **24** B6
Luhuo *China* **58** B3
Lui ➔ *Angola* **84** F3
Luiana *Angola* **88** B3
Luiana ➔ *Angola* **85** H4
Luichow Pen. = Leizhou
  Bandao *China* **58** G7

Luimneach = Limerick
  Ireland **12** D3
Luing *U.K.* **13** E3
Luino *Italy* **40** C5
Luís Correia *Brazil* **125** D10
Luiza *Dem. Rep. of the Congo* **84** F4
Luizi *Dem. Rep. of the Congo* **86** D2
Luján *Argentina* **126** C4
Lujiang *China* **59** B11
Lukang *Taiwan* **59** E13
Lukanga Swamp *Zambia* **87** E2
Lukavac *Bos.-H.* **28** F3
Lukenie ➔
  Dem. Rep. of the Congo **84** E3
Lŭki *Bulgaria* **45** E8
Lukolela
  Dem. Rep. of the Congo **86** D1
Lukosi *Zimbabwe* **87** F2
Lukovë *Albania* **44** G3
Lukovit *Bulgaria* **45** C8
Łuków *Poland* **31** G9
Lukoyanov *Russia* **34** C7
Lukusuzi △ *Zambia* **87** E3
Luleå *Sweden* **8** D20
Luleälven ➔ *Sweden* **8** D20
Lüleburgaz *Turkey* **45** E11
Luliang *China* **58** E4
Lulima *Dem. Rep. of the Congo* **86** C2
Luling *China* **116** G6
Lulong *China* **57** E10
Lulonga ➔
  Dem. Rep. of the Congo **84** D3
Lulua ➔
  Dem. Rep. of the Congo **84** E4
Luma *Amer. Samoa* **91** b
Lumajang *Indonesia* **63** H15
Lumār *Iran* **73** F12
Lumbala N'guimbo *Angola* **85** G4
Lumberton *U.S.A.* **117** D15
Lumsden *Canada* **103** C8
Lumsden *N.Z.* **91** F2
Lumut *Malaysia* **65** K3
Lumut, Tanjung *Indonesia* **62** E3
Luna *India* **68** H3
Lunan *China* **58** E4
Lunavada *India* **68** H5
Lunca *Romania* **29** C10
Lunca Corbului *Romania* **29** F9
Lund *Sweden* **11** J7
Lundazi *Zambia* **87** E3
Lunderskov *Denmark* **11** J3
Lundi ➔ *Zimbabwe* **87** G3
Lundu *Malaysia* **62** D3
Lundy *U.K.* **15** F3
Lüneburg *Germany* **24** B6
Lüneburg Heath =
  Lüneburger Heide
  Germany **24** B6
Lüneburger Heide *Germany* **24** B6
Lunel *France* **21** E8
Lünen *Germany* **24** D3
Lunenburg *Canada* **105** D7
Lunéville *France* **19** D13
Lunga ➔ *Zambia* **87** E2
Lunga Lunga *Kenya* **86** C4
Lungi *S. Leone* **82** D2
Lunglei *India* **67** H18
Luni *India* **68** G5
Luni ➔ *India* **68** G4
Luninets = Luninyets
  Belarus **23** B14
Luning *U.S.A.* **108** G4
Lunino *Russia* **34** D7
Luninyets *Belarus* **23** B14
Lunkaransar *India* **68** E5
Lunsar *S. Leone* **82** D2
Lunsemfwa ➔ *Zambia* **87** E3
Lunsemfwa Falls *Zambia* **87** E2
Luo He ➔ *China* **56** G6
Luocheng *China* **58** E7
Luochuan *China* **56** G5
Luoci *China* **58** E4
Luodian *China* **58** E6
Luoding *China* **59** F8
Luofu *Dem. Rep. of the Congo* **86** C2
Luohe *China* **56** H8
Luojiang *China* **58** B5
Luonan *China* **56** G6
Luoning *China* **56** G6
Luoshan *China* **59** A10
Luotian *China* **59** B10
Luoxiao Shan *China* **59** D10
Luoyang *China* **56** H4
Luoyuan *China* **59** D12
Luozigou *China* **57** C16
Lupeni *Romania* **29** E8
Lupilichi *Mozam.* **87** E4
Lupoing *China* **58** E5
Luquan *China* **58** E4
Luque *Paraguay* **126** B4
Luquillo, Sierra de *Puerto Rico* **121** d
Lúras *Italy* **42** B2
Luray *U.S.A.* **113** F14
Lure *France* **19** E13
Lurgan *U.K.* **12** B5
Lúrio *Mozam.* **87** E5

Lusaka *Zambia* **87** F2
Lusaka □ *Zambia* **87** F2
Lusambo
  Dem. Rep. of the Congo **86** C1
Lusangaye
  Dem. Rep. of the Congo **86** C2
Luseland *Canada* **103** C7
Lusenga Plain △ *Zambia* **87** D2
Lushan *Henan, China* **56** H7
Lushan *Sichuan, China* **58** B4
Lushi *China* **56** G6
Lushnjë *Albania* **44** F3
Lushoto *Tanzania* **86** C4
Lushui *China* **58** E2
Lüshun *China* **57** E11
Lusignan *France* **20** B4
Lusigny-sur-Barse *France* **19** D11
Lusk *U.S.A.* **108** E11
Lussac-les-Châteaux *France* **20** B4
Lustenau *Austria* **26** D2
Lūt, Dasht-e *Iran* **71** D8
Luta = Dalian *China* **57** E11
Lutherstadt Wittenberg
  Germany **24** D8
Luton *U.K.* **15** F7
Luton □ *U.K.* **15** F7
Lutsel K'e *Canada* **103** A6
Lutsk *Ukraine* **23** C13
Lutto = Lotta ➔ *Europe* **8** B24
Lützow Holmbukta *Antarctica* **5** C4
Lutzputs *S. Africa* **88** D3
Luuq *Somali Rep.* **75** G3
Luverne *Ala., U.S.A.* **117** F11
Luverne *Minn., U.S.A.* **112** D5
Luvua *Dem. Rep. of the Congo* **87** D2
Luvua ➔
  Dem. Rep. of the Congo **86** D2
Luvuvhu ➔ *S. Africa* **89** C5
Luwegu ➔ *Tanzania* **87** D4
Luwero *Uganda* **86** B3
Luwuk *Indonesia* **63** E6
Luxembourg *Lux.* **17** E6
Luxembourg □ *Belgium* **17** E5
Luxembourg ■ *Europe* **17** E5
Luxembourg ✈ (LUX) *Lux.* **17** E6
Luxeuil-les-Bains *France* **19** E13
Luxi *Hunan, China* **59** C8
Luxi *Yunnan, China* **58** E4
Luxi *Yunnan, China* **58** E2
Luxor = El Uqsur *Egypt* **80** B3
Luy-de-Béarn ➔ *France* **20** E3
Luy-de-France ➔ *France* **20** E3
Luyi *China* **56** H8
Luz-St-Sauveur *France* **20** F4
Luzern *Switz.* **25** H4
Luzern □ *Switz.* **25** H3
Luzhai *China* **58** E7
Luzhany *Ukraine* **29** B10
Luzhi *China* **58** D5
Luzhou *China* **58** C5
Luziânia *Brazil* **125** G9
Lužnice ➔ *Czech Rep.* **26** B7
Luzon *Phil.* **61** D4
Luzon Strait *Asia* **59** G13
Luzy *France* **19** F10
Luzzi *Italy* **43** C9
Lviv *Ukraine* **33** D13
Lviv □ *Ukraine* **33** H2
Lvov = Lviv *Ukraine* **23** D13
Lwówek *Poland* **31** F3
Lwówek Śląski *Poland* **31** G2
Lyakhavichy *Belarus* **23** B14
Lyakhovskiye, Ostrova
  Russia **53** B15
Lyaki = Läki *Azerbaijan* **35** K8
Lyal I. *Canada* **114** B4
Lyaskovets *Bulgaria* **45** C9
Lyasnaya *Belarus* **31** F10
Lybster *U.K.* **13** C5
Lycaonia *Turkey* **72** D5
Lychen *Germany* **24** B9
Lychkova *Russia* **32** D7
Lycia *Turkey* **47** E11
Lyckeby ➔ *Sweden* **11** H9
Lycksele *Sweden* **8** D18
Lycosura *Greece* **46** D4
Lydda = Lod *Israel* **74** D3
Lydenburg *S. Africa* **89** D5
Lydia *Turkey* **47** C10
Lydney *U.K.* **15** F5
Lydynia ➔ *Poland* **31** F7
Lyell *N.Z.* **91** D4
Lyell I. *Canada* **102** C2
Lyepyel *Belarus* **32** E5
Lygnern *Sweden* **11** G6
Lykens *U.S.A.* **115** F8
Lyman *Ukraine* **29** E14
Lyman *U.S.A.* **108** F8
Lymanske *Ukraine* **29** D14
Lyme B. *U.K.* **15** G4
Lyme Regis *U.K.* **15** G5
Lymington *U.K.* **15** G6
Łyna ➔ *Poland* **30** D8
Lynchburg *U.S.A.* **113** G14
Lynd ➔ *Australia* **94** B3
Lynd Ra. *Australia* **95** D4
Lynden *Canada* **114** C4
Lynden *U.S.A.* **110** B4
Lyndhurst *Australia* **95** E2

Lyndon ➔ *Australia* **93** D1
Lyndonville *N.Y., U.S.A.* **114** C6
Lyndonville *Vt., U.S.A.* **115** B12
Lyngen *Norway* **8** B19
Lynher Reef *Australia* **92** C3
Lynn *U.S.A.* **115** D14
Lynn Canal *U.S.A.* **106** D12
Lynn Haven *U.S.A.* **117** F12
Lynn Lake *Canada* **103** B8
Lynnwood *U.S.A.* **110** C4
Lynton *U.K.* **15** F4
Lynx L. *Canada* **103** A7
Lyon *France* **21** C8
Lyon St-Exupery ✈ (LYS)
  France **21** C9
Lyonnais *France* **21** C8
Lyons = Lyon *France* **21** C8
Lyons *Ga., U.S.A.* **117** E13
Lyons *Kans., U.S.A.* **112** C5
Lyons *N.Y., U.S.A.* **114** C4
Lyons ➔ *Australia* **93** E2
Lyons Falls *U.S.A.* **115** C9
Lyozna *Belarus* **32** E6
Lys = Leie ➔ *Belgium* **17** C3
Lysá nad Labem *Czech Rep.* **26** A7
Lysekil *Sweden* **11** F5
Lysi *Cyprus* **49** D12
Lyskovo *Russia* **34** B7
Lystrup *Denmark* **11** H4
Lysva *Russia* **18** C10
Lysvik *Sweden* **10** D7
Lysychansk *Ukraine* **33** H10
Lytham St. Anne's *U.K.* **14** D4
Lytton *Canada* **102** C4
Lyuban *Russia* **32** C6
Lyubertsy *Russia* **32** E9
Lyubim *Russia* **32** C11
Lyubimets *Bulgaria* **45** E10
Lyuboml *Ukraine* **31** G11
Lyubotyn *Ukraine* **33** H8
Lyubytino *Russia* **32** C7
Lyudinovo *Russia* **32** F8

M

M.R. Stefanik, Bratislava ✈
  (BTS) *Slovak Rep.* **27** C10
Ma ➔ *Vietnam* **58** H5
Ma'adaba *Jordan* **74** E4
Maamba *Zambia* **88** B4
Ma'ān *Jordan* **74** E4
Ma'ān □ *Jordan* **74** F5
Maanselkä *Finland* **8** E23
Ma'anshan *China* **59** B12
Maarianhamina =
  Mariehamn *Finland* **9** F18
Ma'arrat an Nu'mān *Syria* **72** E7
Maas ➔ *Neths.* **17** C4
Maaseik *Belgium* **17** C5
Maasin *Phil.* **63** F6
Maastricht *Neths.* **17** D5
Maave *Mozam.* **89** C5
Mababe Depression
  Botswana **88** B3
Mabalane *Mozam.* **89** C5
Mabel L. *Canada* **102** C5
Mabenge
  Dem. Rep. of the Congo **86** B1
Maberly *Canada* **115** B8
Mabesi, L. *S. Leone* **82** D2
Mabian *China* **58** C4
Mabil *Ethiopia* **81** E4
Mablethorpe *U.K.* **14** D8
Mably *France* **19** F11
Maboma
  Dem. Rep. of the Congo **86** B2
Mabonto *S. Leone* **82** D2
Mabrouk *Mali* **83** B4
Mabuasehube △ *Botswana* **88** D3
Mabuiag *Australia* **94** a
Mac Bac *Vietnam* **65** H6
Macachín *Argentina* **126** D3
Macaé *Brazil* **127** A7
Macael *Spain* **39** H2
McAlester *U.S.A.* **116** D7
McAllen *U.S.A.* **116** H5
MacAlpine L. *Canada* **100** D11
Macamic *Canada* **104** C4
Macao = Macau *China* **59** F9
Macão *Portugal* **37** F3
Macapá *Brazil* **125** C8
Macarao △ *Venezuela* **121** D6
McArthur ➔ *Australia* **94** B2
McArthur, Port *Australia* **94** B2
Macau *Brazil* **125** E11
Macau *China* **59** F9
McBride *Canada* **102** C4
McCall *U.S.A.* **108** D5
McCamey *U.S.A.* **116** F3
McCammon *U.S.A.* **108** E7
McCarran Int., Las
  Vegas ✈ (LAS) *U.S.A.* **111** J11
McCauley I. *Canada* **102** C2
McCleary *U.S.A.* **110** C3
Macclenny *U.S.A.* **117** F13
Macclesfield *U.K.* **14** D5
M'Clintock Chan. *Canada* **100** C11
McClintock Ra. *Australia* **92** C4

McCloud *U.S.A.* **108** F2
McCluer I. *Australia* **92** B5
McClure *U.S.A.* **114** F7
McClure, L. *U.S.A.* **110** H6
M'Clure Str. *Canada* **101** C8
McClusky *U.S.A.* **112** B3
McComb *U.S.A.* **117** F9
McCook *U.S.A.* **112** E3
McCreary *Canada* **103** C9
McCullough Mt. *U.S.A.* **111** K11
McCusker ➔ *Canada* **103** B7
McDermitt *U.S.A.* **108** F5
McDonald *U.S.A.* **114** F4
Macdonald, L. *Australia* **92** D4
McDonald Is. *Ind. Oc.* **3** G13
MacDonnell Ranges
  Australia **92** D5
MacDowell L. *Canada* **104** B1
Macduff *U.K.* **13** D6
Maceda *Spain* **36** C3
Macedonia *U.S.A.* **114** E3
Macedonia ■ *Europe* **44** E5
Maceió *Brazil* **125** E11
Maceira *Portugal* **36** F2
Macerata *Italy* **41** E10
McFarland *U.S.A.* **111** K7
McFarlane ➔ *Canada* **103** B7
Macfarlane, L. *Australia* **95** E2
McGehee *U.S.A.* **116** E9
McGill *U.S.A.* **108** G6
Macgillycuddy's Reeks
  Ireland **12** E2
McGraw *U.S.A.* **115** D8
McGregor *U.S.A.* **112** D8
McGregor Ra. *Australia* **95** D3
McGuire, Mt. *Australia* **94** b
Mach *Pakistan* **68** E2
Māch Kowr *Iran* **71** E9
Machado = Jiparaná ➔
  Brazil **124** E6
Machagai *Argentina* **126** B3
Machakos *Kenya* **86** C4
Machala *Ecuador* **124** D3
Machanga *Mozam.* **89** C6
Machattie, L. *Australia* **94** C2
Machault *France* **19** C11
Machava *Mozam.* **89** D5
Machece *Mozam.* **89** C6
Macheke *Zimbabwe* **89** B5
Macheng *China* **59** B10
Machero *Spain* **37** F6
Machhu ➔ *India* **68** H4
Machias *Maine, U.S.A.* **113** C20
Machias *N.Y., U.S.A.* **114** D6
Machichi ➔ *Canada* **103** B10
Machico *Madeira* **48** D3
Machilipatnam *India* **67** L12
Machiques *Venezuela* **124** A4
Machu Picchu *Peru* **124** F4
Machynlleth *U.K.* **15** E4
Macia *Mozam.* **89** D5
Maciejowice *Poland* **31** G8
McIlwraith Ra. *Australia* **94** A3
Măcin *Romania* **29** E13
Macina *Mali* **82** C4
McInnes L. *Canada* **103** C10
McIntosh *U.S.A.* **112** C3
McIntosh, L. *S. Leone* **82** D2
Macintosh Ra. *Australia* **93** E4
Macintyre ➔ *Australia* **95** D5
Macizo Galaico *Spain* **36** C3
Maçka *Turkey* **73** B8
Mackay *Australia* **94** K7
Mackay *U.S.A.* **108** E7
MacKay ➔ *Canada* **102** E6
Mackay, L. *Australia* **92** D4
McKay Ra. *Australia* **92** D3
McKeesport *U.S.A.* **114** F5
McKenna *U.S.A.* **110** D4
Mackenzie *Canada* **102** B4
Mackenzie *U.S.A.* **117** C1C
Mackenzie ➔ *Australia* **94** C4
Mackenzie ➔ *Canada* **100** D5
McKenzie ➔ *U.S.A.* **108** D2
Mackenzie Bay *Canada* **98** C6
Mackenzie City = Linden
  Guyana **124** B7
Mackenzie King I. *Canada* **101** B3
Mackenzie Mts. *Canada* **100** E6
Mackinac, Straits of *U.S.A.* **107** F23
Mackinaw City *U.S.A.* **113** C11
McKinlay *Australia* **94** C3
McKinlay ➔ *Australia* **94** C3
McKinley, Mt. *U.S.A.* **100** E1
McKinley Sea *Arctic* **4** A7
McKinney *U.S.A.* **116** E6
Mackinnon Road *Kenya* **86** C4
McKittrick *U.S.A.* **111** K7
Macklin *Canada* **103** C7
Macksville *Australia* **95** E5
McLaughlin *U.S.A.* **112** C3
Maclean *Australia* **95** D5
McLean *U.S.A.* **116** D4
McLeansboro *U.S.A.* **112** F9
Maclear *S. Africa* **89** E4

Maclear, C. *Malawi* **87** E3
Macleay ➔ *Australia* **95** E5
McLennan *Canada* **102** B5
McLeod ➔ *Canada* **102** C5
MacLeod, L. *Australia* **93** D1
MacLeod B. *Canada* **103** A7
MacLeod Lake *Canada* **102** C4
McLoughlin, Mt. *U.S.A.* **108** E2
McMechen *U.S.A.* **114** G4
McMinnville *Oreg., U.S.A.* **108** D2
McMinnville *Tenn., U.S.A.* **117** D12
McMurdo *Antarctica* **5** D11
McMurdo Sd. *Antarctica* **5** D11
McMurray = Fort
  McMurray *Canada* **102** B3
McMurray *U.S.A.* **110** B4
Maçobere *Mozam.* **87** E3
Macodoene *Mozam.* **89** C6
Macomb *U.S.A.* **112** E8
Macomer *Italy* **42** B1
Mâcon *France* **19** F11
Macon *Ga., U.S.A.* **117** E13
Macon *Miss., U.S.A.* **117** E10
Macon *Mo., U.S.A.* **112** F7
Macossa *Mozam.* **87** F3
Macoun L. *Canada* **103** B8
Macovane *Mozam.* **89** C6
McPherson *U.S.A.* **112** F5
McPherson Pk. *U.S.A.* **111** L7
McPherson Ra. *Australia* **95** D5
Macquarie ➔ *Australia* **95** E4
Macquarie Harbour *Australia* **95** G4
Macquarie Is. *Pac. Oc.* **96** N7
Macquarie Ridge *S. Ocean* **5** B10
MacRobertson Land
  Antarctica **5** D6
Macroom *Ireland* **12** E3
MacTier *Canada* **114** A5
Macubela *Mozam.* **87** F4
Macugnaga *Italy* **40** C4
Macuira △ *Colombia* **121** D5
Macuiza *Mozam.* **87** F3
Macumba ➔ *Australia* **95** D2
Macuro *Venezuela* **125** K15
Macusani *Peru* **124** F4
Macuse *Mozam.* **87** F4
Macuspana *Mexico* **119** D6
Macusse *Angola* **88** B3
Mada ➔ *Nigeria* **83** D6
Ma'dabā □ *Jordan* **74** D4
Madadeni *S. Africa* **89** D5
Madagali *Nigeria* **83** C7
Madagascar ■ *Africa* **89** C8
Madā'in Sālih *Si. Arabia* **70** E3
Madama *Niger* **79** D8
Madame, I. *Canada* **105** C7
Madan *Bulgaria* **45** E8
Madang *Papua N. G.* **90** B7
Madaoua *Niger* **83** C6
Madara *Nigeria* **83** C7
Madaripur *Bangla.* **67** H17
Madauk *Burma* **67** L20
Madawaska *Canada* **114** A7
Madawaska ➔ *Canada* **114** A7
Madaya *Burma* **67** H20
Madbar *Sudan* **81** F3
Maddalena *Italy* **42** A2
Maddaloni *Italy* **43** A7
Madeira *Atl. Oc.* **48** D3
Madeira ➔ *Brazil* **124** D7
Madeleine, Îs. de la *Canada* **105** C7
Maden *Turkey* **73** C8
Madera *Mexico* **118** B3
Madera *Calif., U.S.A.* **110** J6
Madera *Pa., U.S.A.* **114** F6
Madha *India* **66** L9
Madhavpur *India* **68** J3
Madhepura *India* **69** F12
Madhubani *India* **69** F12
Madhupur *India* **69** G12
Madhya Pradesh □ *India* **68** J8
Madidi ➔ *Bolivia* **124** F5
Madikeri *India* **66** N9
Madikwe △ *S. Africa* **89** D5
Madimba
  Dem. Rep. of the Congo **84** E3
Ma'din *Syria* **73** E8
Madina *Mali* **82** C3
Madinani *Ivory C.* **82** D3
Madinat al Malik Khālid al
  Askarīyah *Si. Arabia* **70** E5
Madīnat ath Thawrah *Syria* **73** E8
Madingou *Congo* **84** E2
Madirovalo *Madag.* **89** B8
Madison *Calif., U.S.A.* **110** G5
Madison *Fla., U.S.A.* **117** F13
Madison *Ind., U.S.A.* **113** F11
Madison *Nebr., U.S.A.* **112** E6
Madison *Ohio, U.S.A.* **114** E3
Madison *S. Dak., U.S.A.* **112** C5
Madison *Wis., U.S.A.* **112** D9
Madison ➔ *U.S.A.* **108** D8
Madison Heights *U.S.A.* **113** G14
Madisonville *Ky., U.S.A.* **112** G10
Madisonville *Tex., U.S.A.* **116** F7
Madista *Botswana* **88** C4
Madiun *Indonesia* **62** F4
Mado Gashi *Kenya* **86** B4

Madoc *Canada* **114** B7
Madon → *France* **19** D13
Madona *Latvia* **32** D4
Madonie *Italy* **42** E6
Madonna di Campíglio *Italy* **40** B7
Madra Daği *Turkey* **47** B9
Madrakah, Ra's al *Oman* **75** D6
Madras = Chennai *India* **66** N12
Madras = Tamil Nadu □ *India* **66** P10
Madras *U.S.A.* **108** D3
Madre, L. *U.S.A.* **116** J6
Madre, Sierra *Phil.* **61** C5
Madre de Dios → *Bolivia* **124** F5
Madre de Dios, I. *Chile* **128** G1
Madre del Sur, Sierra *Mexico* **119** D5
Madre Occidental, Sierra *Mexico* **118** B3
Madre Oriental, Sierra *Mexico* **118** C5
Madri *India* **68** G5
Madrid *Spain* **36** E7
Madrid *U.S.A.* **115** B9
Madrid □ *Spain* **36** E7
Madrid Barajas ✈ (MAD) *Spain* **36** E7
Madridejos *Spain* **37** F7
Madrigal de las Altas Torres *Spain* **36** D6
Madrona, Sierra *Spain* **37** G6
Madroñera *Spain* **37** F5
Madu *Sudan* **81** E2
Madula *Dem. Rep. of the Congo* **86** B2
Madura *Australia* **93** F4
Madura *Indonesia* **63** G15
Madura, Selat *Indonesia* **63** G15
Madurai *India* **66** Q11
Madurantakam *India* **66** N11
Madzhalis *Russia* **35** J8
Mae Chan *Thailand* **64** B2
Mae Hong Son *Thailand* **64** C2
Mae Khlong → *Thailand* **64** F3
Mae Phrik *Thailand* **64** D2
Mae Ping △ *Thailand* **64** F2
Mae Ramat *Thailand* **64** D2
Mae Rim *Thailand* **64** C2
Mae Sai *Thailand* **58** G2
Mae Sot *Thailand* **64** D2
Mae Suai *Thailand* **58** H2
Mae Tha *Thailand* **64** C2
Mae Wong △ *Thailand* **64** E2
Mae Yom △ *Thailand* **64** C3
Maebashi *Japan* **55** F9
Maella *Spain* **38** D5
Maesteg *U.K.* **15** F4
Maestra, Sierra *Cuba* **120** B4
Maevatanana *Madag.* **89** B8
Mafeking = Mafikeng *S. Africa* **88** D4
Mafeking *Canada* **103** C8
Maféré *Ivory C.* **82** D4
Mafeteng *Lesotho* **88** D4
Maffra *Australia* **95** F4
Mafia I. *Tanzania* **86** D4
Mafra *Brazil* **127** B6
Mafra *Portugal* **37** G1
Mafungabusi Plateau *Zimbabwe* **87** F2
Magadan *Russia* **53** D16
Magadi *Kenya* **86** C4
Magadi, L. *Kenya* **86** C4
Magaliesburg *S. Africa* **89** D4
Magallanes, Estrecho de *Chile* **128** G2
Magaluf *Spain* **39** F7
Magangué *Colombia* **124** B4
Magaria *Niger* **83** C6
Magburaka *S. Leone* **82** D2
Magdagachi *Russia* **53** D13
Magdalen Is. = Madeleine, Îs. de la *Canada* **105** C7
Magdalena *Argentina* **126** D4
Magdalena *Bolivia* **124** F6
Magdalena *U.S.A.* **109** J10
Magdalena → *Colombia* **124** A4
Magdalena → *Mexico* **118** A2
Magdalena, B. *Mexico* **118** C2
Magdalena, I. *Mexico* **118** C2
Magdalena, Llano de *Mexico* **118** C2
Magdalena de Kino *Mexico* **118** A2
Magdeburg *Germany* **24** C7
Magdelaine Cays *Australia* **94** B5
Magdub *Sudan* **81** E2
Magee *U.S.A.* **117** F10
Magelang *Indonesia* **62** F4
Magellan's Str. = Magallanes, Estrecho de *Chile* **128** G2
Magenta *Italy* **40** C5
Magenta, L. *Australia* **93** F2
Magerøya *Norway* **8** A21
Maggia → *Switz.* **25** J4
Maggiorasca, Mte. *Italy* **40** D6
Maggiore, Lago *Italy* **40** B5
Maggotty *Jamaica* **120** a
Maghâgha *Egypt* **80** B3

Maghama *Mauritania* **82** B2
Magherafelt *U.K.* **12** B5
Maghreb *N. Afr.* **78** B5
Magione *Italy* **42** E6
Magistralnyy *Russia* **53** D11
Maglaj *Bos.-H.* **28** F3
Magliano in Toscana *Italy* **41** F8
Máglie *Italy* **43** B11
Magnac-Laval *France* **20** B5
Magnetic Pole (North) *Canada* **4** A2
Magnetic Pole (South) *Antarctica* **5** C9
Magnisia □ *Greece* **46** B5
Magnitogorsk *Russia* **52** D6
Magnolia *Ark., U.S.A.* **116** E8
Magnolia *Miss., U.S.A.* **117** F9
Magny-en-Vexin *France* **19** C8
Mago *Fiji* **91** a
Mago △ *Ethiopia* **81** F4
Magog *Canada* **115** A12
Magoro *Uganda* **86** B3
Magoša = Famagusta *Cyprus* **49** D12
Magoulades *Greece* **49** A3
Magoye *Zambia* **87** F2
Magpie, L. *Canada* **105** B7
Magrath *Canada* **102** D6
Magre → *Spain* **39** F4
Magrur *Sudan* **81** E3
Magrur, Wadi → *Sudan* **81** D2
Magta Lahjar *Mauritania* **82** B2
Magu *Tanzania* **86** C3
Maguan *China* **58** F5
Maguarinho, C. *Brazil* **125** D9
Magude *Mozam.* **89** D5
Magurski △ *Poland* **31** J8
Maguse L. *Canada* **103** A9
Maguse Pt. *Canada* **103** A10
Magvana *India* **68** H3
Magwe *Burma* **67** J19
Magwe *Sudan* **81** G3
Magyarország = Hungary ■ *Europe* **27** D12
Maha Sarakham *Thailand* **64** D4
Mahābād *Iran* **73** D11
Mahabharat Lekh *Nepal* **69** E10
Mahabo *Madag.* **89** C7
Mahadeo Hills *India* **69** H8
Mahaffey *U.S.A.* **114** F6
Mahagi *Dem. Rep. of the Congo* **86** B3
Mahajamba → *Madag.* **89** B8
Mahajamba, Helodranon' i *Madag.* **89** B8
Mahajan *India* **68** E5
Mahajanga *Madag.* **89** B8
Mahajanga □ *Madag.* **89** B8
Mahajilo → *Madag.* **89** B8
Mahakam → *Indonesia* **62** E5
Mahalapye *Botswana* **88** C4
Mahale Mts. *Tanzania* **86** D3
Mahale Mts. △ *Tanzania* **86** D2
Maḥallāt *Iran* **71** C6
Māhān *Iran* **71** D8
Mahan → *India* **69** H10
Mahanadi → *India* **67** J15
Mahananda → *India* **69** G12
Mahanoro *Madag.* **89** B8
Mahanoy City *U.S.A.* **115** F8
Maharashtra □ *India* **66** J9
Mahasham, W. → *Egypt* **74** E3
Mahasoa *Madag.* **89** C8
Mahasolo *Madag.* **89** B8
Mahattat ash Shīdīyah *Jordan* **74** F4
Mahattat 'Unayzah *Jordan* **74** E4
Mahavavy → *Madag.* **89** B8
Mahaxay *Laos* **64** D5
Mahbubnagar *India* **66** L10
Mahda *U.A.E.* **71** E8
Maḥḍah *Oman* **71** E7
Mahdia *Tunisia* **79** A8
Mahe *India* **69** C8
Mahé *Seychelles* **85** b
Mahé ✈ (SEZ) *Seychelles* **85** b
Mahébourg *Mauritius* **85** d
Mahendragarh *India* **68** E7
Mahendranagar *Nepal* **69** E9
Mahenge *Tanzania* **87** D4
Maheno *N.Z.* **91** F3
Mahesana *India* **68** H5
Maheshwar *India* **68** H6
Mahgawan *India* **69** F8
Mahi → *India* **68** H5
Mahia Pen. *N.Z.* **91** C7
Mahilyow *Belarus* **23** B16
Mahilyow □ *Belarus* **32** E6
Mahina *Tahiti* **91** d
Mahinerangi, L. *N.Z.* **91** F2
Mahmiya *Sudan* **81** D3
Mahmud Kot *Pakistan* **68** D4
Mahmudia *Romania* **29** E14
Mahmudiye *Turkey* **47** B12
Mahmutbey *Turkey* **45** E12
Māhneshān *Iran* **73** D13
Mahnomen *U.S.A.* **112** B6
Mahoba *India* **69** G8
Mahón = Maó *Spain* **48** B11

Mahon, Menorca ✈ (MAH) *Spain* **38** F9
Mahone Bay *Canada* **105** D7
Mahopac *U.S.A.* **115** E11
Mahuta *Nigeria* **83** C5
Mahuva *India* **68** J4
Mahya Daği *Turkey* **45** E11
Mai-Ndombe, L. *Dem. Rep. of the Congo* **84** E3
Mai Thon, Ko *Thailand* **65** a
Maia *Portugal* **36** D2
Maials *Spain* **38** D5
Maîche *France* **19** E13
Maicuru → *Brazil* **125** D8
Máida *Italy* **43** D9
Maidan Khula *Afghan.* **68** C3
Maidenhead *U.K.* **15** F8
Maidstone *Canada* **103** C7
Maidstone *U.K.* **15** F8
Maiduguri *Nigeria* **83** C7
Maiella △ *Italy* **41** F11
Maigatari *Nigeria* **83** C6
Maigh Nuad = Maynooth *Ireland* **12** C5
Maignelay Montigny *France* **19** C9
Maigo *Phil.* **61** G5
Maigudo *Ethiopia* **81** F4
Maihar *India* **69** G9
Maikala Ra. *India* **67** J12
Maiko △ *Dem. Rep. of the Congo* **86** C2
Mailani *India* **69** E9
Maillezais *France* **20** B3
Mailsi *Pakistan* **68** E5
Main → *Germany* **25** F4
Main → *U.K.* **12** B5
Main Channel *Canada* **114** A3
Main Range △ *Australia* **95** D5
Main Ridge *Trin. & Tob.* **125** J16
Mainburg *Germany* **25** G7
Maine *France* **18** D6
Maine □ *U.S.A.* **113** C19
Maine → *Ireland* **12** D2
Maine, G. of □ *U.S.A.* **113** D19
Maine-et-Loire □ *France* **18** E6
Maïne-Soroa *Niger* **83** C7
Maingkwan *Burma* **67** F20
Mainistir an Corann = Midleton *Ireland* **12** E3
Mainit, L. *Phil.* **61** G6
Mainland *Orkney, U.K.* **13** C5
Mainland *Shet., U.K.* **13** A7
Mainpuri *India* **69** F8
Maintal *Germany* **25** E4
Maintenon *France* **19** D8
Maintirano *Madag.* **89** B7
Mainz *Germany* **25** E4
Maio *C. Verde Is.* **78** b
Maipú *Argentina* **126** D4
Maiquetía *Venezuela* **124** A5
Máira → *Italy* **40** D4
Mairabari *India* **67** F18
Maisí *Cuba* **121** B5
Maisi, Pta. de *Cuba* **121** B5
Maitland *N.S.W., Australia* **95** E5
Maitland *S. Austral., Australia* **95** E2
Maitland → *Canada* **114** C3
Maitri *Antarctica* **5** D3
Maiyema *Nigeria* **83** C5
Maiyuan *China* **59** E11
Maíz, Is. del *Nic.* **120** D3
Maizuru *Japan* **55** G7
Majalengka *Indonesia* **63** G13
Majene *Indonesia* **63** E5
Majete △ *Malawi* **87** F3
Majevica *Bos.-H.* **28** F3
Maji *Ethiopia* **81** F4
Majiang *China* **58** D6
Majorca = Mallorca *Spain* **48** B10
Majuro *Marshall Is.* **96** G9
Maka *Senegal* **82** C2
Makaha *Zimbabwe* **89** B5
Makak *Cameroon* **83** E7
Makalamabedi *Botswana* **88** C3
Makale *Indonesia* **63** E5
Makalu-Barun △ *Nepal* **69** F12
Makamba *Burundi* **86** C2
Makari *Cameroon* **83** C7
Makarikari = Makgadikgadi Salt Pans *Botswana* **88** C4
Makarov Basin *Arctic* **4** A
Makarova *Russia* **53** D11
Makarska *Croatia* **41** E14
Makaryev *Russia* **34** B6
Makasar = Ujung Pandang *Indonesia* **63** F5
Makasar, Selat *Indonesia* **63** E5
Makasar, Str. of = Makasar, Selat *Indonesia* **63** E5
Makat = Maqat *Kazakhstan* **52** E6
Makedonija = Macedonia ■ *Europe* **44** E5
Makeni *S. Leone* **82** D2
Makeyevka = Makiyivka *Ukraine* **33** H9
Makgadikgadi △ *Botswana* **88** C3

Makgadikgadi Salt Pans *Botswana* **88** C4
Makhachkala *Russia* **35** J8
Makhado = Louis Trichardt *S. Africa* **89** C4
Makham, Ao *Thailand* **65** a
Makharadze = Ozurgeti *Georgia* **35** K5
Makhfar al Buşayyah *Iraq* **70** D5
Makhmūr *Iraq* **73** E10
Makian *Indonesia* **63** D7
Makindu *Kenya* **86** C4
Makīnsk *Kazakhstan* **52** D8
Makira = San Cristóbal *Solomon Is.* **90** C9
Makiv *Ukraine* **29** B11
Makiyivka *Ukraine* **33** H9
Makkah *Si. Arabia* **80** C4
Makkovik *Canada* **105** A8
Makó *Hungary* **28** D5
Mako *Senegal* **82** C2
Makogai *Fiji* **91** a
Makokou *Gabon* **84** D2
Makongo *Dem. Rep. of the Congo* **86** B2
Makoro *Dem. Rep. of the Congo* **86** B2
Maków Mazowiecki *Poland* **31** F8
Maków Podhalański *Poland* **31** J6
Makra *Greece* **46** E6
Makrai *India* **68** H7
Makran Coast Range *Pakistan* **66** G4
Makrana *India* **68** F6
Makrany *Belarus* **31** G11
Makri *Greece* **45** F9
Makrigialos *Greece* **49** D7
Mākū *Iran* **73** C11
Makunda *Botswana* **88** C3
Makung *Taiwan* **59** F12
Makurazaki *Japan* **55** J5
Makurdi *Nigeria* **83** D6
Makushin Volcano *U.S.A.* **106** E6
Makūyeh *Iran* **71** D7
Makwassie *S. Africa* **88** D4
Makwiro *Zimbabwe* **89** B5
Mâl *Mauritania* **82** B2
Mal B. *Ireland* **12** D2
Mala = Mallow *Ireland* **12** D3
Mala, Pta. *Panama* **120** E3
Mala Belözërka *Ukraine* **33** J8
Malá Fatra △ *Slovak Rep.* **27** B12
Mala Kapela *Croatia* **41** D12
Mala Panew → *Poland* **31** H4
Mala Vyska *Ukraine* **33** H6
Malabang *Phil.* **61** H6
Malabar Coast *India* **66** P9
Malabon *Phil.* **61** D4
Malabu *Nigeria* **83** D7
Malacca, Straits of *Indonesia* **65** L3
Malacky *Slovak Rep.* **27** C10
Malad City *U.S.A.* **108** E7
Maladeta *Spain* **38** C5
Maladzyechna *Belarus* **23** A14
Málaga *Spain* **37** J6
Málaga □ *Spain* **37** J6
Malagarasi *Tanzania* **86** D3
Malagarasi → *Tanzania* **86** D2
Malagasy Rep. = Madagascar ■ *Africa* **89** C8
Malagón *Spain* **37** F7
Malagón → *Spain* **37** H3
Malahide *Ireland* **12** C5
Malaimbandy *Madag.* **89** C8
Malaita *Solomon Is.* **90** B9
Malakâl *Sudan* **81** F3
Malakand *Pakistan* **68** B4
Malakula *Vanuatu* **90** C9
Malakwal *Pakistan* **68** C5
Malamala *Indonesia* **63** E6
Malanda *Australia* **94** B4
Malang *Indonesia* **62** F4
Malanga *Mozam.* **87** E4
Malangen *Norway* **8** B18
Malanje *Angola* **84** F3
Mälaren *Sweden* **10** E11
Malargüe *Argentina* **126** D2
Malartic *Canada* **104** C4
Malaryta *Belarus* **31** G11
Malaspina Glacier *U.S.A.* **106** D11
Malatya *Turkey* **73** C8
Malatya □ *Turkey* **72** C7
Malawi ■ *Africa* **87** E3
Malawi, L. *Africa* **87** E3
Malay Pen. *Asia* **65** J3
Malaya Belözërka = Mala Belözërka *Ukraine* **33** J8
Malaya Vishera *Russia* **32** C7
Malaya Viska = Mala Vyska *Ukraine* **33** H6
Malaybalay *Phil.* **61** G6
Malāyer *Iran* **73** E13
Malaysia ■ *Asia* **65** K4
Malazgirt *Turkey* **73** C10
Mala ✪ *Australia* **92** D5
Malbaza *Niger* **83** C6
Malbon *Australia* **94** C3
Malbooma *Australia* **95** E1
Malbork *Poland* **30** D6
Malcésine *Italy* **40** C7

Malchin *Germany* **24** B8
Malchow *Germany* **24** B8
Malcolm *Australia* **93** E3
Malcolm, Pt. *Australia* **93** F3
Malczyce *Poland* **31** G3
Maldah *India* **69** G13
Maldegem *Belgium* **17** C3
Malden *Mass., U.S.A.* **115** D13
Malden *Mo., U.S.A.* **112** G9
Malden I. *Kiribati* **97** H12
Maldives ■ *Ind. Oc.* **50** H9
Maldon *U.K.* **15** F8
Maldonado *Uruguay* **127** C5
Maldonado, Pta. *Mexico* **119** D5
Malè *Italy* **40** B7
Malé *Maldives* **50** H8
Malé Karpaty *Slovak Rep.* **27** C10
Maleas, Akra *Greece* **46** E5
Malebo, Pool *Africa* **84** E3
Malegaon *India* **66** J9
Malei *Mozam.* **87** F4
Malek *Sudan* **81** F3
Malek Kandī *Iran* **73** D12
Malela *Dem. Rep. of the Congo* **86** C2
Malema *Mozam.* **87** E4
Maleme *Greece* **49** D5
Mälerås *Sweden* **11** H9
Malerkotla *India* **68** D6
Males *Greece* **49** D7
Malesherbes *France* **19** D9
Maleshevska Planina *Europe* **44** E7
Malesina *Greece* **46** C5
Malestroit *France* **18** E4
Malfa *Italy* **43** D7
Malgobek *Russia* **35** J7
Malgomaj *Sweden* **8** D17
Malgrat de Mar *Spain* **38** D7
Malha *Sudan* **81** D2
Malhargarh *India* **68** G6
Malheur → *U.S.A.* **108** D5
Malheur L. *U.S.A.* **108** E4
Mali ■ *Guinea* **82** C2
Mali ■ *Africa* **82** B4
Mali → *Burma* **67** G20
Mali Kanal *Serbia* **28** E4
Mali Kyun *Burma* **64** F2
Malia *Greece* **49** D7
Malia, Kolpos *Greece* **49** D7
Malibu *U.S.A.* **111** L8
Maliku *Indonesia* **63** E6
Malili *Indonesia* **63** E6
Målilla *Sweden* **11** G9
Malimba, Mts. *Dem. Rep. of the Congo* **86** D2
Malin Hd. *Ireland* **12** A4
Malin Pen. *Ireland* **12** A4
Malindi *Kenya* **86** C5
Malindi Marine △ *Kenya* **86** C5
Malines = Mechelen *Belgium* **17** C4
Malino *Indonesia* **63** D6
Malinyi *Tanzania* **87** D4
Malipo *China* **58** F5
Maliq *Albania* **44** F4
Malita *Phil.* **63** C7
Maliwun *Burma* **65** G2
Maliya *India* **68** H4
Maljenik *Serbia* **44** B5
Malka Mari △ *Kenya* **86** B5
Malkara *Turkey* **45** F10
Malkinia Górna *Poland* **31** F9
Malko Tŭrnovo *Bulgaria* **45** E11
Mallacoota Inlet *Australia* **95** F4
Mallaig *U.K.* **13** D3
Mallaoua *Niger* **83** C6
Mallawan *India* **69** F9
Mallawi *Egypt* **80** B3
Mallemort *France* **21** E9
Málles Venosta *Italy* **40** B7
Mallicolo = Malakula *Vanuatu* **90** C9
Mallorca *Spain* **48** B10
Mallorytown *Canada* **115** B9
Mallow *Ireland* **12** D3
Malmbäck *Sweden* **11** G8
Malmberget *Sweden* **8** C19
Malmédy *Belgium* **17** D6
Malmesbury *S. Africa* **88** E2
Malmivaara = Malmberget *Sweden* **8** C19
Malmköping *Sweden* **10** E10
Malmö *Sweden* **11** J7
Malmslätt *Sweden* **11** F9
Malmyzh *Russia* **34** B10
Malnaş *Romania* **29** D10
Malo Konare *Bulgaria* **45** D8
Maloarkhangelsk *Russia* **33** F9
Malolo *Fiji* **91** a
Malolotja △ *Swaziland* **89** D5
Malolos *Phil.* **63** B6
Malombe L. *Malawi* **87** E4
Malomice *Poland* **31** G2
Malomir *Bulgaria* **45** D10
Malone *U.S.A.* **115** B10
Malong *China* **58** E4
Małopolskie □ *Poland* **31** J7
Malorad *Bulgaria* **44** C7
Måløy *Norway* **8** F11
Maloyaroslovets *Russia* **32** E9
Malpaso *Canary Is.* **48** G1

Malpaso, Presa = Netzahualcóyotl, Presa *Mexico* **119** D6
Malpelo, I. de *Colombia* **124** C1
Malpica de Bergantiños *Spain* **36** B2
Malpur *India* **68** H5
Malpura *India* **68** F6
Mals = Málles Venosta *Italy* **40** B7
Malta *Idaho, U.S.A.* **108** E7
Malta *Mont., U.S.A.* **108** B10
Malta ■ *Europe* **49** D2
Maltahöhe *Namibia* **88** C2
Maltepe *Turkey* **45** F13
Malton *Canada* **114** C5
Malton *U.K.* **14** C7
Maluku *Indonesia* **63** E7
Maluku □ *Indonesia* **63** E7
Maluku Sea = Molucca Sea *Indonesia* **63** E6
Malumfashi *Nigeria* **83** C6
Malung *Sweden* **10** D7
Malungsfors *Sweden* **10** D7
Maluwe *Ghana* **82** D4
Malvan *India* **66** L8
Malvern *U.S.A.* **116** D8
Malvern Hills *U.K.* **15** E5
Malvinas, Is. = Falkland Is. ☑ *Atl. Oc.* **128** G5
Malwal *Sudan* **81** F3
Malý Dunaj → *Slovak Rep.* **27** D11
Malya *Tanzania* **86** C3
Malye Derbety *Russia* **35** G7
Malyn *Ukraine* **23** C15
Malyy Lyakhovskiy, Ostrov *Russia* **53** B15
Malyy Taymyr, Ostrov *Russia* **53** B11
Mama *Russia* **53** D12
Mamadysh *Russia* **34** C10
Mamanguape *Brazil* **125** E11
Mamanuca Group *Fiji* **91** a
Mamarr Mitlā *Egypt* **74** E1
Mamasa *Indonesia* **63** E5
Mambasa *Dem. Rep. of the Congo* **86** B2
Mamberamo → *Indonesia* **63** E9
Mambilima Falls *Zambia* **87** E2
Mambirima *Dem. Rep. of the Congo* **87** E2
Mambo *Tanzania* **86** C4
Mambrui *Kenya* **86** C5
Mamburao *Phil.* **61** E4
Mamedkala *Russia* **73** A13
Mameigwess L. *Canada* **104** B2
Mamers *France* **18** D7
Mamfé *Cameroon* **83** D6
Mammoth *U.S.A.* **109** K8
Mammoth Cave △ *U.S.A.* **112** G10
Mamonovo *Russia* **30** D6
Mamoré → *Bolivia* **124** F5
Mamou *Guinea* **82** C2
Mamoudzou *Mayotte* **85** a
Mampikony *Madag.* **89** B8
Mampong *Ghana* **83** D4
Mamry, Jezioro *Poland* **30** D8
Mamuju *Indonesia* **63** E5
Mamuno *Botswana* **88** C3
Mamuras *Albania* **44** E3
Man *Ivory C.* **82** D3
Man, I. of *U.K.* **14** C3
Man-Bazar *India* **69** H12
Man Na *Burma* **67** H20
Mänä *U.S.A.* **107** L8
Mana → *Fr. Guiana* **125** B8
Mana Pools △ *Zimbabwe* **87** F2
Manaar, G. of = Mannar, G. of *Asia* **66** Q11
Manacapuru *Brazil* **124** D6
Manacor *Spain* **48** B10
Manado *Indonesia* **63** D6
Managua *Nic.* **120** D2
Managua, L. de *Nic.* **120** D2
Manakara *Madag.* **89** C8
Manali *India* **68** C7
Manama = Al Manāmah *Bahrain* **71** E6
Manambao → *Madag.* **89** B7
Manambato *Madag.* **89** A8
Manambolo → *Madag.* **89** B7
Manambolosy *Madag.* **89** B8
Mananara *Madag.* **89** B8
Mananara → *Madag.* **89** C8
Mananara △ *Madag.* **89** B8
Mananjary *Madag.* **89** C8
Manankoro *Mali* **82** C3
Manantali, L. de *Mali* **82** C2
Manantenina *Madag.* **89** C8
Manaos = Manaus *Brazil* **124** D7
Manapire → *Venezuela* **124** B5
Manapouri *N.Z.* **91** F1
Manapouri, L. *N.Z.* **91** F1
Manaqil *Sudan* **81** E3
Manār, Jabal *Yemen* **75** E3
Manaravolo *Madag.* **89** C8
Manas *China* **60** B3
Manas → *India* **67** F17
Manaslu *Nepal* **69** E11
Manasquan *U.S.A.* **115** F10

Manassa *U.S.A.* **109** H11
Manatí *Puerto Rico* **121** d
Manaung *Burma* **67** K18
Manaus *Brazil* **124** D7
Manavgat *Turkey* **72** D4
Manawan L. *Canada* **103** B8
Manay *Phil.* **61** H7
Manbij *Syria* **72** D7
Mancha Real *Spain* **37** H7
Manche □ *France* **18** C5
Manchegorsk *Russia* **52** C4
Manchester *U.K.* **14** D5
Manchester *Calif., U.S.A.* **110** G3
Manchester *Conn., U.S.A.* **115** E12
Manchester *Ga., U.S.A.* **117** E12
Manchester *Iowa, U.S.A.* **112** D8
Manchester *Ky., U.S.A.* **113** G12
Manchester *N.H., U.S.A.* **115** D13
Manchester *N.Y., U.S.A.* **114** D7
Manchester *Pa., U.S.A.* **115** F8
Manchester *Tenn., U.S.A.* **117** D11
Manchester *Vt., U.S.A.* **115** C11
Manchester Int. ✈ (MAN)
  U.K. **14** D5
Manchester L. *Canada* **103** A7
Manchhar L. *Pakistan* **68** F2
Manchuria = Dongbei *China* **54** A5
Manchurian Plain *China* **50** D14
Manciano *Italy* **41** F8
Mancifa *Ethiopia* **81** F5
Mand → *India* **69** J10
Mand → *Iran* **71** D7
Manda *Ludewe, Tanzania* **87** E3
Manda *Mbeya, Tanzania* **86** D3
Manda *Mbeya, Tanzania* **87** D3
Mandabé *Madag.* **89** C7
Mandaguari *Brazil* **127** A5
Mandah = Töhöm *Mongolia* **56** B5
Mandal *Norway* **9** G12
Mandala, Puncak *Indonesia* **63** E10
Mandalay *Burma* **67** J20
Mandale = Mandalay
  Burma **67** J20
Mandalgarh *India* **68** G6
Mandalgovĭ *Mongolia* **56** B4
Mandalī *Iraq* **73** F11
Mandan *U.S.A.* **112** B3
Mandaon *Phil.* **61** E5
Mandar, Teluk *Indonesia* **63** E5
Mándas *Italy* **42** C2
Mandaue *Phil.* **61** F5
Mandelieu-la-Napoule
  France **21** E10
Mandera *Kenya* **86** B5
Mandeville *Jamaica* **120** a
Mandi *India* **68** D7
Mandi Burewala *Pakistan* **68** D5
Mandi Dabwali *India* **68** E6
Mandiana *Guinea* **82** C3
Mandioli *Indonesia* **63** E7
Mandla *India* **69** H9
Mando *Denmark* **11** J2
Mandorah *Australia* **92** B5
Mandoto *Madag.* **89** B8
Mandoudi *Greece* **46** C5
Mandra *Greece* **46** C5
Mandra *Pakistan* **68** C5
Mandraki *Greece* **47** E9
Mandrare → *Madag.* **89** D8
Mandritsara *Madag.* **89** B8
Mandronarivo *Madag.* **89** C8
Mandsaur *India* **68** G6
Mandurah *Australia* **93** F2
Mandúria *Italy* **43** B10
Mandvi *India* **68** H3
Mandya *India* **66** N10
Mandzai *Pakistan* **68** D2
Mané *Burkina Faso* **83** C4
Maneh *Iran* **71** B8
Manengouba, Mts. *Cameroon* **83** E6
Manera *Madag.* **89** C7
Manérbio *Italy* **40** C7
Maneroo Cr. → *Australia* **94** C3
Manfalût *Egypt* **80** B3
Manfredónia *Italy* **41** G12
Manfredónia, G. di *Italy* **41** G13
Manga *Burkina Faso* **83** C4
Manga *Niger* **83** C7
Mangabeira, Chapada das
  Brazil **125** F9
Mangaia *Cook Is.* **97** K12
Mangalia *Romania* **29** G13
Mangalore *India* **66** N9
Mangaluru = Mangalore
  India **66** N9
Mangan *India* **69** F13
Mangawan *India* **69** G9
Mangaweka *N.Z.* **91** C5
Manggar *Indonesia* **62** E3
Manggawitu *Indonesia* **63** E8
Mangghystaū Tübegi
  Kazakhstan **52** E6
Manggis *Indonesia* **63** J18
Mangindrano *Madag.* **89** A8
Mangkalihat, Tanjung
  Indonesia **63** D5
Mangkururrpa ☺ *Australia* **92** D4
Mangla *Pakistan* **68** C5

Mangla Dam *Pakistan* **69** C5
Manglaur *India* **68** E7
Manglisi *Georgia* **35** K7
Mangnai *China* **60** C4
Mango *Togo* **83** C5
Mango *Tonga* **91** c
Mangoche *Malawi* **87** E4
Mangoky → *Madag.* **89** C7
Mangole *Indonesia* **63** E6
Mangombe
  Dem. Rep. of the Congo **86** C2
Mangonui *N.Z.* **91** A4
Mangoro → *Madag.* **89** B8
Mangrol *Mad. P., India* **68** J4
Mangrol *Raj., India* **68** G6
Mangualde *Portugal* **36** E3
Mangueira, L. da *Brazil* **127** C5
Mangum *U.S.A.* **116** D5
Manguri *Australia* **95** A1
Mangyshlak, Poluostrov =
  Mangghystaū Tübegi
  Kazakhstan **52** E6
Manhattan *U.S.A.* **112** F5
Manhiça *Mozam.* **89** D5
Mania → *Madag.* **89** B8
Maniago *Italy* **41** B9
Manica *Mozam.* **89** B5
Manica □ *Mozam.* **89** B5
Manicaland □ *Zimbabwe* **87** F3
Manicoré *Brazil* **124** E6
Manicouagan → *Canada* **105** C6
Manicouagan, Rés. *Canada* **105** B6
Maniema □
  Dem. Rep. of the Congo **86** C2
Manīfah *Si. Arabia* **71** E6
Manifold, C. *Australia* **94** C5
Maniganggo *China* **58** B2
Manigotagan *Canada* **103** C9
Manigotagan → *Canada* **103** C9
Manihari *India* **69** G12
Manihiki *Cook Is.* **97** J11
Manihiki Plateau *Pac. Oc.* **97** J11
Manika, Plateau de la
  Dem. Rep. of the Congo **87** E2
Manikpur *India* **69** G9
Manila *Phil.* **61** D4
Manila *U.S.A.* **108** F9
Manila B. *Phil.* **61** D4
Manilla *Australia* **95** E5
Manimpé *Mali* **82** C3
Maningrida *Australia* **94** A1
Maninian *Ivory C.* **82** C3
Manipur □ *India* **67** G19
Manipur → *Burma* **67** H19
Manisa *Turkey* **47** C9
Manisa □ *Turkey* **47** C9
Manistee *U.S.A.* **112** C10
Manistee → *U.S.A.* **112** C10
Manistique *U.S.A.* **112** C10
Manitoba □ *Canada* **103** B9
Manitoba, L. *Canada* **103** C9
Manitou *Canada* **103** D9
Manitou, L. *Canada* **105** B6
Manitou Is. *U.S.A.* **113** C10
Manitou L. *Canada* **103** C7
Manitou Springs *U.S.A.* **108** G11
Manitoulin I. *Canada* **104** C3
Manitouwadge *Canada* **104** C2
Manitowoc *U.S.A.* **112** C10
Manizales *Colombia* **124** B3
Manja *Madag.* **89** C7
Manjacaze *Mozam.* **89** C5
Manjakandriana *Madag.* **89** B8
Manjhand *Pakistan* **68** G3
Manjimup *Australia* **93** F2
Manjo *Cameroon* **83** E6
Manjra → *India* **66** K10
Mankato *Kans., U.S.A.* **112** F4
Mankato *Minn., U.S.A.* **112** C6
Mankayane *Swaziland* **89** D5
Mankera *Pakistan* **68** C4
Mankim *Cameroon* **83** D7
Mankono *Ivory C.* **82** D3
Mankota *Canada* **103** D7
Manlay = Üydzin *Mongolia* **56** B4
Manlleu *Spain* **38** C7
Manmad *India* **66** J9
Mann Ranges *Australia* **93** E5
Manna *Indonesia* **62** E2
Mannahill *Australia* **95** E3
Mannar *Sri Lanka* **66** Q11
Mannar, G. of *Asia* **66** Q11
Mannar I. *Sri Lanka* **66** Q11
Mannheim *Germany* **25** F4
Manning *Canada* **102** B5
Manning *Oreg., U.S.A.* **110** E3
Manning *S.C., U.S.A.* **117** E14
Mannu → *Italy* **42** C2
Mannu, C. *Italy* **42** B1
Mannum *Australia* **95** E2
Mano *S. Leone* **82** D2
Mano → *Liberia* **82** D2
Mano River *Liberia* **82** D2
Manohar *India* **69** H11
Manokwari *Indonesia* **63** E8
Manolada *Greece* **46** C3
Manombo *Madag.* **89** C7
Manono
  Dem. Rep. of the Congo **86** D2

Manono *Samoa* **91** b
Manoppello *Italy* **41** F11
Manorhamilton *Ireland* **12** B3
Manosque *France* **21** E9
Manotick *Canada* **115** A9
Manouane → *Canada* **105** C5
Manouane, L. *Canada* **105** B5
Manp'o *N. Korea* **57** D14
Manpojin = Manp'o
  N. Korea **57** D14
Manpur *Chhattisgarh, India* **69** H10
Manpur *Mad. P., India* **68** H6
Manresa *Spain* **38** D6
Mansa *Gujarat, India* **68** H5
Mansa *Punjab, India* **68** E6
Mansa *Zambia* **87** E2
Mansa Konko *Gambia* **82** C1
Mânsâsen *Sweden* **10** A8
Mansehra *Pakistan* **68** B5
Mansel I. *Canada* **101** E15
Mansfield *Australia* **95** F4
Mansfield *U.K.* **14** D6
Mansfield, L. *Australia* **94** C4
Mansfield *Mass., U.S.A.* **115** D13
Mansfield *Ohio, U.S.A.* **114** F2
Mansfield *Pa., U.S.A.* **114** E7
Mansfield *Tex., U.S.A.* **116** E6
Mansfield, Mt. *U.S.A.* **115** B12
Mansilla de las Mulas *Spain* **36** C5
Mansle *France* **20** C4
Mansôa *Guinea-Biss* **82** C1
Manson Creek *Canada* **102** B4
Manta *Ecuador* **124** D2
Mantadia △ *Madag.* **89** B8
Mantare *Tanzania* **86** C3
Manteca *U.S.A.* **110** H5
Manteo *U.S.A.* **117** D17
Mantes-la-Jolie *France* **19** D8
Manthani *India* **66** K11
Manti *U.S.A.* **108** G8
Mantiquera, Serra da
  Brazil **127** A7
Manton *U.S.A.* **113** C11
Mantorp *Sweden* **11** F9
Mántova *Italy* **40** C7
Mänttä *Finland* **32** A3
Mantua = Mántova *Italy* **40** C7
Manturovo *Russia* **34** A7
Manú *Peru* **124** F4
Manú → *Peru* **124** F4
Manu'a Is. *Amer. Samoa* **91** b
Manui *Indonesia* **63** E6
Manukau *N.Z.* **91** B5
Manuripi → *Bolivia* **124** F5
Manyallatuk ☺ *Australia* **92** B5
Manyani *Kenya* **86** C4
Manyara, L. *Tanzania* **86** C4
Manyara □ *Tanzania* **86** C4
Manyas *Turkey* **45** F11
Manyava *Ukraine* **29** B9
Manych → *Russia* **35** G5
Manych-Gudilo, Ozero
  Russia **35** G6
Manyonga → *Tanzania* **86** C3
Manyoni *Tanzania* **86** D3
Manzai *Pakistan* **68** C4
Manzala, Bahra el *Egypt* **80** H7
Manzanar △ *U.S.A.* **110** J7
Manzanares *Spain* **37** F7
Manzaneda *Spain* **36** C3
Manzanillo *Cuba* **120** B4
Manzanillo *Mexico* **118** D4
Manzanillo, Pta. *Panama* **120** E4
Manzano Mts. *U.S.A.* **109** J10
Manzariyeh *Iran* **71** C6
Manzhouli *China* **60** B6
Manzini *Swaziland* **89** D5
Manzur Vadisi △ *Turkey* **70** B3
Mao *Chad* **79** F9
Maó *Spain* **48** B11
Maoke, Pegunungan
  Indonesia **63** E9
Maolin *China* **57** C12
Maoming *China* **59** G8
Maopi T'ou *China* **59** G13
Maouri, Dallol → *Niger* **83** C5
Maoxian *China* **58** B4
Maoxing *China* **57** B13
Mapam Yumco *China* **69** D9
Mapastepec *Mexico* **119** D6
Maphrao, Ko *Thailand* **65** a
Mapia, Kepulauan *Indonesia* **63** D8
Mapimí *Mexico* **118** B4
Mapimí, Bolsón de *Mexico* **118** B4
Maping *China* **59** B9
Mapinga *Tanzania* **86** D4
Mapinhane *Mozam.* **89** C6
Maple Creek *Canada* **103** D7
Maple Valley *U.S.A.* **110** C4
Mapleton *U.S.A.* **108** D2
Mapoon ☺ *Australia* **94** A3
Mapuera → *Brazil* **124** D7
Mapulanguene *Mozam.* **89** C5
Mapungubwe △ *S. Africa* **87** G2
Maputo *Mozam.* **89** D5
Maputo □ *Mozam.* **89** D5

Maputo, B. de *Mozam.* **89** D5
Maputo △ *Mozam.* **89** D5
Maqat *Kazakhstan* **52** E6
Maqiaohe *China* **57** B16
Maqnā *Si. Arabia* **70** D2
Maqteïr *Mauritania* **78** D3
Maquan He =
  Brahmaputra → *Asia* **69** H13
Maqueda *Spain* **36** E6
Maquela do Zombo *Angola* **84** F3
Maquinchao *Argentina* **128** E3
Maquoketa *U.S.A.* **112** D8
Mar *Canada* **114** B3
Mar, Serra do *Brazil* **127** B6
Mar Chiquita, L. *Argentina* **126** C3
Mar del Plata *Argentina* **126** D4
Mar Menor *Spain* **39** H4
Mara *Tanzania* **86** C3
Mara □ *Tanzania* **86** C3
Maraã *Brazil* **124** D5
Maraa *Tahiti* **91** d
Marabá *Brazil* **125** E9
Maraboon, L. *Australia* **94** C4
Maracá, I. de *Brazil* **125** C8
Maracaibo *Venezuela* **124** A4
Maracaibo, L. de *Venezuela* **124** B4
Maracaju *Brazil* **127** A4
Maracas Bay Village
  Trin. & Tob. **125** K15
Maracay *Venezuela* **124** A5
Maracena *Spain* **37** H7
Marādah *Libya* **79** C9
Maradi *Niger* **83** C6
Maradi □ *Niger* **83** C6
Marāgheh *Iran* **73** D12
Marāh *Si. Arabia* **70** E5
Marahoue △ *Ivory C.* **82** D3
Marais du Cotentin et du
  Bessin △ *France* **20** B3
Marais Poitevin, Val de
  Sèvre et Vendée △ *France* **20** B3
Marajó, I. de *Brazil* **125** D9
Marākand *Iran* **70** D5
Marakele △ *S. Africa* **89** E4
Maralal *Kenya* **86** B4
Maralinga *Australia* **93** F5
Maralinga Tjarutja ☺
  Australia **93** E5
MaramaRaereğlisi *Turkey* **45** F11
Marambio *Antarctica* **5** C18
Maramureş □ *Romania* **29** C9
Maran *Malaysia* **65** L4
Marana *U.S.A.* **109** K8
Maranboy *Australia* **92** B5
Maranchón *Spain* **38** D2
Marand *Iran* **73** C11
Marang *Malaysia* **65** K4
Maranguape *Brazil* **125** D11
Maranhão = São Luís *Brazil* **125** D10
Maranhão □ *Brazil* **125** E9
Marano, L. di *Italy* **41** C10
Maranoa → *Australia* **95** D4
Marañón → *Peru* **124** D4
Marão *Mozam.* **89** C5
Maraş = Kahramanmaraş
  Turkey **72** D7
Mărăşeşti *Romania* **29** E12
Maratea *Italy* **43** C8
Marateca *Portugal* **37** G2
Marathasa *Cyprus* **49** E11
Marathokambos *Greece* **47** D8
Marathon *Australia* **94** C3
Marathon *Canada* **104** C2
Marathon *N.Y., U.S.A.* **115** D8
Marathon *Tex., U.S.A.* **116** F3
Marathónas *Greece* **46** C5
Marathóvouno *Cyprus* **49** D12
Maratua *Indonesia* **63** D5
Maraval *Trin. & Tob.* **125** K15
Maravatío *Mexico* **118** D4
Marawi City *Phil.* **61** H6
Marawih *Si. Arabia* **80** G4
Marbella *Spain* **37** J6
Marble Bar *Australia* **92** D2
Marble Falls *U.S.A.* **116** F5
Marblehead *Mass., U.S.A.* **115** D14
Marblehead *U.S.A.* **114** E2
Marburg *Germany* **24** E4
Marca, Pta. do *Angola* **85** H2
Marcal → *Hungary* **28** C2
Marcali *Hungary* **28** D2
Marcaria *Italy* **40** C7
Mărcăuţi *Moldova* **29** B12
March *U.K.* **15** E8
Marche *France* **20** B5
Marche □ *Italy* **41** E10
Marche-en-Famenne
  Belgium **17** D5
Marchena *Spain* **37** H5
Marches = Marche □ *Italy* **41** E10
Marchesale △ *Italy* **43** D9
Marciana Marina *Italy* **40** F7
Marcianise *Italy* **43** A7
Marcigny *France* **19** F11
Marcillat-en-Combraille
  France **19** F9
Marck *France* **19** B8

Marckolsheim *France* **19** D14
Marco Island *U.S.A.* **117** J14
Marcos Juárez *Argentina* **126** C3
Mărculeşti *Moldova* **29** C13
Marcus Baker, Mt. *U.S.A.* **106** C10
Marcus I. = Minami-Tori-
  Shima *Pac. Oc.* **96** F7
Marcy, Mt. *U.S.A.* **115** B11
Mardan *Pakistan* **68** B5
Mardarivka *Ukraine* **29** C14
Mardie *Australia* **92** D2
Mardin *Turkey* **73** D9
Mårdsjö *Sweden* **10** A9
Marecchia → *Italy* **41** D9
Maree, L. *U.K.* **13** D3
Mareeba *Australia* **94** B4
Mareetsane *S. Africa* **88** D4
Maremma *Italy* **41** F8
Maremma △ *Italy* **40** F8
Maréna *Kayes, Mali* **82** C2
Maréna *Koulikouro, Mali* **82** C3
Marengo *U.S.A.* **112** E7
Marennes *France* **20** C2
Marerano *Madag.* **89** C7
Maréttimo *Italy* **42** E5
Mareuil *France* **20** C4
Marfa *U.S.A.* **116** F2
Marfa Pt. *Malta* **49** D1
Marganets = Marhanets
  Ukraine **33** J8
Margaret → *Australia* **92** C4
Margaret Bay *Canada* **102** C3
Margaret L. *Canada* **102** B5
Margaret River *Australia* **93** F2
Margarita, I. de *Venezuela* **124** A6
Margariti *Greece* **46** B2
Margaritovo *Russia* **54** C7
Margate *S. Africa* **89** E5
Margate *U.K.* **15** F9
Margeride, Mts. de la *France* **20** D7
Margherita di Savóia *Italy* **43** A9
Margherita Pk. *Uganda* **86** B3
Marghilon *Uzbekistan* **52** E8
Marghita *Romania* **28** C7
Margonin *Poland* **31** F4
Margosatubig *Phil.* **61** H5
Marguerite *Canada* **102** C4
Marhanets *Ukraine* **33** J8
Mari El □ *Russia* **34** B8
Mari Indus *Pakistan* **68** C4
Mari Republic = Mari El □
  Russia **34** B8
María, Sa. de *Spain* **39** H2
María de la Salut *Spain* **48** B10
María Elena *Chile* **126** A2
María Grande *Argentina* **126** C4
Maria I. *N. Terr., Australia* **94** A2
Maria I. *Tas., Australia* **95** G4
Maria Island △ *Australia* **95** G4
Maria van Diemen, C. *N.Z.* **91** A4
Mariager *Denmark* **11** H3
Mariager Fjord *Denmark* **11** H4
Mariakani *Kenya* **86** C4
Mariala △ *Australia* **95** D4
Marian *Australia* **94** b
Marian L. *Canada* **102** A5
Mariana Trench *Pac. Oc.* **96** F6
Marianna *Ark., U.S.A.* **117** D9
Marianna *Fla., U.S.A.* **117** F12
Mariannelund *Sweden* **11** G9
Mariánské Lázně *Czech Rep.* **26** B5
Marias → *U.S.A.* **108** C8
Marias, Islas *Mexico* **118** C3
Mariato, Punta *Panama* **120** E3
Mariazell *Austria* **26** D8
Maribo *Denmark* **11** K5
Maribor *Slovenia* **41** B12
Marico → *Africa* **88** C4
Maricopa *Ariz., U.S.A.* **109** K7
Maricopa *Calif., U.S.A.* **111** K7
Maridī *Sudan* **81** G2
Maridī, Wadi → *Sudan* **81** F2
Marié → *Brazil* **124** D5
Marie Byrd Land *Antarctica* **5** D14
Marie-Galante *Guadeloupe* **120** b
Mariecourt =
  Kangiqsujuaq *Canada* **101** E17
Mariefred *Sweden* **10** E11
Mariehamn *Finland* **9** F18
Marieholm *Sweden* **11** J7
Mariembourg *Belgium* **17** D4
Marienbad = Mariánské
  Lázně *Czech Rep.* **26** B5
Marienberg *Germany* **24** E9
Mariental *Namibia* **88** C2
Marienville *U.S.A.* **114** E5
Marietta *Ga., U.S.A.* **117** E11
Marietta *Ohio, U.S.A.* **113** F13
Marieville *Canada* **115** A11
Mariga → *Nigeria* **83** D6
Marignane *France* **21** E9
Marihatag *Phil.* **61** E7
Mariinsk *Russia* **52** D9
Mariinskiy Posad *Russia* **34** B8
Marijampolė *Lithuania* **30** D10
Marijampolės □ *Lituania* **30** D10
Marília *Brazil* **127** A6

Marín *Spain* **36** C2
Marina *U.S.A.* **110** J5
Marinduque *Phil.* **63** B6
Marine City *U.S.A.* **114** D2
Marineo *Italy* **42** E6
Marinette *U.S.A.* **112** C10
Maringá *Brazil* **127** A5
Marinha Grande *Portugal* **36** F2
Marino *Italy* **41** G9
Marion *Ala., U.S.A.* **117** E11
Marion *Ill., U.S.A.* **112** G9
Marion *Ind., U.S.A.* **113** E11
Marion *Iowa, U.S.A.* **112** D8
Marion *Kans., U.S.A.* **112** F5
Marion *N.C., U.S.A.* **117** D13
Marion *Ohio, U.S.A.* **113** E12
Marion *S.C., U.S.A.* **117** D15
Marion *Va., U.S.A.* **113** G13
Marion, L. *U.S.A.* **117** E14
Mariposa *U.S.A.* **110** H7
Mariscal Estigarribia
  Paraguay **126** A3
Maritime Alps =
  Maritimes, Alpes *Europe* **21** D11
Maritimes, Alpes *Europe* **21** D11
Maritsa = Evros → *Greece* **72** B2
Maritsa *Greece* **49** C10
Mariupol *Ukraine* **33** J9
Mariusa △ *Venezuela* **121** E7
Marīvān *Iran* **73** E12
Marj 'Uyūn *Lebanon* **74** B4
Marka *Si. Arabia* **80** D5
Marka Somali Rep. **75** G3
Markam *China* **58** C2
Markaryd *Sweden* **11** H7
Markdale *Canada* **114** B4
Marked Tree *U.S.A.* **117** D9
Markelsdorfer Huk *Germany* **24** A7
Market Drayton *U.K.* **14** E5
Market Harborough *U.K.* **15** E7
Market Rasen *U.K.* **14** D7
Markham *Canada* **114** C5
Markham, Mt. *Antarctica* **5** E11
Marki *Poland* **31** F8
Märkische Schweiz △
  Germany **24** C10
Markkleeberg *Germany* **24** D8
Markleeville *U.S.A.* **110** G7
Markopoulo *Greece* **46** C5
Markovac *Serbia* **44** B5
Markovo *Russia* **53** C17
Markoye *Burkina Faso* **83** C5
Marks *Russia* **34** E8
Marksville *U.S.A.* **116** F3
Markt Schwaben *Germany* **25** G7
Marktoberdorf *Germany* **25** H6
Marktredwitz *Germany* **25** E8
Marl *Germany* **24** D3
Marla *Australia* **95** D1
Marlbank *Canada* **114** B7
Marlboro *U.S.A.* **115** E11
Marlborough *Australia* **94** C4
Marlborough *U.K.* **15** F6
Marlborough *U.S.A.* **115** D13
Marlborough Downs *U.K.* **15** F6
Marle *France* **19** C10
Marlin *U.S.A.* **116** F6
Marlow *Germany* **24** A8
Marlow *U.K.* **15** F7
Marlow *U.S.A.* **116** D6
Marmagao *India* **66** M3
Marmande *France* **20** D4
Marmara *Turkey* **45** F11
Marmara, Sea of =
  Marmara Denizi *Turkey* **45** F12
Marmara Denizi *Turkey* **45** F12
Marmara Gölü *Turkey* **47** C10
Marmaris *Turkey* **47** E10
Marmaris Limanı *Turkey* **47** E10
Marmion, Mt. *Australia* **93** E2
Marmion L. *Canada* **104** C1
Marmolada, Mte. *Italy* **41** B8
Marmolejo *Spain* **37** G6
Marmora *Canada* **114** B7
Mármora, La *Italy* **42** C2
Marmugao = Marmagao
  India **66** M8
Marnay *France* **19** E12
Marne *Germany* **24** B5
Marne □ *France* **19** D11
Marne → *France* **19** D9
Marneuli *Georgia* **35** K7
Maro Reef *U.S.A.* **107** K5
Maroala *Madag.* **89** B8
Maroantsetra *Madag.* **89** B8
Maroelaboom *Namibia* **88** B2
Marofandilia *Madag.* **89** C7
Marojejy △ *Madag.* **89** A8
Marolambo *Madag.* **89** C8
Maromandia *Madag.* **89** A8
Maromokotro *Madag.* **89** A8
Marondera *Zimbabwe* **87** F3
Maroni → *Fr. Guiana* **125** B8
Maronia *Greece* **45** F9
Maronne → *France* **20** C5
Maroochydore *Australia* **95** D5
Maroona *Australia* **95** F3
Maros → *Hungary* **28** D5
Marosakoa *Madag.* **89** B8

Maroseranana *Madag.* 89 B8
Maróstica *Italy* 41 C8
Marotandrano *Madag.* 89 B8
Marotaolano *Madag.* 89 A8
Maroua *Cameroon* 83 C7
Marovato *Madag.* 89 B8
Marovoay *Madag.* 89 B8
Marquard *S. Africa* 88 D4
Marquesas Fracture Zone
  Pac. Oc. 97 H15
Marquesas Is. = Marquises,
  Îs. *French Polynesia* 97 H14
Marquette *U.S.A.* 112 B10
Marquis *St. Lucia* 121 f
Marquise *France* 19 B8
Marquises, Îs.
  French Polynesia 97 H14
Marra, Djebel *Sudan* 79 F10
Marra, Gebel *Sudan* 81 F2
Marracuene *Mozam.* 89 D5
Marradi *Italy* 41 D8
Marrakech *Morocco* 78 B4
Marratxí *Spain* 38 F7
Marrawah *Australia* 95 G3
Marree *Australia* 95 D2
Marrero *U.S.A.* 117 G9
Marrimane *Mozam.* 89 C5
Marromeu *Mozam.* 89 B6
Marromeu △ *Mozam.* 89 B6
Marroquí, Punta *Spain* 37 K5
Marrowie Cr. → *Australia* 95 E4
Marrubane *Mozam.* 87 F4
Marrúbiu *Italy* 42 C1
Marrupa *Mozam.* 87 E4
Mars Hill *U.S.A.* 113 B20
Marsá 'Alam *Egypt* 80 C3
Marsá Matrûh *Egypt* 80 A2
Marsá Sha'b *Sudan* 80 C4
Marsabit *Kenya* 86 B4
Marsabit △ *Kenya* 86 B4
Marsala *Italy* 42 E5
Marsalforn *Malta* 49 C1
Mârşani *Romania* 29 F9
Marsberg *Germany* 24 D4
Marsciano *Italy* 41 F9
Marsden *Australia* 95 E4
Marseillan *France* 20 E7
Marseille *France* 21 E9
Marseille-Marignane ✈
  (MRS) *France* 21 E9
Marseilles = Marseille *France* 21 E9
Marsh I. *U.S.A.* 116 G9
Marshall *Liberia* 82 D2
Marshall *Ark., U.S.A.* 116 D8
Marshall *Mich., U.S.A.* 113 D11
Marshall *Minn., U.S.A.* 112 C6
Marshall *Mo., U.S.A.* 112 F7
Marshall *Tex., U.S.A.* 116 E7
Marshall → *Australia* 94 C2
Marshall Is. ■ *Pac. Oc.* 90 A10
Marshalltown *U.S.A.* 112 D8
Marshbrook *Zimbabwe* 89 B5
Marshfield *Mo., U.S.A.* 112 G7
Marshfield *Vt., U.S.A.* 115 B12
Marshfield *Wis., U.S.A.* 112 C8
Marshûn *Iran* 71 B6
Mársico Nuovo *Italy* 43 B8
Märsta *Sweden* 10 E11
Marstal *Denmark* 11 K4
Marstrand *Sweden* 11 G5
Mart *U.S.A.* 116 F6
Marta → *Italy* 41 F8
Martaban *Burma* 67 L20
Martaban, G. of *Burma* 67 L20
Martano *Italy* 43 B11
Martapura *Kalimantan,*
  Indonesia 62 E4
Martapura *Sumatera,*
  Indonesia 62 E2
Marte *Nigeria* 83 C7
Marte R. Gómez, Presa
  Mexico 119 B5
Martel *France* 20 D5
Martelange *Belgium* 17 E5
Martellago *Italy* 41 C9
Martés, Sierra *Spain* 39 F4
Martfű *Hungary* 28 C5
Martha's Vineyard *U.S.A.* 115 E14
Martigné-Ferchaud *France* 18 E5
Martigny *Switz.* 25 J3
Martigues *France* 21 E9
Martin *Slovak Rep.* 27 B11
Martin *S. Dak., U.S.A.* 112 D3
Martin *Tenn., U.S.A.* 117 C10
Martín → *Spain* 38 D4
Martin L. *U.S.A.* 117 E12
Martina Franca *Italy* 43 B10
Martinborough *N.Z.* 91 D5
Martinez *Calif., U.S.A.* 110 G4
Martinez *Ga., U.S.A.* 117 E13
Martinique ☑ *W. Indies* 120 c
Martinique Passage
  W. Indies 121 C7
Martino *Greece* 46 C5
Martinópolis *Brazil* 127 A5
Martin's Bay *Barbados* 121 g
Martins Ferry *U.S.A.* 114 F4
Martinsberg *Austria* 26 C8
Martinsburg *Pa., U.S.A.* 114 F6

Martinsburg *W. Va., U.S.A.* 113 F15
Martinsicuro *Italy* 41 F10
Martinsville *Ind., U.S.A.* 112 F10
Martinsville *Va., U.S.A.* 113 G14
Marton *N.Z.* 91 D5
Martorell *Spain* 38 D6
Martos *Spain* 37 H7
Martuni *Armenia* 35 K7
Martu ✿ *Australia* 92 D3
Maru *Nigeria* 83 C6
Marudi *Malaysia* 62 D4
Marugame *Japan* 55 G6
Marunga *Angola* 88 B3
Marungu, Mts.
  Dem. Rep. of the Congo 86 D3
Maruwa ✿ *Australia* 92 D4
Marv Dasht *Iran* 71 D7
Marvast *Iran* 71 D7
Marvejols *France* 20 D7
Marvel Loch *Australia* 93 F2
Marwar *India* 68 G5
Mary *Turkmenistan* 71 B9
Maryborough = Port
  Laoise *Ireland* 12 C4
Maryborough *Queens.,*
  Australia 95 D5
Maryborough *Vic., Australia* 95 F3
Maryfield *Canada* 103 D8
Maryland ☐ *U.S.A.* 113 F15
Maryland Junction *Zimbabwe* 87 F3
Maryport *U.K.* 14 C4
Mary's Harbour *Canada* 105 B8
Marystown *Canada* 105 C8
Marysville *Calif., U.S.A.* 110 F5
Marysville *Kans., U.S.A.* 112 F5
Marysville *Mich., U.S.A.* 114 D2
Marysville *Ohio, U.S.A.* 113 E12
Marysville *Wash., U.S.A.* 110 B4
Maryville *Mo., U.S.A.* 112 E6
Maryville *Tenn., U.S.A.* 117 D13
Marzúq *Libya* 79 C8
Marzúq, Idehan *Libya* 79 D8
Masada *Israel* 74 D4
Masahunga *Tanzania* 86 C3
Masai *Malaysia* 65 d
Masai Mara △ *Kenya* 86 C4
Masai Steppe *Tanzania* 86 C4
Masaka *Uganda* 86 C3
Masâl *Iran* 73 D12
Masalembo, Kepulauan
  Indonesia 62 F4
Masalima, Kepulauan
  Indonesia 62 F5
Masallı *Azerbaijan* 73 C13
Masamba *Indonesia* 63 E6
Masan *S. Korea* 57 G15
Masandam, Ra's *Oman* 71 E8
Masasi *Tanzania* 87 E4
Masaya *Nic.* 120 D2
Masba *Nigeria* 83 C7
Masbate *Phil.* 61 E5
Máscali *Italy* 43 E8
Mascara *Algeria* 78 A6
Mascota *Mexico* 118 C4
Masela *Indonesia* 63 F7
Maseru *Lesotho* 88 D4
Mashaba *Zimbabwe* 87 G3
Mashābih *Si. Arabia* 70 E3
Mashan *China* 58 F7
Mashar *Sudan* 81 F2
Mashatu △ *Botswana* 89 C4
Mashegu *Nigeria* 83 D6
Masherbrum *Pakistan* 69 B7
Mashhad *Iran* 71 B8
Mashi *Nigeria* 83 C6
Mashiz *Iran* 71 D8
Māshkel, Hāmūn-i- *Pakistan* 71 D9
Mashki Chāh *Pakistan* 66 E3
Mashonaland *Zimbabwe* 85 H6
Mashonaland Central ☐
  Zimbabwe 89 B5
Mashonaland East ☐
  Zimbabwe 89 B5
Mashonaland West ☐
  Zimbabwe 89 B4
Mashrakh *India* 69 F11
Masi Manimba
  Dem. Rep. of the Congo 84 E3
Masig *Australia* 94 a
Masindi *Uganda* 86 B3
Masindi Port *Uganda* 86 B3
Masinga Res. *Kenya* 86 C4
Maşīrah, Jazīrat *Oman* 75 C6
Maşīrah, Khalīj *Oman* 75 C6
Masisi *Dem. Rep. of the Congo* 86 C2
Masjed Soleyman *Iran* 71 D6
Mask, L. *Ireland* 12 C2
Maskin *Oman* 71 F8
Maslen Nos *Bulgaria* 45 D11
Maslinica *Croatia* 41 E13
Masnou = El Masnou *Spain* 38 D7
Masoala, Tanjon' i *Madag.* 89 B9
Masoala △ *Madag.* 89 B9
Masoarivo *Madag.* 89 B7
Masohi = Amahai *Indonesia* 63 E7
Masomeloka *Madag.* 89 C8

Mason *Nev., U.S.A.* 110 G7
Mason *Tex., U.S.A.* 116 F5
Mason City *U.S.A.* 112 D7
Maspalomas *Canary Is.* 48 G4
Maspalomas, Pta. *Canary Is.* 48 G4
Masqat *Oman* 75 C6
Masr el Gedida *Egypt* 80 H7
Massa *Italy* 40 D7
Massa Maríttima *Italy* 40 E7
Massachusetts ☐ *U.S.A.* 115 D13
Massachusetts B. *U.S.A.* 115 D14
Massafra *Italy* 43 B10
Massakory *Chad* 79 F9
Massanella *Spain* 48 B9
Massangena *Mozam.* 89 C5
Massango *Angola* 84 F3
Massat *France* 20 F5
Massawa = Mitsiwa *Eritrea* 81 D4
Massena *U.S.A.* 115 B10
Massenya *Chad* 79 F9
Masset *Canada* 102 C2
Masseube *France* 20 E4
Massiac *France* 20 C7
Massiah Street *Barbados* 121 g
Massif Central *France* 20 D7
Massif des Bauges △ *France* 19 G13
Massigui *Mali* 82 C3
Massillon *U.S.A.* 114 F3
Massinga *Mozam.* 89 C6
Massingir *Mozam.* 89 C5
Masson-Angers *Canada* 115 A9
Masson I. *Antarctica* 5 C7
Maştağa *Azerbaijan* 35 K10
Mastanli = Momchilgrad
  Bulgaria 45 E9
Masterton *N.Z.* 91 D5
Mastic *U.S.A.* 115 F12
Mastuj *Pakistan* 69 A5
Mastung *Pakistan* 66 E5
Mastūrah *Si. Arabia* 80 C4
Masty *Belarus* 23 B13
Masuda *Japan* 55 G5
Masuku = Franceville *Gabon* 84 E2
Masurian Lakes =
  Mazurski, Pojezierze
  Poland 30 E7
Masvingo *Zimbabwe* 87 G3
Masvingo ☐ *Zimbabwe* 87 G3
Maswa △ *Tanzania* 86 C3
Maşyâf *Syria* 72 E7
Mat → *Albania* 44 E3
Mata-au = Clutha → *N.Z.* 91 G2
Matabeleland *Zimbabwe* 85 H5
Matabeleland North ☐
  Zimbabwe 87 F2
Matabeleland South ☐
  Zimbabwe 87 G2
Matachel → *Spain* 37 G4
Matachewan *Canada* 104 C3
Matadi *Dem. Rep. of the Congo* 84 F2
Matagalpa *Nic.* 120 D2
Matagami *Canada* 104 C4
Matagami, L. *Canada* 104 C4
Matagorda B. *U.S.A.* 116 G6
Matagorda I. *U.S.A.* 116 G6
Mataiea *Tahiti* 91 d
Matak *Indonesia* 62 D3
Matala *Greece* 49 E6
Matam *Senegal* 82 B2
Matam ☐ *Senegal* 82 B2
Matameye *Niger* 83 C6
Matamoros *Campeche,*
  Mexico 119 D6
Matamoros *Coahuila, Mexico* 118 B4
Matamoros *Tamaulipas,*
  Mexico 119 B5
Ma'ţan as Sarra *Libya* 79 D10
Matandu → *Tanzania* 87 D3
Matane *Canada* 105 C6
Matang *China* 58 F5
Matankari *Niger* 83 C5
Matanomadh *India* 68 H3
Matanzas *Cuba* 120 B3
Matapa *Botswana* 88 C3
Matapédia *Canada* 105 C6
Matapo △ *Zimbabwe* 87 G2
Matara *Sri Lanka* 66 S12
Mataram *Indonesia* 62 F5
Matarani *Peru* 124 D4
Mataranka *Australia* 92 B5
Matarma, Rās *Egypt* 74 E1
Mataró *Spain* 38 D7
Matarraña → *Spain* 38 D5
Mataruška Banja *Serbia* 44 C4
Matatiele *S. Africa* 89 E4
Mataura *N.Z.* 91 G2
Matavai, B. de *Tahiti* 91 d
Matehuala *Mexico* 118 C4
Mateke Hills *Zimbabwe* 87 G3
Matelot *Trin. & Tob.* 125 K15
Matera *Italy* 43 B9
Matese, Monti del *Italy* 43 A7
Matese △ *Italy* 43 A7
Mátészalka *Hungary* 28 C7
Matetsi *Zimbabwe* 87 F2

Matfors *Sweden* 10 B11
Matha *France* 20 C3
Matheniko △ *Uganda* 86 B3
Mathis *U.S.A.* 116 G6
Mathraki *Greece* 49 A3
Mathura *India* 68 F7
Mati *Phil.* 61 H7
Matiakoali *Burkina Faso* 83 C5
Matiali *India* 69 F13
Matías Romero *Mexico* 119 D5
Matibane *Mozam.* 87 E5
Matiri Ra. *N.Z.* 91 D4
Matjiesfontein *S. Africa* 88 E3
Matla → *India* 69 J13
Matlamanyane *Botswana* 88 B4
Matli *Pakistan* 68 G3
Matlock *U.K.* 14 D6
Matna *Sudan* 81 E4
Mato Grosso ☐ *Brazil* 125 F8
Mato Grosso, Planalto do
  Brazil 125 G8
Mato Grosso do Sul ☐ *Brazil* 125 G8
Matobo = Matapo △
  Zimbabwe 87 G2
Matochkin Shar, Proliv
  Russia 52 B6
Matopo Hills *Zimbabwe* 87 G2
Matopos *Zimbabwe* 87 G2
Matosinhos *Portugal* 36 D2
Matour *France* 19 F11
Matroosberg *S. Africa* 88 E2
Matsena *Nigeria* 83 C7
Matsesta *Russia* 35 J4
Matsu Tao *Taiwan* 59 E13
Matsue *Japan* 55 G6
Matsum, Ko *Thailand* 65 b
Matsumae *Japan* 54 D10
Matsumoto *Japan* 55 F9
Matsusaka *Japan* 55 G8
Matsuura *Japan* 55 H4
Matsuyama *Japan* 55 H6
Mattagami → *Canada* 104 B3
Mattancheri *India* 66 Q10
Mattawa *Canada* 104 C4
Matterhorn *Switz.* 25 K3
Mattersburg *Austria* 27 D9
Matthew Town *Bahamas* 121 B5
Matthews Ridge *Guyana* 124 B6
Mattice *Canada* 104 C3
Mattituck *U.S.A.* 115 F12
Mattò *Japan* 55 F8
Mattoon *U.S.A.* 112 F9
Matuba *Mozam.* 89 C5
Matucana *Peru* 124 F3
Matuku *Fiji* 91 a
Matūn = Khowst *Afghan.* 68 C3
Matura B. *Trin. & Tob.* 125 K15
Maturín *Venezuela* 124 B6
Matusadona △ *Zimbabwe* 87 F2
Matveyev Kurgan *Russia* 33 J10
Matxitxako, C. *Spain* 38 B2
Mau *Mad. P., India* 69 F8
Mau *Ut. P., India* 69 G10
Mau *Ut. P., India* 69 G9
Mau Escarpment *Kenya* 86 C4
Mau Ranipur *India* 69 G8
Maua *Kenya* 86 C4
Maúa *Mozam.* 87 E4
Maubeuge *France* 19 B10
Maubin *Burma* 67 L19
Maubourguet *France* 20 E4
Maud, Pt. *Australia* 92 D1
Maud Rise *S. Ocean* 5 C3
Maude *Australia* 95 E3
Maudin Sun *Burma* 67 M19
Maués *Brazil* 124 D7
Mauganj *India* 69 G9
Maughold Hd. *I. of Man* 14 C3
Maug uio *France* 20 E7
Maui *U.S.A.* 107 L8
Maulamyaing = Moulmein
  Burma 67 L20
Maule ☐ *Chile* 126 D1
Mauléon-Licharre *France* 20 E3
Maumee *U.S.A.* 113 E12
Maumee → *U.S.A.* 113 E12
Maumere *Indonesia* 63 F6
Maumusson, Pertuis de
  France 20 C2
Maun *Botswana* 88 C3
Mauna Kea *U.S.A.* 107 M8
Mauna Loa *U.S.A.* 107 M8
Maunath Bhanjan = Mau
  India 69 G10
Maungaraki *Fiji* 91 a
Maungdaw *Burma* 67 J18
Maungu *Kenya* 86 C4
Maupin *U.S.A.* 108 D3
Maure-de-Bretagne *France* 18 E5
Maurepas, L. *U.S.A.* 117 F9
Maures *France* 21 E10
Mauriac *France* 20 C6
Maurice, L. *Australia* 93 E5
Mauricie △ *Canada* 104 C5
Maurienne *France* 21 C10
Mauritania ■ *Africa* 78 E3
Mauritius ■ *Ind. Oc.* 85 d
Mauron *France* 18 D4

Maurs *France* 20 D6
Mauston *U.S.A.* 112 D8
Mauterndorf *Austria* 26 D6
Mauthen *Austria* 26 E6
Mauvezin *France* 20 E4
Mauzé-sur-le-Mignon *France* 20 B3
Mavli *India* 68 G5
Mavrovë *Albania* 44 F3
Mavrovo △ *Macedonia* 44 E4
Mavuradonha Mts. *Zimbabwe* 87 F3
Mawa *Dem. Rep. of the Congo* 86 B2
Mawai *India* 69 H9
Mawana *India* 68 E7
Mawand *Pakistan* 68 E3
Mawat *Iraq* 73 E11
Mawjib, W. al → *Jordan* 74 D4
Mawk Mai *Burma* 67 J20
Mawlaik *Burma* 67 H19
Mawlamyine = Moulmein
  Burma 67 L20
Mawqaq *Si. Arabia* 70 E4
Mawson Base *Antarctica* 5 C6
Mawson Coast *Antarctica* 5 C6
Max *U.S.A.* 112 B3
Maxcanú *Mexico* 119 C6
Maxesibeni *S. Africa* 89 E4
Maxhamish L. *Canada* 102 B4
Maxixe *Mozam.* 89 C6
Maxville *Canada* 115 A10
Maxwell *U.S.A.* 110 F4
Maxwelton *Australia* 94 C3
May, C. *U.S.A.* 113 F16
May Pen *Jamaica* 120 a
Maya → *Russia* 53 D14
Maya Mts. *Belize* 119 D7
Mayaguana *Bahamas* 121 B5
Mayagüez *Puerto Rico* 121 d
Mayahi *Niger* 83 C6
Mayāmey *Iran* 71 B7
Mayang *China* 58 D7
Mayanup *Australia* 93 F2
Mayapán *Mexico* 119 C7
Mayarí *Cuba* 121 B4
Mayaro B. *Trin. & Tob.* 125 K16
Maybell *U.S.A.* 108 F9
Maybole *U.K.* 13 F4
Maychew *Ethiopia* 81 E4
Maydān *Iraq* 73 E11
Maydan *Ukraine* 29 B8
Maydī *Yemen* 81 D5
Mayen *Germany* 25 E3
Mayenne *France* 18 D6
Mayenne ☐ *France* 18 D6
Mayenne → *France* 18 E6
Mayer *U.S.A.* 109 J7
Mayerthorpe *Canada* 102 C5
Mayfield *Ky., U.S.A.* 112 G9
Mayfield *N.Y., U.S.A.* 115 C10
Mayhill *U.S.A.* 109 K11
Maykop *Russia* 35 H5
Maymyo *Burma* 64 A1
Maynard *Mass., U.S.A.* 115 D13
Maynard *Wash., U.S.A.* 110 C4
Maynard Hills *Australia* 93 E2
Mayne → *Australia* 94 C3
Maynooth *Canada* 114 A7
Maynooth *Ireland* 12 C5
Mayo *Canada* 100 E4
Mayo ☐ *Ireland* 12 C2
Mayo Daga *Nigeria* 83 D7
Mayo Faran *Nigeria* 83 D7
Mayon Volcano *Phil.* 61 E5
Mayor I. *N.Z.* 91 B6
Mayorga *Spain* 36 C5
Mayotte ☑ *Ind. Oc.* 85 a
Mayraira Pt. *Phil.* 61 B4
Maysān ☐ *Iraq* 70 D5
Mayskiy *Russia* 35 J7
Maysville *U.S.A.* 113 F12
Mayu *Indonesia* 63 D7
Mayville *N. Dak., U.S.A.* 112 B5
Mayville *N.Y., U.S.A.* 114 D5
Mayya *Russia* 53 C14
Mazabuka *Zambia* 87 F2
Mazagán = El Jadida *Morocco* 78 B4
Mazagão *Brazil* 125 D8
Mazamet *France* 20 E6
Mazán *Peru* 124 D4
Māzandarān ☐ *Iran* 71 B7
Mazapil *Mexico* 118 C4
Mazar *Mexico* 118 B3
Mazar del Vallo *Italy* 42 E5
Mazarrón *Spain* 39 H3
Mazarrón, G. de *Spain* 39 H3
Mazaruni → *Guyana* 124 B7
Mazatán *Mexico* 118 B2
Mazatenango *Guatemala* 120 D1
Mazatlán *Mexico* 118 C3
Mažeikiai *Lithuania* 30 B9
Māzhān *Iran* 71 C8
Mazīnān *Iran* 71 B8
Mazoe *Mozam.* 87 F3
Mazoe → *Mozam.* 87 F3
Mazowe *Zimbabwe* 87 F3
Mazowieckie ☐ *Poland* 31 F8
Mazrūb *Sudan* 81 E2
Mazu Dao *China* 59 D12
Mazurski, Pojezierze *Poland* 30 E7

Mazyr *Belarus* 23 B15
Mba *Fiji* 91 a
Mbaba *Senegal* 82 C1
Mbabane *Swaziland* 89 D5
Mbagne *Mauritania* 82 B2
Mbaïki *C.A.R.* 84 D3
Mbala *Zambia* 87 D3
Mbalabala *Zimbabwe* 89 C4
Mbale *Uganda* 86 B3
Mbalmayo *Cameroon* 83 E7
Mbam → *Cameroon* 83 E7
Mbamba Bay *Tanzania* 87 E3
Mbandaka
  Dem. Rep. of the Congo 84 D3
Mbanga *Cameroon* 83 E6
Mbanza Congo *Angola* 84 F2
Mbanza Ngungu
  Dem. Rep. of the Congo 84 F2
Mbarangandu *Tanzania* 87 D4
Mbarara *Uganda* 86 C3
Mbatto *Ivory C.* 82 D4
Mbengga = Beqa *Fiji* 91 a
Mbenkuru → *Tanzania* 87 D4
Mberengwa *Zimbabwe* 87 G2
Mberengwa, Mt. *Zimbabwe* 87 G2
Mberubu *Nigeria* 83 D6
Mbesuma *Zambia* 87 E3
Mbeya *Tanzania* 87 D3
Mbeya ☐ *Tanzania* 87 D3
Mbhashe → *S. Africa* 89 E4
M'bili *Sudan* 81 F2
Mbinga *Tanzania* 87 E4
Mbini = Río Muni ☐
  Eq. Guin. 84 D2
Mbizi *Zimbabwe* 87 G3
Mboki *C.A.R.* 81 F2
M'bonge *Cameroon* 83 E6
Mboro *Senegal* 82 B1
Mbouda *Cameroon* 83 D7
M'boukou, L. de *Cameroon* 83 D7
Mboune *Senegal* 82 C2
Mbour *Senegal* 82 C1
Mbout *Mauritania* 82 B2
Mbuji-Mayi
  Dem. Rep. of the Congo 86 D1
Mbulu *Tanzania* 86 C4
Mburucuyá *Argentina* 126 B4
Mburucuyá △ *Argentina* 126 B4
Mchinja *Tanzania* 87 D4
Mchinji *Malawi* 87 E3
Mdantsane *S. Africa* 89 E4
Mead, L. *U.S.A.* 111 J12
Meade *U.S.A.* 112 G3
Meade River = Atqasuk
  U.S.A. 106 A8
Meadow Lake *Canada* 103 C7
Meadow Lake △ *Canada* 103 C7
Meadow Valley Wash →
  U.S.A. 111 J12
Meadville *U.S.A.* 114 E4
Meaford *Canada* 114 B4
Mealhada *Portugal* 36 E2
Mealpaeg L. *Canada* 105 C8
Mealy Mts. *Canada* 105 B8
Meander River *Canada* 102 B5
Meares, C. *U.S.A.* 108 D1
Mearim → *Brazil* 125 D10
Meath ☐ *Ireland* 12 C5
Meath Park *Canada* 103 C7
Meaulne *France* 19 F9
Meaux *France* 19 D9
Mebechi-Gawa → *Japan* 54 D10
Mebulu, Tanjung *Indonesia* 63 K18
Mecanhelas *Mozam.* 87 F4
Mecca = Makkah *Si. Arabia* 80 C4
Mecca *U.S.A.* 111 M10
Mechanicsburg *U.S.A.* 114 F8
Mechanicville *U.S.A.* 115 D11
Mechara *Ethiopia* 81 F5
Mechelen *Belgium* 17 C4
Mecheria *Algeria* 78 B5
Mechernich *Germany* 24 E2
Mechetinskaya *Russia* 35 G5
Mecidiye *Turkey* 45 F10
Mecitözü *Turkey* 72 B6
Mecklenburg *Germany* 22 B7
Mecklenburg-
  Vorpommern ☐ *Germany* 24 B7
Mecklenburger Bucht
  Germany 24 A7
Meconta *Mozam.* 87 E4
Mecsek *Hungary* 28 D3
Mecubúri *Mozam.* 87 E4
Mecubúri → *Mozam.* 87 E5
Mecúfi *Mozam.* 87 E5
Meda *Portugal* 36 E3
Medan *Indonesia* 62 D1
Médanos de Coro △
  Venezuela 121 D5
Medanosa, Pta. *Argentina* 128 F3
Mede *Italy* 40 C5
Médéa *Algeria* 78 A6
Mededa *Bos.-H.* 28 G4
Medellín *Colombia* 124 B3
Medelpad *Sweden* 10 B10
Medemblik *Neths.* 17 B5
Mederdra *Mauritania* 82 B1
Medford *Mass., U.S.A.* 115 D13

Medford *Oreg., U.S.A.* **108** E2
Medford *Wis., U.S.A.* **112** C8
Medgidia *Romania* **29** F13
Medi *Sudan* **81** F3
Media Agua *Argentina* **126** C2
Media Luna *Argentina* **126** C2
Medianeira *Brazil* **127** B5
Mediaş *Romania* **29** D9
Medicina *Italy* **41** D8
Medicine Bow *U.S.A.* **108** F10
Medicine Bow Mts. *U.S.A.* **108** F10
Medicine Bow Pk. *U.S.A.* **108** F10
Medicine Hat *Canada* **103** D6
Medicine Lake *U.S.A.* **108** B11
Medicine Lodge *U.S.A.* **112** G4
Medina = Al Madīnah
   Si. Arabia **70** E3
Medina *N. Dak., U.S.A.* **112** B4
Medina *N.Y., U.S.A.* **114** C6
Medina *Ohio, U.S.A.* **114** E3
Medina ➤ *U.S.A.* **116** G5
Medina de Pomar *Spain* **36** C7
Medina de Rioseco *Spain* **36** D5
Medina del Campo *Spain* **36** D6
Médina Gounas *Senegal* **82** C2
Medina L. *U.S.A.* **116** G5
Medina Sidonia *Spain* **37** J5
Medinaceli *Spain* **38** D2
Medinipur *India* **69** H12
Mediterranean Sea *Europe* **6** H7
Médoc *France* **20** C3
Medulin *Croatia* **41** D10
Medveda *Serbia* **44** D5
Medvedevo *Russia* **34** B8
Medveditsa ➤ *Tver, Russia* **32** D9
Medveditsa ➤ *Volgograd,
   Russia* **34** F6
Medvedok *Russia* **34** B10
Medvezhi, Ostrava *Russia* **53** B17
Medvezhyegorsk *Russia* **52** C4
Medway □ *U.K.* **15** F8
Medway ➤ *U.K.* **15** F8
Medzev *Slovak Rep.* **27** C13
Medzilaborce *Slovak Rep.* **27** B14
Medžitlija *Macedonia* **44** F5
Meekatharra *Australia* **93** E2
Meeker *U.S.A.* **108** F10
Meersburg *Germany* **25** H5
Meerut *India* **68** E7
Meeteetse *U.S.A.* **108** D9
Mega *Ethiopia* **81** G4
Megalo *Ethiopia* **81** F5
Megalo Horio *Greece* **47** E9
Megalonisos *Greece* **46** D6
Megalopoli *Greece* **46** D4
Meganisi *Greece* **46** C2
Megasini *India* **69** J12
Megdovas = Tavropos ➤
   Greece **46** B3
Megève *France* **21** C10
Meghalaya □ *India* **67** G17
Meghezez *Ethiopia* **81** F4
Meghna ➤ *Bangla.* **67** H17
Megion *Russia* **52** C8
Mégiscane, L. *Canada* **104** C4
Megiste *Greece* **47** E11
Megisti *Greece* **47** E11
Megra *Russia* **32** B9
Mehadia *Romania* **28** F7
Meharry, Mt. *Australia* **92** D2
Mehedeby *Sweden* **10** D11
Mehedinţi □ *Romania* **28** F7
Meheisa *Sudan* **80** D3
Mehlville *U.S.A.* **112** F8
Mehndawal *India* **69** F10
Mehr Jān *Iran* **71** C7
Mehrābād *Iran* **73** D12
Mehrabān *Iran* **73** C12
Mehrān *Iran* **73** F12
Mehrān ➤ *Iran* **71** E7
Mehrgarh *Pakistan* **68** E2
Mehrīz *Iran* **71** D7
Mehun-sur-Yèvre *France* **19** E9
Mei Jiang ➤ *China* **59** E11
Mei Xian *China* **56** G4
Meicheng *China* **59** C12
Meichengzhen *China* **59** C8
Meichuan *China* **59** B10
Meighen I. *Canada* **101** B12
Meigu *China* **58** C4
Meihekou *China* **57** C13
Meiktila *Burma* **67** J19
Meinerzhagen *Germany* **24** D3
Meiningen *Germany* **24** E6
Meira, Serra de *Spain* **36** B3
Meiringen *Switz.* **25** J4
Meishan *China* **58** B4
Meissen *Germany* **24** D9
Meissner *Germany* **24** D5
Meissner-Kaufunger
   Wald △ *Germany* **24** D5
Meitan *China* **58** D6
Meizhou *China* **59** E11
Meja *India* **69** G10
Mejillones *Chile* **126** A1
Mekdela *Ethiopia* **81** E4
Mekele *Ethiopia* **81** E4
Mekerghene, Sebkra *Algeria* **78** C6

Mékhé *Senegal* **82** B1
Mekhtar *Pakistan* **66** D6
Meknès *Morocco* **78** B4
Meko *Nigeria* **83** D5
Mekong ➤ *Asia* **65** H6
Mekongga *Indonesia* **63** E6
Mekrou ➤ *Benin* **83** C5
Mekvari = Kür ➤
   Azerbaijan **73** C13
Mel *Italy* **41** B9
Melagiri Hills *India* **66** N10
Melaka *Malaysia* **65** L4
Melalap *Malaysia* **62** C5
Melambes *Greece* **49** D6
Melanesia *Pac. Oc.* **96** H7
Melanesian Basin *Pac. Oc.* **96** G8
Melaya *Indonesia* **63** J17
Melbourne *Australia* **95** F4
Melbourne *U.S.A.* **117** G14
Melchor Múzquiz *Mexico* **118** B4
Melchor Ocampo *Mexico* **118** C4
Méldola *Italy* **41** D9
Meldorf *Germany* **24** A5
Melegnano *Italy* **40** C6
Melenci *Serbia* **28** E5
Melenki *Russia* **34** C5
Mélèzes ➤ *Canada* **104** A5
Melfi *Italy* **43** B8
Melfort *Canada* **103** C8
Melfort *Zimbabwe* **87** F3
Melgaço *Portugal* **36** C2
Melgar de Fernamental
   Spain **36** C6
Melhus *Norway* **8** E14
Melide *Spain* **36** C2
Meligales *Greece* **46** D3
Melilla *N. Afr.* **78** A5
Melilli *Italy* **43** E8
Melipilla *Chile* **126** C1
Melissa *Canada* **114** A5
Melissa, Akra *Greece* **49** D6
Melissa Oros *Greece* **47** D8
Melita *Canada* **103** D8
Mélito di Porto Salvo *Italy* **43** E8
Melitopol *Ukraine* **33** J8
Melk *Austria* **26** C8
Mellan Fryken *Sweden* **10** E7
Mellansel *Sweden* **8** E18
Mellbystrand *Sweden* **11** H6
Melle *France* **20** B3
Melle *Germany* **24** C4
Mellen *U.S.A.* **112** B8
Mellerud *Sweden* **11** F6
Mellette *U.S.A.* **112** C4
Mellid = Melide *Spain* **36** C2
Mellieha *Malta* **49** D1
Mellit *Sudan* **81** E2
Mellrichstadt *Germany* **24** E6
Melnik *Bulgaria* **44** E7
Mělník *Czech Rep.* **26** A7
Melnytsya Podilska *Ukraine* **29** 311
Melo *Uruguay* **127** C5
Melolo *Indonesia* **63** F6
Melouprey *Cambodia* **64** F5
Melrhir, Chott *Algeria* **78** B7
Melrose *Australia* **95** E4
Melrose *U.K.* **13** F6
Melrose *Minn., U.S.A.* **112** C6
Melrose *N. Mex., U.S.A.* **109** J12
Melstone *U.S.A.* **108** C10
Melsungen *Germany* **24** D5
Melton Mowbray *U.K.* **14** E7
Melun *France* **19** D9
Melut *Sudan* **81** E3
Melville *Canada* **103** C8
Melville, C. *Australia* **94** A3
Melville, L. *Canada* **105** B8
Melville B. *Australia* **94** A2
Melville B. *Greenland* **101** B19
Melville I. *Australia* **92** B5
Melville I. *Canada* **101** B9
Melville Pen. *Canada* **101** D15
Melvin, L. *Ireland* **12** B3
Mélykút *Hungary* **28** D4
Memaliaj *Albania* **44** F3
Memba *Mozam.* **87** E5
Memboro *Indonesia* **92** A2
Membrilla *Spain* **37** G7
Memel = Klaipėda *Lithuania* **30** C8
Memel *S. Africa* **89** D4
Memmingen *Germany* **25** H6
Mempawah *Indonesia* **62** D3
Memphis *Egypt* **80** J7
Memphis *Mich., U.S.A.* **114** D2
Memphis *Tenn., U.S.A.* **117** D9
Memphis *Tex., U.S.A.* **116** D4
Memphrémagog, L.
   N. Amer. **115** B12
Mena *Ukraine* **33** G7
Mena *U.S.A.* **116** D7
Mena ➤ *Ethiopia* **81** F5
Menai Strait *U.K.* **14** D3
Ménaka *Mali* **83** B5
Menan = Chao Phraya ➤
   Thailand **64** F3
Menarandra ➤ *Madag.* **89** D7
Menard *U.S.A.* **116** F5
Menard Fracture Zone
   Pac. Oc. **97** M18

Menawashei *Sudan* **81** E1
Mendaña Fracture Zone
   Pac. Oc. **97** J18
Mendawai ➤ *Indonesia* **62** E4
Mende *France* **20** D7
Mendebo Mts. *Ethiopia* **81** F4
Mendeleyev Ridge *Arctic* **4** B17
Menden *Germany* **24** D3
Menderes *Turkey* **47** C9
Mendhar *India* **69** C6
Mendi *Ethiopia* **81** F4
Mendip Hills *U.K.* **15** F5
Mendocino *U.S.A.* **108** G2
Mendocino, C. *U.S.A.* **108** F1
Mendocino Fracture Zone
   Pac. Oc. **97** D13
Mendota *Calif., U.S.A.* **110** J6
Mendota *Ill., U.S.A.* **112** E9
Mendoyo *Indonesia* **63** J17
Mendoza *Argentina* **126** C2
Mendoza □ *Argentina* **126** C2
Mene Grande *Venezuela* **124** B4
Menemen *Turkey* **47** C9
Menen *Belgium* **17** D3
Menfi *Italy* **42** E5
Mengdingjie *China* **58** F2
Mengeš *Slovenia* **41** B11
Menggala *Indonesia* **62** E3
Menghai *China* **58** G3
Mengíbar *Spain* **37** H7
Mengjin *China* **56** G7
Mengla *China* **58** G3
Menglian *China* **58** F2
Mengshan *China* **59** E8
Mengyin *China* **57** G9
Mengzhe *China* **58** F3
Mengzi *China* **58** F4
Menihek *Canada* **105** B6
Menihek L. *Canada* **105** B6
Menin = Menen *Belgium* **17** D3
Menindee *Australia* **95** E3
Menindee L. *Australia* **95** E3
Meningie *Australia* **95** F2
Menjangan, Pulau *Indonesia* **63** J17
Menlo Park *U.S.A.* **110** H4
Menminee *U.S.A.* **112** C10
Menominee ➤ *U.S.A.* **112** C10
Menomonie *U.S.A.* **112** C9
Menongue *Angola* **85** G3
Menorca *Spain* **48** B11
Menorca ✈ (MAH) *Spain* **38** F9
Mentakab *Malaysia* **65** L4
Mentawai, Kepulauan
   Indonesia **62** E1
Menton *France* **21** E11
Mentor *U.S.A.* **114** E3
Menzies *Australia* **93** E3
Meob B. *Namibia* **88** C1
Me'ona *Israel* **74** B4
Meoqui *Mexico* **118** B3
Mepaco *Mozam.* **87** F3
Meppel *Neths.* **17** B6
Meppen *Germany* **24** C3
Mequinenza *Spain* **38** D5
Mequinenza, Embalse de
   Spain **38** D5
Mer *France* **18** E8
Merak *Indonesia* **63** F12
Meramangye, L. *Australia* **93** E5
Meran = Merano *Italy* **41** B8
Merano *Italy* **41** B8
Merate *Italy* **40** C6
Merauke *Indonesia* **63** F10
Merbein *Australia* **95** E3
Merbuk, Gunung *Indonesia* **63** J17
Merca = Marka *Somali Rep.* **75** G3
Mercantour △ *France* **21** D10
Mercato Saraceno *Italy* **41** E9
Merced *U.S.A.* **110** H6
Merced ➤ *U.S.A.* **110** H6
Merced Pk. *U.S.A.* **110** H7
Mercedes *Corrientes,
   Argentina* **126** B4
Mercedes *San Luis, Argentina* **126** C2
Mercedes *Uruguay* **126** C4
Merceditas *Chile* **126** B1
Mercer *N.Z.* **91** B5
Mercer *U.S.A.* **114** E4
Mercer Island *U.S.A.* **110** C4
Mercury *U.S.A.* **111** J11
Mercy, C. *Canada* **101** E19
Merdignac *France* **18** D4
Mere *U.K.* **15** F5
Meredith, C. *Falk. Is.* **128** G4
Meredith, L. *U.S.A.* **116** D4
Merefa *Ukraine* **33** H9
Merei *Romania* **29** E11
Merga = Nukheila *Sudan* **80** D2
Mergui *Burma* **64** F2
Mergui Arch. = Myeik
   Kyunzu *Burma* **65** G1
Méribel-les-Allues *France* **21** C10
Meriç *Turkey* **45** F10
Meriç ➤ *Turkey* **45** F10
Mérida *Mexico* **119** C7
Mérida *Spain* **37** G4
Mérida *Venezuela* **124** B4

Mérida, Cord. de *Venezuela* **124** B4
Meriden *U.K.* **15** E6
Meriden *U.S.A.* **115** E12
Meridian *Calif., U.S.A.* **110** F5
Meridian *Idaho, U.S.A.* **108** E5
Meridian *Miss., U.S.A.* **117** E10
Mérignac *France* **20** D3
Merinda *Australia* **94** C4
Mering *Germany* **25** G6
Meringa *Nigeria* **83** C7
Merir *Pac. Oc.* **63** D8
Merirumã *Brazil* **125** C8
Merkel *U.S.A.* **116** E4
Mermaid Reef *Australia* **92** C2
Merowe *Sudan* **80** D3
Merowe Dam *Sudan* **80** D3
Merredin *Australia* **93** F2
Merrick *U.K.* **13** F4
Merrickville *Canada* **115** B9
Merrill *Oreg., U.S.A.* **108** E3
Merrill *Wis., U.S.A.* **112** C9
Merrimack ➤ *U.S.A.* **115** D14
Merriman *U.S.A.* **112** D3
Merritt *Canada* **102** C4
Merritt Island *U.S.A.* **117** G14
Merriwa *Australia* **95** E5
Merry I. *Canada* **104** A4
Merryville *U.S.A.* **116** F8
Mersa Fatma *Eritrea* **81** E5
Mersch *Lux.* **17** E6
Merse ➤ *Italy* **41** E8
Mersea I. *U.K.* **15** F8
Merseburg *Germany* **24** D7
Mersey ➤ *U.K.* **14** D4
Merseyside □ *U.K.* **14** D4
Mersin = İçel *Turkey* **72** D6
Mersing *Malaysia* **65** L4
Merta *India* **68** F6
Merta Road *India* **68** F5
Merthyr Tydfil *U.K.* **15** F4
Merthyr Tydfil □ *U.K.* **15** F4
Merti *Kenya* **86** B4
Mértola *Portugal* **37** H3
Mertzon *U.S.A.* **116** F4
Méru *France* **19** C9
Meru *Kenya* **86** B4
Meru *Tanzania* **86** C4
Meru △ *Kenya* **86** B4
Merville *France* **19** B9
Méry-sur-Seine *France* **19** D10
Merzifon *Turkey* **72** B6
Merzig *Germany* **25** F2
Mesa *U.S.A.* **109** K8
Mesa Verde △ *U.S.A.* **109** H9
Mesagne *Italy* **43** B10
Mesanagros *Greece* **49** C9
Mesaoría *Cyprus* **49** D12
Meschede *Germany* **24** D4
Mescit *Turkey* **73** B9
Mesfinto *Ethiopia* **81** E4
Mesgouez, L. *Canada* **104** B5
Meshchovsk *Russia* **32** E8
Meshed = Mashhad *Iran* **71** B8
Meshgīn Shahr *Iran* **73** C12
Meshoppen *U.S.A.* **115** E8
Meshra er Req *Sudan* **81** F2
Mesilinka ➤ *Canada* **102** B4
Meslay-du-Maine *France* **18** E6
Mesocco *Switz.* **25** J5
Mesologi *Greece* **46** C3
Mesongi *Greece* **49** B3
Mesopotamia = Al Jazirah
   Iraq **73** E10
Mesopotamia *U.S.A.* **114** E4
Mesopotamo *Greece* **46** B2
Mesoraca *Italy* **43** C9
Mésou Volímais = Volimes
   Greece **46** D2
Mesquite *U.S.A.* **109** H6
Messaad *Algeria* **78** B6
Messac *France* **18** E5
Messalo ➤ *Mozam.* **87** E4
Messaména *Cameroon* **83** E7
Messara, Kolpos *Greece* **49** D6
Messina = Musina *S. Africa* **89** C5
Messina *Italy* **43** D8
Messina, Str. di *Italy* **43** D8
Messini *Greece* **46** D4
Messinia □ *Greece* **46** D3
Messiniakos Kolpos *Greece* **46** E4
Messkirch *Germany* **25** H5
Messlingen *Sweden* **10** B6
Mesta = Nestos ➤ *Europe* **45** E8
Mesta, Akra *Greece* **47** C7
Mestanza *Spain* **37** G6
Mestre *Italy* **41** C9
Mesudiye *Turkey* **72** B7
Meta □ *S. Amer.* **124** D5
Meta Incognita Pen. *Canada*
   101 E18
Metabetchouan *Canada* **105** C5
Metairie *U.S.A.* **117** G9
Metalici, Munţii *Romania* **28** D7
Metaline Falls *U.S.A.* **108** B5
Metallifere, Colline *Italy* **40** E8
Metán *Argentina* **126** B3
Metangula *Mozam.* **87** E3
Metauro ➤ *Italy* **41** E10
Metcalfe *Canada* **115** A9

Metema *Ethiopia* **81** E4
Metengobalame *Mozam.* **87** E3
Methana *Greece* **46** D5
Methoni *Greece* **46** D3
Methven *N.Z.* **91** E3
Metil *Mozam.* **87** F4
Metkovets *Bulgaria* **44** C7
Metković *Croatia* **41** E14
Metlakatla *U.S.A.* **100** F5
Metropolis *U.S.A.* **112** G9
Metropolitana □ *Chile* **126** C1
Metsovo *Greece* **46** B3
Metu *Ethiopia* **81** F4
Metz *France* **19** C13
Metzingen *Germany* **25** G5
Meulaboh *Indonesia* **62** D1
Meulan *France* **19** C9
Meung-sur-Loire *France* **19** E8
Meureudu *Indonesia* **62** C1
Meurthe ➤ *France* **19** D13
Meurthe-et-Moselle □
   France **19** D13
Meuse □ *France* **19** C12
Meuse ➤ *Europe* **17** D5
Meuselwitz *Germany* **24** D8
Meuung-sur-Loire = Meung-sur-Loire
Mexborough *U.K.* **14** D6
Mexia *U.S.A.* **116** F6
Mexiana, I. *Brazil* **125** D9
Mexicali *Mexico* **111** N11
Mexican Plateau *Mexico* **98** G9
Mexican Water *U.S.A.* **109** H9
México *Mexico* **119** D5
Mexico *Maine, U.S.A.* **115** B14
Mexico *Mo., U.S.A.* **112** F8
Mexico *N.Y., U.S.A.* **115** C8
México □ *Mexico* **119** D5
Mexico ■ *Cent. Amer.* **118** C4
México, Ciudad de *Mexico* **119** D5
Mexico, G. of *Cent. Amer.* **119** C7
Mexico B. *U.S.A.* **115** C8
Meydān-e Naftūn *Iran* **71** D6
Meydani, Ra's-e *Iran* **71** E8
Meyenburg *Germany* **24** B8
Meyers Chuck *U.S.A.* **102** B2
Meymac *France* **20** C6
Meymaneh *Afghan.* **66** B4
Meyrueis *France* **20** D7
Meyssac *France* **20** C5
Meyzieu *France* **21** C8
Mezdra *Bulgaria* **44** C7
Mèze *France* **20** E7
Mezen *Russia* **52** C5
Mezen ➤ *Russia* **6** B14
Mézenc, Mt. *France* **21** D8
Mezeş, Munţii *Romania* **28** C8
Mezha ➤ *Russia* **32** E6
Mezhdurechensk *Russia* **52** D9
Mezhdurechenskiy *Russia* **52** D7
Mézidon-Canon *France* **18** C6
Mézières-en-Bremne *France* **20** B5
Mézilhac *France* **21** D8
Mézin *France* **20** D4
Mezőberény *Hungary* **28** D6
Mezőfalva *Hungary* **28** D3
Mezőhegyes *Hungary* **28** D6
Mezőkovácsháza *Hungary* **28** D5
Mezőkövesd *Hungary* **28** C5
Mézos *France* **20** D2
Mezőtúr *Hungary* **28** C5
Mezquital *Mexico* **118** C4
Mezzolombardo *Italy* **40** B8
Mfolozi ➤ *S. Africa* **89** D5
Mgeta *Tanzania* **87** D4
Mglin *Russia* **33** F7
Mhlaba Hills *Zimbabwe* **87** F3
Mhow *India* **68** H6
Miahuatlán *Mexico* **119** D5
Miajadas *Spain* **37** F5
Miami *Fla., U.S.A.* **117** J14
Miami *Okla., U.S.A.* **116** C7
Miami *Tex., U.S.A.* **116** D4
Miami Beach *U.S.A.* **117** J14
Mian Xian *China* **56** H4
Mianchi *China* **56** G6
Miāndarreh *Iran* **71** C7
Mīāndowāb *Iran* **73** D12
Miandrivazo *Madag.* **89** B8
Mīāneh *Iran* **73** D12
Mianning *China* **58** C4
Mianwali *Pakistan* **68** C4
Mianyang *China* **58** B5
Miaoli *Taiwan* **59** E13
Miarinarivo *Antananarivo,
   Madag.* **89** B8
Miarinarivo *Toamasina,
   Madag.* **39** B8
Miariraveratra *Madag.* **89** C8
Miass *Russia* **52** D7
Miastko *Poland* **30** E3
Miasto Poland* **30** E3
Mica *S. Africa* **89** C5
Micăsasa *Romania* **29** D9
Michalovce *Slovak Rep.* **27** C14
Michigan □ *U.S.A.* **113** C11
Michigan, L. *U.S.A.* **112** D10
Michigan City *U.S.A.* **112** E10
Michika *Nigeria* **83** C7
Michipicoten I. *Canada* **104** C2

Michoacán □ *Mexico* **118** D4
Michurin *Bulgaria* **45** D11
Michurinsk *Russia* **34** D5
Micoud *St. Lucia* **121** f
Micronesia *Pac. Oc.* **96** G7
Micronesia, Federated
   States of ■ *Pac. Oc.* **90** A8
Mid-Pacific Seamounts
   Pac. Oc. **96** F3
Midai *Indonesia* **62** D3
Midale *Canada* **103** D8
Middelburg *Neths.* **17** C3
Middelburg *Eastern Cape,
   S. Africa* **88** E4
Middelburg *Mpumalanga,
   S. Africa* **89** D4
Middelfart *Denmark* **11** J3
Middelpos *S. Africa* **88** E3
Middelwit *S. Africa* **88** C4
Middle Alkali L. *U.S.A.* **108** F3
Middle America Trench =
   Guatemala Trench
   Pac. Oc. **98** H10
Middle Bass I. *U.S.A.* **114** E2
Middle East *Asia* **50** E5
Middle Fork Feather ➤
   U.S.A. **110** F5
Middle I. *Australia* **93** F3
Middle Loup ➤ *U.S.A.* **112** E4
Middleboro *U.S.A.* **115** E14
Middleburg *Fla., U.S.A.* **117** F14
Middleburg *Pa., U.S.A.* **114** F7
Middleburgh *U.S.A.* **115** D10
Middlebury *U.S.A.* **115** B11
Middlefield *U.S.A.* **114** E3
Middlemount *Australia* **94** C4
Middleport *N.Y., U.S.A.* **114** C6
Middleport *Ohio, U.S.A.* **113** F12
Middlesboro *U.S.A.* **113** G12
Middlesbrough *U.K.* **14** C6
Middlesbrough □ *U.K.* **14** C6
Middlesex *Belize* **120** C2
Middlesex *N.J., U.S.A.* **115** F10
Middlesex *N.Y., U.S.A.* **114** D7
Middleton *Australia* **94** C3
Middleton *Canada* **105** D6
Middleton Cr. ➤ *Australia* **94** C3
Middleton I. *U.S.A.* **106** D10
Middletown *U.K.* **12** B5
Middletown *Calif., U.S.A.* **110** G4
Middletown *Conn., U.S.A.* **115** E12
Middletown *N.Y., U.S.A.* **115** E10
Middletown *Ohio, U.S.A.* **113** F11
Middletown *Pa., U.S.A.* **115** F8
Midge Point *Australia* **94** b
Midhurst *Canada* **114** B5
Midhurst *U.K.* **15** G7
Midi, Canal du ➤ *France* **20** E5
Midi d'Ossau, Pic du *France* **20** F3
Midi-Pyrénées □ *France* **20** E5
Midland *Austral a* **93** F2
Midland *Canada* **114** B5
Midland *Calif., U.S.A.* **111** M12
Midland *Mich., U.S.A.* **113** D11
Midland *Pa., U.S.A.* **114** F4
Midland *Tex., U.S.A.* **116** F3
Midlands □ *Zimbabwe* **87** F2
Midleton *Ireland* **12** E3
Midlothian □ *U.K.* **13** F5
Midnapore = Medinipur
   India **69** H12
Midongy, Tangorombohitr'
   i *Madag.* **89** C8
Midongy Atsimo *Madag.* **89** C8
Midou ➤ *France* **20** E3
Midouze ➤ *France* **20** E3
Midsayap *Phil.* **61** H6
Midtjylland □ *Denmark* **11** H2
Midu *China* **58** E3
Midway Is. *Pac. Oc.* **107** K4
Midway Wells *U.S.A.* **111** N11
Midwest *U.S.A.* **107** G22
Midwest *Wyo., U.S.A.* **108** E10
Midwest City *U.S.A.* **116** D6
Midyat *Turkey* **73** D9
Midzŏr *Bulgaria* **44** C6
Mie □ *Japan* **55** G8
Miechów *Poland* **31** H7
Miedwie, Jezioro *Poland* **31** E1
Międzybórz *Poland* **31** G4
Międzychód *Poland* **31** F2
Międzylesie *Poland* **31** H3
Międzyrzec Podlaski *Poland* **31** G9
Międzyrzecz *Poland* **31** F2
Międzyzdroje *Poland* **30** E1
Miejska Górka *Poland* **31** G3
Miélan *France* **20** E4
Mielec *Poland* **31** H8
Mienga *Angola* **88** B2
Miercurea-Ciuc *Romania* **29** D10
Miercurea Sibiului *Romania* **29** E8
Mieres *Spain* **36** B5
Mieroszów *Poland* **31** H3
Mieso *Ethiopia* **81** F5
Mieszkowice *Poland* **31** F1
Mifflintown *U.S.A.* **114** F7
Mifraz Hefa *Israel* **74** C4
Migennes *France* **19** E10
Migliarino *Italy* **41** D8

Migliarino-San Rossore-
  Massaciuccoli △ *Italy* **40** E7
Migori *Kenya* **86** C3
Miguel Alemán, Presa
  Mexico **119** D5
Miguelturra *Spain* **37** G7
Mihăileni *Romania* **29** C11
Mihăilești *Romania* **29** F10
Mihailovca *Moldova* **29** D13
Mihalgazi *Turkey* **47** A12
Mihaliççık *Turkey* **72** C5
Mihara *Japan* **55** G6
Miheşu de Cîmpie *Romania* **29** D9
Mijas *Spain* **37** J6
Mikese *Tanzania* **86** D4
Mikha-Tskhakaya =
  Senaki *Georgia* **35** J6
Mikhailovka =
  Mykhaylivka *Ukraine* **33** J8
Mikhaylov *Russia* **32** E10
Mikhaylovka *Russia* **34** E6
Mikhaylovgrad =
  Montana *Bulgaria* **44** C7
Mikhaylovka *Russia* **34** E6
Mikhnevo *Russia* **32** E9
Mikines *Greece* **46** D4
Mikkeli *Finland* **32** B4
Mikkwa →~ *Canada* **102** B6
Mikniya *Sudan* **81** D3
Mikołajki *Poland* **30** E8
Míkonos = Mykonos *Greece* **47** D7
Mikri Prespa, L. *Greece* **44** F5
Mikro Derio *Greece* **45** E10
Mikstat *Poland* **31** G4
Mikulov *Czech Rep.* **27** C9
Mikumi *Tanzania* **86** D4
Mikumi △ *Tanzania* **86** D4
Milaca *U.S.A.* **112** C7
Milagro *Ecuador* **124** D3
Milagros *Phil.* **61** E5
Milan = Milano *Italy* **40** C6
Milan *Mo., U.S.A.* **112** E7
Milan *Tenn., U.S.A.* **117** D10
Milange *Mozam.* **87** F4
Milano *Italy* **40** C6
Milano Linate ✈ (LIN) *Italy* **40** C6
Milanoa *Madag.* **89** A8
Milâs *Turkey* **47** D9
Milatos *Greece* **49** D7
Milazzo *Italy* **43** D8
Milbank *U.S.A.* **112** C5
Milbanke Sd. *Canada* **102** C3
Milden *Canada* **103** C7
Mildenhall *U.K.* **15** E8
Mildmay *Canada* **114** B3
Mildura *Australia* **95** E3
Mile *China* **58** E4
Miles *Australia* **95** D5
Miles City *U.S.A.* **108** C11
Milestone *Canada* **103** D8
Mileto *Italy* **43** D9
Miletto, Mte. *Italy* **43** A7
Miletus *Turkey* **47** D9
Milevsko *Czech Rep.* **26** B7
Milford *Calif., U.S.A.* **110** E6
Milford *Conn., U.S.A.* **115** E11
Milford *Del., U.S.A.* **113** F16
Milford *Mass., U.S.A.* **115** D13
Milford *N.H., U.S.A.* **115** D13
Milford *N.Y., U.S.A.* **115** D10
Milford *Pa., U.S.A.* **115** E10
Milford *Utah, U.S.A.* **108** G7
Milford Haven *U.K.* **15** F2
Milford Sd. *N.Z.* **91** F1
Milford Sound *N.Z.* **91** F1
Milḥ, Baḥr al = Razāzah,
  Buḥayrat ar *Iraq* **73** F10
Milicz *Poland* **31** G4
Milies *Greece* **46** B5
Milikapiti *Australia* **92** B5
Miling *Australia* **93** F2
Militello in Val di Catánia
  Italy **43** E7
Milk, Wadi el →~ *Sudan* **80** D3
Milk River *Canada* **102** D6
Mill →~ *U.S.A.* **114** D1
Mill I. *Antarctica* **5** C8
Mill I. *Canada* **101** E16
Mill Valley *U.S.A.* **110** H4
Millárs →~ *Spain* **38** F4
Millau *France* **20** D7
Millbridge *Canada* **114** B7
Millbrook *Canada* **114** B6
Millbrook *Ala., U.S.A.* **117** E11
Millbrook *N.Y., U.S.A.* **115** E11
Mille Lacs, L. des *Canada* **104** C1
Mille Lacs L. *U.S.A.* **112** B7
Milledgeville *U.S.A.* **117** E13
Millen *U.S.A.* **117** E14
Millennium I. = Caroline I.
  Kiribati **97** H12
Miller *U.S.A.* **112** C4
Miller Lake *Canada* **114** A3
Millerovo *Russia* **35** F5
Millersburg *Ohio, U.S.A.* **114** F3
Millersburg *Pa., U.S.A.* **114** F8
Millerton *U.S.A.* **115** E11
Millerton L. *U.S.A.* **110** J7
Millet *St. Lucia* **121** f

Millevaches, Plateau de
  France **20** C6
Millheim *U.S.A.* **114** F7
Millicent *Australia* **95** F3
Millington *U.S.A.* **117** D10
Millinocket *U.S.A.* **113** C19
Millmerran *Australia* **95** D5
Millom *U.K.* **14** C4
Mills L. *Canada* **102** A5
Millsboro *U.S.A.* **114** G5
Millstream Chichester △
  Australia **92** D2
Millstreet *Ireland* **12** D2
Milltown Malbay *Ireland* **12** D2
Millville *N.J., U.S.A.* **113** F16
Millville *Pa., U.S.A.* **115** E8
Millwood L. *U.S.A.* **116** E8
Milna *Croatia* **41** E13
Milne →~ *Australia* **94** C2
Milne *U.K.* **13** C19
Milo *U.S.A.* **113** C19
Milo →~ *Guinea* **82** D3
Milon, Akra *Greece* **49** C10
Milos *Greece* **46** E6
Miłosław *Poland* **31** F4
Milot *Albania* **44** E3
Milparinka *Australia* **95** D3
Milpitas *U.S.A.* **110** H5
Miltenberg *Germany* **25** F5
Milton *N.S., Canada* **105** D7
Milton *Ont., Canada* **114** C5
Milton *N.Z.* **91** G2
Milton *Calif., U.S.A.* **110** G6
Milton *Fla., U.S.A.* **117** F11
Milton *Pa., U.S.A.* **114** F8
Milton *Vt., U.S.A.* **115** B11
Milton-Freewater *U.S.A.* **108** D4
Milton Keynes *U.K.* **15** E7
Milton Keynes □ *U.K.* **15** E7
Miluo *China* **59** C9
Milverton *Canada* **114** C4
Milwaukee *U.S.A.* **112** D10
Milwaukee Deep *Atl. Oc.* **121** C6
Milwaukie *U.S.A.* **110** E4
Mim *Ghana* **82** D4
Mimili *Australia* **93** E5
Mimizan *France* **20** D2
Mimoň *Czech Rep.* **26** A7
Min Jiang →~ *Fujian, China* **59** E12
Min Jiang →~ *Sichuan, China* **58** C5
Min Xian *China* **56** G3
Mina' Jabal 'Alī *U.A.E.* **71** E7
Mina Pirquitas *Argentina* **126** A2
Mīnā Su'ud *Si. Arabia* **71** D6
Mīnā'al Aḥmadī *Kuwait* **71** D6
Minago →~ *Canada* **103** C9
Minaki *Canada* **103** D10
Minamata *Japan* **55** H5
Minami-Arapusa △ *Japan* **55** G9
Minami-Tori-Shima *Pac. Oc.* **96** E7
Minas *Uruguay* **127** C4
Minas, Sierra de las
  Guatemala **120** C2
Minas Basin *Canada* **105** C7
Minas de Riotinto *Spain* **37** H4
Minas Gerais □ *Brazil* **125** G9
Minatitlán *Mexico* **119** D6
Minbu *Burma* **67** J19
Minchinabad *Pakistan* **68** D5
Mincio →~ *Italy* **40** C7
Minčol *Slovak Rep.* **27** B13
Mindanao *Phil.* **61** H6
Mindanao Sea = Bohol Sea
  Phil. **63** C6
Mindanao Trench *Pac. Oc.* **61** F7
Mindel →~ *Germany* **25** G6
Mindelheim *Germany* **25** G6
Mindelo *C. Verde Is.* **78** b
Minden *Canada* **114** B6
Minden *Germany* **24** C4
Minden *La., U.S.A.* **116** E8
Minden *Nev., U.S.A.* **110** G7
Mindibungu = Billiluna
  Australia **92** C4
Mindiptana *Indonesia* **63** F10
Mindoro *Phil.* **61** E4
Mindoro Str. *Phil.* **61** E4
Mine *Japan* **55** G5
Minehead *U.K.* **15** F4
Mineola *N.Y., U.S.A.* **115** F11
Mineola *Tex., U.S.A.* **116** E7
Mineral King *U.S.A.* **110** J8
Mineral Wells *U.S.A.* **116** E5
Mineralnyye Vody *Russia* **35** H6
Miners Bay *Canada* **114** B6
Minersville *U.S.A.* **115** F8
Minerva *N.Y., U.S.A.* **115** C11
Minerva *Ohio, U.S.A.* **114** F3
Minervino Murge *Italy* **43** A9
Minetto *U.S.A.* **115** C8
Mingäçevir *Azerbaijan* **35** K8
Mingäçevir Su Anbarı
  Azerbaijan **35** K8
Mingan *Canada* **105** B7
Mingechaur = Mingäçevir
  Azerbaijan **35** K8
Mingechaurskoye
  Vdkhr. = Mingäçevir Su
  Anbarı *Azerbaijan* **35** K8
Mingela *Australia* **94** B4

Mingenew *Australia* **93** E2
Mingera Cr. →~ *Australia* **94** C2
Minggang *China* **59** A10
Mingguang *China* **59** A11
Mingin *Burma* **67** H19
Mingir *Moldova* **29** D13
Minglanilla *Spain* **39** F3
Minglun *China* **58** E7
Mingo Junction *U.S.A.* **114** F4
Mingora *Pakistan* **69** B5
Mingorría *Spain* **36** E6
Mingshan *China* **58** B4
Mingteke Daban =
  Mintaka Pass *Pakistan* **69** A6
Mingxi *China* **59** D11
Mingyuegue *China* **57** C15
Minho = Miño →~ *Spain* **36** D2
Minhou *China* **59** E12
Miničevo *Serbia* **28** G7
Minidoka *U.S.A.* **108** E7
Minigwal, L. *Australia* **93** E3
Minilya →~ *Australia* **93** D1
Minilya Roadhouse *Australia* **93** D1
Minipi L. *Canada* **105** B7
Minjilang *Australia* **92** B5
Mink L. *Canada* **102** A5
Minkammen *Sudan* **81** F3
Minna *Nigeria* **83** D6
Minneapolis *Kans., U.S.A.* **112** F5
Minneapolis *Minn., U.S.A.* **112** C7
Minnedosa *Canada* **103** C9
Minnesota □ *U.S.A.* **112** B6
Minnesota →~ *U.S.A.* **112** C7
Minnewaukan *U.S.A.* **112** A4
Minnipa *Australia* **95** E2
Minnitaki L. *Canada* **104** C1
Mino *Japan* **55** G8
Miño *Spain* **36** B2
Miño →~ *Spain* **36** D2
Minoa *Greece* **47** F7
Minorca = Menorca *Spain* **48** B11
Minot *U.S.A.* **112** A3
Minqin *China* **56** E2
Minqing *China* **59** D12
Minsen *Germany* **24** B3
Minsk *Belarus* **23** B14
Minsk □ *Belarus* **32** F4
Mińsk Mazowiecki *Poland* **31** F8
Mintabie *Australia* **95** D1
Mintaka Pass *Pakistan* **69** A6
Minto *Canada* **105** C6
Minto, L. *Canada* **104** A5
Minton *Canada* **103** D8
Minturn *U.S.A.* **108** G10
Minturno *Italy* **42** A6
Minudasht *Iran* **71** B8
Minûf *Egypt* **80** H7
Minusinsk *Russia* **53** D10
Minutang *India* **67** E20
Minvoul *Gabon* **84** D2
Minya el Qamḥ *Egypt* **80** H7
Minya Konka = Gongga
  Shan *China* **58** C3
Mionica *Bos.-H.* **28** F3
Mionica *Serbia* **44** B4
Miquelon *Canada* **104** C4
Miquelon *St-P. & M.* **105** C8
Mir *Niger* **83** C7
Mīr Kūh *Iran* **71** E8
Mīr Shahdād *Iran* **71** E8
Mira *Italy* **41** C9
Mira *Portugal* **36** E2
Mira →~ *Portugal* **37** H2
Mira por vos Cay *Bahamas* **121** B5
Mirabella Eclano *Italy* **43** A7
Mirabello, Kolpos *Greece* **49** D7
Mirader-Río Azul △
  Guatemala **120** C2
Miraj *India* **66** L9
Miram Shah *Pakistan* **68** C4
Miramar *Argentina* **126** D4
Miramar *Mozam.* **89** C6
Miramas *France* **21** E8
Mirambeau *France* **20** C3
Miramichi *Canada* **105** C6
Miramichi B. *Canada* **105** C7
Miramont-de-Guyenne
  France **20** D4
Miranda *Brazil* **125** H7
Miranda →~ *Brazil* **124** G7
Miranda de Ebro *Spain* **38** C2
Miranda do Corvo *Portugal* **36** E2
Miranda do Douro *Portugal* **36** D4
Mirande *France* **20** E4
Mirandela *Portugal* **36** D3
Mirándola *Italy* **40** D8
Mirandópolis *Brazil* **127** A5
Mirango *Malawi* **87** E3
Mirani *Australia* **94** b
Mirano *Italy* **41** C9
Miras *Albania* **44** F4
Mirassol *Brazil* **127** A6
Mirbāṭ *Oman* **75** D5
Mirear *Egypt* **80** C4
Mirebeau *France* **18** F7
Mirebeau-sur-Bèze *France* **19** E12
Mirecourt *France* **19** D13
Mires *Greece* **49** D6
Mirgorod = Myrhorod
  Ukraine **33** H7

Miri *Malaysia* **62** D4
Miriam Vale *Australia* **94** C5
Miribel *France* **19** G11
Mirim, L. *S. Amer.* **127** C5
Miriuwung Gajerrong ⊛
  Australia **92** C4
Mīrjāveh *Iran* **71** D9
Mirnyy *Antarctica* **5** C14
Mirnyy *Russia* **53** C12
Mirokhan *Pakistan* **68** F3
Mirond L. *Canada* **103** B8
Mirosławiec *Poland* **30** E3
Mirpur *Pakistan* **69** C5
Mirpur Batoro *Pakistan* **68** G3
Mirpur Bibiwari *Pakistan* **68** E2
Mirpur Khas *Pakistan* **68** G3
Mirpur Sakro *Pakistan* **68** G2
Mirria *Niger* **83** C6
Mirsk *Poland* **31** H2
Mirtağ *Turkey* **70** B4
Mirtoo Sea *Greece* **46** D5
Miryang *S. Korea* **57** G15
Mirzaani *Georgia* **35** K8
Mirzapur *India* **69** G10
Mirzapur-cum-
  Vindhyachal = Mirzapur
  India **69** G10
Misantla *Mexico* **119** D5
Misawa *Japan* **54** D10
Miscou I. *Canada* **105** C7
Mish'āb, Ra's al *Si. Arabia* **71** D6
Mishamo *Tanzania* **86** D3
Mishan *China* **54** B5
Mishawaka *U.S.A.* **112** E10
Mishbih, Gebel *Egypt* **80** C3
Mishima *Japan* **55** G9
Misión *Mexico* **111** N10
Misiones □ *Argentina* **127** B5
Misiones □ *Paraguay* **126** B4
Miskah *Si. Arabia* **70** E4
Miskitos, Cayos *Nic.* **120** D3
Miskolc *Hungary* **28** B5
Misoke *Dem. Rep. of the Congo* **86** C2
Misool *Indonesia* **63** E8
Miṣr = Egypt ■ *Africa* **80** B3
Miṣrātah *Libya* **79** B9
Missanabie *Canada* **104** C3
Missinaibi →~ *Canada* **104** B3
Missinaibi L. *Canada* **104** C3
Mission *Canada* **102** D4
Mission *S. Dak., U.S.A.* **112** D3
Mission *Tex., U.S.A.* **116** H5
Mission Beach *Australia* **94** B4
Mission Viejo *U.S.A.* **111** M9
Missira *Senegal* **82** C1
Missisa L. *Canada* **104** B2
Missisicabi →~ *Canada* **104** B4
Mississippi →~ *Canada* **104** D3
Mississauga *Canada* **114** C5
Mississippi □ *U.S.A.* **117** E10
Mississippi →~ *U.S.A.* **117** G10
Mississippi L. *Canada* **115** A8
Mississippi River Delta
  U.S.A. **117** G10
Mississippi Sd. *U.S.A.* **117** F10
Missoula *U.S.A.* **108** C6
Missouri □ *U.S.A.* **112** F7
Missouri →~ *U.S.A.* **112** F8
Missouri City *U.S.A.* **116** G7
Missouri Valley *U.S.A.* **112** E6
Mist *U.S.A.* **110** E3
Mistassibi →~ *Canada* **105** B5
Mistassini *Canada* **105** C5
Mistassini →~ *Canada* **105** C5
Mistassini, L. *Canada* **104** B5
Mistastin L. *Canada* **105** A7
Mistelbach *Austria* **27** C9
Misterbianco *Italy* **43** E8
Mistinibi, L. *Canada* **105** A7
Mistissini *Canada* **105** C5
Mistretta *Italy* **43** E7
Misty L. *Canada* **103** B8
Misurata = Miṣrātah *Libya* **79** B9
Mît Ghamr *Egypt* **80** H7
Mitande *Mozam.* **87** E4
Mitatib *Sudan* **81** D4
Mitchell *Australia* **95** D4
Mitchell *Canada* **114** C3
Mitchell *Nebr., U.S.A.* **112** E2
Mitchell *Oreg., U.S.A.* **108** D3
Mitchell *S. Dak., U.S.A.* **112** D4
Mitchell →~ *Australia* **94** B3
Mitchell, Mt. *U.S.A.* **117** D13
Mitchell-Alice Rivers △
  Australia **94** B3
Mitchell Ra. *Australia* **94** A2
Mitchelstown *Ireland* **12** D3
Mitha Tiwana *Pakistan* **68** C5
Mithi *Pakistan* **68** G3
Mithimna *Greece* **47** B8
Mithrao *Pakistan* **68** F3
Mitilíni *Greece* **47** B8
Mitilinii *Greece* **47** D8
Mitla Pass = Mamarr Mitlā
  Egypt **74** E1
Mito *Japan* **55** F10
Mitrofanovka *Russia* **33** H10
Mitrovica = Kosovska
  Mitrovica *Kosovo* **44** D4

Mitsamiouli *Comoros Is.* **85** a
Mitsinjo *Madag.* **89** B8
Mitsiwa *Eritrea* **81** D4
Mitsiwa Channel *Eritrea* **81** D5
Mitsukaidō *Japan* **55** F9
Mittagong *Australia* **95** E5
Mittelberg *Austria* **26** D3
Mittelfranken □ *Germany* **25** F6
Mittellandkanal →~ *Germany* **24** C4
Mittenwalde *Germany* **24** C9
Mittersill *Austria* **26** D5
Mitterteich *Germany* **25** F8
Mittimatalik = Pond Inlet
  Canada **101** C16
Mittweida *Germany* **24** E8
Mitú *Colombia* **124** C4
Mitumba *Tanzania* **86** D3
Mitumba, Mts.
  Dem. Rep. of the Congo **86** D2
Mitwaba
  Dem. Rep. of the Congo **87** D2
Mityana *Uganda* **86** B3
Mixteco →~ *Mexico* **119** D5
Miyagi □ *Japan* **54** E10
Miyah, W. el →~ *Egypt* **80** C3
Miyah, W. el →~ *Syria* **70** C3
Miyake-Jima *Japan* **55** G9
Miyako *Japan* **54** E10
Miyako-Jima *Japan* **55** M2
Miyako-Rettō *Japan* **55** M2
Miyakonojō *Japan* **55** J5
Miyān Rahan *Iran* **73** E12
Miyani *India* **68** J3
Miyanoura-Dake *Japan* **55** J5
Miyazaki *Japan* **55** J5
Miyazaki □ *Japan* **55** H5
Miyazu *Japan* **55** G7
Miyet, Bahr el = Dead Sea
  Asia **74** D3
Miyi *China* **58** D4
Miyoshi *Japan* **55** G6
Miyun *China* **56** D9
Miyun Shuiku *China* **57** D9
Mizan Teferi *Ethiopia* **81** F4
Mizdah *Libya* **79** B8
Mizen Hd. *Cork, Ireland* **12** E2
Mizen Hd. *Wicklow, Ireland* **12** D5
Mizhhirya *Ukraine* **29** B8
Mizhi *China* **56** F6
Mizil *Romania* **29** F11
Mizoram □ *India* **67** H18
Mizpe Ramon *Israel* **74** E3
Mizusawa *Japan* **54** E10
Mjällby *Sweden* **11** H8
Mjöbäck *Sweden* **11** G6
Mjölby *Sweden* **11** F9
Mjörn *Sweden* **11** G6
Mjøsa *Norway* **8** F14
Mkata *Tanzania* **86** D4
Mkhaya △ *Swaziland* **89** D5
Mkhuze △ *S. Africa* **89** D4
Mkokotoni *Tanzania* **86** D4
Mkomazi *Tanzania* **86** C4
Mkomazi →~ *S. Africa* **89** E5
Mkomazi △ *Tanzania* **86** C4
Mkulwe *Tanzania* **87** D3
Mkushi *Zambia* **87** E2
Mkushi River *Zambia* **87** E2
Mkuze *S. Africa* **89** D5
Mladá Boleslav *Czech Rep.* **26** A7
Mladenovac *Serbia* **44** B4
Mlala Hills *Tanzania* **86** D3
Mlange = Mulanje, Mt.
  Malawi **87** F4
Mlava →~ *Serbia* **44** B5
Mława *Poland* **31** E7
Mlawula △ *Swaziland* **89** D5
Mljet *Croatia* **41** F14
Mljet △ *Croatia* **41** F14
Mljetski Kanal *Croatia* **41** F14
Młynary *Poland* **30** D6
Mme *Cameroon* **83** D7
Mnichovo Hradiště
  Czech Rep. **26** A7
Mo i Rana *Norway* **8** C16
Moa *Australia* **94** a
Moa *Cuba* **121** B4
Moa *Indonesia* **63** F7
Moa →~ *S. Leone* **82** D2
Moab *U.S.A.* **108** G9
Moala *Fiji* **91** a
Moama *Australia* **95** F3
Moamba *Mozam.* **89** D5
Moapa *U.S.A.* **111** J12
Moate *Ireland* **12** C4
Moba *Dem. Rep. of the Congo* **86** D2
Mobārakābād *Iran* **71** D7
Mobaye *C.A.R.* **84** D4
Mobayi *Dem. Rep. of the Congo* **84** D4
Moberly *U.S.A.* **112** F7
Moberly Lake *Canada* **102** B4
Mobile *U.S.A.* **117** F10
Mobile B. *U.S.A.* **117** F11
Möbő *Sweden* **10** E12
Mobridge *U.S.A.* **112** C3
Moc Chau *Vietnam* **64** B5
Moc Hoa *Vietnam* **65** G5

Mocabe Kasari
  Dem. Rep. of the Congo **87** D2
Moçambique =
  Mozambique ■ *Africa* **87** F4
Moçambique *Mozam.* **87** F5
Mocanaqua *U.S.A.* **115** E8
Moce *Fiji* **91** a
Mochima △ *Venezuela* **121** D7
Mochos *Greece* **49** D7
Mochudi *Botswana* **88** C4
Mocimboa da Praia *Mozam.* **87** E5
Mociu *Romania* **29** D9
Möckeln *Sweden* **11** H8
Mockfjärd *Sweden* **10** D8
Moclips *U.S.A.* **110** C2
Mocoa *Colombia* **124** C3
Mococa *Brazil* **127** A6
Mocorito *Mexico* **118** B3
Moctezuma *Mexico* **118** B3
Moctezuma →~ *Mexico* **119** C5
Mocuba *Mozam.* **87** F4
Modane *France* **21** C10
Modasa *India* **68** H5
Modder →~ *S. Africa* **88** D3
Modderrivier *S. Africa* **88** D3
Módena *Italy* **40** D7
Modena *U.S.A.* **109** H7
Modesto *U.S.A.* **110** H6
Módica *Italy* **43** F7
Modimolle *S. Africa* **89** C4
Modjadjiskloof *S. Africa* **89** C5
Mödling *Austria* **27** C9
Modo *Sudan* **81** F3
Modra *Slovak Rep.* **27** C10
Modriča *Bos.-H.* **28** F3
Moe *Australia* **95** F4
Moebase *Mozam.* **87** F4
Moëlan-sur-Mer *France* **18** E3
Moengo *Suriname* **125** B8
Moffat *U.K.* **13** F5
Moga *India* **68** D6
Mogadishu = Muqdisho
  Somali Rep. **75** G4
Mogador = Essaouira
  Morocco **78** B4
Mogadouro *Portugal* **36** D4
Mogalakwena →~ *S. Africa* **89** C4
Mogami-Gawa →~ *Japan* **54** E10
Mogán *Canary Is.* **48** G4
Mogaung *Burma* **67** G20
Mogente = Moixent *Spain* **39** G4
Mogho *Ethiopia* **81** G5
Mogi das Cruzes *Brazil* **127** A6
Mogi-Guaçu →~ *Brazil* **127** A6
Mogi-Mirim *Brazil* **125** H9
Mogielnica *Poland* **31** G7
Mogige *Ethiopia* **81** F4
Mogilev = Mahilyow
  Belarus **23** B16
Mogilev-Podolskiy =
  Mohyliv-Podilskyy
  Ukraine **29** B12
Mogilno *Poland* **31** F4
Mogincual *Mozam.* **87** F5
Mogliano Véneto *Italy* **41** C9
Mogocha *Russia* **53** D12
Mogok *Burma* **67** H20
Mogollon Rim *U.S.A.* **109** J8
Mógoro *Italy* **42** C1
Mograt *Sudan* **80** D3
Moguer *Spain* **37** H4
Mogumber *Australia* **93** F2
Mogwadi →~ *S. Africa* **89** C4
Mohács *Hungary* **28** E3
Mohales Hoek *Lesotho* **88** E4
Mohall *U.S.A.* **112** A3
Moḥammadābād *Iran* **71** C8
Mohammedia *Morocco* **78** B4
Mohana →~ *India* **69** G11
Mohanlalganj *India* **69** F9
Mohave, L. *U.S.A.* **111** K12
Mohawk →~ *U.S.A.* **115** D11
Moheda *Sweden* **11** G8
Mohéli *Comoros Is.* **85** a
Mohenjodaro *Pakistan* **68** F3
Moher, Cliffs of *Ireland* **12** D2
Mohicanville Res. *U.S.A.* **114** F2
Möhne →~ *Germany* **24** D3
Mohns Ridge *Arctic* **4** B7
Mohoro *Tanzania* **86** D4
Mohsenābād *Iran* **71** B8
Mohyliv-Podilskyy *Ukraine* **29** B12
Moia *Sudan* **81** F3
Moidart, L. *U.K.* **13** E3
Moineşti *Romania* **29** D11
Moira →~ *Canada* **114** B7
Moirans *France* **21** C9
Moirans-en-Montagne
  France **19** F12
Moisaküla *Estonia* **32** C3
Moisie *Canada* **105** B6
Moisie →~ *Canada* **105** B6
Moissac *France* **20** D5
Moita *Portugal* **37** G2
Moixent *Spain* **39** G4
Möja *Sweden* **10** E12
Mojácar *Spain* **39** H3
Mojados *Spain* **36** D6
Mojave *U.S.A.* **111** K8

Mojave △ *U.S.A.* **111** K11
Mojave Desert *U.S.A.* **111** L10
Mojiang *China* **58** F3
Mojjo ⇒ *Ethiopia* **81** F5
Mojkovac *Montenegro* **44** D3
Mojo *Bolivia* **126** A2
Mojo *Ethiopia* **81** F4
Mojokerto *Indonesia* **63** G15
Mokai *N.Z.* **91** C5
Mokambo
 Dem. Rep. of the Congo **87** E2
Mokameh *India* **69** G11
Mokau *N.Z.* **91** C5
Mokelumne ⇒ *U.S.A.* **110** G5
Mokelumne Hill *U.S.A.* **110** G6
Mokhotlong *Lesotho* **89** D4
Möklinta *Sweden* **10** D10
Mokoan, L. *Australia* **95** C4
Mokokchung *India* **67** F19
Mokolo *Cameroon* **83** C7
Mokolo ⇒ *S. Africa* **89** C4
Mokopane *S. Africa* **89** C4
Mokpo *S. Korea* **57** G14
Mokra Gora *Europe* **44** D4
Mokronog *Slovenia* **41** C12
Moksha ⇒ *Russia* **34** C6
Mokshan *Russia* **34** D7
Mokwa *Nigeria* **83** D6
Mol *Belgium* **17** C5
Mola di Bari *Italy* **43** A10
Molai *Greece* **46** E4
Molale *Ethiopia* **81** E4
Molara *Italy* **42** B2
Molat *Croatia* **41** D11
Molchanovo *Russia* **52** D9
Mold *U.K.* **14** D4
Moldava nad Bodvou
 Slovak Rep. **27** C14
Moldavia = Moldova ■
 Europe **29** C13
Moldavia *Romania* **29** D12
Molde *Norway* **8** E12
Moldova ■ *Europe* **29** C13
Moldova Nouă *Romania* **28** F6
Moldoveanu, Vf. *Romania* **29** E9
Moldovița *Romania* **29** C10
Mole ⇒ *U.K.* **15** F7
Mole △ *Ghana* **83** D4
Molepolole *Botswana* **88** C4
Molfetta *Italy* **43** A9
Molina de Aragón *Spain* **38** E3
Molina de Segura *Spain* **39** G3
Moline *U.S.A.* **112** E8
Molinella *Italy* **41** D8
Molinos *Argentina* **126** B2
Moliro *Dem. Rep. of the Congo* **86** D3
Moliterno *Italy* **43** B8
Molkom *Sweden* **10** E7
Mölle *Sweden* **11** H6
Molledo *Spain* **36** B6
Mollendo *Peru* **124** G4
Mollerin, L. *Australia* **93** F2
Mollerussa *Spain* **38** D5
Mollina *Spain* **37** H6
Mölln *Germany* **24** B6
Mölltorp *Sweden* **11** F8
Mölnlycke *Sweden* **11** G6
Molo *Kenya* **86** C4
Molochansk *Ukraine* **33** J8
Molochnoye, Ozero *Ukraine* **33** J8
Molodechno =
 Maladzyechna *Belarus* **23** A14
Molodezhnaya *Antarctica* **5** C9
Molodove *Ukraine* **29** D14
Moloka'i *U.S.A.* **107** L8
Molokai Fracture Zone
 Pac. Oc. **97** E15
Molong *Australia* **95** E4
Molopo ⇒ *Africa* **88** D3
Molos *Greece* **46** E4
Molsheim *France* **19** D14
Molson L. *Canada* **103** C9
Molteno *S. Africa* **88** E4
Molu *Indonesia* **63** F8
Molucca Sea *Indonesia* **63** E6
Moluccas = Maluku
 Indonesia **63** E7
Moma *Dem. Rep. of the Congo* **86** C1
Moma *Mozam.* **87** F4
Mombasa *Kenya* **86** C4
Mombetsu *Japan* **54** B11
Mombuey *Spain* **36** C4
Momchilgrad *Bulgaria* **45** E9
Momi *Dem. Rep. of the Congo* **86** C2
Mompós *Colombia* **124** B4
Møn *Denmark* **11** K6
Mon □ *Burma* **67** L20
Mona, Canal de la = Mona
 Passage *W. Indies* **121** C6
Mona, Isla *Puerto Rico* **121** C6
Mona, Pta. *Costa Rica* **120** E3
Mona Passage *W. Indies* **121** C6
Monaca *U.S.A.* **114** F4
Monaco ■ *Europe* **21** E11
Monadhliath Mts. *U.K.* **13** D4
Monadnock, Mt. *U.S.A.* **115** D12
Monaghan *Ireland* **12** B5
Monaghan □ *Ireland* **12** B5
Monahans *U.S.A.* **116** F3

Monapo *Mozam.* **87** E5
Monar, L. *U.K.* **13** D3
Monarch Mt. *Canada* **102** C3
Monashee Mts. *Canada* **102** C5
Monasterevin *Ireland* **12** C4
Monastir = Bitola *Macedonia* **44** E5
Monastir *Tunisia* **79** A8
Moncada *Phil.* **61** D4
Moncalieri *Italy* **40** D4
Moncalvo *Italy* **40** C5
Moncão *Portugal* **36** C2
Moncarapacho *Portugal* **37** H3
Moncayo, Sierra del *Spain* **38** D3
Monchegorsk *Russia* **8** C25
Mönchengladbach *Germany* **24** D2
Monchique *Portugal* **37** H2
Moncks Corner *U.S.A.* **117** E14
Monclova *Mexico* **118** B4
Moncontour *France* **18** D4
Moncton *Canada* **105** C7
Mondariz *Spain* **36** C2
Mondego ⇒ *Portugal* **36** E2
Mondego, C. *Portugal* **36** E2
Mondeodo *Indonesia* **63** E6
Mondeville *France* **18** C6
Mondolfo *Italy* **41** E9
Mondoñedo *Spain* **36** B3
Mondovì *Italy* **40** D4
Mondragon = Arrasate *Spain* **38** B2
Mondragon *Phil.* **61** E6
Mondragone *Italy* **42** A6
Mondrain I. *Australia* **93** F3
Moneague *Jamaica* **120** a
Monemvasia *Greece* **46** E5
Moneron, Ostrov *Russia* **54** A10
Monessen *U.S.A.* **114** F5
Monesterio *Spain* **37** G4
Monestier-de-Clermont
 France **21** D9
Monett *U.S.A.* **112** G7
Moneymore *U.K.* **12** B5
Monfalcone *Italy* **41** C10
Monflanquin *France* **20** D4
Monforte *Portugal* **37** F3
Monforte de Lemos *Spain* **36** C3
Mong Cai *Vietnam* **64** B6
Mong Hsu *Burma* **58** G2
Mong Kung *Burma* **67** J20
Mong Nai *Burma* **67** J20
Mong Pawk *Burma* **67** H21
Mong Ping *Burma* **58** G2
Mong Ton *Burma* **67** J21
Mong Wa *Burma* **67** J22
Mong Yai *Burma* **67** H21
Mongalla *Sudan* **81** F3
Mongers, L. *Australia* **93** E2
Monghyr = Munger *India* **69** G12
Mongibello = Etna *Italy* **43** E7
Mongo *Chad* **79** F9
Mongo ⇒ *S. Leone* **82** D2
Mongolia ■ *Asia* **53** E10
Mongolia, Plateau of *Asia* **50** D12
Mongonu *Nigeria* **83** C7
Mongu *Zambia* **85** H4
Môngua *Angola* **88** B2
Monifieth *U.K.* **13** E6
Monistrol-sur-Loire *France* **21** C8
Monkey Bay *Malawi* **87** E4
Monkey Mia *Australia* **93** E1
Monkey River *Belize* **119** D7
Mońki *Poland* **30** E9
Monkland *Canada* **115** A10
Monkoto
 Dem. Rep. of the Congo **84** E4
Monkton *Canada* **114** C3
Monmouth *U.K.* **15** F5
Monmouth *Ill., U.S.A.* **112** E8
Monmouth *Oreg., U.S.A.* **108** D2
Monmouthshire □ *U.K.* **15** F5
Mono ⇒ *Togo* **83** D5
Mono, Pta. *Nic.* **120** D3
Mono L. *U.S.A.* **110** H7
Monolith *U.S.A.* **111** K8
Monolithos *Greece* **49** C9
Monongahela *U.S.A.* **114** F5
Monópoli *Italy* **43** B10
Monor *Hungary* **28** C4
Monos I. *Trin. & Tob.* **125** K15
Monóvar *Spain* **39** G4
Monreal del Campo *Spain* **38** E3
Monreale *Italy* **42** D6
Monroe *Ga., U.S.A.* **117** E13
Monroe *La., U.S.A.* **116** E8
Monroe *Mich., U.S.A.* **113** E12
Monroe *N.C., U.S.A.* **117** D14
Monroe *N.Y., U.S.A.* **115** E10
Monroe *Utah, U.S.A.* **108** G7
Monroe *Wash., U.S.A.* **110** C5
Monroe *Wis., U.S.A.* **112** D9
Monroe City *U.S.A.* **112** F8
Monroeton *U.S.A.* **115** E8
Monroeville *Ala., U.S.A.* **117** F11
Monroeville *Pa., U.S.A.* **114** F5
Monrovia *Liberia* **82** D2
Mons *Belgium* **17** D3
Møns Klint *Denmark* **11** K6
Monsaraz *Portugal* **37** G3
Monse *Indonesia* **63** E6
Monségur *France* **20** D4

Monsélice *Italy* **41** C8
Mönsterås *Sweden* **11** G10
Mont Cenis, Col du *France* **21** C10
Mont-de-Marsan *France* **20** E3
Mont-Joli *Canada* **105** C6
Mont-Laurier *Canada* **104** C4
Mont-Louis *Canada* **105** C6
Mont Peko △ *Ivory C.* **82** D3
Mont-roig del Camp *Spain* **38** D5
Mont-St-Michel, Le *France* **18** D5
Mont Sangbé △ *Ivory C.* **82** D3
Mont-Tremblant △ *Canada* **104** C5
Montabaur *Germany* **24** E3
Montagnac *France* **20** E7
Montagnana *Italy* **41** C8
Montagu *S. Africa* **88** E3
Montagu I. *Antarctica* **5** B1
Montague *Canada* **105** C7
Montague, I. *Mexico* **118** A2
Montague I. *U.S.A.* **106** D10
Montague Ra. *Australia* **93** E2
Montague Sd. *Australia* **92** B4
Montaigu *France* **18** F5
Montalbán *Spain* **38** E4
Montalbano Iónico *Italy* **43** B9
Montalbo *Spain* **38** F2
Montalcino *Italy* **41** E8
Montalegre *Portugal* **36** D3
Montalto *Italy* **43** D8
Montalto di Castro *Italy* **41** F8
Montalto Uffugo *Italy* **43** C9
Montalvo *U.S.A.* **111** L7
Montamarta *Spain* **36** D5
Montana *Bulgaria* **44** C7
Montana *Peru* **124** E4
Montana □ *Bulgaria* **44** C7
Montana □ *U.S.A.* **108** C9
Montaña Clara, I. *Canary Is.* **48** E6
Montañas de Malaga △
 Spain **37** J6
Montánchez *Spain* **37** F4
Montargil *Portugal* **37** F2
Montargis *France* **19** E9
Montauban *France* **20** D5
Montauk *U.S.A.* **115** E13
Montauk Pt. *U.S.A.* **115** E13
Montbard *France* **19** E11
Montbarrey *France* **19** E12
Montbéliard *France* **19** E13
Montblanc *Spain* **38** D6
Montbrison *France* **21** C8
Montcalm, Pic de *France* **20** F5
Montceau-les-Mines *France* **19** F11
Montcenis *France* **21** B8
Montclair *U.S.A.* **115** F10
Montcornet *France* **19** C11
Montcuq *France* **20** D5
Montdidier *France* **19** C9
Monte Albán *Mexico* **119** D5
Monte Alegre *Brazil* **125** D8
Monte Azul *Brazil* **125** G10
Monte-Carlo *Monaco* **21** E11
Monte Caseros *Argentina* **126** C4
Monte Comán *Argentina* **126** C2
Monte Cristi *Dom. Rep.* **121** C5
Monte Cucco △ *Italy* **41** E9
Monte Lindo ⇒ *Paraguay* **126** A4
Monte Patria *Chile* **126** C1
Monte Quemado *Argentina* **126** B3
Monte Redondo *Portugal* **36** F2
Monte Rio *U.S.A.* **110** G4
Monte San Giovanni
 Campano *Italy* **42** A6
Monte San Savino *Italy* **41** E8
Monte Sant' Ángelo *Italy* **41** G12
Monte Santu, C. di *Italy* **42** B2
Monte Sibillini △ *Italy* **41** F10
Monte Subasio △ *Italy* **41** E9
Monte Vista *U.S.A.* **109** H10
Monteagudo *Argentina* **127** B5
Montealegre del Castillo
 Spain **39** G3
Montebello *Canada* **104** C5
Montebello Iónico *Italy* **43** E8
Montebello Is. *Australia* **92** D2
Montebelluna *Italy* **41** C9
Montebourg *France* **18** C5
Montecarlo *Argentina* **127** B5
Montecastrilli *Italy* **41** F9
Montecatini Terme *Italy* **40** E7
Montecristi *Ecuador* **124** D2
Montecristo *Italy* **40** F7
Montefalco *Italy* **41** F9
Montefiascone *Italy* **41** F9
Monterío *Spain* **37** H7
Montegiórgio *Italy* **41** E10
Montego Bay *Jamaica* **120** a
Montehermoso *Spain* **36** E4
Montejícar *Spain* **37** H7
Montélimar *France* **21** D8
Montella *Italy* **43** B8
Montellano *Italy* **37** J5
Montello *U.S.A.* **108** F6
Montemor-o-Novo *Portugal* **37** G2
Montemor-o-Velho *Portugal* **36** E2

Montemorelos *Mexico* **119** B5
Montendre *France* **20** C3
Montenegro *Brazil* **127** B5
Montenegro ■ *Europe* **44** D3
Montenero di Bisáccia *Italy* **41** G11
Montepuez *Mozam.* **87** E4
Montepuez ⇒ *Mozam.* **87** E5
Montepulciano *Italy* **41** E8
Montereale *Italy* **41** F10
Montereau-Faut-Yonne
 France **19** D9
Monterey *U.S.A.* **110** J5
Monterey B. *U.S.A.* **110** J5
Montería *Colombia* **124** B3
Monteros *Argentina* **126** B2
Monterotondo *Italy* **41** F9
Monterrey *Mexico* **118** B4
Montes Azules △ *Mexico* **119** D6
Montes Claros *Brazil* **125** G10
Montesano *U.S.A.* **110** D3
Montesano sulla
 Marcellana *Italy* **43** B8
Montesárchio *Italy* **43** A7
Montescaglioso *Italy* **43** B9
Montesilvano *Italy* **41** F11
Montesinho △ *Portugal* **36** D4
Montevarchi *Italy* **41** E8
Montevideo *Uruguay* **127** C4
Montevideo *U.S.A.* **112** C6
Montezuma *U.S.A.* **112** E7
Montezuma Castle △ *U.S.A.* **109** J8
Montfaucon *France* **18** E5
Montfaucon-d'Argonne
 France **19** C12
Montfaucon-en-Velay *France* **21** C8
Montfort-le-Gesnois *France* **18** D7
Montfort-sur-Meu *France* **18** D5
Montfragüe △ *Spain* **36** F5
Montgenèvre *France* **21** D10
Montgomery *U.K.* **15** E4
Montgomery *Ala., U.S.A.* **117** E11
Montgomery *Pa., U.S.A.* **114** E8
Montgomery *W. Va., U.S.A.* **113** F13
Montgomery City *U.S.A.* **112** F8
Montguyon *France* **20** C3
Monthermé *France* **19** C11
Monthey *Switz.* **25** J2
Monthois *France* **19** C11
Monti *Italy* **42** B2
Monti Lucrétili △ *Italy* **41** F9
Monti Picentini △ *Italy* **43** B8
Monti Simbruini △ *Italy* **41** G10
Monticelli d'Ongina *Italy* **40** C6
Monticello *Ark., U.S.A.* **116** E9
Monticello *Fla., U.S.A.* **117** F13
Monticello *Ind., U.S.A.* **112** E10
Monticello *Iowa, U.S.A.* **112** D8
Monticello *Ky., U.S.A.* **113** G11
Monticello *Minn., U.S.A.* **112** C7
Monticello *Miss., U.S.A.* **117** F9
Monticello *N.Y., U.S.A.* **115** E10
Monticello *Utah, U.S.A.* **109** H9
Montichiari *Italy* **40** C7
Montier-en-Der *France* **19** D11
Montignac *France* **20** C5
Montigny-les-Metz *France* **19** C13
Montigny-sur-Aube *France* **19** E11
Montijo *Portugal* **37** G2
Montijo *Spain* **37** G4
Montilla *Spain* **37** H6
Montivilliers *France* **18** C7
Montluçon *France* **19** F9
Montmagny *Canada* **105** C5
Montmarault *France* **19** F9
Montmartre *Canada* **103** C8
Montmédy *France* **19** C12
Montmélian *France* **21** C10
Montmirail *France* **19** D10
Montmoreau-St-Cybard
 France **20** C4
Montmorillon *France* **20** B4
Montmort-Lucy *France* **19** D10
Monto *Australia* **94** C5
Montoire-sur-le-Loir *France* **18** E7
Montongbuwoh *Indonesia* **63** K19
Montório al Vomano *Italy* **41** F10
Montoro *Spain* **37** G6
Montour Falls *U.S.A.* **114** D8
Montoursville *U.S.A.* **114** E8
Montpelier *Idaho, U.S.A.* **108** E8
Montpelier *Vt., U.S.A.* **115** B12
Montpellier *France* **20** E7
Montpezat-de-Quercy *France* **20** D5
Montpon-Ménestérol *France* **20** D4
Montréal *France* **20** D5
Montreal ⇒ *Canada* **104** B3
Montréal *Aude, France* **20** E6
Montréal *Gers, France* **20** E4
Montreal L. *Canada* **103** C7
Montreal Lake *Canada* **103** C7
Montredon-Labessonnié
 France **20** E6
Montréjeau *France* **20** E4
Montrésor *France* **18** E8
Montret *France* **19** F12
Montreuil *Pas-de-Calais,
 France* **19** B8
Montreuil *Seine-St-Denis,
 France* **19** D9
Montreuil-Bellay *France* **18** E6

Montreux *Switz.* **25** J2
Montrevel-en-Bresse *France* **19** F12
Montrichard *France* **18** E8
Montrose *U.K.* **13** E6
Montrose *Colo., U.S.A.* **108** G10
Montrose *Pa., U.S.A.* **115** E9
Monts, Pte. des *Canada* **105** C6
Montsalvy *France* **20** D6
Montsant, Serra de *Spain* **38** D6
Montsauche-les-Settons
 France **19** E11
Montsec, Serra del *Spain* **38** C5
Montseny △ *Spain* **38** D7
Montserrat *Spain* **38** D6
Montserrat ☑ *W. Indies* **121** C7
Montuenga *Spain* **36** D6
Montuiri *Spain* **48** B9
Monywa *Burma* **67** H19
Monza *Italy* **40** C6
Monze *Zambia* **87** F2
Monze, C. *Pakistan* **68** G2
Monzón *Spain* **38** D5
Mooers *U.S.A.* **115** B11
Mooi ⇒ *S. Africa* **89** D5
Mooi River *S. Africa* **89** D4
Moomba *Australia* **95** A3
Moonah ⇒ *Australia* **94** C2
Moonda, L. *Australia* **94** D3
Moonie *Australia* **95** D5
Moonie ⇒ *Australia* **95** D4
Moonta *Australia* **95** E2
Moora *Australia* **93** F2
Moorcroft *U.S.A.* **108** D11
Moore ⇒ *Australia* **93** F2
Moore, L. *Australia* **93** E2
Moore Falls *Canada* **114** B6
Moore Park *Australia* **94** C5
Moore Res. *U.S.A.* **115** B13
Moore River △ *Australia* **93** F2
Moorea *French Polynesia* **91** d
Moorefield *U.S.A.* **113** F14
Moorfoot Hills *U.K.* **13** F5
Moorhead *U.S.A.* **112** B5
Moormerland *Germany* **24** B3
Moorpark *U.S.A.* **111** L8
Moorreesburg *S. Africa* **88** E2
Moose ⇒ *Canada* **104** B3
Moose ⇒ *U.S.A.* **115** C9
Moose Creek *Canada* **115** A10
Moose Factory *Canada* **104** B3
Moose Jaw *Canada* **103** C7
Moose Jaw ⇒ *Canada* **103** C7
Moose Lake *Canada* **103** C8
Moose Lake *U.S.A.* **112** B7
Moose Mountain △ *Canada* **103** D8
Moosehead L. *U.S.A.* **113** C19
Mooselookmeguntic L.
 U.S.A. **115** B14
Moosilauke, Mt. *U.S.A.* **115** B13
Moosomin *Canada* **103** C8
Moosonee *Canada* **104** B3
Moosup *U.S.A.* **115** E13
Mopane *S. Africa* **89** C4
Mopeia Velha *Mozam.* **87** F4
Mopipi *Botswana* **88** C3
Mopoi *C.A.R.* **86** A2
Mopti *Mali* **82** C4
Mopti □ *Mali* **82** C4
Moqatta *Sudan* **81** E4
Moqor *Afghan.* **68** C2
Moquegua *Peru* **124** G4
Mór *Hungary* **28** C3
Móra *Cameroon* **83** C7
Mora *Spain* **37** F7
Mora *Sweden* **10** C8
Mora *Minn., U.S.A.* **112** C7
Mora *N. Mex., U.S.A.* **109** J11
Mora de Rubielos *Spain* **38** E4
Móra d'Ebre *Spain* **38** D5
Móra la Nova *Spain* **38** D5
Morača ⇒ *Montenegro* **44** D3
Moradabad *India* **69** E8
Morafenobe *Madag.* **89** B7
Morag *Poland* **30** E6
Moral de Calatrava *Spain* **37** G7
Moraleja *Spain* **36** E4
Moramanga *Madag.* **89** B8
Moran *Kans., U.S.A.* **112** G6
Moran *Wyo., U.S.A.* **108** E8
Moranbah *Australia* **94** C4
Morang = Biratnagar *Nepal* **69** F12
Morano Cálabro *Italy* **43** C9
Morant Bay *Jamaica* **120** a
Morant Cays *Jamaica* **120** C4
Morant Pt. *Jamaica* **120** a
Morar *India* **68** F8
Morar, L. *U.K.* **13** E3
Moratalla *Spain* **39** G3
Moratuwa *Sri Lanka* **66** R11
Morava ⇒ *Slovak Rep.* **27** C9
Moravia *U.S.A.* **115** D8
Moravian Hts. =
 Českomoravská
 Vrchovina *Czech Rep.* **26** B8
Moravica ⇒ *Serbia* **44** C4
Moravița *Romania* **28** E6

Moravská Třebová
 Czech Rep. **27** B9
Moravské Budějovice
 Czech. Rep. **26** B8
Morawa *Australia* **93** E2
Morawhanna *Guyana* **124** B7
Moray □ *U.K.* **13** D5
Moray Firth *U.K.* **13** D5
Morbach *Germany* **25** F3
Morbegno *Italy* **40** B6
Morbi *India* **68** H4
Morbihan □ *France* **18** E4
Mörbylånga *Sweden* **11** H10
Morcenx *France* **20** D3
Morcone *Italy* **43** A7
Mordelles *France* **18** D5
Morden *Canada* **103** D9
Mordoğan *Turkey* **47** C8
Mordovian Republic =
 Mordvinia □ *Russia* **34** C7
Mordovo *Russia* **34** D5
Mordvinia □ *Russia* **34** C7
Mordy *Poland* **31** F9
Moreau ⇒ *U.S.A.* **112** C3
Morebeng *S. Africa* **89** C4
Morecambe *U.K.* **14** C5
Morecambe B. *U.K.* **14** C5
Moree *Australia* **95** D4
Morehead *U.S.A.* **113** F12
Morehead City *U.S.A.* **117** D16
Morel ⇒ *India* **68** F7
Morelia *Mexico* **118** D4
Morella *Australia* **94** C3
Morella *Spain* **38** E4
Morelos *Mexico* **118** B3
Morelos □ *Mexico* **119** D5
Moremi △ *Botswana* **88** B3
Morena *India* **68** F8
Morena, Sierra *Spain* **37** G7
Moreni *Romania* **29** F10
Moreno Valley *U.S.A.* **111** M10
Moresby I. *Canada* **102** C2
Morestel *France* **21** C9
Moreton I. *Australia* **95** D5
Moreton Island △ *Australia* **95** D5
Moreuil *France* **19** C9
Morez *France* **19** F13
Morgan *U.S.A.* **108** F8
Morgan City *U.S.A.* **116** G9
Morgan Hill *U.S.A.* **110** H5
Morganfield *U.S.A.* **112** G10
Morganton *U.S.A.* **117** D14
Morgantown *U.S.A.* **113** F14
Morgenzon *S. Africa* **89** D4
Morges *Switz.* **25** J2
Morghak *Iran* **71** D8
Morgongåva *Sweden* **10** E10
Morhange *France* **19** D13
Morhar ⇒ *India* **69** G11
Mori *Italy* **40** C7
Mori *Japan* **54** C10
Moriarty *U.S.A.* **109** J10
Moribaya *Guinea* **82** D3
Morice L. *Canada* **102** C3
Moriki *Nigeria* **83** C6
Morinville *Canada* **102** C6
Morioka *Japan* **54** E10
Moris *Mexico* **118** B3
Morlaàs *France* **20** E3
Morlaix *France* **18** D3
Mörlunda *Sweden* **11** G9
Mormanno *Italy* **43** C8
Mormant *France* **19** D9
Mornington *Australia* **95** F4
Mornington, I. *Chile* **128** F1
Mornington I. *Australia* **94** B2
Mornos ⇒ *Greece* **46** E4
Moro *Pakistan* **68** F2
Moro *Sudan* **81** E3
Moro ⇒ *Pakistan* **68** E2
Moro G. *Phil.* **61** H5
Morocco ■ *N. Afr.* **78** B4
Morogoro *Tanzania* **86** D4
Morogoro □ *Tanzania* **86** D4
Moroleón *Mexico* **118** C4
Morombe *Madag.* **89** C7
Moron *Argentina* **126** C4
Morón *Cuba* **120** B4
Mörön *Mongolia* **53** E11
Morón de Almazán *Spain* **38** D2
Morón de la Frontera *Spain* **37** H5
Morona ⇒ *Peru* **124** D3
Morondava *Madag.* **89** C7
Morondo *Ivory C.* **82** D3
Morongo Valley *U.S.A.* **111** L10
Moroni *Comoros Is.* **85** a
Moroni *U.S.A.* **108** G8
Moronou *Ivory C.* **82** D4
Morotai *Indonesia* **63** D7
Moroto *Uganda* **86** B3
Moroto, Mt. *Uganda* **86** B3
Morozov *Bulgaria* **45** D9
Morozovsk *Russia* **35** F5
Morpeth *Canada* **114** D3
Morpeth *U.K.* **14** B6
Morphou *Cyprus* **49** D11
Morphou Bay *Cyprus* **49** D11
Morrilton *U.S.A.* **116** D8
Morrinhos *Brazil* **125** G9

Morrinsville *N.Z.* **91** B5
Morris *Canada* **103** D9
Morris *Ill., U.S.A.* **112** E9
Morris *Minn., U.S.A.* **112** C6
Morris *N.Y., U.S.A.* **115** D9
Morris *Pa., U.S.A.* **114** E7
Morris, Mt. *Australia* **93** E5
Morris Jesup, Kap *Greenland* **98** A16
Morrisburg *Canada* **115** B9
Morristown *Ariz., U.S.A.* **109** K7
Morristown *N.J., U.S.A.* **115** F10
Morristown *N.Y., U.S.A.* **115** B9
Morristown *Tenn., U.S.A.* **117** C13
Morrisville *N.Y., U.S.A.* **115** D9
Morrisville *Pa., U.S.A.* **115** F10
Morrisville *Vt., U.S.A.* **115** B12
Morro, Pta. de *Chile* **126** B1
Morro Bay *U.S.A.* **110** K6
Morro del Jable *Canary Is.* **48** F5
Morro Jable, Pta. de *Canary Is.* **48** F5
Morrocoy △ *Venezuela* **121** D6
Morrosquillo, G. de *Colombia* **120** E4
Mörrum *Sweden* **11** H8
Morrumbene *Mozam.* **89** C6
Mörrumsån → *Sweden* **11** H8
Mors *Denmark* **11** H2
Morshansk *Russia* **34** D5
Mörsil *Sweden* **10** A7
Mortagne → *France* **19** D13
Mortagne-au-Perche *France* **18** D7
Mortagne-sur-Gironde *France* **20** C3
Mortagne-sur-Sèvre *France* **18** F6
Mortain *France* **18** D6
Mortara *Italy* **40** C5
Morteau *France* **19** E13
Morteros *Argentina* **126** C3
Mortlach *Canada* **103** C7
Mortlake *Australia* **95** F3
Morton *Tex., U.S.A.* **116** E3
Morton *Wash., U.S.A.* **110** D4
Moruga *Trin. & Tob.* **125** K15
Morundah *Australia* **95** E4
Moruya *Australia* **95** F5
Morvan *France* **19** E11
Morven △ *France* **19** E11
Morven *Australia* **95** D4
Morvern *U.K.* **13** E3
Morwell *Australia* **95** F4
Moryń *Poland* **31** F1
Morzine *France* **19** F13
Mosalsk *Russia* **32** E8
Mosbach *Germany* **25** F5
Mošćenice *Croatia* **41** C11
Mosciano Sant' Ángelo *Italy* **41** F10
Moscos Is. *Burma* **64** F1
Moscow = Moskva *Russia* **32** E9
Moscow *Idaho, U.S.A.* **108** C5
Moscow *Pa., U.S.A.* **115** E9
Mosel → *Europe* **19** B14
Moselle = Mosel → *Europe* **19** B14
Moselle □ *France* **19** D13
Moses Lake *U.S.A.* **108** C4
Mosgiel *N.Z.* **91** F4
Moshaweng → *S. Africa* **88** D3
Moshchnyy, Ostrov *Russia* **32** B4
Moshi *Tanzania* **86** C4
Moshi → *Nigeria* **83** D5
Moshupa *Botswana* **88** C4
Mosina *Poland* **31** F3
Mosjøen *Norway* **8** D15
Moskenesøya *Norway* **8** C15
Moskenstraumen *Norway* **8** C15
Moskva *Russia* **32** E9
Moskva □ *Russia* **32** D9
Moskva → *Russia* **32** E10
Moslavačka Gora *Croatia* **41** C13
Mosomane *Botswana* **88** C4
Mosonmagyaróvár *Hungary* **28** C2
Mošorin *Serbia* **28** E5
Mospino *Ukraine* **33** J9
Mosquera *Colombia* **124** C3
Mosquero *U.S.A.* **109** J12
Mosqueruela *Spain* **38** E4
Mosquitia *Honduras* **120** C3
Mosquito Coast = Mosquitia *Honduras* **120** C3
Mosquito Creek L. *U.S.A.* **114** E4
Mosquito L. *Canada* **103** A8
Mosquitos, G. de los *Panama* **120** E3
Moss *Norway* **9** G14
Moss Vale *Australia* **95** E5
Mossaka *Congo* **84** E3
Mossbank *Canada* **103** D7
Mossburn *N.Z.* **91** F2
Mosselbaai *S. Africa* **88** E3
Mossendjo *Congo* **84** E2
Mossgiel *Australia* **95** E3
Mossingen *Germany* **25** G5
Mossman *Australia* **94** B4
Mossoró *Brazil* **125** E11
Mossuril *Mozam.* **87** E5
Most *Czech Rep.* **26** A6
Mosta *Malta* **49** D1
Mostaganem *Algeria* **78** A6
Mostar *Bos.-H.* **28** C2
Mostardas *Brazil* **127** C5

Mostiska = Mostyska *Ukraine* **31** J10
Móstoles *Spain* **36** E7
Mosty = Masty *Belarus* **23** B13
Mostyska *Ukraine* **31** J10
Mosul = Al Mawşil *Iraq* **73** D10
Mota *Ethiopia* **81** E4
Mota del Cuervo *Spain* **39** F2
Mota del Marqués *Spain* **36** D5
Motagua → *Guatemala* **120** C2
Motala *Sweden* **11** F9
Motaze *Mozam.* **89** C5
Moţca *Romania* **29** C11
Moth *India* **69** G8
Motherwell *U.K.* **13** F5
Motihari *India* **69** F11
Motilla del Palancar *Spain* **39** F3
Motnik *Slovenia* **41** B11
Motovun *Croatia* **41** C10
Motozintla de Mendoza *Mexico* **119** D6
Motril *Spain* **37** J7
Motru *Romania* **28** F7
Motru → *Romania* **29** F8
Mott *U.S.A.* **112** B2
Móttola *Italy* **43** B10
Motueka *N.Z.* **91** D4
Motueka → *N.Z.* **91** D4
Motul *Mexico* **119** C7
Mouchalagane → *Canada* **105** B6
Mouding *China* **58** E3
Moudjeria *Mauritania* **82** B2
Moudon *Switz.* **25** J2
Moudros *Greece* **47** B7
Mouhoun = Black Volta → *Africa* **82** D4
Mouila *Gabon* **84** E2
Moulamein *Australia* **95** F3
Moule à Chique, C. *St. Lucia* **121** f
Mouliana *Greece* **49** D7
Moulins *France* **19** F10
Moulmein *Burma* **67** L20
Moulouya, O. → *Morocco* **78** B5
Moultrie *U.S.A.* **117** F13
Moultrie, L. *U.S.A.* **117** E14
Mound City *Mo., U.S.A.* **112** E6
Mound City *S. Dak., U.S.A.* **112** C3
Moundou *Chad* **79** G9
Moundsville *U.S.A.* **114** G4
Moung *Cambodia* **64** F4
Mount Airy *U.S.A.* **117** C14
Mount Albert *Canada* **114** B5
Mount Aspiring △ *N.Z.* **91** F2
Mount Barker *S. Austral., Australia* **95** F2
Mount Barker *W. Austral., Australia* **93** F2
Mount Barnett Roadhouse *Australia* **92** C4
Mount Bellew Bridge *Ireland* **12** C3
Mount Brydges *Canada* **114** D3
Mount Burr *Australia* **95** F3
Mount Carmel = Ha Karmel △ *Israel* **74** C4
Mount Carmel *Ill., U.S.A.* **112** F10
Mount Carmel *Pa., U.S.A.* **115** F8
Mount Clemens *U.S.A.* **114** D2
Mount Coolon *Australia* **94** C4
Mount Darwin *Zimbabwe* **87** F3
Mount Desert I. *U.S.A.* **113** C19
Mount Dora *U.S.A.* **117** G14
Mount Ebenezer *Australia* **93** E5
Mount Edziza △ *Canada* **102** B2
Mount Elgon △ *E. Afr.* **86** B3
Mount Field △ *Australia* **95** G4
Mount Fletcher *S. Africa* **89** E4
Mount Forest *Canada* **114** C4
Mount Frankland △ *Australia* **93** F2
Mount Frederick ☉ *Australia* **92** C4
Mount Gambier *Australia* **95** F3
Mount Garnet *Australia* **94** B4
Mount Holly *U.S.A.* **115** G10
Mount Holly Springs *U.S.A.* **114** F7
Mount Hope *N.S.W., Australia* **95** E4
Mount Hope *S. Austral., Australia* **95** E2
Mount Isa *Australia* **94** C2
Mount James ☉ *Australia* **93** D2
Mount Jewett *U.S.A.* **114** E6
Mount Kaputar △ *Australia* **95** E5
Mount Kenya △ *Kenya* **86** C4
Mount Kisco *U.S.A.* **115** E11
Mount Laguna *U.S.A.* **111** N10
Mount Larcom *Australia* **94** C5
Mount Lofty Ranges *Australia* **95** E2
Mount Magnet *Australia* **93** E2
Mount Maunganui *N.Z.* **91** B6
Mount Molloy *Australia* **94** B4
Mount Morgan *Australia* **94** C5
Mount Morris *U.S.A.* **114** D7
Mount Pearl *Canada* **105** C9
Mount Penn *U.S.A.* **115** F9
Mount Perry *Australia* **95** D5
Mount Pleasant *Iowa, U.S.A.* **112** E8
Mount Pleasant *Mich., U.S.A.* **113** D11
Mount Pleasant *Pa., U.S.A.* **114** F5

Mount Pleasant *S.C., U.S.A.* **117** E15
Mount Pleasant *Tenn., U.S.A.* **117** D11
Mount Pleasant *Tex., U.S.A.* **116** E7
Mount Pleasant *Utah, U.S.A.* **108** G8
Mount Pocono *U.S.A.* **115** E9
Mount Rainier △ *U.S.A.* **110** D5
Mount Revelstoke △ *Canada* **102** C5
Mount Robson △ *Canada* **102** C5
Mount St. Helens △ *U.S.A.* **110** D4
Mount Selinda *Zimbabwe* **89** C5
Mount Shasta *U.S.A.* **108** F2
Mount Signal *U.S.A.* **111** N11
Mount Sterling *Ill., U.S.A.* **112** F8
Mount Sterling *Ky., U.S.A.* **113** F12
Mount Surprise *Australia* **94** B3
Mount Union *U.S.A.* **114** F7
Mount Upton *U.S.A.* **115** D9
Mount Vernon *Ill., U.S.A.* **112** F9
Mount Vernon *Ind., U.S.A.* **112** G10
Mount Vernon *N.Y., U.S.A.* **115** F11
Mount Vernon *Ohio, U.S.A.* **114** F2
Mount Vernon *Wash., U.S.A.* **110** B4
Mount William △ *Australia* **95** G4
Mounta, Akra *Greece* **46** C2
Mountain Ash *U.K.* **15** F4
Mountain Center *U.S.A.* **111** M10
Mountain City *Nev., U.S.A.* **108** F6
Mountain City *Tenn., U.S.A.* **117** C14
Mountain Dale *U.S.A.* **115** E10
Mountain Grove *U.S.A.* **112** G7
Mountain Home *Ark., U.S.A.* **116** D8
Mountain Home *Idaho, U.S.A.* **108** E6
Mountain Iron *U.S.A.* **112** B7
Mountain Pass *U.S.A.* **111** K11
Mountain View *Ark., U.S.A.* **116** D8
Mountain View *Calif., U.S.A.* **110** H4
Mountain Zebra △ *S. Africa* **88** E4
Mountainair *U.S.A.* **109** J10
Mountlake Terrace *U.S.A.* **110** C4
Mountmellick *Ireland* **12** C4
Mountrath *Ireland* **12** D4
Moura *Australia* **94** C4
Moura *Brazil* **124** D6
Moura *Portugal* **37** G3
Mourão *Portugal* **37** G3
Mourdi, Dépression du *Chad* **79** E10
Mourdiah *Mali* **82** C3
Mourenx *France* **20** E3
Mouri *Ghana* **83** D4
Mourilyan *Australia* **94** B4
Mourmelon-le-Grand *France* **19** C11
Mourne → *U.K.* **12** B4
Mourne Mts. *U.K.* **12** B5
Mournies *Greece* **49** D6
Mouscron *Belgium* **17** D3
Moussa 'Ali *Djibouti* **81** E5
Moussoro *Chad* **79** F9
Mouthe *France* **19** F13
Moûtiers *France* **21** C10
Moutong *Indonesia* **63** D6
Mouy *France* **19** C9
Mouzaki *Greece* **46** B3
Mouzon *France* **19** C12
Movas *Mexico* **118** B3
Moville *Ireland* **12** A4
Mowandjum *Australia* **92** C3
Moy → *Ireland* **12** B2
Moya *Comoros Is.* **85** a
Moyale *Ethiopia* **86** B4
Moyale *Kenya* **81** G4
Moyamba *S. Leone* **82** D2
Moyen Atlas *Morocco* **78** B4
Moyo *Indonesia* **62** F5
Moyobamba *Peru* **124** E3
Moyowosi △ *Tanzania* **86** C3
Moyyero → *Russia* **53** C11
Moyynqum *Kazakhstan* **52** E8
Moyynty *Kazakhstan* **52** E8
Mozambique = Moçambique *Mozam.* **87** F5
Mozambique ■ *Africa* **87** F4
Mozambique Chan. *Africa* **89** B7
Mozdok *Russia* **35** J7
Mozdūrān *Iran* **71** B9
Mozhaysk *Russia* **32** E9
Mozhga *Russia* **34** B11
Mozhnābād *Iran* **71** C9
Mozirje *Slovenia* **41** B11
Mozyr = Mazyr *Belarus* **23** B15
Mpanda *Tanzania* **86** D3
Mpésoba *Mali* **82** C3
Mphoeng *Zimbabwe* **87** G2
Mpika *Zambia* **87** E3
Mpulungu *Zambia* **87** D3
Mpumalanga *S. Africa* **89** D5
Mpumalanga □ *S. Africa* **89** D5
Mpwapwa *Tanzania* **86** D4
Mqanduli *S. Africa* **89** E4

Mqinvartsveri = Kazbek *Russia* **35** J7
Mrągowo *Poland* **30** E8
Mramor *Serbia* **44** C5
Mrkonjić Grad *Bos.-H.* **28** F2
Mrkopalj *Croatia* **41** C11
Mrocza *Poland* **31** E4
Msaken *Tunisia* **79** A8
Msambansovu *Zimbabwe* **87** F3
M'sila = Algeria *Algeria* **78** A6
Msoro *Zambia* **87** E3
Msta → *Russia* **32** C6
Mstislavl = Mstsislaw *Belarus* **23** A16
Mstsislaw *Belarus* **23** A16
Mszana Dolna *Poland* **31** J7
Mszczonów *Poland* **31** G7
Mtama *Tanzania* **87** E4
Mtamvuna = Mthamvuna → *S. Africa* **89** E5
Mthamvuna → *S. Africa* **89** E5
Mthatha *S. Africa* **89** E4
Mtilikwe → *Zimbabwe* **87** G3
Mtirala △ *Georgia* **35** K6
Mtito Andei *Kenya* **86** C4
Mtsensk *Russia* **32** F9
Mtskheta *Georgia* **35** K7
Mtubatuba *S. Africa* **89** D5
Mtwalume *S. Africa* **89** E5
Mtwara-Mikindani *Tanzania* **87** E5
Mu Gia, Deo *Vietnam* **64** D5
Mu Ko Chang △ *Thailand* **65** G4
Mu Us Shamo *China* **56** E5
Muang Chiang Rai = Chiang Rai *Thailand* **58** H2
Muang Khong *Laos* **64** E5
Muang Lamphun *Thailand* **64** C2
Muang Mai *Thailand* **65** a
Muang Pak Beng *Laos* **58** H3
Muar *Malaysia* **65** L4
Muarabungo *Indonesia* **62** E2
Muaraenim *Indonesia* **62** E2
Muarajuloi *Indonesia* **62** E4
Muarakaman *Indonesia* **62** E5
Muaratebo *Indonesia* **62** E2
Muaratembesi *Indonesia* **62** E2
Muaratewe *Indonesia* **62** E4
Mubarakpur *India* **69** F10
Mubarraz = Al Mubarraz *Si. Arabia* **71** E6
Mubende *Uganda* **86** B3
Mubi *Nigeria* **83** C7
Mucajaí → *Brazil* **124** C6
Muchachos, Roque de los *Canary Is.* **48** F2
Mücheln *Germany* **24** D7
Muchinga Mts. *Zambia* **87** E3
Muchkapskiy *Russia* **34** E6
Muchuan *China* **58** C5
Muck *U.K.* **13** E2
Muckadilla *Australia* **95** D4
Muckaty ☉ *Australia* **94** B1
Muckle Flugga *U.K.* **13** A8
Mucur *Turkey* **72** C6
Mucuri *Brazil* **125** G11
Mucusso *Angola* **88** B3
Muda → *Canary Is.* **48** F6
Mudanjiang *China* **57** B15
Mudanya *Turkey* **45** F12
Muddy Cr. → *U.S.A.* **108** G8
Mudgee *Australia* **95** E4
Mudjatik → *Canada* **103** B7
Mudurnu *Turkey* **72** B4
Muecate *Mozam.* **87** E4
Mueda *Mozam.* **87** E4
Mueller Ranges *Australia* **92** C4
Muende *Mozam.* **87** E3
Muerto, Mar *Mexico* **119** D6
Mufu Shan *China* **59** C10
Mufulira *Zambia* **87** E2
Mufumbiro Range *Africa* **86** C2
Mugardos *Spain* **36** B2
Muge → *Portugal* **37** F2
Múggia *Italy* **41** C10
Mughal Sarai *India* **69** G10
Mughayrā' *Si. Arabia* **70** D3
Mugi *Japan* **55** H7
Mugia = Muxía *Spain* **36** B1
Mugila, Mts. *Dem. Rep. of the Congo* **86** D2
Muğla *Turkey* **47** D10
Muğla □ *Turkey* **47** D10
Muglad *Sudan* **81** E2
Müglizh *Bulgaria* **45** D9
Mugu *Nepal* **69** E10
Muhala *Congo* **86** D2
Muhammad, Râs *Egypt* **70** E2
Muhammad Qol *Sudan* **80** C4
Muhammadabad *India* **69** F10
Muhesi → *Tanzania* **86** D4
Mühlacker *Germany* **25** G4
Mühldorf *Germany* **25** G8
Mühlhausen *Germany* **24** D6
Mühlig Hofmann fjell *Antarctica* **5** D3
Muhos *Finland* **8** D21
Mühlviertel *Austria* **26** C7
Muhu *Estonia* **32** C2
Muhutwe *Tanzania* **86** C3

Muine Bheag *Ireland* **12** D5
Muineachán = Monaghan *Ireland* **12** B5
Muir, L. *Australia* **93** F2
Muir of Ord *U.K.* **13** D4
Mujeres, I. *Mexico* **120** B2
Mujnak = Muynak *Uzbekistan* **52** E6
Muka, Tanjung *Malaysia* **65** c
Mukah *Malaysia* **62** D4
Mukandwara *India* **68** G6
Mukawwa, Geziret *Egypt* **70** F2
Mukawwar *Sudan* **80** C4
Mukdahan *Thailand* **64** D5
Mukden = Shenyang *China* **57** D12
Mukerian *India* **68** D6
Mukhavets *Belarus* **31** F10
Mukhtolovo *Russia* **34** C6
Mukinbudin *Australia* **93** F2
Mukishi *Dem. Rep. of the Congo* **87** D1
Mukomuko *Indonesia* **62** E2
Mukono *Uganda* **86** B3
Muktsar *India* **68** D6
Mukur = Moqor *Afghan.* **68** C2
Mukutuwa → *Canada* **103** C9
Mukwela *Zambia* **87** F2
Mula *Spain* **39** G3
Mula → *Pakistan* **68** F2
Mulange *Dem. Rep. of the Congo* **86** C2
Mulanje, Mt. *Malawi* **87** F4
Mulchatna → *U.S.A.* **106** D8
Mulchén *Chile* **126** D1
Mulde → *Germany* **24** D8
Mule Creek Junction *U.S.A.* **108** E11
Muleba *Tanzania* **86** C3
Mulegé *Mexico* **118** B2
Muleshoe *U.S.A.* **116** D3
Muletta, Gara *Ethiopia* **81** F5
Mulgrave *Canada* **105** C7
Mulgrave I. = Badu *Australia* **94** a
Mulhacén *Spain* **37** H7
Mülheim *Germany* **24** D2
Mulhouse *France* **19** E14
Muli *China* **58** D3
Mulifanua *Samoa* **91** b
Muling *China* **57** B16
Muling → *China* **57** B16
Mull *U.K.* **13** E3
Mull, Sound of *U.K.* **13** E3
Mullach Íde = Malahide *Ireland* **12** C5
Mullaittivu *Sri Lanka* **66** Q12
Mullen *U.S.A.* **112** D3
Mullengudgery *Australia* **95** B4
Mullens *U.S.A.* **113** G13
Muller, Pegunungan *Indonesia* **62** D4
Mullet Pen. *Ireland* **12** B1
Mullewa *Australia* **93** E2
Müllheim *Germany* **25** H3
Mulligan → *Australia* **94** D2
Mullingar *Ireland* **12** C4
Mullins *U.S.A.* **117** D15
Mullsjö *Sweden* **11** G7
Mullumbimby *Australia* **95** D5
Mulobezi *Zambia* **87** F2
Mulonga Plain *Zambia* **85** H4
Mulroy B. *Ireland* **12** A4
Multan *Pakistan* **68** D4
Mulumbe, Mts. *Dem. Rep. of the Congo* **87** D2
Mulvane *U.S.A.* **112** G5
Mulwad *Sudan* **80** D3
Mulwala, L. *Australia* **95** C4
Mumbai *India* **66** K8
Mumbwa *Zambia* **87** F2
Mumias *Kenya* **86** C4
Mumra *Russia* **35** H8
Mun → *Thailand* **64** E5
Muna *Indonesia* **63** F6
Munabao *India* **68** G3
Munamagi *Estonia* **32** D4
Muncan *Indonesia* **63** K18
Muncar *Indonesia* **63** J17
München *Germany* **25** G7
Müncheberg *Germany* **24** C10
München *Germany* **25** G7
München-Gladbach = Mönchengladbach *Germany* **24** D2
Muncho Lake *Canada* **102** B3
Munch'ŏn *N. Korea* **57** E14
Muncie *U.S.A.* **113** E11
Muncoonie L. West *Australia* **94** D2
Mundabbera *Australia* **95** D5
Munday *U.S.A.* **116** E5
Mundemba *Cameroon* **83** D6
Münden *Germany* **24** D5
Münden △ *Germany* **24** D5

Mundiwindi *Australia* **92** D3
Mundo → *Spain* **39** G2
Mundo Novo *Brazil* **125** F10
Mundra *India* **68** H3
Mundrabilla *Australia* **93** F4
Munera *Spain* **39** F2
Mungallala *Australia* **95** D4
Mungallala Cr. → *Australia* **95** D4
Mungana *Australia* **94** B3
Mungaoli *India* **68** G8
Mungari *Mozam.* **87** F3
Mungbere *Dem. Rep. of the Congo* **86** B2
Mungeli *India* **69** H9
Munger *India* **69** G12
Mungerannie *Australia* **95** A2
Mungilli ☉ *Australia* **93** E3
Mungkan Kandju △ *Australia* **94** A3
Mungkarta ☉ *Australia* **94** C1
Munich = München *Germany* **25** G7
Munising *U.S.A.* **112** B10
Munka-Ljungby *Sweden* **11** H6
Munkebo *Denmark* **11** J4
Munkedal *Sweden* **11** F5
Munkfors *Sweden* **10** E7
Munku-Sardyk *Russia* **53** D11
Münnerstadt *Germany* **25** E6
Munnsville *U.S.A.* **115** D9
Muñoz Gamero, Pen. *Chile* **128** G2
Munroe L. *Canada* **103** B9
Munsan *S. Korea* **57** F14
Munster *France* **19** D14
Münster *Niedersachsen, Germany* **24** C6
Münster *Nordrhein-Westfalen, Germany* **24** D3
Munster □ *Ireland* **12** D3
Muntadgin *Australia* **93** F2
Muntele Mare, Vf. *Romania* **29** D8
Muntok *Indonesia* **62** E3
Munzur Dağları *Turkey* **73** C8
Muong Beng *Laos* **58** F3
Muong Boum *Vietnam* **58** F4
Muong Et *Laos* **64** B5
Muong Hai *Laos* **58** G3
Muong Hiem *Laos* **64** B4
Muong Houn *Laos* **58** G3
Muong Hung *Vietnam* **58** G4
Muong Kau *Laos* **64** E5
Muong Khao *Laos* **64** C4
Muong Khoua *Laos* **58** G4
Muong Liep *Laos* **64** C4
Muong May *Laos* **64** E6
Muong Ngeun *Laos* **58** G3
Muong Ngoi *Laos* **58** G4
Muong Nhie *Vietnam* **58** F4
Muong Nong *Laos* **64** D6
Muong Ou Tay *Laos* **58** F3
Muong Oua *Laos* **64** C3
Muong Peun *Laos* **58** G4
Muong Phalane *Laos* **64** D5
Muong Phieng *Laos* **64** C3
Muong Phine *Laos* **64** D6
Muong Sai *Laos* **58** G3
Muong Saiapoun *Laos* **64** C3
Muong Sen *Vietnam* **64** C5
Muong Sing *Laos* **58** G3
Muong Son *Laos* **58** G4
Muong Soui *Laos* **64** C4
Muong Va *Laos* **58** G4
Muong Xia *Vietnam* **64** B5
Muonio *Finland* **8** C20
Muonio älv → *Finland* **8** C20
Muonionjoki = Muonioälven = Muonionjoki → *Finland* **8** C20
Muonionjoki → *Finland* **8** C20
Mupa → *Mozam.* **87** F4
Muping *China* **57** F11
Mupoi *Sudan* **81** F2
Muqaddam, Wadi → *Sudan* **80** D3
Muqdisho *Somali Rep.* **75** G4
Mur → *Austria* **27** E9
Mûr-de-Bretagne *France* **18** D4
Muradiye *Manisa, Turkey* **47** C9
Muradiye *Van, Turkey* **73** C10
Murakami *Japan* **54** E9
Muralag = Prince of Wales I. *Australia* **94** a
Murallón, Cerro *Chile* **128** F2
Muranda *Rwanda* **86** C2
Murang'a *Kenya* **86** C4
Murashi *Russia* **52** D5
Murat *France* **20** C6
Murat → *Turkey* **73** C9
Murat Dağı *Turkey* **47** C11
Muratlı *Turkey* **45** E11
Murato *France* **21** F13
Murau *Austria* **26** D7
Murava *Belarus* **31** F11
Muravera *Italy* **42** C2
Murayama *Japan* **54** E10
Murça *Portugal* **36** D3
Murchison → *Australia* **93** E1
Murchison, Mt. *Antarctica* **5** D11
Murchison Falls *Uganda* **86** B3

Murchison Falls △ *Uganda* **86** B3
Murchison Ra. *Australia* **94** C1
Murchison Rapids *Malawi* **87** F3
Murchison Roadhouse
  Australia **93** E1
Murcia *Spain* **39** G3
Murcia □ *Spain* **39** H3
Murdo *U.S.A.* **112** D3
Murdoch Pt. *Australia* **94** A3
Mürefte *Turkey* **45** F11
Mureş □ *Romania* **29** D9
Mureş ⇒ *Romania* **28** D5
Mureşul = Mureş ⇒
  Romania **28** D5
Muret *France* **20** E5
Murewa *Zimbabwe* **89** B5
Murfreesboro *N.C., U.S.A.* **117** C16
Murfreesboro *Tenn., U.S.A.* **117** D11
Murgap = Murghob
  Tajikistan **52** F8
Murgap ⇒ *Turkmenistan* **71** B9
Murgenella *Australia* **92** B5
Murgeni *Romania* **29** D13
Murgha Kibzai *Pakistan* **68** D3
Murghob *Tajikistan* **52** F8
Murgon *Australia* **95** D5
Muri *India* **69** H11
Muria *Indonesia* **63** G14
Muriaé *Brazil* **127** A7
Murias de Paredes *Spain* **36** C4
Muriel Mine *Zimbabwe* **87** F3
Müritz *Germany* **24** B8
Müritz △ *Germany* **24** B8
Murliganj *India* **69** G12
Murmansk *Russia* **8** B25
Murmashi *Russia* **8** B25
Murnau *Germany* **25** H7
Muro *France* **21** F12
Muro *Spain* **48** B10
Muro, C. de *France* **21** G12
Muro de Alcoy *Spain* **39** G4
Muro Lucano *Italy* **43** B8
Murom *Russia* **34** C6
Muros *Spain* **36** C1
Muros e Noya, Ría de ⇒
  Spain **36** C1
Muroto *Japan* **55** H7
Muroto-Misaki *Japan* **55** H7
Murovani Kurylivtsi
  Ukraine **29** B12
Murowana Goślina *Poland* **31** F3
Murphy *U.S.A.* **108** E5
Murphys *U.S.A.* **110** G6
Murrat *Sudan* **80** D2
Murrat Wells *Sudan* **80** C3
Murray *Australia* **94** a
Murray *Ky., U.S.A.* **112** G9
Murray *Utah, U.S.A.* **108** F8
Murray ⇒ *Australia* **95** F2
Murray, L. *U.S.A.* **117** D14
Murray Bridge *Australia* **95** F2
Murray Fracture Zone
  Pac. Oc. **97** D14
Murray Harbour *Canada* **105** C7
Murray River △ *Australia* **95** E3
Murraysburg *S. Africa* **88** E3
Murree *Pakistan* **68** C5
Murrieta *U.S.A.* **111** M9
Murro di Porco, Capo *Italy* **43** F3
Murrumbidgee ⇒ *Australia* **95** E3
Murrumburrah *Australia* **95** E4
Murrurundi *Australia* **95** E5
Murshid *Sudan* **80** C3
Murshidabad *India* **69** G13
Murska Sobota *Slovenia* **41** B13
Murtle L. *Canada* **102** C5
Murtoa *Australia* **95** F3
Murtosa *Portugal* **36** E2
Murungu *Tanzania* **86** C3
Mururoa *French Polynesia* **97** K14
Murwara *India* **69** H9
Murwillumbah *Australia* **95** D5
Mürz ⇒ *Austria* **26** D8
Mürzzuschlag *Austria* **26** D8
Muş *Turkey* **73** C9
Muş □ *Turkey* **73** C9
Mûsa, Gebel *Egypt* **70** D2
Musa Khel *Pakistan* **68** D3
Mūsa Qal'eh *Afghan.* **66** C4
Musafirkhana *India* **69** F9
Musā'idah *Iraq* **73** H12
Musala *Bulgaria* **44** D7
Musala *Indonesia* **62** D1
Musan *N. Korea* **57** C15
Musangu
  Dem. Rep. of the Congo **87** E1
Musasa *Tanzania* **86** C3
Musay'īd *Qatar* **71** E6
Muscat = Masqat *Oman* **75** C6
Muscatine *U.S.A.* **112** E8
Muscle Shoals *U.S.A.* **117** D11
Musgezi =
  Unsengedsi ⇒ *Zimbabwe* **87** F3
Musgrave Harbour *Canada* **105** C9
Musgrave Ranges *Australia* **93** E5
Mushie *Dem. Rep. of the Congo* **84** E3
Mushin *Nigeria* **83** D5
Musi ⇒ *Indonesia* **62** E2

Musina *S. Africa* **89** C5
Muskeg ⇒ *Canada* **102** A4
Muskegon *U.S.A.* **112** D10
Muskegon ⇒ *U.S.A.* **112** D10
Muskegon Heights *U.S.A.* **112** D10
Muskogee *U.S.A.* **116** D7
Muskoka, L. *Canada* **114** B5
Muskoka Falls *Canada* **114** B5
Muskwa ⇒ *Canada* **102** B4
Muslīmiyah *Syria* **70** B3
Musmar *Sudan* **80** D4
Musofu *Zambia* **87** E2
Musoma *Tanzania* **86** C3
Musquaro, L. *Canada* **105** B7
Musquodoboit Harbour
  Canada **105** D7
Musselburgh *U.K.* **13** F5
Musselshell ⇒ *U.S.A.* **108** C10
Mussende *Angola* **84** G3
Mussidan *France* **20** C4
Mussomeli *Italy* **42** E6
Mussoorie *India* **68** D8
Mussuco *Angola* **88** B2
Mustafakemalpaşa *Turkey* **45** F12
Mustang *Nepal* **69** E10
Musters, L. *Argentina* **128** F3
Musudan *N. Korea* **57** D15
Muswellbrook *Australia* **95** E5
Muszyna *Poland* **31** J7
Mût *Egypt* **80** B2
Mut *Turkey* **72** D5
Mutanda *Mozam.* **89** C5
Mutanda *Zambia* **87** E2
Mutare *Zimbabwe* **87** F3
Mutawintji △ *Australia* **95** E3
Mutha *Kenya* **86** C4
Muting *Indonesia* **63** F10
Mutki = Mirtağ *Turkey* **70** B4
Mutoko *Zimbabwe* **89** B5
Mutomo *Kenya* **86** C4
Mutoray *Russia* **53** C11
Mutsamudu *Comoros Is.* **85** a
Mutshatsha
  Dem. Rep. of the Congo **87** E1
Mutsu *Japan* **54** D10
Mutsu-Wan *Japan* **54** D10
Muttaburra *Australia* **94** C3
Muttalip *Turkey* **47** B12
Mutton I. *Ireland* **12** D2
Mutuáli *Mozam.* **87** E4
Mutum Biyu *Nigeria* **83** D7
Mutumba *Burundi* **86** C2
Muweilih *Egypt* **74** E3
Muxía *Spain* **36** B1
Muy Muy *Nic.* **120** D2
Muyinga *Burundi* **86** C3
Muynak *Uzbekistan* **52** E6
Muyunkum, Peski =
  Moyynqum *Kazakhstan* **52** E8
Muzaffarabad *Pakistan* **69** B5
Muzaffargarh *Pakistan* **68** D4
Muzaffarnagar *India* **68** E7
Muzaffarpur *India* **69** F11
Muzafirpur *Pakistan* **68** D3
Muzhi *Russia* **52** C7
Muzillac *France* **18** E4
Muzūra *Egypt* **80** J7
Mvôlô *Sudan* **81** F2
Mvuma *Zimbabwe* **87** F3
Mvurwi *Zimbabwe* **87** F3
Mwabvi △ *Malawi* **87** F3
Mwadui *Tanzania* **86** C3
Mwali = Mohéli *Comoros Is.* **85** a
Mwambo *Tanzania* **87** E5
Mwandi *Zambia* **87** F1
Mwanza
  Dem. Rep. of the Congo **86** D2
Mwanza *Tanzania* **86** C3
Mwanza *Zambia* **87** F1
Mwanza □ *Tanzania* **86** C3
Mwaya *Tanzania* **87** D3
Mweelrea *Ireland* **12** C2
Mweka *Dem. Rep. of the Congo* **84** E4
Mwene-Ditu
  Dem. Rep. of the Congo **84** F4
Mwenezi *Zimbabwe* **87** G3
Mwenezi ⇒ *Mozam.* **87** G3
Mwenga
  Dem. Rep. of the Congo **86** C2
Mweru, L. *Zambia* **87** D2
Mweru Wantipa △ *Zambia* **87** D2
Mweza Range *Zimbabwe* **87** G3
Mwilambwe
  Dem. Rep. of the Congo **86** D2
Mwimbi *Tanzania* **87** D3
Mwingi *Kenya* **86** C4
Mwinilunga *Zambia* **87** E1
My Tho *Vietnam* **65** G6
Myajlar *India* **68** F4
Myanaung *Burma* **67** K19
Myanmar = Burma ■ *Asia* **67** J20
Myaungmya *Burma* **67** L19
Mycenæ = Mikines *Greece* **46** D4
Myedna *Belarus* **31** G10
Myeik Kyunzu *Burma* **65** G1
Myerstown *U.S.A.* **115** F8
Myingyan *Burma* **67** J19
Myitkyina *Burma* **67** E20
Myjava *Slovak Rep.* **27** C10

Mykhaylivka *Ukraine* **33** J8
Mykines *Færoe Is.* **8** E9
Mykolayiv *Ukraine* **33** J7
Mykolayiv □ *Ukraine* **33** J6
Mykonos *Greece* **47** D7
Mymensingh *Bangla.* **67** G17
Mynydd Du *U.K.* **15** F4
Mýrdalsjökull *Iceland* **8** E4
Myrhorod *Ukraine* **33** H7
Myrtle Beach *U.S.A.* **117** E15
Myrtle Creek *U.S.A.* **108** E2
Myrtle Point *U.S.A.* **108** E1
Myrtou *Cyprus* **49** D12
Mysia *Turkey* **45** G11
Myślenice *Poland* **31** J6
Myślibórz *Poland* **31** F1
Mysłowice *Poland* **31** H6
Mysore = Karnataka □
  India **66** N10
Mysore *India* **66** N10
Mystic *U.S.A.* **115** E13
Mysuru = Mysore *India* **66** N10
Myszków *Poland* **31** H6
Myszyniec *Poland* **30** E8
Mytishchi *Russia* **32** E9
Mývatn *Iceland* **8** D5
Mže ⇒ *Czech Rep.* **26** B6
Mzimba *Malawi* **87** E3
Mzimkulu ⇒ *S. Africa* **89** E5
Mzimvubu ⇒ *S. Africa* **89** E4
Mzuzu *Malawi* **87** E3

N

Na Clocha Liatha =
  Greystones *Ireland* **12** C5
Na Hearadh = Harris *U.K.* **13** D2
Na Noi *Thailand* **64** C3
Na Phao *Laos* **64** D5
Na Sam *Vietnam* **58** F6
Na San *Vietnam* **64** B5
Na Thon *Thailand* **65** b
Na'am *Sudan* **81** F2
Na'am ⇒ *Sudan* **81** F2
Naantali *Finland* **32** B1
Naas *Ireland* **12** C5
Nababeep *S. Africa* **88** D2
Nabadwip = Navadwip
  India **69** H13
Nabawa *Australia* **93** E1
Nabberu, L. *Australia* **93** E3
Nabburg *Germany* **25** F8
Naberezhnyye Chelny
  Russia **34** C11
Nabeul *Tunisia* **79** A8
Nabha *India* **68** D7
Nabīd *Iran* **71** D8
Nabire *Indonesia* **63** E9
Nabisar *Pakistan* **68** G3
Nabisipi ⇒ *Canada* **105** B7
Nabiswera *Uganda* **86** B3
Nāblus = Nābulus *West Bank* **74** C4
Naboomspruit *S. Africa* **89** C4
Nabou *Burkina Faso* **82** C4
Nabouwalu *Fiji* **91** a
Nabua *Phil.* **61** E5
Nābulus *West Bank* **74** C4
Nacala *Mozam.* **87** E5
Nacaome *Honduras* **120** D2
Nacaroa *Mozam.* **87** E4
Naches *U.S.A.* **108** C3
Naches ⇒ *U.S.A.* **110** D6
Nachicapau, L. *Canada* **105** A6
Nachingwea *Tanzania* **87** E4
Nachna *India* **68** F4
Náchod *Czech Rep.* **26** A9
Nacimiento, L. *U.S.A.* **110** K6
Naco *Mexico* **118** A3
Nacogdoches *U.S.A.* **116** F7
Nácori Chico *Mexico* **118** B3
Nacozari de García *Mexico* **118** A3
Nacula *Fiji* **91** a
Nådendal = Naantali *Finland* **32** B1
Nadi *Fiji* **91** a
Nadi *Sudan* **81** C5
Nadiad *India* **68** H5
Nădlac *Romania* **28** D5
Nador *Morocco* **78** B5
Nadur *Malta* **49** C1
Nadūshan *Iran* **71** C7
Nadvirna *Ukraine* **29** B9
Nadvornaya = Nadvirna
  Ukraine **29** B9
Nadym *Russia* **52** C8
Nadym ⇒ *Russia* **52** C8
Nærbø *Norway* **9** G11
Næstved *Denmark* **11** J5
Nafada *Nigeria* **83** C7
Nafpaktos *Greece* **46** C3
Nafplio *Greece* **46** D4
Naft-e Safid *Iran* **71** D6
Naftshahr *Iran* **73** E11
Nafud Desert = An Nafūd
  Si. Arabia **73** D4
Nag Hammâdi *Egypt* **80** B3
Naga *Phil.* **61** E5
Nagagami ⇒ *Canada* **104** B3
Nagahama *Japan* **55** G8

Nagai *Japan* **54** E10
Nagaland □ *India* **67** G19
Nagano *Japan* **55** F9
Nagano □ *Japan* **55** F9
Nagaoka *Japan* **55** F9
Nagaon = Nowgong *India* **67** F18
Nagappattinam *India* **66** P11
Nagar ⇒ *Bangla.* **69** G13
Nagar Parkar *Pakistan* **68** G4
Nagasaki *Japan* **55** H4
Nagasaki □ *Japan* **55** H4
Nagato *Japan* **55** G5
Nagaur *India* **68** F5
Nagda *India* **68** H6
Nagercoil *India* **66** Q10
Nagina *India* **69** E8
Nagīneh *Iran* **71** C8
Nagir *Pakistan* **69** A6
Naglarby *Sweden* **10** D9
Nagles Mts. *Ireland* **12** D3
Nagod *India* **69** G9
Nagold *Germany* **25** G4
Nagold ⇒ *Germany* **25** G4
Nagoorin *Australia* **94** C5
Nagorno-Karabakh □
  Azerbaijan **73** C12
Nagornyy *Russia* **53** D13
Nagoya *Japan* **55** G8
Nagpur *India* **66** J11
Nagua *Dom. Rep.* **121** C6
Naguabo *Puerto Rico* **121** d
Nagurunguru ☺ *Australia* **92** C4
Nagyatád *Hungary* **28** D2
Nagyecsed *Hungary* **28** C7
Nagykálló *Hungary* **28** C6
Nagykanizsa *Hungary* **28** D2
Nagykáta *Hungary* **28** C4
Nagykőrös *Hungary* **28** C4
Naha *Japan* **55** L3
Nahan *India* **68** D7
Nahanni △ *Canada* **102** A4
Nahanni Butte *Canada* **102** A4
Nahargarh *Mad. P., India* **68** G6
Nahargarh *Raj., India* **68** G7
Nahariyya *Israel* **74** C4
Nahāvand *Iran* **73** E13
Nahe ⇒ *Germany* **25** F3
Nahīrne *Ukraine* **29** C13
Nahîya, W. ⇒ *Egypt* **80** B3
Nahuel Huapi, L. *Argentina* **128** E2
Nahuelbuta △ *Chile* **126** D1
Nai Yong *Thailand* **65** a
Naicá *Mexico* **118** B3
Naicam *Canada* **103** C8
Naikoon △ *Canada* **102** C2
Naila *Germany* **25** E7
Naimisharanya *India* **69** F9
Naimona'nyi Feng *Nepal* **69** D9
Nain *Canada* **105** A7
Nā'īn *Iran* **71** C7
Naini Tal *India* **69** E8
Nainpur *India* **69** H9
Naintré *France* **18** F7
Nainwa *India* **68** G6
Naipu *Romania* **29** F10
Nairai *Fiji* **91** a
Nairn *U.K.* **13** D5
Nairobi *Kenya* **86** C4
Nairobi △ *Kenya* **86** C4
Naissaar *Estonia* **32** C3
Naita, Mt. *Ethiopia* **81** F4
Naitaba *Fiji* **91** a
Naivasha *Kenya* **86** C4
Naivasha, L. *Kenya* **86** C4
Najac *France* **20** D5
Najaf = An Najaf *Iraq* **73** G11
Najafābād *Iran* **71** C6
Najd *Si. Arabia* **75** B3
Nájera *Spain* **38** C2
Najerilla ⇒ *Spain* **38** C2
Najibabad *India* **68** E8
Najin *N. Korea* **57** C16
Najmah *Si. Arabia* **71** E6
Najrān *Si. Arabia* **75** D3
Naju *S. Korea* **57** G14
Nakadōri-Shima *Japan* **55** H4
Nakalagba
  Dem. Rep. of the Congo **86** B2
Nakambé = White
  Volta ⇒ *Ghana* **83** D4
Nakaminato *Japan* **55** F10
Nakamura *Japan* **55** H6
Nakano *Japan* **55** F9
Nakano-Shima *Japan* **55** K4
Nakashibetsu *Japan* **54** C12
Nakfa *Eritrea* **81** D4
Nakfa △ *Eritrea* **81** D4
Nakha Yai, Ko *Thailand* **65** a
Nakhichevan = Naxçıvan
  Azerbaijan **73** C11
Nakhichevan Rep. =
  Naxçıvan □ *Azerbaijan* **73** C11
Nakhl *Egypt* **74** F2
Nakhl-e Taqī *Iran* **71** E7
Nakhodka *Russia* **54** C6
Nakhon Nayok *Thailand* **64** E3
Nakhon Pathom *Thailand* **64** F3
Nakhon Phanom *Thailand* **64** D5
Nakhon Ratchasima *Thailand* **64** E4

Nakhon Sawan *Thailand* **64** E3
Nakhon Si Thammarat
  Thailand **65** H3
Nakhon Thai *Thailand* **64** D3
Nakhtarana *India* **68** H3
Nakina *Canada* **104** B2
Naklo nad Notecią *Poland* **31** E4
Nako *Burkina Faso* **82** C4
Nakodar *India* **68** D6
Nakskov *Denmark* **11** K5
Naktong ⇒ *S. Korea* **57** G15
Nakuru *Kenya* **86** C4
Nakuru, L. *Kenya* **86** C4
Nakusp *Canada* **102** C5
Nal *Pakistan* **68** F2
Nal ⇒ *Pakistan* **68** G1
Nalázi *Mozam.* **89** C5
Nalchik *Russia* **35** J6
Nałęczów *Poland* **31** G9
Nalerigu *Ghana* **83** C4
Nalgonda *India* **66** L11
Nalhati *India* **69** G12
Naliya *India* **68** H3
Nallamalai Hills *India* **66** M11
Nallıhan *Turkey* **72** B4
Nalón ⇒ *Spain* **36** B4
Nalubaale Dam *Uganda* **86** B3
Nam Can *Vietnam* **65** H5
Nam Co *China* **60** C4
Nam Dinh *Vietnam* **58** G6
Nam Du, Hon *Vietnam* **65** H5
Nam Nao △ *Thailand* **64** D3
Nam Ngum Res. *Laos* **64** C4
Nam-Phan *Vietnam* **65** G6
Nam Phong *Thailand* **64** D4
Nam Tha *Laos* **58** G3
Nam Tok *Thailand* **64** E2
Namacunde *Angola* **88** B2
Namacurra *Mozam.* **87** F4
Namak, Daryācheh-ye *Iran* **71** C7
Namak, Kavir-e *Iran* **71** C8
Namakzār, Daryācheh-ye
  Iran **71** C9
Namaland *Namibia* **88** C2
Namanga *Kenya* **86** C4
Namangan *Uzbekistan* **52** E8
Namapa *Mozam.* **87** E4
Namaqualand *S. Africa* **88** D2
Namasagali *Uganda* **86** B3
Namber *Indonesia* **63** E8
Nambour *Australia* **95** D5
Nambouwalu =
  Nabouwalu *Fiji* **91** a
Nambucca Heads *Australia* **95** E5
Nambung △ *Australia* **93** F2
Namche Bazar *Nepal* **69** F12
Namchonjŏm =
  Nam-ch'on *N. Korea* **57** E14
Namecunda *Mozam.* **87** E4
Namenalala *Fiji* **91** a
Nameponda *Mozam.* **87** F4
Náměšt' nad Oslavou
  Czech Rep. **27** B9
Námestovo *Slovak Rep.* **27** B12
Nametil *Mozam.* **87** F4
Namew L. *Canada* **103** C8
Namgia *India* **69** D8
Namhkam *Burma* **58** E1
Namialo *Mozam.* **87** E4
Namib Desert *Namibia* **88** C2
Namib-Naukluft △ *Namibia* **88** C2
Namibe *Angola* **85** H2
Namibe □ *Angola* **88** B1
Namibia ■ *Africa* **88** C2
Namibwoestyn = Namib
  Desert *Namibia* **88** C2
Namīn *Iran* **73** C13
Namlea *Indonesia* **63** E7
Namoi ⇒ *Australia* **95** E4
Nampa *U.S.A.* **108** E5
Nampala *Mali* **82** B3
Nampo *N. Korea* **57** E13
Nampō-Shotō *Japan* **55** J10
Nampula *Mozam.* **87** F4
Namrole *Indonesia* **63** E7
Namse Shankou *China* **69** E10
Namsen ⇒ *Norway* **8** D14
Namsos *Norway* **8** D14
Namtok Chat Trakan △
  Thailand **64** D3
Namtok Mae Surin △
  Thailand **64** C2
Namtsy *Russia* **53** C13
Namtu *Burma* **67** H20
Namtumbo *Tanzania* **87** E4
Namu *Canada* **102** C3
Namuka-i-Lau *Fiji* **91** a
Namur *Belgium* **17** D4
Namur □ *Belgium* **17** D4
Namuruputh *Kenya* **86** B4
Namutoni *Namibia* **88** B2
Namwala *Zambia* **87** F2
Namwon *S. Korea* **57** G14
Namyang *N. Korea* **57** C15
Namysłów *Poland* **31** G4
Namu *Canada* **102** C3

Nan-ch'ang = Nanchang
  China **59** C10
Nan Ling *China* **59** E8
Nan Xian *China* **59** C9
Nana *Romania* **29** F11
Nana Kru *Liberia* **82** E3
Nanaimo *Canada* **102** D4
Nānākuli *U.S.A.* **107** L8
Nanam *N. Korea* **57** D15
Nanan *China* **59** E12
Nanango *Australia* **95** D5
Nan'ao *China* **59** F11
Nanao *Japan* **55** F8
Nanbu *China* **58** B6
Nanchang *China* **59** C10
Nancheng *China* **59** D11
Nanching = Nanjing *China* **59** A12
Nanchong *China* **58** B6
Nanchuan *China* **58** C6
Nancy *France* **19** D13
Nanda Devi *India* **69** D8
Nanda Devi △ *India* **69** D8
Nanda Kot *India* **69** D8
Nandan *China* **58** E6
Nandan *Japan* **55** G7
Nanded *India* **66** K10
Nandewar Ra. *Australia* **95** E5
Nandi = Nadi *Fiji* **91** a
Nandi *Zimbabwe* **87** G3
Nandigram *India* **69** H12
Nandurbar *India* **66** J9
Nandyal *India* **66** M11
Nanfeng *Guangdong, China* **59** F8
Nanfeng *Jiangxi, China* **59** D11
Nang Rong *Thailand* **64** E4
Nanga-Eboko *Cameroon* **83** E7
Nanga Parbat *Pakistan* **69** B6
Nangade *Mozam.* **87** E4
Nangapinoh *Indonesia* **62** E4
Nangarhār □ *Afghan.* **66** B7
Nangatayap *Indonesia* **62** E4
Nangbéto, L. de *Togo* **83** D5
Nangeya Mts. *Uganda* **86** B3
Nangis *France* **19** D10
Nangong *China* **56** F3
Nanhua *China* **58** E3
Nanhuang *China* **57** F11
Nanhui *China* **59** B13
Nanisivik *Canada* **101** C15
Nanjeko *Zambia* **87** F1
Nanji Shan *China* **59** D13
Nanjian *China* **58** E3
Nanjiang *China* **58** A6
Nanjing *Fujian, China* **59** E11
Nanjing *Jiangsu, China* **59** A12
Nanjirinji *Tanzania* **87** D4
Nankana Sahib *Pakistan* **68** D5
Nankang *China* **59** E10
Nanking = Nanjing *China* **59** A12
Nankoku *Japan* **55** H6
Nanling *China* **59** B12
Nanning *China* **58** F7
Nannup *Australia* **93** F2
Nanpan Jiang ⇒ *China* **58** E6
Nanpara *India* **69** F9
Nanpi *China* **56** E9
Nanping *Fujian, China* **59** D12
Nanping *Henan, China* **59** C9
Nanri Dao *China* **59** E12
Nanripe *Mozam.* **87** E4
Nansei-Shotō =
  Ryūkyū-rettō *Japan* **55** M3
Nansen Basin *Arctic* **4** A10
Nansen Sd. *Canada* **101** A3
Nanshan I. *S. China Sea* **62** B5
Nansio *Tanzania* **86** C3
Nant *France* **20** D7
Nantawarrirna ☺ *Australia* **95** B2
Nanterre *France* **19** D9
Nantes *France* **18** E5
Nantiat *France* **20** B5
Nanticoke *U.S.A.* **115** E8
Nanton *Canada* **102** C6
Nantong *China* **59** A13
Nant'ou *Taiwan* **59** F13
Nantua *France* **19** F12
Nantucket *U.S.A.* **113** E18
Nantucket I. *U.S.A.* **113** E18
Nantulo *Mozam.* **87** E4
Nantwich *U.K.* **14** D5
Nanty Glo *U.S.A.* **114** F6
Nanuku Passage *Fiji* **91** a
Nanuque *Brazil* **125** G10
Nanusa, Kepulauan
  Indonesia **63** D7
Nanutarra Roadhouse
  Australia **92** D2
Nanxi *China* **58** C5
Nanxiong *China* **59** E10
Nanyang *China* **56** H7
Nanyi Hu *China* **59** B12
Nanyuki *Kenya* **86** B4
Nanzhang *China* **59** B8
Nao, C. de la *Spain* **39** G5
Naococane, L. *Canada* **105** B5
Naoussa *Cyclades, Greece* **47** D7
Naoussa *Imathia, Greece* **44** F6
Naozhou Dao *China* **59** G8
Napa *U.S.A.* **110** G4

Napa → *U.S.A.* **110** G4
Napanee *Canada* **114** B8
Napanoch *U.S.A.* **115** E10
Nape *Laos* **64** C5
Nape Pass = Keo Neua,
  Deo *Vietnam* **64** C5
Napier *N.Z.* **91** C6
Napier Broome B. *Australia* **92** B4
Napier Pen. *Australia* **94** A2
Napierville *Canada* **115** A11
Naples = Nápoli *Italy* **43** B7
Naples *U.S.A.* **117** H14
Napo *China* **58** F5
Napo → *Peru* **124** D4
Napoleon *N. Dak., U.S.A.* **112** B4
Napoleon *Ohio, U.S.A.* **113** E11
Nápoli *Italy* **43** B7
Nápoli, G. di *Italy* **43** B7
Nápoli Capodichino ✈
  (NAP) *Italy* **43** B7
Napopo *Dem. Rep. of the Congo* **86** B2
Naqâda *Egypt* **80** B3
Naqadeh *Iran* **73** D11
Naqb, Ra's an *Jordan* **74** F4
Naqqâsh *Iran* **71** C6
Nara *Japan* **55** G7
Nara *Mali* **82** B3
Nara □ *Japan* **55** G8
Nara Canal *Pakistan* **68** G3
Nara Visa *U.S.A.* **109** J12
Naracoorte *Australia* **95** F3
Naradhan *Australia* **95** E4
Naraini *India* **69** G9
Naranjos *Mexico* **119** C5
Narasapur *India* **67** L12
Narathiwat *Thailand* **65** J3
Narayangadh = Bharatpur
  Nepal **69** F11
Narayanganj *Bangla.* **67** H17
Narayanpet *India* **66** L10
Narberth *U.K.* **15** F3
Narbonne *France* **20** E7
Narcea → *Spain* **36** B4
Nardīn *Iran* **71** B7
Nardò *Italy* **43** B11
Narembeen *Australia* **93** F2
Narendranagar *India* **68** D8
Nares Str. *Arctic* **101** B18
Naretha *Australia* **93** F3
Narew → *Poland* **31** F7
Nari → *Pakistan* **68** F2
Narin *Afghan.* **66** A6
Narindra, Helodranon' i
  Madag. **89** A8
Narita *Japan* **55** G10
Nariva Swamp *Trin. & Tob.* **125** K15
Närke *Sweden* **10** E8
Narmada → *India* **68** J5
Narman *Turkey* **73** B9
Narnaul *India* **68** E7
Narni *Italy* **41** F9
Naro *Ghana* **82** C4
Naro Fominsk *Russia* **32** E9
Narodnaya *Russia* **6** B17
Narok *Kenya* **86** C4
Narón *Spain* **36** B2
Narooma *Australia* **95** F5
Narowal *Pakistan* **68** C6
Narrabri *Australia* **95** E4
Narran → *Australia* **95** D4
Narrandera *Australia* **95** E4
Narromine *Australia* **95** E4
Narrogin *Australia* **93** F2
Narrow Hills △ *Canada* **103** C8
Narsimhapur *India* **69** H8
Narsinghgarh *India* **68** H7
Nartes, L. e *Albania* **44** F3
Nartkala *Russia* **35** J6
Naruto *Japan* **55** G7
Narva *Estonia* **32** C5
Narva → *Russia* **32** C4
Narva Bay = Narva Laht
  Estonia **9** G22
Narva Laht *Estonia* **9** G22
Narvik *Norway* **8** B17
Narvskoye Vdkhr. *Russia* **32** C5
Narwana *India* **68** E7
Narwiański △ *Poland* **31** F9
Narwinbi ☼ *Australia* **94** B2
Naryan-Mar *Russia* **52** C6
Narym *Russia* **52** D9
Naryn *Kyrgyzstan* **52** E8
Naryn Qum *Kazakhstan* **35** G9
Nasa *Norway* **8** C16
Nasau *Fiji* **91** a
Năsăud *Romania* **29** C9
Nasca = Nazca *Peru* **124** F4
Naseby *N.Z.* **91** F3
Naselle *U.S.A.* **110** D3
Naser, Buheirat en *Egypt* **80** C3
Nashik = Nasik *India* **66** K8
Nashua *Mont., U.S.A.* **108** B10
Nashua *N.H., U.S.A.* **115** D13
Nashville *Ark., U.S.A.* **116** E8
Nashville *Ga., U.S.A.* **117** F13
Nashville *Tenn., U.S.A.* **117** C11
Našice *Croatia* **28** E3
Nasielsk *Poland* **31** F7
Nasik *India* **66** K8

Nasipit *Phil.* **61** G6
Nasir *Sudan* **81** F3
Nasirabad *India* **68** F6
Nasirabad *Pakistan* **68** E3
Nasiri = Ahvāz *Iran* **71** D6
Nasiriyah = An Nāşirīyah
  Iraq **70** D5
Naskaupi → *Canada* **105** B7
Naso *Italy* **43** D7
Naşrābād *Iran* **71** C6
Naşrīān-e Pā'īn *Iran* **70** C5
Nass → *Canada* **102** C3
Nassarawa *Nigeria* **83** D6
Nassarawa □ *Nigeria* **83** D6
Nassau *Bahamas* **120** A4
Nassau, L. = Naser,
  Buheirat en *Egypt* **80** C3
Nassian *Ivory C.* **82** D4
Nässjö *Sweden* **11** G8
Nastapoka → *Canada* **104** A4
Nastapoka, Is. *Canada* **104** A4
Nasugbu *Phil.* **61** D4
Näsum *Sweden* **11** H8
Näsviken *Sweden* **10** C10
Nata *Botswana* **88** C4
Nata → *Botswana* **88** C4
Natal *Brazil* **125** E11
Natal *Indonesia* **62** D1
Natal Drakensberg △
  S. Africa **89** D4
Natalinci *Serbia* **28** F5
Naţanz *Iran* **71** C6
Natashquan *Canada* **105** B7
Natashquan → *Canada* **105** B7
Natchez *U.S.A.* **116** F9
Natchitoches *U.S.A.* **116** F8
Natewa B. *Fiji* **91** a
Nathalia *Australia* **95** F4
Nathdwara *India* **68** G5
Nati, Pta. *Spain* **48** A10
Natimuk *Australia* **95** F3
Nation → *Canada* **102** B4
National City *U.S.A.* **111** N9
Natitingou *Benin* **83** C5
Natividad, I. *Mexico* **118** B1
Natkyizin *Burma* **64** E1
Natron, L. *Tanzania* **86** C4
Natrona Heights *U.S.A.* **114** F5
Natrûn, W. el → *Egypt* **80** H7
Nättraby *Sweden* **11** H9
Natukanaoka Pan *Namibia* **88** B2
Natuna Besar, Kepulauan
  Indonesia **62** D3
Natuna Is. = Natuna Besar,
  Kepulauan *Indonesia* **62** D3
Natuna Selatan,
  Kepulauan *Indonesia* **62** D3
Natural Bridge *U.S.A.* **115** B9
Natural Bridges △ *U.S.A.* **109** H9
Naturaliste, C. *Tas., Australia* **95** G4
Naturaliste, C. *W. Austral.,
  Australia* **93** F2
Naturaliste Plateau *Ind. Oc.* **96** L3
Nau Qala *Afghan.* **68** B3
Naucelle *France* **20** D6
Nauders *Austria* **26** E3
Nauen *Germany* **24** C7
Naugatuck *U.S.A.* **115** E11
Naujaat = Repulse Bay
  Canada **101** D14
Naujoji Akmenė *Lithuania* **30** B9
Naumburg *Germany* **24** D7
Nauru ■ *Pac. Oc.* **90** B9
Naushahra = Nowshera
  Pakistan **66** C8
Naushahro *Pakistan* **68** F3
Naushon I. *U.S.A.* **115** E14
Nausori *Fiji* **91** a
Nauta *Peru* **124** D4
Nautanwa *India* **69** F10
Naute △ *Namibia* **88** D2
Nautla *Mexico* **119** C5
Nava *Mexico* **118** B4
Nava *Spain* **36** B5
Nava del Rey *Spain* **36** D5
Navadwip *India* **69** H13
Navahermosa *Spain* **37** F6
Navahrudak *Belarus* **23** B13
Navajo Res. *U.S.A.* **109** H10
Navalcarnero *Spain* **36** E6
Navalmoral de la Mata *Spain* **36** F5
Navalvillar de Pela *Spain* **37** F5
Navan = An Uaimh *Ireland* **12** C5
Navapolatsk *Belarus* **32** E5
Navarin, Mys *Russia* **53** C18
Navarino, I. *Chile* **128** H3
Navarra □ *Spain* **38** C3
Navarre *U.S.A.* **114** F3
Navarro → *U.S.A.* **110** F3
Navas de San Juan *Spain* **37** G7
Navasota *U.S.A.* **116** F6
Navassa I. *W. Indies* **121** C5
Nävekvarn *Sweden* **11** F10
Naver → *U.K.* **13** C4
Navia *Spain* **36** B4
Navia → *Spain* **36** B4
Navia de Suarna = A Pobre
  Spain **36** C3

Navibandar *India* **68** J3
Navidad *Chile* **126** C1
Naviraí *Brazil* **127** A5
Naviti *Fiji* **91** a
Navlakhi *India* **68** H4
Navlya *Russia* **33** F8
Nāvodari *Romania* **29** F13
Navoiy *Uzbekistan* **52** E7
Navojoa *Mexico* **118** B3
Navolato *Mexico* **118** C3
Navrongo *Ghana* **83** C4
Navsari *India* **66** J8
Navua *Fiji* **91** a
Nawa Kot *Pakistan* **68** E4
Nawab Khan *Pakistan* **68** D3
Nawabganj *Ut. P., India* **69** F9
Nawabganj *Ut. P., India* **69** E8
Nawabshah *Pakistan* **68** F3
Nawada *India* **69** G11
Nawakot *Nepal* **69** F11
Nawalgarh *India* **68** F6
Nawanshahr *India* **69** C6
Nawar, Dasht-i- *Afghan.* **68** C3
Nawi *Sudan* **80** D3
Nawoiy = Navoiy *Uzbekistan* **52** E7
Naxçıvan *Azerbaijan* **73** C11
Naxçıvan □ *Azerbaijan* **73** C11
Naxos *Greece* **47** D7
Nay *France* **20** E3
Nay, Mui *Vietnam* **62** B3
Nāy Band *Būshehr, Iran* **71** E7
Nāy Band *Khorāsān, Iran* **71** C8
Nayakhan *Russia* **53** C16
Nayarit □ *Mexico* **118** C4
Nayau *Fiji* **91** a
Nayong *China* **58** D5
Nayoro *Japan* **54** B11
Naypyidaw *Burma* **64** C1
Nayyāl, W. → *Si. Arabia* **70** D3
Nazar Kahrizi *Iran* **73** D12
Nazaré *Brazil* **125** F11
Nazaré *Portugal* **37** F1
Nazareth = Nazerat *Israel* **74** C4
Nazareth *U.S.A.* **115** F9
Nazarovo *Russia* **53** D10
Nazas *Mexico* **118** B4
Nazas → *Mexico* **118** B4
Nazca *Peru* **124** F4
Nazca Ridge *Pac. Oc.* **97** K19
Naze *Japan* **55** K4
Naze, The *U.K.* **15** F9
Nazerat *Israel* **74** C4
Nāzīk *Iran* **73** C11
Nazilli *Turkey* **47** D10
Nazinon = Red Volta →
  Africa **83** C4
Nazko *Canada* **102** C4
Nazko → *Canada* **102** C4
Nāzlu *Iran* **73** D11
Nazret *Ethiopia* **81** F4
Nchanga *Zambia* **87** E2
Ncheu *Malawi* **87** E3
Ndala *Tanzania* **86** C3
Ndalatando *Angola* **84** F2
Ndali *Benin* **83** D5
Ndareda *Tanzania* **86** C4
Ndélé *C.A.R.* **84** C4
Ndiael △ *Senegal* **82** B1
Ndikinimeki *Cameroon* **83** E7
N'Dioum *Senegal* **82** B2
Ndjamena *Chad* **79** F8
Ndola *Zambia* **87** E2
Ndomo → *S. Africa* **89** D5
Ndoto Mts. *Kenya* **86** B4
Nduguti *Tanzania* **86** C3
Nea Alikarnassos *Greece* **47** F7
Nea Anchialos *Greece* **46** B4
Nea Epidavros *Greece* **46** D5
Nea Ionia *Greece* **46** B4
Nea Kalikratia *Greece* **44** F7
Nea Makri *Greece* **46** C5
Nea Moudania *Greece* **44** F7
Nea Peramos *Attiki, Greece* **46** C5
Nea Peramos *Kavala, Greece* **45** F8
Nea Visa *Greece* **45** E10
Nea Zichni *Greece* **44** E7
Neagh, Lough *U.K.* **12** B5
Neah Bay *U.S.A.* **110** B2
Neale, L. *Australia* **92** D5
Neales → *Australia* **95** D2
Neamţ □ *Romania* **29** C11
Neapoli *Kozani, Greece* **44** F5
Neapoli *Kriti, Greece* **49** D7
Neapoli *Lakonia, Greece* **46** E5
Near Is. *U.S.A.* **106** E2
Neath *U.K.* **15** F4
Neath Port Talbot □ *U.K.* **15** F4
Nebbi *Uganda* **86** B3
Nebbou *Burkina Faso* **83** C4
Nebelat el Hagana *Sudan* **81** E2
Nebine Cr. → *Australia* **95** D4
Nebitdag = Balkanabat
  Turkmenistan **71** B7
Nebo *Australia* **94** C4
Nebolchy *Russia* **32** C7
Nebraska □ *U.S.A.* **112** E4
Nebraska City *U.S.A.* **112** E6
Nébrodi, Monti *Italy* **43** E7

Necedah *U.S.A.* **112** C8
Nechako → *Canada* **102** C4
Neches → *U.S.A.* **116** G8
Nechisar △ *Ethiopia* **81** F4
Neckar → *Germany* **25** F4
Neckartal-Odenwald △
  Germany **25** F5
Necker I. *U.S.A.* **107** L7
Necochea *Argentina* **126** D4
Neda *Spain* **36** B2
Neda → *Greece* **46** D3
Nedelino *Bulgaria* **45** E9
Nedelišće *Croatia* **41** B13
Nederland =
  Netherlands ■ *Europe* **17** C5
Nedroboyivtsi *Ukraine* **29** B11
Needles *Canada* **102** D5
Needles *U.S.A.* **111** L12
Needles, The *U.K.* **15** G6
Neembucú □ *Paraguay* **126** B4
Neemuch = Nimach *India* **68** G6
Neenah *U.S.A.* **112** C9
Neepawa *Canada* **103** C9
Neftçala *Azerbaijan* **73** C13
Neftegorsk *Krasnodar, Russia* **35** H4
Neftegorsk *Sakhalin, Russia* **53** D15
Neftekumsk *Russia* **35** H7
Nefteyugansk *Russia* **52** C8
Nefyn *U.K.* **14** E3
Négala *Mali* **82** C3
Negapatam =
  Nagapattinam *India* **66** P11
Neqāb *Iran* **71** C8
Negaunee *U.S.A.* **112** B10
Negele *Oromiya, Ethiopia* **81** F4
Negele *Oromiya, Ethiopia* **81** F4
Negev Desert = Hanegev
  Israel **74** E4
Negoiul, Vf. *Romania* **29** D9
Negombo *Sri Lanka* **66** R11
Negotin *Serbia* **44** B6
Negotino *Macedonia* **44** E6
Negra, Peña *Spain* **36** C4
Negra, Pta. *Mauritania* **78** D2
Negra, Pta. *Peru* **124** E2
Negrais, C. = Maudin Sun
  Burma **67** M19
Negreşti *Romania* **29** D12
Negreşti-Oaş *Romania* **29** C8
Negril *Jamaica* **120** a
Negro → *Argentina* **128** E4
Negro → *Brazil* **124** D7
Negro → *Uruguay* **126** C4
Negros *Phil.* **61** G5
Negru Vodă *Romania* **29** G13
Neguac *Canada* **105** C6
Nehalem → *U.S.A.* **110** E3
Nehāvand *Iran* **71** C6
Nehbandān *Iran* **71** D9
Nehoiu *Romania* **29** E11
Nei Monggol Zizhiqu □
  China **56** D7
Neiafu *Tonga* **91** c
Neiges, Piton des *Réunion* **85** c
Neijiang *China* **58** C5
Neillsville *U.S.A.* **112** C8
Neilton *U.S.A.* **108** C2
Neiqiu *China* **56** F8
Neiva *Colombia* **124** C3
Neixiang *China* **56** H6
Nejanilini L. *Canada* **103** B9
Nejd = Najd *Si. Arabia* **75** B3
Nejo *Ethiopia* **81** F4
Nekā *Iran* **71** B7
Nekemte *Ethiopia* **81** F4
Nèkheb *Egypt* **80** B3
Neksø *Denmark* **11** J9
Nelas *Portugal* **36** E3
Nelia *Australia* **94** C3
Nelidovo *Russia* **32** D7
Neligh *U.S.A.* **112** D4
Nelkan *Russia* **53** D14
Nellore *India* **66** M11
Nelson *Canada* **102** D5
Nelson *N.Z.* **91** D4
Nelson *U.K.* **14** D5
Nelson *Ariz., U.S.A.* **109** J7
Nelson *Nev., U.S.A.* **111** K12
Nelson → *Canada* **103** C9
Nelson, C. *Australia* **95** F3
Nelson, Estrecho *Chile* **128** G2
Nelson Forks *Canada* **102** B4
Nelson House *Canada* **103** B9
Nelson L. *Canada* **103** B8
Nelson Lakes △ *N.Z.* **91** D4
Nelspoort *S. Africa* **88** E3
Nelspruit *S. Africa* **89** D5
Néma *Mauritania* **82** B3
Neman = Nemunas →
  Lithuania **30** C8
Neman *Russia* **30** C9
Nembe *Nigeria* **83** E6
Nembrala *Indonesia* **92** B3
Nemea *Greece* **46** D4
Nemeiben L. *Canada* **103** B7
Nemërçkë, Mal *Albania* **44** F4
Nemira, Vf. *Romania* **29** D11
Nemiscau *Canada* **104** B4
Nemiscau, L. *Canada* **104** B4

Nemours *France* **19** D9
Nemrut Daği △ *Turkey* **73** C8
Nemšová *Slovak Rep.* **27** C11
Nemunas → *Lithuania* **30** C8
Nemuro *Japan* **54** C12
Nemuro-Kaikyō *Japan* **54** C12
Nen Jiang → *China* **57** B13
Nenagh *Ireland* **12** D3
Nenana *U.S.A.* **106** C10
Nenasi *Malaysia* **65** L4
Nene → *U.K.* **15** E8
Nenita *Greece* **47** C8
Nenjiang *China* **60** B7
Neno *Malawi* **87** F3
Neo Chori *Greece* **46** C3
Neochori *Greece* **46** B2
Neodesha *U.S.A.* **112** G6
Neon Petritsi *Greece* **44** E7
Neora Valley △ *India* **69** F13
Neosho *U.S.A.* **112** G6
Neosho → *U.S.A.* **116** C7
Nepal ■ *Asia* **69** F11
Nepalganj *Nepal* **69** E9
Nepalganj Road *India* **69** E9
Nephi *U.S.A.* **108** G8
Nephin *Ireland* **12** B2
Nephin Beg Range *Ireland* **12** B2
Nepi *Italy* **41** F9
Nepomuk *Czech Rep.* **26** B6
Neptune *U.S.A.* **115** F10
Neqāb *Iran* **71** C8
Nera → *Italy* **41** F9
Nera → *Romania* **28** F6
Nérac *France* **20** D4
Nerang *Australia* **95** D5
Nerastro, Sarīr *Libya* **79** D10
Nerchinsk *Russia* **53** D12
Nereju *Romania* **29** E11
Nerekhta *Russia* **32** D11
Neresnytsya *Ukraine* **29** B8
Néret, L. *Canada* **105** B5
Neretvanski Kanal *Croatia* **41** E14
Neringa *Lithuania* **30** D8
Neris → *Lithuania* **32** E3
Nerja *Spain* **37** J7
Nerl → *Russia* **32** D11
Nerpio *Spain* **39** G2
Nerva *Spain* **37** H4
Nervi *Italy* **40** D6
Neryungri *Russia* **53** D13
Nescopeck *U.S.A.* **115** E8
Nesebŭr *Bulgaria* **45** D11
Neskantaga *Canada* **104** B2
Ness, L. *U.K.* **13** D4
Ness City *U.S.A.* **112** F4
Nesterov *Russia* **30** D9
Nesterov *Ukraine* **23** C12
Nestório *Greece* **44** F5
Nestos → *Europe* **45** E8
Nesvady *Slovak Rep.* **27** D11
Nesvizh = Nyasvizh *Belarus* **23** B14
Netanya *Israel* **74** C3
Netarhat *India* **69** H11
Nete → *Belgium* **17** C4
Netherdale *Australia* **94** b
Netherlands ■ *Europe* **17** C5
Netherlands Antilles ☑
  W. Indies **124** A5
Neto → *Italy* **43** C10
Netrang *India* **68** J5
Nettancourt *France* **19** D11
Nettetal *Germany* **24** D2
Nettilling L. *Canada* **101** D17
Nettuno *Italy* **42** A5
Netzahualcóyotl, Presa
  Mexico **119** D6
Neu-Isenburg *Germany* **25** E4
Neu-Ulm *Germany* **25** G6
Neubrandenburg *Germany* **24** B9
Neubukow *Germany* **24** A7
Neuburg *Germany* **25** G7
Neuchâtel *Switz.* **25** J2
Neuchâtel □ *Switz.* **25** J2
Neuchâtel, Lac de *Switz.* **25** J2
Neudau *Austria* **26** D9
Neuenhagen *Germany* **24** C9
Neuenhaus *Germany* **24** C2
Neuf-Brisach *France* **19** D14
Neufahrn *Bayern, Germany* **25** G8
Neufchâteau *Belgium* **17** E5
Neufchâteau *France* **19** D12
Neufchâtel-en-Bray *France* **18** C8
Neufchâtel-sur-Aisne
  France **19** C11
Neuhaus *Germany* **24** B6
Neuillé-Pont-Pierre *France* **18** E7
Neuilly-St-Front *France* **19** C10
Neukalen *Germany* **24** B8
Neumarkt *Germany* **25** F7
Neumayer *Antarctica* **5** D17
Neumünster *Germany* **24** A5
Neung-sur-Beuvron *France* **19** E8
Neunkirchen *Austria* **26** D9
Neunkirchen *Germany* **25** F3
Neuquén *Argentina* **128** D3
Neuquén □ *Argentina* **126** D2

Neuruppin *Germany* **24** C8
Neusäss *Germany* **25** G6
Neuse → *U.S.A.* **117** D16
Neusiedl *Austria* **27** D9
Neusiedl See *Austria* **27** D9
Neusiedler
  See-Seewinkel △ *Austria* **27** D9
Neuss *Germany* **24** D2
Neussargues-Moissac *France* **20** C7
Neustadt *Bayern, Germany* **25** F8
Neustadt *Bayern, Germany* **25** G7
Neustadt *Bayern, Germany* **25** G7
Neustadt *Bayern, Germany* **25** F6
Neustadt *Bayern, Germany* **25** F7
Neustadt *Brandenburg,
  Germany* **24** C8
Neustadt *Hessen, Germany* **24** E5
Neustadt *Niedersachsen,
  Germany* **24** C5
Neustadt *Rhld.-Pfz., Germany* **25** F4
Neustadt *Sachsen, Germany* **24** D10
Neustadt *Schleswig-Holstein,
  Germany* **24** A6
Neustadt *Thüringen, Germany* **24** E7
Neustrelitz *Germany* **24** B9
Neuvic *France* **20** C6
Neuville-sur-Saône *France* **21** C3
Neuvy-le-Roi *France* **18** E7
Neuvy-St-Sépulchre *France* **19** F8
Neuvy-sur-Barangeon
  France **19** E9
Neuwerk *Germany* **24** B4
Neuwied *Germany* **24** E3
Neva → *Russia* **32** C6
Nevada *Iowa, U.S.A.* **112** D7
Nevada *Mo., U.S.A.* **112** G6
Nevada □ *U.S.A.* **108** G5
Nevada City *U.S.A.* **110** F6
Nevado, Cerro *Argentina* **126** D2
Nevado de Colima =
  Volcán de Colima △
  Mexico **118** D4
Nevado de Tres Cruces △
  Chile **126** B2
Nevel *Russia* **32** D5
Nevelsk *Russia* **53** E15
Nevers *France* **19** F10
Nevertire *Australia* **95** E4
Nevesinje *Bos.-H.* **44** C2
Neville *Canada* **103** D7
Nevinnomyssk *Russia* **35** H6
Nevis *St. Kitts & Nevis* **121** C7
Nevrokop = Gotse Delchev
  Bulgaria **44** E7
Nevşehir *Turkey* **72** C6
Nevşehir □ *Turkey* **72** C6
Nevskoye *Russia* **30** D9
New → *U.S.A.* **113** F13
New Aiyansh *Canada* **102** B3
New Albany *Ind., U.S.A.* **113** F11
New Albany *Miss., U.S.A.* **117** H10
New Albany *Pa., U.S.A.* **115** E8
New Amsterdam *Guyana* **124** B7
New Baltimore *U.S.A.* **114** D2
New Bedford *U.S.A.* **115** E14
New Berlin *N.Y., U.S.A.* **115** D9
New Berlin *Pa., U.S.A.* **114** F8
New Bern *U.S.A.* **117** D16
New Bethlehem *U.S.A.* **114** F5
New Bight *Bahamas* **121** B4
New Bloomfield *U.S.A.* **114** F7
New Boston *U.S.A.* **116** F7
New Braunfels *U.S.A.* **116** G5
New Brighton *N.Z.* **91** E4
New Brighton *U.S.A.* **114** F4
New Britain *Papua N. G.* **90** B8
New Britain *U.S.A.* **115** E12
New Brunswick *U.S.A.* **115** F10
New Brunswick □ *Canada* **105** C6
New Bussa *Nigeria* **83** D5
New Caledonia ☑ *Pac. Oc.* **90** D9
New Caledonia Trough
  Pac. Oc. **96** L8
New Castile = Castilla-La
  Mancha □ *Spain* **37** F7
New Castle *Ind., U.S.A.* **113** F11
New Castle *Pa., U.S.A.* **114** F4
New City *U.S.A.* **115** E11
New Concord *U.S.A.* **114** G3
New Cumberland *U.S.A.* **114** F4
New Cuyama *U.S.A.* **111** L7
New Delhi *India* **68** E7
New Denver *Canada* **102** D5
New Don Pedro Res. *U.S.A.* **110** H6
New England *U.S.A.* **107** G25
New England *N. Dak., U.S.A.* **112** B2
New England Ra. *Australia* **95** E5
New Forest △ *U.K.* **15** G6
New Galloway *U.K.* **13** F4
New Glasgow *Canada* **105** C7
New Guinea *Oceania* **90** B6
New Halfa = Halfa al
  Jadidah *Sudan* **81** D4
New Hamburg *Canada* **114** C4
New Hampshire □ *U.S.A.* **115** C13
New Hampton *U.S.A.* **112** D8
New Hanover *S. Africa* **89** D5
New Hartford *U.S.A.* **115** C9
New Haven *Conn., U.S.A.* **115** E12
New Haven *Mich., U.S.A.* **114** D2

New Haven N.Y., U.S.A. 115 C8
New Hazelton Canada 102 B3
New Hebrides =
Vanuatu ■ Pac. Oc. 90 C9
New Holland U.S.A. 115 F8
New Iberia U.S.A. 116 F9
New Ireland Papua N. G. 90 B8
New Jersey □ U.S.A. 113 F16
New Kensington U.S.A. 114 F5
New Lexington U.S.A. 113 F10
New Liskeard Canada 104 C4
New London Conn., U.S.A. 115 E12
New London Ohio, U.S.A. 114 E2
New London Wis., U.S.A. 112 C9
New Madrid U.S.A. 112 G9
New Martinsville U.S.A. 113 F13
New Meadows U.S.A. 108 D5
New Melones L. U.S.A. 110 H6
New Mexico □ U.S.A. 109 J11
New Milford Conn., U.S.A. 115 E11
New Milford Pa., U.S.A. 115 E9
New Moore I. Ind. Oc. 69 J13
New Norcia Australia 93 F2
New Norfolk Australia 95 G4
New Orleans U.S.A. 117 G9
New Philadelphia U.S.A. 114 F3
New Plymouth N.Z. 91 C5
New Plymouth U.S.A. 108 E5
New Port Richey U.S.A. 117 G13
New Providence Bahamas 120 A4
New Quay U.K. 15 E3
New Radnor U.K. 15 E4
New Richmond Canada 105 C6
New Richmond U.S.A. 112 C7
New River Gorge △ U.S.A. 113 G13
New Roads U.S.A. 116 F9
New Rochelle U.S.A. 115 F11
New Rockford U.S.A. 112 B4
New Romney U.K. 15 G8
New Ross Ireland 12 D5
New Salem U.S.A. 112 B3
New Scone = Scone U.K. 13 E5
New Siberian I. = Novaya
Sibir, Ostrov Russia 53 B16
New Siberian Is. =
Novosibirskiye Ostrova
Russia 53 B15
New Smyrna Beach U.S.A. 117 G14
New South Wales □
Australia 95 E4
New Tecumseth = Alliston
Canada 114 B5
New Town U.S.A. 112 B2
New Tredegar U.K. 15 F4
New Ulm U.S.A. 112 C6
New Waterford Canada 105 C7
New Westminster Canada 110 A4
New York U.S.A. 115 F11
New York □ U.S.A. 115 D9
New York J.F. Kennedy
Int. ✈ (JFK) U.S.A. 115 F11
New Zealand ■ Oceania 91 D6
Newaj → India 68 G7
Newala Tanzania 87 E4
Newark Del., U.S.A. 113 F16
Newark N.J., U.S.A. 115 F10
Newark N.Y., U.S.A. 114 C7
Newark Ohio, U.S.A. 114 F2
Newark Liberty Int. ✈
(EWR) U.S.A. 115 F10
Newark-on-Trent U.K. 14 D7
Newark Valley U.S.A. 115 D8
Newberg U.S.A. 108 D2
Newberry Mich., U.S.A. 113 B11
Newberry S.C., U.S.A. 117 D14
Newberry Springs U.S.A. 111 L10
Newboro L. Canada 115 B8
Newbridge = Droichead
Nua Ireland 12 C5
Newburgh Canada 114 B8
Newburgh U.S.A. 115 E10
Newbury U.K. 15 F6
Newbury N.H., U.S.A. 115 B12
Newbury Vt., U.S.A. 115 B12
Newburyport U.S.A. 115 D14
Newcastle Australia 95 E5
Newcastle N.B., Canada 105 C6
Newcastle Ont., Canada 104 D4
Newcastle S. Africa 89 D4
Newcastle U.K. 12 B6
Newcastle Calif., U.S.A. 110 G5
Newcastle Wyo., U.S.A. 108 D11
Newcastle Emlyn U.K. 15 E3
Newcastle Ra. Australia 92 C5
Newcastle-under-Lyme U.K. 14 D5
Newcastle-upon-Tyne U.K. 14 C6
Newcastle Waters Australia 94 B1
Newcastle West Ireland 12 D2
Newcomb U.S.A. 115 C10
Newcomerstown U.S.A. 114 F3
Newdegate Australia 93 F2
Newell Australia 94 B4
Newell U.S.A. 112 C2
Newenham, C. U.S.A. 106 D7
Newfane U.S.A. 114 C6
Newfield U.S.A. 115 D8
Newfound L. U.S.A. 115 C13
Newfoundland Canada 105 C8
Newfoundland U.S.A. 115 E9

Newfoundland &
Labrador □ Canada 105 B8
Newhaven U.K. 15 G8
Newkirk U.S.A. 116 C6
Newlyn U.K. 15 G2
Newman Australia 92 D2
Newman U.S.A. 110 H5
Newmarket Canada 114 B5
Newmarket Ireland 12 D2
Newmarket U.K. 15 E8
Newmarket U.S.A. 115 C14
Newnan U.S.A. 117 E12
Newport I. of W., U.K. 15 G6
Newport Newport, U.K. 15 F5
Newport Ark., U.S.A. 116 D9
Newport Ky., U.S.A. 113 F11
Newport N.H., U.S.A. 115 C12
Newport N.Y., U.S.A. 115 C9
Newport Oreg., U.S.A. 108 D1
Newport Pa., U.S.A. 114 F7
Newport R.I., U.S.A. 115 E13
Newport Tenn., U.S.A. 117 D13
Newport Vt., U.S.A. 115 B12
Newport Wash., U.S.A. 108 B5
Newport □ U.K. 15 F4
Newport Beach U.S.A. 111 M9
Newport News U.S.A. 113 G15
Newport Pagnell U.K. 15 E7
Newquay U.K. 15 G2
Newry U.K. 12 B5
Newry Islands △ Australia 94 b
Newton Ill., U.S.A. 112 F9
Newton Iowa, U.S.A. 112 E7
Newton Kans., U.S.A. 112 F5
Newton Mass., U.S.A. 115 D13
Newton Miss., U.S.A. 117 E10
Newton N.C., U.S.A. 117 D14
Newton N.J., U.S.A. 115 E10
Newton Tex., U.S.A. 116 F8
Newton Abbot U.K. 15 G4
Newton Aycliffe U.K. 14 C6
Newton Falls N.Y., U.S.A. 115 B10
Newton Falls Ohio, U.S.A. 114 E4
Newton Stewart U.K. 13 G4
Newtonmore U.K. 13 D4
Newtown U.K. 15 E4
Newtownabbey U.K. 12 B6
Newtownards U.K. 12 B6
Newtownbarry = Bunclody
Ireland 12 D5
Newtownstewart U.K. 12 B4
Newville U.S.A. 114 F7
Nexon France 20 C5
Neya Russia 34 A6
Neyrīz Iran 71 D7
Neyshābūr Iran 71 B8
Nezhin = Nizhyn Ukraine 33 G6
Nezperce U.S.A. 108 C5
Nezvysko Ukraine 29 B10
Ngaanyatjarra ☼ Australia 92 D4
Ngabang Indonesia 62 D3
Ngabordamlu, Tanjung
Indonesia 63 F8
N'Gage Angola 84 F3
Ngala Nigeria 83 C7
Ngaliwurru Nungali ☼
Australia 92 D5
Ngalurrtju ☼ Australia 92 D5
Ngambé Centre, Cameroon 83 D7
Ngambé Littoral, Cameroon 83 E7
Ngami Depression Botswana 88 C3
Ngamo Zimbabwe 87 F2
Nganbéto, L. de Togo 83 D5
Ngangala Sudan 81 G3
Nganglong Kangri China 69 C9
Ngao Thailand 64 C2
Ngaoundéré Cameroon 84 C2
Ngapara N.Z. 91 F3
Ngara Tanzania 86 C3
Ngarluma ☼ Australia 92 D2
Ngawi Indonesia 63 G14
Ngcobo S. Africa 89 E4
Ngeru Uganda 86 B3
Nghia Lo Vietnam 58 G5
Ngoboli Sudan 81 G3
Ngoma Malawi 87 E3
Ngomahura Zimbabwe 87 G3
Ngomba Tanzania 87 D3
Ngomeni, Ras Kenya 86 C5
Ngong Kenya 86 C4
Ngop Sudan 81 F3
Ngoring Hu China 60 C4
Ngorkou Mali 82 B4
Ngorongoro Tanzania 86 C4
Ngorongoro △ Tanzania 86 C4
Ngozi Burundi 86 C2
Ngudu Tanzania 86 C3
Nguigmi Niger 79 F8
Nguila Cameroon 83 E7
Nguiu Australia 92 B5
Ngukurr Australia 94 A1
Ngundu Zimbabwe 87 G3
Ngunga Tanzania 86 C3
Nguru Nigeria 83 C7
Nguru Mts. Tanzania 86 D4
Ngusi Malawi 87 E3
Nguyen Binh Vietnam 58 F5
Nha Trang Vietnam 65 F7

Nhacoongo Mozam. 89 C6
Nhamaabué Mozam. 87 F4
Nhamundá → Brazil 125 D7
Nhangulaze, L. Mozam. 89 C5
Nharnuwangga, Wajarri
and Ngarlawangga ☼
Australia 93 D2
Nhill Australia 95 F3
Nho Quan Vietnam 58 G5
Nhulunbuy Australia 94 A2
Nia-nia Dem. Rep. of the Congo 86 B2
Niafounké Mali 82 B4
Niagara Falls Canada 114 C5
Niagara Falls U.S.A. 114 C6
Niagara-on-the-Lake
Canada 114 C5
Niah Malaysia 62 D4
Niamey Niger 83 C5
Niamtougou Togo 83 D5
Niandan-Koro Guinea 82 C3
Nianforando Guinea 82 D2
Niangara
Dem. Rep. of the Congo 86 B2
Niangay, L. Mali 82 B4
Niangbo Ivory C. 82 D3
Niangoloko Burkina Faso 82 C4
Niantic U.S.A. 115 E12
Niaro Sudan 81 E3
Nias Indonesia 62 D1
Niassa □ Mozam. 87 E4
Niassa △ Mozam. 87 E4
Nibāk Si. Arabia 71 E7
Nibe Denmark 11 H3
Nicaragua ■ Cent. Amer. 120 D2
Nicaragua, L. de Nic. 120 D2
Nicastro Italy 43 D9
Nice France 21 E11
Nice-Côte-d'Azur ✈ (NCE)
France 21 E11
Niceville U.S.A. 117 F11
Nichicun, L. Canada 105 B5
Nicholás, Canal W. Indies 120 B3
Nicholasville U.S.A. 113 G11
Nichols U.S.A. 115 D8
Nicholson Australia 92 C4
Nicholson U.S.A. 115 E9
Nicholson → Australia 94 B2
Nicholson L. Canada 103 A8
Nicholson Ra. Australia 93 E2
Nicholville U.S.A. 115 B10
Nicobar Is. Ind. Oc. 51 H11
Nicola Canada 102 C4
Nicolls Town Bahamas 120 A4
Nicosia Cyprus 49 D12
Nicosia Italy 43 E7
Nicótera Italy 43 D8
Nicoya Costa Rica 120 D2
Nicoya, G. de Costa Rica 120 E3
Nicoya, Pen. de Costa Rica 120 E2
Nida Lithuania 30 D8
Nidd → U.K. 14 D6
Nidda Germany 25 E5
Nidda → Germany 25 E4
Nidwalden □ Switz. 25 J4
Nidzica Poland 31 E7
Niebüll Germany 24 A4
Nied → Germany 19 C13
Niederaula Germany 24 E5
Niederbayern □ Germany 25 G8
Niederbronn-les-Bains
France 19 D14
Niedere Tauern Austria 26 D7
Niederlausitz Germany 24 D9
Niederösterreich □ Austria 26 C8
Niedersachsen □ Germany 24 C4
Niedersächsisches
Wattenmeer △ Germany 24 B3
Niekerkshoop S. Africa 88 D3
Niellé Ivory C. 82 D3
Niemba Dem. Rep. of the Congo 86 D2
Niemen = Nemunas →
Lithuania 30 C8
Niemodlin Poland 31 H4
Nienburg Germany 24 C5
Niepołomice Poland 31 H7
Niers → Germany 24 D1
Niesky Germany 24 D10
Nieszawa Poland 31 F5
Nieu Bethesda S. Africa 88 E3
Nieuw Amsterdam
Suriname 125 B7
Nieuw Nickerie Suriname 125 B7
Nieuwoudtville S. Africa 88 E2
Nieuwpoort Belgium 17 C2
Nieves, Pico de las Canary Is. 48 G4
Nièvre □ France 19 E10
Niga Mali 82 C3
Niğde Turkey 72 D6
Niğde □ Turkey 72 D6
Nigel S. Africa 89 D4
Niger □ Nigeria 83 D6
Niger ■ W. Afr. 83 B7
Niger → W. Afr. 83 D6
Niger Delta Africa 83 E6
Nigeria ■ W. Afr. 83 D6
Nighasin India 69 E9
Nightcaps N.Z. 91 F2
Nigrita Greece 44 F7

Nihoa U.S.A. 107 L7
Nihon = Japan ■ Asia 55 G8
Nii-Jima Japan 55 G9
Niigata Japan 54 F9
Niigata □ Japan 55 F9
Niihama Japan 55 H6
Ni'ihau U.S.A. 107 L7
Niimi Japan 55 G6
Niitsu Japan 54 F9
Níjar Spain 39 E2
Nijil Jordan 74 E4
Nijkerk Neths. 17 B5
Nijmegen Neths. 17 C5
Nijverdal Neths. 17 B6
Nīk Pey Iran 73 D13
Nike Nigeria 83 D6
Nikel Russia 8 B24
Nikiniki Indonesia 92 A3
Nikití Greece 44 F7
Nikiti Benin 83 D5
Nikkō Japan 55 F9
Nikkō △ Japan 55 F9
Nikolayev = Mykolayiv
Ukraine 33 J7
Nikolayevsk Russia 34 E7
Nikolayevsk-na-Amur
Russia 53 D15
Nikolsk Russia 34 D8
Nikolskoye Russia 53 D17
Nikopol Bulgaria 45 C8
Nikopol Ukraine 33 J8
Nikopolis Greece 46 B2
Niksar Turkey 72 B7
Nīkshahr Iran 71 E9
Nikšić Montenegro 44 D2
Nîl, Nahr en → Africa 80 H7
Nîl el Abyad → Sudan 81 D3
Nîl el Azraq → Sudan 81 D3
Nila Indonesia 63 F7
Niland U.S.A. 111 M11
Nile = Nîl, Nahr en → Africa 80 H7
Nile Delta Egypt 80 H7
Niles Mich., U.S.A. 112 E10
Niles Ohio, U.S.A. 114 E4
Nilüfer → Turkey 45 F12
Nim Ka Thana India 68 F6
Nimach India 68 G6
Nimba, Mts. Africa 82 D3
Nimbahera India 68 G6
Nîmes France 21 E8
Nimfaíon, Ákra = Pines,
Akra Greece 45 F8
Nimmitabel Australia 95 F4
Nimule Sudan 81 G3
Nimule △ Sudan 81 G3
Nin Croatia 41 D12
Nīnawā Iraq 73 D10
Nīnawā □ Iraq 70 B4
Nindigully Australia 95 D4
Nineveh = Nīnawā Iraq 73 D10
Ning Xian China 56 G4
Ning'an China 57 B15
Ningaloo Marine △ Australia 92 D1
Ningbo China 59 C13
Ningcheng China 57 D10
Ningde China 59 D12
Ningdu China 59 D10
Ninggang China 59 D9
Ningguo China 59 B12
Ninghai China 59 C13
Ninghua China 59 D11
Ningi Nigeria 83 C6
Ningjin China 56 F8
Ningjing Shan China 58 C2
Ninglang China 58 D3
Ningling China 56 G8
Ningming China 58 F6
Ningnan China 58 D4
Ningpo = Ningbo China 59 C13
Ningqiang China 56 H4
Ningshan China 56 H5
Ningsia Hui A.R. = Ningxia
Huizu Zizhiqu □ China 56 F4
Ningwu China 56 E7
Ningxia Huizu Zizhiqu □
China 56 F4
Ningxiang China 59 C9
Ningyang China 56 G9
Ningyuan China 59 E8
Ninh Binh Vietnam 58 G5
Ninh Giang Vietnam 64 B6
Ninh Hoa Vietnam 64 F7
Ninh Ma Vietnam 64 F7
Nini-Suhien △ Ghana 82 D4
Ninove Belgium 17 D4
Nioaque Brazil 127 A4
Niobrara U.S.A. 112 D4
Niobrara → U.S.A. 112 D4
Niokolo-Koba △ Senegal 82 C2
Niono Mali 82 C3
Nionsamoridougou Guinea 82 D3
Nioro du Rip Senegal 82 C1
Nioro du Sahel Mali 82 B3
Niort France 20 B3
Nipawin Canada 103 C8
Nipigon Canada 104 C2
Nipigon, L. Canada 104 C2

Nipishish L. Canada 105 B7
Nipissing, L. Canada 104 C4
Nipomo U.S.A. 111 K6
Nippon = Japan ■ Asia 55 G8
Nipton U.S.A. 111 K11
Niquelândia Brazil 125 F9
Nīr Iran 73 C12
Nirasaki Japan 55 G9
Nirmal India 66 K11
Nirmali India 69 F12
Niš Serbia 44 C5
Nisa Portugal 37 F3
Nišava → Serbia 44 C5
Niscemi Italy 43 E7
Nishino'omote Japan 55 J5
Nishinomiya Japan 55 G7
Nishiwaki Japan 55 G7
Niška Banja Serbia 44 C6
Niskibi → Canada 104 A2
Nisko Poland 31 H9
Nisqually → U.S.A. 110 C4
Nisporeni Moldova 29 C13
Nissaki Greece 49 A3
Nissan → Sweden 11 H6
Nissum Bredning Denmark 11 H2
Nissum Fjord Denmark 11 H2
Nistru = Dnister → Europe 23 E16
Nisutlin → Canada 102 A2
Nitchequon Canada 105 B5
Niterói Brazil 127 A7
Nith → Canada 114 C4
Nith → U.K. 13 F5
Nitmiluk △ Australia 92 B5
Nitra Slovak Rep. 27 C11
Nitra → Slovak Rep. 27 D11
Nitriansky □ Slovak Rep. 27 C11
Nittenau Germany 25 F8
Niuafo'ou Tonga 91 c
Niue Pac. Oc. 97 J11
Niulan Jiang → China 58 D4
Niut Indonesia 62 D4
Niutou Shan China 59 C13
Niuzhuang China 57 D12
Nivala Finland 8 E21
Nivelles Belgium 17 D4
Nivernais France 19 E10
Niverville Canada 103 D9
Niwas India 69 H9
Nixa U.S.A. 112 G7
Nixon U.S.A. 116 G6
Nizamabad India 66 K11
Nizamghat India 67 E19
Nizhnaya Russia 53 C17
Nizhnekamsk Russia 34 C10
Nizhnevartovsk Russia 52 C8
Nizhneudinsk Russia 53 D10
Nizhniy Bestyakh Russia 53 C13
Nizhniy Chir Russia 35 F6
Nizhniy Lomov Russia 34 D6
Nizhniy Novgorod Russia 34 B7
Nizhniy Novgorod □ Russia 34 B7
Nizhniy Tagil Russia 52 D6
Nizhyn Ukraine 33 G6
Nizina Mazowiecka Poland 31 F8
Nizip Turkey 72 D7
Nízké Tatry Slovak Rep. 27 C12
Nízké Tatry △ Slovak Rep. 27 C12
Nízký Jeseník Czech Rep. 27 B10
Nizwā Oman 75 C6
Nizza Monferrato Italy 40 D5
Njakwa Malawi 87 E3
Njanji Zambia 87 E3
Njazidja = Grande Comore
Comoros Is. 85 a
Njegoš Montenegro 44 D2
Njinjo Tanzania 87 D4
Njombe Tanzania 87 D3
Njombe → Tanzania 86 D4
Nkambe Cameroon 83 D7
Nkana Zambia 87 E2
Nkandla S. Africa 89 D5
Nkawkaw Ghana 83 D4
Nkayi Zimbabwe 87 F2
Nkhotakota Malawi 87 E3
Nkhotakota △ Malawi 87 E3
Nkondwe Tanzania 86 D3
Nkongsamba Cameroon 83 E6
Nkoteng Cameroon 83 E7
Nkurenkuru Namibia 88 B2
Nkwanta Ghana 82 D4
Nmai → Burma 58 F2
Noakhali Bangla. 67 H17
Nobel Canada 114 A4
Nobeoka Japan 55 H5
Noblejas Spain 36 F7
Noblesville U.S.A. 112 E10
Noboribetsu Japan 54 C10
Noccundra Australia 95 D3
Noce → Italy 40 B8
Nocera Inferiore Italy 43 B7
Nocera Umbra Italy 41 E9
Noci Italy 43 B10
Nocona U.S.A. 116 E6
Nocrich Romania 29 E9

Noda Japan 55 F9
Nogales Mexico 118 A2
Nogales U.S.A. 109 L8
Nogaro France 20 E3
Nogat → Poland 30 D6
Nōgata Japan 55 H5
Nogent France 19 D12
Nogent-le-Rotrou France 18 D7
Nogent-sur-Seine France 19 D10
Noggara Ethiopia 81 E4
Noggerup Australia 93 F2
Noginsk Moskva, Russia 32 E10
Noginsk Tunguska, Russia 53 C10
Nogliki Russia 53 D15
Nogoa → Australia 94 C4
Nogoyá Argentina 126 C4
Nógrád □ Hungary 28 C4
Noguera Pallaresa → Spain 38 D5
Noguera Ribagorçana →
Spain 38 D5
Nohar India 68 E6
Nohfelden Germany 25 F3
Nohta India 69 H8
Noia Spain 36 C2
Noire, Montagne France 20 E6
Noires, Mts. France 18 D3
Noirétable France 20 C7
Noirmoutier, Î. de France 18 F4
Noirmoutier-en-l'Île France 18 F4
Nojane Botswana 88 C3
Nojima-Zaki Japan 55 G9
Nok Kundi Pakistan 66 E3
Nok Ta Phao, Ko Thailand 65 b
Nokaneng Botswana 88 B3
Nokia Finland 32 B2
Nokomis Canada 103 C8
Nokomis L. Canada 103 B8
Nola C.A.R. 84 D3
Nola Italy 43 B7
Nolay France 19 F11
Noli, C. di Italy 40 D5
Nolinsk Russia 34 B9
Noma Omuramba →
Namibia 88 B3
Nombre de Dios Panama 120 E4
Nome U.S.A. 106 C6
Nomo-Zaki Japan 55 H4
Nomuka Tonga 91 c
Nomuka Group Tonga 91 c
Nonacho L. Canada 103 A7
Nonancourt France 18 D8
Nonda Australia 94 C3
None Italy 40 D4
Nong Chang Thailand 64 E2
Nong Het Laos 64 C4
Nong Khai Thailand 64 D4
Nong'an China 57 B13
Nongoma S. Africa 89 D5
Nongsa Indonesia 65 d
Nonsan S. Korea 57 F14
Nonthaburi Thailand 64 F3
Nontron France 20 C4
Nonza France 21 F13
Noonamah Australia 92 B5
Noondie, L. Australia 93 E2
Noonkanbah ☼ Australia 92 C3
Noord Brabant □ Neths. 17 C5
Noord Holland □ Neths. 17 B4
Noordbeveland Neths. 17 C3
Noordoostpolder Neths. 17 B5
Noordwijk Neths. 17 B4
Noosa Heads Australia 95 D5
Nootka I. Canada 102 D3
Nopiming → Canada 103 C9
Nora Eritrea 81 D5
Nora Sweden 10 E9
Noralee Canada 102 C3
Noranda =
Rouyn-Noranda Canada 104 C4
Norberg Sweden 10 D9
Nórcia Italy 41 F10
Norco U.S.A. 111 M9
Nord □ Cameroon 83 D7
Nord □ France 19 B10
Nord-Kivu □
Dem. Rep. of the Congo 86 C2
Nord-Ostsee-Kanal Germany 24 A5
Nord-Ouest □ Cameroon 83 D7
Nord-Pas-de-Calais □ France 19 B9
Nordaustlandet Svalbard 4 B9
Nordborg Denmark 11 J3
Nordby Denmark 11 J2
Norddeich Germany 24 B3
Norddegg Canada 102 C5
Norden Germany 24 B3
Nordenham Germany 24 B4
Norderney Germany 24 B3
Norderstedt Germany 24 B6
Nordfjord Norway 8 F11
Nordfriesische Inseln
Germany 24 A4
Nordhausen Germany 24 D6
Nordhorn Germany 24 C3
Nordøyar Færoe Is. 8
Nördinge-Nol Sweden 11 G6
Nordingrå Sweden 10 B12
Nordjylland □ Denmark 11 G3
Nordkapp Norway 8 A21

Nordkapp *Svalbard* **4** A9
Nordkinnhalvøya *Norway* **8** A22
Nördlicher Teutoburger
  Wald-Wiehengebirge △
  Germany **24** C4
Nördlingen *Germany* **25** G6
Nordrhein-Westfalen □
  Germany **24** D3
Nordstrand *Germany* **24** A4
Nordvik *Russia* **53** B12
Nore → *Ireland* **12** D4
Noreland *Canada* **114** B6
Norfolk = Simcoe *Canada* **114** D4
Norfolk *N.Y., U.S.A.* **115** B10
Norfolk *Nebr., U.S.A.* **112** D5
Norfolk *Va., U.S.A.* **113** G15
Norfolk □ *U.K.* **15** E8
Norfolk Broads △ *U.K.* **15** E9
Norfolk I. *Pac. Oc.* **90** D9
Norfolk Ridge *Pac. Oc.* **96** K8
Norfork L. *U.S.A.* **116** C8
Norge = Norway ■ *Europe* **8** E14
Norilsk *Russia* **53** C9
Norma, Mt. *Australia* **94** C3
Normal *U.S.A.* **112** E9
Norman *U.S.A.* **116** D6
Norman → *Australia* **94** B3
Norman Wells *Canada* **100** D6
Normanby → *Australia* **94** A3
Normandie-Maine △ *France* **18** D6
Normandin *Canada* **104** C5
Normanhurst, Mt. *Australia* **93** E3
Normanton *Australia* **94** B3
Normétal *Canada* **104** C4
Norquay *Canada* **103** C8
Norquinco *Argentina* **128** E2
Norra Dellen *Sweden* **10** C10
Norra Kvill △ *Sweden* **11** G9
Norra Ulvön *Sweden* **10** A12
Norrahammar *Sweden* **11** G8
Norrbottens län □ *Sweden* **8** C19
Nørre Åby *Denmark* **11** J3
Nørre Alslev *Denmark* **11** K5
Nørresundby *Denmark* **11** G3
Norrhult-Klavreström
  Sweden **11** G9
Norris Point *Canada* **105** C8
Norristown *U.S.A.* **115** F9
Norrköping *Sweden* **11** F10
Norrland *Sweden* **8** E16
Norrsundet *Sweden* **10** D11
Norrtälje *Sweden* **10** E12
Norseman *Australia* **93** F3
Norsk *Russia* **53** D14
Norte, Pta. del *Canary Is.* **48** G2
Norte, Serra do *Brazil* **124** F7
North, C. *Canada* **105** C7
North Adams *U.S.A.* **115** D11
North America **98** F10
North Arm *Canada* **102** A5
North Augusta *U.S.A.* **117** E14
North Australian Basin
  Ind. Oc. **92** B2
North Ayrshire □ *U.K.* **13** F4
North Bass I. *U.S.A.* **114** E2
North Battleford *Canada* **103** C7
North Bay *Canada* **104** C4
North Belcher Is. *Canada* **104** A4
North Bend *Oreg., U.S.A.* **108** E1
North Bend *Pa., U.S.A.* **114** E7
North Bend *Wash., U.S.A.* **110** C5
North Bennington *U.S.A.* **115** D11
North Berwick *U.K.* **13** E6
North Berwick *U.S.A.* **115** C14
North Bruce *Canada* **114** B3
North C. *Canada* **105** C7
North C. *N.Z.* **91** A4
North Canadian → *U.S.A.* **116** D7
North Canton *U.S.A.* **114** F3
North Cape = Nordkapp
  Norway **8** A21
North Caribou L. *Canada* **104** B1
North Carolina □ *U.S.A.* **117** D15
North Cascades △ *U.S.A.* **108** B3
North Channel *Canada* **104** C3
North Channel *U.K.* **13** F3
North Charleston *U.S.A.* **117** E15
North Chicago *U.S.A.* **112** D10
North Collins *U.S.A.* **114** D6
North Creek *U.S.A.* **115** C11
North Dakota □ *U.S.A.* **112** B3
North Downs *U.K.* **15** F8
North East *U.S.A.* **114** D5
North East Frontier
  Agency = Arunachal
  Pradesh □ *India* **67** F19
North East Lincolnshire □
  U.K. **14** D7
North Eastern □ *Kenya* **86** B5
North Esk → *U.K.* **13** E6
North European Plain *Europe* **6** E10
North Foreland *U.K.* **15** F9
North Fork *U.S.A.* **110** H7
North Fork American →
  U.S.A. **110** G5
North Fork Feather →
  U.S.A. **110** F5
North Fork Grand →
  U.S.A. **112** C2
North Fork Red → *U.S.A.* **116** D5

North Frisian Is. =
  Nordfriesische Inseln
  Germany **24** A4
North Gower *Canada* **115** A9
North Hd. *Australia* **93** F1
North Henik L. *Canada* **103** A9
North Highlands *U.S.A.* **110** G5
North Horr *Kenya* **86** B4
North I. *Kenya* **86** B4
North I. *N.Z.* **91** C5
North I. *Seychelles* **85** b
North Kingsville *U.S.A.* **114** E4
North Kitui △ *Kenya* **86** C4
North Knife → *Canada* **103** B10
North Koel → *India* **69** G10
North Korea ■ *Asia* **57** E14
North Lakhimpur *India* **67** F19
North Lanarkshire □ *U.K.* **13** F5
North Las Vegas *U.S.A.* **111** J11
North Lincolnshire □ *U.K.* **14** D7
North Little Rock *U.S.A.* **116** D8
North Loup → *U.S.A.* **112** E4
North Luangwa △ *Zambia* **87** E3
North Magnetic Pole *Canada* **4** A2
North Mankato *U.S.A.* **112** C6
North Minch *U.K.* **13** C3
North Moose L. *Canada* **103** C8
North Myrtle Beach *U.S.A.* **117** E15
North Nahanni → *Canada* **102** A4
North Olmsted *U.S.A.* **114** E3
North Ossetia □ *Russia* **35** J7
North Pagai, I. = Pagai
  Utara, Pulau *Indonesia* **62** E2
North Palisade *U.S.A.* **110** H8
North Platte *U.S.A.* **112** E3
North Platte → *U.S.A.* **112** E3
North Pole *Arctic* **4** A
North Portal *Canada* **103** D8
North Powder *U.S.A.* **108** D5
North Pt. *Barbados* **121** g
North Pt. *Trin. & Tob.* **125** J16
North Pt. *U.S.A.* **114** A1
North Rhine Westphalia =
  Nordrhein-Westfalen □
  Germany **24** D3
North River *Canada* **105** B8
North Ronaldsay *U.K.* **13** B6
North Saskatchewan →
  Canada **103** C7
North Sea *Europe* **6** D6
North Seal → *Canada* **103** B9
North Slope *U.S.A.* **106** B9
North Somerset □ *U.K.* **15** F5
North Sydney *Canada* **105** C7
North Syracuse *U.S.A.* **115** C8
North Taranaki Bight *N.Z.* **91** C5
North Thompson → *Canada* **102** C4
North Tonawanda *U.S.A.* **114** C6
North Troy *U.S.A.* **115** B12
North Twin I. *Canada* **104** B4
North Tyne → *U.K.* **14** B5
North Uist *U.K.* **13** D1
North Vancouver *Canada* **110** A3
North Vernon *U.S.A.* **113** F11
North Wabasca L. *Canada* **102** B6
North Walsham *U.K.* **14** E9
North West =
  Severo-Zapadnyy □ *Russia* **52** C4
North-West □ *S. Africa* **88** D4
North West C. *Australia* **92** D1
North West Frontier □
  Pakistan **68** C4
North West Highlands *U.K.* **13** D4
North West River *Canada* **105** B7
North Western □ *Zambia* **87** E2
North Wildwood *U.S.A.* **113** F16
North York Moors *U.K.* **14** C7
North York Moors △ *U.K.* **14** C7
North Yorkshire □ *U.K.* **14** C6
Northallerton *U.K.* **14** C6
Northam *Australia* **93** F2
Northam *S. Africa* **88** C4
Northampton *Australia* **93** E1
Northampton *U.K.* **15** E7
Northampton *Mass., U.S.A.* **115** D12
Northampton *Pa., U.S.A.* **115** F9
Northamptonshire □ *U.K.* **15** E7
Northbridge *U.S.A.* **115** D13
Northbrook *Canada* **114** B7
Northcliffe *Australia* **93** F2
Northeast Pacific Basin
  Pac. Oc. **97** D13
Northeast Providence
  Chan. *W. Indies* **120** A4
Northeim *Germany* **24** D6
Northern □ *Limpopo* □
  S. Africa **89** C4
Northern □ *Ghana* **83** D4
Northern □ *Malawi* **87** E3
Northern □ *S. Leone* **82** D2
Northern □ *Zambia* **87** E2
Northern Areas □ *Pakistan* **69** A5
Northern Cape □ *S. Africa* **88** D3
Northern Circars *India* **67** L13
Northern Indian L. *Canada* **103** B9
Northern Ireland □ *U.K.* **12** B5
Northern Lau Group *Fiji* **91** a
Northern Light L. *Canada* **104** C1
Northern Marianas ☒
  Pac. Oc. **96** F6

Northern Province □
  S. Africa **89** C4
Northern Range *Trin. & Tob.*
  125 K15
Northern Sporades *Greece* **46** B5
Northern Territory □
  Australia **92** D5
Northfield *Minn., U.S.A.* **112** C7
Northfield *Vt., U.S.A.* **115** B12
Northgate *Canada* **103** D8
Northland □ *N.Z.* **91** A4
Northome *U.S.A.* **112** B6
Northport *Ala., U.S.A.* **117** E11
Northport *Wash., U.S.A.* **108** B5
Northumberland, C. *Australia* **95** F3
Northumberland Is. *Australia* **94** C4
Northumberland Str.
  Canada **105** C7
Northville *U.S.A.* **115** C10
Northwest Pacific Basin
  Pac. Oc. **96** D3
Northwest Providence
  Channel *W. Indies* **120** A4
Northwest Territories □
  Canada **100** B8
Northwich *U.K.* **14** D5
Northwood *Iowa, U.S.A.* **112** D7
Northwood *N. Dak., U.S.A.* **112** B5
Norton *U.S.A.* **112** F4
Norton *Zimbabwe* **87** F3
Norton Sd. *U.S.A.* **106** C7
Nortorf *Germany* **24** A5
Norwalk *Calif., U.S.A.* **111** M8
Norwalk *Conn., U.S.A.* **115** E11
Norwalk *Iowa, U.S.A.* **112** E7
Norwalk *Ohio, U.S.A.* **114** E2
Norway *Maine, U.S.A.* **113** C18
Norway *Mich., U.S.A.* **112** C10
Norway ■ *Europe* **8** E14
Norway House *Canada* **103** C9
Norwegian B. *Canada* **101** B14
Norwegian Basin *Atl. Oc.* **4** C7
Norwegian Sea *Atl. Oc.* **4** C7
Norwich *Canada* **114** D4
Norwich *U.K.* **15** E9
Norwich *Conn., U.S.A.* **115** E12
Norwich *N.Y., U.S.A.* **115** D9
Norwood *Canada* **114** B7
Norwood *U.S.A.* **115** B10
Nosappu-Misaki *Japan* **54** C12
Noshiro *Japan* **54** D10
Nosivka *Ukraine* **33** G6
Nosovka = Nosivka *Ukraine* **33** G6
Noşratābād *Iran* **71** D8
Noss Hd. *U.K.* **13** C5
Nossebro *Sweden* **11** F6
Nossob → *S. Africa* **88** D3
Nossombougou *Mali* **82** C3
Nosy Barren *Madag.* **85** H8
Nosy Bé *Madag.* **85** G9
Nosy Boraha *Madag.* **89** B8
Nosy Lava *Madag.* **89** A8
Nosy Varika *Madag.* **89** C8
Noteć → *Poland* **31** F2
Notikewin → *Canada* **102** B5
Notio Aigaio □ *Greece* **47** E7
Notios Aiyaíon = Notio
  Aigaio □ *Greece* **47** E7
Notios Evvoikos Kolpos
  Greece **46** C5
Noto *Italy* **43** F8
Noto, G. di *Italy* **43** F8
Notodden *Norway* **9** G13
Notre Dame B. *Canada* **105** C8
Notre-Dame-de-Koartac =
  Quaqtaq *Canada* **101** E18
Notre-Dame-des-Bois
  Canada **115** A13
Notre-Dame-d'Ivugivic =
  Ivujivik *Canada* **101** E16
Notre-Dame-du-Nord
  Canada **104** C4
Notsé *Togo* **83** D5
Nottawasaga B. *Canada* **114** B4
Nottaway → *Canada* **104** B4
Nottingham *U.K.* **14** E6
Nottingham, City of □ *U.K.* **14** E6
Nottingham I. *Canada* **101** E16
Nottinghamshire □ *U.K.* **14** D6
Nottoway → *U.S.A.* **113** G15
Notwane → *Botswana* **88** C4
Nouâdhibou *Mauritania* **78** D2
Nouâdhibou, Râs *Mauritania* **78** D2
Nouakchott *Mauritania* **82** B1
Nouâmghâr *Mauritania* **82** B1
Nouméa *N. Cal.* **90** D9
Nouna *Burkina Faso* **82** C4
Noupoort *S. Africa* **88** E3
Nouveau Comptoir =
  Wemindji *Canada* **104** B4
Nouvelle Amsterdam, Î.
  Ind. Oc. **3** F13
Nouvelle-Calédonie = New
  Caledonia □ *Pac. Oc.* **90** D9
Nouzonville *France* **19** C11
Nová Baňa *Slovak Rep.* **27** C11
Nová Bystřice *Czech Rep.* **26** B8
Nova Esperança *Brazil* **127** A5
Nova Friburgo *Brazil* **127** A7

Nova Gorica *Slovenia* **41** C10
Nova Gradiška *Croatia* **28** E2
Nova Iguaçu *Brazil* **127** A7
Nova Iorque *Brazil* **125** E10
Nova Kakhovka *Ukraine* **33** J7
Nova Lamego *Guinea-Biss.* **82** C2
Nova Lusitânia *Mozam.* **87** F3
Nova Mambone *Mozam.* **89** C6
Nova Odesa *Ukraine* **33** J6
Nová Paka *Czech Rep.* **26** A8
Nova Pavova *Serbia* **28** F5
Nova Scotia □ *Canada* **105** C7
Nova Siri *Italy* **43** B9
Nova Sofala *Mozam.* **89** C5
Nova Ushytsya *Ukraine* **29** B12
Nova Varoš *Serbia* **44** C3
Nova Venécia *Brazil* **125** G10
Nova Zagora *Bulgaria* **45** D10
Novaci *Macedonia* **44** E5
Novaci *Romania* **29** E8
Novafeltria *Italy* **41** E9
Novannenskiy =
  Novoannenskiy *Russia* **34** E6
Novar *Canada* **114** A5
Novara *Italy* **40** C5
Novato *U.S.A.* **110** G4
Novaya Kakhovka = Nova
  Kakhovka *Ukraine* **33** J7
Novaya Kazanka =
  Zhangaqala *Kazakhstan* **35** F9
Novaya Ladoga *Russia* **32** B7
Novaya Lyalya *Russia* **52** D7
Novaya Sibir, Ostrov *Russia* **53** B16
Novaya Zemlya *Russia* **52** B6
Nové Město *Slovak Rep.* **27** C10
Nové Město na Moravě
  Czech Rep. **26** B9
Nové Město nad Metují
  Czech Rep. **27** A9
Nové Zámky *Slovak Rep.* **27** C11
Novelda *Spain* **39** G4
Novellara *Italy* **40** D7
Noventa Vicentina *Italy* **41** C8
Novgorod *Russia* **32** C6
Novgorod □ *Russia* **32** C7
Novgorod-Severskiy =
  Novhorod-Siverskyy
  Ukraine **33** G7
Novhorod-Siverskyy *Ukraine* **33** G7
Novi Bečej *Serbia* **28** E5
Novi Iskar *Bulgaria* **44** D7
Novi Kneževac *Serbia* **28** D5
Novi Lígure *Italy* **40** D5
Novi Pazar *Bulgaria* **45** C11
Novi Pazar *Serbia* **44** C4
Novi Sad *Serbia* **28** E4
Novi Slankamen *Serbia* **28** E5
Novi Travnik *Bos.-H.* **28** F2
Novi Vinodolski *Croatia* **41** C11
Novigrad *Istra, Croatia* **41** C10
Novigrad *Zadar, Croatia* **41** D12
Novigradsko More *Croatia* **41** D12
Novo Hamburgo *Brazil* **127** B5
Novo Ivanivka *Ukraine* **29** E14
Novo Mesto *Slovenia* **41** C12
Novo Miloševo *Serbia* **28** E5
Novoaleksandrovsk *Russia* **35** H5
Novoaleksandrovskaya =
  Novoaleksandrovsk
  Russia **35** H5
Novoaltaysk *Russia* **52** D9
Novoannenskiy *Russia* **34** E6
Novoazovsk *Ukraine* **33** J10
Novocheboksarsk *Russia* **34** B8
Novocherkassk *Russia* **35** G5
Novodevichye *Russia* **34** D9
Novodvinsk *Russia* **52** C5
Novogrudok =
  Navahrudak *Belarus* **23** B13
Novohrad-Volynskyy
  Ukraine **23** C14
Novokachalinsk *Russia* **54** B5
Novokhopersk *Russia* **34** E5
Novokuybyshevsk *Russia* **34** D9
Novokuznetsk *Russia* **52** D9
Novolazarevskaya *Antarctica* **5** D3
Novomirgorod *Ukraine* **33** H6
Novomoskovsk *Russia* **32** E10
Novomoskovsk *Ukraine* **33** H8
Novopolotsk =
  Navapolatsk *Belarus* **32** E5
Novorossiysk *Russia* **33** K9
Novorybnoye *Russia* **53** B11
Novorzhev *Russia* **32** D5
Novosej *Albania* **44** E4
Novoselytsya *Ukraine* **29** B11
Novoshakhtinsk *Russia* **33** J10
Novosibirsk *Russia* **52** D9
Novosibirskiye Ostrova
  Russia **53** B15
Novosil *Russia* **32** E10
Novosokolniki *Russia* **32** D6
Novotitarovskaya *Russia* **35** H4
Novotroitsk *Russia* **52** D6
Novoukrayinka *Ukraine* **33** H6
Novouljanovsk *Russia* **34** C9
Novouzensk *Russia* **34** E9
Novovolynsk *Ukraine* **31** H11
Novovoronezhsky *Russia* **33** G10
Novoyavoriske *Ukraine* **31** J10

Novozybkov *Russia* **33** F6
Novska *Croatia* **41** C14
Nový Bor *Czech Rep.* **26** A7
Nový Bydžov *Czech Rep.* **26** A8
Nový Dvor *Belarus* **31** F11
Nový Jičín *Czech Rep.* **27** B11
Novyy Afon *Georgia* **35** J5
Novyy Buh *Ukraine* **33** J7
Novyy Oskol *Russia* **33** G9
Novyy Port *Russia* **52** C8
Novyy Urengoy *Russia* **52** C8
Nowa Deba *Poland* **31** H8
Nowa Ruda *Poland* **31** H3
Nowa Sarzyna *Poland* **31** H9
Nowa Sól *Poland* **31** G2
Nowata *U.S.A.* **116** C7
Nowbaran *Iran* **71** C6
Nowe *Poland* **30** E5
Nowe Miasteczko *Poland* **31** G2
Nowe Miasto *Poland* **31** G7
Nowe Miasto Lubawskie
  Poland **30** E6
Nowe Skalmierzyce *Poland* **31** G4
Nowe Warpno *Poland* **30** E1
Nowghab *Iran* **71** C8
Nowgong *Assam, India* **67** F18
Nowgong *Mad. P., India* **69** G8
Nowogard *Poland* **30** E2
Nowogród *Poland* **31** E8
Nowogród Bobrzanski
  Poland **31** G2
Nowogrodziec *Poland* **31** G2
Nowra *Australia* **95** E5
Nowshera *Pakistan* **66** C8
Nowy Dwór Gdański *Poland* **30** D6
Nowy Sącz *Poland* **31** J7
Nowy Staw *Poland* **30** D6
Nowy Targ *Poland* **31** J7
Nowy Tomyśl *Poland* **31** F3
Nowy Wiśnicz *Poland* **31** J7
Noxen *U.S.A.* **115** E8
Noyabr'sk *Russia* **52** C8
Noyant *France* **18** E7
Noyers *France* **19** E10
Noyon *France* **19** C9
Noyon *Mongolia* **56** C2
Nozay *France* **18** E5
Nqutu *S. Africa* **89** D5
Nsanje *Malawi* **87** F4
Nsawam *Ghana* **83** D4
Nseluka *Zambia* **87** E3
Nsomba *Zambia* **87** E2
Nsukka *Nigeria* **83** D6
Ntaria ☼ *Australia* **92** D5
Ntui *Cameroon* **83** E7
Ntungamo *Uganda* **86** C3
Nu Jiang → *China* **58** D2
Nu Shan *China* **58** E2
Nuba Mts. = Nubah,
  Jibalan *Sudan* **81** E3
Nubah, Jibalan *Sudan* **81** E3
Nubia *Africa* **76** D7
Nubian Desert = Nûbiya,
  Es Sahrâ en *Sudan* **80** C3
Nûbiya, Es Sahrâ en *Sudan* **80** C3
Nubledo *Spain* **36** B5
Nuboai *Indonesia* **63** E9
Nucet *Romania* **28** D7
Nueces → *U.S.A.* **116** H6
Nueltin L. *Canada* **103** A9
Nuestra Señora del Rosario
  de Caá-Catí *Argentina* **126** B4
Nueva Carteya *Spain* **37** H6
Nueva Ciudad Guerrero
  Mexico **119** B5
Nueva Gerona *Cuba* **120** B3
Nueva Palmira *Uruguay* **126** C4
Nueva Rosita *Mexico* **118** B4
Nueva San Salvador *El Salv.* **120** D2
Nueva Tabarca *Spain* **39** G4
Nuéve de Julio *Argentina* **126** D3
Nuevitas *Cuba* **120** B4
Nuevo, G. *Argentina* **128** E4
Nuevo Casas Grandes
  Mexico **118** A3
Nuevo Laredo *Mexico* **119** B5
Nuevo León □ *Mexico* **118** C5
Nuevo Rocafuerte *Ecuador* **124** D3
Nugget Pt. *N.Z.* **91** G2
Nugrus, Gebel *Egypt* **80** C3
Nuhaka *N.Z.* **91** C6
Nuits-St-Georges *France* **19** E11
Nukey Bluff *Australia* **95** E2
Nukhayb *Iraq* **73** F10
Nukheila *Sudan* **80** D2
Nuku Hiva *French Polynesia* **97** H13
Nuku'alofa *Tonga* **91** b
Nukus *Uzbekistan* **52** E6
Nulato *U.S.A.* **106** C8
Nules *Spain* **38** F4
Nullagine *Australia* **92** D3
Nullagine → *Australia* **92** D3
Nullarbor *Australia* **95** F5
Nullarbor △ *Australia* **93** F2
Nullarbor Plain *Australia* **93** F4

Numalla, L. *Australia* **95** D3
Numan *Nigeria* **83** D7
Numata *Japan* **55** F9
Numatinna → *Sudan* **81** F2
Numaykoos Lake △ *Canada* **103** B9
Numazu *Japan* **55** G9
Numbulwar *Australia* **94** A2
Numfoor *Indonesia* **63** E8
Numurkah *Australia* **95** F4
Nunaksaluk I. *Canada* **105** A7
Nunap Isua *Greenland* **98** D15
Nunavik *Greenland* **101** C21
Nunavut □ *Canada* **101** D15
Nunda *U.S.A.* **114** D7
Nuneaton *U.K.* **15** E6
Nungarin *Australia* **93** F2
Nungo *Mozam.* **87** E4
Nungwe *Tanzania* **86** C3
Nunivak I. *U.S.A.* **106** C6
Nunkun *India* **69** C7
Núoro *Italy* **42** B2
Nür *Iran* **71** B7
Nūrābād *Hormozgān, Iran* **71** E8
Nūrābād *Lorestān, Iran* **73** E12
Nure → *Italy* **40** C6
Nuremberg = Nürnberg
  Germany **25** F7
Nuri *Mexico* **118** B3
Nuri *Sudan* **80** D3
Nuriootpa *Australia* **95** E2
Nūristān □ *Afghan.* **66** B7
Nurlat *Russia* **34** C10
Nurmes *Finland* **8** E23
Nürnberg *Germany* **25** F7
Nurpur *Pakistan* **68** D4
Nurra, La *Italy* **42** B1
Nurran, L. = Terewah, L.
  Australia **95** D4
Nurrari Lakes *Australia* **93** E5
Nurri *Italy* **42** C2
Nürtingen *Germany* **25** G5
Nurzec → *Poland* **31** F9
Nus *Italy* **40** C4
Nusa Barung *Indonesia* **63** H15
Nusa Dua *Indonesia* **63** K18
Nusa Kambangan *Indonesia* **63** G13
Nusa Tenggara Barat □
  Indonesia **62** F5
Nusa Tenggara Timur □
  Indonesia **63** F6
Nusaybin *Turkey* **73** D9
Nushki *Pakistan* **68** E2
Nuuk *Greenland* **99** C14
Nuupere, Pte. *Moorea* **91** d
Nuwakot *Nepal* **69** E10
Nuwayb'ī, W. an →
  Si. Arabia **74** F3
Nuweiba' *Egypt* **70** D2
Nuwerus *S. Africa* **88** E2
Nuweveldberge *S. Africa* **88** E3
Nuyts, Pt. *Australia* **93** G2
Nuyts Arch. *Australia* **95** E1
Nxai Pan △ *Botswana* **88** B3
Nxaunxau *Botswana* **88** B3
Nyaake *Liberia* **82** E3
Nyabing *Australia* **93** F2
Nyack *U.S.A.* **115** E11
Nyagan *Russia* **52** C7
Nyahanga *Tanzania* **86** C3
Nyahua *Tanzania* **86** D3
Nyahururu *Kenya* **86** B4
Nyainqêntanglha Shan
  China **60** C4
Nyakanazi *Tanzania* **86** C3
Nyakrom *Ghana* **83** D4
Nyâlâ *Sudan* **81** E1
Nyamandhlovu *Zimbabwe* **87** F2
Nyambiti *Tanzania* **86** C3
Nyamira *Kenya* **86** B4
Nyamlell *Sudan* **81** F2
Nyamwaga *Tanzania* **86** C3
Nyandekwa *Tanzania* **86** C3
Nyanding → *Sudan* **81** F3
Nyandoma *Russia* **32** B11
Nyanga △ *Zimbabwe* **87** F3
Nyangana *Namibia* **88** B3
Nyanguge *Tanzania* **86** C3
Nyankpala *Ghana* **83** D4
Nyanza *Rwanda* **86** C2
Nyanza □ *Kenya* **86** C3
Nyanza-Lac *Burundi* **86** C2
Nyaponges *Sudan* **81** F3
Nyasa, L. = Malawi, L. *Africa* **87** E3
Nyasvizh *Belarus* **23** B14
Nyazura *Zimbabwe* **87** F3
Nyazwidzi → *Zimbabwe* **87** G3
Nyborg *Denmark* **11** J4
Nybro *Sweden* **11** H9
Nyda *Russia* **52** C8
Nyeboe Land *Greenland* **101** A20
Nyeri *Kenya* **86** C4
Nyerol *Sudan* **81** F3
Nyhammar *Sweden* **10** D8
Nyíka △ *Malawi* **87** E3
Nyimba *Zambia* **87** E3
Nyinahin *Ghana* **82** D4
Nyíradony *Hungary* **28** C7
Nyírbátor *Hungary* **28** C7
Nyíregyháza *Hungary* **28** C7
Nyiru, Mt. *Kenya* **86** B4

Nykarleby =
   Uusikaarlepyy *Finland* **8** E20
Nykøbing *Nordjylland,*
   Denmark **11** H2
Nykøbing *Sjælland, Denmark* **11** K5
Nykøbing *Sjælland, Denmark* **11** J5
Nyköping *Sweden* **11** F11
Nykroppa *Sweden* **10** E8
Nykvarn *Sweden* **10** E11
Nyland *Sweden* **10** A11
Nylstroom = Modimolle
   S. Africa **89** C4
Nymagee *Australia* **95** E4
Nymboida △ *Australia* **95** D5
Nymburk *Czech Rep.* **26** A8
Nynäshamn *Sweden* **11** F11
Nyngan *Australia* **95** E4
Nyoma Rap *India* **69** C8
Nyoman = Nemunas ➤
   Lithuania **30** C8
Nyon *Switz.* **25** J2
Nyong ➤ *Cameroon* **83** E6
Nyons *France* **21** D9
Nyou *Burkina Faso* **83** C4
Nýrsko *Czech Rep.* **26** B6
Nysa *Poland* **31** H4
Nysa ➤ *Europe* **24** C10
Nysa Kłodzka ➤ *Poland* **31** H4
Nysäter *Sweden* **10** E6
Nyslott = Savonlinna *Finland* **32** B5
Nyssa *U.S.A.* **108** E5
Nystad = Uusikaupunki
   Finland **32** B1
Nysted *Denmark* **11** K5
Nyunzu *Dem. Rep. of the Congo* **86** D2
Nyurba *Russia* **53** C12
Nyzhankovychi *Ukraine* **31** J9
Nyzhnohirskyy *Ukraine* **33** K8
Nyzhny Vorota *Ukraine* **28** B8
Nzébéla *Guinea* **82** D3
Nzega *Tanzania* **86** C3
Nzérékoré *Guinea* **82** D3
Nzeto *Angola* **84** F2
Nzilo, Chutes de
   Dem. Rep. of the Congo **87** E2
N'zo ➤ *Ivory C.* **82** D3
N'zo △ *Ivory C.* **82** D3
Nzubuka *Tanzania* **86** C3
Nzwani = Anjouan
   Comoros Is. **85** a

O

O Barco *Spain* **36** C4
O Carballiño *Spain* **36** C2
O Corgo *Spain* **36** C3
O Le Pupū Pu'e △ *Samoa* **91** b
O Pino *Spain* **36** C2
O Porriño *Spain* **36** C2
Ō-Shima *Hokkaidō, Japan* **54** D9
Ō-Shima *Shizuoka, Japan* **55** G9
Oa, Mull of *U.K.* **13** F2
Oacoma *U.S.A.* **112** D4
Oahe, L. *U.S.A.* **112** C3
Oahe Dam *U.S.A.* **112** C3
O'ahu *U.S.A.* **107** L8
Oak Harbor *U.S.A.* **110** B4
Oak Hill *U.S.A.* **113** G13
Oak Island *U.S.A.* **117** E15
Oak Ridge *U.S.A.* **117** C12
Oak View *U.S.A.* **111** L7
Oakan-Dake *Japan* **54** C12
Oakdale *Calif., U.S.A.* **110** H6
Oakdale *La., U.S.A.* **116** F8
Oakes *U.S.A.* **112** B4
Oakesdale *U.S.A.* **108** C5
Oakey *Australia* **95** D5
Oakfield *U.S.A.* **114** C6
Oakham *U.K.* **15** E7
Oakhurst *U.S.A.* **110** H7
Oakland *Calif., U.S.A.* **110** H4
Oakland *Pa., U.S.A.* **115** E9
Oakley *Idaho, U.S.A.* **108** E7
Oakley *Kans., U.S.A.* **112** F3
Oakover ➤ *Australia* **92** D3
Oakridge *U.S.A.* **108** E2
Oakville *Canada* **114** C5
Oakville *U.S.A.* **110** D3
Oamaru *N.Z.* **91** F3
Oancea *Romania* **29** E12
Oasi Faunistica di
   Vendicari △ *Italy* **43** F8
Oasis *Calif., U.S.A.* **110** H9
Oasis *Calif., U.S.A.* **111** M10
Oates Land *Antarctica* **5** C11
Oatman *U.S.A.* **111** K12
Oaxaca *Mexico* **119** D5
Oaxaca □ *Mexico* **119** D5
Ob ➤ *Russia* **52** C7
Oba *Canada* **104** C3
Obala *Cameroon* **83** E7
Obama *Japan* **55** G7
Oban *Nigeria* **83** D6
Oban *U.K.* **13** E3
Obbia = Hobyo *Somali Rep.* **75** F4
Oberá *Argentina* **127** B4
Oberammergau *Germany* **25** H7
Oberasbach *Germany* **25** F6
Oberbayern □ *Germany* **25** G7
Oberdrauburg *Austria* **26** E5

Obere Donau △ *Germany* **25** G5
Oberer Bayerischer
   Wald △ *Germany* **25** F8
Oberfranken □ *Germany* **25** E7
Oberhausen *Germany* **24** D2
Oberkirch *Germany* **25** G4
Oberlausitz *Germany* **24** D10
Oberlin *Kans., U.S.A.* **112** F3
Oberlin *La., U.S.A.* **116** K8
Oberlin *Ohio, U.S.A.* **114** E2
Obernai *France* **19** D14
Oberndorf *Germany* **25** G4
Oberon *Australia* **95** E4
Oberösterreich □ *Austria* **26** C7
Oberpfalz □ *Germany* **25** F8
Oberpfälzer Wald *Germany* **25** F8
Oberpfälzer Wald △ *Germany* **25** F8
Oberstdorf *Germany* **25** H6
Obertyn *Ukraine* **29** B10
Oberursel *Germany* **25** E4
Oberwart *Austria* **27** D9
Obi, Kepulauan *Indonesia* **63** E7
Obiaruku *Nigeria* **83** D6
Óbidos *Brazil* **125** D7
Óbidos *Portugal* **37** F1
Obihiro *Japan* **54** C11
Obilatu *Indonesia* **63** E7
Obilnoye *Russia* **35** G7
Obing *Germany* **25** G8
Objat *France* **20** C5
Obluchye *Russia* **53** E14
Obninsk *Russia* **32** E9
Obo *C.A.R.* **86** A2
Obock *Djibouti* **81** E5
Obodivka *Ukraine* **29** B14
Oborniki *Poland* **31** F3
Oborniki Śląskie *Poland* **31** G3
Oboyan *Russia* **33** G9
Obozerskaya = Obozerskiy
   Russia **52** C5
Obozerskiy *Russia* **52** C5
Obrenovac *Serbia* **44** B4
Obrovac *Croatia* **41** D12
Obruk *Turkey* **72** C5
Obrzycko *Poland* **31** F3
Observatory Inlet *Canada* **102** B3
Obshchi Syrt *Russia* **6** E16
Obskaya Guba *Russia* **52** C8
Obuasi *Ghana* **83** D4
Obubra *Nigeria* **83** D6
Obudu *Nigeria* **83** D6
Obwalden □ *Switz.* **25** J4
Obzor *Bulgaria* **45** D11
Ocala *U.S.A.* **117** G13
Ocampo *Chihuahua, Mexico* **118** B3
Ocampo *Tamaulipas, Mexico* **119** C5
Ocaña *Spain* **36** F7
Occidental, Cordillera
   Colombia **124** C3
Occidental, Grand Erg
   Algeria **78** B6
Ocean City *Md., U.S.A.* **113** F16
Ocean City *N.J., U.S.A.* **113** F16
Ocean City *Wash., U.S.A.* **110** C2
Ocean Falls *Canada* **102** C3
Ocean I. = Banaba *Kiribati* **96** H8
Ocean Park *U.S.A.* **110** D2
Oceano *U.S.A.* **111** K6
Oceanport *U.S.A.* **115** F10
Oceanside *U.S.A.* **111** M9
Ochagavía *Spain* **38** C3
Ochakiv *Ukraine* **33** J6
Ochamchira *Georgia* **35** J5
Ochi, Óros *Greece* **46** D5
Ochil Hills *U.K.* **13** E5
Ocho Rios *Jamaica* **120** a
Ochsenfurt *Germany* **25** F6
Ochsenhausen *Germany* **25** G5
Ocilla *U.S.A.* **117** F13
Ockelbo *Sweden* **10** D10
Ocmulgee ➤ *U.S.A.* **117** F13
Ocna Mureş *Romania* **29** D8
Ocna Sibiului *Romania* **29** E9
Ocnele Mari *Romania* **29** E9
Ocniţa *Moldova* **29** B12
Oconee ➤ *U.S.A.* **117** F13
Oconomowoc *U.S.A.* **112** D9
Oconto *U.S.A.* **112** C10
Oconto Falls *U.S.A.* **112** C9
Ocosingo *Mexico* **119** D6
Ocotal *Nic.* **120** D2
Ocotlán *Jalisco, Mexico* **118** C4
Ocotlán *Oaxaca, Mexico* **119** D5
Ocreza ➤ *Portugal* **37** F3
Ócsa *Hungary* **28** C4
Octeville *France* **18** C5
Oda *Ghana* **83** D4
Ōda *Japan* **55** G6
Oda, J. *Sudan* **80** C4
Ódáðahraun *Iceland* **8** D5
Ódaejin *N. Korea* **56** D4
Ödåkra *Sweden* **11** H6
Odate *Japan* **54** D10
Odawara *Japan* **55** G9
Odda *Norway* **9** F12
Odder *Denmark* **11** J4
Odei ➤ *Canada* **103** B9
Odemira *Portugal* **37** H2
Ödemiş *Turkey* **47** C9
Odendaalsrus *S. Africa* **88** D4

Odensbacken *Sweden* **10** E9
Odense *Denmark* **11** J4
Odenwald = Neckartal-
   Odenwald △ *Germany* **25** F5
Odenwald *Germany* **25** F5
Oder ➤ *Europe* **24** B10
Oder-Havel Kanal *Germany* **24** C10
Oderzo *Italy* **41** C9
Odesa *Ukraine* **33** J6
Odesa □ *Ukraine* **33** J5
Ödeshög *Sweden* **11** F8
Odessa = Odesa *Ukraine* **33** J6
Odessa *Canada* **115** B8
Odessa *Tex., U.S.A.* **116** F3
Odessa *Wash., U.S.A.* **108** C4
Odiakwe *Botswana* **88** C4
Odiel ➤ *Spain* **37** H4
Odienné *Ivory C.* **82** D3
Odintsovo *Russia* **32** E9
Odiongan *Phil.* **61** E4
Odobeşti *Romania* **29** E12
Odolanów *Poland* **31** G4
O'Donnell *U.S.A.* **116** E4
O'Donnell Pt. *Canada* **114** A4
Odorheiu Secuiesc *Romania* **29** D10
Odoyevo *Russia* **32** F9
Odra = Oder ➤ *Europe* **24** B10
Odra ➤ *Spain* **36** C6
Odžaci *Serbia* **28** E4
Odžak *Bos.-H.* **28** E3
Odzi *Zimbabwe* **89** B5
Odzi ➤ *Zimbabwe* **89** B5
Oebisfelde *Germany* **24** C6
Oeiras *Brazil* **125** E10
Oeiras *Portugal* **37** G1
Oelrichs *U.S.A.* **112** D2
Oelsnitz *Germany* **25** E8
Oelwein *U.S.A.* **112** D8
Oeno I. *Pac. Oc.* **97** K14
Oenpelli = Gunbalanya
   Australia **92** B5
Oetz *Austria* **26** D3
Of *Turkey* **73** B9
Ofanto ➤ *Italy* **43** A9
Offa *Nigeria* **83** D5
Offaly □ *Ireland* **12** C4
Offenbach *Germany* **25** E4
Offenburg *Germany* **25** G3
Officer Cr. ➤ *Australia* **93** E5
Offida *Italy* **41** F10
Ofidousa *Greece* **47** E8
Ofolanga *Tonga* **91** c
Ofotfjorden *Norway* **8** B17
Ofu *Amer. Samoa* **91** b
Ōfunato *Japan* **54** E10
Oga *Japan* **54** E9
Oga-Hantō *Japan* **54** E9
Ogaden *Ethiopia* **75** F3
Ōgaki *Japan* **55** G8
Ogallala *U.S.A.* **112** E3
Ogasawara Gunto *Pac. Oc.* **51** F16
Ogbomosho *Nigeria* **83** D5
Ogden *U.S.A.* **108** F8
Ogdensburg *U.S.A.* **115** B9
Ogea Driki *Fiji* **91** a
Ogea Levu *Fiji* **91** a
Ogeechee ➤ *U.S.A.* **117** F14
Ogilby *U.S.A.* **111** N12
Oglio ➤ *Italy* **40** C7
Óglio Nord △ *Italy* **40** C6
Óglio Sud △ *Italy* **40** C7
Ogmore *Australia* **94** C4
Ognon ➤ *France* **19** E12
Ogoja *Nigeria* **83** D6
Ogoki *Canada* **104** B2
Ogoki ➤ *Canada* **104** B2
Ogoki L. *Canada* **104** B2
Ogoki Res. *Canada* **104** B2
Ogooué ➤ *Gabon* **84** E1
Ogowe = Ogooué ➤ *Gabon* **84** E1
Ogr = Sharafa *Sudan* **81** E2
Ograźden *Macedonia* **44** E6
Ogre *Latvia* **32** D3
Ogrein *Sudan* **80** D3
Ogulin *Croatia* **41** C12
Ogun □ *Nigeria* **83** D5
Ogurচinskiy, Ostrov
   Turkmenistan **71** B7
Oguta *Nigeria* **83** D6
Ogüzeli *Turkey* **72** D7
Ogwashi-Uku *Nigeria* **83** D6
Ogwe *Nigeria* **83** E6
Ohai *N.Z.* **91** F2
Ohakune *N.Z.* **91** C5
Ohata *Japan* **54** D10
Ohau, L. *N.Z.* **91** F2
Ohio □ *U.S.A.* **114** F2
Ohio ➤ *U.S.A.* **112** G9
Ohře ➤ *Czech Rep.* **26** A7
Ohre ➤ *Germany* **24** C7
Ohrid *Macedonia* **44** E4
Ohridsko Jezero *Macedonia* **44** E4
Ohrigstad *S. Africa* **89** C5
Öhringen *Germany* **25** F5
Oi Qu *China* **58** C3
Oiapoque *Brazil* **125**
Oikou *China* **57** E9
Oil City *U.S.A.* **114** E5

Oil Springs *Canada* **114** D2
Oildale *U.S.A.* **111** K7
Oinousa = Inousses *Greece* **47** C8
Oise □ *France* **19** C9
Oise ➤ *France* **19** C9
Oiseaux du Djoudj △ *Senegal* **82** B1
Oistins *Barbados* **121** g
Oistins B. *Barbados* **121** g
Ōita *Japan* **55** H5
Ōita □ *Japan* **55** H5
Oiticica *Brazil* **125** E10
Ojai *U.S.A.* **111** L7
Ojcowski △ *Poland* **31** H6
Ojinaga *Mexico* **118** B4
Ojiya *Japan* **55** F9
Ojo Caliente *Mexico* **118** C4
Ojo de Liebre, L. *Mexico* **118** B2
Ojos del Salado, Cerro
   Argentina **126** B2
Oka *Nigeria* **83** D5
Oka ➤ *Russia* **34** B7
Okaba *Indonesia* **63** F9
Okahandja *Namibia* **88** C2
Okanagan L. *Canada* **102** D5
Okandja *Gabon* **84** E2
Okanogan *U.S.A.* **108** B4
Okanogan ➤ *U.S.A.* **108** B4
Okanogan Range *N. Amer.* **102** D5
Okány *Hungary* **28** D6
Okapi △
   Dem. Rep. of the Congo **86** B2
Okaputa *Namibia* **88** C2
Okara *Pakistan* **68** D5
Okaukuejo *Namibia* **88** B2
Okavango Delta *Botswana* **88** B3
Okavango Swamp =
   Okavango Delta *Botswana* **88** B3
Okaya *Japan* **55** F9
Okayama *Japan* **55** G6
Okayama □ *Japan* **55** G6
Okazaki *Japan* **55** G8
Oke-Iho *Nigeria* **83** D5
Okeechobee *U.S.A.* **117** H14
Okeechobee, L. *U.S.A.* **117** H14
Okefenokee △ *U.S.A.* **117** F13
Okefenokee Swamp *U.S.A.* **117** F13
Okehampton *U.K.* **15** G4
Okene *Nigeria* **83** D6
Oker ➤ *Germany* **24** C6
Okha *India* **68** H3
Okha *Russia* **53** D15
Okhotsk *Russia* **53** D15
Okhotsk, Sea of *Asia* **53** D15
Okhotskiy Perevoz *Russia* **53** C14
Okhtyrka *Ukraine* **33** G8
Oki-Shotō *Japan* **55** F6
Ōkigwi *Nigeria* **83** D6
Okija *Nigeria* **83** D6
Okinawa *Japan* **55** L3
Okinawa □ *Japan* **55** L4
Okinawa-Guntō *Japan* **55** L4
Okinawa-Jima *Japan* **55** L4
Okino-erabu-Shima *Japan* **55** L4
Okitipupa *Nigeria* **83** D5
Oklahoma □ *U.S.A.* **116** D6
Oklahoma City *U.S.A.* **116** D6
Okmulgee *U.S.A.* **116** D7
Oknitsa = Ocniţa *Moldova* **29** B12
Oko, W. ➤ *Sudan* **80** C4
Okolo *Uganda* **86** B3
Okolona *U.S.A.* **117** E10
Okombahe *Namibia* **88** C2
Okonek *Poland* **30** E3
Okotoks *Canada* **102** C6
Okrika *Nigeria* **83** E6
Oksibil *Indonesia* **63** E10
Ólimbos, Óros = Olympos
   Oros *Greece* **44** F6
Oktyabrsk = Qandyaghash
   Kazakhstan **52** E6
Oktyabrsk *Russia* **34** D9
Oktyabrskiy = Aktsyabrski
   Belarus **23** B15
Oktyabrskiy *Kamchatka,*
   Russia **53** D16
Oktyabrskiy *Rostov, Russia* **35** G5
Oktyabrskoy Revolyutsii,
   Ostrov *Russia* **53** B10
Oktyabrskoye = Zhovtneve
   Ukraine **33** J7
Okulovka *Russia* **32** C7
Okuru *N.Z.* **91** E2
Okushiri-Tō *Japan* **54** C9
Okwa ➤ *Botswana* **88** C3
Ola *Russia* **53** D16
Ólafsfjörður *Iceland* **8** C4
Ólafsvík *Iceland* **8** D2
Olaine *Latvia* **30** B10
Olancha *U.S.A.* **111** J8
Olancha Pk. *U.S.A.* **111** J8
Olanchito *Honduras* **120** C2
Öland *Sweden* **11** H10
Ölands norra udde *Sweden* **11** G11
Ölands södra udde *Sweden* **11** H10
Olargues *France* **20** E6
Olary *Australia* **95** E3

Olathe *U.S.A.* **112** F6
Olavarría *Argentina* **126** D3
Oława *Poland* **31** H4
Olbernhau *Germany* **24** E9
Ólbia *Italy* **42** B2
Ólbia, G. di *Italy* **42** B2
Olching *Germany* **25** G7
Olcott *U.S.A.* **114** C6
Old Bahama Chan. =
   Bahama, Canal Viejo de
   W. Indies **120** B4
Old Baldy Pk. = San
   Antonio, Mt. *U.S.A.* **111** L9
Old Bridge *U.S.A.* **115** F10
Old Castile = Castilla y
   Leon □ *Spain* **36** D6
Old Crow *Canada* **100** D4
Old Dale *U.S.A.* **111** L11
Old Forge *N.Y., U.S.A.* **115** C10
Old Forge *Pa., U.S.A.* **115** E9
Old Mapoon ◎ *Australia* **94** A3
Old Perlican *Canada* **105** C9
Old Shinyanga *Tanzania* **86** C3
Old Speck Mt. *U.S.A.* **115** B14
Old Town *U.S.A.* **113** C19
Old Washington *U.S.A.* **114** F3
Old Wives L. *Canada* **103** C7
Oldbury *U.K.* **15** F5
Oldcastle *Ireland* **12** C4
Oldeani *Tanzania* **86** C4
Oldenburg
   Schleswig-Holstein, Germany **24** A6
Oldenburg
   Niedersachsen,
   Germany **24** B4
Oldenzaal *Neths.* **17** B6
Oldham *U.K.* **14** D5
Oldman ➤ *Canada* **102** D6
Oldmeldrum *U.K.* **13** D6
Olds *Canada* **102** C6
Olduvai Gorge *Tanzania* **86** C4
Oldziyt *Mongolia* **56** B5
Olean *U.S.A.* **114** D6
Olecko *Poland* **30** D9
Oléggio *Italy* **40** C5
Oleiros *Portugal* **36** F3
Oleiros *Spain* **36** B2
Olekma ➤ *Russia* **53** C13
Olekminsk *Russia* **53** C13
Oleksandriya *Kirovohrad,*
   Ukraine **33** H7
Oleksandriya *Rivne, Ukraine* **23** C14
Oleksandrovka *Ukraine* **33** H7
Olema *U.S.A.* **110** G4
Olenegorsk *Russia* **8** B25
Olenek *Russia* **53** C12
Olenek ➤ *Russia* **53** B13
Olenino *Russia* **32** D7
Oléron, Î. d' *France* **20** C2
Olesk *Ukraine* **31** G11
Oleśnica *Poland* **31** G4
Olesno *Poland* **31** H5
Olevsk *Ukraine* **23** C14
Olga, L. *Canada* **104** C4
Olgas, The = Kata Tjuta
   Australia **93** E5
Ölgiy *Mongolia* **52** E9
Ølgod *Denmark* **11** J2
Olhão *Portugal* **37** H3
Olhopil *Ukraine* **29** B14
Olhovatka *Russia* **30** D9
Olib *Croatia* **41** D11
Oliena *Italy* **42** B2
Oliete *Spain* **38** D4
Olifants = Elefantes ➤ *Africa* **89** C5
Olifants ➤ *Namibia* **88** C2
Olifantshoek *S. Africa* **88** D3
Ólimbos *Greece* **47** F9
Ólimbos, Óros = Olympos
   Oros *Greece* **44** F6
Olímpia *Brazil* **127** A6
Olinda *Brazil* **125** E12
Olite *Spain* **38** C3
Oliva *Argentina* **126** C3
Oliva *Spain* **39** G4
Oliva, Punta del *Spain* **36** B5
Oliva de la Frontera *Spain* **37** G4
Olivares, Cerro los *Argentina* **126** C2
Olivares de Júcar *Spain* **38** F2
Olive Branch *U.S.A.* **117** D10
Olivehurst *U.S.A.* **110** G5
Oliveira de Azeméis *Portugal* **36** E2
Oliveira do Douro *Portugal* **36** D2
Olivenza *Spain* **37** G3
Oliver *Canada* **102** D5
Oliver L. *Canada* **103** B8
Olivet *France* **19** E8
Olkhovka *Russia* **34** F7
Olkusz *Poland* **31** H6
Ollagüe *Chile* **126** A2
Olmaliq *Uzbekistan* **52** E7
Olmedo *Spain* **36** D6
Olmeto *France* **21** G12
Olney *Ill., U.S.A.* **112** F9
Olney *Tex., U.S.A.* **116** E5
Olofström *Sweden* **11** H8
Oloitokitok *Kenya* **86** C4
Oloma *Cameroon* **83** E7
Olomane ➤ *Canada* **105** B7

Olomouc *Czech Rep.* **27** B10
Olomoucký □ *Czech Rep.* **27** B10
Olonets *Russia* **32** B7
Olongapo *Phil.* **61** D4
Olonne-sur-Mer *France* **20** E2
Oloron, Gave d' ➤ *France* **20** E2
Oloron-Ste-Marie *France* **20** E3
Olosega *Amer. Samoa* **91** b
Olosenga = Swains I.
   Amer. Samoa **97** J11
Olot *Spain* **38** C7
Olovo *Bos.-H.* **28** F3
Olovyannaya *Russia* **53** D12
Oloy ➤ *Russia* **53** C16
Olsberg *Germany* **24** D4
Olshammar *Sweden* **11** F8
Olshanka *Ukraine* **33** H6
Olshany *Ukraine* **33** G8
Olsztyn *Poland* **30** E7
Olsztynek *Poland* **30** E7
Olt □ *Romania* **29** F9
Olt ➤ *Romania* **29** G9
Olten *Switz.* **25** H3
Olteniţa *Romania* **29** F11
Olton *U.S.A.* **116** D3
Oltu *Turkey* **73** B9
Oluan Pi *Taiwan* **59** G13
Olula del Rio *Spain* **39** H2
Olur *Turkey* **73** B10
Olutanga *Phil.* **61** H5
Olvega *Spain* **38** D2
Olvera *Spain* **37** J5
Olymbos *Cyprus* **49** D12
Olympos Oros *Greece* **44** F6
Olympia *Greece* **46** D3
Olympia *U.S.A.* **110** D4
Olympic △ *U.S.A.* **110** C3
Olympic Dam *Australia* **95** E2
Olympic Mts. *U.S.A.* **110** C3
Olympus *Cyprus* **49** E11
Olympus, Mt. = Olymbos
   Oros *Greece* **44** F6
Olympus, Mt. = Uludağ
   Turkey **45** F13
Olympus, Mt. *U.S.A.* **110** C3
Olyphant *U.S.A.* **115** E9
Olyutorskiy, Mys *Russia* **53** D18
Om ➤ *Russia* **52** D8
Om Hajer *Eritrea* **81** E4
Om Koi *Thailand* **64** D2
Ōma *Japan* **54** D10
Ōmachi *Japan* **55** F8
Omae-Zaki *Japan* **55** G9
Ōmagari *Japan* **54** E10
Omagh *U.K.* **12** B4
Omagh □ *U.K.* **12** B4
Omaha *U.S.A.* **112** E6
Omak *U.S.A.* **108** B4
Omalos *Greece* **49** D5
Oman ■ *Asia* **75** C6
Oman, G. of *Asia* **71** E8
Omaruru *Namibia* **88** C2
Omaruru ➤ *Namibia* **88** C1
Omate *Peru* **124** D4
Ombai, Selat *Indonesia* **63** F6
Omboué *Gabon* **84** E1
Ombrone ➤ *Italy* **40** F8
Omdurmân *Sudan* **81** D3
Omegna *Italy* **40** C5
Omemee *Canada* **114** B6
Omeonga
   Dem. Rep. of the Congo **86** C1
Ometepe, I. de *Nic.* **120** D2
Ometepec *Mexico* **119** D5
Ominato *Japan* **54** D10
Omineca ➤ *Canada* **102** B4
Omineca Mts. *Canada* **102** B3
Omiš *Croatia* **41** E13
Omišalj *Croatia* **41** C11
Omitara *Namibia* **88** C2
Ōmiya = Saitama *Japan* **55** G9
Omme Å ➤ *Denmark* **11** J2
Ommen *Neths.* **17** B6
Ömnögovi □ *Mongolia* **56** C3
Omo ➤ *Ethiopia* **81** F4
Omo △ *Ethiopia* **81** F4
Omo Valley *Ethiopia* **81** F4
Omodeo, L. *Italy* **42** B1
Omodhos *Cyprus* **49** E11
Omoko *Nigeria* **83** D6
Omolon ➤ *Russia* **53** C16
Omono-Gawa ➤ *Japan* **54** E10
Ompha *Canada* **115** B8
Omsk *Russia* **52** D8
Omsukchan *Russia* **53** C16
Ōmu *Japan* **54** B11
Omul, Vf. *Romania* **29** E10
Omulew ➤ *Poland* **31** E8
Ōmura *Japan* **55** H4
Omuramba Omatako ➤
   Namibia **88** B2
Omuramba Ovambo ➤
   Namibia **88** B2
Ōmurtag *Bulgaria* **45** C10
Ōmuta *Japan* **55** H5
Oña *Spain* **36** C7
Onaga *U.S.A.* **112** F6
Onalaska *U.S.A.* **112** D8
Onancock *U.S.A.* **113** G16
Onang *Indonesia* **63** E5

Onangue, L. *Gabon* **84** E2
Onaping L. *Canada* **104** C3
Oñati *Spain* **38** B2
Onavas *Mexico* **118** B3
Onawa *U.S.A.* **112** D5
Oncócua *Angola* **88** B1
Onda *Spain* **38** F4
Ondangwa *Namibia* **88** B2
Ondarroa *Spain* **38** B2
Ondava → *Slovak Rep.* **27** C14
Ondjiva *Angola* **88** B2
Ondo *Nigeria* **83** D5
Ondo □ *Nigeria* **83** D6
Öndörshil *Mongolia* **56** B5
Öndverðarnes *Iceland* **8** D2
One Arm Point *Australia* **92** C3
One Arm Point ⊚ *Australia* **92** C3
One Tree *Australia* **95** E3
Oneata *Fiji* **91** a
Onega *Russia* **52** C4
Onega → *Russia* **6** C13
Onega, L. = Onezhskoye Ozero *Russia* **32** B8
Oneida *U.S.A.* **115** C9
Oneida L. *U.S.A.* **115** C9
O'Neill *U.S.A.* **112** D4
Onekotan, Ostrov *Russia* **53** E16
Onema *Dem. Rep. of the Congo* **86** C1
Oneonta *U.S.A.* **115** D9
Oneşti *Romania* **29** D11
Onezhskoye Ozero *Russia* **32** B8
Ongarue *N.Z.* **91** C5
Ongea Levu = Ogea Levu *Fiji* **91** a
Ongers → *S. Africa* **88** E3
Ongerup *Australia* **93** F2
Ongjin *N. Korea* **57** F13
Ongkharak *Thailand* **64** E3
Ongniud Qi *China* **57** C10
Ongoka *Dem. Rep. of the Congo* **86** C2
Ongole *India* **66** M12
Ongon = Havirga *Mongolia* **56** B7
Oni *Georgia* **35** J6
Onida *U.S.A.* **112** C4
Onilahy → *Madag.* **89** C7
Onitsha *Nigeria* **83** D6
Ono *Fiji* **91** a
Onoda *Japan* **55** G5
Ons, I. de *Spain* **36** C2
Onsala *Sweden* **11** G6
Onslow *Australia* **92** D2
Onslow B. *U.S.A.* **117** D16
Ontake-San *Japan* **55** G8
Ontario *Calif., U.S.A.* **111** L9
Ontario *Oreg., U.S.A.* **108** D5
Ontario □ *Canada* **104** B2
Ontario, L. *N. Amer.* **114** C7
Ontinyent *Spain* **39** G4
Ontonagon *U.S.A.* **112** B9
Ontur *Spain* **39** G3
Onyx *U.S.A.* **111** K8
Oodnadatta *Australia* **95** D2
Ooldea *Australia* **93** F5
Oombulgurri *Australia* **92** C4
Oombulgurri ⊚ *Australia* **92** C4
Oorindi *Australia* **94** C3
Oost-Vlaanderen □ *Belgium* **17** C3
Oostende *Belgium* **17** C2
Oosterhout *Neths.* **17** C4
Oosterschelde → *Neths.* **17** C4
Oosterwolde *Neths.* **17** B6
Ootacamund = Udagamandalam *India* **66** P10
Ootsa L. *Canada* **102** C3
Ooty = Udagamandalam *India* **66** P10
Op Luang △ *Thailand* **64** C2
Opaka *Bulgaria* **45** C10
Opala *Dem. Rep. of the Congo* **86** C1
Opalenica *Poland* **31** F3
Opan *Bulgaria* **45** D9
Opanake *Sri Lanka* **66** R12
Opasatika *Canada* **104** C3
Opasquia ○ *Canada* **104** B1
Opatija *Croatia* **41** C11
Opatów *Poland* **31** H8
Opava *Czech Rep.* **27** B10
Opelika *U.S.A.* **117** E12
Opelousas *U.S.A.* **116** F8
Opémisca, L. *Canada* **104** C5
Opheim *U.S.A.* **108** B10
Ophthalmia Ra. *Australia* **92** D2
Opi *Nigeria* **83** D6
Opinaca → *Canada* **104** B4
Opinaca, Rés. *Canada* **104** B4
Opinnagau → *Canada* **104** B3
Opiscotéo, L. *Canada* **105** B6
Opobo *Nigeria* **83** E6
Opochka *Russia* **32** D5
Opoczno *Poland* **31** G7
Opol *Phil.* **61** G6
Opole *Poland* **31** H4
Opole Lubelskie *Poland* **31** G8
Opolskie □ *Poland* **31** H5
Oponono L. *Namibia* **88** B2
Oporto = Porto *Portugal* **36** D2
Opotiki *N.Z.* **91** C6
Opp *U.S.A.* **117** F11
Oppdal *Norway* **8** E13
Óppido Mamertina *Italy* **43** D8
Opportunity *U.S.A.* **108** C5

Oprişor *Romania* **28** F8
Oprtalj *Croatia* **41** C10
Opua *N.Z.* **91** A5
Opunake *N.Z.* **91** C4
Opuzen *Croatia* **41** E14
Ora *Cyprus* **49** E12
Oracle *U.S.A.* **109** K8
Oradea *Romania* **28** D2
Öræfajökull *Iceland* **8** D5
Orahovac *Kosovo* **44** D4
Orahovica *Croatia* **28** E2
Orai *India* **69** G8
Oraison *France* **21** E9
Oral = Zhayyq → *Kazakhstan* **6** F16
Oral *Kazakhstan* **34** E10
Oran *Algeria* **78** A5
Orange *Australia* **95** E4
Orange *France* **21** D8
Orange *Calif., U.S.A.* **111** M9
Orange *Mass., U.S.A.* **115** D12
Orange *Tex., U.S.A.* **116** F8
Orange *Va., U.S.A.* **113** F14
Orange → *S. Africa* **88** D2
Orange, C. *Brazil* **124** B4
Orange Cove *U.S.A.* **110** J7
Orange Free State = Free State □ *S. Africa* **88** D4
Orange Grove *U.S.A.* **116** H6
Orange Walk *Belize* **119** D7
Orangeburg *U.S.A.* **117** E14
Orangeville *Canada* **114** C4
Orango *Guinea-Biss.* **82** C1
Orani *Phil.* **61** D4
Oranienburg *Germany* **24** C9
Oranje = Orange → *S. Africa* **88** D2
Oranjemund *Namibia* **88** D2
Oranjerivier *S. Africa* **88** D3
Oranjestad *Aruba* **121** D5
Orapa *Botswana* **85** J5
Oras *Phil.* **61** E6
Orašje *Bos.-H.* **28** E3
Orăştie *Romania* **29** E8
Orava → *Slovak Rep.* **27** B12
Orava, Vodna nádriž *Slovak Rep.* **27** B12
Oraviţa *Romania* **28** E6
Orb → *France* **20** E7
Orba → *Italy* **40** D5
Ørbæk *Denmark* **11** J4
Orbe *Switz.* **25** J2
Orbec *France* **18** C7
Orbetello *Italy* **41** F8
Órbigo → *Spain* **36** C5
Orbisonia *U.S.A.* **114** F7
Orbost *Australia* **95** F4
Örbyhus *Sweden* **10** D11
Órcia → *Italy* **41** F8
Orco → *Italy* **40** C4
Ord *U.S.A.* **112** E4
Ord → *Australia* **92** C4
Ord, Mt. *Australia* **92** C4
Ord Mts. *U.S.A.* **111** L10
Ordenes = Ordes *Spain* **36** B2
Orderville *U.S.A.* **109** H7
Ordes *Spain* **36** B2
Ordesa y Monte Perido △ *Spain* **38** C4
Ording = St-Peter-Ording *Germany* **24** A4
Ordos = Mu Us Shamo *China* **56** E5
Ordu *Turkey* **72** B7
Ordu □ *Turkey* **72** B7
Ordubad *Azerbaijan* **73** C12
Órdua Álava, *Spain* **38** D2
Orduña *Granada, Spain* **37** H7
Ordway *U.S.A.* **108** G12
Ordzhonïkïdze *Ukraine* **33** J8
Ore *Dem. Rep. of the Congo* **86** B2
Ore Mts. = Erzgebirge *Germany* **24** E8
Orebić *Croatia* **41** F14
Örebro *Sweden* **10** E9
Örebro län □ *Sweden* **10** E8
Orecchiella △ *Italy* **40** D7
Oregon *U.S.A.* **112** D9
Oregon □ *U.S.A.* **108** E3
Oregon City *U.S.A.* **110** E4
Oregon Dunes △ *U.S.A.* **108** E1
Öregrund *Sweden* **10** D12
Öregrundsgrepen *Sweden* **10** D12
Orekhov = Orikhiv *Ukraine* **33** J8
Orekhovo-Zuyevo *Russia* **32** E10
Orel *Russia* **33** F9
Orel □ *Russia* **33** F9
Orel → *Ukraine* **33** H8
Orellana, Canal de *Spain* **37** F5
Orellana la Vieja *Spain* **37** F5

Orem *U.S.A.* **108** F8
Ören *Turkey* **47** D9
Orenburg *Russia* **52** D6
Orencik *Turkey* **47** B11
Orense = Ourense *Spain* **36** C3
Orepuki *N.Z.* **91** G1
Orestes Pereyra *Mexico* **118** B3
Orestiada *Greece* **45** E10
Øresund *Europe* **11** J6
Orfanos Kolpos *Greece* **44** F7
Orford Ness *U.K.* **15** E9
Organ Pipe Cactus △ *U.S.A.* **109** K7
Organos, Pta. de los *Canary Is.* **48** F2
Organyà *Spain* **38** C6
Orgaz *Spain* **37** F7
Orgeyev = Orhei *Moldova* **29** C13
Orhaneli *Turkey* **45** G12
Orhaneli → *Turkey* **45** G12
Orhangazi *Turkey* **45** F13
Orhei *Moldova* **29** C13
Orhon Gol → *Mongolia* **53** D11
Ória *Italy* **43** B10
Oriental, Cordillera *Colombia* **124** B4
Oriental, Grand Erg *Algeria* **78** B7
Orientale □ *Dem. Rep. of the Congo* **86** B2
Oriente *Argentina* **126** D3
Orihuela *Spain* **39** G4
Orihuela del Tremedal *Spain* **38** E3
Orikhiv *Ukraine* **33** J8
Orikum *Albania* **44** F3
Orillia *Canada* **114** B5
Orinoco → *Venezuela* **124** B6
Orion *Canada* **103** D6
Oriskany *U.S.A.* **115** C9
Orissa □ *India* **67** K14
Orissaare *Estonia* **32** C2
Oristano *Italy* **42** C1
Oristano, G. di *Italy* **42** C1
Orizaba *Mexico* **119** D5
Orizaba, Pico de *Mexico* **119** D5
Orizare *Bulgaria* **45** D11
Orjen *Bos.-H.* **44** D2
Orjiva *Spain* **37** J7
Orkanger *Norway* **8** E13
Örkelljunga *Sweden* **11** H7
Örken *Sweden* **11** G9
Örkény *Hungary* **28** C4
Orkla → *Norway* **8** E13
Orkney *S. Africa* **88** D4
Orkney □ *U.K.* **13** B5
Orkney Is. *U.K.* **13** B6
Orland *U.S.A.* **110** F4
Orlando *U.S.A.* **117** G14
Orlando, C. d' *Italy* **43** D7
Orléanais *France* **19** E9
Orléans *France* **19** E8
Orleans *U.S.A.* **115** B12
Orléans, Î. d' *Canada* **105** C5
Orlice → *Czech Rep.* **26** A8
Orlivka *Ukraine* **29** E13
Orlov *Slovak Rep.* **27** B13
Orlov Gay *Russia* **34** E9
Orlová *Czech Rep.* **27** B11
Orlovat *Serbia* **28** E5
Orly, Paris ✈ (ORY) *France* **19** D9
Ormara *Pakistan* **66** G4
Ormea *Italy* **40** D4
Ormília *Greece* **44** F7
Ormoc *Phil.* **61** F6
Ormond *N.Z.* **91** C6
Ormond Beach *U.S.A.* **117** G14
Ormož *Slovenia* **41** B13
Ormskirk *U.K.* **14** D5
Ormstown *Canada* **115** A11
Ornans *France* **19** E13
Orne □ *France* **18** D7
Orne → *France* **18** C6
Orneta *Poland* **30** D7
Ornö *Sweden* **10** E12
Örnsköldsvik *Sweden* **10** A12
Oro *N. Korea* **57** D14
Oro → *Mexico* **118** B3
Oro Grande *U.S.A.* **111** L9
Oro Valley *U.S.A.* **109** K8
Orobie, Alpi *Italy* **40** B6
Orobie Bergamasche △ *Italy* **40** C6
Orobie Valtellinesi △ *Italy* **40** B6
Orocué *Colombia* **124** C4
Orodara *Burkina Faso* **82** C4
Orodo *Nigeria* **83** D6
Orofino *U.S.A.* **108** C5
Orohena, Mt. *Tahiti* **91** d
Orol Dengizi = Aral Sea *Asia* **52** E7
Oromiya □ *Ethiopia* **81** F5
Oromocto *Canada* **105** C6
Oron *Nigeria* **83** E6
Orono *Canada* **114** C6
Orono *U.S.A.* **113** C19
Oronsay *U.K.* **13** E2
Oropesa *Spain* **36** F5
Orosei *Italy* **42** B2
Orosei, G. di *Italy* **42** B2
Orosháza *Hungary* **28** D5
Oroszlány *Hungary* **28** C3
Orotukan *Russia* **53** C16
Oroville *Calif., U.S.A.* **110** F5

Oroville *Wash., U.S.A.* **108** B4
Oroville, L. *U.S.A.* **110** F5
Orrefors *Sweden* **11** H9
Orroroo *Australia* **95** E2
Orrville *U.S.A.* **114** F3
Orsa *Sweden* **10** C8
Orsara di Púglia *Italy* **43** A8
Orsasjön *Sweden* **10** C8
Orsha *Belarus* **32** E6
Orsk *Russia* **52** D6
Orşova *Romania* **28** F7
Ørsted *Denmark* **11** H4
Ørsundsbro *Sweden* **10** E11
Orta *Turkey* **72** B5
Orta, L. d' *Italy* **40** C5
Orta Nova *Italy* **43** A8
Ortaca *Turkey* **47** E10
Ortakent *Turkey* **47** D9
Ortaklar *Turkey* **47** D9
Ortaköy *Çorum, Turkey* **72** B6
Ortaköy *Niğde, Turkey* **72** C6
Orte *Italy* **41** F9
Ortegal, C. *Spain* **36** B3
Orthez *France* **20** E3
Ortigueira *Spain* **36** B3
Orting *U.S.A.* **110** C4
Ortisei *Italy* **41** B8
Ortles *Italy* **40** B7
Ortón → *Bolivia* **124** F5
Ortona *Italy* **41** F11
Ortonville *U.S.A.* **112** C5
Orūmīyeh *Iran* **73** D11
Orūmīyeh, Daryācheh-ye *Iran* **73** D11
Orune *Italy* **42** B2
Oruro *Bolivia* **124** G5
Orust *Sweden* **11** F5
Oruzgān □ *Afghan.* **66** C5
Orvault *France* **18** E5
Orvieto *Italy* **41** F9
Orwell *Ohio, U.S.A.* **114** E4
Orwell *Vt., U.S.A.* **115** C11
Orwell → *U.K.* **15** E9
Orwigsburg *U.S.A.* **115** F8
Oryakhovo *Bulgaria* **44** C7
Orynyn *Ukraine* **29** B11
Oryol = Orel *Russia* **33** F9
Orzinuovi *Italy* **40** C6
Orzyc → *Poland* **31** F8
Orzysz *Poland* **30** E8
Osa *Russia* **52** D6
Osa, Pen. de *Costa Rica* **120** E3
Osage *U.S.A.* **112** D7
Osage → *U.S.A.* **112** F8
Osage City *U.S.A.* **112** F6
Ōsaka *Japan* **55** G7
Osan *S. Korea* **57** F14
Osawatomie *U.S.A.* **112** F6
Osborne *U.S.A.* **112** F4
Osby *Sweden* **11** H7
Osceola *Ark., U.S.A.* **117** D10
Osceola *Iowa, U.S.A.* **112** E7
Oschatz *Germany* **24** D9
Oschersleben *Germany* **24** C7
Óschiri *Italy* **42** B2
Oscoda *U.S.A.* **114** B1
Osečina *Serbia* **44** B3
Ösel = Saaremaa *Estonia* **32** C2
Osery *Russia* **32** E10
Osgoode *Canada* **115** A9
Osh *Kyrgyzstan* **52** E8
Oshakati *Namibia* **85** H3
Oshawa *Canada* **114** C6
Oshigambo *Namibia* **88** B2
Oshkosh *Nebr., U.S.A.* **112** E2
Oshkosh *Wis., U.S.A.* **112** C9
Oshmyany = Ashmyany *Belarus* **23** A13
Oshnovïyeh *Iran* **73** D11
Oshogbo *Nigeria* **83** D5
Oshtorīnān *Iran* **73** E13
Oshwe *Dem. Rep. of the Congo* **84** E3
Osi *Nigeria* **83** D6
Osiezek *Poland* **31** G3
Osijek *Croatia* **28** E3
Ósilo *Italy* **42** B1
Ósimo *Italy* **41** E10
Osintorf *Belarus* **32** E6
Osipovichi = Asipovichy *Belarus* **23** B15
Osiyan *India* **68** F5
Osizweni *S. Africa* **89** D5
Oskaloosa *U.S.A.* **112** E7
Oskarshamn *Sweden* **11** G10
Öskemen *Kazakhstan* **52** E9
Oskol → *Ukraine* **33** H9
Osku *Iran* **73** D12
Oslo *Norway* **9** G14
Oslob *Phil.* **61** G5
Oslofjorden *Norway* **9** G14
Osmanabad *India* **66** K10
Osmancık *Turkey* **72** B6
Osmaniye *Turkey* **72** D7
Osmanlı *Turkey* **45** E10
Ösmo *Sweden* **10** F11
Osnabrück *Germany* **24** C4

Ośno Lubuskie *Poland* **31** F1
Osoblaha *Czech Rep.* **27** A10
Osogovska Planina *Macedonia* **44** D6
Osor *Italy* **41** D11
Osório *Brazil* **127** B5
Osorno *Chile* **128** E2
Osorno *Spain* **36** C6
Osorno, Vol. *Chile* **128** D2
Osoyoos *Canada* **102** D5
Osøyro *Norway* **8** F11
Ospika → *Canada* **102** B4
Oss *Neths.* **17** C5
Ossa, Mt. *Australia* **95** G4
Ossa, Oros *Greece* **46** B4
Ossa de Montiel *Spain* **39** G2
Ossabaw I. *U.S.A.* **117** F14
Osse → *France* **20** D4
Osse → *Nigeria* **83** D6
Ossi *Italy* **42** B1
Ossining *U.S.A.* **115** E11
Ossipee *U.S.A.* **115** C13
Ossokmanuan L. *Canada* **105** B7
Ossora *Russia* **53** D17
Ostashkov *Russia* **32** D7
Ostavall *Sweden* **10** B9
Oste → *Germany* **24** B5
Ostend = Oostende *Belgium* **17** C2
Oster *Ukraine* **23** C16
Österbotten = Pohjanmaa *Finland* **8** E20
Osterburg *Germany* **24** C7
Osterburg *U.S.A.* **114** F6
Osterburken *Germany* **25** F5
Österbybruk *Sweden* **10** D11
Österbymo *Sweden* **11** G9
Österdalälven *Sweden* **10** C7
Østerdalen *Norway* **10** C4
Österfärnebo *Sweden* **10** D10
Österforse *Sweden* **10** A11
Östergötlands län □ *Sweden* **11** F9
Osterholz-Scharmbeck *Germany* **24** B4
Østerild *Denmark* **11** G2
Östermyra = Seinäjoki *Finland* **8** E20
Osterode *Germany* **24** D6
Østervåla *Sweden* **10** D11
Östhammar *Sweden* **10** D12
Óstia, Lido di *Italy* **41** G9
Ostíglia *Italy* **41** C8
Östmark *Sweden* **10** D6
Östra Husby *Sweden* **11** F10
Ostrava *Czech Rep.* **27** B11
Ostravský □ *Czech Rep.* **27** B10
Ostróda *Poland* **30** E6
Ostrogozhsk *Russia* **33** G10
Ostroh *Ukraine* **23** C14
Ostrołęka *Poland* **31** E8
Ostrov *Bulgaria* **45** C8
Ostrov *Czech Rep.* **26** A5
Ostrov *Romania* **29** F12
Ostrov *Russia* **32** D5
Ostrów Lubelski *Poland* **31** G9
Ostrów Mazowiecka *Poland* **31** F8
Ostrów Wielkopolski *Poland* **31** G4
Ostrowiec-Świętokrzyski *Poland* **31** H8
Ostrožac *Bos.-H.* **28** E3
Ostrzeszów *Poland* **31** G4
Ostseebad Kühlungsborn *Germany* **24** A7
Osttirol □ *Austria* **26** E5
Ostuni *Italy* **43** B10
Osum → *Albania* **44** F4
Osŭm → *Bulgaria* **45** C8
Ōsumi-Kaikyō *Japan* **55** J5
Ōsumi-Shotō *Japan* **55** J5
Osun □ *Nigeria* **83** D5
Osuna *Spain* **37** H5
Oswegatchie → *U.S.A.* **115** B9
Oswego *U.S.A.* **115** C8
Oswego → *U.S.A.* **115** C8
Oswestry *U.K.* **14** E4
Oświęcim *Poland* **31** H6
Otaci *Moldova* **29** B11
Otago □ *N.Z.* **91** F2
Otago Harbour *N.Z.* **91** F3
Otaheite B. *Trin. & Tob.* **125** K15
Otaki *N.Z.* **91** D5
Otaru *Japan* **54** C10
Otaru-Wan = Ishikari-Wan *Japan* **54** C10
Otava → *Czech Rep.* **26** B7
Otavalo *Ecuador* **124** C3
Otavi *Namibia* **88** B2
Otchinjau *Angola* **88** B1
Otego *U.S.A.* **115** D9
Otelec *Romania* **28** E5
Otelnuk, L. *Canada* **105** A6
Oţelu Roşu *Romania* **28** E7
Othello *U.S.A.* **108** C4
Othoni *Greece* **46** B1
Othris, Oros *Greece* **46** B4
Oti → *Africa* **83** D5
Oti △ *Togo* **83** C5
Otish, Mts. *Canada* **105** B5
Otjiwarongo *Namibia* **88** C2
Oto Tolu Group *Tonga* **91** c
Otočac *Croatia* **41** D11
Otoineppu *Japan* **54** B11
Otok *Croatia* **41** E13
Otopeni, Bucureşti ✈ (OTP) *Romania* **29** F11
Otorohanga *N.Z.* **91** C5
Otoskwin → *Canada* **104** B2
Otra → *Norway* **9** G13
Otradnyy *Russia* **34** D10
Otranto *Italy* **43** B11
Otranto, C. d' *Italy* **43** B11
Otranto, Str. of *Italy* **43** B11
Otrokovice *Czech Rep.* **27** B10
Otse *S. Africa* **88** D4
Otsego L. *U.S.A.* **115** D10
Ōtsu *Japan* **55** G7
Ōtsuki *Japan* **55** G9
Ottawa = Outaouais → *Canada* **104** C5
Ottawa *Canada* **115** A9
Ottawa *Ill., U.S.A.* **112** E9
Ottawa *Kans., U.S.A.* **112** F7
Ottawa Is. *Canada* **101** F15
Ottélé *Cameroon* **83** E7
Ottensheim *Austria* **26** C7
Otter Cr. → *U.S.A.* **115** B11
Otter Lake *Canada* **114** A5
Otterndorf *Germany* **24** B4
Otterup *Denmark* **11** J4
Otterville *Canada* **114** D4
Ottery St. Mary *U.K.* **15** G4
Otto Beit Bridge *Zimbabwe* **87** F2
Ottosdal *S. Africa* **88** D4
Ottumwa *U.S.A.* **112** E7
Otu *Nigeria* **83** D6
Otukpa *Nigeria* **83** D6
Oturkpo *Nigeria* **83** D6
Otway, B. *Chile* **128** G2
Otway, C. *Australia* **95** F3
Otwock *Poland* **31** F8
Otyniya *Ukraine* **29** B9
Ötztaler Ache → *Austria* **26** D3
Ötztaler Alpen *Austria* **26** E3
Ou → *Laos* **64** B4
Ou Neua *Laos* **58** F3
Ou-Sammyaku *Japan* **54** E10
Ouachita → *U.S.A.* **116** F9
Ouachita, L. *U.S.A.* **116** D8
Ouachita Mts. *U.S.A.* **116** D7
Ouagadougou *Burkina Faso* **83** C4
Ouahigouya *Burkina Faso* **82** C4
Ouahran = Oran *Algeria* **78** A5
Oualâta *Mauritania* **82** B3
Ouallam *Niger* **83** C5
Ouallene *Algeria* **78** D6
Ouarâne *Mauritania* **78** D3
Ouargaye *Burkina Faso* **83** C5
Ouargla *Algeria* **78** B7
Ouarkoye *Burkina Faso* **82** C4
Ouarra → *C.A.R.* **84** C4
Ouarzazate *Morocco* **78** B4
Ouassouas *Mali* **83** B5
Ouatagouna *Mali* **83** B5
Oubangi → *Dem. Rep. of the Congo* **84** E3
Ouche → *France* **19** E12
Ouddorp *Neths.* **17** C3
Oude Rijn → *Neths.* **17** B4
Oudeïka *Mali* **83** B4
Oudon → *France* **18** E5
Oudtshoorn *S. Africa* **88** E3
Ouella *Niger* **83** C5
Ouellé *Ivory C.* **82** D4
Ouémé → *Benin* **83** D5
Ouessa *Burkina Faso* **82** C4
Ouessant, Î. d' *France* **18** D1
Ouesso *Congo* **84** D3
Ouest □ *Cameroon* **83** D7
Ouest, Pte. de l' *Canada* **105** C7
Ouezzane *Morocco* **78** B4
Ougarou *Burkina Faso* **83** C5
Oughter, L. *Ireland* **12** B4
Oughterard *Ireland* **12** C2
Ouidah *Benin* **83** D5
Ouidi *Niger* **83** C7
Ouistreham *France* **18** C6
Oujda *Morocco* **78** B5
Oujeft *Mauritania* **82** A2
Oulainen *Finland* **8** D21
Oulins *France* **21** C8
Oulu *Finland* **8** D21
Oulujärvi *Finland* **8** D22
Oulujoki → *Finland* **8** D21
Oulx *Italy* **40** C3
Oum Chalouba *Chad* **79** E10
Oum Hadjer *Chad* **79** F9
Oumé *Ivory C.* **82** D3
Ounasjoki → *Finland* **8** C21
Ounguati *Namibia* **88** C2

Ounianga Kébir Chad 79 E10
Our ➤ Lux. 17 E6
Oura, Akra Greece 47 C8
Ouranoupoli Greece 44 F7
Ourârene Niger 83 B6
Ouray U.S.A. 109 G10
Ourcq ➤ France 19 C10
Ourense Spain 36 C3
Ourense □ Spain 36 C3
Ouricuri Brazil 125 E10
Ourinhos Brazil 127 A6
Ourique Portugal 37 H2
Ouro Fino Brazil 127 A6
Ouro-Ndia Mali 82 B4
Ouro Prêto Brazil 127 A7
Ouro Sogui Senegal 82 B2
Oursi Burkina Faso 83 C4
Ourthe ➤ Belgium 17 D5
Ouse ➤ E. Sussex, U.K. 15 G8
Ouse ➤ N. Yorks., U.K. 14 D7
Oust France 20 F5
Oust ➤ France 18 E4
Outamba-Kilimi △ S. Leone 82 D2
Outaouais ➤ Canada 104 C5
Outardes ➤ Canada 105 C6
Outeiro de Rei Spain 36 B3
Outer Hebrides U.K. 13 D1
Outes = A Serra de Outes
  Spain 36 C2
Outjo Namibia 88 C2
Outlook Canada 103 C7
Outokumpu Finland 8 E23
Outreau France 19 B8
Ouvèze ➤ France 21 E8
Ouyen Australia 95 F3
Ouzouer-le-Marché France 19 E8
Ovada Italy 40 D5
Ovalau Fiji 91 a
Ovalle Chile 126 C1
Ovamboland Namibia 88 B2
Ovanåker Sweden 10 C9
Ovar Portugal 36 E2
Overath Germany 24 E3
Overflakkee Neths. 17 C4
Overijssel □ Neths. 17 B6
Overland Park U.S.A. 112 F6
Overlander Roadhouse
  Australia 93 E1
Overton U.S.A. 111 J12
Övertorneå Sweden 8 C20
Överum Sweden 11 F10
Ovid U.S.A. 115 D8
Ovidiopol Ukraine 33 J6
Ovidiu Romania 29 F13
Oviedo Spain 36 B5
Oviksfjällen Sweden 10 A7
Ovīšrags Latvia 30 A8
Ovoot Mongolia 56 B7
Övör Hangay □ Mongolia 56 B2
Ovoro Nigeria 83 D6
Øvre Årdal Norway 8 F12
Övre Fryken Sweden 10 E7
Ovruch Ukraine 23 C15
Owaka N.Z. 91 G2
Owambo = Ovamboland
  Namibia 88 B2
Owasco L. U.S.A. 115 D8
Owase Japan 55 G8
Owatonna U.S.A. 112 C7
Owbeh Afghan. 66 B3
Owego U.S.A. 115 D8
Owen Falls Dam =
  Nalubaale Dam Uganda 86 B3
Owen Sound Canada 114 B4
Owen Stanley Ra.
  Papua N. G. 90 B7
Oweniny ➤ Ireland 12 B2
Owens ➤ U.S.A. 110 J9
Owens L. U.S.A. 111 J9
Owensboro U.S.A. 112 G10
Owerri Nigeria 83 D6
Owl ➤ Canada 103 B10
Owo Nigeria 83 D6
Owosso U.S.A. 113 D11
Owyhee U.S.A. 108 F5
Owyhee ➤ U.S.A. 108 E5
Owyhee, L. U.S.A. 108 E5
Ox Mts. = Slieve Gamph
  Ireland 12 B3
Öxarfjörður Iceland 8 C5
Oxbow Canada 103 D8
Oxelösund Sweden 11 F11
Oxford N.Z. 91 E4
Oxford U.K. 15 F6
Oxford Mass., U.S.A. 115 D13
Oxford Miss., U.S.A. 117 D10
Oxford N.C., U.S.A. 117 C15
Oxford N.Y., U.S.A. 115 D9
Oxford Ohio, U.S.A. 113 F11
Oxford L. Canada 103 C9
Oxfordshire □ U.K. 15 F6
Oxia Greece 46 C3
Oxie Sweden 11 J7
Oxilithos Greece 46 C6
Oxnard U.S.A. 111 L7
Oxsjövälen Sweden 10 B7
Oxus = Amudarya ➤
  Uzbekistan 52 E6
Oya Malaysia 62 D4
Oyama Japan 55 F9

Oyambre △ Spain 36 B6
Oyem Gabon 84 D2
Oyen Canada 103 C6
Oykel ➤ U.K. 13 D4
Oymyakon Russia 53 C15
Oyo Nigeria 83 D5
Oyo Sudan 80 C4
Oyo □ Nigeria 83 D5
Oyonnax France 19 F12
Oyster Bay U.S.A. 115 F11
Ōyūbari Japan 54 C11
Ōzalp Turkey 73 C10
Ozamiz Phil. 61 G5
Ozark Ala., U.S.A. 117 F12
Ozark Ark., U.S.A. 116 D8
Ozark Mo., U.S.A. 112 G7
Ozark Plateau U.S.A. 112 G8
Ozarks, L. of the U.S.A. 112 F7
Ożarów Poland 31 H8
Özd Hungary 28 B5
Ozernovskiy Russia 53 D16
Ozernoye Russia 34 E10
Ozero Svityaz Ukraine 31 G10
Ozersk Russia 30 D8
Ozette, L. U.S.A. 110 B2
Ozieri Italy 42 B2
Ozimek Poland 31 H5
Ozinki Russia 34 E9
Ozona U.S.A. 116 F4
Ozorków Poland 31 G6
Ozren Bos.-H. 28 G3
Ozuluama Mexico 119 C5
Ozun Romania 29 E10
Ozurgeti Georgia 35 K5

P

Pa Burkina Faso 82 C4
Pa-an Burma 67 L20
Pa Mong Dam Thailand 64 D4
Pa Sak ➤ Thailand 64 E3
Paamiut Greenland 4 C5
Paar ➤ Germany 25 G7
Paarl S. Africa 88 E2
Pab Hills Pakistan 68 F2
Pabianice Poland 31 G6
Pabna Bangla. 67 G16
Pabo Uganda 86 B3
Pacaja ➤ Brazil 125 D8
Pacaraima, Sa. S. Amer. 124 C6
Pacasmayo Peru 124 E3
Paceco Italy 42 E5
Pachia Greece 47 E7
Pachino Italy 43 F8
Pachitea ➤ Peru 124 E4
Pachmarhi India 69 H8
Pachnes Greece 49 D6
Pachpadra India 68 G5
Pachuca Mexico 119 C5
Pacific Antarctic Ridge
  Pac. Oc. 5 B13
Pacific Grove U.S.A. 110 J5
Pacific Ocean 97 G14
Pacific Rim △ Canada 110 B2
Pacifica U.S.A. 110 H4
Pacitan Indonesia 63 H14
Packwood U.S.A. 110 D5
Pacov Czech Rep. 26 B8
Pacy-sur-Eure France 18 C8
Padaido, Kepulauan
  Indonesia 63 E9
Padang Riau, Indonesia 65 M4
Padang Sumatera Barat,
  Indonesia 62 E2
Padang Endau Malaysia 65 L4
Padangpanjang Indonesia 62 E2
Padangsidempuan Indonesia 62 D1
Padborg Denmark 11 K3
Paddle Prairie Canada 102 B5
Paderborn Germany 24 D4
Padeș, Vf. Romania 28 E7
Padma India 69 G11
Pádova Italy 41 C8
Padra India 68 H5
Padrauna India 69 F10
Padre I. U.S.A. 116 H6
Padre Island △ U.S.A. 116 H6
Padrón Spain 36 C2
Padstow U.K. 15 G3
Padua = Pádova Italy 41 C8
Paducah Ky., U.S.A. 112 G9
Paducah Tex., U.S.A. 116 D4
Padul Spain 37 H7
Paea Tahiti 91 d
Paeroa N.Z. 91 B5
Paesana Italy 40 D4
Pafúri Mozam. 89 C5
Pag Croatia 41 D12
Paga Ghana 83 C4
Pagadian Phil. 61 H5
Pagai Selatan, Pulau
  Indonesia 62 E2
Pagai Utara, Pulau Indonesia 62 E2
Pagalu = Annobón Atl. Oc. 77 G4
Pagara India 69 G9
Pagastikos Kolpos Greece 46 B5
Pagatan Indonesia 62 E5
Page U.S.A. 109 H8

Pagėgiai Lithuania 30 C8
Paget, Mt. S. Georgia 128 G9
Pago Pago Amer. Samoa 91 b
Pagosa Springs U.S.A. 109 H10
Pagwa River Canada 104 B2
Pāhala U.S.A. 107 M8
Pahang □ Malaysia 65 L4
Pahiatua N.Z. 91 D5
Pahokee U.S.A. 117 H⁴4
Pahrump U.S.A. 111 J11
Pahute Mesa U.S.A. 110 H10
Pai Thailand 64 C2
Paicines U.S.A. 110 J5
Paide Estonia 32 C3
Paignton U.K. 15 G4
Paiho Taiwan 59 F13
Päijänne Finland 32 B3
Pailani India 69 G9
Pailin Cambodia 64 F4
Paimpol France 18 D3
Painan Indonesia 62 E2
Painesville U.S.A. 114 E3
Paint Hills = Wemindji
  Canada 104 B4
Paint L. Canada 103 B9
Painted Desert U.S.A. 109 H8
Paintsville U.S.A. 113 G12
País Vasco □ Spain 38 C2
Paisley Canada 114 33
Paisley U.K. 13 F4
Paisley U.S.A. 108 E3
Paita Peru 124 E2
Paiva ➤ Portugal 36 D2
Paizhou China 59 E9
Pajares Spain 36 B5
Pajares, Puerto de Spain 36 C5
Pajęczno Poland 31 G5
Pak Lay Laos 64 C3
Pak Phanang Thailand 65 H3
Pak Sane Laos 64 C4
Pak Song Laos 64 E6
Pak Suong Laos 58 H4
Pakaur India 69 G12
Pakch'ŏn N. Korea 57 E13
Pakenham Canada 115 A8
Pakhuis S. Africa 88 E2
Pakistan ■ Asia 68 E4
Pakkading Laos 64 C4
Paklenica △ Croatia 41 D12
Pakokku Burma 67 J19
Pakość Poland 31 F5
Pakowki L. Canada 103 D6
Pakpattan Pakistan 68 D5
Pakrac Croatia 28 E2
Pakruojis Lithuania 30 C10
Paks Hungary 28 D3
Paktīā □ Afghan. 66 C6
Paktīkā □ Afghan. 66 C6
Pakwach Uganda 86 B3
Pakxe Laos 64 E5
Pal Lahara India 69 J11
Pala Chad 79 G9
Pala Dem. Rep. of the Congo 86 D2
Pala U.S.A. 111 M9
Palabek Uganda 86 B3
Palacios U.S.A. 116 G6
Palafrugell Spain 38 D8
Palagiano Italy 43 B10
Palagonía Italy 43 F8
Palagruža Croatia 41 F13
Palaiseau France 19 D9
Palakkad = Palghat India 66 P10
Palam India 66 K10
Palamas Greece 46 B4
Palamós Spain 38 D8
Palampur India 68 C7
Palamut Turkey 47 C9
Palana Australia 95 F4
Palana Russia 53 D16
Palanan Phil. 61 C5
Palanan Pt. Phil. 61 C5
Palandri Pakistan 69 C5
Palanga Lithuania 30 C8
Palangkaraya Indonesia 62 E4
Palani Hills India 66 P10
Palanpur India 68 G5
Palapye Botswana 88 C4
Palas Pakistan 69 B5
Palas de Rei Spain 36 C3
Palasponga India 69 J11
Palatka Russia 53 C16
Palatka U.S.A. 117 G14
Palau Italy 42 A2
Palau ■ Palau 90 A6
Palauk Burma 64 F2
Palawan Phil. 61 G3
Palayankottai India 66 Q10
Palazzo, Pte. France 21 F12
Palazzo San Gervásio Italy 43 B8
Palazzolo Acréide Italy 43 E7
Paldiski Estonia 32 C3
Pale Bos.-H. 28 G3
Palekastro Greece 49 D8
Paleleh Indonesia 63 D6
Palembang Indonesia 62 E2
Palencia Spain 36 C6
Palencia □ Spain 36 C6
Palenque Mexico 119 D6
Paleochora Greece 49 D5
Paleokastritsa Greece 49 A3

Paleometokho Cyprus 49 D12
Paleopoli Greece 46 D6
Palermo Italy 42 D6
Palermo U.S.A. 108 G3
Palermo ✈ (PMO) Italy 42 D6
Paleros Greece 46 C2
Palestina Chile 128 A3
Palestine Asia 74 D4
Palestine U.S.A. 116 F7
Palestrina Italy 41 G9
Palghat India 66 P10
Palgrave, Mt. Australia 92 D2
Pali India 68 G5
Palikir Micronesia 96 G7
Palinuro Italy 43 B8
Palinuro, C. Italy 43 B8
Paliouri, Akra Greece 44 G7
Palisades Res. U.S.A. 108 E8
Paliseul Belgium 17 E5
Palitana India 68 J4
Palizada Mexico 119 D6
Palk Bay Asia 66 Q11
Palk Strait Asia 66 Q11
Palkānah Iraq 70 C5
Palkot India 69 H11
Pallanza = Verbánia Italy 40 C5
Pallarenda Australia 94 B4
Pallasovka Russia 34 E8
Pallës, Bishti i Albania 44 E3
Pallinup ➤ Australia 93 F2
Pallisa Uganda 86 B3
Pallu India 68 E6
Palm Bay U.S.A. 117 G14
Palm Beach U.S.A. 117 H14
Palm Coast U.S.A. 117 G14
Palm Desert U.S.A. 111 M10
Palm-Grove △ Australia 94 C4
Palm Is. Australia 94 B4
Palm Springs U.S.A. 111 M10
Palma Mozam. 87 E5
Palma, B. de Spain 48 B9
Palma de Mallorca Spain 48 B9
Palma de Mallorca ✈
  (PMI) Spain 39 B9
Palma del Río Spain 37 H5
Palma di Montechiaro Italy 42 E6
Palma Nova = Palmanova
  Spain 48 B9
Palma Soriano Cuba 120 B4
Palmanova Spain 48 B9
Palmares Brazil 125 E11
Palmarola Italy 42 B5
Palmas Brazil 127 B5
Palmas, C. Liberia 82 E3
Pálmas, G. di Italy 42 D1
Palmdale U.S.A. 111 L8
Palmeira das Missões Brazil 127 B5
Palmeira dos Índios Brazil 125 E11
Palmela Portugal 37 G2
Palmer Antarctica 5 C17
Palmer U.S.A. 100 E2
Palmer ➤ Australia 94 B3
Palmer Arch. Antarctica 5 C17
Palmer Lake U.S.A. 108 G11
Palmer Land Antarctica 5 D18
Palmerston Australia 92 B5
Palmerston Canada 114 C4
Palmerston N.Z. 91 F3
Palmerston North N.Z. 91 D5
Palmerton U.S.A. 115 F9
Palmetto U.S.A. 117 H13
Palmi Italy 43 D8
Palmira Argentina 126 C2
Palmira Colombia 124 C3
Palmyra = Tudmur Syria 73 E8
Palmyra Mo., U.S.A. 112 F8
Palmyra N.J., U.S.A. 115 F9
Palmyra N.Y., U.S.A. 114 C7
Palmyra Pa., U.S.A. 115 F8
Palmyra Is. Pac. Oc. 97 G11
Palo Alto U.S.A. 110 H4
Palo Seco Trin. & Tob. 125 K15
Palo Verde Costa Rica 120 D2
Palo Verde △ Costa Rica 120 D2
Paloich Sudan 81 E3
Palomar Mt. U.S.A. 111 M10
Palompon Phil. 61 F6
Palopo Indonesia 63 E6
Palos, C. de Spain 39 H4
Palos de la Frontera Spain 37 H4
Palos Verdes, Pt. U.S.A. 111 M8
Palos Verdes Estates U.S.A. 111 M8
Pålsboda Sweden 10 E9
Palu Indonesia 63 E5
Palu Turkey 73 C9
Paluke Liberia 82 D3
Paluma Ra. Australia 94 B4
Paluzza Italy 41 B10
Palwal India 68 E7
Pama Burkina Faso 83 C5
Pama △ Burkina Faso 83 C5
Pamanukan Indonesia 63 G12
Pamekasan Indonesia 63 G15
Pamenang Indonesia 63 J19
Pamiers France 20 E5
Pamir Tajikistan 52 F8
Pamlico ➤ U.S.A. 117 D16
Pamlico Sd. U.S.A. 117 D17
Pampa U.S.A. 116 D4

Pampa de las Salinas
  Argentina 126 C2
Pampanua Indonesia 63 E6
Pampas Argentina 126 D3
Pampas Peru 124 F4
Pamplona Colombia 124 B4
Pamplona-Iruña Spain 38 C3
Pampoenpoort S. Africa 88 E3
Pamukçu Turkey 47 B9
Pamukkale Turkey 47 D11
Pan de Azúcar Chile 126 A2
Pan de Azúcar △ Chile 126 B1
Pan Xian China 58 E5
Pana U.S.A. 112 F9
Panabo Phil. 61 H6
Panaca U.S.A. 109 H6
Panagyurishte Bulgaria 45 D8
Panaitan Indonesia 63 G11
Panaji India 66 M8
Panamá Panama 120 E4
Panama ■ Cent. Amer. 120 E4
Panamá, G. de Panama 120 E4
Panama, Isthmus of
  Cent. Amer. 98 J12
Panama Basin Pac. Oc. 97 G19
Panama Canal Panama 120 E4
Panama City U.S.A. 117 F12
Panamint Range U.S.A. 111 J9
Panamint Springs U.S.A. 111 J9
Panão Peru 124 E3
Panaon I. Phil. 61 F6
Panare Thailand 65 J3
Panarea Italy 43 D8
Panaro ➤ Italy 41 D8
Panay Phil. 61 F5
Panay G. Phil. 63 B6
Panayarvi △ Russia 8 C24
Pančevo Serbia 44 B5
Panch'iao Taiwan 59 E13
Panciu Romania 29 E11
Pancorbo, Desfiladero Spain 36 C7
Panda Mozam. 89 C5
Pandan Malaysia 65 d
Pandan Antique, Phil. 61 F5
Pandan Catanduanes, Phil. 61 D6
Pandan, Selat Singapore 65 d
Pandan Tampoi = Tampoi
  Malaysia 65 d
Pandegelang Indonesia 63 G12
Pandhana India 68 J7
Pandharpur India 66 L9
Pando Uruguay 127 C4
Pando, L. = Hope, L.
  Australia 95 D2
Pandokratoras Greece 49 A3
Pandora Costa Rica 120 E3
Pandrup Denmark 11 G3
Panevéggio-Pale di San
  Martino △ Italy 41 B8
Panevėžys Lithuania 32 E3
Panfilovo Russia 34 E6
Pang-Long Burma 67 H21
Pang Sida △ Thailand 64 E4
Pang-Yang Burma 67 H21
Panga Dem. Rep. of the Congo 86 B2
Pangaíon Óros Greece 45 F8
Pangalanes, Canal des =
  Ampangalana,
  Lakandranon' Madag. 89 C8
Pangani Tanzania 86 D4
Pangani ➤ Tanzania 86 D4
Pangar Djeréme △ Cameroon 83 D7
Pangfou = Bengbu China 57 H9
Pangil Dem. Rep. of the Congo 86 C2
Pangkah, Tanjung
  Indonesia 63 G15
Pangkajene Indonesia 63 E5
Pangkalanbrandan Indonesia 62 D1
Pangkalanbuun Indonesia 62 E4
Pangkalpinang Indonesia 62 E3
Pangkor, P. Malaysia 65 K3
Pangnirtung Canada 101 D18
Pangody Russia 52 C8
Pangong Tso = Bangong
  Co China 69 C8
Panguitch U.S.A. 109 H7
Pangutaran Group Phil. 61 H4
Panhandle U.S.A. 116 D4
Pani Mines India 68 H5
Pania-Mutombo
  Dem. Rep. of the Congo 86 D1
Panikota I. India 68 J4
Panipat India 68 E7
Panjal Range = Pir Panjal
  Range India 68 C7
Panjang, Hon Vietnam 65 H4
Panjgur Pakistan 66 F4
Panjim = Panaji India 66 M8
Panjin China 57 D12
Panjnad ➤ Pakistan 68 E4
Panjnad Barrage Pakistan 68 E4
Panjwai Afghan. 68 D1
Pankshin Nigeria 83 D6
Panmunjŏm N. Korea 57 F14
Panna India 69 G8
Panna △ India 69 G8
Panna Hills India 69 G9
Pannawonica Australia 92 D2

Pannga, Tanjung Indonesia 63 K19
Pannirtuuq = Pangnirtung
  Canada 101 D18
Pano Akil Pakistan 68 F3
Pano Lefkara Cyprus 49 E12
Pano Panayia Cyprus 49 E11
Panorama Brazil 127 A5
Panormos Greece 49 D6
Pansemal India 68 J6
Panshan = Panjin China 57 D12
Panshi China 57 C14
Pantanal Brazil 124 H7
Pantano de Centla △
  Mexico 119 D6
Pantar Indonesia 63 F6
Pante Macassar E. Timor 63 F6
Pantelleria Italy 42 F4
Pantón Spain 36 C3
Panyam Nigeria 83 D6
Panyu China 59 F9
Panzhihua China 58 D3
Páola Italy 43 C9
Paola Malta 49 D2
Paola U.S.A. 112 F6
Paonia U.S.A. 108 G10
Paopao Moorea 91 d
Paoting = Baoding China 56 E8
Paot'ou = Baotou China 56 D6
Paoua C.A.R. 84 C3
Pápa Hungary 28 C2
Papa Stour U.K. 13 A7
Papa Westray U.K. 13 B6
Papagayo ➤ Mexico 119 D5
Papagayo, G. de Costa Rica 120 D2
Papakura N.Z. 91 B5
Papantla Mexico 119 C5
Papar Malaysia 62 C5
Papara Tahiti 91 d
Paparoa △ N.Z. 91 E3
Papas, Akra Greece 46 C3
Papeete Tahiti 91 d
Papenburg Germany 24 B3
Papenoo Tahiti 91 d
Papenoo ➤ Tahiti 91 d
Papetoai Moorea 91 d
Paphlagonia Turkey 72 B5
Paphos Cyprus 49 E11
Papikio Oros Greece 45 E9
Paposo Chile 126 B1
Papoutsa Cyprus 49 E12
Papua □ Indonesia 63 E9
Papua, G. of Papua N. G. 90 B7
Papua New Guinea ■
  Oceania 90 B7
Papudo Chile 126 C1
Papuk Croatia 28 E2
Papun Burma 67 K20
Papunya Australia 92 D5
Pará = Belém Brazil 125 D9
Pará □ Brazil 125 D8
Paraburdoo Australia 92 D2
Paracale Phil. 61 D5
Paracatu Brazil 125 G9
Paracel Is. S. China Sea 62 A4
Parachilna Australia 95 E2
Parachinar Pakistan 68 C4
Paracín Serbia 44 C5
Paradas Spain 37 H5
Paradela Spain 36 C3
Paradip India 67 J15
Paradise Calif., U.S.A. 110 F5
Paradise Nev., U.S.A. 111 J11
Paradise ➤ Canada 105 B8
Paradise Hill Canada 103 C7
Paradise River Canada 105 B8
Paradise Valley U.S.A. 108 F5
Paradisi Greece 49 C10
Parado Indonesia 63 F5
Paragould U.S.A. 117 C9
Paragua ➤ Venezuela 124 B6
Paraguaçu ➤ Brazil 125 F11
Paraguaçu Paulista Brazil 127 A5
Paraguaná, Pen. de
  Venezuela 124 A5
Paraguarí Paraguay 126 B4
Paraguarí □ Paraguay 126 B4
Paraguay ■ S. Amer. 126 A4
Paraguay ➤ Paraguay 126 B4
Paraíba = João Pessoa
  Brazil 125 E12
Paraíba □ Brazil 125 E11
Paraíba do Sul ➤ Brazil 127 A7
Parainen Finland 32 B2
Paraíso Mexico 119 D6
Parak Iran 71 E7
Parakhino Paddubye Russia 32 C7
Paralimni Cyprus 49 D12
Paralio Astros Greece 46 D4
Paramaribo Suriname 125 B7
Paramithia Greece 46 B2
Páramos del Batallón y La
  Negra △ Venezuela 121 E5
Paramushir, Ostrov Russia 53 D16
Paran ➤ Israel 74 E4
Paraná Argentina 126 C3
Paraná Brazil 125 F9
Paraná □ Brazil 127 A5
Paraná ➤ Argentina 126 C4

Paranaguá *Brazil* **127** B6
Paranaíba *Brazil* **125** G8
Paranaíba ➤ *Brazil* **125** H8
Paranapanema ➤ *Brazil* **127** A5
Paranapiacaba, Serra do *Brazil* **127** A6
Paranas *Phil.* **61** F6
Paranavaí *Brazil* **127** A5
Parang *Maguindanao, Phil.* **63** C6
Parang *Sulu, Phil.* **61** J4
Parângul Mare, Vf. *Romania* **29** E8
Paraparaumu *N.Z.* **91** D5
Paraspori, Akra *Greece* **47** F9
Paray-le-Monial *France* **19** F11
Parbati ➤ *Mad. P., India* **68** G7
Parbati ➤ *Raj., India* **68** F7
Parbhani *India* **66** K10
Parchim *Germany* **24** B7
Parczew *Poland* **31** G9
Pardes Hanna-Karkur *Israel* **74** C3
Pardilla *Spain* **36** D7
Pardo ➤ *Bahia, Brazil* **125** G11
Pardo ➤ *Mato Grosso, Brazil* **127** A5
Pardoo Roadhouse *Australia* **92** D2
Pardubice *Czech Rep.* **26** A8
Pardubický □ *Czech Rep.* **26** B8
Pare *Indonesia* **63** G15
Pare Mts. *Tanzania* **86** C4
Parecis, Serra dos *Brazil* **124** F7
Paredes de Nava *Spain* **36** C6
Paren *Russia* **53** C17
Parent *Canada* **104** C5
Parent, L. *Canada* **104** C4
Parentis-en-Born *France* **20** D2
Parepare *Indonesia* **63** E5
Parfino *Russia* **32** D6
Parga *Greece* **46** B2
Pargas = Parainen *Finland* **32** B2
Pargo, Pta. do *Madeira* **48** D2
Parham *Canada* **115** B8
Paria ➤ *U.S.A.* **109** H8
Paria, G. de *Venezuela* **125** K14
Pariaguán *Venezuela* **124** B6
Paricutín, Cerro *Mexico* **118** D4
Parigi *Indonesia* **63** E6
Parika *Guyana* **124** B7
Parikia *Greece* **47** D7
Parikkala *Finland* **32** B5
Parima, Serra *Brazil* **124** C6
Parinari *Peru* **124** D4
Pariñas, Pta. *Peru* **122** D2
Parincea *Romania* **29** D12
Parintins *Brazil* **125** D7
Pariparit Kyun *Burma* **67** M18
Paris *Canada* **114** C4
Paris *France* **19** D9
Paris *Idaho, U.S.A.* **108** E8
Paris *Ky., U.S.A.* **113** F11
Paris *Tenn., U.S.A.* **117** C10
Paris *Tex., U.S.A.* **116** E7
Paris, Ville de □ *France* **19** D9
Paris Charles de Gaulle ✈ (CDG) *France* **19** D9
Paris Orly ✈ (ORY) *France* **19** D9
Parish *U.S.A.* **115** C8
Parishville *U.S.A.* **115** B10
Pariti *Indonesia* **92** B3
Park *U.S.A.* **110** B4
Park City *U.S.A.* **112** G5
Park Falls *U.S.A.* **112** C8
Park Head *Canada* **114** B3
Park Hills *U.S.A.* **112** G8
Park Range *U.S.A.* **108** F10
Park Rapids *U.S.A.* **112** B6
Park River *U.S.A.* **112** A5
Park Rynie *S. Africa* **89** E5
Parkã Bandar *Iran* **71** E8
Parkano *Finland* **32** A2
Parker *Ariz., U.S.A.* **111** L12
Parker *Pa., U.S.A.* **114** E5
Parker Dam *U.S.A.* **111** L12
Parkersburg *U.S.A.* **113** F13
Parkes *Australia* **95** E4
Parkfield *U.S.A.* **110** K6
Parkhill *Canada* **114** C3
Parkland *U.S.A.* **110** C4
Parkston *U.S.A.* **112** D5
Parksville *Canada* **102** D4
Parkway *U.S.A.* **110** G5
Parla *Spain* **36** E7
Pârliţa *Moldova* **29** C12
Parma *Italy* **40** D7
Parma *Idaho, U.S.A.* **108** E5
Parma *Ohio, U.S.A.* **114** E3
Parma ➤ *Italy* **40** D7
Parnaguá *Brazil* **125** F10
Parnaíba *Brazil* **125** D10
Parnaíba ➤ *Brazil* **125** D10
Parnassós *Greece* **46** C4
Parnitha *Greece* **46** C5
Parnitha △ *Greece* **46** C5
Parnonas Oros *Greece* **46** D4
Pärnu *Estonia* **32** C3
Paro Dzong *Bhutan* **69** F13
Paroo ➤ *Australia* **95** E3
Paros *Greece* **47** D7
Parowan *U.S.A.* **109** H7
Parpaillon *France* **21** D10
Parral *Chile* **126** D1

Parras *Mexico* **118** B4
Parrett ➤ *U.K.* **15** F4
Parris I. *U.S.A.* **117** E14
Parrsboro *Canada* **105** C7
Parry I. *Canada* **114** A4
Parry Channel *Canada* **101** C13
Parry Is. *Canada* **101** B10
Parry Sound *Canada* **114** A5
Parsābād *Iran* **73** C13
Parsaloi *Kenya* **86** B4
Parsberg *Germany* **25** F7
Parsęta ➤ *Poland* **30** D2
Parsnip ➤ *Canada* **102** B4
Parsons *U.S.A.* **112** G6
Parsons Ra. *Australia* **94** A2
Partanna *Italy* **42** E5
Partenio △ *Italy* **43** B7
Parthenay *France* **18** F6
Partinico *Italy* **42** D6
Partizansk *Russia* **54** C6
Partizánske *Slovak Rep.* **27** C11
Partridge I. *Canada* **104** A2
Partry Mts. *Ireland* **12** C2
Paru ➤ *Brazil* **125** D8
Parvān □ *Afghan.* **66** B6
Parvatipuram *India* **67** K13
Parvatsar *India* **68** F6
Påryd *Sweden* **11** H9
Parys *S. Africa* **88** D4
Pas, Pta. des *Spain* **48** C7
Pas, The *Canada* **103** C8
Pas-de-Calais □ *France* **19** B9
Pasada *Spain* **36** B5
Pasadena *Canada* **105** C8
Pasadena *Calif., U.S.A.* **111** L8
Pasadena *Tex., U.S.A.* **116** G7
Pasaje ➤ *Argentina* **126** B3
Pasar *Indonesia* **63** J17
Pasay *Phil.* **61** D4
Pascagoula *U.S.A.* **117** F10
Pascagoula ➤ *U.S.A.* **117** F10
Paşcani *Romania* **29** C11
Pasco *U.S.A.* **108** C4
Pasco I. *Australia* **92** D2
Pascoag *U.S.A.* **115** E13
Pascua, I. de *Chile* **97** K17
Pasewalk *Germany* **24** B9
Pasfield L. *Canada* **103** B7
Pasha ➤ *Russia* **32** B7
Pasinler *Turkey* **73** C9
Pasir Mas *Malaysia* **65** J4
Pasir Panjang *Singapore* **65** d
Pasir Putih *Malaysia* **65** K4
Pasirian *Indonesia* **63** H15
Pasirkuning *Indonesia* **62** E2
Påskallavik *Sweden* **11** G10
Paskūh *Iran* **71** E9
Pasłęk *Poland* **30** D6
Pasłęka ➤ *Poland* **30** D6
Pasley, C. *Australia* **93** F3
Pašman *Croatia* **41** E12
Pasni *Pakistan* **66** G3
Paso Bravo △ *Paraguay* **126** A4
Paso Cantinela *Mexico* **111** N11
Paso de Indios *Argentina* **128** E3
Paso de los Libres *Argentina* **126** B4
Paso de los Toros *Uruguay* **126** C4
Paso Robles *U.S.A.* **110** K6
Paspébiac *Canada* **105** C6
Pasrur *Pakistan* **68** C6
Passage East *Ireland* **12** D5
Passage West *Ireland* **12** E3
Passaic *U.S.A.* **115** F10
Passau *Germany* **25** G9
Passero, C. *Italy* **43** F8
Passo Fundo *Brazil* **127** B5
Passos *Brazil* **125** H9
Passow *Germany* **24** B10
Passy *France* **21** C10
Pastavy *Belarus* **32** E4
Pastaza ➤ *Peru* **124** D3
Pasto *Colombia* **124** C3
Pastrana *Spain* **38** E2
Pasuruan *Indonesia* **63** G15
Pasym *Poland* **30** E7
Pásztó *Hungary* **28** C4
Patagonia *Argentina* **128** F3
Patagonia *U.S.A.* **109** L8
Patambar *Iran* **71** D9
Patan = Lalitapur *Nepal* **69** F11
Patan = Somnath *India* **68** J4
Patan *India* **68** H5
Patani *Indonesia* **63** D7
Pătârlagele *Romania* **29** E11
Pataudi *India* **68** E7
Patchewollock *Australia* **95** F3
Patchogue *U.S.A.* **115** F11
Pate *Kenya* **86** C5
Patea *N.Z.* **91** C5
Pategi *Nigeria* **83** D6
Patensie *S. Africa* **88** E3
Paternion *Austria* **26** E6
Paternò *Italy* **43** E7
Pateros *U.S.A.* **108** B4
Paterson *U.S.A.* **115** F10
Paterson Ra. *Australia* **92** D3
Pathankot *India* **68** C6

Pathfinder Res. *U.S.A.* **108** E10
Pathiu *Thailand* **65** G2
Pathum Thani *Thailand* **64** E3
Pati *Indonesia* **63** G14
Patía ➤ *Colombia* **124** C3
Patiala *Punjab, India* **68** D7
Patiala *U. P., India* **69** F8
Patine Kouka *Senegal* **82** C2
Patitiri *Greece* **47** D7
Patkai Bum *India* **67** F19
Patmos *Greece* **47** D8
Patna *India* **69** G11
Patnos *Turkey* **73** C10
Pato Branco *Brazil* **127** B5
Patonga, Ao *Thailand* **65** a
Patonga *Uganda* **86** B3
Patos *Albania* **44** F3
Patos *Brazil* **125** E11
Patos, L. dos *Brazil* **127** C5
Patos, Río de los ➤ *Argentina* **126** C2
Patos de Minas *Brazil* **125** G9
Patquía *Argentina* **126** C2
Patra *Greece* **46** C3
Patraikos Kolpos *Greece* **46** C3
Patras = Patra *Greece* **46** C3
Patriot Hills *Antarctica* **5** E16
Patrocínio *Brazil* **125** G9
Pattada *Italy* **42** B2
Pattani *Thailand* **65** J3
Pattaya *Thailand* **64** F3
Patten *U.S.A.* **113** B19
Patterson *Calif., U.S.A.* **110** H5
Patterson *La., U.S.A.* **116** G9
Patterson, Mt. *U.S.A.* **110** G7
Patti *Punjab, India* **68** D6
Patti *Ut. P., India* **69** G10
Patti *Italy* **43** D7
Patton *U.S.A.* **114** F6
Patuakhali *Bangla.* **67** H17
Patuanak *Canada* **103** B7
Patuca ➤ *Honduras* **120** C3
Patuca, Punta *Honduras* **120** C3
Patuca △ *Honduras* **120** D2
Pătulele *Romania* **28** F7
Patvinsuo △ *Finland* **8** E24
Pau *France* **20** E3
Pau, Gave de ➤ *France* **20** E2
Paudash *Canada* **114** B7
Pauillac *France* **20** C3
Pauk *Burma* **67** J19
Paul I. *Canada* **105** A7
Paul Smiths *U.S.A.* **115** B10
Paulatuk *Canada* **100** D7
Paulhan *France* **20** E7
Paulista *Brazil* **125** E12
Paulistana *Brazil* **125** E10
Paulo Afonso *Brazil* **125** E11
Paulpietersburg *S. Africa* **89** D5
Pauls Valley *U.S.A.* **116** D6
Pauma Valley *U.S.A.* **111** M10
Pauri *India* **69** D8
Pāveh *Iran* **73** E12
Pavelets *Russia* **32** F10
Pavia *Italy* **40** C6
Pavilion *U.S.A.* **114** D6
Pavilly *France* **18** C7
Pāvilosta *Latvia* **30** B8
Pavlikeni *Bulgaria* **45** C9
Pavlodar *Kazakhstan* **52** D8
Pavlograd = Pavlohrad *Ukraine* **33** H8
Pavlohrad *Ukraine* **33** H8
Pavlovo *Russia* **34** C6
Pavlovsk *Russia* **34** E5
Pavlovskaya *Russia* **35** G4
Pavlovskiy-Posad *Russia* **32** E10
Pavullo nel Frignano *Italy* **40** D7
Pawai, Pulau *Singapore* **65** d
Pawayan *India* **69** E9
Pawhuska *U.S.A.* **116** C6
Pawling *U.S.A.* **115** E11
Pawnee *U.S.A.* **116** C6
Pawnee City *U.S.A.* **112** E5
Pawtucket *U.S.A.* **115** E13
Paxi *Greece* **46** B2
Paximadia *Greece* **49** E6
Paxton *U.S.A.* **112** E9
Payakumbuh *Indonesia* **62** E2
Payerne *Switz.* **25** J2
Payette *U.S.A.* **108** D5
Paymogo *Spain* **37** H3
Payne Bay = Kangirsuk *Canada* **101** F18
Payne L. *Canada* **101** F17
Paynes Find *Australia* **93** E2
Paynesville *Liberia* **82** D2
Paynesville *U.S.A.* **112** C6
Pays de la Loire □ *France* **18** E6
Paysandú *Uruguay* **126** C4
Payson *Ariz., U.S.A.* **109** J8
Payson *Utah, U.S.A.* **108** F8
Paz ➤ *Guatemala* **120** D1
Paz, B. de la *Mexico* **118** C2
Pāzanān *Iran* **71** D6
Pazar *Turkey* **73** B9
Pazarcık *Turkey* **72** D7
Pazardzhik *Bulgaria* **45** D8

Pazarköy *Turkey* **47** B9
Pazarlar *Turkey* **47** C11
Pazaryeri *Turkey* **47** B11
Pazaryolu *Turkey* **73** B9
Pazin *Croatia* **41** C10
Pčinja ➤ *Macedonia* **44** E5
Pe Ell *U.S.A.* **110** D3
Peabody *U.S.A.* **115** D14
Peace ➤ *Canada* **102** B6
Peace Point *Canada* **102** B6
Peace River *Canada* **102** B5
Peach Springs *U.S.A.* **109** J7
Peachland *Canada* **102** D5
Peachtree City *U.S.A.* **117** E12
Peak, The = Kinder Scout *U.K.* **14** D6
Peak Charles △ *Australia* **93** F3
Peak District △ *U.K.* **14** D6
Peak Hill *Australia* **95** E4
Peak Ra. *Australia* **94** C4
Peake Cr. ➤ *Australia* **95** D2
Peale, Mt. *U.S.A.* **108** G9
Pearblossom *U.S.A.* **111** L9
Pearl ➤ *U.S.A.* **117** F10
Pearl and Hermes Reef *U.S.A.* **107** K4
Pearl River = Zhu Jiang ➤ *China* **59** F9
Pearl River *U.S.A.* **115** E10
Pearsall *U.S.A.* **116** G5
Pearson Int. Toronto ✈ (YYZ) *Canada* **114** C5
Peary Land *Greenland* **4** A6
Pease ➤ *U.S.A.* **116** D5
Peawanuck *Canada* **104** A2
Pebane *Mozam.* **87** F4
Pebas *Peru* **124** D4
Pebble Beach *U.S.A.* **110** J5
Peć = Kosovo *U.K.* **44** D4
Péccioli *Italy* **40** E7
Pechea *Romania* **29** E12
Pechenga *Russia* **8** B24
Pechenizhyn *Ukraine* **29** B9
Pechiguera, Pta. *Canary Is.* **48** F6
Pechnezhskoye Vdkhr. *Ukraine* **33** G9
Pechora *Russia* **52** C6
Pechora ➤ *Russia* **6** B16
Pechorskaya Guba *Russia* **52** C6
Pechory *Russia* **32** D4
Pecica *Romania* **28** D6
Pecka *Serbia* **44** B3
Pecos *N. Mex., U.S.A.* **109** J11
Pecos *Tex., U.S.A.* **116** F3
Pecos ➤ *U.S.A.* **116** G4
Pécs *Hungary* **28** D3
Pedasí *Panama* **120** E3
Pedder, L. *Australia* **95** G4
Peddie *S. Africa* **89** E4
Pedernales *Dom. Rep.* **121** C5
Pedieos ➤ *Cyprus* **49** D12
Pedirka Desert *Australia* **95** A1
Pedra Azul *Brazil* **125** G10
Pedra Lume *C. Verde Is.* **78** b
Pedregner *Spain* **39** G5
Pedreiras *Brazil* **125** D10
Pedro Afonso *Brazil* **125** E9
Pedro Cays *Jamaica* **120** C4
Pedro de Valdivia *Chile* **126** A2
Pedro Juan Caballero *Paraguay* **127** A4
Pedro Muñoz *Spain* **37** F8
Pedrógão Grande *Portugal* **36** F2
Pee Dee = Great Pee Dee ➤ *U.S.A.* **117** E15
Peebinga *Australia* **95** E3
Peebles *U.K.* **13** F5
Peekskill *U.S.A.* **115** E11
Peel *I. of Man* **14** C3
Peel ➤ *Australia* **95** E5
Peel ➤ *Canada* **100** D5
Peel Sd. *Canada* **100** C12
Peene ➤ *Germany* **24** A9
Peera Peera Poolanna L. *Australia* **95** D2
Peerless Lake *Canada* **102** B6
Peers *Canada* **102** C5
Pegasus Bay *N.Z.* **91** E4
Peggau *Austria* **26** D8
Pegnitz *Germany* **25** F7
Pegnitz ➤ *Germany* **25** F6
Pego *Spain* **39** G4
Pegu *Burma* **67** L20
Pegu Yoma *Burma* **67** K20
Pehčevo *Macedonia* **44** E6
Pehlivanköy *Turkey* **45** E10
Pehuajó *Argentina* **126** D3
Pei Xian = Pizhou *China* **56** G9
Peikang *Taiwan* **59** F13
Peine *Chile* **126** A2
Peine *Germany* **24** C6
Peip'ing = Beijing *China* **56** E9
Peipus, L. = Chudskoye, Ozero *Russia* **32** C4
Peissenberg *Germany* **25** H7
Peitz *Germany* **24** D10
Peixe *Brazil* **125** F9
Peixe ➤ *Brazil* **125** H8

Pek ➤ *Serbia* **44** B5
Pekalongan *Indonesia* **62** F3
Pekan *Malaysia* **65** L4
Pekan Nenas *Malaysia* **65** d
Pekanbaru *Indonesia* **62** D2
Pekin *U.S.A.* **112** E9
Peking = Beijing *China* **56** E9
Pekutatan *Indonesia* **63** J17
Pela *Greece* **44** F6
Péla *Guinea* **82** D3
Pelabuhan Klang *Malaysia* **65** L3
Pelabuhan Ratu, Teluk *Indonesia* **63** G12
Pelabuhanratu *Indonesia* **63** G12
Pélagos = Kira Panagia *Greece* **46** B6
Pelaihari *Indonesia* **62** E4
Pelat, Mt. *France* **21** D10
Pelcyzce *Poland* **31** E2
Peleaga, Vf. *Romania* **28** E7
Pelée, Mt. *Martinique* **120** c
Pelee, Pt. *Canada* **104** E4
Pelee I. *Canada* **114** E2
Pelekech *Kenya* **86** B4
Peleng *Indonesia* **63** E6
Pélézi *Ivory C.* **82** D3
Pelhřimov *Czech Rep.* **26** B8
Pelican *U.S.A.* **102** B1
Pelican L. *Canada* **103** C8
Pelican Narrows *Canada* **103** B8
Pelister △ *Macedonia* **44** F5
Pelješac *Croatia* **41** F13
Pelkosenniemi *Finland* **8** C22
Pella *S. Africa* **88** D2
Pella *U.S.A.* **112** E7
Pella □ *Greece* **44** F6
Pello *Finland* **8** C20
Pellworm *Germany* **24** A4
Pelly ➤ *Canada* **100** B1
Pelly Bay *Canada* **101** D14
Peloponnese □ *Greece* **46** D4
Peloritani, Monti *Italy* **43** D8
Pelorus Sd. *N.Z.* **91** D4
Pelotas *Brazil* **127** C5
Pelotas ➤ *Brazil* **127** B5
Pelovo *Bulgaria* **45** C8
Pelplin *Poland* **30** E5
Pelvoux, Massif du *France* **21** D10
Pemalang *Indonesia* **63** G13
Pemanggil, Pulau *Malaysia* **65** L5
Pematangsiantar *Indonesia* **62** D1
Pemba *Mozam.* **87** E5
Pemba *Zambia* **87** F2
Pemba Channel *Tanzania* **86** D4
Pemba I. *Tanzania* **86** D4
Pemberton *Australia* **93** F2
Pemberton *Canada* **102** C4
Pembina ➤ *Canada* **102** C6
Pembroke *Canada* **104** C4
Pembroke *U.K.* **15** F3
Pembrokeshire □ *U.K.* **15** F3
Pembrokeshire Coast △ *U.K.* **15** F2
Pen-y-Ghent *U.K.* **14** C5
Peña, Sierra de la *Spain* **38** C4
Peña de Francia, Sierra de la *Spain* **36** E4
Penafiel *Portugal* **36** D2
Peñafiel *Spain* **36** D6
Peñaflor *Spain* **37** H5
Penal *Trin. & Tob.* **125** K15
Peñalara *Spain* **36** E7
Penamacôr *Portugal* **36** E3
Penang = Pinang *Malaysia* **65** c
Penápolis *Brazil* **127** A6
Peñaranda de Bracamonte *Spain* **36** E5
Peñarroya *Spain* **38** E4
Peñarroya-Pueblonuevo *Spain* **37** G5
Penarth *U.K.* **15** F4
Peñas, C. de *Spain* **36** B5
Peñas, G. de *Chile* **128** F2
Peñas de San Pedro *Spain* **39** G3
Peñas del Chache *Canary Is.* **48** E6
Peñausende *Spain* **36** D5
Pench △ *India* **69** J8
Pench'i = Benxi *China* **57** D12
Pend Oreille ➤ *U.S.A.* **108** B5
Pend Oreille, L. *U.S.A.* **108** B5
Pendalofos *Greece* **44** F5
Pendembu *Eastern, S. Leone* **82** D2
Pendembu *Northern, S. Leone* **82** D2
Pender B. *Australia* **92** C3
Pendik *Turkey* **45** F13
Pendjari ➤ *Benin* **83** C5
Pendjari △ *Benin* **83** C5
Pendleton *U.S.A.* **108** D4
Pendra *India* **69** H9
Peneda-Gerês △ *Portugal* **36** D2
Penedo *Brazil* **125** F11
Penelokan *Indonesia* **63** J18
Penetanguishene *Canada* **114** B5
Penfield *U.S.A.* **114** E6
Pengalengan *Indonesia* **63** G12
Penge *Kasai-Or., Dem. Rep. of the Congo* **86** D1
Penge *Sud-Kivu, Dem. Rep. of the Congo* **86** C2
P'enghu Ch'üntou *Taiwan* **59** F12

Penglai *China* **57** F11
Pengshan *China* **58** B4
Pengshui *China* **58** C7
Penguin *Australia* **95** G4
Pengxi *China* **58** B5
Pengze *China* **59** C11
Penhalonga *Zimbabwe* **87** F3
Peniche *Portugal* **37** F1
Penicuik *U.K.* **13** F5
Penida, Nusa *Indonesia* **62** F5
Peninnes, Alpes = Pennine, Alpi *Alps* **25** E3
Peninsular Malaysia □ *Malaysia* **65** L4
Peñíscola *Spain* **38** E5
Penitente, Serra do *Brazil* **125** E9
Pēnjwīn *Iraq* **73** E11
Penkridge *U.K.* **14** E5
Penmarch *France* **18** E2
Penmarch, Pte. de *France* **18** E2
Penn Hills *U.S.A.* **114** F5
Penn Yan *U.S.A.* **114** D7
Penna, Punta della *Italy* **41** F11
Pennant *Canada* **103** C7
Penne *Italy* **41** F10
Penner ➤ *India* **66** M12
Pennine, Alpi *Alps* **25** J3
Pennines *U.K.* **14** C5
Pennington *U.S.A.* **110** F5
Pennington ➤ *Nigeria* **83** E6
Pennino, Mte. *Italy* **41** E9
Pennsburg *U.S.A.* **115** F9
Pennsylvania □ *U.S.A.* **113** E15
Penny *Canada* **102** C4
Peno *Russia* **32** D7
Penobscot ➤ *U.S.A.* **113** C19
Penobscot B. *U.S.A.* **113** C19
Penola *Australia* **95** F3
Penong *Australia* **93** F5
Penonomé *Panama* **120** E3
Penrhyn *Cook Is.* **97** H12
Penrith *Australia* **95** E5
Penrith *U.K.* **14** C5
Penryn *U.K.* **15** G2
Pensacola *U.S.A.* **117** F11
Pensacola Mts. *Antarctica* **5** E1
Pense *Canada* **103** C8
Penshurst *Australia* **95** F3
Penticton *Canada* **102** D5
Pentland *Australia* **94** C4
Pentland Firth *U.K.* **13** C5
Pentland Hills *U.K.* **13** F5
Pentland Hills △ *U.K.* **13** F5
Penza *Russia* **34** D7
Penza □ *Russia* **34** D7
Penzance *U.K.* **15** G2
Penzberg *Germany* **25** H7
Penzhino *Russia* **53** C17
Penzhinskaya Guba *Russia* **53** C17
Penzhou *China* **58** B4
Penzlin *Germany* **24** B9
Peoria *Ariz., U.S.A.* **109** K7
Peoria *Ill., U.S.A.* **112** E9
Pepacton Res. *U.S.A.* **115** D10
Pepani ➤ *S. Africa* **88** D3
Pepel *S. Leone* **82** D2
Peqin *Albania* **44** E3
Pera Hd. *Australia* **94** A3
Perabumilih *Indonesia* **62** E2
Perachora *Greece* **46** C4
Perak ➤ *Malaysia* **65** K3
Perales del Alfambra *Spain* **38** E4
Perales del Puerto *Spain* **36** E4
Perama *Kerkyra, Greece* **49** A3
Perama *Kriti, Greece* **49** D6
Perancak *Indonesia* **63** J17
Peräpohjola *Finland* **8** C22
Perast *Montenegro* **44** D2
Percé *Canada* **105** C7
Perche *France* **18** D8
Perche □ *France* **18** D7
Perchtoldsdorf *Austria* **27** C9
Percival Lakes *Australia* **92** D4
Percy *France* **18** D5
Percy Is. *Australia* **94** C5
Perdido, Mte. *Spain* **38** C5
Perdu, Mt. = Perdido, Mte. *Spain* **38** C5
Perechyn *Ukraine* **28** B7
Perehinske *Ukraine* **29** B9
Pereira *Colombia* **124** C3
Perelazovskiy *Russia* **35** F6
Perenjori *Australia* **93** E2
Peresecina *Moldova* **29** C13
Pereslavl-Zalesskiy *Russia* **32** D10
Peretu *Romania* **29** F10
Pereyaslav-Khmelnytskyy *Ukraine* **33** G6
Pereyma *Ukraine* **29** B14
Pérez, I. *Mexico* **119** C7
Perg *Austria* **26** C7
Pergamino *Argentina* **126** C3
Pergau ➤ *Malaysia* **65** K3
Pérgine Valsugana *Italy* **41** B8
Pérgola *Italy* **41** E9
Perham *U.S.A.* **112** B6
Perhentian, Kepulauan *Malaysia* **65** K4
Peri ➤ *Turkey* **73** C8
Periam *Romania* **28** D5

Péribonka ⇸ *Canada* 105 C5
Péribonka, L. *Canada* 105 B5
Perico *Argentina* 126 A2
Pericos *Mexico* 118 B3
Périers *France* 18 C5
Périgord *France* 20 D4
Périgord-Limousin △ *France* 20 C4
Périgueux *France* 20 C4
Perijá, Sierra de *Colombia* 124 B4
Perijá △ *Venezuela* 121 E5
Peristera *Greece* 46 B5
Peristerona ⇸ *Cyprus* 49 D12
Perito Moreno *Argentina* 128 F2
Perivol = Dragovishtitsa *Bulgaria* 44 D6
Perkasie *U.S.A.* 115 F9
Perković *Croatia* 41 E13
Perlas, Arch. de las *Panama* 120 E4
Perlas, Punta de *Nic.* 120 D3
Perleberg *Germany* 24 B7
Perlez *Serbia* 28 E5
Perm *Russia* 52 D6
Përmet *Albania* 44 F4
Pernambuco = Recife *Brazil* 125 E12
Pernambuco □ *Brazil* 125 E11
Pernatty Lagoon *Australia* 95 E2
Pernik *Bulgaria* 44 D7
Peron Is. *Australia* 92 B5
Peron Pen. *Australia* 93 E1
Péronne *France* 19 C9
Perosa Argentina *Italy* 40 D4
Perow *Canada* 102 C3
Perpignan *France* 20 F6
Perris *U.S.A.* 111 M9
Perros-Guirec *France* 18 D3
Perry Fla., U.S.A. 117 F13
Perry Ga., U.S.A. 117 E13
Perry Iowa, U.S.A. 112 E6
Perry N.Y., U.S.A. 114 D7
Perry Okla., U.S.A. 116 C6
Perryton *U.S.A.* 116 C4
Perryville *U.S.A.* 112 G9
Persan *France* 19 C9
Persberg *Sweden* 10 E8
Perşembe *Turkey* 72 B7
Persepolis *Iran* 71 D7
Pershotravensk *Ukraine* 23 C14
Persia = Iran ■ *Asia* 71 C7
Persian Gulf *Asia* 71 E6
Perstorp *Sweden* 11 H7
Pertek *Turkey* 73 C8
Perth *Australia* 93 F2
Perth *Canada* 115 B8
Perth *U.K.* 13 E5
Perth & Kinross □ *U.K.* 13 E5
Perth Amboy *U.S.A.* 115 F10
Perth-Andover *Canada* 105 C6
Perth Basin *Ind. Oc.* 96 L2
Pertuis *France* 21 E9
Pertusato, C. *France* 21 G13
Peru *Ind., U.S.A.* 112 E10
Peru *N.Y., U.S.A.* 115 B11
Peru ■ *S. Amer.* 124 D4
Peru Basin *Pac. Oc.* 97 J18
Peru-Chile Trench *Pac. Oc.* 124 G3
Perúgia *Italy* 41 E9
Perušić *Croatia* 41 D12
Pervomaysk *Russia* 34 C6
Pervomaysk *Ukraine* 33 H6
Pervouralsk *Russia* 52 D6
Pésaro *Italy* 41 E9
Pescadores = P'enghu Ch'üntou *Taiwan* 59 F12
Pescara *Italy* 41 F11
Pescara ⇸ *Italy* 41 F11
Peschanokopskoye *Russia* 35 G5
Péscia *Italy* 40 E7
Pescina *Italy* 41 F10
Peshawar *Pakistan* 68 B4
Peshkopi *Albania* 44 E4
Peshtera *Bulgaria* 45 D8
Peshtigo *U.S.A.* 112 C10
Peski *Russia* 34 E6
Pêso da Régua *Portugal* 36 D3
Pesqueira *Brazil* 125 E11
Pessac *France* 20 D3
Pest □ *Hungary* 28 C4
Pestovo *Russia* 32 C8
Pestravka *Russia* 34 D9
Petah Tiqwa *Israel* 74 C3
Petalídi *Greece* 46 E3
Petaling Jaya *Malaysia* 65 L3
Petaloudes *Greece* 49 C10
Petaluma *U.S.A.* 110 G4
Pétange *Lux.* 17 E5
Petaro *Pakistan* 68 G3
Petas *Greece* 46 B3
Petatlán *Mexico* 118 D4
Petauke *Zambia* 87 E3
Petawawa *Canada* 104 C4
Petén Itzá, L. *Guatemala* 120 C2
Peter I. *Br. Virgin Is.* 121 e
Peter I. Øy *Antarctica* 5 C16
Peter Pond L. *Canada* 103 B7
Peterbell *Canada* 104 C3
Peterborough *Australia* 95 E2
Peterborough *Canada* 114 B6
Peterborough *U.K.* 15 E7
Peterborough *U.S.A.* 115 D13

Peterborough □ *U.K.* 15 E7
Peterculter *U.K.* 13 D6
Peterhead *U.K.* 13 D7
Peterlee *U.K.* 14 C6
Petermann Gletscher *Greenland* 101 A20
Petermann Ranges *Australia* 93 E5
Petermann ☼ *Australia* 93 E4
Petersburg *Alaska, U.S.A.* 100 F5
Petersburg *Pa., U.S.A.* 114 F6
Petersburg *Va., U.S.A.* 113 G15
Petersburg *W. Va., U.S.A.* 113 F14
Petersfield *U.K.* 15 F7
Petershagen *Germany* 24 C4
Petília Policastro *Italy* 43 C9
Petit-Canal *Guadeloupe* 120 b
Petit Goâve *Haiti* 121 C5
Petit Lac Manicouagan *Canada* 105 B6
Petit-Mécatina ⇸ *Canada* 105 B8
Petit-Mécatina, Î. du *Canada* 105 B8
Petit Piton *St. Lucia* 121 f
Petit-Saguenay *Canada* 105 C5
Petit Saint Bernard, Col du *Italy* 21 C11
Petitcodiac *Canada* 105 C6
Petite Terre, Îles de la *Guadeloupe* 120 b
Petitot ⇸ *Canada* 102 A4
Petitsikapau L. *Canada* 105 B6
Petlad *India* 68 H5
Peto *Mexico* 119 C7
Petone *N.Z.* 91 D5
Petorca *Chile* 126 C1
Petoskey *U.S.A.* 113 C11
Petra *Jordan* 74 E4
Petra *Spain* 48 B10
Petra, Ostrova *Russia* 53 B12
Petra Velikogo, Zaliv *Russia* 54 C6
Petre, Pt. *Canada* 114 C7
Petrel = Petrer *Spain* 39 G4
Petrer *Spain* 39 G4
Petreto-Bicchisano *France* 21 G12
Petrich *Bulgaria* 44 E7
Petrified Forest △ *U.S.A.* 109 J9
Petrijanec *Croatia* 41 B13
Petrikov = Pyetrikaw *Belarus* 23 B15
Petrila *Romania* 29 E8
Petrinja *Croatia* 41 C13
Petrodvorets *Russia* 32 C5
Petrolândia *Brazil* 125 E11
Petrolia *Canada* 114 D2
Petrolina *Brazil* 125 E10
Petropavl *Kazakhstan* 52 D7
Petropavlovsk = Petropavl *Kazakhstan* 52 D7
Petropavlovsk-Kamchatskiy *Russia* 53 D16
Petropavlovskiy = Akhtubinsk *Russia* 35 F8
Petrópolis *Brazil* 127 A7
Petroşani *Romania* 29 E8
Petrova Gora *Croatia* 41 C12
Petrovac *Montenegro* 44 D2
Petrovac *Serbia* 44 B5
Petrovaradin *Serbia* 28 E4
Petrovsk *Russia* 34 D7
Petrovsk-Zabaykalskiy *Russia* 53 D11
Petrovskaya *Russia* 33 K9
Petrovskiy *Russia* 32 B8
Petrus Steyn *S. Africa* 89 D4
Petrusburg *S. Africa* 88 D4
Petzeck *Austria* 26 E5
Peumo *Chile* 126 C1
Peureulak *Indonesia* 62 D1
Pevek *Russia* 53 C18
Peveragno *Italy* 40 D4
Peyrehorade *France* 20 E2
Peyruis *France* 21 D9
Pézenas *France* 20 E7
Pezinok *Slovak Rep.* 27 C10
Pfaffenhofen *Germany* 25 G7
Pfälzerwald △ *Germany* 25 F5
Pfarrkirchen *Germany* 25 G8
Pfeffenhausen *Germany* 25 G7
Pforzheim *Germany* 25 G4
Pfullendorf *Germany* 25 H5
Pfungstadt *Germany* 25 F4
Pha Taem △ *Thailand* 64 E5
Phaestos *Greece* 49 D6
Phagwara *India* 68 D6
Phala *Botswana* 88 C4
Phalera = Phulera *India* 68 F6
Phalodi *India* 68 F5
Phalsbourg *France* 19 D14
Phaluai, Ko *Thailand* 65 b
Phan *Thailand* 64 C2
Phan Rang *Vietnam* 65 G7
Phan Ri = Hoa Da *Vietnam* 65 G7
Phan Si Pan *Vietnam* 64 A4
Phan Thiet *Vietnam* 65 G7
Phanae *Greece* 47 C7
Phanat Nikhom *Thailand* 64 F3
Phangan, Ko *Thailand* 65 H3
Phangnga *Thailand* 65 H2
Phangnga, Ao *Thailand* 65 a
Phanom Sarakham *Thailand* 64 F3

Phaphund *India* 69 F8
Pharenda *India* 69 F10
Pharr *U.S.A.* 116 H5
Phatthalung *Thailand* 65 J3
Phayao *Thailand* 64 C2
Phelps *U.S.A.* 114 D7
Phelps L. *Canada* 103 B8
Phenix City *U.S.A.* 117 E12
Phet Buri *Thailand* 64 F2
Phetchabun *Thailand* 64 D3
Phetchabun, Thiu Khao *Thailand* 64 D3
Phetchaburi = Phet Buri *Thailand* 64 F2
Phi Phi, Ko *Thailand* 65 J2
Phiafay *Laos* 64 E6
Phichai *Thailand* 64 D3
Phichit *Thailand* 64 D3
Philadelphia *Miss. U.S.A.* 117 E10
Philadelphia *N.Y., U.S.A.* 115 B9
Philadelphia *Pa., U.S.A.* 115 G9
Philip *U.S.A.* 112 C3
Philip Smith Mts. *U.S.A.* 106 B10
Philippi *U.S.A.* 113 F13
Philippi L. *Australia* 94 C2
Philippeville *Belgium* 17 D4
Philippine Basin *Pac. Oc.* 96 F5
Philippine Sea *Pac. Oc.* 61 C6
Philippine Trench = Mindanao Trench *Pac. Oc.* 61 F7
Philippines ■ *Asia* 61 F5
Philippolis *S. Africa* 88 E4
Philippopolis = Plovdiv *Bulgaria* 45 D8
Philipsburg *Canada* 115 A11
Philipsburg *Mont., U.S.A.* 108 C7
Philipsburg *Pa., U.S.A.* 114 F6
Philipstown = Daingean *Ireland* 12 C4
Philipstown *S. Africa* 88 E3
Phillip I. *Australia* 95 F4
Phillips *U.S.A.* 112 C8
Phillipsburg *Kans., U.S.A.* 112 F4
Phillipsburg *N.J., U.S.A.* 115 F9
Philmont *U.S.A.* 115 D11
Philomath *U.S.A.* 108 D2
Phimai *Thailand* 64 E4
Phitsanulok *Thailand* 64 D3
Phnom Kulen △ *Cambodia* 64 F5
Phnom Penh *Cambodia* 65 G5
Phnom Penh = Phnom Penh *Cambodia* 65 G5
Phoenicia *U.S.A.* 115 D10
Phoenix *Mauritius* 85 d
Phoenix *Ariz., U.S.A.* 109 K7
Phoenix *N.Y., U.S.A.* 115 C8
Phoenix Is. *Kiribati* 96 H10
Phoenixville *U.S.A.* 115 F9
Phon *Thailand* 64 E4
Phon Tiou *Laos* 64 D5
Phong ⇸ *Thailand* 64 D4
Phong Saly *Laos* 58 G4
Phong Tho *Vietnam* 64 A4
Phonhong *Laos* 64 C4
Phonum *Thailand* 65 H2
Phothararm *Thailand* 64 F2
Phra Nakhon Si Ayutthaya *Thailand* 64 E3
Phra Pradaeng *Thailand* 64 F3
Phra Thong, Ko *Thailand* 65 H2
Phrae *Thailand* 64 C3
Phrom Phiram *Thailand* 64 D3
Phrygia *Turkey* 72 C4
Phu Bia *Laos* 64 C4
Phu Chong-Na Yoi △ *Thailand* 64 E5
Phu Dien *Vietnam* 64 C5
Phu Hin Rang Kla △ *Thailand* 64 D3
Phu Kradung △ *Thailand* 64 D3
Phu Loi *Laos* 64 B4
Phu Luang △ *Thailand* 64 D3
Phu Ly *Vietnam* 58 G5
Phu Phan △ *Thailand* 64 D4
Phu Quoc, Dao *Vietnam* 65 G4
Phu Tho *Vietnam* 58 G5
Phu Wiang △ *Thailand* 64 D4
Phuc Yen *Vietnam* 58 G5
Phuket *Thailand* 65 a
Phuket, Ko *Thailand* 65 a
Phul *India* 68 D6
Phulad *India* 68 F5
Phulchari *Bangla.* 69 G13
Phulera *India* 68 F6
Phulpur *India* 69 F9
Phun Phin *Thailand* 65 H2
Phuntsholing *Bhutan* 69 F13
Piacenza *Italy* 40 C6
Piai, Tanjung *Malaysia* 65 d
Pian Cr. ⇸ *Australia* 95 E4
Pian-Upe △ *Uganda* 86 B3
Piana *France* 21 F12
Pianella *Italy* 41 F11
Pianosa *Puglia, Italy* 41 F12
Pianosa *Toscana, Italy* 40 F7
Piapot *Canada* 103 D7
Pias *Portugal* 37 G3

Piaseczno *Poland* 31 F8
Piaski *Poland* 31 G9
Piastów *Poland* 31 F7
Piatra *Romania* 29 G10
Piatra Craiului △ *Romania* 29 E10
Piatra Neamţ *Romania* 29 D11
Piatra Olt *Romania* 29 F9
Piauí □ *Brazil* 125 E10
Piauí ⇸ *Brazil* 125 E10
Piave ⇸ *Italy* 41 C9
Piazza Ármerina *Italy* 43 E7
Pia ☼ *Australia* 93 E2
Pibor ⇸ *Sudan* 81 F3
Pibor Post *Sudan* 81 F3
Picardie □ *France* 19 C10
Picardie, Plaine de *France* 19 C9
Picardy = Picardie □ *France* 19 C10
Picayune *U.S.A.* 117 F10
Picerno *Italy* 43 B8
Pichhor *India* 69 G8
Pichilemu *Chile* 126 C1
Pichor *India* 68 G8
Pickerel L. *Canada* 104 C1
Pickering *U.K.* 14 C7
Pickering, Vale of *U.K.* 14 C7
Pickle Lake *Canada* 104 B1
Pickwick L. *U.S.A.* 117 D10
Pico *Azores* 78 a
Pico Bonito △ *Honduras* 120 C2
Pico Truncado *Argentina* 128 F3
Picos *Brazil* 125 E10
Picos de Europa △ *Spain* 36 B6
Picton *Canada* 114 B7
Picton *N.Z.* 91 D5
Pictou *Canada* 105 C7
Picture Butte *Canada* 102 D6
Pictured Rocks △ *U.S.A.* 112 B10
Picún Leufú *Argentina* 128 D3
Pidbuzh *Ukraine* 31 J10
Pidurutalagala *Sri Lanka* 66 R12
Piechowice *Poland* 31 H2
Piedimonte Matese *Italy* 43 A7
Piedmont = Piemonte □ *Italy* 40 D3
Piedmont *Ala., U.S.A.* 117 E12
Piedmont *S.C., U.S.A.* 98 F11
Piedra ⇸ *Spain* 38 D3
Piedrabuena *Spain* 37 G6
Piedrahita *Spain* 36 E5
Piedralaves *Spain* 36 E6
Piedras Blancas *Spain* 36 B5
Piedras Negras *Mexico* 118 B4
Piekary Śląskie *Poland* 31 H5
Pieksämäki *Finland* 32 A4
Pielinen *Finland* 8 E23
Piemonte □ *Italy* 40 D5
Pienaarsrivier *S. Africa* 89 D4
Pieniężno *Poland* 30 D7
Pieninský △ *Europe* 27 B13
Pieńsk *Poland* 31 G2
Piercefield *U.S.A.* 115 B10
Pierceland *Canada* 103 C7
Pieria □ *Greece* 44 F6
Pierpont *U.S.A.* 114 E4
Pierre *U.S.A.* 112 C4
Pierre-Buffière *France* 20 C5
Pierre-de-Bresse *France* 19 F12
Pierrefonds *Canada* 115 A11
Pierrefontaine-les-Varans *France* 19 E13
Pierrefort *France* 20 D6
Pierrelatte *France* 21 D8
Pierreville *Trin. & Tob.* 125 K16
Pieštany *Slovak Rep.* 27 C10
Piesting ⇸ *Austria* 27 C9
Pieszyce *Poland* 31 H3
Piet Retief *S. Africa* 89 D5
Pietarsaari *Finland* 8 E20
Pietermaritzburg *S. Africa* 89 D5
Pietersburg = Polokwane *S. Africa* 89 C4
Pietragalla *Italy* 43 B8
Pietrasanta *Italy* 40 E7
Pietroşiţa *Romania* 29 E10
Pietrosul, Vf. *Maramureş, Romania* 29 C9
Pietrosul, Vf. *Suceava, Romania* 29 C10
Pieve di Cadore *Italy* 41 B9
Pieve di Teco *Italy* 40 D4
Pievepélago *Italy* 40 D7
Pigadítsa *Greece* 44 G5
Pigeon L. *Canada* 114 B6
Piges *Greece* 46 B3
Piggott *U.S.A.* 117 C9
Pigna *Italy* 40 E4
Pigüe *Argentina* 126 D3
Pihani *India* 69 F9
Pihlajavesi *Finland* 32 B5
Pijijiapan *Mexico* 119 D6
Pikalevo *Russia* 32 C8
Pikangikum *Canada* 103 C10
Pikes Peak *U.S.A.* 108 G11
Piketberg *S. Africa* 88 E2
Pikeville *U.S.A.* 113 G12
Pikou *China* 57 E12
Pikwitonei *Canada* 103 B9
Pila *Poland* 31 E9
Pila *Spain* 39 G3
Pilanesberg △ *S. Africa* 88 D4

Pilani *India* 68 E6
Pilar *Paraguay* 126 B4
Pilar de la Horadada *Spain* 39 H4
Pilat △ *France* 21 C8
Pilawa *Poland* 31 G8
Pilaya ⇸ *Bolivia* 124 H6
Pilbara *Australia* 92 D2
Pilcomayo ⇸ *Paraguay* 126 B4
Pilea *Greece* 44 F6
Pilgrim's Rest *S. Africa* 89 C5
Pilgrimstad *Sweden* 10 B9
Pili *Greece* 47 E9
Pilibhit *India* 69 E8
Pilica ⇸ *Poland* 31 G8
Pílio, Oros *Greece* 46 B5
Pilipinas = Philippines ■ *Asia* 61 F5
Pilis *Hungary* 28 C4
Pilisvörösvár *Hungary* 28 C3
Pilkhana *India* 68 E7
Pilliga *Australia* 95 E4
Pílos *Greece* 46 E3
Pilot Mound *Canada* 103 D9
Pilot Point *U.S.A.* 116 E6
Pilot Rock *U.S.A.* 108 D4
Pilsen = Plzeň *Czech Rep.* 26 B6
Pilštanj *Slovenia* 41 B12
Pilzno *Poland* 31 J8
Pima *U.S.A.* 109 K9
Pimba *Australia* 95 E2
Pimenta Bueno *Brazil* 124 F6
Pimentel *Peru* 124 E3
Pin Valley △ *India* 68 D7
Pina de Ebro *Spain* 38 D4
Pinamalayan *Phil.* 61 E4
Pinang *Malaysia* 65 c
Pinar, C. des *Spain* 48 310
Pinar del Río *Cuba* 120 B3
Pınarbaşı *Çanakkale, Turkey* 47 B8
Pınarbaşı *Kayseri, Turkey* 72 C7
Pınarhisar *Turkey* 45 E11
Pinatubo, Mt. *Phil.* 61 D3
Pinawa *Canada* 103 D9
Pincehely *Hungary* 28 D3
Pinchang *China* 58 B6
Pincher Creek *Canada* 102 D6
Pinchi L. *Canada* 102 C4
Pinckneyville *U.S.A.* 112 F9
Pińczów *Poland* 31 H7
Pindar *Australia* 93 E2
Pindera Downs ☼ *Australia* 95 A3
Pindi Gheb *Pakistan* 68 C5
Pindiga *Nigeria* 83 D7
Pindos △ *Greece* 46 B3
Pindos Oros *Greece* 46 B3
Pindus Mts. = Pindos Oros *Greece* 46 B3
Pine ⇸ *B.C., Canada* 102 B4
Pine ⇸ *Sask., Canada* 103 B7
Pine Bluff *U.S.A.* 116 D8
Pine Bluffs *U.S.A.* 108 F11
Pine City *U.S.A.* 112 C7
Pine Cr. ⇸ *U.S.A.* 114 E7
Pine Creek *Australia* 92 B5
Pine Falls *Canada* 103 C9
Pine Flat L. *U.S.A.* 110 J7
Pine Grove *U.S.A.* 115 F8
Pine Hill *Australia* 94 C4
Pine Pass *Canada* 102 B4
Pine Point *Canada* 102 A6
Pine Ridge *U.S.A.* 112 D3
Pine River *Canada* 103 C8
Pine River *U.S.A.* 112 B6
Pine Valley *U.S.A.* 111 N10
Pinecrest *U.S.A.* 110 G6
Pinedale *Calif., U.S.A.* 110 J7
Pinedale *Wyo., U.S.A.* 108 E9
Pinega ⇸ *Russia* 52 C5
Pinehouse L. *Canada* 103 B7
Pineimuta ⇸ *Canada* 104 B1
Pinerolo *Italy* 40 D4
Pines, Akra *Greece* 45 F8
Pineto *Italy* 41 F11
Pinetop-Lakeside *U.S.A.* 109 J9
Pinetown *S. Africa* 89 D5
Pineville *U.S.A.* 116 F8
Piney *France* 19 D11
Ping ⇸ *Thailand* 64 E3
Pingaring *Australia* 93 F2
Pingba *China* 58 D6
Pingbian *China* 58 F4
Pingchuan *China* 56 F3
Pingding *China* 56 F7
Pingdingshan *China* 56 H7
Pingdong *Taiwan* 59 F13
Pingdu *China* 57 F10
Pingelly *Australia* 93 F2
Pingguo *China* 58 F6
Pinghe *China* 59 E11
Pinghu *China* 59 B13
Pingjiang *China* 59 C9
Pingle *China* 59 E8
Pingli *China* 58 A7
Pingliang *China* 56 G4
Pinglu *China* 56 E9
Pingluo *China* 56 F4
Pingnan *Fujian, China* 59 D12

Pingnan *Guangxi Zhuangzu, China* 59 F8
Pingquan *China* 57 D10
Pingrup *Australia* 93 F2
Pingshan *China* 58 C5
Pingtan *China* 59 E12
Pingtang *China* 58 E6
P'ingtung *Taiwan* 59 F13
Pingwu *China* 56 H3
Pingxiang *Guangxi Zhuangzu, China* 58 F6
Pingxiang *Jiangxi, China* 59 D9
Pingyao *China* 56 F7
Pingyi *China* 57 G9
Pingyuan *Guangdong, China* 59 E10
Pingyuan *Shandong, China* 56 F9
Pingyuanjie *China* 58 F4
Pinhal Novo *Portugal* 37 G2
Pinheiro *Brazil* 125 D9
Pinheiro Machado *Brazil* 127 C5
Pinhel *Portugal* 36 E3
Pini *Indonesia* 62 D1
Pinios ⇸ *Ilia, Greece* 46 D3
Pinios ⇸ *Trikala, Greece* 46 B4
Pinjarra *Australia* 93 F2
Pink Mountain *Canada* 102 B4
Pinkafeld *Austria* 27 D9
Pinnacles △ *U.S.A.* 110 J5
Pinnaroo *Australia* 95 F3
Pinneberg *Germany* 24 B5
Pinon Hills *U.S.A.* 111 L9
Pinos *Mexico* 118 C4
Pinos, Mt. *U.S.A.* 111 L7
Pinos Pt. *U.S.A.* 109 H3
Pinos Puente *Spain* 37 H7
Pinrang *Indonesia* 63 E5
Pins, Pte. aux *Canada* 114 D3
Pinsk *Belarus* 23 B14
Pintados *Chile* 124 H5
Pinyang *China* 59 D13
Pinyug *Russia* 52 C5
Pioche *U.S.A.* 109 H6
Piombino *Italy* 40 F7
Piombino, Canale di *Italy* 40 F7
Pioner, Ostrov *Russia* 53 B10
Pionerskiy *Russia* 30 D7
Pionki *Poland* 31 G8
Piopiotaki = Milford Sd. *N.Z.* 91 F1
Piorini, L. *Brazil* 124 D6
Piotrków Trybunalski *Poland* 31 G6
Piove di Sacco *Italy* 41 C9
Pip *Iran* 71 E9
Pipar *India* 68 F5
Pipar Road *India* 68 F5
Piparia *Mad. P., India* 68 H8
Piparia *Mad. P., India* 68 J7
Piperi *Greece* 46 B6
Pipestone *U.S.A.* 112 D5
Pipestone ⇸ *Canada* 104 B2
Pipestone Cr. ⇸ *Canada* 103 D8
Piplan *Pakistan* 68 C4
Piploda *India* 68 H6
Pipmuacan, Rés. *Canada* 105 C5
Pippingarra *Australia* 92 D2
Pipriac *France* 18 E5
Piqua *U.S.A.* 113 E11
Piquiri ⇸ *Brazil* 127 A5
Pir Panjal Range *India* 68 C7
Pir Sohrâb *Iran* 71 E9
Pira *Benin* 83 D5
Piracicaba *Brazil* 127 A6
Piracuruca *Brazil* 125 D10
Pirae *Tahiti* 91 d
Piraeus = Pireas *Greece* 46 D5
Piraiévs = Pireas *Greece* 46 D5
Pirajuí *Brazil* 127 A6
Piram I. *India* 68 J5
Piran *Slovenia* 41 C10
Pirané *Argentina* 126 B4
Pirano = Piran *Slovenia* 41 C10
Pīränshahr *Iran* 73 D11
Pirapora *Brazil* 125 G10
Pirawa *India* 68 G7
Pirdop *Bulgaria* 45 D8
Pireas *Greece* 46 D5
Pirgi *Greece* 47 C7
Pirgos *Ilia, Greece* 46 D3
Pirgos *Kriti, Greece* 47 F7
Pirgovo *Bulgaria* 45 C9
Piribebuy *Paraguay* 126 B4
Pirimapun *Indonesia* 63 F9
Pirin △ *Bulgaria* 44 E7
Pirin Planina *Bulgaria* 44 E7
Pirineos = Pyrénées *Europe* 20 F4
Piripiri *Brazil* 125 D10
Pirlangimpi *Australia* 92 B5
Pirmasens *Germany* 25 F3
Pirna *Germany* 24 C9
Pirot *Serbia* 44 C6
Piru *Indonesia* 63 E7
Piru *U.S.A.* 111 L8
Piryatin = Pyryatyn *Ukraine* 33 E7
Pisa *Italy* 40 E7
Pisa ⇸ *Poland* 31 E8
Pisagne *Italy* 40 C7
Pisa, Firenze ✈ (PSA) *Italy* 40 E7
Pisagua *Chile* 124 G4
Pisarovina *Croatia* 41 C12

Pisco *Peru* **124** F3
Piscu *Romania* **29** E12
Písek *Czech Rep.* **26** B7
Pishan *China* **60** C2
Pishcha *Ukraine* **31** G10
Pishchanka *Ukraine* **29** B13
Pīshīn *Iran* **71** E9
Pishin *Pakistan* **68** D2
Pishin Lora ⇀ *Pakistan* **68** E1
Pisidia *Turkey* **72** D4
Pising *Indonesia* **63** F6
Pismo Beach *U.S.A.* **111** K6
Piso, L. *Liberia* **82** D2
Pissila *Burkina Faso* **83** C4
Pissis, Cerro *Argentina* **126** B2
Pissos *France* **20** D3
Pissouri *Cyprus* **49** E11
Pisticci *Italy* **43** B9
Pistóia *Italy* **40** E7
Pistol B. *Canada* **103** A10
Pisuerga ⇀ *Spain* **36** D6
Pisz *Poland* **30** E8
Pit ⇀ *U.S.A.* **108** F2
Pita *Guinea* **82** C2
Pitarpunga L. *Australia* **95** E3
Pitcairn I. *Pac. Oc.* **97** K14
Pitch L. *Trin. & Tob.* **125** K15
Piteå *Sweden* **8** D19
Piteälven ⇀ *Sweden* **8** D19
Piterka *Russia* **34** E8
Piteşti *Romania* **29** F9
Pithapuram *India* **67** L13
Pithara *Australia* **93** F2
Pithio *Greece* **45** E11
Pithiviers *France* **19** D9
Pithoragarh *India* **69** E9
Pithoro *Pakistan* **68** G3
Pitigliano *Italy* **41** F8
Pitkyaranta *Russia* **32** B6
Pitlochry *U.K.* **13** E5
Pitsilia *Cyprus* **49** E12
Pitt I. *Canada* **102** C3
Pittsburg *Calif., U.S.A.* **110** G5
Pittsburg *Kans., U.S.A.* **112** G6
Pittsburg *Tex., U.S.A.* **116** E7
Pittsburgh *U.S.A.* **114** F5
Pittsfield *Ill., U.S.A.* **112** F8
Pittsfield *Maine, U.S.A.* **113** C19
Pittsfield *Mass., U.S.A.* **115** D11
Pittsfield *N.H., U.S.A.* **115** C13
Pittston *U.S.A.* **115** E9
Pittsworth *Australia* **95** D5
Pituri ⇀ *Australia* **94** C2
Piura *Peru* **124** E2
Piva ⇀ *Montenegro* **44** C2
Piwniczna *Poland* **31** J7
Pixley *U.S.A.* **110** K7
Pizhou *China* **56** G9
Pizzo *Italy* **43** D9
Placentia *Canada* **105** C9
Placentia B. *Canada* **105** C9
Placer *Masbate, Phil.* **61** F5
Placer *Surigao N., Phil.* **61** G6
Placerville *U.S.A.* **110** G6
Placetas *Cuba* **120** B4
Plačkovica *Macedonia* **44** E6
Plainfield *N.J., U.S.A.* **115** F10
Plainfield *Ohio, U.S.A.* **114** F3
Plainfield *Vt., U.S.A.* **115** B12
Plains *Mont., U.S.A.* **108** C6
Plains *Tex., U.S.A.* **116** E3
Plainview *Nebr., U.S.A.* **112** D5
Plainview *Tex., U.S.A.* **116** D4
Plainwell *U.S.A.* **113** D11
Plaisance *France* **20** E4
Plaistow *U.S.A.* **115** D13
Plaka *Greece* **47** B7
Plaka, Ákra *Greece* **49** D8
Plakenska Planina *Macedonia* **44** E5
Planá *Czech Rep.* **26** B5
Plana Cays *Bahamas* **121** B5
Planada *U.S.A.* **110** H6
Plancoët *France* **18** D4
Plandište *Serbia* **28** E6
Plano *U.S.A.* **116** E6
Plant City *U.S.A.* **117** G13
Plasencia *Spain* **36** E4
Plaški *Croatia* **41** C12
Plaster City *U.S.A.* **111** N11
Plaster Rock *Canada* **105** C6
Plastun *Russia* **54** B8
Plasy *Czech Rep.* **26** B6
Plata, Río de la ⇀ *S. Amer.* **126** C4
Plátani ⇀ *Italy* **42** E6
Platanos *Greece* **49** D5
Plateau □ *Nigeria* **83** D6
Platte *U.S.A.* **112** D4
Platte ⇀ *Mo., U.S.A.* **112** F6
Platte ⇀ *Nebr., U.S.A.* **112** E6
Platteville *U.S.A.* **112** D9
Plattling *Germany* **25** G8
Plattsburgh *U.S.A.* **115** B11
Plattsmouth *U.S.A.* **112** E6
Plau *Germany* **24** B8
Plauen *Germany* **24** E8
Plauer See *Germany* **24** B8
Plav *Montenegro* **44** D3
Plavinas *Latvia* **32** D3

Plavnica *Montenegro* **44** D3
Plavno *Croatia* **41** D13
Plavsk *Russia* **32** F9
Playa Blanca *Canary Is.* **48** F6
Playa Blanca Sur *Canary Is.* **48** F6
Playa de las Americas
 Canary Is. **48** F3
Playa de Mogán *Canary Is.* **48** G4
Playa del Carmen *Mexico* **119** C7
Playa del Inglés *Canary Is.* **48** G4
Playa Esmerelda *Canary Is.* **48** F5
Playgreen L. *Canada* **103** C9
Pleasant Bay *Canada* **105** C7
Pleasant Hill *U.S.A.* **110** H4
Pleasant Mount *U.S.A.* **115** E9
Pleasanton *Calif., U.S.A.* **110** H5
Pleasanton *Tex., U.S.A.* **116** G5
Pleasantville *N.J., U.S.A.* **113** F16
Pleasantville *Pa., U.S.A.* **114** E5
Pléaux *France* **20** C6
Plei Ku *Vietnam* **64** F7
Plélan-le-Grand *France* **18** D4
Pléneuf-Val-André *France* **18** D4
Pleniţa *Romania* **29** F8
Plenty *Australia* **94** C2
Plenty, B. of *N.Z.* **91** B6
Plentywood *U.S.A.* **108** B11
Plérin *France* **18** D4
Plessisville *Canada* **105** C5
Plestin-les-Grèves *France* **18** D3
Pleszew *Poland* **31** G4
Pleternica *Croatia* **28** E2
Plétipi, L. *Canada* **105** B5
Pleven *Bulgaria* **45** C8
Plevlja *Montenegro* **44** C3
Plevna *Canada* **114** B4
Plitvička Jezera △ *Croatia* **41** D12
Pljevlja *Croatia* **41** D12
Pločnice *Italy* **42** B1
Ploče *Croatia* **44** C1
Plöckenpass *Italy* **41** B9
Plöckenstein *Germany* **25** G9
Ploemeur *France* **18** E3
Ploërmel *France* **18** E4
Ploieşti *Romania* **29** F11
Plomari *Greece* **47** C8
Plombières-les-Bains *France* **19** E13
Plomin *Croatia* **41** C11
Plön *Germany* **24** A6
Plonge, Lac la *Canada* **103** B7
Płońsk *Poland* **31** F7
Plopeni *Romania* **29** E10
Plopişului, Munţii *Romania* **28** C7
Płoty *Poland* **30** E2
Plouaret *France* **18** D3
Plouay *France* **18** E3
Ploučnice ⇀ *Czech Rep.* **26** A7
Ploudalmézeau *France* **18** D2
Plouescat *France* **18** D2
Plougasnou *France* **18** D3
Plougastel-Daoulas *France* **18** D2
Plouguerneau *France* **18** D2
Plouha *France* **18** D4
Plouhinec *France* **18** E2
Plovdiv *Bulgaria* **45** D8
Plovdiv □ *Bulgaria* **45** D8
Plum *U.S.A.* **114** F5
Plum I. *U.S.A.* **115** E12
Plumas *U.S.A.* **110** F6
Plummer *U.S.A.* **108** C5
Plumridge Lakes *Australia* **93** E4
Plumtree *Zimbabwe* **87** G2
Plunge *Lithuania* **30** C8
Pluvigner *France* **18** E3
Plužine *Montenegro* **44** C2
Plymouth *Trin. & Tob.* **125** J16
Plymouth *U.K.* **15** G3
Plymouth *Calif., U.S.A.* **110** G6
Plymouth *Ind., U.S.A.* **112** E10
Plymouth *Mass., U.S.A.* **115** E14
Plymouth *N.C., U.S.A.* **117** D16
Plymouth *N.H., U.S.A.* **115** C13
Plymouth *Pa., U.S.A.* **115** E9
Plymouth *Wis., U.S.A.* **112** D10
Plympton-Wyoming =
 Wyoming *Canada* **114** D2
Plynlimon = Pumlumon
 Fawr *U.K.* **15** E4
Plyusa *Russia* **32** C5
Plyusa ⇀ *Russia* **32** C5
Plzeň *Czech Rep.* **26** B6
Plzeňský □ *Czech Rep.* **26** B6
Pmere Nyente ☉ *Australia* **94** C2
Pniewy *Poland* **31** F3
Pô *Burkina Faso* **83** C4
Po ⇀ *Italy* **41** D9
Po, Foci del *Italy* **41** D9
Pô △ *Burkina Faso* **83** C4
Po Hai = Bo Hai *China* **57** E10
Pobé *Benin* **83** D5
Pobé *Burkina Faso* **83** C4
Pobeda *Russia* **53** C15
Pobedy, Pik *Kyrgyzstan* **52** E8
Pobiedziska *Poland* **31** F4
Pobladura del Valle *Spain* **36** C5
Pocahontas *Ark., U.S.A.* **117** D9
Pocahontas *Iowa, U.S.A.* **112** D6
Pocatello *U.S.A.* **108** E7

Počátky *Czech Rep.* **26** B8
Pochep *Russia* **33** F7
Pochinki *Russia* **34** C7
Pochinok *Russia* **32** E7
Pöchlarn *Austria* **26** C8
Pocking *Germany* **25** G9
Pocomoke City *U.S.A.* **113** F16
Poços de Caldas *Brazil* **127** A6
Podbořany *Czech Rep.* **26** A6
Poddębice *Poland* **31** G5
Poděbrady *Czech Rep.* **26** A8
Podensac *France* **20** D3
Podenzano *Italy* **40** D6
Podgorač *Croatia* **28** E3
Podgorica *Montenegro* **44** D3
Podgorie *Albania* **44** F4
Podilska Vysochyna
 Ukraine **29** B13
Podkarpackie □ *Poland* **31** H9
Podkova *Bulgaria* **45** E9
Podlapača *Croatia* **41** D12
Podlaskie □ *Poland* **31** E10
Podoleni *Romania* **29** D11
Podolínec *Slovak Rep.* **27** B13
Podolsk *Russia* **32** E9
Podor *Senegal* **82** B1
Podporozhye *Russia* **32** B8
Podu Iloaiei *Romania* **29** C11
Podu Turcului *Romania* **29** D12
Podujevo *Kosovo* **44** D5
Pofadder *S. Africa* **88** D2
Poggiardo *Italy* **43** B11
Poggibonsi *Italy* **40** E8
Póggio Mirteto *Italy* **41** F9
Pogoanele *Romania* **29** F11
Pogorzela *Poland* **31** G4
Pogradec *Albania* **44** F4
Pogranichnyy *Russia* **54** B5
Poh *Indonesia* **63** E6
Pohang *S. Korea* **57** F15
Pohjanmaa *Finland* **8** E20
Pohnpei *Micronesia* **96** G7
Pohorelá *Slovak Rep.* **27** C13
Pohořelice *Czech Rep.* **27** C9
Pohorje *Slovenia* **41** B12
Pohri *India* **68** G6
Poiana Mare *Romania* **28** G8
Poiana Ruscăi, Munţii
 Romania **28** E7
Poiana Stampei *Romania* **29** C10
Poinsett, C. *Antarctica* **5** C8
Point Arena *U.S.A.* **110** G3
Point Baker *U.S.A.* **102** B2
Point Fortin *Trin. & Tob.* **125** K15
Point Hope *U.S.A.* **106** B6
Point L. *Canada* **100** D9
Point Lisas *Trin. & Tob.* **125** K15
Point Pedro *Sri Lanka* **66** Q12
Point Pelee △ *Canada* **114** E2
Point Pleasant *N.J., U.S.A.* **115** F10
Point Pleasant *W. Va.,
 U.S.A.* **113** F12
Point Reyes ⇀ *U.S.A.* **110** G2
Pointe-à-Pitre *Guadeloupe* **120** b
Pointe-au-Pic = La Malbaie
 Canada **105** C5
Pointe-Claire *Canada* **115** A11
Pointe-Gatineau *Canada* **115** A9
Pointe-Noire *Congo* **84** E2
Pointe-Noire *Guadeloupe* **120** b
Poio *Spain* **36** C2
Poipet *Cambodia* **64** F4
Poirino *Italy* **40** D4
Poisonbush Ra. *Australia* **92** D3
Poissonnier Pt. *Australia* **92** C2
Poitiers *France* **18** F7
Poitou *France* **20** B3
Poitou-Charentes □ *France* **20** B4
Poix-de-Picardie *France* **19** C8
Poix-Terron *France* **19** C11
Pojoaque *U.S.A.* **109** J10
Pokaran *India* **68** F4
Pokataroo *Australia* **95** D4
Pokhara *Nepal* **69** E10
Pokhvistnevo *Russia* **34** D11
Poko *Dem. Rep. of the Congo* **86** B2
Poko *Sudan* **81** F3
Pokrov *Russia* **32** E10
Pokrovsk *Russia* **53** C13
Pokrovskoye *Russia* **33** J10
Pol-e Dokhtar *Iran* **73** F12
Pol-e Zahāb *Iran* **73** E11
Pola = Pula *Croatia* **41** D10
Pola *Russia* **32** D7
Pola de Allande *Spain* **36** B4
Pola de Lena *Spain* **36** B5
Pola de Siero *Spain* **36** B5
Pola de Somiedo *Spain* **36** B4
Polacca *U.S.A.* **109** J8
Polan *Iran* **71** E9
Poland ■ *Europe* **31** C10
Polanica-Zdrój *Poland* **31** H3
Połaniec *Poland* **31** H8
Polanów *Poland* **30** D3
Polar Bear △ *Canada* **104** A2
Polatlı *Turkey* **72** C5

Polatsk *Belarus* **32** E5
Polcura *Chile* **126** D1
Polczyn-Zdrój *Poland* **30** E3
Poldasht *Iran* **73** C11
Polessk *Russia* **30** D8
Polesye = Pripet Marshes
 Europe **23** B15
Polgár *Hungary* **28** C6
Poli *Cameroon* **83** C7
Policastro, G. di *Italy* **43** C8
Police *Poland* **30** E1
Police, Pte. *Seychelles* **85** b
Polichnitos *Greece* **47** B8
Polička *Czech Rep.* **27** B9
Policoro *Italy* **43** B9
Poliegos *Greece* **46** E6
Poligiros *Greece* **44** F7
Polignano a Mare *Italy* **43** A9
Poligny *France* **19** F12
Polillo Is. *Phil.* **61** D5
Polillo Strait *Phil.* **61** D4
Polis *Cyprus* **49** D11
Polístena *Italy* **43** D9
Polk *U.S.A.* **114** E5
Polkowice *Poland* **31** G3
Polla *Italy* **43** B8
Pollachi *India* **66** P10
Pollença *Spain* **48** B10
Pollença, B. de *Spain* **48** B10
Póllica *Italy* **43** B8
Pollino, Mte. *Italy* **43** C9
Pollino △ *Italy* **43** C9
Polna *Russia* **32** C5
Polnovat *Russia* **52** C7
Pology *Ukraine* **33** J9
Polokwane *S. Africa* **89** C4
Polokwane ⇀ *S. Africa* **89** C5
Polonne *Ukraine* **23** C14
Polonnoye = Polonne
 Ukraine **23** C14
Polski Trŭmbesh *Bulgaria* **45** C9
Polsko Kosovo *Bulgaria* **45** C9
Polson *U.S.A.* **108** C6
Poltár *Slovak Rep.* **27** C12
Poltava *Ukraine* **33** H8
Poltava ⇀ *Ukraine* **33** G7
Põltsamaa *Estonia* **32** C3
Polunochnoye *Russia* **52** C7
Põlva *Estonia* **32** C4
Polyana *Ukraine* **28** B7
Polyarny *Russia* **8** B25
Polyarnyye Zori *Russia* **8** C25
Polynesia *Pac. Oc.* **97** F11
Polynésie française =
 French Polynesia ☑
 Pac. Oc. **97** J13
Pomarance *Italy* **40** E7
Pombal *Portugal* **36** F2
Pombia *Greece* **49** E6
Pomene *Mozam.* **89** C6
Pomeroy *U.K.* **15** B5
Pomeroy *Ohio, U.S.A.* **113** F12
Pomeroy *Wash., U.S.A.* **108** C5
Pomézia *Italy* **42** A5
Pomichna *Ukraine* **33** H6
Pomío, L. de *Bolivia* **124** E6
Pomona *Australia* **95** D5
Pomona *U.S.A.* **111** L9
Pomorie *Bulgaria* **45** D11
Pomorskie □ *Poland* **30** D5
Pomorskie, Pojezierze *Poland* **30** E3
Pomos *Cyprus* **49** D11
Pomos, C. *Cyprus* **49** D11
Pompano Beach *U.S.A.* **117** H14
Pompei *Italy* **43** B7
Pompey *France* **19** D13
Pompeys Pillar *U.S.A.* **108** D10
Pompeys Pillar △ *U.S.A.* **108** D10
Pompton Lakes *U.S.A.* **115** F10
Ponape = Pohnpei *Micronesia* **96** G7
Ponask L. *Canada* **104** B1
Ponca *U.S.A.* **112** D5
Ponca City *U.S.A.* **116** C6
Ponce *Puerto Rico* **121** d
Ponchatoula *U.S.A.* **117** F9
Poncheville, L. *Canada* **104** B4
Pond *U.S.A.* **111** K7
Pond Inlet *Canada* **101** C16
Pondicherry = Puducherry
 India **66** P11
Ponds, I. of *Canada* **105** B8
Ponferrada *Spain* **36** C4
Pongo, Wadi ⇀ *Sudan* **81** F2
Poniatowa *Poland* **31** G9
Poniec *Poland* **31** G3
Ponikva *Slovenia* **41** B12
Ponnani *India* **66** P9
Ponoka *Canada* **102** C6
Ponorogo *Indonesia* **63** G14
Pons = Ponts *Spain* **38** D6
Pons *France* **20** C3
Ponsul ⇀ *Portugal* **36** F3
Pont-à-Mousson *France* **19** D13
Pont-Audemer *France* **18** C7
Pont-Aven *France* **18** E3
Pont Canavese *Italy* **40** C4
Pont-d'Ain *France* **19** F12
Pont-de-Roide *France* **19** E13
Pont-de-Salars *France* **20** D6
Pont-de-Vaux *France* **19** F11
Pont-de-Veyle *France* **19** F11

Pont-du-Château *France* **19** G10
Pont-l'Abbé *France* **18** E2
Pont-l'Évêque *France* **18** C7
Pont-St-Esprit *France* **21** D8
Pont-St-Martin *Italy* **40** C4
Pont-Ste-Maxence *France* **19** C9
Pont-sur-Yonne *France* **19** D10
Ponta Delgada *Azores* **78** a
Ponta do Sol *Madeira* **48** D3
Ponta Grossa *Brazil* **127** B5
Ponta Porã *Brazil* **127** A4
Pontacq *France* **20** E3
Pontailler-sur-Saône *France* **19** E12
Pontarlier *France* **19** F13
Pontassieve *Italy* **41** E8
Pontaumur *France* **20** C6
Pontcharra *France* **21** C10
Pontchartrain, L. *U.S.A.* **117** F9
Pontchâteau *France* **18** E4
Ponte da Barca *Portugal* **36** D2
Ponte de Sor *Portugal* **37** F2
Ponte dell'Ólio *Italy* **40** D6
Ponte di Legno *Italy* **40** B7
Ponte do Lima *Portugal* **36** D2
Ponte do Pungué *Mozam.* **87** F3
Ponte-Leccia *France* **21** F13
Ponte nelle Alpi *Italy* **41** B9
Ponte Nova *Brazil* **127** A7
Ponteareas *Spain* **36** C2
Pontebba *Italy* **41** B10
Ponteceso *Spain* **36** B1
Pontecorvo *Italy* **42** A6
Pontedeume *Spain* **36** B2
Ponteix *Canada* **103** D7
Pontevedra *Spain* **36** C2
Pontevedra □ *Spain* **36** C2
Pontevedra, R. de ⇀ *Spain* **36** C2
Pontevico *Italy* **40** C7
Pontiac *Ill., U.S.A.* **112** E9
Pontiac *Mich., U.S.A.* **113** D12
Pontian Kechil *Malaysia* **65** d
Pontianak *Indonesia* **62** E3
Pontine Mts. = Kuzey
 Anadolu Dağları *Turkey* **72** B7
Pontínia *Italy* **42** A6
Pontivy *France* **18** D4
Pontoise *France* **19** C9
Ponton ⇀ *Canada* **102** B5
Pontorson *France* **18** D5
Pontrémoli *Italy* **40** D6
Pontrieux *France* **18** D3
Ponts *Spain* **38** D6
Pontypool *Canada* **114** B6
Pontypool *U.K.* **15** F4
Ponza *Italy* **42** B5
Ponziane, Ísole *Italy* **42** B5
Poochera *Australia* **95** E1
Poole *U.K.* **15** G6
Poole □ *U.K.* **15** G6
Poona = Pune *India* **66** K8
Pooncarie *Australia* **95** E3
Poopelloe L. *Australia* **95** E3
Popayán *Colombia* **124** C3
Poperinge *Belgium* **17** D2
Popiltah L. *Australia* **95** E3
Popio L. *Australia* **95** E3
Poplar *U.S.A.* **108** B11
Poplar ⇀ *Canada* **103** C9
Poplar Bluff *U.S.A.* **112** G8
Poplarville *U.S.A.* **117** F10
Popocatépetl, Volcán
 Mexico **119** D5
Pópoli *Italy* **41** F10
Popovača *Croatia* **41** C13
Popovo *Bulgaria* **45** C10
Poppberg *Germany* **25** F7
Poppi *Italy* **41** E8
Poprad *Slovak Rep.* **27** B13
Poprad ⇀ *Slovak Rep.* **27** B13
Porali ⇀ *Pakistan* **68** G2
Porbandar *India* **68** J3
Porcher I. *Canada* **102** C2
Porcuna *Spain* **37** H6
Porcupine ⇀ *Canada* **103** B8
Porcupine ⇀ *U.S.A.* **100** D2
Porcupine Gorge △ *Australia* **94** C3
Pordenone *Italy* **41** C9
Pordim *Bulgaria* **45** C8
Poreč *Croatia* **41** C10
Poretskoye *Russia* **34** C8
Pori *Finland* **32** B1
Pori *Greece* **46** F5
Porkhov *Russia* **32** C5
Porlamar *Venezuela* **124** A6
Porlezza *Italy* **40** B6
Porma ⇀ *Spain* **36** C5
Pornic *France* **18** E4
Poronaysk *Russia* **53** E15
Poros *Greece* **46** D5
Poroshiri-Dake *Japan* **54** C11
Poroszló *Hungary* **28** C5
Poroto Mts. *Tanzania* **87** D3

Porpoise B. *Antarctica* **5** C9
Porquerolles, Î. de *France* **21** F10
Porrentruy *Switz.* **25** H3
Porreres *Spain* **48** B10
Port Alberni *Canada* **102** D3
Port Alfred *S. Africa* **88** E4
Port Alice *Canada* **102** C3
Port Allegany *U.S.A.* **114** E6
Port Allen *U.S.A.* **116** F9
Port Alma *Australia* **94** C5
Port Alma *Canada* **114** D2
Port Angeles *U.S.A.* **110** B3
Port Antonio *Jamaica* **120** a
Port Aransas *U.S.A.* **116** H6
Port Arthur *Australia* **95** G4
Port Arthur *U.S.A.* **116** G8
Port au Choix *Canada* **105** B8
Port au Port B. *Canada* **105** C8
Port-au-Prince *Haiti* **121** C5
Port Augusta *Australia* **95** E2
Port Austin *U.S.A.* **114** B2
Port Bell *Uganda* **86** B3
Port Bergé Vaovao *Madag.* **89** B8
Port Blandford *Canada* **105** C9
Port-Bouët *Ivory C.* **82** D4
Port Bradshaw *Australia* **94** A2
Port Broughton *Australia* **95** E2
Port Bruce *Canada* **114** D4
Port Burwell *Canada* **114** D4
Port Canning *India* **69** H13
Port Carling *Canada* **114** A5
Port-Cartier *Canada* **105** B6
Port Chalmers *N.Z.* **91** F3
Port Charlotte *U.S.A.* **117** H13
Port Chester *U.S.A.* **115** F11
Port Clements *Canada* **102** C2
Port Clinton *U.S.A.* **113** E12
Port Colborne *Canada* **114** D5
Port Coquitlam *Canada* **110** A4
Port Credit *Canada* **114** C5
Port-Cros △ *France* **21** F10
Port Curtis *Australia* **94** C5
Port d'Alcúdia *Spain* **48** B10
Port Dalhousie *Canada* **114** C5
Port d'Andratx *Spain* **48** B9
Port Darwin *Australia* **92** B5
Port Darwin *Falk. Is.* **128** G5
Port Davey *Australia* **95** G4
Port-de-Bouc *France* **21** E8
Port-de-Paix *Haiti* **121** C5
Port de Pollença *Spain* **48** B10
Port de Sóller *Spain* **48** B9
Port Dickson *Malaysia* **65** L3
Port Douglas *Australia* **94** B4
Port Dover *Canada* **114** D4
Port Edward *Canada* **102** C2
Port Elgin *Canada* **114** B3
Port Elizabeth *S. Africa* **88** E4
Port Ellen *U.K.* **13** F2
Port-en-Bessin-Huppain
 France **18** C6
Port Erin *I. of Man* **14** C3
Port Essington *Australia* **92** B5
Port Ewen *U.S.A.* **115** E11
Port Fairy *Australia* **95** F3
Port Fouâd = Bûr Fuad *Egypt* **80** H8
Port Gamble *U.S.A.* **110** C4
Port-Gentil *Gabon* **84** E1
Port Germein *Australia* **95** E2
Port Ghalib *Egypt* **70** E2
Port Gibson *U.S.A.* **116** F9
Port Glasgow *U.K.* **13** F4
Port Harcourt *Nigeria* **83** E6
Port Hardy *Canada* **102** C3
Port Harrison = Inukjuak
 Canada **101** F16
Port Hawkesbury *Canada* **105** C7
Port Hedland *Australia* **92** D2
Port Henry *U.S.A.* **115** B11
Port Hood *Canada* **105** C7
Port Hope *Canada* **114** C6
Port Hope *U.S.A.* **114** C2
Port Hope Simpson *Canada* **105** B8
Port Hueneme *U.S.A.* **111** L7
Port Huron *U.S.A.* **114** D2
Port Iliç *Azerbaijan* **73** C13
Port Jefferson *U.S.A.* **115** F11
Port Jervis *U.S.A.* **115** E10
Port Katon *Russia* **33** J10
Port Kelang = Pelabuhan
 Klang *Malaysia* **65** L3
Port Kenny *Australia* **95** E1
Port-la-Nouvelle *France* **20** E7
Port Lairge = Waterford
 Ireland **12** D4
Port Laoise *Ireland* **12** C4
Port Lavaca *U.S.A.* **116** G6
Port Leyden *U.S.A.* **115** C9
Port Lincoln *Australia* **95** E2
Port Loko *S. Leone* **82** D2
Port Louis *France* **18** E3
Port-Louis *Guadeloupe* **120** b
Port Louis *Mauritius* **85** d
Port MacDonnell *Australia* **95** F3
Port McNeill *Canada* **102** C3
Port Macquarie *Australia* **95** E5
Port Maria *Jamaica* **120** a

Port Matilda *U.S.A.* **114** F6
Port McNicoll *Canada* **114** B5
Port Mellon *Canada* **102** D4
Port-Menier *Canada* **105** C7
Port Moody *Canada* **110** A4
Port Morant *Jamaica* **120** a
Port Moresby *Papua N. G.* **90** B7
Port Musgrave *Australia* **94** A3
Port-Navalo *France* **18** E4
Port Neches *U.S.A.* **116** G8
Port Nolloth *S. Africa* **88** D2
Port Nouveau-Québec =
    Kangiqsualujjuaq *Canada*
    101 F18
Port of Climax *Canada* **103** D7
Port of Coronach *Canada* **103** D7
Port of Spain *Trin. & Tob.* **121** D7
Port Orange *U.S.A.* **117** G14
Port Orchard *U.S.A.* **110** C4
Port Orford *U.S.A.* **108** E1
Port Pegasus *N.Z.* **91** G1
Port Perry *Canada* **114** B6
Port Phillip B. *Australia* **95** F3
Port Pirie *Australia* **95** E2
Port Renfrew *Canada* **110** B2
Port Roper *Australia* **94** A2
Port Rowan *Canada* **114** D4
Port Safaga = Bûr Safâga
    Egypt **70** E2
Port Said = Bûr Sa'îd *Egypt* **80** H8
Port St. Joe *U.S.A.* **117** G12
Port St. Johns =
    Umzimvubu *S. Africa* **89** E4
Port-St-Louis-du-Rhône
    France **21** E8
Port St. Lucie *U.S.A.* **117** H14
Port-Ste-Marie *France* **20** D4
Port Sanilac *U.S.A.* **114** C2
Port Severn *Canada* **114** B5
Port Shepstone *S. Africa* **89** E5
Port Simpson *Canada* **102** C2
Port Stanley = Stanley
    Falk. Is. **128** G5
Port Stanley *Canada* **114** D3
Port Sudan = Bûr Sûdân
    Sudan **80** D4
Port Sulphur *U.S.A.* **117** G10
Port-sur-Saône *France* **19** E13
Port Talbot *U.K.* **15** F4
Port Taufiq = Bûr Taufiq
    Egypt **80** J8
Port Townsend *U.S.A.* **110** B4
Port-Vendres *France* **20** F7
Port Vila *Vanuatu* **90** C9
Port Vladimir *Russia* **8** B25
Port Wakefield *Australia* **95** E2
Port Washington *U.S.A.* **112** D10
Porta Orientalis *Romania* **23** F12
Portacloy *Ireland* **12** B2
Portadown *U.K.* **12** B5
Portaferry *U.K.* **12** B6
Portage *Pa., U.S.A.* **114** F6
Portage *Wis., U.S.A.* **112** D9
Portage la Prairie *Canada* **103** D9
Portageville *U.S.A.* **112** G9
Portalegre □ *Portugal* **37** F3
Portalegre *Portugal* **37** F3
Portales *U.S.A.* **109** J12
Portarlington *Ireland* **12** C4
Portbou *Spain* **38** C8
Portel *Portugal* **37** G3
Portela, Lisboa ✈ (LIS)
    Portugal **37** G1
Porter L. *N.W.T., Canada* **103** A7
Porter L. *Sask., Canada* **103** B7
Porterville *S. Africa* **88** E2
Porterville *U.S.A.* **110** J8
Portes-lès-Valence *France* **21** D8
Porthcawl *U.K.* **15** F4
Porthill *U.S.A.* **108** B5
Porthmadog *U.K.* **14** E3
Portile de Fier *Europe* **28** F7
Portimão *Portugal* **37** H2
Portishead *U.K.* **15** F5
Portiței, Gura *Romania* **29** F14
Portknockie *U.K.* **13** D6
Portland *N.S.W., Australia* **95** E5
Portland *Vic., Australia* **95** F3
Portland *Canada* **115** B8
Portland *Conn., U.S.A.* **115** E12
Portland *Maine, U.S.A.* **113** D18
Portland *Mich., U.S.A.* **113** D11
Portland *Oreg., U.S.A.* **110** E4
Portland *Pa., U.S.A.* **115** F9
Portland *Tex., U.S.A.* **116** H6
Portland, I. of *U.K.* **15** G5
Portland B. *Australia* **95** F3
Portland Bight *Jamaica* **120** a
Portland Bill *U.K.* **15** G5
Portland Canal *Canada* **102** B2
Portland Int. ✈ (PDX)
    U.S.A. **110** E4
Portland Pt. *Jamaica* **120** a
Portmadoc = Porthmadog
    U.K. **14** E3
Portmore *Jamaica* **120** a
Porto *France* **21** F12
Porto *Portugal* **36** D2
Porto □ *Portugal* **36** D2
Porto, G. de *France* **21** F12

Pôrto Alegre *Brazil* **127** C5
Porto Azzurro *Italy* **40** F7
Porto Colom *Spain* **48** B10
Porto Cristo *Spain* **48** B10
Pôrto de Moz *Brazil* **125** D8
Porto Empédocle *Italy* **42** E6
Porto Esperança *Brazil* **124** G7
Porto Franco *Brazil* **125** E9
Porto Inglês *C. Verde Is.* **78** b
Porto Mendes *Brazil* **127** A5
Porto Moniz *Madeira* **48** D2
Pôrto Murtinho *Brazil* **124** H7
Porto Nacional *Brazil* **125** F9
Porto-Novo *Benin* **83** D5
Porto Primavera, Represa
    Brazil **127** A5
Porto San Giórgio *Italy* **41** E10
Porto Sant' Elpídio *Italy* **41** E10
Porto Santo, I. de *Madeira* **78** B2
Porto Santo Stéfano *Italy* **40** F8
Porto São José *Brazil* **127** A5
Porto Seguro *Brazil* **125** G11
Pôrto Tolle *Italy* **41** D9
Porto Tórres *Italy* **42** B1
Porto União *Brazil* **127** B5
Porto-Vecchio *France* **21** G13
Pôrto Velho *Brazil* **124** E6
Pôrto Walter *Brazil* **124** E4
Portobelo *Panama* **120** E4
Portoferráio *Italy* **40** F7
Portogruaro *Italy* **41** C9
Portola *U.S.A.* **110** F6
Portomaggiore *Italy* **41** D8
Portopetro *Spain* **48** B10
Portoscuso *Italy* **42** C1
Portovénere *Italy* **40** D6
Portoviejo *Ecuador* **124** D2
Portpatrick *U.K.* **13** G3
Portree *U.K.* **13** D2
Portrush *U.K.* **12** A5
Portsmouth *Dominica* **121** C7
Portsmouth *U.K.* **15** G6
Portsmouth *N.H., U.S.A.* **115** C14
Portsmouth *Ohio, U.S.A.* **113** F12
Portsmouth *R.I., U.S.A.* **115** E13
Portsmouth *Va., U.S.A.* **113** G15
Portsmouth □ *U.K.* **15** G6
Portsoy *U.K.* **13** D6
Portstewart *U.K.* **12** A5
Porttipahdan tekojärvi
    Finland **8** B22
Portugal ■ *Europe* **36** F3
Portugalete *Spain* **38** B1
Portumna *Ireland* **12** C3
Portville *U.S.A.* **114** D6
Poruma *Australia* **94** a
Porvenir *Chile* **128** G2
Porvoo *Finland* **32** B3
Porzuna *Spain* **37** F6
Posada *Italy* **42** B2
Posada ➔ *Italy* **42** B2
Posadas *Argentina* **127** B4
Posadas *Spain* **37** H5
Poschiavo *Switz.* **25** J6
Posets *Spain* **38** C5
Posht-e Badam *Iran* **71** C7
Posídium *Greece* **47** F9
Poso *Indonesia* **63** E6
Posof *Turkey* **73** B10
Posse *Brazil* **125** F9
Possession I. *Antarctica* **5** D11
Pössneck *Germany* **24** E7
Possum Kingdom L. *U.S.A.* **116** E5
Post *U.S.A.* **116** E4
Post Falls *U.S.A.* **108** C5
Postavy = Pastavy *Belarus* **32** E4
Poste-de-la-Baleine =
    Kuujjuarapik *Canada* **104** A4
Postmasburg *S. Africa* **88** D3
Postojna *Slovenia* **41** C11
Poston *U.S.A.* **111** M12
Postville *Canada* **105** B8
Posyet *Russia* **54** C5
Potamos *Antikythira, Greece* **46** F5
Potamos *Kythira, Greece* **46** F4
Potchefstroom *S. Africa* **88** D4
Potcoava *Romania* **29** F9
Poteau *U.S.A.* **116** D7
Poteet *U.S.A.* **116** G5
Potenza *Italy* **43** B8
Potenza ➔ *Italy* **41** E10
Potenza Picena *Italy* **41** E10
Poteriteri, L. *N.Z.* **91** G1
Potgietersrus = Mokopane
    S. Africa **89** C4
Poti *Georgia* **35** J5
Potiskum *Nigeria* **83** C7
Potlogi *Romania* **29** F10
Potomac ➔ *U.S.A.* **113** F14
Potosí *Bolivia* **124** G5
Potosi Mt. *U.S.A.* **111** K11
Pototan *Phil.* **61** F5
Potrerillos *Chile* **126** B2
Potsdam *Germany* **24** C9
Potsdam *U.S.A.* **115** B10
Pottenstein *Germany* **25** F7
Pottersville *U.S.A.* **115** C11
Pottstown *U.S.A.* **115** F9
Pottsville *U.S.A.* **115** F8
Pottuvil *Sri Lanka* **66** R12

P'otzu *Taiwan* **59** F13
Pouancé *France* **18** E5
Pouce Coupé *Canada* **102** B4
Poughkeepsie *U.S.A.* **115** E11
Pouilly-sur-Loire *France* **19** E9
Poulaphouca Res. *Ireland* **12** C5
Poulsbo *U.S.A.* **110** C4
Poultney *U.S.A.* **115** C11
Poulton-le-Fylde *U.K.* **14** D5
Pouso Alegre *Brazil* **127** A6
Pout *Senegal* **82** C1
Pouthisat *Cambodia* **64** F4
Pouytenga *Burkina Faso* **83** C4
Pouzauges *France* **18** F6
Pova de Santa Iria *Portugal* **37** G1
Považská Bystrica
    Slovak Rep. **27** B11
Poverty B. *N.Z.* **91** C7
Pøvlen *Serbia* **44** B3
Póvoa de Lanhosa *Portugal* **36** D2
Póvoa de Varzim *Portugal* **36** D2
Povorino *Russia* **34** E6
Povorotnyy, Mys *Russia* **54** C6
Povungnituk = Puvirnituq
    Canada **101** E16
Powassan *Canada* **104** C4
Poway *U.S.A.* **111** N9
Powder ➔ *U.S.A.* **108** C11
Powder River *U.S.A.* **108** E10
Powell *U.S.A.* **108** D9
Powell, L. *U.S.A.* **109** H8
Powell River *Canada* **102** D4
Powers *U.S.A.* **112** C10
Pownal *U.S.A.* **115** D11
Powys □ *U.K.* **15** E4
Poyang Hu *China* **59** C11
Poyarkovo *Russia* **53** E13
Poysdorf *Austria* **27** C9
Poza de la Sal *Spain* **36** C7
Poza Rica *Mexico* **119** C5
Pozantı *Turkey* **72** D6
Pozarevac *Serbia* **44** B5
Pozazal, Puerto *Spain* **36** C6
Požega *Croatia* **28** E2
Požega *Serbia* **44** C4
Poznań *Poland* **31** F3
Poznań ✈ (POZ) *Poland* **31** F3
Pozo *U.S.A.* **111** K6
Pozo Alcón *Spain* **37** H8
Pozo Almonte *Chile* **124** H5
Pozo Colorado *Paraguay* **126** A4
Pozoblanco *Spain* **37** G6
Pozzallo *Italy* **43** F7
Pozzomaggiore *Italy* **42** B1
Pozzuoli *Italy* **43** B7
Pra ➔ *Ghana* **83** D4
Prabuty *Poland* **30** E6
Prača *Bos.-H.* **28** G3
Prachatice *Czech Rep.* **26** B6
Prachin Buri *Thailand* **64** F3
Prachuap Khiri Khan
    Thailand **65** G2
Pradelles *France* **20** D7
Prades *France* **20** F6
Prado *Brazil* **125** G11
Prado del Rey *Spain* **37** J5
Pragersko *Slovenia* **41** B12
Prague = Praha *Czech Rep.* **26** A7
Praha *Czech Rep.* **26** A7
Praha ✈ (PRG) *Czech Rep.* **26** A7
Prahecq *France* **20** B3
Prahova □ *Romania* **29** E10
Prahova ➔ *Romania* **29** F10
Prahovo *Serbia* **44** B6
Praia *C. Verde Is.* **78** b
Praia a Mare *Italy* **43** C8
Praid *Romania* **29** D10
Prainha *Brazil* **125** D8
Prainha Nova *Brazil* **124** E6
Prairie *Australia* **94** C3
Prairie *U.S.A.* **108** D4
Prairie City *U.S.A.* **108** D4
Prairie Dog Town Fork
    Red ➔ *U.S.A.* **116** D5
Prairie du Chien *U.S.A.* **112** D8
Prairies, L. of the *Canada* **103** C8
Pramanda *Greece* **46** B3
Prampram *Ghana* **83** D4
Pran Buri *Thailand* **64** F2
Prang *Ghana* **83** D4
Prapat *Indonesia* **62** D1
Praslin *Seychelles* **85** b
Prasonísi, Ákra *Greece* **49** D9
Prästmon *Sweden* **10** A11
Praszka *Poland* **31** G5
Prata *Brazil* **125** G9
Pratabpur *India* **69** H10
Pratapgarh *Raj., India* **68** G6
Pratapgarh *Ut. P., India* **69** G9
Pratas Is. = Dongsha Dao
    S. China Sea **59** G11
Prato *Italy* **40** E8
Prátola Peligna *Italy* **41** F10
Prats-de-Mollo-la-Preste
    France **20** F6
Pratt *U.S.A.* **112** G4
Prattville *U.S.A.* **117** E11
Pravdinsk *Kaliningrad, Russia* **30** D8
Pravdinsk *Nizhniy Novgorod,
    Russia* **34** B6

Pravets *Bulgaria* **44** D7
Pravia *Spain* **36** B4
Praya *Indonesia* **62** F5
Prayag = Allahabad *India* **69** G9
Pré-en-Pail *France* **18** D6
Preble *U.S.A.* **115** D8
Precipice △ *Australia* **95** D5
Precordillera *Argentina* **126** C2
Predáppio *Italy* **41** D8
Predazzo *Italy* **41** B8
Predeal *Romania* **29** E10
Predejane *Serbia* **44** D6
Preeceville *Canada* **103** C8
Preetz *Germany* **24** A6
Pregolya ➔ *Russia* **30** D7
Pregrada *Croatia* **41** B12
Preili *Latvia* **32** D4
Preko *Croatia* **41** D12
Prelog *Croatia* **41** B13
Prémery *France* **19** E10
Premià de Mar *Spain* **38** D7
Premont *U.S.A.* **116** H5
Premuda *Croatia* **41** D11
Prentice *U.S.A.* **112** C8
Prenzlau *Germany* **24** B9
Preobrazheniye *Russia* **54** C6
Preparis North Channel
    Ind. Oc. **67** M18
Preparis South Channel
    Ind. Oc. **67** M18
Přerov *Czech Rep.* **27** B10
Prescott *Canada* **115** B9
Prescott *Ariz., U.S.A.* **109** J7
Prescott *Ark., U.S.A.* **116** E8
Prescott Valley *U.S.A.* **109** J7
Preservation Inlet *N.Z.* **91** G1
Preševo *Serbia* **44** D5
Presho *U.S.A.* **112** D3
Presicce *Italy* **43** C11
Presidencia de la Plaza
    Argentina **126** B4
Presidencia Roque Saenz
    Peña *Argentina* **126** B3
Presidente Epitácio *Brazil* **125** H8
Presidente Hayes □
    Paraguay **126** A4
Presidente Prudente *Brazil* **127** A5
Presidio *Mexico* **118** B4
Presidio *U.S.A.* **116** G2
Preslav *Bulgaria* **45** C10
Preslavska Planina *Bulgaria* **45** C10
Prešov *Slovak Rep.* **27** B14
Prešovský □ *Slovak Rep.* **27** B13
Prespa, L. = Prespansko
    Jezero *Macedonia* **44** F5
Prespa △ *Greece* **44** F5
Prespansko Jezero *Macedonia* **44** F5
Presque I. *U.S.A.* **114** D4
Presque Isle *U.S.A.* **113** B19
Prestatyn *U.K.* **14** D4
Prestea *Ghana* **82** D4
Presteigne *U.K.* **15** E5
Přeštice *Czech Rep.* **26** B6
Preston *Canada* **114** C4
Preston *U.K.* **14** D5
Preston *Idaho, U.S.A.* **108** E8
Preston *Minn., U.S.A.* **112** D7
Preston, C. *Australia* **92** D2
Prestonsburg *U.S.A.* **113** G12
Prestranda *Norway* **10** E3
Prestwick *U.K.* **13** F4
Pretoria *S. Africa* **89** D4
Preuilly-sur-Claise *France* **18** F7
Preveza *Greece* **46** C2
Preveza □ *Greece* **46** B2
Prey Veng *Cambodia* **65** G5
Priazovskoye *Ukraine* **33** J8
Pribilof Is. *U.S.A.* **106** D6
Priboj *Serbia* **44** C3
Příbram *Czech Rep.* **26** B7
Price *U.S.A.* **108** G8
Price I. *Canada* **102** C3
Prichard *U.S.A.* **117** F10
Priego *Spain* **38** E2
Priego de Córdoba *Spain* **37** H6
Priekule *Latvia* **30** B8
Priekule *Lithuania* **30** C8
Prien *Germany* **25** H8
Prienai *Lithuania* **30** D10
Prieska *S. Africa* **88** D3
Priest L. *U.S.A.* **108** B5
Priest River *U.S.A.* **108** B5
Priest Valley *U.S.A.* **110** J6
Prievidza *Slovak Rep.* **27** C11
Prijedor *Bos.-H.* **41** D13
Prijepolje *Serbia* **44** C3
Prikaspiyskaya
    Nizmennost = Caspian
    Depression *Eurasia* **35** G9
Prikro *Ivory C.* **82** D4
Prikubanskaya
    Nizmennost *Russia* **35** H4
Prilep *Macedonia* **44** E5
Priluki = Pryluky *Ukraine* **33** G7
Prime Seal I. *Australia* **95** G4
Primo Tapia *Mexico* **111** N10
Primorsk *Kaliningrad, Russia* **30** D6

Primorsk *St. Petersburg,
    Russia* **32** B5
Primorskiy Kray □ *Russia* **54** B7
Primorsko *Bulgaria* **45** D11
Primorsko-Akhtarsk *Russia* **33** J10
Primorskoye *Ukraine* **33** J9
Primrose L. *Canada* **103** C7
Prince Albert *S. Africa* **88** E3
Prince Albert *Canada* **103** C7
Prince Albert △ *Canada* **103** C7
Prince Albert Mts. *Antarctica* **5** D11
Prince Albert Pen. *Canada* **100** A8
Prince Albert Sd. *Canada* **100** A9
Prince Alfred, C. *Antarctica* **4** B1
Prince Charles I. *Canada* **101** D16
Prince Charles Mts. *Antarctica* **5** D6
Prince Edward Fracture
    Zone *Ind. Oc.* **5** A4
Prince Edward I. □ *Canada* **105** C7
Prince Edward Is. *Ind. Oc.* **3** G11
Prince George *Canada* **102** C4
Prince of Wales, C. *U.S.A.* **106** B6
Prince of Wales I. *Australia* **94** A3
Prince of Wales I. *Canada* **100** C12
Prince of Wales I. *U.S.A.* **100** F5
Prince of Wales Icefield
    Canada **101** B16
Prince of Wales Str. *Canada* **100** C8
Prince Patrick I. *Canada* **101** B8
Prince Regent Inlet *Canada* **101** C14
Prince Rupert *Canada* **102** C2
Prince William Sd. *U.S.A.* **100** E2
Princes Town *Trin. & Tob.* **125** K15
Princess Charlotte B.
    Australia **94** A3
Princess Elizabeth Trough
    S. Ocean **5** C7
Princess May Ranges
    Australia **92** C4
Princess Royal I. *Canada* **102** C3
Princeton *Canada* **102** D4
Princeton *Calif., U.S.A.* **110** F4
Princeton *Ill., U.S.A.* **112** E9
Princeton *Ind., U.S.A.* **112** F10
Princeton *Ky., U.S.A.* **112** G10
Princeton *Mo., U.S.A.* **112** E7
Princeton *N.J., U.S.A.* **115** F10
Princeton *W. Va., U.S.A.* **113** G13
Príncipe *São Tomé & Príncipe* **76** F4
Príncipe da Beira *Brazil* **124** F6
Prineville *U.S.A.* **108** D3
Prins Harald Kyst *Antarctica* **5** D4
Prinsesse Astrid Kyst
    Antarctica **5** D3
Prinsesse Ragnhild Kyst
    Antarctica **5** D4
Prinzapolca *Nic.* **120** D3
Prior, C. *Spain* **36** B2
Priozersk *Russia* **32** B5
Pripet = Prypyat ➔ *Europe* **23** C16
Pripet Marshes *Europe* **23** B15
Pripyat Marshes = Pripet
    Marshes *Europe* **23** B15
Pripyats = Prypyat ➔
    Europe **23** C16
Prislop, Pasul *Romania* **29** C9
Pristen *Russia* **33** G9
Priština *Kosovo* **44** D5
Pritzwalk *Germany* **24** B8
Privas *France* **21** D8
Priverno *Italy* **42** A6
Privolzhsk *Russia* **34** B5
Privolzhskaya
    Vozvyshennost *Russia* **34** E7
Privolzhskiy *Russia* **34** E8
Privolzhskiy □ *Russia* **34** B10
Privolzhye *Russia* **34** D9
Priyutnoye *Russia* **35** G6
Prizren *Kosovo* **44** D4
Prizzi *Italy* **42** E6
Prnjavor *Bos.-H.* **28** F2
Probolinggo *Indonesia* **63** G15
Prochowice *Poland* **31** G3
Proctor *U.S.A.* **115** C11
Proddatur *India* **66** M11
Prodhromos *Cyprus* **49** E11
Proença-a-Nova *Portugal* **36** F3
Profilia *Greece* **49** C9
Profondeville *Belgium* **17** D4
Progreso *Coahuila, Mexico* **118** B4
Progreso *Yucatán, Mexico* **119** C7
Progress *Antarctica* **5** C12
Progress *Russia* **53** E13
Prokhladnyy *Russia* **35** J7
Prokletije *Albania* **44** D3
Prokopyevsk *Russia* **52** D9
Prokuplje *Serbia* **44** C5
Proletarsk *Russia* **35** G5
Proletarskaya = Proletarsk
    Russia **35** G5
Prome *Burma* **67** K19
Prophet ➔ *Canada* **102** B4
Prophet River *Canada* **102** B4
Propriá *Brazil* **125** F11
Propriano *France* **21** G12
Proserpine *Australia* **94** b
Prosna ➔ *Poland* **31** G4
Prospect *U.S.A.* **115** C9
Prosser *U.S.A.* **108** C4

Prostějov *Czech Rep.* **27** B10
Prostki *Poland* **30** E9
Proston *Australia* **95** D5
Proszowice *Poland* **31** H7
Proti *Greece* **46** D3
Provadiya *Bulgaria* **45** C11
Provence *France* **21** E9
Provence-Alpes-Côte
    d'Azur □ *France* **21** D10
Providence *Ky., U.S.A.* **112** G10
Providence *R.I., U.S.A.* **115** E13
Providence Bay *Canada* **104** C3
Providence Mts. *U.S.A.* **111** K11
Providencia, I. de *Colombia* **120** D3
Provideniya *Russia* **53** C19
Provincetown *U.S.A.* **113** D18
Provins *France* **19** D10
Provo *U.S.A.* **108** F8
Provost *Canada* **103** C6
Prozor *Bos.-H.* **28** G2
Prrenjas *Albania* **44** E4
Prudhoe Bay *U.S.A.* **106** A10
Prudhoe I. *Australia* **94** C4
Prud'homme *Canada* **103** C7
Prudnik *Poland* **31** H4
Prüm *Germany* **25** E2
Prundu *Romania* **29** F11
Pruszcz Gdański *Poland* **30** D5
Pruszków *Poland* **31** F7
Prut ➔ *Romania* **29** E13
Pruzhany *Belarus* **23** B13
Prvić *Croatia* **41** D11
Prydz B. *Antarctica* **5** C6
Pryluky *Ukraine* **33** G7
Pryor *U.S.A.* **116** C7
Prypyat ➔ *Europe* **23** C16
Przasnysz *Poland* **31** E7
Przedbórz *Poland* **31** G6
Przedecz *Poland* **31** F5
Przemków *Poland* **31** G2
Przemyśl *Poland* **31** J9
Przeworsk *Poland* **31** H9
Przewóz *Poland* **31** G1
Przhevalsk = Karakol
    Kyrgyzstan **52** E8
Przysucha *Poland* **31** G7
Psachna *Greece* **46** C5
Psara *Greece* **47** C7
Psathoura *Greece* **46** B6
Psel ➔ *Ukraine* **33** H7
Pserimos *Greece* **47** E9
Psiloritis, Oros *Greece* **49** D6
Psira *Greece* **49** D7
Pskov *Russia* **32** D5
Pskov □ *Russia* **32** D5
Pskovskoye, Ozero *Russia* **32** D5
Psunj *Croatia* **28** E2
Pteleos *Greece* **46** B4
Ptich = Ptsich ➔ *Belarus* **23** B15
Ptichia = Vidos *Greece* **49** A3
Ptolemaida *Greece* **44** F5
Ptsich ➔ *Belarus* **23** B15
Ptuj *Slovenia* **41** B12
Ptujska Gora *Slovenia* **41** B12
Pu Xian *China* **56** F6
Pua *Thailand* **64** C3
Puán *Argentina* **126** D3
Pu'an *China* **58** E5
Pu'apu'a *Samoa* **91** b
Pubei *China* **58** F7
Pucallpa *Peru* **124** E4
Pucheng *China* **59** D12
Pucheni *Romania* **29** E10
Puchheim *Germany* **25** G7
Puch'on = Bucheon *S. Korea* **57** F14
Púchov *Slovak Rep.* **27** B11
Pucioasa *Romania* **29** E10
Pučišća *Croatia* **41** E13
Puck *Poland* **30** D5
Pucka, Zatoka *Poland* **30** D5
Puçol *Spain* **39** F4
Pudasjärvi *Finland* **8** D22
Puding *China* **58** D5
Pudozh *Russia* **32** B9
Pudu = Suizhou *China* **59** B9
Puducherry *India* **66** P11
Pudukkottai *India* **66** P11
Puebla *Mexico* **119** D5
Puebla □ *Mexico* **119** D5
Puebla de Alcocer *Spain* **37** G5
Puebla de Don Fadrique
    Spain **39** H2
Puebla de Don Rodrigo *Spain* **37** F6
Puebla de Guzmán *Spain* **37** H3
Puebla de la Calzada *Spain* **37** G4
Puebla de Sanabria *Spain* **36** C4
Puebla de Trives = Pobra
    de Trives *Spain* **36** C3
Pueblo *U.S.A.* **108** G11
Puelches *Argentina* **126** D2
Puelén *Argentina* **126** D2
Puente Alto *Chile* **126** C1
Puente-Genil *Spain* **37** H6
Puente la Reina *Spain* **38** C3
Puente San Miguel *Spain* **36** B6
Puenteareas = Ponteareas
    Spain **36** C2
Puentedeume =
    Pontedeume *Spain* **36** B2

Puentes de Garcia
  Rodriguez = As Pontes
  de García Rodríguez *Spain* **36** B3
Pu'er *China* **58** F3
Puerca, Pta. *Puerto Rico* **121** d
Puerco → *U.S.A.* **109** J10
Puerto Aisén *Chile* **128** F2
Puerto Ángel *Mexico* **119** D5
Puerto Arista *Mexico* **119** D6
Puerto Armuelles *Panama* **120** E3
Puerto Ayacucho *Venezuela* **124** B5
Puerto Barrios *Guatemala* **120** C2
Puerto Bermejo *Argentina* **126** B4
Puerto Bermúdez *Peru* **124** F4
Puerto Bolívar *Ecuador* **124** D3
Puerto Cabello *Venezuela* **124** A5
Puerto Cabezas *Nic.* **120** D3
Puerto Cabo Gracias á Dios
  Nic. **120** D3
Puerto Carreño *Colombia* **124** B5
Puerto Castilla *Honduras* **120** C2
Puerto Chicama *Peru* **124** E3
Puerto Coig *Argentina* **128** G3
Puerto Cortés *Honduras* **120** C2
Puerto Cumarebo *Venezuela* **124** A5
Puerto de Alcudia = Port
  d'Alcúdia *Spain* **48** B10
Puerto de Cabrera *Spain* **48** B9
Puerto de Gran Tarajal
  Canary Is. **48** F5
Puerto de la Cruz *Canary Is.* **48** F3
Puerto de los Angeles △
  Mexico **118** C3
Puerto de Mazarrón *Spain* **39** H3
Puerto de Pozo Negro
  Canary Is. **48** F6
Puerto de Sóller = Port de
  Sóller *Spain* **48** B9
Puerto de Somosierra *Spain* **36** D7
Puerto del Carmen *Canary Is.* **48** F6
Puerto del Rosario *Canary Is.* **48** F6
Puerto Deseado *Argentina* **128** F3
Puerto Escondido *Mexico* **119** D5
Puerto Heath *Bolivia* **124** F5
Puerto Inírida *Colombia* **124** C5
Puerto Juárez *Mexico* **119** C7
Puerto La Cruz *Venezuela* **124** A6
Puerto Leguízamo *Colombia* **124** D4
Puerto Lempira *Honduras* **120** C3
Puerto Libertad *Mexico* **118** B2
Puerto Limón *Colombia* **124** C4
Puerto Lobos *Argentina* **128** E3
Puerto Lumbreras *Spain* **39** H3
Puerto Madryn *Argentina* **128** E3
Puerto Maldonado *Peru* **124** F5
Puerto Manatí *Cuba* **120** B4
Puerto Montt *Chile* **128** E2
Puerto Morazán *Nic.* **120** D2
Puerto Morelos *Mexico* **119** C7
Puerto Natales *Chile* **128** G2
Puerto Oscuro *Chile* **126** C1
Puerto Padre *Cuba* **120** B4
Puerto Páez *Venezuela* **124** B5
Puerto Peñasco *Mexico* **118** A2
Puerto Pinasco *Paraguay* **126** A4
Puerto Plata *Dom. Rep.* **121** C5
Puerto Pollensa = Port de
  Pollença *Spain* **48** B10
Puerto Princesa *Phil.* **61** G3
Puerto Quepos *Costa Rica* **120** E3
Puerto Real *Spain* **37** J4
Puerto Rico *Canary Is.* **48** G4
Puerto Rico ☐ *W. Indies* **121** d
Puerto Rico Trench *Atl. Oc.* **121** C6
Puerto San Julián *Argentina* **128** F3
Puerto Santa Cruz *Argentina* **128** G3
Puerto Sastre *Paraguay* **126** A4
Puerto Serrano *Spain* **37** J5
Puerto Suárez *Bolivia* **124** G7
Puerto Vallarta *Mexico* **118** C3
Puerto Varas *Chile* **128** E2
Puerto Wilches *Colombia* **124** B4
Puertollano *Spain* **37** G6
Pueu *Tahiti* **91** d
Pueyrredón, L. *Argentina* **128** F2
Púez Odle △ *Italy* **41** B8
Puffin I. *Ireland* **12** E1
Pugachev *Russia* **34** D9
Pugal *India* **68** E5
Puge *China* **58** D4
Puge *Tanzania* **86** C3
Puget Sound *U.S.A.* **108** C2
Puget-Théniers *France* **21** E10
Púglia ☐ *Italy* **43** A9
Pugōdong *N. Korea* **57** C16
Pugu *Tanzania* **86** D4
Pūgūnzī *Iran* **71** E8
Pui *Romania* **28** E8
Puieşti *Romania* **29** D12
Puig Major *Spain* **48** B9
Puigcerdà *Spain* **38** C6
Puigmal *Spain* **38** C7
Puigpunyent *Spain* **48** B9
Puijiang *China* **58** C6
Puisaye, Collines de la
  France **19** E10
Puiseaux *France* **19** D9
Pujehun *S. Leone* **82** D2
Pujiang *China* **59** C12
Pujols *France* **20** D3

Pujon-ho *N. Korea* **57** D14
Pukaki, L. *N.Z.* **91** F3
Pukapuka *Cook Is.* **97** J11
Pukaskwa △ *Canada* **104** C2
Pukatawagan *Canada* **103** B8
Pukchin *N. Korea* **57** D13
Pukch'ŏng *N. Korea* **57** D15
Pukë *Albania* **44** D3
Pukekohe *N.Z.* **91** B5
Pukhrayan *India* **69** F8
Pukou *China* **59** A12
Pula *Croatia* **41** D10
Pula *Italy* **42** C1
Pulacayo *Bolivia* **124** H5
Pulai *Malaysia* **65** d
Pulandian *China* **57** E11
Pulaski *N.Y., U.S.A.* **115** C8
Pulaski *Tenn., U.S.A.* **117** D11
Pulaski *Va., U.S.A.* **113** G13
Pulau → *Indonesia* **63** F9
Puławy *Poland* **31** G8
Pulga *U.S.A.* **110** F5
Pulicat L. *India* **66** N12
Pullman *U.S.A.* **108** C5
Pulog, Mt. *Phil.* **61** C4
Pultusk *Poland* **31** F8
Pülümür *Turkey* **73** C8
Pumlumon Fawr *U.K.* **15** E4
Puná, I. *Ecuador* **124** D2
Punaauia *Tahiti* **91** d
Punakaiki *N.Z.* **91** E3
Punakha Dzong *Bhutan* **67** F16
Punasar *India* **68** F5
Punata *Bolivia* **124** G5
Punch *India* **69** C6
Punch → *Pakistan* **68** C5
Punda Maria *S. Africa* **89** C5
Pune *India* **66** K8
P'ungsan *N. Korea* **57** D15
Pungue, Ponte de *Mozam.* **87** F3
Puning *China* **59** F11
Punjab ☐ *India* **68** D7
Punjab ☐ *Pakistan* **68** E6
Puno *Peru* **124** G4
Punpun → *India* **69** G11
Punta, Cerro de *Puerto Rico* **121** d
Punta Alta *Argentina* **128** D4
Punta Arenas *Chile* **128** G2
Punta del Díaz *Chile* **126** B1
Punta del Hidalgo *Canary Is.* **48** F3
Punta Gorda *Belize* **119** D7
Punta Gorda *U.S.A.* **117** H13
Punta Prieta *Mexico* **118** B2
Punta Prima *Spain* **48** B11
Punta Umbría *Spain* **37** H4
Puntarenas *Costa Rica* **120** E3
Puntland *Somali Rep.* **75** F4
Punto Fijo *Venezuela* **124** A4
Punxsutawney *U.S.A.* **114** F6
Pupuan *Indonesia* **63** J18
Puqi *China* **59** C9
Puquio *Peru* **124** F4
Pur → *Russia* **52** C8
Puracé, Vol. *Colombia* **124** C3
Puračić *Bos.-H.* **28** F3
Puralia = Puruliya *India* **69** H12
Puranpur *India* **69** E9
Purbeck, Isle of *U.K.* **15** G5
Purcell *U.S.A.* **116** D6
Purcell Mts. *Canada* **102** D5
Purdy *Canada* **114** A7
Puri *India* **67** K14
Purmerend *Neths.* **17** B4
Purnia *India* **69** G12
Purnululu △ *Australia* **92** C4
Pursat = Pouthisat *Cambodia* **64** F4
Purukcahu *Indonesia* **62** E4
Puruliya *India* **69** H12
Purus → *Brazil* **124** D6
Puruvesi *Finland* **32** B5
Purvis *U.S.A.* **117** F10
Pŭrvomay *Bulgaria* **45** D9
Purwa *India* **69** F9
Purwakarta *Indonesia* **63** G12
Purwo, Tanjung *Indonesia* **63** K18
Purwodadi *Indonesia* **63** G14
Purwokerto *Indonesia* **63** G13
Puryŏng *N. Korea* **57** C15
Pusa *India* **69** G11
Pusan = Busan *S. Korea* **57** G15
Pushkin *Russia* **32** C6
Pushkino *Moskva, Russia* **32** D9
Pushkino *Saratov, Russia* **34** E8
Püspökladány *Hungary* **28** C6
Pustoshka *Russia* **32** D5
Puszczykowo *Poland* **31** F3
Put-in-Bay *U.S.A.* **114** E2
Putahow L. *Canada* **103** B8
Putao *Burma* **67** F20
Putaruru *N.Z.* **91** C5
Putbus *Germany* **24** A9
Putian *China* **59** E12
Putignano *Italy* **43** B10
Puting, Tanjung *Indonesia* **62** E4
Putlitz *Germany* **24** B8
Putna *Romania* **29** C10
Putna → *Romania* **29** D11
Putnam *U.S.A.* **115** E13
Putnok *Hungary* **28** B5
Putorana, Gory *Russia* **53** C10

Putrajaya *Malaysia* **65** L3
Puttalam *Sri Lanka* **66** Q11
Puttgarden *Germany* **24** A7
Püttlingen *Germany* **25** F2
Putumayo → *S. Amer.* **124** D5
Putuo *China* **59** C14
Putussibau *Indonesia* **62** D4
Putyla *Ukraine* **29** B10
Puvirnituq *Canada* **101** E16
Puy-de-Dôme *France* **20** C6
Puy-de-Dôme ☐ *France* **20** C7
Puy-l'Évêque *France* **20** D5
Puyallup *U.S.A.* **110** C4
Puyang *China* **56** G8
Puylaurens *France* **20** E6
Pūzeh Rīg *Iran* **71** E8
Puzhaykove *Ukraine* **29** B14
Pwani ☐ *Tanzania* **86** D4
Pweto *Dem. Rep. of the Congo* **87** D2
Pwllheli *U.K.* **14** E3
Pyana → *Russia* **34** C8
Pyaozero, Ozero *Russia* **8** C24
Pyapon *Burma* **67** L19
Pyasina → *Russia* **53** B9
Pyatigorsk *Russia* **35** H6
Pyatykhatky *Ukraine* **33** H7
Pydna *Greece* **44** F6
Pyè = Prome *Burma* **67** K19
Pyeongtaek *S. Korea* **57** F14
Pyetrikaw *Belarus* **23** B15
Pyhäjoki *Finland* **8** D21
Pyinmana *Burma* **67** K20
Pyla, C. *Cyprus* **49** E12
Pymatuning Res. *U.S.A.* **114** E4
Pyŏktong *N. Korea* **57** D13
Pyŏnggang *N. Korea* **57** E14
P'yŏngsong *N. Korea* **57** E13
P'yŏngyang *N. Korea* **57** E13
Pyote *U.S.A.* **116** F3
Pyramid L. *U.S.A.* **108** F4
Pyramid Pk. *U.S.A.* **111** J10
Pyramids *Egypt* **80** J7
Pyrénées *Europe* **20** F4
Pyrénées △ *France* **20** F3
Pyrénées-Atlantiques ☐
  France **20** E3
Pyrénées-Orientales ☐
  France **20** F6
Pyryatyn *Ukraine* **33** G7
Pyrzyce *Poland* **31** E1
Pyskowice *Poland* **31** H5
Pytalovo *Russia* **32** D4
Pyu *Burma* **67** K20
Pyzdry *Poland* **31** F4

Q

Qaanaaq *Greenland* **101** B18
Qabirri → *Azerbaijan* **35** K8
Qachasnek *S. Africa* **89** E4
Qādisiyah, Buhayrat al *Iraq* **73** E10
Qa'el Jafr *Jordan* **74** E5
Qa'emābād *Iran* **71** D9
Qa'emshahr *Iran* **71** B7
Qagan Nur *China* **56** C8
Qahar Youyi Zhongqi *China* **56** D7
Qahremānshahr =
  Kermānshāh *Iran* **73** E12
Qaidam Pendi *China* **60** C4
Qaiyara *Iraq* **73** E10
Qajarīyeh *Iran* **71** D6
Qala, Ras il *Malta* **49** C1
Qala-i-Jadid = Spīn Būldak
  Afghan. **68** D2
Qala Point = Qala, Ras il
  Malta **49** C1
Qala Viala *Pakistan* **68** D2
Qala Yangi *Afghan.* **68** B2
Qal'at al Akhḍar *Si. Arabia* **70** E3
Qal'at Bīshah *Si. Arabia* **80** D5
Qal'at Dīzah *Iraq* **73** D11
Qal'at Şāliḥ *Iraq* **70** D5
Qal'at Sukkar *Iraq* **73** G12
Qalyūb *Egypt* **80** H7
Qamani'tuaq = Baker Lake
  Canada **100** E12
Qamdo *China* **58** B1
Qamea *Fiji* **91** a
Qamruddin Karez *Pakistan* **68** D3
Qandahār = Kandahār
  Afghan. **66** D4
Qandahār = Kandahār ☐
  Afghan. **66** D4
Qandyaghash *Kazakhstan* **52** E6
Qapān *Iran* **71** B7
Qapshaghay *Kazakhstan* **52** E8
Qaqortoq *Greenland* **4** C5
Qâra *Egypt* **80** B2
Qara Dāgh *Iraq* **73** E11
Qara Qash → *China* **69** B8
Qarabutaq *Kazakhstan* **52** E7
Qaraçala *Azerbaijan* **35** L9
Qaraghandy *Kazakhstan* **52** E8
Qaraghayly *Kazakhstan* **52** E8
Qārah *Si. Arabia* **70** D4
Qarah Āghāj *Iran* **73** D12
Qaraqosh *Iraq* **73** D10
Qarataū *Ongtüstik Qazaqstan,
  Kazakhstan* **52** E7
Qarataū *Zhambyl, Kazakhstan* **52** E8

Qarazhal *Kazakhstan* **52** E8
Qardho *Somali Rep.* **75** F4
Qardud *Sudan* **81** E2
Qareh → *Iran* **73** C12
Qareh Tekān *Iran* **71** B6
Qarnein *U.A.E.* **71** E7
Qarqan He → *China* **60** C3
Qarqaraly *Kazakhstan* **52** E8
Qarrasa *Sudan* **81** E3
Qarshi *Uzbekistan* **52** F7
Qartabā *Lebanon* **74** A4
Qārūh *Kuwait* **71** D6
Qaryat al Gharab *Iraq* **70** D5
Qaryat al 'Ulyā *Si. Arabia* **70** E5
Qasr 'Amra *Jordan* **70** D3
Qaşr-e Qand *Iran* **71** E9
Qaşr-e Shīrīn *Iran* **73** E11
Qasr Farâfra *Egypt* **80** B2
Qatanā *Syria* **74** B5
Qatar ■ *Asia* **71** E6
Qatlīsh *Iran* **71** B8
Qattâra *Egypt* **80** A2
Qattâra, Munkhafed el *Egypt* **80** B2
Qattâra Depression =
  Qattâra, Munkhafed el
  Egypt **80** B2
Qausiuittuq = Resolute
  Canada **101** C13
Qawām al Ḥamzah = Al
  Ḥamzah *Iraq* **70** D5
Qāyen *Iran* **71** C8
Qazaqstan =
  Kazakhstan ■ *Asia* **52** E8
Qazax *Azerbaijan* **35** K7
Qazımämmäd *Azerbaijan* **35** K9
Qazvīn *Iran* **71** B6
Qazvīn ☐ *Iran* **71** B6
Qeissan *Sudan* **81** E3
Qena *Egypt* **80** B3
Qena, W. → *Egypt* **80** B3
Qeqertarsuaq *Greenland* **4** C5
Qeqertarsuaq *Greenland* **98** C14
Qeshlāq *Iran* **73** E12
Qeshm *Iran* **71** E8
Qeydār *Iran* **73** D13
Qeys *Iran* **71** E7
Qezel Owzen → *Iran* **71** B6
Qezi'ot *Israel* **74** E3
Qi Xian *China* **56** G8
Qian Gorlos *China* **57** B13
Qian Xian *China* **56** G5
Qiancheng *China* **58** D7
Qianjiang *Guangxi Zhuangzu,
  China* **58** F7
Qianjiang *Hubei, China* **59** B9
Qianjiang *Sichuan, China* **58** C7
Qianshan *China* **59** B11
Qianwei *China* **58** C4
Qianxi *China* **58** D6
Qianyang *Hunan, China* **59** D8
Qianyang *Shaanxi, China* **56** G4
Qianyang *Zhejiang, China* **59** B12
Qiaojia *China* **58** D4
Qichun *China* **59** B10
Qidong *Hunan, China* **59** D9
Qidong *Jiangsu, China* **59** B13
Qijiang *China* **58** C6
Qikiqtarjuaq *Canada* **101** D19
Qila Saifullāh *Pakistan* **68** D3
Qilian Shan *China* **60** C4
Qimen *China* **59** C11
Qin He → *China* **56** G7
Qin Jiang →
  Guangxi Zhuangzu, China **58** F7
Qin Jiang → *Jiangxi, China* **59** D10
Qin Ling = Qinling Shandi
  China **56** H5
Qin'an *China* **56** G3
Qing Xian *China* **56** E9
Qingcheng *China* **57** F9
Qingdao *China* **57** F11
Qingfeng *China* **56** G8
Qinghai ☐ *China* **60** C4
Qinghai Hu *China* **60** C5
Qinghecheng *China* **57** D13
Qinghemen *China* **57** D11
Qingjian *China* **56** F6
Qingjiang = Huaiyin *China* **57** H10
Qingliu *China* **59** D11
Qinglong *China* **59** E5
Qingping *China* **58** D6
Qingpu *China* **59** B13
Qingshui *China* **56** G4
Qingshuihe *China* **56** E6
Qingtian *China* **59** C13
Qingtongxia Shuiku *China* **56** F3
Qingxi *China* **58** D7
Qingxu *China* **56** F7
Qingyang *Anhui, China* **59** B11
Qingyang *Gansu, China* **56** F4
Qingyi Jiang → *China* **58** C4
Qingyuan *Guangdong, China* **59** F9
Qingyuan *Liaoning, China* **57** C13
Qingyuan *Zhejiang, China* **59** D12
Qingyun *China* **57** F9
Qingzhen *China* **58** D6
Qinhuangdao *China* **57** E10
Qinling Shandi *China* **56** H5
Qinshui *China* **56** G7

Qinyuan *China* **56** F7
Qinzhou *China* **58** G7
Qionghai *China* **64** C8
Qionglai *China* **58** B4
Qionglai Shan *China* **58** B4
Qiongzhou Haixia *China* **64** B8
Qiqihar *China* **53** E13
Qiraīya, W. → *Egypt* **74** E3
Qiryat Ata *Israel* **74** C4
Qiryat Gat *Israel* **74** D3
Qiryat Mal'akhi *Israel* **74** D3
Qiryat Shemona *Israel* **74** B4
Qiryat Yam *Israel* **74** C4
Qishan *China* **56** G4
Qitai *China* **60** B3
Qitaihe *China* **54** B5
Qiubei *China* **58** E5
Qixia *China* **57** F11
Qiyang *China* **59** D8
Qızılağac Körfäzi *Azerbaijan* **73** C13
Qojūr *Iran* **73** C11
Qom *Iran* **71** C6
Qom ☐ *Iran* **71** C6
Qomolangma Feng =
  Everest, Mt. *Nepal* **69** E12
Qomsheh *Iran* **71** D6
Qoqek = Tacheng *China* **60** B3
Qoqon = Qŭqon *Uzbekistan* **52** E8
Qoraqalpoghistan ☐
  Uzbekistan **52** E6
Qorveh *Iran* **73** E12
Qostanay *Kazakhstan* **52** D7
Qoţūr *Iran* **73** C11
Qu Jiang → *China* **58** B6
Qu Xian *China* **58** B6
Quabbin Res. *U.S.A.* **115** D12
Quairading *Australia* **93** F2
Quakenbrück *Germany* **24** C3
Quakertown *U.S.A.* **115** F9
Qualicum Beach *Canada* **102** D4
Quambatook *Australia* **95** F3
Quambone *Australia* **95** E4
Quamby *Australia* **94** C3
Quan Long = Ca Mau
  Vietnam **65** H5
Quanah *U.S.A.* **116** D5
Quang Ngai *Vietnam* **64** E7
Quang Tri *Vietnam* **64** D6
Quang Yen *Vietnam* **58** G6
Quannan *China* **59** E10
Quantock Hills *U.K.* **15** F4
Quanzhou *Fujian, China* **59** E12
Quanzhou
  Guangxi Zhuangzu, China **59** E8
Qu'Appelle → *Canada* **103** C8
Quaqtaq *Canada* **101** E18
Quaraí *Brazil* **126** C4
Quarré-les-Tombes *France* **19** E11
Quarteira *Portugal* **37** H2
Quartu Sant'Élena *Italy* **42** C2
Quartzsite *U.S.A.* **111** M12
Quatre Bornes *Mauritius* **85** d
Quatsino Sd. *Canada* **102** C3
Quba *Azerbaijan* **35** K9
Qūchān *Iran* **71** B8
Queanbeyan *Australia* **95** F4
Québec *Canada* **105** C5
Québec ☐ *Canada* **105** C6
Quebo *Guinea-Biss.* **82** C2
Quebrada del Condorito △
  Argentina **126** C3
Quedlinburg *Germany* **24** D7
Queen Alexandra Ra.
  Antarctica **5** E11
Queen Charlotte City
  Canada **102** C2
Queen Charlotte Is. *Canada* **102** C2
Queen Charlotte Sd. *Canada* **102** C3
Queen Charlotte Strait
  Canada **102** C3
Queen Elizabeth △ *Uganda* **86** C3
Queen Elizabeth ☐ *U.K.* **13** E4
Queen Elizabeth Is. *Canada* **101** B13
Queen Mary Land *Antarctica* **5** D7
Queen Maud G. *Canada* **100** D11
Queen Maud Land =
  Dronning Maud Land
  Antarctica **5** D3
Queen Maud Mts. *Antarctica* **5** E13
Queens Channel *Australia* **92** C4
Queenscliff *Australia* **95** F3
Queensland ☐ *Australia* **94** C3
Queenstown *Australia* **95** G4
Queenstown *N.Z.* **91** F2
Queenstown *Singapore* **65** d
Queenstown *S. Africa* **88** E4
Queets *U.S.A.* **110** C2
Queguay Grande →
  Uruguay **126** C4
Queimadas *Brazil* **125** F11
Quelimane *Mozam.* **87** F4
Quellón *Chile* **128** E2
Quelpart = Jeju-do *S. Korea* **57** H14
Queluz *Portugal* **37** G1
Quemado *N. Mex., U.S.A.* **109** J9
Quemado *Tex., U.S.A.* **116** G4
Quemoy = Chinmen *Taiwan* **59** E13
Quemú-Quemú *Argentina* **126** D3
Quequén *Argentina* **126** D4
Querétaro *Mexico* **118** C4

Querétaro ☐ *Mexico* **118** C5
Querfurt *Germany* **24** D7
Quérigut *France* **20** F6
Quesada *Spain* **37** H7
Queshan *China* **56** H8
Quesnel *Canada* **102** C4
Quesnel → *Canada* **102** C4
Quesnel L. *Canada* **102** C4
Questa *U.S.A.* **109** H11
Questembert *France* **18** E4
Quetico △ *Canada* **104** C1
Quetta *Pakistan* **68** D2
Queyras △ *France* **21** D10
Quezaltenango *Guatemala* **120** D1
Quezon City *Phil.* **61** D4
Qufār *Si. Arabia* **70** E4
Qui Nhon *Vietnam* **64** F7
Quibala *Angola* **84** G3
Quibaxe *Angola* **84** F2
Quibdó *Colombia* **124** B3
Quiberon *France* **18** E3
Quiberon, Presqu'île de
  France **18** E3
Quickborn *Germany* **24** B5
Quiet L. *Canada* **102** A2
Quiindy *Paraguay* **126** B4
Quilá *Mexico* **118** C3
Quilán, C. *Chile* **128** E2
Quilcene *U.S.A.* **110** C4
Quilimarí *Chile* **126** C1
Quilino *Argentina* **126** C3
Quillabamba *Peru* **124** F4
Quillagua *Chile* **126** A2
Quillan *France* **20** F6
Quilmes *Argentina* **126** C4
Quilon *India* **66** Q10
Quilpie *Australia* **95** D3
Quilpué *Chile* **126** C1
Quilua *Mozam.* **87** F4
Quimilí *Argentina* **126** B3
Quimper *France* **18** E2
Quimperlé *France* **18** E3
Quinault → *U.S.A.* **110** C2
Quincy *Calif., U.S.A.* **110** F6
Quincy *Fla., U.S.A.* **117** F12
Quincy *Ill., U.S.A.* **112** F8
Quincy *Mass., U.S.A.* **115** D14
Quincy *Wash., U.S.A.* **108** C4
Quines *Argentina* **126** C2
Quinga *Mozam.* **87** F5
Quingey *France* **19** E12
Quinhámel *Guinea-Biss.* **82** C1
Quintana de la Serena *Spain* **37** G5
Quintana Roo ☐ *Mexico* **119** D7
Quintanar de la Orden *Spain* **37** F7
Quintanar de la Sierra *Spain* **38** D2
Quintanar del Rey *Spain* **39** F3
Quintero *Chile* **126** C1
Quintin *France* **18** D4
Quinto *Spain* **38** D4
Quípar → *Spain* **39** G3
Quirihue *Chile* **126** D1
Quirimbas △ *Mozam.* **87** E5
Quirindi *Australia* **95** E5
Quirinópolis *Brazil* **125** G9
Quiroga *Spain* **36** C3
Quissac *France* **21** E8
Quissanga *Mozam.* **87** E5
Quissico *Mozam.* **89** C5
Quitilipi *Argentina* **126** B3
Quitman *U.S.A.* **117** F13
Quito *Ecuador* **124** D3
Quixadá *Brazil* **125** D11
Quixaxe *Mozam.* **87** F5
Qujing *China* **58** E4
Qulan *Kazakhstan* **52** E8
Qul'ân, Jazā'ir *Egypt* **70** E2
Qulsary *Kazakhstan* **52** E6
Qumbu *S. Africa* **89** E4
Qŭnghirot *Uzbekistan* **52** E6
Qu'nyido *China* **58** B2
Quoin I. *Australia* **92** B4
Quoin Pt. *S. Africa* **88** E2
Quorn *Australia* **95** E2
Qŭqon *Uzbekistan* **52** E8
Qurein *Sudan* **81** E3
Qurimbas *Mozam.* **87** E5
Qurnat as Sawdā' *Lebanon* **74** A5
Qûs *Egypt* **80** B3
Qusar *Azerbaijan* **35** K9
Quşaybā' *Si. Arabia* **70** E4
Quşaybah *Iraq* **73** E9
Quseir *Egypt* **70** E2
Qūshchī *Iran* **73** D11
Quthing *Lesotho* **89** E4
Qūţīābād *Iran* **71** C6
Quwo *China* **56** G6
Quyang *China* **56** E8
Quynh Nhai *Vietnam* **64** B4
Quyon *Canada* **115** A8
Quzhou *China* **59** C12
Quzi *China* **56** F4
Qvareli *Georgia* **35** K7
Qyzylorda *Kazakhstan* **52** E7

R

Ra, Ko *Thailand* **65** H2
Raab *Austria* **26** C6
Raahe *Finland* **8** D21
Raalte *Neths.* **17** B6
Raasay *U.K.* **13** D2
Raasay, Sd. of *U.K.* **13** D2
Rab *Croatia* **41** D11
Raba *Indonesia* **63** F5
Rába → *Hungary* **28** C2
Raba → *Poland* **31** H7
Rabaçal → *Portugal* **36** D3
Rabah *Nigeria* **83** C6
Rabai *Kenya* **86** C4
Rabak *Sudan* **81** E3
Rabastens *France* **20** E5
Rabastens-de-Bigorre *France* **20** E4
Rabat = Victoria *Malta* **49** C1
Rabat *Malta* **49** D1
Rabat *Morocco* **78** B4
Rabaul *Papua N. G.* **90** B8
Rabbit Flat *Australia* **92** D5
Rabbit Lake Mine *Canada* **103** B8
Rabi *Fiji* **91** a
Rābigh *Si. Arabia* **75** C2
Rabka *Poland* **31** J6
Râbniţa *Moldova* **29** C14
Rābor *Iran* **71** D8
Rabwah = Chenab Nagar
　Pakistan **68** D5
Rača *Serbia* **44** B4
Răcăciuni *Romania* **29** D11
Răcăşdia *Romania* **28** F6
Racconigi *Italy* **40** D4
Race, C. *Canada* **105** C9
Rach Gia *Vietnam* **65** G5
Rachid *Mauritania* **82** B2
Raciąż *Poland* **31** F7
Racibórz *Poland* **31** H5
Racichy *Belarus* **30** E10
Racine *U.S.A.* **112** D10
Rackerby *U.S.A.* **110** F5
Radama, Nosy *Madag.* **89** A8
Radama, Saikanosy *Madag.* **89** A8
Radan *Serbia* **44** D5
Rădăuţi *Romania* **29** C10
Rădăuţi-Prut *Romania* **29** B11
Radbuza → *Czech Rep.* **26** B6
Radcliff *U.S.A.* **113** G11
Radeberg *Germany* **24** D9
Radebeul *Germany* **24** D9
Radeče *Slovenia* **41** B12
Radekhiv *Ukraine* **23** C13
Radekhiv = Radekhiv
　Ukraine **23** C13
Radenthein *Austria* **26** E6
Radew → *Poland* **30** D2
Radford *U.S.A.* **113** G13
Radhanpur *India* **68** H4
Radhwa, Jabal *Si. Arabia* **70** E3
Radika → *Macedonia* **44** E4
Radisson *Qué., Canada* **104** B4
Radisson *Sask., Canada* **103** C7
Radium Hot Springs *Canada* **102** C5
Radlje ob Dravi *Slovenia* **41** B12
Radnevo *Bulgaria* **45** D9
Radnice *Czech Rep.* **26** B6
Radnor Forest *U.K.* **15** E4
Radolfzell *Germany* **25** H4
Radom *Poland* **31** G8
Radomka → *Poland* **31** G8
Radomsko *Poland* **31** G6
Radomyshl *Ukraine* **23** C15
Radomyśl Wielki *Poland* **31** H8
Radoszyce *Poland* **31** G7
Radoviš *Macedonia* **44** E6
Radovljica *Slovenia* **41** B11
Radstadt *Austria* **26** D6
Radstock, C. *Australia* **95** E1
Răducăneni *Romania* **29** D12
Raduša *Macedonia* **44** D5
Raduzhnyy *Russia* **52** C8
Radvanichy *Belarus* **31** F11
Radviliškis *Lithuania* **30** C10
Radville *Canada* **103** D8
Raḑwá, J. *Si. Arabia* **80** C4
Radymno *Poland* **31** J9
Radzanów *Poland* **31** F7
Radziejów *Poland* **31** F5
Radzyń Chełmiński *Poland* **30** E5
Radzyń Podlaski *Poland* **31** G9
Rae *Canada* **102** A5
Rae Bareli *India* **69** F9
Rae Isthmus *Canada* **101** D14
Raeren *Belgium* **17** D6
Raeside, L. *Australia* **93** E3
Raetihi *N.Z.* **91** C5
Rafaela *Argentina* **126** C3
Rafah *Gaza Strip* **74** D3
Rafai *C.A.R.* **86** B1
Raffadali *Italy* **42** E6
Raffili *Sudan* **81** F2
Rafina *Greece* **46** C6
Rafsanjān *Iran* **71** D8
Raft Pt. *Australia* **92** C3
Râgă *Sudan* **81** F2
Raga → *Sudan* **81** F2

Ragachow *Belarus* **23** B16
Ragag *Sudan* **81** E1
Ragama *Sri Lanka* **66** R11
Ragged, Mt. *Australia* **93** F3
Ragged Pt. *Barbados* **121** c
Raghunathpalli *India* **69** H11
Raghunathpur *India* **69** H12
Raglan *N.Z.* **91** B5
Ragusa *Italy* **43** F7
Raha *Indonesia* **63** E6
Rahad, Nahr ed → *Sudan* **81** E3
Rahaeng = Tak *Thailand* **64** D2
Rahat, Ḥarrat *Si. Arabia* **80** C5
Rahatgarh *India* **69** H8
Rahden *Germany* **24** C4
Raheita *Eritrea* **81** E5
Rahimyar Khan *Pakistan* **68** E4
Rāhjerd *Iran* **71** C6
Rahole △ *Kenya* **86** B4
Rahon *India* **68** D7
Raiatéa, Î. *French Polynesia* **97** J12
Raichur *India* **66** L10
Raiganj *India* **69** G13
Raigarh *India* **67** J13
Raikot *India* **68** D6
Railton *Australia* **95** G4
Rainbow Bridge △ *U.S.A.* **109** H8
Rainbow Lake *Canada* **102** B5
Rainier *U.S.A.* **110** D4
Rainier, Mt. *U.S.A.* **110** D5
Rainy L. *Canada* **103** D10
Rainy River *Canada* **103** D10
Raippaluoto *Finland* **8** E19
Raipur *India* **67** J12
Ra'is *Si. Arabia* **80** C4
Raisen *India* **68** H8
Raisio *Finland* **32** B2
Raj Nandgaon *India* **67** J12
Raj Nilgiri *India* **69** J12
Raja, Ujung *Indonesia* **62** D1
Raja Ampat, Kepulauan
　Indonesia **63** E8
Rajahmundry *India* **67** L12
Rajaji △ *India* **68** D8
Rajang → *Malaysia* **62** D4
Rajanpur *Pakistan* **68** E4
Rajapalaiyam *India* **66** Q10
Rajasthan □ *India* **68** F5
Rajasthan Canal = Indira
　Gandhi Canal *India* **68** F5
Rajauri *India* **69** C6
Rajgarh *Mad. P., India* **68** G7
Rajgarh *Raj., India* **68** E7
Rajgarh *Raj., India* **68** E6
Rajgir *India* **69** G11
Rajgród *Poland* **30** E9
Rajkot *India* **68** H4
Rajmahal Hills *India* **69** G12
Rajpipla *India* **66** J8
Rajpur *India* **68** H6
Rajpura *India* **68** D7
Rajsamand = Kankroli *India* **68** G5
Rajshahi *Bangla.* **67** G16
Rajshahi □ *Bangla.* **69** G13
Rajula *India* **68** J4
Rakaia *N.Z.* **91** E4
Rakaia → *N.Z.* **91** E4
Rakan, Ra's *Qatar* **71** E6
Rakaposhi *Pakistan* **69** A6
Rakata, Pulau *Indonesia* **62** F3
Rakhiv *Ukraine* **29** B9
Rakhni *Pakistan* **68** D3
Rakhni → *Pakistan* **68** E3
Rakhny-Lisovi *Ukraine* **29** B13
Rakiraki *Fiji* **91** a
Rakitnoye *Russia* **54** B7
Rakitovo *Bulgaria* **45** E8
Rakiura = Stewart I. *N.Z.* **91** G1
Rakiura △ *N.Z.* **91** G1
Rakoniewice *Poland* **31** F3
Rakops *Botswana* **88** C3
Rakovica *Croatia* **41** D12
Rakovník *Czech Rep.* **26** A6
Rakovski *Bulgaria* **45** D8
Rakvere *Estonia* **32** C4
Raleigh *U.S.A.* **117** D15
Ralik Chain *Pac. Oc.* **96** G8
Ralja *Serbia* **44** B4
Ralls *U.S.A.* **116** E4
Ralston *U.S.A.* **114** E8
Ram → *Canada* **102** A4
Rām Allāh *West Bank* **74** D4
Rama *Nic.* **120** D3
Ramacca *Italy* **43** E7
Ramakona *India* **69** J8
Ramales de la Victoria *Spain* **36** B7
Rāmallāh = Rām Allāh
　West Bank **74** D4
Raman *Thailand* **65** J3
Ramanathapuram *India* **66** Q11
Ramanetaka, B. de *Madag.* **89** A8
Ramanujganj *India* **69** H10
Ramat Gan *Israel* **74** C3
Ramatlhabama *S. Africa* **88** D4
Ramban *India* **69** C6
Rambervillers *France* **19** D13
Rambi = Rabi *Fiji* **91** a
Rambipuji *Indonesia* **63** H15

Rambouillet *France* **19** D8
Rame Hd. *Australia* **95** F4
Ramechhap *Nepal* **69** F12
Ramenskoye *Russia* **32** E10
Ramganga → *India* **69** F8
Ramgarh *Jharkhand, India* **69** H11
Ramgarh *Raj., India* **68** F6
Ramgarh *Raj., India* **68** F4
Rāmhormoz *Iran* **71** D6
Ramīān *Iran* **71** B7
Ramingining *Australia* **94** A2
Ramla *Israel* **74** D3
Ramlu *Eritrea* **81** E5
Ramm = Rum *Jordan* **74** F4
Ramm, Jabal *Jordan* **74** F4
Râmna → *Romania* **29** E12
Ramnad =
　Ramanathapuram *India* **66** Q11
Ramnagar
　Jammu & Kashmir, India **69** C6
Ramnagar *Uttarakhand, India* **69** E8
Ramnäs *Sweden* **10** E10
Râmnicu Sărat *Romania* **29** E12
Râmnicu Vâlcea *Romania* **29** E9
Ramnous *Greece* **46** C6
Ramon *Russia* **33** G10
Ramona *U.S.A.* **111** M10
Ramonville-St-Agne *France* **20** E5
Ramore *Canada* **104** C3
Ramos → *Nigeria* **83** D6
Ramotswa *Botswana* **88** C4
Rampur *H.P., India* **68** D7
Rampur *Mad. P., India* **68** H5
Rampur *Ut. P., India* **69** E8
Rampur Hat *India* **69** G12
Rampura *India* **68** G6
Ramrama Tola *India* **69** J8
Ramree I. *Burma* **67** K19
Rāmsar *Iran* **71** B6
Ramsey *I. of Man* **14** C3
Ramsey *U.S.A.* **115** E10
Ramsey L. *Canada* **104** C3
Ramsgate *U.K.* **15** F9
Ramsjö *Sweden* **10** B9
Ramstein *Germany* **25** F3
Ramtek *India* **66** J11
Ramu *Kenya* **86** B5
Ramvik *Sweden* **10** B11
Rana Pratap Sagar Dam
　India **68** G6
Ranaghat *India* **69** H13
Ranahu *Pakistan* **68** G3
Ranau *Malaysia* **62** C5
Rancagua *Chile* **126** C1
Rancheria → *Canada* **102** A3
Ranchester *U.S.A.* **108** D10
Ranchi *India* **69** H11
Rancho Cordova *U.S.A.* **110** G5
Rancho Cucamonga *U.S.A.* **111** L9
Randalstown *U.K.* **12** B5
Randan *France* **19** F10
Randazzo *Italy* **43** E7
Randers *Denmark* **11** H4
Randers Fjord *Denmark* **11** H4
Randfontein *S. Africa* **89** D4
Randle *U.S.A.* **110** D5
Randolph *Mass., U.S.A.* **115** D13
Randolph *N.Y., U.S.A.* **114** D6
Randolph *Utah, U.S.A.* **108** F8
Randolph *Vt., U.S.A.* **115** C12
Randsburg *U.S.A.* **111** K9
Råneälven → *Sweden* **8** D20
Rangae *Thailand* **65** J3
Rangaunu B. *N.Z.* **91** A4
Range, The *Zimbabwe* **87** F3
Rangeley *U.S.A.* **115** B14
Rangeley L. *U.S.A.* **115** B14
Rangely *U.S.A.* **108** F9
Ranger *U.S.A.* **116** E5
Rangia *India* **67** F17
Rangiora *N.Z.* **91** E4
Rangitaiki → *N.Z.* **91** B6
Rangitata → *N.Z.* **91** E3
Rangitoto ke te tonga =
　D'Urville I. *N.Z.* **91** D4
Rangkasbitung *Indonesia* **63** G12
Rangon → *Burma* **67** L20
Rangoon *Burma* **67** L20
Rangpur *Bangla.* **67** G16
Rangsang *Indonesia* **65** M4
Rangsit *Thailand* **65** J3
Ranibennur *India* **66** M9
Raniganj *Ut. P., India* **69** F9
Raniganj *W. Bengal, India* **67** H15
Ranikhet *India* **69** E8
Raniwara *India* **68** G5
Rāniyah *Iraq* **73** D11
Ranka *India* **69** H10
Ranken → *Australia* **94** C2
Rankin *U.S.A.* **116** F4
Rankin Inlet *Canada* **100** E13
Rankins Springs *Australia* **95** E4
Rankweil *Austria* **26** D2
Rannoch, L. *U.K.* **13** E4
Rannoch Moor *U.K.* **13** E4
Ranobe, Helodranon' i
　Madag. **89** C7
Ranohira *Madag.* **89** C8

Ranomafana *Toamasina,
　Madag.* **89** B8
Ranomafana *Toliara, Madag.* **89** C8
Ranomena *Madag.* **89** C8
Ranong *Thailand* **65** H2
Ranotsara Nord *Madag.* **89** C8
Rantabe *Madag.* **89** B8
Rantauprapat *Indonesia* **62** D1
Rantemario *Indonesia* **63** E5
Ranthambore △ *India* **68** F7
Rantoul *U.S.A.* **112** E9
Ranum *Denmark* **11** H3
Ranyah, W. → *Si. Arabia* **80** C5
Raohe *China* **54** A7
Raon l'Étape *France* **19** D13
Raoping *China* **59** F11
Raoyang *China* **56** E8
Rap, Ko *Thailand* **65** b
Rapa *French Polynesia* **97** K13
Rapa Nui = Pascua, I. de
　Chile **97** K17
Rapallo *Italy* **40** D6
Rapar *India* **68** H4
Rāpch *Iran* **71** E8
Rapel, Lago *Chile* **126** C1
Raper, C. *Canada* **101** D18
Rapid City *U.S.A.* **112** C2
Rapid River *U.S.A.* **112** C10
Rapla *Estonia* **32** C3
Rapti → *India* **69** F10
Rapu Rapu I. *Phil.* **61** E6
Raqaba ez Zarqa → *Sudan* **81** F2
Raqqa = Ar Raqqah *Syria* **73** E9
Raquette → *U.S.A.* **115** B10
Raquette Lake *U.S.A.* **115** C10
Rara △ *Nepal* **69** E10
Rarotonga *Cook Is.* **97** K12
Ras Abu Soma *Egypt* **80** B3
Ra's al 'Ayn *Syria* **73** D9
Ra's al Khaymah *U.A.E.* **71** E7
Ra's aţ Ţib *Tunisia* **76** C5
Râs el Mâ *Mali* **82** B4
Râs Ghârib *Egypt* **80** B3
Râs Muhammad △ *Egypt* **80** B3
Râs Sudr *Egypt* **80** B3
Rasa, Pta. *Argentina* **126** E4
Rasca, Pta. de la *Canary Is.* **48** G3
Raseiniai *Lithuania* **30** C10
Rashad *Sudan* **81** E3
Rashi *Egypt* **80** H7
Rashīd, Masabb *Egypt* **80** H7
Rashmi *India* **68** G6
Rasht *Iran* **73** D13
Rasi Salai *Thailand* **64** E5
Raška *Serbia* **44** C4
Râsnov *Romania* **29** E10
Rason L. *Australia* **93** E3
Raşova *Romania* **29** F12
Rasovo *Bulgaria* **44** C7
Rasra *India* **69** G10
Rasskazovo *Russia* **34** D5
Rast *Romania* **29** G8
Rastatt *Germany* **25** G4
Rastede *Germany* **24** B4
Răstoliţa *Romania* **29** D9
Rasul *Pakistan* **68** C5
Raszków *Poland* **31** G4
Rat → *Canada* **103** D9
Rat Buri *Thailand* **64** F2
Rat Islands *U.S.A.* **106** E3
Rat L. *Canada* **103** B9
Ratak Chain *Pac. Oc.* **96** G8
Rătan *Sweden* **10** B9
Ratangarh *India* **68** E6
Raţāwī *Iraq* **70** D5
Rath *India* **69** G8
Rath Luirc *Ireland* **12** D3
Rathangan *Ireland* **12** C4
Rathdrum *Ireland* **12** D5
Rathenow *Germany* **24** C8
Rathkeale *Ireland* **12** D3
Rathlin I. *U.K.* **12** A5
Rathmelton *Ireland* **12** A4
Ratibor = Racibórz *Poland* **31** H5
Rätikon *Austria* **26** D2
Ratingen *Germany* **24** D2
Ratlam *India* **68** H6
Ratmanova Ostrov *Russia* **106** B6
Ratnagiri *India* **66** L8
Ratodero *Pakistan* **68** F3
Raton *U.S.A.* **109** H11
Ratten *Austria* **26** D8
Rattray Hd. *U.K.* **13** D7
Rättvik *Sweden* **10** D9
Ratz, Mt. *Canada* **102** B2
Ratzeburg *Germany* **24** B6
Raub *Malaysia* **65** L3
Rauch *Argentina* **126** D4
Raudales *Mexico* **119** D6
Raufarhöfn *Iceland* **8** C6
Raufoss *Norway* **8** F14
Raukumara Ra. *N.Z.* **91** C6
Rauma *Finland* **32** B1
Raumo = Rauma *Finland* **32** B1
Raung, Gunung *Indonesia* **63** J17
Raurkela *India* **69** H11

Rausu-Dake *Japan* **54** B12
Răut → *Moldova* **29** C14
Rava-Ruska *Ukraine* **31** H10
Rava Russkaya =
　Rava-Ruska *Ukraine* **31** H10
Ravalli *U.S.A.* **108** C6
Ravānsar *Iran* **73** E12
Ravanusa *Italy* **42** E6
Rāvar *Iran* **71** D8
Ravena *U.S.A.* **115** D11
Ravenna *Italy* **41** D9
Ravenna *Nebr., U.S.A.* **112** E4
Ravenna *Ohio, U.S.A.* **114** E3
Ravensburg *Germany* **25** H5
Ravenshoe *Australia* **94** B4
Ravensthorpe *Australia* **93** F3
Ravenswood *Australia* **94** C4
Ravenswood *U.S.A.* **113** F13
Ravi → *Pakistan* **68** D4
Ravna Gora *Croatia* **41** C11
Ravna Reka *Serbia* **44** B5
Ravne na Koroškem
　Slovenia **41** B11
Rawa Mazowiecka *Poland* **31** G7
Rawalpindi *Pakistan* **68** C5
Rawang *Malaysia* **65** L3
Rawene *N.Z.* **91** A4
Rawicz *Poland* **31** G3
Rawka → *Poland* **31** F7
Rawlinna *Australia* **93** F4
Rawlins *U.S.A.* **108** F10
Rawlinson Ra. *Australia* **93** D4
Rawson *Argentina* **128** E3
Raxaul *India* **69** F11
Ray *U.S.A.* **112** A2
Ray, C. *Canada* **105** C8
Ray Mts. *U.S.A.* **106** B9
Raya Ring, Ko *Thailand* **65** a
Rayadurg *India* **66** M10
Rayagada *India* **67** K13
Raychikhinsk *Russia* **53** E13
Rāyen *Iran* **71** D8
Rayleigh *U.K.* **15** F8
Raymond *Canada* **102** D6
Raymond *Calif., U.S.A.* **110** H7
Raymond *N.H., U.S.A.* **115** C13
Raymond *Wash., U.S.A.* **110** D3
Raymondville *U.S.A.* **116** H6
Raymore *Canada* **103** C8
Rayón *Mexico* **118** B2
Rayong *Thailand* **64** F3
Raystown L. *U.S.A.* **114** F6
Rayville *U.S.A.* **116** E9
Raz, Pte. du *France* **18** D2
Razan *Iran* **73** E13
Razāzah, Buḥayrat ar *Iraq* **73** F10
Razazah, L. = Razāzah,
　Buḥayrat ar *Iraq* **73** F10
Razdelna *Bulgaria* **45** C11
Razdel'naya = Rozdilna
　Ukraine **29** D15
Razdolnoye *Russia* **54** C5
Razdolnoye *Ukraine* **33** K7
Razeh *Iran* **71** C6
Razgrad *Bulgaria* **45** C10
Razim, Lacul *Romania* **29** F14
Razlog *Bulgaria* **44** E7
Razmak *Pakistan* **68** C3
Re, Cu Lao *Vietnam* **64** E7
Ré, Î. de *France* **20** B2
Reading *U.K.* **15** F7
Reading *U.S.A.* **115** F9
Reading □ *U.K.* **15** F7
Realicó *Argentina* **126** D3
Réalmont *France* **20** E6
Ream *Cambodia* **65** G4
Ream △ *Cambodia* **65** G4
Reata *Mexico* **118** B4
Reay Forest *U.K.* **13** C4
Rebais *France* **19** D10
Rebecca, L. *Australia* **93** F3
Rebi *Indonesia* **63** F8
Rebiana *Libya* **79** D10
Rebiana, Sahrâ' *Libya* **79** D10
Reboly *Russia* **8** E24
Rebun-Tō *Japan* **54** B10
Recanati *Italy* **41** E10
Recaş *Romania* **28** E6
Recco *Italy* **40** D6
Recherche, Arch. of the
　Australia **93** F3
Rechna Doab *Pakistan* **68** D5
Rechytsa *Belarus* **23** B16
Recife *Brazil* **125** E12
Recife *Seychelles* **85** b
Recklinghausen *Germany* **17** C6
Reconquista *Argentina* **126** B4
Recreo *Argentina* **126** B2
Recz *Poland* **31** E2
Red → *U.S.A.* **116** F9
Red Bank *U.S.A.* **115** F10
Red Bay *Canada* **105** B8
Red Bluff *U.S.A.* **108** F2
Red Bluff Res. *U.S.A.* **109** L12
Red Cliffs *Australia* **95** E3
Red Cloud *U.S.A.* **112** E4
Red Creek *U.S.A.* **115** C8
Red Deer *Canada* **102** C6
Red Deer → *Alta., Canada* **103** C7

Red Deer → *Man., Canada* **103** C8
Red Deer L. *Canada* **103** C8
Red Hook *U.S.A.* **115** E11
Red Indian L. *Canada* **105** C8
Red L. *Canada* **103** C10
Red Lake *Canada* **103** C10
Red Lake Falls *U.S.A.* **112** B6
Red Lake Road *Canada* **103** C10
Red Lodge *U.S.A.* **108** D9
Red Mountain *U.S.A.* **111** K9
Red Oak *U.S.A.* **112** E7
Red River of the North →
　N. Amer. **112** A5
Red Rock *Canada* **104** C2
Red Rock, L. *U.S.A.* **112** E7
Red Rocks Pt. *Australia* **93** F4
Red Sea *Asia* **75** C2
Red Slate Mt. *U.S.A.* **110** H8
Red Sucker L. *Canada* **104** B1
Red Tower Pass = Turnu
　Roşu, P. *Romania* **29** E9
Red Volta → *Africa* **83** C4
Red Wing *U.S.A.* **112** C7
Reda *Poland* **30** D5
Redang *Malaysia* **65** K4
Redange *Lux.* **17** E5
Redcar *U.K.* **14** C6
Redcar & Cleveland □ *U.K.* **14** C7
Redcliff *Canada* **108** AE
Redcliffe *Australia* **95** D5
Redcliffe, Mt. *Australia* **93** E3
Reddersburg *S. Africa* **88** D4
Redding *U.S.A.* **108** F2
Redditch *U.K.* **15** E6
Redfield *U.S.A.* **112** C4
Redford *U.S.A.* **115** B11
Redhead *Trin. & Tob.* **125** K16
Redkino *Russia* **32** D9
Redlands *U.S.A.* **111** M9
Redmond *Oreg., U.S.A.* **108** D3
Redmond *Wash., U.S.A.* **110** C4
Redon *France* **18** E4
Redonda *Antigua & B.* **121** C7
Redondela *Spain* **36** C2
Redondo *Portugal* **37** G3
Redondo Beach *U.S.A.* **111** M8
Redoubt Volcano *U.S.A.* **106** C9
Redruth *U.K.* **15** G2
Redvers *Canada* **103** D8
Redwater *Canada* **102** C6
Redwood *U.S.A.* **115** B9
Redwood △ *U.S.A.* **108** F1
Redwood City *U.S.A.* **110** H4
Redwood Falls *U.S.A.* **112** C6
Ree, L. *Ireland* **12** C3
Reed City *U.S.A.* **113** D11
Reed L. *Canada* **103** C8
Reedley *U.S.A.* **110** J7
Reedsburg *U.S.A.* **112** D8
Reedsport *U.S.A.* **108** E1
Reedsville *U.S.A.* **114** F7
Reefton *N.Z.* **91** E3
Rees *Germany* **24** D2
Reese → *U.S.A.* **108** F5
Refahiye *Turkey* **73** C8
Reftele *Sweden* **11** G7
Refugio *U.S.A.* **116** G6
Rega → *Poland* **30** D2
Regalbuto *Italy* **43** E7
Regana, C. de *Spain* **48** B9
Regen *Germany* **25** G9
Regen → *Germany* **25** F8
Regensburg *Germany* **25** F8
Regenstauf *Germany* **25** F8
Reggâne = Zaouiet
　Reggâne *Algeria* **78** C6
Reggello *Italy* **41** E8
Réggio di Calábria *Italy* **43** D8
Réggio nell'Emília *Italy* **40** D7
Reghin *Romania* **29** D9
Regina *Canada* **103** C8
Regina Beach *Canada* **103** C8
Registro *Brazil* **127** A6
Reguengos de Monsaraz
　Portugal **37** G3
Rehar → *India* **69** H10
Rehli *India* **69** H8
Rehoboth *Namibia* **88** C2
Rehovot *Israel* **74** D3
Reichenbach *Germany* **24** E8
Reid *Australia* **93** F4
Reidsville *U.S.A.* **117** C15
Reigate *U.K.* **15** F7
Reille *Spain* **49** F7
Reims *France* **19** C11
Reina Adelaida, Arch. *Chile* **128** G2
Reina Sofía, Tenerife ✈
　(TFS) *Canary Is.* **48** F3
Reinbek *Germany* **24** B6
Reindeer I. *Canada* **103** C9
Reindeer L. *Canada* **103** B8
Reinga, C. *N.Z.* **91** A4
Reinosa *Spain* **36** B6
Reitz *S. Africa* **89** D4
Reivilo *S. Africa* **88** D3
Rejaf *Sudan* **81** G3
Rejmyre *Sweden* **11** F9
Rejowiec Fabryczny *Poland* **31** G10
Reka → *Slovenia* **41** C11

Rekovac *Serbia* **44** C5
Reliance *Canada* **103** A7
Rémalard *France* **18** D7
Remanso *Brazil* **125** E10
Remarkable, Mt. *Australia* **95** E2
Rembang *Indonesia* **63** G14
Remedios *Panama* **120** E3
Remeshk *Iran* **71** E8
Remetea *Romania* **29** D10
Remich *Lux.* **17** E6
Remiremont *France* **19** D13
Remo *Ethiopia* **81** F5
Remontnoye *Russia* **35** G6
Remoulins *France* **21** E8
Remscheid *Germany* **17** C7
Ren Xian *China* **56** F8
Rendang *Indonesia* **63** J18
Rende *Italy* **43** C9
Rendina *Greece* **46** B3
Rendsburg *Germany* **24** A5
Renfrew *Canada* **115** A8
Renfrewshire □ *U.K.* **13** F4
Rengat *Indonesia* **62** E2
Rengo *Chile* **126** C1
Renhua *China* **59** E9
Renhuai *China* **58** D6
Reni = Taranagar *India* **68** E6
Reni *Ukraine* **29** E13
Renk *Sudan* **81** E3
Renmark *Australia* **95** E3
Rennell Sd. *Canada* **102** C2
Renner Springs *Australia* **94** B1
Rennes *France* **18** D5
Rennick Glacier *Antarctica* **5** D21
Rennie L. *Canada* **103** A7
Reno *U.S.A.* **110** F7
Reno ~ *Italy* **41** D9
Renovo *U.S.A.* **114** E7
Renqiu *China* **56** E9
Rens *Denmark* **11** K3
Renshou *China* **58** C5
Rensselaer *Ind., U.S.A.* **112** E10
Rensselaer *N.Y., U.S.A.* **115** D11
Renton *U.S.A.* **110** C4
Renukoot *India* **69** G10
Réo *Burkina Faso* **82** C4
Reocín = Puente San
    Miguel *Spain* **36** B6
Reotipur *India* **69** G10
Répcelak *Hungary* **28** C2
Republic *Mo., U.S.A.* **112** G7
Republic *Wash., U.S.A.* **108** B4
Republican ~ *U.S.A.* **112** F5
Repulse B. *Australia* **94** b
Repulse Bay *Canada* **101** D14
Requena *Peru* **124** E4
Requena *Spain* **39** F3
Réquista *France* **20** D6
Reşadiye *Muğla, Turkey* **47** E9
Reşadiye *Tokat, Turkey* **72** B7
Reşadiye Yarımadası *Turkey* **47** E9
Resavica *Serbia* **44** B5
Resen *Macedonia* **44** E5
Reserve *U.S.A.* **109** K9
Resht = Rasht *Iran* **73** D13
Resistencia *Argentina* **126** B4
Reşiţa *Romania* **28** E6
Resko *Poland* **30** E2
Reso = Raisio *Finland* **32** B2
Resolute *Canada* **101** C13
Resolution I. *Canada* **101** E19
Resolution I. *N.Z.* **91** F1
Ressano Garcia *Mozam.* **89** D5
Reston *Canada* **103** D8
Reszel *Poland* **30** D8
Retalhuleu *Guatemala* **120** D1
Retenue, L. de
    Dem. Rep. of the Congo **87** E2
Retezat, Munţii *Romania* **28** E8
Retezat △ *Romania* **28** E7
Retford *U.K.* **14** D7
Rethel *France* **19** C11
Rethem *Germany* **24** C5
Rethímno *Greece* **49** D6
Rethímno □ *Greece* **49** D6
Reti *Pakistan* **68** E3
Retiche, Alpi *Switz.* **25** J6
Retiers *France* **18** E5
Retortillo *Spain* **36** E4
Retournac *France* **21** C8
Rétság *Hungary* **28** C4
Réunion ☑ *Ind. Oc.* **85** c
Reus *Spain* **38** D6
Reuterstadt Stavenhagen
    Germany **24** B8
Reutlingen *Germany* **25** G5
Reutte *Austria* **26** D3
Reval = Tallinn *Estonia* **32** C3
Revel *France* **20** E6
Revelganj *India* **69** G11
Revelstoke *Canada* **102** C5
Reventazón *Peru* **124** E2
Revigny-sur-Ornain *France* **19** D11
Revillagigedo, Is. de *Pac. Oc.* **118** D2
Revin *France* **19** C11
Revúca *Slovak Rep.* **27** C13
Revuè ~ *Mozam.* **87** F3
Rewa *India* **69** G9
Rewari *India* **68** E7
Rexburg *U.S.A.* **108** E8

Rey *Iran* **71** C6
Rey, I. del *Panama* **120** E4
Rey, L. del *Mexico* **118** B4
Rey Malabo *Eq. Guin.* **83** E6
Reyðarfjörður *Iceland* **8** D6
Reyes, Pt. *U.S.A.* **110** H3
Reyhanlı *Turkey* **72** D7
Reykjahlíð *Iceland* **8** D5
Reykjanes *Iceland* **8** E2
Reykjavík *Iceland* **8** D3
Reynolds Ra. *Australia* **92** D5
Reynoldsville *U.S.A.* **114** E6
Reynosa *Mexico* **119** B5
Rēzekne *Latvia* **32** D4
Rezina *Moldova* **29** C13
Rezovo *Bulgaria* **45** D12
Rezvān *Iran* **71** E8
Rezvānshahr *Iran* **73** D13
Rgotina *Serbia* **44** B6
Rhayader *U.K.* **15** E4
Rheda-Wiedenbrück
    Germany **24** D4
Rhede *Germany* **24** D2
Rhein ~ *Europe* **17** C6
Rhein-Main-Donau-Kanal
    Germany **25** F7
Rhein-Ruhr, Düsseldorf ✈
    (DUS) *Germany* **24** D2
Rhein-Taunus △ *Germany* **25** E4
Rhein-Westerwald △
    Germany **24** E3
Rheinbach *Germany* **24** E2
Rheine *Germany* **24** C3
Rheinfelden *Germany* **25** H3
Rheinhessen-Pfalz □
    Germany **25** F3
Rheinland-Pfalz □ *Germany* **25** E2
Rheinsberg *Germany* **24** B8
Rhin = Rhein ~ *Europe* **17** C6
Rhine = Rhein ~ *Europe* **17** C6
Rhinebeck *U.S.A.* **115** E11
Rhineland-Palatinate =
    Rheinland-Pfalz □
    Germany **25** E2
Rhinelander *U.S.A.* **112** C9
Rhinns Pt. *U.K.* **13** F2
Rhino Camp *Uganda* **86** B3
Rhir, Cap *Morocco* **78** B4
Rho *Italy* **40** C6
Rhode Island □ *U.S.A.* **115** E13
Rhodes *Greece* **49** C10
Rhodes ✈ (RHO) *Greece* **47** E10
Rhodope Mts. = Rhodopi
    Planina *Bulgaria* **45** E8
Rhodopi Planina *Bulgaria* **45** E8
Rhön *Germany* **24** E5
Rhondda *U.K.* **15** F4
Rhondda Cynon Taff □ *U.K.* **15** F4
Rhône □ *France* **21** C8
Rhône ~ *France* **21** E8
Rhône-Alpes □ *France* **21** C9
Rhum *U.K.* **13** E2
Rhyl *U.K.* **14** D4
Ri-Aba *Eq. Guin.* **83** E6
Ria Formosa *Portugal* **37** H3
Riachão *Brazil* **125** E9
Riangnom *Sudan* **81** F3
Riaño *Spain* **36** C6
Rians *France* **21** E9
Riansáres ~ *Spain* **37** F7
Riasi *India* **69** C6
Riau □ *Indonesia* **62** E2
Riau, Kepulauan *Indonesia* **62** D2
Riau Arch. = Riau,
    Kepulauan *Indonesia* **62** D2
Riaza *Spain* **36** D7
Riaza ~ *Spain* **36** D7
Riba de Saelices *Spain* **38** E2
Riba-roja de Túria *Spain* **39** F4
Ribadavia *Spain* **36** C2
Ribadeo *Spain* **36** B3
Ribadesella *Spain* **36** B5
Ribado *Nigeria* **83** D7
Ribao *Cameroon* **83** D7
Ribas = Ribes de Freser *Spain* **38** C7
Ribas do Rio Pardo *Brazil* **125** H8
Ribauè *Mozam.* **87** E4
Ribble ~ *U.K.* **14** D5
Ribe *Denmark* **11** J2
Ribeauvillé *France* **19** D14
Ribécourt-Dreslincourt
    France **19** C9
Ribeira = Santa Uxía de
    Ribeira *Spain* **36** C2
Ribeira Brava *Madeira* **48** D2
Ribeira Grande *C. Verde Is.* **78** b
Ribeirão Prêto *Brazil* **127** A6
Ribemont *France* **19** C10
Ribera *Italy* **42** E6
Ribérac *France* **20** C4
Riberalta *Bolivia* **124** F5
Ribes de Freser *Spain* **38** C7
Ribnica *Slovenia* **41** C11
Ribnitz-Damgarten *Germany* **24** A8
Říčany *Czech Rep.* **26** B7
Riccarton *N.Z.* **91** E4
Riccia *Italy* **43** A7
Riccione *Italy* **41** E9
Rice *U.S.A.* **111** L12
Rice L. *Canada* **114** B6

Rice Lake *U.S.A.* **112** C8
Rich, C. *Canada* **114** B4
Richard Toll *Senegal* **82** B1
Richards Bay *S. Africa* **89** D5
Richardson ~ *Canada* **103** B6
Richardson Lakes *U.S.A.* **113** C18
Richardson Springs *U.S.A.* **110** F5
Riche, C. *Australia* **93** F2
Richelieu *France* **18** E7
Richey *U.S.A.* **108** C11
Richfield *U.S.A.* **108** G7
Richfield Springs *U.S.A.* **115** D10
Richford *U.S.A.* **115** B12
Richibucto *Canada* **105** C7
Richland *Ga., U.S.A.* **117** E12
Richland *Wash., U.S.A.* **108** C4
Richland Center *U.S.A.* **112** D8
Richlands *U.S.A.* **113** G13
Richmond *Australia* **94** C3
Richmond *N.Z.* **91** D4
Richmond *U.K.* **14** C6
Richmond *Calif., U.S.A.* **110** H4
Richmond *Ind., U.S.A.* **113** F11
Richmond *Ky., U.S.A.* **113** G11
Richmond *Mich., U.S.A.* **114** D2
Richmond *Mo., U.S.A.* **112** F7
Richmond *Tex., U.S.A.* **116** G7
Richmond *Utah, U.S.A.* **108** F8
Richmond *Va., U.S.A.* **113** G15
Richmond *Vt., U.S.A.* **115** B12
Richmond Hill *Canada* **114** C5
Richmond Ra. *Australia* **95** D5
Richmondville *U.S.A.* **115** D10
Richtersveld △ *S. Africa* **88** D2
Richville *U.S.A.* **115** B9
Richwood *U.S.A.* **113** F13
Ricla *Spain* **38** D3
Ridder = Leninogorsk
    Kazakhstan **52** D9
Riddlesburg *U.S.A.* **114** F6
Ridgecrest *U.S.A.* **111** K9
Ridgefield *Conn., U.S.A.* **115** E11
Ridgefield *Wash., U.S.A.* **110** E4
Ridgeland *Miss., U.S.A.* **117** E9
Ridgeland *S.C., U.S.A.* **117** E14
Ridgetown *Canada* **114** D3
Ridgewood *U.S.A.* **115** F10
Ridgway *U.S.A.* **114** E6
Riding Mountain △ *Canada* **103** C9
Ridley, Mt. *Australia* **93** F3
Riebeek-Oos *S. Africa* **88** E4
Ried *Austria* **26** C6
Riedlingen *Germany* **25** G5
Riedstadt *Germany* **25** F4
Rienza ~ *Italy* **41** B8
Riesa *Germany* **24** D9
Riesi *Italy* **43** E7
Riet ~ *S. Africa* **88** D3
Rietavas *Lithuania* **30** C8
Rietbron *S. Africa* **88** E3
Rietfontein *Namibia* **88** C3
Rieti *Italy* **41** F9
Rieupeyroux *France* **20** D6
Riez *France* **21** E10
Rif = Er Rif *Morocco* **78** A5
Riffe L. *U.S.A.* **110** D4
Rifle *U.S.A.* **108** G10
Rift Valley *Africa* **76** G7
Rift Valley ~ *Kenya* **86** B4
Rīga *Latvia* **30** B11
Rīga ✈ (RIX) *Latvia* **30** B10
Riga, G. of *Latvia* **30** A10
Rigacikun *Nigeria* **83** C6
Rīgān *Iran* **71** D8
Rīgas Jūras Līcis = Riga, G.
    of *Latvia* **30** A10
Rigaud *Canada* **115** A10
Rigby *U.S.A.* **108** E8
Rīgestān *Afghan.* **66** D4
Riggins *U.S.A.* **108** D5
Rignac *France* **20** D6
Rigolet *Canada* **105** B8
Rigu *Ghana* **83** D4
Rihand Dam *India* **69** G10
Riihimäki *Finland* **32** B3
Riiser-Larsen-halvøya
    Antarctica **5** C4
Riiser-Larsen Ice Shelf
    S. Ocean **5** D2
Riiser-Larsen Sea *S. Ocean* **5** C4
Rijau *Nigeria* **83** C6
Rijeka *Croatia* **41** C11
Rijeka Crnojevića *Montenegro* **44** D3
Rijssen *Neths.* **17** B6
Rika ~ *Ukraine* **29** B8
Rike *Ethiopia* **81** E4
Rikuchū-Kaigan △ *Japan* **54** E11
Rikuzentakada *Japan* **54** E10
Rila *Bulgaria* **44** D7
Rila Planina *Bulgaria* **44** D7
Riley *U.S.A.* **108** E4
Rima ~ *Nigeria* **83** C6
Rimah, Wadi ar ~ *Si. Arabia* **70** E4
Rimau, Pulau *Malaysia* **65** c
Rimavská Sobota
    Slovak Rep. **27** C13
Rimbey *Canada* **102** C6
Rimbo *Sweden* **10** E12
Rimersburg *U.S.A.* **114** E5
Rimforsa *Sweden* **11** F9

Rimi *Nigeria* **83** C6
Rímini *Italy* **41** D9
Rimouski *Canada* **105** C6
Rimrock *U.S.A.* **110** D5
Rinca *Indonesia* **63** F5
Rincón de la Victoria *Spain* **37** J6
Rincón de Romos *Mexico* **118** C4
Rinconada *Argentina* **126** A2
Rind ~ *India* **69** G9
Ringarum *Sweden* **11** F10
Ringas *India* **68** F6
Ringe *Denmark* **11** J4
Ringgold Is. *Fiji* **91** a
Ringim *Nigeria* **83** C6
Ringkøbing *Denmark* **11** H2
Ringkøbing Fjord *Denmark* **11** H2
Ringsjön *Sweden* **11** J7
Ringsted *Denmark* **11** J5
Ringvassøya *Norway* **8** B18
Ringwood *U.S.A.* **115** E10
Rinia *Greece* **47** D7
Rinjani *Indonesia* **62** F5
Rinteln *Germany* **24** C5
Río, Punta del *Spain* **39** J2
Rio Branco *Brazil* **124** E5
Río Branco *Uruguay* **127** C5
Río Bravo *Mexico* **119** B5
Río Bravo △ N. Amer. **118** B4
Río Bravo del Norte ~
    Mexico **119** B5
Río Brilhante *Brazil* **127** A5
Río Claro *Brazil* **127** A6
Río Claro *Trin. & Tob.* **121** D7
Río Colorado *Argentina* **128** D4
Río Cuarto *Argentina* **126** C3
Rio das Pedras *Mozam.* **89** C6
Rio de Janeiro *Brazil* **127** A7
Rio de Janeiro □ *Brazil* **127** A7
Rio do Sul *Brazil* **127** B6
Río Dulce △ *Guatemala* **120** C2
Río Gallegos *Argentina* **128** G3
Rio Grande *Argentina* **128** G3
Rio Grande *Brazil* **127** C5
Río Grande *Mexico* **118** C4
Río Grande *Puerto Rico* **121** d
Rio Grande ~ *N. Amer.* **116** J6
Río Grande City *U.S.A.* **116** H5
Río Grande de Santiago ~
    Mexico **118** C3
Rio Grande do Norte □
    Brazil **125** E11
Rio Grande do Sul □ *Brazil* **127** C5
Río Lagartos *Mexico* **119** C7
Rio Largo *Brazil* **125** E11
Rio Maior *Portugal* **37** F2
Rio Marina *Italy* **40** F7
Río Mulatos *Bolivia* **124** G5
Río Muni □ *Eq. Guin.* **84** D2
Rio Negro *Brazil* **127** B6
Rio Pardo *Brazil* **127** C5
Río Pilcomayo △ *Argentina* **126** B4
Río Platano △ *Honduras* **120** C3
Rio Rancho *U.S.A.* **109** J10
Río Segundo *Argentina* **126** C3
Río Tercero *Argentina* **126** C3
Rio Tinto *Portugal* **36** D2
Rio Verde *Brazil* **125** G8
Río Verde *Mexico* **119** C5
Rio Vista *U.S.A.* **110** G5
Ríobamba *Ecuador* **124** D3
Ríohacha *Colombia* **124** A4
Riom *France* **20** C7
Riom-ès-Montagnes *France* **20** C6
Rion-des-Landes *France* **20** E3
Rionero in Vúlture *Italy* **43** B8
Rioni ~ *Georgia* **35** J5
Ríos *Spain* **36** D3
Ríosucio *Colombia* **124** B3
Riou L. *Canada* **103** B7
Rioz *France* **19** E13
Ripatransone *Italy* **41** F10
Ripley *Canada* **114** B3
Ripley *Calif., U.S.A.* **111** M12
Ripley *N.Y., U.S.A.* **114** D5
Ripley *Tenn., U.S.A.* **117** D10
Ripley *W. Va., U.S.A.* **113** F13
Ripoll *Spain* **38** C7
Ripon *U.K.* **14** C6
Ripon *Calif., U.S.A.* **110** H5
Ripon *Wis., U.S.A.* **112** D9
Riposto *Italy* **43** E8
Risan *Montenegro* **44** D2
Riscle *France* **20** E3
Rishā', W. ar ~ *Si. Arabia* **70** E5
Rishiri-Rebun-Sarobetsu △
    Japan **54** B10
Rishiri-Tō *Japan* **54** B10
Rishon le Ziyyon *Israel* **74** D3
Risle ~ *France* **18** C7
Risnjak △ *Croatia* **41** C11
Rison *U.S.A.* **116** D8
Risør *Norway* **9** G13
Rita Blanca Cr. ~ *U.S.A.* **116** D3
Riti *Nigeria* **83** D6
Rittman *U.S.A.* **114** F3
Ritzville *U.S.A.* **108** C4
Riva del Garda *Italy* **40** C7
Riva Lígure *Italy* **40** E4

Rivadavia *B. Aires, Argentina* **126** D3
Rivadavia *Mendoza,
    Argentina* **126** C2
Rivadavia *Salta, Argentina* **126** A3
Rivadavia *Chile* **126** B1
Rivarolo Canavese *Italy* **40** C4
Rivas *Nic.* **120** D2
Rivash *Iran* **71** C8
Rivera *Argentina* **126** D3
Rivera *Uruguay* **127** C4
Riverbank *U.S.A.* **110** H6
Riverdale *U.S.A.* **110** J7
Riverhead *U.S.A.* **115** F12
Riverhurst *Canada* **103** C7
Rivers *Canada* **103** C8
Rivers □ *Nigeria* **83** E6
Rivers Inlet *Canada* **102** C3
Riversdale *Canada* **114** B3
Riversdale *S. Africa* **88** E3
Riverside *U.S.A.* **111** M9
Riverton *Australia* **95** E2
Riverton *Canada* **103** C9
Riverton *N.Z.* **91** G2
Riverton *U.S.A.* **108** E9
Rives *France* **21** C9
Rivesaltes *France* **20** F6
Riviera *U.S.A.* **111** K12
Riviera di Levante *Italy* **40** D6
Riviera di Ponente *Italy* **40** D5
Rivière-au-Renard *Canada* **105** C7
Rivière-du-Loup *Canada* **105** C6
Rivière-Pentecôte *Canada* **105** C6
Rivière-Pilote *Martinique* **120** c
Rivière St-Paul *Canada* **105** B8
Rivière-Salée *Martinique* **120** c
Rivne *Odesa, Ukraine* **29** D14
Rivne *Rivne, Ukraine* **23** C14
Rivne □ *Ukraine* **23** C14
Rívoli *Italy* **40** C4
Rívoli B. *Australia* **95** F3
Rixheim *France* **19** E14
Riyadh = Ar Riyāḍ *Si. Arabia* **70** E5
Riyadh al Khabrā' *Si. Arabia* **70** E4
Riza *Greece* **47** A4
Rize *Turkey* **73** B9
Rize □ *Turkey* **73** B9
Rizhao *China* **57** G10
Rizokarpaso *Cyprus* **49** D13
Rizzuto, C. *Italy* **43** D10
Rjukan *Norway* **9** G13
Rkîz, L. *Mauritania* **82** B1
Ro *Greece* **47** E11
Roa *Spain* **36** D7
Road Town *Br. Virgin Is.* **121** e
Roan Plateau *U.S.A.* **108** G9
Roanne *France* **19** F11
Roanoke *Ala., U.S.A.* **117** E12
Roanoke *Va., U.S.A.* **113** G14
Roanoke ~ *U.S.A.* **117** D16
Roanoke I. *U.S.A.* **117** D17
Roanoke Rapids *U.S.A.* **117** C16
Roatán *Honduras* **120** C2
Robāt *Iran* **73** E12
Robāt Sang *Iran* **71** C8
Robāţkarīm *Iran* **71** C6
Robbins I. *Australia* **95** G4
Róbbio *Italy* **40** C5
Robe ~ *Australia* **92** D2
Röbel *Germany* **24** B8
Robert Bourassa, Rés.
    Canada **104** B4
Robert Lee *U.S.A.* **116** F4
Robertsdale *U.S.A.* **114** F6
Robertsganj *India* **69** G10
Robertson *S. Africa* **88** E2
Robertson I. *Antarctica* **5** C18
Robertson Ra. *Australia* **92** D3
Robertsport *Liberia* **82** D2
Robertstown *Australia* **95** E2
Roberval *Canada* **105** C5
Robeson Chan. *N. Amer.* **101** A19
Robesonia *U.S.A.* **115** F8
Robi *Ethiopia* **81** F4
Robinson *U.S.A.* **112** F10
Robinson ~ *Australia* **94** B2
Robinson Crusoe I. *Pac. Oc.* **122** F2
Robinson Ra. *Australia* **93** E2
Robinvale *Australia* **95** E3
Robledo *Spain* **39** G2
Roblin *Canada* **103** C8
Roboré *Bolivia* **124** G7
Robson, Mt. *Canada* **102** C5
Robstown *U.S.A.* **116** H6
Roca, C. da *Portugal* **37** G1
Roca Partida, I. *Mexico* **118** D2
Rocamadour *France* **20** D5
Rocas, I. *Brazil* **125** D12
Rocca San Casciano *Italy* **41** D8
Roccadáspide *Italy* **43** B8
Roccastrada *Italy* **41** F8
Roccella Iónica *Italy* **43** D9
Rocciamelone, Monte =
    Roche Melon *Italy* **21** C11
Rocha *Uruguay* **127** C5
Roche Melon *Italy* **21** C11
Rochechouart *France* **20** C4

Rochefort *Belgium* **17** D5
Rochefort *France* **20** C3
Rochefort-en-Terre *France* **18** E4
Rochelle *U.S.A.* **112** E9
Rocher River *Canada* **102** A6
Rocheservière *France* **18** F5
Rochester *U.K.* **15** F8
Rochester *Ind., U.S.A.* **112** E10
Rochester *Minn., U.S.A.* **112** C7
Rochester *N.H., U.S.A.* **115** C14
Rochester *N.Y., U.S.A.* **114** C7
Rociu *Romania* **29** F10
Rock ~ *Canada* **102** A3
Rock, The *Australia* **95** F4
Rock Creek *U.S.A.* **114** E4
Rock Falls *U.S.A.* **112** E9
Rock Hill *U.S.A.* **117** D14
Rock Island *U.S.A.* **112** E8
Rock Port *U.S.A.* **112** E6
Rock Rapids *U.S.A.* **112** D5
Rockall *Atl. Oc.* **6** D3
Rock Sound *Bahamas* **120** B4
Rock Springs *Mont., U.S.A.* **108** C10
Rock Springs *Wyo., U.S.A.* **108** F9
Rock Valley *U.S.A.* **112** D5
Rockdale *Tex., U.S.A.* **116** F6
Rockdale *Wash., U.S.A.* **110** C5
Rockeby =
    Kandju △ *Australia* **94** A3
Rockefeller Plateau
    Antarctica **5** E14
Rockford *U.S.A.* **112** D9
Rockglen *Canada* **103** D7
Rockhampton *Australia* **94** C5
Rockingham *Australia* **93** F2
Rockingham *N.C., U.S.A.* **117** D15
Rockingham *Vt., U.S.A.* **115** C12
Rockingham B. *Australia* **94** B4
Rocklake *U.S.A.* **112** A4
Rockland *Canada* **115** A9
Rockland *Idaho, U.S.A.* **108** E7
Rockland *Maine, U.S.A.* **113** C19
Rockland *Mich., U.S.A.* **112** B9
Rocklin *U.S.A.* **110** G5
Rockmart *U.S.A.* **117** D12
Rockport *Mass., U.S.A.* **115** D14
Rockport *Tex., U.S.A.* **116** G6
Rocksprings *U.S.A.* **116** F4
Rockville *Conn., U.S.A.* **115** E12
Rockville *Md., U.S.A.* **113** F15
Rockwall *U.S.A.* **116** E6
Rockwell City *U.S.A.* **112** D7
Rockwood *Canada* **114** C4
Rockwood *Maine, U.S.A.* **113** C19
Rockwood *Tenn., U.S.A.* **117** D12
Rocky Ford *U.S.A.* **108** G12
Rocky Gully *Australia* **93** F2
Rocky Harbour *Canada* **105** C8
Rocky Island L. *Canada* **104** C3
Rocky Lane *Canada* **102** B5
Rocky Mount *U.S.A.* **117** D16
Rocky Mountain △ *U.S.A.* **108** F11
Rocky Mountain House
    Canada **102** C6
Rocky Mts. *N. Amer.* **108** B6
Rocky Point *Namibia* **88** B2
Rocroi *France* **19** C11
Rod *Pakistan* **66** E3
Roda *Greece* **49** A3
Rødby *Denmark* **11** K5
Rødbyhavn *Denmark* **11** K5
Roddickton *Canada* **105** B8
Rødding *Denmark* **11** J3
Rødekro *Denmark* **11** J3
Rodeby *Sweden* **11** H9
Rödekro *Denmark* **11** J3
Rodenkirchen *Germany* **24** B4
Rodez *France* **20** D6
Ródhos = Rhodes *Greece* **49** C10
Rodi Gargánico *Italy* **41** G12
Rodia *Greece* **49** D7
Rodna *Romania* **29** C9
Rodna ◎ *Australia* **92** D5
Rodnei, Munţii *Romania* **29** C9
Rodney *Canada* **114** D3
Rodney, C. *N.Z.* **91** B5
Rodniki *Russia* **34** B5
Rodolivos *Greece* **44** F7
Rodonit, Kepi i *Albania* **44** E3
Rodopi □ *Greece* **45** E9
Rodopos *Greece* **49** D5
Rodrigues *Ind. Oc.* **3** E13
Roe ~ *U.K.* **12** A5
Roebling *U.S.A.* **115** F10
Roebourne *Australia* **92** D2
Roebuck B. *Australia* **92** C3
Roebuck Roadhouse
    Australia **92** C3
Roermond *Neths.* **17** C6
Roes Welcome Sd. *Canada* **101** E14
Roeselare *Belgium* **17** D3
Rogachev = Ragachow
    Belarus **23** B16
Rogačica *Serbia* **44** B3
Rogagua, L. *Bolivia* **124** F5
Rogaška Slatina *Slovenia* **41** B12
Rogatec *Slovenia* **41** B12
Rogatica *Bos.-H.* **28** G4
Rogatyn *Ukraine* **23** D13
Rogers *U.S.A.* **116** C7

Rogers City U.S.A. **113** C12
Rogersville Canada **105** C6
Roggan → Canada **104** B4
Roggan L. Canada **104** B4
Roggeveen Basin Pac. Oc. **97** L18
Roggiano Gravina Italy **43** C9
Rogliano France **21** F13
Rogliano Italy **43** C9
Rogoaguado, L. Bolivia **124** F5
Rogojampi Indonesia **63** J17
Rogoźno Poland **31** F3
Rogue → U.S.A. **108** E1
Rohan France **18** D4
Rohri Pakistan **68** F3
Rohri Canal Pakistan **68** F3
Rohtak India **68** E7
Roi Et Thailand **64** D4
Roja Latvia **30** A9
Rojas Argentina **126** C3
Rojişte Romania **29** F8
Rojo, C. Mexico **119** C5
Rokan → Indonesia **62** D2
Rokel → S. Leone **82** D2
Rokiškis Lithuania **32** E3
Rokitno Russia **33** G8
Rokycany Czech Rep. **26** B6
Rolândia Brazil **127** A5
Rolla Mo., U.S.A. **112** G8
Rolla N. Dak., U.S.A. **112** A4
Rolleston Australia **94** C4
Rollingstone Australia **94** B4
Rom Sudan **81** F3
Roma Australia **95** D4
Roma Italy **41** G9
Roma Sweden **11** G12
Roma Fiumicino ✈ (FCO)
     Italy **41** G9
Roma-Los Saenz U.S.A. **116** H5
Romain, C. U.S.A. **117** E15
Romaine → Canada **105** B7
Roman Bulgaria **44** C7
Roman Romania **29** D11
Roman-Kosh, Gora Ukraine **33** K8
Romanche → France **21** C9
Romang Indonesia **63** F7
Români Egypt **74** E1
Romania ■ Europe **29** D10
Romanija Bos.-H. **28** G3
Romano, Cayo Cuba **120** B4
Romans-sur-Isère France **21** C9
Romanshorn Switz. **25** H5
Romanzof C. U.S.A. **106** C6
Rombari Sudan **81** G3
Romblon Phil. **61** E5
Rome = Roma Italy **41** G9
Rome Ga., U.S.A. **117** D12
Rome N.Y., U.S.A. **115** C9
Rome Pa., U.S.A. **115** E8
Rometta Italy **43** D8
Romilly-sur-Seine France **19** D10
Romney U.S.A. **113** F14
Romney Marsh U.K. **15** F8
Romny Ukraine **33** G7
Rømø Denmark **11** J2
Romodan Ukraine **33** G7
Romodanovo Russia **34** C7
Romont Switz. **25** J2
Romorantin-Lanthenay
     France **19** E8
Romsdalen Norway **8** E12
Romsey U.K. **15** G6
Ron Vietnam **64** D6
Rona U.K. **13** D3
Ronan U.S.A. **108** C6
Roncador, Cayos Colombia **120** D3
Roncador, Serra do Brazil **125** F8
Ronciglione Italy **41** F9
Ronco → Italy **41** D9
Ronda Spain **37** J5
Ronda, Serranía de Spain **37** J5
Rondane Norway **8** F13
Rondônia □ Brazil **124** F6
Rondonópolis Brazil **125** G8
Rondu Pakistan **69** B6
Rong, Koh Cambodia **65** G4
Rong Jiang → China **58** E7
Rong Xian
     Guangxi Zhuangzu, China **59** F8
Rong Xian Sichuan, China **58** C5
Rong'an China **58** E7
Rongchang China **58** C5
Ronge, L. la Canada **103** B7
Rongjiang China **58** E7
Rongshui China **58** E7
Rønne Denmark **11** J8
Ronne Ice Shelf Antarctica **5** D18
Ronneby Sweden **11** H9
Ronnebyån → Sweden **11** H9
Rönneshytta Sweden **11** F9
Ronsard, C. Australia **93** D1
Ronse Belgium **17** D3
Roodepoort S. Africa **89** D4
Roof Butte U.S.A. **109** H9
Rooiboklaagte → Namibia **88** C3
Rooniu, Mt. Tahiti **91** d
Roorkee India **68** E7
Roosendaal Neths. **17** C4
Roosevelt U.S.A. **108** F9

Roosevelt → Brazil **124** E6
Roosevelt, Mt. Canada **102** B3
Roosevelt I. Antarctica **5** D12
Ropczyce Poland **31** H8
Roper → Australia **94** A2
Roper Bar Australia **94** A1
Roper River = St.
     Vidgeon's ◌ Australia **94** A1
Roque Pérez Argentina **126** D4
Roquefort France **20** D3
Roquemaure France **21** D8
Roquetas de Mar Spain **39** J2
Roquetes Spain **38** E5
Roquevaire France **21** E9
Roraima □ Brazil **124** C6
Roraima, Mt. Venezuela **124** B6
Røros Norway **8** E14
Rorschach Switz. **25** H5
Ros Comáin = Roscommon
     Ireland **12** C3
Rosa Zambia **87** D3
Rosa, Monte Europe **40** C4
Rosal de la Frontera Spain **37** H3
Rosalia U.S.A. **108** C5
Rosamond U.S.A. **111** L8
Rosans France **21** D9
Rosario Argentina **126** C3
Rosário Brazil **125** D10
Rosario Baja Calif., Mexico **118** B1
Rosario Sinaloa, Mexico **118** C3
Rosario Paraguay **126** A4
Rosario de la Frontera
     Argentina **126** B3
Rosario de Lerma Argentina **126** A2
Rosario del Tala Argentina **126** C4
Rosário do Sul Brazil **127** C5
Rosarito Mexico **111** N9
Rosarno Italy **43** D8
Rosas = Roses Spain **38** C8
Roscoe U.S.A. **115** E10
Roscoff France **18** D3
Roscommon Ireland **12** C3
Roscommon □ Ireland **12** C3
Roscrea Ireland **12** D4
Rose → Australia **94** A2
Rose, L. Bahamas **121** B5
Rose Belle Mauritius **85** d
Rose Blanche Canada **105** C8
Rose Hill Mauritius **85** d
Rose Pt. Canada **102** C2
Rose Valley Canada **103** C8
Roseau Dominica **121** C7
Roseau U.S.A. **112** A6
Rosebery Australia **95** G4
Rosebud S. Dak., U.S.A. **112** D3
Rosebud Tex., U.S.A. **116** F6
Roseburg U.S.A. **108** E2
Rosedale U.S.A. **117** E9
Rosehearty U.K. **13** D6
Roseires Res. Sudan **79** F12
Roseland U.S.A. **110** G4
Rosemary Canada **102** C6
Rosenberg U.S.A. **116** G7
Rosendaël France **19** A9
Rosenheim Germany **25** H8
Roses Spain **38** C8
Roses, G. de Spain **38** C8
Roseto degli Abruzzi Italy **41** F11
Rosetown Canada **103** C7
Rosetta = Rashîd Egypt **80** H7
Roseville Calif., U.S.A. **110** G5
Roseville Mich., U.S.A. **114** D2
Roseville Pa., U.S.A. **115** E8
Rosewood Australia **95** D5
Roshkhvār Iran **71** C8
Rosières-en-Santerre France **19** C9
Rosignano Maríttimo Italy **40** E7
Rosignol Guyana **124** B7
Roşiori de Vede Romania **29** F10
Rositsa Bulgaria **45** C11
Rositsa → Bulgaria **45** C9
Roskilde Denmark **11** J6
Roskovec Albania **44** F4
Roslavl Russia **32** F7
Rosmaninhal Portugal **36** F3
Rosmead S. Africa **88** E4
Røsnæs Denmark **11** J4
Rosolini Italy **43** F7
Rosporden France **18** E3
Ross Australia **95** G4
Ross N.Z. **91** E3
Ross Béthio Mauritania **82** B1
Ross Dependency Antarctica **5** D12
Ross I. Antarctica **5** D11
Ross Ice Shelf Antarctica **5** E12
Ross L. U.S.A. **108** B3
Ross Mhic Thriúin = New
     Ross Ireland **12** D5
Ross-on-Wye U.K. **15** F5
Ross River Australia **94** C1
Ross River Canada **102** A2
Ross Sea Antarctica **5** D11
Rossall Pt. U.K. **14** D4
Rossan Pt. Ireland **12** B3
Rossano Italy **43** C9
Rossburn Canada **103** C8
Rosseau Canada **114** A5
Rosseau, L. Canada **114** A5
Rosses, The Ireland **12** A3
Rossignol, L. Canada **104** B5

Rossignol L. Canada **105** D6
Rossiya = Russia ■ Eurasia **53** C11
Rossland Canada **102** D5
Rosslare Ireland **12** D5
Rosslare Harbour Ireland **12** D5
Rosslau Germany **24** C8
Rossmore Canada **114** B7
Rosso Mauritania **82** B1
Rosso, C. France **21** F12
Rossosh Russia **33** G10
Rossvatnet Norway **8** D16
Røst Norway **8** C15
Rosthern Canada **103** C7
Rostock Germany **24** A8
Rostov Don, Russia **33** J10
Rostov Yaroslavl, Russia **32** D10
Rostov □ Russia **35** F5
Rostrenen France **18** D3
Roswell Ga., U.S.A. **117** D12
Roswell N. Mex., U.S.A. **109** K11
Rota Spain **37** J4
Rotan U.S.A. **116** E4
Rotenburg Hessen, Germany **24** E5
Rotenburg Niedersachsen,
     Germany **24** B5
Roth Germany **25** F7
Rothaargebirge Germany **24** D4
Rothaargebirge △ Germany **24** E4
Rothenburg ob der Tauber
     Germany **25** F6
Rother → U.K. **15** G8
Rothera Antarctica **5** C17
Rotherham U.K. **14** D6
Rothes U.K. **13** D5
Rothesay Canada **105** C6
Rothesay U.K. **13** F3
Roti Indonesia **63** F6
Rotja, Pta. Spain **39** G6
Roto Australia **95** E4
Rotondo, Mte. France **21** F13
Rotoroa, L. N.Z. **91** D4
Rotorua N.Z. **91** C6
Rotorua, L. N.Z. **91** C6
Rott → Germany **25** G9
Rottenburg Germany **25** G4
Rottenmann Austria **26** D7
Rotterdam Neths. **17** C4
Rotterdam U.S.A. **115** D10
Rottne Sweden **11** G8
Rottnest I. Australia **93** F2
Rottumeroog Neths. **17** A6
Rottweil Germany **25** G4
Rotuma Fiji **90** C10
Roubaix France **19** B10
Roudnice nad Labem
     Czech Rep. **26** A7
Rouen France **18** C8
Rouergue France **20** D5
Rouillac France **20** C3
Rouleau Canada **103** C8
Roulpmaulpma ◌ Australia **92** D5
Round I. Mauritius **85** d
Round Mountain U.S.A. **108** G5
Round Mt. Australia **95** E5
Round Rock U.S.A. **116** F6
Roundup U.S.A. **108** C9
Rousay U.K. **13** B5
Rouses Point U.S.A. **115** B11
Rouseville U.S.A. **114** E5
Rousse = Ruse Bulgaria **45** C9
Roussenski Lom → Bulgaria **45** C10
Roussillon Isère, France **21** C8
Roussillon Pyrénées-Or.,
     France **20** F6
Rouxville S. Africa **88** E4
Rouyn-Noranda Canada **104** C4
Rovaniemi Finland **8** C21
Rovato Italy **40** C7
Rovenki Ukraine **33** H10
Rovereto Italy **40** C8
Rovigo Italy **41** C8
Rovinj Croatia **41** C10
Rovno = Rivne Ukraine **23** C14
Rovnoye Russia **34** E8
Rovuma = Ruvuma →
     Tanzania **87** E5
Row'ān Iran **71** C6
Rowena Australia **95** D4
Rowley I. Canada **101** D16
Rowley Shoals Australia **92** C2
Roxa Guinea-Biss. **82** C1
Roxas Capiz, Phil. **61** F5
Roxas Isabela, Phil. **61** C4
Roxas Mind. Or., Phil. **61** E4
Roxboro U.S.A. **117** C15
Roxborough Trin. & Tob. **125** J16
Roxburgh N.Z. **91** F2
Roxbury N.Y., U.S.A. **115** D10
Roxbury Pa., U.S.A. **114** F7
Roxby Downs Australia **95** E2
Roxen Sweden **11** F9
Roy Mont., U.S.A. **108** C9
Roy N. Mex., U.S.A. **109** J11
Roy Utah, U.S.A. **108** F7
Royal Bardia △ Nepal **69** E9
Royal Canal Ireland **12** C4
Royal Chitwan △ Nepal **69** F11
Royal Geographical Society
     Is. Canada **100** D11
Royal Leamington Spa U.K. **15** E6

Royal Natal △ S. Africa **89** D4
Royal Tunbridge Wells U.K. **15** F8
Royale, Isle U.S.A. **112** B9
Royan France **20** C2
Roye France **19** C9
Royston U.K. **15** E7
Rozay-en-Brie France **19** D9
Rozdilna Ukraine **23** E16
Rozhnyativ Ukraine **29** D15
Rozhyshche Ukraine **23** C13
Rožmitál pod Třemšínem
     Czech Rep. **26** B6
Rožňava Slovak Rep. **27** C13
Rozogi Poland **30** E8
Rozoy-sur-Serre France **19** C11
Roztoczański △ Poland **31** H10
Rozzano Italy **40** C6
Rrëshen Albania **44** E3
Rrogozhine Albania **44** E3
Rtanj Serbia **44** C5
Rtishchevo Russia **34** D6
Rúa = A Rúa Spain **36** C3
Ruacaná Namibia **88** B1
Ruaha △ Tanzania **86** D3
Ruahine Ra. N.Z. **91** C6
Ruapehu N.Z. **91** C5
Ruapuke I. N.Z. **91** G2
Ruâq, W. → Egypt **74** F2
Rub' al Khālī Si. Arabia **75** D4
Rubeho Mts. Tanzania **86** D4
Rubezhnoye = Rubizhne
     Ukraine **33** H10
Rubh a' Mhail U.K. **13** F2
Rubha Hunish U.K. **13** D2
Rubha Robhanais = Lewis,
     Butt of U.K. **13** C2
Rubí Spain **38** D7
Rubicon → U.S.A. **110** G5
Rubicone → Italy **41** D9
Rubik Albania **44** E3
Rubino Ivory C. **82** D4
Rubio Venezuela **124** B4
Rubizhne Ukraine **33** H10
Rubondo △ Tanzania **86** C3
Rubtsovsk Russia **52** D9
Ruby L. U.S.A. **108** F6
Ruby Mts. U.S.A. **108** F6
Rubyvale Australia **94** C4
Rucheng China **59** E9
Ruciane-Nida Poland **30** E8
Rūd Sar Iran **71** B6
Ruda Sweden **11** G10
Ruda Śląska Poland **31** H5
Rudall Australia **95** E2
Rudall → Australia **92** D3
Rudall River △ Australia **92** D3
Rudbar Iran **71** B6
Rüdersdorf Germany **24** C9
Rudewa Tanzania **87** E3
Rudkøbing Denmark **11** K4
Rudky Ukraine **31** J10
Rudna Poland **31** G3
Rudnik Bulgaria **45** D11
Rudnik Poland **31** H9
Rudnik Serbia **44** B4
Rudnya Russia **32** E6
Rudnyy Kazakhstan **52** D7
Rudo Bos.-H. **28** G4
Rudolfa, Ostrov Russia **52** A6
Rudolstadt Germany **24** E7
Rudong China **59** A13
Rudozem Bulgaria **45** E8
Rudyard U.S.A. **113** B11
Rue France **19** B8
Ruenya → Africa **87** F3
Rufa'a Sudan **81** E3
Ruffling Pt. Br. Virgin Is. **121** e
Rufiji → Tanzania **86** D4
Rufino Argentina **126** C3
Rufisque Senegal **82** C1
Rufunsa Zambia **87** F2
Rugao China **59** A13
Rugby U.K. **15** E6
Rugby U.S.A. **112** A4
Rügen Germany **24** A9
Rügen △ Germany **24** A9
Rugles France **18** D7
Ruhengeri Rwanda **86** C2
Ruhla Germany **24** E6
Ruhland Germany **24** D9
Ruhnu Estonia **30** A10
Ruhr → Germany **24** D2
Ruhuhu → Tanzania **87** E3
Rui'an China **59** D13
Ruichang China **59** C10
Ruidoso U.S.A. **109** K11
Ruijin China **59** E10
Ruili China **58** E1
Ruivo, Pico Madeira **48** D3
Ruj Bulgaria **44** D6
Rujen Macedonia **44** D6
Rujm Tal'at al Jamā'ah
     Jordan **74** E4
Ruk Pakistan **68** F3
Rukhla Pakistan **68** C4
Ruki → Dem. Rep. of the Congo **84** E3
Rukwa □ Tanzania **86** D3

Rukwa, L. Tanzania **86** D3
Rulenge Burundi **86** C3
Rulhieres, C. Australia **92** B4
Rum = Rhum U.K. **13** E2
Rum Jordan **74** F4
Rum Cay Bahamas **121** B5
Rum Jungle Australia **92** B5
Ruma Serbia **28** E4
Ruma △ Kenya **86** C3
Rumāḥ Si. Arabia **70** E5
Rumania = Romania ■
     Europe **29** D10
Rumaylah Iraq **70** D5
Rumbêk Sudan **81** F2
Rumburk Czech Rep. **26** A7
Rumford U.S.A. **115** B14
Rumia Poland **30** D5
Rumilly France **21** C9
Rumoi Japan **54** C10
Rumonge Burundi **86** C2
Rumphi Malawi **87** E3
Rumson U.S.A. **115** F11
Rumula Australia **94** B4
Rumuruti Kenya **86** B4
Runan China **56** H8
Runanga N.Z. **91** E3
Runaway, C. N.Z. **91** B6
Runaway Bay Jamaica **120** a
Runcorn U.K. **14** D5
Rundu Namibia **88** B2
Rungwa Tanzania **86** D3
Rungwa → Tanzania **86** D3
Rungwa △ Tanzania **86** D3
Rungwe Tanzania **87** D3
Rungwe, Mt. Tanzania **84** F6
Runka Nigeria **83** C6
Runn Sweden **10** D9
Runton Ra. Australia **92** D3
Ruokolahti Finland **32** B5
Ruoqiang China **60** C3
Rupa India **67** F18
Rupar India **68** D7
Rupat Indonesia **62** D2
Rupea Romania **29** D10
Rupen → India **68** H4
Rupert U.S.A. **108** E7
Rupert → Canada **104** B4
Rupert B. Canada **104** B4
Rupert House =
     Waskaganish Canada **104** B4
Rupsa India **69** J12
Rur → Germany **24** D1
Rurrenabaque Bolivia **124** F5
Rus → Spain **39** F2
Rusambo Zimbabwe **87** F3
Rusape Zimbabwe **87** F3
Ruschuk = Ruse Bulgaria **45** C9
Ruse Bulgaria **45** C9
Ruse □ Bulgaria **45** C10
Ruşeţu Romania **29** F12
Rush Ireland **12** C5
Rushan China **57** F11
Rushden U.K. **15** E7
Rushmore, Mt. U.S.A. **112** D2
Rushville Ill., U.S.A. **112** E8
Rushville Ind., U.S.A. **113** F11
Rushville Nebr., U.S.A. **112** D2
Russas Brazil **125** D11
Russell Canada **103** C8
Russell Kans., U.S.A. **112** F4
Russell N.Y., U.S.A. **115** B9
Russell Pa., U.S.A. **114** E5
Russell Cave △ U.S.A. **117** D12
Russell L. Man., Canada **103** B8
Russell L. N.W.T., Canada **102** A5
Russellkonda India **67** K14
Russellville Ala., U.S.A. **117** D11
Russellville Ark., U.S.A. **116** D8
Russellville Ky., U.S.A. **112** G10
Rüsselsheim Germany **25** F4
Russi Italy **41** D9
Russia ■ Eurasia **53** C11
Russian → U.S.A. **110** G3
Rust Austria **27** D9
Rustam Shahr Pakistan **68** F2
Rustavi Georgia **35** K7
Rustenburg S. Africa **88** D4
Ruston U.S.A. **116** E8
Rutana Burundi **86** C3
Rute Spain **37** H6
Ruteng Indonesia **63** F6
Rutenga Zimbabwe **87** G3
Ruth U.S.A. **114** C2
Rutherford U.S.A. **110** G4
Rutland U.S.A. **115** C12
Rutland □ U.K. **15** E7
Rutland Water U.K. **15** E7
Rutledge → Canada **103** A6
Rutledge L. Canada **103** A6
Rutqa, W. → Syria **73** E9
Rutshuru
     Dem. Rep. of the Congo **86** C2
Ruvo di Púglia Italy **43** A9
Ruvu Tanzania **86** D4
Ruvu → Tanzania **86** D4
Ruvuma □ Tanzania **87** E4
Ruvuma → Tanzania **87** E5
Ruwais U.A.E. **71** E7
Ruwenzori Africa **86** B2
Ruwenzori △ Uganda **86** B2

Ruya → Zimbabwe **89** B5
Ruyigi Burundi **86** C3
Ruyuan China **59** E9
Ruzayevka Russia **34** C7
Ružhevo Konare Bulgaria **45** D8
Ružomberok Slovak Rep. **27** B12
Ruzyne, Praha ✈ (PRG)
     Czech Rep. **26** A7
Rwanda ■ Africa **86** C3
Ryakhovo Bulgaria **45** C10
Ryan, L. U.K. **13** G3
Ryazan Russia **32** E10
Ryazan □ Russia **34** C4
Ryazhsk Russia **32** F11
Rybachiy Russia **30** C7
Rybachiy Poluostrov Russia **8** B25
Rybinsk Russia **32** C10
Rybinskoye Vdkhr. Russia **32** C10
Rybnik Poland **31** H5
Rybnitsa = Râbniţa Moldova **29** C14
Rybnoye Russia **32** E10
Rychnov nad Kněžnou
     Czech Rep. **27** A9
Rychwał Poland **31** F5
Rycroft Canada **102** B5
Ryd Sweden **11** H8
Rydaholm Sweden **11** H8
Ryde U.K. **15** G6
Ryderwood U.S.A. **110** D3
Rydzyna Poland **31** G3
Rye U.K. **15** G8
Rye → U.K. **14** C7
Rye Bay U.K. **15** G8
Rye Patch Res. U.S.A. **108** F4
Ryegate U.S.A. **108** C9
Ryki Poland **31** G8
Ryley Canada **102** C6
Rylsk Russia **33** G8
Rylstone Australia **95** E4
Rymanów Poland **31** J8
Ryn Poland **30** E8
Ryn Peski = Naryn Qum
     Kazakhstan **35** G9
Ryōtsu Japan **54** E9
Rypin Poland **31** E6
Ryssby Sweden **11** H8
Ryūgasaki Japan **55** G10
Ryukyu Is. = Ryūkyū-rettō
     Japan **55** M3
Ryūkyū-rettō Japan **55** M3
Rzepin Poland **31** F1
Rzeszów Poland **31** H8
Rzhev Russia **32** D8

S

Sa Thailand **64** C3
Sa Cabaneta Spain **48** B9
Sa Canal Spain **48** C7
Sa Conillera Spain **48** C7
Sa Dec Vietnam **65** G5
Sa Dragonera Spain **48** B9
Sa Kaeo Thailand **64** F4
Sa Mesquida Spain **48** B11
Sa Pa Vietnam **64** A4
Sa Pobla Spain **38** F8
Sa Savina Spain **48** C7
Sa'ādatābād Fārs, Iran **71** D7
Sa'ādatābād Hormozgān, Iran **71** D7
Sa'ādatābād Kermān, Iran **71** D7
Saale → Germany **24** D7
Saaler Bodden Germany **24** A8
Saalfeld Germany **24** E7
Saalfelden Austria **26** D5
Saane → Switz. **25** H3
Saanich Canada **110** B3
Saar → Europe **17** E6
Saar-Hunsrück △ Germany **25** F2
Saarbrücken Germany **25** F2
Saarburg Germany **25** F2
Saaremaa Estonia **32** C2
Saarijärvi Finland **8** E21
Saariselkä Finland **8** B23
Saarland □ Germany **25** F2
Saarlouis Germany **25** F2
Saatlı Azerbaijan **73** C13
Sab 'Ābar Syria **72** F7
Saba W. Indies **121** C7
Šabac Serbia **44** B3
Sabadell Spain **38** D7
Sabah □ Malaysia **62** C5
Sabak Malaysia **65** L3
Sabalān, Kūhhā-ye Iran **73** C12
Sabalana, Kepulauan
     Indonesia **63** F5
Sábana de la Mar Dom. Rep. **121** C6
Sábanalarga Colombia **124** A4
Sabang Indonesia **62** C1
Şabanözü Turkey **72** B5
Săbăoani Romania **29** C11
Sabarmati → India **68** H5
Sabattis U.S.A. **115** B10
Sabáudia Italy **42** A6
Saberania Indonesia **63** E9
Sabhā Libya **79** C8
Sabi → India **68** F7
Sabidana, J. Sudan **80** D4
Sabie S. Africa **89** D5
Sabinal Mexico **118** A3

Sabinal *U.S.A.* **116** G5
Sabiñánigo *Spain* **38** C4
Sabinar, Punta del *Spain* **39** J2
Sabinas *Mexico* **118** B4
Sabinas ➤ *Mexico* **118** B4
Sabinas Hidalgo *Mexico* **118** B4
Sabine ➤ *U.S.A.* **116** G8
Sabine L. *U.S.A.* **116** G8
Sabine Pass *U.S.A.* **116** G8
Sabinov *Slovak Rep.* **27** B14
Sabirabad *Azerbaijan* **35** K9
Sablayan *Phil.* **61** E4
Sable *Canada* **105** A6
Sable, C. *Canada* **105** D6
Sable, C. *U.S.A.* **120** A3
Sable I. *Canada* **105** D8
Sablé-sur-Sarthe *France* **18** E6
Sabonkafi *Niger* **83** C6
Sabor ➤ *Portugal* **36** D3
Sabou *Burkina Faso* **82** C4
Sabres *France* **20** D3
Sabrina Coast *Antarctica* **5** C9
Sabugal *Portugal* **36** E3
Sabulubbek *Indonesia* **62** E1
Sabuncu *Turkey* **47** B12
Sabzevār *Iran* **71** B8
Sabzvārān = Jiroft *Iran* **71** D8
Sac City *U.S.A.* **112** D6
Sacedón *Spain* **38** E2
Săcele *Romania* **29** E10
Sacheon *S. Korea* **57** G15
Sachigo ➤ *Canada* **104** A2
Sachigo, L. *Canada* **104** B1
Sachimbo *Angola* **84** F4
Sachkhere *Georgia* **35** J6
Sachsen □ *Germany* **24** D7
Sachsen-Anhalt □ *Germany* **24** D7
Sächsische Schweiz △
    Germany **24** E10
Sacile *Italy* **41** C9
Sackets Harbor *U.S.A.* **115** C8
Sackville *Canada* **105** C7
Saco Maine, *U.S.A.* **115** C14
Saco Mont., *U.S.A.* **108** B10
Sacramento *U.S.A.* **110** G5
Sacramento ➤ *U.S.A.* **110** G5
Sacramento Mts. *U.S.A.* **109** K11
Sacramento Valley *U.S.A.* **110** G5
Sacratif, C. *Spain* **37** J7
Săcueni *Romania* **28** C7
Sada *Spain* **36** B2
Sada-Misaki *Japan* **55** H6
Sádaba *Spain* **38** C3
Sadabad *India* **68** F8
Sadani *Tanzania* **86** D4
Sadani △ *Tanzania* **86** D4
Sadao *Thailand* **65** J3
Sadd el Aali *Egypt* **80** C3
Saddle Mt. *U.S.A.* **110** E3
Sade *Nigeria* **83** C7
Sadimi *Dem. Rep. of the Congo* **87** D1
Sadiola *Mali* **82** C2
Sa'dīyah, Hawr as *Iraq* **73** F12
Sado *Japan* **54** F9
Sado ➤ *Portugal* **37** G2
Sadon *Russia* **35** J6
Sadovoye *Russia* **35** G7
Sadra *India* **68** H5
Sadri *India* **68** G5
Sæby *Denmark* **11** G4
Saegertown *U.S.A.* **114** E4
Saelices *Spain* **38** F8
Safaalan *Turkey* **45** E12
Safaga *Egypt* **80** B3
Şafājah *Si. Arabia* **70** E3
Šafárikovo = Tornaľa
    Slovak Rep. **27** C13
Safata B. *Samoa* **91** b
Säffle *Sweden* **10** E6
Safford *U.S.A.* **109** K9
Saffron Walden *U.K.* **15** E8
Safi *Morocco* **78** B4
Safiābād *Iran* **71** B8
Safid Dasht *Iran* **71** C6
Safid Kūh *Afghan.* **66** B3
Safid Rūd ➤ *Iran* **71** B6
Safipur *India* **69** F9
Şafītā *Syria* **72** E7
Safonovo *Russia* **32** E7
Safranbolu *Turkey* **72** B5
Saft Rashīn *Egypt* **80** J7
Safune *Samoa* **91** b
Şafwān *Iraq* **70** D5
Sag Harbor *U.S.A.* **115** F12
Saga *Japan* **55** H5
Saga □ *Japan* **55** H5
Sagae *Japan* **54** E10
Sagaing *Burma* **67** J19
Sagala *Mali* **82** C3
Sagamore *U.S.A.* **114** F5
Saganaga L. *Canada* **112** A8
Sagar *Karnataka, India* **66** M9
Sagar *Mad. P., India* **69** H8
Sagara, L. *Tanzania* **86** D3
Sagarmatha = Everest, Mt.
    Nepal **69** E12
Sagarmatha △ *Nepal* **69** F12
Sagay *Phil.* **61** F5
Saginaw *U.S.A.* **113** D12

Saginaw B. *U.S.A.* **113** D12
Sagleipie *Liberia* **82** D3
Saglouc = Salluit *Canada* **101** E16
Sagone *France* **21** F12
Sagone, G. de *France* **21** F12
Sagres *Portugal* **37** J2
Sagua la Grande *Cuba* **120** B3
Saguache *U.S.A.* **108** G10
Saguaro △ *U.S.A.* **109** K8
Saguenay ➤ *Canada* **105** C5
Sagunt *Spain* **38** F4
Sagunto = Sagunt *Spain* **38** F4
Sagwara *India* **68** H6
Sahaba *Sudan* **80** D3
Sahagún *Spain* **36** C5
Şaham al Jawlān *Syria* **74** C4
Sahamandrevo *Madag.* **89** C8
Sahand, Kūh-e *Iran* **73** D12
Sahara *Africa* **78** D6
Saharan Atlas = Saharien,
    Atlas *Algeria* **78** B6
Saharanpur *India* **68** E7
Saharien, Atlas *Algeria* **78** B6
Saharsa *India* **69** G12
Sahasinaka *Madag.* **89** C8
Sahaswan *India* **69** E8
Saheira, W. el ➤ *Egypt* **74** E2
Sahel *Africa* **78** E5
Sahel, Canal du *Mali* **82** C3
Sahibganj *India* **69** G12
Sāḥilīyah *Iraq* **73** F10
Sahiwal *Pakistan* **68** D5
Şaḥneh *Iran* **73** E12
Sahrawi = Western
    Sahara ■ *Africa* **78** D3
Sahuaripa *Mexico* **118** B3
Sahuarita *U.S.A.* **109** L8
Sahuayo de Díaz *Mexico* **118** C4
Šahy *Slovak Rep.* **27** C11
Sai ➤ *India* **69** G10
Sai Buri *Thailand* **65** J3
Sai Twong △ *Thailand* **64** E3
Sai Yok △ *Thailand* **64** E2
Saibai I. *Australia* **94** a
Sa'id Bundās *Sudan* **79** G10
Sa'īdābād = Sīrjān *Iran* **71** D7
Sa'īdābād *Iran* **71** B7
Sa'īdīyeh *Iran* **71** B6
Saidpur *Bangla.* **67** G16
Saidpur *India* **69** G10
Saidu Sharif *Pakistan* **69** B5
Saignes *France* **20** C6
Saigō *Japan* **55** F6
Saigon = Thanh Pho Ho
    Chi Minh *Vietnam* **65** G6
Saijō *Japan* **55** H6
Saikai △ *Japan* **55** H4
Saikanosy Masoala *Madag.* **89** B9
Saikhoa Ghat *India* **67** F19
Saiki *Japan* **55** H6
Sā'īl *Si. Arabia* **70** E4
Sailana *India* **68** H6
Saillans *France* **21** D9
Sailolof *Indonesia* **63** E8
Saimaa *Finland* **32** B5
Saimbeyli *Turkey* **72** D7
Saimen = Saimaa *Finland* **32** B5
Şa'in Dezh *Iran* **73** D12
St. Abb's Head *U.K.* **13** F6
St-Affrique *France* **20** E6
St-Agrève *France* **21** C8
St-Aignan *France* **18** E8
St. Alban's *Canada* **105** C8
St. Albans *U.K.* **15** F7
St. Albans *Vt., U.S.A.* **115** B11
St. Albans *W. Va., U.S.A.* **113** F13
St. Albert *Canada* **102** C6
St-Amand-en-Puisaye
    France **19** E10
St-Amand-les-Eaux *France* **19** B10
St-Amand-Montrond *France* **19** F9
St-Amarin *France* **19** E14
St-Amour *France* **19** F12
St-André *Réunion* **85** c
St-André-de-Cubzac *France* **20** D3
St-André-les-Alpes *France* **21** E10
St. Andrew's *Canada* **105** C8
St. Andrews *U.K.* **13** E6
St-Anicet *Canada* **115** A10
St. Annes *Canada* **103** D9
St. Ann's B. *Canada* **105** C7
St. Ann's Bay *Jamaica* **120** a
St. Anthony *Canada* **105** B8
St. Anthony *U.S.A.* **108** E8
St-Antoine *Canada* **105** C6
St-Antonin-Noble-Val *France* **20** D5
St. Arnaud *Australia* **95** F3
St-Astier *France* **20** C4
St-Aubin-du-Cormier *France* **18** D5
St-Augustin *Canada* **105** B8
St-Augustin ➤ *Canada* **105** B8
St. Augustine *U.S.A.* **117** G14
St-Aulaye *France* **20** C4
St. Austell *U.K.* **15** G3
St-Avold *France* **19** C13
St. Barbe *Canada* **105** B8
St-Barthélemy *W. Indies* **121** C7
St-Béat *France* **20** F4
St. Bees Hd. *U.K.* **14** C4

St. Bees I. *Australia* **94** b
St-Benoît *Réunion* **85** c
St-Benoît-du-Sault *France* **20** B5
St-Bonnet-en-Champsaur
    France **21** D10
St-Brevin-les-Pins *France* **18** E4
St-Brice-en-Coglès *France* **18** D5
St. Bride's, Pte. de *France* **18** E4
St. Brides B. *U.K.* **15** F2
St-Brieuc *France* **18** D4
St-Calais *France* **18** E7
St-Cast-le-Guildo *France* **18** D4
St. Catharines *Canada* **114** C5
St. Catherines I. *U.S.A.* **117** F14
St. Catherine's Pt. *U.K.* **15** G6
St-Céré *France* **20** D5
St-Cergue *Switz.* **25** J2
St-Cernin *France* **20** C6
St-Chamond *France* **21** C8
St. Charles Ill., *U.S.A.* **112** E9
St. Charles *Md., U.S.A.* **113** F15
St. Charles *Mo., U.S.A.* **112** F9
St. Charles I. *N. Amer.* **114** D2
St-Chély-d'Apcher *France* **20** D7
St-Chinian *France* **20** E6
St. Christopher-Nevis = St.
    Kitts & Nevis ■ *W. Indies* **121** C7
St-Ciers-sur-Gironde *France* **20** C3
St. Clair *Mich., U.S.A.* **114** D2
St. Clair *Pa., U.S.A.* **115** F8
St. Clair ➤ *U.S.A.* **114** D2
St. Clair, L. *N. Amer.* **114** D2
St. Clairsville *U.S.A.* **114** F4
St-Claud *France* **20** C4
St. Claude *Canada* **103** D9
St-Claude *France* **19** F12
St. Clears *U.K.* **15** F3
St-Clet *Canada* **115** A10
St. Cloud *Fla., U.S.A.* **117** G14
St. Cloud *Minn., U.S.A.* **112** C6
St-Cricq, C. *Australia* **93** E1
St. Croix *U.S. Virgin Is.* **121** C7
St. Croix ➤ *U.S.A.* **112** C7
St. Croix Falls *U.S.A.* **112** C7
St-Cyprien *France* **20** F7
St-Cyr-sur-Mer *France* **21** E9
St. David's *Canada* **105** C8
St. David's *U.K.* **15** F1
St. David's Head *U.K.* **15** F2
St-Denis *France* **19** D9
St-Denis *Réunion* **85** c
St-Denis ✈ (RUN) *Réunion* **85** c
St-Dié *France* **19** D13
St-Dizier *France* **19** D11
St-Égrève *France* **21** C9
St. Elias, Mt. *U.S.A.* **100** E3
St. Elias Mts. *N. Amer.* **102** A1
St-Éloy-les-Mines *France* **19** F9
St-Émilion *France* **20** D3
St-Étienne *France* **21** C8
St-Étienne-de-Tinée *France* **21** D10
St-Étienne-du-Rouvray
    France **18** C8
St. Eugène *Canada* **115** A10
St. Eustatius *W. Indies* **121** C7
St-Exupery, Lyon ✈ (LYS)
    France **21** C9
St-Fargeau *France* **19** E10
St-Félicien *Canada* **104** C5
St-Florent *France* **21** F13
St-Florent, G. de *France* **21** F13
St-Florent-sur-Cher *France* **19** F9
St-Florentin *France* **19** E10
St-Flour *France* **20** C7
St. Francis *Canada* **112** F3
St. Francis ➤ *U.S.A.* **117** D9
St. Francis, C. *S. Africa* **88** E3
St. Francisville *U.S.A.* **116** F9
St-François, L. *Canada* **115** A10
St-Fulgent *France* **18** F5
St-Gabriel *Canada* **104** C5
St. Gallen = Sankt Gallen
    Switz. **25** H5
St-Galmier *France* **19** G11
St-Gaudens *France* **20** E4
St-Gaultier *France* **18** F8
St-Gengoux-le-National
    France **19** F11
St-Geniez-d'Olt *France* **20** D6
St. George *Australia* **95** D4
St. George *N.B., Canada* **105** C6
St. George *Ont., Canada* **114** C4
St. George *S.C., U.S.A.* **117** E14
St. George *Utah, U.S.A.* **109** H7
St. George, C. *Canada* **105** C8
St. George, C. *U.S.A.* **117** G12
St. George I. *U.S.A.* **106** D6
St. George Ra. *Australia* **92** C4
St. George's *Canada* **105** C8
St-Georges *Canada* **105** C5
St. George's *Grenada* **121** D7
St. George's B. *Canada* **105** C8
St. Georges Basin *N.S.W.,
    Australia* **95** F5
St. Georges Basin
    W. Austral., Australia **92** C4
St. George's Channel *Europe* **12** E6
St. George's Hd. *Australia* **95** F5
St-Georges-lès-
    Baillargeaux *France* **20** B4

St-Germain-de-Calberte
    France **20** D7
St-Germain-en-Laye *France* **19** D9
St-Germain-Lembron *France* **20** C7
St-Gervais-d'Auvergne
    France **19** F9
St-Gervais-les-Bains *France* **21** C10
St-Gildas, Pte. de *France* **18** E4
St-Gilles *France* **21** E8
St-Girons *Ariège, France* **20** F5
St-Girons *Landes, France* **20** E2
St. Gotthard P. = San
    Gottardo, P. del *Switz.* **25** J4
St. Helena *Atl. Oc.* **76** H3
St. Helena *U.S.A.* **108** G2
St. Helena, Mt. *U.S.A.* **110** G4
St. Helena B. *S. Africa* **88** E2
St. Helens *Australia* **95** G4
St. Helens *U.K.* **14** D5
St. Helens *U.S.A.* **110** E4
St. Helens, Mt. *U.S.A.* **110** D4
St. Helier *U.K.* **15** H5
St-Herblain *France* **18** E5
St-Hilaire-du-Harcouët
    France **18** D5
St-Hippolyte *France* **19** E13
St-Hippolyte-du-Fort *France* **20** E7
St-Honoré-les-Bains *France* **19** F10
St-Hubert *Belgium* **17** D5
St-Hubert *Canada* **115** A11
St-Hyacinthe *Canada* **104** C5
St. Ignace *U.S.A.* **113** C11
St. Ignace I. *Canada* **104** C2
St. Ignatius *U.S.A.* **108** C6
St-Imier *Switz.* **25** H2
St. Ives *Cambs., U.K.* **15** E7
St. Ives *Corn., U.K.* **15** G2
St-James *France* **18** D5
St. James *U.S.A.* **112** D6
St-Jean ➤ *Canada* **105** B7
St-Jean, L. *Canada* **105** C5
St-Jean-d'Angély *France* **20** C3
St-Jean-de-Braye *France* **19** E8
St-Jean-de-Luz *France* **20** E2
St-Jean-de-Maurienne
    France **21** C10
St-Jean-de-Monts *France* **18** F4
St-Jean-du-Gard *France* **20** D7
St-Jean-en-Royans *France* **21** C9
St-Jean-Pied-de-Port *France* **20** E2
St-Jean-Port-Joli *Canada* **105** C5
St-Jean-sur-Richelieu
    Canada **115** A11
St-Jérôme *Canada* **104** C5
St. John *Canada* **105** C6
St. John *U.S.A.* **112** F4
St. John ➤ *N. Amer.* **113** C20
St. John, C. *Canada* **105** C8
St. John I. *U.S. Virgin Is.* **121** e
St. John's *Antigua & B.* **121** C7
St. John's *Canada* **105** C9
St. Johns *Ariz., U.S.A.* **109** J9
St. Johns *Mich., U.S.A.* **113** D11
St. Johns ➤ *U.S.A.* **117** F14
St. John's Pt. *Ireland* **12** B3
St. Johnsbury *U.S.A.* **115** B12
St. Johnsville *U.S.A.* **115** C10
St. Joseph *Canada* **114** C3
St. Joseph *Martinique* **120** c
St-Joseph *Réunion* **85** c
St. Joseph *La., U.S.A.* **116** F9
St. Joseph *Mo., U.S.A.* **112** F6
St. Joseph ➤ *U.S.A.* **112** D10
St. Joseph, I. *Canada* **104** C3
St. Joseph, L. *Canada* **104** B1
St-Jovite *Canada* **104** C5
St-Juéry *France* **20** E6
St-Julien-Chapteuil *France* **21** C8
St-Julien-de-Vouvantes
    France **18** E5
St-Julien-en-Genevois
    France **19** F13
St-Junien *France* **20** C4
St-Just-en-Chaussée *France* **19** C9
St-Just-en-Chevalet *France* **20** C7
St. Kilda *U.K.* **13** D7
St. Kitts & Nevis ■ *W. Indies* **121** C7
St. Laurent *Canada* **103** C9
St-Laurent-de-la-Salanque
    France **20** F6
St-Laurent-du-Pont *France* **21** C9
St-Laurent-en-Grandvaux
    France **19** F12
St-Laurent-Médoc *France* **20** C3
St. Lawrence *Australia* **94** C4
St. Lawrence *Canada* **105** C8
St. Lawrence ➤ *Canada* **105** C6
St. Lawrence, Gulf of *Canada* **105** C7
St. Lawrence I. *U.S.A.* **106** C5
St. Lawrence Islands △
    Canada **115** B9
St. Léonard *Canada* **105** C6
St-Léonard-de-Noblat *France* **20** C5
St-Leu *Réunion* **85** c
St. Lewis ➤ *Canada* **105** B8
St-Lô *France* **18** C5
St-Louis *France* **19** E14
St-Louis *Guadeloupe* **120** b
St-Louis *Réunion* **85** c

St. Louis *Senegal* **82** B1
St. Louis *U.S.A.* **112** F8
St. Louis □ *Senegal* **82** B2
St. Louis ➤ *U.S.A.* **112** B7
St-Loup-sur-Semouse
    France **19** E13
St-Luc *Canada* **115** A11
St. Lucia ■ *W. Indies* **121** f
St. Lucia, L. *S. Africa* **89** D5
St. Lucia Channel *W. Indies* **121** D7
St. Maarten ☑ *W. Indies* **121** C7
St. Magnus B. *U.K.* **13** A7
St-Maixent-l'École *France* **20** B3
St-Malo *France* **18** D4
St-Malo, G. de *France* **18** D4
St-Mandrier-sur-Mer *France* **21** E9
St-Marc *Haiti* **121** C5
St-Marcellin *France* **21** C9
St-Marcouf, Îs. *France* **18** C5
St. Maries *U.S.A.* **108** C5
St-Martin ☑ *W. Indies* **121** C7
St. Martin, L. *Canada* **103** C9
St-Martin-de-Crau *France* **21** E8
St-Martin-de-Ré *France* **20** B2
St-Martin-d'Hères *France* **21** C9
St-Martin-Vésubie *France* **21** D11
St. Martins *Barbados* **121** g
St-Martory *France* **20** E4
St. Mary Pk. *Australia* **95** E2
St. Marys *Australia* **95** G4
St. Marys *Canada* **114** C3
St. Mary's Corn., *U.K.* **15** H1
St. Mary's *Orkney, U.K.* **13** C6
St. Marys *Ga., U.S.A.* **117** F14
St. Marys *Pa., U.S.A.* **114** E6
St. Mary's, C. *Canada* **105** C9
St. Mary's B. *Canada* **105** C9
St. Mary's Bay *Canada* **105** D6
St-Mathieu, Pte. *France* **18** D2
St. Matthew I. *U.S.A.* **106** C5
St-Maurice ➤ *Canada* **104** C5
St-Maximin-la-Ste-Baume
    France **21** E9
St-Médard-en-Jalles *France* **20** D3
St-Méen-le-Grand *France* **18** D4
St-Mihiel *France* **19** D12
St-Nazaire *France* **18** E4
St. Neots *U.K.* **15** E7
St-Nicolas-de-Port *France* **19** D13
St-Omer *France* **19** B9
St-Palais-sur-Mer *France* **20** C2
St-Pamphile *Canada* **105** C6
St-Pardoux-la-Rivière *France* **20** C4
St-Pascal *Canada* **105** C6
St. Paul *Canada* **102** C6
St-Paul *France* **21** D9
St-Paul *Réunion* **85** c
St. Paul *Minn., U.S.A.* **112** C7
St. Paul *Nebr., U.S.A.* **112** E4
St-Paul ➤ *Canada* **109** J9
St-Paul ➤ *Liberia* **82** D2
St. Paul, I. *Ind. Oc.* **3** F13
St-Paul-de-Fenouillet *France* **20** F6
St. Paul I. *Canada* **105** C7
St. Paul I. *U.S.A.* **106** D5
St-Paul-lès-Dax *France* **20** E2
St-Péray *France* **21** D8
St. Peter *U.S.A.* **112** C7
St. Peter-Ording *Germany* **24** A4
St. Peter Port *U.K.* **15** H5
St. Peters *N.S., Canada* **105** C7
St. Peters *P.E.I., Canada* **105** C7
St. Petersburg =
    Sankt-Peterburg *Russia* **32** C6
St. Petersburg *U.S.A.* **117** H13
St-Philbert-de-Grand-Lieu
    France **18** E5
St-Phillippe *Réunion* **85** c
St-Pie *Canada* **115** A12
St-Pierre *Martinique* **120** c
St-Pierre *Réunion* **85** c
St-Pierre *St-P. & M.* **105** C8
St-Pierre, L. *Canada* **104** C5
St-Pierre-d'Oléron *France* **20** C2
St-Pierre-en-Port *France* **18** C7
St-Pierre-et-Miquelon ☑
    N. Amer. **105** C8
St-Pierre-le-Moûtier *France* **19** F10
St-Pierre-sur-Dives *France* **18** C6
St-Pol-de-Léon *France* **18** D3
St-Pol-sur-Mer *France* **19** A9
St-Pol-sur-Ternoise *France* **19** B9
St-Pons *France* **20** E6
St-Pourçain-sur-Sioule
    France **19** F10
St-Priest *France* **21** C8
St-Quay-Portrieux *France* **18** D4
St-Quentin *Canada* **105** C6
St-Quentin *France* **19** C10
St-Rambert-d'Albon *France* **21** C8
St-Raphaël *France* **21** E10
St. Regis *U.S.A.* **108** C6
St. Regis Falls *U.S.A.* **115** B10
St-Renan *France* **18** D2
St-Saëns *France* **18** C8
St-Savin *France* **20** B4
St-Savinien *France* **20** C3

St. Sebastien, Tanjon' i
    Madag. **89** A8
St-Seine-l'Abbaye *France* **19** E11
St-Sernin-sur-Rance *France* **20** E6
St-Sever *France* **20** E3
St-Siméon *Canada* **105** C6
St. Simons I. *U.S.A.* **117** F14
St. Simons Island *U.S.A.* **117** F14
St. Stephen *Canada* **105** C6
St-Sulpice *France* **20** E5
St-Sulpice-Laurière *France* **20** B5
St-Sulpice-les-Feuilles *France* **20** B5
St-Syprien = St-Cyprien
    France **20** F7
St-Thégonnec *France* **18** D3
St. Thomas *Canada* **114** D3
St. Thomas I. *U.S. Virgin Is.* **121** e
St-Tite *Canada* **104** C5
St-Tropez *France* **21** E10
St-Troud = St. Truiden
    Belgium **17** D5
St. Truiden *Belgium* **17** D5
St-Vaast-la-Hougue *France* **18** C5
St-Valery-en-Caux *France* **18** C7
St-Valéry-sur-Somme *France* **19** B8
St-Vallier *France* **19** F11
St-Vallier-de-Thiey *France* **21** E10
St-Varent *France* **18** F6
St-Vaury *France* **20** B5
St. Vidgeon's ◎ *Australia* **94** A1
St. Vincent = São Vicente
    C. Verde Is. **78** b
St. Vincent *Italy* **40** C4
St. Vincent, G. *Australia* **95** F2
St. Vincent & the
    Grenadines ■ *W. Indies* **121** D7
St-Vincent-de-Tyrosse *France* **20** E2
St. Vincent Passage
    W. Indies **121** D7
St-Vith *Belgium* **17** D6
St-Vivien-de-Médoc *France* **20** C2
St. Walburg *Canada* **103** C7
St-Yrieix-la-Perche *France* **20** C5
Ste-Adresse *France* **18** C7
Ste-Agathe-des-Monts
    Canada **104** C5
Ste-Anne *Guadeloupe* **120** b
Ste-Anne *Seychelles* **85** b
Ste-Anne, L. *Canada* **105** B6
Ste-Anne-des-Monts *Canada* **105** C6
Ste-Croix *Switz.* **25** J2
Ste-Énimie *France* **20** D7
Ste-Foy-la-Grande *France* **20** D4
Ste. Genevieve *U.S.A.* **112** G8
Ste-Hermine *France* **18** B2
Ste-Livrade-sur-Lot *France* **20** D4
Ste-Marguerite ➤ *Canada* **105** B6
Ste-Marie *Canada* **105** C5
Ste-Marie *Martinique* **120** c
Ste-Marie *Réunion* **85** c
Ste-Marie, Ile = Nosy
    Boraha *Madag.* **89** B8
Ste-Marie-aux-Mines
    France **19** D14
Ste-Maure-de-Touraine
    France **18** E7
Ste-Maxime *France* **21** E10
Ste-Menehould *France* **19** C11
Ste-Mère-Église *France* **18** C5
Ste-Rose *Guadeloupe* **120** b
Ste-Rose *Réunion* **85** c
Ste. Rose du Lac *Canada* **103** C9
Ste-Savine *France* **19** D11
Ste-Sigolène *France* **21** C8
Saintes *France* **20** C3
Saintes, Îs. des *Guadeloupe* **120** b
Stes-Maries-de-la-Mer *France* **21** E8
Saintfield *U.K.* **12** B6
Saintonge *France* **20** C3
Saipan *N. Marianas* **96** F6
Sairang *India* **67** H18
Sairecábur, Cerro *Bolivia* **126** A2
Saitama *Japan* **55** G9
Saitama □ *Japan* **55** F9
Saiteli = Kadınhanı *Turkey* **72** C5
Saiṭi *Moldova* **29** D14
Saiyid *Pakistan* **68** D5
Saja-Besaya △ *Spain* **36** B6
Sajama *Bolivia* **124** G5
Sajó ➤ *Hungary* **28** C6
Sajószentpéter *Hungary* **28** B5
Sajum *India* **69** C8
Sak ➤ *S. Africa* **88** E3
Saka *Kenya* **86** B4
Sakaba *Nigeria* **83** C6
Sakai *Japan* **55** G7
Sakaide *Japan* **55** G6
Sakaiminato *Japan* **55** G6
Sakākah *Si. Arabia* **70** D4
Sakakawea, L. *U.S.A.* **112** B3
Sakami *Canada* **104** B4
Sakami, L. *Canada* **104** B4
Sâkâne, 'Erg i-n *Mali* **83** A4
Sakania *Dem. Rep. of the Congo* **87** E2
Sakaraha *Madag.* **89** C7
Sakartvelo = Georgia ■ *Asia* **35** J6
Sakarya *Turkey* **72** B4
Sakarya □ *Turkey* **72** B4
Sakarya ➤ *Turkey* **72** B4

Sakashima-Guntō *Japan* **55** M2
Sakassou *Ivory C.* **82** D3
Sakata *Japan* **54** E9
Sakchu *N. Korea* **57** D13
Sakeny ➤ *Madag.* **89** C8
Sakété *Benin* **83** D5
Sakha □ *Russia* **53** C14
Sakhalin *Russia* **53** D15
Sakhalinskiy Zaliv *Russia* **53** D15
Şaki *Azerbaijan* **35** K8
Šakiai *Lithuania* **30** D10
Sakon Nakhon *Thailand* **64** D5
Sakri *India* **69** F12
Sakrivier *S. Africa* **88** E3
Sakskøbing *Denmark* **11** K5
Sakti *India* **69** H10
Sakuma *Japan* **55** G8
Sakurai *Japan* **55** G7
Saky *Ukraine* **33** K7
Sal ➤ *Russia* **35** G5
Sal ➤ *Russia* **35** G5
Sal Rei *C. Verde Is.* **78** b
Sala *Eritrea* **81** D4
Sala ➤ *Eritrea* **81** D4
Sala *Sweden* **10** E10
Sala ➤ *Eritrea* **81** D4
Sala Consilina *Italy* **43** B8
Sala-y-Gómez *Pac. Oc.* **97** K17
Sala y Gómez Ridge *Pac. Oc.* **97** K18
Salaberry-de-Valleyfield
  Canada **115** A10
Salacgrīva *Latvia* **30** A11
Salada, L. *Mexico* **109** K6
Saladas *Argentina* **126** B4
Saladillo *Argentina* **126** D4
Salado ➤ *B. Aires, Argentina* **126** D4
Salado ➤ *La Pampa,*
  Argentina **128** D3
Salado ➤ *Santa Fe,*
  Argentina **126** C3
Salado ➤ *Mexico* **116** H5
Salaga *Ghana* **83** D4
Şalāḩ *Syria* **74** C5
Şalāḩ ad Dīn □ *Iraq* **70** C4
Sălaj □ *Romania* **28** C8
Salakos *Greece* **49** C9
Salala *Liberia* **82** D2
Salala *Sudan* **80** C4
Salālah *Oman* **75** D5
Salamanca *Chile* **126** C1
Salamanca *Spain* **36** E5
Salamanca *U.S.A.* **114** D6
Salamanca □ *Spain* **36** E5
Salāmatābād *Iran* **70** C5
Salamina *Greece* **46** D5
Salamis *Cyprus* **49** D12
Salar de Atacama *Chile* **126** A2
Salar de Uyuni *Bolivia* **124** H5
Sălard *Romania* **28** C7
Salas *Spain* **36** B4
Salas de los Infantes *Spain* **36** C7
Salatiga *Indonesia* **63** G14
Salaverry *Peru* **124** E3
Salawati *Indonesia* **63** E8
Salaya *India* **68** H3
Salayar *Indonesia* **63** F6
Salazar ➤ *Spain* **38** C3
Salbris *France* **19** E9
S'Albufera *Spain* **48** B10
Salcia *Romania* **29** G9
Sălciua *Romania* **29** D8
Salcombe *U.K.* **15** G4
Saldaña *Spain* **36** C6
Saldanha *S. Africa* **88** E2
Saldanha B. *S. Africa* **88** E2
Saldus *Latvia* **30** B9
Saldus □ *Latvia* **30** B9
Sale *Australia* **95** F4
Sale *Italy* **40** D5
Salé *Morocco* **78** B4
Sale *U.K.* **14** D5
Salekhard *Russia* **52** C7
Salelolologa *Samoa* **91** b
Salem *India* **66** P11
Salem *Ill., U.S.A.* **112** F9
Salem *Ind., U.S.A.* **112** F10
Salem *Mass., U.S.A.* **115** D14
Salem *Mo., U.S.A.* **112** G8
Salem *N.H., U.S.A.* **115** D13
Salem *N.J., U.S.A.* **113** F16
Salem *N.Y., U.S.A.* **115** C11
Salem *Ohio, U.S.A.* **114** F4
Salem *Oreg., U.S.A.* **108** D2
Salem *S. Dak., U.S.A.* **112** D5
Salem *Va., U.S.A.* **113** G13
Salemi *Italy* **42** E5
Sälen *Sweden* **10** D7
Salernes *France* **21** E10
Salerno *Italy* **43** B7
Salerno, G. di *Italy* **43** B7
Salford *U.K.* **14** D5
Salgir ➤ *Ukraine* **33** K8
Salgótarján *Hungary* **28** B4
Salgueiro *Brazil* **125** E11
Salibabu *Indonesia* **63** D7
Salibea = Salybia
  Trin. & Tob. **125** K15
Salida *U.S.A.* **107** H18
Salies-de-Béarn *France* **20** E3

Salihli *Turkey* **72** C3
Salihorsk *Belarus* **23** B14
Salima *Malawi* **85** G6
Salina *Italy* **43** D7
Salina *Kans., U.S.A.* **112** F5
Salina *Utah, U.S.A.* **108** G8
Salina Cruz *Mexico* **119** D5
Salina di Margherita di
  Savoia ➤ *Italy* **43** A9
Salinas *Brazil* **125** G10
Salinas *Ecuador* **124** D2
Salinas *U.S.A.* **110** J5
Salinas ➤ *Guatemala* **119** D6
Salinas ➤ *U.S.A.* **110** J5
Salinas, B. de *Nic.* **120** D2
Salinas, Pampa de las
  Argentina **126** C2
Salinas Ambargasta
  Argentina **126** B3
Salinas de Hidalgo *Mexico* **118** C4
Salinas Grandes *Argentina* **126** C3
Salinas Pueblo Missions △
  U.S.A. **109** J10
Salinas Valley *U.S.A.* **110** J5
Saline ➤ *Ark., U.S.A.* **116** E8
Saline ➤ *Kans., U.S.A.* **112** F5
Saline di Trapani e
  Paceco △ *Italy* **42** E5
Salines, C. de ses *Spain* **48** B10
Salinópolis *Brazil* **125** D9
Salins-les-Bains *France* **19** F12
Salir *Portugal* **37** H2
Salisbury *Australia* **95** E2
Salisbury *U.K.* **15** F6
Salisbury *Md., U.S.A.* **113** F16
Salisbury *N.C., U.S.A.* **117** D14
Salisbury I. *Canada* **101** E16
Salisbury Plain *U.K.* **15** F6
Săliște *Romania* **29** E8
Salka *Nigeria* **83** C5
Şalkhad *Syria* **74** C5
Salkove *Ukraine* **29** B14
Salla *Finland* **8** C23
Sallanches *France* **21** C10
Sallent *Spain* **38** D6
Salles *France* **20** D3
Salles-Curan *France* **20** D6
Salling *Denmark* **11** H2
Salliq = Coral Harbour
  Canada **101** E15
Sallisaw *U.S.A.* **116** D7
Sallom *Sudan* **80** D4
Salluit *Canada* **101** E16
Salmān Pak *Iraq* **73** G11
Salmās *Iran* **73** C11
Salmerón *Spain* **38** E2
Salmo *Canada* **102** D5
Salmon *U.S.A.* **108** D7
Salmon ➤ *Canada* **102** C4
Salmon ➤ *U.S.A.* **108** D5
Salmon Arm *Canada* **102** C5
Salmon Gums *Australia* **93** F3
Salmon Pt. *Canada* **114** C7
Salmon River Mts. *U.S.A.* **108** D6
Salmon River Res. *U.S.A.* **115** C9
Salo *Finland* **32** B2
Salò *Italy* **40** C7
Salobreña *Spain* **37** J7
Salome *U.S.A.* **111** M13
Salon *India* **69** F9
Salon-de-Provence *France* **21** E9
Salonica = Thessaloniki
  Greece **44** F6
Salonta *Romania* **28** D6
Salor ➤ *Spain* **37** F3
Salou *Spain* **38** D6
Salou, C. de *Spain* **38** D6
Saloum ➤ *Senegal* **82** C1
Salpausselkä *Finland* **32** B4
Salsacate *Argentina* **126** C2
Salses *France* **20** F6
Salsk *Russia* **35** G5
Salso ➤ *Italy* **42** E6
Salsomaggiore Terme *Italy* **40** D6
Salt *Spain* **38** D7
Salt ➤ *Canada* **102** B6
Salt ➤ *U.S.A.* **109** K7
Salt Fork Red ➤ *U.S.A.* **116** D5
Salt L. *Australia* **95** E3
Salt Lake City *U.S.A.* **108** F8
Salt Range *Pakistan* **68** C5
Salta *Argentina* **126** A2
Salta □ *Argentina* **126** A2
Saltara *Italy* **41** E9
Saltash *U.K.* **15** G3
Saltburn by the Sea *U.K.* **14** C7
Saltcoats *U.K.* **13** F4
Saltee Is. *Ireland* **12** D5
Saltfjellet *Norway* **8** C16
Saltfjorden *Norway* **8** C16
Saltholm *Denmark* **11** J6
Saltillo *Mexico* **118** B4
Salto *Argentina* **126** C3
Salto *Uruguay* **126** C4
Salto del Guaíra *Paraguay* **127** A5
Salton City *U.S.A.* **111** M11
Salton Sea *U.S.A.* **111** M11
Saltpond *Ghana* **83** D4
Saltsburg *U.S.A.* **114** F5
Saltsjöbaden *Sweden* **10** E12

Saluda ➤ *U.S.A.* **117** D14
Salūm *Egypt* **80** A2
Salûm, Khâlig el *Egypt* **80** A2
Salur *India* **67** K13
Saluzzo *Italy* **40** D4
Salvador *Brazil* **125** F11
Salvador *Canada* **103** C7
Salvador, El ■ *Cent. Amer.* **120** D2
Salvador, L. *U.S.A.* **117** G9
Salvaterra de Magos *Portugal* **37** F2
Sálvora, I. de *Spain* **36** C2
Salyan *Azerbaijan* **73** C13
Salybia *Trin. & Tob.* **125** K15
Salza ➤ *Austria* **26** D7
Salzach ➤ *Austria* **26** C5
Salzburg *Austria* **26** D6
Salzburg □ *Austria* **26** D6
Salzgitter *Germany* **24** C6
Salzkotten *Germany* **24** D4
Salzwedel *Germany* **24** C7
Sam *India* **68** F4
Sam Neua *Laos* **58** G5
Sam Ngao *Thailand* **64** D2
Sam Rayburn Res. *U.S.A.* **116** F7
Sam Son *Vietnam* **64** C5
Sam Teu *Laos* **64** C5
Sama de Langreo =
  Langreo *Spain* **36** B5
Samagaltay *Russia* **53** D10
Samales Group *Phil.* **61** J5
Samâlût *Egypt* **80** B3
Samana *India* **68** D7
Samana Cay *Bahamas* **121** B5
Samandağ *Turkey* **72** D6
Samandira *Turkey* **45** F13
Samanga *Tanzania* **87** D4
Samangān □ *Afghan.* **66** B5
Samangwa
  Dem. Rep. of the Congo **86** C1
Samani *Japan* **54** C11
Samanli Dağları *Turkey* **45** F13
Samar *Phil.* **61** F6
Samara *Russia* **34** D10
Samara ➤ *Russia* **34** D10
Samara ➤ *Ukraine* **33** H8
Samaria = Shōmrōn
  West Bank **74** C4
Samaria △ *Greece* **49** D5
Samarinda *Indonesia* **62** E5
Samarkand = Samarqand
  Uzbekistan **52** F7
Samarqand *Uzbekistan* **52** F7
Sāmarrā' *Iraq* **73** E10
Samastipur *India* **69** G11
Samaxı *Azerbaijan* **35** K9
Samba *Dem. Rep. of the Congo* **86** C2
Samba *India* **69** C6
Sambalpur *India* **67** J14
Sambar, Tanjung *Indonesia* **62** E4
Sambas *Indonesia* **62** D3
Sambava *Madag.* **89** A9
Sambawizi *Zimbabwe* **87** F2
Sambhajinagar =
  Aurangabad *India* **66** K9
Sambhal *India* **69** E8
Sambhar *India* **68** F6
Sambhar L. *India* **68** F6
Sambiase *Italy* **43** D9
Sambir *Ukraine* **31** D12
Sambor *Cambodia* **64** F6
Samborombón, B. *Argentina* **126** D4
Sambuca di Sicilia *Italy* **42** E6
Samburu △ *Kenya* **86** B4
Samcheok *S. Korea* **57** F15
Same *Tanzania* **86** C4
Samer *France* **19** B8
Samfya *Zambia* **87** E2
Sami *Greece* **46** C2
Şämkir *Azerbaijan* **35** K8
Şamlı *Turkey* **47** B9
Sāmnah *Si. Arabia* **70** E3
Samo Alto *Chile* **126** C1
Samoa ■ *Pac. Oc.* **91** b
Samobor *Croatia* **41** C12
Samoëns *France* **19** F13
Samokov *Bulgaria* **44** D7
Šamorín *Slovak Rep.* **27** C10
Samorogouan *Burkina Faso* **82** C4
Samos *Greece* **47** D8
Samoš *Serbia* **28** E5
Samos *Spain* **36** C3
Samos □ *Greece* **47** D8
Samothráki = Mathraki
  Greece **49** A3
Samothraki *Greece* **45** F9
Samoylovka *Russia* **34** E6
Sampa *Ghana* **82** D4
Sampacho *Argentina* **126** C3
Sampalan *Indonesia* **63** K18
Sampang *Indonesia* **63** G15
Samper de Calanda *Spain* **38** D4
Sampéyre *Italy* **40** D4
Sampit *Indonesia* **62** E4
Sampit, Teluk *Indonesia* **62** E4
Samrong *Cambodia* **64** E4
Samrong *Thailand* **64** E3
Samsø *Denmark* **11** J4
Samsø Bælt *Denmark* **11** J4
Samsun *Turkey* **72** B7

Samsun □ *Turkey* **72** B7
Samtredia *Georgia* **35** J6
Samui, Ko *Thailand* **65** b
Samur ➤ *Russia* **35** K9
Samurskiy Khrebet *Russia* **35** K8
Samusole
  Dem. Rep. of the Congo **87** E1
Samut Prakan *Thailand* **64** F3
Samut Songkhram *Thailand* **64** F3
Samwari *Pakistan* **68** E2
San *Mali* **82** C4
San ➤ *Cambodia* **64** F5
San ➤ *Poland* **31** H8
San Adrián *Spain* **38** C3
San Adrián, C. de *Spain* **36** B2
San Agustin, C. *Phil.* **61** H7
San Agustín de Valle Fértil
  Argentina **126** C2
San Ambrosio *Pac. Oc.* **122** F3
San Andreas *U.S.A.* **110** G6
San Andres *Phil.* **61** E6
San Andrés, I. de *Caribbean* **120** D3
San Andrés del Rabanedo
  Spain **36** C5
San Andres Mts. *U.S.A.* **109** K10
San Andrés Tuxtla *Mexico* **119** D5
San Angelo *U.S.A.* **116** F4
San Anselmo *U.S.A.* **110** H4
San Antonio *Belize* **119** D7
San Antonio *Chile* **126** C1
San Antonio *Phil.* **61** D4
San Antonio *N. Mex., U.S.A.*
  109 K10
San Antonio *Tex., U.S.A.* **116** G5
San Antonio ➤ *U.S.A.* **116** G6
San Antonio, C. *Argentina* **126** D4
San Antonio, C. de *Cuba* **120** B3
San Antonio, C. de *Spain* **39** G5
San Antonio, Mt. *U.S.A.* **111** L9
San Antonio de los Baños
  Cuba **120** B3
San Antonio de los Cobres
  Argentina **126** A2
San Antonio Oeste
  Argentina **128** E4
San Arcángelo *Italy* **43** B9
San Ardo *U.S.A.* **110** J6
San Augustín *Canary Is.* **48** G4
San Augustine *U.S.A.* **116** F7
San Bartolomé *Canary Is.* **48** F6
San Bartolomé de Tirajana
  Canary Is. **48** G4
San Bartolomeo in Galdo
  Italy **43** A8
San Benedetto del Tronto
  Italy **41** F10
San Benedetto Po *Italy* **40** C7
San Benedicto, I. *Mexico* **118** D2
San Benito *U.S.A.* **116** H6
San Benito ➤ *U.S.A.* **110** J5
San Benito Mt. *U.S.A.* **110** J6
San Bernardino *U.S.A.* **111** L9
San Bernardino Mts. *U.S.A.*
  111 L10
San Bernardino Str. *Phil.* **61** E6
San Bernardo *Chile* **126** C1
San Bernardo, I. de *Colombia* **124** B3
San Blas *Mexico* **118** B3
San Blas, Arch. de *Panama* **120** E4
San Blas, C. *U.S.A.* **117** G12
San Bonifacio *Italy* **41** C8
San Borja *Bolivia* **124** F5
San Buenaventura =
  Ventura *U.S.A.* **111** L7
San Buenaventura *Mexico* **118** B4
San Carlos = Sant Carles
  Spain **48** B8
San Carlos *Argentina* **126** C2
San Carlos *Chile* **126** D1
San Carlos *Baja Calif. S.,*
  Mexico **118** C2
San Carlos *Coahuila, Mexico* **118** B4
San Carlos *Nic.* **120** D3
San Carlos *Pangasinan, Phil.* **61** D4
San Carlos *Uruguay* **127** C5
San Carlos *U.S.A.* **109** K8
San Carlos *Venezuela* **124** B5
San Carlos de Bariloche
  Argentina **128** E2
San Carlos de Bolívar
  Argentina **126** D3
San Carlos de la Rápita =
  Sant Carles de la Ràpita
  Spain **38** E5
San Carlos del Zulia
  Venezuela **124** B4
San Carlos L. *U.S.A.* **109** K8
San Cataldo *Italy* **42** E6
San Celoni = Sant Celoni
  Spain **38** D7
San Clemente *Chile* **126** D1
San Clemente *Spain* **39** F2
San Clemente *U.S.A.* **111** M9
San Clemente I. *U.S.A.* **111** N8
San Cristóbal = Es Migjorn
  Gran *Spain* **48** B11
San Cristóbal *Argentina* **126** C3
San Cristóbal *Dom. Rep.* **121** C5
San Cristóbal *Solomon Is.* **90** C9

San Cristóbal *Venezuela* **124** B4
San Cristóbal de las Casas
  Mexico **119** D6
San Damiano d'Asti *Italy* **40** D5
San Daniele del Friuli *Italy* **41** B10
San Diego *Calif., U.S.A.* **111** N9
San Diego *Tex., U.S.A.* **116** H5
San Diego, C. *Argentina* **128** G3
San Diego de la Unión
  Mexico **118** C4
San Diego Int. ✈ (SAN)
  U.S.A. **111** N9
San Dimitri, Ras *Malta* **49** C1
San Dimitri Point = San
  Dimitri, Ras *Malta* **49** C1
San Donà di Piave *Italy* **41** C9
San Estanislao *Paraguay* **126** A4
San Esteban de Gormaz
  Spain **38** D1
San Felice Circeo *Italy* **42** A6
San Felice sul Panaro *Italy* **41** D8
San Felipe *Chile* **126** C1
San Felipe *Mexico* **118** A2
San Felipe *Venezuela* **124** A5
San Felipe ➤ *U.S.A.* **111** M11
San Félix *Chile* **126** B1
San Félix *Pac. Oc.* **122** F2
San Fernando = Sant
  Ferran *Spain* **48** C7
San Fernando *Chile* **126** C1
San Fernando *Mexico* **119** C5
San Fernando *La Union, Phil.* **61** C4
San Fernando *Pampanga,*
  Phil. **61** D4
San Fernando *Spain* **37** J4
San Fernando *Trin. & Tob.* **125** D7
San Fernando *U.S.A.* **111** L8
San Fernando de Apure
  Venezuela **124** B5
San Fernando de Atabapo
  Venezuela **124** C5
San Fernando di Púglia *Italy* **43** A9
San Francisco *Argentina* **126** C3
San Francisco *U.S.A.* **110** H4
San Francisco ➤ *U.S.A.* **109** K9
San Francisco, C. de
  Colombia **122** C3
San Francisco, Paso de
  S. Amer. **126** B2
San Francisco de Macorís
  Dom. Rep. **121** C5
San Francisco del Monte de
  Oro *Argentina* **126** C2
San Francisco del Oro
  Mexico **118** B3
San Francisco Int. ✈ (SFO)
  U.S.A. **110** H4
San Francisco Javier = Sant
  Francesc de Formentera
  Spain **48** C7
San Fratello *Italy* **43** D7
San Gabriel *Chile* **126** C1
San Gabriel Chilac *Mexico* **119** D5
San Gabriel Mts. *U.S.A.* **111** L9
San Gavino Monreale *Italy* **42** C1
San German *Puerto Rico* **121** d
San Gimignano *Italy* **41** E8
San Giórgio di Nogaro *Italy* **41** C10
San Giórgio Iónico *Italy* **43** B10
San Giovanni Bianco *Italy* **40** C6
San Giovanni in Fiore *Italy* **43** C9
San Giovanni in Persiceto
  Italy **41** D3
San Giovanni Rotondo *Italy* **41** G12
San Giovanni Valdarno *Italy* **41** E8
San Giuliano Terme *Italy* **40** E7
San Gorgonio Mt. *U.S.A.* **111** L10
San Gottardo, P. del *Switz.* **25** J4
San Gregorio *Uruguay* **127** C4
San Gregorio *U.S.A.* **110** H4
San Guillermo △ *Argentina* **126** B2
San Guiseppe Jato *Italy* **42** E6
San Ignacio *Belize* **119** D7
San Ignacio *Bolivia* **124** G6
San Ignacio *Mexico* **118** B2
San Ignacio *Paraguay* **126** B4
San Ignacio, L. *Mexico* **118** B2
San Ildefonso, C. *Phil.* **61** D5
San Isidro *Argentina* **126** C4
San Isidro *Phil.* **61** H7
San Jacinto *U.S.A.* **111** M10
San Jaime = Sant Jaume
  Spain **48** B11
San Javier *Misiones,*
  Argentina **127** B5
San Javier *Santa Fe,*
  Argentina **126** C4
San Javier *Bolivia* **124** G6
San Javier *Chile* **126** D1
San Javier *Spain* **39** H4
San Jerónimo Taviche
  Mexico **119** D5
San Joaquin *U.S.A.* **110** J6
San Joaquin ➤ *U.S.A.* **110** G5
San Joaquin Valley *U.S.A.* **110** J6
San Jon *U.S.A.* **109** J12
San Jordi = Sant Jordi *Spain* **48** B9
San Jorge *Argentina* **126** C3
San Jorge, B. *Mexico* **118** A2
San Jorge, G. *Argentina* **128** F3

San José = San Josep *Spain* **48** C7
San José *Argentina* **126** C4
San José *Costa Rica* **120** E3
San José *Guatemala* **120** D1
San Jose *Mind. Occ., Phil.* **61** E4
San Jose *Nueva Ecija, Phil.* **61** D4
San Jose *U.S.A.* **110** H5
San Jose ➤ *U.S.A.* **109** J10
San José, I. *Mexico* **118** C3
San José de Buenavista *Phil.* **63** B6
San José de Chiquitos
  Bolivia **124** G6
San José de Feliciano
  Argentina **126** C4
San José de Jáchal *Argentina* **126** C2
San José de Mayo *Uruguay* **126** C4
San José del Cabo *Mexico* **118** C3
San José del Guaviare
  Colombia **124** C4
San Josep *Spain* **48** C7
San Juan *Argentina* **126** C2
San Juan *Phil.* **61** F6
San Juan *Puerto Rico* **121** d
San Juan *Trin. & Tob.* **125** K15
San Juan □ *Argentina* **126** C2
San Juan ➤ *Argentina* **126** C2
San Juan ➤ *Nic.* **120** D3
San Juan ➤ *U.S.A.* **109** H8
San Juan Bautista = Sant
  Joan de Labritja *Spain* **48** B8
San Juan Bautista *Paraguay* **126** B4
San Juan Bautista *U.S.A.* **110** J5
San Juan Capistrano *U.S.A.* **111** M9
San Juan Cr. ➤ *U.S.A.* **110** J5
San Juan de Guadelupe
  Mexico **118** C4
San Juan de la Costa *Mexico* **118** C2
San Juan de los Lagos
  Mexico **118** C4
San Juan de los Morros
  Venezuela **124** B5
San Juan del Norte *Nic.* **120** D3
San Juan del Norte, B. de
  Nic. **120** D3
San Juan del Río *Mexico* **119** C5
San Juan del Sur *Nic.* **120** D2
San Juan I. *U.S.A.* **110** B3
San Juan Island △ *U.S.A.* **110** B4
San Juan Mts. *U.S.A.* **109** H10
San Just, Sierra de *Spain* **38** E4
San Justo *Argentina* **126** C3
San Kamphaeng *Thailand* **64** C2
San Lázaro, C. *Mexico* **118** C2
San Leandro *U.S.A.* **110** H4
San Leonardo de Yagüe
  Spain **38** D1
San Lorenzo = Sant Llorenç
  des Cardassar *Spain* **48** B10
San Lorenzo *Argentina* **126** C3
San Lorenzo *Ecuador* **124** C3
San Lorenzo *Paraguay* **126** B4
San Lorenzo ➤ *Mexico* **118** C3
San Lorenzo, I. *Mexico* **118** B2
San Lorenzo, Mte. *Argentina* **128** F2
San Lorenzo de la Parrilla
  Spain **38** F2
San Lorenzo de Morunys =
  Sant Llorenç de Morunys
  Spain **38** C6
San Lucas = Cabo San
  Lucas *Mexico* **118** C3
San Lucas *Bolivia* **124** H5
San Lucas *Mexico* **118** B2
San Lucas *U.S.A.* **110** J5
San Lucas, C. *Mexico* **118** C3
San Lúcido *Italy* **43** C9
San Luis *Argentina* **126** C2
San Luis *Cuba* **120** B3
San Luis *Guatemala* **120** C2
San Luis *Ariz., U.S.A.* **109** K6
San Luis *Colo., U.S.A.* **109** H11
San Luis *Mexico* **118** B2
San Luis, I. *Mexico* **118** B2
San Luis, Sierra de *Argentina* **126** C2
San Luis de la Paz *Mexico* **118** C4
San Luis Obispo *U.S.A.* **111** K6
San Luis Potosí *Mexico* **118** C4
San Luis Potosí □ *Mexico* **118** C4
San Luis Res. *U.S.A.* **110** H5
San Luis Río Colorado
  Mexico **118** A2
San Manuel *U.S.A.* **109** K8
San Marco, C. *Italy* **42** C1
San Marco Argentano *Italy* **43** C9
San Marco in Lámis *Italy* **41** G12
San Marcos *Guatemala* **120** D1
San Marcos *Calif., U.S.A.* **111** M9
San Marcos *Tex., U.S.A.* **116** G6
San Marcos, I. *Mexico* **118** B2
San Marino *San Marino* **41** E9
San Marino ■ *Europe* **41** E9
San Martín *Antarctica* **5** C17
San Martín *Argentina* **126** C2
San Martín ➤ *Bolivia* **124** F6
San Martín, L. *Argentina* **128** F2
San Martín de la Vega *Spain* **36** E7
San Martín de los Andes
  Argentina **128** E2
San Martín de
  Valdeiglesias *Spain* **36** E6

San Mateo = Sant Mateu
Baleares, Spain **48** B7
San Mateo = Sant Mateu
Valencia, Spain **38** E5
San Mateo *Phil.* **61** C4
San Mateo *U.S.A.* **110** H4
San Matías *Bolivia* **124** G7
San Matías, G. *Argentina* **128** E4
San Miguel = Sant Miquel
Spain **48** B7
San Miguel *El Salv.* **120** D2
San Miguel *Panama* **120** E4
San Miguel *U.S.A.* **110** K6
San Miguel → *Bolivia* **124** F6
San Miguel de Tucumán
Argentina **126** B2
San Miguel del Monte
Argentina **126** D4
San Miguel I. *U.S.A.* **111** L6
San Miniato *Italy* **40** E7
San Nicolás *Canary Is.* **48** G4
San Nicolas *Phil.* **61** B4
San Nicolás de los Arroyos
Argentina **126** C3
San Nicolas I. *U.S.A.* **111** M7
San Onofre *U.S.A.* **111** M9
San Pablo *Bolivia* **126** A2
San Pablo *Phil.* **61** D4
San Pablo *U.S.A.* **110** H4
San Páolo di Civitate *Italy* **41** G12
San Pedro *B. Aires, Argentina* **126** C4
San Pedro *Misiones,*
Argentina **127** B5
San Pedro *Chile* **126** C1
San Pedro *Ivory C.* **82** E3
San Pedro *Mexico* **118** C2
San Pedro □ *Paraguay* **126** A4
San Pedro → *Chihuahua,*
Mexico **118** B3
San Pedro → *Nayarit,*
Mexico **118** C3
San Pedro → *U.S.A.* **109** K8
San Pedro, Pta. *Chile* **126** B1
San Pedro, Sierra de *Spain* **37** F4
San Pedro Channel *U.S.A.* **111** M8
San Pedro de Atacama *Chile* **126** A2
San Pedro de Jujuy
Argentina **126** A3
San Pedro de las Colonias
Mexico **118** B4
San Pedro de Macorís
Dom. Rep. **121** C6
San Pedro del Norte *Nic.* **120** D3
San Pedro del Paraná
Paraguay **126** B4
San Pedro del Pinatar *Spain* **39** H4
San Pedro Mártir, Sierra
Mexico **118** A1
San Pedro Mártir △ *Mexico* **118** A1
San Pedro Ocampo =
Melchor Ocampo *Mexico* **118** C4
San Pedro Pochutla *Mexico* **119** D5
San Pedro Sula *Honduras* **120** C2
San Pedro Tututepec
Mexico **119** D5
San Pietro *Italy* **42** C1
San Pietro Vernótico *Italy* **43** B11
San Rafael *Argentina* **126** C2
San Rafael *Calif., U.S.A.* **110** H4
San Rafael *N. Mex., U.S.A.* **109** J10
San Rafael Mt. *U.S.A.* **111** L7
San Rafael Mts. *U.S.A.* **111** L7
San Ramón de la Nueva
Orán *Argentina* **126** A3
San Remo *Italy* **40** E4
San Roque *Argentina* **126** B4
San Roque *Spain* **37** J5
San Rosendo *Chile* **126** D1
San Saba *U.S.A.* **116** F5
San Salvador *El Salv.* **120** D2
San Salvador de Jujuy
Argentina **126** A3
San Salvador I. *Bahamas* **121** B5
San Salvo *Italy* **41** F11
San Sebastián = Donostia-
San Sebastián *Spain* **38** B3
San Sebastián *Argentina* **128** G3
San Sebastián *Puerto Rico* **121** d
San Sebastián de la
Gomera *Canary Is.* **48** F2
San Serra = Son Serra *Spain* **48** B10
San Serverino Marche *Italy* **41** E10
San Severo *Italy* **41** G12
San Simeon *U.S.A.* **110** K5
San Simon *U.S.A.* **109** K9
San Stéfano di Cadore *Italy* **41** B9
San Stino di Livenza *Italy* **41** C9
San Telmo *Mexico* **118** A1
San Tiburcio *Mexico* **118** C4
San Valentin, Mte. *Chile* **128** F2
San Vicente de Alcántara
Spain **37** F3
San Vicente de Cañete *Peru* **124** F3
San Vicente de la Barquera
Spain **36** B6
San Vincenzo *Italy* **40** E7
San Vito *Costa Rica* **120** E3
San Vito *Italy* **42** C2
San Vito, C. *Italy* **42** D5

San Vito al Tagliamento
Italy **41** C9
San Vito Chietino *Italy* **41** F11
San Vito dei Normanni *Italy* **43** B10
Sana' *Yemen* **75** D3
Sana → *Bos.-H.* **41** C13
Sanaba *Burkina Faso* **82** C4
Sanae IV *Antarctica* **5** D2
Şanâfir *Si. Arabia* **80** B3
Sanaga → *Cameroon* **83** E6
Sanak I. *U.S.A.* **106** E7
Sanaloa, Presa *Mexico* **118** C3
Sanana *Indonesia* **63** E7
Sanand *India* **68** H5
Sanandaj *Iran* **73** E12
Sanandita *Bolivia* **126** A3
Sanary-sur-Mer *France* **21** E9
Sanawad *India* **68** H7
Sancellas = Sencelles *Spain* **48** B9
Sancergues *France* **19** E9
Sancerre *France* **19** E9
Sancerrois, Collines du
France **19** E9
Sancha He → *China* **58** D6
Sanchahe *China* **57** B14
Sánchez *Dom. Rep.* **121** C6
Sanchor *India* **68** G4
Sancoins *France* **19** F9
Sancti Spíritus *Cuba* **120** B4
Sancy, Puy de *France* **20** C6
Sand = Polokwane →
S. Africa **89** C5
Sand Hills *U.S.A.* **112** D3
Sand Lakes △ *Canada* **103** B9
Sand Springs *U.S.A.* **116** C6
Sanda *Japan* **55** G7
Sandakan *Malaysia* **62** C5
Sandan = Sambor *Cambodia* **64** F6
Sandanski *Bulgaria* **44** E7
Sandaré *Mali* **82** C2
Sandared *Sweden* **11** G6
Sandarne *Sweden* **10** C11
Sanday *U.K.* **13** B6
Sande *Norway* **10** E4
Sandefjord *Norway* **9** G14
Sanders *U.S.A.* **109** J9
Sanderson *U.S.A.* **116** F3
Sandersville *U.S.A.* **117** E13
Sandfire Roadhouse *Australia* **92** C3
Sandfly L. *Canada* **103** B7
Sandfontein *Namibia* **88** C2
Sandhammaren *Sweden* **11** J8
Sandheads, The *India* **69** J13
Sandía *Peru* **124** F5
Sandıklı *Turkey* **47** C12
Sandila *India* **69** F9
Sandnes *Norway* **9** G11
Sandnessjøen *Norway* **8** C15
Sandoa *Dem. Rep. of the Congo* **84** F4
Sandomierz *Poland* **31** H8
Sândominic *Romania* **29** D10
Sandover → *Australia* **94** C2
Sandoway = Thandwe
Burma **67** K19
Sandoy *Færoe Is.* **8** F9
Sandpoint *U.S.A.* **108** B5
Sandray *U.K.* **13** E1
Sandringham *U.K.* **14** E8
Sandstone *Australia* **93** E2
Sandu *China* **58** E6
Sandusky *Mich., U.S.A.* **114** C2
Sandusky *Ohio, U.S.A.* **114** E2
Sandveld *Namibia* **88** C3
Sandvig *Denmark* **11** J8
Sandviken *Sweden* **10** D10
Sandwich, C. *Australia* **94** B4
Sandwich B. *Canada* **105** B8
Sandwich B. *Namibia* **88** C1
Sandy *Oreg., U.S.A.* **110** E4
Sandy *Pa., U.S.A.* **114** E6
Sandy *Utah, U.S.A.* **108** F8
Sandy Bay *Canada* **103** B8
Sandy Bight *Canada* **103** B8
Sandy C. *Queens., Australia* **94** C5
Sandy C. *Tas., Australia* **95** G3
Sandy Cay *Bahamas* **121** B4
Sandy Cr. → *Australia* **95** B4
Sandy Cr. → *U.S.A.* **108** F9
Sandy Creek *U.S.A.* **115** C8
Sandy L. *Canada* **104** B1
Sandy Lake *Canada* **104** B1
Sandy Valley *U.S.A.* **111** K11
Sânfjällets △ *Sweden* **10** B7
Sanford *Fla., U.S.A.* **117** G14
Sanford *Maine, U.S.A.* **115** C14
Sanford *N.C., U.S.A.* **117** D15
Sanford → *Australia* **93** E2
Sanford, Mt. *U.S.A.* **100** E3
Sang-i-Masha *Afghan.* **68** C2
Sanga *Mozam.* **87** E4
Sanga → *Congo* **84** E3
Sangamner *India* **66** K9
Sangān *Iran* **71** C9
Sanganeb Atoll △ *Sudan* **80** D4
Sangar *Afghan.* **68** C1
Sangar *Russia* **53** C13
Sangar Sarai *Afghan.* **68** B4
Sangareddi *Guinea* **82** C2
Sangarh → *Pakistan* **68** D3
Sangasso *Mali* **82** C3

Sangatte *France* **19** B8
Sangāw *Iraq* **73** E11
Sangay *Ecuador* **124** D3
Sangbé *Cameroon* **83** D7
Sange *Dem. Rep. of the Congo* **86** D2
Sangeang *Indonesia* **63** F5
Sângeorz-Băi *Romania* **29** C9
Sanger *U.S.A.* **110** J7
Sangerhausen *Germany* **24** D7
Sanggan He → *China* **56** E9
Sanggau *Indonesia* **62** D4
Sanghar *Pakistan* **68** F3
Sangihe, Kepulauan
Indonesia **63** D7
Sangihe, Pulau *Indonesia* **63** D7
Sangju *S. Korea* **57** F15
Sangkapura *Indonesia* **62** F4
Sangkhla Buri *Thailand* **64** E2
Sangkulirang *Indonesia* **62** D5
Sangla *Pakistan* **68** D5
Sangli *India* **66** L9
Sangmélima *Cameroon* **83** E7
Sango *Zimbabwe* **87** F3
Sangod *India* **68** G7
Sangre de Cristo Mts. *U.S.A.*
109 H11
Sangre Grande *Trin. & Tob.* **125** K15
Sangro → *Italy* **41** F11
Sangrur *India* **68** D6
Sangudo *Canada* **102** C6
Sangue → *Brazil* **124** F7
Sangüesa *Spain* **38** C3
Sanguinaires, Îs. *France* **21** G12
Sangzhi *China* **59** C8
Sanhala *Ivory C.* **82** C3
Sanibel *U.S.A.* **117** H13
Sanikiluaq *Canada* **104** A4
Sanin-Kaigan △ *Japan* **55** G7
Sanirajak = Hall Beach
Canada **101** D15
Sanjawi *Pakistan* **68** D3
Sanje *Uganda* **86** C3
Sanjiang *China* **58** E7
Sanjo *Japan* **54** F9
Sankh → *India* **69** H11
Sankt Andrä *Austria* **26** E7
Sankt Anton *Austria* **25** H6
Sankt Augustin *Germany* **24** E3
Sankt Blasien *Germany* **25** H4
Sankt Gallen *Switz.* **25** H5
Sankt Gallen □ *Switz.* **25** H5
Sankt Goar *Germany* **25** E3
Sankt Ingbert *Germany* **25** F3
Sankt Johann im Pongau
Austria **26** D6
Sankt Johann in Tirol
Austria **26** D5
Sankt Michel = Mikkeli
Finland **32** B4
Sankt Moritz *Switz.* **25** J5
Sankt-Peterburg *Russia* **32** C6
Sankt Pölten *Austria* **26** C8
Sankt Ulrich = Ortisei *Italy* **41** B8
Sankt Valentin *Austria* **26** C7
Sankt Veit an der Glan
Austria **26** E7
Sankt Wendel *Germany* **25** F3
Sankt Wolfgang *Austria* **26** D6
Sankuru →
Dem. Rep. of the Congo **84** E4
Sanliurfa *Turkey* **73** D8
Sanliurfa □ *Turkey* **73** D8
Sanlúcar de Barrameda *Spain* **37** J4
Sanluri *Italy* **42** C1
Sânmartin *Romania* **29** D10
Sanmen *China* **59** C13
Sanmenxia *China* **56** G6
Sanming *China* **59** D11
Sannicandro Gargánico
Italy **41** G12
Sânnicolau Mare *Romania* **28** D5
Sannieshof *S. Africa* **88** D4
Sannîn, J. *Lebanon* **74** B4
Sanniquellie *Liberia* **82** D3
Sannûr, W. → *Egypt* **80** B3
Sanok *Poland* **31** J9
Sanquhar *U.K.* **13** F5
Sans Souci *Trin. & Tob.* **125** K16
Sansanding *Mali* **82** C3
Sansané *Niger* **83** C5
Sansepolcro *Italy* **41** E9
Sansha *China* **59** D13
Sanshui *China* **59** F9
Sanski Most *Bos.-H.* **41** D13
Sansui *China* **58** D7
Sant Antoni de Portmany
Spain **48** C7
Sant Boi de Llobregat *Spain* **38** D7
Sant Carles *Spain* **48** B8
Sant Carles de la Ràpita
Spain **38** E5
Sant Celoni *Spain* **38** D7
Sant Elm *Spain* **48** B9
Sant Feliu de Guíxols *Spain* **38** D8
Sant Feliu de Llobregat *Spain* **38** D7
Sant Ferran *Spain* **48** C7
Sant Francesc de
Formentera *Spain* **48** C7
Sant Jaume *Spain* **48** B11

Sant Joan *Spain* **48** B10
Sant Joan d'Alacant *Spain* **39** G4
Sant Joan de Labritja *Spain* **48** B8
Sant Jordi *Ibiza, Spain* **48** C7
Sant Jordi *Mallorca, Spain* **48** B9
Sant Jordi, G. de *Spain* **38** E6
Sant Llorenç de Morunys
Spain **38** C6
Sant Llorenç del Munt y
l'Obac □ *Spain* **38** D7
Sant Llorenç des Cardassar
Spain **48** B10
Sant Mateu *Baleares, Spain* **48** B7
Sant Mateu *Valencia, Spain* **38** E5
Sant Miquel *Spain* **48** B7
Sant Salvador *Spain* **48** B10
Sant Vicent del Raspeig
Spain **39** G4
Sant' Ágata Militello *Italy* **43** D7
Santa Agnès *Spain* **48** B7
Santa Ana *Bolivia* **124** F5
Santa Ana *El Salv.* **120** D2
Santa Ana *Mexico* **118** A2
Santa Ana *U.S.A.* **111** M9
Sant' Ángelo Lodigiano *Italy* **40** C6
Sant' Antíoco *Italy* **42** C1
Santa Bárbara *Chile* **126** D1
Santa Bárbara *Honduras* **120** D2
Santa Bárbara *Mexico* **118** B3
Santa Bárbara *Spain* **38** E5
Santa Barbara *U.S.A.* **111** L7
Santa Bárbara, Mt. *Spain* **39** H2
Santa Barbara Channel
U.S.A. **111** L7
Santa Barbara I. *U.S.A.* **111** M7
Santa Catalina, Gulf of
U.S.A. **111** N9
Santa Catalina, I. *Mexico* **118** B2
Santa Catalina I. *U.S.A.* **111** M8
Santa Catarina □ *Brazil* **127** B6
Santa Catarina, I. de *Brazil* **127** B6
Santa Caterina di Pittinuri
Italy **42** B1
Santa Caterina Villarmosa
Italy **43** E7
Santa Cecília *Brazil* **127** B5
Santa Clara *Cuba* **120** B4
Santa Clara *Calif., U.S.A.* **110** H5
Santa Clara *N.Y., U.S.A.* **115** B10
Santa Clara *Utah, U.S.A.* **109** H7
Santa Clara de Olimar
Uruguay **127** C5
Santa Clara Valley *U.S.A.* **110** J5
Santa Clarita *U.S.A.* **111** L8
Santa Clotilde *Peru* **124** D4
Santa Coloma de Farners
Spain **38** D7
Santa Coloma de Gramenet
Spain **38** D7
Santa Comba *Spain* **36** B2
Santa Croce Camerina *Italy* **43** F7
Santa Croce di Magliano
Italy **41** G11
Santa Cruz *Bolivia* **124** G6
Santa Cruz *Chile* **126** C1
Santa Cruz *Costa Rica* **120** D2
Santa Cruz *Madeira* **48** D3
Santa Cruz *Phil.* **61** D4
Santa Cruz *U.S.A.* **110** J4
Santa Cruz → *Argentina* **128** G3
Santa Cruz de la Palma
Canary Is. **48** F2
Santa Cruz de la Palma ✈
(SPC) *Canary Is.* **48** F2
Santa Cruz de Mudela *Spain* **37** G7
Santa Cruz de Tenerife
Canary Is. **48** F3
Santa Cruz del Norte *Cuba* **120** B3
Santa Cruz del Retamar
Spain **36** E6
Santa Cruz del Sur *Cuba* **120** B4
Santa Cruz do Rio Pardo
Brazil **127** A6
Santa Cruz do Sul *Brazil* **127** B5
Santa Cruz I. *U.S.A.* **111** M7
Santa Cruz Is. *Solomon Is.* **90** C9
Santa Cruz Mts. *Jamaica* **120** a
Santa Domingo, Cay
Bahamas **120** B4
Sant' Egídio alla Vibrata
Italy **41** F10
Santa Elena *Argentina* **126** C4
Santa Elena, C. *Costa Rica* **120** D2
Sant' Eufémia, G. di *Italy* **43** D9
Santa Eulària des Riu *Spain* **48** C8
Santa Fé *Argentina* **126** C3
Santa Fé *Spain* **37** H7
Santa Fe *U.S.A.* **109** J11
Santa Fé □ *Argentina* **126** C3
Santa Fé do Sul *Brazil* **125** H8
Santa Filomena *Brazil* **125** E9
Santa Fiora *Italy* **41** F8
Santa Gertrudis *Spain* **48** C7
Santa Giustina *Italy* **41** B9
Santa Inês *Brazil* **125** F11
Santa Inés *Spain* **37** G5
Santa Inés, I. *Chile* **128** G2
Santa Isabel *Argentina* **126** D2
Santa Isabel do Morro
Brazil **125** F8

Santa Lucía *Corrientes,*
Argentina **126** B4
Santa Lucía *San Juan,*
Argentina **126** C2
Santa Lucía *Spain* **39** H4
Santa Lucia Range *U.S.A.* **110** K5
Santa Luzia *C. Verde Is.* **78** b
Santa Lucía *Uruguay* **126** C4
Santa Margalida *Spain* **48** B10
Santa Margarita *Argentina* **126** D3
Santa Margarita *U.S.A.* **110** K6
Santa Margarita → *U.S.A.* **111** M9
Santa Margarita, I. *Mexico* **118** C2
Santa Margherita *Italy* **42** D1
Santa Margherita Ligure
Italy **40** D6
Santa María *Argentina* **126** B2
Santa Maria *Azores* **78** a
Santa Maria *Brazil* **127** B5
Santa Maria *C. Verde Is.* **78** b
Santa Maria *Phil.* **61** C4
Santa Maria *U.S.A.* **111** L6
Santa María → *Mexico* **118** A3
Santa María, B. de *Mexico* **118** B3
Santa Maria, C. de *Portugal* **37** J3
Santa Maria Cápua Vétere
Italy **43** A7
Santa Maria da Feira
Portugal **36** E2
Santa Maria da Vitória
Brazil **125** F10
Santa María del Camí *Spain* **48** B9
Santa Maria di Léuca, C.
Italy **43** C11
Santa María la Real de
Nieva *Spain* **36** D6
Santa Marinella *Italy* **41** F8
Santa Marta *Colombia* **124** A4
Santa Marta, Sierra
Nevada de *Colombia* **124** A4
Santa Marta de Tormes *Spain* **36** E5
Santa Marta Grande, C.
Brazil **127** B6
Santa Marta Ortigueira,
Ría de *Spain* **36** B3
Santa Maura = Lefkada
Greece **46** C2
Santa Monica *U.S.A.* **111** M8
Santa Monica Mts. △
U.S.A. **111** L8
Santa Olalla *Spain* **36** E6
Santa Olalla del Cala *Spain* **37** H4
Santa Paula *U.S.A.* **111** L7
Santa Pola *Spain* **39** G4
Santa Ponça *Spain* **48** B9
Santa Rosa *La Pampa,*
Argentina **126** D3
Santa Rosa *San Luis,*
Argentina **126** C2
Santa Rosa *Brazil* **127** B5
Santa Rosa *Calif., U.S.A.* **110** G4
Santa Rosa *N. Mex., U.S.A.* **109** J11
Santa Rosa and San Jacinto
Mts. △ *U.S.A.* **111** M10
Santa Rosa de Copán
Honduras **120** D2
Santa Rosa de Río Primero
Argentina **126** C3
Santa Rosa del Sara *Bolivia* **124** G6
Santa Rosa I. *Calif., U.S.A.* **111** M6
Santa Rosa I. *Fla., U.S.A.* **117** F11
Santa Rosa Range *U.S.A.* **108** F5
Santa Rosalía *Mexico* **118** B2
Santa Sylvina *Argentina* **126** B3
Santa Tecla = Nueva San
Salvador *El Salv.* **120** D2
Santa Teresa *Argentina* **126** C3
Santa Teresa *Australia* **94** C1
Santa Teresa *Mexico* **119** B5
Santa Teresa △ *Uruguay* **127** C5
Santa Teresa di Riva *Italy* **43** E8
Santa Teresa Gallura *Italy* **42** A2
Santa Teresita *Argentina* **126** D4
Santa Uxía de Ribeira *Spain* **36** C2
Santa Vitória do Palmar
Brazil **127** C5
Santa Ynez → *U.S.A.* **111** L6
Santa Ynez Mts. *U.S.A.* **111** L6
Santa Ysabel *U.S.A.* **111** M10
Santadi *Italy* **42** C1
Santaella *Spain* **37** H6
Santai *China* **58** B5
Santana *Madeira* **48** D3
Sântana *Romania* **28** D6
Santana, Coxilha de *Brazil* **127** C4
Santana do Livramento
Brazil **127** C4
Santander *Spain* **36** B7
Santander Jiménez *Mexico* **119** C5
Santanilla, Is. *Honduras* **120** C3
Santanyí *Spain* **48** B10
Santaquin *U.S.A.* **108** G8
Santarcángelo di Romagna
Italy **41** D9
Santarém *Brazil* **125** D8
Santarém *Portugal* **37** F2
Santarém □ *Portugal* **37** F2
Santaren Channel *W. Indies* **120** B4
Santee *U.S.A.* **111** N10
Santee → *U.S.A.* **117** E15

Santéramo in Colle *Italy* **43** B9
Santerno → *Italy* **41** D8
Santhià *Italy* **40** C5
Santi-Quaranta = Sarandë
Albania **44** G3
Santiago = Río Grande de
Santiago → *Mexico* **118** C3
Santiago = São Tiago
C. Verde Is. **78** b
Santiago *Brazil* **127** B5
Santiago *Canary Is.* **48** F2
Santiago *Chile* **126** C1
Santiago *Panama* **120** E3
Santiago *Phil.* **61** C4
Santiago → *Peru* **124** D3
Santiago, Punta de *Eq. Guin.* **83** E6
Santiago de Compostela
Spain **36** C2
Santiago de Cuba *Cuba* **120** C4
Santiago de los Caballeros
Dom. Rep. **121** C5
Santiago del Estero
Argentina **126** B3
Santiago del Estero □
Argentina **126** B3
Santiago del Teide *Canary Is.* **48** F3
Santiago do Cacém *Portugal* **37** G2
Santiago Ixcuintla *Mexico* **118** C3
Santiago Jamiltepec *Mexico* **119** D5
Santiago Papasquiaro
Mexico **118** C3
Santiago Pinotepa
Nacional *Mexico* **119** D5
Santiaguillo, L. de *Mexico* **118** C4
Santiaguila *Mali* **82** C3
Santillana del Mar *Spain* **36** B6
Santisteban del Puerto *Spain* **37** G7
Santo Amaro *Brazil* **125** F11
Santo Anastácio *Brazil* **127** A5
Santo André *Brazil* **127** A6
Santo Ângelo *Brazil* **127** B5
Santo Antão *C. Verde Is.* **78** b
Santo Antônio do Içá *Brazil* **124** D5
Santo Antônio do Leverger
Brazil **125** G7
Santo Domingo *Dom. Rep.* **121** C6
Santo Domingo *Baja Calif.,*
Mexico **118** A1
Santo Domingo
Baja Calif. S., Mexico **118** B2
Santo Domingo *Nic.* **120** D3
Santo Domingo de la
Calzada *Spain* **38** C2
Santo Domingo de los
Colorados *Ecuador* **124** D3
Santo Domingo Pueblo
U.S.A. **109** J10
Santo Stéfano di Camastro
Italy **43** D7
Santo Tirso *Portugal* **36** D2
Santo Tomás *Mexico* **118** A1
Santo Tomás *Peru* **124** F4
Santo Tomé *Argentina* **127** B4
Santo Tomé de Guayana =
Ciudad Guayana
Venezuela **124** B6
Santomera *Spain* **39** G3
Santoña *Spain* **36** B7
Santorini *Greece* **47** E7
Santos *Brazil* **127** A6
Santos, Sierra de los *Spain* **37** G5
Santos Dumont *Brazil* **127** A7
Santuario de Aves Laguna
Colorada △ *Bolivia* **126** A2
Sanur *Indonesia* **63** K18
Sanwer *India* **68** H6
Sanxenxo *Spain* **36** C2
Sanya *China* **64** C7
Sanyuan *China* **56** G5
São Bartolomeu de
Messines *Portugal* **37** H2
São Bernardo do Campo
Brazil **127** A6
São Borja *Brazil* **127** B4
São Brás de Alportel *Portugal* **37** H3
São Carlos *Brazil* **127** A6
São Cristóvão *Brazil* **125** F11
São Domingos *Brazil* **125** F9
São Domingos *Guinea-Biss.* **82** C1
São Filipe *C. Verde Is.* **78** b
São Francisco *Brazil* **125** G10
São Francisco → *Brazil* **125** F11
São Francisco do Sul *Brazil* **127** B6
São Gabriel *Brazil* **127** C5
São Gonçalo *Brazil* **127** A7
Sao Hill *Tanzania* **87** D4
São João *Guinea-Biss.* **82** C1
São João da Boa Vista *Brazil* **127** A6
São João da Madeira *Portugal* **36** E2
São João da Pesqueira
Portugal **36** D3
São João del Rei *Brazil* **127** A7
São João do Araguaia *Brazil* **125** E9
São João do Piauí *Brazil* **125** E10
São Joaquim *Brazil* **125** G10
São Joaquim △ *Brazil* **127** B6
São Jorge *Azores* **78** a
São Jorge, Pta. de *Madeira* **48** D3
São José *Brazil* **127** B5
São José do Norte *Brazil* **127** C5

São José do Rio Preto *Brazil* **127** A6
São José dos Campos *Brazil* **127** A6
São Leopoldo *Brazil* **127** B5
São Lourenço *Brazil* **127** A6
São Lourenço ➤ *Brazil* **125** G7
São Lourenço, Pta. de
  Madeira **48** D3
São Lourenço do Sul *Brazil* **127** C5
São Luís *Brazil* **125** D10
São Luís Gonzaga *Brazil* **127** B5
São Marcos ➤ *Brazil* **125** G9
São Marcos, B. de *Brazil* **125** D10
São Martinho da Cortiça
  Portugal **36** E2
São Mateus *Brazil* **125** G11
São Mateus do Sul *Brazil* **127** B5
São Miguel *Azores* **78** a
São Miguel do Oeste *Brazil* **127** B5
São Nicolau *C. Verde Is.* **78** b
São Paulo *Brazil* **127** A6
São Paulo □ *Brazil* **127** A6
São Paulo de Olivença
  Brazil **124** D5
São Pedro do Sul *Portugal* **36** E2
São Roque *Madeira* **48** D3
São Roque, C. de *Brazil* **125** E11
São Sebastião, I. de *Brazil* **127** A6
São Sebastião do Paraíso
  Brazil **127** A6
São Teotónio *Portugal* **37** H2
São Tiago *C. Verde Is.* **78** b
São Tomé *São Tomé & Príncipe* **76** F4
São Tomé, C. de *Brazil* **127** A7
São Tomé & Príncipe ■
  Africa **76** F4
São Vicente *Brazil* **127** A6
São Vicente *C. Verde Is.* **78** b
São Vicente *Madeira* **48** D2
São Vicente, C. de *Portugal* **37** H1
Saona, I. *Dom. Rep.* **121** C6
Saône ➤ *France* **19** F6
Saône-et-Loire □ *France* **19** F11
Saonek *Indonesia* **63** E8
Sapam, Ao *Thailand* **65** a
Sapanca *Turkey* **72** B4
Saparua *Indonesia* **63** E7
Sapele *Nigeria* **83** D6
Sapelo I. *U.S.A.* **117** F14
Sapes *Greece* **45** E9
Saphane *Turkey* **47** B11
Sapi △ *Zimbabwe* **87** F2
Sapo △ *Liberia* **82** D3
Sapone *Burkina Faso* **83** C4
Saposoa *Peru* **124** E3
Sapotskina *Belarus* **30** E10
Sapouy *Burkina Faso* **83** C4
Sapozhok *Russia* **34** D5
Sapphire *Australia* **94** C4
Sappho *U.S.A.* **110** B2
Sapporo *Japan* **54** C10
Sapri *Italy* **43** B8
Sapulpa *U.S.A.* **116** D6
Saqqez *Iran* **73** D12
Sar Dasht
  Āzarbāyjān-e Gharbī, Iran **73** D11
Sar Dasht *Khuzestān, Iran* **71** C6
Sar-e Pol □ *Afghan.* **66** B4
Sar Gachīneh = Yāsūj *Iran* **71** D6
Sar Planina *Macedonia* **44** E4
Sara *Burkina Faso* **82** C4
Sara *Phil.* **61** F5
Šara △ *Serbia* **44** D5
Sara Buri = Saraburi *Thailand* **64** E3
Sarāb *Iran* **73** D12
Sarābādī *Iraq* **70** C5
Sarābleh *Iran* **73** F12
Saraburi *Thailand* **64** E3
Saradiya *India* **68** J4
Saraféré *Mali* **82** B4
Saragossa = Zaragoza *Spain* **38** D4
Saraguro *Ecuador* **124** D3
Sarahs *Turkmenistan* **71** B9
Sarai Naurang *Pakistan* **68** C4
Saraikela *India* **69** H11
Saraiu *Romania* **29** F13
Sarajevo *Bos.-H.* **28** G3
Sarakhs = Sarahs
  Turkmenistan **71** B9
Saran, Gunung *Indonesia* **62** E4
Saranac Lake *U.S.A.* **115** B10
Saranac Lakes *U.S.A.* **115** B10
Saranda *Tanzania* **86** D3
Sarandë *Albania* **44** G3
Sarandí del Yí *Uruguay* **127** C4
Sarandí Grande *Uruguay* **126** C4
Sarangani B. *Phil.* **61** J6
Sarangani Is. *Phil.* **61** J6
Sarangarh *India* **67** J13
Saransk *Russia* **34** C7
Sarapul *Russia* **52** D6
Sarasota *U.S.A.* **117** H13
Sarata *Ukraine* **29** D14
Sarata ➤ *Ukraine* **29** E14
Saratoga *Calif., U.S.A.* **110** H4
Saratoga *Wyo., U.S.A.* **108** F10
Saratoga △ *U.S.A.* **115** D11
Saratoga L. *U.S.A.* **115** C11
Saratoga Springs *U.S.A.* **115** C11
Saratok *Malaysia* **62** D4

Saratov *Russia* **34** E7
Saratov □ *Russia* **34** E8
Sarāvān *Iran* **71** E9
Saravane *Laos* **64** E6
Sarawak □ *Malaysia* **62** D4
Saray *Tekirdağ, Turkey* **45** E11
Saray *Van, Turkey* **73** C11
Saraya *Senegal* **82** C2
Saraycık *Turkey* **47** B11
Saraýköy *Turkey* **47** D10
Saraylar *Turkey* **45** F11
Sarayönü *Turkey* **72** C5
Sarbāz *Iran* **71** E9
Sarbīsheh *Iran* **71** C8
Sárbogárd *Hungary* **28** D3
Sarca ➤ *Italy* **40** C7
Sarcelles *France* **19** D9
Sarda ➤ *India* **69** F9
Sardarshahr *India* **68** E6
Sardegna □ *Italy* **42** B1
Sardhana *India* **68** E7
Sardina, Pta. *Canary Is.* **48** F4
Sardinia = Sardegna □ *Italy* **42** B1
Sardis *Turkey* **47** C10
Sārdūīyeh = Dar Mazār *Iran* **71** D8
Saren *Indonesia* **63** J18
Sarentino *Italy* **41** B8
Sarera, G. of *Indonesia* **90** B6
Saréyamou *Mali* **82** B4
Sargodha *Pakistan* **68** C5
Sarh *Chad* **79** G9
Sarhala *Ivory C.* **82** D3
Sārī *Iran* **71** B7
Sari d'Orcino *France* **21** F12
Saria *Greece* **47** F9
Saria *India* **69** J10
Sariab *Pakistan* **68** D2
Sarıbeyler *Turkey* **47** B9
Sarıgöl *Turkey* **72** C3
Sarıkamış *Turkey* **73** B10
Sarıkaya *Turkey* **72** C6
Sarikei *Malaysia* **62** D4
Sarıköy *Turkey* **45** F11
Sarila *India* **69** G8
Sarina *Australia* **94** C4
Sariñena *Spain* **38** D4
Sarıoğlan *Turkey* **72** C6
Sarita *U.S.A.* **116** H6
Sariwŏn *N. Korea* **57** E13
Sariyar Baraji *Turkey* **72** B4
Sarıyer *Turkey* **45** E13
Sarız *Turkey* **72** C7
Sarju ➤ *India* **69** F9
Sark *U.K.* **15** H5
Sarkad *Hungary* **28** D6
Sarkari Tala *India* **68** F4
Şarkışla *Turkey* **72** C7
Şarköy *Turkey* **45** F11
Sarlat-la-Canéda *France* **20** D5
Sărmăşag *Romania* **28** C7
Sărmaşu *Romania* **28** D9
Sarmi *Indonesia* **63** E9
Sarmiento *Argentina* **128** F3
Sarmizegetusa *Romania* **28** E7
Särna *Sweden* **10** C7
Sarnano *Italy* **41** E10
Sarnen *Switz.* **25** J4
Sarnia *Canada* **114** D2
Sarno *Italy* **43** B7
Sarnthein = Sarentino *Italy* **41** B8
Särö *Sweden* **11** G5
Sarolangun *Indonesia* **62** E2
Saronikos Kolpos *Greece* **46** D5
Saronno *Italy* **40** C6
Saros Körfezi *Turkey* **45** F10
Sárospatak *Hungary* **28** B6
Sarpsborg *Norway* **9** G14
Sarqan *Kazakhstan* **52** E8
Sarracín *Spain* **36** C7
Sarralbe *France* **19** D14
Sarre = Saar ➤ *Europe* **17** E6
Sarre *Italy* **40** C4
Sarre-Union *France* **19** D14
Sarrebourg *France* **19** D14
Sarreguemines *France* **19** C14
Sarria *Spain* **36** C3
Sarrión *Spain* **38** E4
Sarro *Mali* **82** C3
Sarsing *Iraq* **73** D10
Sarstedt *Germany* **24** C5
Sartène *France* **21** G12
Sarthe □ *France* **18** D7
Sarthe ➤ *France* **18** E6
Sartilly *France* **18** D5
Saruhanlı *Turkey* **47** C9
Saruna ➤ *Pakistan* **68** F2
Sārūq *Iran* **71** C6
Sarvar *India* **68** F6
Sarvestān *Iran* **71** D7
Särvfjället *Sweden* **10** B7
Särviz ➤ *Hungary* **28** D3
Sary-Tash *Kyrgyzstan* **52** F8
Sarych, Mys *Ukraine* **33** K7
Saryshagan *Kazakhstan* **52** E8
Sarzana *Italy* **40** D6
Sarzeau *France* **18** E4

Sasar, Gir *India* **68** J4
Sasaram *India* **69** G11
Sasebo *Japan* **55** H4
Saser Kangri *India* **69** B7
Saskatchewan □ *Canada* **103** C7
Saskatchewan ➤ *Canada* **103** C8
Saskatoon *Canada* **103** C7
Saskylakh *Russia* **53** B12
Saslaya △ *Nic.* **120** D2
Sasolburg *S. Africa* **89** D4
Sason *Turkey* **73** C9
Sasovo *Russia* **34** C5
Sassandra *Ivory C.* **82** E3
Sassandra ➤ *Ivory C.* **82** E3
Sássari *Italy* **42** B1
Sassie *Australia* **94** a
Sassnitz *Germany* **24** A9
Sasso Marconi *Italy* **41** D8
Sassocorvaro *Italy* **41** E9
Sassoferrato *Italy* **41** E9
Sasstown *Liberia* **82** E3
Sassuolo *Italy* **40** D7
Sástago *Spain* **38** D4
Sasyk, Ozero *Ukraine* **29** E14
Sata-Misaki *Japan* **55** J5
Satadougou *Mali* **82** C2
Satakunda = Satakunta
  Finland **32** B2
Satakunta *Finland* **32** B2
Satama-Soukoura *Ivory C.* **82** D4
Satara *India* **66** L8
Satara *S. Africa* **89** C5
Satbarwa *India* **69** H11
Satevó *Mexico* **118** B3
Satilla ➤ *U.S.A.* **117** F14
Satmala Hills
  Andhra Pradesh, India **66** K11
Satmala Hills *Maharashtra,
  India* **66** J9
Satna *India* **69** G9
Šator *Bos.-H.* **41** D13
Sátoraljaújhely *Hungary* **28** B6
Satpura △ *India* **68** H8
Satpura Ra. *India* **66** J10
Satrup *Germany* **24** A5
Satsuna-Shotō *Japan* **55** K5
Sattahip *Thailand* **64** F3
Satu Mare *Romania* **28** C7
Satu Mare □ *Romania* **28** C8
Satui *Indonesia* **62** E5
Satun *Thailand* **65** J3
Satupa'itea *Samoa* **91** b
Saturnina ➤ *Brazil* **124** F7
Sauce *Argentina* **126** C4
Sauceda *Mexico* **118** B4
Saucillo *Mexico* **118** B3
Sauda *Norway* **9** G12
Sauðárkrókur *Iceland* **8** D4
Saudi Arabia ■ *Asia* **70** B3
Sauerland *Germany* **22** C4
Saugeen ➤ *Canada* **114** B3
Saugerties *U.S.A.* **115** D11
Saugues *France* **20** D7
Saugus *U.S.A.* **111** L8
Saujon *France* **20** C3
Sauk Centre *U.S.A.* **112** C6
Sauk Rapids *U.S.A.* **112** C6
Saulgau *Germany* **25** G5
Saulieu *France* **19** E11
Sault *France* **21** D9
Sault Ste. Marie *Canada* **104** C3
Sault Ste. Marie *U.S.A.* **113** B11
Saumlaki *Indonesia* **63** F8
Saumur *France* **18** E6
Saunders, C. *N.Z.* **91** F3
Saunders I. *Antarctica* **5** B1
Saunders Pt. *Australia* **93** E4
Sauri *Nigeria* **83** C6
Saurimo *Angola* **84** F4
Sausalito *U.S.A.* **110** H4
Sauveterre-de-Béarn *France* **20** E3
Sauzé-Vaussais *France* **20** B4
Savá *Honduras* **120** C2
Sava *Italy* **43** B10
Sava ➤ *Serbia* **28** F5
Savage *U.S.A.* **108** C11
Savage I. = Niue *Pac. Oc.* **97** J11
Savage River *Australia* **95** G4
Savai'i *Samoa* **91** b
Savalou *Benin* **83** D5
Savane *Mozam.* **87** F4
Savanna *U.S.A.* **112** D8
Savanna-la-Mar *Jamaica* **120** a
Savannah *Ga., U.S.A.* **117** D11
Savannah *Mo., U.S.A.* **112** F6
Savannah *Tenn., U.S.A.* **117** D10
Savannah ➤ *U.S.A.* **117** E14
Savannakhet *Laos* **64** D5
Savant L. *Canada* **104** B1
Savant Lake *Canada* **104** B1
Savarkundla = Kundla *India* **68** J4
Săvârşin *Romania* **28** D7
Savaştepe *Turkey* **47** B9
Savé *Benin* **83** D5
Save ➤ *France* **20** E5
Save ➤ *Mozam.* **89** C5
Sāveh *Iran* **71** C6
Savelugu *Ghana* **83** D4

Savenay *France* **18** E5
Săveni *Romania* **29** C11
Saverdun *France* **20** E5
Saverne *France* **19** D14
Savigliano *Italy* **40** D4
Savigny-sur-Braye *France* **18** E7
Sávio ➤ *Italy* **41** D9
Savoie □ *France* **21** C10
Savolax = Savo *Finland* **8** E22
Savona *Italy* **40** D5
Savona *U.S.A.* **114** D7
Savonlinna *Finland* **32** B5
Savoy = Savoie □ *France* **21** C10
Şavşat *Turkey* **73** B10
Sävsjö *Sweden* **11** G8
Savur *Turkey* **70** B4
Savusavu *Fiji* **91** a
Savusavu B. *Fiji* **91** a
Sawahlunto *Indonesia* **62** E2
Sawai *Indonesia* **63** E7
Sawai Madhopur *India* **68** G7
Sawaleke *Fiji* **91** a
Sawang Daen Din *Thailand* **64** D4
Sawankhalok *Thailand* **64** D2
Sawara *Japan* **55** G10
Sawatch Range *U.S.A.* **108** G10
Sawel Mt. *U.K.* **12** B4
Sawi *Thailand* **65** G2
Sawla *Ghana* **82** D4
Sawmills *Zimbabwe* **87** F2
Sawtooth △ *U.S.A.* **108** D6
Sawtooth Range *U.S.A.* **108** D6
Sawu *Indonesia* **63** F6
Sawu Sea *Indonesia* **63** F6
Saxby ➤ *Australia* **94** B3
Saxmundham *U.K.* **15** E9
Saxony = Sachsen □
  Germany **24** E9
Saxony, Lower =
  Niedersachsen □ *Germany* **24** C4
Saxton *U.S.A.* **114** F6
Say *Mali* **83** C5
Say *Niger* **83** C5
Saya *Nigeria* **83** D5
Sayabec *Canada* **105** C6
Sayaboury *Laos* **64** C3
Sayán *Peru* **124** F3
Sayan, Vostochnyy *Russia* **53** D10
Sayan, Zapadnyy *Russia* **53** D10
Sayanogorsk *Russia* **53** D10
Saydā *Lebanon* **74** B4
Sayhandulaan = Oldziyt
  Mongolia **56** B5
Sayḩūt *Yemen* **75** D5
Saykhin *Kazakhstan* **35** F8
Saylac *Somali Rep.* **75** E3
Saynshand = Buyant-Uhaa
  Mongolia **60** B6
Sayre *Okla., U.S.A.* **116** D5
Sayre *Pa., U.S.A.* **115** E8
Sayreville *U.S.A.* **115** F10
Sayula *Mexico* **118** D4
Sayward *Canada* **102** C3
Sazanit *Albania* **44** F7
Sázava ➤ *Czech Rep.* **26** B7
Sazin *Pakistan* **69** B5
Sazlıka ➤ *Bulgaria* **45** E9
Scaër *France* **18** D3
Scafell Pike *U.K.* **14** C4
Scalea *Italy* **43** C8
Scalloway *U.K.* **13** A7
Scalpay *U.K.* **13** D3
Scandia *Canada* **102** C6
Scandiano *Italy* **40** D7
Scandicci *Italy* **41** E8
Scandinavia *Europe* **8** E15
Scansano *Italy* **41** F8
Scapa Flow *U.K.* **13** C5
Scappoose *U.S.A.* **110** E4
Scaramia, Capo *Italy* **43** F7
Scarba *U.K.* **13** E3
Scarborough *Trin. & Tob.* **121** D7
Scarborough *U.K.* **14** C7
Scariff I. *Ireland* **12** E1
Scarp *U.K.* **13** C1
Scarpe-Escaut △ *France* **19** B10
Scebeli = Shabeelle ➤
  Somali Rep. **75** G3
Schaal See *Germany* **24** B6
Schaalsee △ *Germany* **24** B6
Schaffhausen *Switz.* **25** H4
Schagen *Neths.* **17** B4
Schaghticoke *U.S.A.* **115** D11
Schärding *Austria* **26** C6
Scharhörn *Germany* **24** B4
Scheessel *Germany* **24** B5
Schefferville *Canada* **105** B6
Schelde ➤ *Belgium* **17** C4
Schell Creek Ra. *U.S.A.* **108** G6
Schellsburg *U.S.A.* **114** F6
Schenectady *U.S.A.* **115** D11
Schenevus *U.S.A.* **115** D10
Scherfede *Germany* **24** D5
Schesslitz *Germany* **25** F7
Schiedam *Neths.* **17** C4
Schiermonnikoog *Neths.* **17** A6

Schiltigheim *France* **19** D14
Schinousa *Greece* **47** E7
Schio *Italy* **41** C8
Schladming *Austria* **26** D6
Schlanders = Silandro *Italy* **40** B7
Schlei ➤ *Germany* **24** A5
Schleiden *Germany* **24** E2
Schleiz *Germany* **24** E7
Schleswig *Germany* **24** A5
Schleswig-Holstein □
  Germany **24** A5
Schlüchtern *Germany* **25** E5
Schmalkalden *Germany* **24** E6
Schmölln *Germany* **24** E8
Schneeberg *Austria* **26** D8
Schneeberg *Germany* **24** E8
Schneverdingen *Germany* **24** B5
Schœlcher *Martinique* **120** c
Schoharie *U.S.A.* **115** D10
Schoharie Cr. ➤ *U.S.A.* **115** D10
Scholls *U.S.A.* **110** E4
Schönberg
  *Mecklenburg-Vorpommern,
  Germany* **24** B6
Schönberg
  Schleswig-Holstein, Germany **24** A6
Schönbuch △ *Germany* **25** G5
Schönebeck *Germany* **24** C7
Schöngau *Germany* **25** H6
Schöningen *Germany* **24** C6
Schopfheim *Germany* **25** H3
Schorndorf *Germany* **25** G5
Schortens *Germany* **24** B3
Schouten I. *Australia* **95** G4
Schouten Is. = Supiori
  Indonesia **63** E9
Schouwen *Neths.* **17** C3
Schramberg *Germany* **25** G4
Schrankogel *Austria* **26** D4
Schreiber *Canada* **104** C2
Schrems *Austria* **26** C8
Schrobenhausen *Germany* **25** G7
Schroffenstein *Namibia* **88** D2
Schroon Lake *U.S.A.* **115** C11
Schruns *Austria* **26** D2
Schuler *Canada* **103** C6
Schumacher *Canada* **104** C3
Schurz *U.S.A.* **108** G4
Schuyler *U.S.A.* **112** E5
Schuylerville *U.S.A.* **115** C11
Schuylkill ➤ *U.S.A.* **115** G9
Schuylkill Haven *U.S.A.* **115** F8
Schwabach *Germany* **25** F7
Schwaben □ *Germany* **25** G6
Schwäbisch-Fränkischer
  Wald △ *Germany* **25** G5
Schwäbisch Gmünd *Germany* **25** G5
Schwäbisch Hall *Germany* **25** F5
Schwäbische Alb *Germany* **25** G5
Schwabmünchen *Germany* **25** G6
Schwalmstadt *Germany* **24** E5
Schwandorf *Germany* **25** F8
Schwaner, Pegunungan
  Indonesia **62** E4
Schwanewede *Germany* **24** B4
Schwarmstedt *Germany* **24** C5
Schwarze Elster ➤ *Germany* **24** D8
Schwarzenberg *Germany* **24** E8
Schwarzrand *Namibia* **88** D2
Schwarzwald *Germany* **25** G4
Schwatka Mts. *U.S.A.* **106** B8
Schwaz *Austria* **26** D4
Schwechat *Austria* **27** C9
Schwechat, Wien ✈ (VIE)
  Austria **27** C9
Schwedt *Germany* **24** B10
Schweinfurt *Germany* **25** E6
Schweiz = Switzerland ■
  Europe **25** J4
Schweizer-Reneke *S. Africa* **88** D4
Schwenningen = Villingen-
  Schwenningen *Germany* **25** G4
Schwerin *Germany* **24** B7
Schweriner See *Germany* **24** B7
Schwetzingen *Germany* **25** F4
Schwyz *Switz.* **25** H4
Schwyz □ *Switz.* **25** H4
Šćedro *Croatia* **41** E13
Sciacca *Italy* **42** E6
Scicli *Italy* **43** F7
Sciliar △ *Italy* **41** B8
Scilla *Italy* **43** D8
Scilly, Isles of *U.K.* **15** H1
Ścinawa *Poland* **31** G3
Scione *Greece* **44** G7
Scioto ➤ *U.S.A.* **113** F12
Scituate *U.S.A.* **115** D14
Scobey *U.S.A.* **108** B11
Scone *Australia* **95** E5
Scone *U.K.* **13** E5
Scordia *Italy* **43** E7
Scoresbysund =
  Ittoqqortoormiit *Greenland* **4** B6
Scornicești *Romania* **29** F9
Scotia *Calif., U.S.A.* **108** F1
Scotia *N.Y., U.S.A.* **115** D11
Scotia Sea *Antarctica* **5** B18
Scotland *Canada* **114** C4
Scotland □ *U.K.* **13** E5

Scott *Antarctica* **5** D11
Scott, C. *Australia* **92** B4
Scott City *U.S.A.* **112** F3
Scott Glacier *Antarctica* **5** C8
Scott I. *Antarctica* **5** C11
Scott Is. *Canada* **102** C3
Scott L. *Canada* **103** B7
Scott Reef *Australia* **92** B3
Scottburgh *S. Africa* **89** E5
Scottdale *U.S.A.* **114** F5
Scottish Borders □ *U.K.* **13** F6
Scotts Valley *U.S.A.* **110** H4
Scottsbluff *U.S.A.* **112** E2
Scottsboro *U.S.A.* **117** D11
Scottsburg *U.S.A.* **113** F11
Scottsdale *Australia* **95** G4
Scottsdale *U.S.A.* **109** K8
Scottsville *Ky., U.S.A.* **112** G10
Scottsville *N.Y., U.S.A.* **114** C7
Scottville *U.S.A.* **112** D10
Scranton *U.S.A.* **115** E9
Scugog, L. *Canada* **114** B6
Sculeni *Moldova* **29** C12
Scunthorpe *U.K.* **14** D7
Scuol Schuls *Switz.* **25** J6
Scutari = Shkodër *Albania* **44** D3
Scutari = Üsküdar *Turkey* **45** F13
Sea Is. *U.S.A.* **117** F14
Seabrook, L. *Australia* **93** F2
Seaford *U.K.* **15** G8
Seaford *U.S.A.* **113** F16
Seaforth *Australia* **94** b
Seaforth *Canada* **114** C3
Seaforth, L. *U.K.* **13** D2
Seagraves *U.S.A.* **116** E3
Seaham *U.K.* **14** C6
Seal ➤ *Canada* **103** B10
Seal L. *Canada* **105** B7
Sealy *U.S.A.* **116** G6
Searchlight *U.S.A.* **111** K12
Searcy *U.S.A.* **116** D9
Searles L. *U.S.A.* **111** K9
Seascale *U.K.* **14** C4
Seaside *Calif., U.S.A.* **110** J5
Seaside *Oreg., U.S.A.* **110** E3
Seaspray *Australia* **95** F4
Seattle *U.S.A.* **110** C4
Seattle-Tacoma Int. ✈
  (SEA) *U.S.A.* **110** C4
Seba *Indonesia* **92** B3
Sebago L. *U.S.A.* **115** C14
Sebago Lake *U.S.A.* **115** C14
Sebastián Vizcaíno, B.
  Mexico **118** B2
Sebastopol = Sevastopol
  Ukraine **33** K7
Sebastopol *U.S.A.* **110** G4
Sebba *Burkina Faso* **83** C5
Sebderat *Eritrea* **81** D4
Sébékoro *Mali* **82** C3
Seben *Turkey* **72** B4
Sebeş *Romania* **29** E8
Sebeşului, Munţii *Romania* **29** E8
Sebewaing *U.S.A.* **113** D12
Sebezh *Russia* **32** D5
Sebha = Sabhā *Libya* **79** C8
Sébi *Mali* **82** B4
Şebinkarahisar *Turkey* **73** B8
Sebiş *Romania* **28** D7
Sebnitz *Germany* **24** E10
Sebring *Fla., U.S.A.* **117** H14
Sebring *Ohio, U.S.A.* **114** F3
Sebringville *Canada* **114** C3
Sebta = Ceuta *N. Afr.* **78** A4
Sebuku *Indonesia* **62** E5
Sebuku, Teluk *Malaysia* **62** D5
Sečanj *Serbia* **28** E5
Secchia ➤ *Italy* **40** C8
Sechelt *Canada* **102** D4
Sechura, Desierto de *Peru* **124** E2
Seclin *France* **19** B10
Secondigny *France* **18** F6
Sečovce *Slovak Rep.* **27** C14
Secretary I. *N.Z.* **91** F1
Secunderabad *India* **66** L11
Security *U.S.A.* **108** C11
Sedalia *U.S.A.* **112** F7
Sedan *France* **19** C11
Sedan *U.S.A.* **112** G5
Sedano *Spain* **36** C7
Sedbergh *U.K.* **14** C5
Seddon *N.Z.* **91** D5
Seddonville *N.Z.* **91** D4
Sedé Boqér *Israel* **74** E3
Sedeh *Fārs, Iran* **71** D7
Sedeh *Khorāsān, Iran* **71** C8
Séderon *France* **21** D9
Sederot *Israel* **74** D3
Sédhiou *Senegal* **82** C1
Sedico *Italy* **41** B9
Sedley *Canada* **103** C8
Sedom *Israel* **109** J8
Sedova, Pik *Russia* **52** B6
Sedro-Woolley *U.S.A.* **110** B4
Šeduva *Lithuania* **30** D10
Sędziszów *Poland* **31** H7
Sędziszów Małopolski *Poland* **31** H8
Seebad Ahlbeck *Germany* **24** B10
Seefeld in Tirol *Austria* **26** D4

Seehausen *Germany* 24 C7
Seeheim *Namibia* 88 D2
Seeheim-Jugenheim *Germany* 25 F4
Seeis *Namibia* 88 C2
Seekoei → *S. Africa* 88 E4
Seeley's Bay *Canada* 115 B8
Seelow *Germany* 24 C10
Sées *France* 18 D7
Seesen *Germany* 24 D6
Seevetal *Germany* 24 B6
Seewinkel = Neusiedler See-Seewinkel △ *Austria* 27 D9
Şefaatli *Turkey* 72 C6
Seferihisar *Turkey* 47 C8
Séféto *Mali* 82 C3
Sefophe *Botswana* 87 G2
Sefwi Bekwai *Ghana* 82 D4
Segamat *Malaysia* 65 L4
Şegarcea *Romania* 29 F8
Ségbana *Benin* 83 C5
Segbwema *S. Leone* 82 D2
Segesta *Italy* 42 E5
Seget *Indonesia* 63 E8
Segonzac *France* 20 C3
Segorbe *Spain* 38 F4
Ségou *Mali* 82 C3
Ségou □ *Mali* 82 C3
Segovia = Coco → *Cent. Amer.* 120 D3
Segovia *Spain* 36 E6
Segovia □ *Spain* 36 E6
Segré *France* 18 E6
Segre → *Spain* 38 D5
Seguam I. *U.S.A.* 106 E5
Séguéla *Ivory C.* 82 D3
Séguélon *Ivory C.* 82 D3
Ségénéga *Burkina Faso* 83 C4
Seguin *U.S.A.* 116 G6
Segundo → *Argentina* 126 C3
Segura → *Spain* 39 G4
Segura, Sierra de *Spain* 39 G2
Seh Konj, Kūh-e *Iran* 71 D8
Seh Qal'eh *Iran* 71 C8
Sehitwa *Botswana* 88 C3
Sehlabathebe △ *Lesotho* 89 D4
Sehore *India* 68 H7
Sehwan *Pakistan* 68 F2
Şeica Mare *Romania* 29 D9
Seikan Tunnel *Japan* 54 D10
Seil *U.K.* 13 E3
Seiland *Norway* 8 A20
Seilhac *France* 20 C5
Seiling *U.S.A.* 116 C5
Seille → *Moselle, France* 19 C13
Seille → *Saône-et-Loire, France* 19 F11
Sein, Î. de *France* 18 D2
Seinäjoki *Finland* 8 E20
Seine → *France* 18 C7
Seine, B. de la *France* 18 C6
Seine-et-Marne □ *France* 19 D10
Seine-Maritime □ *France* 18 C7
Seine-St-Denis □ *France* 19 D9
Seini *Romania* 29 C8
Seirijai *Lithuania* 30 D10
Seistan = Sīstān *Asia* 71 D9
Seistan, Daryācheh-ye = Sīstan, Daryācheh-ye *Iran* 71 D9
Sejerø *Denmark* 11 J5
Sejerø Bugt *Denmark* 11 J5
Sejny *Poland* 30 D10
Seka *Ethiopia* 81 F4
Sekayu *Indonesia* 62 E2
Seke *Tanzania* 86 C3
Sekenke *Tanzania* 86 C3
Seki *Turkey* 47 E11
Sekondi-Takoradi *Ghana* 82 E4
Sekota *Ethiopia* 81 E4
Seksna *Russia* 32 C10
Sekudai *Malaysia* 65 d
Sekuma *Botswana* 88 C3
Selah *U.S.A.* 108 C3
Selama *Malaysia* 65 K3
Selárgius *Italy* 42 C2
Selaru *Indonesia* 63 F8
Selatan, Selat *Malaysia* 65 c
Selawik L. *U.S.A.* 106 B7
Selb *Germany* 25 E8
Selby *U.K.* 14 D6
Selby *U.S.A.* 112 C3
Selca *Croatia* 41 E13
Selçuk *Turkey* 47 D9
Selden *U.S.A.* 112 F3
Sele → *Italy* 43 B7
Selebi-Phikwe *Botswana* 89 C4
Selemdzha → *Russia* 53 D13
Selendi *Manisa, Turkey* 47 C10
Selendi *Manisa, Turkey* 47 C9
Selenga = Selenge Mörön → *Asia* 60 A5
Selenge Mörön → *Asia* 60 A5
Selenicë *Albania* 44 F3
Selenter See *Germany* 24 A6
Sélestat *France* 19 D14
Seletan, Tanjung *Indonesia* 62 E4
Selevac *Serbia* 44 B4
Sélibabi *Mauritania* 82 B2
Seliger, Ozero *Russia* 32 D7
Seligman *U.S.A.* 109 J7
Şelim *Turkey* 73 B10
Selîma *Sudan* 80 C2
Selimiye *Turkey* 47 D9
Selinda Spillway → *Botswana* 88 B3
Sélingué, L. de *Mali* 82 C3
Selinsgrove *U.S.A.* 114 F8
Selizharovo *Russia* 32 D7
Selkirk *Man., Canada* 103 C9
Selkirk *Ont., Canada* 114 D5
Selkirk *U.K.* 13 F6
Selkirk I. = Horse I. *Canada* 103 C9
Selkirk Mts. *Canada* 100 G8
Sellafield *U.K.* 14 C4
Sellama *Sudan* 81 E2
Sellia *Greece* 49 D6
Sellières *France* 19 F12
Sells *U.S.A.* 109 L8
Sellye *Hungary* 28 E2
Selma *Ala., U.S.A.* 117 E11
Selma *Calif., U.S.A.* 110 J7
Selma *N.C., U.S.A.* 117 D15
Selmer *U.S.A.* 117 D10
Selongey *France* 19 E12
Selous ⌂ *Tanzania* 87 D4
Selowandoma Falls *Zimbabwe* 87 G3
Selpele *Indonesia* 63 E8
Selsey Bill *U.K.* 15 G7
Seltso *Russia* 32 F8
Seltz *France* 19 D15
Selu *Indonesia* 63 F8
Sélune → *France* 18 D5
Selva = La Selva del Camp *Spain* 38 D6
Selva *Argentina* 126 B3
Selva *Spain* 48 B9
Selva Lancandona = Montes Azules ⌂ *Mexico* 119 D6
Selvagens, Ilhas *Madeira* 78 B2
Selvas *Brazil* 124 E5
Selwyn L. *Canada* 103 B8
Selwyn Mts. *Canada* 100 E5
Selwyn Ra. *Australia* 94 C3
Selyatyn *Ukraine* 29 C10
Seman → *Albania* 44 F3
Semarang *Indonesia* 62 F4
Sembabule *Uganda* 86 C3
Sembawang *Singapore* 65 d
Sembung *Indonesia* 63 J18
Şemdinli *Turkey* 73 D11
Sémé *Senegal* 82 B2
Semeih *Sudan* 81 E3
Semenanjung Blambangan *Indonesia* 63 K17
Semenov *Russia* 34 B7
Semenovka *Chernihiv, Ukraine* 33 F7
Semenovka *Kremenchuk, Ukraine* 33 H7
Semeru *Indonesia* 63 H15
Semey *Kazakhstan* 52 D9
Semikarakorskiy *Russia* 35 G5
Semiluki *Russia* 33 G10
Seminoe Res. *U.S.A.* 108 E10
Seminole *Okla., U.S.A.* 116 D6
Seminole *Tex., U.S.A.* 116 E3
Seminole Draw → *U.S.A.* 116 E3
Semipalatinsk = Semey *Kazakhstan* 52 D9
Semirara Is. *Phil.* 61 F4
Semisopochnoi I. *U.S.A.* 106 E3
Semitau *Indonesia* 62 D4
Semliki △ *Uganda* 86 B3
Semmering P. *Austria* 26 D8
Semnān *Iran* 71 C7
Semnān □ *Iran* 71 C7
Semporna *Malaysia* 63 D5
Semuda *Indonesia* 62 E4
Semur-en-Auxois *France* 19 E11
Sen → *Cambodia* 64 F5
Senā *Iran* 71 D6
Sena *Mozam.* 87 F4
Sena Madureira *Brazil* 124 E5
Senador Pompeu *Brazil* 125 E11
Senaki *Georgia* 35 J6
Senang, Pulau *Singapore* 65 d
Senanga *Zambia* 85 H4
Senatobia *U.S.A.* 117 D10
Sencelles *Spain* 48 B9
Sendafa *Ethiopia* 81 F4
Sendai *Kagoshima, Japan* 55 J5
Sendai *Miyagi, Japan* 54 E10
Sendai-Wan *Japan* 54 E10
Senden *Bayern, Germany* 25 G6
Senden *Nordrhein-Westfalen, Germany* 24 D3
Sendhwa *India* 68 J6
Sene → *Ghana* 83 D4
Senec *Slovak Rep.* 27 C10
Seneca *U.S.A.* 117 D13
Seneca Falls *U.S.A.* 115 D8
Seneca L. *U.S.A.* 114 D8
Senecaville L. *U.S.A.* 114 G3
Senegal ■ *W. Afr.* 82 C2
Sénégal → *W. Afr.* 82 B1
Senegambia *Africa* 76 E2
Senekal *S. Africa* 89 D4
Senftenberg *Germany* 24 D10
Senga Hill *Zambia* 87 D3
Senge Khambab = Indus → *Pakistan* 68 G2
Sengerema *Tanzania* 86 C3
Sengiley *Russia* 34 D9
Sengua → *Zimbabwe* 87 F2
Senhor-do-Bonfim *Brazil* 125 F10
Senica *Slovak Rep.* 27 C10
Senigállia *Italy* 41 E10
Senio → *Italy* 41 D9
Senirkent *Turkey* 47 C12
Senise *Italy* 43 B9
Senj *Croatia* 41 D11
Senja *Norway* 8 B17
Senkaku-Shotō *E. China Sea* 55 M1
Senkuang *Indonesia* 65 d
Senlis *France* 19 C9
Senmonorom *Cambodia* 64 F6
Sennâr *Sudan* 81 E3
Sennâr □ *Sudan* 81 E3
Senneterre *Canada* 104 C4
Senno *Belarus* 32 E5
Sénnori *Italy* 42 B1
Seno *Laos* 64 D5
Senonches *France* 18 D8
Senorbì *Italy* 42 C2
Senožeče *Slovenia* 41 C11
Senqu = Orange → *S. Africa* 88 D2
Sens *France* 19 D10
Senta *Serbia* 28 E5
Sentani *Indonesia* 63 E10
Sentery = Lubao *Dem. Rep. of the Congo* 86 D2
Sentinel *U.S.A.* 109 K7
Šentjur *Slovenia* 41 B12
Sentosa *Singapore* 65 d
Senya Beraku *Ghana* 83 D4
Seo de Urgel = La Seu d'Urgell *Spain* 38 C6
Seogwipo *S. Korea* 57 H14
Seohara *India* 69 E8
Seonath → *India* 69 J10
Seondha *India* 69 F8
Seongnam *S. Korea* 57 F14
Seoni *India* 69 H8
Seoni Malwa *India* 68 H8
Seonsan *S. Korea* 57 F15
Seosan *S. Korea* 57 F14
Seoul *S. Korea* 57 F14
Sepīdān *Iran* 71 D7
Sep'o *N. Korea* 57 E14
Sępólno Krajeńskie *Poland* 30 E4
Sepone *Laos* 64 D6
Sępopol *Poland* 30 D8
Sept-Îles *Canada* 105 B6
Septemvri *Bulgaria* 45 D8
Sepúlveda *Spain* 36 D7
Sequeros *Spain* 36 E4
Sequim *U.S.A.* 110 B3
Sequoia △ *U.S.A.* 110 J8
Serafimovich *Russia* 34 F6
Seraing *Belgium* 17 D5
Serakhis → *Cyprus* 49 D11
Seram *Indonesia* 63 E7
Seram Sea *Indonesia* 63 E7
Serampore = Shrirampur *India* 69 H13
Seranantsara *Madag.* 89 B8
Serang *Indonesia* 63 G12
Serangoon *Singapore* 65 d
Serasan *Indonesia* 62 D3
Seravezza *Italy* 40 E7
Şerbettar *Turkey* 45 E10
Serbia ■ *Europe* 44 C4
Şercaia *Romania* 29 E10
Serdar *Turkmenistan* 71 B8
Serdo *Ethiopia* 81 E5
Serdobsk *Russia* 34 D7
Sered' *Slovak Rep.* 27 C10
Seredka *Russia* 32 C5
Serednye *Ukraine* 28 B7
Şereflikoçhisar *Turkey* 72 C5
Seregno *Italy* 40 C6
Seremban *Malaysia* 65 L3
Serengeti △ *Tanzania* 86 C3
Serengeti Plain *Tanzania* 86 C4
Serenje *Zambia* 87 E3
Seret → *Ukraine* 29 B10
Sereth = Siret → *Romania* 29 E12
Sergach *Russia* 34 C7
Sergen *Turkey* 45 E11
Sergeya Kirova, Ostrova *Russia* 53 B10
Sergino *Russia* 52 C7
Sergipe □ *Brazil* 125 F11
Sergiyev Posad *Russia* 32 D10
Serhetabat *Turkmenistan* 71 C9
Seria *Brunei* 62 D4
Serian *Malaysia* 62 D4
Seriate *Italy* 40 C6
Seribu, Kepulauan *Indonesia* 62 F3
Sericho *Kenya* 86 B4
Sérifontaine *France* 19 C8
Serifos *Greece* 46 D6
Sérignan *France* 20 E7
Serigny → *Canada* 105 A6
Serik *Turkey* 72 D4
Seringapatam Reef *Australia* 92 B3
Serinhisar *Turkey* 47 D11
Seririt *Indonesia* 63 J17
Serishābād *Iran* 70 C5
Serkout *Algeria* 78 D7
Sermaize-les-Bains *France* 19 D11
Sermata *Indonesia* 63 F7
Sermersuaq *Greenland* 101 B19
Sérmide *Italy* 41 D8
Sernovodsk *Russia* 34 D10
Sernur *Russia* 34 B9
Serock *Poland* 31 F8
Serón *Spain* 39 H2
Serós *Spain* 38 D5
Serov *Russia* 52 D7
Serowe *Botswana* 88 C4
Serpa *Portugal* 37 H3
Serpeddí, Punta *Italy* 42 C2
Serpentara *Italy* 42 C2
Serpentine Lakes *Australia* 93 E4
Serpent's Mouth = Sierpe, Bocas de la *Venezuela* 125 L15
Serpis → *Spain* 39 G4
Serpneve *Ukraine* 29 D14
Serpukhov *Russia* 32 E9
Serra da Estrela ⌂ *Portugal* 36 E3
Serra do Navio *Brazil* 125 C8
Serra San Bruno *Italy* 43 D9
Serradilla *Spain* 36 F4
Serramanna *Italy* 42 C1
Serranía San Luís △ *Paraguay* 126 A4
Serranía San Rafael △ *Paraguay* 127 B4
Serras d'Aire e Candeeiros ⌂ *Portugal* 37 F2
Serravalle Scrívia *Italy* 40 D5
Serre-Ponçon, L. de *France* 21 D10
Serres *France* 21 D9
Serres *Greece* 44 E7
Serres □ *Greece* 44 E7
Serrezuela *Argentina* 126 C2
Serrinha *Brazil* 125 F11
Sersale *Italy* 43 C9
Sertã *Portugal* 36 F2
Sertanópolis *Brazil* 127 A5
Sêrtar *China* 58 A3
Serua *Indonesia* 63 F8
Serui *Indonesia* 63 E9
Serule *Botswana* 88 C4
Servia *Greece* 44 F6
Serzedelo *Portugal* 36 D2
Ses Salines *Spain* 48 B10
Sese Is. *Uganda* 86 C3
Sesepe *Indonesia* 63 E7
Sesfontein *Namibia* 88 B1
Sesheke *Zambia* 88 B3
Sésia → *Italy* 40 C5
Sesimbra *Portugal* 37 G1
S'Espalmador *Spain* 48 C7
S'Espardell *Spain* 48 C7
Sessa Aurunca *Italy* 42 A6
S'Estanyol *Spain* 48 B9
Sestao *Spain* 38 B2
Sesto Calende *Italy* 40 C5
Sesto San Giovanni *Italy* 40 C6
Sestri Levante *Italy* 40 D6
Sestriere *Italy* 40 D3
Sestroretsk *Russia* 32 B6
Sestrunj *Croatia* 41 D11
Sestu *Italy* 42 C2
Setana *Japan* 54 C9
Sète *France* 20 E7
Sete Lagoas *Brazil* 125 G10
Sétif *Algeria* 78 A7
Setit → *Sudan* 81 E4
Seto *Japan* 55 G8
Setonaikai *Japan* 55 G6
Setonaikai △ *Japan* 55 G6
Settat *Morocco* 78 B4
Séttimo Torinese *Italy* 40 C4
Setting L. *Canada* 103 C9
Settle *U.K.* 14 C5
Settlement, The *Br. Virgin Is.* 121 e
Settlers *S. Africa* 89 C4
Setúbal *Portugal* 37 G2
Setúbal □ *Portugal* 37 G2
Setúbal, B. de *Portugal* 37 G2
Seugne → *France* 20 C3
Seul, Lac *Canada* 104 B1
Seurre *France* 19 F12
Sevan *Armenia* 35 K7
Sevan, Ozero = Sevana Lich *Armenia* 35 K7
Sevana Lich *Armenia* 35 K7
Sevastopol *Ukraine* 33 K7
Seven Sisters *Canada* 102 C3
Sever → *Spain* 37 F3
Sévérac-le-Château *France* 20 D7
Severn → *Canada* 104 A2
Severn → *U.K.* 15 F5
Severnaya Zemlya *Russia* 53 B11
Severo-Kurilsk *Russia* 53 D16
Severo-Yeniseyskiy *Russia* 53 C10
Severo-Zapadnyy □ *Russia* 52 C4
Severobaykalsk *Russia* 53 D11
Severočeský □ *Czech Rep.* 26 A7
Severodonetsk = Syeverodonetsk *Ukraine* 33 H10
Severodvinsk *Russia* 52 C4
Severomoravský □ *Czech Rep.* 27 B10
Severomorsk *Russia* 8 B25
Seversk *Russia* 52 D9
Sevier → *U.S.A.* 108 G7
Sevier Desert *U.S.A.* 108 G7
Sevier L. *U.S.A.* 108 G7
Sevilla *Spain* 37 H5
Sevilla □ *Spain* 37 H5
Seville = Sevilla *Spain* 37 H5
Sevlievo *Bulgaria* 45 C9
Sevnica *Slovenia* 41 B12
Sèvre-Nantaise → *France* 18 E5
Sèvre-Niortaise → *France* 20 B3
Sevsk *Russia* 33 F8
Sewa → *S. Leone* 82 D2
Sewani *India* 68 E6
Seward *Alaska, U.S.A.* 100 E2
Seward *Nebr., U.S.A.* 112 E5
Seward *Pa., U.S.A.* 114 F5
Seward Peninsula *U.S.A.* 106 B6
Sewell *Chile* 126 C1
Sewer *Indonesia* 63 F8
Sewickley *U.S.A.* 114 F4
Sexsmith *Canada* 102 B5
Seychelles ■ *Ind. Oc.* 85 b
Seyðisfjörður *Iceland* 8 D7
Seydişehir *Turkey* 72 D4
Seydvān *Iran* 73 C11
Seyhan → *Turkey* 72 D6
Seyhan Barajı *Turkey* 72 D6
Seyitgazi *Turkey* 47 B12
Seyitömer *Turkey* 47 B11
Seym → *Ukraine* 33 G7
Seymen *Turkey* 45 E11
Seymour *Australia* 95 F4
Seymour *S. Africa* 89 E4
Seymour *Conn., U.S.A.* 115 E11
Seymour *Ind., U.S.A.* 113 F11
Seymour *Tex., U.S.A.* 116 E5
Seyne *France* 21 D10
Seyssel *France* 21 C9
Sežana *Slovenia* 41 C10
Sézanne *France* 19 D10
Sezze *Italy* 42 A6
Sfântu Gheorghe *Covasna, Romania* 29 E10
Sfântu Gheorghe *Tulcea, Romania* 29 F14
Sfântu Gheorghe, Braţul → *Romania* 29 F14
Sfax *Tunisia* 79 B8
Sha Xi → *China* 59 D12
Sha Xian *China* 59 D11
Shaanxi □ *China* 56 G5
Shaba = Katanga □ *Dem. Rep. of the Congo* 86 D2
Shaba ⌂ *Kenya* 86 B4
Shabeelle → *Somali Rep.* 75 G3
Shabestar *Iran* 73 C11
Shabla *Bulgaria* 45 C12
Shabogamo L. *Canada* 105 B6
Shabunda *Dem. Rep. of the Congo* 86 C2
Shache *China* 60 C2
Shackleton Fracture Zone *S. Ocean* 5 B18
Shackleton Ice Shelf *Antarctica* 5 C8
Shackleton Inlet *Antarctica* 5 E11
Shādegān *Iran* 71 D6
Shadi *China* 59 D10
Shadi *India* 69 C7
Shadrinsk *Russia* 52 D7
Shadyside *U.S.A.* 114 G4
Shaffa *Nigeria* 83 C7
Shafter *U.S.A.* 111 K7
Shaftesbury *U.K.* 15 F5
Shaftsbury *U.S.A.* 115 D11
Shagamu *Nigeria* 83 D5
Shagram *Pakistan* 69 A5
Shah Alam *Malaysia* 65 L3
Shah Alizai *Pakistan* 68 E2
Shah Bunder *Pakistan* 68 G2
Shahabad *Punjab, India* 68 D7
Shahabad *Raj., India* 68 G7
Shahabad *Ut. P., India* 69 F8
Shahadpur *Pakistan* 68 G3
Shahbā' *Syria* 74 C5
Shahdād *Iran* 71 D8
Shahdād, Namakzār-e *Iran* 71 D8
Shahdadkot *Pakistan* 68 F2
Shahdol *India* 69 H9
Shahe *China* 56 F8
Shahganj *India* 69 F10
Shahgarh *India* 68 F3
Shahjahanpur *India* 69 F8
Shahpur = Salmās *Iran* 73 C11
Shahpur *India* 68 H7
Shahpur *Baluchistan, Pakistan* 68 E3
Shahpur *Punjab, Pakistan* 68 C5
Shahpur Chakar *Pakistan* 68 F3
Shahpura *Mad. P., India* 69 H9
Shahpura *Raj., India* 68 G6
Shahr-e Bābak *Iran* 71 D7
Shahr-e Kord *Iran* 71 C6
Shāhrakht *Iran* 71 C9
Shahrezā = Qomsheh *Iran* 71 D6
Shahrig *Pakistan* 68 D2
Shāhrud = Emāmrūd *Iran* 71 B7
Shahukou *China* 56 D7
Shaikhabad *Afghan.* 68 B3
Shajapur *India* 68 H7
Shakargarh *Pakistan* 68 C6
Shakawe *Botswana* 88 B3
Shaker Heights *U.S.A.* 114 E3
Shakhtersk *Russia* 53 E15
Shakhty *Russia* 35 G5
Shakhunya *Russia* 34 B8
Shaki *Nigeria* 83 D5
Shākir *Egypt* 80 B3
Shaksam Valley *Asia* 69 A7
Shala, L. *Ethiopia* 81 F4
Shali *Russia* 35 J7
Shalkar Köli *Kazakhstan* 34 E10
Shallow Lake *Canada* 114 B3
Shalqar *Kazakhstan* 52 E6
Shalskiy *Russia* 32 B8
Shaluli Shan *China* 58 B2
Shām *Iran* 71 E8
Shām, Bādiyat ash *Asia* 70 C3
Shamâl Bahr el Ghazal □ *Sudan* 81 F2
Shamâl Dârfûr □ *Sudan* 81 E2
Shamâl Kordofân □ *Sudan* 81 E3
Shamâl Sînî □ *Egypt* 74 E2
Shamattawa *Canada* 104 A1
Shamattawa → *Canada* 104 A2
Shambe *Sudan* 81 F3
Shambe △ *Sudan* 81 F3
Shambu *Ethiopia* 81 F4
Shamīl *Iran* 71 E8
Shamkhor = Şämkir *Azerbaijan* 35 K8
Shāmkūh *Iran* 71 C8
Shamli *India* 68 E7
Shammar, Jabal *Si. Arabia* 70 E4
Shamo = Gobi *Asia* 56 C6
Shamo, L. *Ethiopia* 81 F4
Shamokin *U.S.A.* 115 F8
Shamrock *Canada* 115 A8
Shamrock *U.S.A.* 116 D4
Shamva *Zimbabwe* 87 F3
Shan □ *Burma* 67 J21
Shan Xian *China* 56 G9
Shanan → *Ethiopia* 81 F5
Shanchengzhen *China* 57 C13
Shāndak *Iran* 71 D9
Shandon *U.S.A.* 110 K6
Shandong □ *China* 57 G10
Shandong Bandao *China* 57 F11
Shandur Pass *Pakistan* 69 A5
Shang Xian = Shangzhou *China* 56 H5
Shangalowe *Dem. Rep. of the Congo* 87 E2
Shangani *Zimbabwe* 89 B4
Shangani → *Zimbabwe* 87 F2
Shangbancheng *China* 57 D10
Shangcheng *China* 59 B10
Shangchuan Dao *China* 59 G9
Shangdu *China* 56 D7
Shanggao *China* 59 C10
Shanghai *China* 59 B13
Shanghai Shi □ *China* 59 B13
Shanghang *China* 59 E11
Shanghe *China* 57 F9
Shanglin *China* 58 F7
Shangnan *China* 56 H6
Shangqiu *China* 56 G8
Shangrao *China* 59 C11
Shangri-La = Zhongdian *China* 58 D2
Shangshui *China* 60 C6
Shangsi *China* 58 F6
Shangyou *China* 59 E10
Shangyu *China* 59 B13
Shangzhi *China* 57 B14
Shangzhou *China* 56 H5
Shanhetun *China* 57 B14
Shani *Nigeria* 83 C7
Shānidar *Iraq* 73 D11
Shanklin *U.K.* 15 G6
Shannon *N.Z.* 91 D5
Shannon → *Ireland* 12 D2
Shannon ✈ (SNN) *Ireland* 12 D3
Shannon, Mouth of the *Ireland* 12 D2
Shannon △ *Australia* 93 F2
Shannonbridge *Ireland* 12 C3
Shansi = Shanxi □ *China* 56 F7
Shantar, Ostrov Bolshoy *Russia* 53 D14
Shantipur *India* 69 H13
Shantou *China* 59 F11
Shantung = Shandong □ *China* 57 G10
Shanwei *China* 59 F10
Shanxi □ *China* 56 F7
Shanyang *China* 56 H5
Shanyin *China* 56 E7
Shaodong *China* 59 D8
Shaoguan *China* 59 E9
Shaoshan *China* 59 D9
Shaowu *China* 59 D11
Shaoxing *China* 59 C13
Shaoyang *Hunan, China* 59 D8
Shaoyang *Hunan, China* 59 D8
Shap *U.K.* 14 C5
Shapinsay *U.K.* 13 B6
Shaqlāwah *Iraq* 73 D11
Shaqq el Gi'eifer → *Sudan* 81 D2
Shaqra' *Si. Arabia* 70 E5
Shaqrā' *Yemen* 75 E4
Sharafa *Sudan* 81 E2
Sharafkhāneh *Iran* 73 C11
Sharashova *Belarus* 31 F11

Sharbot Lake *Canada* **115** B8
Sharhorod *Ukraine* **29** B13
Shari *Japan* **54** C12
Sharjah = Ash Shāriqah
  U.A.E. **71** E7
Shark B. *Australia* **93** E1
Shark Bay △ *Australia* **93** E1
Sharm el Sheikh *Egypt* **80** B3
Sharon *Canada* **114** B5
Sharon *Mass., U.S.A.* **115** D13
Sharon *Pa., U.S.A.* **114** E4
Sharon Springs *Kans., U.S.A.* **112** F3
Sharon Springs *N.Y., U.S.A.*
  115 D10
Sharp Pt. *Australia* **94** A3
Sharpe L. *Canada* **104** B1
Sharpsville *U.S.A.* **114** E4
Sharq el Istiwa'iya □ *Sudan* **81** G3
Sharqi, Al Jabal ash *Lebanon* **74** B5
Sharya *Russia* **34** A7
Shasha *Ethiopia* **81** F4
Shashemene *Ethiopia* **81** F4
Shashi *Botswana* **89** C4
Shashi *China* **59** B9
Shashi ➤ *Africa* **87** G2
Shasta, Mt. *U.S.A.* **108** F2
Shasta L. *U.S.A.* **108** F2
Shatawi *Sudan* **81** E3
Shatsk *Russia* **34** C5
Shatsk *Ukraine* **31** G10
Shatsky Rise *Pac. Oc.* **96** D7
Shatskyi △ *Ukraine* **31** G10
Shatt al Arab *Asia* **71** D6
Shatura *Russia* **32** F10
Shaumyani = Shulaveri
  Georgia **35** K7
Shaunavon *Canada* **103** D7
Shaver L. *U.S.A.* **110** H7
Shaw ➤ *Australia* **92** D2
Shaw I. *Australia* **94** b
Shawanaga *Canada* **114** A4
Shawangunk Mts. *U.S.A.* **115** E10
Shawano *U.S.A.* **112** C9
Shawinigan *Canada* **104** C5
Shawmari, J. ash *Jordan* **74** E5
Shawnee *U.S.A.* **116** D6
Shay Gap *Australia* **92** D3
Shayang *China* **59** B9
Shaybārā *Si. Arabia* **70** E3
Shayib el Banat, Gebel *Egypt* **80** B3
Shaykh, J. ash *Lebanon* **74** B4
Shaykh Miskīn *Syria* **74** C5
Shaykh Sa'd *Iraq* **73** F12
Shāzand *Iran* **71** C6
Shchekino *Russia* **32** E9
Shchigry *Russia* **33** G9
Shchors *Ukraine* **33** G6
Shchūchīnsk *Kazakhstan* **52** D8
She Xian *Anhui, China* **59** C12
She Xian *Hebei, China* **56** F7
Shebekino *Russia* **33** G9
Shebele = Shabeelle ➤
  Somali Rep. **75** G3
Sheboygan *U.S.A.* **112** D10
Shebshi Mts. *Nigeria* **83** D7
Shediac *Canada* **105** C7
Sheelin, L. *Ireland* **12** C4
Sheenjek ➤ *U.S.A.* **106** B11
Sheep Haven *Ireland* **12** A4
Sheep Range *U.S.A.* **111** J11
Sheerness *U.K.* **15** F8
Sheet Harbour *Canada* **105** D7
Sheffield *U.K.* **14** D6
Sheffield *Ala., U.S.A.* **117** D11
Sheffield *Mass., U.S.A.* **115** D11
Sheffield *Pa., U.S.A.* **114** E5
Shehojele *Ethiopia* **81** E4
Shehong *China* **58** B5
Sheikh Zayed, Qana es *Egypt* **80** C3
Sheikh Zayed Canal =
  Sheikh Zayed, Qana es
  Egypt **80** C3
Sheikhpura *India* **69** G11
Shek Hasan *Ethiopia* **81** E4
Shekhupura *Pakistan* **68** D5
Sheki = Şaki *Azerbaijan* **35** K8
Shelburne *N.S., Canada* **105** D6
Shelburne *Ont., Canada* **114** B4
Shelburne *U.S.A.* **115** B11
Shelburne B. *Australia* **94** A3
Shelburne Falls *U.S.A.* **115** D12
Shelby *Mich., U.S.A.* **112** D10
Shelby *Miss., U.S.A.* **117** E9
Shelby *Mont., U.S.A.* **108** B8
Shelby *N.C., U.S.A.* **117** D14
Shelby *Ohio, U.S.A.* **114** F2
Shelbyville *Ill., U.S.A.* **112** F9
Shelbyville *Ind., U.S.A.* **113** F11
Shelbyville *Ky., U.S.A.* **113** F11
Shelbyville *Tenn., U.S.A.* **117** D11
Sheldon *U.S.A.* **112** D6
Sheldrake *Canada* **105** B7
Shelengo, Khawr ➤ *Sudan* **81** E2
Shelikhova, Zaliv *Russia* **53** D16
Shelikof Strait *U.S.A.* **106** D9
Shell Lakes *Australia* **93** E4
Shellbrook *Canada* **103** C7
Shellharbour *Australia* **95** E5
Shelon ➤ *Russia* **32** C6
Shelter I. *U.S.A.* **115** E12

Shelton *Conn., U.S.A.* **115** E11
Shelton *Wash., U.S.A.* **110** C3
Shemakha = Şamaxı
  Azerbaijan **35** K9
Shëmri *Albania* **44** D4
Shemsi *Sudan* **80** D2
Shen Xian *China* **56** F8
Shenandoah *Iowa, U.S.A.* **112** E6
Shenandoah *Pa., U.S.A.* **115** F8
Shenandoah *Va., U.S.A.* **113** F14
Shenandoah ➤ *U.S.A.* **113** F15
Shenandoah △ *U.S.A.* **113** F14
Shenchi *China* **56** E7
Shendam *Nigeria* **83** D6
Shendī *Sudan* **81** D3
Shenge *S. Leone* **82** D2
Shengfang *China* **56** E9
Shëngjergj *Albania* **44** E3
Shëngjin *Albania* **44** E3
Shengzhou *China* **59** C13
Shenjingzi *China* **57** B13
Shenmu *China* **56** E6
Shennongjia *China* **59** B8
Shenqiu *China* **56** H8
Shensi = Shaanxi □ *China* **56** G5
Shenyang *China* **57** D12
Shenzhen *China* **59** F10
Sheo *India* **68** F4
Sheopur Kalan *India* **68** G7
Shepetivka *Ukraine* **23** C14
Shepparton *Australia* **95** F4
Sheppey, I. of *U.K.* **15** F8
Shepton Mallet *U.K.* **15** F5
Sheqi *China* **56** H7
Sher Qila *Pakistan* **69** A6
Sherab *Sudan* **81** E1
Sherborne *U.K.* **15** G5
Sherbro ➤ *S. Leone* **82** D2
Sherbro I. *S. Leone* **82** D2
Sherbrooke *N.S., Canada* **105** C7
Sherbrooke *Qué., Canada* **115** A13
Sherburne *U.S.A.* **115** D9
Shereik *Sudan* **80** D3
Shergarh *India* **68** F5
Sherghati *India* **69** G11
Sheridan *Ark., U.S.A.* **116** D8
Sheridan *Wyo., U.S.A.* **108** D10
Sheringham *U.K.* **14** E9
Sherkin I. *Ireland* **12** E2
Sherkot *India* **69** E8
Sherlovaya Gora *Russia* **53** D12
Sherman *N.Y., U.S.A.* **114** D5
Sherman *Tex., U.S.A.* **116** E6
Sherpur *India* **69** G10
Sherridon *Canada* **103** B8
Sherwood Forest *U.K.* **14** D6
Sherwood Park *Canada* **102** C6
Sheslay ➤ *Canada* **102** B2
Shethanei L. *Canada* **103** B9
Shetland □ *U.K.* **13** A7
Shetland Is. *U.K.* **13** A7
Shetrunji ➤ *India* **68** J5
Shevchenkovo *Ukraine* **29** E14
Shevisheh *Iran* **73** E12
Shewa *Ethiopia* **81** F4
Shewa Gimira *Ethiopia* **81** F4
Shey-Phoksundo △ *Nepal* **69** E10
Sheyenne ➤ *U.S.A.* **112** B5
Shiashkotan, Ostrov *Russia* **53** E16
Shibām *Yemen* **75** D4
Shibata *Japan* **54** F9
Shibecha *Japan* **54** C12
Shibetsu *Japan* **54** B11
Shibin el Kôm *Egypt* **80** H7
Shibin el Qanâtir *Egypt* **80** H7
Shibing *China* **58** D7
Shibogama L. *Canada* **104** B2
Shibushi *Japan* **55** J5
Shicheng *China* **59** D11
Shickshinny *U.S.A.* **115** E8
Shickshock Mts. =
  Chic-Chocs, Mts. *Canada* **105** C6
Shidao *China* **57** F12
Shidian *China* **58** E2
Shido *Japan* **55** G7
Shiel, L. *U.K.* **13** E3
Shield, C. *Australia* **94** A2
Shīeli *Kazakhstan* **52** E7
Shifang *China* **58** B5
Shiga □ *Japan* **55** G8
Shigu *China* **58** D2
Shiguaigou *China* **56** D6
Shihchiachuangi =
  Shijiazhuang *China* **56** E8
Shihezi *China* **60** B3
Shijak *Albania* **44** E3
Shijiazhuang *China* **56** E8
Shijiu Hu *China* **59** B12
Shikarpur *India* **68** E8
Shikarpur *Pakistan* **68** F3
Shikohabad *India* **69** F8
Shikoku □ *Japan* **55** H6
Shikoku-Sanchi *Japan* **55** H6
Shikotan, Ostrov *Asia* **53** E15
Shikotsu-Ko *Japan* **54** C10
Shikotsu-Tōya △ *Japan* **54** C10
Shiliguri *India* **67** F16
Shiliu = Changjiang *China* **64** C7
Shilka *Russia* **53** D12
Shilka ➤ *Russia* **53** D13

Shillelagh *Ireland* **12** D5
Shillington *U.S.A.* **115** F9
Shillong *India* **67** G17
Shilo *West Bank* **74** C4
Shilong *China* **59** F9
Shilou *China* **56** F6
Shilovo *Russia* **34** C5
Shimabara *Japan* **55** H5
Shimada *Japan* **55** G9
Shimane □ *Japan* **55** G6
Shimanovsk *Russia* **53** D13
Shimba Hills △ *Kenya* **86** C4
Shimbiris *Somali Rep.* **75** E4
Shimen *China* **59** C8
Shimenjie *China* **59** C11
Shimian *China* **58** C4
Shimizu *Japan* **55** G9
Shimla *India* **68** D7
Shimodate *Japan* **55** F9
Shimoga *India* **66** N9
Shimoni *Kenya* **86** C4
Shimonoseki *Japan* **55** H5
Shimsk *Russia* **32** C6
Shin, L. *U.K.* **13** C4
Shinan *China* **58** F7
Shinano-Gawa ➤ *Japan* **55** F9
Shināş *Oman* **71** E8
Shīndand *Afghan.* **66** C3
Shinglehouse *U.S.A.* **114** E6
Shingū *Japan* **55** H7
Shingwidzi *S. Africa* **89** C5
Shinjō *Japan* **54** E10
Shinkafe *Nigeria* **83** C6
Shinkolobwe
  Dem. Rep. of the Congo **84** G5
Shinshār *Syria* **74** A5
Shinyanga *Tanzania* **86** C3
Shinyanga □ *Tanzania* **86** C3
Shio-no-Misaki *Japan* **55** H7
Shiogama *Japan* **54** E10
Shiojiri *Japan* **55** F8
Shipchenski Prokhod
  Bulgaria **45** D9
Shiping *China* **58** F4
Shippagan *Canada* **105** C7
Shippensburg *U.S.A.* **114** F7
Shippenville *U.S.A.* **114** E5
Shiprock *U.S.A.* **109** H9
Shiqian *China* **58** D7
Shiqma, N. ➤ *Israel* **74** D3
Shiquan *China* **56** H5
Shiquan He = Indus ➤
  Pakistan **68** G2
Shīr Kūh *Iran* **71** D7
Shiragami-Misaki *Japan* **54** D10
Shirakawa *Fukushima, Japan* **55** F10
Shirakawa *Gifu, Japan* **55** F8
Shirane-San *Gumma, Japan* **55** F9
Shirane-San *Yamanashi, Japan* **55** G9
Shiraoi *Japan* **54** C10
Shīrāz *Iran* **71** D7
Shirbīn *Egypt* **80** H7
Shire ➤ *Africa* **87** F4
Shiretoko-Misaki *Japan* **54** B12
Shirinab ➤ *Pakistan* **68** D2
Shiriya-Zaki *Japan* **54** D10
Shiroishi *Japan* **54** E10
Shiroro Res. *Nigeria* **83** D6
Shirshov Ridge *Pac. Oc.* **96** B8
Shīrvān *Iran* **71** B8
Shirwa, L. = Chilwa, L.
  Malawi **87** F4
Shishaldin Volcano *U.S.A.* **106** E7
Shishi *China* **59** E12
Shishou *China* **59** C9
Shitai *China* **59** B11
Shithāthah *Iraq* **73** G10
Shivamogga = Shimoga
  India **66** N9
Shivpuri *India* **68** G7
Shixian *China* **57** C15
Shixing *China* **59** E10
Shiyan *China* **59** A8
Shiyata *Egypt* **80** B2
Shizhu *China* **58** C7
Shizong *China* **58** E5
Shizuishan *China* **56** E4
Shizuoka *Japan* **55** G9
Shizuoka □ *Japan* **55** G9
Shkhara *Georgia* **73** A10
Shklov = Shklow *Belarus* **23** A16
Shklow *Belarus* **23** A16
Shkodër *Albania* **44** D3
Shkumbini ➤ *Albania* **44** E3
Shmidta, Ostrov *Russia* **53** A10
Shō-Gawa ➤ *Japan* **55** F8
Shoal L. *Canada* **103** D9
Shoal Lake *Canada* **103** C8
Shōdo-Shima *Japan* **55** G7
Shōmrōn *West Bank* **74** C4
Shoreham *U.S.A.* **115** C11
Shoreham by Sea *U.K.* **15** G7
Shori ➤ *Pakistan* **68** E3
Shorkot *Pakistan* **68** D4
Shorkot Road *Pakistan* **68** D5
Shoshone *Calif., U.S.A.* **111** K10
Shoshone *Idaho, U.S.A.* **108** E6
Shoshone L. *U.S.A.* **108** D8

Shoshone Mts. *U.S.A.* **108** G5
Shoshong *Botswana* **88** C4
Shoshoni *U.S.A.* **108** E9
Shostka *Ukraine* **33** G7
Shot *Iran* **73** C11
Shou Xian *China* **59** A11
Shouchang *China* **59** C12
Shouguang *China* **57** F10
Shouning *China* **59** D12
Shouyang *China* **56** F7
Show Low *U.S.A.* **109** J8
Showak *Sudan* **81** E4
Shpola *Ukraine* **33** H6
Shpykiv *Ukraine* **29** B13
Shqipëria = Albania ■
  Europe **44** E4
Shreveport *U.S.A.* **116** E8
Shrewsbury *U.K.* **15** E5
Shri Mohangarh *India* **68** F4
Shrirampur *India* **69** H13
Shropshire □ *U.K.* **15** E5
Shū *Kazakhstan* **52** E8
Shuangbai *China* **58** E3
Shuangcheng *China* **57** B14
Shuangfeng *China* **59** D9
Shuanggou *China* **57** G9
Shuangjiang *China* **58** F2
Shuangliao *China* **57** C12
Shuangshanzi *China* **57** D10
Shuangyang *China* **57** C13
Shuangyashan *China* **60** B8
Shubrâ el Kheima *Egypt* **80** H7
Shubrâ Khit *Egypt* **80** H7
Shucheng *China* **59** B11
Shugozero *Russia* **32** C8
Shuguri Falls *Tanzania* **87** D4
Shuiji *China* **59** D12
Shuiye *China* **56** F8
Shujalpur *India* **68** H7
Shukpa Kunzang *India* **69** B8
Shulan *China* **57** B14
Shulaveri *Georgia* **35** K7
Shule *China* **60** C2
Shumagin Is. *U.S.A.* **106** D7
Shumen *Bulgaria* **45** C10
Shumerlya *Russia* **34** C8
Shumikha *Russia* **52** D7
Shunchang *China* **59** D11
Shunde *China* **59** F9
Shungay *Kazakhstan* **35** F8
Shungnak *U.S.A.* **106** B8
Shuo Xian = Shuozhou
  China **56** E7
Shuozhou *China* **56** E7
Shūr ➤ *Fārs, Iran* **71** D7
Shūr ➤ *Kermān, Iran* **71** D8
Shūr ➤ *Yazd, Iran* **71** D7
Shūr Āb *Iran* **71** C6
Shūr Gaz *Iran* **71** D8
Shūrāb *Iran* **71** C8
Shūrjestān *Iran* **71** D7
Shurugwi *Zimbabwe* **87** F3
Shūsf *Iran* **71** D9
Shūsh *Iran* **73** F13
Shūshtar *Iran* **71** D6
Shuswap L. *Canada* **102** C5
Shute Harbour △ *Australia* **94** b
Shuya *Russia* **34** B5
Shuyang *China* **57** G10
Shūzū *Iran* **71** D7
Shwebo *Burma* **67** H19
Shwegu *Burma* **67** G20
Shweli ➤ *Burma* **67** H20
Shymkent *Kazakhstan* **52** E7
Shyok *India* **69** B8
Shyok ➤ *Pakistan* **69** B6
Shyroke *Odesa, Ukraine* **29** E15
Shyroke *Ternopil, Ukraine* **28** B8
Si Kiang = Xi Jiang ➤ *China* **59** F9
Si Lanna △ *Thailand* **64** C2
Si Nakarin Res. *Thailand* **64** E2
Si-ngan = Xi'an *China* **56** G5
Si Prachan *Thailand* **64** E3
Si Racha *Thailand* **64** F3
Si Xian *China* **57** H9
Siachen Glacier *Asia* **69** B7
Sīāh Chashmeh *Iran* **73** C11
Siahaf ➤ *Pakistan* **68** E3
Siahan Range *Pakistan* **66** F4
Siaksriindrapura *Indonesia* **62** D2
Sialkot *Pakistan* **68** C6
Siam = Thailand ■ *Asia* **64** E4
Sian = Xi'an *China* **56** G5
Sian Ka'an △ *Mexico* **119** D7
Sianów *Poland* **30** D3
Siantan *Indonesia* **62** D3
Sīāreh *Iran* **71** D9
Siargao I. *Phil.* **61** G7
Siari *Pakistan* **69** B7
Siasi *Phil.* **63** C6
Siasi I. *Phil.* **61** J4
Siatista *Greece* **44** F5
Siau *Indonesia* **63** D7
Šiauliai *Lithuania* **30** C10
Šiauliai □ *Lithuania* **30** C10
Siazan = Siyäzän *Azerbaijan* **35** K9
Sibâi, Gebel el *Egypt* **70** E2
Sibang *Indonesia* **63** K18
Sibayi, L. *S. Africa* **89** D5
Sibdu *Sudan* **81** E2

Šibenik *Croatia* **41** E12
Siberia = Sibirskiy □ *Russia* **53** D10
Siberia *Russia* **4** D3
Siberut *Indonesia* **62** E1
Sibi *Pakistan* **68** E2
Sibil = Oksibil *Indonesia* **63** E10
Sibiloi △ *Kenya* **86** B4
Sibirskiy □ *Russia* **53** D10
Sibirtsevo *Russia* **54** B5
Sibiti *Congo* **84** E2
Sibiu *Romania* **29** E9
Sibiu □ *Romania* **29** E9
Sibley *La., U.S.A.* **116** E8
Sibley *Minn., U.S.A.* **112** D6
Sibolga *Indonesia* **62** D1
Siborongborong *Indonesia* **65** L2
Sibsagar *India* **67** F19
Sibu *Malaysia* **62** D4
Sibuco *Phil.* **61** H5
Sibuguey B. *Phil.* **61** H5
Sibut *C.A.R.* **84** C3
Sibutu *Phil.* **63** D5
Sibutu Group *Phil.* **61** J3
Sibutu Passage *E. Indies* **61** J4
Sibuyan I. *Phil.* **61** E5
Sibuyan Sea *Phil.* **61** E5
Sic *Romania* **29** D8
Sicamous *Canada* **102** C5
Siccus ➤ *Australia* **95** E2
Sichon *Thailand* **65** H2
Sichuan □ *China* **58** B5
Sichuan Pendi *China* **58** B5
Sicilia *Italy* **43** E7
Sicily = Sicilia *Italy* **43** E7
Sicily, Str. of *Medit. S.* **42** E4
Sico ➤ *Honduras* **120** C3
Sicuani *Peru* **124** F4
Sid *Serbia* **28** E4
Šid *Serbia* **28** E4
Sidamo *Ethiopia* **81** G4
Sidaouet *Niger* **83** B6
Sidari *Greece* **49** A3
Siddhapur *India* **68** H5
Siddipet *India* **66** K11
Sidensjö *Sweden* **10** A12
Sidéradougou *Burkina Faso* **82** C4
Siderno *Italy* **43** D9
Sideros, Akra *Greece* **49** D8
Sidhauli *India* **69** F9
Sidhi *India* **69** G9
Sīdi Abd el Rahmân *Egypt* **80** A2
Sīdi Barrâni *Egypt* **80** A2
Sidi-bel-Abbès *Algeria* **78** A5
Sīdi Haneish *Egypt* **80** A2
Sidi Ifni *Morocco* **78** C3
Sīdi Omar *Egypt* **80** A1
Sidikalang *Indonesia* **65** L2
Sidirokastro *Greece* **44** E7
Sidlaw Hills *U.K.* **13** E5
Sidley, Mt. *Antarctica* **5** D14
Sidmouth *U.K.* **15** G4
Sidmouth, C. *Australia* **94** A3
Sidney *Canada* **110** B3
Sidney *Mont., U.S.A.* **108** C11
Sidney *N.Y., U.S.A.* **115** D9
Sidney *Nebr., U.S.A.* **112** E2
Sidney *Ohio, U.S.A.* **113** E11
Sidney Lanier, L. *U.S.A.* **117** D12
Sido *Mali* **82** C3
Sidoarjo *Indonesia* **63** G15
Sidon = Saydā *Lebanon* **74** B4
Sidra, G. of = Surt, Khalīj
  Libya **79** B9
Siedlce *Poland* **31** F9
Sieg ➤ *Germany* **24** E3
Siegburg *Germany* **24** E3
Siegen *Germany* **24** E4
Siem Pang *Cambodia* **64** E6
Siem Reap = Siemreab
  Cambodia **64** F4
Siemiatycze *Poland* **31** F9
Siemreab *Cambodia* **64** F4
Siena *Italy* **41** E8
Sieniawa *Poland* **31** H9
Sieradz *Poland* **31** G5
Sieraków *Poland* **31** F3
Sierck-les-Bains *France* **19** C13
Sierning *Austria* **26** C7
Sierpc *Poland* **31** F6
Sierpe, Bocas de la *Venezuela*
  125 L15
Sierra Blanca *U.S.A.* **116** F2
Sierra Blanca Peak *U.S.A.* **109** K11
Sierra City *U.S.A.* **110** F6
Sierra Colorada *Argentina* **128** E3
Sierra de Agalta △ *Honduras* **120** C2
Sierra de Aracena y Picas
  de Aroche △ *Spain* **37** H4
Sierra de Bahoruco △
  Dom. Rep. **121** C5
Sierra de Baza △ *Spain* **39** H2
Sierra de Castril △ *Spain* **39** H2
Sierra de Espuña △ *Spain* **39** H3
Sierra de Grazalema △ *Spain* **37** J5
Sierra de Gredos △ *Spain* **36** E5
Sierra de Hornachuelos △
  Spain **37** H5
Sierra de Huétor △ *Spain* **37** H7
Sierra de La Culata △
  Venezuela **121** E5
Sierra de Lancandón △
  Guatemala **120** C1

Sierra de las Nieves △ *Spain* **37** J6
Sierra de las Quijadas △
  Argentina **126** C2
Sierra de María-Los
  Vélez △ *Spain* **39** H2
Sierra de San Luis △
  Venezuela **121** D6
Sierra de San Pedro Mártir,
  Parque Nac. △ *Mexico* **118** A1
Sierra de Yeguas *Spain* **37** H6
Sierra del São Mamede △
  Portugal **37** F3
Sierra Gorda *Chile* **126** A2
Sierra Leone ■ *W. Afr.* **82** D2
Sierra Madre *Mexico* **119** D6
Sierra Madre Occidental
  Mexico **118** B3
Sierra Madre Oriental
  Mexico **118** C5
Sierra Mágina △ *Spain* **37** H7
Sierra Mojada *Mexico* **118** B4
Sierra Nevada *Spain* **37** H7
Sierra Nevada *U.S.A.* **110** H8
Sierra Nevada △ *Spain* **37** H7
Sierra Nevada △ *Venezuela* **121** E5
Sierra Nevada de Santa
  Marta △ *Colombia* **121** D5
Sierra Norte de Sevilla △
  Spain **37** H5
Sierra Subbéticas △ *Spain* **37** H6
Sierra Vista *U.S.A.* **109** L3
Sierras de Cardeña y
  Montoro △ *Spain* **37** G6
Sierras de Cazorla, Segura
  y las Villas △ *Spain* **39** J2
Sierraville *U.S.A.* **110** F6
Sierre *Switz.* **25** J3
Sifani *Ethiopia* **81** E5
Sifié *Ivory C.* **82** D3
Sifnos *Greece* **46** E6
Sifton *Canada* **103** C8
Sifton Pass *Canada* **102** B3
Sig *Algeria* **78** A5
Sigatoka *Fiji* **91** a
Sigean *France* **20** E6
Sighetu-Marmaţiei *Romania* **29** C8
Sighişoara *Romania* **29** D9
Sigli *Indonesia* **62** C1
Siglufjörður *Iceland* **3** C4
Sigmaringen *Germany* **25** G5
Signa *Italy* **40** E8
Signakhi = Tsnori *Georgia* **35** K7
Signal de Botrang *Belgium* **17** D6
Signal Pk. *U.S.A.* **111** M12
Signy I. *Antarctica* **5** C18
Signy-l'Abbaye *France* **19** C11
Sígsig *Ecuador* **124** D3
Sigtuna *Sweden* **10** E11
Sigüenza *Spain* **38** D2
Siguiri *Guinea* **82** C3
Sigulda *Latvia* **32** D3
Sihora *India* **69** H9
Sihui *China* **59** F9
Siikajoki ➤ *Finland* **8** D21
Siilinjärvi *Finland* **8** E22
Siirt *Turkey* **73** D9
Siirt □ *Turkey* **73** D9
Sijarira Ra. = Chizarira
  Zimbabwe **87** F2
Sika *India* **68** H3
Sikanni Chief ➤ *Canada* **102** B4
Sikao *Thailand* **65** J2
Sikar *India* **68** F6
Sikasso *Mali* **82** C3
Sikasso □ *Mali* **82** C3
Sikeston *U.S.A.* **112** G9
Sikhote Alin, Khrebet *Russia* **54** B8
Sikhote Alin Ra. = Sikhote
  Alin, Khrebet *Russia* **54** B8
Sikia *Greece* **44** F7
Sikinos *Greece* **47** E7
Sikkim □ *India* **67** F16
Siklós *Hungary* **28** E3
Sil ➤ *Spain* **36** C3
Silacayoapan *Mexico* **119** D5
Šilalė *Lithuania* **30** C10
Silandro *Italy* **40** B7
Silawad *India* **68** J6
Silay *Phil.* **61** F5
Silba *Croatia* **41** D11
Silchar *India* **67** G18
Şile *Turkey* **45** E13
Siler City *U.S.A.* **117** D15
Silesia = Śląsk *Poland* **22** C9
Silgarhi Doti *Nepal* **69** E9
Silghat *India* **67** F18
Silhouette *Seychelles* **85** b
Sili *Burkina Faso* **82** C4
Silifke *Turkey* **72** D5
Siliguri = Shiliguri *India* **67** F16
Siling Co *China* **60** C3
Silistea Nouă *Romania* **29** F10
Silistra *Bulgaria* **45** B11
Silivri *Turkey* **45** E12
Siljan *Sweden* **10** D8
Siljansnäs *Sweden* **10** D8
Silkeborg *Denmark* **11** H3
Silkwood *Australia* **94** B4
Silla *Spain* **39** F4
Sillajhuay, Cordillera *Chile* **124** G5

Sillamäe *Estonia* 32 C4
Sillé-le-Guillaume *France* 18 D6
Silleda *Spain* 36 C2
Silloth *U.K.* 14 C4
Silo *Greece* 45 E9
Siloam Springs *U.S.A.* 116 C7
Silopi *Turkey* 73 D10
Silsbee *U.S.A.* 116 F7
Siluko *Nigeria* 83 D6
Šilutė *Lithuania* 30 C8
Silvan *Turkey* 73 C9
Silvani *India* 69 H8
Silver City *U.S.A.* 109 K9
Silver Cr. → *U.S.A.* 108 E4
Silver Creek *U.S.A.* 114 D5
Silver L. *U.S.A.* 110 G6
Silver Lake *Calif., U.S.A.* 111 K10
Silver Lake *Oreg., U.S.A.* 108 E3
Silverdalen *Sweden* 11 G9
Silvermine Mts. *Ireland* 12 D3
Silverton *Colo., U.S.A.* 109 H10
Silverton *Tex., U.S.A.* 116 D4
Silves *Portugal* 37 H2
Silvi Marina *Italy* 41 F11
Silvies → *U.S.A.* 108 E4
Silvrettahorn *Switz.* 26 C2
Silwa Bahari *Egypt* 80 C3
Silz *Austria* 26 D3
Simaltala *India* 69 G12
Simanggang = Sri Aman *Malaysia* 62 D4
Simao *China* 58 F3
Simard, L. *Canada* 104 C4
Şīmareh → *Iran* 73 F12
Simav *Turkey* 47 B10
Simav → *Turkey* 45 F12
Simav Dağları *Turkey* 47 B10
Simba *Tanzania* 86 C4
Simbach *Germany* 25 G9
Simbirsk = Ulyanovsk *Russia* 34 C9
Simbo *Tanzania* 86 C2
Simcoe *Canada* 114 D4
Simcoe, L. *Canada* 114 B5
Simdega *India* 69 H11
Simeonovgrad *Bulgaria* 45 D9
Simeria *Romania* 28 E8
Simeto → *Italy* 43 E8
Simeulue *Indonesia* 62 D1
Simferopol *Ukraine* 33 K8
Simi *Greece* 47 E9
Simi Valley *U.S.A.* 111 L8
Simien Mts. △ *Ethiopia* 81 E4
Simikot *Nepal* 69 E9
Simineh → *Iran* 73 D11
Simitli *Bulgaria* 44 E7
Simla = Shimla *India* 68 D7
Simlångsdalen *Sweden* 11 H7
Şimleu-Silvaniei *Romania* 28 C7
Simlipal △ *India* 69 J12
Simmern *Germany* 25 F3
Simmie *Canada* 103 D7
Simmler *U.S.A.* 111 K7
Simnas *Lithuania* 30 D10
Simo älv = Simojoki → *Finland* 8 D21
Simojoki → *Finland* 8 D21
Simojovel *Mexico* 119 D6
Simonette → *Canada* 102 B5
Simonstown *S. Africa* 88 E2
Simontornya *Hungary* 28 D3
Simpang Empat *Malaysia* 65 c
Simplonpass *Switz.* 25 J4
Simplontunnel *Switz.* 25 J4
Simpson Desert *Australia* 94 D2
Simpson Desert △ *Australia* 94 C2
Simpson Pen. *Canada* 101 D14
Simrishamn *Sweden* 11 J8
Simsbury *U.S.A.* 115 E12
Simushir, Ostrov *Russia* 53 E16
Sin Cowe I. *S. China Sea* 62 C4
Sina Dhago *Somali Rep.* 75 F4
Sinabang *Indonesia* 62 D1
Sinai = Es Sînâ' *Egypt* 74 F3
Sinai, Mt. = Mûsa, Gebel *Egypt* 70 D2
Sinaia *Romania* 29 E10
Sinaloa □ *Mexico* 118 C3
Sinaloa de Leyva *Mexico* 118 B3
Sinalunga *Italy* 41 E8
Sinan *China* 58 D7
Sînandrei *Romania* 28 E6
Sinarades *Greece* 49 A3
Sincan *Turkey* 72 B2
Sincanlı *Turkey* 47 C12
Sincelejo *Colombia* 124 B3
Sinch'ang *N. Korea* 57 D15
Sinch'ŏn *N. Korea* 57 E13
Sinclair *U.S.A.* 108 F10
Sinclair Mills *Canada* 102 C4
Sinclair's B. *U.K.* 13 C5
Sinclairville *U.S.A.* 114 D5
Sincorá, Serra do *Brazil* 125 F10
Sind = Sindh □ *Pakistan* 68 G3
Sind → *Jammu & Kashmir, India* 69 B6
Sind → *Mad. P., India* 69 F8
Sind Sagar Doab *Pakistan* 68 D4
Sindal *Denmark* 11 G4
Sindangan *Phil.* 61 G5
Sindangbarang *Indonesia* 63 G12

Sinde *Zambia* 87 F2
Sindelfingen *Germany* 25 G4
Sindh = Indus → *Pakistan* 68 G2
Sindh □ *Pakistan* 68 G3
Sındırgı *Turkey* 47 B10
Sindou *Burkina Faso* 82 C3
Sindri *India* 69 H12
Sine → *Senegal* 82 C1
Sinegorskiy *Russia* 35 G5
Sinekli *Turkey* 45 E12
Sinelnikovo = Synelnykove *Ukraine* 33 H8
Sinendé *Benin* 83 C5
Sines *Portugal* 37 H2
Sines, C. de *Portugal* 37 H2
Sineu *Spain* 48 B10
Sinfra *Ivory C.* 82 D3
Sing Buri *Thailand* 64 E3
Singa *Sudan* 81 E3
Singalila △ *India* 69 F13
Singapore ■ *Asia* 65 d
Singapore, Straits of *Asia* 65 d
Singapore Changi ✈ (SIN) *Singapore* 65 M4
Singaraja *Indonesia* 62 F5
Singatoka = Sigatoka *Fiji* 91 a
Singen *Germany* 25 H4
Singida *Tanzania* 86 C3
Singida □ *Tanzania* 86 D3
Singkaling Hkamti *Burma* 67 G19
Singkang *Indonesia* 63 E6
Singkawang *Indonesia* 62 D3
Singkep *Indonesia* 62 E2
Singkil *Indonesia* 65 L1
Singleton *Australia* 95 E5
Singleton, Mt. *N. Terr., Australia* 92 D5
Singleton, Mt. *W. Austral., Australia* 93 E2
Singö *Sweden* 10 D12
Singoli *India* 68 G6
Singora = Songkhla *Thailand* 65 J3
Sinhŭng *N. Korea* 57 D14
Siniscóla *Italy* 42 B2
Sinj *Croatia* 41 E13
Sinjai *Indonesia* 63 F6
Sinjajevina *Montenegro* 44 D3
Sinjar *Iraq* 73 D9
Sinjār, Jabal *Iraq* 73 D9
Sinkat *Sudan* 80 D4
Sinkiang = Xinjiang Uygur Zizhiqu □ *China* 60 B3
Sinko *Guinea* 82 D3
Sinmak *N. Korea* 57 E14
Sinmi-do *N. Korea* 57 E13
Sínnai *Italy* 42 C2
Sinnamary *Fr. Guiana* 125 B8
Sinni → *Italy* 43 B9
Sinnuris *Egypt* 80 J7
Sinoie, Lacul *Romania* 29 F13
Sinop *Turkey* 72 A6
Sinop □ *Turkey* 72 B6
Sinor *India* 68 J5
Sinp'o *N. Korea* 57 E15
Sinsheim *Germany* 25 F4
Sinsk *Russia* 53 C13
Sintang *Indonesia* 62 D4
Sinton *U.S.A.* 116 G6
Sintra *Portugal* 37 G1
Sintra-Cascais △ *Portugal* 37 G1
Sinŭiju *N. Korea* 57 D13
Sinyukha → *Ukraine* 33 H6
Si'umu *Samoa* 91 b
Siuna *Nic.* 120 D3
Siuri *India* 69 H12
Siutghiol, Lacul *Romania* 29 F13
Sīvand *Iran* 71 D7
Sivas *Turkey* 72 C7
Sivas □ *Turkey* 72 C7
Sivaslı *Turkey* 47 C11
Siverek *Turkey* 73 D8
Sivrihisar *Turkey* 72 C4
Sîwa *Egypt* 80 B2
Sîwa, El Wâhât es *Egypt* 80 B2
Siwa Oasis = Sîwa, El Wâhât es *Egypt* 80 B2
Siwalik Range *Nepal* 69 F10
Siwan *India* 69 F11
Siwana *India* 68 G5
Six Cross Roads *Barbados* 121 g
Sixmilebridge *Ireland* 12 D3
Sixth Cataract *Sudan* 81 D3
Siyah Kuh, Kavīr-e *Iran* 71 C7
Siyâl, Jazâ'ir *Egypt* 80 C4
Siyäzän *Azerbaijan* 35 K9
Siziwang Qi *China* 56 D6
Sjælland *Denmark* 11 J5
Sjælland □ *Denmark* 11 J5
Sjællands Odde *Denmark* 11 J5
Sjenica *Serbia* 44 C3
Sjöbo *Sweden* 11 J7
Sjötofta *Sweden* 11 G7
Sjötorp *Sweden* 11 F8
Sjumen = Shumen *Bulgaria* 45 C10
Sjuntorp *Sweden* 11 F6
Skadarsko Jezero *Europe* 44 D3
Skadarsko Jezero △ *Montenegro* 44 D3
Skadovsk *Ukraine* 33 J7
Skælskør *Denmark* 11 J5
Skærbæk *Denmark* 11 J2

Sirakoro *Mali* 82 C3
Şiran *Turkey* 73 B8
Sirasso *Ivory C.* 82 D3
Sirathu *India* 69 G9
Sīrdān *Iran* 73 D13
Sire *Ethiopia* 81 F4
Siren *U.S.A.* 112 C7
Sirente-Velino △ *Italy* 41 F10
Sirer *Spain* 48 C7
Siret *Romania* 29 C11
Siret → *Romania* 29 E12
Sirghāyā *Syria* 74 B5
Şiria *Romania* 28 D6
Sirinat △ *Thailand* 65 a
Sirino, Mte. *Italy* 43 B8
Sīrjān *Iran* 71 D7
Sirmaur *India* 69 G9
Sirmilik △ *Canada* 101 C15
Sirna *Greece* 47 E9
Şirnak *Turkey* 73 D10
Sirohi *India* 68 G5
Sironj *India* 68 G7
Síros = Ermoupoli *Greece* 46 D6
Sirr, Nafud as *Si. Arabia* 70 E5
Sirretta Pk. *U.S.A.* 111 K8
Sīrrī *Iran* 71 E7
Sirsa *India* 68 E6
Sirsa → *India* 69 F8
Siruela *Spain* 37 G5
Sirvān → *Iran* 73 E12
Sisak *Croatia* 41 C13
Sisaket *Thailand* 64 E5
Sisante *Spain* 39 F2
Sisargas, Is. *Spain* 36 B2
Sishen *S. Africa* 88 D3
Sishui *Henan, China* 56 G7
Sishui *Shandong, China* 57 G9
Sisian *Armenia* 73 C12
Sisipuk L. *Canada* 103 B8
Sisophon *Cambodia* 64 F4
Sisseton *U.S.A.* 112 C5
Sissonne *France* 19 C10
Sisters *U.S.A.* 108 D3
Sisters, The *Seychelles* 85 b
Siswa Bazar *India* 69 F10
Sitakili *Mali* 82 C2
Sitamarhi *India* 69 F11
Sitampiky *Madag.* 89 B8
Sitapur *India* 69 F9
Siteki *Swaziland* 89 D5
Sitges *Spain* 38 D6
Sithonia *Greece* 44 F7
Sitia *Greece* 49 D8
Sitito-Ozima Ridge *Pac. Oc.* 96 E6
Sitka *U.S.A.* 102 B1
Sitoti *Botswana* 88 C3
Sitra *Egypt* 80 B2
Sittang Myit → *Burma* 67 L20
Sittard *Neths.* 17 C5
Sittensen *Germany* 24 B5
Sittingbourne *U.K.* 15 F8
Sittona *Eritrea* 81 E4
Sittoung = Sittang Myit → *Burma* 67 L20
Sittwe *Burma* 67 J18
Situbondo *Indonesia* 63 G16
Siuna *Nic.* 120 D3

Skaftafell *Iceland* 8 D5
Skaftafell △ *Iceland* 8 D5
Skagafjörður *Iceland* 8 D4
Skagastølstindane *Norway* 8 F12
Skagaströnd *Iceland* 8 D3
Skagen *Denmark* 11 G4
Skagern *Sweden* 10 E8
Skagerrak *Denmark* 11 G2
Skagit → *U.S.A.* 110 B4
Skagway *U.S.A.* 100 F4
Skala-Podilska *Ukraine* 29 B11
Skalat *Ukraine* 23 D13
Skalbmierz *Poland* 31 H7
Skálica *Slovak Rep.* 27 C10
Skalni Dol = Kamenyak *Bulgaria* 45 C10
Skanderborg *Denmark* 11 H3
Skåne *Sweden* 11 J7
Skåne län □ *Sweden* 11 H7
Skaneateles *U.S.A.* 115 D8
Skaneateles L. *U.S.A.* 115 D8
Skänninge *Sweden* 11 F9
Skärblacka *Sweden* 11 F9
Skardu *Pakistan* 69 B6
Skåre *Sweden* 10 E7
Skärhamn *Sweden* 11 G5
Skarszewy *Poland* 30 D5
Skaryszew *Poland* 31 G8
Skarżysko-Kamienna *Poland* 31 G7
Skattkärr *Sweden* 10 E7
Skattungbyn *Sweden* 10 C8
Skawina *Poland* 31 J6
Skebobruk *Sweden* 10 E12
Skeena → *Canada* 102 C2
Skeena Mts. *Canada* 102 B3
Skegness *U.K.* 14 D8
Skeldon = Corriverton *Guyana* 124 B7
Skeleton Coast *Namibia* 85 J2
Skeleton Coast △ *Namibia* 88 C1
Skellefteå *Sweden* 8 C19
Skellefteälven → *Sweden* 8 D19
Skelleftehamn *Sweden* 8 D19
Skender Vakuf *Bos.-H.* 28 F2
Skerries, The *U.K.* 14 D3
Skhidnytsya *Ukraine* 31 J10
Skhiza *Greece* 46 E3
Ski *Norway* 9 G14
Skiathos *Greece* 46 B5
Skibbereen *Ireland* 12 E2
Skiddaw *U.K.* 14 C4
Skidegate *Canada* 102 C2
Skidra *Greece* 44 F6
Skien *Norway* 9 G13
Skierniewice *Poland* 31 G7
Skihist, Mt. *Canada* 102 C4
Skikda *Algeria* 78 A7
Skillingaryd *Sweden* 11 G8
Skillinge *Sweden* 11 J8
Skilloura *Cyprus* 49 D12
Skinari, Akra *Greece* 46 C2
Skinnskatteberg *Sweden* 10 E9
Skipton *U.K.* 14 D5
Skiring, C. *Senegal* 82 C1
Skirmish Pt. *Australia* 94 A1
Skiropoula *Greece* 46 C6
Skiros *Greece* 46 C6
Skivarp *Sweden* 11 J7
Skive *Denmark* 11 H3
Skjálfandafljót → *Iceland* 8 D5
Skjálfandi *Iceland* 8 C5
Skjern *Denmark* 11 J2
Skjern → *Denmark* 11 J2
Skoczów *Poland* 31 J5
Škofja Loka *Slovenia* 41 B11
Skoghall *Sweden* 10 E7
Skogstorp *Sweden* 10 E10
Skoki *Poland* 31 F4
Skole *Ukraine* 23 D12
Skopelos *Greece* 46 B5
Skópi *Greece* 49 D8
Skopin *Russia* 32 F10
Skopje *Macedonia* 44 E5
Skopje ✈ (SKP) *Macedonia* 44 E5
Skórcz *Poland* 30 E5
Skørping *Denmark* 11 H3
Skövde *Sweden* 11 F7
Skovorodino *Russia* 53 D13
Skowhegan *U.S.A.* 113 C19
Skradin *Croatia* 41 E12
Skrea *Sweden* 11 H6
Skrunda *Latvia* 30 B9
Skrwa → *Poland* 31 F6
Skuleskogen △ *Sweden* 10 A12
Skull *Ireland* 12 E2
Skultorp *Sweden* 11 F7
Skultuna *Sweden* 10 E10
Skunk → *U.S.A.* 112 E8
Skuodas *Lithuania* 30 B8
Skurup *Sweden* 11 J7
Skutskär *Sweden* 10 D11
Skvyra *Ukraine* 23 D15
Skwierzyna *Poland* 31 F2
Skye *U.K.* 13 D2
Skykomish *U.S.A.* 108 C3
Skyros = Skiros *Greece* 46 C6

Skyttorp *Sweden* 10 D11
Slade Point *Australia* 94 b
Slade Pt. *Australia* 94 b
Slættaratindur *Færoe Is.* 8 E9
Slagelse *Denmark* 11 J5
Slamet *Indonesia* 63 G13
Slane *Ireland* 12 C5
Slaney → *Ireland* 12 D5
Slangberge *S. Africa* 88 E3
Slănic *Romania* 29 E10
Slano *Croatia* 44 D1
Slantsy *Russia* 32 C5
Slaný *Czech Rep.* 26 A7
Slask *Poland* 22 C9
Slatina *Croatia* 28 E2
Slatina *Romania* 29 F9
Slatina Timiş *Romania* 28 E7
Slatington *U.S.A.* 115 F9
Slaton *U.S.A.* 116 E4
Slave → *Canada* 102 A6
Slave Coast *W. Afr.* 83 D5
Slave Lake *Canada* 102 B6
Slave Pt. *Canada* 102 A5
Slavgorod *Russia* 52 D8
Slavinja *Serbia* 44 C6
Slavkov u Brna *Czech Rep.* 27 B9
Slavkovský Les △ *Czech Rep.* 26 A5
Slavonija *Europe* 28 E3
Slavonski Brod *Croatia* 28 E3
Slavsk *Russia* 30 C8
Slavska *Ukraine* 29 B8
Slavskoye *Russia* 30 D7
Slavuta *Ukraine* 23 C14
Slavyanka *Russia* 54 C5
Slavyanovo *Bulgaria* 45 C8
Slavyansk = Slovyansk *Ukraine* 33 H9
Slavyansk-na-Kubani *Russia* 33 K10
Slawa *Poland* 31 G3
Slawharad *Belarus* 23 B16
Sławno *Poland* 30 D3
Slawoborze *Poland* 30 E2
Sleaford *U.K.* 14 D7
Sleaford B. *Australia* 95 E2
Sleat, Sd. of *U.K.* 13 D3
Sleeper Is. *Canada* 101 F15
Sleeping Bear Dunes △ *U.S.A.* 112 C10
Sleepy Eye *U.S.A.* 112 C6
Slemon L. *Canada* 102 A5
Ślesin *Poland* 31 F5
Slide Mt. *U.S.A.* 115 E10
Slidell *U.S.A.* 117 F10
Sliema *Malta* 49 D2
Slieve Aughty *Ireland* 12 C3
Slieve Bloom *Ireland* 12 C4
Slieve Donard *U.K.* 12 B6
Slieve Gamph *Ireland* 12 B3
Slieve Gullion *U.K.* 12 B5
Slieve League *Ireland* 12 B3
Slieve Mish *Ireland* 12 D2
Slievenamon *Ireland* 12 D4
Sligeach = Sligo *Ireland* 12 B3
Sligo *Ireland* 12 B3
Sligo *U.S.A.* 114 E5
Sligo □ *Ireland* 12 B3
Sligo B. *Ireland* 12 B3
Slippery Rock *U.S.A.* 114 E4
Slite *Sweden* 11 G12
Slīteres △ *Latvia* 30 A9
Sliven *Bulgaria* 45 D10
Slivnitsa *Bulgaria* 44 D7
Sljeme *Croatia* 41 C12
Sloan *U.S.A.* 111 K11
Sloansville *U.S.A.* 115 D10
Slobidka *Ukraine* 29 C14
Slobozia *Moldova* 29 D14
Slobozia *Argeş, Romania* 29 F10
Slobozia *Ialomiţa, Romania* 29 F12
Slocan *Canada* 102 D5
Slomniki *Poland* 31 H7
Slonim *Belarus* 23 B13
Slough *U.K.* 15 F7
Slough □ *U.K.* 15 F7
Sloughhouse *U.S.A.* 110 G5
Slovak Rep. ■ *Europe* 27 C13
Slovakia = Slovak Rep. ■ *Europe* 27 C13
Slovenian Ore Mts. = Slovenské Rudohorie *Slovak Rep.* 27 C12
Slovenia ■ *Europe* 41 C11
Slovenija = Slovenia ■ *Europe* 41 C11
Slovenj Gradec *Slovenia* 41 B12
Slovenska = Slovak Rep. ■ *Europe* 27 C13
Slovenska Bistrica *Slovenia* 41 B12
Slovenske Konjice *Slovenia* 41 B12
Slovenské Rudohorie *Slovak Rep.* 27 C12
Slovenský Raj △ *Slovak Rep.* 27 C13
Slovyansk *Ukraine* 33 H9
Słowiński △ *Poland* 30 D4
Słubice *Poland* 31 F1
Sluch → *Ukraine* 23 C14

Sluis *Neths.* 17 C3
Slŭnchev Bryag *Bulgaria* 45 D11
Slunj *Croatia* 41 C12
Słupca *Poland* 31 F4
Słupia → *Poland* 30 D3
Słupsk *Poland* 30 D4
Slurry *S. Africa* 88 D4
Slutsk *Belarus* 23 B14
Slyne Hd. *Ireland* 12 C1
Slyudyanka *Russia* 53 D11
Småland *Sweden* 11 G9
Smålandsfarvandet *Denmark* 11 J5
Smålandsstenar *Sweden* 11 G7
Smalltree L. *Canada* 103 A8
Smallwood Res. *Canada* 105 B7
Smarhon *Belarus* 23 A14
Smarje *Slovenia* 41 B12
Smartt Syndicate Dam *S. Africa* 88 E3
Smartville *U.S.A.* 110 F5
Smeaton *Canada* 103 C8
Smedby *Sweden* 11 H10
Smederevo *Serbia* 44 B4
Smederevska Palanka *Serbia* 44 B4
Smedjebacken *Sweden* 10 D9
Smela = Smila *Ukraine* 33 H6
Smerwick Harbour *Ireland* 12 D1
Smethport *U.S.A.* 114 E6
Smidovich *Russia* 53 E14
Śmigiel *Poland* 31 F3
Smila *Ukraine* 33 H6
Smilyan *Bulgaria* 45 E8
Smith *Canada* 102 B6
Smith Center *U.S.A.* 112 F4
Smith I. *Canada* 101 E16
Smith Islands △ *Australia* 94 b
Smith River → *U.S.A.* 108 F2
Smithburne → *Australia* 94 B3
Smithers *Canada* 102 C3
Smithfield *S. Africa* 89 E4
Smithfield *N.C., U.S.A.* 117 D15
Smithfield *Utah, U.S.A.* 108 F8
Smiths Falls *Canada* 115 B9
Smithton *Australia* 95 G4
Smithville *Canada* 114 C5
Smithville *U.S.A.* 116 F6
Smoke Creek Desert *U.S.A.* 108 F4
Smoky → *Canada* 102 B5
Smoky Bay *Australia* 95 E1
Smoky Hill → *U.S.A.* 112 F5
Smoky Hills *U.S.A.* 112 F4
Smoky Lake *Canada* 102 C6
Smøla *Norway* 8 E13
Smolensk *Russia* 32 E7
Smolensk □ *Russia* 32 E7
Smolikas, Oros *Greece* 44 F4
Smolník *Slovak Rep.* 27 C13
Smolyan *Bulgaria* 45 E8
Smooth Rock Falls *Canada* 104 C3
Smoothstone L. *Canada* 103 C7
Smorgon = Smarhon *Belarus* 23 A14
Smotrych *Ukraine* 29 B11
Smotrych → *Ukraine* 29 B11
Smulţi *Romania* 29 E12
Smyadovo *Bulgaria* 45 C11
Smygehamn *Sweden* 11 J7
Smyrna = İzmir *Turkey* 47 C9
Smyrna *U.S.A.* 113 F16
Snæfell *Iceland* 8 D6
Snaefell *I. of Man* 14 C3
Snæfellsjökull *Iceland* 8 D2
Snake → *U.S.A.* 108 C4
Snake I. *Australia* 95 F4
Snake Range *U.S.A.* 108 G6
Snake River Plain *U.S.A.* 108 E7
Snasahögarna *Sweden* 10 A6
Snåsavatnet *Norway* 8 D15
Snedsted *Denmark* 11 H2
Sneek *Neths.* 17 A5
Sneem *Ireland* 12 E2
Sneeuberge *S. Africa* 88 E3
Snejbjerg *Denmark* 11 H2
Snelling *U.S.A.* 110 H6
Snezhnoye *Ukraine* 33 J10
Sněžka *Europe* 31 A8
Snežnik *Slovenia* 41 C11
Śniadowo *Poland* 31 E8
Sniardwy, Jezioro *Poland* 30 E9
Śnieżka *Europe* 26 A8
Snigirevka = Snihurivka *Ukraine* 33 J7
Snihurivka *Ukraine* 33 J7
Snina *Slovak Rep.* 27 C15
Snizort, L. *U.K.* 13 D2
Snøhetta *Norway* 8 E13
Snohomish *U.S.A.* 110 C4
Snoqualmie Pass *U.S.A.* 110 C5
Snoul *Cambodia* 65 F6
Snover *U.S.A.* 114 C2
Snow Hill *U.S.A.* 113 F16
Snow Lake *Canada* 103 C8
Snow Mt. *Calif., U.S.A.* 110 F4
Snow Mt. *Maine, U.S.A.* 115 A14
Snow Shoe *U.S.A.* 114 E7
Snowbird L. *Canada* 103 A8
Snowdon *U.K.* 14 D3
Snowdonia △ *U.K.* 14 D4
Snowdrift = Łutsel K'e *Canada* 103 A6

Snowdrift ➤ *Canada* 103 A6
Snowflake *U.S.A.* 109 J8
Snowshoe Pk. *U.S.A.* 108 B6
Snowtown *Australia* 95 E2
Snowville *U.S.A.* 108 F7
Snowy ➤ *Australia* 95 F4
Snowy Mt. *U.S.A.* 115 C10
Snowy Mts. *Australia* 95 F4
Snug Corner *Bahamas* 121 B5
Snug Harbour *Canada* 114 A4
Snyatyn *Ukraine* 29 B10
Snyder *Okla., U.S.A.* 116 D5
Snyder *Tex., U.S.A.* 116 E4
Soahanina *Madag.* 89 B7
Soalala *Madag.* 89 B8
Soaloka *Madag.* 89 B8
Soamanonga *Madag.* 89 C7
Soan ➤ *Pakistan* 68 C4
Soanierana-Ivongo *Madag.* 89 B8
Soanindraniny *Madag.* 89 B8
Şoarş *Romania* 29 E9
Soavina *Madag.* 89 C8
Soavinandriana *Madag.* 89 B8
Sob ➤ *Ukraine* 29 B14
Soba *Nigeria* 83 C6
Sobat, Nahr ➤ *Sudan* 81 F3
Soběslav *Czech Rep.* 26 B7
Sobhapur *India* 68 H8
Sobinka *Russia* 32 E11
Sobótka *Poland* 31 H3
Sobra *Croatia* 41 F14
Sobradinho, Represa de
  Brazil 125 E10
Sobral *Brazil* 125 D10
Sobrance *Slovak Rep.* 27 C15
Sobreira Formosa *Portugal* 36 F3
Soc Giang *Vietnam* 58 F6
Soc Trang *Vietnam* 65 H5
Soča ➤ *Europe* 26 E6
Socastee *U.S.A.* 117 E15
Sochaczew *Poland* 31 F7
Soch'e = Shache *China* 60 C2
Sochi *Russia* 35 J4
Sochos *Greece* 44 F7
Société, Îs. de la
  French Polynesia 97 J12
Society Is. = Société, Îs. de
  la *French Polynesia* 97 J12
Socompa, Portezuelo de
  Chile 126 A2
Socorro *N. Mex., U.S.A.* 109 J10
Socorro *Tex., U.S.A.* 116 F1
Socorro, I. *Mexico* 118 D2
Socotra *Yemen* 75 E5
Socovos *Spain* 39 G3
Socuéllamos *Spain* 39 F2
Soda L. *U.S.A.* 109 J5
Soda Plains *India* 69 B8
Soda Springs *U.S.A.* 108 E8
Sodankylä *Finland* 8 C22
Soddy-Daisy *U.S.A.* 117 D12
Söderala *Sweden* 10 C10
Söderåsen △ *Sweden* 11 H7
Söderbärke *Sweden* 10 D9
Söderfors *Sweden* 10 D11
Söderhamn *Sweden* 10 C11
Söderköping *Sweden* 11 F10
Södermanland *Sweden* 9 G17
Södermanlands län □
  Sweden 10 E10
Södertälje *Sweden* 10 E11
Sodiri *Sudan* 81 E2
Sodo *Ethiopia* 81 F4
Södra Dellen *Sweden* 10 C10
Södra Finnskoga *Sweden* 10 D6
Södra Sandby *Sweden* 11 J7
Södra Ulvön *Sweden* 10 B12
Södra Vi *Sweden* 11 G9
Sodus *U.S.A.* 114 C7
Sodwana Bay △ *S. Africa* 89 D5
Soe *Indonesia* 92 A3
Soekmekaar = Morebeng
  S. Africa 89 C4
Soest *Germany* 24 D4
Soest *Neths.* 17 B5
Sofades *Greece* 46 B4
Sofala □ *Mozam.* 89 B5
Sofara *Mali* 82 C4
Sofia = Sofiya *Bulgaria* 44 D7
Sofia ➤ *Madag.* 89 B8
Sofievka *Ukraine* 33 H7
Sofiko *Greece* 46 D5
Sofiya *Bulgaria* 44 D7
Sofiya □ *Bulgaria* 44 D7
Sofiya ✈ (SOF) *Bulgaria* 44 D7
Sofrana *Greece* 47 E8
Sõfu-Gan *Japan* 55 K10
Sogakofe *Ghana* 83 D5
Sogamoso *Colombia* 124 B4
Sogār *Iran* 71 E8
Sögel *Germany* 24 C3
Sogndalsfjøra *Norway* 8 F12
Søgne *Norway* 9 G12
Sognefjorden *Norway* 8 F11
Söğüt *Bilecik, Turkey* 47 A12
Söğüt *Burdur, Turkey* 47 D11
Söğüt Dağı *Turkey* 47 D11
Söğütköy *Turkey* 47 E10
Soh *Iran* 71 C6

Sohâg *Egypt* 80 B3
Sohagpur *India* 68 H8
Soignies *Belgium* 17 D4
Soin *Burkina Faso* 82 C4
Soira *Eritrea* 81 E4
Soissons *France* 19 C10
Sōja *Japan* 55 G6
Sojat *India* 68 G5
Sok ➤ *Russia* 34 D10
Sokal *Ukraine* 23 C13
Sokcho *S. Korea* 57 E15
Söke *Turkey* 47 D9
Sokelo *Dem. Rep. of the Congo* 87 D1
Sokhumi *Georgia* 35 J5
Soko Banja *Serbia* 44 C5
Sokodé *Togo* 83 D5
Sokol *Russia* 32 C11
Sokolac *Bos.-H.* 28 G3
Sokółka *Poland* 31 E10
Sokolo *Ségou, Mali* 82 C3
Sokolo *Sikasso, Mali* 82 C3
Sokolov *Czech Rep.* 26 A5
Sokołów Małopolski *Poland* 31 H9
Sokołów Podlaski *Poland* 31 F9
Sokoły *Poland* 31 F9
Sokoto *Nigeria* 83 C6
Sokoto □ *Nigeria* 83 C6
Sokoto ➤ *Nigeria* 83 C6
Sokyrnytsya *Ukraine* 29 B8
Sokyryany *Ukraine* 29 B12
Sol Iletsk *Russia* 52 D6
Sola ➤ *Poland* 31 H6
Solai *Kenya* 86 B4
Solan *India* 68 D7
Solana Beach *U.S.A.* 111 N9
Solano *Phil.* 61 C4
Solapur *India* 66 L9
Solca *Romania* 29 C10
Solda Gölü *Turkey* 47 D11
Soldăneşti *Moldova* 29 C13
Soldeu *Andorra* 38 C6
Soldotna *U.S.A.* 100 E1
Soléa *Cyprus* 49 D12
Solec Kujawski *Poland* 31 E5
Soledad *Colombia* 124 A4
Soledad *U.S.A.* 110 J5
Soledad *Venezuela* 124 B6
Solent, The *U.K.* 15 G6
Solenzara *France* 21 G13
Solesmes *France* 19 B10
Solfonntaggen *Norway* 9 F12
Solhan *Turkey* 73 C9
Soligorsk = Salihorsk
  Belarus 23 B14
Solihull *U.K.* 15 E6
Solikamsk *Russia* 52 D6
Solila *Madag.* 89 C8
Solimões = Amazonas ➤
  S. Amer. 125 D8
Solin *Croatia* 41 E13
Solingen *Germany* 24 D3
Söll *Austria* 25 H8
Sollebrunn *Sweden* 11 F6
Sollefteå *Sweden* 10 A11
Sollentuna *Sweden* 10 E11
Sóller *Spain* 48 B9
Sollerön *Sweden* 10 D8
Solling *Germany* 24 D5
Solling-Vogler △ *Germany* 24 D5
Solnechnogorsk *Russia* 32 D9
Solo ➤ *Indonesia* 63 G15
Solofra *Italy* 43 B7
Sologne *France* 19 E8
Solok *Indonesia* 62 E2
Sololá *Guatemala* 120 D1
Sololo *Kenya* 86 B4
Solomon, N. Fork ➤ *U.S.A.* 112 F4
Solomon, S. Fork ➤ *U.S.A.* 112 F4
Solomon Is. ■ *Pac. Oc.* 90 B8
Solomon Rise *Pac. Oc.* 96 G7
Solon *China* 60 B7
Solon Springs *U.S.A.* 112 B8
Solor *Indonesia* 63 F6
Solotcha *Russia* 32 E10
Solothurn *Switz.* 25 H3
Solothurn □ *Switz.* 25 H3
Solotvyn *Ukraine* 29 B9
Solsona *Spain* 38 C6
Solt *Hungary* 28 D4
Šolta *Croatia* 41 E13
Solţānābād *Khorāsān, Iran* 71 C8
Solţānābād *Khorāsān, Iran* 71 B8
Soltau *Germany* 24 C5
Soltsy *Russia* 32 C6
Solunska Glava *Macedonia* 44 E5
Solvang *U.S.A.* 111 L6
Solvay *U.S.A.* 115 C8
Sölvesborg *Sweden* 11 H8
Solway Firth *U.K.* 14 C4
Solwezi *Zambia* 87 E2
Sõma *Japan* 54 F10
Soma *Turkey* 47 B9
Somabhula *Zimbabwe* 89 B4
Somali Pen. *Africa* 76 F8
Somali Rep. ■ *Africa* 75 F4
Somalia = Somali Rep. ■
  Africa 75 F4
Somaliland □ *Somali Rep.* 75 F4
Sombernon *France* 19 E11

Sombor *Serbia* 28 E4
Sombra *Canada* 114 D2
Sombrerete *Mexico* 118 C4
Sombrero *Anguilla* 121 C7
Şomcuta Mare *Romania* 29 C8
Somdari *India* 68 G5
Someido ➤ *Spain* 36 B4
Somers *U.S.A.* 108 B6
Somerset *Ky., U.S.A.* 113 G11
Somerset *Mass., U.S.A.* 115 E13
Somerset *Pa., U.S.A.* 114 F5
Somerset □ *U.K.* 15 F5
Somerset East *S. Africa* 88 E4
Somerset I. *Canada* 100 C13
Somerset West *S. Africa* 88 E2
Somersworth *U.S.A.* 115 C14
Somerton *U.S.A.* 109 K6
Somerville *U.S.A.* 115 F10
Someş ➤ *Romania* 28 C7
Someşul Mare ➤ *Romania* 29 C8
Somme □ *France* 19 C9
Somme ➤ *France* 19 B8
Somme, B. de la *France* 18 B8
Sommen *Jönköping, Sweden* 11 F8
Sommen *Östergötland, Sweden* 11 F9
Sommepy-Tahure *France* 19 C11
Sömmerda *Germany* 24 D7
Sommesous *France* 19 D11
Sommières *France* 21 E8
Somnath *India* 68 J4
Somogy □ *Hungary* 28 D2
Somogyszob *Hungary* 28 D2
Somosomo *Fiji* 91 a
Somosomo Str. *Fiji* 91 a
Somoto *Nic.* 120 D2
Sompolno *Poland* 31 F5
Somport, Tunnel de *Spain* 38 C4
Son ➤ *India* 69 G11
Son Ha *Vietnam* 64 E7
Son Hoa *Vietnam* 64 F7
Son La *Vietnam* 58 B4
Son Morrell *Spain* 48 B10
Son Rapinya *Spain* 48 B9
Son Sardina *Spain* 48 B9
Son Sera *Spain* 48 B10
Son Servera *Spain* 38 F8
Son Tay *Vietnam* 58 G5
Soná *Panama* 120 E3
Sonamarg *India* 69 B6
Sonamukhi *India* 69 H12
Sonar ➤ *India* 69 G8
Sondags ➤ *S. Africa* 88 E4
Sóndalo *Italy* 40 B7
Sondar *India* 69 C6
Sønder Felding *Denmark* 11 J2
Sønder Omme *Denmark* 11 J2
Sønderborg *Denmark* 11 K3
Sondershausen *Germany* 24 D6
Sóndrio *Italy* 40 B6
Sone *Mozam.* 87 F3
Sonepur *India* 67 J13
Song *Nigeria* 83 D7
Song *Thailand* 64 C3
Song Cau *Vietnam* 64 F7
Song Hong ➤ *Vietnam* 58 F5
Song Xian *China* 56 G7
Songan *Indonesia* 63 J18
Songea *Tanzania* 87 E4
Songeons *France* 19 C8
Songhua Hu *China* 57 C14
Songhua Jiang ➤ *China* 60 B8
Songimvelo △ *S. Africa* 89 D5
Songjiang *China* 59 B13
Songjin = Kimch'aek
  N. Korea 57 D15
Songkan *China* 58 C6
Songkhla *Thailand* 65 J3
Songming *China* 58 E4
Songnim *N. Korea* 57 E13
Songo *Mozam.* 87 F3
Songo *Sudan* 79 G10
Songpan *China* 58 A4
Songtao *China* 58 C7
Songwe *Dem. Rep. of the Congo* 86 C2
Songwe ➤ *Africa* 87 D3
Songxi *China* 59 D12
Songzi *China* 59 B8
Sonhat *India* 69 H10
Sonid Youqi *China* 56 C7
Sonipat *India* 68 E7
Sonkach *India* 68 H7
Sonkovo *Russia* 32 D9
Sonmiani *Pakistan* 68 G2
Sonmiani B. *Pakistan* 68 G2
Sono ➤ *Brazil* 125 E9
Sonoma *U.S.A.* 110 G4
Sonora *Calif., U.S.A.* 110 H6
Sonora *Tex., U.S.A.* 116 F4
Sonora □ *Mexico* 118 B2
Sonora ➤ *Mexico* 118 B2
Sonoran Desert *U.S.A.* 111 L12
Sonoyta *Mexico* 118 A2
Sonqor *Iran* 73 E12
Sonseca *Spain* 37 F7
Sonsonate *El Salv.* 120 D2
Sonstorp *Sweden* 11 F9
Sonthofen *Germany* 25 H6
Soochow = Suzhou *China* 59 B13

Sooke *Canada* 110 B3
Soomaaliya = Somali
  Rep. ■ *Africa* 75 F4
Sop Hao *Laos* 58 G5
Sop Prap *Thailand* 64 D2
Sopelana *Spain* 38 B2
Sopi *Indonesia* 63 D7
Sopo, Nahr ➤ *Sudan* 81 F2
Sopot *Bulgaria* 45 D8
Sopot *Poland* 30 D5
Sopot *Serbia* 44 B4
Sopotnica *Macedonia* 44 E5
Sopron *Hungary* 28 C1
Sopur *India* 69 B6
Sora *Italy* 41 G10
Sorah *Pakistan* 68 F3
Soraon *India* 69 G9
Sorbas *Spain* 39 H2
Sörbygden *Sweden* 10 B10
Sord = Swords *Ireland* 12 C5
Sore *France* 20 D3
Sorel-Tracy *Canada* 104 C5
Soresina *Italy* 40 C6
Sörforsa *Sweden* 10 C10
Sörgono *Italy* 42 B2
Sorgues *France* 21 D8
Sorgun *Turkey* 72 C6
Soria *Spain* 38 D2
Soria □ *Spain* 38 D2
Soriano *Uruguay* 126 C4
Soriano nel Cimino *Italy* 41 F9
Sorkh, Kuh-e *Iran* 71 C8
Sorkheh *Iran* 71 C7
Sorø *Denmark* 11 J5
Soro *Guinea* 82 C3
Soroca *Moldova* 29 B13
Sorocaba *Brazil* 127 A6
Soroki = Soroca *Moldova* 29 B13
Sorong *Indonesia* 63 E8
Soroni *Greece* 49 C10
Soroti *Uganda* 86 B3
Sørøya *Norway* 8 A20
Sørøysundet *Norway* 8 A20
Sorraia ➤ *Portugal* 37 G2
Sorrell *Australia* 95 G4
Sorrento *Italy* 43 B7
Sorsele *Sweden* 8 D17
Sörsjön *Sweden* 10 C7
Sorso *Italy* 42 B1
Sorsogon *Phil.* 61 E6
Sortavala *Russia* 32 B5
Sortino *Italy* 43 E8
Sortland *Norway* 8 B16
Sortot *Sudan* 80 D3
Sorvizhi *Russia* 34 B9
Sos del Rey Católico *Spain* 38 C3
Soscumica, L. *Canada* 104 B4
Sösdala *Sweden* 11 H7
Sosna ➤ *Russia* 33 F10
Sosnovka *Kirov, Russia* 34 B10
Sosnovka *Tambov, Russia* 34 D5
Sosnovyy Bor *Russia* 32 C5
Sosnowiec *Poland* 31 H6
Sospel *France* 21 E11
Sossus Vlei *Namibia* 88 C2
Šoštanj *Slovenia* 41 B12
Sösura *N. Korea* 57 C16
Sot ➤ *India* 69 F8
Sotavento *C. Verde Is.* 78 b
Sotik *Kenya* 86 C4
Sotkamo *Finland* 8 D23
Soto del Barco *Spain* 36 B4
Soto la Marina *Mexico* 119 C5
Soto la Marina ➤ *Mexico* 119 C5
Soto y Amío *Spain* 36 C5
Sotouboua *Togo* 83 D5
Sotrondio *Spain* 36 B5
Sotuta *Mexico* 119 C7
Souanké *Congo* 84 D2
Soubré *Ivory C.* 82 D3
Souda *Greece* 49 D6
Soudas, Ormos *Greece* 49 D6
Souderton *U.S.A.* 115 F9
Soufli *Greece* 45 E10
Soufrière *Guadeloupe* 120 b
Soufrière *St. Lucia* 121 f
Soufrière Bay *Dominica* 121 f
Souillac *France* 20 D5
Souilly *France* 19 C12
Soukhouma *Laos* 64 E5
Sŏul = Seoul *S. Korea* 57 F14
Soulac-sur-Mer *France* 20 C2
Soulougou *Burkina Faso* 83 C5
Soultz-sous-Forêts *France* 19 D14
Sound, The = Øresund
  Europe 11 J6
Sound, The *U.K.* 15 G3
Sounio, Akra *Greece* 46 D6
Sources, Mt. aux *Lesotho* 89 D4
Soure *Brazil* 125 D9
Soure *Portugal* 36 E2
Souris *Man., Canada* 103 D8
Souris *P.E.I., Canada* 105 C7
Souris ➤ *N. Amer.* 112 A4
Sourou ➤ *Africa* 82 C4
Sourpi *Greece* 46 B5
Sousa *Brazil* 125 E11
Sousel *Portugal* 37 G3

Sousse *Tunisia* 79 A8
Soustons *France* 20 E2
Sout ➤ *S. Africa* 88 E2
South Africa ■ *Africa* 88 E3
South America 122 E5
South Aulatsivik I. *Canada* 105 A7
South Australia □ *Australia* 95 E2
South Australian Basin
  Ind. Oc. 96 L4
South Ayrshire □ *U.K.* 13 F4
South Baldy Pk. *U.S.A.* 109 J10
South Bass I. *U.S.A.* 114 E2
South Bend *Ind., U.S.A.* 112 E10
South Bend *Wash., U.S.A.* 110 D3
South Boston *U.S.A.* 113 G14
South Branch *Canada* 105 C8
South Brook *Canada* 105 C8
South Bruny I. *Australia* 95 G4
South Carolina □ *U.S.A.* 117 E14
South Charleston *U.S.A.* 113 F13
South China Sea *Asia* 62 C4
South Cumberland Is. △
  Australia 94 b
South Dakota □ *U.S.A.* 112 C4
South Dayton *U.S.A.* 114 D5
South Deerfield *U.S.A.* 115 D12
South Downs *U.K.* 15 G7
South East C. *Australia* 95 G4
South East Is. *Australia* 93 F3
South Esk ➤ *U.K.* 13 E6
South Fiji Basin *Pac. Oc.* 96 K9
South Foreland *U.K.* 15 F9
South Fork American ➤
  U.S.A. 110 G5
South Fork Feather ➤
  U.S.A. 110 F5
South Fork Grand ➤
  U.S.A. 112 C2
South Fork Milk ➤ *U.S.A.* 108 B10
South Fork Republican ➤
  U.S.A. 112 E3
South Georgia *Antarctica* 128 G9
South Gloucestershire □
  U.K. 15 F5
South Hadley *U.S.A.* 115 D12
South Haven *U.S.A.* 112 D10
South Henik L. *Canada* 103 A9
South Horr *Kenya* 86 B4
South I. *Kenya* 86 B4
South I. *N.Z.* 91 F3
South Indian Lake *Canada* 103 B9
South Invercargill *N.Z.* 91 G2
South Island △ *Kenya* 86 B4
South Kitui △ *Kenya* 86 C4
South Knife ➤ *Canada* 103 B10
South Koel ➤ *India* 69 H11
South Korea ■ *Asia* 57 G15
South Lake Tahoe *U.S.A.* 110 G6
South Lanarkshire □ *U.K.* 13 F5
South Loup ➤ *U.S.A.* 112 E4
South Luangwa △ *Zambia* 87 E3
South Magnetic Pole
  Antarctica 5 C9
South Milwaukee *U.S.A.* 112 D10
South Molton *U.K.* 15 F4
South Moose L. *Canada* 103 C8
South Nahanni ➤ *Canada* 102 A4
South Nation ➤ *Canada* 115 A9
South Natuna Is. = Natuna
  Selatan, Kepulauan
  Indonesia 62 D3
South Negril Pt. *Jamaica* 120 a
South Orkney Is. *Antarctica* 5 C18
South Ossetia □ *Georgia* 35 J7
South Otselic *U.S.A.* 115 D9
South Pagai, I. = Pagai
  Selatan, Pulau *Indonesia* 62 E2
South Paris *U.S.A.* 115 B14
South Pittsburg *U.S.A.* 117 D12
South Platte ➤ *U.S.A.* 112 E3
South Pole *Antarctica* 5 E
South Porcupine *Canada* 104 C3
South Portland *U.S.A.* 113 D18
South Pt. *Barbados* 121 g
South Pt. *U.S.A.* 114 B1
South River *Canada* 104 C4
South River *U.S.A.* 115 F10
South Ronaldsay *U.K.* 13 C6
South Rukuru ➤ *Malawi* 87 E3
South Sandwich Is. *Antarctica* 5 B1
South Sandwich Trench
  Atl. Oc. 5 B1
South Saskatchewan ➤
  Canada 103 C7
South Seal ➤ *Canada* 103 B9
South Shetland Is. *Antarctica* 5 C18
South Shields *U.K.* 14 C6
South Sioux City *U.S.A.* 112 D5
South Sister *U.S.A.* 108 D3
South Talpatti = New
  Moore I. *Ind. Oc.* 69 J13
South Taranaki Bight *N.Z.* 91 C5
South Tasman Rise *S. Ocean* 5 A10
South Thompson ➤ *Canada* 102 C4
South Twin I. *Canada* 104 B4
South Tyne ➤ *U.K.* 14 C5
South Uist *U.K.* 13 D1
South Valley *U.S.A.* 109 J10
South Wellesley Is. *Australia* 94 B2
South West C. *Australia* 95 G4

South West C. *N.Z.* 91 G1
South Williamsport *U.S.A.* 114 E8
South Yorkshire □ *U.K.* 14 D6
Southampton *Canada* 114 B3
Southampton *U.K.* 15 G6
Southampton *U.S.A.* 115 F12
Southampton □ *U.K.* 15 G6
Southampton I. *Canada* 101 E15
Southaven *U.S.A.* 117 D9
Southbank *Canada* 102 C3
Southbridge *N.Z.* 91 E4
Southbridge *U.S.A.* 115 D12
Southend *Canada* 103 B8
Southend-on-Sea *U.K.* 15 F8
Southend-on-Sea □ *U.K.* 15 F8
Southern = Janub □ *Sudan* 81 F2
Southern = Yedebub
  Biheroch Bihereseboch
  na Hizboch □ *Ethiopia* 81 F4
Southern = Yuzhnyy □
  Russia 35 H5
Southern □ *Malawi* 87 F4
Southern □ *S. Leone* 82 D2
Southern □ *Zambia* 87 F2
Southern Alps *N.Z.* 91 E3
Southern Cross *Australia* 93 F2
Southern Indian L. *Canada* 103 B9
Southern Lau Group *Fiji* 91 a
Southern Ocean *Antarctica* 5 C6
Southern Pines *U.S.A.* 117 D15
Southern Uplands *U.K.* 13 F5
Southington *U.S.A.* 115 E12
Southland □ *N.Z.* 91 F1
Southold *U.S.A.* 115 E12
Southport *Australia* 95 D5
Southport *U.K.* 14 D4
Southport *U.S.A.* 114 D8
Southwest △ *Australia* 95 G4
Southwest Pacific Basin
  Pac. Oc. 5 A12
Southwold *U.K.* 15 E9
Southwood △ *Australia* 95 D5
Soutpansberg *S. Africa* 89 C4
Souvigny *France* 19 F10
Sovata *Romania* 29 D10
Soverato *Italy* 43 D9
Sovetsk *Kaliningrad, Russia* 30 D8
Sovetsk *Kirov, Russia* 34 B9
Sovetskaya Gavan *Russia* 53 E15
Soviciille *Italy* 41 E8
Soweto *S. Africa* 89 D4
Sowma'eh Sarā *Iran* 73 D13
Sōya-Kaikyō = La Perouse
  Str. *Asia* 54 B11
Sōya-Misaki *Japan* 54 B10
Soyaux *France* 20 C4
Soyo *Angola* 84 F2
Sozh ➤ *Belarus* 23 B16
Sozopol *Bulgaria* 45 D11
Spa *Belgium* 17 D5
Spain ■ *Europe* 7 H5
Spalding *Australia* 95 E2
Spalding *U.K.* 14 E7
Spanaway *U.S.A.* 110 C4
Spangler *U.S.A.* 114 F6
Spaniard *Canada* 104 C3
Spanish Fork *U.S.A.* 108 F8
Spanish Town *Br. Virgin Is.* 121 e
Spanish Town *Jamaica* 120 a
Sparks *U.S.A.* 110 F7
Sparreholm *Sweden* 10 E10
Sparta = Sparti *Greece* 46 D4
Sparta *Mich., U.S.A.* 113 D11
Sparta *N.J., U.S.A.* 115 E10
Sparta *Wis., U.S.A.* 112 D8
Spartanburg *U.S.A.* 117 D14
Sparti *Greece* 46 D4
Spartivento, C. *Calabria, Italy* 43 E9
Spartivento, C. *Sard., Italy* 42 D1
Sparwood *Canada* 102 D6
Spas-Demensk *Russia* 32 E7
Spas-Klepiki *Russia* 32 E11
Spass Dalniy *Russia* 54 B6
Spassk-Ryazanskiy *Russia* 32 E11
Spatha, Akra *Greece* 49 D5
Spatsizi ➤ *Canada* 102 B3
Spatsizi Plateau
  Wilderness △ *Canada* 102 B3
Spean ➤ *U.K.* 13 E4
Spearfish *U.S.A.* 112 C3
Spearman *U.S.A.* 116 C4
Speculator *U.S.A.* 115 C10
Speia *Moldova* 29 D14
Speightstown *Barbados* 121 g
Speke Gulf *Tanzania* 86 C3
Spello *Italy* 41 F9
Spence Bay = Taloyoak
  Canada 100 D13
Spencer *Idaho, U.S.A.* 108 D7
Spencer *Iowa, U.S.A.* 112 D6
Spencer *N.Y., U.S.A.* 115 D8
Spencer *Nebr., U.S.A.* 112 D4
Spencer, C. *Australia* 95 F2
Spencer B. *Namibia* 88 D1
Spencer G. *Australia* 95 E2
Spencerville *Canada* 115 B9
Spennymoor *U.K.* 14 C6
Spenser Mts. *N.Z.* 91 E4
Spentrup *Denmark* 11 H4

Sperchios → Greece 46 C4
Sperrin Mts. U.K. 12 B5
Spessart Germany 25 F5
Spetses Greece 46 D5
Spey → U.K. 13 D5
Speyer Germany 25 F4
Spezand Pakistan 68 E2
Spezzano Albanese Italy 43 C9
Spiddle Ireland 12 C2
Spiekeroog Germany 24 B3
Spiez Switz. 25 J3
Spili Greece 49 D6
Spilimbergo Italy 41 B9
Spīn Būldak Afghan. 68 D2
Spinalonga Greece 49 D7
Spinazzola Italy 43 B9
Spineni Romania 29 F9
Spinifex ○ Australia 93 E4
Spirit Lake U.S.A. 110 D4
Spirit River Canada 102 B5
Spiritwood Canada 103 C7
Spišská Nová Ves
  Slovak Rep. 27 C13
Spišské Podhradie
  Slovak Rep. 27 B13
Spital Austria 26 D7
Spithead U.K. 15 G6
Spittal an der Drau Austria 26 E6
Spitzbergen = Svalbard Arctic 4 B8
Spjelkavik Norway 8 E12
Split Croatia 41 E13
Split ✕ (SPU) Croatia 41 E13
Split L. Canada 103 B9
Split Lake Canada 103 B9
Splitski Kanal Croatia 41 E13
Splügenpass Switz. 25 J5
Spofford U.S.A. 116 G4
Spokane U.S.A. 108 C5
Spoleto Italy 41 F9
Spooner U.S.A. 112 C8
Sporyy Navolok, Mys Russia 52 B7
Sprague U.S.A. 108 C5
Spratly I. S. China Sea 62 C4
Spratly Is. S. China Sea 62 C4
Spray U.S.A. 108 D4
Spreča → Bos.-H. 28 F3
Spree → Germany 24 C9
Spreewald Germany 24 D9
Spremberg Germany 24 D10
Sprengisandur Iceland 8 D4
Spring City U.S.A. 115 F9
Spring Creek U.S.A. 108 F6
Spring Garden U.S.A. 110 F6
Spring Hall Barbados 121 g
Spring Hill U.S.A. 117 G13
Spring Mts. U.S.A. 111 J11
Spring Valley Calif., U.S.A. 111 N10
Spring Valley Nev., U.S.A. 111 J11
Springbok S. Africa 88 D2
Springboro U.S.A. 114 E4
Springdale Canada 105 C8
Springdale U.S.A. 116 C7
Springe Germany 24 C5
Springer U.S.A. 109 H11
Springerville U.S.A. 109 J9
Springfield Canada 114 D4
Springfield N.Z. 91 E3
Springfield Colo., U.S.A. 109 H12
Springfield Ill., U.S.A. 112 F9
Springfield Mass., U.S.A. 115 D12
Springfield Mo., U.S.A. 112 G7
Springfield Ohio, U.S.A. 113 F12
Springfield Oreg., U.S.A. 108 D2
Springfield Tenn., U.S.A. 117 C11
Springfield Vt., U.S.A. 115 C12
Springfontein S. Africa 88 E4
Springhill Canada 105 C7
Springhill U.S.A. 116 E8
Springhouse Canada 102 C4
Springs S. Africa 89 D4
Springsure Australia 94 C4
Springvale U.S.A. 115 C14
Springville Calif., U.S.A. 110 J8
Springville N.Y., U.S.A. 114 D6
Springville Utah, U.S.A. 108 F8
Springwater U.S.A. 114 D7
Spruce-Creek U.S.A. 114 F6
Spruce Knob-Seneca
  Rocks △ U.S.A. 113 F14
Spruce Mt. U.S.A. 115 B12
Sprucedale Canada 114 A5
Spur U.S.A. 116 E4
Spurn Hd. U.K. 14 D8
Spuž Montenegro 44 D3
Spuzzum Canada 102 D4
Squam L. U.S.A. 115 C13
Squamish Canada 102 D4
Square Islands Canada 105 B8
Squillace, G. di Italy 43 D9
Squinzano Italy 43 B11
Squires, Mt. Australia 93 E4
Srbac Bos.-H. 28 E2
Srbica Kosovo 44 D4
Srbija = Serbia ■ Europe 44 C4
Srbobran Serbia 28 E4
Sre Ambel Cambodia 65 G4
Sre Khtum Cambodia 65 F6
Sre Umbell = Sre Ambel
  Cambodia 65 G4

Srebrenica Bos.-H. 28 F4
Sredinny Ra. = Sredinnyy
  Khrebet Russia 53 D17
Sredinnyy Khrebet Russia 53 D17
Središče Slovenia 41 B13
Sredna Gora Bulgaria 45 D8
Srednekolymsk Russia 53 C16
Sredni Rodopi Bulgaria 45 E8
Srednogorie Bulgaria 45 D8
Śrem Poland 31 F4
Sremska Mitrovica Serbia 28 F4
Sremski Karlovci Serbia 28 E4
Srepok → Cambodia 64 F6
Sretensk Russia 53 D12
Sri Aman Malaysia 62 D4
Sri Lanka ■ Asia 66 R12
Srikakulam India 67 K13
Srinagar India 69 B6
Środa Śląska Poland 31 G3
Środa Wielkopolski Poland 31 F4
Srono Indonesia 63 J17
Srpska Crnja Serbia 28 E5
Srpski Itebej Serbia 28 E5
Ssese Is. = Sese Is. Uganda 86 C3
Staaten → Australia 94 B3
Staaten River △ Australia 94 B3
Staberhuk Germany 24 A7
Stade Germany 24 B5
Stadskanaal Neths. 17 A6
Stadtallendorf Germany 24 E5
Stadthagen Germany 24 C5
Stadtlohn Germany 24 D2
Stadtroda Germany 24 E7
Staffa U.K. 13 E2
Staffanstorp Sweden 11 J7
Stafford U.K. 14 E5
Stafford U.S.A. 112 G4
Stafford Springs U.S.A. 115 E12
Staffordshire □ U.K. 14 E5
Stagnone Italy 42 E5
Stagnone di Marsala △ Italy 42 E5
Staines U.K. 15 F7
Stainz Austria 26 E8
Stakhanov Ukraine 33 H10
Stalać Serbia 44 C5
Stalida Greece 49 D7
Stallarholmen Sweden 10 E11
Ställdalen Sweden 10 E8
Stalowa Wola Poland 31 H9
Stalybridge U.K. 14 D5
Stamford Australia 94 C3
Stamford U.K. 15 E7
Stamford Conn., U.S.A. 115 E11
Stamford N.Y., U.S.A. 115 D10
Stamford Tex., U.S.A. 116 E5
Stampriet Namibia 88 C2
Stamps U.S.A. 116 E8
Stančevo = Kalipetrovo
  Bulgaria 45 B11
Standerton S. Africa 89 D4
Standish U.S.A. 113 D12
Stanford S. Africa 88 E2
Stanford U.S.A. 108 C8
Stånga Sweden 11 G12
Stanger S. Africa 89 D5
Stängselåsen =
  Salpausselkä Finland 32 B4
Stanišić Serbia 28 E4
Stanislaus → U.S.A. 110 H5
Stanisławów Poland 31 F8
Stanley Australia 95 G4
Stanley Falk. Is. 128 G5
Stanley U.K. 14 C6
Stanley Idaho, U.S.A. 108 D6
Stanley N. Dak., U.S.A. 112 A2
Stanley N.Y., U.S.A. 114 D7
Stanley Mission Canada 103 B8
Stannards U.S.A. 114 D7
Stanovoy Khrebet Russia 53 D14
Stanovoy Ra. = Stanovoy
  Khrebet Russia 53 D14
Stansmore Ra. Australia 92 D4
Stansted, London ✕ (STN)
  U.K. 15 F8
Stanthorpe Australia 95 D5
Stanton U.S.A. 116 E4
Stanwood U.S.A. 110 B4
Staples Canada 114 D2
Staples U.S.A. 112 B6
Stapleton U.S.A. 112 E3
Stąporków Poland 31 G7
Star City Canada 103 C8
Star Lake U.S.A. 115 B9
Stará L'ubovňa Slovak Rep. 27 B13
Stara Moravica Serbia 28 E4
Stara Pazova Serbia 28 E4
Stara Planina Bulgaria 44 C7
Stara Sil Ukraine 31 J9
Stará Turá Slovak Rep. 27 C10
Stara Ushytsya Ukraine 29 B12
Stara Zagora Bulgaria 45 D9
Starachowice Poland 31 G8
Staraya Russa Russia 32 D6
Starbuck I. Kiribati 97 H12
Starchiojd Romania 29 E11
Starcke △ Australia 94 A2
Stargard Szczeciński Poland 30 E2
Stari Bar Montenegro 44 D3
Stari Trg Slovenia 41 C12
Staritsa Russia 32 D8

Starke U.S.A. 117 G13
Starkville U.S.A. 117 E10
Starnberg Germany 25 H7
Starnberger See Germany 25 H7
Starobilsk Ukraine 33 H10
Starodub Russia 33 F7
Starogard Gdański Poland 30 E5
Starokonstantinov =
  Starokonstyantyniv
  Ukraine 23 D14
Starokonstyantyniv Ukraine 23 D14
Starokozache Ukraine 29 D14
Starominskaya Russia 33 J10
Staroshcherbinovskaya
  Russia 33 J10
Start Pt. U.K. 15 G4
Stary Sącz Poland 31 J7
Staryy Biryuzyak Russia 35 H8
Staryy Chartoriysk Ukraine 23 C13
Staryy Krym Ukraine 33 K8
Staryy Oskol Russia 33 G9
Staryy Sambir Ukraine 31 J9
Stassfurt Germany 24 D7
Staszów Poland 31 H8
State College U.S.A. 114 F7
Stateline U.S.A. 110 G7
Staten, I. = Estados, I. de
  Los Argentina 128 G4
Staten I. U.S.A. 115 F10
Statesboro U.S.A. 117 E14
Statesville U.S.A. 117 D14
Statia = St. Eustatius
  W. Indies 121 C7
Stauffer U.S.A. 111 L7
Staunton Ill., U.S.A. 112 F9
Staunton Va., U.S.A. 113 F14
Stavanger Norway 9 G11
Staveley N.Z. 91 E3
Stavelot Belgium 17 D5
Stavern Norway 9 G14
Stavoren Neths. 17 B5
Stavropol Russia 35 H6
Stavropol □ Russia 35 G6
Stavros Cyprus 49 D11
Stavros Kriti, Greece 49 D6
Stavros Thessaloniki, Greece 44 F7
Stavros, Akra Greece 49 D6
Stavroupoli Greece 45 E8
Stawell Australia 95 F3
Stawell → Australia 94 C3
Stawiski Poland 30 E9
Stawiszyn Poland 31 G5
Stayner Canada 114 B4
Stayton U.S.A. 108 D2
Steamboat Springs U.S.A. 108 F10
Steblevë Albania 44 E4
Steele U.S.A. 112 B4
Steelton U.S.A. 114 F8
Steen River Canada 102 B5
Steens Mt. U.S.A. 108 E4
Steenwijk Neths. 17 B6
Steep Pt. Australia 93 E1
Steep Rock Canada 103 C9
Ştefan Vodă Moldova 29 D14
Ştefăneşti Romania 29 C12
Stefanie △ Ethiopia 81 G4
Stefanie L. = Chew Bahir
  Ethiopia 81 G4
Stefansson Bay Antarctica 5 C5
Stefansson I. Canada 101 C10
Stege Denmark 11 K6
Steierdorf Germany 25 F6
Steigerwald Germany 25 F6
Steigerwald △ Germany 25 F6
Steilacoom U.S.A. 110 C4
Steilrandberge Namibia 88 B1
Steinbach Canada 103 D9
Steinfurt Germany 24 C3
Steinhausen Namibia 88 C2
Steinheim Germany 24 D5
Steinhuder Meer Germany 24 C5
Steinhuder Meer △ Germany 24 C5
Steinkjer Norway 8 D14
Steinkopf S. Africa 88 D2
Steinwald △ Germany 25 F8
Stellarton Canada 105 C7
Stellenbosch S. Africa 88 E2
Stelvio, Paso dello Italy 40 B7
Stenay France 19 C12
Stendal Germany 24 C7
Stende Latvia 30 A9
Stenhamra Sweden 10 E11
Stenshuvud △ Sweden 11 J8
Stenstorp Sweden 11 F7
Stenungsund Sweden 11 F5
Steornabhaigh =
  Stornoway U.K. 13 C2
Stepanakert = Xankändi
  Azerbaijan 73 C12
Stepanavan Armenia 35 K7
Stephens Creek Australia 95 E3
Stephens I. Canada 102 C2
Stephens L. Canada 103 B9
Stephenville Canada 105 C8
Stephenville U.S.A. 116 E5
Stepnica Poland 30 E1
Steppe Asia 50 C7
Sterea Ellas □ Greece 46 C4
Sterkstroom S. Africa 88 E4

Sterling Colo., U.S.A. 108 F12
Sterling Ill., U.S.A. 112 E9
Sterling Kans., U.S.A. 112 F4
Sterling City U.S.A. 116 F4
Sterling Heights U.S.A. 113 D12
Sterling Run U.S.A. 114 E6
Sterlitamak Russia 52 D6
Sternberg Germany 24 B7
Šternberk Czech Rep. 27 B10
Sterzing = Vipiteno Italy 41 B8
Stettin = Szczecin Poland 30 E1
Stettiner Haff Germany 24 B10
Stettler Canada 102 C6
Steubenville U.S.A. 114 F4
Stevenage U.K. 15 F7
Stevens Point U.S.A. 112 C9
Stevenson U.S.A. 110 E5
Stevenson → Australia 95 D2
Stevenson L. Canada 103 C9
Stevensville U.S.A. 108 C6
Stevns Klint Denmark 11 J6
Stewart Canada 102 B3
Stewart U.S.A. 110 F7
Stewart → Canada 100 E4
Stewart, C. Australia 94 A1
Stewart, I. Chile 128 G2
Stewart I. N.Z. 91 G1
Stewarts Point U.S.A. 110 G3
Stewartville U.S.A. 112 D7
Stewiacke Canada 105 C7
Steynsburg S. Africa 88 E4
Steyr Austria 26 C7
Steyr → Austria 26 C7
Steytlerville S. Africa 88 E3
Stia Italy 41 E8
Stigler U.S.A. 116 D7
Stigliano Italy 43 B9
Stigtomta Sweden 11 F10
Stikine → Canada 102 B2
Stilfontein S. Africa 88 D4
Stilida Greece 46 C4
Stillwater N.Z. 91 E3
Stillwater N.Y., U.S.A. 115 D11
Stillwater Okla., U.S.A. 116 C6
Stillwater Range U.S.A. 108 G4
Stillwater Res. U.S.A. 115 C9
Stilo, Pta. Italy 43 D9
Stilwell U.S.A. 116 D7
Stînga Nistrului □ Moldova 29 C14
Ştip Macedonia 44 E6
Stira Greece 46 C6
Stirling Canada 114 B7
Stirling U.K. 13 E5
Stirling □ U.K. 13 E4
Stirling Ra. Australia 93 F2
Stirling Range △ Australia 93 F2
Stittsville Canada 115 A9
Stjernøya Norway 8 A20
Stjørdalshalsen Norway 8 E14
Stockach Germany 25 H5
Stockaryd Sweden 11 G8
Stockerau Austria 27 C9
Stockholm Sweden 10 E12
Stockholm Arlanda ✕
  (ARN) Sweden 10 E12
Stockholms län □ Sweden 10 E12
Stockport U.K. 14 D5
Stocksbridge U.K. 14 D6
Stockton Calif., U.S.A. 110 H5
Stockton Kans., U.S.A. 112 F4
Stockton Mo., U.S.A. 112 G7
Stockton-on-Tees U.K. 14 C6
Stockton-on-Tees □ U.K. 14 C6
Stockton Plateau U.S.A. 116 F3
Stoczek Łukowski Poland 31 G8
Stöde Sweden 10 B10
Stoeng Treng Cambodia 64 F5
Stoer, Pt. of U.K. 13 C3
Stogovo Macedonia 44 E4
Stoholm Denmark 11 H3
Stoke-on-Trent U.K. 14 D5
Stoke-on-Trent □ U.K. 14 D5
Stokes → Australia 93 F3
Stokes Bay Canada 114 B3
Stokes Pt. Australia 95 G3
Stokes Ra. Australia 92 C5
Stokksnes Iceland 8 D6
Stokmarknes Norway 8 B16
Stolac Bos.-H. 44 C1
Stolberg Germany 24 E2
Stolbovoy, Ostrov Russia 53 B14
Stolbtsy = Stowbtsy Belarus 23 B14
Stolin Belarus 23 C14
Stöllet Sweden 10 D7
Stolnici Romania 29 F9
Stomio Greece 49 D5
Ston Croatia 41 F14
Stone U.K. 14 E5
Stoneboro U.S.A. 114 E4
Stonehaven U.K. 13 E6
Stonehenge Australia 94 C3
Stonehenge U.K. 15 F6
Stonewall Canada 103 C9
Stony I. U.S.A. 115 C8
Stony L. Man., Canada 103 B9
Stony L. Ont., Canada 114 B6
Stony Point U.S.A. 115 E11
Stony Pt. U.S.A. 115 C8
Stony Rapids Canada 103 B7

Stony Tunguska =
  Tunguska,
  Podkamennaya →
  Russia 53 C10
Stonyford U.S.A. 110 F4
Stopnica Poland 31 H7
Storå Sweden 10 E9
Storå → Denmark 11 H2
Stora Gla Sweden 10 E6
Stora Le Sweden 10 E5
Stora Lulevatten Sweden 8 C18
Storavan Sweden 8 D18
Stord Norway 9 G11
Store Bælt Denmark 11 J4
Store Heddinge Denmark 11 J6
Store Mosse △ Sweden 11 G7
Storebro Sweden 11 G9
Storfors Sweden 10 E8
Storlien Sweden 10 A6
Storm B. Australia 95 G4
Storm Lake U.S.A. 112 D6
Stormberge S. Africa 88 E4
Stormsrivier S. Africa 88 E3
Stornoway U.K. 13 C2
Storo Italy 40 C7
Storozhinets =
  Storozhynets Ukraine 29 B10
Storozhynets Ukraine 29 B10
Storrs U.S.A. 115 E12
Storsjön Gävleborg, Sweden 10 D10
Storsjön Jämtland, Sweden 10 B7
Storsjön Jämtland, Sweden 10 A8
Storuman Sweden 8 D17
Storuman, L. Sweden 8 D17
Storvik Sweden 10 D10
Storvreta Sweden 10 E11
Stouffville Canada 114 C5
Stoughton Canada 103 D8
Stour → Dorset, U.K. 15 G6
Stour → Kent, U.K. 15 F9
Stour → Suffolk, U.K. 15 F9
Stourbridge U.K. 15 E5
Stout L. Canada 103 C10
Stove Pipe Wells Village
  U.S.A. 111 J9
Støvring Denmark 11 H3
Stow U.S.A. 114 E3
Stowbtsy Belarus 23 B14
Stowmarket U.K. 15 E9
Strabane U.K. 12 B4
Stracin Macedonia 44 D6
Stradella Italy 40 C6
Strahan Australia 95 G4
Strajitsa Bulgaria 45 C9
Strakonice Czech Rep. 26 B6
Straldzha Bulgaria 45 D10
Stralsund Germany 24 A9
Strand S. Africa 88 E2
Stranda Møre og Romsdal,
  Norway 8 E12
Stranda Nord-Trøndelag,
  Norway 8 E14
Strandby Denmark 11 G4
Strangford L. U.K. 12 B6
Strängnäs Sweden 10 E11
Stranorlar Ireland 12 B4
Stranraer U.K. 13 G3
Strasbourg Canada 103 C8
Strasbourg France 19 D14
Strasburg Germany 24 B9
Strășeni Moldova 29 C13
Strässa Sweden 10 E9
Stratford Canada 114 C4
Stratford N.Z. 91 C5
Stratford Calif., U.S.A. 110 J7
Stratford Conn., U.S.A. 115 E11
Stratford Tex., U.S.A. 116 C3
Stratford-upon-Avon U.K. 15 E6
Strath Spey U.K. 13 D5
Strathalbyn Australia 95 F2
Strathaven U.K. 13 F4
Strathcona △ Canada 102 D3
Strathmore Canada 102 C6
Strathmore U.K. 13 E5
Strathnaver Canada 102 C4
Strathpeffer U.K. 13 D4
Strathroy Canada 114 D3
Strathy Pt. U.K. 13 C4
Strattanville U.S.A. 114 E5
Stratton U.S.A. 115 A14
Stratton Mt. U.S.A. 115 C12
Straubing Germany 25 G8
Straumnes Iceland 8 C2
Strausberg Germany 24 C9
Strawberry → U.S.A. 108 F8
Strážnice Czech Rep. 27 C10
Streaky B. Australia 95 E1
Streaky Bay Australia 95 E1
Streator U.S.A. 112 E9
Středočeský □ Czech Rep. 26 B7
Streetsboro U.S.A. 114 E3
Streetsville Canada 114 C5
Strehaia Romania 29 F8
Strelcha Bulgaria 45 D8
Streng → Cambodia 64 F4
Stresa Italy 40 C5
Streymoy Føroe Is. 8 E9

Strezhevoy Russia 52 C8
Stříbro Czech Rep. 26 A6
Strilky Ukraine 31 J9
Strimonas → Greece 44 F7
Strofades Greece 46 D3
Strokestown Ireland 12 C3
Stroma U.K. 13 C5
Stromberg-Heuchelberg △
  Germany 25 F4
Strómboli Italy 43 D8
Stromeferry U.K. 13 D3
Stromness U.K. 13 C5
Strömsbruk Sweden 10 C11
Stromsburg U.S.A. 112 E5
Strömsnäsbruk Sweden 11 H7
Strömstad Sweden 11 F5
Strömsund Sweden 8 E16
Strongili Greece 47 E11
Stróngoli Italy 43 C10
Strongsville U.S.A. 114 E3
Stronie Śląskie Poland 31 H3
Stronsay U.K. 13 B6
Stropkov Slovak Rep. 27 B14
Stroud U.K. 15 F5
Stroud Road Australia 95 E5
Stroudsburg U.S.A. 115 F9
Stroumbi Cyprus 49 E11
Štrpce Kosovo 44 D5
Struer Denmark 11 H2
Struga Macedonia 44 E4
Strugi Krasnyye Russia 32 C5
Strumica Macedonia 44 E6
Strumica → Europe 44 E7
Strumok Ukraine 29 E14
Struthers U.S.A. 114 E4
Stryama → Bulgaria 45 D8
Stryker U.S.A. 108 B6
Stryków Poland 31 G6
Stryy Ukraine 23 D12
Strzegom Poland 31 H3
Strzelce Krajeńskie Poland 31 F2
Strzelce Opolskie Poland 31 H5
Strzelecki Cr. → Australia 95 D2
Strzelecki Desert Australia 95 D3
Strzelin Poland 31 H4
Strzelno Poland 31 F5
Strzybnica Poland 31 H5
Strzyżów Poland 31 J8
Stuart Fla., U.S.A. 117 H14
Stuart Nebr., U.S.A. 112 D4
Stuart → Canada 102 C4
Stuart Bluff Ra. Australia 92 D5
Stuart I. U.S.A. 106 C7
Stuart L. Canada 102 C4
Stuart Ra. Australia 95 D1
Stubbekøbing Denmark 11 K6
Stuben Austria 26 D3
Studen Kladenets, Yazovir
  Bulgaria 45 E9
Studenka Czech Rep. 27 B11
Stugun Sweden 10 A9
Stuhr Germany 24 B4
Stull L. Canada 104 B1
Stung Treng = Stoeng
  Treng Cambodia 64 F5
Stupart → Canada 104 A1
Stupava Slovak Rep. 27 C10
Stupino Russia 32 E10
Sturge I. Antarctica 5 C11
Sturgeon B. Canada 103 C9
Sturgeon Bay U.S.A. 112 C10
Sturgeon Falls Canada 104 C4
Sturgeon L. Alta., Canada 102 B5
Sturgeon L. Ont., Canada 104 C1
Sturgeon L. Ont., Canada 114 B6
Sturgis Canada 103 C8
Sturgis Mich., U.S.A. 113 E11
Sturgis S. Dak., U.S.A. 112 C3
Sturkö Sweden 11 H9
Šturovo Slovak Rep. 27 D11
Sturt △ Australia 95 D3
Sturt Cr. → Australia 92 C4
Sturt Stony Desert Australia 95 D3
Stutterheim S. Africa 88 E4
Stuttgart Germany 25 G5
Stuttgart U.S.A. 116 D9
Stuttgart Echterdingen ✕
  (STR) Germany 25 G5
Stuyvesant U.S.A. 115 D11
Stykkishólmur Iceland 8 D2
Styria = Steiermark □
  Austria 26 D8
Styrsö Sweden 11 G5
Su Xian = Suzhou China 56 H9
Suakin Sudan 80 D4
Suakin Archipelago Sudan 80 D4
Suan N. Korea 57 E14
Suar India 69 E8
Şubā Si. Arabia 70 E2
Subang Indonesia 63 G12
Subansiri → India 67 F18
Subarnarekha → India 69 H12
Subay', Urūq Si. Arabia 80 C5
Subayhah Si. Arabia 70 D3
Subcetate Romania 28 E8
Subi Indonesia 62 D3
Subiaco Italy 41 G10
Subic B. Phil. 61 D4
Subotica Serbia 28 D4

Suceava *Romania* **29** C11
Suceava □ *Romania* **29** C10
Suceava → *Romania* **29** C11
Sucha-Beskidzka *Poland* **31** J6
Suchan = Partizansk *Russia* **54** C6
Suchań *Poland* **31** E2
Suchedniów *Poland* **31** G7
Suchil *Mexico* **118** C4
Suchou = Suzhou *China* **59** B13
Süchow = Xuzhou *China* **57** G9
Suchowola *Poland* **30** E10
Suck → *Ireland* **12** C3
Sucre *Bolivia* **124** G5
Sućuraj *Croatia* **41** E14
Sucuríu → *Brazil* **125** H8
Sud □ *Cameroon* **83** E7
Sud, Pte. du *Canada* **105** C7
Sud-Kivu □
  Dem. Rep. of the Congo **86** C2
Sud-Ouest □ *Cameroon* **83** D6
Sud-Ouest, Pte. *Canada* **105** C7
Sud Ouest, Pte. *Mauritius* **85** d
Suda → *Russia* **32** C9
Sudak *Ukraine* **33** K8
Sudan *U.S.A.* **116** D3
Sudan ■ *Africa* **81** E3
Sudbury *Canada* **104** C3
Sudbury *U.K.* **15** E8
Sŭdd *Sudan* **81** F3
Sudeifel = Deutsch-
  Luxemburgischer △
  Germany **25** F2
Süderbrarup *Germany* **24** A5
Süderlügum *Germany* **24** A4
Süderoogsand *Germany* **24** A4
Sudeten Mts. = Sudety
  Europe **27** A9
Sudety *Europe* **27** A9
Südheide △ *Germany* **24** C6
Suðuroy *Færoe Is.* **8** F9
Sudi *Tanzania* **87** E4
Sudirman, Pegunungan
  Indonesia **63** E9
Sudiți *Romania* **29** F12
Sudogda *Russia* **34** C5
Sudong, Pulau *Singapore* **65** d
Sudova Vyshnya *Ukraine* **31** J10
Sudzha *Russia* **33** G8
Sue → *Sudan* **81** F2
Sueca *Spain* **39** F4
Süedinenie *Bulgaria* **45** D8
Suemez I. *U.S.A.* **102** B2
Suez = El Suweis *Egypt* **80** J8
Suez, G. of = Suweis,
  Khalîg el *Egypt* **80** J8
Suez Canal = Suweis, Qanâ
  es *Egypt* **80** H8
Suffield *Canada* **102** C6
Suffolk *U.S.A.* **113** G15
Suffolk □ *U.K.* **15** E9
Şufiān *Iran* **73** C11
Şugag *Romania* **29** E8
Sugar Grove *U.S.A.* **114** E5
Sugarcreek *U.S.A.* **114** E5
Sugarive → *India* **69** F12
Suğla Gölü *Turkey* **72** D5
Sugluk = Salluit *Canada* **101** E16
Suhaia, Lacul *Romania* **29** G10
Şuḩār *Oman* **71** E8
Sühbaatar □ *Mongolia* **56** B8
Suhl *Germany* **24** E6
Şuḥut *Turkey* **47** C12
Sui *Pakistan* **68** E3
Sui Xian *China* **56** G8
Šuica *Bos.-H.* **28** G2
Suichang *China* **59** C12
Suichuan *China* **59** D10
Suide *China* **56** F6
Suifenhe *China* **57** B16
Suihua *China* **60** B7
Suijiang *China* **58** C4
Suining *Hunan, China* **59** D8
Suining *Jiangsu, China* **57** H9
Suining *Sichuan, China* **58** B5
Suiping *China* **56** H7
Suippes *France* **19** C11
Suir → *Ireland* **12** D4
Suisse = Switzerland ■
  Europe **25** J4
Suisun City *U.S.A.* **110** G4
Suixi *China* **59** G8
Suiyang *Guizhou, China* **58** D6
Suiyang *Heilongjiang, China* **57** B16
Suizhong *China* **57** D11
Suizhou *China* **59** B9
Sujangarh *India* **68** F6
Sukabumi *Indonesia* **63** G12
Sukadana *Indonesia* **62** E4
Sukagawa *Japan* **55** F10
Sukaraja *Indonesia* **62** E4
Sukawati *Indonesia* **63** K18
Sukch'ŏn *N. Korea* **57** E13
Sukhindol *Bulgaria* **45** C9
Sukhinichi *Russia* **32** E8
Sukhona → *Russia* **52** D4
Sukhothai *Thailand* **64** D2
Sukhumi = Sokhumi *Georgia* **35** J5
Sukkur *Pakistan* **68** F3
Sukkur Barrage *Pakistan* **68** F3

Sukovo *Serbia* **44** C6
Sukri → *India* **68** G4
Sukumo *Japan* **55** H6
Sukunka → *Canada* **102** B4
Sula *Ukraine* **33** H7
Sula, Kepulauan *Indonesia* **63** E7
Sulaco → *Honduras* **120** C2
Sulaiman Range *Pakistan* **68** D3
Sulak → *Russia* **35** J8
Sulakyurt *Turkey* **72** B5
Sūlār *Iran* **71** D6
Sulawesi *Indonesia* **63** E6
Sulawesi Barat □ *Indonesia* **63** E5
Sulawesi Sea = Celebes Sea
  Indonesia **63** D6
Sulawesi Selatan □ *Indonesia* **63** E6
Sulawesi Tengah □ *Indonesia* **63** E6
Sulawesi Tenggara □
  Indonesia **63** E6
Sulawesi Utara □ *Indonesia* **63** D6
Sulechów *Poland* **31** F2
Sulęcin *Poland* **31** F2
Suleja *Nigeria* **83** D6
Sulejów *Poland* **31** G6
Sulejówek *Poland* **31** F8
Süleymanlı *Turkey* **47** C9
Sulima *S. Leone* **82** D2
Sulina *Romania* **29** E14
Sulina, Brațul → *Romania* **29** E14
Sulingen *Germany* **24** C4
Sulița *Romania* **29** C11
Sulitjelma *Norway* **8** C17
Sułkowice *Poland* **31** J6
Sullana *Peru* **124** D2
Süller *Turkey* **47** C11
Sullivan *Ill., U.S.A.* **112** F9
Sullivan *Ind., U.S.A.* **112** F10
Sullivan *Mo., U.S.A.* **112** F8
Sullivan Bay *Canada* **102** C3
Sullivan I. = Lanbi Kyun
  Burma **65** G2
Sullom Voe *U.K.* **13** A7
Sully-sur-Loire *France* **19** E9
Sulmierzyce *Poland* **31** G4
Sulmona *Italy* **41** F10
Sulphur *La., U.S.A.* **116** F8
Sulphur *Okla., U.S.A.* **116** D6
Sulphur Pt. *Canada* **102** A6
Sulphur Springs *U.S.A.* **116** E7
Sultan *Canada* **104** C3
Sultan *U.S.A.* **110** C5
Sultan Dağları *Turkey* **72** C4
Sultan Hamud *Kenya* **86** C4
Sultanābād = Arāk *Iran* **71** C6
Sultanhisar *Turkey* **47** D10
Sultançiçi *Turkey* **45** F11
Sultaniye *Turkey* **45** F12
Sultanpur *Mad. P., India* **68** H8
Sultanpur *Punjab, India* **68** D6
Sultanpur *Ut. P., India* **69** F10
Sulu Arch. *Phil.* **61** J4
Sulu Sea *E. Indies* **61** H4
Sülüklü *Turkey* **72** C5
Sululta *Ethiopia* **81** F4
Suluova *Turkey* **72** B6
Sulūq *Libya* **79** B10
Sulzbach *Germany* **25** F3
Sulzbach-Rosenberg
  Germany **25** F7
Sulzberger Ice Shelf
  Antarctica **5** E13
Sumalata *Indonesia* **63** D6
Sumampa *Argentina* **126** B3
Sumatera *Indonesia* **62** D2
Sumatera Barat □ *Indonesia* **62** E2
Sumatera Utara □ *Indonesia* **62** D1
Sumatra = Sumatera
  Indonesia **62** D2
Šumava △ *Czech Rep.* **26** C6
Sumba *Indonesia* **63** F5
Sumba, Selat *Indonesia* **63** F5
Sumbawa *Indonesia* **62** F5
Sumbawa Besar *Indonesia* **62** F5
Sumbawanga *Tanzania* **84** F6
Sumbe *Angola* **84** G2
Sumbu △ *Zambia* **87** D3
Sumburgh Hd. *U.K.* **13** B7
Sumdeo *India* **69** D8
Sumdo *China* **69** B8
Sumedang *Indonesia* **63** G12
Sumen = Shumen *Bulgaria* **45** C10
Sümeg *Hungary* **28** D2
Sumeih *Sudan* **81** F2
Sumenep *Indonesia* **63** G15
Sumgait = Sumqayıt
  Azerbaijan **35** K9
Sumiswald *Switz.* **25**
Summer L. *U.S.A.* **108** E3
Summerland *Canada* **102** D5
Summerside *Canada* **105** C7
Summersville *U.S.A.* **113** F13
Summerville *Ga., U.S.A.* **117** D12
Summerville *S.C., U.S.A.* **117** E14
Summit Lake *Canada* **102** C4
Summit Peak *U.S.A.* **109** H10
Sumner *Iowa, U.S.A.* **112** D7
Sumner *Wash., U.S.A.* **110** C4
Sumoto *Japan* **55** G7
Šumperk *Czech Rep.* **27** B9

Sumqayıt *Azerbaijan* **35** K9
Sumter *U.S.A.* **117** E14
Sumy *Ukraine* **33** G8
Sumy □ *Ukraine* **33** G7
Sun City *S. Africa* **88** D4
Sun City *Ariz., U.S.A.* **109** K7
Sun City *Calif., U.S.A.* **111** M9
Sun City Center *U.S.A.* **117** H13
Sun Lakes *U.S.A.* **109** K8
Sun Valley *U.S.A.* **108** E6
Sunagawa *Japan* **54** C10
Sunan *N. Korea* **57** E13
Sunart, L. *U.K.* **13** E3
Sunburst *U.S.A.* **108** B8
Sunbury *Australia* **95** F3
Sunbury *U.S.A.* **115** F8
Sunchales *Argentina* **126** C3
Suncheon *S. Korea* **57** G14
Suncho Corral *Argentina* **126** B3
Sunch'on *N. Korea* **57** E13
Suncook *U.S.A.* **115** C13
Sunda, Selat *Indonesia* **62** F3
Sunda Is. *Indonesia* **96** H2
Sunda Str. = Sunda, Selat
  Indonesia **62** F3
Sunda Trench = Java
  Trench *Ind. Oc.* **62** F3
Sundance *Canada* **103** B10
Sundance *U.S.A.* **108** D11
Sundar Nagar *India* **68** D7
Sundarbans *Asia* **67** J16
Sundarbans □ *Pakistan* **69** J13
Sundargarh *India* **67** H14
Sundays = Sondags →
  S. Africa **88** E4
Sunderland *Canada* **114** B5
Sunderland *U.K.* **14** C6
Sundown △ *Australia* **95** D5
Sundre *Canada* **102** C6
Sunds *Denmark* **11** H3
Sundsvall *Sweden* **10** B11
Sundsvallsbukten *Sweden* **10** B11
Sung Hei *Vietnam* **65** G6
Sungai Acheh *Malaysia* **65** c
Sungai Kolok *Thailand* **65** J3
Sungai Lembing *Malaysia* **65** L4
Sungai Petani *Malaysia* **65** K3
Sungaigerong *Indonesia* **62** E2
Sungailiat *Indonesia* **62** E3
Sungaipenuh *Indonesia* **62** E2
Sungari = Songhua
  Jiang → *China* **60** B8
Songhua Chiang =
  Songhua Jiang → *China* **60** B8
Sungikai *Sudan* **81** E2
Sungurlu *Turkey* **72** B6
Sunja *Croatia* **41** C13
Sunland Park *U.S.A.* **109** L10
Sunnansjö *Sweden* **10** D8
Sunndalsøra *Norway* **8** E13
Sunne *Sweden* **10** E7
Sunnemo *Sweden* **10** E7
Sunnyside *U.S.A.* **108** C4
Sunnyvale *U.S.A.* **110** H4
Sunrise Manor *U.S.A.* **111** J11
Suntar *Russia* **53** C12
Sunyani *Ghana* **82** D4
Suomenselkä *Finland* **8** E21
Suomi = Finland ■ *Europe* **8** E22
Suomussalmi *Finland* **8** D23
Suoyarvi *Russia* **32** A7
Supai *U.S.A.* **109** H7
Supaul *India* **69** F12
Superior *Ariz., U.S.A.* **109** K8
Superior *Mont., U.S.A.* **108** C6
Superior *Nebr., U.S.A.* **112** E5
Superior *Wis., U.S.A.* **112** B7
Superior, L. *N. Amer.* **104** C2
Supetar *Croatia* **41** E13
Suphan Buri *Thailand* **64** E3
Suphan Dağı *Turkey* **73** C10
Supiori *Indonesia* **63** E9
Supraśl *Poland* **31** E10
Supraśl → *Poland* **31** E10
Supung Shuiku *China* **57** D13
Süq ash Shuyūkh *Iraq* **70** D5
Süq Suwayq *Si. Arabia* **70** E3
Suqian *China* **57** H10
Suquţra = Socotra *Yemen* **75** E5
Sūr *Lebanon* **74** B4
Şūr *Oman* **75** C6
Sur, Pt. *U.S.A.* **110** J5
Sura → *Russia* **34** C8
Surab *Pakistan* **68** E2
Suraia *Romania* **29** E12
Surakarta *Indonesia* **62** F4
Šurany *Slovak Rep.* **27** C11
Surat *Australia* **95** D4
Surat *India* **66** J8
Suratgarh *India* **68** E5
Surat Thani *Thailand* **65** H2
Suratgarh *India* **68** E5
Suraxanı *Azerbaijan* **35** K10
Şuraymilā *Si. Arabia* **70** E5
Suraż *Poland* **31** F9
Surazh *Belarus* **32** E6

Surazh *Russia* **33** F7
Surduc *Romania* **29** C8
Surduc Pasul *Romania* **29** E8
Surdulica *Serbia* **44** D6
Surendranagar *India* **68** H4
Surf *U.S.A.* **111** L6
Surfers Paradise *Australia* **95** D5
Surgères *France* **20** B3
Surgut *Russia* **52** C8
Sùria *Spain* **38** D6
Suriapet *India* **66** L11
Surigao *Phil.* **61** G6
Surigao Strait *Phil.* **61** F6
Surin *Thailand* **64** E4
Surin Nua, Ko *Thailand* **65** H1
Surinam = Suriname ■
  S. Amer. **125** C7
Suriname ■ *S. Amer.* **125** C7
Suriname → *Suriname* **125** B7
Sûrmaq *Iran* **71** D7
Sürmene *Turkey* **73** B9
Surovikino *Russia* **35** F6
Surrey *Canada* **110** A4
Surrey □ *U.K.* **15** F7
Sursand *India* **69** F11
Sursar → *India* **69** F12
Sursee *Switz.* **25** H4
Sursk *Russia* **34** D7
Surskoye *Russia* **34** C8
Surt *Libya* **79** B9
Surt, Khalīj *Libya* **79** B9
Surte *Sweden* **11** G6
Surtsey *Iceland* **8** E3
Sürüç *Turkey* **73** D8
Suruga-Wan *Japan* **55** G9
Susa *Italy* **40** C4
Susà → *Denmark* **11** J5
Süsah *Libya* **79** B10
Sušac *Croatia* **41** F13
Susaki *Japan* **55** H6
Susanville *U.S.A.* **108** F3
Susch *Switz.* **25** J6
Susleni *Moldova* **29** C13
Susner *India* **68** H7
Susong *China* **59** B11
Susquehanna *U.S.A.* **115** E9
Susquehanna → *U.S.A.* **115** G8
Susques *Argentina* **126** A2
Sussex *Canada* **105** C6
Sussex *U.S.A.* **115** E10
Sussex, E. □ *U.K.* **15** G8
Sussex, W. □ *U.K.* **15** G7
Sustut → *Canada* **102** B3
Susuman *Russia* **53** C15
Susunu *Indonesia* **63** E8
Susurluk *Turkey* **47** B10
Susuz *Turkey* **73** B10
Susz *Poland* **30** E6
Sütçüler *Turkey* **72** D4
Şuțești *Romania* **29** E12
Sutherland *S. Africa* **88** E3
Sutherland *U.K.* **13** C4
Sutherland *U.S.A.* **112** E3
Sutherland Falls *N.Z.* **91** F1
Sutherlin *U.S.A.* **108** E2
Suthri *India* **68** H3
Sutjeska △ *Bos.-H.* **28** G3
Sutlej → *Pakistan* **68** E4
Sutter *U.S.A.* **110** F5
Sutter Buttes *U.S.A.* **110** F5
Sutter Creek *U.S.A.* **110** G6
Sutton *Canada* **115** A12
Sutton *Nebr., U.S.A.* **112** E6
Sutton *W. Va., U.S.A.* **113** F13
Sutton → *Canada* **104** A3
Sutton Coldfield *U.K.* **15** E6
Sutton in Ashfield *U.K.* **14** D6
Sutton L. *Canada* **104** B3
Suttor → *Australia* **94** C4
Suttsu *Japan* **54** C10
Sutwik I. *U.S.A.* **106** D8
Suva *Fiji* **91** a
Suva Gora *Macedonia* **44** E5
Suva Planina *Serbia* **44** C6
Suva Reka *Kosovo* **44** D4
Suvorov *Russia* **32** E9
Suvorov Is. = Suwarrow Is.
  Cook Is. **97** J11
Suvorove *Ukraine* **29** E13
Suvorovo *Bulgaria* **45** C11
Suwałki *Poland* **30** D9
Suwannaphum *Thailand* **64** E4
Suwannee → *U.S.A.* **117** G13
Suwanose-Jima *Japan* **55** K4
Suwarrow Is. *Cook Is.* **97** J11
Suwayqiyah, Hawr as *Iraq* **73** G12
Suweis, Khalîg el *Egypt* **80** J8
Suweis, Qanâ es *Egypt* **80** H8
Suwon *S. Korea* **57** F14
Suzdal *Russia* **32** D11
Suzhou *Anhui, China* **56** H9
Suzhou *Jiangsu, China* **59** B13
Suzu *Japan* **55** F8
Suzu-Misaki *Japan* **55** F8

Suzuka *Japan* **55** G8
Suzzara *Italy* **40** D7
Svalbard *Arctic* **4** B8
Svalbard Radio =
  Longyearbyen *Svalbard* **4** B8
Svalöv *Sweden* **11** J7
Svalyava *Ukraine* **28** B7
Svaneke *Denmark* **11** J9
Svängsta *Sweden* **11** H8
Svanskog *Sweden* **10** E6
Svappavaara *Sweden* **8** C19
Svärdsjö *Sweden* **10** D9
Svartå *Sweden* **10** E8
Svartisen *Norway* **8** C15
Svartvik *Sweden* **10** B11
Svatove *Ukraine* **33** H10
Svatovo = Svatove *Ukraine* **33** H10
Svay Chek *Cambodia* **64** F4
Svay Rieng *Cambodia* **65** G5
Svealand *Sweden* **10** D9
Svedala *Sweden* **11** J7
Sveg *Sweden* **10** B8
Svendborg *Denmark* **11** J4
Svenljunga *Sweden* **11** G7
Svenstavik *Sweden* **10** B8
Svenstrup *Denmark* **11** H3
Sverdlovsk *Ukraine* **33** H10
Sverdrup Chan. *Canada* **101** B12
Sverdrup Is. *Canada* **98** B10
Sverige = Sweden ■ *Europe* **9** H16
Svetac *Croatia* **41** E12
Sveti Nikola, Prokhad *Europe* **44** C6
Sveti Nikole *Macedonia* **44** E5
Sveti Rok *Croatia* **41** D12
Svetlaya *Russia* **54** A9
Svetlogorsk =
  Svyetlahorsk *Belarus* **23** B15
Svetlogorsk *Russia* **30** D7
Svetlograd *Russia* **35** H6
Svetlovodsk = Svitlovodsk
  Ukraine **33** H7
Svetlyy *Russia* **30** D7
Svidník *Slovak Rep.* **27** B14
Svilaja Planina *Croatia* **41** E13
Svilajnac *Serbia* **44** B5
Svilengrad *Bulgaria* **45** E10
Svir → *Russia* **32** B7
Sviritsa *Russia* **32** B7
Svishtov *Bulgaria* **45** C9
Svislach *Belarus* **31** E11
Svitava → *Czech Rep.* **27** B9
Svitavy *Czech Rep.* **27** B9
Svitlovodsk *Ukraine* **33** H7
Svizzera = Switzerland ■
  Europe **25** J4
Svobodnyy *Russia* **53** D13
Svoge *Bulgaria* **44** D7
Svolvær *Norway* **8** B16
Svratka → *Czech Rep.* **27** B9
Svrljig *Serbia* **44** C5
Svyetlahorsk *Belarus* **23** B15
Swabian Alps =
  Schwäbische Alb *Germany* **25** G5
Swaffham *U.K.* **15** E8
Swains I. *Amer. Samoa* **97** J11
Swainsboro *U.S.A.* **117** E13
Swakop → *Namibia* **88** C2
Swakopmund *Namibia* **88** C1
Swale → *U.K.* **14** C6
Swan → *Austral.ia* **93** F2
Swan → *Canada* **103** C8
Swan Hill *Australia* **95** F3
Swan Hills *Canada* **102** C5
Swan Is. = Santanilla, Is.
  Honduras **120** C3
Swan L. *Man., Canada* **103** C6
Swan L. *Ont., Canada* **104** B1
Swan Ra. *U.S.A.* **108** C7
Swan River *Canada* **103** C8
Swanage *U.K.* **15** G6
Swansea *Austral.ia* **95** G4
Swansea *Canada* **114** C5
Swansea *U.K.* **15** F4
Swansea □ *U.K.* **15** F3
Swartberge *S. Africa* **88** E3
Swartmodder *S. Africa* **88** D3
Swartnossob → *Namibia* **88** C2
Swartruggens *S. Africa* **88** D4
Swastika *Canada* **104** C3
Swat → *Pakistan* **69** B5
Swatow = Shantou *China* **59** F11
Swaziland ■ *Africa* **89** D5
Sweden ■ *Europe* **9** H16
Swedru *Ghana* **83** D4
Sweet Grass *U.S.A.* **108** B8
Sweet Home *U.S.A.* **108** D2
Sweetwater *Nev., U.S.A.* **110** G7
Sweetwater *Tenn., U.S.A.* **117** D12
Sweetwater *Tex., U.S.A.* **116** E4
Sweetwater → *U.S.A.* **108** E10
Swellendam *S. Africa* **88** E3
Swider → *Poland* **31** F8
Świdnica *Poland* **31** H3
Świdnik *Poland* **31** G9
Świdwin *Poland* **30** E2
Świebodzice *Poland* **31** H3
Świebodzin *Poland* **31** F2
Świecie *Poland* **30** E5
Świerzawa *Poland* **31** G2

Świętokrzyski △ *Poland* **31** H7
Świętokrzyskie □ *Poland* **31** H7
Świętokrzyskie, Góry *Poland* **31** H7
Swift Current *Canada* **103** C7
Swift Current → *Canada* **103** C7
Swilly, L. *Ireland* **12** A4
Swindon *U.K.* **15** F6
Swindon □ *U.K.* **15** F6
Swinemünde =
  Świnoujście *Poland* **30** E1
Swinford *Ireland* **12** C3
Świnoujście *Poland* **30** E1
Switzerland ■ *Europe* **25** J4
Swords *Ireland* **12** C5
Swoyerville *U.S.A.* **115** E9
Syasstroy *Russia* **32** B7
Sychevka *Russia* **32** E7
Syców *Poland* **31** G4
Syddanmark □ *Denmark* **11** J2
Sydenham → *Canada* **114** D2
Sydney *Australia* **95** E5
Sydney *Canada* **105** C7
Sydney L. *Canada* **103** C10
Sydney Mines *Canada* **105** C7
Sydproven = Alluitsup Paa
  Greenland **4** C5
Sydra, G. of = Surt, Khalīj
  Libya **79** B9
Syeverodonetsk *Ukraine* **33** H10
Syke *Germany* **24** C4
Sykesville *U.S.A.* **114** E6
Syktyvkar *Russia* **52** C6
Sylacauga *U.S.A.* **117** E11
Sylarna *Sweden* **8** E15
Sylhet *Bangla.* **67** G17
Sylhet □ *Bangla.* **67** G17
Sylt *Germany* **24** A4
Sylvan Beach *U.S.A.* **115** C9
Sylvan Lake *Canada* **102** C6
Sylvania *Ga., U.S.A.* **117** E14
Sylvania *Ohio, U.S.A.* **113** E12
Sylvester *U.S.A.* **117** F13
Sym *Russia* **52** C9
Synelnykove *Ukraine* **33** H8
Synevyr *Ukraine* **29** B8
Synevyrska Polyana *Ukraine* **29** B8
Synnot Ra. *Australia* **92** C4
Synyak *Ukraine* **28** B7
Syowa *Antarctica* **5** C5
Syracuse *Kans., U.S.A.* **112** G3
Syracuse *N.Y., U.S.A.* **115** C8
Syracuse *Nebr., U.S.A.* **112** E5
Syrdarya → *Kazakhstan* **52** E7
Syria ■ *Asia* **73** E8
Syrian Desert = Shām,
  Bādiyat ash *Asia* **70** C3
Syros = Ermoupoli *Greece* **46** D6
Sysslebäck *Sweden* **10** D6
Syzran *Russia* **34** D9
Szabolcs-Szatmár-Bereg □
  Hungary **28** B6
Szadek *Poland* **31** G5
Szamocin *Poland* **31** E4
Szamos → *Hungary* **28** B7
Szamotuły *Poland* **31** F3
Százraz → *Hungary* **28** D6
Szarvas *Hungary* **28** D5
Százhalombatta *Hungary* **28** C3
Szczawnica *Poland* **31** J7
Szczecin *Poland* **30** E1
Szczecinek *Poland* **30** E3
Szczeciński, Zalew =
  Stettiner Haff *Germany* **24** B10
Szczekociny *Poland* **31** H6
Szczucin *Poland* **31** H8
Szczuczyn *Poland* **30** E9
Szczyrk *Poland* **31** J6
Szczytna *Poland* **31** H3
Szczytno *Poland* **30** E7
Szechuan = Sichuan Basin =
  Pendi *China* **58** B5
Szechwan = Sichuan □
  China **58** B5
Szécsény *Hungary* **28** B4
Szeged *Hungary* **28** D5
Szeghalom *Hungary* **28** C6
Székesfehérvár *Hungary* **28** C3
Szekszárd *Hungary* **28** D3
Szendrő *Hungary* **28** B5
Szentendre *Hungary* **28** C4
Szentes *Hungary* **28** D5
Szentgotthárd *Hungary* **28** D1
Szentlőrinc *Hungary* **28** D3
Szerencs *Hungary* **28** B6
Szigetszentmiklós *Hungary* **28** C4
Szigetvár *Hungary* **28** D2
Szikszó *Hungary* **28** B5
Szklarska Poręba *Poland* **31** H2
Szkwa → *Poland* **31** E8
Szlichtyngowa *Poland* **31** G3
Szob *Hungary* **28** C3
Szolnok *Hungary* **28** C5
Szombathely *Hungary* **28** C1
Szprotawa *Poland* **31** G2
Sztum *Poland* **30** E6
Sztutowo *Poland* **30** D6
Szydłowiec *Poland* **31** G7
Szypliszki *Poland* **30** D10

T

Ta Khli *Thailand* **64** E3
Ta Khli Khok *Thailand* **64** E3
Ta Lai *Vietnam* **65** G6
Tab *Hungary* **28** D3
Tabacal *Argentina* **126** A3
Tabaco *Phil.* **61** E5
Tabagné *Ivory C.* **82** D4
Tabanan *Indonesia* **63** K18
Tabankort *Niger* **83** B5
Ţabas *Khorāsān, Iran* **71** C9
Ţabas *Yazd, Iran* **71** C8
Tabasará, Serranía de
  Panama **120** E3
Tabasco □ *Mexico* **119** D6
Tabāsīn *Iran* **71** D8
Tabatinga, Serra da *Brazil* **125** F10
Taber *Canada* **102** D6
Taberg *Sweden* **11** G8
Tabla *Niger* **83** C5
Tablas *Phil.* **61** E5
Tablas de Daimiel △ *Spain* **37** F7
Tablas Strait *Phil.* **61** E4
Table, Pte. de la *Réunion* **85** c
Table B. *Canada* **105** B8
Table B. *S. Africa* **88** E2
Table Mountain △ *S. Africa* **88** E2
Table Mt. *S. Africa* **88** E2
Table Rock L. *U.S.A.* **112** G7
Tabletop, Mt. *Australia* **94** C4
Tábor *Czech Rep.* **26** B7
Tabora *Tanzania* **86** D3
Tabora □ *Tanzania* **86** D3
Tabou *Ivory C.* **82** E3
Tabrīz *Iran* **73** C12
Tabuaeran *Kiribati* **97** G12
Tabuenca *Spain* **38** D3
Tabūk *Si. Arabia* **70** D3
Tabūk □ *Si. Arabia* **70** E3
Taburno-Camposauro △
  Italy **43** A7
Täby *Sweden* **10** E12
Tacámbaro de Codallos
  Mexico **118** D4
Tacheng *China* **60** B3
Tach'i *Taiwan* **59** E13
Tachia *Taiwan* **59** E13
Tach'ing Shan = Daqing
  Shan *China* **56** D6
Tachov *Czech Rep.* **26** B5
Tácina ↠ *Italy* **43** D9
Tacloban *Phil.* **61** F6
Tacna *Peru* **124** G4
Tacoma *U.S.A.* **110** C4
Tacuarembó *Uruguay* **127** C4
Tademaït, Plateau du *Algeria* **78** C6
Tadio, L. *Ivory C.* **82** D3
Tadjoura *Djibouti* **81** E5
Tadjoura, Golfe de *Djibouti* **81** E5
Tadmor *N.Z.* **91** D4
Tadoule L. *Canada* **103** B9
Tadoussac *Canada* **105** C6
Tadrés ↠ *Niger* **83** B6
Tadzhikistan =
  Tajikistan ■ *Asia* **52** F8
Taegu = Daegu *S. Korea* **57** G15
Taegwan *N. Korea* **57** D13
Taejŏn = Daejeon *S. Korea* **57** F14
Taen, Ko *Thailand* **65** b
Tafalla *Spain* **38** C3
Tafar *Sudan* **81** F2
Tafelbaai = Table B. *S. Africa* **88** E2
Tafermaar *Indonesia* **63** F8
Tafí Viejo *Argentina* **126** B2
Tafīhān *Iran* **71** D7
Tafiré *Ivory C.* **82** D3
Tafo *Ghana* **83** D4
Tafresh *Iran* **71** C6
Taft *Iran* **71** D7
Taft *Phil.* **61** F6
Taft *U.S.A.* **111** K7
Taftan *Pakistan* **66** E2
Taftān, Kūh-e *Iran* **71** D9
Taga *Samoa* **91** b
Taga Dzong *Bhutan* **67** F16
Taganrog *Russia* **33** J10
Taganrogskiy Zaliv *Russia* **33** J10
Tagânt □ *Mauritania* **82** B3
Tagatay *Phil.* **61** D4
Tagbilaran *Phil.* **61** G5
Tággia *Italy* **40** E4
Tagish *Canada* **102** A2
Tagish L. *Canada* **102** A2
Tagliacozzo *Italy* **41** F10
Tagliamento ↠ *Italy* **41** C10
Táglio di Po *Italy* **41** D9
Tago *Phil.* **61** G7
Tagomago *Spain* **48** B8
Tagourâret *Mauritania* **82** B3
Taguatinga *Brazil* **125** F10
Tagudin *Phil.* **61** C4
Tagum *Phil.* **61** H6
Tagus = Tejo ↠ *Europe* **37** F2
Tahakopa *N.Z.* **91** G2
Tahan, Gunung *Malaysia* **65** K4
Tahat *Algeria* **78** D7
Täherī *Iran* **71** E7
Tahiti *French Polynesia* **91** d

Tahiti, I. *Tahiti* **91** d
Tahlequah *U.S.A.* **116** D7
Tahoe, L. *U.S.A.* **110** G6
Tahoe City *U.S.A.* **110** F6
Tahoka *U.S.A.* **116** E4
Tahoua *Niger* **83** C6
Tahrūd *Iran* **71** D8
Tahsis *Canada* **102** D3
Tahta *Egypt* **80** B3
Tahtaköprü *Turkey* **45** G13
Tahtalı Dağları *Turkey* **72** C7
Tahulandang *Indonesia* **63** D7
Tahuna *Indonesia* **63** D7
Taï *Ivory C.* **82** D3
Taï △ *Ivory C.* **82** D3
Tai Hu *China* **59** B12
Tai Rom Yen △ *Thailand* **65** H2
Tai Shan *China* **57** F9
Tai'an *China* **57** F9
Taiarapu, Presqu'île de *Tahiti* **91** d
Taibei = T'aipei *Taiwan* **59** E13
Taibique *Canary Is.* **48** G2
Taibus Qi *China* **56** D8
Taicang *China* **59** B13
Taichung = T'aichung
  Taiwan **59** E13
Taieri ↠ *N.Z.* **91** G3
Taigu *China* **56** F7
Taihang Shan *China* **56** G7
Taihape *N.Z.* **91** C5
Taihe *Anhui, China* **56** H8
Taihe *Jiangxi, China* **59** D10
Taihu *China* **59** B11
Taijiang *China* **58** D7
Taikang *China* **56** G8
Tailem Bend *Australia* **95** F2
Tailfingen *Germany* **25** G5
T'ailuko *Taiwan* **59** E13
Tain *U.K.* **13** D4
T'ainan *Taiwan* **59** F13
Taining *China* **59** D11
T'aipei *Taiwan* **59** E13
Taiping *China* **59** B12
Taiping *Malaysia* **65** K3
Taipingzhen *China* **56** H6
Tairbeart = Tarbert *U.K.* **13** D2
Taishan *China* **59** F9
Taishun *China* **59** D12
Taitao, Pen. de *Chile* **128** F2
T'aitung *Taiwan* **59** F13
Taivalkoski *Finland* **8** D23
Taiwan ■ *Asia* **59** F13
Taiwan Strait *Asia* **59** E12
Taixing *China* **59** A13
Taiyara *Sudan* **81** E3
Taiyiba *Israel* **74** C4
Taiyuan *China* **56** F7
Taizhong = T'aichung
  Taiwan **59** E13
Taizhou *China* **59** A12
Taizhou Liedao *China* **59** C13
Ta'izz *Yemen* **75** E3
Tājābād *Iran* **71** D7
Tajikistan ■ *Asia* **52** F8
Tajima *Japan* **55** F9
Tajo = Tejo ↠ *Europe* **37** F2
Tajrīsh *Iran* **71** C6
Tak *Thailand* **64** D2
Takāb *Iran* **73** D12
Takachiho *Japan* **55** H5
Takachu *Botswana* **88** C3
Takada *Japan* **55** F9
Takahagi *Japan* **55** F10
Takaka *N.Z.* **91** D4
Takamaka *Seychelles* **85** b
Takamatsu *Japan* **55** G7
Takaoka *Japan* **55** F8
Takapuna *N.Z.* **91** B5
Takasaki *Japan* **55** F9
Takatsuki *Japan* **55** G7
Takaungu *Kenya* **86** C4
Takayama *Japan* **55** F8
Take-Shima *Japan* **55** J5
Takefu *Japan* **55** G8
Takengon *Indonesia* **62** D1
Takeo *Japan* **55** H5
Tåkern *Sweden* **11** F8
Takh *India* **69** C7
Takhmau *Cambodia* **65** G5
Takht-Sulaiman *Pakistan* **68** D3
Takiéta *Niger* **83** C6
Takikawa *Japan* **54** C10
Takla L. *Canada* **102** B3
Takla Landing *Canada* **102** B3
Takla Makan *China* **60** C3
Taklamakan Shamo =
  Takla Makan *China* **60** C3
Taksimo *Russia* **53** D12
Taku ↠ *Canada* **102** B2
Takua Pa *Thailand* **65** H2
Takua Thung *Thailand* **65** a
Takum *Nigeria* **83** D6

Tal Halāl *Iran* **71** D7
Tala *Uruguay* **127** C4
Talachyn *Belarus* **32** E5
Talacogan *Phil.* **61** G6
Talagang *Pakistan* **68** C5
Talagante *Chile* **126** C1
Talak *Niger* **83** B6
Talamanca, Cordillera de
  Cent. Amer. **120** E3
Talampaya △ *Argentina* **126** B2
Talara *Peru* **124** D2
Talas *Kyrgyzstan* **52** E8
Talas *Turkey* **72** C6
Talâta *Egypt* **74** E1
Talata Mafara *Nigeria* **83** C6
Talaud, Kepulauan *Indonesia* **63** D7
Talaud Is. = Talaud,
  Kepulauan *Indonesia* **63** D7
Talavera de la Reina *Spain* **36** F6
Talavera la Real *Spain* **37** G4
Talayan *Phil.* **61** H6
Talayuela *Spain* **36** F5
Talbandh *India* **69** H12
Talbert, Sillon de *France* **18** D3
Talbot, C. *Australia* **92** B4
Talbragar ↠ *Australia* **95** E4
Talca *Chile* **126** D1
Talcahuano *Chile* **126** D1
Talcher *India* **67** J14
Talcho *Niger* **83** C5
Taldy Kurgan =
  Taldyqorghan *Kazakhstan* **52** E8
Taldyqorghan *Kazakhstan* **52** E8
Tālesh *Iran* **73** D13
Tālesh, Kūhhā-ye *Iran* **73** D13
Talguharai *Sudan* **80** D4
Tali Post *Sudan* **81** F3
Taliabu *Indonesia* **63** E6
Talihina *U.S.A.* **116** D7
Talisayan *Phil.* **61** G6
Taliwang *Indonesia* **62** F5
Talkha *Egypt* **80** H7
Tall 'Afar *Iraq* **73** D10
Tall Kalakh *Syria* **74** A5
Tall Kayf *Iraq* **73** D10
Talla *Egypt* **80** B3
Talladega *U.S.A.* **117** E11
Tallahassee *U.S.A.* **117** F12
Tallangatta *Australia* **95** F4
Tallard *France* **21** D10
Tålberg *Sweden* **10** D9
Tallering Pk. *Australia* **93** E2
Talli *Pakistan* **68** E3
Tallinn *Estonia* **32** C3
Tallmadge *U.S.A.* **114** E3
Tallulah *U.S.A.* **116** E9
Tălmaciu *Romania* **29** E9
Talmont-St-Hilaire *France* **20** B2
Talnakh *Russia* **53** C9
Talne *Ukraine* **33** H6
Talnoye = Talne *Ukraine* **33** H6
Talodi *Sudan* **81** E3
Talovaya *Russia* **34** E5
Taloyoak *Canada* **100** D13
Talpa de Allende *Mexico* **118** C4
Talparo *Trin. & Tob.* **125** K15
Talsi *Latvia* **30** A9
Talsi □ *Latvia* **30** A9
Taltal *Chile* **126** B1
Taltson ↠ *Canada* **102** A6
Talwood *Australia* **95** D4
Talyawalka Cr. ↠ *Australia* **95** E3
Tam Ky *Vietnam* **64** E7
Tam Quan *Vietnam* **64** E7
Tama *U.S.A.* **112** E7
Tama △ *Ethiopia* **81** F4
Tama Abu, Banjaran
  Malaysia **62** D5
Tamale *Ghana* **83** D4
Taman *Russia* **33** K9
Taman Negara △ *Malaysia* **65** K4
Tamani *Mali* **82** C3
Tamano *Japan* **55** G6
Tamanrasset *Algeria* **78** D7
Tamaqua *U.S.A.* **115** F9
Tamar ↠ *U.K.* **15** G3
Tamarin *Mauritius* **85** d
Tamarinda *Spain* **48** B10
Tamarite de Litera *Spain* **38** D5
Tamashima *Japan* **55** G6
Tamási *Hungary* **28** D3
Tamaské *Niger* **83** C6
Tamatave = Toamasina
  Madag. **89** B8
Tamaulipas □ *Mexico* **119** C5
Tamaulipas, Sierra de
  Mexico **119** C5
Tamazula *Mexico* **118** C3
Tamazunchale *Mexico* **119** C5
Tamba-Dabatou *Guinea* **82** C2
Tambach *Kenya* **86** B4
Tambacounda *Senegal* **82** C2
Tambacounda □ *Senegal* **82** C2
Tambelan, Kepulauan
  Indonesia **62** D3
Tambellup *Australia* **93** F2
Tambo *Australia* **94** C4
Tambo de Mora *Peru* **124** F3

Tambohorano *Madag.* **89** B7
Tambora *Indonesia* **62** F5
Tamboura *C.A.R.* **81** F2
Tambov *Russia* **34** D5
Tambov □ *Russia* **34** D5
Tambre ↠ *Spain* **36** C2
Tambuku *Indonesia* **63** G15
Tamburâ *Sudan* **81** F2
Tâmchekket *Mauritania* **82** B2
Tâmega ↠ *Portugal* **36** D2
Tamenglong *India* **67** G18
Tamiahua, L. de *Mexico* **119** C5
Tamil Nadu □ *India* **66** P10
Tamis ↠ *Serbia* **28** F5
Tamiya *Egypt* **80** J7
Tamluk *India* **69** H12
Tammerfors = Tampere
  Finland **32** B2
Tammisaari *Finland* **32** B2
Tämnaren *Sweden* **10** D11
Tampa *U.S.A.* **117** H13
Tampa, Tanjung *Indonesia* **63** K19
Tampa B. *U.S.A.* **117** H13
Tampere *Finland* **32** B2
Tampico *Mexico* **119** C5
Tampin *Malaysia* **65** L4
Tampoi *Malaysia* **65** d
Tamsweg *Austria* **26** D6
Tamu *Burma* **67** G19
Tamuja ↠ *Spain* **37** F4
Tamworth *Australia* **95** E5
Tamworth *Canada* **114** B8
Tamworth *U.K.* **15** E6
Tan An *Vietnam* **65** G6
Tan Chau *Vietnam* **65** G5
Tan-Tan *Morocco* **78** C3
Tana ↠ *Kenya* **86** C5
Tana ↠ *Norway* **8** A23
Tana, L. *Ethiopia* **81** E4
Tana River Primate △ *Kenya* **86** C5
Tanabe *Japan* **55** H7
Tanafjorden *Norway* **8** A23
Tanaga I. *U.S.A.* **106** E4
Tanahbala *Indonesia* **62** E1
Tanahgrogot *Indonesia* **62** E5
Tanahjampea *Indonesia* **63** F6
Tanahmasa *Indonesia* **62** E1
Tanahmerah *Indonesia* **63** F10
Tanakpur *India* **69** E9
Tanakura *Japan* **55** F10
Tanami Desert *Australia* **92** C5
Tanana *U.S.A.* **106** B9
Tanana ↠ *U.S.A.* **100** D1
Tananarive =
  Antananarivo *Madag.* **89** B8
Tánaro ↠ *Italy* **40** D5
Tancheng *China* **57** G10
Tanch'ŏn *N. Korea* **57** D15
Tanda *Ut. P., India* **69** F10
Tanda *Ut. P., India* **69** E8
Tanda *Ivory C.* **82** D4
Tandag *Phil.* **61** G7
Tandaia *Tanzania* **87** D3
Tăndărei *Romania* **29** F12
Tandaué *Angola* **88** B2
Tandil *Argentina* **126** D4
Tandil, Sa. del *Argentina* **126** D4
Tandlianwala *Pakistan* **68** D5
Tando Adam *Pakistan* **68** G3
Tando Allahyar *Pakistan* **68** G3
Tando Bago *Pakistan* **68** G3
Tando Mohommed Khan
  Pakistan **68** G3
Tandou L. *Australia* **95** E3
Tandoureh △ *Iran* **71** B8
Tandragee *U.K.* **16** B5
Tandsjöborg *Sweden* **10** C8
Tane-ga-Shima *Japan* **55** J5
Taneatua *N.Z.* **91** C6
Tanen Tong Dan = Dawna
  Ra. *Burma* **64** D2
Tanew ↠ *Poland* **31** H9
Tanezrouft *Algeria* **78** D6
Tang, Koh *Cambodia* **65** G4
Tang, Ra's-e *Iran* **71** E8
Tang Krasang *Cambodia* **64** F5
Tanga *Tanzania* **86** D4
Tanga □ *Tanzania* **86** D4
Tanganyika, L. *Africa* **86** D3
Tangaza *Nigeria* **83** C5
Tanger *Morocco* **78** A4
Tangerang *Indonesia* **63** G12
Tangerhütte *Germany* **24** C7
Tangermünde *Germany* **24** C7
Tanggu *China* **57** E9
Tanggula Shan *China* **60** C4
Tanghe *China* **56** H7
Tanghla Range =
  Tanggula Shan *China* **60** C4
Tangier = Tanger *Morocco* **78** A4
Tangorin *Australia* **94** C3
Tangorombohitr'i Makay
  Madag. **89** C8
Tangshan *China* **57** E10
Tangtou *China* **57** G10
Tanguen-Dassouri
  Burkina Faso **83** C4
Tanguiéta *Benin* **83** C5
Tangxi *China* **59** C12

Tangyan He ↠ *China* **58** C7
Tanimbar, Kepulauan
  Indonesia **63** F8
Tanimbar Is. = Tanimbar,
  Kepulauan *Indonesia* **63** F8
Taninthari = Tenasserim
  Burma **65** F2
Tanjay *Phil.* **61** G5
Tanjong Malim *Malaysia* **65** L3
Tanjong Pelepas *Malaysia* **65** d
Tanjore = Thanjavur *India* **66** P11
Tanjung *Bali, Indonesia* **63** J19
Tanjung *Kalimantan, Indonesia* **62** E5
Tanjung Tokong *Malaysia* **65** c
Tanjungbalai *Indonesia* **62** D1
Tanjungbatu *Indonesia* **62** D5
Tanjungkarang
  Telukbetung = Bandar
  Lampung *Indonesia* **62** F3
Tanjungpandan *Indonesia* **62** E3
Tanjungpinang *Indonesia* **62** D2
Tanjungredeb *Indonesia* **62** D5
Tanjungselor *Indonesia* **62** D5
Tank *Pakistan* **68** C4
Tankhala *India* **68** J5
Tannersville *U.S.A.* **115** E9
Tannis Bugt *Denmark* **11** G4
Tannu Ola *Asia* **53** D10
Tannum Sands *Australia* **94** C5
Tano ↠ *Ghana* **82** D4
Tanon Str. *Phil.* **61** F5
Tanout *Niger* **83** C6
Tanshui *Taiwan* **59** E13
Tansilla *Burkina Faso* **82** C4
Tanta *Egypt* **80** H7
Tantoyuca *Mexico* **119** C5
Tantung = Dandong *China* **57** D13
Taolanaro *Madag.* **89** D8
Taole *China* **56** E4
Taonan *China* **57** B12
Taormina *Italy* **43** E8
Taos *U.S.A.* **109** H11
Taoudenni *Mali* **78** D5
Taoyuan *China* **59** C8
T'aoyüan *Taiwan* **59** E13
Tapa *Estonia* **32** C3
Tapa Shan = Daba Shan
  China **58** B7
Tapachula *Mexico* **119** E6
Tapah *Malaysia* **65** K3
Tapajós ↠ *Brazil* **125** D8
Tapaktuan *Indonesia* **62** D1
Tapanahoni ↠ *Suriname* **125** C8
Tapanui *N.Z.* **91** F2
Tapauá ↠ *Brazil* **124** E6
Tapes *Brazil* **127** C5
Tapeta *Liberia* **82** D3
Taphan Hin *Thailand* **64** D3
Tapia de Casariego *Spain* **36** B4
Tapirapecó, Serra *Venezuela* **124** C6
Tapo-Capara △ *Venezuela* **121** E5
Tapolca *Hungary* **28** D2
Tapti ↠ *India* **66** J8
Tapuae-o-Uenuku *N.Z.* **91** E4
Tapul Group *Phil.* **61** J4
Tapurucuará *Brazil* **124** D5
Taqtaq *Iraq* **73** E11
Taquara *Brazil* **127** B5
Taquari ↠ *Brazil* **124** D7
Tara *Australia* **95** D5
Tara *Canada* **114** B3
Tara ↠ *Russia* **52** D8
Tara *Zambia* **87** F2
Tara ↠ *Montenegro* **44** C2
Tara △ *Serbia* **44** C3
Taraba □ *Nigeria* **83** D7
Taraba ↠ *Nigeria* **83** D7
Tarābulus *Lebanon* **74** A4
Tarābulus *Libya* **79** B8
Tarābulus N. Afr. *79* B8
Taracha *Taraclia, Moldova* **29** E13
Taraclia *Tighina, Moldova* **29** D14
Taradehi *India* **69** H8
Tarajalejo *Canary Is.* **48** F5
Tarakan *Indonesia* **62** D5
Tarakit, Mt. *Kenya* **86** B4
Tarama-Jima *Japan* **55** M2
Taran, Mys *Russia* **30** D7
Taranagar *India* **68** E6
Taranaki □ *N.Z.* **91** C5
Taranaki, Mt. *N.Z.* **91** C5
Tarancón *Spain* **38** E1
Tarangire △ *Tanzania* **86** C4
Taransay *U.K.* **13** D1
Táranto *Italy* **43** B10
Táranto, G. di *Italy* **43** B10
Tarapacá *Colombia* **124** D5
Tarapacá □ *Chile* **126** A2
Tarapoto *Peru* **124** E3

Tarare *France* **21** C8
Tararua Ra. *N.Z.* **91** D5
Tarascon *France* **21** E8
Tarascon-sur-Ariège *France* **20** F5
Tarashcha *Ukraine* **23** D16
Tarauacá *Brazil* **124** E4
Tarauacá ↠ *Brazil* **124** E5
Taravao *Tahiti* **91** d
Taravao, Isthme de *Tahiti* **91** d
Tarawa *Kiribati* **96** G9
Tarawera *N.Z.* **91** C6
Tarawera, L. *N.Z.* **91** C6
Taraz *Kazakhstan* **52** E8
Tarazona *Spain* **38** D3
Tarazona de la Mancha
  Spain **39** F3
Tarbagatay, Khrebet
  Kazakhstan **52** E9
Tarbat Ness *U.K.* **13** D5
Tarbela Dam *Pakistan* **68** B5
Tarbert *Ireland* **12** D2
Tarbert *Argyll & Bute, U.K.* **13** F3
Tarbert *W. Isles, U.K.* **13** D2
Tarbes *France* **20** E4
Tarboro *U.S.A.* **117** D16
Tărcău, Munţii *Romania* **29** D11
Tarcento *Italy* **41** B10
Tarcoola *Australia* **95** E1
Tarcoon *Australia* **95** E4
Tardets-Sorholus *France* **20** E3
Tardoire ↠ *France* **20** C4
Taree *Australia* **95** E5
Tarfa, W. el ↠ *Egypt* **80** B3
Tarfaya *Morocco* **78** C2
Târgovişte *Romania* **29** F10
Târgu Bujor *Romania* **29** E12
Târgu Cărbuneşti *Romania* **29** F8
Târgu Frumos *Romania* **29** C12
Târgu Jiu *Romania* **29** E8
Târgu Lăpuş *Romania* **29** C8
Târgu Mureş *Romania* **29** D9
Târgu Neamţ *Romania* **29** C11
Târgu Ocna *Romania* **29** D11
Târgu Secuiesc *Romania* **29** E11
Târguşor *Romania* **29** F13
Târhăus, Vf. *Romania* **29** D11
Ţarif *U.A.E.* **71** E7
Tarifa *Spain* **37** J5
Tarija *Bolivia* **126** A3
Tarija □ *Bolivia* **126** A3
Tariku ↠ *Indonesia* **63** E9
Tarim Basin = Tarim Pendi
  China **52** F9
Tarim He ↠ *China* **60** C3
Tarim Pendi *China* **52** F9
Taritatu ↠ *Indonesia* **63** E9
Tarka ↠ *S. Africa* **88** E4
Tarka La *Bhutan* **69** F13
Tarkastad *S. Africa* **88** E4
Tarkhankut, Mys *Ukraine* **33** K7
Tarko Sale *Russia* **52** C8
Tarkwa *Ghana* **82** D4
Tarlac *Phil.* **61** D4
Tarm *Denmark* **11** J2
Tarma *Peru* **124** F3
Tarmiya *Iraq* **73** G11
Tarn □ *France* **20** E6
Tarn ↠ *France* **20** D5
Tarn-et-Garonne □ *France* **20** D5
Tarna ↠ *Hungary* **28** C4
Târnava Mare ↠ *Romania* **29** D8
Târnava Mică ↠ *Romania* **29** D8
Târnăveni *Romania* **29** D9
Tarnica *Poland* **31** J9
Tarnobrzeg *Poland* **31** H8
Tarnogród *Poland* **31** H9
Tarnos *France* **20** E2
Târnova *Moldova* **29** B12
Târnova *Romania* **28** E6
Tarnów *Poland* **31** H8
Tarnowskie Góry *Poland* **31** H5
Tärnsjö *Sweden* **10** D10
Tãro ↠ *Italy* **40** C7
Ţārom *Iran* **71** D7
Taroom *Australia* **95** D4
Taroudannt *Morocco* **78** B4
Tarp *Germany* **24** A5
Tarpon Springs *U.S.A.* **117** G13
Tarquínia *Italy* **41** F8
Tarrafal *C. Verde Is.* **78** b
Tarragona *Spain* **38** D6
Tarragona □ *Spain* **38** D6
Tarraleah *Australia* **95** G4
Tarrasa = Terrassa *Spain* **38** D7
Tàrrega *Spain* **38** D6
Tarrytown *U.S.A.* **115** E11
Tårs *Denmark* **11** G4
Tarsus *Turkey* **72** D6
Tartagal *Argentina* **126** A3
Tärtär *Azerbaijan* **35** K8
Tärtär ↠ *Azerbaijan* **35** K8
Tartas *France* **20** E3
Ţarţūs *Syria* **72** E6
Ţarţūs □ *Syria* **72** E7
Tarumizu *Japan* **55** J5
Tarussa *Russia* **32** E9

Tarutao = Ko Tarutao △ Thailand 65 J2
Tarutao, Ko Thailand 65 J2
Tarutung Indonesia 62 D1
Tarutyne Ukraine 29 D14
Tarvísio Italy 41 B10
Taseko ➤ Canada 102 C4
Tash-Kömür Kyrgyzstan 52 E8
Tash-Kumyr = Tash-Kömür Kyrgyzstan 52 E8
Tashauz = Dashoguz Turkmenistan 52 E6
Tashi Chho Dzong = Thimphu Bhutan 67 F16
Tashk, Daryācheh-ye Iran 71 D7
Tashkent = Toshkent Uzbekistan 52 E7
Tashtagol Russia 52 D9
Tasiilaq Greenland 4 C6
Tasik Kenyir Malaysia 65 K4
Tasikmalaya Indonesia 63 G13
Tåsinge Denmark 11 J4
Tåsjön Sweden 8 D16
Task Niger 83 C7
Taskan Russia 53 C16
Taşkent Turkey 72 D5
Taşköprü Turkey 72 B6
Taşlâc Moldova 29 C14
Taşliçay Turkey 73 C10
Tasman B. N.Z. 91 D4
Tasman Basin Pac. Oc. 96 M7
Tasman Mts. N.Z. 91 D4
Tasman Pen. Australia 95 G4
Tasman Sea Pac. Oc. 90 E9
Tasmania □ Australia 95 G4
Tasmanian Wilderness World Heritage Area △ Australia 95 G4
Tăşnad Romania 28 C7
Taşova Turkey 72 B7
Tassili n'Ajjer Algeria 78 C7
Tassili-Oua-n-Ahaggar Algeria 78 D7
Tassili Tin-Rerhoh Algeria 83 A5
Tasuj Iran 73 C11
Tat Ton △ Thailand 64 E4
Tata Hungary 28 C3
Tata Morocco 78 C4
Tatabánya Hungary 28 C3
Tatahouine Tunisia 79 B8
Tataouine Tunisia 79 B8
Tatar Republic = Tatarstan □ Russia 34 C10
Tatarbunary Ukraine 29 E14
Tatarsk Russia 52 D8
Tatarskiy Proliv Russia 53 E15
Tatarstan □ Russia 34 C10
Tatatua, Pte. Tahiti 91 d
Tateyama Japan 55 G9
Tathlina L. Canada 102 A5
Tathra Australia 95 F4
Tatinnai L. Canada 103 A9
Tatla Lake Canada 102 C4
Tatlısu Turkey 45 F11
Tatnam, C. Canada 103 B10
Tatra = Tatry Slovak Rep. 27 B13
Tatransky △ Slovak Rep. 27 B13
Tatry Slovak Rep. 27 B13
Tatshenshini ➤ Canada 102 B1
Tatsuno Japan 55 G7
Tatta Pakistan 68 G2
Tatuí Brazil 127 A6
Tatum U.S.A. 109 K12
Tat'ung = Datong China 56 D7
Tatvan Turkey 73 C10
Ta'ū Amer. Samoa 91 b
Taubaté Brazil 127 A6
Tauberbischofsheim Germany 25 F5
Taucha Germany 24 D8
Tauern Austria 22 E7
Tauern-tunnel Austria 26 D8
Taufikia Sudan 81 F3
Taulé France 18 D3
Taumarunui N.Z. 91 C5
Taumaturgo Brazil 124 E4
Taung S. Africa 88 D3
Taungdwingyi Burma 67 J19
Taunggyi Burma 67 J20
Taungup Burma 67 K19
Taunsa Pakistan 68 D4
Taunsa Barrage Pakistan 68 D4
Taunton U.K. 15 F4
Taunton U.S.A. 115 E13
Taunus Germany 25 E4
Taupo N.Z. 91 C6
Taupo, L. N.Z. 91 C5
Tauragė Lithuania 30 C9
Tauragė □ Lithuania 30 C9
Tauranga N.Z. 91 B6
Tauranga Harb. N.Z. 91 B6
Taureau, Rés. Canada 104 C5
Taurianova Italy 43 D9
Taurus Mts. = Toros Dağları Turkey 72 D5
Tauste Spain 38 D3
Tautira Tahiti 91 d
Tauz = Tovuz Azerbaijan 35 K7
Tavas Turkey 47 D11

Tavastehus = Hämeenlinna Finland 32 B3
Tavda Russia 52 D7
Tavda ➤ Russia 52 D7
Taverner B. Canada 101 D17
Tavernes de la Valldigna Spain 39 F4
Taveta Kenya 86 C4
Taveuni Fiji 91 a
Taviano Italy 43 C11
Tavignano ➤ France 21 F13
Tavira Portugal 37 H3
Tavistock Canada 114 C4
Tavistock U.K. 15 G3
Tavolara Italy 42 B2
Távora ➤ Portugal 36 D3
Tavoy Burma 64 E2
Tavrichanka Russia 54 C5
Tavropos ➤ Greece 46 B3
Tavşanlı Turkey 47 B11
Tavua Fiji 91 a
Tavuki Fiji 91 a
Taw ➤ U.K. 15 F3
Tawa ➤ India 68 H8
Tawas City U.S.A. 113 C12
Tawau Malaysia 62 D5
Taweisha Sudan 81 E2
Tawi-Tawi Phil. 63 C6
Tawu Taiwan 59 F13
Tāwūq Iraq 73 E11
Taxco Mexico 119 D5
Taxila Pakistan 68 C5
Tay ➤ U.K. 13 E5
Tay, Firth of U.K. 13 E5
Tay, L. Australia 93 F3
Tay, L. U.K. 13 E4
Tay △ U.K. 13 E5
Tay Ninh Vietnam 65 G6
Tayabamba Peru 124 E3
Tayabas Bay Phil. 61 E4
Taygetos Oros Greece 46 D4
Taylakova Russia 52 D8
Taylor Canada 102 B4
Taylor Nebr., U.S.A. 112 E4
Taylor Pa., U.S.A. 115 E9
Taylor Tex., U.S.A. 116 F6
Taylor, Mt. U.S.A. 109 J10
Taylorville U.S.A. 112 F9
Taymā Si. Arabia 70 E3
Taymyr, Oz. Russia 53 B11
Taymyr, Poluostrov Russia 53 B11
Tayport U.K. 13 E6
Tayrona △ Colombia 121 D5
Tayshet Russia 53 D10
Taytay Phil. 61 F3
Täyyebād Iran 71 C9
Täyyebād □ Iran 71 C9
Taz ➤ Russia 52 C8
Taza Morocco 78 B5
Taza Khurmātū Iraq 73 E11
Tazawa-Ko Japan 54 E10
Tazerbo Libya 79 C10
Tazin ➤ Canada 103 B7
Tazin L. Canada 103 B7
Tazovskiy Russia 52 C8
Tbilisi Georgia 35 K7
Tchad = Chad ■ Africa 79 F8
Tchad, L. Chad 79 F8
Tchaourou Benin 83 D5
Tch'eng-tou = Chengdu China 58 B5
Tchentlo L. Canada 102 B4
Tchetti Benin 83 D5
Tchibanga Gabon 84 E2
Tchien Liberia 82 D3
Tchin Tabaraden Niger 83 B6
Tch'ong-k'ing = Chongqing China 58 C6
Tczew Poland 30 D5
Te Anau, L. N.Z. 91 F1
Te Aroha N.Z. 91 B5
Te Awamutu N.Z. 91 C5
Te Ika a Maui = North I. N.Z. 91 C5
Te Kuiti N.Z. 91 C5
Te-n-Dghâmcha, Sebkhet Mauritania 82 B1
Te Puke N.Z. 91 B6
Te Waewae B. N.Z. 91 G1
Te Wai Pounamu = South I. N.Z. 91 F3
Teaca Romania 29 D9
Teague U.S.A. 116 F6
Teahupoo Tahiti 91 d
Teano Italy 43 A7
Teapa Mexico 119 D6
Teba Spain 37 J6
Tebakang Malaysia 62 D4
Tébarat Niger 83 C6
Teberda Russia 35 J5
Teberu Malaysia 65 d
Tébessa Algeria 78 A7
Tebicuary ➤ Paraguay 126 B4
Tebingtinggi Riau, Indonesia 62 E2
Tebingtinggi Sumatera Utara, Indonesia 62 D1
Tebulos Georgia 35 J7
Tecate Mexico 111 N10
Tecer Dağları Turkey 72 C7
Tech ➤ France 20 F7

Techiman Ghana 82 D4
Techirghiol Romania 29 F13
Tecka Argentina 128 E2
Tecomán Mexico 118 D4
Tecopa U.S.A. 111 K10
Tecoripa Mexico 118 B3
Tecuala Mexico 118 C3
Tecuci Romania 29 E12
Tecumseh Canada 114 D2
Tecumseh Mich., U.S.A. 113 D12
Tecumseh Okla., U.S.A. 116 D6
Tedzhen = Tejen Turkmenistan 52 F7
Tees ➤ U.K. 14 C6
Tees B. U.K. 14 C6
Teeswater Canada 114 C3
Tefé Brazil 124 D6
Tefenni Turkey 47 D11
Tegal Indonesia 62 F3
Tegallalang Indonesia 63 J18
Tegalsari Indonesia 63 J17
Tegel, Berlin ✈ (TXL) Germany 24 C9
Tegernsee Germany 25 H7
Teggiano Italy 43 B8
Tegid, L. = Bala, L. U.K. 14 E4
Tegina Nigeria 83 C6
Tegucigalpa Honduras 120 D2
Teguidda i-n-Tessoum Niger 83 B6
Tehachapi U.S.A. 111 K8
Tehachapi Mts. U.S.A. 111 L8
Tehamiyam Sudan 80 D4
Tehilla Sudan 80 D4
Téhini Ivory C. 82 D4
Tehoru Indonesia 63 E7
Tehrān Iran 71 C6
Tehrān □ Iran 71 C6
Tehri India 69 D8
Tehuacán Mexico 119 D5
Tehuantepec Mexico 119 D5
Tehuantepec, G. de Mexico 119 D5
Tehuantepec, Istmo de Mexico 119 D6
Teide, Pico de Canary Is. 48 F3
Teifi ➤ U.K. 15 E3
Teigebyen Norway 10 D5
Teign ➤ U.K. 15 G4
Teignmouth U.K. 15 G4
Teiuş Romania 29 D8
Teixeira Pinto Guinea-Biss. 82 C1
Tejam India 69 E9
Tejen Turkmenistan 52 F7
Tejen ➤ Turkmenistan 71 B9
Tejo ➤ Europe 37 D2
Tejon Pass U.S.A. 111 L8
Tekamah U.S.A. 112 E5
Tekapo, L. N.Z. 91 E3
Tekax Mexico 119 C7
Teke Turkey 45 E13
Tekeli Kazakhstan 52 E8
Tekeze ➤ Ethiopia 81 E4
Tekija Serbia 44 B6
Tekirdağ Turkey 45 F11
Tekirdağ □ Turkey 45 E11
Tekirova Turkey 47 E12
Tekkali India 67 K14
Tekke Turkey 72 B7
Tekman Turkey 73 C9
Tekoa U.S.A. 108 C5
Tekong Besar, Pulau Singapore 65 d
Tel Aviv ✈ (TLV) Israel 74 C3
Tel Aviv-Yafo Israel 74 C3
Tel Lakhish Israel 74 D3
Tel Megiddo Israel 74 C4
Tela Honduras 120 C2
Telanaipura = Jambi Indonesia 62 E2
Telašćica △ Croatia 41 E12
Telavi Georgia 35 J7
Telč Czech Rep. 26 B8
Telciu Romania 29 C9
Telde Canary Is. 48 G4
Telegraph Creek Canada 102 B2
Telekhany = Tsyelyakhany Belarus 23 B13
Telemark Norway 9 G12
Telemsés Niger 83 B5
Telén Argentina 126 D2
Teleng Iran 71 E9
Teleño Spain 36 C4
Teleorman □ Romania 29 G10
Teleorman ➤ Romania 29 G10
Teles Pires ➤ Brazil 124 E7
Telescope Pk. U.S.A. 111 J9
Teletaye Mali 83 B5
Telford and Wrekin □ U.K. 14 E5
Telfs Austria 26 D4
Télimélé Guinea 82 C2
Teljo, J. Sudan 81 E2
Telkwa Canada 102 C3
Tell City U.S.A. 112 G10
Teller U.S.A. 106 B6
Tellicherry India 66 P9
Telluride U.S.A. 109 H10
Teloloapán Mexico 119 D5
Telpos Iz Russia 6 C17

Telsen Argentina 128 E3
Telšiai Lithuania 30 C9
Telšiai □ Lithuania 30 C9
Teltow Germany 24 C9
Teluk Anson = Teluk Intan Malaysia 65 K3
Teluk Bahang Malaysia 65 c
Teluk Betung = Bandar Lampung Indonesia 62 F3
Teluk Intan Malaysia 65 K3
Teluk Kumbar Malaysia 65 c
Telukbutun Indonesia 62 D3
Telukdalem Indonesia 62 D1
Tema Ghana 83 D5
Temagami, L. Canada 104 C3
Temax Mexico 119 C7
Temba S. Africa 89 D4
Tembagapura Indonesia 63 E9
Tembe Dem. Rep. of the Congo 86 C2
Tembe △ S. Africa 89 D5
Tembleque Spain 36 F7
Temblor Range U.S.A. 111 K7
Teme ➤ U.K. 15 E5
Temecula U.S.A. 111 M9
Temengor, Tasik Malaysia 65 K3
Temerloh Malaysia 65 L4
Temir Kazakhstan 52 E6
Temirtau Russia 52 D9
Temiscamie ➤ Canada 105 B5
Témiscaming Canada 104 C4
Témiscamingue, L. Canada 104 C4
Temnikov Russia 34 C6
Temo ➤ Italy 42 B1
Temosachic Mexico 118 B3
Tempe U.S.A. 109 K8
Témpio Pausánia Italy 42 B2
Tempiute U.S.A. 110 H11
Temple U.S.A. 116 F6
Temple B. Australia 94 A3
Templemore Ireland 12 D4
Templeton U.S.A. 110 K6
Templeton ➤ Australia 94 C2
Templin Germany 24 B9
Tempoal de Sánchez Mexico 119 C5
Temryuk Russia 33 K9
Temska ➤ Serbia 44 C6
Temuco Chile 128 D2
Temuka N.Z. 91 F3
Tenabo Mexico 119 C6
Tenaha U.S.A. 116 F7
Tenakee Springs U.S.A. 102 B1
Tenali India 67 L12
Tenancingo de Degollado Mexico 119 D5
Tenango del Valle Mexico 119 D5
Tenaro, Akra Greece 46 E4
Tenasserim Burma 65 F2
Tenasserim □ Burma 64 F2
Tenby U.K. 15 F3
Tenda, Colle di France 21 D11
Tendaho Ethiopia 81 E5
Tende France 21 D11
Tendelti Sudan 81 E3
Tendukhera India 69 H8
Tendrovska Kosa Ukraine 33 J6
Teneguía, Volcanes de Canary Is. 48 F2
Teneida Egypt 80 B2
Tenenkou Mali 82 C4
Ténéré Niger 83 B7
Ténéré, Erg du Niger 79 E8
Tenerife Canary Is. 48 F3
Tenerife, Pico Canary Is. 48 G1
Tenerife Norte ✈ (TFN) Canary Is. 48 F3
Tenerife Sur ✈ (TFS) Canary Is. 48 F3
Teng Xian Guangxi Zhuangzu, China 59 F8
Teng Xian Shandong, China 57 G9
Tengah, Kepulauan Indonesia 62 F5
Tengchong China 58 D1
Tengchowfu = Penglai China 57 F11
Tenggarong Indonesia 62 E5
Tenggol, Pulau Malaysia 65 K4
Tengiz Köli Kazakhstan 52 D7
Tenhult Sweden 11 G8
Teniente Enciso △ Paraguay 126 A3
Teniente Rodolfo Marsh Antarctica 5 C18
Tenino U.S.A. 110 D4
Tenkasi India 66 Q10
Tenke Katanga, Dem. Rep. of the Congo 87 E2
Tenke Katanga, Dem. Rep. of the Congo 87 E2
Tenkodogo Burkina Faso 83 C4
Tenna ➤ Italy 41 E10
Tennant Creek Australia 94 B1
Tennessee □ U.S.A. 117 D11
Tennessee ➤ U.S.A. 117 C10
Teno, Pta. de Canary Is. 48 F3
Tenom Malaysia 62 C5
Tenosique Mexico 119 D6
Tenryū-Gawa ➤ Japan 55 G8
Tenterden U.K. 15 F8
Tenterfield Australia 95 D5
Teo = A Ramallosa Spain 36 C2

Teófilo Otoni Brazil 125 G10
Tepa Indonesia 63 F7
Tepalcatepec ➤ Mexico 118 D4
Tepecik Bursa, Turkey 45 F12
Tepecik Kütahya, Turkey 47 B11
Tepehuanes Mexico 118 B3
Tepelenë Albania 44 F4
Tepic Mexico 118 C4
Teplá Czech Rep. 26 B5
Teplice Czech Rep. 26 A6
Teploca, C. Mexico 118 A2
Teplyk Ukraine 29 B14
Tepoca, C. Mexico 118 A2
Tequila Mexico 118 C4
Ter ➤ Spain 38 C8
Ter Apel Neths. 17 B7
Téra Niger 83 C5
Tera ➤ Spain 36 D5
Teraina Kiribati 97 G12
Terakeka Sudan 81 F3
Terang Australia 95 F3
Terang, Teluk Indonesia 63 K19
Terazit, Massif de Niger 83 A6
Tercan Turkey 73 C9
Tercero ➤ Argentina 126 C3
Terebovlya Ukraine 23 D13
Teregova Romania 28 E7
Terek ➤ Russia 35 J8
Terepaima △ Venezuela 121 E6
Tereshka ➤ Russia 34 E8
Teresina Brazil 125 E10
Terespol Poland 31 F10
Teresva Ukraine 29 B8
Terewah, L. Australia 95 D4
Terges ➤ Portugal 37 H3
Tergnier France 19 C10
Terlizzi Italy 43 A9
Termas de Río Hondo Argentina 126 B3
Terme Turkey 72 B7
Termez = Termiz Uzbekistan 52 F7
Términi Imerese Italy 42 E6
Términos, L. de Mexico 119 D6
Termiz Uzbekistan 52 F7
Térmoli Italy 41 F12
Ternate Indonesia 63 D7
Terneuzen Neths. 17 C3
Terney Russia 54 B8
Terni Italy 41 F9
Ternitz Austria 26 D9
Ternivka Ukraine 29 B14
Ternopil Ukraine 23 D13
Ternopil □ Ukraine 33 H3
Ternopol = Ternopil Ukraine 23 D13
Terowie Australia 95 E2
Terpni Greece 44 D5
Terra Bella U.S.A. 111 K7
Terra Nova △ Canada 105 C9
Terrace Canada 102 C3
Terrace Bay Canada 104 C2
Terracina Italy 42 A6
Terralba Italy 42 C1
Terrasini Italy 42 D6
Terrassa Spain 38 D7
Terrasson-la-Villedieu France 20 C5
Terre Haute U.S.A. 112 F10
Terrebonne B. U.S.A. 117 G9
Terrecht Mali 83 B5
Terrell U.S.A. 116 E6
Terrenceville Canada 105 C9
Terry U.S.A. 108 C11
Terryville U.S.A. 115 E11
Tersko-Kumskiy Kanal Russia 35 H7
Tertenia Italy 42 C2
Terter = Tärtär ➤ Azerbaijan 35 K8
Teruel Spain 38 E3
Teruel □ Spain 38 E4
Tervel Bulgaria 45 C11
Tervola Finland 8 C21
Teryaweynya L. Australia 95 E3
Tešanj Bos.-H. 28 F7
Teseney Eritrea 81 D4
Teshio-Gawa ➤ Japan 54 B10
Tešica Serbia 44 C5
Tesiyn Gol ➤ Mongolia 60 A4
Teslić Bos.-H. 28 F2
Teslin Canada 102 A2
Teslin ➤ Canada 102 A2
Teslin L. Canada 102 A2
Tessalit Mali 83 A5
Tessaoua Niger 83 C6
Tessin Germany 24 A8
Tessit Mali 83 B5
Test ➤ U.K. 15 F6
Testa del Gargano Italy 41 G13
Testigos, Is. Los Venezuela 121 D7
Tét Hungary 28 C3
Tét ➤ France 20 F7
Tetachuck L. Canada 102 C3
Tetas, Pta. Chile 126 A1
Tete Mozam. 87 F3
Tete □ Mozam. 87 F3

Teterev ➤ Ukraine 23 C16
Teterow Germany 24 B8
Teteven Bulgaria 45 D8
Tethul ➤ Canada 102 A6
Tetiyev Ukraine 23 D15
Teton ➤ U.S.A. 108 C8
Tétouan Morocco 78 A4
Tetovo Macedonia 44 D4
Tetufera, Mt. Tahiti 91 d
Tetyushi Russia 34 C9
Teuco ➤ Argentina 126 B3
Teulada Italy 42 D1
Teulon Canada 103 C9
Teun Indonesia 63 F7
Teuri-Tō Japan 54 B10
Teutoburger Wald Germany 24 C4
Tevere ➤ Italy 41 G9
Tevere △ Italy 41 F9
Teverya Israel 74 C4
Teviot ➤ U.K. 13 F6
Tewantin Australia 95 D5
Tewkesbury U.K. 15 F5
Texada I. Canada 102 D4
Texarkana Ark., U.S.A. 116 E7
Texarkana Tex., U.S.A. 116 E7
Texas Australia 95 D5
Texas □ U.S.A. 116 F5
Texas City U.S.A. 116 G7
Texel Neths. 17 A4
Texline U.S.A. 116 C3
Texoma, L. U.S.A. 116 E6
Teyateyaneng Lesotho 85 K5
Teykovo Russia 32 D11
Teza ➤ Russia 34 B5
Tezin Afghan. 68 B3
Teziutlán Mexico 119 D5
Tezzeron L. Canada 102 C4
Tha-anne ➤ Canada 103 A10
Tha Deua Laos 64 D4
Tha Deua Laos 64 C3
Tha Li Thailand 64 D3
Tha Pla Thailand 64 D3
Tha Rua Thailand 64 E3
Tha Sala Thailand 65 H2
Tha Song Yang Thailand 64 D1
Thaba Putsoa Lesotho 89 D4
Thabana Ntlenyana Lesotho 89 D4
Thabazimbi S. Africa 89 C4
Thādiq Si. Arabia 70 E5
Thai Binh Vietnam 58 G6
Thai Muang Thailand 65 H2
Thai Nguyen Vietnam 58 G5
Thailand ■ Asia 64 E4
Thailand, G. of Asia 65 G3
Thakhek Laos 64 D5
Thal Pakistan 68 C4
Thal Desert Pakistan 68 D4
Thala La = Hkakabo Razi Burma 67 E20
Thalabarivat Cambodia 64 F5
Thalassery = Tellicherry India 66 P9
Thallon Australia 95 D4
Thalu, Ko Thailand 65 b
Thalwil Switz. 25 H4
Thames N.Z. 91 B5
Thames ➤ Canada 114 D2
Thames ➤ U.K. 15 F8
Thames ➤ U.S.A. 115 E12
Thames Estuary U.K. 15 F8
Thamesford Canada 114 C4
Thamesville Canada 114 D3
Than India 68 H4
Than Uyen Vietnam 64 B4
Thana Gazi India 68 F7
Thandla India 68 H6
Thandwe Burma 67 K19
Thane India 66 K8
Thanesar India 68 D7
Thanet, I. of U.K. 15 F9
Thangool Australia 94 C5
Thanh Hoa Vietnam 64 C5
Thanh Hung Vietnam 65 H5
Thanh Pho Ho Chi Minh Vietnam 65 G6
Thanh Thuy Vietnam 64 A5
Thanjavur India 66 P11
Thanlwin = Salween ➤ Burma 67 L20
Thann France 19 E14
Thano Bula Khan Pakistan 68 G2
Thaolintoa L. Canada 103 A9
Thaon-les-Vosges France 19 D13
Thap Lan △ Thailand 64 E4
Thap Sakae Thailand 65 G2
Thap Than Thailand 64 E2
Thar Desert India 68 F5
Tharad India 68 G4
Thargomindah Australia 95 D3
Tharp Fracture Zone S. Ocean 5 B14
Tharrawaddy Burma 67 L19
Tharthār, Buhayrat ath Iraq 73 E10
Tharthar, L. = Tharthār, Buhayrat ath Iraq 73 E10
Tharthār, W. ath ➤ Iraq 73 E10
Thasopoula Greece 45 F8
Thasos Greece 45 F8
That Khe Vietnam 58 F6

Thatcher *Ariz., U.S.A.* 109 K9
Thatcher *Colo., U.S.A.* 109 H11
Thaton *Burma* 67 L20
Thau, Bassin de *France* 20 E7
Thaungdut *Burma* 67 G19
Thayer *U.S.A.* 112 G8
Thayetmyo *Burma* 67 K19
Thazi *Burma* 67 J20
Thbeng Meanchey *Cambodia* 64 F5
The Broads *U.K.* 14 E9
The Everglades *U.S.A.* 117 J14
The Gulf = Persian Gulf *Asia* 71 E6
The Hague =
  's-Gravenhage *Neths.* 17 B4
The Pas *Canada* 103 C8
The Wash *U.K.* 14 E8
The Weald *U.K.* 15 F8
Thebes = Thiva *Greece* 46 C5
Thebes *Egypt* 80 B3
Thedford *U.S.A.* 112 E3
Theebine *Australia* 95 D5
Thekulthili L. *Canada* 103 A7
Thelon ➤ *Canada* 103 A8
Thénezay *France* 18 F6
Thenon *France* 20 C5
Theodore *Australia* 94 C5
Theodore *Canada* 103 C8
Theodore *U.S.A.* 117 F10
Theodore Roosevelt △
  U.S.A. 112 B2
Theodore Roosevelt L.
  U.S.A. 109 K8
Thepha *Thailand* 65 J3
Thérain ➤ *France* 19 C9
Theresa *U.S.A.* 115 B9
Thermopolis *U.S.A.* 108 E9
Thermopylae *Greece* 46 C4
Thesprotia □ *Greece* 46 B2
Thessalon *Canada* 104 C3
Thessalonica, Gulf of =
  Thessaloniki Kolpos *Greece* 44 F6
Thessaloniki *Greece* 44 F6
Thessaloniki □ *Greece* 44 F7
Thessaloniki ✈ (SKG) *Greece* 44 F7
Thessaloniki Kolpos *Greece* 44 F6
Thessaly □ *Greece* 46 B4
Thetford *U.K.* 15 E8
Thetford Mines *Canada* 105 C5
Theun ➤ *Laos* 64 C5
Theunissen *S. Africa* 88 D4
Thevenard *Australia* 95 E1
Thiamis ➤ *Greece* 46 B2
Thibeville *France* 18 C7
Thibodaux *U.S.A.* 117 G9
Thicket Portage *Canada* 103 B9
Thief River Falls *U.S.A.* 112 A5
Thiel Mts. *Antarctica* 5 E16
Thiene *Italy* 41 C8
Thiérache *France* 19 C10
Thiers *France* 20 C7
Thiès *Senegal* 82 C1
Thiès □ *Senegal* 82 C1
Thiesi *Italy* 42 B1
Thika *Kenya* 86 C4
Thille-Boubacar *Senegal* 82 B1
Thimphu *Bhutan* 67 F16
Thina ➤ *S. Africa* 89 E4
Þingvallavatn *Iceland* 8 D3
Thionville *France* 19 C13
Thira = Santorini *Greece* 47 E7
Thirasia *Greece* 47 E7
Third Cataract *Sudan* 80 D3
Thirsk *U.K.* 14 C6
Thiruvananthapuram =
  Trivandrum *India* 66 Q10
Thisted *Denmark* 11 H2
Thistle I. *Australia* 95 F2
Thithia = Cicia *Fiji* 91 a
Thiva *Greece* 46 C5
Thiviers *France* 20 C4
Thizy *France* 19 F11
Þjórsá ➤ *Iceland* 8 E3
Thlewiaza ➤ *Canada* 103 A10
Thmar Puok *Cambodia* 64 F4
Tho Vinh *Vietnam* 64 C5
Thoa ➤ *Canada* 103 A7
Thoen *Thailand* 64 D2
Thoeng *Thailand* 64 C3
Thohoyandou *S. Africa* 85 J6
Tholdi *Pakistan* 69 B7
Thomas *U.S.A.* 116 D5
Thomas, L. *Australia* 95 D2
Thomas Hubbard, C. *Canada* 101 A13
Thomaston *U.S.A.* 117 E12
Thomasville *Ala., U.S.A.* 117 F11
Thomasville *Ga., U.S.A.* 117 F13
Thomasville *N.C., U.S.A.* 117 D14
Thompson *Canada* 103 B9
Thompson *U.S.A.* 115 E9
Thompson ➤ *Canada* 102 C4
Thompson ➤ *U.S.A.* 112 F7
Thompson Falls *U.S.A.* 108 C6
Thompson Pk. *U.S.A.* 108 F2
Thompson Springs *U.S.A.* 108 G9
Thompsontown *U.S.A.* 114 F7
Thomson *U.S.A.* 117 E13
Thomson ➤ *Australia* 94 C3
Thônes *France* 21 C10
Thong Yang *Thailand* 65 b

Thonon-les-Bains *France* 19 F13
Thoothukudi = Tuticorin
  India 66 Q11
Thorez *Ukraine* 33 H10
Þórisvatn *Iceland* 8 D4
Thornaby on Tees *U.K.* 14 C6
Thornbury *Canada* 114 B4
Thorne *U.K.* 14 D7
Thornton *Canada* 114 B5
Thornton *U.S.A.* 108 G11
Thorold *Canada* 114 C5
Þórshöfn *Iceland* 8 C6
Thouarcé *France* 18 E6
Thouars *France* 18 F6
Thouet ➤ *France* 18 E6
Thouin, C. *Australia* 92 D2
Thousand Islands *U.S.A.* 115 B9
Thousand Oaks *U.S.A.* 111 L8
Thrace *Turkey* 45 F10
Thrace, Sea of *Greece* 45 F8
Three Forks *U.S.A.* 108 D8
Three Gorges Dam *China* 59 B8
Three Hills *Canada* 102 C6
Three Hummock I. *Australia* 95 G3
Three Pagodas Pass *Asia* 64 E2
Three Points, C. *Ghana* 82 E4
Three Rivers *Calif., U.S.A.* 110 J8
Three Rivers *Tex., U.S.A.* 116 G5
Three Springs *Australia* 93 E2
Thrissur = Trichur *India* 66 P10
Throssell, L. *Australia* 93 E3
Throssell Ra. *Australia* 93 D3
Thrushton △ *Australia* 95 D4
Thua ➤ *Kenya* 86 C4
Thuan Hoa *Vietnam* 65 H5
Thubun Lakes *Canada* 103 A6
Thueyts *France* 21 D8
Thuin *Belgium* 17 D4
Thuir *France* 20 F6
Thule = Qaanaaq *Greenland* 101 B18
Thule Air Base =
  Uummannaq *Greenland* 101 B18
Thun *Switz.* 25 J3
Thunder B. *U.S.A.* 114 B1
Thunder Bay *Canada* 104 C2
Thunersee *Switz.* 25 J3
Thung Salaeng Luang △
  Thailand 64 D3
Thung Song *Thailand* 65 H2
Thunkar *Bhutan* 67 F17
Thuong Tra *Vietnam* 64 D6
Thur ➤ *Switz.* 25 H5
Thurgau □ *Switz.* 25 H5
Thüringen □ *Germany* 24 D6
Thüringer Wald *Germany* 24 E6
Thuringowa △ *Australia* 94 B4
Thurles *Ireland* 12 D4
Thurn P. *Austria* 26 D5
Thurrock □ *U.K.* 15 F8
Thursday I. *Australia* 94 A3
Thurso *Canada* 104 C4
Thurso *U.K.* 13 C5
Thurso ➤ *U.K.* 13 C5
Thurston I. *Antarctica* 5 D16
Thury-Harcourt *France* 18 D6
Thutade L. *Canada* 102 B3
Thy *Denmark* 11 H2
Thyborøn *Denmark* 11 H2
Thyolo *Malawi* 87 F4
Ti-n-Amzi ➤ *Niger* 83 B5
Ti-n-Barraouene, O. ➤
  Africa 83 B5
Ti-n-Zaouatene *Algeria* 83 B5
Ti-Tree *Australia* 94 C1
Tiadiaye *Senegal* 82 C1
Tian Shan *Asia* 60 B3
Tianchang *China* 59 A12
Tiandeng *China* 58 F6
Tiandong *China* 58 F6
Tian'e *China* 58 E6
Tianhe *China* 58 E7
Tianjin *China* 57 E9
Tiankoura *Burkina Faso* 82 C4
Tianlin *China* 58 E6
Tianmen *China* 59 B9
Tianquan *China* 58 B4
Tianshifu *China* 57 D13
Tianshui *China* 56 G3
Tiantai *China* 59 C13
Tianyang *China* 58 F6
Tianyar *Indonesia* 63 J18
Tianzhen *China* 56 D8
Tianzhu *China* 58 D7
Tianzhuangtai *China* 57 D12
Tiarei *Tahiti* 91 d
Tiaret *Algeria* 78 A6
Tiassalé *Ivory C.* 82 D4
Tibagi *Brazil* 127 A5
Tibagi ➤ *Brazil* 127 A5
Tibastī, Sarīr *Libya* 79 D9
Tibati *Cameroon* 83 D7
Tibe *Ethiopia* 81 F4
Tiber = Tevere ➤ *Italy* 41 G9
Tiber Res. *U.S.A.* 108 B8
Tiberias = Teverya *Israel* 74 C4
Tiberias, L. = Yam
  Kinneret *Israel* 74 C4
Tibesti *Chad* 79 D9

Tibet = Xizang Zizhiqu □
  China 60 C3
Tibet, Plateau of *Asia* 50 E10
Tibiao *Phil.* 61 F5
Tibiri *Niger* 83 C6
Tibnī *Syria* 73 E8
Tibooburra *Australia* 95 D3
Tibro *Sweden* 11 F8
Tiburón, I. *Mexico* 118 B2
Ticao I. *Phil.* 61 E5
Tîchît *Mauritania* 82 B3
Ticho *Ethiopia* 81 F4
Ticino □ *Switz.* 25 J4
Ticino ➤ *Italy* 25 J4
Ticleni *Romania* 29 F8
Ticul *Mexico* 119 C7
Tidaholm *Sweden* 11 F8
Tidan *Sweden* 11 F8
Tiddim *Burma* 67 H18
Tidioute *U.S.A.* 114 E5
Tidjikja *Mauritania* 82 B2
Tidore *Indonesia* 63 D7
Tiébissou *Ivory C.* 82 D3
Tiefa *China* 57 C12
Tiel *Neths.* 17 C5
Tiel *Senegal* 82 C1
Tieling *China* 57 C12
Tielt *Belgium* 17 C3
Tien Shan = Tian Shan *Asia* 60 B3
Tien-tsin = Tianjin *China* 57 E9
Tien Yen *Vietnam* 64 B6
T'ienching = Tianjin *China* 57 E9
Tienen *Belgium* 17 D4
Tientsin = Tianjin *China* 57 E9
Tieri *Australia* 94 C4
Tierp *Sweden* 10 D11
Tierra Amarilla *Chile* 126 B1
Tierra Amarilla *U.S.A.* 109 H10
Tierra Colorada *Mexico* 119 D5
Tierra de Barros *Spain* 37 G4
Tierra de Campos *Spain* 36 C6
Tierra del Fuego, I. Grande
  de *Argentina* 128 G3
Tiétar ➤ *Spain* 36 F4
Tietê ➤ *Brazil* 127 A5
Tiffin *U.S.A.* 113 E12
Tifton *U.S.A.* 117 F13
Tifu *Indonesia* 63 E7
Tiga Res. *Nigeria* 83 C6
Tighina *Moldova* 29 D14
Tigil *Russia* 53 D16
Tignish *Canada* 105 C7
Tigray □ *Ethiopia* 81 E4
Tigre ➤ *Peru* 124 D3
Tigre ➤ *Venezuela* 124 B6
Tigris = Dijlah, Nahr ➤
  Asia 70 D5
Tigveni *Romania* 29 E9
Tigyaing *Burma* 67 H20
Tîh, Gebel el *Egypt* 80 B3
Tihāmah *Asia* 75 D3
Tijara *India* 68 F7
Tijuana *Mexico* 111 N9
Tikal *Guatemala* 120 C2
Tikal △ *Guatemala* 120 C2
Tikamgarh *India* 69 G8
Tikaré *Burkina Faso* 83 C4
Tikchik Lakes *U.S.A.* 106 D8
Tikhoretsk *Russia* 35 H5
Tikhvin *Russia* 32 C5
Tikirarjuaq = Whale Cove
  Canada 103 A10
Tikmehdāsh *Iran* 73 D12
Tiko *Cameroon* 83 E6
Tikrīt *Iraq* 73 E10
Tiksi *Russia* 53 B13
Tilamuta *Indonesia* 63 D6
Tilburg *Neths.* 17 C5
Tilbury *Canada* 114 D2
Tilbury *U.K.* 15 F8
Tilcara *Argentina* 126 A2
Tilden *U.S.A.* 112 D5
Tilemsi, Vallée du *Mali* 83 B5
Tilhar *India* 69 F8
Tilichiki *Russia* 53 C17
Tilissos *Greece* 49 D7
Till ➤ *U.K.* 14 B5
Tillabéri *Niger* 83 C5
Tillamook *U.S.A.* 108 D2
Tillberga *Sweden* 10 E10
Tillia *Niger* 83 B5
Tillsonburg *Canada* 114 D4
Tillyeria *Cyprus* 49 D11
Tilogne *Senegal* 82 B2
Tilos *Greece* 47 E9
Tilpa *Australia* 95 E3
Tilt ➤ *U.K.* 13 E5
Tilton *U.S.A.* 115 C13
Tiltonsville *U.S.A.* 114 F4
Tim *Denmark* 11 H2
Tima *Egypt* 80 B3
Timanfaya △ *Canary Is.* 48 F6
Timaru *N.Z.* 91 F3
Timashëvo *Russia* 34 D10
Timashevsk *Russia* 35 H4
Timau *Kenya* 86 B4

Timbaki *Greece* 49 D6
Timbedgha *Mauritania* 82 B3
Timber Creek *Australia* 92 C5
Timber Lake *U.S.A.* 112 C3
Timber Mt. *U.S.A.* 110 H10
Timbo *Guinea* 82 C2
Timbo *Liberia* 82 D3
Timbué, Ponta *Mozam.* 87 F4
Timbuktu = Tombouctou
  Mali 82 B4
Timeïaouine *Algeria* 83 A5
Timétrin *Mali* 83 B4
Timétrine, Mts. *Mali* 83 B4
Timfi Oros *Greece* 46 B2
Timfristos, Oros *Greece* 46 C3
Timi *Cyprus* 49 E11
Tîmia *Niger* 83 B6
Timimoun *Algeria* 78 C6
Timiris, Râs *Mauritania* 82 B1
Timiş = Tamis ➤ *Serbia* 28 F5
Timiş □ *Romania* 28 E6
Timişoara *Romania* 28 E6
Timmersdala *Sweden* 11 F7
Timmins *Canada* 104 C3
Timok ➤ *Serbia* 44 B6
Timoleague *Ireland* 12 E3
Timor *Asia* 63 F7
Timor Leste = East
  Timor ■ *Asia* 63 F7
Timor Sea *Ind. Oc.* 92 B4
Timrå *Sweden* 10 B11
Tin Can Bay *Australia* 95 D5
Tin Ethisane *Mali* 83 B4
Tin Gornai *Mali* 83 B4
Tin Mt. *U.S.A.* 110 J9
Tina = Thina ➤ *S. Africa* 89 E4
Tina, Khalîg el *Egypt* 74 D1
Tinaca Pt. *Phil.* 61 J6
Tinajo *Canary Is.* 48 F6
Tinca *Romania* 28 D6
Tindal *Australia* 92 B5
Tindouf *Algeria* 78 C4
Tinée ➤ *France* 21 E11
Tineo *Spain* 36 B4
Tinfunque △ *Paraguay* 126 A3
Ting Jiang ➤ *China* 59 E11
Tinggi, Pulau *Malaysia* 65 L5
Tingi Mts. *S. Leone* 82 D2
Tinglev *Denmark* 11 K3
Tingo Maria *Peru* 124 E3
Tingrela *Ivory C.* 82 C3
Tingsryd *Sweden* 11 H9
Tingstäde *Sweden* 11 G12
Tinh Bien *Vietnam* 65 G5
Tinian *N. Marianas* 96 F6
Tinkisso ➤ *Guinea* 82 C3
Tinnevelly = Tirunelveli
  India 66 Q10
Tinogasta *Argentina* 126 B2
Tinos *Greece* 47 D7
Tiñoso, C. *Spain* 39 H3
Tinpahar *India* 69 G12
Tîntâne *Mauritania* 82 B2
Tintina *Argentina* 126 B3
Tintinara *Australia* 95 F3
Tintioulé *Guinea* 82 C3
Tinto ➤ *Spain* 37 H4
Tiobraid Árran = Tipperary
  Ireland 12 D3
Tioga *N. Dak., U.S.A.* 112 A2
Tioga *Pa., U.S.A.* 114 E7
Tioman, Pulau *Malaysia* 65 L5
Tione di Trento *Italy* 40 B7
Tionesta *U.S.A.* 114 E5
Tior *Sudan* 81 F3
Tipperary *Ireland* 12 D3
Tipperary □ *Ireland* 12 D4
Tipton *Calif., U.S.A.* 110 J7
Tipton *Iowa, U.S.A.* 112 E8
Tipton Mt. *U.S.A.* 111 K12
Tiptonville *U.S.A.* 117 C10
Tīrān *Iran* 71 C6
Tîrân *Si. Arabia* 80 B3
Tiranë *Albania* 44 E3
Tiranë ✈ (TIA) *Albania* 44 E3
Tirano *Italy* 40 B7
Tirari Desert *Australia* 95 D2
Tiraspol *Moldova* 29 D14
Tirdout *Mali* 83 B4
Tire *Turkey* 47 C9
Tirebolu *Turkey* 73 B8
Tiree *U.K.* 13 E2
Tiree, Passage of *U.K.* 13 E2
Tîrgoviște = Târgoviște
  Romania 29 F10
Tîrgu Jiu = Târgu Jiu
  Romania 29 E8
Tîrgu Mureş = Târgu
  Mureş *Romania* 29 D9
Tirich Mir *Pakistan* 66 A7
Tiriolo *Italy* 43 D9
Tiriro *Guinea* 82 C3
Tiritiri o te Moana =
  Southern Alps *N.Z.* 91 E3
Tirnavos *Greece* 46 B4
Tirodi *India* 66 J11
Tirol □ *Austria* 26 D3

Tirschenreuth *Germany* 25 F8
Tirso ➤ *Italy* 42 C1
Tirstrup *Denmark* 11 H4
Tiruchchirappalli *India* 66 P11
Tirunelveli *India* 66 Q10
Tiruppur *India* 66 P10
Tirupati *India* 66 N11
Tiruvannamalai *India* 66 N11
Tisa ➤ *Serbia* 28 E5
Tisa *India* 68 C7
Tisa ➤ *Serbia* 28 E5
Tisdale *Canada* 103 C8
Tishomingo *U.S.A.* 116 D6
Tisjön *Sweden* 10 D7
Tisnaren *Sweden* 11 F9
Tišnov *Czech Rep.* 27 B9
Tisovec *Slovak Rep.* 27 C12
Tisza = Tisa ➤ *Serbia* 28 E5
Tiszaföldvár *Hungary* 28 D5
Tiszafüred *Hungary* 28 C5
Tiszalök *Hungary* 28 B6
Tiszavasvári *Hungary* 28 C6
Tit-Ary *Russia* 53 B13
Titaguas *Spain* 38 F3
Titao *Burkina Faso* 83 C4
Titel *Serbia* 28 E5
Tithwal *Pakistan* 69 B5
Titicaca, L. *S. Amer.* 124 G5
Titisee *Germany* 25 H4
Titiwa *Nigeria* 83 C7
Tito *Italy* 43 B8
Titova Korenica *Croatia* 41 D12
Titu *Romania* 29 F10
Titule *Dem. Rep. of the Congo* 86 B2
Titusville *Fla., U.S.A.* 117 G14
Titusville *Pa., U.S.A.* 114 E5
Tivaouane *Senegal* 82 C1
Tivat *Montenegro* 44 D2
Tivedens △ *Sweden* 11 F8
Tiverton *Canada* 114 B3
Tiverton *U.K.* 15 G4
Tívoli *Italy* 41 G9
Tiwi ◎ *Australia* 92 B5
Tiyo *Eritrea* 81 E5
Tizi-Ouzou *Algeria* 78 A6
Tizimín *Mexico* 119 C7
Tiznit *Morocco* 78 C4
Tjæreborg *Denmark* 11 J2
Tjällmo *Sweden* 11 F9
Tjeggelvas *Sweden* 8 C17
Tjibon = Cirebon *Indonesia* 62 F3
Tjirebon = Cirebon *Indonesia* 62 F3
Tjïrkarli ◎ *Australia* 93 E4
Tjluring *Indonesia* 63 J17
Tjörn *Sweden* 11 F5
Tjukayirla Roadhouse
  Australia 93 E3
Tjurabalan ◎ *Australia* 92 C4
Tkibuli = Tqibuli *Georgia* 35 J6
Tkvarcheli = Tqvarcheli
  Georgia 35 J5
Tlacotalpan *Mexico* 119 D5
Tlahualilo de Zaragoza
  Mexico 118 B4
Tlaquepaque *Mexico* 118 C4
Tlaxcala *Mexico* 119 D5
Tlaxcala □ *Mexico* 119 D5
Tlaxiaco *Mexico* 119 D5
Tlemcen *Algeria* 78 B5
Tlumach *Ukraine* 29 B10
Tłuszcz *Poland* 31 F8
Tlyarata *Russia* 35 J8
Toamasina *Madag.* 89 B8
Toamasina □ *Madag.* 89 B8
Toay *Argentina* 126 D3
Toba *China* 58 B1
Toba *Japan* 55 G8
Toba, Danau *Indonesia* 62 D1
Toba Kakar *Pakistan* 68 D3
Toba Tek Singh *Pakistan* 68 D5
Tobago *Trin. & Tob.* 121 D7
Tobarra *Spain* 39 G3
Tobelo *Indonesia* 63 D7
Tobermory *Canada* 114 A3
Tobermory *U.K.* 13 E2
Tobi *Pac. Oc.* 63 D8
Tobin, L. *Australia* 92 D4
Tobin, L. *Canada* 103 C8
Toblach = Dobbiaco *Italy* 41 B9
Toboali *Indonesia* 62 E3
Tobol ➤ *Russia* 52 D7
Toboli *Indonesia* 63 E6
Tobolsk *Russia* 52 D7
Tobor *Senegal* 82 C1
Tobruk = Tubruq *Libya* 79 B10
Tobyhanna *U.S.A.* 115 E9
Tobyl = Tobol ➤ *Russia* 52 D7
Tocantinópolis *Brazil* 125 E9
Tocantins □ *Brazil* 125 F9
Tocantins ➤ *Brazil* 125 D9
Toccoa *U.S.A.* 117 D13
Toce ➤ *Italy* 40 C5
Tochi ➤ *Pakistan* 68 C4
Tochigi *Japan* 55 F9
Tochigi □ *Japan* 55 F9

Tocina *Spain* 37 H5
Töcksfors *Sweden* 10 E5
Toco *Trin. & Tob.* 125 K16
Toconao *Chile* 126 A2
Tocopilla *Chile* 126 A1
Tocumwal *Australia* 95 F4
Tocuyo ➤ *Venezuela* 124 A5
Todd ➤ *Australia* 94 C2
Todeli *Indonesia* 63 E6
Todenyang *Kenya* 86 B4
Todgarh *India* 68 G5
Todi *Italy* 41 F9
Todos os Santos, B. de *Brazil* 125 F11
Todos Santos *Mexico* 118 C2
Todtnau *Germany* 25 H3
Toe Hd. *U.K.* 13 D1
Toecé *Burkina Faso* 83 C4
Tofield *Canada* 102 C6
Tofino *Canada* 102 D3
Töfsingdalens △ *Sweden* 10 B6
Tofua *Tonga* 91 c
Tōgane *Japan* 55 G10
Togba *Mauritania* 82 B2
Togian, Kepulauan *Indonesia* 63 E6
Togliatti *Russia* 34 D9
Togo ■ *W. Afr.* 83 D5
Togtoh *China* 56 D6
Tohiea, Mt. *Moorea* 91 d
Tohma ➤ *Turkey* 72 C8
Tōhoku □ *Japan* 54 E10
Töhöm *Mongolia* 56 B5
Toinya *Sudan* 81 F2
Toiyabe Range *U.S.A.* 108 G5
Tojikiston = Tajikistan ■
  Asia 52 F8
Tojo *Indonesia* 63 E6
Tōjō *Japan* 55 G6
Tok *U.S.A.* 100 E3
Tokachi-Dake *Japan* 54 C11
Tokachi-Gawa ➤ *Japan* 54 C11
Tokaj *Hungary* 28 B6
Tokala *Indonesia* 63 E6
Tōkamachi *Japan* 55 F9
Tokanui *N.Z.* 91 G2
Tokar *Sudan* 80 D4
Tokara-Rettō ➤ *Japan* 55 K4
Tokarahi *N.Z.* 91 F3
Tokashiki-Shima *Japan* 55 L3
Tokat *Turkey* 72 B7
Tokat □ *Turkey* 72 B7
Tŏkch'ŏn *N. Korea* 57 E14
Tokdo *Asia* 55 F5
Tokeland *U.S.A.* 110 D3
Tokelau Is. *Pac. Oc.* 96 H10
Tokmak *Kyrgyzstan* 52 E8
Tokmak *Ukraine* 33 J8
Toko Ra. *Australia* 94 C2
Tokoro-Gawa ➤ *Japan* 54 B12
Toku *Tonga* 91 c
Tokuno-Shima *Japan* 55 L4
Tokushima *Japan* 55 G7
Tokushima □ *Japan* 55 H7
Tokuyama *Japan* 55 G5
Tōkyō *Japan* 55 G9
Tolaga Bay *N.Z.* 91 C7
Tolbukhin = Dobrich
  Bulgaria 45 C11
Toledo *Brazil* 127 A5
Toledo *Spain* 36 F6
Toledo *Ohio, U.S.A.* 113 E12
Toledo *Oreg., U.S.A.* 108 D2
Toledo *Wash., U.S.A.* 108 C2
Toledo, Montes de *Spain* 37 F6
Toledo Bend Res. *U.S.A.* 116 F8
Tolentino *Italy* 41 E10
Tolfa *Italy* 41 F8
Tolga *Australia* 94 B4
Toliara *Madag.* 89 C7
Toliara □ *Madag.* 89 C8
Tolima *Colombia* 124 C3
Tolitoli *Indonesia* 63 D6
Tolkmicko *Poland* 30 D6
Tollarp *Sweden* 11 J7
Tollensee *Germany* 24 B9
Tollhouse *U.S.A.* 110 H7
Tolmachevo *Russia* 32 C5
Tolmezzo *Italy* 41 B10
Tolmin *Slovenia* 41 B10
Tolna *Hungary* 28 D3
Tolna □ *Hungary* 28 D3
Tolo, Teluk *Indonesia* 63 E6
Tolochin = Talachyn *Belarus* 32 E5
Tolosa *Spain* 38 B2
Tolox *Spain* 37 J6
Toluca *Mexico* 119 D5
Tolyatti = Togliatti *Russia* 34 D9
Tom Burke *S. Africa* 89 C4
Tom Price *Australia* 92 D2
Toma *Burkina Faso* 82 C4
Tomah *U.S.A.* 112 D8
Tomahawk *U.S.A.* 112 C9
Tomai *Moldova* 29 D13
Tomakomai *Japan* 54 C10
Tomales *U.S.A.* 110 G4
Tomales B. *U.S.A.* 110 G3
Tomanivi *Fiji* 91 a
Tomar *Portugal* 37 F2
Tomaros, Oros *Greece* 46 B2
Tomarza *Turkey* 72 C6

Tomashevka *Belarus* **31** G10
Tomashpil *Ukraine* **29** B13
Tomaszów Lubelski *Poland* **31** H10
Tomaszów Mazowiecki
  Poland **31** G7
Tomatlán *Mexico* **118** D3
Tombadonkéa *Guinea* **82** C2
Tombador, Serra do *Brazil* **124** F7
Tombe *Sudan* **81** F3
Tombigbee ↝ *U.S.A.* **117** F11
Tombouctou *Mali* **82** B4
Tombouctou □ *Mali* **82** B4
Tombstone *U.S.A.* **109** L8
Tombua *Angola* **88** B1
Tomé *Chile* **126** D1
Tomelilla *Sweden* **11** J7
Tomelloso *Spain* **37** F7
Tomini *Indonesia* **63** D6
Tomini, Teluk *Indonesia* **63** E6
Tominian *Mali* **82** C4
Tomiño *Spain* **36** D2
Tomintoul *U.K.* **13** D5
Tomislavgrad *Bos.-H.* **28** G2
Tomkinson Ranges *Australia* **93** E4
Tommot *Russia* **53** D13
Tomnop Ta Suos *Cambodia* **65** G5
Tomo ↝ *Colombia* **124** B5
Toms Place *U.S.A.* **110** H8
Toms River *U.S.A.* **115** G10
Tomsk *Russia* **52** D9
Tomtabacken *Sweden* **11** G8
Tona *Spain* **38** D7
Tonalá *Chiapas, Mexico* **119** D6
Tonalá *Jalisco, Mexico* **118** C4
Tonale, Passo del *Italy* **40** B7
Tonantins *Brazil* **124** D5
Tonasket *U.S.A.* **108** B4
Tonawanda *U.S.A.* **114** D6
Tonb *Iran* **71** E7
Tonbridge *U.K.* **15** F3
Tondano *Indonesia* **63** D6
Tondela *Portugal* **36** E2
Tønder *Denmark* **11** K2
Tondi Kiwindi *Niger* **83** C5
Tondibi *Mali* **83** B4
Tondoro *Namibia* **88** B2
Tone ↝ *Australia* **93** F2
Tone-Gawa ↝ *Japan* **55** F9
Tonekābon *Iran* **71** B6
Tong Xian *China* **56** E9
Tong-Yeong *S. Korea* **57** G15
Tonga *Cameroon* **83** E7
Tôngâ *Sudan* **81** F3
Tonga ■ *Pac. Oc.* **91** c
Tonga Trench *Pac. Oc.* **96** J10
Tongaat *S. Africa* **89** D5
Tong'an *China* **59** E12
Tongareva = Penrhyn
  Cook Is. **97** H12
Tongariro △ *N.Z.* **91** C5
Tongatapu *Tonga* **91** c
Tongatapu Group *Tonga* **91** c
Tongbai *China* **59** A9
Tongcheng *Anhui, China* **59** B11
Tongcheng *Hubei, China* **59** C9
Tongchuan *China* **56** G5
Tongdao *China* **58** D7
Tongeren *Belgium* **17** D5
Tonggu *China* **59** C10
Tonghai *China* **58** E4
Tonghua *China* **57** D13
Tongjiang *China* **58** B6
Tongjosŏn Man *N. Korea* **57** E15
Tongking, G. of = Tonkin,
  G. of *Asia* **64** C7
Tongliang *China* **58** C6
Tongliao *China* **57** C12
Tongling *China* **59** B11
Tonglu *China* **59** C12
Tongnan = Anyue *China* **58** B5
Tongobory *Madag.* **89** C7
Tongoy *Chile* **126** C1
Tongren *China* **58** D7
Tongres = Tongeren *Belgium* **17** D5
Tongsa Dzong *Bhutan* **67** F17
Tongshi *China* **64** C7
Tongue *U.K.* **13** C4
Tongue ↝ *U.S.A.* **108** C11
Tongwei *China* **56** G3
Tongxiang *China* **59** B13
Tongxin *China* **56** F3
Tongyang *N. Korea* **57** E14
Tongyu *China* **57** B12
Tongzi *China* **58** C6
Tonj *Sudan* **81** F2
Tonj ↝ *Sudan* **81** F2
Tonk *India* **68** F6
Tonkawa *U.S.A.* **116** C6
Tonkin = Bac Phan *Vietnam* **58** G5
Tonkin, G. of *Asia* **64** C7
Tonle Sap *Cambodia* **64** F5
Tonnay-Charente *France* **20** C3
Tonneins *France* **20** D4
Tonnerre *France* **19** E10
Tönning *Germany* **24** A4
Tono *Japan* **54** E10
Tonopah *U.S.A.* **109** G5
Tonosí *Panama* **120** E3
Tons ↝ *Haryana, India* **68** D7

Tons ↝ *Ut. P., India* **69** F10
Tønsberg *Norway* **9** G14
Tonto △ *U.S.A.* **109** K8
Tonumea *Tonga* **91** c
Tonya *Turkey* **73** B8
Toobanna *Australia* **94** B4
Toodyay *Australia* **93** F2
Tooele *U.S.A.* **108** F7
Toompine *Australia* **95** D3
Toora *Australia* **95** F4
Toora-Khem *Russia* **53** D10
Toowoomba *Australia* **95** D5
Top Springs *Australia* **92** C5
Topalu *Romania* **29** F13
Topaz *U.S.A.* **110** G7
Topeka *U.S.A.* **112** F6
Topľa ↝ *Slovak Rep.* **27** C14
Topley *Canada* **102** C3
Toplica ↝ *Serbia* **44** C5
Toplița *Romania* **29** D10
Topocalma, Pta. *Chile* **126** C1
Topock *U.S.A.* **111** L12
Topola *Serbia* **44** B4
Topolčani *Macedonia* **44** E5
Topoľčany *Slovak Rep.* **27** C11
Topolnitsa ↝ *Bulgaria* **45** D8
Topolobampo *Mexico* **118** B3
Topoloveni *Romania* **29** F10
Topolovgrad *Bulgaria* **45** D10
Topolváțu Mare *Romania* **28** E6
Topozero, Ozero *Russia* **8** D25
Toppenish *U.S.A.* **108** C3
Topraisar *Romania* **29** F13
Topusko *Croatia* **41** C12
Torà *Spain* **38** D6
Tora Kit *Sudan* **81** E3
Toraka Vestale *Madag.* **89** B7
Torata *Peru* **124** G4
Torbalı *Turkey* **47** C9
Torbat-e Heydārīyeh *Iran* **71** C8
Torbat-e Jām *Iran* **71** C9
Torbay *Canada* **105** C9
Torbay □ *U.K.* **15** G4
Torbjörntorp *Sweden* **11** F7
Tordesillas *Spain* **36** D6
Torekov *Sweden* **11** H6
Torelló *Spain* **38** C7
Toreno *Spain* **36** C4
Torfaen □ *U.K.* **15** F4
Torgau *Germany* **24** D8
Torgelow *Germany* **24** B10
Torhamn *Sweden* **11** H9
Torhout *Belgium* **17** C3
Tori *Ethiopia* **81** F3
Tori-Shima *Japan* **55** J10
Torigni-sur-Vire *France* **18** C6
Torija *Spain* **38** E1
Torilla Pen. *Australia* **94** C5
Torino *Italy* **40** C4
Torit *Sudan* **81** G3
Torkamān *Iran* **73** D12
Torkovichi *Russia* **32** C6
Tormac *Romania* **28** E6
Tormes ↝ *Spain* **36** D4
Tornado Mt. *Canada* **102** D6
Tornal'a *Slovak Rep.* **27** C13
Torneå = Tornio *Finland* **8** D21
Torneälven ↝ *Europe* **8** D21
Tornetråsk *Sweden* **8** B18
Torngat Mts. *Canada* **101** F19
Tornio *Finland* **8** D21
Tornionjoki =
  Torneälven ↝ *Europe* **8** D21
Tornquist *Argentina* **126** D3
Toro *Baleares, Spain* **48** B11
Toro *Zamora, Spain* **36** D5
Torö *Sweden* **11** F11
Toro, Cerro del *Chile* **126** B2
Toro ↝ *Uganda* **86** C3
Toro Pk. *U.S.A.* **111** M10
Torodi *Niger* **83** C5
Törökszentmiklós *Hungary* **28** C5
Toronto *Canada* **114** C5
Toronto *U.S.A.* **114** F4
Toronto Lester B. Pearson
  Int. ✈ (YYZ) *Canada* **114** C5
Toropets *Russia* **32** D6
Tororo *Uganda* **86** B3
Toros Dağları *Turkey* **72** D5
Torpa *India* **69** H11
Torquay *U.K.* **15** G4
Torquemada *Spain* **36** C6
Torrance *U.S.A.* **111** M8
Torrão *Portugal* **37** G2
Torre Annunziata *Italy* **43** B7
Torre de Moncorvo *Portugal* **36** D3
Torre del Campo *Spain* **37** H7
Torre del Greco *Italy* **43** B7
Torre del Mar *Spain* **37** J6
Torre-Pacheco *Spain* **39** H4
Torre Péllice *Italy* **40** D4
Torreblanca *Spain* **38** E5
Torrecampo *Spain* **37** G6
Torrecilla en Cameros *Spain* **38** C2
Torredembarra *Spain* **38** D6
Torredonjimeno *Spain* **37** H7
Torrejón de Ardoz *Spain* **36** E7
Torrejoncillo *Spain* **36** F4

Torrelaguna *Spain* **36** E7
Torrelavega *Spain* **36** B6
Torremaggiore *Italy* **41** G12
Torremolinos *Spain* **37** J6
Torrens, L. *Australia* **95** E2
Torrens Cr. ↝ *Australia* **94** C4
Torrens Creek *Australia* **94** C4
Torrent *Spain* **39** F4
Torrenueva *Spain* **37** G7
Torreón *Mexico* **118** B4
Torreperogil *Spain* **37** G7
Torres *Brazil* **127** B5
Torres *Mexico* **118** B2
Torres Novas *Portugal* **37** F2
Torres Strait *Australia* **94** a
Torres Vedras *Portugal* **37** F1
Torrevieja *Spain* **39** H4
Torrey *U.S.A.* **108** G8
Torridge ↝ *U.K.* **15** G3
Torridon, L. *U.K.* **13** D3
Torrijos *Spain* **36** F6
Tørring *Denmark* **11** J3
Torrington *Conn., U.S.A.* **115** E11
Torrington *Wyo., U.S.A.* **108** E11
Torroella de Montgrí *Spain* **38** C8
Torrox *Spain* **37** J7
Torsås *Sweden* **11** H9
Torsby *Sweden* **10** D6
Torshälla *Sweden* **10** E10
Tórshavn *Færoe Is.* **8** E9
Torslanda *Sweden* **11** G5
Torsö *Sweden* **11** F7
Tortola *Br. Virgin Is.* **121** e
Tórtoles de Esgueva *Spain* **36** D6
Tortolì *Italy* **42** C2
Tortona *Italy* **40** D5
Tortorici *Italy* **43** D7
Tortosa *Spain* **38** E5
Tortosa, C. *Spain* **38** E5
Tortosendo *Portugal* **36** E3
Tortue, Î. de la *Haiti* **121** B5
Tortuguero △ *Costa Rica* **120** D3
Tortum *Turkey* **73** B9
Torūd *Iran* **71** C7
Torul *Turkey* **73** B8
Toruń *Poland* **31** E5
Torun *Ukraine* **29** B8
Tory Hill *Canada* **114** B6
Tory I. *Ireland* **12** A3
Torysa ↝ *Slovak Rep.* **27** C14
Torzhok *Russia* **32** D8
Torzym *Poland* **31** F2
Tosa *Japan* **55** H6
Tosa-Shimizu *Japan* **55** H6
Tosa-Wan *Japan* **55** H6
Toscana □ *Italy* **40** E8
Toscano, Arcipelago *Italy* **40** F7
Toshka *Egypt* **80** C3
Toshka, Buheirat en *Egypt* **80** C3
Toshka Lakes = Toshka,
  Buheirat en *Egypt* **80** C3
Toshkent *Uzbekistan* **52** E7
Tosno *Russia* **32** C6
Tossa de Mar *Spain* **38** D7
Tösse *Sweden* **11** F6
Tostado *Argentina* **126** B3
Tostedt *Germany* **24** B5
Tostón, Pta. de *Canary Is.* **48** F5
Tosu *Japan* **55** H5
Tosya *Turkey* **72** B6
Totana *Spain* **39** H3
Totebo *Sweden* **11** G10
Toteng *Botswana* **88** C3
Tôtes *France* **18** C8
Tótkomlós *Hungary* **28** D5
Totma *Russia* **52** D5
Totnes *U.K.* **15** G4
Totness *Suriname* **125** B7
Toto *Nigeria* **83** D6
Totonicapán *Guatemala* **120** D1
Totoya, I. *Fiji* **91** a
Totten Glacier *Antarctica* **5** C8
Tottenham *Australia* **95** E4
Tottenham *Canada* **114** B5
Tottori *Japan* **55** G7
Tottori □ *Japan* **55** G7
Touâret *Niger* **83** A6
Touba *Ivory C.* **82** D3
Touba *Senegal* **82** C1
Toubkal, Djebel *Morocco* **78** B4
Toucy *France* **19** E10
Tougan *Burkina Faso* **82** C4
Touggourt *Algeria* **78** B7
Tougouri *Burkina Faso* **83** C4
Tougué *Guinea* **82** C2
Toukoto *Mali* **82** C3
Toul *France* **19** D12
Toulepleu *Ivory C.* **82** D3
Touliu *Taiwan* **59** F13
Toulon *France* **21** E9
Toulouse *France* **20** E5
Toulouse Blagnac ✈ (TLS)
  France **20** E5
Toummo *Niger* **79** D8
Toumodi *Ivory C.* **82** D3
Tounan *Taiwan* **59** F13
Toungo *Nigeria* **83** D7
Toungoo *Burma* **67** K20
Touques ↝ *France* **18** C7

Touraine *France* **18** E7
Tourcoing *France* **19** B10
Touriñán, C. *Spain* **36** B1
Tournai *Belgium* **17** D3
Tournan-en-Brie *France* **19** D9
Tournay *France* **20** E4
Tournon-St-Martin *France* **18** F7
Tournon-sur-Rhône *France* **21** C8
Tournus *France* **19** F11
Tours *France* **18** E7
Toussoro, Mt. *C.A.R.* **84** C4
Touws ↝ *S. Africa* **88** E3
Touwsrivier *S. Africa* **88** E3
Tovarkovskiy *Russia* **32** F10
Tovste *Ukraine* **29** B10
Tovuz *Azerbaijan* **35** K7
Towada *Japan* **54** D10
Towada-Hachimantai △
  Japan **54** D10
Towada-Ko *Japan* **54** D10
Towanda *U.S.A.* **115** E8
Towang *India* **67** F18
Tower *U.S.A.* **112** B7
Towerhill Cr. ↝ *Australia* **94** C3
Towner *U.S.A.* **112** A3
Townsend *U.S.A.* **108** C8
Townshend I. *Australia* **94** C5
Townsville *Australia* **94** B4
Towot *Sudan* **81** F3
Towraghondī *Afghan.* **66** B3
Towson *U.S.A.* **113** F15
Towuti, Danau *Indonesia* **63** E6
Toya-Ko *Japan* **54** C10
Toyama *Japan* **55** F8
Toyama □ *Japan* **55** F8
Toyama-Wan *Japan* **55** F8
Toyapakeh *Indonesia* **63** K18
Toyohashi *Japan* **55** G8
Toyokawa *Japan* **55** G8
Toyonaka *Japan* **55** G7
Toyooka *Japan* **55** G7
Toyota *Japan* **55** G8
Tozeur *Tunisia* **78** B7
Tqibuli *Georgia* **35** J6
Tqvarcheli *Georgia* **35** J5
Trá Lí = Tralee *Ireland* **12** D2
Trá Mhór = Tramore *Ireland* **12** D4
Tra On *Vietnam* **65** H5
Trabancos ↝ *Spain* **36** D5
Traben-Trarbach *Germany* **25** F3
Trabzon *Turkey* **73** B8
Trabzon □ *Turkey* **73** B8
Tracadie *Canada* **105** C7
Tracy *Canada* **105** C7
Tracy *Calif., U.S.A.* **110** H5
Tracy *Minn., U.S.A.* **112** C6
Tradate *Italy* **40** C5
Trade Town *Liberia* **82** D3
Trafalgar, C. *Spain* **37** J4
Tragonhisi *Greece* **47** D7
Traian *Brăila, Romania* **29** E12
Traian *Tulcea, Romania* **29** E13
Trail *Canada* **102** D5
Trainor L. *Canada* **102** A4
Trákhonas *Cyprus* **49** D12
Tralee *Ireland* **12** D2
Tralee B. *Ireland* **12** D2
Tramore *Ireland* **12** D4
Tramore B. *Ireland* **12** D4
Tramuntana, Serra de *Spain* **48** B9
Tran Ninh, Cao Nguyen *Laos* **64** C4
Tranås *Sweden* **11** F8
Tranbjerg *Denmark* **11** H4
Trancas *Argentina* **126** B2
Trancoso *Portugal* **36** E3
Tranebjerg *Denmark* **11** J4
Tranemo *Sweden* **11** G7
Trang *Thailand* **65** J2
Trangahy *Madag.* **89** B7
Trangan *Indonesia* **63** F8
Trangie *Australia* **95** E4
Trångsviken *Sweden* **10** A7
Trani *Italy* **43** A9
Tranoroa *Madag.* **89** C8
Tranqueras *Uruguay* **127** C4
Transantarctic Mts.
  Antarctica **5** E12
Transcarpathia =
  Zakarpattya □ *Ukraine* **29** B3
Transilvania *Romania* **29** D9
Transilvanian Alps =
  Carpații Meridionali
  Romania **29** E9
Transnistria = Stînga
  Nistrului □ *Moldova* **29** C14
Transtrand *Sweden* **10** C7
Transtrandsfjällen *Sweden* **10** C6
Transylvania =
  Transilvania *Romania* **29** D9
Trápani *Italy* **42** D5
Trapper Pk. *U.S.A.* **108** D6
Traralgon *Australia* **95** F4
Trarza □ *Mauritania* **82** B2
Trasacco *Italy* **41** G10
Trăscău, Munții *Romania* **29** D8
Trasimeno, L. *Italy* **41** E9
Träslövsläge *Sweden* **11** G6
Trasvase Tajo-Segura,
  Canal de *Spain* **38** E2
Trat *Thailand* **65** F4

Tratani ↝ *Pakistan* **68** E3
Traun *Austria* **26** C7
Traunreut *Germany* **25** H8
Traunsee *Austria* **26** D6
Traunstein *Germany* **25** H8
Travellers L. *Australia* **95** E3
Travemünde *Germany* **24** B6
Travers, Mt. *N.Z.* **91** E4
Traverse City *U.S.A.* **113** C11
Travis, L. *U.S.A.* **116** F6
Travnik *Bos.-H.* **28** F2
Trawbreaga B. *Ireland* **12** A4
Trbovlje *Slovenia* **41** B12
Trbovuša *Slovenia* **41** B12
Trébbia ↝ *Italy* **40** C6
Trebel ↝ *Germany* **24** B9
Trébeurden *France* **18** D3
Trebević △ *Bos.-H.* **28** G3
Třebíč *Czech Rep.* **26** B8
Trebinje *Bos.-H.* **44** D3
Trebisacce *Italy* **43** C9
Trebišnjica ↝ *Bos.-H.* **44** D2
Trebišov *Slovak Rep.* **27** C14
Trebižat ↝ *Bos.-H.* **41** E14
Trebnje *Slovenia* **41** C12
Trěboň *Czech Rep.* **26** B8
Trebonne *Australia* **94** B4
Třeboňsko △ *Czech Rep.* **26** B7
Trebujena *Spain* **37** J4
Trecate *Italy* **40** C5
Tregaron *U.K.* **15** E4
Tregnago *Italy* **41** C8
Tregrosse Is. *Australia* **94** B5
Tréguier *France* **18** D3
Trégunc *France* **18** E3
Treherne *Canada* **103** D9
Tréia *Italy* **41** E10
Treignac *France* **20** C5
Treinta y Tres *Uruguay* **127** C5
Treis-karden *Germany* **25** E3
Treklyano *Bulgaria* **44** D6
Trelawney *Zimbabwe* **89** B5
Trélazé *France* **18** E6
Trelew *Argentina* **128** E3
Trélissac *France* **20** C4
Trelleborg *Sweden* **11** J7
Tremadog Bay *U.K.* **14** E3
Trémiti *Italy* **41** F12
Tremonton *U.S.A.* **108** F7
Tremp *Spain* **38** C5
Trenche ↝ *Canada* **104** C5
Trenčianský □ *Slovak Rep.* **27** C11
Trenčín *Slovak Rep.* **27** C11
Trenggalek *Indonesia* **63** H14
Trenque Lauquen *Argentina* **126** D3
Trent ↝ *Canada* **114** B7
Trent ↝ *U.K.* **14** D7
Trentino-Alto Adige □ *Italy* **41** B8
Trento *Italy* **40** B8
Trenton *Canada* **114** B7
Trenton *Mo., U.S.A.* **112** E7
Trenton *N.J., U.S.A.* **115** F10
Trenton *Nebr., U.S.A.* **112** E3
Trepassey *Canada* **105** C9
Trepuzzi *Italy* **43** B11
Tres Arroyos *Argentina* **126** D3
Três Corações *Brazil* **127** A6
Três Lagoas *Brazil* **125** H8
Tres Lomas *Argentina* **126** D3
Tres Montes, C. *Chile* **128** F1
Tres Pinos *U.S.A.* **110** J5
Três Pontas *Brazil* **127** A6
Tres Puentes *Chile* **126** B1
Tres Puntas, C. *Argentina* **128** F3
Três Rios *Brazil* **127** A7
Tres Valles *Mexico* **119** D5
Tresco *U.K.* **15** H1
Treska ↝ *Macedonia* **44** E5
Treskavica *Bos.-H.* **28** G3
Trespaderne *Spain* **36** C7
Tresticklan △ *Sweden* **11** F5
Trets *France* **21** E9
Treuchtlingen *Germany* **25** G6
Treuenbrietzen *Germany* **24** C8
Trevi *Italy* **41** F9
Trevínca, Peña *Spain* **36** C4
Treviso *Italy* **41** C9
Trévoux *France* **21** C8
Trgovište *Serbia* **44** D6
Triabunna *Australia* **95** G4
Tribal Areas □ *Pakistan* **68** C4
Tribsees *Germany* **24** A8
Tribulation, C. *Australia* **94** B4
Tribune *U.S.A.* **112** F3
Tricárico *Italy* **43** B9
Tricase *Italy* **43** C11
Trichinopoly =
  Tiruchchirappalli *India* **66** P11
Trichur *India* **66** P10
Trichy = Tiruchchirappalli
  India **66** P11
Trida *Australia* **95** E4
Trier *Germany* **25** F2
Trieste *Italy* **41** C10
Trieste, G. di *Italy* **41** C10

Trieux ↝ *France* **18** D3
Triggiano *Italy* **43** A9
Triglav *Slovenia* **41** B10
Triglavski △ *Slovenia* **41** B10
Trigno ↝ *Italy* **41** F11
Trigueros *Spain* **37** H4
Trikala *Greece* **46** B3
Trikala □ *Greece* **46** B3
Trikeri *Greece* **46** B5
Trikomo *Cyprus* **49** D12
Trikora, Puncak *Indonesia* **63** E9
Trilj *Croatia* **41** E13
Trillo *Spain* **38** E2
Trim *Ireland* **12** C5
Trimmu Dam *Pakistan* **68** D5
Trincomalee *Sri Lanka* **66** C12
Trindade *Brazil* **125** G9
Trindade, I. *Atl. Oc.* **2** F8
Třinec *Czech Rep.* **27** B11
Trinidad *Bolivia* **124** F6
Trinidad *Cuba* **120** B4
Trinidad *Trin. & Tob.* **121** D7
Trinidad *Uruguay* **126** C4
Trinidad *U.S.A.* **109** H11
Trinidad ↝ *Mexico* **119** E5
Trinidad & Tobago ■
  W. Indies **121** D7
Trinitápoli *Italy* **43** A9
Trinity *Canada* **105** C9
Trinity *U.S.A.* **116** F7
Trinity ↝ *Calif., U.S.A.* **108** F2
Trinity ↝ *Tex., U.S.A.* **116** G7
Trinity B. *Canada* **105** C9
Trinity Hills *Trin. & Tob.* **125** K15
Trinity Is. *U.S.A.* **106** D9
Trinity Range *U.S.A.* **108** F4
Trinkitat *Sudan* **80** D4
Trino *Italy* **40** C5
Trinway *U.S.A.* **114** F2
Triolet *Mauritius* **85** d
Trionto, C. *Italy* **43** C9
Triora *Italy* **40** D4
Tripoli = Tarābulus *Lebanon* **74** A4
Tripoli = Tarābulus *Libya* **79** B8
Tripoli *Greece* **46** D4
Tripolitania = Tarābulus
  N. Afr. **79** B8
Tripura □ *India* **67** H18
Tripylos *Cyprus* **49** E11
Trischen *Germany* **24** A4
Tristan da Cunha *Atl. Oc.* **77** K2
Trisul *India* **69** D8
Trivandrum *India* **66** Q10
Trivento *Italy* **41** G11
Trizin *Greece* **46** D5
Trnava *Slovak Rep.* **27** C10
Trnavský □ *Slovak Rep.* **27** C10
Troarn *France* **18** C6
Trochu *Canada* **102** C6
Trodely I. *Canada* **104** B4
Trogir *Croatia* **41** E13
Troglav *Croatia* **41** E13
Tróia *Italy* **43** A8
Troilus, L. *Canada* **104** B5
Troina *Italy* **43** E7
Trois-Pistoles *Canada* **105** C6
Trois-Rivières *Canada* **104** C5
Trois-Rivières *Guadeloupe* **120** b
Troisdorf *Germany* **24** E3
Troitsk *Russia* **52** D7
Troitsko Pechorsk *Russia* **52** C6
Troitskoye *Russia* **35** G7
Trölladyngja *Iceland* **8** D5
Trollhättan *Sweden* **11** F6
Trollheimen *Norway* **8** E13
Trombetas ↝ *Brazil* **125** D7
Tromsø *Norway* **8** B18
Tron *Thailand* **64** D2
Trona *U.S.A.* **111** K9
Tronador, Mte. *Argentina* **128** E2
Trøndelag *Norway* **8** D14
Trondheim *Norway* **8** E14
Trondheimsfjorden *Norway* **8** E14
Trönninge *Sweden* **11** H6
Tronto ↝ *Italy* **41** F10
Troodos *Cyprus* **49** E11
Troon *U.K.* **13** F4
Tropea *Italy* **43** D8
Tropic *U.S.A.* **109** H7
Tropojë *Albania* **44** D4
Trosa *Sweden* **11** F11
Trostan *U.K.* **12** A5
Trostberg *Germany* **25** G8
Trostyanets *Sumy, Ukraine* **33** G8
Trostyanets *Vinnytsʹka,
  Ukraine* **29** B14
Trou Gras Pt. *St. Lucia* **121** f
Trout ↝ *Canada* **102** A5
Trout L. *N.W.T., Canada* **102** A4
Trout L. *Ont., Canada* **103** C10
Trout Lake *Canada* **102** B6
Trout Lake *U.S.A.* **110** E5
Trout River *Canada* **105** C8
Trout Run *U.S.A.* **114** E7
Trouville-sur-Mer *France* **18** C7
Trowbridge *U.K.* **15** F5
Troy *Turkey* **47** B8
Troy *Ala., U.S.A.* **117** F12
Troy *Kans., U.S.A.* **112** F6
Troy *Mo., U.S.A.* **112** F8

Troy Mont., U.S.A. 108 B6
Troy N.Y., U.S.A. 115 D11
Troy Ohio, U.S.A. 113 E11
Troy Pa., U.S.A. 115 E8
Troyan Bulgaria 45 D8
Troyes France 19 D11
Trpanj Croatia 41 E14
Trstenik Serbia 44 C5
Trubchevsk Russia 33 F7
Truchas Pk. U.S.A. 109 J11
Trucial States = United
   Arab Emirates ■ Asia 71 F7
Truckee U.S.A. 110 F6
Trudfront Russia 35 H8
Trudovoye Russia 54 C6
Trujillo Honduras 120 C2
Trujillo Peru 124 E3
Trujillo Spain 37 F5
Trujillo U.S.A. 109 J11
Trujillo Venezuela 124 B4
Truk Micronesia 96 G7
Trumann U.S.A. 117 D9
Trumansburg U.S.A. 115 D8
Trumbull, Mt. U.S.A. 109 H7
Trŭn Bulgaria 44 D6
Trun France 18 D7
Trundle Australia 95 E4
Trung-Phan = Annam
   Vietnam 64 E7
Truro Canada 105 C7
Truro U.K. 15 G2
Truskavets Ukraine 23 D12
Trůstenik Bulgaria 45 C8
Trustrup Denmark 11 H4
Trutch Canada 102 B4
Truth or Consequences
   U.S.A. 109 K10
Trutnov Czech Rep. 26 A8
Truyère → France 20 D6
Tryavna Bulgaria 45 D9
Tryonville U.S.A. 114 E5
Trzcianka Poland 31 E3
Trzciel Poland 31 F2
Trzcińsko Zdrój Poland 31 F1
Trzebiatów Poland 30 D2
Trzebiez Poland 30 E1
Trzebnica Poland 31 G4
Trzemeszno Poland 31 F4
Tržič Slovenia 41 B11
Tsagan Aman Russia 35 G8
Tsamandas Greece 46 B2
Tsandi Namibia 88 B1
Tsaratanana Madag. 89 B8
Tsaratanana, Mt. de =
   Maromokotro Madag. 89 A8
Tsaratanana △ Madag. 89 A8
Tsarevo Bulgaria 45 D9
Tsau Botswana 88 C3
Tsavo Kenya 86 C4
Tsavo East △ Kenya 86 C4
Tsavo West △ Kenya 86 C4
Tsebrykove Ukraine 33 J6
Tsentralnyy □ Russia 34 D4
Tses Namibia 88 D2
Tsetserleg Mongolia 60 B5
Tsévié Togo 83 D5
Tshabong Botswana 88 D3
Tshane Botswana 88 C3
Tshela Dem. Rep. of the Congo 84 E2
Tshesebe Botswana 89 C4
Tshibeke
   Dem. Rep. of the Congo 86 C2
Tshibinda
   Dem. Rep. of the Congo 86 C2
Tshikapa
   Dem. Rep. of the Congo 84 F4
Tshilenge
   Dem. Rep. of the Congo 86 D1
Tshinsenda
   Dem. Rep. of the Congo 87 E2
Tshofa Dem. Rep. of the Congo 86 D2
Tshwane = Pretoria S. Africa 89 D4
Tshwane Botswana 88 C3
Tsigara Botswana 88 C4
Tsihombe Madag. 89 D8
Tsiigehtchic Canada 100 D5
Ts'il-os △ Canada 102 C4
Tsimlyansk Russia 35 G6
Tsimlyansk Res. =
   Tsimlyanskoye Vdkhr.
   Russia 35 F6
Tsimlyanskoye Vdkhr.
   Russia 35 F6
Tsinan = Jinan China 56 F9
Tsineng S. Africa 88 D3
Tsinghai = Qinghai □ China 60 C4
Tsingtao = Qingdao China 57 F11
Tsingy de Bemaraha △
   Madag. 89 B8
Tsingy de Namoraka △
   Madag. 89 B8
Tsinjoarivo Madag. 89 B8
Tsinjomitondraka Madag. 89 B8
Tsirigo = Kythira Greece 46 E5
Tsiroanomandidy Madag. 89 B8
Tsiteli-Tsqaro Georgia 35 K8
Tsitondroina Madag. 89 C8
Tsitsikamma △ S. Africa 88 E3
Tsivilsk Russia 34 C8

Tsivory Madag. 89 C8
Tskhinvali Georgia 35 J7
Tsna → Russia 34 C6
Tsnori Georgia 35 K7
Tso Moriri, L. India 69 C8
Tsobis Namibia 88 B2
Tsodilo Hill Botswana 88 B3
Tsogttsetsiy = Baruunsuu
   Mongolia 56 C3
Tsolo S. Africa 89 E4
Tsomo S. Africa 89 E4
Tsu Japan 55 G8
Tsu L. Canada 102 A6
Tsuchiura Japan 55 F10
Tsuen Wan China 59 F10
Tsugaru-Kaikyō Japan 54 D10
Tsumeb Namibia 88 B2
Tsumis Namibia 88 C2
Tsuruga Japan 55 G8
Tsurugi-San Japan 55 H7
Tsuruoka Japan 54 E9
Tsushima Gifu, Japan 55 G8
Tsushima Nagasaki, Japan 55 G4
Tsuyama Japan 55 G7
Tsvetkovo Ukraine 33 H6
Tsyelyakhany Belarus 23 B13
Tua → Portugal 36 D3
Tuaim = Tuam Ireland 12 C3
Tual Indonesia 63 F8
Tualatin U.S.A. 110 E4
Tuam Ireland 12 C3
Tuamotu, Îs.
   French Polynesia 97 J13
Tuamotu Arch. =
   Tuamotu, Îs.
   French Polynesia 97 J13
Tuamotu Ridge Pac. Oc. 97 K14
Tuan Giao Vietnam 64 B4
Tuanfeng China 59 B10
Tuanxi China 58 D6
Tuao Phil. 61 C4
Tuapse Russia 35 H4
Tuas Singapore 65 d
Tuatapere N.Z. 91 G1
Tuba City U.S.A. 109 H8
Tuban Indonesia 63 G15
Tubani Botswana 88 C3
Tubarão Brazil 127 B6
Tūbās West Bank 74 C4
Tubas → Namibia 88 C2
Tübingen Germany 25 G5
Tubou Fiji 91 a
Tubruq Libya 79 B10
Tubuaï, Îs. French Polynesia 97 K13
Tuc Trung Vietnam 65 G6
Tucacas Venezuela 124 A5
T'uch'ang Taiwan 59 E13
Tuchitua Canada 102 A3
Tuchodi → Canada 102 B4
Tuchola Poland 30 E4
Tuchów Poland 31 J8
Tuckanarra Australia 93 E2
Tucson U.S.A. 109 K8
Tucumán □ Argentina 126 B2
Tucumcari U.S.A. 109 J12
Tucupita Venezuela 124 B6
Tucuruí Brazil 125 D9
Tucuruí, Represa de Brazil 125 D9
Tuczno Poland 31 E3
Tudela Spain 38 C3
Tudmur Syria 73 E8
Tudor, L. Canada 105 A6
Tudora Romania 29 C11
Tuella → Portugal 36 D3
Tufanbeyli Turkey 72 C7
Tugela → S. Africa 89 D5
Tuguegarao Phil. 61 C4
Tugur Russia 53 D14
Tui Spain 36 C2
Tuineje Canary Is. 48 F5
Tukangbesi, Kepulauan
   Indonesia 63 F6
Tukarak I. Canada 104 A4
Tukayyid Iraq 70 D5
Tūkh Egypt 80 H7
Tukhlya Ukraine 29 B8
Tukobo Ghana 82 D4
Tuktoyaktuk Canada 100 D5
Tuktut Nogait △ Canada 100 D7
Tukums Latvia 30 B10
Tukums □ Latvia 30 B10
Tukuyu Tanzania 87 D3
Tula Hidalgo, Mexico 119 C5
Tula Tamaulipas, Mexico 119 C5
Tula Nigeria 83 D7
Tula Russia 32 E9
Tula □ Russia 32 F9
Tulach Mhór = Tullamore
   Ireland 12 C4
Tulancingo Mexico 119 C5
Tulare Serbia 44 D5
Tulare U.S.A. 110 J7
Tulare Lake Bed U.S.A. 110 K7
Tularosa U.S.A. 109 K10
Tulbagh S. Africa 88 E2
Tulcán Ecuador 124 C3
Tulcea Romania 29 E13
Tulcea □ Romania 29 E13
Tulchyn Ukraine 29 B9
Tüledi Araldary Kazakhstan 35 H10

Tūleh Iran 71 C7
Tulemalu L. Canada 103 A9
Tulgheş Romania 29 D10
Tuli Zimbabwe 87 G2
Tulia U.S.A. 116 D4
Tuliszków Poland 31 F5
Tulita Canada 100 E6
Ţülkarm West Bank 74 C4
Tulla Ireland 12 D3
Tullahoma U.S.A. 117 D11
Tullamore Australia 95 E4
Tullamore Ireland 12 C4
Tulle France 20 C5
Tulln Austria 26 C9
Tullow Ireland 12 D5
Tullus Sudan 81 E1
Tully Australia 94 B4
Tully U.S.A. 115 D8
Tulnici Romania 29 E11
Tulovo Bulgaria 45 D9
Tulsa U.S.A. 116 C7
Tulsequah Canada 102 B2
Tulu Milki Ethiopia 81 F4
Tulu Welel Ethiopia 81 F3
Tuluá Colombia 124 C3
Tuluceşti Romania 29 E13
Tulun Russia 53 D11
Tulungagung Indonesia 63 H14
Tuma Russia 32 E11
Tuma → Nic. 120 D3
Tumacacori △ U.S.A. 109 L8
Tumaco Colombia 124 C3
Tumakuru = Tumkur India 66 N10
Tumatumari Guyana 124 B7
Tumba Sweden 10 E11
Tumba, L.
   Dem. Rep. of the Congo 84 E3
Tumbarumba Australia 95 F4
Tumbaya Argentina 126 A2
Tumbes Peru 124 D2
Tumbler Ridge Canada 102 B4
Tumbur Sudan 81 G3
Tumbwe
   Dem. Rep. of the Congo 87 E2
Tumby Bay Australia 95 E2
Tumd Youqi China 56 D6
Tumen China 54 C4
Tumen Jiang → China 57 C16
Tumeremo Venezuela 124 B6
Tumkur India 66 N10
Tump Pakistan 66 F3
Tumpat Malaysia 65 J4
Tumu Ghana 82 C4
Tumucumaque, Serra
   Brazil 125 C8
Tumut Australia 95 F4
Tumwater U.S.A. 110 C4
Tuna India 68 H4
Tunadal Sweden 10 B11
Tunapuna Trin. & Tob. 125 K15
Tunas de Zaza Cuba 120 B4
Tunbridge Wells = Royal
   Tunbridge Wells U.K. 15 F8
Tunçbilek Turkey 47 B11
Tunceli Turkey 73 C8
Tunceli □ Turkey 73 C8
Tuncurry Australia 95 E5
Tundla India 68 F8
Tundubai Sudan 80 D2
Tunduru Tanzania 87 E4
Tundzha → Bulgaria 45 C10
Tunga Nic. 120 D3
Tungabhadra → India 66 M11
Tungaru Sudan 81 E3
Tungla Nic. 120 D3
Tungsha Tao = Dongsha
   Dao S. China Sea 59 G11
Tungshih Taiwan 59 E13
Tungsten Canada 102 A3
Tunguska, Nizhnyaya →
   Russia 53 C9
Tunguska,
   Podkamennaya →
   Russia 53 C10
Tunica U.S.A. 117 D9
Tunis Tunisia 78 A7
Tunis ✈ (TUN) Tunisia 42 F3
Tunisia ■ Africa 79 A7
Tunja Colombia 124 B4
Tunkhannock U.S.A. 115 E9
Tunliu China 56 F7
Tunnel Creek △ Australia 92 C4
Tunnsjøen Norway 8 D15
Tunø Denmark 11 J4
Tunungayualok I. Canada 105 A7
Tunuyán Argentina 126 C2
Tunuyán → Argentina 126 C2
Tunxi = Huangshan China 59 B12
Tuo Jiang → China 58 C5
Tuolumne U.S.A. 110 H6
Tuolumne → U.S.A. 110 H5
Ţüp Ăghāj Iran 73 D12
Tupã Brazil 127 A5
Tupelo U.S.A. 117 D10
Tupik Russia 32 E7
Tupinambaras, I. Brazil 124 D7
Tupiza Bolivia 126 A2
Tupižnica Serbia 44 C6
Tupman U.S.A. 111 K7
Tupper Canada 102 B4
Tupper L. U.S.A. 115 B10

Tupper Lake U.S.A. 115 B10
Tüpqarghan Muyis
   Kazakhstan 35 H10
Tupungato, Cerro S. Amer. 126 C2
Tuquan China 57 B11
Túquerres Colombia 124 C3
Tura Russia 53 C11
Turabah Ḥā'il, Si. Arabia 70 D4
Turabah Makkah, Si. Arabia 80 C5
Tūrān Iran 71 C8
Turan Russia 53 D10
Ţurayf Si. Arabia 70 D3
Turbacz Poland 31 J7
Turbe Bos.-H. 28 F2
Turčianske Teplice
   Slovak Rep. 27 C11
Turcoaia Romania 29 E13
Turda Romania 29 D8
Turek Poland 31 F5
Turén Venezuela 124 B5
Turfan = Turpan China 60 B3
Turgeon → Canada 104 C4
Türgovishte Bulgaria 45 C10
Turgut Turkey 47 D10
Turgutlu Turkey 47 C9
Turgwe → Zimbabwe 89 C5
Turhal Turkey 72 B7
Turia → Spain 39 F4
Turiaçu Brazil 125 D9
Turiaçu → Brazil 125 D9
Turiec → Slovak Rep. 27 B11
Turin = Torino Italy 40 C4
Turka Ukraine 31 J10
Turkana, L. Africa 86 B4
Türkeli Turkey 45 F11
Turkestan = Türkistan
   Kazakhstan 52 E7
Túrkeve Hungary 28 C5
Turkey ■ Eurasia 72 C7
Turkey Creek = Warmun
   Australia 92 C4
Turki Russia 34 D6
Türkistan Kazakhstan 52 E7
Türkmenabat Turkmenistan 71 B9
Türkmenbashi Turkmenistan 71 A7
Turkmenistan ■ Asia 52 F6
Türkmenli Turkey 47 B8
Türkoğlu Turkey 72 D7
Turks & Caicos Is. ☑
   W. Indies 121 B5
Turks Island Passage
   W. Indies 121 B5
Turku Finland 32 B2
Turkwel → Kenya 86 B4
Turlock U.S.A. 110 H6
Turnagain Australia 94 a
Turnagain → Canada 102 B3
Turnagain, C. N.Z. 91 D6
Turneffe Is. Belize 119 D7
Turner U.S.A. 108 B9
Turner Pt. Australia 94 A1
Turner Valley Canada 102 C6
Turners Falls U.S.A. 115 D12
Turner's Pen. S. Leone 82 D2
Turnhout Belgium 17 C4
Türnitz Austria 26 D8
Turnor L. Canada 103 B7
Turnov Czech Rep. 26 A8
Tŭrnovo = Veliko Tŭrnovo
   Bulgaria 45 C9
Turnu Măgurele Romania 29 G9
Turnu Roşu, P. Romania 29 E9
Turobin Poland 31 H9
Turpan China 60 B3
Turrës, Kala e Albania 44 E3
Turriff U.K. 13 D6
Tursãq Iraq 73 F11
Tursi Italy 43 B9
Turtle Head I. Australia 94 A3
Turtle Is. S. Leone 82 D2
Turtle L. Canada 103 C7
Turtle Lake U.S.A. 112 B3
Turtleford Canada 103 C7
Turuépano △ Venezuela 121 D7
Turukhansk Russia 53 C9
Turzovka Slovak Rep. 27 B11
Tuscaloosa U.S.A. 117 E11
Tuscánia Italy 41 F8
Tuscany = Toscana □ Italy 40 E8
Tuscarawas → U.S.A. 114 F3
Tuscarora Mt. U.S.A. 114 F7
Tuscola Ill., U.S.A. 112 F9
Tuscola Tex., U.S.A. 116 E5
Tuscumbia U.S.A. 117 D11
Tuskegee U.S.A. 117 E12
Tuszyn Poland 31 G6
Tutak Turkey 73 C10
Tutayev Russia 32 D10
Tuticorin India 66 Q11
Tutin Serbia 44 D4
Tutóia Brazil 125 D10
Tutong Brunei 62 D4
Tutova → Romania 29 D12
Tutrakan Bulgaria 45 B10
Tutshi L. Canada 102 B2
Tuttle Creek L. U.S.A. 112 F5
Tuttlingen Germany 25 H4
Tutuala E. Timor 63 F7
Tutuila Amer. Samoa 91 b
Tutume Botswana 85 J5
Tutun Egypt 80 J7

Tuva □ Russia 53 D10
Tuvalu ■ Pac. Oc. 90 B10
Tuvuca Fiji 91 a
Tuxer Alpen Austria 26 D4
Tuxpan Mexico 119 C5
Tuxtla Gutiérrez Mexico 119 D6
Tuy = Tui Spain 36 C2
Tuy An Vietnam 64 F7
Tuy Duc Vietnam 65 F6
Tuy Hoa Vietnam 64 F7
Tuy Phong Vietnam 65 G7
Tuya L. Canada 102 B2
Tuyen Hoa Vietnam 64 D6
Tuyen Quang Vietnam 58 G5
Tūysarkān Iran 73 E13
Tuz Gölü Turkey 72 C5
Ţūz Khurmātū Iraq 73 E11
Tuzi Montenegro 44 D3
Tuzigoot △ U.S.A. 109 J7
Tuzla Bos.-H. 28 F3
Tuzla Turkey 73 B10
Tuzluca Turkey 73 B10
Tuzly Ukraine 29 E15
Tvååker Sweden 11 G6
Tvardiţa Moldova 29 D13
Tver Russia 32 D8
Tver □ Russia 32 D8
Tvrdošin Slovak Rep. 27 B12
Tvrdošovce Slovak Rep. 27 C11
Tvŭrditsa Bulgaria 45 D9
Twain U.S.A. 110 E5
Twain Harte U.S.A. 110 G6
Twardogóra Poland 31 G4
Tweed → Canada 114 B7
Tweed → U.K. 13 F6
Tweed Heads Australia 95 D5
Tweedsmuir △ Canada 102 C3
Twentynine Palms U.S.A. 111 L10
Twillingate Canada 105 C9
Twin Bridges U.S.A. 108 D7
Twin Falls Canada 105 B7
Twin Falls U.S.A. 108 E6
Twin Valley U.S.A. 112 B6
Twinsburg U.S.A. 114 E3
Twistringen Germany 24 C4
Twitchell Res. U.S.A. 111 L6
Two Harbors U.S.A. 112 B8
Two Hills Canada 102 C6
Two Rivers U.S.A. 112 C10
Two Rocks Australia 93 F2
Twofold B. Australia 95 F4
Tyachiv Ukraine 23 D12
Tychy Poland 31 H5
Tyczyn Poland 31 J9
Tykocin Poland 31 E9
Tyler Minn., U.S.A. 112 C5
Tyler Tex., U.S.A. 116 E7
Tyligul → Ukraine 33 J6
Týmanivka Ukraine 29 B13
Týn nad Vltavou Czech Rep. 26 B7
Tynda Russia 53 D13
Tyndall U.S.A. 112 D5
Tyne → U.K. 14 C6
Tyne & Wear □ U.K. 14 B6
Týnec nad Sázavou
   Czech Rep. 26 B7
Tynemouth U.K. 14 B6
Tyre = Sūr Lebanon 74 B4
Tyresta △ Sweden 10 E12
Tyrifjorden Norway 9 F14
Tyringe Sweden 11 H7
Tyrnyauz Russia 35 J6
Tyrol = Tirol □ Austria 26 D3
Tyrone S. Africa 89 D4
Tyrone □ U.K. 12 B4
Tyrrell → Australia 95 F3
Tyrrell, L. Australia 95 F3
Tyrrell L. Canada 103 A7
Tyrrhenian Sea Medit. S. 6 G8
Tysfjorden Norway 8 B17
Tysmenytsya Ukraine 29 B9
Tystberga Sweden 11 F11
Tytuvenai Lithuania 30 C10
Tyub Karagan, Mys =
   Tüpqarghan Muyis
   Kazakhstan 35 H10
Tyuleni, Ostrova = Tüledi
   Araldary Kazakhstan 35 H10
Tyuleniy S. Africa 35 H8
Tyuleniy, Mys Azerbaijan 35 K10
Tyumen Russia 52 D7
Tywi → U.K. 15 F3
Tywyn U.K. 15 E3
Tzaneen S. Africa 89 C5
Tzermiado Greece 49 D7
Tzoumérka, Óros =
   Athamanon Oros Greece 46 B3
Tzukong = Zigong China 58 C5

U

U.S.A. = United States of
   America ■ N. Amer. 107 H20
U.S. Virgin Is. ☑ W. Indies 121 e
Uanle Uen = Wanleweyne
   Somali Rep. 75 G3
Uatumã → Brazil 124 D7
Uaupés Brazil 124 C4
Uaupés → Brazil 124 C4
Uaxactún Guatemala 120 C2

Ub Serbia 44 B4
Ubá Brazil 127 A7
Uba Nigeria 83 C7
Ubaitaba Brazil 125 F11
Ubangi = Oubangi →
   Dem. Rep. of the Congo 84 E3
Ubauro Pakistan 68 E3
Ubaye → France 21 D10
Ubayyiḍ, W. al → Iraq 73 F10
Ube Japan 55 H5
Úbeda Spain 37 G7
Uberaba Brazil 125 G9
Uberlândia Brazil 125 G9
Überlingen Germany 25 H5
Ubiaja Nigeria 83 D6
Ubin, Pulau Singapore 65 d
Ubolratna Res. Thailand 64 D4
Ubombo S. Africa 89 D5
Ubon Ratchathani Thailand 64 E5
Ubondo Dem. Rep. of the Congo 86 C2
Ubort → Belarus 23 B15
Ubrique Spain 37 J5
Ubud Indonesia 63 J18
Ubundu Dem. Rep. of the Congo 86 C2
Ucar Azerbaijan 73 B12
Ucayali → Peru 124 D4
Uchab Namibia 88 B2
Uchiura-Wan Japan 54 C10
Uchquduq Uzbekistan 52 E7
Uchte Germany 24 C4
Uchur → Russia 53 D14
Uckermark Germany 24 B9
Ucluelet Canada 102 D3
Uda → Russia 53 D14
Udachnyy Russia 53 C12
Udagamandalam India 66 P10
Udainagar India 68 H7
Udaipur India 68 G5
Udaipur Garhi Nepal 69 F12
Udala India 69 J12
Udawalawe △ Sri Lanka 66 R12
Udbina Croatia 41 D12
Uddeholm Sweden 10 D7
Udhampur India 69 C6
Udi Nigeria 83 D6
Údine Italy 41 B10
Udintsev Fracture Zone
   S. Ocean 5 B13
Udmurtia □ Russia 52 D6
Udon Thani Thailand 64 D4
Udong Cambodia 65 G5
Udskaya Guba Russia 53 D14
Udu Pt. Fiji 91 a
Udupi India 66 N9
Udvoy Balkan Bulgaria 45 D10
Udzungwa △ Tanzania 86 D4
Udzungwa Range Tanzania 87 D4
Ueckermünde Germany 24 B10
Ueda Japan 55 F9
Uedineniya, Os. Russia 4 B12
Uele → Dem. Rep. of the Congo 84 D4
Uelen Russia 53 C19
Uelzen Germany 24 C6
Uetersen Germany 24 B5
Uetze Germany 24 C6
Ufa Russia 52 D6
Uffenheim Germany 25 F6
Ugab → Namibia 88 C1
Ugalla → Tanzania 86 D3
Ugalla River △ Tanzania 86 D3
Uganda ■ Africa 86 B3
Ugento Italy 43 C11
Ugep Nigeria 83 D6
Ughelli Nigeria 83 D6
Ugie S. Africa 89 E4
Uíge Spain 37 J7
Ugine France 21 C10
Uglegorsk Russia 53 E15
Uglich Russia 32 D10
Ugljan Croatia 41 D12
Ugljane Croatia 41 E13
Ugolnye Kopi Russia 53 C18
Ugra → Russia 32 E9
Ugŭrchin Bulgaria 45 C8
Uh → Slovak Rep. 27 C15
Uherské Hradiště Czech Rep. 27 B10
Uherský Brod Czech Rep. 27 B10
Úhlava → Czech Rep. 26 B6
Uhlenhorst Namibia 88 C2
Uhrichsville U.S.A. 114 F3
Uibhist a Deas = South Uist
   U.K. 13 D1
Uibhist a Tuath = North
   Uist U.K. 13 D1
Uig U.K. 13 D2
Uíge Angola 84 F2
Uiha Tonga 90 c
Uijeongbu S. Korea 57 F14
Uiju N. Korea 57 D13
Uinta Mts. U.S.A. 108 F8
Uis Namibia 88 C1
Uiseong S. Korea 57 F15
Uitenhage S. Africa 88 E4
Uithuizen Neths. 17 A6
Ujazd Poland 31 H5

Újfehértó Hungary 28 C6
Ujh → India 68 C6
Uji-guntō Japan 55 J4
Ujjain India 68 H6
Ujście Poland 31 E3
Újszász Hungary 28 C5
Ujung Pandang Indonesia 63 F5
Uka Russia 53 D17
Ukara I. Tanzania 86 C3
Uke-Shima Japan 55 K4
Ukerewe I. Tanzania 86 C3
Ukholovo Russia 34 D5
Ukhrul India 67 G19
Ukhta Russia 52 C6
Ukiah U.S.A. 110 F3
Ukmergė Lithuania 32 E3
Ukraine ■ Europe 33 H7
Ukwi Botswana 88 C3
Ula Turkey 72 D3
Ulaan-Uul Mongolia 56 B6
Ulaanbaatar Mongolia 53 E11
Ulaangom Mongolia 60 A4
Ulaanjirem Mongolia 56 B3
Ulak I. U.S.A. 106 E4
Ulamba Dem. Rep. of the Congo 87 D1
Ulan Bator = Ulaanbaatar
    Mongolia 53 E11
Ulan Erge Russia 35 G7
Ulan Khol Russia 35 H8
Ulan Ude Russia 53 D11
Ulanhad = Chifeng China 57 C10
Ulanów Poland 31 H9
Ulaş Sivas, Turkey 72 C7
Ulaş Tekirdağ, Turkey 45 E11
Ulaya Morogoro, Tanzania 86 D4
Ulaya Tabora, Tanzania 86 C3
Ulcinj Montenegro 44 E3
Ulco S. Africa 88 D3
Ule älv = Oulujoki →
    Finland 8 D21
Ule träsk = Oulujärvi Finland 8 D22
Uleåborg = Oulu Finland 8 D21
Ulefoss Norway 9 G13
Ulëz Albania 44 E3
Ulfborg Denmark 11 H2
Ulhasnagar India 66 K8
Uliastay Mongolia 60 B4
Uljin S. Korea 57 F15
Uljma Serbia 28 E6
Ulla → Spain 36 C2
Ulladulla Australia 95 F5
Ullapool U.K. 13 D3
Ullared Sweden 11 G6
Ulldecona Spain 38 E5
Ulleungdo S. Korea 55 F5
Ullswater Canada 114 A5
Ullswater U.K. 14 C5
Ulm Germany 25 G5
Ulmarra Australia 95 D5
Ulmeni Buzău, Romania 29 E11
Ulmeni Maramureş, Romania 29 C8
Ulonguè Mozam. 87 E3
Ulricehamn Sweden 11 G7
Ulrika Sweden 11 F9
Ulsan S. Korea 57 G15
Ulsta U.K. 13 A7
Ulster □ U.K. 12 B5
Ulstrem Bulgaria 45 D10
Ulubat Gölü Turkey 45 F12
Ulubey Turkey 47 C11
Uluborlu Turkey 47 C12
Uluçinar Turkey 72 D6
Uludağ Turkey 45 F13
Uludağ △ Turkey 45 F13
Uludere Turkey 73 D10
Uluguru Mts. Tanzania 86 D4
Ulukışla Turkey 72 D6
Ulungur He → China 60 B3
Uluru Australia 93 E5
Uluru-Kata Tjuta △ Australia 93 E5
Ulutau Kazakhstan 52 E7
Uluwatu Indonesia 63 K18
Ulva U.K. 13 E2
Ulverston U.K. 14 C4
Ulverstone Australia 95 G4
Ulya Russia 53 D15
Ulyanovo Russia 30 D9
Ulyanovsk Russia 34 C9
Ulyanovsk □ Russia 34 C9
Ulyasutay = Uliastay
    Mongolia 60 B4
Ulysses Kans., U.S.A. 112 G3
Ulysses Pa., U.S.A. 114 E7
Ulysses, Mt. Canada 102 B4
Umag Croatia 41 C10
Umala Bolivia 124 G5
'Umān = Oman ■ Asia 75 C6
Uman Ukraine 23 D16
Umaria India 69 H9
Umarkot Pakistan 68 G3
Umarpada India 68 J5
Umatilla U.S.A. 108 D4
Umba Russia 52 C6
Umbagog L. U.S.A. 115 B13
Umbakumba Australia 94 A2
Umbértide Italy 41 E9
Umbrella Mts. N.Z. 91 F2
Umbria □ Italy 41 F9
Umeå Sweden 8 E19
Umeälven → Sweden 8 E19

Umera Indonesia 63 E7
Umfuli → Zimbabwe 87 F2
Umfurudzi △ Zimbabwe 87 F3
Umgusa Zimbabwe 87 F2
Umgwenya → Mozam. 89 D5
Umiujaq Canada 104 A4
Umka Serbia 44 B4
Umkomaas S. Africa 89 E5
Umlazi S. Africa 85 L6
Umm ad Daraj, J. Jordan 74 C4
Umm al Khashab Si. Arabia 80 D5
Umm al Qaywayn U.A.E. 71 E7
Umm al Qittayn Jordan 74 C5
Umm Arda Sudan 81 D3
Umm Bāb Qatar 71 E6
Umm Badr Sudan 81 E2
Umm Bel Sudan 81 E2
Umm Birkah Si. Arabia 80 B4
Umm Boim Sudan 81 F2
Umm Dam Sudan 81 E3
Umm Debi Sudan 81 D3
Umm Durban Sudan 81 D3
Umm Durman =
    Omdurmân Sudan 81 D3
Umm el Fahm Israel 74 C4
Umm Gafala Sudan 81 E2
Umm Gimala Sudan 81 E2
Umm Inderaba Sudan 80 D3
Umm Keddada Sudan 81 E2
Umm Koweika Sudan 81 E3
Umm Lajj Si. Arabia 70 E3
Umm Merwa Sudan 80 D3
Umm Qantur Sudan 81 E3
Umm Qasr Iraq 70 D5
Umm Qurein Sudan 81 F2
Umm Ruwaba Sudan 81 E3
Umm Saiyala Sudan 81 E3
Umm Shutur Sudan 81 F2
Umm Sidr Sudan 81 E2
Umm Urūmah Si. Arabia 80 B4
Umm Zehetir Egypt 80 J8
Umnak I. U.S.A. 106 E6
Umniati → Zimbabwe 87 F2
Umpqua → U.S.A. 108 E1
Umreth India 68 H5
Umtata = Mthatha S. Africa 89 E4
Umuahia Nigeria 83 D6
Umuarama Brazil 127 A5
Umvukwe Ra. Zimbabwe 87 F3
Umzimvubu S. Africa 89 E4
Umzingwane → Zimbabwe 87 G2
Umzinto = eMuziwezinto
    S. Africa 89 E5
Una India 68 J4
Una → Bos.-H. 41 D13
Unac → Bos.-H. 41 D13
Unadilla U.S.A. 115 D9
Unalakleet U.S.A. 106 C7
Unalaska U.S.A. 106 E6
Unalaska I. U.S.A. 106 E6
'Unayzah Si. Arabia 70 E4
'Unayzah, J. Asia 73 F8
Uncastillo Spain 38 C3
Uncía Bolivia 124 G5
Uncompahgre Peak U.S.A. 108 G10
Uncompahgre Plateau
    U.S.A. 108 G9
Undara Volcanic △ Australia 94 B3
Unden Sweden 11 F8
Underbool Australia 95 F3
Undersaker Sweden 10 A7
Underwood Canada 114 B3
Unecha Russia 33 F7
Ungarie Australia 95 E4
Ungarra Australia 95 E2
Ungava, Pén. d' Canada 101 F17
Ungava B. Canada 101 F18
Ungeny = Ungheni Moldova 29 C12
Unggi N. Korea 57 C16
Ungheni Moldova 29 C12
Unguala → Ethiopia 81 F5
Ungwana B. Kenya 86 C5
Ungwatiri Sudan 81 D4
Uni Russia 34 B10
União da Vitória Brazil 127 B5
Uničov Czech Rep. 27 B10
Uniejów Poland 31 G5
Unije Croatia 41 D11
Unimak I. U.S.A. 106 E7
Unimak Pass. U.S.A. 106 E7
Union Miss., U.S.A. 117 E10
Union Mo., U.S.A. 112 F9
Union S.C., U.S.A. 117 D14
Union City Calif., U.S.A. 110 H4
Union City N.J., U.S.A. 115 F10
Union City Pa., U.S.A. 114 E5
Union City Tenn., U.S.A. 117 C10
Union Dale U.S.A. 115 E9
Union Gap U.S.A. 108 C3
Union Springs Ala., U.S.A. 117 E12
Union Springs N.Y., U.S.A. 115 D8
Uniondale S. Africa 88 E3
Uniontown U.S.A. 113 F14
Unionville U.S.A. 112 E7
Unirea Romania 29 F12
United Arab Emirates ■ Asia 71 F7
United Kingdom ■ Europe 16 E6
United States of America ■
    N. Amer. 107 H20

Unity Canada 103 C7
Universales, Mtes. Spain 38 E3
University Park U.S.A. 109 K10
University Place U.S.A. 110 C4
Unjha India 68 H5
Unna Germany 24 D3
Unnao India 69 F9
Unc, Ilha Guinea-Biss. 82 C1
Unsengedsi → Zimbabwe 87 F3
Unst U.K. 13 A8
Unstrut → Germany 24 D7
Unterfranken □ Germany 25 F5
Unterschleissheim Germany 25 G7
Unuk → Canada 102 B2
Ünye Turkey 72 B7
Urzen-Amakusa △ Japan 55 H5
Unzha Russia 34 A7
Unzha → Russia 34 B6
Uozu Japan 55 F8
Upata Venezuela 124 B6
Upemba, L.
    Dem. Rep. of the Congo 87 D2
Upemba △
    Dem. Rep. of the Congo 87 D2
Upernavik Greenland 4 B5
Upington S. Africa 88 D3
Upleta India 68 J4
'Upolu Samoa 91 b
Upper → Ghana 83 C4
Upper Alkali L. U.S.A. 108 F3
Upper Arrow L. Canada 102 C5
Upper Daly ⊙ Australia 92 B5
Upper Darby U.S.A. 113 F16
Upper Foster L. Canada 103 B7
Upper Hutt N.Z. 91 D5
Upper Klamath L. U.S.A. 108 E3
Upper Lake U.S.A. 110 F4
Upper Liard Canada 102 A3
Upper Manzanilla
    Trin. & Tob. 125 K15
Upper Missouri Breaks △
    U.S.A. 108 C9
Upper Musquodoboit
    Canada 105 C7
Upper Red L. U.S.A. 112 A6
Upper Sandusky U.S.A. 113 E12
Upper Volta = Burkina
    Faso ■ Africa 82 C4
Upphärad Sweden 11 F6
Uppland Sweden 10 D11
Upplands-Väsby Sweden 10 E11
Uppsala Sweden 10 E11
Uppsala län □ Sweden 10 D11
Upshi India 69 C7
Upton U.S.A. 108 D11
Uqsuqtuuq = Gjoa Haven
    Canada 100 D12
Ur Iraq 70 D5
Urad Qianqi China 56 D5
Urakawa Japan 54 C11
Ural = Uralskiy □ Russia 52 C7
Ural → Zhayyq → Kazakhstan 6 F16
Ural Australia 95 E4
Ural Mts. = Uralskie Gory
    Eurasia 6 C17
Uralla Australia 95 E5
Uralsk = Oral Kazakhstan 34 E10
Uralskie Gory Eurasia 6 C17
Uralskiy □ Russia 52 C7
Urambo Tanzania 86 D3
Urandangi Australia 94 C2
Uranium City Canada 103 B7
Urapuntja = Utopia Australia 94 C1
Uraricoera → Brazil 124 C6
Urasoe Japan 55 L3
Urawa = Saitama Japan 55 G9
Uray Russia 52 C7
'Uray'irah Si. Arabia 71 E6
Urbana Ill., U.S.A. 112 E9
Urbana Ohio, U.S.A. 113 E12
Urbandale U.S.A. 112 E7
Urbánia Italy 41 E9
Urbel → Spain 36 C7
Urbino Italy 41 E9
Urbión, Picos de Spain 38 C2
Urcos Peru 124 F4
Urdinarrain Argentina 126 C4
Urdos France 20 F3
Ure → U.K. 14 C6
Uren Russia 34 B7
Urengoy Russia 52 C8
Ures Mexico 118 B2
Urewera △ N.Z. 91 C6
Urfa = Şanlıurfa Turkey 73 D8
Urganch Uzbekistan 52 E7
Urgench = Urganch
    Uzbekistan 52 E7
Ürgüp Turkey 72 C6
Uri India 69 B6
Uri □ Switz. 25 J4
Uribia Colombia 124 A4
Uricani Romania 28 E8
Uriondo Bolivia 126 A3
Urique Mexico 118 B3
Urique → Mexico 118 B3
Urk Neths. 17 B5
Urla Turkey 47 C8
Urlaţi Romania 29 F11
Urmia = Orūmīyeh Iran 73 D11

Uromi Nigeria 83 D6
Uroševac Kosovo 44 D5
Uroyan, Montanas de
    Puerto Rico 121 d
Urrampinyi Iltjiltarri ⊙
    Australia 92 D5
Urshult Sweden 11 H8
Ursula Lithuania 32 E3
Uruaçu Brazil 125 F9
Uruapan Mexico 118 D4
Urubamba → Peru 124 F4
Urucará Brazil 124 D7
Uruçuí Brazil 125 E10
Uruguai → Brazil 127 B5
Uruguaiana Brazil 126 B4
Uruguay ■ S. Amer. 126 C4
Uruguay → S. Amer. 126 C4
Urumchi = Ürümqi China 52 E9
Ürümqi China 52 E9
Uruna ⊙ Australia 92 D5
Urup → Russia 35 H5
Urup, Ostrov Russia 53 E16
Uryupinsk Russia 34 E5
Ürzhar Kazakhstan 52 E9
Urzhum Russia 34 B9
Urziceni Romania 29 F11
Usa → Russia 52 C6
Uşak Turkey 47 C11
Uşak □ Turkey 47 C11
Usakos Namibia 88 C2
Uşçe Serbia 44 C4
Usedom Germany 24 B10
Usedom → Germany 24 B10
Useless Loop Australia 93 E1
'Usfān Si. Arabia 80 C4
Ushakova, Ostrov Russia 53 A8
Ushakovo Russia 30 D7
Ushant = Ouessant, Î. d'
    France 18 D1
Ushashi Tanzania 86 C3
Ushat Sudan 81 F2
'Ushayrah Ar Riyāḍ, Si. Arabia 70 E5
'Ushayrah Makkah, Si. Arabia 80 C5
Ushibuka Japan 55 H5
Üshtöbe Kazakhstan 52 E8
Ushuaia Argentina 128 G3
Ushumun Russia 53 D13
Ushytsya → Ukraine 29 B12
Usinsk Russia 52 C6
Usk Canada 102 C3
Usk → U.K. 15 F5
Uska India 69 F10
Üsküdar Turkey 45 F13
Uslar Germany 24 D5
Usman Russia 33 F10
Usoke Tanzania 86 D3
Usolye-Sibirskoye Russia 53 D11
Usoro Nigeria 83 D6
Uspallata, P. de Argentina 126 C2
Ussel France 20 C6
Usson-du-Poitou France 20 B4
Ussuriysk Russia 54 C5
Ussurka Russia 54 B6
Ust-Buzulukskaya Russia 34 E6
Ust-Chaun Russia 53 C18
Ust-Chorna Ukraine 29 B8
Ust-Donetskiy Russia 35 G5
Ust-Ilimsk Russia 53 D11
Ust-Ishim Russia 52 D8
Ust-Kamchatsk Russia 53 D17
Ust-Kamenogorsk =
    Öskemen Kazakhstan 52 E9
Ust-Khayryuzovo Russia 53 D16
Ust-Kut Russia 53 D11
Ust-Kuyga Russia 53 B14
Ust-Labinsk Russia 35 H4
Ust-Luga Russia 32 C5
Ust-Maya Russia 53 C14
Ust-Mil Russia 53 D14
Ust-Nera Russia 53 C15
Ust-Nyukzha Russia 53 D13
Ust-Olenek Russia 53 B12
Ust-Omchug Russia 53 C15
Ust-Port Russia 52 C9
Ust-Tsilma Russia 52 C6
Ust-Urt = Ustyurt Plateau
    Asia 52 E6
Ustaritz France 20 E2
Ustecký □ Czech Rep. 26 A7
Uster Switz. 25 H4
Ústí nad Labem Czech Rep. 26 A7
Ústí nad Orlicí Czech Rep. 27 B9
Ústica Italy 42 E6
Ustinov = Izhevsk Russia 52 D6
Ustka Poland 30 D3
Ustroń Poland 31 J5
Ustrzyki Dolne Poland 31 J9
Ustyluh Ukraine 31 H11
Ustyurt Plateau Asia 52 E6
Ustyuzhna Russia 32 C9
Usu China 60 B3
Usuki Japan 55 H5
Usulután El Salv. 120 D2
Usumacinta → Mexico 119 D6
Usumbura = Bujumbura
    Burundi 86 C2
Usure Tanzania 86 C3
Usutuo → Mozam. 89 D5
Uta Indonesia 63 E9
Utah □ U.S.A. 108 G8
Utah L. U.S.A. 108 F8

Utansjö Sweden 10 B11
Utara, Selat Malaysia 65 c
Utarni India 68 F4
Utatlan Guatemala 120 C1
Ute Creek → U.S.A. 109 J12
Utebo Spain 38 D3
Utena Lithuania 32 E3
Utete Tanzania 86 D4
Uthai Thani Thailand 64 E3
Uthal Pakistan 68 G2
Utiariti Brazil 124 F7
Utica N.Y., U.S.A. 115 C9
Utica Ohio, U.S.A. 114 F2
Utiel Spain 39 F3
Utikuma L. Canada 102 B5
Utila Honduras 120 C2
Utō Sweden 10 F12
Utopia Australia 94 C1
Utraula India 69 F10
Utrecht Neths. 17 B5
Utrecht S. Africa 89 D5
Utrecht □ Neths. 17 B5
Utrera Spain 37 H5
Utsjoki → Finland 8 B22
Utsunomiya Japan 55 F9
Uttar Pradesh □ India 69 F9
Uttaradit Thailand 64 D3
Uttarakhand □ India 69 D8
Utterson Canada 114 A5
Uttoxeter U.K. 14 E6
Utuado Puerto Rico 121 d
Uummannaq Avannaarsua,
    Greenland 101 B18
Uummannaq Kitaa, Greenland 4 B5
Uummannarsuaq = Nunap
    Isua Greenland 98 D15
Uusikaarlepyy Finland 8 E20
Uusikaupunki Finland 32 B1
Uva Russia 34 B11
Uvac → Serbia 44 C3
Uvalde U.S.A. 116 G5
Uvarovo Russia 34 E6
Uvat Russia 52 D7
Uvinza Tanzania 86 D3
Uvira Dem. Rep. of the Congo 86 C2
Uvs Nuur Mongolia 60 A4
'Uwairidh, Ḥarrat al
    Si. Arabia 70 E3
Uwajima Japan 55 H6
Uwanda Tanzania 86 D3
Uweinat, Jebel Sudan 80 C1
Uxbridge Canada 114 B5
Uxin Qi China 56 E5
Uxmal Mexico 119 C7
Üydzin Mongolia 56 B4
Uyo Nigeria 83 D6
Üyüklü Tepe Turkey 47 D9
Uyûn Mûsa Egypt 74 F1
Uyuni Bolivia 124 H5
Uzbekistan ■ Asia 52 E7
Uzboy → Turkmenistan 71 B7
Uzen, Bolshoi = Uzen,
    Mal → Kazakhstan 35 F9
Uzen, Mal → Kazakhstan 35 F9
Uzerche France 20 C5
Uzès France 21 D8
Uzh → Ukraine 23 C16
Uzhgorod = Uzhhorod
    Ukraine 28 B7
Uzhhorod Ukraine 28 B7
Uzhok Ukraine 28 B7
Užice Serbia 44 C3
Üzümlü Turkey 47 C11
Uzunköprü Turkey 45 E10
Uzunkuyu Turkey 47 C8

V

Vaal → S. Africa 88 D3
Vaal Dam S. Africa 89 D4
Vaalbos △ S. Africa 88 D3
Vaalwater S. Africa 89 C4
Vaasa Finland 8 E19
Vabre France 20 E6
Vác Hungary 28 C4
Vacaria Brazil 127 B5
Vacata Fiji 91 a
Vacaville U.S.A. 110 G5
Vaccarès, Étang de France 21 E8
Vach = Vakh → Russia 52 C8
Vache, Î. à Haiti 121 C5
Vacoas Mauritius 85 d
Vadakara = Badagara India 66 P9
Väddö Sweden 10 D12
Vadnagar India 68 H5
Vado Lígure Italy 40 D5
Vadodara India 68 H5
Vadsø Norway 8 A23
Vadstena Sweden 11 F8
Vaduz Liech. 25 H5
Værøy Norway 8 C15
Vágar Færoe Is. 8 E9
Vaggeryd Sweden 11 G8
Vaghia Greece 46 C5
Vagia, Akra Greece 49 C10
Vagney France 19 D13
Vagnhärad Sweden 11 F11
Vado Lígure Italy 40 D5
Vágos Portugal 36 E2
Vågsfjorden Norway 8 B17
Váh → Slovak Rep. 27 D11
Vahsel B. Antarctica 5 D1
Váhtjer = Gällivare Sweden 8 C19
Vaï Greece 49 D8
Vaiges France 18 D6
Vaihingen Germany 25 G4
Vaihiria, L. Tahiti 91 d
Vail U.S.A. 107 H18
Vailly-sur-Aisne France 19 C10
Vairao Tahiti 91 d
Vaisali → India 69 F8
Vaison-la-Romaine France 21 D9
Vaitogi Amer. Samoa 91 b
Vakarel Bulgaria 44 D7
Vakfikebir Turkey 73 B8
Vakh → Russia 52 C8
Vakhtan Russia 34 B8
Vál Hungary 28 C3
Val-de-Marne □ France 19 D9
Val-d'Isère France 21 C10
Val-d'Oise □ France 19 C9
Val-d'Or Canada 104 C4
Val Grande △ Italy 40 B5
Val Marie Canada 103 D7
Val Thorens France 21 C10
Valaam Russia 32 B6
Valadares Portugal 36 D2
Valahia Romania 29 F9
Valais □ Switz. 25 J3
Valais, Alpes du Switz. 25 J3
Valandovo Macedonia 44 E6
Valašské Meziříčí Czech Rep. 27 B10
Valatie U.S.A. 115 D11
Valaxa Greece 46 C6
Vålberg Sweden 10 E7
Valbo Sweden 10 D10
Valbondione Italy 40 B7
Vălcani Romania 28 D5
Vâlcea □ Romania 29 F9
Valcheta Argentina 128 E3
Valdagno Italy 41 C8
Valdahon France 19 E13
Valdai Hills = Valdayskaya
    Vozvyshennost Russia 32 D7
Valday Russia 32 D7
Valdayskaya
    Vozvyshennost Russia 32 D7
Valdeazogues → Spain 37 G6
Valdecañas, Embalse de
    Spain 36 F5
Valdemarsvik Sweden 11 F10
Valdemoro Spain 38 E7
Valdepeñas Spain 37 G7
Valderaduey → Spain 36 D5
Valderice Italy 42 D5
Valderrobres Spain 38 E5
Valdés, Pen. Argentina 128 E4
Valdez U.S.A. 100 E2
Valdivia Chile 128 D2
Valdivia Abyssal Plain
    S. Ocean 5 B1
Valdobbiádene Italy 41 C8
Valdosta U.S.A. 117 F13
Valdoviño Spain 36 B2
Valdres Norway 8 F13
Vale Georgia 35 K6
Vale U.S.A. 108 E5
Vale of Glamorgan □ U.K. 15 F4
Valea lui Mihai Romania 28 C7
Valea Mărului Romania 29 E12
Valemount Canada 102 C5
Valença Brazil 125 F11
Valença Portugal 36 C2
Valença do Piauí Brazil 125 E10
Valençay France 19 E8
Valence France 21 D8
Valence d'Agen France 20 D4
Valencia Phil. 61 H6
Valencia Spain 39 F4
Valencia Trin. & Tob. 125 K15
Valencia U.S.A. 109 J10
Valencia Venezuela 124 A5
Valencia □ Spain 39 F4
Valencia ✈ (VLC) Spain 39 F4
Valencia, G. de Spain 39 F5
Valencia de Alcántara Spain 37 F3
Valencia de Don Juan Spain 36 C5
Valencia I. Ireland 12 E1
Valenciennes France 19 B10
Văleni Romania 29 F9
Vălenii de Munte Romania 29 E11
Valensole France 21 E9
Valentigney France 19 E13
Valentim, Sa. do Brazil 125 E10
Valentin Russia 54 C7
Valentine Nebr., U.S.A. 112 D3
Valentine Tex., U.S.A. 116 F2
Valenza Italy 40 C5
Valera Venezuela 124 B4
Valga Estonia 32 D4
Valguarnera Caropepe Italy 43 E7
Valier U.S.A. 108 B7
Valjevo Serbia 44 B3
Valka Latvia 32 D4

Vall de Uxó = La Vall
d'Uixó *Spain* **38** F4
Valla *Sweden* **10** E10
Valladolid *Mexico* **119** C7
Valladolid *Spain* **36** D6
Valladolid □ *Spain* **36** D6
Vallata *Italy* **43** A8
Valldemossa *Spain* **48** B9
Valle d'Aosta □ *Italy* **40** C4
Valle de Aran *Spain* **38** C5
Valle de la Pascua *Venezuela* **124** B5
Valle de las Palmas *Mexico* **111** N10
Valle de Santiago *Mexico* **118** C4
Valle de Zaragoza *Mexico* **118** B3
Valle del Ticino △ *Italy* **40** C6
Valle Fértil, Sierra del
Argentina **126** C2
Valle Gran Rey *Canary Is.* **48** F2
Valle Hermoso *Mexico* **119** B5
Valle Nacional *Mexico* **119** D5
Valledupar *Colombia* **124** A4
Vallehermoso *Canary Is.* **48** F2
Vallejo *U.S.A.* **110** G4
Vallenar *Chile* **126** B1
Vallentuna *Sweden* **10** E12
Valleraugue *France* **20** D7
Vallet *France* **18** E5
Valletta *Malta* **49** D2
Valley Center *U.S.A.* **111** M9
Valley City *U.S.A.* **112** B5
Valley Falls *Oreg., U.S.A.* **108** E3
Valley Falls *R.I., U.S.A.* **115** E13
Valley of Flowers △ *India* **69** D8
Valley of the Kings *Egypt* **80** B3
Valley Springs *U.S.A.* **110** G6
Valley View *U.S.A.* **115** F8
Valley Wells *U.S.A.* **111** K11
Valleyview *Canada* **102** B5
Valli di Comácchio *Italy* **41** D9
Vallimanca, Arroyo
Argentina **126** D4
Vallo della Lucánia *Italy* **43** B8
Vallon-Pont-d'Arc *France* **21** D8
Vallorbe *Switz.* **25** J2
Valls *Spain* **38** D6
Valmaseda = Balmaseda
Spain **38** B1
Valmiera *Latvia* **32** D3
Valnera *Spain* **36** B7
Valognes *France* **18** C5
Valona = Vlorë *Albania* **44** F3
Valongo *Portugal* **36** D2
Valozhyn *Belarus* **23** A14
Valpaços *Portugal* **36** D3
Valparaíso *Chile* **126** C1
Valparaíso *Mexico* **118** C4
Valparaiso *U.S.A.* **112** E10
Valparaíso □ *Chile* **126** C1
Valpovo *Croatia* **28** E3
Valréas *France* **21** D9
Vals *Switz.* **25** J5
Vals → *S. Africa* **88** D4
Vals, Tanjung *Indonesia* **63** F9
Vals-les-Bains *France* **21** D8
Valsad *India* **68** J8
Valtellina *Italy* **40** B6
Valuyki *Russia* **33** G10
Valverde *Canary Is.* **48** G2
Valverde del Camino *Spain* **37** H4
Valverde del Fresno *Spain* **36** E4
Vama *Romania* **29** C10
Vamdrup *Denmark* **11** J3
Våmhus *Sweden* **10** C8
Vamizi, I. *Mozam.* **87** E5
Vammala *Finland* **32** B2
Vamos *Greece* **49** D6
Van *Turkey* **73** C10
Van □ *Turkey* **73** C10
Van, L. = Van Gölü *Turkey* **73** C10
Van Alstyne *U.S.A.* **116** E6
Van Blommestein Meer
Suriname **125** C7
Van Buren *Canada* **105** C6
Van Buren *Ark., U.S.A.* **116** D7
Van Buren *Maine, U.S.A.* **113** B20
Van Buren *Mo., U.S.A.* **112** G8
Van Canh *Vietnam* **64** F7
Van Diemen, C. *N. Terr.,
Australia* **92** B5
Van Diemen, C. *Queens.,
Australia* **94** B2
Van Diemen G. *Australia* **92** B5
Van Gölü *Turkey* **73** C10
Van Horn *U.S.A.* **116** F2
Van Ninh *Vietnam* **64** F7
Van Rees, Pegunungan
Indonesia **63** E9
Van Wert *U.S.A.* **113** E11
Van Yen *Vietnam* **58** G5
Van Zylsrus *S. Africa* **88** D3
Vanadzor *Armenia* **35** K7
Vanavara *Russia* **53** C11
Vancouver *Canada* **110** A3
Vancouver *U.S.A.* **110** E4
Vancouver, C. *Australia* **93** G2
Vancouver I. *Canada* **110** B2
Vancouver Int. ✈ (YVR)
Canada **110** A3
Vanda = Vantaa *Finland* **32** B3
Vandalia *Ill., U.S.A.* **112** F9

Vandalia *Mo., U.S.A.* **112** F8
Vandenberg Village *U.S.A.* **111** L6
Vandergrift *U.S.A.* **114** F5
Vanderhoof *Canada* **102** C4
Vanderkloof Dam *S. Africa* **88** E3
Vanderlin I. *Australia* **94** B2
Vänern *Sweden* **11** F6
Vänersborg *Sweden* **11** F6
Vang Vieng *Laos* **64** C4
Vanga *Kenya* **86** C4
Vangaindrano *Madag.* **89** C8
Vanguard *Canada* **103** D7
Vanino *Russia* **53** E15
Vânju Mare *Romania* **28** F7
Vankleek Hill *Canada* **115** A10
Vännäs *Sweden* **8** E18
Vannes *France* **18** E4
Vannøya *Norway* **8** A18
Vanoise, Massif de la *France* **21** C10
Vanrhynsdorp *S. Africa* **88** E2
Vansbro *Sweden* **10** D8
Vansittart B. *Australia* **92** B4
Vansittart I. *Canada* **101** D15
Vantaa *Finland* **32** B3
Vanua Balavu *Fiji* **91** a
Vanua Levu *Fiji* **91** a
Vanua Vatu *Fiji* **91** a
Vanuatu ■ *Pac. Oc.* **90** C9
Vanwyksvlei *S. Africa* **88** E3
Vapnyarka *Ukraine* **29** B13
Var □ *France* **21** E10
Var → *France* **21** E11
Vara *Sweden* **11** F6
Varades *France* **18** E5
Varáita → *Italy* **40** D7
Varalé *Ivory C.* **82** D4
Varallo *Italy* **40** C5
Varāmīn *Iran* **71** C6
Varāmīn *Iran* **71** B6
Varanasi *India* **69** G10
Varangerfjorden *Norway* **8** A23
Varangerhalvøya *Norway* **8** A23
Varano, Lago di *Italy* **41** G12
Varaždin *Croatia* **41** B13
Varazze *Italy* **40** D5
Varberg *Sweden* **11** G6
Vardak □ *Afghan.* **66** B6
Vardar = Axios → *Greece* **44** F6
Varde *Denmark* **11** J2
Varde Å → *Denmark* **11** J2
Vardenis *Armenia* **35** K7
Vardø *Norway* **8** A24
Varel *Germany* **24** B4
Varella, Mui *Vietnam* **64** F7
Varéna *Lithuania* **32** E3
Varennes-sur-Allier *France* **19** F10
Varennes-Vauzelles *France* **19** E10
Vareš *Bos.-H.* **28** F3
Varese *Italy* **40** C5
Vârfurile *Romania* **28** D7
Vårgårda *Sweden* **11** F6
Varginha *Brazil* **127** A6
Vargön *Sweden* **11** F6
Varillas *Chile* **126** A1
Varkaus *Finland* **32** A4
Värmdölandet *Sweden* **10** E12
Värmeln *Sweden* **10** E6
Värmlands län □ *Sweden* **10** E6
Värmlandsbro *Sweden* **10** E7
Varna *Bulgaria* **45** C11
Varna □ *Bulgaria* **45** C11
Värnamo *Sweden* **11** G8
Varnsdorf *Czech Rep.* **26** A7
Várpalota *Hungary* **28** C3
Vars *Canada* **115** A9
Vars *France* **21** D10
Varto *Turkey* **73** C9
Varvarin *Serbia* **44** C5
Varysburg *U.S.A.* **114** D6
Varzaneh *Iran* **71** C7
Varzaqān *Iran* **73** C12
Varzi *Italy* **40** D6
Varzo *Italy* **40** B5
Varzy *France* **19** E10
Vas □ *Hungary* **28** C1
Vasa = Vaasa *Finland* **8** E19
Vasa Barris → *Brazil* **125** F11
Vascão → *Portugal* **37** H3
Vaşcău *Romania* **28** D7
Vascongadas = País
Vasco □ *Spain* **38** C2
Vashkivtsi *Ukraine* **29** B10
Vasht = Khāsh *Iran* **71** D9
Vasilevichi *Belarus* **23** B15
Vasiliki *Greece* **46** C2
Vasiliko *Greece* **46** C5
Vasilkov = Vasylkiv *Ukraine* **23** C16
Vaslui *Romania* **29** D12
Vaslui □ *Romania* **29** D12
Väsman *Sweden* **10** D9
Vassar *Canada* **103** D9
Vassar *U.S.A.* **113** D12
Västerås *Sweden* **10** E10
Västerbotten *Sweden* **8** D19
Västerdalälven → *Sweden* **10** D8
Västergötland *Sweden* **11** F7
Västerhaninge *Sweden* **10** E12
Västervik *Sweden* **11** G10
Västmanland *Sweden* **9** G17

Västmanlands län □ *Sweden* **10** E10
Vasto *Italy* **41** F11
Västra Götalands Län □
Sweden **11** F6
Vasvár *Hungary* **28** C1
Vasylivka *Ukraine* **29** E13
Vasylkiv *Ukraine* **23** C16
Vatan *France* **19** E8
Vatersay *U.K.* **13** E1
Vathia *Greece* **46** E4
Vati *Greece* **49** C9
Vatican City ■ *Europe* **41** G9
Vaticano, C. *Italy* **43** D8
Vatili *Cyprus* **49** D12
Vatin *Serbia* **28** E6
Vatiu = Atiu *Cook Is.* **97** J12
Vatnajökull *Iceland* **8** D5
Vatoa *Fiji* **91** a
Vatolakkos *Greece* **49** D5
Vatoloha *Madag.* **89** B8
Vatomandry *Madag.* **89** B8
Vatra-Dornei *Romania* **29** C10
Vatrak → *India* **68** H5
Vättern *Sweden* **11** F8
Vatu Vara *Fiji* **91** a
Vatulele *Fiji* **91** a
Vaucluse □ *France* **21** E9
Vaucouleurs *France* **19** D12
Vaud □ *Switz.* **25** J2
Vaudreuil-Dorion *Canada* **115** A10
Vaughn *Mont., U.S.A.* **108** C8
Vaughn *N. Mex., U.S.A.* **109** J11
Vaujours L. *Canada* **104** A5
Vaupés = Uaupés → *Brazil* **124** C5
Vaupés □ *Colombia* **124** C4
Vauvert *France* **21** E8
Vauxhall *Canada* **102** C6
Vav *India* **68** G4
Vavatenina *Madag.* **89** B8
Vava'u *Tonga* **91** c
Vava'u Group *Tonga* **91** c
Vavoua *Ivory C.* **82** D3
Vawkavysk *Belarus* **23** B13
Vaxholm *Sweden* **10** E12
Växjö *Sweden* **11** H8
Vaygach, Ostrov *Russia* **52** C7
Veaikevárri = Svappavaara
Sweden **8** C19
Vechelde *Germany* **24** C6
Vechta *Germany* **24** C4
Vechte → *Neths.* **17** B6
Vecsés *Hungary* **28** C4
Veddige *Sweden* **11** G6
Vedea → *Romania* **29** G10
Vedi *Armenia* **73** C11
Vedia *Argentina* **126** C3
Vedrette di Ries-Aurina △
Italy **41** B9
Vedum *Sweden* **11** F7
Veendam *Neths.* **17** A6
Veenendaal *Neths.* **17** B5
Vefsna → *Norway* **8** D15
Vega *Norway* **8** D14
Vega *U.S.A.* **116** D3
Vega Baja *Puerto Rico* **121** d
Vegadeo *Spain* **36** B3
Vegoritida, L. *Greece* **44** F5
Vegreville *Canada* **102** C6
Veinge *Sweden* **11** H7
Veisiejai *Lithuania* **30** D10
Vejbystrand *Sweden* **11** H6
Vejen *Denmark* **11** J3
Vejer de la Frontera *Spain* **37** J5
Vejle *Denmark* **11** J3
Vejle Fjord *Denmark* **11** J3
Vela Luka *Croatia* **41** F13
Velas, C. *Costa Rica* **120** D2
Velasco, Sierra de *Argentina* **126** B2
Velay, Mts. du *France* **20** D7
Velbert *Germany* **24** D3
Velddrif *S. Africa* **88** E2
Velebit △ *Croatia* **41** D12
Velebit Planina *Croatia* **41** D12
Velebitski Kanal *Croatia* **41** D11
Veleka → *Bulgaria* **45** D11
Velenče-itó *Hungary* **28** C3
Velenje *Slovenia* **41** B12
Veles *Macedonia* **44** E5
Velestino *Greece* **44** E4
Vélez-Málaga *Spain* **37** J6
Vélez Rubio *Spain* **39** H2
Velhas → *Brazil* **125** G10
Velika *Croatia* **28** E2
Velika Gorica *Croatia* **41** C13
Velika Kapela *Croatia* **41** C12
Velika Kladuša *Bos.-H.* **41** C12
Velika Kruša *Kosovo* **44** D4
Velika Morava → *Serbia* **44** B5
Velika Plana *Serbia* **44** B5
Velikaya → *Russia* **32** D5
Velikaya Kema *Russia* **54** B4
Velike Lašče *Slovenia* **41** C11
Veliki Jastrebac *Serbia* **44** C5
Veliki Kanal *Serbia* **28** E4
Veliki Popović *Serbia* **44** B5
Velikiye Luki *Russia* **32** D6
Veliko Gradište *Serbia* **44** B5
Veliko Tŭrnovo *Bulgaria* **45** C9

Velikonda Range *India* **66** M11
Vélingara *Kolda, Senegal* **82** C2
Vélingara *Louga, Senegal* **82** B2
Velingrad *Bulgaria* **44** D7
Velino, Mte. *Italy* **41** F10
Velizh *Russia* **32** E6
Velké Karlovice *Czech Rep.* **27** B11
Velké Meziříčí *Czech Rep.* **26** B9
Veľký Javorník *Slovak Rep.* **27** B11
Veľký Krtíš *Slovak Rep.* **27** C12
Veľký Meder *Slovak Rep.* **27** D10
Veľký Tribeč *Slovak Rep.* **27** C11
Velletri *Italy* **42** A5
Vellinge *Sweden* **11** J6
Vellmar *Germany* **24** D5
Vellore *India* **66** N11
Velopoula *Greece* **46** E5
Velsk *Russia* **32** B11
Velten *Germany* **24** C9
Veluwezoom △ *Neths.* **17** B6
Velva *U.S.A.* **112** A3
Velvendos *Greece* **44** F6
Vemb *Denmark* **11** H2
Vemdalen *Sweden* **10** B7
Ven *Sweden* **11** J6
Venado *Mexico* **118** C4
Venado Tuerto *Argentina* **126** C3
Venafro *Italy* **43** A7
Venarey-les-Laumes *France* **19** E11
Venaría *Italy* **40** C4
Venčane *Serbia* **44** B4
Vence *France* **21** E11
Vendas Novas *Portugal* **37** G2
Vendée □ *France* **18** F5
Vendée → *France* **18** F5
Vendéen, Bocage *France* **20** B2
Vendeuvre-sur-Barse
France **19** D11
Vendôme *France* **18** E8
Vendrell = El Vendrell *Spain* **38** D6
Vendsyssel *Denmark* **11** G4
Vendychany *Ukraine* **29** B12
Venelles *France* **21** E9
Véneta, L. *Italy* **41** C9
Véneto □ *Italy* **41** C9
Venev *Russia* **32** E10
Venézia *Italy* **41** C9
Venézia, G. di *Italy* **41** C10
Venezuela ■ *S. Amer.* **124** B5
Venezuela, G. de *Venezuela* **124** A4
Vengurla *India* **66** M8
Venice = Venézia *Italy* **41** C9
Venice *U.S.A.* **117** H13
Vénissieux *France* **21** C9
Venjansjön *Sweden* **10** D8
Venkatapuram *India* **67** K12
Venlo *Neths.* **17** C6
Vennachar Junction *Canada* **114** A7
Vennesla *Norway* **9** G12
Venosa *Italy* **43** B8
Venray *Neths.* **17** C6
Venta → *Latvia* **30** A8
Venta de Baños *Spain* **36** D6
Venta de Cardeña =
Cardeña *Spain* **37** G6
Ventana, Punta de la
Mexico **118** C3
Ventana, Sa. de la *Argentina* **126** D3
Ventersburg *S. Africa* **88** D4
Venterstad *S. Africa* **88** E4
Ventimíglia *Italy* **40** E4
Ventnor *U.K.* **15** G6
Ventoténe *Italy* **42** B6
Ventoux, Mt. *France* **21** D9
Ventspils *Latvia* **30** A8
Ventspils □ *Latvia* **30** A8
Ventuarí → *Venezuela* **124** C5
Ventucopa *U.S.A.* **111** L7
Ventura *U.S.A.* **111** L7
Vénus, Pte. *Tahiti* **91** d
Venus B. *Australia* **95** F4
Venustiano Carranza
Mexico **118** A1
Vera *Argentina* **126** B3
Vera *Spain* **39** H3
Veracruz *Mexico* **119** D5
Veracruz □ *Mexico* **119** D5
Veraval *India* **68** J4
Verbánia *Italy* **40** C5
Verbicaro *Italy* **43** C8
Verbier *Switz.* **25** J3
Vercelli *Italy* **40** C5
Verchovchevo *Ukraine* **33** H8
Vercors △ *France* **21** D9
Verdalsøra *Norway* **8** E14
Verde → *Argentina* **128** E3
Verde → *Goiás, Brazil* **125** G8
Verde → *Mato Grosso do Sul,
Brazil* **125** H8
Verde → *Chihuahua, Mexico* **118** B3
Verde → *Oaxaca, Mexico* **119** D5
Verde → *Veracruz, Mexico* **118** C4
Verde → *Paraguay* **126** A4

Verde → *U.S.A.* **106** J17
Verde, Cay *Bahamas* **120** B4
Verde Island Pass *Phil.* **61** E4
Verden *Germany* **24** C5
Verdi *U.S.A.* **110** F7
Verdon → *France* **21** E10
Verdon → *France* **21** E9
Verdun *France* **19** C12
Verdun-sur-le-Doubs *France* **19** F12
Vereeniging *S. Africa* **89** D4
Verga, C. *Guinea* **82** C2
Vergara *Uruguay* **127** C5
Vergato *Italy* **40** D8
Vergemont Cr. → *Australia* **94** C3
Vergennes *U.S.A.* **115** B11
Vergt *France* **20** C4
Veria *Greece* **44** F6
Verín *Spain* **36** D3
Verkhnedvinsk =
Vyerkhnyadzvinsk *Belarus* **32** E4
Verkhnetulomskoye
Vdkhr. *Russia* **8** B24
Verkhnevilyuysk *Russia* **53** C13
Verkhniy Baskunchak
Russia **35** F8
Verkhovye *Russia* **33** F9
Verkhovyna *Ukraine* **29** B9
Verkhoyansk *Russia* **53** C14
Verkhoyansk Ra. =
Verkhoyanskiy Khrebet
Russia **53** C13
Verkhoyanskiy Khrebet
Russia **53** C13
Vermenton *France* **19** E10
Vermilion *Canada* **103** C6
Vermilion *U.S.A.* **114** E2
Vermilion → *Canada* **103** C6
Vermilion B. *U.S.A.* **116** G9
Vermilion Bay *Canada* **103** D10
Vermilion L. *U.S.A.* **112** B7
Vermillion *U.S.A.* **112** D5
Vermillion → *Canada* **104** C5
Vermont □ *U.S.A.* **115** C12
Vermosh *Albania* **44** D3
Vernadsky *Antarctica* **5** C17
Vernal *U.S.A.* **108** F9
Vernalis *U.S.A.* **110** H5
Vernazza *Italy* **40** D6
Verner *Canada* **104** C3
Verneuil-sur-Avre *France* **18** D7
Verneukpan *S. Africa* **88** E3
Vernier *Switz.* **25** J2
Vérnio *Italy* **40** D8
Vernon *Canada* **102** C5
Vernon *France* **18** C8
Vernon *U.S.A.* **116** D5
Vernonia *U.S.A.* **110** E3
Vero Beach *U.S.A.* **117** H14
Véroia = Veria *Greece* **44** F6
Véroli *Italy* **41** G10
Verona *Canada* **115** B8
Verona *Italy* **40** C7
Versailles *France* **19** D9
Versmold *Germany* **24** C4
Vert, C. *Senegal* **82** C1
Vertou *France* **18** E5
Vertus *France* **19** D11
Verulam *S. Africa* **89** D5
Verviers *Belgium* **17** D5
Vervins *France* **19** C10
Veržej *Slovenia* **41** B13
Verzy *France* **19** C11
Vescovato *France* **21** F13
Veselí nad Lužnicí *Czech Rep.* **26** B7
Veselie *Bulgaria* **45** D11
Veselovskoye Vdkhr. *Russia* **35** G5
Veshenskaya *Russia* **34** F5
Vesle → *France* **19** C10
Vesoul *France* **19** E13
Vessigebro *Sweden* **11** H6
Vesterålen *Norway* **8** B16
Vestfjorden *Norway* **8** C16
Vestmannaeyjar *Iceland* **8** E3
Vestspitsbergen *Svalbard* **4** B8
Vestvågøya *Norway* **8** B15
Vesuvio *Italy* **43** B7
Vesuvius, Mt. = Vesuvio
Italy **43** B7
Vesyegonsk *Russia* **32** C9
Veszprém *Hungary* **28** C2
Veszprém □ *Hungary* **28** C2
Vésztő *Hungary* **28** D6
Vetlanda *Sweden* **11** G9
Vetluga *Russia* **34** B7
Vetlugu → *Russia* **34** B7
Vetluzhskiy *Kostroma, Russia* **34** A7
Vetluzhskiy
Nizhniy Novgorod, Russia **34** B7
Vetovo *Bulgaria* **45** C10
Vetralla *Italy* **41** F9
Vetren *Bulgaria* **45** D8
Vettore, Mte. *Italy* **41** F10
Veurne *Belgium* **17** C2
Veveno → *Sudan* **81** F3
Vevey *Switz.* **25** J2
Vevi *Greece* **44** F5
Veynes *France* **21** D9
Veys *Iran* **71** D6

Vézelay *France* **19** E10
Vézelise *France* **19** D13
Vézère → *France* **20** D4
Vezhen *Bulgaria* **45** D8
Vi Thanh *Vietnam* **65** H5
Viacha *Bolivia* **124** G5
Viadana *Italy* **40** D7
Viamão *Brazil* **127** C5
Viana *Brazil* **125** D10
Viana *Spain* **38** C2
Viana do Alentejo *Portugal* **37** G3
Viana do Bolo *Spain* **36** C3
Viana do Castelo *Portugal* **36** D2
Viana do Castelo □ *Portugal* **36** D2
Vianden *Lux.* **17** E6
Viangchan = Vientiane *Laos* **64** D4
Vianópolis *Brazil* **125** G9
Vianos *Greece* **49** D7
Viar → *Spain* **37** H5
Viaréggio *Italy* **40** E7
Viaur → *France* **20** D5
Vibble *Sweden* **11** G12
Vibo Valéntia *Italy* **43** D9
Viborg *Denmark* **11** H3
Vibraye *France* **18** D7
Vic *Spain* **38** D7
Vic, Étang de *France* **20** E7
Vic-en-Bigorre *France* **20** E4
Vic-Fezensac *France* **20** E4
Vic-le-Comte *France* **19** G10
Vic-sur-Cère *France* **20** D6
Vícar *Spain* **39** J2
Vicenza *Italy* **41** C8
Vich = Vic *Spain* **38** D7
Vichada → *Colombia* **124** C5
Vichuga *Russia* **34** B5
Vichy *France* **19** F10
Vicksburg *Ariz., U.S.A.* **111** M13
Vicksburg *Miss., U.S.A.* **117** E9
Vico *France* **21** F12
Vico, L. di *Italy* **41** F9
Vico del Gargano *Italy* **41** G12
Vicovu de Sus *Romania* **29** C10
Victor *India* **68** J4
Victor Harbor *Australia* **95** F2
Victoria *Argentina* **126** C3
Victoria *Canada* **110** B3
Victoria *Chile* **128** D2
Victoria *Guinea* **82** C2
Victoria *Malta* **49** C1
Victoria *Phil.* **61** D4
Victoria *Romania* **29** E9
Victoria *Seychelles* **85** b
Victoria *Kans., U.S.A.* **112** F4
Victoria *Tex., U.S.A.* **116** G6
Victoria □ *Australia* **95** F3
Victoria → *Australia* **92** C4
Victoria, Grand L. *Canada* **104** C4
Victoria, L. *Africa* **86** C3
Victoria, L. *Australia* **95** E3
Victoria, Mt. *Burma* **67** J18
Victoria Beach *Canada* **103** C9
Victoria de Durango =
Durango *Mexico* **118** C4
Victoria de las Tunas = Las
Tunas *Cuba* **120** B4
Victoria Falls *Zimbabwe* **87** F2
Victoria Harbour *Canada* **114** B5
Victoria I. *Canada* **100** C9
Victoria L. *Canada* **105** C8
Victoria Ld. *Antarctica* **5** D11
Victoria Nile → *Uganda* **86** B3
Victoria Pk. *Belize* **119** D7
Victoria River *Australia* **92** C5
Victoria Str. *Canada* **100** D11
Victoria West *S. Africa* **88** E3
Victorias *Phil.* **61** F5
Victoriaville *Canada* **105** C5
Victorica *Argentina* **126** D2
Victorville *U.S.A.* **111** L9
Vicuña *Chile* **126** C1
Vicuña Mackenna
Argentina **126** C3
Vidal *Calif., U.S.A.* **111** L12
Vidal *Calif., U.S.A.* **111** L12
Vidalia *U.S.A.* **117** E13
Vidamlya *Belarus* **31** F10
Vidauban *France* **21** E10
Videbæk *Denmark* **11** H2
Videle *Romania* **29** F10
Vidigueira *Portugal* **37** G3
Vidin *Bulgaria* **44** C6
Vidio, C. *Spain* **36** B4
Vidisha *India* **68** H7
Vidos *Greece* **49** A3
Vidra *Romania* **29** E11
Viduša *Bos.-H.* **44** D2
Viechtach *Germany* **25** F8
Viedma *Argentina* **128** E4
Viedma, L. *Argentina* **128** E2
Vieira do Minho *Portugal* **36** D2
Vielha *Spain* **38** C5
Vielha = Vielha *Spain* **38** C5
Vielsalm *Belgium* **17** D5
Vienenburg *Germany* **24** D6
Vieng Pou Kha *Laos* **58** G3
Vienna = Wien *Austria* **27** C9

Vienna *Canada* **114** D4
Vienna *Ill., U.S.A.* **112** G9
Vienna *Mo., U.S.A.* **112** F8
Vienne *France* **21** C8
Vienne □ *France* **20** B4
Vienne ➤ *France* **18** E7
Vientiane *Laos* **64** D4
Vientos, Paso de los
  Caribbean **121** C5
Vieques *Puerto Rico* **121** d
Vierge Pt. *St. Lucia* **121** f
Viernheim *Germany* **25** F4
Viersen *Germany* **24** D2
Vierwaldstättersee *Switz.* **25** J4
Vierzon *France* **19** E9
Vieste *Italy* **41** G13
Viet Tri *Vietnam* **64** B5
Vietnam ■ *Asia* **64** C6
Vieux-Boucau-les-Bains
  France **20** E2
Vieux Fort *St. Lucia* **121** f
Vif *France* **21** C9
Vigan *Phil.* **61** C4
Vigévano *Italy* **40** C5
Vigia *Brazil* **125** D9
Viglas, Akra *Greece* **49** D9
Vignemalle *France* **20** F3
Vigneulles-lès-
  Hattonchâtel *France* **19** D12
Vignola *Italy* **40** D8
Vigo *Spain* **36** C2
Vigo, Ría de *Spain* **36** C2
Vigsø Bugt *Denmark* **11** G2
Vihiers *France* **18** E6
Vihowa *Pakistan* **68** D4
Vihowa ➤ *Pakistan* **68** D4
Vijayawada *India* **67** L12
Vijosë *Albania* **44** F3
Vík *Iceland* **8** E4
Vika *Sweden* **10** D8
Vikarbyn *Sweden* **10** D9
Vikeke = Viqueque *E. Timor* **63** F7
Viken *Skåne, Sweden* **11** H6
Viken *Västra Götaland, Sweden* **11** F8
Viking *Canada* **102** C6
Vikmanshyttan *Sweden* **10** D9
Vikna *Norway* **8** D14
Vikos-Aoos △ *Greece* **46** B2
Vila da Maganja *Mozam.* **87** F4
Vila da Ribeira Brava
  C. Verde Is. **78** b
Vila de Rei *Portugal* **36** F2
Vila do Bispo *Portugal* **37** H2
Vila do Conde *Portugal* **36** D2
Vila Franca de Xira *Portugal* **37** G2
Vila Gamito *Mozam.* **87** E3
Vila Gomes da Costa *Mozam.* **89** C5
Vila Machado *Mozam.* **87** F3
Vila Mouzinho *Mozam.* **87** E3
Vila Nova de Famalicão
  Portugal **36** D2
Vila Nova de Fos Côa
  Portugal **36** D3
Vila Nova de Gaia *Portugal* **36** D2
Vila Nova de Ourém *Portugal* **36** F2
Vila Pouca de Aguiar
  Portugal **36** D3
Vila Real *Portugal* **36** D3
Vila-Real *Spain* **38** F4
Vila Real □ *Portugal* **36** D3
Vila Real de Santo António
  Portugal **37** H3
Vila-seca *Spain* **38** D6
Vila Vasco da Gama *Mozam.* **87** E3
Vila Velha *Brazil* **127** A7
Vila Viçosa *Portugal* **37** G3
Vilafranca del Maestrat *Spain* **38** E4
Vilafranca del Penedès *Spain* **38** D6
Vilagarcía de Arousa *Spain* **36** C2
Vilaine ➤ *France* **18** E4
Vilanandro, Tanjona *Madag.* **89** B7
Vilanculos *Mozam.* **89** C6
Vilanova i la Geltrú *Spain* **38** D6
Vilar Formoso *Portugal* **36** E4
Vilasaca-Salou = Vila-seca
  Spain **38** D6
Vilbjerg *Denmark* **11** H2
Vilcheka, Ostrov *Russia* **52** B6
Vilcheka, Zemlya *Russia* **4** A11
Vilches *Spain* **37** G7
Vileyka *Belarus* **23** A14
Vilhelmina *Sweden* **8** D17
Vilhena *Brazil* **124** F6
Viliya = Neris ➤ *Lithuania* **32** E3
Viljandi *Estonia* **32** C3
Vilkaviškis *Lithuania* **30** D10
Vilkija *Lithuania* **30** C10
Vilkitskogo, Proliv *Russia* **53** B11
Vilkovo = Vylkove *Ukraine* **29** E14
Villa Abecia *Bolivia* **126** A2
Villa Ana *Argentina* **126** B4
Villa Angela *Argentina* **126** B3
Villa Bella *Bolivia* **124** F5
Villa Cañás *Argentina* **126** C3
Villa Constitución *Argentina* **126** C3
Villa de Arriaga *Mexico* **118** C4
Villa de María *Argentina* **126** B3
Villa de Méndez *Mexico* **119** B5
Villa del Río *Spain* **37** H6
Villa Dolores *Argentina* **126** C2

Villa Frontera *Mexico* **118** B4
Villa Gesell *Argentina* **126** D4
Villa Guillermina *Argentina* **126** B4
Villa Hayes *Paraguay* **126** B4
Villa Hidalgo *Mexico* **119** C5
Villa Iris *Argentina* **126** D3
Villa María *Argentina* **126** C3
Villa Mazán *Argentina* **126** B2
Villa Minozzo *Italy* **40** D7
Villa Montes *Bolivia* **126** A3
Villa Ocampo *Argentina* **126** B4
Villa Ocampo *Mexico* **118** B3
Villa Ojo de Agua *Argentina* **126** B3
Villa San Giovanni *Italy* **43** D8
Villa San Martín *Argentina* **126** B3
Villa Santina *Italy* **41** B9
Villa Unión *Mexico* **118** C3
Villablino *Spain* **36** C4
Villacarlos *Spain* **48** B11
Villacarriedo *Spain* **36** B7
Villacarrillo *Spain* **37** G7
Villacastín *Spain* **36** E6
Villach *Austria* **26** E6
Villacidro *Italy* **42** C1
Villada *Spain* **36** C6
Villadiego *Spain* **36** C6
Villadóssola *Italy* **40** B5
Villafeliche *Spain* **38** D3
Villafranca *Spain* **38** C3
Villafranca de Bonany *Spain* **48** B10
Villafranca de los Barros
  Spain **37** G4
Villafranca de los
  Caballeros *Spain* **37** F7
Villafranca del Cid =
  Vilafranca del Maestrat
  Spain **38** E4
Villafranca del Panadés =
  Vilafranca del Penedès
  Spain **38** D6
Villafranca di Verona *Italy* **40** C7
Villafranca Tirrena *Italy* **43** D8
Villagrán *Mexico* **119** C5
Villaguay *Argentina* **126** C4
Villaharta *Spain* **37** G6
Villahermosa *Mexico* **119** D6
Villahermosa *Spain* **39** G2
Villaines-la-Juhel *France* **18** D6
Villajoyosa *Spain* **39** G4
Villalba *Spain* **36** B3
Villalba de Guardo *Spain* **36** C6
Villalón de Campos *Spain* **36** C5
Villalpando *Spain* **36** D5
Villaluenga de la Sagra *Spain* **36** E7
Villamanán *Spain* **36** C5
Villamartín *Spain* **37** J5
Villamayor de Santiago *Spain* **38** F2
Villamblard *France* **20** C4
Villanova Monteleone *Italy* **42** B1
Villanueva *U.S.A.* **109** J11
Villanueva de Castellón *Spain* **39** F4
Villanueva de Córdoba *Spain* **37** G6
Villanueva de la Fuente
  Spain **39** G2
Villanueva de la Serena
  Spain **37** G5
Villanueva de la Sierra *Spain* **36** E4
Villanueva de los Castillejos
  Spain **37** H3
Villanueva de los Infantes
  Spain **37** G7
Villanueva del Arzobispo
  Spain **39** G2
Villanueva del Fresno *Spain* **37** G3
Villanueva y Geltrú =
  Vilanova i la Geltrú *Spain* **38** D6
Villaputzu *Italy* **42** C2
Villaquilambre *Spain* **36** C5
Villar del Arzobispo *Spain* **38** F4
Villar del Rey *Spain* **37** F4
Villard-de-Lans *France* **21** C9
Villarramiel *Spain* **36** C6
Villarreal = Vila-Real *Spain* **38** F4
Villarrica *Chile* **128** D2
Villarrica *Paraguay* **126** B4
Villarrobledo *Spain* **39** F2
Villarroya de la Sierra *Spain* **38** D3
Villarrubia de los Ojos *Spain* **37** F7
Villars-les-Dombes *France* **19** F12
Villasayas *Spain* **38** D2
Villaseco de los Gamitos
  Spain **36** D4
Villasimíus *Italy* **42** C2
Villastar *Spain* **38** E3
Villatobas *Spain* **36** F7
Villavicencio *Argentina* **126** C2
Villavicencio *Colombia* **124** C4
Villaviciosa *Spain* **36** B5
Villazón *Bolivia* **126** A2
Ville-Marie *Canada* **104** C4
Ville Platte *U.S.A.* **116** F8
Villedieu-les-Poêles *France* **18** D5
Villefort *France* **20** D7
Villefranche-de-Lauragais
  France **20** E5
Villefranche-de-Rouergue
  France **20** D6
Villefranche-du-Périgord
  France **20** D5

Villefranche-sur-Saône
  France **21** C8
Villel *Spain* **38** E3
Villemur-sur-Tarn *France* **20** E5
Villena *Spain* **39** G4
Villenauxe-la-Grande
  France **19** D10
Villenave-d'Ornon *France* **20** D3
Villeneuve-d'Ascq *France* **19** B10
Villeneuve-l'Archevêque
  France **19** D10
Villeneuve-lès-Avignon
  France **21** E8
Villeneuve-sur-Allier *France* **19** F10
Villeneuve-sur-Lot *France* **20** D4
Villeneuve-sur-Yonne
  France **19** D10
Villeréal *France* **20** D4
Villers-Bocage *France* **18** C6
Villers-Cotterêts *France* **19** C10
Villers-sur-Mer *France* **18** C6
Villersexel *France* **19** E13
Villerupt *France* **19** C12
Villeurbanne *France* **21** C8
Villiers *S. Africa* **89** D4
Villingen-Schwenningen
  Germany **25** G4
Villmanstrand =
  Lappeenranta *Finland* **32** B5
Vilna *Canada* **102** C6
Vilnius *Lithuania* **32** E3
Vils *Austria* **25** H5
Vils ➤ *Bayern, Germany* **25** G9
Vils ➤ *Bayern, Germany* **25** F7
Vilsbiburg *Germany* **25** G8
Vilshofen *Germany* **25** G9
Vilusi *Montenegro* **44** D2
Vilvoorde *Belgium* **17** D4
Vilyuchinsk *Russia* **53** D16
Vilyuy ➤ *Russia* **53** C13
Vilyuysk *Russia* **53** C13
Vimianzo *Spain* **36** B1
Vimioso *Portugal* **36** D4
Vimmerby *Sweden* **11** G9
Vimoutiers *France* **18** D7
Vímperk *Czech Rep.* **26** B6
Viña del Mar *Chile* **126** C1
Vinaròs *Spain* **38** E5
Vincennes *U.S.A.* **112** F10
Vincennes Bay *S. Ocean* **5** C8
Vincent *U.S.A.* **111** L8
Vinchina *Argentina* **126** B2
Vindelälven ➤ *Sweden* **8** E18
Vindeln *Sweden* **8** D18
Vinderup *Denmark* **11** H2
Vindhya Ra. *India* **68** H7
Vineland *U.S.A.* **113** F16
Vinga *Romania* **28** D6
Vingåker *Sweden* **10** E9
Vinh *Vietnam* **64** C5
Vinh Linh *Vietnam* **64** D6
Vinh Long *Vietnam* **65** G5
Vinh Yen *Vietnam* **58** G5
Vinhais *Portugal* **36** D3
Vinica *Croatia* **41** B13
Vinica *Macedonia* **44** E6
Vinica *Slovenia* **41** C12
Vinita *U.S.A.* **116** C7
Vinkovci *Croatia* **28** E3
Vinnitsa = Vinnytsya
  Ukraine **23** D15
Vinnytsya *Ukraine* **23** D15
Vinnytsya □ *Ukraine* **33** H5
Vinslöv *Sweden* **11** H7
Vinson Massif *Antarctica* **5** D16
Vinton *Calif., U.S.A.* **110** F6
Vinton *Iowa, U.S.A.* **112** D7
Vinton *La., U.S.A.* **116** F8
Vințu de Jos *Romania* **29** D8
Viöl *Germany* **24** A5
Violet Valley ۞ *Australia* **92** C4
Viotia □ *Greece* **46** C5
Vipava *Slovenia* **41** C10
Vipiteno *Italy* **41** B8
Viqueque *E. Timor* **63** F7
Vir *Croatia* **41** D12
Virac *Phil.* **61** E6
Virachey *Cambodia* **64** F6
Virachey △ *Cambodia* **64** E6
Virago Sd. *Canada* **102** C2
Viramgam *India* **68** H5
Viranşehir *Turkey* **73** D8
Virawah *Pakistan* **68** G4
Virbalis *Lithuania* **30** D9
Virden *Canada* **103** D8
Vire *France* **13** D6
Vire ➤ *France* **18** C5
Vírgenes, C. *Argentina* **128** G3
Virgin ➤ *U.S.A.* **109** H6
Virgin Gorda *Br. Virgin Is.* **121** e
Virgin Is. (British) ☑
  W. Indies **121** e
Virgin Is. (U.S.) ☑ *W. Indies* **121** e
Virgin Islands △
  U.S. Virgin Is. **121** C7
Virginia *S. Africa* **88** D4
Virginia *U.S.A.* **112** B7
Virginia □ *U.S.A.* **113** G14

Virginia Beach *U.S.A.* **113** F16
Virginia City *Mont., U.S.A.* **108** D8
Virginia City *Nev., U.S.A.* **110** F7
Virginia Falls *Canada* **102** A3
Virginiatown *Canada* **104** C4
Virje *Croatia* **41** B13
Viroqua *U.S.A.* **112** D8
Virovitica *Croatia* **28** E2
Virpazar *Montenegro* **44** D3
Virpur *India* **68** J4
Virserum *Sweden* **11** G9
Virton *Belgium* **17** E5
Virudunagar *India* **66** Q10
Virunga △
  Dem. Rep. of the Congo **86** B2
Vis *Croatia* **41** E13
Visalia *U.S.A.* **110** J7
Visayan Sea *Phil.* **61** F5
Visby *Sweden* **11** G12
Viscount Melville Sd.
  Canada **101** C10
Visé *Belgium* **17** D5
Vise, Ostrov *Russia* **52** B8
Višegrad *Bos.-H.* **28** G4
Viseu *Brazil* **125** D9
Viseu *Portugal* **36** E3
Viseu □ *Portugal* **36** E3
Vişeu de Sus *Romania* **29** C9
Vishakhapatnam *India* **67** L13
Vişina *Romania* **29** G9
Vişineşti *Moldova* **29** D13
Visingsö *Sweden* **11** F8
Viskafors *Sweden* **11** G6
Viskan ➤ *Sweden* **11** G6
Viški Kanal *Croatia* **41** E13
Vislanda *Sweden* **11** H8
Visnagar *India* **68** H5
Višnja Gora *Slovenia* **41** C11
Viso, Mte. *Italy* **40** D4
Viso del Marqués *Spain* **37** G7
Visoko *Bos.-H.* **28** G3
Visokoi I. *Antarctica* **5** B1
Visp *Switz.* **25** J3
Vissefjärda *Sweden* **11** H9
Visselhövede *Germany* **24** C5
Vissenbjerg *Denmark* **11** J4
Vista *U.S.A.* **111** M9
Vistonida, L. *Greece* **45** E9
Vistonikos, Ormos =
  Vistonida, L. *Greece* **45** E9
Vistula = Wisła ➤ *Poland* **30** D5
Vit ➤ *Bulgaria* **45** C8
Vitanje *Slovenia* **41** B12
Vitebsk = Vitsyebsk *Belarus* **32** E6
Viterbo *Italy* **41** F9
Vitez *Bos.-H.* **28** G7
Viti Levu *Fiji* **91** a
Vitigudino *Spain* **36** D4
Vitim *Russia* **53** D12
Vitim ➤ *Russia* **53** D12
Vitina *Bos.-H.* **41** E14
Vitina *Greece* **45** E9
Vítkov *Czech Rep.* **27** B10
Vitória *Brazil* **125** H10
Vitória da Conquista *Brazil* **125** F10
Vitória de Santo Antão
  Brazil **125** E11
Vitoria-Gasteiz *Spain* **38** C2
Vitória *Italy* **43** F7
Vitória *Veneto, Italy* **41** C9
Vitré *France* **18** D5
Vitry-le-François *France* **19** D11
Vitry-sur-Seine *France* **19** D9
Vitsand *Sweden* **10** D7
Vitsi, Oros *Greece* **44** F5
Vitsyebsk *Belarus* **32** E5
Vitsyebsk □ *Belarus* **32** E5
Vittangi *Sweden* **11** H7
Vitteaux *France* **19** E11
Vittel *France* **19** D12
Vittória *Italy* **43** F7
Vittório Véneto *Italy* **41** C9
Vittsjö *Sweden* **11** H7
Viveiro *Spain* **36** B3
Vivian *U.S.A.* **116** E8
Viviers *France* **21** D8
Vivonne *France* **20** B4
Viwa *Fiji* **91** a
Vizcaíno, Desierto de
  Mexico **118** B2
Vizcaíno, Sierra *Mexico* **118** B2
Vizcaya □ *Spain* **38** B2
Vize *Turkey* **45** E11
Vizianagaram *India* **67** K13
Vizille *France* **21** C9
Viziñada *Croatia* **41** C10
Vizinga *Russia* **29** E12
Vizzini *Italy* **43** E7
Vlaardingen *Neths.* **17** C4
Vlachiotis *Greece* **46** D2
Vlădeasa, Vf. *Romania* **28** D7
Vladičin Han *Serbia* **44** D6
Vladikavkaz *Russia* **35** J7
Vladimir *Russia* **32** D11
Vladimir □ *Russia* **34** B5
Vladimir Volynskiy =
  Volodymyr-Volynskyy
  Ukraine **23** C13
Vladimirci *Serbia* **44** B3
Vladimirovac *Serbia* **28** E5
Vladimirovka *Russia* **35** F8

Vladimirovo *Bulgaria* **44** C7
Vladislavovka *Ukraine* **33** K8
Vladivostok *Russia* **54** C5
Vlăhița *Romania* **29** D11
Vlasenica *Bos.-H.* **28** F3
Vlašić *Bos.-H.* **28** F2
Vlašim *Czech Rep.* **26** B7
Vlasinsko Jezero *Serbia* **44** D6
Vlasotince *Serbia* **44** D6
Vlieland *Neths.* **17** A4
Vlissingen *Neths.* **17** C3
Vlorë *Albania* **44** F3
Vlorës, Gjiri i *Albania* **44** F3
Vltava ➤ *Czech Rep.* **26** A7
Vo Dat *Vietnam* **65** G6
Vobarno *Italy* **40** C7
Voćin *Croatia* **28** E2
Vöcklabruck *Austria* **26** C6
Vodice *Croatia* **41** E12
Vodňany *Czech Rep.* **26** B7
Vodnjan *Croatia* **41** D10
Voe *U.K.* **13** A7
Vogan *Togo* **83** D5
Vogel Pk. *Nigeria* **83** D7
Vogelkop = Doberai,
  Jazirah *Indonesia* **63** E8
Vogelsberg *Germany* **24** E5
Voghera *Italy* **40** D6
Vohibinany *Madag.* **89** B8
Vohilava *Madag.* **89** C8
Vohimarina = Iharana
  Madag. **89** A9
Vohimena, Tanjon' i *Madag.* **89** D8
Vohipeno *Madag.* **89** C8
Voi *Kenya* **86** C4
Void-Vacon *France* **19** D12
Voineşti *Iaşi, Romania* **29** C12
Voineşti *Prahova, Romania* **29** E10
Voinjama *Liberia* **82** D3
Voiron *France* **21** C9
Voisey B. *Canada* **105** A7
Voitsberg *Austria* **26** D8
Vojens *Denmark* **11** J3
Vojmsjön *Sweden* **8** D17
Vojnić *Croatia* **41** C12
Vojnik *Italy* **41** B12
Vojvodina □ *Serbia* **28** E5
Vokhtoga *Russia* **32** C11
Volary *Czech Rep.* **26** C6
Volborg *U.S.A.* **108** D11
Volcán de Colima △ *Mexico* **118** D4
Volcano Is. = Kazan-Rettō
  Pac. Oc. **96** E6
Volcans △ *Rwanda* **86** C2
Volcans d'Auvergne ○
  France **20** C6
Volchansk = Vovchansk
  Ukraine **33** G9
Volchya ➤ *Ukraine* **33** H8
Volda *Norway* **8** E12
Volga = Privolzhskiy □
  Russia **34** B10
Volga *Russia* **32** C10
Volga ➤ *Russia* **35** G9
Volga Hts. = Privolzhskaya
  Vozvyshennost *Russia* **34** E7
Volgo-Baltiyskiy Kanal
  Russia **32** B9
Volgo-Donskoy Kanal *Russia* **35** F7
Volgodonsk *Russia* **35** G6
Volgograd *Russia* **35** F7
Volgograd □ *Russia* **34** F7
Volgogradskoye Vdkhr.
  Russia **34** E8
Volgorechensk *Russia* **34** B5
Volimes *Greece* **46** D2
Volintiri *Moldova* **29** D14
Volissos *Greece* **47** C7
Volkach *Germany* **25** F6
Völkermarkt *Austria* **26** E7
Volkhov *Russia* **32** B7
Volkhov ➤ *Russia* **32** B7
Völklingen *Germany* **25** F2
Volkovysk = Vawkavysk
  Belarus **23** B13
Volksrust *S. Africa* **89** D4
Volnansk *Ukraine* **33** H8
Volnovakha *Ukraine* **33** J9
Volochanka *Russia* **53** B10
Volodarsk *Russia* **34** B6
Volodymyr-Volynskyy
  Ukraine **23** C13
Vologda *Russia* **32** C10
Vologda □ *Russia* **32** B10
Volokolamsk *Russia* **32** D8
Volokonovka *Russia* **33** G9
Volos *Greece* **46** B4
Volosovo *Russia* **32** C5
Volovets *Ukraine* **29** B8
Volovo *Russia* **32** F10
Volozhin = Valozhyn
  Belarus **23** A14
Volsk *Russia* **34** D8
Volta □ *Ghana* **83** D5
Volta ➤ *Ghana* **83** D5
Volta, L. *Ghana* **83** D5
Volta Blanche = White
  Volta ➤ *Ghana* **83** D4
Volta Redonda *Brazil* **127** A7
Voltaire, C. *Australia* **92** B4

Volterra *Italy* **40** E7
Voltri *Italy* **40** D5
Volturno ➤ *Italy* **42** A6
Volvi, L. *Greece* **44** F7
Volyn □ *Ukraine* **33** G3
Volyně *Czech Rep.* **26** B6
Volzhsk *Russia* **34** C9
Volzhskiy *Russia* **35** F7
Vomo *Fiji* **91** a
Vondrozo *Madag.* **89** C8
Vonitsa *Greece* **46** C2
Vopnafjörður *Iceland* **8** D6
Vorarlberg □ *Austria* **26** D2
Voras Oros *Greece* **44** F5
Vorbasse *Denmark* **11** J3
Vorchdorf *Austria* **26** C6
Vorderrhein ➤ *Switz.* **25** J5
Vordingborg *Denmark* **11** J5
Vorë *Albania* **44** E3
Voreio Aigaio □ *Greece* **47** C7
Voreppe *France* **21** C9
Vori *Greece* **46** F6
Vorios Evoikos Kolpos *Greece* **46** C5
Vorkuta *Russia* **52** C7
Vormsi *Estonia* **32** C2
Vorona ➤ *Russia* **34** E6
Voronezh *Russia* **33** G10
Voronezh *Ukraine* **33** G7
Voronezh □ *Russia* **34** E4
Voronezh ➤ *Russia* **33** G10
Vorontsovo-
  Aleksandrovskoye =
  Zelenokumsk *Russia* **35** H6
Vorpommersche
  Boddenlandschaft △
  Germany **24** A8
Vorskla ➤ *Ukraine* **33** H8
Võrts Järv *Estonia* **32** C4
Võru *Estonia* **32** D4
Vosges *France* **19** D14
Vosges □ *France* **19** D13
Vosges du Nord △ *France* **19** D14
Voskopojë *Albania* **44** F4
Voskresensk *Russia* **32** E10
Voskresenskoye *Russia* **34** B7
Voss *Norway* **8** F12
Vostok *Antarctica* **5** D8
Vostok I. *Kiribati* **97** J12
Votice *Czech Rep.* **26** B7
Votsuri-Shima *Japan* **55** M1
Vouga ➤ *Portugal* **36** E2
Vouillé *France* **18** F7
Vouxa, Akra *Greece* **49** D5
Vouzela *Portugal* **36** E2
Vouziers *France* **19** C11
Vovchansk *Ukraine* **33** G9
Vowchyn *Belarus* **31** F10
Voyageurs △ *U.S.A.* **112** A7
Voynitsa *Russia* **8** D24
Voyvozh *Russia* **52** C6
Vozhe, Ozero *Russia* **32** B10
Vozhega *Russia* **32** B11
Voznesensk *Ukraine* **33** J6
Voznesenye *Russia* **32** B8
Vrå *Denmark* **11** G3
Vráble *Slovak Rep.* **27** C11
Vraćevšnica *Serbia* **44** B4
Vrachneika *Greece* **46** C3
Vrancea □ *Romania* **29** E11
Vrancei, Munţii *Romania* **29** E11
Vrangel *Russia* **54** C6
Vranjska Banja *Serbia* **44** D6
Vranje *Serbia* **44** D5
Vranov nad Topľou
  Slovak Rep. **27** C14
Vransko *Slovenia* **41** B11
Vransko Jezero *Croatia* **41** E12
Vrapčište *Macedonia* **44** E4
Vratsa *Bulgaria* **44** C7
Vrbas *Serbia* **28** E4
Vrbas ➤ *Bos.-H.* **28** E2
Vrbnik *Croatia* **41** C11
Vrbovec *Croatia* **41** C13
Vrbovsko *Croatia* **41** C12
Vrchlabí *Czech Rep.* **26** A8
Vrede *S. Africa* **89** D4
Vredefort *S. Africa* **88** D4
Vreden *Germany* **24** C2
Vredenburg *S. Africa* **88** E1
Vredendal *S. Africa* **88** E2
Vretstorp *Sweden* **10** E8
Vrgorac *Croatia* **41** E14
Vrhnika *Slovenia* **41** C11
Vríði *Ivory C.* **82** D4
Vrigstad *Sweden* **11** G8
Vrisses *Greece* **49** D6
Vrnograč *Bos.-H.* **41** C12
Vrpolje *Croatia* **28** E3
Vršac *Serbia* **28** E6
Vrsacki Kanal *Serbia* **28** E5
Vrútky *Slovak Rep.* **27** B11
Vryburg *S. Africa* **88** D3
Vryheid *S. Africa* **89** D5
Vsetín *Czech Rep.* **27** B11
Vu Liet *Vietnam* **64** C5
Vŭcha ➤ *Bulgaria* **45** D8

Vučitrn *Kosovo* **44** D4
Vukovar *Croatia* **28** E3
Vuktyl *Russia* **52** C6
Vulcan *Canada* **102** C6
Vulcan *Romania* **29** E8
Vulcaneşti *Moldova* **29** E13
Vulcano *Italy* **43** D7
Vŭlchedruma *Bulgaria* **44** C7
Vulkaneshty = Vulcaneşti
  Moldova **29** E13
Vunduzi ➤ *Mozam.* **87** F3
Vunidawa *Fiji* **91** a
Vunisea *Fiji* **91** a
Vŭrbitsa *Bulgaria* **45** D10
Vurshets *Bulgaria* **44** C7
Vutcani *Romania* **29** D12
Vuya *Sudan* **81** F2
Vuzlove *Ukraine* **28** B7
Vwaza △ *Malawi* **87** E3
Vyartsilya *Russia* **32** A6
Vyatka = Kirov *Russia* **52** D5
Vyatka ➤ *Russia* **34** C10
Vyatskiye Polyany *Russia* **34** B10
Vyazemskiy *Russia* **53** E14
Vyazma *Russia* **32** E8
Vyazniki *Russia* **34** B6
Vyborg *Russia* **32** B5
Vychegda ➤ *Russia* **52** C5
Vychodné Beskydy *Europe* **27** B15
Vyerkhnyadzvinsk *Belarus* **32** E4
Vyhoda *Ukraine* **29** B8
Vyksa *Russia* **34** C6
Vylkove *Ukraine* **29** E14
Vylok *Ukraine* **28** B8
Vynohradiv *Ukraine* **28** B8
Vyrnwy, L. *U.K.* **14** E4
Vyshhiv *Ukraine* **29** B8
Vyshkove *Ukraine* **29** B8
Vyshniy Volochek *Russia* **32** D8
Vyshzha = imeni 26
  Bakinskikh Komissarov
  Turkmenistan **71** B7
Vyškov *Czech Rep.* **27** B9
Vysokaye *Belarus* **31** F10
Vysoké Mýto *Czech Rep.* **27** B9
Vysokovsk *Russia* **32** D9
Vyšší Brod *Czech Rep.* **26** C7
Vytegra *Russia* **32** B9
Vyzhnytsya *Ukraine* **29** B10
Vyzhnytsya △ *Ukraine* **29** B10

W

W du Benin △ *Benin* **83** C5
W du Burkina Faso △
  Burkina Faso **83** C4
W du Niger △ *Niger* **83** C5
W.A.C. Bennett Dam
  Canada **102** B4
Wa *Ghana* **82** C4
Waal ➤ *Neths.* **17** C5
Waalwijk *Neths.* **17** C5
Waanyi-Garawa ◎ *Australia* **94** B2
Waat *Sudan* **81** F3
Wabakimi △ *Canada* **104** B2
Wabana *Canada* **105** C9
Wabasca ➤ *Canada* **102** B5
Wabasca-Desmarais *Canada* **102** B6
Wabash *U.S.A.* **113** E11
Wabash ➤ *U.S.A.* **112** G9
Wabi ➤ *Ethiopia* **81** F5
Wabigoon L. *Canada* **103** D10
Wabowden *Canada* **103** C9
Wąbrzeźno *Poland* **31** E5
Wabu Hu *China* **59** A11
Wabuk Pt. *Canada* **104** A2
Wabush *Canada* **105** B6
Wąchock *Poland* **31** G8
Wächtersbach *Germany* **25** E5
Waco *U.S.A.* **116** F6
Waconichi, L. *Canada* **104** B5
Wad Ban Naqa *Sudan* **81** D3
Wad Banda *Sudan* **81** E2
Wad el Haddad *Sudan* **81** E3
Wad en Nau *Sudan* **81** E3
Wad Hamid *Sudan* **81** D3
Wad Medanî *Sudan* **81** E3
Wad Thana *Pakistan* **68** F2
Wadai *Africa* **76** E5
Wadayama *Japan* **55** G7
Waddeneilanden *Neths.* **17** A5
Waddenzee *Neths.* **17** A5
Waddi, Chappal *Nigeria* **83** D7
Waddington *U.S.A.* **115** B9
Waddington, Mt. *Canada* **102** C3
Waddy Pt. *Australia* **95** C5
Wadebridge *U.K.* **15** G3
Wadena *Canada* **103** C8
Wadena *U.S.A.* **112** B6
Wädenswil *Switz.* **25** H4
Wadern *Germany* **25** F2
Wadeye *Australia* **92** B4
Wadhams *Canada* **102** C3
Wadhwan *India* **68** H4
Wādī as Sīr *Jordan* **74** D4
Wâdi Gemâl, J. *Egypt* **80** C4
Wadi Halfa *Sudan* **80** C3
Wadi Rum △ *Jordan* **74** F4
Wadian *China* **59** A9

Wadlew *Poland* **31** G6
Wadowice *Poland* **31** J6
Wadsworth *Nev., U.S.A.* **108** G4
Wadsworth *Ohio, U.S.A.* **114** E3
Waegwan *S. Korea* **57** G15
Wafangdian *China* **57** E11
Wafrah *Kuwait* **70** D5
Wagait ◎ *Australia* **92** B5
Wageningen *Neths.* **17** C5
Wager B. *Canada* **101** D14
Wagga Wagga *Australia* **95** F4
Waghete *Indonesia* **63** E9
Wagin *Australia* **93** F2
Wagner *U.S.A.* **112** D4
Wagon Mound *U.S.A.* **109** H11
Wagoner *U.S.A.* **116** D7
Wągrowiec *Poland* **31** F4
Wah *Pakistan* **68** C5
Wahai *Indonesia* **63** E7
Wâhid *Egypt* **74** E1
Wahni *Ethiopia* **81** E4
Wahoo *U.S.A.* **112** E5
Wahpeton *U.S.A.* **112** B5
Waialua *U.S.A.* **107** L8
Waiau ➤ *N.Z.* **91** E4
Waibeem *Indonesia* **63** E8
Waiblingen *Germany* **25** G5
Waidhofen an der Thaya
  Austria **26** C8
Waidhofen an der Ybbs
  Austria **26** D8
Waigeo *Indonesia* **63** E8
Waihi *N.Z.* **91** B5
Waihou ➤ *N.Z.* **91** B5
Waika *Dem. Rep. of the Congo* **86** C2
Waikabubak *Indonesia* **63** F5
Waikaremoana, L. *N.Z.* **91** C6
Waikari *N.Z.* **91** E4
Waikato ➤ *N.Z.* **91** B5
Waikelo *Indonesia* **92** A2
Waikerie *Australia* **95** E3
Waikokopu *N.Z.* **91** C6
Waikouaiti *N.Z.* **91** F3
Waimakariri ➤ *N.Z.* **91** E4
Waimate *N.Z.* **91** F3
Waingapu ➤ *India* **66** K11
Waingapu *Indonesia* **63** F6
Waini ➤ *Guyana* **124** B7
Wainuiomata *N.Z.* **91** D5
Wainwright *Canada* **103** C6
Wainwright *U.S.A.* **106** A7
Waiouru *N.Z.* **91** C5
Waipara *N.Z.* **91** E4
Waipawa *N.Z.* **91** C6
Waipiro *N.Z.* **91** C7
Waipoua Forest *N.Z.* **91** A4
Waipu *N.Z.* **91** A5
Waipukurau *N.Z.* **91** D6
Wairakei *N.Z.* **91** C6
Wairarapa, L. *N.Z.* **91** D5
Wairoa *N.Z.* **91** C6
Waitaki ➤ *N.Z.* **91** F3
Waitangi *N.Z.* **91** A5
Waitara *N.Z.* **91** C5
Waitomo Caves *N.Z.* **91** C5
Waitsburg *U.S.A.* **108** C4
Waiuku *N.Z.* **91** B5
Wajima *Japan* **55** F8
Wajir *Kenya* **86** B5
Waka *Ethiopia* **81** F4
Wakasa *Japan* **55** G7
Wakasa-Wan *Japan* **55** G7
Wakatipu, L. *N.Z.* **91** F2
Wakaw *Canada* **103** C7
Wakaya *Fiji* **91** a
Wakayama *Japan* **55** G7
Wakayama □ *Japan* **55** H7
Wake Forest *U.S.A.* **117** D15
Wake I. *Pac. Oc.* **96** F8
WaKeeney *U.S.A.* **112** F4
Wakefield *Jamaica* **120** a
Wakefield *N.Z.* **91** D4
Wakefield *U.K.* **14** D6
Wakefield *Mass., U.S.A.* **115** D13
Wakefield *Mich., U.S.A.* **112** B9
Wakkanai *Japan* **54** B10
Wakkerstroom *S. Africa* **89** D5
Wakool *Australia* **95** F3
Wakool ➤ *Australia* **95** F3
Wakre *Indonesia* **63** E8
Wakuach, L. *Canada* **105** A6
Walagunya ◎ *Australia* **92** D3
Walamba *Zambia* **87** E2
Wałbrzych *Poland* **31** H3
Walbury Hill *U.K.* **15** F6
Walcha *Australia* **95** E5
Walcott *U.S.A.* **108** F10
Wałcz *Poland* **31** E3
Waldbröl *Germany* **24** E3
Waldburg Ra. *Australia* **93** D2
Waldeck *Germany* **24** D5
Walden *Colo., U.S.A.* **108** F10
Walden *N.Y., U.S.A.* **115** E10
Waldkirch *Germany* **25** G3
Waldkirchen *Germany* **25** G9
Waldkraiburg *Germany* **25** G8
Waldport *U.S.A.* **108** D1
Waldron *U.S.A.* **116** D7
Waldviertel *Austria* **26** C8

Walebing *Australia* **93** F2
Walembele *Ghana* **82** C4
Walensee *Switz.* **25** H5
Wales □ *U.K.* **15** E3
Wales I. *Canada* **101** D14
Walewale *Ghana* **83** C4
Walgett *Australia* **95** E4
Walgreen Coast *Antarctica* **5** D15
Walker *U.S.A.* **112** B6
Walker, L. *Canada* **105** B6
Walker L. *Canada* **103** C9
Walker L. *U.S.A.* **108** G4
Walkerston *Australia* **94** b
Walkerton *Canada* **114** B3
Wall *U.S.A.* **112** C2
Walla Walla *U.S.A.* **108** C4
Wallace *Idaho, U.S.A.* **108** C6
Wallace *N.C., U.S.A.* **117** D16
Wallaceburg *Canada* **114** D2
Wallachia = Valahia
  Romania **29** F9
Wallal *Australia* **95** D4
Wallam Cr. ➤ *Australia* **95** D4
Wallambin, L. *Australia* **93** F2
Wallangarra *Australia* **95** D5
Wallaroo *Australia* **95** E2
Walldürn *Germany* **25** F5
Wallenhorst *Germany* **24** C4
Wallenpaupack, L. *U.S.A.* **115** E9
Wallingford *Conn., U.S.A.* **115** E12
Wallingford *Vt., U.S.A.* **115** C12
Wallis & Futuna, Is. *Pac. Oc.* **90** C11
Wallowa *U.S.A.* **108** D5
Wallowa Mts. *U.S.A.* **108** D5
Walls *U.K.* **13** A7
Walls of Jerusalem △
  Australia **95** G4
Wallula *U.S.A.* **108** C4
Wallumbilla *Australia* **95** D4
Walmsley L. *Canada* **103** A7
Walney, I. of *U.K.* **14** C4
Walnut Canyon △ *U.S.A.* **109** J8
Walnut Creek *U.S.A.* **110** H4
Walnut Ridge *U.S.A.* **117** C9
Walpole *Australia* **93** F2
Walpole *U.S.A.* **115** D13
Walpole-Nornalup △
  Australia **93** G2
Wals *Austria* **26** D5
Walsall *U.K.* **15** E6
Walsenburg *U.S.A.* **109** H11
Walsh *U.S.A.* **109** H12
Walsh ➤ *Australia* **94** B3
Walsingham *Canada* **114** D4
Walsrode *Germany* **24** C5
Walter F. George Res.
  U.S.A. **117** F12
Walterboro *U.S.A.* **117** E14
Walters *U.S.A.* **116** D5
Waltershausen *Germany* **24** E6
Waltham *U.S.A.* **115** D13
Waltman *U.S.A.* **108** E10
Walton *U.S.A.* **115** D9
Walton-on-the-Naze *U.K.* **15** F9
Walvis Bay *Namibia* **88** C1
Walvisbaai = Walvis Bay
  Namibia **88** C1
Wamba *Dem. Rep. of the Congo* **86** B2
Wamba *Kenya* **86** B4
Wamba *Nigeria* **83** D6
Wambardi ◎ *Australia* **92** C5
Wamego *U.S.A.* **112** F5
Wamena *Indonesia* **63** E9
Wampana Karlantijpa ◎
  Australia **92** C5
Wampaya ◎ *Australia* **94** B2
Wampsville *U.S.A.* **115** C9
Wamsutter *U.S.A.* **108** F10
Wamulan *Indonesia* **63** E7
Wan Xian *China* **56** E8
Wana *Pakistan* **68** C3
Wanaaring *Australia* **95** D3
Wanaka *N.Z.* **91** F2
Wanaka, L. *N.Z.* **91** F2
Wan'an *China* **59** D10
Wanapitei L. *Canada* **104** C3
Wandel Sea = McKinley
  Sea *Arctic* **4** A7
Wandérama *Ivory C.* **82** D4
Wanderer *Zimbabwe* **87** F3
Wandhari *Pakistan* **68** F2
Wanding *China* **58** E2
Wandoan *Australia* **95** D4
Wanfu *China* **57** D12
Wang ➤ *Thailand* **64** D2
Wang Kai *Sudan* **81** F2
Wang Noi *Thailand* **64** E3
Wang Saphung *Thailand* **64** D3
Wang Thong *Thailand* **64** D3
Wanga *Dem. Rep. of the Congo* **86** B2
Wangal *Indonesia* **63** F8
Wanganella *Australia* **95** F3
Wanganui *N.Z.* **91** C5
Wangaratta *Australia* **95** F4
Wangary *Australia* **95** E2
Wangcang *China* **58** A6
Wangcheng *China* **59** C9
Wangdu *China* **56** E8
Wangen *Germany* **25** H5
Wangerooge *Germany* **24** B3

Walebing *Australia* **93** F2
Wangiwangi *Indonesia* **63** F6
Wangjiang *China* **59** B11
Wangmo *China* **58** E6
Wangolodougou *Ivory C.* **82** D3
Wangqing *China* **57** C15
Wanimiyn ◎ *Australia* **92** C5
Wanjina Wunggurr
  Wilinggin ◎ *Australia* **92** C4
Wankaner *India* **68** H4
Wanless *Canada* **103** C8
Wanleweyne *Somali Rep.* **75** G3
Wannian *China* **59** C11
Wanning *China* **64** C8
Wannoo Billabong
  Roadhouse *Australia* **93** E2
Wanon Niwat *Thailand* **64** D4
Wanquan *China* **56** D8
Wanrong *China* **56** G6
Wanshan *China* **58** D7
Wanshengchang *China* **58** C6
Wantage *U.K.* **15** F6
Wanxian *China* **58** B7
Wanyuan *China* **58** A7
Wanzai *China* **59** C10
Wapakoneta *U.S.A.* **113** E11
Wapato *U.S.A.* **108** C3
Wapawekka L. *Canada* **103** C8
Wapikopa L. *Canada* **104** B2
Wapiti ➤ *Canada* **102** B5
Wappingers Falls *U.S.A.* **115** E11
Wapsipinicon ➤ *U.S.A.* **112** E8
Wapusk △ *Canada* **103** B10
Warab *Sudan* **81** F2
Warab □ *Sudan* **81** F2
Warakurna *Australia* **93** D4
Warangal *India* **66** L11
Waraseoni *India* **69** J9
Waratah *Australia* **95** G4
Waratah B. *Australia* **95** F4
Warburg *Germany* **24** D5
Warburton *Vic., Australia* **95** F4
Warburton *W. Austral.,
  Australia* **93** E4
Warburton ➤ *Australia* **95** D2
Warburton Groove *Australia* **95** A2
Warburton Ra. *Australia* **93** E4
Warburton ◎ *Australia* **93** E4
Ward *N.Z.* **91** D5
Ward ➤ *Australia* **95** D4
Ward Mt. *U.S.A.* **110** H8
Warden *S. Africa* **89** D4
Wardha *India* **66** J11
Wardha ➤ *India* **66** K11
Wardsville *Canada* **114** D3
Ware *U.K.* **15** F8
Ware *U.S.A.* **115** D12
Waregem *Belgium* **17** D3
Wareham *U.S.A.* **115** E14
Waremme *Belgium* **17** D5
Waren *Germany* **24** B8
Warendorf *Germany* **24** D4
Warialda *Australia* **95** D5
Wariap *Indonesia* **63** E8
Warin Chamrap *Thailand* **64** E5
Warka *Poland* **31** G8
Warkopi *Indonesia* **63** E8
Warm Springs *U.S.A.* **109** G5
Warman *Canada* **103** C7
Warmbad = Bela Bela
  S. Africa **89** C4
Warmbad *Namibia* **88** D2
Warmińsko-Mazurskie □
  Poland **30** D8
Warminster *U.K.* **15** F5
Warminster *U.S.A.* **115** F9
Warmun *Australia* **92** C4
Warnemünde *Germany* **24** A8
Warner Mts. *U.S.A.* **108** F3
Warner Robins *U.S.A.* **117** E13
Warnow ➤ *Germany* **24** A8
Waroona *Australia* **93** F2
Warrabri = Alekarenge
  Australia **94** C1
Warracknabeal *Australia* **95** F3
Warragul *Australia* **95** F4
Warrego ➤ *Australia* **95** E4
Warrego Ra. *Australia* **94** C4
Warren *Australia* **95** E4
Warren *Ark., U.S.A.* **116** E8
Warren *Mich., U.S.A.* **113** D12
Warren *Minn., U.S.A.* **112** A5
Warren *Ohio, U.S.A.* **114** E4
Warren *Pa., U.S.A.* **114** E5
Warrenpoint *U.K.* **12** B5
Warrensburg *Mo., U.S.A.* **112** F7
Warrensburg *N.Y., U.S.A.* **115** C11
Warrenton *S. Africa* **88** D3
Warrenton *U.S.A.* **110** D3
Warri *Nigeria* **83** D6
Warrington *U.K.* **14** D5
Warrington *U.S.A.* **117** F11
Warrnambool *Australia* **95** F3
Warroad *U.S.A.* **112** A6
Warruwi *Australia* **94** A1
Warsa *Indonesia* **63** E9
Warsak Dam *Pakistan* **68** B4
Warsaw = Warszawa *Poland* **31** F8
Warsaw *Ind., U.S.A.* **113** E11
Warsaw *N.Y., U.S.A.* **114** D6

Warsaw *Ohio, U.S.A.* **114** F3
Warstein *Germany* **24** D4
Warszawa *Poland* **31** F8
Warszawa ✈ (WAW) *Poland* **31** F7
Warta *Poland* **31** G5
Warta ➤ *Poland* **31** F1
Warthe = Warta ➤ *Poland* **31** F1
Waru *Indonesia* **63** E8
Warumungu ◎ *Australia* **94** B1
Warwick *Australia* **95** D5
Warwick *U.K.* **15** E6
Warwick *N.Y., U.S.A.* **115** E10
Warwick *R.I., U.S.A.* **115** E13
Warwickshire □ *U.K.* **15** E6
Wasaga Beach *Canada* **114** B4
Wasagaming *Canada* **103** C9
Wasatch Ra. *U.S.A.* **108** F8
Wasbank *S. Africa* **89** D5
Wasco *Calif., U.S.A.* **111** K7
Wasco *Oreg., U.S.A.* **108** D3
Waseca *U.S.A.* **112** C7
Wasekamio L. *Canada* **103** B7
Wash, The *U.K.* **14** E8
Washago *Canada* **114** B5
Washburn *N. Dak., U.S.A.* **112** B3
Washburn *Wis., U.S.A.* **112** B8
Washim *India* **66** J10
Washington *U.K.* **14** C6
Washington *D.C., U.S.A.* **113** F15
Washington *Ga., U.S.A.* **117** E13
Washington *Ind., U.S.A.* **112** F10
Washington *Iowa, U.S.A.* **112** E8
Washington *Mo., U.S.A.* **112** F8
Washington *N.C., U.S.A.* **117** D16
Washington *N.J., U.S.A.* **115** F10
Washington *Pa., U.S.A.* **114** F4
Washington *Utah, U.S.A.* **109** H7
Washington □ *U.S.A.* **108** C3
Washington, Mt. *U.S.A.* **115** B13
Washington Court House
  U.S.A. **113** F12
Washington I. *U.S.A.* **112** C10
Washougal *U.S.A.* **110** E4
Washpool △ *Australia* **95** D5
Wasian *Indonesia* **63** E8
Wasilków *Poland* **31** E10
Wasilla *U.S.A.* **100** E2
Wasior *Indonesia* **63** E8
Wāsiṭ □ *Iraq* **73** F11
Waskaganish *Canada* **104** B4
Waskaiowaka L. *Canada* **103** B9
Waskesiu Lake *Canada* **103** C7
Wasserburg *Germany* **25** G8
Wasserkuppe *Germany* **24** E5
Wassy *France* **19** D11
Waswanipi *Canada* **104** C4
Waswanipi, L. *Canada* **104** C4
Watampone *Indonesia* **63** E6
Watamu *Kenya* **86** C5
Watarrka △ *Australia* **92** D5
Water Park Pt. *Australia* **94** C5
Water Valley *U.S.A.* **117** D10
Waterberg Plateau △
  Namibia **88** C2
Waterberge *S. Africa* **89** C4
Waterbury *Conn., U.S.A.* **115** E11
Waterbury *Vt., U.S.A.* **115** B12
Waterbury L. *Canada* **103** B8
Waterdown *Canada* **114** C5
Waterford *Canada* **114** D4
Waterford *Calif., U.S.A.* **110** H6
Waterford *Pa., U.S.A.* **114** E5
Waterford *Ireland* **12** D4
Waterford □ *Ireland* **12** D4
Waterford Harbour *Ireland* **12** D5
Waterhen L. *Canada* **103** C9
Waterloo *Belgium* **17** D4
Waterloo *Ont., Canada* **114** C4
Waterloo *Qué., Canada* **115** A12
Waterloo *S. Leone* **82** D2
Waterloo *Ill., U.S.A.* **112** F8
Waterloo *Iowa, U.S.A.* **112** D7
Waterloo *N.Y., U.S.A.* **114** D8
Watermeet *U.S.A.* **112** B9
Waterton Lakes △ *Canada* **102** D6
Watertown *Conn., U.S.A.* **115** E11
Watertown *N.Y., U.S.A.* **115** C9
Watertown *S. Dak., U.S.A.* **112** C6
Watertown *Wis., U.S.A.* **112** D9
Waterval-Boven *S. Africa* **89** D5
Waterville *Maine, U.S.A.* **113** C19
Waterville *N.Y., U.S.A.* **115** D9
Waterville *Pa., U.S.A.* **114** E7
Waterville *Wash., U.S.A.* **108** C3
Watervliet *U.S.A.* **115** D11
Wates *Indonesia* **63** G14
Watford *Canada* **114** D3
Watford *U.K.* **15** F7
Watford City *U.S.A.* **112** B2
Wathaman ➤ *Canada* **103** B8
Wathaman L. *Canada* **103** B8
Watheroo *Australia* **93** F2
Watheroo △ *Australia* **93** F2
Wating *China* **56** G4
Watkins Glen *U.S.A.* **114** D8
Watling I. = San Salvador
  I. *Bahamas* **121** B5

Watonga *U.S.A.* **116** D5
Watrous *Canada* **103** C7
Watrous *U.S.A.* **109** J11
Watsa *Dem. Rep. of the Congo* **86** B2
Watseka *U.S.A.* **112** E10
Watson *Canada* **103** C8
Watson Lake *Canada* **102** A3
Watsontown *U.S.A.* **114** E8
Watsonville *U.S.A.* **110** J5
Wattiwarriganna Cr. ➤
  Australia **95** D2
Wattwil *Switz.* **25** H5
Watuata = Batuata *Indonesia* **63** F6
Watubela, Kepulauan
  Indonesia **63** E8
Watubela Is. = Watubela,
  Kepulauan *Indonesia* **63** E8
Wau = Wâw *Sudan* **81** F2
Waubamik *Canada* **114** A4
Waubay *U.S.A.* **112** C5
Wauchope *N.S.W., Australia* **95** E5
Wauchope *N. Terr., Australia* **94** C1
Wauchula *U.S.A.* **117** H14
Waukarlycarly, L. *Australia* **92** D3
Waukegan *U.S.A.* **112** D10
Waukesha *U.S.A.* **112** D9
Waukon *U.S.A.* **112** D8
Waupaca *U.S.A.* **112** C9
Waupun *U.S.A.* **112** D9
Waurika *U.S.A.* **116** D6
Wausau *U.S.A.* **112** C9
Wautoma *U.S.A.* **112** C9
Wauwatosa *U.S.A.* **112** D9
Wave Hill = Kalkarindji
  Australia **92** C5
Wave Rock △ *Australia* **93** F2
Waveney ➤ *U.K.* **15** E9
Waverley *N.Z.* **91** C5
Waverly *Iowa, U.S.A.* **112** D7
Waverly *N.Y., U.S.A.* **115** E8
Wavre *Belgium* **17** D4
Wâw *Sudan* **81** F2
Wāw al Kabīr *Libya* **79** C9
Wawa *Canada* **104** C3
Wawa *Nigeria* **83** D5
Wawa *Sudan* **80** C3
Wawanesa *Canada* **103** D9
Wawona *U.S.A.* **110** H7
Waxahachie *U.S.A.* **116** E6
Way, L. *Australia* **93** E3
Waya *Fiji* **91** a
Waycross *U.S.A.* **117** F13
Wayi *Sudan* **81** F3
Wayland *U.S.A.* **114** D7
Wayne *Nebr., U.S.A.* **112** D5
Wayne *W. Va., U.S.A.* **113** F12
Waynesboro *Ga., U.S.A.* **117** E13
Waynesboro *Miss., U.S.A.* **117** F10
Waynesboro *Pa., U.S.A.* **113** F15
Waynesboro *Va., U.S.A.* **113** F14
Waynesburg *U.S.A.* **113** F13
Waynesville *U.S.A.* **117** D13
Waynoka *U.S.A.* **116** C5
Wazirabad *Pakistan* **68** C6
Waziristan *Pakistan* **68** C4
Wda ➤ *Poland* **30** E5
We *Indonesia* **62** C1
Weald, The *U.K.* **15** F8
Wear ➤ *U.K.* **14** C6
Weatherford *Okla., U.S.A.* **116** D5
Weatherford *Tex., U.S.A.* **116** E6
Weaverville *U.S.A.* **108** F2
Webb City *U.S.A.* **112** G6
Webequie *Canada* **104** B2
Webo = Nyaake *Liberia* **82** E4
Webster *Mass., U.S.A.* **115** D13
Webster *N.Y., U.S.A.* **114** C7
Webster *S. Dak., U.S.A.* **112** C5
Webster City *U.S.A.* **112** D7
Webster Springs *U.S.A.* **113** F13
Webuye *Kenya* **86** B3
Weda *Indonesia* **63** D7
Weda, Teluk *Indonesia* **63** D7
Weddell Abyssal Plain
  S. Ocean **5** C2
Weddell I. *Falk. Is.* **128** G4
Weddell Sea *Antarctica* **5** D1
Wedderburn *Australia* **95** F3
Wedel *Germany* **24** B5
Wedemark *Germany* **24** C5
Wedgeport *Canada* **105** D4
Wedza *Zimbabwe* **87** F3
Wee Waa *Australia* **95** E4
Weed *U.S.A.* **108** F2
Weed Heights *U.S.A.* **110** G7
Weedsport *U.S.A.* **115** C8
Weedville *U.S.A.* **114** E6
Weenen *S. Africa* **89** D5
Weener *Germany* **24** B3
Weert *Neths.* **17** C5
Węgierska-Górka *Poland* **31** J6
Węgliniec *Poland* **31** G2
Wegorzewo *Poland* **30** D8
Wegorzyno *Poland* **30** E2
Węgrów *Poland* **31** F9
Wehda □ *Sudan* **81** F3
Wei He ➤ *Hebei, China* **56** F8
Wei He ➤ *Shaanxi, China* **56** G6
Weichang *China* **57** D9
Weichuan *China* **56** G7

Weida Germany 24 E8
Weiden Germany 25 F8
Weifang China 57 F10
Weihai China 57 F12
Weil Germany 25 H3
Weilburg Germany 24 E4
Weilheim Germany 25 H7
Weimar Germany 24 E7
Weinan China 56 65
Weingarten Germany 25 F4
Weinheim Germany 25 F4
Weining China 58 D5
Weipa Australia 94 A3
Weir → Australia 95 D4
Weir → Canada 103 B10
Weir River Canada 103 B10
Weirton U.S.A. 114 F4
Weiser U.S.A. 108 D5
Weishan Shandong, China 57 G9
Weishan Yunnan, China 58 E3
Weissenburg Germany 25 F6
Weissenfels Germany 24 D7
Weisswasser Germany 24 D10
Wéitra Austria 26 C7
Weixi China 58 D2
Weixin China 58 D5
Weiyuan China 56 G3
Weiz Austria 26 D8
Weizhou Dao China 58 G7
Wejherowo Poland 30 D5
Wekusko L. Canada 103 C9
Welch U.S.A. 113 G13
Weldya Ethiopia 81 E4
Welega Ethiopia 81 F3
Welford △ Australia 94 D3
Welkite Ethiopia 81 F4
Welkom S. Africa 88 D4
Welland Canada 114 D5
Welland → U.K. 15 E7
Wellesley Is. Australia 94 B2
Wellesley Islands ○ Australia 94 B2
Wellingborough U.K. 15 E7
Wellington Australia 95 E4
Wellington Canada 114 C7
Wellington N.Z. 91 D5
Wellington S. Africa 88 E2
Wellington Somst., U.K. 15 G4
Wellington Telford & Wrekin, U.K. 15 E5
Wellington Colo., U.S.A. 108 F11
Wellington Kans., U.S.A. 112 G5
Wellington Nev., U.S.A. 110 G7
Wellington Ohio, U.S.A. 114 E2
Wellington Tex., U.S.A. 116 D4
Wellington, I. Chile 128 F2
Wellington, L. Australia 95 E4
Wellington Chan. Canada 101 C13
Wells U.K. 15 F5
Wells Maine, U.S.A. 115 C14
Wells N.Y., U.S.A. 115 C10
Wells Nev., U.S.A. 108 F6
Wells, L. Australia 93 E3
Wells, Mt. Australia 92 C4
Wells Gray △ Canada 102 C4
Wells-next-the-Sea U.K. 14 E8
Wells River U.S.A. 115 B12
Wellsboro U.S.A. 114 E7
Wellsburg U.S.A. 114 F4
Wellsville N.Y., U.S.A. 114 D7
Wellsville Ohio, U.S.A. 114 F4
Wellsville Utah, U.S.A. 108 F8
Wellton U.S.A. 109 K6
Welmel, Wabi → Ethiopia 81 F5
Welo Ethiopia 81 E4
Wels Austria 26 C7
Welshpool U.K. 15 E4
Welwyn Garden City U.K. 15 F7
Wem U.K. 14 E5
Wembere → Tanzania 86 C3
Wemindji Canada 104 B4
Wemyss Canada 115 B8
Wen Xian China 56 G7
Wenatchee U.S.A. 108 C3
Wenchang China 64 C8
Wencheng China 59 D13
Wenchi Ghana 82 D4
Wenchow = Wenzhou China 59 D13
Wenchuan China 58 B4
Wenden U.S.A. 111 M13
Wendeng China 57 F12
Wendesi Indonesia 63 E8
Wendo Ethiopia 81 F4
Wendover U.S.A. 108 F6
Weng'an China 58 D6
Wengcheng China 59 E9
Wengen Switz. 19 F14
Wengyuan China 59 E10
Wenjiang China 58 B4
Wenling China 59 C13
Wenlock → Australia 94 A3
Wenshan China 58 F5
Wenshang China 56 G9
Wenshui China 56 F7
Wensleydale U.K. 14 C6
Wensu China 60 B3
Wensum → U.K. 14 E8
Wentworth Australia 95 E3
Wentzel L. Canada 102 B6
Wenut Indonesia 63 E8

Wenxi China 56 G6
Wenxian China 56 H3
Wenzhou China 59 D13
Weott U.S.A. 108 F2
Wepener S. Africa 88 D4
Werda Botswana 88 D3
Werdau Germany 24 E8
Werder Germany 24 C8
Werdohl Germany 24 D3
Wereilu Ethiopia 81 E4
Weri Indonesia 63 E8
Werneck Germany 25 F6
Wernigerode Germany 24 D6
Werra → Germany 24 D5
Werrimull Australia 95 E3
Werris Creek Australia 95 E5
Wertach → Germany 25 G6
Wertheim Germany 25 F5
Wertingen Germany 25 G6
Wesel Germany 24 D2
Weser → Germany 24 B4
Weser-Ems □ Germany 24 C3
Weserbergland Germany 24 C5
Weserbergland Schaumburg Hameln △ Germany 24 C5
Wesiri Indonesia 63 F7
Weslaco U.S.A. 116 H6
Weslemkoon L. Canada 114 A7
Wesleyville Canada 105 C9
Wesleyville U.S.A. 114 D4
Wessel, C. Australia 94 A2
Wessel Is. Australia 94 A2
Wesselburen Germany 24 A4
Wessington Springs U.S.A. 112 C4
West □ U.S.A. 116 F6
West → U.S.A. 115 D12
West Allis U.S.A. 112 D9
West Antarctica Antarctica 5 D15
West Baines → Australia 92 C4
West Bank ■ Asia 74 C4
West Bend U.S.A. 112 D9
West Bengal □ India 69 H13
West Berkshire □ U.K. 15 F6
West Beskids = Západné Beskydy Europe 27 B12
West Branch U.S.A. 113 C11
West Branch Susquehanna → U.S.A. 115 F8
West Bromwich U.K. 15 E6
West Burra U.K. 13 A7
West Canada Cr. → U.S.A. 115 C10
West Caroline Basin Pac. Oc. 96 G5
West Chazy U.S.A. 115 B11
West Chester U.S.A. 115 G9
West Coast □ Namibia 88 C1
West Coast △ S. Africa 88 E2
West Columbia U.S.A. 116 G7
West Covina U.S.A. 111 L9
West Des Moines U.S.A. 112 E7
West Dunbartonshire □ U.K. 13 F4
West End Bahamas 120 A4
West Falkland Falk. Is. 128 G4
West Fargo U.S.A. 112 B6
West Fiji Basin Pac. Oc. 96 J9
West Fjord = Vestfjorden Norway 8 C16
West Fork Trinity → U.S.A. 116 E6
West Frankfort U.S.A. 112 G9
West Grand L. U.S.A. 113 C20
West Hartford U.S.A. 115 E12
West Haven U.S.A. 115 E12
West Hazleton U.S.A. 115 F9
West Helena U.S.A. 117 D9
West Hurley U.S.A. 115 E10
West Ice Shelf Antarctica 5 C7
West Indies Cent. Amer. 121 D7
West Jordan U.S.A. 108 F8
West Linn U.S.A. 110 E4
West Lorne Canada 114 D3
West Lothian □ U.K. 13 F5
West Lunga → Zambia 87 E1
West MacDonnell △ Australia 92 D5
West Mariana Basin Pac. Oc. 96 F5
West Memphis U.S.A. 117 D9
West Midlands □ U.K. 15 E6
West Mifflin U.S.A. 114 F5
West Milford U.S.A. 115 E10
West Milton U.S.A. 114 E8
West Monroe U.S.A. 116 E8
West Newton U.S.A. 114 F5
West Nicholson Zimbabwe 87 G2
West Odessa U.S.A. 116 F3
West Palm Beach U.S.A. 117 H14
West Plains U.S.A. 112 G8
West Point Miss., U.S.A. 117 E10
West Point N.Y., U.S.A. 115 E11
West Point Nebr., U.S.A. 112 E5
West Point Va., U.S.A. 113 G15
Weott I. Canada 104 B4
West Pt. = Ouest, Pte. de l' Canada 105 C7
West Pt. Australia 95 F2
West Road → Canada 102 C4
West Rutland U.S.A. 115 C11
West Schelde = Westerschelde → Neths. 17 C3
West Seneca U.S.A. 114 D6

West Siberian Plain Russia 50 B9
West Sussex □ U.K. 15 G7
West-Terschelling Neths. 17 A5
West Valley City U.S.A. 108 F8
West Virginia □ U.S.A. 113 F13
West-Vlaanderen □ Belgium 17 D2
West Walker → U.S.A. 110 G7
West Wyalong Australia 95 E4
West Yellowstone U.S.A. 108 D8
West Yorkshire □ U.K. 14 D6
Westall, Pt. Australia 95 E1
Westbrook U.S.A. 113 D18
Westbury Australia 95 G4
Westby U.S.A. 108 B11
Westend U.S.A. 111 K9
Westerland Germany 24 A4
Westerly U.S.A. 115 E13
Western □ Ghana 82 D4
Western □ Kenya 86 B3
Western □ S. Leone 82 D2
Western □ Zambia 87 F1
Western Australia □ Australia 93 E2
Western Cape □ S. Africa 88 E3
Western Dvina = Daugava → Latvia 32 D3
Western Ghats India 66 N9
Western Isles □ U.K. 13 D1
Western Sahara ■ Africa 78 D3
Western Samoa = Samoa ■ Pac. Oc. 91 b
Western Sierra Madre = Madre Occidental, Sierra Mexico 118 B3
Westernport U.S.A. 113 F14
Westerschelde → Neths. 17 C3
Westerstede Germany 24 B3
Westerwald Germany 24 E3
Westfield Mass., U.S.A. 115 D12
Westfield N.Y., U.S.A. 114 D5
Westfield Pa., U.S.A. 114 E7
Westhill U.K. 13 D6
Westhope U.S.A. 112 A3
Westland △ N.Z. 91 E3
Westland Bight N.Z. 91 E3
Westlock Canada 102 C6
Westmar Australia 95 D4
Westmeath □ Ireland 12 C4
Westminster Calif., U.S.A. 111 M8
Westminster Colo., U.S.A. 108 G11
Westminster Md., U.S.A. 113 F15
Westmont U.S.A. 114 F6
Westmoreland Barbados 121 g
Westmorland U.S.A. 111 M11
Weston Oreg., U.S.A. 108 D4
Weston W. Va., U.S.A. 113 F13
Weston I. Canada 104 B4
Weston-super-Mare U.K. 15 F5
Westover U.S.A. 114 F6
Westport Canada 115 B8
Westport Ireland 12 C2
Westport N.Z. 91 D3
Westport N.Y., U.S.A. 115 B11
Westport Oreg., U.S.A. 110 D3
Westport Wash., U.S.A. 110 D2
Westray Canada 103 C8
Westray U.K. 13 B5
Westree Canada 104 C3
Westville U.S.A. 110 F6
Westwood U.S.A. 108 F3
Wetar Indonesia 63 F7
Wetaskiwin Canada 102 C6
Wete Tanzania 84 F7
Wetherby U.K. 14 D6
Wethersfield U.S.A. 115 E12
Wetteren Belgium 17 D3
Wetzlar Germany 24 E4
Wewoka U.S.A. 116 D6
Wexford Ireland 12 D5
Wexford □ Ireland 12 D5
Wexford Harbour Ireland 12 D5
Weyburn Canada 103 D8
Weyer Markt Austria 26 D7
Weyhe Germany 24 C4
Weyib → Ethiopia 81 F5
Weymouth Canada 105 D6
Weymouth U.K. 15 G5
Weymouth U.S.A. 115 D14
Weymouth, C. Australia 94 A3
Wha Ti Canada 100 B8
Whakaari N.Z. 91 B6
Whakatane N.Z. 91 B6
Whale = Baleine → Canada 105 A6
Whale Cove Canada 103 A10
Whales, B. of Antarctica 5 D12
Whalsay U.K. 13 A8
Whangamata N.Z. 91 B5
Whangamomona N.Z. 91 C5
Whanganui N.Z. 91 C5
Whangarei N.Z. 91 A5
Whangarei Harb. N.Z. 91 A5
Wharekauri = Chatham Is. Pac. Oc. 96 M10
Wharfe → U.K. 14 D6
Wharfedale U.K. 14 C5
Wharton N.J., U.S.A. 115 F10
Wharton Pa., U.S.A. 114 E6
Wharton Tex., U.S.A. 116 L7
Wharton Basin Ind. Oc. 96 K1
Wheatland Calif., U.S.A. 110 G5

Wheatland Wyo., U.S.A. 108 E11
Wheatley Canada 114 D2
Wheaton Md., U.S.A. 113 F15
Wheaton Minn., U.S.A. 112 C5
Wheelbarrow Pk. U.S.A. 110 H10
Wheeler Oreg., U.S.A. 108 D2
Wheeler Tex., U.S.A. 116 D4
Wheeler → Canada 105 A6
Wheeler L. U.S.A. 117 D11
Wheeler Pk. N. Mex., U.S.A. 109 H11
Wheeler Pk. Nev., U.S.A. 108 G6
Wheeler Ridge U.S.A. 111 L8
Wheelersburg U.S.A. 113 F12
Wheeling U.S.A. 114 F4
Whernside U.K. 14 C5
Whiddy I. Ireland 12 E2
Whim Creek Australia 92 D2
Whiskey Jack L. Canada 103 B8
Whiskeytown-Shasta-Trinity △ U.S.A. 108 F2
Whistleduck Cr. → Australia 94 C2
Whistler Canada 102 C4
Whitby Canada 114 C6
Whitby U.K. 14 C7
White → Ark., U.S.A. 116 E9
White → Ind., U.S.A. 112 F10
White → S. Dak., U.S.A. 112 D4
White → Tex., U.S.A. 116 E4
White → Utah, U.S.A. 108 F9
White → Vt., U.S.A. 115 C12
White → Wash., U.S.A. 110 C4
White, L. Australia 92 D4
White B. Canada 105 C8
White Bird U.S.A. 108 D5
White Butte U.S.A. 112 B2
White City U.S.A. 108 E2
White Cliffs Australia 95 E3
White Desert = Es Sahrâ al Beida Egypt 80 B2
White Hall U.S.A. 112 F8
White Haven U.S.A. 115 E9
White Horse, Vale of U.K. 15 F6
White I. = Whakaari N.Z. 91 B6
White L. Canada 115 A8
White L. U.S.A. 116 G8
White Lake Canada 115 A8
White Mountain Peak U.S.A. 109 H4
White Mts. Calif., U.S.A. 110 H8
White Mts. N.H., U.S.A. 115 B13
White Mts. △ Australia 94 C4
White Nile = Nîl el Abyad → Sudan 81 D3
White Nile Dam = Khazzân Jabal al Awliyâ Sudan 81 D3
White Otter L. Canada 104 C1
White Pass U.S.A. 110 D5
White Plains U.S.A. 115 E11
White River Canada 104 C2
White River U.S.A. 112 D3
White Rock Canada 110 A4
White Rock U.S.A. 109 J10
White Russia = Belarus ■ Europe 23 B14
White Sands △ U.S.A. 109 K10
White Sea = Beloye More Russia 52 B6
White Sulphur Springs Mont., U.S.A. 108 C8
White Sulphur Springs W. Va., U.S.A. 113 G13
White Swan U.S.A. 110 D6
White Volta → Ghana 83 D4
Whitecliffs N.Z. 91 E3
Whitecourt Canada 102 C5
Whiteface Mt. U.S.A. 115 B11
Whitefield U.S.A. 115 B13
Whitefish U.S.A. 108 B6
Whitefish B. U.S.A. 104 C3
Whitefish L. Canada 103 A7
Whitefish Pt. U.S.A. 113 B11
Whitegull, L. = Goélands, L. aux Canada 105 A7
Whitehall Mich., U.S.A. 112 D10
Whitehall Mont., U.S.A. 108 D7
Whitehall N.Y., U.S.A. 115 C11
Whitehall Wis., U.S.A. 112 C8
Whitehaven U.K. 14 C4
Whitehorse Canada 102 A1
Whitemark Australia 95 G4
Whiteplains Liberia 82 D2
Whiteriver U.S.A. 109 K9
Whitesand → Canada 102 A5
Whitesands S. Africa 88 E3
Whitesboro N.Y., U.S.A. 115 C9
Whitesboro Tex., U.S.A. 116 E6
Whiteshell △ Canada 103 D9
Whiteville U.S.A. 117 D15
Whitewater U.S.A. 112 D9
Whitewater Baldy U.S.A. 109 K9
Whitewater L. Canada 104 B2
Whitewood Australia 94 C3
Whitewood Canada 103 C8
Whithorn U.K. 13 G4
Whitianga N.Z. 91 B5
Whitman U.S.A. 115 D14
Whitney Canada 114 A6
Whitney, Mt. U.S.A. 110 J8
Whitney Point U.S.A. 115 D9

Whitstable U.K. 15 F9
Whitsunday I. Australia 94 b
Whitsunday Islands △ Australia 94 b
Whittier Alaska, U.S.A. 106 C10
Whittier Calif., U.S.A. 111 M8
Whittlesea Australia 95 F4
Wholdaia L. Canada 103 A8
Whyalla Australia 95 E2
Wiang Kosai △ Thailand 64 D2
Wiang Sa Thailand 64 C3
Wiarton Canada 114 B3
Wiawso Ghana 82 D4
Wiay U.K. 13 D1
Wiązów Poland 31 H4
Wibaux U.S.A. 108 C11
Wichian Buri Thailand 64 E3
Wichita U.S.A. 112 G5
Wichita Falls U.S.A. 116 E5
Wick U.K. 13 C5
Wickenburg U.S.A. 109 K7
Wickepin Australia 93 F2
Wickham Australia 92 D2
Wickham, C. Australia 95 F3
Wickliffe U.S.A. 114 E3
Wicklow Ireland 12 D5
Wicklow □ Ireland 12 D5
Wicklow Hd. Ireland 12 D6
Wicklow Mts. △ Ireland 12 C5
Widawa → Poland 31 G5
Widawka → Poland 31 G5
Widgeegoara Cr. → Australia 95 D4
Widgiemooltha Australia 93 F3
Widnes U.K. 14 D5
Więcbork Poland 31 E4
Wiehengebirge = Nördlicher Teutoburger Wald-Wiehengebirge △ Germany 24 C4
Wiehl Germany 24 E3
Wiek Germany 24 A9
Wielbark Poland 30 E7
Wieleń Poland 31 F3
Wielichowo Poland 31 F3
Wieliczka Poland 31 J7
Wielkopolski △ Poland 31 F3
Wielkopolskie □ Poland 31 F4
Wieluń Poland 31 G5
Wien Austria 27 C9
Wien-Schwechat ✈ (VIE) Austria 27 C9
Wiener Neustadt Austria 27 D9
Wieprz → Poland 31 G8
Wieprza → Poland 30 D3
Wieruszów Poland 31 G5
Wiesbaden Germany 25 E4
Wiesental Germany 25 F4
Wiesloch Germany 25 F4
Wiesmoor Germany 24 B3
Wieżyca Poland 30 D5
Wigan U.K. 14 D5
Wiggins Colo., U.S.A. 108 F11
Wiggins Miss., U.S.A. 117 F10
Wight, I. of U.K. 15 G6
Wigston U.K. 15 E6
Wigton U.K. 14 C4
Wigtown U.K. 13 G4
Wigtown B. U.K. 13 G4
Wik and Wikway People ○ Australia 94 A3
Wil Switz. 25 H5
Wilamowice Poland 31 J6
Wilber U.S.A. 112 E5
Wilberforce Canada 114 A6
Wilberforce, C. Australia 94 A2
Wilburton U.S.A. 116 D7
Wilcannia Australia 95 E3
Wilcox U.S.A. 114 E6
Wildbad Germany 25 G4
Wildeshausen Germany 24 C4
Wildon Austria 26 E8
Wildrose U.S.A. 111 J9
Wildspitze Austria 26 E3
Wilga → Poland 31 G8
Wilge → S. Africa 89 D4
Wilhelm II Coast Antarctica 5 C7
Wilhelmsburg Austria 26 C8
Wilhelmshaven Germany 24 B4
Wilhelmstal Namibia 88 C2
Wilkes-Barre U.S.A. 115 E9
Wilkes Land Antarctica 5 D9
Wilkie Canada 103 C7
Wilkinsburg U.S.A. 114 F5
Wilkinson Lakes Australia 93 E5
Willandra Creek → Australia 95 E4
Willapa B. U.S.A. 108 C1
Willapa Hills U.S.A. 110 D3
Willard U.S.A. 108 F8
Willare Bridge Roadhouse Australia 92 C3
Willcox U.S.A. 109 K9
Willemstad Neth. Ant. 121 D6
William → Canada 103 B7

William 'Bill' Dannelly Res. U.S.A. 117 E11
William Creek Australia 95 D2
Williams Australia 93 F2
Williams Ariz., U.S.A. 109 J7
Williams Calif., U.S.A. 110 F4
Williams Harbour Canada 105 B8
Williams Lake Canada 102 C4
Williamsburg Ky., U.S.A. 113 G11
Williamsburg Pa., U.S.A. 114 F6
Williamsburg Va., U.S.A. 113 G15
Williamson N.Y., U.S.A. 114 C7
Williamson W. Va., U.S.A. 113 G12
Williamsport U.S.A. 114 E7
Williamston U.S.A. 117 D16
Williamstown Australia 95 F3
Williamstown Ky., U.S.A. 113 F11
Williamstown Mass., U.S.A. 115 D11
Williamstown N.Y., U.S.A. 115 C9
Willimantic U.S.A. 115 E12
Willingboro U.S.A. 113 E16
Williston S. Africa 88 E3
Williston Fla., U.S.A. 117 G13
Williston N. Dak., U.S.A. 112 A2
Williston L. Canada 102 B4
Willits U.S.A. 108 G2
Willmar U.S.A. 112 C6
Willmore Wilderness △ Canada 102 C5
Willoughby U.S.A. 114 E3
Willow Bunch Canada 103 D7
Willow L. Canada 102 A5
Willow Wall, The China 57 C12
Willowick U.S.A. 114 E3
Willowlake → Canada 102 A4
Willowmore S. Africa 88 E3
Willows U.S.A. 110 F4
Willowvale = Gatyana S. Africa 89 E4
Wills, L. Australia 92 D4
Wills Cr. → Australia 94 C3
Willsboro U.S.A. 115 B11
Willunga Australia 95 F2
Wilmette U.S.A. 112 D10
Wilmington Australia 95 E2
Wilmington Del., U.S.A. 113 F16
Wilmington N.C., U.S.A. 117 D16
Wilmington Ohio, U.S.A. 113 F12
Wilmington Vt., U.S.A. 115 D12
Wilmslow U.K. 14 D5
Wilpena Cr. → Australia 95 E2
Wilsall U.S.A. 108 D8
Wilson N.C., U.S.A. 117 D16
Wilson N.Y., U.S.A. 114 C6
Wilson Pa., U.S.A. 115 F9
Wilson → Australia 92 C4
Wilson Bluff Australia 93 F4
Wilson Inlet Australia 93 G2
Wilsons Promontory Australia 95 F4
Wilster Germany 24 B5
Wilton U.S.A. 112 B3
Wilton → Australia 94 A1
Wiltshire □ U.K. 15 F6
Wiltz Lux. 17 E5
Wiluna Australia 93 E3
Wimborne Minster U.K. 15 G6
Wimereux France 19 E8
Wimmera → Australia 95 F3
Winam G. Kenya 86 C3
Winburg S. Africa 88 D4
Winchendon U.S.A. 115 D12
Winchester U.K. 15 F5
Winchester Conn., U.S.A. 115 E11
Winchester Idaho, U.S.A. 108 C5
Winchester Ind., U.S.A. 113 E11
Winchester Ky., U.S.A. 113 G11
Winchester N.H., U.S.A. 115 D12
Winchester Nev., U.S.A. 111 J11
Winchester Tenn., U.S.A. 117 D11
Winchester Va., U.S.A. 113 F14
Wind → U.S.A. 108 E9
Wind Cave △ U.S.A. 112 D2
Wind River Range U.S.A. 108 E9
Windamere, L. Australia 95 B4
Windau = Ventspils Latvia 30 A8
Windber U.S.A. 114 F6
Winder U.S.A. 117 E13
Windermere U.K. 14 C5
Windhoek Namibia 88 C2
Windidda Australia 93 E3
Windischgarsten Austria 26 D7
Windjana Gorge △ Australia 92 C3
Windom U.S.A. 112 D6
Windorah Australia 94 D3
Window Rock U.S.A. 109 J9
Windrush → U.K. 15 F6
Windsor Australia 95 E5
Windsor N.S., Canada 105 D7
Windsor Ont., Canada 114 D2
Windsor U.K. 15 F7
Windsor Calif., U.S.A. 108 G2
Windsor Colo., U.S.A. 108 F11
Windsor Conn., U.S.A. 115 E12
Windsor Mo., U.S.A. 112 F7
Windsor N.Y., U.S.A. 115 D9
Windsor Vt., U.S.A. 115 C12
Windsor & Maidenhead □ U.K. 15 F7

Windsorton *S. Africa* **88** D3
Windward Is. *W. Indies* **121** D7
Windward Passage =
  Vientos, Paso de los
  Caribbean **121** C5
Winefred L. *Canada* **103** B6
Winejok *Sudan* **81** F2
Winfield *U.S.A.* **112** G5
Wingate Mts. *Australia* **92** B5
Wingellina = Irrunytju
  Australia **93** E4
Wingham *Australia* **95** E5
Wingham *Canada* **114** C3
Winisk → *Canada* **104** A2
Winisk L. *Canada* **104** B2
Wink *U.S.A.* **116** F3
Winkler *Canada* **103** D9
Winklern *Austria* **26** E5
Winlock *U.S.A.* **110** D4
Winneba *Ghana* **83** D4
Winnebago, L. *U.S.A.* **112** D9
Winnecke Cr. → *Australia* **92** C5
Winnemucca *U.S.A.* **108** F5
Winnemucca L. *U.S.A.* **108** F4
Winner *U.S.A.* **112** D4
Winnett *U.S.A.* **108** C9
Winnfield *U.S.A.* **116** F8
Winnibigoshish, L. *U.S.A.* **112** B6
Winnipeg *Canada* **103** D9
Winnipeg → *Canada* **103** C9
Winnipeg, L. *Canada* **103** C9
Winnipeg Beach *Canada* **103** C9
Winnipegosis *Canada* **103** C9
Winnipegosis L. *Canada* **103** C9
Winnipesaukee, L. *U.S.A.* **115** C13
Winnisquam L. *U.S.A.* **115** C13
Winnsboro *La., U.S.A.* **116** E9
Winnsboro *S.C., U.S.A.* **117** D14
Winnsboro *Tex., U.S.A.* **116** E7
Winokapau, L. *Canada* **105** B7
Winona *Minn., U.S.A.* **112** C8
Winona *Miss., U.S.A.* **117** E10
Winooski *U.S.A.* **115** B11
Winooski → *U.S.A.* **115** B11
Winschoten *Neths.* **17** A7
Winsen *Germany* **24** B6
Winsford *U.K.* **14** D5
Winslow = Bainbridge
  Island *U.S.A.* **110** C2
Winslow *U.S.A.* **109** J8
Winsted *U.S.A.* **115** E11
Winston-Salem *U.S.A.* **117** C14
Winter Garden *U.S.A.* **117** G14
Winter Haven *U.S.A.* **117** G14
Winter Park *U.S.A.* **117** G14
Winterberg *Germany* **24** D4
Winterhaven *U.S.A.* **111** N12
Winters *U.S.A.* **110** G5
Winterset *U.S.A.* **112** E6
Wintersville *U.S.A.* **114** F4
Winterswijk *Neths.* **17** C6
Winterthur *Switz.* **25** H4
Winthrop *U.S.A.* **108** B3
Winton *Australia* **94** C3
Winton *N.Z.* **91** G2
Wipper → *Germany* **24** D7
Wirlyajarrayi ☼ *Australia* **92** D5
Wirrulla *Australia* **95** E1
Wisbech *U.K.* **15** E8
Wisconsin □ *U.S.A.* **112** C9
Wisconsin → *U.S.A.* **112** D8
Wisconsin Rapids *U.S.A.* **112** C9
Wisdom *U.S.A.* **108** D7
Wiseman *U.S.A.* **106** B9
Wishaw *U.K.* **13** F5
Wishek *U.S.A.* **112** B4
Wisła *Poland* **31** J5
Wisła → *Poland* **30** D5
Wisłok → *Poland* **31** H9
Wisłoka → *Poland* **31** H8
Wismar *Germany* **24** B7
Wisner *U.S.A.* **112** E5
Wissant *France* **19** B8
Wissembourg *France* **19** C14
Wisznice *Poland* **31** G10
Witbank = eMalahleni
  S. Africa **89** D4
Witdraai *S. Africa* **88** D3
Witham *U.K.* **15** F8
Witham → *U.K.* **14** E7
Withernsea *U.K.* **14** D8
Witjira ☼ *Australia* **95** D2
Witkowo *Poland* **31** F4
Witless Bay *Canada* **105** C9
Witney *U.K.* **15** F6
Witnica *Poland* **31** F1
Witnossob → *Namibia* **88** D3
Witrivier *S. Africa* **89** D5
Wittdün *Germany* **24** A4
Witten *Germany* **24** D3
Wittenberge *Germany* **24** B7
Wittenburg *Germany* **24** B7
Wittenheim *France* **19** E14
Wittenoom *Australia* **92** D2
Wittingen *Germany* **24** C6
Wittlich *Germany* **25** F2
Wittmund *Germany* **24** B3
Wittow *Germany* **24** A9
Wittstock *Germany* **24** B8
Witu *Kenya* **86** C5

Witvlei *Namibia* **88** C2
Witzenhausen *Germany* **24** D5
Wiwon *N. Korea* **57** D14
Wkra → *Poland* **31** F7
Władysławowo *Poland* **30** D5
Wleń *Poland* **31** G2
Wlingi *Indonesia* **63** H15
Włocławek *Poland* **31** F6
Włodawa *Poland* **31** G10
Włoszczowa *Poland* **31** H6
Woburn *U.S.A.* **115** D13
Wodian *China* **56** H7
Wodonga *Australia* **95** F4
Wodzisław Śląski *Poland* **31** H5
Wœrth *France* **19** D14
Woinbogoin *China* **58** A2
Woippy *France* **19** C13
Wojcieszów *Poland* **31** H2
Wokam *Indonesia* **63** F8
Woking *U.K.* **15** F7
Wokingham *U.K.* **15** F7
Wokingham □ *U.K.* **15** F7
Wolbrom *Poland* **31** H6
Woldegk *Germany* **24** B9
Wolf → *Canada* **102** A2
Wolf Creek *U.S.A.* **108** C7
Wolf L. *Canada* **102** A2
Wolf Point *U.S.A.* **108** B11
Wolfe Creek Crater △
  Australia **92** C4
Wolfe I. *Canada* **115** B8
Wolfeboro *U.S.A.* **115** C13
Wolfen *Germany* **24** D8
Wolfenbüttel *Germany* **24** C6
Wolfratshausen *Germany* **25** H7
Wolfsberg *Austria* **26** E7
Wolfsburg *Germany* **24** C6
Wolgast *Germany* **24** A9
Wolhusen *Switz.* **25** H4
Wolin *Poland* **30** E1
Woliński △ *Poland* **30** E1
Wollaston, Is. *Chile* **128** H3
Wollaston L. *Canada* **103** B8
Wollaston Lake *Canada* **103** B8
Wollaston Pen. *Canada* **100** D9
Wollongong *Australia* **95** E5
Wolmaransstad *S. Africa* **88** D4
Wolmirstedt *Germany* **24** C7
Wołomin *Poland* **31** F8
Wołów *Poland* **31** G3
Wolseley *S. Africa* **88** E2
Wolsey *U.S.A.* **112** C4
Wolstenholme, C. *Canada* **98** C12
Wolsztyn *Poland* **31** F3
Wolvega *Neths.* **17** B6
Wolverhampton *U.K.* **15** E5
Wondai *Australia* **95** D5
Wongalarroo L. *Australia* **95** E3
Wongan Hills *Australia* **93** F2
Wonju *S. Korea* **57** F14
Wonosari *Indonesia* **63** G14
Wonosobo *Indonesia* **63** G13
Wonowon *Canada* **102** B4
Wŏnsan *N. Korea* **57** E14
Wonthaggi *Australia* **95** F4
Wood Buffalo △ *Canada* **102** B6
Wood Is. *Australia* **92** C3
Wood L. *Canada* **103** B8
Woodah, I. *Australia* **94** A2
Woodbourne *U.S.A.* **115** E10
Woodbridge *Canada* **114** C5
Woodbridge *U.K.* **15** E9
Woodburn *Australia* **95** A5
Woodburn *U.S.A.* **108** D2
Woodenbong *Australia* **95** D5
Woodend *Australia* **95** F3
Woodford *Australia* **95** D5
Woodfords *U.S.A.* **110** G7
Woodlake *U.S.A.* **110** J7
Woodland *Calif., U.S.A.* **110** G5
Woodland *Maine, U.S.A.* **113** C20
Woodland *Pa., U.S.A.* **114** F6
Woodland *Wash., U.S.A.* **110** E4
Woodland Caribou △
  Canada **103** C10
Woodlands *Singapore* **65** d
Woodlands, The *U.S.A.* **116** F7
Woodonga *Australia* **95** F4
Woodridge *Canada* **103** D9
Woodroffe, Mt. *Australia* **93** E5
Woods, L. *Australia* **94** B1
Woods, L. of the *Canada* **103** D10
Woods, L. of the *U.S.A.* **107** F21
Woods Bay *Canada* **114** A5
Woodstock *Australia* **94** B4
Woodstock *N.B., Canada* **105** C6
Woodstock *Ont., Canada* **114** C4
Woodstock *U.K.* **15** F6
Woodstock *Ill., U.S.A.* **112** D9
Woodstock *N.Y., U.S.A.* **115** D10
Woodstock *Vt., U.S.A.* **115** C12
Woodsville *U.S.A.* **115** B13
Woodville *N.Z.* **91** D5
Woodville *Miss., U.S.A.* **116** F9
Woodville *Tex., U.S.A.* **116** F7
Woodward *U.S.A.* **116** C5
Woody *U.S.A.* **111** K8
Woody → *Canada* **103** C8

Woolacombe *U.K.* **15** F3
Woolamai, C. *Australia* **95** F4
Wooler *U.K.* **14** B5
Woolgoolga *Australia* **95** E5
Woomera *Australia* **95** E2
Woonsocket *R.I., U.S.A.* **115** E13
Woonsocket *S. Dak., U.S.A.* **112** C4
Wooramel → *Australia* **93** E1
Wooramel Roadhouse
  Australia **93** E1
Wooroonooran △ *Australia* **94** B4
Wooster *U.S.A.* **114** F3
Worcester *S. Africa* **88** E2
Worcester *U.K.* **15** E5
Worcester *Mass., U.S.A.* **115** D13
Worcester *N.Y., U.S.A.* **115** D10
Worcestershire □ *U.K.* **15** E5
Wörgl *Austria* **26** D5
Workington *U.K.* **14** C4
Worksop *U.K.* **14** D6
Workum *Neths.* **17** B5
Worland *U.S.A.* **108** D10
Wormhout *France* **19** B9
Worms *Germany* **25** F4
Worsley *Canada* **102** B5
Wörth *Germany* **25** F8
Wortham *U.S.A.* **116** F6
Wörther See *Austria* **26** E7
Worthing *Barbados* **121** g
Worthing *U.K.* **15** G7
Worthington *Minn., U.S.A.* **112** D6
Worthington *Pa., U.S.A.* **114** F5
Wosi *Indonesia* **63** E7
Wote *Kenya* **86** C4
Wotjalum ☼ *Australia* **92** C3
Wotjobaluk ☼ *Australia* **95** C3
Wou-han = Wuhan *China* **59** B10
Wousi = Wuxi *China* **59** B13
Wowoni *Indonesia* **63** E6
Wrangel I. = Vrangelya,
  Ostrov *Russia* **53** B18
Wrangell *U.S.A.* **102** B2
Wrangell Mts. *U.S.A.* **100** E3
Wrath, C. *U.K.* **13** C3
Wray *U.S.A.* **108** F12
Wrekin, The *U.K.* **15** E5
Wrens *U.S.A.* **117** E13
Wrexham *U.K.* **14** D4
Wrexham □ *U.K.* **14** D5
Wriezen *Germany* **24** C10
Wright = Paranas *Phil.* **61** F6
Wright *Fla., U.S.A.* **117** F11
Wright *Wyo., U.S.A.* **108** E11
Wright Pt. *Canada* **114** C3
Wrightson, Mt. *U.S.A.* **109** L8
Wrightwood *U.S.A.* **111** L9
Wrigley *Canada* **100** E7
Wrocław *Poland* **31** G4
Wronki *Poland* **31** F3
Września *Poland* **31** F4
Wschowa *Poland* **31** G3
Wu Jiang → *China* **58** C6
Wu'an *China* **56** F8
Wubalawun ☼ *Australia* **92** C5
Wubin *Australia* **93** F2
Wubu *China* **56** F6
Wuchang *China* **57** B14
Wucheng *China* **56** F9
Wuchuan *Guangdong, China* **59** G8
Wuchuan *Guizhou, China* **58** C7
Wuchuan
  Nei Monggol Zizhiqu, China **56** D6
Wudi *China* **57** F9
Wuding *China* **58** E4
Wuding He → *China* **56** F6
Wudinna *Australia* **95** E2
Wudu *China* **56** H3
Wufeng *China* **59** B8
Wugang *China* **59** D8
Wugong China Shan *China* **59** D9
Wugullar = Beswick
  Australia **92** B5
Wuhan *China* **59** B10
Wuhe *China* **57** H9
Wuhsi = Wuxi *China* **59** B13
Wuhu *China* **59** B12
Wujiang *China* **59** B13
Wukari *Nigeria* **83** D6
Wulajie *China* **57** B14
Wulanbulang *China* **56** D6
Wular L. *India* **69** B6
Wulehe *Ghana* **83** D5
Wulian *China* **57** G10
Wuliang Shan *China* **58** E3
Wuliaru *Indonesia* **63** F8
Wuling Shan *China* **58** C7
Wulong *China* **58** C6
Wulumuchi = Ürümqi *China* **52** E9
Wum *Cameroon* **83** D7
Wuming *China* **58** F7
Wun Rog *Sudan* **81** F2
Wundanyi *Kenya* **86** C4
Wuning *China* **59** C10
Wunnummin L. *Canada* **104** B2
Wunsiedel *Germany* **25** E8
Wuntho *Burma* **67** H19
Wupatki ☼ *U.S.A.* **109** J8
Wuping *China* **59** E11
Wuppertal *Germany* **24** D3

Wuppertal *S. Africa* **88** E2
Wuqing *China* **57** E9
Wurralibi ☼ *Australia* **94** B2
Wurtsboro *U.S.A.* **115** E10
Würzburg *Germany* **25** F5
Wurzen *Germany* **24** D8
Wushan *China* **56** G3
Wushishi *Nigeria* **83** D6
Wutach → *Germany* **25** H4
Wutai *China* **56** E7
Wuting = Huimin *China* **57** F9
Wutong *China* **59** E8
Wutonghaolai *China* **57** C11
Wutongqiao *China* **58** C4
Wuwei *Anhui, China* **59** B11
Wuwei *Gansu, China* **60** C5
Wuxi *Jiangsu, China* **59** B13
Wuxi *Sichuan, China* **58** B7
Wuxiang *China* **56** F7
Wuxuan *China* **58** F7
Wuxue *China* **59** C10
Wuyang *China* **56** H7
Wuyi *Hebei, China* **56** F8
Wuyi *Zhejiang, China* **59** C12
Wuyi Shan *China* **59** D11
Wuyishan *China* **59** D12
Wuyo *Nigeria* **83** C7
Wuyuan *Jiangxi, China* **59** C11
Wuyuan
  Nei Monggol Zizhiqu, China **56** D5
Wuzhai *China* **56** E6
Wuzhi Shan *China* **64** C7
Wuzhong *China* **56** E4
Wuzhou *China* **59** F8
Wyaaba Cr. → *Australia* **94** B3
Wyalkatchem *Australia* **93** F2
Wyalusing *U.S.A.* **115** E8
Wyandotte *U.S.A.* **113** D12
Wyandra *Australia* **95** D4
Wyangala, L. *Australia* **95** E4
Wyara, L. *Australia* **95** D3
Wycheproof *Australia* **95** F3
Wycliffe Well *Australia* **94** C1
Wye → *U.K.* **15** F5
Wyemandoo *Australia* **93** E2
Wyk *Germany* **24** A4
Wymondham *U.K.* **15** E9
Wymore *U.S.A.* **112** E5
Wyndham *Australia* **92** C4
Wyndham *N.Z.* **91** G2
Wynne *U.S.A.* **117** D9
Wynyard *Australia* **95** G4
Wynyard *Canada* **103** C8
Wyola L. *Australia* **93** E5
Wyoming *Canada* **114** D2
Wyoming □ *U.S.A.* **108** E10
Wyomissing *U.S.A.* **115** F9
Wyong *Australia* **95** E5
Wyrzysk *Poland* **31** E4
Wysoka *Poland* **31** E4
Wysokie *Poland* **31** H9
Wysokie Mazowieckie
  Poland **31** F9
Wyszków *Poland* **31** F8
Wyszogród *Poland* **31** F7
Wytheville *U.S.A.* **113** G13
Wyżyna Małopolska *Poland* **31** H7

X

Xaafuun *Somali Rep.* **75** E5
Xaafuun, Ras *Somali Rep.* **75** E5
Xaçmaz *Azerbaijan* **35** K9
Xai-Xai *Mozam.* **89** D5
Xainza *China* **60** C3
Xalapa *Mexico* **119** D5
Xallas → *Spain* **36** C1
Xangongo *Angola* **88** B2
Xankändi *Azerbaijan* **73** C12
Xanlar *Azerbaijan* **35** K8
Xanten *Germany* **24** D2
Xanthi *Greece* **45** E8
Xanthi □ *Greece* **45** E8
Xanthos *Turkey* **47** E11
Xanxerê *Brazil* **127** B5
Xapuri *Brazil* **124** F5
Xar Moron He → *China* **57** C11
Xarrê *Albania* **44** G4
Xátiva *Spain* **39** G4
Xau, L. *Botswana* **88** C3
Xavantina *Brazil* **127** A5
Xenia *U.S.A.* **113** F12
Xeropotamos → *Cyprus* **49** E11
Xertigny *France* **19** D13
Xhora *S. Africa* **89** E4
Xhumo *Botswana* **88** C3
Xi Jiang → *China* **59** F9
Xi Xian *Henan, China* **59** A10
Xi Xian *Shanxi, China* **56** F6
Xia Xian *China* **56** G6
Xiachengzi *China* **57** B16
Xiachuan Dao *China* **59** G9
Xiaguan *China* **60** D3
Xiajiang *China* **59** D10
Xiajin *China* **56** F9
Xiamen *China* **59** E12
Xi'an *China* **56** G5
Xian Xian *China* **56** E9
Xianfeng *China* **58** C7

Xiang Jiang → *China* **59** C9
Xiangcheng *Henan, China* **56** H8
Xiangcheng *Henan, China* **56** H7
Xiangcheng *Sichuan, China* **58** C2
Xiangdu *China* **58** F6
Xiangfan *China* **59** A9
Xianggang = Hong
  Kong □ *China* **59** F10
Xianghuang Qi *China* **56** C7
Xiangning *China* **56** G6
Xiangquan *China* **56** F7
Xiangquan He = Sutlej →
  Pakistan **68** E3
Xiangshan *China* **59** C13
Xiangshui *China* **57** G10
Xiangtan *China* **59** D9
Xiangxiang *China* **59** D9
Xiangyin *China* **59** C9
Xiangyun *China* **58** E3
Xiangzhou *China* **58** F7
Xianju *China* **59** C13
Xianning *China* **59** C10
Xianshui He → *China* **58** B3
Xiantao *China* **59** B9
Xianyang *China* **56** G5
Xianyou *China* **59** E12
Xiao Hinggan Ling *China* **60** B7
Xiao Xian *China* **56** G9
Xiaofeng *China* **59** B12
Xiaogan *China* **59** B9
Xiaojin *China* **58** B4
Xiaolan *China* **59** F9
Xiaoshan *China* **59** B13
Xiaoyi *China* **56** F6
Xiapu *China* **59** D12
Xiawa *China* **57** C11
Xiayi *China* **56** G9
Xichang *China* **58** D4
Xichong *China* **58** B5
Xichou *China* **58** E5
Xichuan *China* **56** H6
Xide *China* **58** C4
Xiemahe *China* **59** B8
Xieng Khouang *Laos* **64** C4
Xifei He → *China* **56** H9
Xifeng *Gansu, China* **56** G4
Xifeng *Guizhou, China* **58** D6
Xifeng *Liaoning, China* **57** C13
Xifengzhen = Xifeng *China* **56** G4
Xigazê *China* **60** D3
Xihe *China* **56** G3
Xihua *China* **56** H8
Xilaganj *Greece* **45** F9
Xiliao He → *China* **57** C12
Xilin *China* **58** E5
Xilinhot *China* **56** C9
Xilokastro *Greece* **46** C4
Ximana *Mozam.* **87** F3
Xime *Guinea-Biss.* **82** C2
Ximeng *China* **58** F2
Xin Jiang → *China* **59** C11
Xin Xian = Xinzhou *China* **56** E7
Xinavane *Mozam.* **89** D5
Xinbin *China* **57** D13
Xincai *China* **59** A10
Xinchang *China* **59** C13
Xincheng *Guangxi Zhuangzu,*
  China **58** E7
Xincheng *Jiangxi, China* **59** D10
Xincun *China* **57** E9
Xindu *China* **58** B5
Xinfeng *Guangdong, China* **59** E10
Xinfeng *Jiangxi, China* **59** D11
Xinfeng *Jiangxi, China* **59** D10
Xinfengjiang Shuiku *China* **59** F10
Xing Xian *China* **56** E6
Xing'an *Guangxi Zhuangzu,*
  China **59** E8
Xingan *Jiangxi, China* **59** D10
Xingcheng *China* **57** D11
Xingguo *China* **59** D10
Xinghe *China* **56** D7
Xinghua *China* **57** H10
Xinghua Wan *China* **59** E12
Xinglong *China* **57** D9
Xingning *China* **59** E10
Xingping *China* **56** G5
Xingren *China* **58** E5
Xingshan *China* **59** B8
Xingtai *China* **56** F8
Xingu → *Brazil* **125** D8
Xingwen *China* **58** C5
Xingyang *China* **56** G7
Xinhe *China* **56** F8
Xinhua *China* **59** D8
Xinhuang *China* **58** D7
Xinhui *China* **59** F9
Xining *China* **60** C5
Xinjian *China* **59** C10
Xinjiang *China* **56** G6
Xinjiang Uygur Zizhiqu □
  China **60** B3
Xinjie *China* **58** D3
Xinjin = Pulandian *China* **57** E11
Xinjin *China* **58** B4
Xinkai He → *China* **57** C12
Xinle *China* **56** E8
Xinlitun *China* **57** D12
Xinlong *China* **58** B3
Xinmin *China* **57** D12

Xinning *China* **59** D8
Xinping *China* **58** E3
Xinshao *China* **59** D8
Xintai *China* **57** G9
Xintian *China* **59** E9
Xinxian *China* **59** B10
Xinxiang *China* **56** G7
Xinxing *China* **59** F9
Xinyang *China* **59** A10
Xinye *China* **59** A9
Xinyi *China* **59** F8
Xinyu *China* **59** D10
Xinzhan *China* **57** C14
Xinzheng *China* **56** G7
Xinzhou *Hainan, China* **64** C7
Xinzhou *Hubei, China* **59** B10
Xinzhou *Shanxi, China* **56** E7
Xinzo de Limia *Spain* **36** C3
Xiongyuecheng *China* **57** D12
Xiping *Henan, China* **56** H8
Xiping *Henan, China* **56** H6
Xiping *Zhejiang, China* **59** C12
Xique-Xique *Brazil* **125** F10
Xisha Qundao = Paracel Is.
  S. China Sea **62** A4
Xishui *Guizhou, China* **58** C6
Xishui *Hubei, China* **59** B10
Xitole *Guinea-Biss.* **82** C2
Xiu Shui → *China* **59** C10
Xiuning *China* **59** C12
Xiuren *China* **59** E8
Xiushan *China* **58** C7
Xiushui *China* **59** C10
Xiuwen *China* **58** D6
Xiuyan *China* **57** D12
Xixabangma Feng *China* **69** E11
Xixia *China* **56** H6
Xixiang *China* **56** H4
Xixón = Gijón *Spain* **36** B5
Xiyang *China* **56** F7
Xizang Zizhiqu □ *China* **60** C3
Xlendi *Malta* **49** C1
Xochob *Mexico* **119** D7
Xu Jiang → *China* **59** D11
Xuan Loc *Vietnam* **65** G6
Xuan'en *China* **58** C7
Xuanhan *China* **58** B6
Xuanhua *China* **56** D8
Xuanwei *China* **58** C5
Xuanzhou *China* **59** B12
Xuchang *China* **56** G7
Xudat *Azerbaijan* **35** K9
Xuefeng Shan *China* **59** D8
Xuejiaping *China* **59** B8
Xun Jiang → *China* **59** F8
Xun Xian *China* **56** G8
Xundian *China* **58** E4
Xunwu *China* **59** E10
Xunyang *China* **56** H5
Xunyi *China* **56** G5
Xupu *China* **59** D8
Xúquer → *Spain* **39** G4
Xushui *China* **56** E8
Xuwen *China* **59** G8
Xuyen Moc *Vietnam* **65** G6
Xuyong *China* **58** C5
Xuzhou *China* **57** G9
Xylophagou *Cyprus* **49** E12

Y

Ya Xian = Sanya *China* **64** C7
Yaamba *Australia* **94** C5
Ya'an *China* **58** C4
Yaapeet *Australia* **95** F3
Yabassi *Cameroon* **83** E6
Yabayo *Ivory C.* **82** D3
Yabelo *Ethiopia* **81** G4
Yabelo △ *Ethiopia* **81** F4
Yablanitsa *Bulgaria* **45** C8
Yablonovyy Khrebet *Russia* **53** D12
Yablonovyy Ra. =
  Yablonovyy Khrebet
  Russia **53** D12
Yabluniv *Ukraine* **29** B9
Yablunytsya *Ukraine* **29** B9
Yabrai Shan *China* **56** E2
Yabrūd *Syria* **74** B5
Yabucoa *Puerto Rico* **121** d
Yacambú △ *Venezuela* **121** E6
Yacheng *China* **64** C7
Yacuiba *Bolivia* **126** A3
Yacuma → *Bolivia* **124** F5
Yadgir *India* **66** L10
Yadkin → *U.S.A.* **117** D14
Yadrin *Russia* **34** C8
Yadua *Fiji* **91** a
Yaeyama-Rettō *Japan* **55** M1
Yagaba *Ghana* **83** C4
Yagasa Cluster *Fiji* **91** a
Yağcılar *Turkey* **47** B10
Yagodnoye *Russia* **53** C15
Yahila *Dem. Rep. of the Congo* **86** B1
Yahk *Canada* **102** D5
Yahotyn *Ukraine* **33** G6
Yahuma
  Dem. Rep. of the Congo **84** D4
Yahyalı *Turkey* **72** C6
Yaita *Japan* **55** F9
Yaiza *Canary Is.* **48** F6

Yajiang *China* 58 B3
Yajua *Nigeria* 83 C7
Yakima *U.S.A.* 108 C3
Yakima → *U.S.A.* 108 C4
Yakishiri-Jima *Japan* 54 B10
Yako *Burkina Faso* 82 C4
Yakobi I. *U.S.A.* 102 B1
Yakoruda *Bulgaria* 44 D7
Yakovlevka *Russia* 54 B6
Yaku-Shima *Japan* 55 J5
Yakumo *Japan* 54 C10
Yakutat *U.S.A.* 100 F4
Yakutat B. *U.S.A.* 106 D11
Yakutia = Sakha □ *Russia* 53 C14
Yakutsk *Russia* 53 C13
Yala *Thailand* 65 J3
Yalata *Australia* 93 F5
Yalata ◎ *Australia* 93 F5
Yalboroo *Australia* 94 b
Yale *U.S.A.* 114 C2
Yalgorup △ *Australia* 93 F2
Yalinga *C.A.R.* 84 C4
Yalkabul, Pta. *Mexico* 119 C7
Yalleroi *Australia* 94 C4
Yalobusha → *U.S.A.* 117 E9
Yalong Jiang → *China* 58 D3
Yalova *Turkey* 45 F13
Yalpirakinu ◎ *Australia* 92 D5
Yalpuh, Ozero *Ukraine* 29 E13
Yalta *Ukraine* 33 K8
Yalu Jiang → *China* 57 E13
Yalvaç *Turkey* 72 C4
Yam *Australia* 94 a
Yam Ha Melaḥ = Dead Sea
    Asia 74 D4
Yam Kinneret *Israel* 74 C4
Yamada *Japan* 55 H5
Yamagata *Japan* 54 E10
Yamagata □ *Japan* 54 E10
Yamaguchi *Japan* 55 G5
Yamaguchi □ *Japan* 55 G5
Yamal, Poluostrov *Russia* 52 B8
Yamal Pen. = Yamal,
    Poluostrov *Russia* 52 B8
Yamanashi □ *Japan* 55 G9
Yamato Ridge *Sea of Japan* 54 E7
Yamba *Australia* 95 D5
Yambarran Ra. *Australia* 92 C5
Yambéring *Guinea* 82 C2
Yâmbiô *Sudan* 81 G2
Yambol *Bulgaria* 45 D10
Yamburg *Russia* 52 C8
Yamdena *Indonesia* 63 F8
Yame *Japan* 55 H5
Yamethin *Burma* 67 J20
Yamma Yamma, L. *Australia* 95 D3
Yamoussoukro *Ivory C.* 82 D3
Yampa → *U.S.A.* 108 F9
Yampi Sd. *Australia* 92 C3
Yampil *Moldova* 23 D15
Yampol = Yampil *Moldova* 23 D15
Yamrat *Nigeria* 83 D6
Yamrukchal = Botev
    Bulgaria 45 D8
Yamuna → *India* 69 G9
Yamunanagar *India* 68 D7
Yamzho Yumco *China* 60 D4
Yan *Nigeria* 83 C7
Yana → *Russia* 53 B14
Yanagawa *Japan* 55 H5
Yanai *Japan* 55 H6
Yan'an *China* 56 F5
Yanbian *China* 58 D3
Yanbu 'al Baḥr *Si. Arabia* 70 F3
Yanchang *China* 56 F6
Yancheng *Henan, China* 56 H8
Yancheng *Jiangsu, China* 57 H11
Yanchep *Australia* 93 F2
Yanchi *China* 56 F4
Yanchuan *China* 56 F6
Yanco Cr. → *Australia* 95 F4
Yandeyarra ◎ *Australia* 92 D2
Yandicoogina *Australia* 92 D2
Yandoon *Burma* 67 L19
Yanfeng *China* 58 E3
Yanfolila *Mali* 82 C3
Yang Xian *China* 56 H4
Yang-yang *S. Korea* 57 E15
Yang-Yang *Senegal* 82 B1
Yangambi
    Dem. Rep. of the Congo 86 B1
Yangbi *China* 58 E2
Yangcheng *China* 56 G7
Yangch'ü = Taiyuan *China* 56 F7
Yangchun *China* 59 F8
Yanggao *China* 56 D7
Yanggu *China* 56 F8
Yangjiang *China* 59 G8
Yangliuqing *China* 57 E9
Yangon = Rangoon *Burma* 67 L20
Yangping *China* 59 B8
Yangpingguan *China* 56 H4
Yangquan *China* 56 F7
Yangshan *China* 59 E9
Yangshuo *China* 58 E8
Yangtse = Chang Jiang →
    China 59 B13
Yangtze Kiang = Chang
    Jiang → *China* 59 B13
Yangudi Rassa △ *Ethiopia* 81 E5
Yangxin *China* 59 C10

Yangyuan *China* 56 D8
Yangzhong *China* 59 A12
Yangzhou *China* 59 A12
Yanhe *China* 58 C7
Yanji *China* 57 C15
Yanjin *China* 58 C5
Yanjing *China* 58 C2
Yankari △ *Nigeria* 83 D7
Yankton *U.S.A.* 112 D5
Yankunytjatjara-
    Antakirinja ◎ *Australia* 95 A1
Yanonge
    Dem. Rep. of the Congo 86 B1
Yanqi *China* 60 B3
Yanqing *China* 56 D8
Yanshan *Hebei, China* 57 E9
Yanshan *Jiangxi, China* 59 C11
Yanshan *Yunnan, China* 58 F5
Yanshou *China* 57 B15
Yantai *China* 57 F11
Yantabulla *Australia* 95 D4
Yantarnyy *Russia* 30 D6
Yanting *China* 58 B5
Yantra → *Bulgaria* 45 C9
Yanuca *Fiji* 91 a
Yanwa *China* 58 D2
Yanyuan *China* 58 D3
Yanzhou *China* 56 G9
Yao Noi, Ko *Thailand* 65 a
Yao Xian *China* 56 G5
Yao Yai, Ko *Thailand* 65 a
Yao'an *China* 58 E3
Yaodu *China* 58 A5
Yaowan *China* 57 G10
Yap *Pac. Oc.* 96 G5
Yapei *Ghana* 83 D4
Yapen *Indonesia* 63 E9
Yapen, Selat *Indonesia* 63 E9
Yapero *Indonesia* 63 E9
Yappar → *Australia* 94 B3
Yapuparra ◎ *Australia* 93 E4
Yaqaga *Fiji* 91 a
Yaqui → *Mexico* 118 B2
Yar-Sale *Russia* 52 C8
Yaraka *Australia* 94 C3
Yaransk *Russia* 34 B8
Yarbasan *Turkey* 47 C10
Yardımcı Burnu *Turkey* 47 E12
Yare → *U.K.* 15 E9
Yaremcha *Ukraine* 29 B9
Yarensk *Russia* 52 C5
Yarfa *Si. Arabia* 80 C4
Yarí → *Colombia* 124 D4
Yarkand = Shache *China* 60 C2
Yarker *Canada* 115 B8
Yarkhun → *Pakistan* 69 A5
Yarlung Ziangbo Jiang =
    Brahmaputra → *Asia* 69 H13
Yarmouth *Canada* 105 D6
Yarmūk → *Syria* 74 C4
Yaroslavl *Russia* 32 D10
Yaroslavl □ *Russia* 32 C10
Yarqa, W. → *Egypt* 74 F2
Yarra Yarra Lakes *Australia* 93 E2
Yarram *Australia* 95 F4
Yarraman *Australia* 95 D5
Yarras *Australia* 95 E5
Yarrie *Australia* 92 D3
Yartsevo *Sib., Russia* 53 C10
Yartsevo *Smolensk, Russia* 32 E7
Yarumal *Colombia* 124 B3
Yasawa *Fiji* 91 a
Yasawa Group *Fiji* 91 a
Yaselda *Belarus* 23 B14
Yasen *Ukraine* 29 B9
Yashi *Nigeria* 83 C6
Yashikera *Nigeria* 83 D5
Yashkul *Russia* 35 G7
Yasin *Pakistan* 69 A5
Yasinovataya *Ukraine* 33 H9
Yasinski, L. *Canada* 104 B4
Yasinya *Ukraine* 29 B9
Yasothon *Thailand* 64 E5
Yass *Australia* 95 E4
Yāsūj *Iran* 71 D6
Yatağan *Turkey* 47 D10
Yatakala *Niger* 83 C5
Yates Center *U.S.A.* 112 G6
Yathkyed L. *Canada* 103 A9
Yatsushiro *Japan* 55 H5
Yatta Plateau *Kenya* 86 C4
Yauco *Puerto Rico* 121 d
Yavarí → *Peru* 124 D4
Yávaros *Mexico* 118 B3
Yavatmal *India* 66 J11
Yavne *Israel* 74 D3
Yavoriv *Ukraine* 31 J10
Yavorov = Yavoriv *Ukraine* 31 J10
Yavuzeli *Turkey* 72 D7
Yawatahama *Japan* 55 H6
Yawri B. *S. Leone* 82 D2
Yaxi *China* 58 D6
Yaxian = Sanya *China* 64 C7
Yayladağı *Turkey* 72 E7
Yazd *Iran* 71 D7
Yazd □ *Iran* 71 D7
Yazd-e Khvāst *Iran* 71 D7
Yazıköy *Turkey* 47 E9
Yazman *Pakistan* 68 E4
Yazoo → *U.S.A.* 117 E9

Yazoo City *U.S.A.* 117 E9
Ybbs *Austria* 26 C8
Ybycuí ◇ *Paraguay* 126 B4
Ybytyruzú ◇ *Paraguay* 127 B4
Ye *Burma* 64 E1
Ye Xian *China* 56 H7
Yebyu *Burma* 64 E2
Yecheon *S. Korea* 57 F15
Yecla *Spain* 39 G3
Yécora *Mexico* 118 B3
Yedashe *Burma* 67 K20
Yedintsy = Edineț *Moldova* 29 B12
Yedseram → *Nigeria* 83 C7
Yefremov *Russia* 32 F10
Yeghegnadzor *Armenia* 73 C11
Yegorlyk → *Russia* 35 G5
Yegorlykskaya *Russia* 35 G5
Yegoryevsk *Russia* 32 E10
Yegros *Paraguay* 126 B4
Yehbuah *Indonesia* 63 J17
Yehuda, Midbar *Israel* 74 D4
Yei *Sudan* 81 G3
Yei, Nahr → *Sudan* 81 F3
Yeji *Ghana* 83 D4
Yejmiadzin *Armenia* 35 K7
Yekaterinburg *Russia* 52 D7
Yelabuga *Russia* 34 C11
Yelan *Russia* 34 E6
Yelarbon *Australia* 95 D5
Yelatma *Russia* 34 C5
Yelets *Russia* 33 F10
Yélimané *Mali* 82 B2
Yelizavetgrad =
    Kirovohrad *Ukraine* 33 H7
Yelizovo *Russia* 53 D16
Yell *U.K.* 13 A7
Yell Sd. *U.K.* 13 A7
Yellow = Huang He →
    China 57 F10
Yellow Sea *China* 57 G12
Yellowhead Pass *Canada* 102 C5
Yellowknife *Canada* 102 A6
Yellowknife → *Canada* 102 A6
Yellowstone → *U.S.A.* 108 C12
Yellowstone △ *U.S.A.* 108 D8
Yellowstone L. *U.S.A.* 108 D8
Yelnya *Russia* 32 E7
Yelsk *Belarus* 23 C15
Yelwa *Nigeria* 83 C5
Yemen ■ *Asia* 75 E3
Yen Bai *Vietnam* 58 G5
Yenagoa *Nigeria* 83 E6
Yenakiyeve *Ukraine* 33 H10
Yenakiyevo = Yenakiyeve
    Ukraine 33 H10
Yenangyaung *Burma* 67 J19
Yenbo = Yanbu 'al Baḥr
    Si. Arabia 70 F3
Yenda *Australia* 95 E4
Yende Millimou *Guinea* 82 D2
Yendéré *Burkina Faso* 82 C4
Yendi *Ghana* 83 D4
Yéni *Niger* 83 C5
Yeni Erenköy = Yialousa
    Cyprus 49 D13
Yenice *Ankara, Turkey* 72 C5
Yenice *Aydın, Turkey* 47 D10
Yenice *Çanakkale, Turkey* 47 B9
Yenice *Edirne, Turkey* 45 F10
Yenice → *Turkey* 72 D6
Yenifoça *Turkey* 47 C8
Yenihisar *Turkey* 47 D9
Yeniköy *Bursa, Turkey* 45 F13
Yeniköy *Çanakkale, Turkey* 47 B8
Yeniköy *Kütahya, Turkey* 47 C11
Yenipazar *Turkey* 47 D10
Yenişehir *Turkey* 45 F13
Yenisey → *Russia* 52 B9
Yeniseysk *Russia* 53 D10
Yeniseyskiy Zaliv *Russia* 52 B9
Yenne *France* 21 C9
Yenotayevka *Russia* 35 G8
Yenyuka *Russia* 53 D13
Yeo → *U.K.* 15 G5
Yeo, L. *Australia* 93 E3
Yeo I. *Canada* 114 A3
Yeoju *S. Korea* 57 F14
Yeola *India* 66 J9
Yeong-wol *S. Korea* 57 F15
Yeongcheon *S. Korea* 57 G15
Yeongdeok *S. Korea* 57 F15
Yeongdeungpo *S. Korea* 57 F14
Yeongdong *S. Korea* 57 F14
Yeongju *S. Korea* 57 F15
Yeosu *S. Korea* 57 G14
Yeotmal = Yavatmal *India* 66 J11
Yeovil *U.K.* 15 G5
Yepes *Spain* 36 F7
Yeppoon *Australia* 94 C5
Yerbent *Turkmenistan* 52 F6
Yerbogachen *Russia* 53 C11
Yerevan *Armenia* 35 K7
Yerington *U.S.A.* 108 G4
Yerkesik *Turkey* 47 D10
Yerköy *Turkey* 72 C6
Yermak *Kazakhstan* 52 D8
Yermo *U.S.A.* 111 L10
Yerólakkos *Cyprus* 49 D12

Yeropol *Russia* 53 C17
Yeroskipos *Cyprus* 49 E11
Yershov *Russia* 34 E9
Yerushalayim = Jerusalem
    Israel/West Bank 74 D4
Yerville *France* 18 C7
Yes Tor *U.K.* 15 G4
Yesan *S. Korea* 57 F14
Yeşilhisar *Turkey* 72 C6
Yeşilırmak → *Turkey* 72 B7
Yeşilkent *Turkey* 72 D7
Yeşilköy *Turkey* 45 F12
Yeşilova *Manisa, Turkey* 47 C10
Yeşilova *Muğla, Turkey* 47 D11
Yesnogorsk *Russia* 32 E9
Yeso *U.S.A.* 109 J11
Yessentuki *Russia* 35 H6
Yessey *Russia* 53 C11
Yeste *Spain* 39 G2
Yetman *Australia* 95 D5
Yeu, Î. d' *France* 18 F4
Yevlakh = Yevlax *Azerbaijan* 35 K8
Yevlax *Azerbaijan* 35 K8
Yevpatoriya *Ukraine* 33 K7
Yeya → *Russia* 33 J10
Yeysk *Russia* 33 J10
Yezd = Yazd *Iran* 71 D7
Yezerishche *Belarus* 32 E5
Ygatimi *Paraguay* 127 A4
Yhati *Paraguay* 126 B4
Yhú *Paraguay* 127 B4
Yí → *Uruguay* 126 C4
Yi 'Allaq, G. *Egypt* 74 E2
Yi He → *China* 57 G10
Yi Xian *Anhui, China* 59 C11
Yi Xian *Hebei, China* 56 E8
Yi Xian *Liaoning, China* 57 D11
Yialiás → *Cyprus* 49 D12
Yialousa *Cyprus* 49 D13
Yibin *China* 58 C5
Yichang *China* 59 B8
Yicheng *Henan, China* 59 B9
Yicheng *Shanxi, China* 56 G6
Yichuan *China* 56 F6
Yichun *Heilongjiang, China* 60 B7
Yichun *Jiangxi, China* 59 D10
Yidu *China* 57 F10
Yidun *China* 58 B2
Yifag *Etaiopia* 81 E4
Yifeng *China* 59 C10
Yijun *China* 56 G5
Yıldız Dağları *Turkey* 45 E11
Yıldızeli *Turkey* 72 C7
Yiliang *Yunnan, China* 58 D5
Yiliang *Yunnan, China* 58 E4
Yilong *China* 58 B6
Yimen *China* 58 E4
Yimianpo *China* 57 B15
Yinchuan *China* 56 E4
Yindarlgooda, L. *Australia* 93 F3
Yindjibarndi ◎ *Australia* 92 D2
Ying He → *China* 56 H9
Ying Xian *China* 56 E7
Yingcheng *China* 59 B9
Yingde *China* 59 E9
Yingjiang *China* 58 E1
Yingjing *China* 58 C4
Yingkou *China* 57 D12
Yingshan *Henan, China* 59 B9
Yingshan *Hubei, China* 59 B10
Yingshan *Sichuan, China* 58 B6
Yingshang *China* 59 A11
Yingtan *China* 59 C11
Yingualyalya ◎ *Australia* 92 C4
Yining *China* 52 E9
Yiningarra ◎ *Australia* 92 D4
Yinjiang *China* 58 C7
Yinmabin *Burma* 67 H19
Yioúra = Giaros *Greece* 46 D6
Yipinglang *China* 58 E3
Yirba Muda *Ethiopia* 81 F4
Yirga Alem *Ethiopia* 81 F4
Yirol *Sudan* 81 F3
Yirrkala *Australia* 94 A2
Yishan *China* 58 E7
Yishui *China* 57 G10
Yishun *Singapore* 65 d
Yitong *China* 57 C13
Yiwu *China* 59 C13
Yixing *China* 59 B12
Yiyang *Henan, China* 56 G7
Yiyang *Hunan, China* 59 C9
Yiyang *Jiangxi, China* 59 C11
Yizhang *China* 59 E9
Yizheng *China* 59 A12
Yli-Kitka *Finland* 8 C23
Yliki, L. *Greece* 46 C5
Ylitornio *Finland* 8 C20
Ylivieska *Finland* 8 D21
Yngaren *Sweden* 11 F10
Yoakum *U.S.A.* 116 G6
Yob △ *Eritrea* 81 D4
Yobe □ *Nigeria* 83 C7
Yoboki *Djibouti* 81 E5
Yog Pt. *Phil.* 63 B6
Yoğuntaş *Turkey* 45 E11
Yogyakarta *Indonesia* 62 F4
Yogyakarta □ *Indonesia* 63 G14
Yoho △ *Canada* 102 C5

Yojoa, L. de *Honduras* 120 D2
Yok Don △ *Vietnam* 64 F6
Yokadouma *Cameroon* 84 D2
Yokkaichi *Japan* 55 G8
Yoko *Cameroon* 83 D7
Yokohama *Japan* 55 G9
Yokosuka *Japan* 55 G9
Yokote *Japan* 54 E10
Yola *Nigeria* 83 D7
Yolaina, Cordillera de *Nic.* 120 D3
Yólöten *Turkmenistan* 71 B9
Yom → *Thailand* 64 E3
Yonago *Japan* 55 G6
Yonaguni-Jima *Japan* 55 M1
Yŏnan *N. Korea* 57 F14
Yonezawa *Japan* 54 F10
Yong Peng *Malaysia* 65 M4
Yong Sata *Thailand* 65 J2
Yongamp'o *N. Korea* 57 E13
Yong'an *China* 59 E11
Yongcheng *China* 56 H9
Yongchuan *China* 58 C5
Yongchun *China* 59 E12
Yongde *China* 58 E2
Yongdeng *China* 56 F2
Yongding *China* 59 E11
Yongfeng *China* 59 D10
Yongfu *China* 58 E7
Yonghe *China* 56 F6
Yŏnghŭng *N. Korea* 57 E14
Yongji *China* 56 G6
Yongjia *China* 59 C13
Yongkang *Yunnan, China* 58 E2
Yongkang *Zhejiang, China* 59 C13
Yongnian *China* 56 F8
Yongning *Guangxi Zhuangzu,*
    China 58 F7
Yongning *Ningxia Huizu,*
    China 56 E4
Yongping *China* 58 E2
Yongqing *China* 56 E9
Yongren *China* 58 D3
Yongshan *China* 58 C4
Yongsheng *China* 58 D3
Yongshun *China* 58 C7
Yongtai *China* 59 E12
Yongxin = Jinggangshan
    China 59 D10
Yongxing *China* 59 D9
Yongxiu *China* 59 C10
Yongzhou *China* 59 D8
Yonibana *S. Leone* 82 D2
Yonkers *U.S.A.* 115 F11
Yonne □ *France* 19 E10
Yonne → *France* 19 D9
York *Australia* 93 F2
York *U.K.* 14 D6
York *Ala., U.S.A.* 117 E10
York *Nebr., U.S.A.* 112 E5
York *Pa., U.S.A.* 113 F15
York, C. *Australia* 94 A3
York, City of □ *U.K.* 14 D6
York, Kap *Greenland* 101 B18
York, Vale of *U.K.* 14 C6
York Sd. *Australia* 92 C4
Yorke Pen. *Australia* 95 E2
Yorkshire Dales △ *U.K.* 14 C5
Yorkshire Wolds *U.K.* 14 C7
Yorkton *Canada* 103 C8
Yorkville *U.S.A.* 110 G3
Yoro *Honduras* 120 C2
Yoron-Jima *Japan* 55 L4
Yorosso *Mali* 82 C3
Yos Sudarso, Pulau =
    Dolak, Pulau *Indonesia* 63 F9
Yosemite △ *U.S.A.* 110 H7
Yosemite Village *U.S.A.* 110 H7
Yoshino-Kumano △ *Japan* 55 H8
Yoshkar Ola *Russia* 34 B8
Yotvata *Israel* 74 F4
You Jiang → *China* 58 F6
You Xian *China* 59 D9
Youbou *Canada* 110 B2
Youghal *Ireland* 12 E4
Youghal B. *Ireland* 12 E4
Youkounkoun *Guinea* 82 C2
Young *Australia* 95 E4
Young *Canada* 103 C7
Young *Uruguay* 126 C4
Young I. *Antarctica* 5 C11
Younghusband, L. *Australia* 95 E2
Younghusband Pen.
    Australia 95 F2
Youngstown *Canada* 103 C6
Youngstown *N.Y., U.S.A.* 114 C5
Youngstown *Ohio, U.S.A.* 114 E4
Youngsville *U.S.A.* 114 E5
Youngwood *U.S.A.* 114 F5
Youxi *China* 59 D12
Youyang *China* 58 C7
Youyu *China* 56 D7
Yozgat *Turkey* 72 C6
Yozgat □ *Turkey* 72 C6
Ypacaraí ◇ *Paraguay* 126 B4
Ypané → *Paraguay* 126 A4
Ypres = Ieper *Belgium* 17 D2
Ypsonas *Cyprus* 49 E11
Yreka *U.S.A.* 108 F2
Yssingeaux *France* 21 C8
Ystad *Sweden* 11 J7
Ysyk-Köl *Kyrgyzstan* 52 E8

Ythan → *U.K.* 13 D7
Ytterhogdal *Sweden* 10 B8
Ytyk-Kyuyel *Russia* 53 C14
Yu Jiang → *China* 58 F7
Yü Shan *Taiwan* 59 F13
Yu Xian = Yuzhou *China* 56 G7
Yu Xian *Hebei, China* 56 E8
Yu Xian *Shanxi, China* 56 E7
Yuan Jiang → *Hunan, China* 59 C8
Yuan Jiang → *Yunnan, China* 58 F4
Yuan'an *China* 59 B8
Yuanjiang *Hunan, China* 59 C9
Yuanjiang *Yunnan, China* 58 F4
Yüanli *Taiwan* 59 E13
Yüanlin *Taiwan* 59 F13
Yuanling *China* 59 C8
Yuanqu *China* 56 G6
Yuanyang *Henan, China* 56 G7
Yuanyang *Yunnan, China* 58 F4
Yuba → *U.S.A.* 110 F5
Yuba City *U.S.A.* 110 F5
Yūbari *Japan* 54 C10
Yubdo *Ethiopia* 81 F4
Yūbetsu *Japan* 54 B11
Yubo *Sudan* 81 F2
Yucatán □ *Mexico* 119 C7
Yucatán, Canal de *Caribbean* 120 B2
Yucatán, Península de
    Mexico 98 H11
Yucatan Basin *Cent. Amer.* 119 D7
Yucatan Channel =
    Yucatán, Canal de
    Caribbean 120 B2
Yucca *U.S.A.* 111 L12
Yucca Valley *U.S.A.* 111 L10
Yucheng *China* 56 F9
Yuci = Jinzhong *China* 56 F7
Yudu *China* 59 E10
Yuechi *China* 58 B6
Yuendumu *Australia* 92 D5
Yuendumu ◎ *Australia* 92 D5
Yueqing *China* 59 C13
Yueqing Wan *China* 59 D13
Yuexi *Anhui, China* 59 B11
Yuexi *Sichuan, China* 58 C4
Yueyang *China* 59 C9
Yugan *China* 59 C11
Yugorenok *Russia* 53 D14
Yuhuan *China* 59 C13
Yúhuan Dao *China* 59 C13
Yujiang *China* 59 C11
Yukhnov *Russia* 32 E8
Yukon *U.S.A.* 116 D6
Yukon → *U.S.A.* 106 C7
Yukon Flats *U.S.A.* 106 B10
Yukon Territory □ *Canada* 100 E5
Yüksekova *Turkey* 73 D11
Yukta *Russia* 53 C11
Yukuhashi *Japan* 55 H5
Yulara *Australia* 93 E5
Yule → *Australia* 92 D2
Yüli *Taiwan* 59 F13
Yulin *Guangxi Zhuangzu, China* 59 F8
Yulin *Hainan, China* 64 C7
Yulin *Shaanxi, China* 56 E5
Yuma *Ariz., U.S.A.* 111 N12
Yuma *Colo., U.S.A.* 108 F12
Yuma, B. de *Dom. Rep.* 121 C6
Yumbe *Uganda* 86 B3
Yumbi *Dem. Rep. of the Congo* 86 C2
Yumen *China* 60 C4
Yumurtalık *Turkey* 72 D6
Yun Gui Gaoyuan *China* 58 E3
Yun Ling *China* 58 D2
Yun Xian *Hubei, China* 59 A8
Yun Xian *Yunnan, China* 58 E3
Yuna *Australia* 93 E2
Yunak *Turkey* 72 C4
Yunan *China* 59 F8
Yuncheng *Henan, China* 56 G8
Yuncheng *Shanxi, China* 56 G6
Yunfu *China* 59 F9
Yungas *Bolivia* 124 G5
Yungay *Chile* 126 D1
Yunhe *China* 59 C12
Yunkai Dashan *China* 59 F8
Yunkanjini ◎ *Australia* 92 D5
Yunlong *China* 58 E2
Yunmeng *China* 59 B9
Yunnan □ *China* 58 E4
Yunquera de Henares *Spain* 38 E1
Yunt Dağı *Turkey* 47 C9
Yunta *Australia* 95 E2
Yunxi *China* 59 H6
Yunxiao *China* 59 F11
Yupanqui Basin *Pac. Oc.* 97 J17
Yuping *China* 58 D6
Yurayagir △ *Australia* 95 D5
Yurga *Russia* 52 D9
Yurimaguas *Peru* 124 E3
Yurkivka *Ukraine* 29 B13
Yurubí △ *Venezuela* 121 D6
Yuryev-Polskiy *Russia* 32 D10
Yuryevets *Russia* 34 B6
Yuscarán *Honduras* 120 D2
Yûsef, Bahr → *Egypt* 80 B3
Yushan *China* 59 C12

Yushanzhen *China* 58 C7
Yushe *China* 56 F7
Yushu *Jilin, China* 57 B14
Yushu *Qinghai, China* 60 C4
Yusufeli *Turkey* 73 B9
Yutai *China* 56 G9
Yutian *China* 57 E9
Yuxarı Qarabağ = Nagorno-Karabakh □ *Azerbaijan* 73 C12
Yuxi *China* 58 E4
Yuyao *China* 59 B13
Yuzawa *Japan* 54 E10
Yuzha *Russia* 34 B6
Yuzhno-Kurilsk *Russia* 53 E15
Yuzhno-Sakhalinsk *Russia* 53 E15
Yuzhno-Sukhokumsk *Russia* 35 H7
Yuzhnyy □ *Russia* 35 H5
Yuzhou *China* 56 G7
Yvelines □ *France* 19 D8
Yverdon-les-Bains *Switz.* 25 J2
Yvetot *France* 18 C7
Yzeure *France* 19 F10

Z

Zaanstad *Neths.* 17 B4
Záb al Kabīr → *Iraq* 73 D10
Záb aş Şaghīr → *Iraq* 73 E10
Žabalj *Serbia* 28 E5
Žabari *Serbia* 44 B5
Zabarjad *Egypt* 80 C4
Zabki *Poland* 31 F8
Ząbkowice Śląskie *Poland* 31 H3
Zabłudów *Poland* 31 F9
Żabno *Poland* 31 H7
Zabol *Iran* 71 D9
Zābol □ *Afghan.* 66 D5
Zāboli *Iran* 71 E9
Zabolotiv *Ukraine* 29 B10
Zabolottya *Ukraine* 31 G11
Zabré *Burkina Faso* 83 C4
Zábřeh *Czech Rep.* 27 B9
Zabrze *Poland* 31 H5
Zabuzhzhya *Ukraine* 31 G10
Zabzuga *Ghana* 83 D5
Zacapa *Guatemala* 120 D2
Zacapu *Mexico* 118 D4
Zacatecas *Mexico* 118 C4
Zacatecas □ *Mexico* 118 C4
Zacatecoluca *El Salv.* 120 D2
Zacharo *Greece* 46 D3
Zachary *U.S.A.* 116 F9
Zachodnio-Pomorskie □ *Poland* 30 E2
Zacoalco de Torres *Mexico* 118 C4
Zacualtipán *Mexico* 119 C5
Zadar *Croatia* 41 D12
Zadawa *Nigeria* 83 C7
Zadetkyi Kyun *Burma* 65 G2
Zadonsk *Russia* 33 F10
Zafarqand *Iran* 71 C7
Zafra *Spain* 37 G4
Žagań *Poland* 31 G2
Zagaoua *Chad* 79 E10
Žagarė *Lithuania* 30 B10
Zagazig *Egypt* 80 H7
Zāgheh *Iran* 71 C6
Zagnanado *Benin* 83 D5
Zagora *Greece* 46 B5
Zagorje *Slovenia* 41 B11
Zagórów *Poland* 31 F4
Zagórz *Poland* 31 J9
Zagreb *Croatia* 41 C12
Zagreb ✈ (ZAG) *Croatia* 41 C13
Zāgros, Kūhhā-ye *Iran* 71 C6
Zagros Mts. = Zāgros, Kūhhā-ye *Iran* 71 C6
Žagubica *Serbia* 44 B5
Zaguinaso *Ivory C.* 82 C3
Zagyva → *Hungary* 28 C5
Zahamena △ *Madag.* 89 B8
Zāhedān *Fārs, Iran* 71 D7
Zāhedān *Sīstān va Balūchestān, Iran* 71 D9
Zahlah *Lebanon* 74 B4
Zahna *Germany* 24 D8
Záhony *Hungary* 28 B7
Zainsk *Russia* 34 C11
Zaïre = Congo → *Africa* 84 F2
Zaječar *Serbia* 44 C6
Zaka *Zimbabwe* 89 C5
Zakamensk *Russia* 53 D11
Zakarpattya □ *Ukraine* 29 B8
Zakataly = Zaqatala *Azerbaijan* 35 K8
Zakhodnaya Dzvina = Daugava → *Latvia* 32 D3
Zākhū *Iraq* 73 D10
Zakinthos = Zakynthos *Greece* 46 D2
Zakopane *Poland* 31 J6
Zakroczym *Poland* 31 F7
Zakros *Greece* 49 D8
Zakynthos *Greece* 46 D2
Zakynthos ○ *Greece* 46 D2
Zala *Ethiopia* 81 F4
Zala □ *Hungary* 28 D1

Zala → *Hungary* 28 D2
Zalaegerszeg *Hungary* 28 D1
Zalakomár *Hungary* 28 D2
Zalalövö *Hungary* 28 D1
Zalamea de la Serena *Spain* 37 G5
Zalamea la Real *Spain* 37 H4
Zalari *Russia* 53 D11
Zalău *Romania* 28 C8
Žalec *Slovenia* 41 B12
Zaleshchiki = Zalishchyky *Ukraine* 29 B10
Zalesye *Russia* 30 D8
Zalew Wiślany *Poland* 30 D6
Zalewo *Poland* 30 E6
Zalingei *Sudan* 79 F10
Zalishchyky *Ukraine* 29 B10
Zama L. *Canada* 102 B5
Zambeke *Dem. Rep. of the Congo* 86 B2
Zambeze → *Africa* 87 F4
Zambezi = Zambeze → *Africa* 87 F4
Zambezi *Zambia* 85 G4
Zambezi △ *Zimbabwe* 87 F2
Zambézia □ *Mozam.* 87 F4
Zambia ■ *Africa* 87 F2
Zamboanga *Phil.* 61 H5
Zambrów *Poland* 31 F9
Zametchino *Russia* 34 D6
Zamfara □ *Nigeria* 83 C6
Zamfara → *Nigeria* 83 C5
Zamora *Mexico* 118 D4
Zamora *Spain* 36 D5
Zamora □ *Spain* 36 D5
Zamość *Poland* 31 H10
Zamtang *China* 58 A3
Zan *Ghana* 83 D4
Záncara → *Spain* 39 F1
Zandvoort *Neths.* 17 B4
Zanesville *U.S.A.* 114 G2
Zangābād *Iran* 70 B5
Zangliveri *Greece* 44 F7
Zangoza = Sangüesa *Spain* 38 C3
Zangue → *Mozam.* 87 F4
Zanjan *Iran* 73 D13
Zanjan □ *Iran* 71 B6
Zanjan → *Iran* 71 B6
Zannone *Italy* 42 B6
Zante = Zakynthos *Greece* 46 D2
Zanthus *Australia* 93 F3
Zanzibar *Tanzania* 86 D4
Zaouiet El-Kala = Bordj Omar Driss *Algeria* 78 C7
Zaouiet Reggâne *Algeria* 78 C6
Zaoyang *China* 59 A9
Zaozhuang *China* 57 G9
Zap Suyu = Záb al Kabīr → *Iraq* 73 D10
Zapadna Morava → *Serbia* 44 C5
Zapadnaya Dvina = Daugava → *Latvia* 32 D3
Zapadnaya Dvina *Russia* 32 D7
Západné Beskydy *Europe* 27 B12
Zapadni Rodopi *Bulgaria* 44 E7
Západočeský □ *Czech Rep.* 26 B6
Zapala *Argentina* 128 D2
Zapaleri, Cerro *Bolivia* 126 A2
Zapata *U.S.A.* 116 H5
Zapatón → *Spain* 37 F4
Zapolyarnyy *Russia* 8 B24
Zapopán *Mexico* 118 C4
Zaporizhzhya *Ukraine* 33 J8
Zaporizhzhya □ *Ukraine* 33 J8
Zaporozhye = Zaporizhzhya *Ukraine* 33 J8
Zaqatala *Azerbaijan* 35 K8
Zara *Turkey* 72 C7
Zaragoza *Coahuila, Mexico* 118 B4
Zaragoza *Nuevo León, Mexico* 119 C5
Zaragoza *Spain* 38 D4
Zaragoza □ *Spain* 38 D4
Zarand *Kermān, Iran* 71 D8
Zarand *Markazī, Iran* 71 C6
Zărandului, Munţii *Romania* 28 D7
Zaranj *Afghan.* 66 D2
Zarasai *Lithuania* 32 E10
Zárate *Argentina* 126 C4
Zarautz *Spain* 38 B2
Zaraysk *Russia* 32 E10
Zard, Kūh-e *Iran* 71 C6
Zāreh *Iran* 71 C6
Zari *Nigeria* 83 C7
Zaria *Nigeria* 83 C6
Zarineh → *Iran* 73 D12
Žarki *Poland* 31 H6
Zarko *Greece* 46 B4
Zarneh *Iran* 70 C5
Zărneşti *Romania* 29 E10
Zaros *Greece* 49 D6
Żarów *Poland* 31 H3
Zarqā', Nahr az → *Jordan* 74 C4
Zarrīn *Iran* 71 C7
Zarrīnābād *Iran* 73 D13
Zaruma *Ecuador* 124 D3
Żary *Poland* 31 G2
Zarza de Granadilla *Spain* 36 E4
Zarzis *Tunisia* 79 B8
Zas *Spain* 36 B2
Zaskar → *India* 69 B7
Zaskar Mts. *India* 69 C7
Zastavna *Ukraine* 29 B10
Zastron *S. Africa* 88 E4

Žatec *Czech Rep.* 26 A6
Zaterechnyy *Russia* 35 H7
Zator *Poland* 31 J6
Zatyshshya *Ukraine* 29 C14
Zavala *Bos.-H.* 44 D1
Zavāreh *Iran* 71 C7
Zave *Zimbabwe* 89 B5
Zavetnoye *Russia* 35 G6
Zavidovići *Bos.-H.* 28 F3
Zavitinsk *Russia* 53 D13
Zavodovski, I. *Antarctica* 5 B1
Zavolzhsk *Russia* 34 B6
Zavolzhye *Russia* 34 B6
Zawadzkie *Poland* 31 H5
Zawichost *Poland* 31 H8
Zawidów *Poland* 31 G2
Zawiercie *Poland* 31 H6
Zāwiyat al Baydā = Al Baydā *Libya* 79 B10
Zāwyet Shammas *Egypt* 80 A2
Zāwyet Um el Rakham *Egypt* 80 A2
Zāwyet Ungeīla *Egypt* 80 A2
Zāyā *Iraq* 70 C5
Zāyandeh → *Iran* 71 C7
Zaysan *Kazakhstan* 52 E9
Zaysan Köli *Kazakhstan* 52 E9
Zayü *China* 58 C1
Zazafotsy *Madag.* 89 C8
Zázrivá *Slovak Rep.* 27 B12
Zbarazh *Ukraine* 23 D13
Zbąszyń *Poland* 31 F2
Zbąszynek *Poland* 31 F2
Zblewo *Poland* 30 E5
Zbruch → 29 B11
Žďár nad Sázavou *Czech Rep.* 26 B8
Zdolbuniv *Ukraine* 23 C14
Ždrelo *Serbia* 44 B5
Zduńska Wola *Poland* 31 G5
Zduny *Poland* 31 G4
Zeballos *Canada* 102 D3
Zebediela *S. Africa* 89 C4
Zebila *Ghana* 83 C4
Zeebrugge *Belgium* 17 C3
Zeehan *Australia* 95 G4
Zeeland □ *Neths.* 17 C3
Zeerust *S. Africa* 88 D4
Zefat *Israel* 74 C4
Zege *Ethiopia* 81 E4
Zeggerene, Iracher *Mali* 83 B5
Zégoua *Mali* 82 C3
Zehak *Iran* 71 D9
Zehdenick *Germany* 24 C9
Zeil, Mt. *Australia* 92 D5
Zeila = Saylac *Somali Rep.* 75 E3
Zeist *Neths.* 17 B5
Zeitz *Germany* 24 D8
Želechów *Poland* 31 G8
Zelena *Ukraine* 29 B9
Zelengora *Bos.-H.* 44 C2
Zelenodolsk *Russia* 34 C9
Zelenogorsk *Russia* 32 B5
Zelenograd *Russia* 32 D9
Zelenogradsk *Russia* 30 D7
Zelenokumsk *Russia* 35 H6
Železná Ruda *Czech Rep.* 26 B6
Železnik *Serbia* 44 B4
Zelienople *U.S.A.* 114 F4
Želiezovce *Slovak Rep.* 27 C11
Zelina *Croatia* 41 C13
Zell *Baden-W., Germany* 25 H3
Zell *Rhld-Pfz., Germany* 25 E3
Zell am See *Austria* 26 D5
Zella-Mehlis *Germany* 24 E6
Zelów *Poland* 31 G6
Zeltweg *Austria* 26 D7
Žemaitija □ *Lithuania* 30 B8
Zémio *C.A.R.* 86 A2
Zempoala *Mexico* 119 D5
Zemun *Serbia* 44 B4
Zengbé *Cameroon* 83 D7
Zengcheng *China* 59 F9
Zenica *Bos.-H.* 28 F3
Žepče *Bos.-H.* 28 F3
Zeraf, Bahr ez → *Sudan* 81 F3
Zerbst *Germany* 24 D8
Żerków *Poland* 31 F4
Zermatt *Switz.* 25 J3
Zernez *Switz.* 25 J6
Zernograd *Russia* 35 G5
Zerqan *Albania* 44 E4
Zestaponi *Georgia* 35 J6
Zetel *Germany* 24 B3
Zeulenroda *Germany* 24 E7
Zeven *Germany* 24 B5
Zevenaar *Neths.* 17 C6
Zévio *Italy* 40 C8
Zeya *Russia* 53 D13
Zeya → *Russia* 53 D13
Zeytinbaği *Turkey* 45 F12
Zeytindağ *Turkey* 47 C9
Zghartā *Lebanon* 74 A4
Zgierz *Poland* 31 G6
Zgorzelec *Poland* 31 G2
Zgurița *Moldova* 29 B13
Zhabinka *Belarus* 23 B13
Zhabokrych *Ukraine* 29 B13
Zhalpaqtal *Kazakhstan* 34 F9
Zhambyl = Taraz *Kazakhstan* 52 E8

Zhangaly *Kazakhstan* 35 G10
Zhangaqala *Kazakhstan* 35 F9
Zhangaqazaly *Kazakhstan* 52 E7
Zhangbei *China* 56 D8
Zhangguangcai Ling *China* 57 B15
Zhangjiagang *China* 59 B13
Zhangjiakou *China* 56 D8
Zhangping *China* 59 E11
Zhangpu *China* 59 E11
Zhangshu *China* 59 C10
Zhangwu *China* 57 C12
Zhangye *China* 60 C5
Zhangzhou *China* 59 E11
Zhanhua *China* 57 F10
Zhänibek *Kazakhstan* 34 F8
Zhanjiang *China* 59 G8
Zhanyi *China* 58 E4
Zhanyu *China* 57 B12
Zhao Xian *China* 56 F8
Zhao'an *China* 59 F11
Zhaocheng *China* 56 F6
Zhaojue *China* 58 C4
Zhaoping *China* 59 E8
Zhaoqing *China* 59 F9
Zhaotong *China* 58 D4
Zhaoyuan *Heilongjiang, China* 57 B13
Zhaoyuan *Shandong, China* 57 F11
Zharkent *Kazakhstan* 52 E9
Zharkovskiy *Russia* 32 E7
Zhashkiv *Ukraine* 23 D16
Zhashui *China* 56 H5
Zhayylma *Kazakhstan* 52 D7
Zhdanov = Mariupol *Ukraine* 33 J9
Zhecheng *China* 56 G8
Zhegao *China* 59 B11
Zhejiang □ *China* 59 C13
Zheleznodorozhnyy *Russia* 30 D8
Zheleznogorsk *Russia* 33 F8
Zheleznogorsk-Ilimskiy *Russia* 53 D11
Zheltyye Vody = Zhovti Vody *Ukraine* 33 H7
Zhen'an *China* 56 H5
Zhenba *China* 58 A6
Zhenfeng *China* 58 E5
Zheng'an *China* 58 C6
Zhengding *China* 56 E8
Zhenghe *China* 59 D12
Zhengyang *China* 59 A10
Zhengyangguan *China* 59 A11
Zhengzhou *China* 56 G7
Zhenhai *China* 59 C13
Zhenjiang *China* 59 A12
Zhenkang *China* 58 F2
Zhenlai *China* 57 B12
Zhenning *China* 58 D5
Zhenping *Henan, China* 56 H7
Zhenping *Shaanxi, China* 58 B7
Zhenxiong *China* 58 D5
Zhenyuan *Gansu, China* 56 G4
Zhenyuan *Guizhou, China* 58 D7
Zherdevka *Russia* 34 E5
Zherebkove *Ukraine* 29 C14
Zherong *China* 59 D12
Zhetiqara *Kazakhstan* 52 D7
Zhezqazghan *Kazakhstan* 52 E7
Zhicheng *China* 59 B8
Zhidan *China* 56 F5
Zhigansk *Russia* 53 C13
Zhigulevsk *Russia* 34 D9
Zhijiang *Hubei, China* 59 B8
Zhijiang *Hunan, China* 58 D7
Zhijin *China* 58 D5
Zhilinda *Russia* 53 C12
Zhilino *Russia* 30 D8
Zhirnovsk *Russia* 34 E7
Zhitomir = Zhytomyr *Ukraine* 23 C15
Zhizdra *Russia* 32 F8
Zhlobin *Belarus* 23 B16
Zhmerynka *Ukraine* 23 D15
Zhob *Pakistan* 68 D3
Zhob → *Pakistan* 68 C3
Zhodzina *Belarus* 23 A15
Zhongdian *China* 58 D2
Zhongdong *China* 58 F6
Zhongdu *China* 58 E7
Zhongning *China* 56 F3
Zhongshan *Antarctica* 5 C6
Zhongshan *Guangdong, China* 59 F9
Zhongshan *Guangxi Zhuangzu, China* 59 E8
Zhongtiao Shan *China* 56 G6
Zhongwei *China* 56 F3
Zhongxiang *China* 59 B9
Zhongyang *China* 56 F6
Zhoranny *Ukraine* 31 G10
Zhosaly *Kazakhstan* 52 E7
Zhoucun *China* 57 F9
Zhouning *China* 59 D12
Zhoushan *China* 59 B14
Zhoushan Dao *China* 59 C14
Zhouzhi *China* 56 G5
Zhovti Vody *Ukraine* 33 H7
Zhovtneve *Lubelskie, Ukraine* 31 H11
Zhovtneve *Mykolayiv, Ukraine* 33 J7
Zhu Jiang → *China* 59 F9

Zhuanghe *China* 57 E12
Zhucheng *China* 57 G10
Zhugqu *China* 56 H3
Zhuhai *China* 59 F9
Zhuji *China* 59 C13
Zhukovka *Russia* 32 F7
Zhumadian *China* 56 H8
Zhuo Xian = Zhuozhou *China* 56 E8
Zhuolu *China* 56 D8
Zhuozhou *China* 56 E8
Zhuozi *China* 56 D7
Zhushan *China* 59 A8
Zhuxi *China* 58 A7
Zhuzhou *China* 59 D9
Zhvanets *Ukraine* 29 B11
Zhytomyr *Ukraine* 23 C15
Zhytomyr □ *Ukraine* 33 G5
Zi Shui → *China* 59 C9
Žiar nad Hronom *Slovak Rep.* 27 C11
Ziarat *Pakistan* 68 D2
Zibo *China* 57 F10
Zichang *China* 56 F5
Zidarovo *Bulgaria* 45 D11
Zidi = Wandhari *Pakistan* 68 F2
Zigey *Burkina Faso* 83 C4
Zigong *China* 58 C5
Ziguéy *Chad* 79 F9
Ziguinchor *Senegal* 82 C1
Ziguinchor □ *Senegal* 82 C1
Zihuatanejo *Mexico* 118 D4
Zijin *China* 59 F10
Zile *Turkey* 72 B6
Zilina *Slovak Rep.* 27 B11
Žilinský □ *Slovak Rep.* 27 B12
Zillah *Libya* 79 C9
Zillertaler Alpen *Austria* 26 D4
Zima *Russia* 53 D11
Zimapán *Mexico* 119 C5
Zimba *Zambia* 87 F2
Zimbabwe *Zimbabwe* 87 G3
Zimbabwe ■ *Africa* 87 F3
Zimmi *S. Leone* 82 D2
Zimnicea *Romania* 29 G10
Zimovniki *Russia* 35 G6
Zinave △ *Mozam.* 89 C5
Zinder *Niger* 83 C6
Zinder □ *Niger* 83 C7
Zinga *Tanzania* 87 D4
Zingaro △ *Italy* 42 D5
Zingst *Germany* 24 A8
Ziniaré *Burkina Faso* 83 C4
Zinnowitz *Germany* 24 A9
Zion △ *U.S.A.* 109 H7
Zirbitzkogel *Austria* 26 D7
Zirc *Hungary* 28 C2
Žiri *Slovenia* 41 B11
Žirje *Croatia* 41 E12
Zirl *Austria* 26 D4
Zirndorf *Germany* 25 F6
Ziros *Greece* 49 D8
Zirreh, Gowd-e *Afghan.* 66 E3
Zisterdorf *Austria* 27 C9
Zitácuaro *Mexico* 118 D4
Žitava → *Slovak Rep.* 27 C11
Žitište *Serbia* 28 E5
Zitong *China* 58 B5
Zitsa *Greece* 46 B2
Zittau *Germany* 24 E10
Zitundo *Mozam.* 89 D5
Ziwa Magharibi = Kagera □ *Tanzania* 86 C3
Ziway *Ethiopia* 81 F4
Ziway, L. *Ethiopia* 81 F4
Zixi *China* 59 D11
Zixing *China* 59 E9
Ziyang *Shaanxi, China* 56 H5
Ziyang *Sichuan, China* 58 B5
Ziyuan *China* 59 D8
Ziyun *China* 58 E6
Zizhong *China* 58 C5
Zizur Mayor *Spain* 38 C3
Zlarin *Croatia* 41 E12
Zlatar *Croatia* 41 B13
Zlatar *Serbia* 44 C3
Zlaté Moravce *Slovak Rep.* 27 C11
Zlatibor *Serbia* 44 C3
Zlatitsa *Bulgaria* 45 D8
Zlatna *Romania* 29 D8
Zlatna Panega *Bulgaria* 45 C8
Zlatni Pyasŭtsi *Bulgaria* 45 C12
Zlatograd *Bulgaria* 45 E9
Zlatoust *Russia* 52 D6
Zletovo *Macedonia* 44 E6
Zlín *Czech Rep.* 27 B10
Zlínský □ *Czech Rep.* 27 B10
Złocieniec *Poland* 30 E3
Złoczew *Poland* 31 G5
Zlot *Serbia* 44 B5
Złotoryja *Poland* 31 G2
Złotów *Poland* 30 E4
Zmeinogorsk *Kazakhstan* 52 D9
Žmigród *Poland* 31 G3
Zmiyev *Ukraine* 33 H9

Znamenka = Znamyanka *Ukraine* 33 H7
Znamensk *Russia* 30 D8
Znamyanka *Ukraine* 33 H7
Žnin *Poland* 31 F4
Znojmo *Czech Rep.* 26 C9
Zobeyrī *Iran* 70 C5
Zobia *Dem. Rep. of the Congo* 86 B2
Zoetermeer *Neths.* 17 B4
Zogang *China* 58 C2
Zogno *Italy* 40 C6
Zogqên *China* 58 A2
Zohreh → *Iran* 71 D6
Zolochiv *Ukraine* 23 D13
Zolotonosha *Ukraine* 33 H7
Zolotyy Potik *Ukraine* 29 B10
Zomba *Malawi* 87 F4
Zongo *Dem. Rep. of the Congo* 84 D3
Zonguldak *Turkey* 72 B4
Zonguldak □ *Turkey* 72 B4
Zongyang *China* 59 B11
Zonqor Pt. *Malta* 49 D2
Zonza *France* 21 G13
Zorgo *Burkina Faso* 83 C4
Zorita *Spain* 37 F5
Zorleni *Romania* 29 D12
Zornitsa *Bulgaria* 45 D10
Zorritos *Peru* 124 D2
Žory *Poland* 31 H5
Zorzor *Liberia* 82 D3
Zossen *Germany* 24 C9
Zou Xiang *China* 56 G9
Zouan-Hounien *Ivory C.* 82 D3
Zouar *Chad* 79 D9
Zouérate = Zouîrât *Mauritania* 78 D3
Zouîrât *Mauritania* 78 D3
Zourika *Niger* 83 B6
Zourma *Burkina Faso* 83 C4
Zoutkamp *Neths.* 17 A6
Zrenjanin *Serbia* 28 E5
Zuarungu *Ghana* 83 C4
Zuba *Nigeria* 83 D6
Zubayr *Yemen* 81 D5
Zubin Potok *Kosovo* 44 D4
Zubtsov *Russia* 32 D8
Zuénoula *Ivory C.* 82 D3
Zuera *Spain* 38 D4
Zufār *Oman* 75 D5
Zug *Switz.* 25 H4
Zugdidi *Georgia* 35 J5
Zugersee *Switz.* 25 H4
Zugspitze *Germany* 25 H6
Zuid-Holland □ *Neths.* 17 C4
Zuidbeveland *Neths.* 17 C3
Zuidhorn *Neths.* 17 A6
Zújar *Spain* 37 H8
Zújar → *Spain* 37 G5
Żukowo *Poland* 30 D5
Zula *Eritrea* 81 D4
Zülpich *Germany* 24 E2
Zumaia *Spain* 38 B2
Zumárraga *Spain* 38 B2
Zumbo *Mozam.* 87 F3
Zummo *Nigeria* 83 D7
Zumpango *Mexico* 119 D5
Zungeru *Nigeria* 83 D6
Zunhua *China* 57 D9
Zuni Pueblo *U.S.A.* 109 J9
Zuo Jiang → *China* 58 F6
Zuozhou *China* 58 F6
Županja *Croatia* 28 E3
Žur *Kosovo* 44 D4
Zurbātīyah *Iraq* 73 F12
Zürich *Switz.* 25 H4
Zürich □ *Switz.* 25 H4
Zürichsee *Switz.* 25 H4
Žuromin *Poland* 31 E6
Zutphen *Neths.* 17 B6
Zuurberg △ *S. Africa* 88 E4
Zūzan *Iran* 71 C8
Žužemberk *Slovenia* 41 C11
Zvečan *Kosovo* 44 D4
Zvenigorodka = Zvenyhorodka *Ukraine* 33 H6
Zvenyhorodka *Ukraine* 33 H6
Zvezdets *Bulgaria* 45 D11
Zvishavane *Zimbabwe* 87 G3
Zvolen *Slovak Rep.* 27 C12
Zvonce *Serbia* 44 D6
Zvornik *Bos.-H.* 28 F4
Zwedru = Tchien *Liberia* 82 D3
Zweibrücken *Germany* 25 F3
Zwenkau *Germany* 24 D8
Zwettl *Austria* 26 C8
Zwickau *Germany* 24 E8
Zwierzyniec *Poland* 31 H9
Zwiesel *Germany* 25 F9
Zwoleń *Poland* 31 G8
Zwolle *Neths.* 17 B6
Zwolle *U.S.A.* 116 F8
Žychlin *Poland* 31 F6
Żyrardów *Poland* 31 F7
Zyryan *Kazakhstan* 52 E9
Zyryanka *Russia* 53 C16
Zyryanovsk = Zyryan *Kazakhstan* 52 E9
Żywiec *Poland* 31 J6

KEY TO EUROPEAN MAP PAGES

Large scale maps
(>1:2 500 000)

Medium scale maps
(1:2 800 000 — 1:9 900 000)

Small scale maps
(<1:10 000 000)

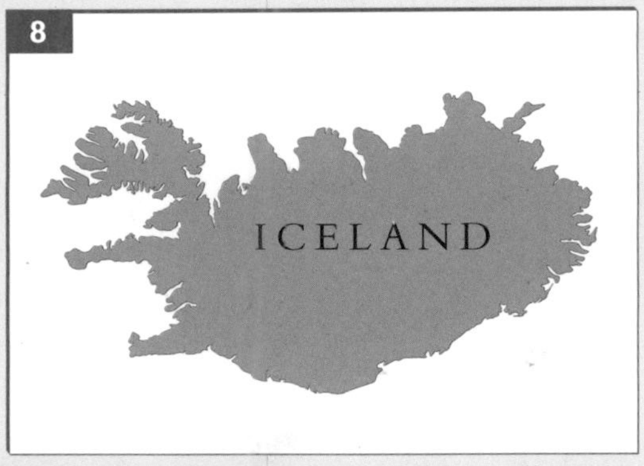

8

ICELAND

Arctic Circle

WORLD COUNTRY INDEX

Afghanistan	66	**G**ermany	24—25	**O**man	75
Albania	44	Ghana	82—83		
Algeria	78	Greece	44—47	**P**akistan	66, 68
Angola	84—85	Greenland	4	Panama	120
Argentina	126, 128	Guadeloupe	120	Papua New Guinea	96
Armenia	73	Guatemala	120	Paraguay	126—127
Australia	92—95	Guinea	82	Peru	124
Austria	26—27	Guinea-Bissau	82	Philippines	61
Azerbaijan	73	Guyana	124	Poland	30—31
				Portugal	36—37
Bahamas	120—121	**H**aiti	121	Puerto Rico	121
Bahrain	71	Honduras	120		
Bangladesh	67	Hungary	28	**Q**atar	71
Barbados	121				
Belarus	32—33	**I**celand	8	**R**omania	28—29
Belgium	17	India	66—69	Russia	32—35, 52—53
Belize	120	Indonesia	62—63	Rwanda	86
Benin	83	Iran	70—71, 73		
Bhutan	67	Iraq	70—71, 73	**S**t. Lucia	121
Bolivia	124	Irish Republic	12	Samoa	91
Bosnia-Herzegovina	41, 44	Israel	74	Saudi Arabia	70—71, 75
Botswana	88	Italy	40—43	Scotland	13
Brazil	124—125, 127	Ivory Coast	82	Senegal	82
Brunei	62			Serbia	28, 44
Bulgaria	44—45	**J**amaica	120	Sierra Leone	82
Burkina Faso	82—83	Japan	54—55	Singapore	65
Burma (Myanmar)	67	Jordan	74	Slovak Republic	27
Burundi	86			Slovenia	41
		Kazakhstan	52	Solomon Is.	96
Cambodia	64—65	Kenya	86	Somali Republic	75
Canary Is.	48	Korea, North	57	South Africa	88—89
Cameroon	83, 84	Korea, South	57	Spain	36—39
Canada	100—105	Kosovo	44	Sri Lanka	66
Central African Republic	84	Kuwait	70—71	Sudan	80—81
Chad	79	Kyrgyzstan	52	Suriname	124—125
Chile	126, 128			Swaziland	89
China	56—60	**L**aos	64	Sweden	8—9
Colombia	124	Latvia	32	Switzerland	25
Congo	84	Lebanon	74	Syria	70, 72—73
Congo, Dem. Rep.		Lesotho	89		
of the	84—85, 86—87	Liberia	82	**T**aiwan	59
Costa Rica	120	Libya	79	Tajikistan	52
Croatia	41	Lithuania	32	Tanzania	86—87
Cuba	120—121	Luxembourg	17	Thailand	64—65
Cyprus	49			Togo	83
Czech Republic	26—27	**M**acedonia	44	Tonga	91
		Madagascar	89	Trinidad and Tobago	125
Denmark	11	Malawi	87	Tunisia	78—79
Djibouti	81	Malaysia	62—63, 65	Turkey	72—73
Dominican Republic	121	Mali	78, 82—83	Turkmenistan	52
		Malta	49		
East Timor	63	Martinique	120	**U**ganda	86
Ecuador	124	Mauritania	78, 82	Ukraine	33
Egypt	80	Mexico	118—119	United Arab Emirates	75
El Salvador	120	Moldova	29	United Kingdom	12—16
England	14—15	Mongolia	60	USA	106—117
Equatorial Guinea	84	Montenegro	44	Uruguay	126—127
Eritrea	80—81	Morocco	78	Uzbekistan	52
Estonia	32	Mozambique	87, 89		
Ethiopia	75, 81			**V**anuatu	96
		Namibia	88	Venezuela	124
Fiji	91	Nepal	69	Vietnam	64—65
Finland	8—9	Netherlands	17		
France	18—21	New Zealand	91	**W**ales	14—15
French Guiana	125	Nicaragua	120		
		Niger	78—79, 83	**Y**emen	75
Gabon	84	Nigeria	83		
Gambia	82	Northern Ireland	12	**Z**ambia	85, 87
Georgia	35	Norway	8—9	Zimbabwe	87

8

16

13

13

13

14

12

22

17

18

IRELAND

UNITED KINGDOM

20

FRAN

36

38

ANDORRA

PORTUGAL

SPAIN

48

ML   6/10   MOROCCO   AL